Ripley's
Believe It or Not!®

Executive VP Norm Deska
VP, Exhibits & Archives Edward Meyer

Publisher Anne Marshall

Editorial Director Rebecca Miles
Senior Researcher & Picture Manager James Proud
Researcher Lucas Stram
Assistant Editor Charlotte Howell
Additional Research Rosie Alexander
Text Geoff Tibballs
Additional Text James Proud
Editors Judy Barratt, Sally McFall
Factchecker Alex Bazlinton
Indexer Hilary Bird

Art Director Sam South
Design Dynamo Design
Reprographics Juice Creative

ISBN: 978-1-60991-000-6

For information regarding permission, write to
VP Intellectual Property
Ripley Entertainment Inc.
Suite 188, 7576 Kingspointe Parkway
Orlando, Florida 32819

Email: publishing@ripleys.com

Manufactured in China
in May/2011 by Leo Paper
1st printing

Library of Congress Cataloging-in-Publication Data

Tibballs, Geoff.
  Ripley's believe it or not!. Strikingly true / [text
Geoff Tibballs].
    p. cm.
  ISBN 978-1-60991-000-6
  1. Curiosities and wonders. I. Title. II. Title:
Strikingly true.
  AG243.T3987 2011
  031.02--dc22

                    2011010342

PUBLISHER'S NOTE
While every effort has been made to verify
the accuracy of the entries in this book, the
Publishers cannot be held responsible for any
errors contained in the work. They would be
glad to receive any information from readers.

WARNING
Some of the stunts and activities in this book
are undertaken by experts and should not
be attempted by anyone without adequate
training and supervision.

Christmas 2011

To Matthew

Love, Ya Ya & Gaps

Ripley's
Believe *It or Not!*®

STRIKINGLY TRUE

Ripley
PUBLISHING
a Jim Pattison Company

contents

Ripley's World 6

Featuring New Museum in South Korea 6, Crazy Contributors 7, Making the Lizardman 8, Ripley's Top 12 Purchases of the Year 9

Believe It! 10

Featuring Diving Horses 14, Sky-high Dining 17, Beard full of Birds 21, Mind-blowing Mummies 22, Tattooed Ladies 26, The Amazing Jumbo 30

page 15

World 34

Featuring March of the Lava 36, Starling Patterns 41, Serious Sandstorm 48, Weeping Glacier 50, Dried-up Niagara Falls 52, Ice Lighthouse 53, River Runs Red 54

page 35

Animals 56

page 241

Featuring Plant Potty 62, Exploding Ants 63, Muscle Hound 67, Spot the Caterpillar 70, Tale of Ripley the Dog 76, Lightning Cow 81, Two-legged Pig 84

Sports 86

Featuring Olympic Oddities 88, Mighty Mouth 92, Airbed Race 94, Climbing Frozen Waterfalls 95, Skiing on Sand 96, Survival Stories 98

Body 102

Featuring Presidential Portraits on a Hair 104, Magnetic Fingers 107, Belly-button Fluff Bears 108, Too Many Toes 109, Major Mite 116, Heavenly Strike 118

Ripley's Oddito

Transport 130

Featuring Lost Squadron 132, GatorBike 134, Parking Problem 135, Sparkling Blades 136, Monster Limo 140, Fake Porsche 142, Inflatable Tanks 143

page 136

Feats 144

Featuring Balloon Ride 149, Wall of Death 150, Human Sparkler 152, Serpent Queen 156, Ripley's Odditorium—Chicago World's Fair 161, Tightrope Terror 169

page 161

Ripley's Odditorium Special Feature

Mysteries 172

Featuring Real Fairies? 175, Extreme Ectoplasm 176, Pod People 178, Bizarre Beach Monster 180, Alien Autopsy 181

page 173

Food 182

Featuring Larvae Soup 187, Squeaky Loaf 189, Chocolate Skulls 190, Cutlery for Dinner 191, Squirrel Beer Bottles 193, Volcano Barbecue 194

Arts 196

Featuring Inflated Animals 198, Tape Jellyfish 202, Carved Pencil Tips 208, Gum Dog 210, Tabletop Landscapes 216, Plastic Penguins 218, Man-made Monsters 220

Science 224

Featuring Self-appendectomy 226, Snake Digestion 228, Hand Grafted onto Foot 229, Invisibility Coat 230

Beyond Belief 232

Featuring Hanged Elephant 234, Headstand on Glass 236, Roadside Angel 237, Dried Shark 240, King of Cobras 241, Car Coffins 242, Saved by Ears 244, Weird Airports 245

Index 246

Smallest Man

Born on June 18, 1993, Junrey Balawing of the Philippines stands just 22 in (56 cm) tall.

RIPLEY'S WORLD

The world of Ripley's is a vast, elaborate machine. There are researchers, curators, archivists and model-makers, as well as editors and correspondents who compile articles and write for the Ripley's Believe It or Not! books. Dedicated and passionate about what they do, these people never tire in their mission to uncover and preserve the unbelievable side of life.

Across the world, 31 museums showcase the Ripley's collection. On display are unforgettable exhibits supplied by the huge central archive that is kept in the vast storage warehouse at Ripley's headquarters in Orlando, Florida. This is also where all of the wax-work sculptures of extraordinary people, past and present, are conceived and lovingly brought to life (see page 8).

Ripley's operates with the energy of its founder, Robert Ripley, who, in 1918, began his quest to uncover the world's most unbelievable true stories.

At the time, he was working as a cartoonist at the *New York Globe*. At first, his column pinpointed unusual achievements in athletics, but he soon broadened his search into every aspect of life. Traveling endlessly to collect material, he covered more than 464,000 mi (747,000 km) in his lifetime, and his enthusiasm for the bizarre was matched only by that of his readership—the mailbags dumped on his desk contained as many as 170,000 letters a week from fans with a curious tale to tell.

RIPLEY'S SOUTH KOREA

The world of Ripley's continued to expand in 2010 when a new Ripley's museum opened on Jeju Island, South Korea. Among the 600 exhibits inside the robot-shaped building is Buzz Aldrin's space suit, a meteorite from Mars, a big piece of the Berlin Wall and a collection of Ripley's South American shrunken heads.

▲ Ripley's gives special certificates to its contributors to recognize their particular achievements. Here, Gary Duschl is presented with a certificate in recognition of his 12-mi-long (19-km) gum-wrapper chain by Ripley's President, Jim Pattison, Jr.

Tell us if you have a strange fact that we should know about

"Ripley's regularly receives all kinds of amazing photographs and stories from around the world. From odd animals to crazy physical feats and curious creations, everything is welcome and the weirder the better. We are waiting to hear from you!"

1 Amanda Kay Wallace made an aluminum-can dress **2** Alex Kendik can bend his legs behind his neck **3** Ray Gonzales can turn his feet backward **4** Al Gliniecki knotted 911 cherry stems with his tongue in one hour **5** Mickey the Spaniel puppy has Mickey Mouse on his fur **6** A flying bird left a perfect impression on Darlene Gabehart's car **7** Denny Calloway's toe was run over by a forklift truck and never treated **8** Brian Jackson can blow up and burst a hot-water bottle in 12.29 seconds

WRITE TO US

BION Research
Ripley Entertainment Inc.,
7576 Kingspointe Parkway, 188,
Orlando, Florida 32819,
U.S.A. (Please include photos where possible)

Follow us on Facebook and Twitter@RipleyWorld

Or send an email to bionresearch@ripleys.com

Contribute via our website www.ripleybooks.com

Go to your phone's APP store for our eye-popping **APPS!**

1 Being immortalized for Ripley's is a messy process!

3 Covering Erik's entire body makes an exact replica for the model

2 Erik spent two days having the casts made

4 Applying finishing touches to Erik's head mold

MAKING THE LIZARDMAN

The Lizardman, also known as Erik Sprague from Austin, Texas, is one of the most iconic individuals featured in *Ripley's Believe It or Not!* A performance artist who has spent years transforming himself into a reptile-man hybrid, Erik's entire body is covered in scaly tattoos, his teeth are filed to a point, he has implants in his forehead and a forked tongue.

Ripley's wanted to immortalize the Lizardman by creating a life-size model to display in the Ripley's museums. Erik was invited to a session with the art team at Ripley's headquarters in Orlando, Florida, where his entire head, and then his body, was covered in silicone and plaster to make a mold. The final figure was formed from a hardwearing resin and has an incredible resemblance to human—or lizard—skin and flesh.

Chocolate wedding favor from Michael Jackson and Lisa-Marie Presley's wedding

Edward's Choice

Ripley's archivist, Edward Meyer, chooses his favorite acquisitions of the year—many of which are featured in this book—and lists the strangest items he bought in 2011.

Top 12 items bought by Ripley's this year

1. Two driftwood sculptures—*A Matter of Time* and *Ocean's 11th Hour*
2. Elephant armor, with replica elephant
3. Imperial jade burial suit from the Han Dynasty of ancient China
4. *Lucy in the Sky with Diamonds*, a Beatles themed art car
5. Series of portraits made from carved telephone books
6. Crucifixion portrait made from toast
7. Giant portraits of Bill and Hillary Clinton painted with hamburger grease
8. Collection of celebrity portraits made from cassette tape
9. Picture of *The Last Supper* made from laundry lint
10. Miniature writings of complete movie scripts making up pictures of scenes or characters from famous movies
11. *Cathedrals of the Sea*, a matchstick oil rig
12. Optimus Prime, a robot-transformer made from car parts

Top 12 strangest things Ripley's bought at auctions in 2011

1. Small piece of the burnt skin of an elephant from the P.T. Barnum museum fire of July 13, 1865, New York City
2. Autographed leather Michael Jackson "Bad" outfit custom-made for his chimpanzee "Bubbles"
3. Marilyn Monroe's handprint from Grauman's Chinese Theater stone slab
4. Handmade 1932 tri-plane prototype aero-car
5. Autographed metal funnel worn as a hat by the Tin Man in the 1939 movie *The Wizard of Oz*
6. Sleeping mask worn by actress Rita Hayworth in the 1940s
7. Inscribed chocolate bar that was a wedding reception favor at Michael Jackson and Lisa-Marie Presley's wedding
8. Series of five flags flown on the Moon during *Apollo* space missions and a vial of Moon dust
9. Dean Cain's *Superman* costume
10. *Apollo* space mission decontamination bootie worn by an astronaut on return to Earth
11. Michael Jackson's plaster werewolf fangs from the original *Thriller* video
12. Elvis Presley's black eyeliner make-up kit

All in a day's work...

The tragic but fascinating story of Mary, the hanged elephant, is featured in this book on page 234. How Ripley's acquired photographic evidence of this terrible event is another story in itself. Edward Meyer, Ripley's archivist, explains...

"As for the photo... The story was featured in a Ripley cartoon in the 1930s, so I knew it well and, in fact, considered it one of the strangest BION stories of all time. Just south of Orlando is where all the circuses "winter," and at least once a year Tampa has a big circus garage sale-auction. I was there to buy a 100-year-old miniature carousel, the kind used by salesmen at the turn of the century to sell actual carousels to different towns. The guy who was selling it tried to get my interest by wooing me with a box of old postcards and photos—he literally gave them to me in exchange for a good lunch. Well, the Mary photo was in this old shoebox! Also in the box was a collection of amazing Major Mite photos [see pages 116–17]."

Ocean's 11th Hour— driftwood sculpture

food

arts

science

beyond belief

believe it!

world

animals

sports

body

transport

feats

mysteries

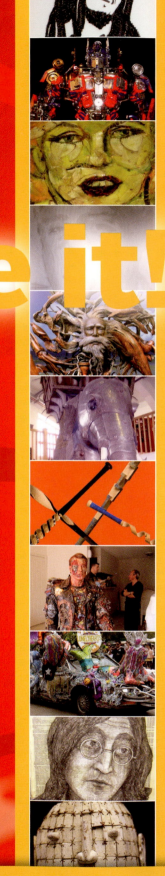

Burger Bill

Ripley's recently bought large portraits of Bill and Hillary Clinton made entirely from burger grease. Created by Washington artist Phil Hansen, the artworks are intended to show just how greasy fast food burgers are. Bill measures 8 x 4 ft (2.4 x 1.2 m) and was made with grease from more than 50 burgers.

Ripley's EXHIBITS

Ripley's Believe It or Not!

Body of Work

A closer look at these images reveals that they are all created using the human body. By painting directly onto skin, artist Craig Tracy of New Orleans, Louisiana, manipulates the natural shape of his models against a meticulously designed background, creating mind-blowing illusions without the use of computer trickery.

Craig uses photographs to plan the image and then models often sit for hours at a time as he applies the paint, with each painting taking on average one day to complete.

Ripley's Ask

How did you start painting on people? *I had been a conventional professional artist for 20 years, but I never felt satisfied with what I was creating. I kept searching for a style or a technique that would not only fulfill and push me, but that would also contribute to the evolution of contemporary art. I was in my mid-thirties before I considered bodypainting as the solution to my creative dilemma. I had painted on several bodies before and the idea of taking bodypainting seriously as fine art made the difference. Only a handful of artists had approached bodypainting as fine art before me, and this allowed for plenty of room to contribute.*

How long can a bodypainting take to complete? *The amount of time that my work takes to produce can vary greatly. Some of my pieces incorporate custom-painted backdrops and these can easily take a full day of work or more to create and complete. Other, simpler images require only a few hours to achieve. My average bodypainting takes about eight hours to complete and about 40 minutes to photograph.*

What do you like about body art as opposed to more conventional painting? *In the past 30 years, I've painted on almost every surface known to man and I can unequivocally state that nothing even comes close to the beauty and complexity of working on the human body. We are the most interesting and sophisticated entity in our known universe. I've chosen to not just artistically represent the human figure, I've purposefully decided to create directly on and with the beauty and soulfulness of the human being.*

BUTTERFLY
Named after the butterfly shape visible on the nose of the panther, *Butterfly* was completed in one mammoth 24-hour session, with only one hour of sleep for Craig and his model.

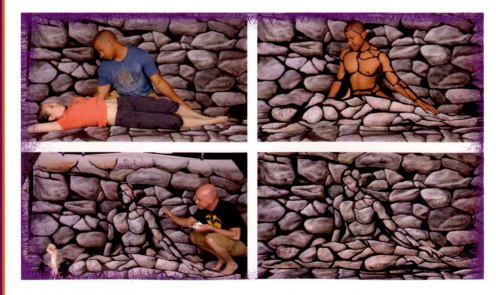

IMMACULATE ▲
Immaculate features a hand-painted and airbrushed background. Once the models are in position, Craig adds the final paint to their body.

Ripley's—
Believe It or Not!®

High Horse

From the 1880s through to the 1970s, one of the most popular shows on the Steel Pier in Atlantic City, New Jersey, was the horse high dive. Highly trained horses, usually ridden by girls, would leap from heights of up to 60 ft (18 m) into a pool 10 ft (3 m) deep. Riders asserted at the time that the horses enjoyed diving, were excellent swimmers and were never forced to jump. However, owing to public pressure, diving horse shows died out in the 1970s and only one show remains—in a scaled-down form—in New York, where a riderless horse named Lightning will jump 10 ft (3 m) into water for a bucket of oats.

roar deal A thief in Germany stole a circus trailer in November 2009, unaware that there was a five-year-old lion in the back. The vehicle was later abandoned with its engine running after crashing into a road sign. Police believe the driver may have panicked on hearing the lion—named Caesar—let out a hungry roar.

double take When Helen MacGregor was sent a 21-year-old postcard of the town in Yorkshire, England, where she grew up, she was amazed to see herself in the center of the photo as a toddler. A friend had sent her the postcard of Otley, unaware that the child pictured in the street scene was Miss MacGregor, then aged three.

mistaken identity The dead body of a 75-year-old man slumped over a chair on the balcony of his third-floor Los Angeles, California, apartment was left undisturbed for several days in October 2009 as neighbors thought it was a Halloween dummy.

money to burn A German snowboarder stranded in the Austrian Alps for six hours in February 2010 was rescued after attracting attention by setting fire to his money. Stuck 33 ft (10 m) above ground after the ski lift was switched off at dusk, Dominik Podolsky was finally spotted by cleaners as he burned the last of his euros.

incriminating evidence An 18-year-old from Philadelphia, Pennsylvania, turned himself in to police in December 2009 for stealing a cell phone—after he took a photo of himself with it and it automatically sent a copy to the owner's e-mail!

close relatives Adopted by different families at a young age, biological brothers Stephen Goosney and Tommy Larkin finally found each other nearly 30 years later—and discovered that for the past seven months they had been living almost directly across the street from each other in Corner Brook, Newfoundland, Canada.

lottery luck Since 1993, Joan Ginther of Las Vegas, Nevada, has won the Texas Lottery four times, each time scooping at least $1 million, with total prize money of more than $20 million. She bought two of her winning tickets at the same store in Bishop, Texas, while visiting her father. Her chances of winning four lottery jackpots were put at more than 200-million-to-one.

classroom relic In June 2010, while cleaning up her classroom before a move, schoolteacher Michelle Eugenio of Peabody, Massachusetts, discovered a colonial-era document dating back to April 1792 among a pile of old books and scraps of paper.

dump dig Sanitation workers in Parsippany, New Jersey, dug through 10 tons of trash at a city dump to successfully recover a wedding ring that had been accidentally thrown away by a couple. Bridget Pericolo had placed the ring in a cup, but her husband of 55 years, Angelo, mistakenly threw it out with the garbage before leaving for work.

spelling mistake The general manager of the Chilean mint was fired after the country's name was spelt incorrectly on thousands of coins. The 2008 batch of 50-peso coins bore the stamp CHIIE, but amazingly the spelling mistake was not spotted until late 2009.

unexpected mourner Brazilian bricklayer Ademir Jorge Goncalves gave friends and family a surprise in November 2009 by turning up at his own funeral. Relatives had identified him as the disfigured victim of a car crash in Parana state, but actually he had been out on a drinking spree and did not hear about his funeral until it was already underway.

BUOYANCY CASTLE

Three men from London, England, invented a bizarre new water sport when they fulfilled an ambition to ride a full-size bouncy castle across Lake Garda in Italy in May 2010. After drifting into the path of a sailing regatta and being redirected by a police launch, adventurers Jack Watkins, Chris Hayes and Dave Sibley completed the 5-mi (8-km) voyage in two hours.

secret stash Calin Tarescu of Alba Iulia, Romania, discovered that his wife had thrown away a pair of his old shoes in which he had stashed $64,000. Police helped him to recover the majority of the money.

hand stolen The mummified hand of a cheating gambler was stolen from a locked cabinet at a pub in Wiltshire, England, in March 2010. The hand, said to have been cut off a gambler caught cheating at the card game whist, was clutching a pack of 18th-century playing cards and is rumored to be cursed.

late appointment Reynolds Smith Jr. was appointed by the Alabama Democratic Party to sit on a party panel in October 2009—even though he had died 11 months earlier!

buried alive After spending hours digging a 10-ft-deep (3-m) tunnel at a beach on Tenerife in Spain's Canary Islands, a 23-year-old German tourist had to be rescued when the sand collapsed and buried him up to his head. He was trapped on the beach for nearly two hours before 15 firefighters were able to free him.

Ripley's REVISITED

FACE PAINT

Lucky Diamond Rich is almost 100 percent covered with tattoos. Every inch of his skin is inked, including his eyelids and the insides of his ears. Lucky's incredibly dense face tattoos have developed over the last few years: He was last featured in *Ripley's Believe It or Not! Expect the Unexpected*, and his amazing transformation can clearly be seen. An international circus and street performer from Adelaide, Australia, Lucky has alloy-capped teeth with which he can perform extreme feats of strength.

FAITHFUL FEET

Hua Chi, a monk at a monastery near Tongren, China, has been coming to exactly the same spot to kowtow at the temple for so many years that perfect footprints have been worn into the wooden floor. For nearly 20 years he has carefully placed his feet to bend down, and lie prostrate, two- to three-thousand times a day, although now that he's over 70 years old, he can manage only a thousand!

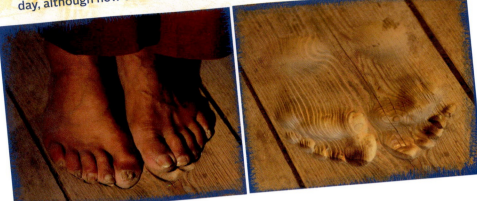

four babies Four sisters from one family each gave birth within four days in 2010. The same obstetrician delivered the babies of Lilian Sepulveda, Saby Pazos and Leslie Pazos at the same Chicago, Illinois, hospital on August 6 and 7, and a fourth sister, Heidi Lopez, gave birth in California on August 9.

200 grandkids During her life, Yitta Schwartz (1917–2010) of Kiryas Joel, New York, had 15 children, more than 200 grandchildren and a staggering total of more than 2,000 living descendants.

cash bonfire Infamous Colombian drug baron Pablo Escobar once burned more than $1.5 million in cash to keep his daughter Manuela warm during a single night on the run. When he realized she was suffering from hypothermia at his mountain hideout, he lit a bonfire using wads of U.S. dollars.

extra time A Thai man spent three extra years behind bars in an Indonesian prison because of a typo in his paperwork. Kamjai Khong Thavorn should have been released in 2007 after serving a 20-year sentence for possessing heroin, but a clerical error wrongly stated his first year in prison as 1997 instead of 1987. The error was not spotted until 2010.

WORKING FLAT OUT

Hurrying to impose new parking restrictions ahead of the 2010 Tall Ships sailing races, council workers in Hartlepool, England, painted yellow lines right over a squashed, dead hedgehog in the road rather than move the animal.

fake workers After adding biometric scanning to record employee attendance in 2009, the city of Delhi, India, discovered 22,853 fake workers on its payroll.

croc monsieur After receiving reports of a 12-ft-long (3.6-m) crocodile circling boats in the English Channel, French authorities banned swimming near Boulogne and broadcast warnings to vacationers in both French and English—only to discover that the reptile was nothing more dangerous than a floating piece of wood.

satan image A family in Budapest, Hungary, abandoned their new-look bathroom after an image of Satan appeared overnight in a tile. Emerging from her first shower in the freshly decorated room, Andrea Csrefko fled in horror when she noticed the horned head of the devil in one of the tiles. The spooky image had not been there when husband Laszlo had put the tiles up and no cleaning detergent was able to remove it.

what fire? A man in Pittsburgh, Pennsylvania, slept while his house caught fire and part of the roof collapsed. It was not until fire crews did a walk-through of the house more than two hours later that he woke up.

document leak A 2,400-page restricted document from Britain's Ministry of Defence giving advice on how to stop documents leaking onto the Internet was itself leaked onto the Internet in 2009.

unique stamp The one-of-a-kind Treskilling Yellow postage stamp is worth about $7.4 million. First issued in Sweden in 1855, it owes its value to the fact that it was printed in yellow by mistake, when the rest of the batch was green. It survives today thanks only to a 14-year-old Swedish schoolboy who rescued it from his grandmother's garbage bin in 1885 and sold it to a dealer for about $1.

end of war Although fighting in World War I finished in 1918, the war did not officially end until October 3, 2010—92 years later—when Germany finally settled its war debt by paying $90 million, which was the last instalment of the reparations imposed on it by the Allies. Germany was forced to pay compensation toward the cost of the war by the 1919 Treaty of Versailles—the bill would have been settled much earlier but Adolf Hitler reneged on the agreement.

High Tea

Waiters serve lunch to two steel workers perched on a girder high above New York City in 1930. The men were working on the construction of the 47-story, 625-ft-high (190-m) Waldorf-Astoria Hotel on Park Avenue.

delayed delivery Gill Smeathers of Northamptonshire, England, received a package in February 2010 that was postmarked November 4, 1982.

inflated numbers During World War II, the 1,100 men of the U.S. Army's 23rd Headquarters Special Troops used inflatable vehicles, sound recordings and fake radio broadcasts to deceive the enemy into thinking they were an army of 30,000 soldiers.

mattress mishap After accidentally throwing away a mattress that her mother had stuffed with $1 million, a Tel Aviv woman searched in vain through Israeli landfill sites containing thousands of tons of garbage. She had bought her mother a new mattress as a surprise.

battle dead In 2010, Brian Freeman, a former Australian army captain, uncovered the forgotten site of a World-War-II battle in Papua New Guinea, with the bodies of three Japanese soldiers still lying where they fell in 1942. Local villagers led him to Eora Creek—the biggest single battle of the Kokoda campaign—where he found the remains of the soldiers, along with their weapons and equipment.

lucky numbers Beating astronomical odds, Ernest Pullen of Bonne Terre, Missouri, won $3 million in two separate lotteries in the space of three months. After picking up $1 million in June 2010, he won another $2 million in September, combining his lucky numbers with numbers he had dreamed about six years earlier when foreseeing that he would one day win a lot of money.

own phone After his cell phone was stolen, a Californian man bought a new one on classifieds website Craigslist, choosing it because it looked just like his old phone. When it arrived, it actually was his old phone and still had his numbers stored. Luckily for the police, the thief had put his return address on the package.

balloon daredevils Early balloonists used highly flammable hydrogen gas instead of hot air or helium. In 1785, the French inventor Jean-Pierre Blanchard and American John Jeffries used an early hydrogen gas balloon to fly across the English Channel between England and France. When Jean-François Pilâtre de Rozier attempted to do the same, his balloon exploded and he became the first to die in an air accident.

Tim on chewing molten lead:

"Fire-eaters have been doing this stunt for over 200 years, and the technique is still a closely guarded secret. Just like fire-eating, it takes years of practice before you can be ready to perform, and even then it is still highly dangerous. First, the metal is melted in a small furnace, and then a small amount (about a tablespoon) is transferred to a spoon. I then take this into my mouth and keep it there until it solidifies completely. After about 30 seconds I spit the nugget out onto a tray or catch it with a pair of thick gloves."

Tim Cockerill, aka The Great Inferno, happily gargles hot molten lead until it cools and hardens into solid metal in his mouth. During the day, Tim is a zoologist at Cambridge University in the U.K.

When he is not working in the lab, or trekking through a jungle to study insects, Tim wows audiences with such stunts as heating his tongue with a blowtorch, swallowing fire, and hammering nails into his head. The Great Inferno has been amazing audiences for 15 years with his extremely painful-looking acts.

The Great Inferno

Tim on the blowtorch stunt:

"The blowtorch stunt is one of the most difficult of the fire-eater's stunts to perform. With a flame that burns at around 1600°C [2,900°F], there is no margin for error—any hesitation would result in a serious burn. There is no real secret here, but the trick is to come at the flame with confidence and respect. This is one stunt that is just as intimidating no matter how many times you perform it!"

Tim on the blockhead stunt:

"The Human Blockhead was invented in the 1930s by sideshow performer Melvin Burkhart, 'The Anatomical Wonder.' What you see is what you get with this stunt—a solid steel nail is hammered all the way into the face. This is not something to be tried by anyone—get the angle wrong and the nail would go straight through the skull and into the brain!"

Ripley's Believe It or Not!®

NAME GAME
Les Cool and Les Hot (above) once worked together as radio repairmen for the Babeck Music Company in Olympia, Washington State. And in another curious name twist, I.M. Wiser and his wife May B. Wiser lived in Washington, D.C., in the 1940s. Mr. Wiser is seen here with "a little Wiser."

R small world In 1980, when Alex and Donna Voutsinas lived in different countries and long before they met and married, they were captured in the same photo at Walt Disney World, Orlando, Florida. Five-year-old Donna was photographed at the same moment as three-year-old Alex, who then lived in Montréal, Canada, was being pushed down Main Street in a stroller by his father.

R same name In 2009, 77-year-old retired policeman Geraint Woolford was admitted to Abergele Hospital in North Wales and placed in a bed next to a 52-year-old Geraint Woolford, unrelated and also a retired policeman! The two men had never met before and checks showed they are the only two people in the whole of Great Britain named Geraint Woolford.

R short journey Six-year-old Heidi Kay Werstler tossed a message in a bottle into the sea at Ocean City, New Jersey, in 1985 and it washed ashore 24 years later at Duck, North Carolina—less than 300 mi (480 km) away.

R spoon dig A female convict used a spoon to dig her way out of a prison in Breda in the Netherlands, in February 2010. Using the spoon, she dug a tunnel under the cellar of the prison's kitchen to the outside world.

R treasure trove A Scottish game warden who bought a metal detector for a new hobby struck gold on his very first treasure hunt, discovering a $1.5 million hoard of Iron-Age jewelry. Five days after taking delivery of the detector and just seven steps into his first hunt, David Booth unearthed four 2,300-year-old items made of pure gold—the most significant discovery ever of Iron-Age metalwork in Scotland.

R force farce The entire police force in a Hungarian town quit after winning more than $15 million on the lottery in 2009. The 15-strong squad in Budaörs resigned immediately after scooping the jackpot.

R shoe thief A second-hand shoe store owner stole more than 1,200 pairs of designer shoes by posing as a mourner at hospitals and funeral homes in South Korea. His victims were genuine friends and relatives of the deceased, who had slipped off their shoes in a traditional demonstration of respect. The thief would remove his own footwear, pay his respects, then put on a more expensive pair and walk off.

R last post A postcard bringing holiday news to a couple in West Yorkshire, England, was delivered in 2009—40 years after it was posted.

R family graduation Chao Muhe, 96, and his grandson Zhao Shuangzhan, 32, both graduated from university in June 2009. Retired lecturer Chao, who enrolled to set an example to his grandson, earned a master's degree in philosophy from the University of South China in Taiwan, while Zhao graduated from Chung Hua University. During the six-year course, Chao never missed a class despite needing to get up at 5 a.m. every day to catch several buses to the university.

R vader raider In July 2010, a man robbed a bank in Setauket, New York State, dressed in the mask and cape of Darth Vader, the villain from the *Star Wars* movies.

R bad timing At Lowestoft, Suffolk, England in 2010, an unlucky 13-year-old boy was struck by lightning at 13.13 on Friday, August 13. Thankfully, he suffered only minor burns and made a full recovery.

R winner winner A store in Winner, South Dakota, sold the winning ticket, worth $232 million, in the drawing of the Powerball Lottery on May 27, 2009.

R thumb find When fisherman Blake Robinson caught a 6½-lb (2.9-kg) lake trout at Flaming Gorge Reservoir, Wyoming, he discovered a human thumb inside it.

R crushed crustacean A lobster became one of the last casualties of World War II when it was blown up inside an unexploded mine in 2009. The crustacean had made its home inside the 600-lb (272-kg) mine that had lay dormant on the seabed off the coast of Dorset, England, for more than 60 years—but when the Royal Navy's bomb disposal unit tried to coax it out before detonating the device, it refused to move and instead delivered a nasty nip to the divers.

R watch returned A pocket watch was returned to the family of Welsh sailor Richard Prichard in 2009—128 years after his death. In 2000, diver Rich Hughes had been exploring the wreck of Prichard's ship—the *Barbara*—that sank in 1881, when he found the watch. After nine years of painstaking research, he was finally able to identify the owner's family and give the watch back.

R Singing Ban With Venezuela suffering from serious water and energy shortages in 2009, the country's President Hugo Chavez ordered his citizens to stop singing in the shower. He hoped the ban would limit the amount of time people spent using water in the bathroom.

SWING THE LIZARD

As a change from roaming the grassland at India's Corbett National Park, an Indian elephant named Madhuri picked up a passing monitor lizard and played with it for several days. With the lizard's tail firmly grasped in her trunk, she carried it with her wherever she went, swinging it around in the air over and over again, sometimes tossing it high and even dropping it before finally letting the dazed reptile go.

Watch the Beardie

Charles Earnshaw of Anchorage, Alaska, displays his "Beards of a Feather" facial hair sculpture at the 2010 U.S. National Beard and Mustache Championships in Bend, Oregon. There were over 200 entrants, and this creation earned him a prize in the freestyle section.

BUDDHIST MONK

Thai Buddhist monk Loung Pordaeng died in 1973, but to this day remains sitting in the Lotus position, the very position in which he died—naturally mummified in a temple on the Thai island of Koh Samui. Two months before he died at the age of 79, Loung believed his death to be imminent and asked that if his body did not decompose could it stay on display in the temple to inspire future generations to follow Buddhism. He meditated in silence for the final week of his life, eating and drinking nothing, and when he died his wishes were carried out. Local monks added a pair of sunglasses when his eyes eventually fell into his head.

ANCIENT TATTOOS

In 2006, a 1,500-year-old, heavily tattooed and very well-preserved female mummy was discovered in a mud-brick pyramid in northern Peru. She was buried with many weapons, leading experts to believe that she could have been a rare warrior queen of the warlike Moche people.

BABY MUMMY

This incredibly well-preserved, mummified body of a young Peruvian child, who died some 6,500 years ago, is one of the oldest mummies ever found, and is hundreds of years older than the earliest known Egyptian mummies. It formed part of the largest collection of mummies ever assembled, which went on display at the California Science Center in Los Angeles in 2010.

⊗ RIPLEY RESEARCH

Mummification—where skin, soft flesh and hair remain on the bones—can preserve the human body for thousands of years. It can be achieved intentionally, such as with the elaborate Egyptian embalming ritual where the organs are removed from the body, or it can occur completely naturally. Natural mummification generally requires a dry atmosphere and a lack of oxygen to keep the natural process of decay at bay.

EGYPTIAN CAT

The ancient Egyptians, who practiced mummification on royal personages, also mummified animals. These underwent the same elaborate treatment as human corpses, with cloth wraps, a large amount of salt and resin. This Egyptian cat is more than 2,000 years old.

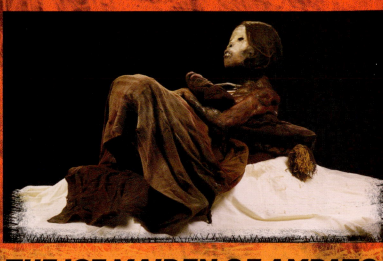

THE ICE MAIDEN OF AMPATO

The frozen, mummified body of a teenage Incan girl was discovered near the 20,700-ft (6,310-m) summit of Mount Ampato, Peru, in 1995. It is thought that she was ritually sacrificed more than 500 years ago. Other mummified children have also been found on the mountain. The "Ice Maiden," as she is known, was removed from the site and is kept under controlled conditions in a Peruvian museum.

Mummies

ANCIENT BEAUTY

In 1934, a Swedish archeologist discovered hundreds of ancient mummies buried under boats in a mysterious cemetery in a remote desert in the Xinjiang region of China. The location, which featured rivers and lakes thousands of years ago, was lost until 2000, and researchers began to excavate the area in 2003. They found the body of a woman thought to have died almost 4,000 years ago, who has become known as the most beautiful mummy in the world, owing to incredibly well-preserved features that even include her eyelashes.

gold rush A huge 220-lb (100-kg) Canadian gold coin was sold at auction to a Spanish company for $4 million in 2010. One of only five $1 million Maple Leaf coins ever produced by the Royal Canadian Mint, it measures 21 in (53 cm) in diameter and is 1¼ in (3 cm) thick.

changing fortunes Brothers Zsolt and Geza Peladi were homeless and living in a cave outside Budapest, Hungary, when they discovered in December 2009 that they were due to inherit part of their grandmother's multi-billion euro fortune.

dummy guard In July 2010, two prisoners escaped from a jail in Argentina that, because of a lack of resources, was using a dummy to man one of its guard towers. Staff had put a prison officer's cap on a football to try to fool the convicts into thinking they were being watched from the tower by a real person.

blood match Eight years after breaking into a house in rural Tasmania, Australia, Peter Cannon was convicted of armed robbery because his DNA matched that of blood found inside a leech at the scene of the crime.

PIGLET BANK
An Internet site is selling a piggy bank made from a real piglet! The brainchild of designer Colin Hart from Belfast, Northern Ireland, the taxidermied pig with a slot in its back costs $4,000 and must be ordered 12 months in advance.

picture perfect When Royal Dutch Navy sergeant Dick de Bruin lost his camera while scuba diving off the Caribbean island of Aruba, he thought he would never see it again. However, seven months later the camera was found 1,130 mi (1,800 km) away by a coastguard at Key West, Florida—and although it was covered in crusty sea growth, it still worked.

remote patrol Burglars who broke into a man's apartment in Midwest City, Oklahoma, were caught via webcam by the man's wife more than 8,000 mi (12,875 km) away in the Philippines. Jim and Maribel Chouinard used the webcam to communicate face-to-face when they were apart.

old student A woman in China became an elementary school pupil at age 102. Ma Xiuxian from Jinan, Shandong Province, started work in a cotton mill at age 13 but had always longed for a proper education. So in 2010—89 years after leaving school—the grandmother went back, joining the grade one class at Weishan Road Elementary School. She uses hearing aids to make sure she can hear the teacher and a magnifying glass to help read text books.

frozen assets In May 2010, the Iowa Court of Appeals ordered the family of Orville Richardson, who died in February 2009 at age 81, to exhume his body so that his head could be cut off and frozen. In 2004, he had signed a contract with an Arizona company and paid $53,500 to have his head placed in cryogenic suspension after his death, but his siblings had buried him instead.

GO SLOW
Road safety campaigners in Canada encouraged motorists to reduce their speed by painting a large 3-D image of a child on to the road outside an elementary school in West Vancouver, British Columbia. The picture of a girl chasing after a ball appeared to come alive when drivers were 100 ft (30 m) away, giving them time to slow down.

ant arsonists A 2009 house fire in Daytona Beach, Florida, was started by ants. Dozens of carpenter ants had built their nest around an electrical box and, when the insects came in contact with the live wiring, they ignited. The resulting flames burst out of the box, set fire to an adjacent desk and then spread to the rest of the house.

dead candidate Carl Robin Geary Sr. was elected mayor of Tracy City, Tennessee, on April 13, 2010, several weeks after he had died.

parallel lives Identical twins Jim Lewis and Jim Springer from Ohio were separated a month after birth, then reunited at age 39. Both had divorced a Linda, married a Betty, had sons named James, driven blue Chevrolets and owned dogs named Toy.

lennon's toilet A toilet once owned by Beatle John Lennon was sold for the grand sum of $14,740 in 2010. The builder who had removed the lavatory from Lennon's Berkshire, England, home in 1971 kept it in his shed for almost 40 years.

granny auction Ten-year-old Zoe Pemberton of Essex, England, put her grandmother Marion Goodall up for sale on eBay in 2009, describing her as "cuddly" but "'annoying." Although the listing was meant as a joke, bidding for the granny reached $30,000 before the auction website took it down.

soap drama A wife from Pune, Maharashtra, India, divorced her husband in August 2009 on the grounds that his refusal to allow her to watch her favorite soap operas on TV amounted to a form of domestic cruelty.

Long Hair

▶ When Tran Van Hay from Vietnam died in February 2010 his hair measured 22 ft (6.7 m) in length and weighed more than 23 lb (10.5 kg). He had not cut his hair for 50 years.

▶ Sardar Pishora Singh from India spent eight years cultivating a 3½-in-long (9-cm) eyebrow hair.

▶ When measured in 2004, Chinese Xie Quiping's hair measured 18 ft (5.5 m) in length. It had been growing for over 30 years without a trim.

▶ Justin Shaw from Miami has hair on his arms that measures 5¾ in (14.6 cm) in length.

▶ Brian Peterkin-Vertanesian from Washington, D.C., has a bizarre single eyebrow hair that has grown to more than 6 in (15 cm) in length.

▶ When Wesley Pemberton of Texas measured his leg hair in 2007, one of them was 6½ in (16.5 cm) long.

▶ Badamsinh Juwansinh Gurjar grew his mustache for 22 years, until it reached a length of 12½ ft (3.8 m).

▶ Norway's Hans Langseth died in 1927 with a beard that measured 17½ ft (5.3 m).

Ear Wig

Radhakant Bajpai has a striking claim to fame: magnificent ear tufts that are longer than the hair on most men's heads, and probably the longest ear hair in the world. When Radhakant's hair was officially measured last, it stretched 5.2 in (13.2 cm), but since then it has more than doubled to a reported 11 in (28 cm). Although some think that his extreme ear hair is odd, Radhakant is very proud of his achievement.

Tattooed Ladies

The tattooed lady was an astonishing and beautiful addition to the circus sideshows, dime museums and carnivals that were found in North America and Europe in the late 19th century. They featured in such shows until the late 20th century, when the last tattooed lady retired, aged 80, in 1995.

TRIBAL CUSTOM

The outlandish stories of Nora Hildebrandt and Irene Woodward (see far right) were perhaps based on the true tale of Olive Oatman. In 1850, as she traveled with her family in a wagon train, they were attacked by Yavapai Indians. She and her sister were the only ones to survive and were sold to the Mojave tribe, who treated Olive kindly but tattooed her chin in keeping with tribal custom. Olive was content with her captors and was reluctant to leave the Mojave tribe when she was "rescued" two years later.

Olive Oatman

Betty Broadbent

TATTOO BARGAIN

As a young girl, Lady Viola had made an agreement with her family that if she trained as a nurse she could do anything she liked afterward. Once qualified, she kept them to their word and got her first tattoo. Often billed as "The Most Beautiful Tattooed Woman in the World," Lady Viola's tattoos included the portraits of six U.S. presidents across her chest. The Capitol decorated her back, the Statue of Liberty and Rock of Ages her legs. During the outdoor season in the 1930s, she worked with the Ringling Brothers Circus, while winter months found her in dime museums, such as Gorman's in Philadelphia. She was still working at the age of 73.

Lady Viola

DISOWNED

Betty was born in 1909. During a girls' weekend in Atlantic City, New Jersey, she got a small tattoo and, as a result, her family disowned her. She claimed she had no other choice but to get more tattoos and make a career out of them. Betty worked with many circuses and was an attraction at the 1939 New York World's Fair with the "John Hix Strange as it Seems" sideshow.

INK REPELLANT

One of the first Western women to be significantly tattooed was Irene Woodward. On her debut in 1882, she scandalized the public with her tattoos, which had previously only been seen on sailors. Inked by her father, Irene maintained (probably not truthfully) that he did it to protect her from being captured by American Indians. Described on one show billboard as "A pretty picturesque specimen of punctured purity," she was a shy and dignified performer.

Irene Woodward

SHOCKING STORY

Every great tattooed lady had a sensational story, and Nora Hildebrandt dramatically claimed that she'd been forcibly tattooed by American Indians while tied to a tree for a year. She even said that Sitting Bull was involved in the murky affair. The truth was a little less scandalous—Nora's father tattooed soldiers fighting in the Civil War and used to practice his designs on his daughter. By the time she began to exhibit herself in 1882, she had 365 tattoos.

Nora Hildebrandt

MARRIAGE OF EQUALS

One night in July 1885, the audience at the Sells Brothers Circus in Burlington, Iowa, got a surprise. During the performance, tattooed Frank de Burgh came into the ring bare-chested to marry Emma Kohl, who wore a revealing costume that showed off her own wonderful designs.

Emma de Burgh

SNAKE CHARMER

In the late 19th and early 20th century, it was fashionable for aristocrats, including women, to be tattooed. Lady Randolph Churchill, Winston Churchill's mother, had a snake tattooed on her wrist. Tattoos then were very expensive. Later, as costs came down, tattooing was adopted by the lower classes and the practice fell out of favor with the social élite.

Nose for Trouble

An anti-landmine organization based in Belgium uses African giant pouched rats to sniff out deadly landmines in Mozambique and Tanzania. The rats' relatively light weight means they are unlikely to explode the mines, even when scratching at the ground to indicate their whereabouts. These super rats, trained with food rewards, can also smell the life-threatening disease tuberculosis, analyzing samples more than 50 times quicker than a laboratory scientist.

surprise visit After nine-year-old Beatrice Delap wrote to Captain Jack Sparrow—Johnny Depp's character in the *Pirates of the Caribbean* movies—asking for help with an uprising against teachers at her school in Greenwich, London, Depp responded by turning up at the school in full pirate costume. The Hollywood star was in the area filming the fourth movie in the series in October 2010 and gave the school 10 minutes' notice that he was on his way.

deadly shock A 70-year-old Indian man was so shocked to receive a bogus receipt for his own cremation service that he suffered a fatal heart attack. Horrified to read that he had supposedly been cremated the week before, dairy farmer Frail Than Singh collapsed with chest pains—and his body was subsequently delivered to the same crematorium in Ghaziabad and given the same serial number, 89, as listed on the fake letter.

unlucky number Superstitious phone company bosses in Bulgaria suspended a jinxed cell phone number—0888 888 888—in 2010 after all three customers to whom it had been assigned over the previous ten years suffered untimely deaths.

identical couples Identical twin brothers married identical twin sisters in a joint wedding ceremony in China. Grooms Yang Kang and Yang Jian sported different haircuts for the ceremony so that people could tell them apart, while brides Zhang Lanxiang and Jiang Juxiang wore differently colored dresses.

ghostly sale Two vials said to contain the spirits of ghosts exorcised from a house in Christchurch, New Zealand, were sold on an online auction site for more than $1,500 in March 2010. The sales pitch claimed that the "holy water" in the vials had dulled the spirits' energy and put them to sleep. To revive them, the buyer would need to pour the contents into a dish and let them "evaporate into your house." The seller, Avie Woodbury, said that once an exorcist's fee had been deducted, the proceeds of the spirit sale would go to an animal welfare group.

sold soul More than 7,000 online shoppers unwittingly agreed to sell their souls in 2010, thanks to a clause in the terms and conditions of a British computer-game retailer. As an April Fool's Day joke to highlight the fact that online shoppers do not read the small print, GameStation added a clause to its contract granting it a "non transferable option to claim, for now and for ever more, your immortal soul."

lucky seven On March 31, 2010, the four-number state lottery in Pennsylvania came up 7-7-7-7 and had a $7.77 million payout!

DEAD RINGER

Biker David Morales Colón of San Juan, Puerto Rico, became a dead ringer for his idol Meat Loaf by attending his own funeral in 2010 on the back of his beloved Honda motorcycle. So that friends could pay their respects at his wake, undertakers mounted his embalmed body carefully on the machine, hiding a series of body braces beneath his clothes and covering his eyes with wraparound sunglasses.

ruff justice In Athens, Georgia, a woman scared off a would-be burglar by acting like a dog. Police said she got on the floor and began scratching at the door and acting like a large dog when the intruder tried turning the door knob—he then ran away.

kept corpses Jean Stevens of Bradford County, Pennsylvania, lived with the corpse of her dead husband for ten years and with the body of her dead twin sister for almost a year. After they died, she had their embalmed bodies dug up and stored at her house. She maintained the immaculately dressed corpses as best she could, spraying sister June with expensive perfume and keeping her on a couch in a spare room while husband James rested on a couch in the garage.

frustrated caller A woman from Clarksville, Tennessee, was arrested in 2009 after she kept calling 911 to complain that a man refused to marry her.

OFF ROAD

Lin Su from China drove his brand new Subaru SUV 100 ft (30 m) into the sea from Sanya beach, Hainan Province, in 2010, before getting out and leaving his vehicle in the waves. He announced that the car was no longer needed, and that he had abandoned it as an offering to the Chinese dragon water god, to ask for respite for recent severe flooding. The Subaru was eventually salvaged from the sea by the police.

confused clergy Two female clerics at the same church in Cambridgeshire, England, share the same three names— Rhiannon Elizabeth Jones. Both are also graduates of the same college.

antique gown When three-month-old George Parfitt was baptized in Devon, England, in 2009, he wore the same antique christening gown that had been used by 20 members of his family since it was made by his great-great-great-grandmother in 1884.

lung stolen Organizers offered $2,000 for the return of a left lung that was stolen from a traveling exhibition of human cadavers in Peru in 2009.

prize catch Barbara and Dennis Gregory of Johannesburg, South Africa, lost their camera when it dropped into the sea from the *Queen Mary 2* cruise ship en route from New York to Southampton in 2008. Sixteen months later, Spanish fisherman Benito Estevez found the camera in his nets and traced the couple after posting the photographs online.

cash stash Four children aged between 10 and 13 who found $20,000 stuffed in a brown envelope on their way to school in Frankfurt, Germany, shared it out among their friends in the playground. After teachers were alerted, police managed to recoup most of the cash.

grim find A Dutch riverboat captain who dropped anchor in the River Danube in Austria had a surprise when he raised it. He hauled up a BMW car—with the dead driver still behind the steering wheel.

prison landing A driver escaping from police officers in Cleveland, Ohio, abandoned his car after a 90-mph (145-km/h) chase and jumped a fence—only to land in the yard of the state women's prison where he was quickly arrested.

all the nines Henry Michael Berendes of Wisconsin was born at 9.09 a.m. on 9–9–09 and weighed 9 lb 9 oz (4.3 kg).

BEARDED MOTHER

Richard Lorenc of Kansas finally tracked down his birth mother in 2010—and discovered that she is a famous bearded lady who as a young girl worked in a circus sideshow. Vivian Wheeler boasts an 11-in-long (28-cm) beard, as a result of inheriting the condition hypertrichosis, also known as werewolf syndrome, which causes the growth of excessive facial hair from an early age.

Jumbo was an African elephant of monumental proportions, and he enjoyed fame on both sides of the Atlantic every bit as huge as his stature. At the end of the 19th century, he drew crowds in the same way that a baseball team would today, won the heart of a queen, and became an advertising superstar, before dying a hero's death.

Jumbomania, as it was called, began in 1861 when the elephant was captured in the French Sudan and then exported to the Jardins des Plantes Zoo in Paris, France. He then moved on to London Zoo, where he became famous for giving rides to visitors. Placed under such unnatural restraints, Jumbo's patience wore thin. The elephant, whose name was based on jumbe, the Swahili word for "chief," became too hot to handle and he was sold to "The Greatest Show on Earth"—the Barnum & Bailey Circus based in the U.S.A. The whole British nation rose up to protest. Crowds converged on the zoo, legal proceedings against the decision began, and Queen Victoria, herself a huge fan, received 100,000 letters appealing for her to intervene. American P.T. Barnum was offered £100,000 in exchange for the precious elephant, but in a moment of huge showbiz drama, the offer was refused. Jumbo was to be shipped out of London for good.

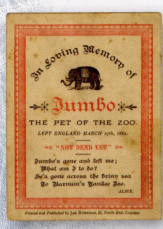

▲ ON LEAVING LONDON ZOO, ALL MANNER OF JUMBO MEMORABILIA APPEARED, EVEN A SPOOF MEMORIAL CARD FROM JUMBO'S "WIFE," ANOTHER ELEPHANT AT THE ZOO.

WHAT HAPPENED TO JUMBO? ▼

After his death, the *New York Times* reported that taxidermists had removed Jumbo's hide—which weighed 1,600 lb (726 kg) and needed 100 tons of salt and 100 lb (45 kg) of elm bark to cure it—and bones. His skeleton was given to New York's Museum of Natural History, and his heart was bought by Cornell University. The rest of his body was cremated. His stuffed hide traveled with the circus until Barnum donated it to Tufts University, near Boston (see left), where Jumbo became the official mascot. He was displayed there until destroyed by a fire in 1975.

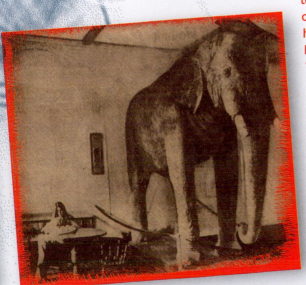

A HEROIC END ▲

On the night of September 15, 1885, the circus was showing in St. Thomas, Ontario. Its 29 elephants had finished their routines and were being led from the big top to their railway cars. Only Jumbo and the smallest elephant, Tom Thumb, remained to take a final bow. Afterward, as they walked back to their carriages, reports say that Jumbo saw Tom Thumb wander onto the railtrack and rushed toward him to lead him to safety. Before he could get there, an unscheduled express train hit Tom. The train derailed, and Jumbo was crushed by the flying wreckage, his skull broken in 100 places. His devoted keeper, Matthew Scott, who had come with Jumbo to the U.S.A. in 1882, stayed with him until he died on the sidings.

www.ripleybooks.com

Fun FUNERALS

- Although Ozella McHargue of St. John, Indiana, died in September 2004, her family gave her a Christmas-themed funeral—with holly, mistletoe and "Rudolph the Red-Nosed Reindeer"—because she loved Christmas so much.

- Ice-cream salesman Derek Greenwood of Rochdale, England, had a funeral cortege of 12 ice-cream vans all playing their jingles on the way to the cemetery.

- For the 2004 funeral of Maine tractor enthusiast Harold Peabody, his son led a procession of antique tractors to the cemetery.

- Arne Shield always wanted a Viking-themed funeral—so his ashes were put on a papier-mâché Viking ship, set ablaze, and cast adrift on Lake Michigan.

- A Queensland, Australia, funeral firm offers the deceased the opportunity to be transported to the cemetery on a Fat Boy Harley-Davidson motorbike hearse.

KICKING THE BUCKET

Gaetano Di Furia's coffin was carried to his funeral in Lincolnshire, England, in the bucket of a JCB digger. His family chose it instead of a traditional hearse because he had always enjoyed driving JCBs at work.

same name Even though he had no connection with the town, Eric Gordon Douglas, of Edinburgh, Scotland, left over $17,000 in his will to Douglas, Isle of Man, simply because it shared his surname.

family church When Daryl McClure married Dean Sutcliffe at St. Michael's and All Angels' Church in Ashton-under-Lyne, Greater Manchester, England, in August 2010, she became the seventh generation of her family to marry at that church. At least 11 members of her family have been married there since 1825, but the connection could date back as far as the 17th century.

long dead Tokyo officials trying to update their list of centenarians in preparation for Japan's Respect for the Elderly Day in September 2010 discovered that the city's "oldest man" had actually died more than 30 years earlier. Police said Sogen Kato, who was born in July 1899 and would therefore have been 111, was discovered lying in his bed in a mummified state, wearing pajamas and covered with a blanket.

you can't hurry love A couple with a combined age of 184 married in England in July 2010. After a four-year courtship, Henry Kerr, 97, tied the knot with 87-year-old Valerie Berkowitz in North London.

body snatchers The New York Police Department towed away an illegally parked funeral van in March 2010—with a corpse inside. Funeral director Paul DeNigris had parked his 2002 Dodge minivan outside the funeral home while he went inside on business, but he returned to find the vehicle—and the body in the back—had been towed to the city pound. He had to rush there to reclaim the corpse and put it on a flight to Miami, where it was headed for cremation.

faint pulse Pronounced dead three hours after suffering a suspected heart attack, Jozef Guzy of Katowice, Poland, was about to be sealed up in a coffin when a funeral director detected a faint pulse. Mr Guzy, 76, was taken to hospital where mystified doctors could find nothing wrong with him, and a few days later he was sent home.

MODEL FATHER

When Paul Challis of Cheshire, England, died aged 38, his widow Maria wanted to keep his memory alive for their two children by creating a life-size cardboard cutout of her late husband to live in the family home. The 6-ft-1-in (1.8-m) 2-D father was a guest at his own funeral and a few weeks later even attended a friend's wedding.

video girlfriend In 2009, a man in Tokyo, Japan, married his animated video-game girlfriend—who exists only in a Nintendo DS game—in a public ceremony complete with a priest, a DJ, and speeches from friends and family.

macabre marriage To mark the end of his bachelor days bridegroom Pat Vincent arrived for his wedding in London, England, in 2009 in a coffin. After marrying Jacqueline Brick, he climbed back into the wooden box and was carried by train to the reception.

age gap A couple who married in Guriceel, Somalia, in 2009 had an age difference of 95 years. Ahmed Muhamed Dore, who claimed to be 112, wed 17-year-old Safia Abdulleh, making him old enough to be her great-great-great grandfather.

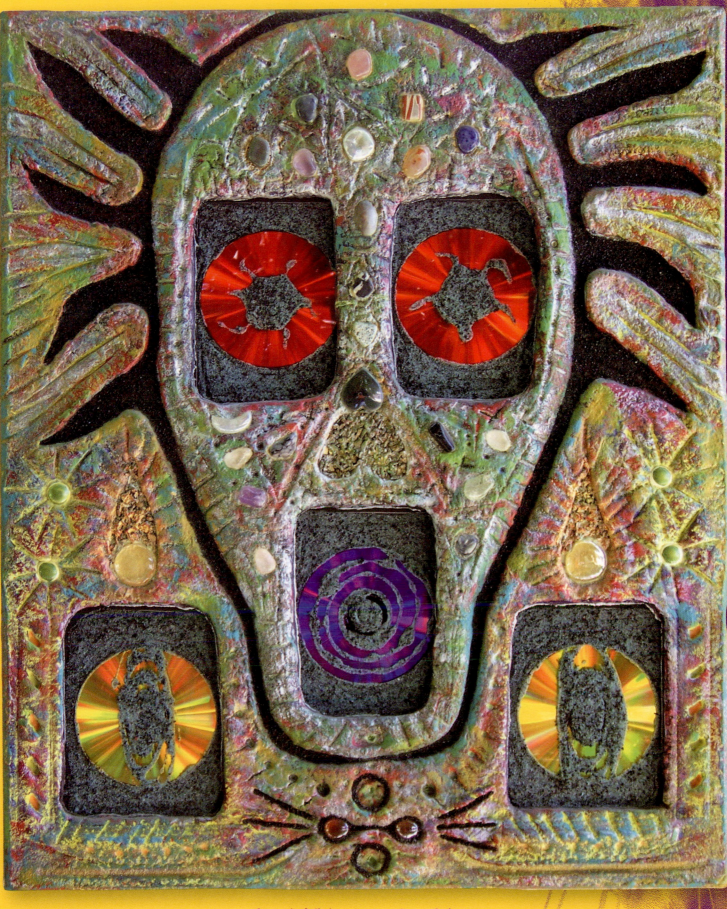

DISH MAN

Artist Daniel Roberto Ortega from San Diego, California, turns the ashes of dead people and pets into cherished works of art. His first human cremation piece included the ashes of his late father. Bereaved relatives or pet owners send the former mortician's assistant ashes and bone fragments, together with a photograph and biography. He mixes the cremated remains into a paste, adds artifacts representing aspects of the subject's life, and then paints the resulting pattern before drying it and applying an acrylic finish.

arts

science

beyond belief

believe it!

world

animals

sports

body

transport

feats

mysteries

food

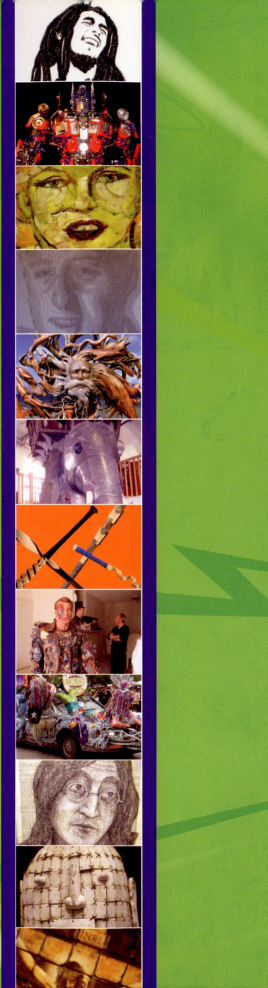

Driftwood Sculpture

Floridian artist Paul Baliker carved this magnificent sculpture from driftwood found at Cedar Key, Florida. *Ocean's 11th Hour* is 8 ft (2.4 m) wide and features 22 endangered ocean creatures encircling Father Time at its center.

Ripley's EXHIBITS

31
32
33
34
35
36
37
38
39
40
41
42
43
44
45
46
47
48
49
50
51
52
53
54
55
56
57
58

Ripley's Believe It or Not!®

March OF THE Lava

The active volcano of Kilauea in Hawaii has been constantly erupting since 1983, and its unstoppable flow of burning lava has devastated hundreds of homes and businesses in its vicinity. Incredibly, it has also gradually extended Hawaii's coastline by an area the size of Washington, D.C.

In 1990, the entire town of Kaimū and part of the town of Kalapana were buried under 50 ft (15 m) of slow-moving lava from Kilauea. Despite the constant threat from the volcano, there are a few Kalapana residents who still choose to live alongside the lava.

Run! These scientists got a little too close when the eruption began in 1983.

sun block When Tambora, a volcano on the island of Sumbawa, Indonesia, erupted in 1815, the 200 million tons of sulfur dioxide gas that were ejected into the atmosphere reduced the amount of sunlight reaching the ground. This caused temperatures to drop dramatically all over the world, resulting in crop failures throughout Europe, and, in 1816, North America's "year without a summer," snow fell in June and New England experienced severe frosts in August.

rapid growth Just a week after it first appeared in a Mexican cornfield in 1943, the volcano Parícutin had reached a height of five stories, and a year later it stood 1,102 ft (336 m) tall.

lava flow Volcanic lava can reach a temperature of 2,300°F (1,250°C) and flow at speeds of up to 62 mph (100 km/h)— that's nearly three times as fast as an Olympic sprinter.

constant eruption Known as the "Lighthouse of the Mediterranean," 3,038-ft-high (926-m) Stromboli, off the coast of Italy, has been erupting almost continuously for over 20,000 years, emitting smoke and lava fragments about every 20 to 40 minutes.

sole survivor The city of St. Pierre (population 30,000) on the French-Caribbean island of Martinique was flattened in 1902 by the eruption of Mount Pelée, leaving just one survivor in the direct path of the volcano— Louis Auguste Cyparis. This man owed his life to the fact that he was being held in a poorly ventilated prison cell. After the disaster he was pardoned and joined the circus, until his death in 1929, as the "Prisoner of St. Pierre," earning a living by locking himself in an exact replica of his cell.

deadly river The 1783 Laki eruption in Iceland sent enough lava spewing from a 15-mi-long (25-km) crack to fill two deep river valleys and cover an area of more than 190 sq mi (500 sq km). The lava river, which was 100 ft (30 m) deep, engulfed villages and released poisonous gases that killed many of those who managed to escape its flow.

nuclear noise The 1883 eruption of Krakatoa, near Java, unleashed the power of 15,000 nuclear bombs with a noise so loud it could be heard nearly 3,100 mi (5,000 km) away. Before the eruption, the island of Krakatoa stood 1,476 ft (450 m) above sea level, but the blast leveled most of the island to 820 ft (250 m) below sea level.

As the lava builds in height, it tears road signs out of the ground before cooling to solid rock.

undersea blast There are at least 1,500 active volcanoes on the surface of the Earth and an estimated 10,000 volcanoes beneath the ocean. When an underwater volcano off the coast of Iceland erupted in 1963, it did so with such force that it punched through the sea and formed the 1-sq-mi (2.7-sq-km) Surtsey Island.

volcano threat Some 500 million people live close to active volcanoes—that's about one in 13 of the world's population. Popocatépetl, nicknamed El Popo, is just 33 mi (53 km) from Mexico City and every year it sends thousands of tons of gas and volcanic ash into the air.

Molten lava oozes toward the house.

The building finally succumbs to the heat.

World
Believe It or Not!®

R **inaccessible inn** Built in the middle of the 17th century, the Old Forge pub on the Knoydart peninsula in Northern Scotland can be reached only by boat or by walking 18 mi (29 km) from the nearest road over hills that rise to 3,500 ft (1,067 m).

R **moon lake** The 39,000-sq-mi (101,000-sq-km) lake on the north pole of Saturn's moon Titan is bigger than Lake Superior and most likely filled with liquid methane and ethane.

R **limestone forest** Water erosion has turned parts of Madagascar's Tsingy de Bemaraha National Park into forests of giant limestone spikes made of fossils and shellfish that died in the sea 200 million years ago.

R **acid drip** Snottites are colonies of bacteria that hang from the ceilings of caves and are similar to stalactites. The bacteria derive their energy from volcanic sulfur compounds and drip sulfuric acid that is as corrosive as battery acid.

R **dam cops** Nevada's Hoover Dam has its own police department whose duties include protecting the dam and safeguarding the lives of visitors and employees.

SPIDER CITY

A gigantic 600-ft-long (183-m) web appeared over the course of two weeks along the banks of a lake in a Texas state park. The unnerving sight at Lake Tawakoni drew more than 3,000 curious visitors on one weekend. Experts believe that the giant web was spun by thousands of spiders from several different species working together to trap as many insects as possible.

R **king carbone** Former flower grower Giorgio Carbone spent nearly 50 years championing the independence of the Italian village of Seborga, which he claimed should be recognized as a separate nation because it had never been formally included in the 19th-century unification of Italy. Proclaiming himself His Tremendousness Giorgio I, he ruled over 360 subjects until his death in 2009. He gave the principality its own currency, stamps, flag and even a Latin motto—*Sub Umbra Sede* ("Sit in the Shade").

R **sewer fat** In a huge underground cleanup of central London in 2010, more than 1,000 tons of putrid fat were removed from sewers—enough fat to fill nine double-decker buses.

DOWN THE DRAIN

This giant chasm in Lake Berryessa, California, is the biggest drain hole in the world, at 30 ft (9 m) in diameter. When the lake reaches capacity, water tips over the lip of the drain and surges down a 700-ft-long (213-m) concrete pipe to exit through the Monticello Dam some 300 ft (91 m) below. Swimming or even boating near the hole is strongly discouraged; in 1997, a swimmer strayed too close and was sucked into the powerful drain. Water gushes through the "glory hole," as locals have named it, at a rate of 362,057 gallons every second—that's enough to fill 15,000 bathtubs. When the lake's level is low, local skateboarders and BMX bikers ride the giant exit pipe.

haunted house Josh Bond of Cuchillo, New Mexico, put his 130-year-old haunted house up for sale on the Internet auction site eBay. The listing offered 1,250 sq ft (115 sq m) of space spread over three bedrooms, an antique wood-burning stove and the spirits of the restless dead.

new ocean A 2005 volcanic eruption caused a 35-mi-long (56-km) rift, 20 ft (6 m) wide in places, to open up in the Ethiopian desert in just days. In 2010, geologists predicted that the rift would slowly become a new ocean, as Africa begins to split in two.

cursing festival Every February, youngsters in the neighboring South Nepalese villages of Parsawa and Laxmipur hurl insults at each other and passersby in a ten-day cursing festival. On the final day of the festival, they set heaps of straw ablaze and celebrate the Hindu festival of Holi, which is marked by raucous "play" fights using powdered colored paints and water.

more singapore Thanks to numerous land reclamation projects, the island city-state of Singapore has 20 percent more land than it did four decades ago.

cargo cult For more than 60 years, villagers on the island of Tanna, Vanuatu, have worshiped "John Frum," an American they believe will one day return with a bounty of cargo. Clan leaders first saw the mysterious figure in the late 1930s and he is said to have appeared before them again during World War II, dressed in white like a Navy seaman. In his honor, the islanders celebrate John Frum Day every February 15.

crystal clouds Noctilucent clouds are formed by ice crystals 50 mi (80 km) above the Earth, on the very edge of space. They reflect sunlight at night, so that they glow.

passion play The village of Oberammergau, Bavaria, Germany, has held a Passion play, depicting the Crucifixion of Jesus, every ten years with few exceptions since 1633, when villagers swore an oath to perform the play every decade after their town was spared from the plague.

tree dwellers Members of the Korowai tribe of Papua New Guinea live in tree houses that are built as high as 150 ft (46 m) off the ground. They reach them by climbing vines or stairs carved into the trunks.

Festival of the Skulls

Every year worshipers in the Bolivian city of La Paz offer gifts of flowers, food and alcohol to the "snub noses"—decorated skulls of their relatives—to thank the dead for protecting the homes of the living. The "Day of the Skulls" festival is part of wider "Day of the Dead" rituals across Latin America, and traditionally entire skeletons were honored in this way.

TAKING A LIBERTY

At 8.45 p.m. on the night of September 22, 2010, New York City photographer Jay Fine took this incredible photo of lightning striking the Statue of Liberty. He spent two hours braving the storm and took more than 80 shots before finally striking lucky. The iconic statue attracts over 600 bolts of lightning each year.

last speaker An ancient dialect called Bo, thought to date back 65,000 years, became extinct in 2010 after Boa Sr., the last person to speak it, died on a remote Indian island. At 85, Boa Sr. was the oldest member of the Great Andamanese Bo tribe before her death in Port Blair, the capital of Andaman and Nicobar Islands.

dual rule The U.S. city of Bristol straddles the borders of Virginia and Tennessee and has two governments, one for each half.

burning river The Cuyahoga River in Ohio was so polluted in the 20th century that it caught fire more than half a dozen times.

volcano video In May 2009, U.S. scientists videotaped an undersea volcanic eruption off the coast of Samoa, 4,000 ft (1,220 m) beneath the surface—the first time a sea floor eruption had been filmed.

rabbit island It cost more than one million dollars to rid the tiny Scottish island of Canna of rats in 2006, and now, less than four years later, it has been overrun with thousands of rabbits—because there are no rats to keep their numbers down! The island's only restaurant has responded by adding a number of rabbit dishes to its menu.

mail boat Since 1916, a boat has been delivering mail to dozens of homes on Lake Geneva, Wisconsin—and because it never stops, teenage carriers are hired to jump off the moving boat, put the mail in mailboxes on the dock, then scurry back on board, hopefully without falling into the lake.

huge hailstone A giant hailstone that fell in Vivian, South Dakota, on the night of July 23, 2010, measured 8 in (20 cm) in diameter, 18½ in (47 cm) in circumference and weighed 1 lb 15 oz (900 g)! This and other ice missiles were so large that some punched holes into roofs big enough for householders to put their arms through, while other hailstones gouged holes in the ground more than an inch deep.

watery grave As drought conditions dried up a pond in Aligarh, Uttar Pradesh, India, in May 2009, 98 human skulls were found at the bottom.

sparsely populated The state of Nevada covers an area about the size of Britain and Ireland combined, but has only 70 towns, whereas the British Isles has more than 40,000.

shifting city The Chilean earthquake of February 27, 2010, moved the city of Concepción about 10 ft (3 m) to the west. The quake was so powerful that it shortened the length of the day by 1.26 microseconds, and even Buenos Aires—840 mi (1,350 km) from Concepción—shifted by 1.5 in (3.8 cm).

Pink Lake

Lake Retba (the Rose Lake), situated 25 mi (40 km) north of Dakar in Senegal, has pink water, which can even turn purple in strong sunshine. The 1-sq-mi (3-sq-km) lake gets its unusual color from unique cyan bacteria in the water and also from its very high salt content.

buried lake At 155 mi (250 km) long and 31 mi (50 km) wide, Lake Vostok is about the same size as Lake Ontario—but lies beneath 2.5 mi (4 km) of Antarctic ice.

ginkgo stink The ginkgo tree species, native to Asia, is so resilient that several survived the atomic bomb blast in Hiroshima, Japan—but its smell is proving its downfall in Iowa City, U.S.A. When the tree drops its seed shells, it produces a sticky mess that smells of rotten eggs, creating a sanitation problem for the city.

floating stump The Old Man of the Lake, a 30-ft-tall (9-m) tree stump, has floated around Crater Lake, Oregon, for more than 100 years. During that time, high winds and waves have caused it to move great distances—in one three-month period of observation in 1938 it traveled more than 62 mi (100 km).

hot water At the bottom of shallow bodies of very salty water, temperatures can reach 176°F (80°C) and stay that way 24 hours a day.

river logjam Over several centuries, a natural logjam in North America's Red River grew to a length of more than 160 mi (256 km). When people began clearing it in the early 1800s, it took 40 years to complete the task.

lightning storm In just one hour on September 9, 2010, Hong Kong was hit by 13,102 lightning strikes. The violent electrical storm contained wind gusts of 62 mph (100 km/h) and caused power cuts that left people trapped in elevators.

widespread snow On February 12, 2010, all of the states in the U.S.A. except Hawaii received some snow.

fog nets Communities in Chile's Atacama Desert use nets to catch the morning fog—the only accessible fresh water in the region. One of the driest places on Earth, it only gets significant rainfall two to four times a century, and in some parts of the desert no rain has ever been recorded.

asteroid blast A 33-ft-wide (10-m) asteroid exploded with the energy of three Hiroshima atom bombs in the atmosphere above Indonesia on October 8, 2009. The asteroid hit the atmosphere at about 45,000 mph (72,000 km/h), causing a blast that was estimated by NASA to be equivalent to 55,000 tons of TNT, and which was heard by monitoring stations 10,000 mi (16,000 km) away. There was no damage on the ground, however, because it occurred at least 9.3 mi (15 km) above the Earth's surface.

life on mars? Huge plumes of methane—a gas that can indicate the presence of living organisms—have been found on the northern side of Mars. The methane may come from live organisms or from the decomposing remains of dead ones.

RIPLEY RESEARCH

In winter, starlings flock in groups of anything from a few thousand to 20 million birds—huge numbers that turn the sky black. Flying at speeds of more than 20 mph (32 km/h) while they search for somewhere safe to roost for the night, they group together to avoid predators such as sparrowhawks and peregrine falcons. In flight, each starling is able to track seven other birds—irrespective of distance—and this is what enables them to maintain such a cohesive overall shape.

STARLING FLOCK

Thousands of starlings in the sky above Taunton in Somerset, England, formed the shape of one giant starling! These acrobatic birds have created many different patterns in the sky, including a rabbit, a rubber duck and a turtle.

Ripley's—
Believe It or Not!®

leaning skyscraper The 530-ft-high (160-m) Capital Gate building in Abu Dhabi leans at an angle of 18 degrees—four times more than Italy's famous Leaning Tower of Pisa. The new 35-story building achieves this angle by using staggered floor plates from the 12th floor up.

towering tent A giant tent 490 ft (150 m) high opened in Astana, Kazakhstan, in 2010. Designed to withstand the nation's extreme variations in temperature, the Khan Shatyr Entertainment Center took four years to build. Made from three layers of transparent plastic, it stands on a 650-ft (200-m) concrete base and houses shops, restaurants, cinemas and even an artificial beach and running track.

security cage After being burgled eight times in six months, 80-year-old Chinese grandmother Ling Wan turned her apartment in Changsha into a giant birdcage. She sealed up the stairs and built an iron cage around the apartment so that the only way in and out is via a ladder that is securely locked on her balcony.

capsule hotels Japan's capsule hotels have rooms that measure roughly 7 x 4 x 3 ft (2.1 x 1.2 x 0.9 m)— not much bigger than a coffin! They are stacked side by side on two levels, with steps providing access to the upper capsule. Some hotels have more than 700 capsules.

light tower The Eiffel Tower in Paris, France, weighs less than a cylinder of air occupying the same dimensions. The force of the wind causes the top of the lightweight metal tower to sway up to 3 in (7.6 cm).

sole occupant Owing to the recession, for three years Les Harrington was the only resident of a 2.4-acre (1-ha) luxury village in Essex, England, that boasted 58 cottages and apartments.

007 tribute For a 2009 New Year's Eve party, James Bond fanatics Simon and Angie Mullane spent four months and $4,500 transforming their Dorset, England, home into a 007 movie set. Guests were greeted at a homemade checkpoint manned by dummies dressed in authentic East German border guard uniforms bought on the Internet, while a Sean Connery mannequin dangled from a real hang glider in the garden.

luxury igloo In January 2010, Jimmy Grey built a luxury, four-room igloo in the yard of his home in Aquilla, Ohio. The igloo had 6-ft-high (1.8-m) ceilings and an entertainment room, complete with cable TV (plugged into an outlet in his garage) and surround-sound stereo.

Container Store

Shoppers visiting the flagship Freitag bag store in Zurich, Switzerland, certainly need a head for heights, as the building is made from a dizzying stack of used steel shipping containers. It consists of 17 containers of which nine form the 85-ft-high (26-m) tower. The recycling theme of the building mirrors the bags sold inside, which are made from such items as old truck tarpaulins, bicycle inner tubes and car seat belts.

TUNNEL VISION

Over a period of four weeks, sculptors Dan Havel and Dean Ruck from Houston, Texas, transformed two connected properties to create a large, tunnel-like vortex, making it look as if the interior of the buildings had exploded. The outer skin of the two houses—made from planks of pine—was peeled off and used to create a 60-ft-long (18-m) spiral, which narrowed to a width of about 2 ft (60 cm) at the far end.

poop light In 2010, a park in Cambridge, Massachusetts, had a street light that was powered by dog poop. Created by artist Matthew Mazzotta, the "Park Spark" project encouraged dog walkers to dump their pets' poop in biodegradable bags and drop it into one of two 500-gal (1,900-l) steel tanks. Microbes in the waste gave off methane gas, which was fed through a second tank to the lamp and burned off.

mecca clock The Royal Mecca Clock, located on a skyscraper in Mecca, Saudi Arabia, has four amazing faces each measuring 151 ft (46 m) in diameter—that's more than six times larger than the faces of London's Big Ben clock. More than 90 million pieces of colored glass mosaic decorate the sides of the clock, which is visible from every part of the city. On special occasions, 16 bands of vertical lights shoot from the clock 6 mi (10 km) into the sky.

lost language The writing on the back of a letter discovered in 2008 by archeologists at a 17th-century dig site reveals a previously unknown language spoken by indigenous peoples in northern Peru. The letter, found under a pile of clay bricks in a collapsed church near Trujillo, shows a column of numbers written in Spanish and translated into a mysterious language that has been extinct for at least 400 years.

home wrecker In February 2010, a man bulldozed his $350,000 Moscow, Ohio, home when a bank claimed it as collateral for outstanding debt.

whistle blowers Officials in Alor Setar, Malaysia, blow whistles loudly at litterbugs in the hope of shaming them into never littering again.

rotating house A rotating house north of Sydney, Australia, guarantees Luke Everingham and his family a different view every time they wake up. The octagonal-shaped house sits on a turntable powered by a small electric motor and controlled by a computer, which allows it to move on demand, completing a full rotation in half an hour.

vast collection The British Museum in London has 80,000 objects on display—but that is only one per cent of its total collection.

railroad room The Washington Hotel in Tokyo, Japan, has created a special room for model railway enthusiasts to sleep in. It includes a grand model of the local area, complete with working railroads. Train lovers can bring their own models or, alternatively, the hotel will happily provide some.

school mascot The mascot of Yuma Union High School in Yuma, Arizona, is a criminal dressed in a prison uniform. It was adopted nearly a century ago after classes were held in a prison building when the original school burned down.

CIGARETTTE HOUSE

A house in Hangzhou, Zhejiang Province, China, is brightly decorated throughout with more than 30,000 empty cigarette packets. The occupant collected them over a period of six years and has even created seats and tables from the empty packs.

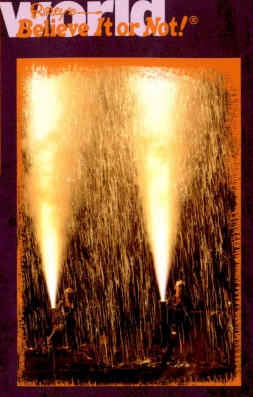

FLAMING FESTIVAL

Each year the city of Toyohashi in Japan hosts an extreme fire festival. Fearless volunteers launch enormous homemade bamboo fireworks, known as *tezutsu hanabi*, which explode inches from their faces. The 300-year-old festival sets off 12,000 fireworks and can draw more than 350 homemade cannons that spew fire up to 65 ft (20 m) into the sky.

luminous beams A mysterious "rain" of vertical luminous beams appeared for nearly an hour in the night sky above Xiamen, China, in July 2010. At first there were just five beams, hanging low in the sky, but soon the number increased to 50. A local observatory confirmed that it was definitely not a meteor shower.

glass elephant Built on top of an old coalminer's washroom, the Glass Elephant in the Maximillianpark, Hamm, Germany—designed in 1984 by artist and architect Horst Rellecke—stands an amazing 115 ft (35 m) tall.

mud volcano A mud volcano in Sidoarjo, East Java, Indonesia, spews enough scalding mud daily to fill 50 Olympic-size swimming pools. Since its first eruption in 2006, it has buried 12 villages.

royal shrine Mehrangarh Fort in Jodhpur, Rajasthan, India, has a shrine bearing carvings of the handprints of royal widows that committed *suttee*—a ceremony in which women were burned alive upon the funeral pyre of their husbands.

falling ice In 2008, a 6-lb (2.7-kg) chunk of ice fell from the sky, crashed through the roof of a home in York Township, Pennsylvania, and hit Mary Ann Foster, who was sleeping, on the head. It turned out to be atmospheric ice, formed when moisture in the atmosphere freezes into small ice balls, which then bump into each other and sometimes attach themselves together to create larger chunks.

underground home Unable to afford a bigger house, retired Chinese miner Chen Xinnian tunneled out a one-bedroom apartment measuring 540-sq-ft (50-sq-m) beneath his existing home in Zhengzhou, Henan Province. The apartment is 20 ft (6 m) underground and is so cool that food does not need to be kept in a refrigerator.

hard wood Ironwood trees—including the black ironwood species that is native to the U.S.A.—have wood so dense that it won't float in water. It sinks instead.

river ritual More than ten million devotees from across the country came to Haridwar, India, in February 2010 for the Kumbh Mela Festival, held here once every 12 years, to bathe in the River Ganges.

desert snow China's largest desert, the Taklamakan, covers approximately 125,000 sq mi (325,000 sq km) and, in January 2008, snow blanketed the entire area for the first time ever.

violent quake On February 7, 1812, a massive earthquake struck near New Madrid, Missouri, and shook so violently that the Mississippi River flowed backward for several hours.

lunar pit Photographs of the Moon taken from the Japanese Kaguya spacecraft revealed a giant pit about 427 ft (130 m) in diameter on the lunar surface—that's large enough to swallow an entire football field.

hanging coffins The Bo people, an ethnic group from China's Sichuan Province that disappeared hundreds of years ago, hung the coffins of their dead on the sides of cliffs. The coffins were lowered on ropes from above to rest on precipices or wooden stakes. Some were hung as high as 425 ft (130 m) above ground, as the belief was that the higher the coffin was placed, the more propitious it was for the dead. The earliest hanging coffins found in the region date back 2,500 years.

CRACKERS

During the Chinese Lantern Festival celebrations in Taiwan, it's customary for onlookers to launch firecrackers at a shirtless man who represents the god of wealth. The more fireworks that hit their intended target, the more successful the firework thrower will become. This dangerous-looking ritual has been performed in the area for over 50 years.

Fire in the Hole

In the middle of a remote desert in Turkmenistan, the Darvaza crater is continually ablaze. The 200-ft-wide (60-m) chasm was created when a sinkhole collapsed under a gas-mining rig in 1971. The miners started a fire to burn off the gas, but it just kept coming and the crater has been burning ever since. If you can stand the heat, it is possible to walk right to the edge of the hole, which is 65 ft (20 m) deep.

Ripley's **world Believe It or Not!**®

Burj Khalifa

The Burj Khalifa, which opened in January 2010, is the tallest structure ever built. At 2,717 ft (828 m) tall, it is more than twice the height of the Empire State Building—the equivalent of 180 giraffes standing on each other's heads. Each of the 160 floors took just three days to build, with the complete tower taking 5½ years to finish, at a cost of $1.5 billion.

▶ The building is designed to minimize twisting in high winds, but it still sways 5 ft (1.5 m) at its highest point. The 656-ft-high (200-m) spire was made from 4,000 tons of steel.

▶ The overall floor area of the building is 3,331,100 sq ft (309,469 sq m), the size of more than 700 basketball courts.

▶ The building is so large that it can take four months for a 30-strong team to clean the surface.

▶ Double-decker elevators ascend at an incredible 40 mph (64 km/h) to the 160th floor. Alternatively, there are 2,909 stairs from the bottom to the top.

▶ The glass on the Burj Khalifa would cover more than 30 football fields.

▶ The tower weighs 551,000 tons when empty. That's about the equivalent of 8,000 U.S. homes piled up on top of each other.

▶ At peak periods the tower uses enough electricity to power almost 20 passenger trains.

▶ Floors 77–108: Over 1,000 apartments. The tower is expected to hold 35,000 people at once—the equivalent of the population of a small town in one building.

▶ The building uses the weight of 26,000 family sedans in reinforced steel, and the exterior stainless-steel cladding weighs as much as 75 Statues of Liberty.

▶ In January 2010, two base jumpers made the highest ever free-fall leap from the 160th floor of the towers, free-falling for 10 seconds before opening their parachutes.

▶ 11,653,840 cubic ft (330,000 cubic m) of concrete were used in the construction of the tower. This is enough to have laid a sidewalk from London to Madrid—a distance of 785 mi (1,263 km).

▶ From the outdoor observation deck on the 124th floor, 1,483 ft (452 m) up, you can see Iran, 50 mi (80 km) away.

▶ Owing to Dubai's desert location, the Burj Khalifa is built to withstand sandstorms and temperatures of up to 118°F (48°C). The building moves up to 3 ft (1 m) as the metal expands in the heat. A water system collects enough condensation from the air conditioning every year to fill 20 Olympic swimming pools.

▶ There is an outside swimming pool on the 76th floor.

The Burj Khalifa is built on desert sand, so the tower's foundations are an incredible 165 ft (50 m) deep, filled with 110,000 tons of concrete. However, by the time of the official opening, the building had already sunk 2.5 in (6.3 cm) into the ground.

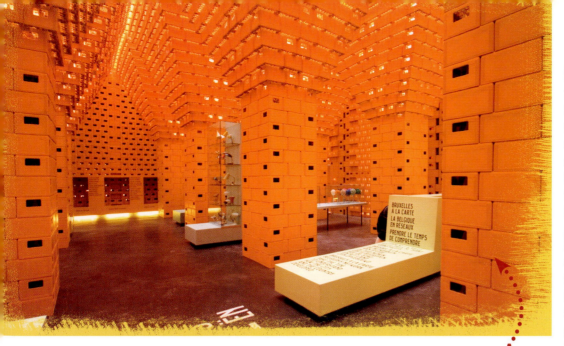

tower highway The 16-story Gate Tower Building in Osaka, Japan, has a highway running through its middle between the fifth and seventh floors. An exit of the Hanshin Expressway passes through as a bridge, held up by supports next to the building. The office block's elevator moves through the vacant floors without stopping between floor four and floor eight.

time for change A giant astronomical clock at Wells Cathedral in Somerset, England, was painstakingly wound by hand for more than 600 years—and from 1919 to 2010 it was operated by five generations of the Fisher family. From 1987, Paul Fisher spent an hour, three times a week, turning the three 550-lb (250-kg) weights about 800 times. The weights were winched up on a pulley system and powered the clock as they descended over the next two days.

gladiator school The University of Regensburg, Germany, has a summer camp in which students live and train like Roman gladiators.

happy harry Harry Hallowes, an Irish tramp who squatted for more than 20 years in one of London's most expensive suburbs, was awarded a plot of land that could be worth up to $6 million. He was given squatters' rights to a patch of land 120 x 60 ft (36 x 18 m) on Hampstead Heath, where he has lived in a tiny shack since 1986.

4,200 clocks The Pentagon, headquarters for the U.S. Department of Defense, has 4,200 wall clocks. Over 200,000 telephone calls are made from the Pentagon every day through phones connected by 100,000 mi (160,000 km) of cable, and although there are 17½ mi (28 km) of corridors, it takes only seven minutes to walk between any two points in the building.

pub crawl Rather than demolish the 124-year-old Birdcage Tavern to make way for a new road tunnel in Auckland, New Zealand, the country's transport authority decided to move the landmark hostelry 130 ft (40 m) up a hill. After the walls were reinforced by inserting carbon-fiber rods, the three-story building was jacked onto concrete rails lubricated with Teflon and liquid silicon, then painstakingly pushed up the hill by hydraulic ramps. The move took two days.

gold machine The Emirates Palace Hotel in Abu Dhabi, U.A.E., has a vending machine that dispenses gold bars—with prices updated to correspond to the world markets every 10 minutes.

rat free A Japanese shipwreck in 1780 inadvertently introduced rats to Rat Island, Alaska, and the island was heavily infested until 2009, when it finally became free of rats again—229 years later.

BEER CRATE HOUSE

Architect Jörn Bihain used 43,000 plastic beer crates to create what he named the "Pavilion of Temporary Happiness," in the grounds of the Atomium building in Brussels, Belgium, in 2008. The vast temporary structure commemorated 50 years since the Atomium was erected at the 1958 Brussels World Fair.

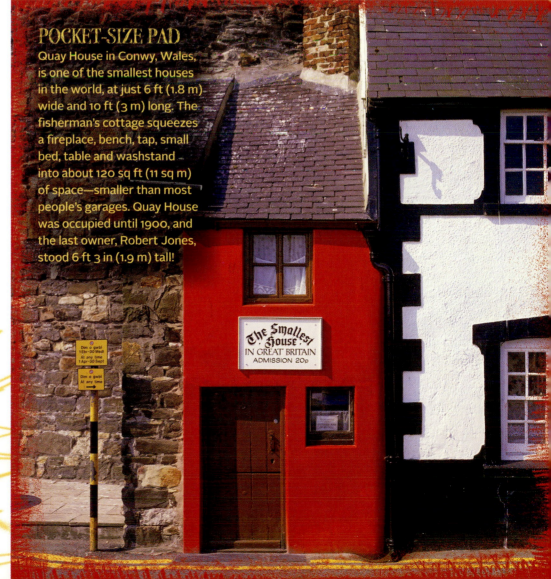

POCKET-SIZE PAD

Quay House in Conwy, Wales, is one of the smallest houses in the world, at just 6 ft (1.8 m) wide and 10 ft (3 m) long. The fisherman's cottage squeezes a fireplace, bench, tap, small bed, table and washstand into about 120 sq ft (11 sq m) of space—smaller than most people's garages. Quay House was occupied until 1900, and the last owner, Robert Jones, stood 6 ft 3 in (1.9 m) tall!

The Smallest House IN GREAT BRITAIN ADMISSION 20p

RIPLEY RESEARCH
The Gobi Desert is expanding into China very rapidly, claiming an area of 3,860 sq mi (10,000 sq km) each year—that's almost four times the size of the state of Rhode Island. The desert is now less than 50 mi (80 km) from Beijing, China, where the largest sandstorms can dump hundreds of thousands of tons of sand on the city.

monster star Scientists from the University of Sheffield, England, have discovered a new star that weighs 265 times the mass of our Sun and is almost 10 million times brighter. The monster star—named R136a1—is believed to be around a million years old and is so bright that if it were located where our Sun is, it would completely fry the Earth within minutes.

disappearing island An island that was at the center of a 30-year dispute between India and Bangladesh disappeared beneath rising seas in 2010. Measuring 2.2 mi (3.5 km) long and 1.9 mi (3 km) wide, uninhabited New Moore Island in the Bay of Bengal had been claimed by both countries—however, environmental experts said that global warming had finally resolved the matter of ownership.

Snow Patrol To prevent bad weather spoiling important Moscow holidays, such as Victory Day and City Day, the Russian Air Force blasts snow clouds from the sky before they can reach the capital. When heavy snow is forecast for a Moscow celebration, airplanes spray liquid nitrogen, silver or cement particles into the cloud mass, forcing the snow to fall on other parts of Russia instead.

painted peak Using water jugs to splash an eco-friendly whitewash onto the rocks, a team of workers in Peru have painted the 15,600-ft-high (4,756-m) Chalon Sombrero mountain white. The peak in the Andes was once home to a sprawling glacier and it is hoped that the newly painted mountain will reflect away sunlight and help cool down the slopes to trigger a re-growth of its ice.

meteorite attack The same house in Gornji Lajici, Bosnia, was hit by meteorites six times in three years between 2007 and 2010. The repeated bombardment of white-hot rocks forced owner Radivoje Lajic to reinforce the roof with a steel girder. He says the chances of being hit by a meteorite once are so small that to be hit six times must mean that he is being targeted by aliens.

windy planet Wind speeds of 4,350 mph (7,000 km/h) were measured in 2010 in the atmosphere of planet HD209458b, which orbits a star in the constellation Pegasus, some 150 light years from Earth. The planet has a temperature of about 1,800°F (1,000°C) on its hot side.

toxic island Owing to the risk of toxic volcanic gases on Miyakejima Island, Japan, residents carry gas masks with them at all times—and sometimes even sleep with them.

fish rain For two days in February 2010, the remote desert town of Lajamanu in Australia's Northern Territory was bombarded with hundreds of small fish falling from rain clouds in the sky—even though it is 326 mi (525 km) from the nearest river.

in the dark A power outage in 2009 left the town of Quipeio, Angola (population 1,000), in the dark for more than two months.

black gold Beverly Hills High School in California has oil wells beneath its grounds, which earn the school hundreds of thousands of dollars in revenue every year.

Sandstorm

A vast sandstorm engulfed the town of Golmud in central China in May 2010 as it roared in from the Gobi Desert at a rate of 70 ft (20 m) a minute. Such storms are increasingly common in this area in springtime and, although often short-lived, they can cause electrical blackouts and cause breathing difficulties in residents.

glowing urine A glowing trail spotted in the night sky above North America in September 2009 was caused by a falling block of astronaut urine. It came from the Space Shuttle *Discovery* which, unable to unload human waste while it was docked to the International Space Station, had then been forced to dump nearly two weeks' worth of waste in one drop.

lightning hotspot An area near the village of Kifuka, in the Democratic Republic of the Congo, has the greatest number of lightning strikes per square kilometer in the world—about 158 a year.

deadly icicles In the winter of 2009 to 2010, Russia's coldest in 30 years, five people were killed and over 150 injured by icicles falling from the rooftops of buildings in St. Petersburg.

space smash A 4.6-billion-year-old meteorite smashed through the windshield of a truck in Grimsby, Ontario, Canada, in September 2009. Minutes beforehand, local astronomers had witnessed a "brilliant fireball," 100 times brighter than a full moon, streaking across the night sky.

starfish graveyard More than 10,000 starfish died on a beach in Norfolk, England, in December 2009 after being washed ashore during a storm. The creatures had gathered in the shallows to feed on mussels, but were swept on to the beach during high tide and quickly perished once they were out of water.

shrinking storm Jupiter's giant storm, the Great Red Spot, shrank by more than 0.6 mi (1 km) per day between 1996 and 2006.

high cloud Morning Glory clouds, which appear regularly over Northern Australia each spring, stand one mile (1.6 km) high and can stretch for hundreds of miles. The clouds are often accompanied by sudden wind squalls and can move at speeds of up to 37 mph (60 km/h).

rocky rain On the distant planet COROT-7b, which is nearly twice the size of Earth, it rains rocks! Scientists from Washington University in St. Louis, Missouri, found that the planet's atmosphere is made up of vaporized rock, and when a weather front moves in, pebbles condense out of the air and rain down on the surface.

bio blitz On a single day in August 2009, a team of 125 scientists and volunteers found more than 1,100 species of life—plants, lichens, mushrooms, bees, bugs, butterflies, worms and bats—in just 2 sq mi (5 sq km) of Yellowstone National Park, including several species not previously known to exist there.

unconquered peak Gangkhar Puensum, a mountain in Bhutan standing 24,836 ft (7,570 m) tall, is the highest unclimbed mountain on the planet.

blown away When Cyclone Olivia hit Australia's Barrow Island in 1996, it created a wind gust of 253 mph (407 km/h).

changing places The moons Janus and Epimetheus are in the same orbit around Saturn, with one a little farther out and slower than the other. The faster moon catches its neighbor every four years and the two moons swap places and the cycle begins again.

single bloom The *Tahina spectabilis* palm tree of Madagascar grows for decades up to a height of more than 50 ft (15 m) before it finally flowers for a single time, then dies.

world
Ripley's Believe It or Not!®

hamster hotel In 2009, a hotel in Nantes, France, offered guests the chance to live like a hamster for a day. Architects Frederic Tabary and Yann Falquerho designed the room to resemble the inside of a hamster's cage, and for $130 a night visitors could feast on hamster grain, get a workout by running in a giant hamster wheel and sleep in piles of hay.

toilet tour German guide Anna Haase runs a different kind of sightseeing tour—instead of showing visitors the traditional sights of Berlin, she takes them on a tour of the city's famous toilets. These range from a historic 19th-century toilet block to a Japanese automatic toilet that costs as much as a small car.

tar lake Covering an area of 100 acres (40 ha) and delving to about 250 ft (80 m) deep at the center, Pitch Lake on the island of Trinidad is filled with liquid asphalt, the result of oil being forced up through the faults on which the lake sits. Despite the highly toxic chemicals, the lake is home to bacterial life.

tunnel network During the Vietnam War (1955–75), Viet Cong soldiers using only hand tools dug a single tunnel network all the way from Saigon to the Cambodian border—a distance of over 150 mi (240 km). They created an underground city with living areas, kitchens, weapons factories and field hospitals, installing large air vents (which were disguised as anthills or termite mounds), baffled vents to dissipate cooking smells, and lethal booby traps. Up to 10,000 people lived underground for years, getting married, giving birth, and only coming out at night to tend to their crops under cover of darkness.

jesus image While looking for holiday destinations on the mapping website Google Earth, Zach Evans from Southampton, England, spotted an outline of the face of Jesus Christ in satellite pictures of a field near Puspokladany, Hungary.

sewage symphony A sewage plant near Berlin, Germany, is breaking down sludge more quickly by playing the music of Mozart to its microbes. The composer's classics are piped in to the plant around the clock via a series of speakers because the sonic patterns of the music help stimulate activity among the tiny organisms, speeding up the breakdown of waste.

bone décor The Sedlec Ossuary in Sedlec, Czech Republic, is a Roman Catholic chapel containing more than 40,000 human skeletons, the bones of which have been arranged to form the chapel's decorations and furnishings.

cave man After living in a 7-ft-wide (2.1-m) cave for 16 years, officials evicted Hilaire Purbrick of Brighton, England, in 2009 because his underground home lacked a second fire exit.

no flow When astronauts cry in space, their tears stay in a ball against their eyes until they are wiped away, because there is no gravity to make them fall naturally.

tough tree A Sabal palm tree with a 6-in-wide (15-cm) hole through its trunk has survived several hurricanes in Estero, Florida.

great hedge The Great Hedge of India was planted across the country by the British in the mid-19th century to prevent salt smuggling. It was a 2,000-mi-long (3,200-km) barrier of living impenetrable thorny hedge that was patrolled by up to 14,000 attendants.

snowball payment For hundreds of years, Scotland's Clan MacIntyre delivered a single snowball in the summer to Clan Campbell as part of a long-standing debt.

WEEPING GLACIER
A human face, appearing to cry, appeared in a glacier in Svalbard, Norway, in 2009. As the ice cap melted, the water poured into the sea, eroding the ice and creating the mysterious shape.

Away from the more organized areas of the catacombs, bones lie scattered in forgotten tunnels.

Secret City

Believe it or not, hidden directly below the busy streets of Paris, France, there are countless secret tunnels and caverns, and millions of human bones.

The city expanded so quickly in the 18th century that cemeteries and mass graves were soon literally overflowing—it is said that the cellar walls of adjoining buildings would ooze with human remains, and disease was rife. To solve the problem, bodies were removed each night and buried in caves adjoining the Parisian sewers. These catacombs—or underground cemeteries—and the tunnels between them were recycled Roman stone quarries that stretched for 500 mi (805 km). It is thought that the bones of six million Parisians are piled up in the catacombs—over half the current live population. It is still possible to wander through the maze of passages that run 65 ft (20 m) below the city streets.

• French resistance troops used the catacombs as a base during World War II, as did occupying German forces. The tunnels also served as air-raid shelters for Parisians seeking refuge from enemy bombing.

• In 1787, the future King Charles X of France held a party in a large cavern deep in the catacombs.

• A gang of thieves was arrested in the catacombs in 1905 after attempting to steal skulls and bones to sell to medical students.

• A team of experts constantly surveys hundreds of miles of the catacombs to prevent any of the caves collapsing, which would potentially cause parts of the city, lying directly above them, to fall into the ground.

• An escaped orangutan perished in the Paris underground tunnels over 200 years ago. Its skeleton is still kept on public display.

• In 1871, 100 rebel soldiers escaped into the catacombs. They got lost in the dark tunnels and were never seen again.

IN THE MEMORY OF PHILIBERT ASPAIRT LOST IN THIS QUARRY ON NOVEMBER 3RD 1793 FOUND ELEVEN YEARS LATER AND BURIED AT THE SAME PLACE ON APRIL 30TH 1804

BURIED ALIVE

In 1793, Philibert Aspairt descended into the catacombs under the hospital where he worked, hoping to steal wine from cellars belonging to monks. His body was found 11 years later, only yards from an exit.

THE GATEWAY TO THE CATACOMBS STATES
"ARRETE! C'EST ICI L'EMPIRE DE LA MORT"
("STOP! HERE IS THE EMPIRE OF DEATH.")

OSSEMENTs DU CIMETIÈRE DES INNOCENTS DÉPOSÉS LE 2 JUILLET 1809

Ripley's Believe It or Not!®

CRAZY KINK

A 7.1-magnitude earthquake near Canterbury, New Zealand, in September 2010 caused rail tracks in the region to buckle alarmingly. A train engineer managed to stop his two engines just 100 ft (30 m) short of this crazy kink. Repairs involved removing the crippled rails and replacing them with new rails that measured about 6½ ft (2 m) shorter than the originals.

ring of fire Three-quarters of the world's active and dormant volcanoes exist within the 25,000-mi (40,000-km) Ring of Fire, situated along the edges of the Pacific Ocean. Among them is Alaska's Mount Redoubt, which erupted in March 2009, sending a plume of smoke nearly 10 mi (16 km) into the air.

shooting spores *Pilobolis* fungi live in animal dung and are less than 0.4 in (1 cm) tall, but they shoot packets of spores up to 6 ft (1.8 m) in the air to reproduce.

meteorite crater Max Rocca, an amateur geologist from Buenos Aires, Argentina, found an ancient meteorite crater 31 mi (50 km) across in the Colombian rainforest—by examining satellite pictures. His interest was aroused after he detected a near-perfect semicircular curve in the Vichada River.

young star On November 7, 2008, 14-year-old amateur astronomer Caroline Moore of Warwick, New York, discovered a supernova—and the exploding star she found (dubbed SN 2008ha) was about 1,000 times dimmer than a typical supernova.

multiple eclipse Solar eclipses are a major phenomenon here on Earth, but the planet Jupiter, because it has 50 confirmed moons, can have multiple eclipses happening simultaneously.

nuclear reactions The Sun's core has enough hydrogen to continue fueling its nuclear reactions for another five billion years.

new cloud Meteorologists believe they have discovered a new type of cloud. The Cloud Appreciation Society has named it *asperatus*, after the Latin word for "rough," on account of its rough and choppy underside. If it becomes officially recognized, it will be the first new cloud type since 1951.

black hole NASA has found a gigantic black hole 100 million times the mass of the Sun, feeding off gas, dust and stars at the center of a galaxy, 50 million light-years away.

toxic lake Argentina's Lake Diamante is filled with thriving bacteria despite being oxygen depleted, hyper-saline, spectacularly toxic and bombarded with ultraviolet radiation.

school climb Erping Village Elementary School in Sichuan Province, China, is built on a platform nearly 10,000 ft (3,050 m) up a remote mountainside. Until 2010, when a new steel stairway was built on the cliff, students could get to school only by climbing a series of rickety, homemade wooden ladders. The school's two teachers had to escort the children up and down the ladders because the journey was so dangerous and exhausting.

DRY RUN

The U.S. side of the mighty Niagara Falls was nearly as dry as a desert for five months in 1969. Engineers stopped the waterfall for the first time in 12,000 years by building a temporary 600-ft-wide (180-m) dam from 27,800 tons of rock and diverting the flow of the Niagara River over the larger Horseshoe Falls on the Canadian side. The work was carried out to remove a large quantity of loose rock from the base of the U.S. side of the Falls, which, if left in place, might eventually prevent the waterfall from flowing at all. To delay the gradual erosion of the U.S. side, faults were also mechanically strengthened. When the task was finished and the dam was blown up, 60,000 gal (227,000 l) of water once again thundered over the U.S. side of the Falls every second.

Ice House

The Cleveland Harbor West Pierhead Lighthouse on the shores of Lake Erie, Ohio, looked more like a fairy-tale castle in December 2010 when it became completely covered in layers of ice. High winds caused waves to crash over the lighthouse, where the water then froze in the bitterly cold temperatures.

phone access Only about one-third of India's population has access to modern sanitation—but nearly half of the population has a cell phone!

narrow house A three-story house in Brighton, East Sussex, England, is just 6 ft (1.8 m) wide. Owners Iain and Rachel Boyle bought the former donkey-cart shed for just $12,000 in 1998, but have turned it into such a stylish home—complete with a mezzanine bedroom—that they now rent it out.

one-way traffic Between 2004 and 2009, nearly 10,000 North Koreans defected to South Korea—while only two people went in the other direction!

hot ash Volcanic avalanches of hot ash, rock fragments and gas—known as pyroclastic flows—can move at 150 mph (240 km/h) and are capable of knocking down and burning everything in their path.

judge numbers India has 11 judges for every million people, while the U.S.A. has 110 per million—ten times as many.

reduced alphabet Rotokas, a language spoken on the island of Bougainville, Papua New Guinea, has only 12 letters in its entire alphabet—they are A, E, G, I, K, O, P, R, S, T, U and V.

boy power China has 32 million more boys under the age of 20 than it has girls.

lonely lighthouse The Stannard Rock lighthouse, Michigan, is the only structure on a large rock 23 mi (37 km) off the coast of Lake Superior. It was staffed for eight decades, until it was finally automated in 1962.

ooh-la-law! In 2010, French politicians finally sought to repeal a 1799 law that banned women in Paris from wearing pants except when riding horses or bicycles.

new ring In 2009, U.S. astronomers discovered a new ring around Saturn that is so large it could hold a billion Earths. The ring is made up of debris from Saturn's distant moon Phoebe.

flood terror In January 2011, torrential rain in the state of Victoria, Australia, killed over 22,000 sheep and 300,000 poultry and led to the formation of an inland lake of floodwater more than 50 mi (80 km) long. Further north in Queensland, the floods submerged an area of land the size of France and Germany combined.

the twitchhiker Paul Smith traveled around the world for free in 30 days relying solely on the goodwill of people using the social networking site Twitter. By accepting free accommodation and transport from his fellow tweeters, he managed to travel from his home in Newcastle upon Tyne, England, to Stewart Island, New Zealand, via Amsterdam, Paris, Frankfurt, New York, Washington, D.C., Chicago, San Francisco, Los Angeles and Auckland.

deadly storm On April 30, 1888, a violent hailstorm dropped ice balls the size of oranges on the city of Moradabad in India, killing 230 people.

Ripley's—
Believe It or Not!®

RIVER RUNS RED

The water rushing over Cameron Falls, Alberta, Canada, turned pinky red following a heavy storm. The phenomenon was caused by high levels of rain that washed a red sediment called argolite from 1,500-million-year-old rocks into the river.

underwater meeting In October 2009, the government of the low-lying islands of the Maldives in the Indian Ocean held an underwater meeting to highlight the dangers of global warming. Dressed in full scuba gear, President Nasheed and ten colleagues took part in the 30-minute meeting at a depth of 20 ft (6 m) off the coast, near the country's capital Malé. Most of the Maldives is barely 3 ft (1 m) above sea level, and scientists fear it could be uninhabitable in fewer than 100 years.

time tunnel Ramchandra Das of Bihar, India, spent 14 years digging a tunnel 33 ft (10 m) long and 13 ft (4 m) wide through a mountain with only a hammer and chisel so that his neighbors could avoid an arduous 4½-mi (7-km) trek around the mountain to work and so that he could park his truck closer to home.

hidden home Sharon Simpson created a luxurious tent home—complete with solar shower and satellite TV—on a busy traffic circle in the center of Derby, England. She lived there unnoticed for five months and moved out only when leaves falling off nearby bushes took away her privacy.

souvenir snowball For more than 30 years, Prena Thomas of Lakeland, Florida, has kept a snowball in her freezer—the souvenir of a rare Florida snowfall. When 2 in (5 cm) of snow fell on the normally balmy state on January 19, 1977, she was so surprised that she collected some of the snow and put it in her freezer.

piping hot The sidewalks of Klamath Falls, Oregon, are kept free from snow and ice—and therefore safe for pedestrians—by hot-water pipes that run underneath them.

new castle Since 1997, some 50 workers in central France have been building a new medieval castle using only the tools and materials that were available in the 13th century. The brainchild of local landowner Michel Guyot, the Château de Guédelon is being built from sandstone, and when it's finished in around 2022 will boast a main tower more than 90 ft (27 m) tall.

BROCKEN SPECTER

Local climbers in the Polish Tatra Mountains believe that if they witness a Brocken Specter—their own giant shadow projected on thick cloud below them—then they are doomed to die on the mountain. The phenomenon is named after the Brocken Mountain in Germany.

jet power The Dubai Fountain, located beside the Burj Khalifa skyscraper in Dubai, is almost 900 ft (275 m) long and can fire jets of water 500 ft (150 m) into the air.

ice man Nicknamed the "Ice man of Ladakh," retired Indian engineer Chewang Norphel has tackled environmental problems by building more than a dozen new glaciers in the Himalayas. He constructs his own glaciers by diverting meltwater through pipes into artificial lakes. Shaded by the mountains and kept in place by dams, the water in the lakes remains frozen until springtime when it melts and feeds the rivers below, which in turn irrigate surrounding farmland. He decided to act after melting glaciers caused floods that destroyed homes and crops.

time travel Russia has no fewer than nine different time zones—and the eastern region of Chukotka (just across the Bering Strait from Alaska) is nine hours ahead of Kaliningrad in the extreme west of the country. There were 11 time zones in Russia until two were scrapped in 2010.

storm hole A Guatemala City clothing factory and an entire traffic intersection were swallowed by a cavernous sinkhole, which suddenly opened up during a tropical storm in 2010. The sinkhole was almost perfectly round and measured 65 ft (20 m) wide and 100 ft (30 m) deep.

purple snow In March 2010, purple snow fell in Stavropol, southern Russia. The unusual coloration was the result of dust from Africa rising in a massive cyclone to layers of the upper atmosphere and then mixing with regular snow clouds over Russia.

Freeze that Fire!

When water was used to put out a burning building in Montreal, Quebec, Canada, in the late 19th century, the air temperature was so cold that the water quickly turned to ice.

St. James Street Fire, Montreal.

science

beyond belief

believe it!

world

animals

sports

body

transport

feats

mysteries

food

arts

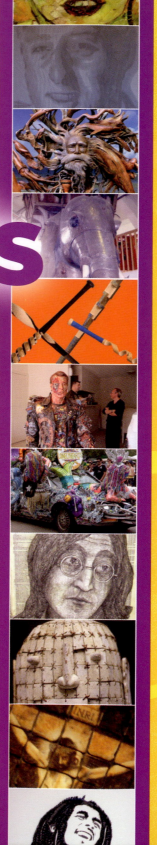

Elephant Armor

Ripley's found this 18th-century Indo-Persian suit of elephant armor, including chain mail eye protectors, in Stratford-upon-Avon, England. Elephants wearing such armor would have carried important warriors into battle in India. This suit would fit an elephant standing over 12 ft (3.6 m) high, and with the howdah—the carriage that sits on the elephant's back—the exhibit is 16 ft (4.9 m) tall overall.

Ripley's EXHIBITS

animals
Ripley's Believe It or Not!®

A Bug's Life

Artist Chris Trueman of Claremont, California, came up with an unusual way to make this portrait of his younger brother dressed up as a cowboy look like an old, yellowed photograph—he used 200,000 dead ants. At first Chris tried to catch the harvester ants himself, but he soon realized that it would take him years to catch enough for the painting. So, he bought the ants live over the Internet and, after killing them, incorporated their bodies into the painting with tweezers and a resin called Galkyd, which has a yellowish color. It took him about two weeks to apply each batch of 40,000 ants to the portrait. The painting was first exhibited at the Alexander Salazar gallery in San Diego, but is now owned by Ripley's and will soon be on display in one of Ripley's 32 museums worldwide.

Ripley's Ask

What is the story behind the original photograph?
I staged and photographed my youngest brother Bryce when he was 6 or 7. I had him dress up in my old cowboy outfit and hold my father's unloaded rifle. He was in my parents' suburban backyard. It was a menacing image, as he pretended to be a cowboy, but was holding a real gun.

Why did you decide to use ants for the image? I was revisiting a specific experience from my childhood. When I was five years old, my younger brother and I attacked an anthill and were bitten by red ants. That was the first time I intentionally tried to harm intelligent life and, more than 25 years later, I decided to return to that experience. Ants ride the line of what we consider intelligent life—if we see them in the kitchen, many of us think little of killing them all. But if we take the time to look at them closely, they are remarkable creatures.

How long did it take to complete? It took several years, not because of the actual labor, but because at one point I started to feel bad about killing all of the ants and I stopped the project for over a year. Then I decided that because I was most of the way done, the first ants would have died in vain if I didn't finish the work, so I decided to continue. It was also quite an expensive work to produce as each shipment of ants would cost $500.

Can you explain how you work the ants into the painting? In the detailed areas I worked with tweezers and would put down a layer of Galkyd resin and then position the ants. In areas where the detail was less specific, I would sprinkle the ants on.

What was the most challenging aspect of this piece of work? The work was challenging from start to finish, finding and acquiring the ants, figuring out what medium to use, getting the right image, working in the details. I also had a hard time carrying through with the project. Some people don't believe me that it was hard to kill them, but I think at that quantity you become hyper-aware of what you are doing.

Red harvester ants are native to the southwestern U.S.A. and are relatively large, measuring $1/2$ in (1.3 cm) long. They are venomous and will give a painful bite!

ESCAPE BID

A Tokyo Zoo worker dressed as an orangutan pretends to make a bid for freedom from his enclosure as part of the zoo's animal escape drill. Staff practice confronting the escapee, as well as surrounding him with nets, before pretending to shoot him with a tranquilizer dart.

monkey smuggler When customs officials at Mexico City International Airport noticed a passenger with a mysterious bulge in his clothing, they discovered that he had 16 live monkeys hidden inside his sweater.

ace ape Following a stint as a painter, where her works fetched up to $3,000, Nonja, an orangutan at Schoenbrunn Zoo, Vienna, Austria, turned her hand to photography. Keepers gave her a digital camera, which issued a fruit treat whenever a picture was taken, and set up a Facebook page for her on which thousands of fans viewed images of her food, her companion and climbing her rope.

eight lives left Sandy LaPierre's pet cat Smoka was found alive—after being buried deep in rubble for 26 days. Sandy had assumed that the cat had perished in the fire that destroyed her apartment in Franklin, Ohio, but almost a month later when demolition crews moved in to tear down what remained of the building, they found Smoka's head sticking out from under 16 ft (5 m) of debris.

parachuting pooches As part of their training, U.S. Army police dogs make parachute jumps, plummeting 12,500 ft (3,800 m) from a military helicopter at speeds of 120 mph (193 km/h).

shrinking sheep A breed of Scottish sheep has shrunk in body size by five percent over the last 24 years—because of climate change. The legs of the Soay sheep have got steadily shorter and their body weight has decreased as milder winters help smaller sheep to survive.

jumping cow Arriving home to find a damaged roof and smashed tiles, a woman in Somerset, England, phoned police to report a burglar—only to discover that the culprit was a cow that had somehow managed to jump 6 ft (1.8 m) up onto the roof.

extra leg Sydney May and Jamison Conley of Big Rapids, Michigan found a five-legged rat while working at a pet store.

bear-faced cheek A 125-lb (57-kg) black bear walked through the automatic doors of a Hayward, Wisconsin, grocery store in October 2009. He climbed 12 ft (3.6 m) onto a shelf in the beer cooler, and sat there happily for an hour before being tranquilized by wildlife authorities.

Lucky Lamb

A lamb in Shangdong Province, China, gets around well and is steady on his feet despite being born with only two legs. Sheep farmer Cui Jinxin would normally have killed the lamb at birth, but she was so moved by his determination to survive that she spared him and kept him as a pet.

spider fossil Scientists discovered a well-preserved, 165-million-year-old spider fossil in Inner Mongolia, China. It closely resembles a family of modern arachnids.

artistic dog Paintings by Sam, a pet dog owned by Mary Stadelbacher of Eastern Shore, Maryland, sell for up to $1,700. Sam has created more than 20 different works of art, each made by holding a tailor-made paintbrush in his mouth.

chimp chefs Chimpanzees in the mountain forests of Guinea, Africa, have been observed fashioning their own cutlery to eat food more comfortably. They have been seen using pieces of stone and wood to chop up their food into bite-size portions—this is the first time such behavior has been witnessed in a nonhuman species.

ticket seller A Chinese zoo recruited a baboon to work as a ticket seller. Tianjin Zoo in Tianjin, northeast China, said the baboon, named Chun Chun, accepted money from visitors, handed them their tickets and gave them their change—but still had to work with a human supervisor because he would only accept 100-yuan banknotes as they are red, his favorite color.

pig voter Pauline Grant took her pig Blossom to her local polling station in East Sussex, England, after the animal was sent a letter by the council asking it to vote at the 2010 general election. Owing to an administrative error, the pig receives several junk letters a month, plus repeated demands for overdue bills.

joyriding bear A bear climbed into an empty car outside a house near Denver, Colorado, honked the horn and knocked the gear shift on the automatic transmission into neutral, sending the vehicle rolling backward 125 ft (38 m) down the driveway into a thicket. The bear was still inside the car when deputies arrived on the scene. They suggested the bear had been attracted by a peanut butter sandwich left on the back seat.

guardian angel Eleven-year-old Austin Forman of Boston Bar, British Columbia, Canada, was saved from a cougar attack by his 18-month-old Golden Retriever, Angel, who leaped in front of the cougar and blocked its path, giving Austin time to escape. Angel survived, too, despite receiving puncture wounds around her head and neck.

DETERMINED DINER

Believe it or not, this incredible photograph shows a python attempting to haul a wallaroo out of a watering hole in Kimberly, Western Australia, in order to eat it. The wallaroo is a marsupial related to the kangaroo and can reach a length of 6½ ft (2 m), while the predator is an olive python, examples of which can stretch over 13 ft (4 m)—making it one of the biggest snakes in Australia.

Snake Stories

- IN 2009, A FAMILY IN KATHERINE, AUSTRALIA, DISCOVERED THAT AN 8-FT (2.5-M) OLIVE PYTHON HAD NOT ONLY EATEN THEIR PET RABBIT OSCAR BUT ALSO TAKEN UP RESIDENCE IN HIS RABBIT HUTCH.

- AN OLIVE PYTHON, MEASURING 6½ FT (2 M) LONG, WAS DISCOVERED TRAPPED INSIDE A WASHING MACHINE IN MIRANDA SEIB'S HOUSE IN BATCHELOR, AUSTRALIA, IN 2008. THE SNAKE HAD SLITHERED UP THROUGH THE PLUMBING.

- THREE MALAYSIAN FISHERMEN GOT MORE THAN THEY BARGAINED FOR WHEN THEY HAULED IN A NET AND DISCOVERED THEY HAD CAUGHT A 22-FT (6.6-M) PYTHON, COMPLETE WITH A 6½-FT-LONG (2-M) MONITOR LIZARD INSIDE ITS STOMACH.

hero hugo A cat saved a neighbor's life by rescuing him from his burning home. Andrew Williams was asleep when the fire broke out in his bungalow in Berkshire, England, and he would almost certainly have died but for his neighbor's cat Hugo coming in through a catflap and waking him by clawing at his face. Hugo and his brother Harvey are regular visitors to the home of cat-lover Mr. Williams.

jack's journey A Whippet-Terrier cross called Jack was reunited with his owners in Sheffield, England, after a marathon 31-hour trek that took him across the M1—one of Britain's busiest expressways—four major roads and miles of treacherous moorland. The dog, who got separated from his owners on a walk, was especially brave considering he suffers from a fear of traffic, and walks with a limp after being knocked down by a truck in 2005.

wasp stings A 53-year-old woman from Attleboro, Massachusetts, survived being stung more than 500 times after falling onto a wasp nest outside her home. Firefighters used a carbon dioxide chemical fire extinguisher to blast the aggressive insects off the woman's body.

plunging parrots A mystery illness caused hundreds of lorikeets to fall out of the sky over Darwin, Northern Territory, Australia, in 2010. The birds appeared groggy and listless, as if they were suffering from a bad hangover, but recovered over a period of a few weeks.

POTTY PLANT

The mountain treeshrew of Malaysia has a handy place to go to the bathroom. There is a particular type of pitcher plant shaped conveniently like a treeshrew-sized toilet bowl that attracts the small creatures with its sweet nectar. And while the shrew feeds on the pitcher's nectar, the plant has been found to extract food of its own from the shrew droppings.

living larders Some members of honeypot ant colonies eat until they are unable to walk. They then become living food storage containers, regurgitating food for their nest mates as needed.

painful ritual To prove they are real men, teenage members of the Setere-Mawe people of Brazil subject themselves to being stung repeatedly by bullet ants, the sting of which is so painful it has been compared to a gunshot wound. For the initiation, boys wear a pair of gloves each laced with hundreds of live bullet ants, stingers pointing inward, for ten minutes—and they must go through this agonizing ritual 20 times.

faithful fowl Of the thousands of pairs of mating swans studied over 40 years at the Wildfowl and Wetlands Trust in Slimbridge, England, only two have ever "divorced" and found new partners.

air miles Arctic terns migrate about 43,000 mi (70,000 km) each year, which, during their lifetime of 30-plus years, works out at a distance equal to three round trips from the Earth to the Moon.

adaptable lungs Elephant seals collapse their lungs before they dive for food and can stay underwater for up to two hours.

population boom Under ideal conditions, a population of five pregnant female German cockroaches could grow to 45 million—in just a year.

Antarctic Escape

In 2005, a lucky gentoo penguin narrowly escaped a pod of hungry killer whales off the coast of Antarctica when it jumped from the water into an inflatable boat full of tourists that happened to be floating nearby. The penguin then swam away, but quickly returned to the boat to escape the lingering whales for a second time.

death dance Male Australian redback spiders, which weigh only one percent as much as females, must dance for well over an hour when approaching a female, otherwise they will be eaten before they can finish mating.

fisherman's luck? While fishing 80 ft (25 m) above the water from a cargo ship off the coast of Queensland, Australia, Filipino engineer Algerico Salise was stung by a tentacle from a thimble-sized irukandji jellyfish. The potentially fatal sting happened when the engineer's face was splashed with seawater that contained the jellyfish as he reeled in a fish. Urgent hospital treatment saved his life.

bird deodorant Scientists in New Zealand are seeking a deodorant for some of the country's smelly birds in a bid to make them less attractive to predators. Unlike their overseas counterparts, birds native to New Zealand did not evolve alongside traditional land mammals, and they emit a strong smell when preening themselves to produce the wax needed to protect their feathers. The kiwi emits a mushroom-like scent, while the kakapo parrot smells like a musty violin case—and these odors attract newly introduced foreign predators.

WHALE WHISPERER

Andrew Armour from the Caribbean island of Dominica is able to pet Scar, a vast sperm whale that he has befriended. The "whale whisperer," as Andrew is known, first encountered Scar as an injured calf ten years ago, and soon struck up a relationship when Scar, now 32 ft (10 m) long, began recognizing his boat. Andrew's unique relationship with Scar and the other whales in his pod gives a rare insight into the behavior of these mysterious animals, which can grow up to 65 ft (20 m) long, weigh more than five school buses and live for 70 years.

lost gator In 2010, a 5-ft-long (1.5-m) freshwater alligator was found swimming with whales 20 mi (32 km) out to sea in the North Atlantic off the coast of Georgia. It is thought the reptile had been washed out to sea from the mouth of the Altamaha River during heavy rains.

thieving spiders Rather than build their own webs, dewdrop spiders steal food or eat the leftovers from the webs of larger spiders.

bifocal bugs The principal eyes of the larvae of the sunburst diving beetle have bifocal lenses. The bifocals have been found in four of the larvae's 12 eyes and allow it to switch its vision from up-close to distance—all the better for seeing and catching its favorite prey, mosquito larvae.

KAMIKAZE CARPENTERS

A species of carpenter ant found in Borneo has a gruesome way to defend its colony. Designated soldier ants wait until a predator is close by and then sacrifice themselves by exploding glands that run along their bodies. These glands contain a sticky poisonous glue that ensnares the would-be invader, but also kills the carpenter ant in the process.

shark rider Attacked by a 14-ft-long (4.3-m) tiger shark off the coast of Hawaii, 68-year-old surfer Jim Rawlinson grabbed its fin, pulled himself on to its back so that he was straddling the shark and then rode it for about 10 seconds. Sliding off the beast's back and watching it swim off, Jim returned to what remained of his board (after the shark had bitten a chunk out of it) and surfed for another 45 minutes before returning to the beach uninjured.

false legs Meadow, a calf born in New Mexico who lost her two back hooves to frostbite, was able to walk again after being fitted with a pair of prosthetic legs by veterinarians at Colorado State University.

boating otter Wolfgang Gettmann of Dusseldorf, Germany, has a pet otter that accompanies him on kayaking trips.

run over twice A Utah railway company worker rescued a stray dog that had been run over by a freight train twice on the same day—April 4, 2010. Although hit by the train's snowplow, the small dog survived and was nursed back to health by Fred Krause and his family.

car wash To raise funds, three African elephants at the Wildlife Safari Park in Winston, Oregon, were taught to wash visitors' cars. For $20 a time, the elephants scrubbed the cars with sponges and rinsed the water off with their trunks.

PAWS FOR THOUGHT

Hope, a cat owned by Nicole Kane from County Carlow, Ireland, has 24 digits—six on each paw.

UNLUCKY PUPPY

Smokey, a 12-week-old Chihuahua puppy from London, Kentucky, survived a freak accident at a garden party that left him with a barbecue fork stuck in his head. Despite having the 3-in-long (8-cm) fork prongs lodged in his brain for three days, veterinarians were eventually able to operate and save Smokey's life, and he was soon back at home with his owners.

Swallowed Diamond When a gem dealer dropped a $20,000 diamond in a Washington, D.C., jewelry shop, it was immediately gobbled up by a dog! The dealer got his diamond back three days later after nature took its course.

vegetarian spider Unlike other spiders, *Bagheera kiplingi*, discovered recently in acacia trees in the forests of Central America, is vegetarian. It is almost exclusively herbivorous, only nibbling on ant larvae for an occasional change of diet. The males are also the only spiders that are known to help the females look after their eggs and young.

hunter hit In January 2010, a 53-year-old hunter in Los Banos, California, was shot and injured by his own dog when it stepped on the trigger of his loaded gun.

sex change A cockerel in Tuscany, Italy, changed sex after a fox raid on his enclosure killed all his hens. Within days of the 2010 raid, the bird that was previously a rooster suddenly started laying eggs and trying to hatch them.

irwin legacy A new, rare species of Australian tree snail has been named *Crikey steveirwini* in honor of the country's famous wildlife advocate, Steve Irwin, who was tragically killed by a stingray barb in 2006.

sixth sense A lost cat found her way to an animal rescue center in Fife, Scotland, despite having a can of cat food stuck on her head! The cat was thought to have been scavenging for food when she came across the discarded can. Unable to see where she was going, she somehow managed to avoid being hit by a car and wandered into the Scottish SPCA unit in Dunfermline where the tin headgear was removed.

frozen journey In January 2010, a dog was rescued by the crew of a Polish ship after being found huddled on an ice floe 15 mi (24 km) out in the Baltic Sea. The shivering dog had floated at least 75 mi (120 km) down the Vistula River and out into the sea as temperatures dipped to below −4°F (−20°C).

domesticated deer Since being abandoned by her mother five years ago, Dillie the deer has shared the Canal Fulton, Ohio, home of the Butera family, where she has learned to turn lights on and off and fetch one of her favorite meals, ice cream, from the refrigerator.

diving dachshund Sergei Gorbunov, a professional diver from Vladivostok, Russia, has taught his pet Dachshund Boniface to scuba dive in a specially built wetsuit, complete with helmet.

high-rise heifer A cow was rescued from the 13th floor of an apartment block in Chelyabinsk, Russia, in 2009. No one knows how it got there, but when fire crews arrived they found it trying to get into an elevator. They decided bring it down the stairs instead.

Alien Monster?

Tomas Rak uses macro photography to make tiny, harmless British jumping spiders look like alien monsters from a horror movie. He scours the country in search of the spiders, which measure just ¼ in (6 mm) long, but can jump six times their own height. Tomas sometimes waits for up to three weeks to get the right shot.

bird slippers A baby African Crowned Crane was able to walk properly after keepers at a wildlife park in Cornwall, England, fitted its feet with a pair of tiny bright green slippers. The hand-reared chick had been born with a slight defect that left it with curled toes, but the slippers helped to straighten them out.

happy reunion Twelve-year-old Brierley Howard was reunited with her pet Labrador dog Iggy in 2010—nearly five years after he vanished. Amazingly, Iggy turned up 130 mi (209 km) away from the family home in Lancashire, England.

bewildered bear An inquisitive black bear in Vermont had a milk can stuck on its head for more than six hours in 2010. After the bear had been seen running around aimlessly, bumping into trees and boulders, rescuers successfully cut the can from the animal's head.

wine buffs Baboons invaded the vineyards in South Africa's Franschhoek Valley in early 2010 and ate thousands of bottles' worth of grapes right from the vines.

fox's revenge A wounded fox turned the tables on a hunter in the Grodno region of Belarus by accidentally putting its paw on the trigger of the hunter's rifle and shooting him. The hunter, who had been trying to finish the animal off with the butt of his rifle, was taken to hospital with a leg wound while the fox made its escape.

slow progress Lottie the tortoise disappeared from her home in Essex, England, in 2008—and was found safe and well nearly two years later, having traveled just 1½ mi (2.4 km).

FEARSOME FURRY FAMILY

In the wild, predators Shere Khan, Baloo and Leo would be mortal enemies, but at the Noah's Ark animal center in Georgia, the 350-lb (159-kg) Bengal tiger, 1,000-lb (454-kg) American black bear and 350-lb (159-kg) African lion live, eat and sleep together in the same custom-built cabin. The three gentle giants, all male, were rescued as a group of cubs in 2001 and their amazing relationship has developed as they've grown up together.

high hound Giant George, a blue Great Dane owned by David Nasser of Tucson, Arizona, stands 43 in (1.1 m) tall from paw to shoulder and weighs 245 lb (111 kg). He eats around 110 lb (50 kg) of food each month and is so tall that some children mistake him for a horse!

bad habits In 2010, Zhora, a chimpanzee at a zoo in Rostov, Russia, was sent to rehab to cure the smoking and beer-drinking habits he had picked up. He used to pester visitors at the zoo for cigarettes and alcohol.

beefy beetles Some male bull-headed dung beetles fight off love rivals by developing the strength to haul loads 1,000 times their own body weight—the equivalent of a human pulling six fully laden double-decker buses.

Lizard Boy

Navratan Harsh is the lizard boy of India, spending most of his time with the creatures, particularly his favorite geckos. In his local village in Rajasthan, he is known as the Gecko King owing to his love for the wild reptiles that he seeks out and trains. Navratan even enjoys the lizards biting his skin, crawling over his face and climbing inside his mouth.

extra teeth Martin Esquivel of Chaparral, New Mexico, owns a Chihuahua dog with two rows of front teeth.

speed queen In 2009, Sarah, a cheetah at the Cincinnati Zoo, Ohio, ran 100 m (109 yards) in 6.13 seconds—three seconds faster than Usain Bolt's best time. Sarah's time was all-the-more impressive because, at eight years old, she is middle-aged in big cat terms.

wasps' nest A giant wasps' nest measuring 6 x 5 ft (1.8 x 1.5 m)—almost as big as a king-size bed—was discovered in the loft of a pub in Southampton, England, in 2010.

rare reptile A two-headed, albino hognose snake was unveiled at a Venice Beach, California, sideshow in June 2010. Todd Ray paid $20,000 for the bizarre serpent—called Lenny and Squiggy—which he saw on an online reptile message board. Each of the snake's heads is fed twice a week.

bravery medal In 2010, a nine-year-old black Labrador dog named Treo was given Britain's Dickin medal—the highest military honor an animal can receive—for his work sniffing out explosives in Afghanistan. The medal has been awarded to more than 60 animals since its inception in 1943, including 32 carrier pigeons, three horses and a cat.

tongue tied Some chameleons have tongues that measure an incredible 4 in (10 cm) longer than their bodies. When at rest, the tongue sits rolled up at the bottom of the chameleon's throat, behind its head.

Artistic Ape For at least 30 minutes a day, Jimmy, a chimpanzee at Niteroi Zoo, Rio de Janeiro, Brazil, dips a brush into plastic paint containers and uses bold, broad strokes to create works of art. His keeper had tried everything to keep him entertained but Jimmy showed little interest in the usual chimp toys until the paints were introduced.

clever crocs Two dwarf crocodiles at an aquarium in Merseyside, England, have been taught to recognize their names. The Cuvier's caiman—named Paleo and Suchus—have also learned to open their mouths when requesting their food.

bat speak Just like people, bats have regional accents. A study of about 30 bat species living in the forests along the coast of New South Wales, Australia, found that their calls varied depending on their location.

MUSCLE HOUND ••••••➤

No, this is not trick photography, and this dog has not been pumping iron. Her oversized muscles are perfectly natural, albeit very unusual. Wendy, from Canada, is a "Bully" whippet, a mutation of the breed that causes muscles to grow to double their normal size, meaning Wendy is twice as heavy as a regular whippet.

Ripley's
Believe It or Not!®
animals

Creepy Cra

They might look like strange extraterrestrial beings, but these creatures, photographed in Germany, are called harvestmen.

Although they look like spiders, harvestmen are actually another type of arachnid, only recently discovered in Europe. Different types of harvestmen often mass together in groups of tens of thousands, moving as one to resemble a single large organism. This seething carpet of tangled legs, which can each span 6 in (15 cm), is thought to deter predators—it also multiplies the effect of the unpleasant odor that harvestmen secrete when under threat.

animals
Believe It or Not!

CLOSE-UPS

Dr. Richard Kirby of the University of Plymouth, England, has taken high-magnification photographs of sea angels (*Clione limacina*), microscopic plankton that live in the ocean around the U.K. Despite their size, they anchor the entire marine food chain by providing fish with food and the world with oxygen, and they also play a key role in the global carbon cycle.

SPOT THE CATERPILLAR

Believe it or not, there's a hungry caterpillar standing on this leaf! The Baron caterpillar—*Euthalia aconthea gurda*—of Southeast Asia is almost invisible against the background of this mango tree leaf in Kuala Lumpur, Malaysia.

doggy stroller Jenny, a pug owned by Ellen Zessin of Portland, Oregon, loves to stand on her hind legs and push her soft toy pugs around the garden in a baby stroller.

underground fish *Stygichthys typhlops*, an extremely rare blind fish that lives underground in Brazil, was recently rediscovered almost 50 years after the only known specimen was collected. Biologists believe that the fish may be a living relict that has survived deep below ground while its relatives above ground became extinct.

stunt baboon Moco, a baboon at China's Changzhou Yancheng Wild Animal Park, is such a talented gymnast and daredevil that he has joined a circus. He specializes in the flying rings but can also perform stunts involving the horizontal bars, parallel bars, balance beam, fire hoops and even bike riding!

draining experience Three weeks after disappearing from Susan Garr's home in Salt Lake City, Utah, Millie, a four-year-old Australian Shepherd mix, was found stuck in a storm drain. Rescue crews freed the dog, whose weight had dropped from 35 lb (16 kg) to 22 lb (10 kg) during her ordeal.

hen-pecked A cockerel and his three hens gained revenge for a series of attacks by killing a young fox that broke into their pen in Essex, England. A table in the corner of the coop had been kicked over, knocking the fox out, allowing Dude the cockerel and hens Izzy, Pongo and Pecky to peck the intruder to death.

giant squid In July 2009, a 19.5-ft-long (6-m) giant squid was caught in the Gulf of Mexico—the first live giant gulf squid captured for more than 50 years.

helpful marking In case anyone has any doubt as to what sort of animal she is, Polly, a tabby kitten owned by Garry and Joan Marsh of Staffordshire, England, has the word "cat" clearly spelled out in her fur on her left side.

long lives Splish and Splash, two goldfish won at a funfair in Gloucestershire, England, by Hayley and Matthew Wright in 1977, were still alive 33 years later.

turtle surprise A monster grouper fish that died after being washed up on a beach in Townsville, Queensland, Australia, was found to have a whole sea turtle inside its stomach. The green turtle had a shell measuring 16 in (40 cm), while the fish, estimated to be 25 years old, weighed a mighty 330 lb (150 kg). Although the cause of the turtle's death was probably the grouper, veterinarians said it was unlikely that the turtle caused the grouper's death.

lucky by name... Lucky, a cat belonging to Keri Hostetler of New York City, survived a 26-story fall from the ledge of her apartment building.

NATURAL HAIRCUT

A manatee living off the coast of Florida receives a natural haircut from dozens of tiny blue gill fish, which crowd around the gentle sea mammal and eat algae, parasites and dead skin off its body.

Herd for Heights

These Alpine ibexes think nothing of climbing the near-vertical face of the Cingino Dam in the Italian Alps to lick minerals from the stones. Alpine ibex have incredible agility and balance, which enable them to cling to the rough rock of the 160-ft-high (49-m) dam with their hooves.

one big eye Although sea urchins don't have actual eyes, they see by using the entire surface of their body as one big eye. They have light-sensitive molecules, mainly in their tube feet and around their spines, and use these to avoid predators or find dark corners to hide in. Therefore, the sea urchins with the most densely packed spines are the ones with the best vision.

greyhound wedding Inseparable greyhounds Pete and Zoe were married in a canine ceremony at an animal shelter in Cambridgeshire, England. The bride wore a specially made dress and afterward she and her spouse devoured a three-tier liver cake. Staff thought a wedding would be a good way to seal the dogs' love for each other and to ensure they would be adopted together.

master of disguise The blue-striped fangblenny, a reef fish found off the coasts of Australia and Indonesia, can change its color at will to mimic other fish so it can get close enough to take a bite.

swallowed soccer ball Bracken, a two-year-old Labrador Retriever owned by John Grant of East Dunbartonshire, Scotland, needed emergency surgery after swallowing a whole toy soccer ball. The deflated ball—measuring 5 in (12 cm) long—had become lodged next to his heart, causing him to cough incessantly.

Scary Ride A tiny kitten that was just a few weeks old survived a 20-mi (32-km) journey in the engine of a car in Perthshire, Scotland. The cat had crawled under the hood of John Kellas' car. When the unsuspecting car-owner heard miaowing the following day, he drove the vehicle to a garage where mechanics found the terrified kitten stuck in a wheel arch. The kitten was given the name Farmer, after the garage that saved it.

ram raid A ram smashed through the glass patio door of a house in Lancashire, England, and ran amok, butting the stove door, knocking over a TV, smashing up furniture and wrecking carpets. It is believed the animal, which had fled from a nearby field and was agitated because of the breeding season, charged at the patio door after seeing his own reflection in the glass.

four wings A guin—a rare hybrid between a chicken and a guinea fowl—was born in Worcestershire, England, in 2010 with four wings. Although the strange chick had two extra wings at the front, it was unable to fly. Lyn Newman had introduced two guinea fowl into her coop to act as lookouts, unaware that they could breed with her hens.

bee careful Ellie, a Labrador Retriever owned by Robert and Sandra Coe of Santee, California, survived after eating a beehive containing pesticides and thousands of dead bees. The inquisitive dog has also eaten wooden toy train tracks and laptop computer keys.

lucky turtle In 1922, a giant turtle amazingly survived being swallowed by a shark. Suffering from nothing worse than cuts and shock, the turtle was rescued and taken to the New York Aquarium where he was named Jonah.

terrible tusks Babirusas, the "deer pigs" of the Indonesian archipelago, have a set of tusks that push straight through their nose and can grow long enough to curve back around and poke a hole in their forehead.

parrot alarm Burglars who broke into a house in London's Docklands in July 2010 were scared off when owner Gennadi Kurkul's green Lory parrot, Kuzya, let out a screech that could be heard several streets away.

bat cave Bracken Cave, near San Antonio, Texas, is home to 20 million bats that feed on more than 100 tons of insects every night.

panda puzzle Giant pandas possess the genes needed to digest meat, but none of the genes required to digest their only significant food source—bamboo.

BEE-STUNG LIPS

The 2010 Clovermead bee beard competition was abuzz with excitement as competitors were loaded with some of the millions of bees kept on the Clovermead farm in Ontario, Canada. A queen bee was attached to each competitor's neck, her smell attracting entire bee colonies. The champion beard belonged to Tibor Szabo, who wore a bee mask that covered his face. He was congratulated by a particularly courageous spectator.

OPEN WIDE

This fearsome deep-sea creature sports what appear to be humanlike teeth at the center of its tentacles. An unusual species of squid, the *Promachoteuthis sulcus* was discovered at a depth of 6,560 ft (2,000 m) in the South Atlantic Ocean. In reality it is far less terrifying than it appears— what look like teeth are fleshy lips around its beak, and this specimen is actually only 1 inch (2.5 cm) long.

ACTUAL SIZE ACTUAL SIZE ACTUAL SIZE ACTUAL SIZE

camel freed Fire crews shoveled mud for several hours to free a 1,500-lb (680-kg) camel that had fallen into an 8-ft-deep (2.4-m) sinkhole in Oregon City, Oregon.

allergic alsatian Joey, a sensitive Alsatian-Collie cross who lives in Hamilton, Scotland, gets a nasty rash if he chases a cat. He is also allergic to running through grass, jumping into water—and all types of food except potatoes and porridge.

beaver attack A large beaver weighing around 42 lb (19 kg) hospitalized fisherman Russ McTindal in 2010 after launching an unprovoked attack on him. The animal swam across Georgia's Chattahoochee River and launched at him, gnawing at his arm while he tried fending it off by hitting it with his fishing rod.

pinocchio frog On a 2008 expedition to West Papua, Indonesia, Australian scientist Paul Oliver found a tree frog with a long nose that points upward while the frog sounds a call.

IDENTITY THEFT

Pet dogs at the Dahe Pet Civilization Park in Zhengzhou, China, went undercover disguised as wild animals in 2010. With the help of some expertly applied paint, a Golden Retriever and a pack of Chow Chows were surprisingly convincing as the endangered tigers and pandas of China.

BEFORE

AFTER

Ripley's Believe It or Not!

full house A 60-year-old woman shared her home in a suburb of Stockholm, Sweden, with her mother, her sister, her son—and 191 cats.

four ears A four-eared kitten was found living at a gas station in Vladivostok, Russia, in 2010. Luntik's second, smaller pair of ears do not have any canals, however, so his hearing is no better than that of the average cat.

fish hospital Patit Paban Halder runs a hospital for pet fish at his home in Chandannagore, West Bengal, India. The fish doctor does his rounds of the 32 aquariums, takes blood samples, checks the patients for fungus and bacteria and even gives them tiny injections.

heat alert A chocolate Labrador trapped in a car in Macungie, Pennsylvania, on a 90°F (32°C) day in July 2010 honked the horn until he was rescued. Max's owner had gone shopping and forgot that the dog was still in the car, but when she heard the sound of the horn she went outside and saw Max sitting in the driver's seat, honking the horn.

ice dive The dagger-shaped bill of the common kingfisher is so sharp that the bird can dive straight through a thin layer of ice to catch fish.

smoking viper Po the viper enjoys two cigarettes a day after picking up on his owner's 20-a-day habit. When Sho Lau of Taipei, Taiwan, casually threw a cigarette butt away, the snake went for it and seemed to enjoy having it in his mouth, subsequently becoming hooked on nicotine.

ankle biters A police officer who was escorting a teenager home following a traffic violation was hospitalized after being attacked by a gang of angry Chihuahuas. The five dogs ran from the boy's home in Fremont, California, and rushed the officer, leaving him with a number of injuries, including bites to his ankle.

ONE EAR

Rabbit breeder Franz-Xaver Noemmer from Egglham, Germany, holds his pet white rabbit born in February 2010 with only one ear.

BAT LINE

More than 130 orphaned bats were wrapped in dusters and hung on clothes lines while they recovered after being rescued from the devastating floods that hit Queensland, Australia, in January 2011. Vulnerable after coming to the ground to feed, the baby bats were picked up by the Australian Bat Clinic and then bottle-fed and housed in the cloths to keep warm.

gallant granny A 60-year-old grandmother fought off an attack from a 5-ft-long (1.5-m) shark by repeatedly punching and kicking it after it had ripped off chunks of her flesh. Paddy Trumbull suffered deep bite wounds and lost a huge amount of blood in the incident, which occurred while she was snorkeling off the coast of Queensland, Australia.

breast-fed calf After a calf's mother died when it was just three days old, Chouthi Bai of Kilchu, Rajasthan, India, saved the young animal's life by breast-feeding it three or four times a day. As well as giving the calf her own milk, Bai supplemented its diet with chapatis and water. Many people in India consider the cow to be a sacred animal.

rooster arrested A rooster was taken into police custody in Benton, Illinois, after it confronted a woman and her child in an aggressive manner. It was the latest in a series of incidents involving the bird, which had been bothering local residents and preventing them from going about their business.

zucchini attack When a 200-lb (91-kg) bear tried to force its way into a house near Frenchtown, Montana, in September 2010, a woman sent the animal fleeing by pelting it with a large zucchini. As the bear stuck its head through the doorway, the woman grabbed a 14-inch-long (35-cm) zucchini from the kitchen counter and hurled the vegetable at the bear, hitting it on the top of its head and causing it to run off.

swallowed glass A German Pointer dog had to undergo emergency surgery after downing a shot of Jägermeister liqueur—and the glass—at a party in Australia. Billy made a full recovery following a three-hour operation to remove the glass from his stomach.

burpless sheep Australian scientists are working on a program to breed sheep that don't burp in a bid to reduce greenhouse gas emissions. The agriculture sector in Australia produces about 16 percent of the country's total emissions, and two-thirds of that figure comes from livestock, chiefly the result of methane being released from the guts of grazing sheep and cattle.

crab crawl The 100 million red crabs living on Christmas Island in the Pacific Ocean walk from the inland forest to the island's shoreline and back in an annual breeding migration. Roads are closed and special tunnels dug as the entire island is turned into a creeping crimson carpet.

food sharing Bonobos—a sister species of chimpanzees—share things just like humans. A scientific study of bonobos in the Democratic Republic of the Congo showed that they voluntarily shared their food with other members of their group, making them the only species known to do this apart from humans.

permanently pregnant European brown hares are capable of being pregnant twice at the same time—and can therefore potentially be permanently pregnant. Researchers in Berlin, Germany, fertilized female hares in late pregnancy and found they became pregnant again about four days before delivery, a phenomenon known as superconception. Simultaneous pregnancies mean the hares can give birth to up to a third more offspring each reproductive season.

clean kitten A kitten had an incredible escape after climbing into a washing machine and going through a full wash cycle. Liz Fear's seven-month-old Burmese cat Suki was soaked, rinsed and then spun dry after climbing in with a load full of dirty clothes at the family home in Melbourne, Australia. Despite her ordeal, Suki was later given a clean bill of health.

cat nap A house fire in Port Townsend, Washington State, was started by a cat that managed to depress a toaster lever while sleeping on top of the toaster oven. The cat, which slept there to avoid the family's dog, escaped unharmed.

Pretty Boy

Despite his bug eyes, crooked mouth and distinctive teeth, Ug, a partially blind two-year-old Pointer cross, proved a big hit with the ladies. April Parker from Doncaster, England, paid £200 ($320) for him— and renamed him Doug—after her two teenage daughters fell in love with him on an animal sanctuary's website.

Ripley's Believe It or Not!

PRETTY IN PINK

This rare, bright pink grasshopper was found in the garden of a house in Havant, England, in July 2010. Grasshoppers are normally green and this one's colorful pigmentation is bad news, as it makes the insect more vulnerable to attack from predators.

RIPLEY RESEARCH

A grasshopper can either be born pink as the result of a genetic mutation or turn pink as an adult because of infection. During the summer, a parasitic worm may enter the insect's body through its food, and this can alter the grasshopper's physiological status and cause it to change color.

dog on wheels Tillman, a five-year-old bulldog owned by Ron Davis of Oxnard, California, can skateboard 325 ft (100 m) in under 20 seconds. The 60-lb (27-kg) dog began skateboarding at the age of nine months and has now mastered it so well that he can do turns and tricks. Tillman has also been trained to surf and snowboard. "He's an adrenaline junkie," says Davis.

yoga bear Santra, a female brown bear at Ahtari Zoo, Finland, performs a 15-minute yoga routine every morning. Visitors watch in amazement as she calmly stretches both legs before balancing on her bottom and pulling them up around her ears.

pigs can fly Scarlet, a Hungarian mangalitza pig, loves to bounce around on a trampoline at her home in Shropshire, England. Gwen Howell discovered her pet's hidden talent after leaving her on the family's trampoline in the garden, and soon the pig was spending 45 minutes a day on it.

swooping hawk Canada Post temporarily suspended mail service to 150 homes in a suburb of Calgary, Alberta, in September 2010 because a hawk repeatedly swooped down from the sky and attacked the postman. The bird was so aggressive it even broke a bike helmet the mail carrier was wearing for protection.

too small An owl chick had an incredible escape at Paignton Zoo, Devon, England, after it fell from its nest and landed right next to an adult lioness. The tawny owls nest in a tree in the lion enclosure, but this one got lucky because the lioness, Indu, decided it was too small to eat.

watch bird Lorenzo the parrot was arrested in Colombia in 2010 for trying to tip off a local drug cartel while police officers carried out an undercover raid. Police suspicions were confirmed when Lorenzo spent the whole of his first morning in custody squawking: "Run, run, you are going to get caught."

Ripley's Help Ripley

When the My Heart's Desire animal rescue group in Louisiana found this abandoned poodle in a ditch, he was in such an unbelievable condition that they named him Ripley, after *Ripley's Believe It or Not!* According to shelter co-director Tracy Lapeyrouse, "You would have never believed there was a dog under there. He didn't even look like a dog. He looked like the elephant man. All you could see was his snout." Ripley's fur was so overgrown and twisted that he couldn't see or even get up and walk.

When *Ripley's Believe It or Not!* heard about Ripley's predicament, they stepped in to help, making a donation to the animal rescue center and pledging to help his new owners cover Ripley's food and grooming expenses. At the shelter, Ripley was shorn of 2 lb 8 oz (1.2 kg) of thick matted hair, given a wash and a feed, and was soon looking like a dog again, ready for adoption.

bionic cat A cat that lost both of his back paws in an accident can run and jump again after being fitted with two bionic legs. The mechanical implants were drilled into Oscar's ankles by British veterinarian Noel Fitzpatrick, and then treated with a substance that allows bone and skin to grow around them. To give Oscar full movement, fake paws were then fitted on "see-saw" joints at the ends of the prosthetics.

mini horse Einstein, a horse born in April 2010 in Barnstead, New Hampshire, weighed just 6 lb (2.7 kg) and stood only 14 in (35 cm) tall at birth.

chewed toe Kiko the Jack Russell terrier saved his owner's life by eating his big toe. After Jerry Douthett of Rockford, Michigan, passed out one day, Kiko sensed an infection festering in his master's right big toe and chewed most of it off. Douthett woke up to find lots of blood and rushed to a nearby hospital where doctors diagnosed him with diabetes with a dangerously high blood-sugar level. A bone infection meant the toe needed to be amputated.

tiny frog A new species of frog found in Borneo measures a tiny 0.4 in (10.2 mm) long as an adult—that's about the size of a fingertip. The micro species *Microhyla nepenthicola*, which was named after a plant that is also found on the island, had been documented before, but scientists had wrongly assumed it was a juvenile of another species of frog instead of an adult in its own right.

SEAGULL SNIPER

A seagull was seen flying around the seaside town of Scarborough, England, for more than a month with a crossbow bolt through its head. Local animal rescue officers tried to catch and treat the bird, but to no avail. The victim of a mystery sniper, the seagull was able to survive because the bolt miraculously missed its brain.

world tour Together with his South African owner Joanne Lefson, Oscar the dog visited five continents and 29 countries in 2009. During their nine-month world tour, Oscar walked on the Great Wall of China, posed beneath the Statue of Liberty and took in such sights as the Eiffel Tower and the Taj Mahal.

swollen tongue Penny, an 18-year-old dog from Paisley, Scotland, nearly suffocated after a freak accident caused her tongue to swell to four times its normal size. She was eating her favorite treat of pig's heart when membrane from the pig's aorta wound itself around the base of her tongue, cutting off the blood supply and causing it to swell up. As she tried to paw her tongue free, blood began gushing from her mouth. Luckily, veterinarian Dermot Mullen managed to separate the aorta from her tongue.

quicker by pigeon A carrier pigeon proved faster than a rural broadband connection in an English race to determine which was more efficient at sending a video from East Yorkshire to Lincolnshire. Rory the pigeon made the journey carrying the five-minute video loaded onto a computer memory card in 80 minutes, reaching his destination while the computer was still uploading the video.

colorful cat Natasha Gregory from Swindon, Wiltshire, England, dyed the white fur of her cat pink with food coloring so that it matched her own pink hair.

BEFORE

AFTER

Toadally Cool

You've heard of leather made from cows, and even alligators and kangaroos, but what about toads? Marino Leather Exports, from Cairns, Australia, has been making bags, purses and hats from giant Cane Toads since 1994. There are now more than 60 items in the range, some using the entire toad, which can grow to a length of 15 in (38 cm)—and that's not counting the legs.

spat out A new species of chameleon was discovered in 2009—inside the mouth of a snake. The tiny lizard, *Kinyongia magomberae*, small enough to sit in the palm of a human hand, was spat out dead by a twig snake that had been disturbed by a scientist in Tanzania's Magombera forest.

croc house Shaun Foggett from Oxford, England, shares his semi-detached house with his fiancée, their three young children and 24 crocodiles and alligators. He spends $12,000 a year feeding the reptiles.

ALIEN FROG

This may look like a weird alien creature, but it is really a close-up of an eye of a sleeping red-eyed tree frog photographed by Igor Siwanowicz at his studio in Munich, Germany. Igor has spent over seven years studying insects and amphibians and has captured such strange natural phenomena as a praying mantis posing like a kung-fu fighter and two stag beetles wrestling.

clever collie Whereas most dogs can recognize about 15 commands, Betsy, a seven-year-old Border Collie in Austria, can recognize more than 340 words. She can also fetch an object after seeing a picture of it.

no hurry At its average speed of 0.03 mph (0.05 km/h), a garden snail would take 34,519 days to slide around the world—that's nearly 95 years.

giant amphibians The giant salamanders of China and Japan can grow to more than 5 ft (1.5 m) in length and live for as long as 50 years.

insect velcro A species of South American ant—*Azteca andreae*—has its own Velcro-like device that enables it to hold on to about 6,000 times its body weight—the equivalent of a domestic cat holding on to a humpback whale. The ant's claws are shaped like hooks and fit neatly into fibrous loops on the undersides of the leaves where it lives, enabling it to trap much bigger insects as prey.

yap nav Taxi driver Andrzej Szymcakowi from Lodz, Poland, decided to switch off his GPS after realizing that Bobo, his Yorkshire Terrier, is better at giving him directions. Bobo, who has traveled in the cab since he was a puppy, knows all the routes. He yaps and raises his right paw to indicate a right turn, lifts his left paw for a left turn, and barks and wags his tail for straight on.

ant invasion Millions of crazy Rasberry ants—a newly recognized species named after Tom Rasberry, an exterminator from Pearland, Texas—have been swarming over the state. They are attracted to electrical equipment and have ruined pumps at sewage pumping stations, fouled computers and gas meters, and caused fire alarms to malfunction. Rasberry had to clear the ants from the Johnson Space Center, one of NASA's major facilities, for fear that they would destroy the computer systems.

gambling rabbit Daisy the pet white rabbit has become a regular at the Prince of Wales pub in Malvern, England, where he enjoys a drink of cider while playing the fruit slot machine. His owner says the rabbit loves the flashing lights.

slippery surface A highway in northern Greece was closed for two hours in May 2010 after millions of frogs emerging from a nearby lake caused three drivers to skid off the road.

goat land-scraping City officials in Chattanooga, Tennessee, use herds of goats to control invasive kudzu vines, one of their favorite foods.

toxic rub Lemurs of Madagascar rub millipedes over their bodies, covering themselves in toxic chemicals, before eating the bugs.

big stink An infestation of stinkbugs hit Brooklyn, New York City, in January 2010. The small, brown flying beetles, which are native to the Far East, emit a smell like rotting cheese when they are squashed or even vacuumed.

golf balls When Chris Morrison from Dunfermline, Scotland, noticed a strange rattling sound coming from the stomach of his black Labrador, Oscar, he took the five-year-old dog to a veterinarian—who removed 13 golf balls from the animal's stomach. One of the balls had been in Oscar's stomach so long that it had turned black and was decomposing.

long journey A cat traveled an amazing 2,000 mi (3,200 km) over a period of two years to track down his owners after they had moved house without him. Ravila Hairova thought her gray cat, Karim, would find the move from Gulistan, Uzbekistan, too traumatic, so she asked neighbors to take him in, but in 2010 she found her bedraggled pet waiting on her doorstep at her new home in Liska, Russia.

in the doghouse A dog named Bruno was found safe and well 20 mi (32 km) away from his home in Gesztered, Hungary, after he and the kennel he was in were sucked into the sky by the wind during a violent storm. Agnes Tamas had chained her pet, whom she has renamed Lucky, to the kennel and could only watch helplessly as the doghouse was lifted up into the air with the animal cowering inside.

PSYCHIC OCTOPUS

Paul the Psychic Octopus became a worldwide celebrity after correctly predicting all of the German national soccer team's results at the 2010 World Cup. Before each match, two plastic boxes, one with a German flag and one with the flag of their opponents, were lowered into his tank at the Oberhausen Sea Life Center in Germany. Each box contained a tasty mussel, and the box that Paul opened first was judged to be the predicted winner. After correctly forecasting five German victories, he upset the nation by choosing Spain to win their semifinal clash. Spain duly defeated Germany, and Paul maintained his 100 percent record by predicting that Spain would beat the Netherlands in the final.

mutant frogs *Riberoria trematodes*, a parasitic flatworm, infects tadpoles, causing them to grow several additional legs as they develop into adult frogs.

defence mechanism In addition to their venomous fangs, many species of tarantula defend themselves with a patch of barbed, inflammatory hairs on their abdomen, which they kick off into the air.

shark fight Fishermen were reeling in a 10-ft-long (3-m) great white shark off the coast of Australia in October 2009 when a second great white—estimated to be 20 ft long (6.1 m)—bit it nearly in half.

sacred whale In February 2010, nearly 10,000 people gathered in a small Vietnam village to pay homage to a 15-ton whale that had died offshore.

croc jailed A cranky crocodile was thrown in jail for three days in 2009 for loitering around the town of Arrkuluk Camp in Australia's Northern Territory. Rangers seized the 6-ft-6-in (2-m) saltwater croc and placed it in a police cell after it had been spotted acting suspiciously near a residential area.

six-legged calf An otherwise healthy calf, born in Leizhou, Guangdong Province, China, in March 2010 had two extra legs—complete with hooves—and a second tail growing out of its back.

water catastrophe An octopus flooded California's Santa Monica Pier Aquarium by swimming to the top of its tank and disassembling the water recycling system's valve—causing around 200 gal (757 l) of seawater to gush on to the floor.

nut house Veined octopuses, found off the coast of Indonesia, occasionally carry empty coconut shells as portable homes.

curious eater Polly, an Australian cattle dog, underwent surgery to remove 1,000 magnets from her stomach. The dog, who took the magnets from the office of her owner, Cathy James of Mickleham, Victoria, had previously swallowed a computer mouse, gardening gloves and several rolls of fax paper.

MATCH	PAUL'S PICK	RESULT	
Germany vs. Australia	Germany	Germany 4	Australia 0
Germany vs. Serbia	Serbia	Serbia 1	Germany 0
Germany vs. Ghana	Germany	Germany 1	Ghana 0
Germany vs. England	Germany	Germany 4	England 1
Germany vs. Argentina	Germany	Germany 4	Argentina 0
Germany vs. Spain	Spain	Spain 1	Germany 0
Germany vs. Uruguay	Germany	Germany 3	Uruguay 2
Netherlands vs. Spain	Spain	Spain 1	Netherlands 0

animals
Ripley's Believe It or Not!®

shell slice When veterinarians at Brazil's Anhembi Morumbi University discovered that a pregnant tortoise was unable to deliver her eggs naturally, they cut away a small square section of her shell with an electric circular saw and safely retrieved the eggs. They then replaced the piece of shell and left the tortoise to recover.

cliff plunge Oscar, a five-year-old Cocker Spaniel owned by Rupert and Emma Brown, survived despite running over the edge of a 120-ft-high (37-m) cliff in Dorset, England. He emerged from his death-defying leap with nothing worse than a slight limp after being rescued from the rocks below by a canoeist who had witnessed the accident.

eggs-hausted A chicken belonging to Chris Schauerman of Honeoye Falls, New York State, laid a 5-oz (140-g) egg (two-and-a-half times normal size), along with five normal eggs—but the stress was so great that the bird died.

splash of color A beluga whale at the Qingdao Polar Ocean World in China paints pictures that sell for hundreds of dollars. Xiao Qiang paints with the brush in his mouth while his keeper holds the paper. Belugas are able to manipulate a brush because they have more soft tissue around their mouth than other whales and the turning of the head to paint is a natural movement that they perform in the wild when cleaning sand from their food.

purr-fect day In an unofficial ceremony, postman Uwe Mitzscherlich, from Possendorf, Germany, "married" his cat Cecilia in May 2010 after being told that the animal did not have long to live. As marrying an animal is illegal in Germany, Uwe paid an actress $395 to officiate at the ceremony.

HUMAN MIMIC

A pet dog in Zhumadian, China, prefers to walk upright on her back legs—just like a human. Owner Zhou Guanshun taught Lu Lu to walk on two legs at the age of four months by holding one of her front paws—and she hasn't stopped since! Even when she rests, Lu Lu chooses to squat on her back legs while keeping her body upright and her front legs off the ground.

royal lineage Queen Elizabeth II has owned more than 30 Corgis, nearly all descended from her first dog, Susan, who died in 1959, and was a gift from her parents on her 18th birthday.

rabbit whisperer Cliff Penrose, of St. Austell, Cornwall, England, has treated hundreds of rabbits with behavioral problems by hypnotizing them. By massaging certain parts of a rabbit's body, particularly the belly, he is able to relax the animal in a matter of seconds. He then "bows" to the rabbit by lowering its head so that it does not feel threatened before shutting its eyelids, leaving it in a trance. He says the rabbit emerges from the trance a happier, more relaxed pet.

mosquito killer In a contest organized by an insect trap company Huang Yuyen, a pig farmer from Taiwan, killed and caught more than four million mosquitoes in a month. Her haul weighed in at just over 3 lb 5 oz (1.5 kg).

sewer snake In 2005, a 10-ft-long (3-m) python lived for three months in a neighborhood sewer system in Manchester, England, moving from toilet to toilet before it was eventually caught.

selective breeding Researchers at Yale University are working to bring back to life a species of giant Galapagos tortoise that became extinct hundreds of years ago. The selective breeding program, based on the D.N.A. of the tortoises' great-great-great-grandchildren, will take over a century to complete owing to the reptiles' long lifespan and the fact that they don't reproduce until they are 20 to 30 years old.

turtle eggs In 2006, scientists in Utah discovered a 75-million-year-old fossil of a pregnant turtle, with a clutch of eggs inside.

CRASH LANDING

A couple on a whale-watching trip off Cape Town, South Africa, got a closer view than they expected when a 40-ton, 33-ft-long (10-m), southern right whale suddenly jumped on to their yacht. After snapping the mast on impact, it thrashed around before sliding back into the water. A species with notoriously bad eyesight, the whale navigates by sound, and as the boat had its engine off, the whale probably hadn't realized it was there.

LIGHTNING STRIKE!

A cow miraculously survived after being struck by lightning near the town of Gladstone in Queensland, Australia. The animal was left with blistering burns and ankle wounds after the bolt apparently entered via its front legs and exited out the back legs. Cows are particularly susceptible to lightning strikes because they graze with all four legs on the ground and eat grass from the ground, where electricity is conducted from the strike.

swooping swan A motorcyclist in Worcestershire, England, suffered a broken collarbone after being knocked off his bike by a low-flying swan.

wire walk At a zoo in Fuzhou, Fujian Province, China, visitors flock in their hundreds to see a goat walking a tightrope while being ridden by a small monkey!

regurgitates fish A performer with the Great Moscow Circus swallows and regurgitates a live fish. Local authorities banned her act when the circus visited Australia in 2010 for being cruel to the fish.

good disguise A zebra's black-and-white stripes are effective camouflage because lions, who hunt them, are colorblind.

uninvited passenger In February 2010, a turkey vulture crashed through the windshield of a helicopter being flown by Paul Appleton over Miami, Florida, and landed on his lap. It sat there until the chopper landed, then flew away. Appleton sustained a scratch to his forehead and the bird partially knocked off his headset and glasses, but luckily it didn't knock his hand from the controls.

▲ The lion approaches the white Toyota and tries the door handle with its teeth.

▲ Curiosity gets the better of the cat as it starts to open the unlocked door.

▲ The lion pulls the door open, leaving the occupants momentarily frozen in fear before they drive off.

ANY CHANCE OF A RIDE?

A couple visiting Lion Safari Park, Johannesburg, South Africa, had the fright of their lives when a 300-lb (136-kg) lion opened the rear door of their car with its teeth. As they drove off, the lion chased the car to the park gates, where a game warden managed to shoo it back into the enclosure.

pet wash Animal owners in Japan can wash their cats and dogs in specially designed washing machines at pet supermarkets. The machines, which are claimed to be entirely safe, give the animals a shampoo, a rinse and a dry in a half-hour cycle for around $10.

bison family The last wild European bison was killed in 1927 and the 3,000 animals alive today are all descendants of 12 captive bison.

secret growl Scientists at San Diego Zoo, California, have discovered that, in addition to the familiar trumpeting call, elephants communicate in a secret language that is largely inaudible to humans. They say two-thirds of the elephants' growling sound is at a frequency too low to be picked up by human ears.

bringing up baby A Chinese woman rocked an abandoned bear cub to sleep each night and put him in diapers so that he didn't soak the wooden box she had made for his bed. Huang Lijie adopted the cub, which she called Hu Niu, at her home in Dandong, Liaoning Province, and fed him milk and baby food four times a day until he was big enough to be released back into the wild.

pink hippo British wildlife photographers Will and Matt Burrard-Lucas were picnicking on the banks of the Mara River in Kenya's Masai Mara game reserve in 2010 when they spotted a pink hippo emerge from the water onto the opposite bank! The animal's rare coloring is a result of leucism, a condition in which pigmentation cells fail to develop properly, causing pale skin color.

missing in action Sabi, a bomb-sniffing dog for the Australian Special Forces in Afghanistan, was lost during a battle in September 2008 and wandered the countryside until an American soldier found her 14 months later.

tortoise masks Following a fire at Poestlingberg Zoo in Linz, Austria, fire crews saved the lives of six giant tortoises by strapping oxygen masks onto their heads. Although the masks were designed for humans, they fitted the 140-lb (63.5-kg) tortoises and prevented them dying from smoke inhalation.

pigeon spy A white pigeon that landed in the Indian state of Punjab, close to the border with Pakistan, was taken to a police station where it was held under armed guard and accused of spying. It had a ring around its foot and a Pakistani phone number and address stamped on its body in red ink, but the message it was suspected of carrying was never found.

TUG-OF-WAR

A thirsty baby elephant that ventured to the edge of a waterhole in South Africa's Kruger National Park got the fright of its life when a lurking crocodile suddenly grabbed it by the trunk. As the croc tried to drag its prey into the water, the baby's distress calls alerted the rest of the herd and they managed to scare off the reptile by trumpeting loudly and stamping their feet.

bear steals teddy A black bear broke into a house in Laconia, New Hampshire, in 2010 and stole a teddy bear! The burglar bear ate a selection of fruit, and drank from the Parkinson family fishbowl, before making off with the stuffed toy after being scared by the sound of the garage door being raised.

lone wolverine Buddy, California's last wolverine, was discovered roaming the Tahoe National Forest in 2008—almost 90 years after the species was declared extinct in the state. He was seen marking his territory to attract a mate—even though the nearest other wolverines are thought to be more than 800 miles (1,290 km) and two states away.

romantic stork A stork named Rodan flies 8,080 mi (13,000 km) each year from South Africa to Brodski Varos, Croatia, to visit his handicapped mate, Malena, who is unable to fly. They have chicks each year and Rodan teaches them to fly. He then takes them with him to South Africa for the winter and returns with them to Malena in the spring.

ink intact Even though it died around 155 million years ago, scientists were still able to extract ink from the fossilized remains of a squid-like creature discovered in a rock in Wiltshire, England. The odds of finding a squid's delicate ink sac intact after so many centuries are put at a billion to one.

rubber crocs Pansteatitis, a disease normally associated with cats, caused the body fat of more than 200 crocodiles in South Africa's Kruger National Park to turn to the consistency of shoe rubber in 2008, eventually killing them. The disease, which results from eating too much rancid fat, led the reptiles' body fat to solidify, leaving them heavy, lethargic and unable to hunt. When their bodies were opened up, the crocodiles' insides were found to be orange, hard and rubbery.

vet trapped A female veterinarian had to be rescued by fire crews in Devon, England, after becoming trapped under a sedated horse. She was called to a farm to treat a horse that was stuck in a fence, but when she sedated it, the animal fell asleep on top of her.

Monster Bug

Giant isopods are a cousin of the humble wood louse and often measure up to 15 in (38 cm) long. They live 1,000–7,000 ft (300–2,100 m) deep in the ocean and can weigh almost 4 lb (1.8 kg). In April 2010, oil workers in the Gulf of Mexico discovered a giant isopod double this size, measuring $2\frac{1}{2}$ ft (76 cm) long!

ACTUAL SIZE!

RIPLEY RESEARCH

The giant isopod is an example of deep-sea gigantism, where creatures living at great depths are often much larger than their shallow-water counterparts. This is thought to be because deep-sea animals need a sturdy body to withstand the colder temperatures and intense pressure in the watery depths, plus the slow pace of life, which delays sexual maturity and results in greater size.

Ripley's
Believe It or Not!®

animals

Balancing Act

A pig in Xincai County, Henan Province, China, can walk despite being born with only its two front legs. Owner Wang Xihai started training the two-legged piglet to walk when it was just a few days old by lifting it up by its tail, and after a month it was able to walk upside down without help. Named by villagers Zhu Jianqiang ("strong-willed pig"), it can balance and move well on its front trotters even though it weighs over 110 lb (50 kg).

R fishing dog A dog in China's Hubei Province has become a local celebrity after taking up fishing. Mr Lin's dog, Ding Ding, had always loved swimming in Donghu Lake, but in 2009 he suddenly started catching live fish. His owner says the dog locates the fish by watching bubbles coming from the water.

R busy beavers A beaver dam in Wood Buffalo National Park, Northern Alberta, Canada, is more than 2,800 ft (850 m) long. The construction, which has been worked on by several generations of beavers since the 1970s, is so big that it can be seen on NASA satellite photographs taken from outer space.

R clever horse Lukas, a 17-year-old thoroughbred horse owned by Karen Murdock of Chino Hills, California, has mastered 35 feats of intelligence—including counting, spelling and shape sorting. He can spell his own name, Karen's name, and that of Karen's husband Doug. Lukas has also learned to nod his head for "yes" and shake it for "no," curtsy, and pretend to be lame.

R rodent infestation Police who raided an apartment in Aachen, Germany, discovered that it was overrun by 300 guinea pigs—and in some rooms the pile of droppings was 4 in (10 cm) high.

R hero buddy Buddy the German Shepherd saved his owner's home by guiding emergency service personnel to the blazing building. The dog was in the Caswell Lakes, Alaska, workshop of his owner, Ben Heinrichs, when a stray spark started a fire. Buddy then ran out, found an Alaskan Trooper at a crossroads and, by running in front of the patrol car, steered him through a series of back roads to the scene of the fire.

R bee line A swarm of 20,000 bees attached themselves to colorful socks and underpants that were hanging on a woman's clothes line in Victoria, Australia.

replica romance Timmy, a 60-year-old tortoise who lives in a sanctuary in Cornwall, England, has fallen in love with a plastic toy tortoise. He never hit it off with other tortoises, but since Tanya the replica was introduced into his enclosure, he has started nuzzling and kissing her and fetching food for her.

thieving octopus Victor Huang was diving off the coast of Wellington, New Zealand, in April 2010 when an octopus suddenly lunged forward and grabbed his bright blue digital camera. The octopus quickly swam off with its booty but, after a five-minute chase, Huang used his speargun to extract the camera from its grasp.

musical fish Diane Rains from Hudson, Wisconsin, owns a goldfish that can play musical instruments, including the glockenspiel and handbells, in perfect time to music playing outside its tank. Jor Jor has been trained to play single notes, chords and four-part harmonies, using its mouth to tug on a string attached to each instrument.

old hen A hen in China is 22 years old—the equivalent of around 400 years in human age. Hens normally live for only seven years, but the bird owned by Yang Shaofu of Yunnan Province has reached three times that age, during which time she has laid over 5,000 eggs.

climbing fish The climbing perch of Africa and Southeast Asia is a fish that can breathe air and use its spiky gill covers and pectoral fins to "walk" on dry land from one body of water to another. It can live out of water for several days and will actually drown if it is held underwater.

drink tears Three species of worker bee drink human tears. Either singly or in groups of up to seven, the bees were observed in Thailand landing on people's lower eyelashes and sipping lachrymation. It is thought the insects have adapted to drink tears as a means of gaining extra protein.

FROGS IN THEIR THROATS

Humans might be divided on eating frog's legs, but they remain very popular in the natural world.

1 Tad and Karen Bacon from Maryland discovered this giant bullfrog snacking on another frog after taking a dip in their swimming pool. Bullfrogs can grow to over 12 in (30 cm) long.

2 Luis Fernando Espin from Ecuador came upon an Amazonian whipsnake slowly devouring a large tree frog. The frog has toxic chemicals in its skin but that didn't prevent the snake from eventually swallowing it whole.

3 A burrowing owl in Florida makes short work of a large frog—legs included.

beyond belief

believe it!

world

animals

sports

body

transport

feats

mysteries

food

arts

science

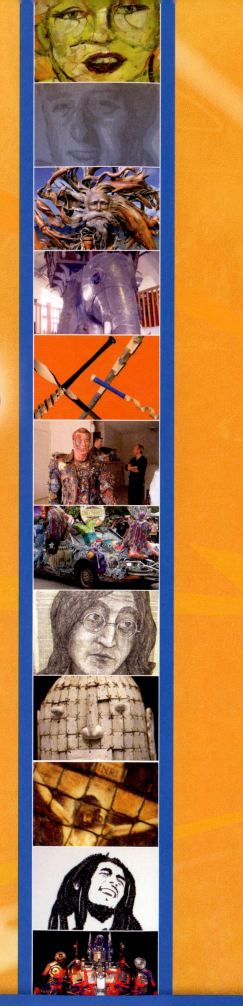

Dutch Baseball

Peter Schuyff takes regular baseball bats and chips away at them until they become elegant pieces of art. The Dutch artist started by carving branches to pass the time in the dark while traveling in Southeast Asia. He moved on to shaping full-size baseball bats when he lived in New York. When a passerby asked what the bats are used for, he replied "Dutch baseball," which became the name of the project. Peter says that his sculptures look like they were made by something between a beaver and a snail!

RIPLEY's EXHIBITS

80
81
82
83
84
85
86
87
88
89
90
91
92
93
94
95
96
97
98
99
100
101
102
103
104
105
106
107

Ripley's Sports
Believe It or Not!®

The modern Olympic Games were established by a Frenchman—Baron de Coubertin—who was inspired by the ancient Greek competition of the same name.

They are hosted by different countries and, with the exception of three cancellations due to world wars (in 1916, 1940 and 1944), have been staged every four years since 1896. Both Summer and Winter Games are held, and today more than 13,000 athletes compete in 400 events representing 35 sports. While every Olympics delivers great tales of sporting prowess, it is perhaps some of the lesser-known tales that are the most remarkable...

THE ANCIENT OLYMPICS

Contested between representatives of several city states and kingdoms, the Ancient Olympics were staged every four years from 776BC until AD393, when Roman Emperor Theodosius banned them on the grounds that they were a pagan ritual. Believe it or not...

- The Emperor Nero of Rome competed in the AD66 Olympics, accompanied by 5,000 bodyguards, and won every event in which he took part.

- All the competitors at the Ancient Olympics were men, and they competed naked.

- Among the more unusual events was a contest for trumpeters.

- Three-time Olympic champions had statues erected in their honor and were offered exemption from taxation.

- Centurions demonstrated their speed and strength in races run in full suits of armor.

- The Pankration, or all-in wrestling, allowed any moves, including strangling your opponent.

- The 2004 Olympic marathon in Athens was raced over the same historic course first run by the messenger Pheidippides in 490BC when he announced the Greek victory over Persia in the Battle of Marathon.

THE EARLY DAYS

big chill The swimming races at the 1896 Athens Olympics were held in the Mediterranean Sea, which was so cold that many competitors, numb from the chill, gave up and had to be rescued by boat.

mystery cox To reduce the weight in their boat, Dutch pair Francois Antoine Brandt and Roelof Klein recruited a young French boy—believed to be about seven years old—to act as their coxswain in the rowing final at the 1900 Paris Olympics. The mystery boy helped them to win the Olympic title but then vanished into thin air and his name was never recorded.

the pits! The track and field events at the 1900 Paris Olympics were staged on rough ground in the Bois de Boulogne—a large park on the edge of the city—where facilities were so basic that the jumpers had to dig their own pits and the obstacles for the men's 400 meters hurdles were 30-ft-long (9-m) telephone poles.

short distance Women were not allowed to compete in track and field events at the Olympics until 1928. However, some collapsed at the end of the 800 meters in that year so they were subsequently banned from running in races beyond 200 meters until 1960.

how far? During the first several modern Olympics, the marathon was an approximate distance. In 1908, the British royal family requested that the marathon start at Windsor Castle so that the royal children could see its start. The distance from Windsor Castle to the Olympic Stadium was 26 miles and 385 yd. In 1924, this distance became the standard length of a marathon.

art prizes No medals were awarded at the 1900 Paris Olympics—winners were given pieces of art instead. At this, the second of the modern Olympics, more athletes than spectators attended the Games.

OLYMPIC ODDITIES

not allowed Harvard University refused to give student James B. Connolly eight weeks' leave of absence in order to compete in the 1896 Olympics in Greece. So he resigned from the university, paid for the voyage himself—and went on to win the triple jump.

wrong anthem At the medal ceremony for the 1964 Tokyo Olympics marathon, won by Abebe Bikila of Ethiopia, the stadium band did not know the Ethiopian national anthem, so they played the Japanese one instead.

first gold India has 17 percent of the world's population, but the country did not win its first individual Olympic title until 2008 when Abhinav Bindra won the 10-meter air rifle shooting event.

bully-off As a reward for winning gold in the women's field hockey tournament at the 1980 Moscow Olympics, every member of the Zimbabwe team was presented with a live ox on their return home.

walk, don't run The three leading competitors in the women's 20-km walk at the 2000 Sydney Olympics were all disqualified for running in the final kilometer, leaving China's Wang Liping to claim an unlikely gold medal.

dirty laundry Competitors at the modern Olympics produce over 2,000,000 lb (907,000 kg) of dirty laundry. A family of four would take an estimated 264 years to get through that much laundry.

nine-hour bout The light-heavyweight Greco-Roman wrestling final at the 1912 Stockholm Olympics between Anders Ahlgren of Sweden and Ivar Böhling of Finland went on for nine hours without a decision being reached. So the judges called it a draw and awarded both men silver medals as neither had defeated his opponent to earn gold.

no gold Long-jumper Robert LeGendre, a 26-year-old graduate from Georgetown University, Washington, D.C., jumped further than anyone else and set a new world record of 25 ft 5½ in (7.76 m) at the 1924 Olympics—but he didn't win a gold medal because he was competing in the pentathlon, where he could finish only third overall.

OLYMPIC HEROES

dislocated arm Konrad von Wangenheim helped Germany's equestrian team to win gold at the 1936 Olympics despite riding with a broken collarbone and his left arm in a sling.

incredible double At the 1924 Paris Olympics, Finland's Paavo Nurmi won the men's 1,500 meters final and then just over an hour later he won the 5,000 meters final, setting Olympic records in both events.

veteran rider At the 2008 Olympics in Beijing, equestrian rider Hiroshi Hoketsu represented Japan at the age of 67. He had also taken part in the Tokyo Olympics—44 years earlier.

heroic horsewoman Despite being paralyzed below the knees after contracting polio, Denmark's Lis Hartel, who had to be helped on and off her horse, won silver medals in the individual dressage event at both the 1952 and 1956 Olympics.

wooden leg American gymnast George Eyser won six medals in one day at the 1904 Olympics in St. Louis, Missouri—three of them gold—despite having a wooden leg. His left leg had been amputated after he was run over by a train. He even won gold in the long horse vault, which he jumped without the help of a springboard.

duck escort Partway through his quarter-final race against Victor Saurin of France at the 1928 Olympics, Australian rower Henry Pearce stopped rowing to allow a family of ducks to pass in single file in front of his boat. He recovered to win the race and later the gold medal, too.

changing hands Hungarian pistol shooter Károly Takács lost his right hand in 1938 when a grenade that he was holding exploded. So he taught himself to shoot left-handed and won a gold medal at the 1948 London Olympics, successfully defending his title four years later in Helsinki.

Sports Ripley's Believe It or Not!®

OLYMPIC HOWLERS

calendar chaos After spending over 16 days at sea, the U.S. team arrived in Athens for the first modern Olympic Games in 1896 believing that they still had 12 days to prepare for the competition. In fact, the Games started the very next day—the Americans had forgotten that Greece still used the Julian calendar and was therefore 12 days in advance.

joined picnic Exhausted by the heat of the 1912 Olympic marathon in Stockholm, Sweden, Japan's Shizo Kanaguri stumbled into the garden of a family who were enjoying a picnic and stayed with them rather than rejoining the race.

lost medal After winning a rowing gold medal at the 1956 Olympics, 18-year-old Russian Vyacheslav Ivanov quickly lost it. He threw the medal into the air in celebration, but it landed in the lake. He dived in but was unable to find it.

hot stuff To prepare himself for the heat of Rome, where he won the 50-km walk at the 1960 Olympics, Britain's Don Thompson kept the heat on at all times in his bathroom for 18 months—and ran up a gas bill of over £9,000. He returned home from his triumph to find that the gas had been cut off.

lost in translation American athlete Loren Murchison was left at the start of the 1920 Olympic men's 100 meters final in Antwerp, Belgium, because he didn't understand French. When the starter said "prêt" ("get set"), Murchison thought that the crouching runners had been told to stand up and was doing so when the starting gun went off.

missing gloves Moments before he was due to fight at the 1992 Barcelona Olympics, Iranian boxer Ali Kazemi was disqualified because he had forgotten his gloves.

feeling crushed Having arrived in Canada in preparation for the 1976 Montreal Olympics, the Czech cycling team lost all of their wheels and spare tires after garbage collectors mistakenly took them away to be crushed.

shot in foot U.S. Lieutenant Sidney Hinds won gold in the free rifle team event at the 1924 Olympics in Paris, shooting a perfect 50—despite having been accidentally shot in the foot partway through the competition when the Belgian rifleman positioned next to him threw his loaded weapon to the ground during an argument with an official.

pot luck Sweden's Svante Rasmuson was set to win the modern pentathlon at the 1984 Olympics until, a few yards from the finish of the cross country, he stumbled over a potted plant, placed there by the Los Angeles organizers to brighten up the course. Italy's Daniele Masala passed him to snatch gold.

UNUSUAL OLYMPIC EVENTS

Vertical rope climb (1896, 1904, 1906, 1924, 1932)
So hard was this event that in 1896 only two of the climbers made it to the top, prompting officials to send the rope back for alterations.

Men's Sailor's 100 meter freestyle (1896)
This event was only open to sailors in the Greek Royal Navy. Only three competitors took place in the event. And the winner was from... Greece!

Long jump for horses (1900)
A horse named *Extra Dry* won at the Paris Olympics with a jump of 20 ft ¼ in (6.1 m)—that's shorter than the men's record in 1901.

Underwater swimming race (1900)
Not the most thrilling visual spectacle, this race was held over 60 meters with competitors being awarded points for each meter swum and time spent underwater.

Pigeon shooting (1900)
Paris 1900 featured the only Olympic event in history at which animals were deliberately harmed—300 live pigeons. Belgium's Leon de Lunden won gold, bagging himself 21 birds.

200m obstacle swimming race (1900)
Held in Paris' River Seine, competitors had to climb over a pole, clamber over a row of boats and then swim under another row of boats.

Pistol dueling (1906)
Participants shot over 20 and 30 meters at mannequins that wore fancy frock coats with bull's-eyes embroidered on the chest.

Tug of war (1900, 1904, 1908, 1912, 1920)
The Ancient Greeks staged the first tug in 500BC, but in modern Olympic rules, a team of eight had to pull the opposition 6 ft (1.8 m) to win. London 1908 saw the sport at its most intense, when America was beaten in just a few short seconds by Great Britain. The unhappy losers accused the British team—all policemen—of wearing illegal spiked boots, so they were offered a rematch, with the British in their socks. They still lost.

FAMOUS OLYMPIANS

● Lieutenant George S. Patton, one of the leading generals during World War II, finished fifth in the modern pentathlon at the 1912 Olympics.

● Johnny Weissmuller of the United States won three gold medals in freestyle swimming at the 1924 Olympics plus a bronze in the men's water polo, and two more swimming golds in 1928—feats that helped him earn a lucrative Hollywood career playing Tarzan.

● Buster Crabbe of the U.S.A. won a swimming gold medal at the 1932 Olympics and also went on to play Tarzan in the movies.

● Britain's Philip Noel-Baker won silver in the 1,500 meters at the 1920 Olympics—and in 1959 was awarded the Nobel Peace Prize.

● Crown Prince (later King) Constantine of Greece won a sailing gold medal at the 1960 Olympics.

● Hollywood actress Geena Davis took part in the trials for the U.S. archery team for the 2000 Olympics.

● Baby care expert Dr. Benjamin Spock was a member of the Yale University eight that won rowing gold for the U.S.A. at the 1924 Olympics.

● Harold Sakata won a weightlifting silver for the U.S. in 1948 before going on to play the evil Oddjob in the James Bond movie *Goldfinger*.

● Princess Anne, daughter of Queen Elizabeth II, was a member of the British equestrian team at the 1976 Montreal Olympics.

REMARKABLE TORCH RELAYS

Tokyo 1964 This torch relay featured the most torchbearers ever used—101,866—comprising a carrier, two reserve runners and up to 20 accompanying people for every kilometer of its land journey.

Grenoble 1968 In the later stages of the relay, a diver swam across the French port of Marseilles holding the torch's flame out of the water.

Mexico City 1968 The relay retraced the steps of Christopher Columbus to the New World and featured one of his direct descendants, Cristóbal Colón de Carbajal, as the last runner on Spanish soil before the torch made its way across the Atlantic.

Montreal 1976 The Canadians organized the transmission of the flame by satellite between Athens and Ottawa by transforming it into a radio signal that was sent by satellite to Canada, where it triggered a laser beam to relight the flame on Canadian soil.

Lillehammer 1994 The flame was transferred between two parachute jumpers—in midair—and then made an impressive entry at the opening ceremony of the Games when it was carried by a ski jumper during his actual jump!

Atlanta 1996 and Sydney 2000
The Olympic torch (but not the flame) was carried into space by astronauts.

SHINE A LIGHT

One of the enduring symbols of the Games is the Olympic flame, which burns for the duration of the competition. A few months before each Games, at the Temple of Hera at Olympia, Greece—the site of the ancient games—a woman in ceremonial robes lights the torch, using just a mirror and the sun. The flame is then carried by relay to the host city, where it ignites the Olympic cauldron in the stadium and burns until the closing ceremony. During its journey, it must never go out. The route to each stadium is often long and tortuous.

In 2004, to celebrate the Games held in Athens, Greece, the torch went on a global tour, covering 48,470 mi (78,000 km) in the hands of some 11,300 torchbearers.

Over the years, it's been carried by dogsled, horseback, camel and canoe, as well as by an army of runners.

When the flame has to travel in an airplane, special security lanterns are used, and every night of its journey the flame is kept burning in custom-made cauldrons, attended by three guards, one of whom must be awake at all times.

Eighteen authentic Olympic torches are displayed in the Ripley's Believe It or Not! Museum in London, England, among them the torch from the Sydney 2000 Olympiad that was carried, lit, underwater by divers near the Great Barrier Reef.

Mighty Mouth
A man in Lagos, Nigeria, lifts a bar carrying 110 lb (50 kg) of iron weights with his mouth!

solo sailor At age 16, Jessica Watson of Queensland, Australia, finished a 210-day, 23,000-nautical-mile (42,600-km), solo, nonstop and unassisted voyage around the world. In her 34-ft-long (10-m) yacht *Ella's Pink Lady*, she battled 39-ft (12-m) swells and a ripped sail and ate 576 chocolate bars.

jail jaunt In June 2009, 194 French inmates made a 1,430-mi (2,300-km) bicycle trip through the country in a prisoners' Tour de France.

head-to-head Croatian tennis player Goran Ivanisevic needed stitches when he tried to head the ball over the net at the 1998 Canadian Open, only to bang heads with his doubles partner Mark Philippoussis, who had tried to do the same thing. Philippoussis got away with only a bruised forehead.

dodgeball tournament In October 2009, more than 235 teams in three divisions competed in a dodgeball tournament in Richmond, Virginia, involving more than 4,000 players.

novice at 90 Ninety-year-old Mary Tattersall from West Yorkshire, England, hit a hole-in-one at a golf course near Bradford in 2010. She had been playing golf for only two years.

world cup miss Spain's international goalkeeper Santiago Cañizares missed the 2002 soccer World Cup after dropping a bottle of aftershave onto his right foot, severing one of his tendons.

board marathon A team of ten wakeboarders (a cross between waterskiing and surfing) completed 1,448 laps of a Cincinnati, Ohio, cable wakeboard park in 24 hours in June 2010. They traveled just over 506 mi (814 km)—roughly the distance from Cincinnati to Atlanta, Georgia.

delayed game Twenty-one years after a 1989 New Jersey high-school hockey championship game between Delbarton and St. Joseph's was canceled because of a measles outbreak, the players—now in their late thirties—finally took to the ice to play the deciding game for charity.

surf club The Palestinian territory's Gaza Strip has its own surf club, which was founded after a Jewish surfer donated a dozen surfboards to the community.

fast match In October 2009, Jo-Wilfried Tsonga of France and Spain's Fernando Verdasco played a tennis match on board a train traveling at 268 mph (431 km/h). The mini-tennis court was laid out in one of Shanghai's high-speed Maglev trains, where the players were traveling faster than their serves.

round-the-world In 2010, 34-year-old Vin Cox from Cornwall, England, cycled 18,225 mi (29,330 km) around the world in just 163 days. Starting and finishing his journey in London, he took 12 plane and boat transfers, crossed six continents—Europe, (northern) Africa, Asia, Australia, South America and North America—and cycled through 17 countries.

big haul In August 2010, Jeff Kolodzinski caught 2,160 fish—mostly small bluegills and perch—from Lake Minnetonka, Minnesota, in a 24-hour period.

one-legged wrestler Michigan-based Zach "Tenacious Z" Gowen, who lost his leg at age eight, made his debut at 19 as a one-legged professional wrestler.

thrown away Jesus Leonardo of Wanaque, New Jersey, earns about $45,000 a year examining discarded horse-racing tickets for winning stubs accidentally thrown away.

insect aside Spotting that an insect had landed on his ball at the 1950 U.S. Open Golf Championship, Lloyd Mangrum of the U.S.A. instinctively picked up the ball and flicked the insect away. However, he was penalized two strokes for his misdemeanor, which ultimately cost him the title.

blind catch Sheila Penfold, a legally blind grandmother from London, England, caught a catfish that weighed in at a whopping 214 lb (97 kg) and measured 8 ft 2 in (2.5 m) long on Spain's Ebro River in January 2010. It took Mrs. Penfold, who stands just 5 ft 3 in (1.6 m) tall, 30 minutes to reel in the monster.

master jockey Since 1974, Canadian jockey Russell Baze has won more than 11,000 horse races. In the space of just two days—October 17 and 18, 2007—he won no fewer than 11 races.

seven out In 2009, in his first game as a pitcher for the St. Louis Cardinals, John Smoltz struck out seven hitters in a row—something he had never managed to do in 708 trips to the mound with his previous team, the Atlanta Braves.

first female In 2010, Kelly Kulick of the U.S.A. became the first woman to qualify for the Professional Bowlers' Association's Tournament of Champions—and she went on to beat an all-male field of 62 to claim the title.

extra load In 2009, former British soldier Kez Dunkley ran the 26.2-mi (42-km) Leicester Marathon in 5 hours 53 minutes with an 84-lb (38-kg) tumble-drier strapped to his back. The previous year he had run the race with a bag of cement on his back.

BIKE CLIMB

In November 2010, Colombian cyclist Javier Zapata rode up the 649 steps of the Piedra del Peñol monolithic formation in Guatapé, Colombia, in just 43 minutes. Zapata is no stranger to epic climbs. In 2003, he rode his bike up the 1,318 stairs of Mexico City's Torre Mayor, the tallest building in Latin America.

Bill emerges from the seawater following his surfing extravaganza with bloodshot eyes and dusted in salt.

SURF'S UP!

Surfer extraordinaire Bill Laity of San Clemente, California, surfed for 26 hours straight at the state's Huntington Beach in November 2010, during which time he caught 147 waves.

Bill paddled his board into the water at 7.24 a.m. on a Saturday morning—he didn't stop surfing until 9.26 a.m. on Sunday!

The super-surfer's fingers appear severely wrinkled as a result of being submerged in the water for 26 hours straight.

AIRBED RACE

At the annual Glen Nevis River Race in Scotland, competitors on inflatable airbeds don helmets and lifejackets to navigate a treacherous 1½-mi (2.4-km) course along the Glen Nevis River, tackling white-water torrents, rapids and even a 30-ft (9-m) waterfall.

bowling star Retired high-school principal Allen Meyer of Toronto, Canada, was still bowling twice a week in a league that he ran at the age of 106.

foul ball After years of attending Philadelphia Phillies baseball games, Steve Monforto made a great grab to catch his first foul ball. He high-fived his three-year-old daughter Emily and handed her the prize ball… which she then threw back over the railing! The family still went home with a ball after Phillies officials saw what happened and took a ball up to him. What's more, spectators threw back every foul ball caught for the remainder of the game so that Emily didn't feel bad for losing her dad the special ball.

extreme hole The "Extreme 19th" hole at the Legend Golf and Safari Resort in Limpopo, South Africa, has a tee-off on a mountain that is accessible only by helicopter—and sits 1,300 ft (400 m) above a green designed in the shape of the continent of Africa. In 2008, Ireland's Padraig Harrington became the first golfer to make a par-3 at this hole.

welly wanging Under the British rules of "welly wanging" (or gum-boot throwing), competitors take a maximum run-up of 42 paces before hurling a size 9, non-steel toecap gum-boot through the air as far as possible. Finland's Jouni Viljanen has hurled a gum boot more than 208 ft (64 m).

anvil blast In the U.S. sport of competitive anvil shooting, participants use black gunpowder to launch 100-lb (45-kg) anvils up to 200 ft (60 m) into the air. One anvil is placed upside down on the ground, the brick-shaped cavity in its underside is filled with gunpowder, and then a second anvil is placed on top of it. A fuse is lit—and the anvil-shooter runs as fast as he can out of the blast radius.

rabbit jumping As well as pioneering show jumping, where horses clear obstacles, Sweden established the sport of rabbit jumping, in which domestic rabbits are trained to jump miniature fences without touching them.

double faults In her first-round ladies' singles match at Wimbledon in 1957, Brazilian tennis player Miss M. de Amorim began by serving 17 consecutive double faults.

flying kayak Miles Daisher of Twin Falls, Idaho, paddles a kayak… across the sky at an altitude of 13,000 ft (4,000 m). The daredevil has invented a new sport, skyaking, a combination of skydiving and kayaking. Sitting in his kayak he jumps from a plane, pulls the chute at about 5,000 ft (1,525 m) and descends at nearly 100 mph (160 km/h), reducing to half that speed as he finally swoops to land spectacularly on water.

solo row In her 19-ft-long (5.8-m) rowboat *Liv*, Katie Spotz, 22, from Mentor, Ohio, rowed solo 2,817 mi (4,533 km) across the Atlantic Ocean from Dakar, Senegal, to Georgetown, Guyana, in just over 70 days in 2010. Previously she has swam the entire 325-mi (520-km) length of the Allegheny River, run 150 mi (240 km) across the Mojave and Colorado deserts and cycled 3,300 mi (5,310 km) across the U.S.A. from Seattle, Washington, to Washington, D.C.

FIERY BULL

In a festival dating back to the 16th century, a Bull of Fire runs through the streets of Medinaceli, Spain. The bull's body is covered in mud to protect it from burns and it wears an iron frame on its horns that bears two torches. The bull is chased through the streets until the torches go out.

Ripley's Believe It or Not!®
sports

R **tennis marathon** At the 2010 Wimbledon Tennis Championships, John Isner of the U.S.A. beat France's Nicolas Mahut in a match that lasted more than 11 hours over three days. The match began at 6.18 p.m. on Tuesday, June 22 and finished at 4.49 p.m. on Thursday, June 24, Isner eventually winning 6-4, 3-6, 6-7, 7-6, 70-68 in a final set that lasted 8 hours 11 minutes.

R **mirror image** U.S. golfer Phil Mickelson is right-handed in everything but golf. He plays left-handed after mirroring his father's right-handed swing as a child.

R **every ground** In February 2010, Scott Poleykett from Kent, England, completed a 50,000-mi (80,000-km) journey to visit every soccer ground—professional and amateur—in England and Wales. In the course of his ten-year mission, he took photographs of 2,547 soccer fields.

R **commentator's nightmare** The finish of an August 2010 race at Monmouth Park, New Jersey, was fought out between horses named *Mywifeknowseverything* and *Thewifedoesn'tknow*. The two horses were unconnected, with separate trainers and owners.

TATTOO TRIBUTE
Colombian soccer fan Felipe Alvarez has had his upper body tattooed to resemble a jersey of his favorite team, Atletico Nacional. The tattoo is in honor of Andrés Escobar, the Colombian player who was shot dead as a result of scoring an own goal, which lost his side the match, while playing against the U.S.A. at the 1994 World Cup. Seen here with Atletico player Victor Aristizábal, Alvarez now has Escobar's number 2 permanently marked on his back.

R **one hand** At 6 ft 10 in (2.1 m) tall, Kevin Laue of Pleasanton, California, received a scholarship to play basketball for Manhattan College despite having only one hand.

R **flying shot** In 2010, Tyler Toney, a student from Texas A&M University, made a basketball shot he threw from a low-flying airplane!

R **atlantic crossing** A four-man crew led by Scotsman Leven Brown overcame 40-ft (12-m) waves, two capsizes and an outbreak of food poisoning to row 3,500 mi (5,600 km) across the Atlantic from New York to the Scilly Isles, which lie off the southwest coast of England, in 43 days in 2010. They were following the route of a Norwegian crew who had made the same crossing in 55 days back in 1896.

R **veteran coach** Soccer coach Ivor Powell finally hung up his boots in 2010—at age 93. A former Welsh international forward, he went on to train more than 9,000 players during his 53-year coaching career.

R **wrestling champs** In 2010, Blair Academy of Blairstown, New Jersey, won its 30th consecutive National Prep School Wrestling Championship.

R **monkey guards** Organizers at the 2010 Commonwealth Games in New Delhi, India, hired monkeys to work as guards at the athletes' village. They hoped that the team of 40 gray langur monkeys would chase off the packs of smaller rhesus monkeys that had been breaking into buildings and stealing from the competitors' quarters.

R **switch hitters** It took 134 years for the Arizona Diamondbacks' Felipe Lopez to become the first baseball player in history to switch-hit homers from both sides of the plate on Opening Day. It took just one inning, in the same 2009 game, for Tony Clark to become the second.

SAND SKIS
Germany's Henrik May prefers to ski on sand rather than snow—and in the Namibian Desert he reached a speed of 57.24 mph (92.12 km/h) while skiing down a 246-ft-high (75-m) dune. He has developed a special type of wax that enables the skis he uses to slide over sand.

flying fish One of the favorites to win the 2010 Missouri River 340—a grueling 340-mi (550-km) canoe and kayak race—Brad Pennington from Houston, Texas, was forced to quit just hours into the event after a 30-lb (13.6-kg) Asian silver carp leaped out of the water and hit him in the head. He described the blow as like being hit with a brick, and it left him with a pounding headache.

tug-of-war Fishing on the Victoria Nile River in Uganda, Tim Smith from Enniskillen, Northern Ireland, landed a 249-lb (113-kg) Nile perch, which at 6 ft (1.8 m) long, was taller than him. He battled for 45 minutes to reel in the monster—and then had to pry his catch from the jaws of a crocodile that launched itself at his tiny boat in a desperate bid to snatch the fish.

soccer saints An executive box at the Hamburg stadium of German soccer club St. Pauli is decorated like a Gothic chapel, complete with stained glass windows, candles, an altar to football and depictions of the team's players as saints.

frozen toe The U.S.A.'s Rulon Gardner, the 2000 Olympic Greco-Roman wrestling gold medallist, lost a toe to frostbite in 2002 and kept it in a jar in his refrigerator for years, apparently to remind him of his mortality.

free throws Perry Dissmore, a pastor from Hartford, Illinois, made 1,968 successful basketball free throws in an hour in September 2010—an average of one throw every 1.8 seconds.

matador fled Matador Christian Hernandez quit his job mid-bullfight in Mexico City in 2010—by running away from the charging bull, jumping over a wall and fleeing the stadium to a chorus of boos.

loyal fan Nesan Sinnadurai, a U.S.-based fan of English soccer club Arsenal, has flown more than 6,000,000 mi (9,600,000 km) supporting the club since 1967. Every other weekend during the soccer season, the Sri Lankan I.T. consultant makes the 9,000-mi (14,500-km) round trip from Columbus, Georgia, to London to watch his favorite team.

blind abseiler Blind extreme sports enthusiast Dean Dunbar abseiled down the 658-ft-high (200-m) Eas a' Chual Aluinn waterfall in Scotland. He has also competed in power boating, mountain biking, sea kayaking and hill running events, bungee jumped from a helicopter and been hurled through the air as a human catapult.

super sprinter Irish sprinter Jason Smyth can run the 100 meters in 10.32 seconds—even though he is legally blind. He suffers from Stargardt's disease, a disorder that has reduced his vision to about ten percent of that of a fully sighted person, but can run so fast that he competed against able-bodied athletes at the 2010 European Championships.

too much yelling Manchester United goalkeeper Alex Stepney dislocated his jaw while shouting at his defenders during a 1975 soccer match against Birmingham City.

Sky Walker

Californian Dean Potter walked across a highline 100 ft (30 m) long and over 1,000 ft (305 m) above the ground in Yosemite National Park in 2009. He walked barefoot, and unattached. Dean has many years of experience on the highline—if he does slip off, he grabs the line with his arms or legs.

www.ripleybooks.com

Believe It or Not!®

Sports Survivors

HOCKEY HORROR

Buffalo Sabres' goaltender Clint Malarchuk narrowly escaped death after a collision caused a player's skate to cut the cartoid artery in his neck during a 1989 hockey match against the St. Louis Blues. If the skate had hit Malarchuk $1/8$ in (3 mm) higher, he would have been dead within 2 minutes. The injury was so horrific that 11 fans fainted and two had heart attacks, while three players vomited on the ice. Malarchuk needed 300 stitches to fix the wound, but was back playing in goal ten days later.

These heroic athletes and fans have the scars to show how sport can be dangerous. Incredibly, all have survived and, believe it or not, returned to the arena for more.

When baseball player Kelly Shoppach of the Cleveland Indians let the bat slip at a game against the Texas Rangers in Arlington, Texas, in 2006, this unfortunate fan failed to notice Shoppach's bat flying straight toward his face. In 2009, Shoppach claimed another victim when he struck a female fan in the face with a foul ball during a game against the Kansas City Royals.

FACEBALL BAT

10 MOST DANGEROUS SPORTS IN THE U.S.A.

(Injuries per year)

1. Basketball 512,213
2. Cycling 485,669
3. Football 418,260
4. Soccer 174,686
5. Baseball 155,898
6. Skateboarding 112,544
7. Trampoline 108,029
8. Softball 106,884
9. Swimming/diving 82,354
10. Horseback riding 73,576

DANGEROUS RING

Celebrating a goal for Swiss team Servette in 2004, recently married Portuguese soccer player Paulo Diogo jumped on the stadium fence and caught his wedding ring on the top. When he jumped off, he left the ring and half his finger behind. To add insult to injury, the referee showed him a yellow card for time wasting as the doctors searched for the missing finger! Although doctors were unable to reattach the digit, Diogo quickly resumed his career.

Ripley's Sports
Believe It or Not!®

UNLUCKY BREAK

Brazilian-born Croatian soccer player Eduardo suffered a horrific broken leg when playing for his club team, Arsenal, in England's Premier League in 2008. A tackle by Birmingham City's Martin Taylor left Eduardo's anklebone sticking through his sock and kept him out of the game for almost a year.

BRUTE FORCE

Spanish matador Julio Aparicio was gored through the neck with such force by a bull in Madrid in 2010 that the end of the animal's horn can be seen coming out of the bullfighter's mouth. The horn went through Aparicio's tongue and penetrated the roof of his mouth. His life was saved after two operations and, incredibly, he returned to the ring two months later.

EDUARDO
9

DIVING BELLE

Seventeen-year-old Columbus, Ohio, diver Chelsea Davis smashed the bridge of her nose on the diving board while competing at the 2005 World Swimming Championships in Montréal, Canada. She was lifted on to a stretcher, her face covered in blood, but she never lost consciousness and was soon back competing.

believe it!

world

animals

sports

body

transport

feats

mysteries

food

arts

science

beyond belief

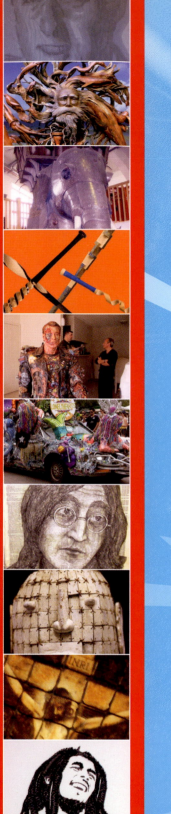

The Terminator

In 2011, Ripley's acquired a life-sized statue of Arnold Schwarzenegger as the Terminator, created by Mexican artist Enrique Ramos. Made from an assortment of materials, including a dead bat, the sculpture is a tribute to Hollywood films and icons, and features images of Spiderman, Homer Simpson, E.T., Jaws and Frankenstein among many others.

Ripley's
EXHIBITS

102
103
104
105
106
107
108
109
110
111
112
113
114
115
116
117
118
119
120
121
122
123
124
125
126
127
128
129

www.ripleybooks.com

body
Ripley's Believe It or Not!®

Thomas Jefferson 1801–1809

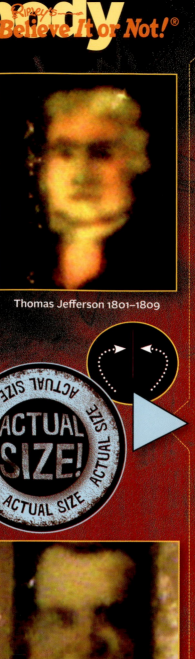

George Washington 1789–1797

John Adams 1797–1801

Thomas Jefferson 1801–1809

James Madison 1809–1817

James Monroe 1817–1825

John Quincy Adams 1825–1829

Andrew Jackson 1829–1837

Martin Van Buren 1837–1841

William Henry Harrison 1841

John Tyler 1841–1845

James K. Polk 1845–1849

Zachary Taylor 1849–1850

Millard Fillmore 1850–1853

Franklin Pierce 1853–1857

James Buchanan 1857–1861

Abraham Lincoln 1861–1865

Andrew Johnson 1865–1869

Ulysses S. Grant 1869–1877

Rutherford B. Hayes 1877–1881

James A. Garfield 1881

Chester A. Arthur 1881–1885

Grover Cleveland 1885–1889 & 1893–1897

Benjamin Harrison 1889–1893

William McKinley 1897–1901

Theodore Roosevelt 1901–1909

William Howard Taft 1909–1913

Woodrow Wilson 1913–1921

Warren G. Harding 1921–1923

Calvin Coolidge 1923–1929

Herbert Hoover 1929–1933

Franklin D. Roosevelt 1933–1945

Harry S. Truman 1945–1953

Dwight D. Eisenhower 1953–1961

John F. Kennedy 1961–1963

Lyndon B. Johnson 1963–1969

Richard Nixon 1969–1974

Gerald Ford 1974–1977

Jimmy Carter 1977–1981

Ronald Reagan 1981–1989

George H. W. Bush 1989–1993

Bill Clinton 1993–2001

George W. Bush 2001–2009

ACTUAL SIZE!

HEADS OF STATE

Chinese micro-artist Jin Y. Hua has painted the face of every President of the U.S.A. from George Washington to George W. Bush—that's 42 portraits—on a single human hair less than ½ in (1.3 cm) long and just 0.0035 in (0.09 mm) thick. Jin uses a brush made from a single rabbit hair to apply the paint.

John F. Kennedy 1961–1963

Lyndon B. Johnson 1963–1969

Richard Nixon 1969–1974

Ronald Reagan 1981–1989

snake twins In June 2009, in Xiaogan, eastern China, Hui Chung gave birth to conjoined twins, who were known as the "snake babies" because they were attached at the waist. The siblings shared one long body with a head at each end, and as they did not have external sexual organs, it was impossible to say what sex they were.

long hair When 79-year-old Tran Van Hay died in Kien Giang, Vietnam, in February 2010, his hair was more than 22 ft (6.7 m) long and weighed 23 lb (10.5 kg). He began to let his hair grow more than 50 years ago, because he often became sick after a haircut. As his hair grew, he balanced it on his head like a basket.

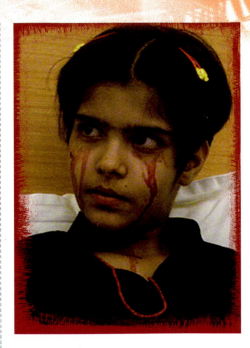

LICK OFF

Actor Nick Afanasiev from California has an incredible role all to himself—as the owner of America's longest tongue! Stretching to an unbelievable 3.5 in (9 cm), it means that Nick can lick his own nose and even his elbow, a bizarre feat that most people find impossible.

BLOOD, SWEAT AND TEARS

Twinkle Dwivedi from Lucknow, India, is one of the strangest and rarest medical cases in the world. From the age of 12, Twinkle began to bleed at random through the skin on any part of her body—without any visible wounds or pain—from the soles of her feet to her eyes. Although the cause of her spontaneous bleeding remains a mystery, experts believe that she may suffer from a blood disorder, or hematohidrosis, an extremely rare but recognized condition where the patient sweats blood through the skin.

miracle escape A Japanese toddler who wandered onto rail tracks in Suzaka City escaped with only scratches after a train came to a halt on top of her. After spotting the girl, the driver applied the emergency brakes and the train stopped with the girl beneath. She survived because she was trapped in the 20-in (50-cm) gap between the train and the tracks.

scorched footprints For two weeks in 2009, Sikeli Nadiri left a trail of scorched footprints on grassland around his home village in Fiji. There was no explanation as to why the grass had burned away beneath his feet, as he had not stepped on any chemicals or anything else that would cause scorching.

dangerous operation In March 2010, U.S. Army medical staff at Bagram airfield in Afghanistan donned armor in the operating room while removing a live high-explosive round from the scalp of a soldier from the Afghan Army.

Ripley's Believe It or Not!®

A Bicycle Made for Two

Although Charles B. Tripp had no arms and Eli Bowen had no legs, they were able to ride a bicycle—together. Known to circus audiences as "The Armless Wonder" and "The Legless Wonder," they simply combined their physical attributes on a tandem bicycle—Tripp pedaling with his legs and Bowen steering with his arms.

Charles B. Tripp was born without arms in 1855 in Woodstock, Ontario, Canada, but soon learned to dress himself and write using his feet. Remarkably, he made his living as a skilled carpenter until joining Barnum's Circus, which was the start of a 50-year career as a performer. He specialized in penmanship, portrait painting and paper cutting—holding the implements between his toes. Around the turn of the century, he developed an interest in photography and became known as "The Armless Photographer." He died in 1939 in Salisbury, North Carolina, at the grand age of 84.

Eli Bowen was born in Ohio in 1844. He was one of ten children, all of whom were able-bodied except for Eli who had seal limbs, or phocomelia, a condition that left him with no legs and with two feet of different sizes growing from his hips. As a child he walked on his arms, perfecting a technique whereby he held wooden blocks in his hands that enabled him to swing his hips between his arms. The strength he gained from this helped him become a talented acrobat and, at the age of 13, he joined his first circus troupe.

Despite his condition, Eli was considered by many to be the most handsome man in showbusiness and, age 26, he married Mattie Haight who was ten years his junior. The couple had four healthy sons. He continued performing into his eighties, and his death, from pleurisy in 1924, was just days before he was due to appear at The Dreamland Circus at Coney Island, New York.

Eli Bowen with his wife and son

Charles Tripp having a cup of tea

swallowed cutlery When 52-year-old Margaret Daalmans went to a hospital in Rotterdam, Holland, complaining of stomach pains, surgeons removed 78 different items of cutlery—including spoons and forks—that she had swallowed.

seven-foot worm Sailing on board the ship *Elizabeth* from Cork, Ireland, to Quebec, Canada, in June 1825, 12-year-old Ellen McCarthy fell ill and coughed up three intestinal worms, the longest of which measured 7 ft 3 in (2.2 m).

Ice Man Wearing just trunks, goggles and a swimming cap, Lewis Pugh of Devon, England, swam 0.62 mi (1 km) across the glacial Pumori Lake, which lies 17,400 ft (5,300 m) up Mount Everest and has a water temperature of just 2°C (36°F). The man, dubbed the "human polar bear," took 22 minutes 51 seconds to breaststroke across the lake. He had to find a delicate balance between going too fast and going too slowly—too quickly he could have lost energy and drowned, but too slowly and he would have suffered hypothermia.

lightning strike Dog-walker Brad Gifford of Kettering, England, had a miraculous escape after he was knocked unconscious, burst both eardrums and exploded into flames when a 300,000-volt bolt of lightning struck him on the ear. The lightning was traveling at 14,000 mph (22,500 km/h) and had heated the air around it to 54,032°F (30,000°C)—five times hotter than the surface of the Sun.

big baby At ten months old, Lei Lei, a baby from Hunan Province, China, weighed 44 lb (20 kg)—equivalent to the weight of an average six-year-old.

parachute plunge When her parachute became entangled seconds after she exited an airplane above South Africa, skydiver Lareece Butler plunged 3,000 ft (915 m) before hitting the ground—she survived with a broken leg, broken pelvis, bruises and concussion.

ate finger In a protest over unpaid wages, a Serbian union official chopped off his finger and ate it. Zoran Bulatovic, a union leader at a textile factory in Novi Pazar, was so angry because some of his fellow workers had not been paid for several years that he used a hacksaw to chop off most of the little finger on his left hand and then ate it to underline the fact that the workers could no longer afford to eat conventional food.

ILLUSTRATED LADY

Julia Gnuse of Foothill Ranch, California, got her first tattoo to cover unsightly blisters on her legs, but she became hooked and now has tattoos over 95 percent of her body, including her face. Known as "The Illustrated Lady," her body drawings include jungle scenes, cartoons and the cast of *Bewitched*.

MAGNETIC FINGERS

By having tiny magnetic implants inserted in their fingers, people are able to pick up metal items, such as paper clips or bottle tops, seemingly by magic. Some people have even had magnets inserted in the backs of their hands or on their ears!

RIPLEY RESEARCH

A small incision is made either at the front or to the side of the fingertip, a tiny dermal elevator is used to separate the layers of the skin, and then the magnet covered in silicone is inserted slightly to the side of the finger pad. The incision is then closed with a stitch. With a finger magnet, people can detect live electrical cables but they can't erase computer hard drives or credit cards or get stuck to refrigerators. The magnets are effective at lifting small items, but this shouldn't be done for longer than 20 minutes at a time in case the skin over the magnet becomes damaged.

ACTUAL SIZE!

BELLY BUTTON BEARS

Artist Rachel Betty Case from Bethlehem, Pennsylvania, turns belly button fluff into tiny bears. She collects the lint from the belly buttons of male friends and sells her cute fluffy creations in small glass jars.

bullet surprise A 35-year-old Polish man who went to a hospital in Bochum, Germany, worried about a small lump on the back of his head, was unaware that he had been shot five years earlier. It was only when doctors removed a .22 caliber bullet that he remembered receiving a blow to the head around midnight at a New Year's Party.

metal muncher Doctors in Cajamarca, Peru, removed 2 lb 3 oz (1 kg) of metal from a man's stomach, including nails, coins, copper wire and scrap metal. Requelme Abanto Alvarado said he had been eating metal for months and had once swallowed 17 5-in (13-cm) nails in one day.

talented toes Since having both arms amputated at age ten after an accident, Liu Wei of Beijing, China, has learned to do everything with his feet. He uses his toes to eat, dress himself, brush his teeth and surf the Internet. He even plays the piano with his toes and earned a standing ovation when he performed on the TV show *China's Got Talent*, which he then went on to win.

not twins In 2010, Angie Cromar from Murray, Utah, found herself pregnant with two babies at the same time—but they weren't twins. She was born with a rare condition called didelphys, meaning two uteruses, and she conceived in both, at odds of one in five million.

long lobes Jian Tianjin, a farmer from Taiwan, has stretchy earlobes that make his ears 6½ in (16 cm) in length. His lobes are so long and flexible that they reach his shoulders and can be wound around his chin.

eight limbs Before having an operation to remove them when he was seven years old, Deepak Paswaan of Bihar, India, had four extra limbs—the result of being born with the arms, legs and buttocks of a parasitic twin protruding from his chest. Although the parasitic twin's arms were small and withered, its legs grew at the same rate as Deepak, meaning the youngster had to carry a heavy weight around.

single handed Despite being born with just one hand, Kevin Shields from Fort William, Scotland, is an accomplished rock climber and has even mastered treacherous ice climbs.

GALL STONES

Doctors in Shenyang, Liaoning Province, China, removed more than 880 stones from the gall bladder of a 67-year-old woman. Mrs. Miao's gall bladder was so full of stones it had swollen to the size of a fist, forcing doctors to remove the whole bladder. They estimated that the stones had been forming inside her for about 20 years.

new language A 13-year-old Croatian girl woke from a 24-hour coma speaking fluent German. The girl was no longer able to speak Croatian but was able to communicate perfectly in German, a language that she had only just started studying at school.

sum girl! A 15-year-old schoolgirl with a love of math was awakened from a coma when her father began asking her simple sums. Vicki Alex of Northamptonshire, England, had been unconscious for three days and had failed to respond to other attempts to stimulate her brain, but after her father's intervention she soon regained full consciousness.

hairy hands Since becoming the first American to undergo a double hand transplant, Jeff Kepner from Augusta, Georgia, has noticed that his new hands are considerably hairier than the rest of his body because the donor had more hair than him.

self-amputation Ramlan, an 18-year-old construction worker who was trapped by a fallen concrete girder in the rubble of a building that collapsed during a 2009 earthquake in Padang, Indonesia, survived by sawing off his own leg.

toddler plunge Two-year-old Zhu Xinping had a miraculous escape after falling from the 21st floor of an apartment block in Jianyang City, Sichuan Province, China. She escaped with nothing worse than a broken leg after landing on a freshly dug pile of soil that cushioned her fall.

large family After giving birth to two sets of quadruplets (in 2004 and 2005), Dale Chalk of Sydney, New South Wales, Australia, had twins in 2009, giving her a total of 11 children under the age of seven.

self-service After badly cutting his leg in an accident at home, a 32-year-old man became so frustrated at having to wait an hour at Sundsvall Hospital in northern Sweden that he picked up a needle and thread and sewed up the cut himself.

tugged off In June 2009, a man from Shenzhen, China, was competing in a game of tug-of-war when he had his hand pulled off.

born twice Doctors in Texas performed prenatal surgery at 25 weeks to remove a grapefruit-sized tumor from Macie McCartney, while she was still inside her mother's womb. The procedure involved pulling out the uterus of mother Keri and then half of Macie. Once free from the tumor, Macie was returned to the womb, where she recovered and grew for another ten weeks before being "born" again.

baby's tail Surgeons in China performed an operation to remove a 5-in-long (13-cm) tail from the body of a four-month-old baby girl. Hong Hong, from China's Anhui Province, was born with the tail, but it quickly doubled in size. X-rays had shown that it was connected to a fatty tumor within her spinal column.

reverse walker Rotating his feet nearly 180 degrees, Bittu Gandhi of Rajkot, Gujarat, India, can walk backward while facing forward!

Too Many Toes

In 2010, doctors at a hospital in Shenyang, China, operated on a six-year-old boy who had eight toes on each foot and 15 fingers owing to a rare genetic mutation known as central polydactyly. After a 6½-hour operation, medics had successfully removed 11 extra digits.

22cm

body
Believe It or Not!®

determined dan Dan Netherland of Gatlinburg, Tennessee, can keep his fingers gripped together while ten people try to pull his arms apart.

tongue typist Legally blind and unable to use his hands, Josh LaRue of New Concord, Ohio, wrote a book by tapping out the words in Morse Code using his tongue.

lucky break When Raymond Curry overturned his car near his home in Northumberland, England, he was rushed to hospital with a fence post speared through his chest. There, doctors were relieved to see that the post had amazingly missed all of his vital organs—and they found a four-leafed clover stuck to his back.

saving lives Ben Kopp, a U.S. Army Ranger Corporal, was killed while saving six soldiers in a firefight and then helped save the lives of 75 others by donating his organs and tissues.

sprouting pea Doctors in Cape Cod, Massachusetts, investigating the cause of a patient's sickness, were stunned to find that he had a pea plant growing in his lung. They believe Ron Sveden, from nearby Brewster, had eaten a pea at some time in the previous couple of months but it had gone down the wrong way, and the seed had split inside him and started to sprout about ½ in (1 cm).

beatle tattoo Beatles fan Rose Ann Belluso of Downington, Pennsylvania, took a sign to Paul McCartney's Philadelphia show in August 2010 asking him to sign her back with a marker pen that she had brought along. After the singer called her up on stage and obliged, she decided to make the inscription permanent the next day by getting a tattoo artist to ink over the signature.

puff, puff... boom! Unlucky Andi Susanto of Indonesia lost six of his teeth when a cigarette he was smoking mysteriously exploded in February 2010.

route 66 Ron Jones of Bartlesville, Oklahoma, gets his kicks out of having Route 66 tattoos all over his body. He has more than 80 tattoos dedicated to destinations along the 2,448-mi (3,940-km) highway, including the Ariston Café in Litchfield, Illinois, and the arch on the Santa Monica Pier in California, which marks the end of the road.

bee therapy Bed-ridden multiple sclerosis sufferer Sami Chugg from Bristol, England, was able to get back on her feet after being stung 1,500 times by bees. The Bee Venom Therapy, carried out over a period of 18 months, involved holding a bee in a pair of tweezers and deliberately stinging an area of skin around her spine.

little miss dynamite Dr. Thienna Ho, 5 ft (1.5 m) tall and weighing barely 95 lb (43 kg), deadlifted 104,846 lb (47,557 kg) in one hour in San Francisco. The barbell she lifted weighed 46 lb (21 kg)—nearly half her body weight. She has previously completed more than 5,000 sumo squats in an hour.

chinese accent After suffering a severe migraine headache in March 2010, Sarah Colwill of Plymouth, Devon, England, suddenly started speaking with a Chinese accent—despite never having been to that country. Doctors say she has Foreign Accent Syndrome, a rare condition that damages the part of the brain that controls speech and word formation.

deep sleep A Polish man woke up from a 19-year coma to find the Communist Party no longer in power and food no longer rationed. After being hit by a train in 1988, railway worker Jan Grzebski also slept through the weddings of four of his children and the births of 11 grandchildren.

head returned Lewis Powell, a conspirator in the assassination of U.S. President Abraham Lincoln, was hanged in 1865 and was buried headless. His skull had been missing for 127 years when it was found in storage in the Smithsonian Museum and returned to the body.

migraine cure In order to relieve crippling migraine headache pains, teenager Melissa Peacock from Bradford, England, has to "drink" her brain fluid every day. At the age of nine she was diagnosed with intracranial hypertension, a condition that causes her body to produce too much spinal fluid. This collects in her skull and pushes on her brain, leaving her with such bad migraines and blurred vision that sometimes she could not walk in a straight line. On nine separate occasions, doctors punctured her skull to drain the fluid, but when it kept returning they decided to fit a tube that siphons fluid from her brain straight into her stomach.

odd reaction Desiree Jennings from Ashburn, Virginia, claimed she couldn't walk forward after suffering a freak reaction to a seasonal flu shot. Her forward motion suddenly became awkward with a twisted gait and she also had difficulty speaking, reading and remembering things—yet the symptoms disappeared when she ran or walked backward.

frozen fingertip After losing her right pinky fingertip in an accident at her home in Davis, California, Deepa Kulkarni took it to doctors—and when they said they were unable to reattach it, she decided to investigate a new procedure called tissue regeneration. Eventually, she persuaded a local doctor to carry out tissue regeneration on her fingertip and after seven weeks of treatment it grew back. However, she still keeps the original fingertip in her freezer.

armless pitcher Tom Willis of San Diego, California, can throw a baseball the entire 60½ ft (18.5 m) distance from the mound to home plate without the ball bouncing—with his feet. Born with no arms, he has used his feet to throw the first pitch of a game at more than ten Major League Baseball stadiums in the U.S.A.

hidden bullet Eighty-three-year-old World-War-II veteran Fred Gough from the West Midlands, England, thought that he was suffering from painful arthritis—until doctors told him in 2010 that a German bullet had been lodged in his hip for the past 66 years.

light lunch U.S. sideshow performer Todd Robbins has chewed and swallowed more than 4,000 lightbulbs.

bunny girl Rabbit-loving grandmother Annette Edwards of Worcester, England, has spent $16,000 on cosmetic surgery to make herself look like Jessica Rabbit, the sultry heroine of the 1988 movie *Who Framed Roger Rabbit?* As well as the surgery, she went on a rabbit-style diet for three months, eating just salads and cereals.

tattoo marathon In December 2009, Nick Thunberg was tattooed for 52 straight hours by body artist Jeremy Brown in Rockford, Illinois.

Self-styled

Etienne Dumont, a journalist from Geneva, Switzerland, has some of the most stunning body modifications in the world. He is tattooed from head to toe with vibrant images including skulls, flowers and animals, but most striking are the designs covering his face and a hole stretched in his chin, held open by a transparent disk through which you can see his teeth. He also has a synthetic horn implant protruding from his scalp and has also used progressively larger disks to stretch his earlobes.

body
Believe It or Not!®

Iron Man

In 1848, a man working on the Vermont railway survived having an iron rod blasted right through his face and out of the top of his skull. Phineas Gage had been using explosives to clear space for the tracks by packing gunpowder into holes in rock with a heavy iron rod when a spark ignited the powder and the rod shot through his head.

Unbelievably, Gage survived this horrific accident and remained physically able for the rest of his life, although damage to his brain significantly altered his character. His injury became famous in medical circles, and contributed to an understanding of how the brain works. Gage returned to work as a coach driver and died in 1860, 12 years after his accident.

Identified as Gage in 2009, this photo shows him with the same 13-lb (6-kg) temping iron that pierced his brain, which he kept as a gruesome souvenir. He lost the sight in his left eye when the rod passed behind it.

R hair insured American football player Troy Polamalu, a defender with the Pittsburgh Steelers, has had his hair insured for $1 million by Lloyd's of London. His 3-ft-long (90-cm) black curls are so famous that he has not cut them since 2000. Although he wears a helmet while playing, his hair is still at risk—in 2006 he was tackled by his ponytail by Larry Johnson of the Kansas City Chiefs after intercepting a pass.

R magnetic disruption Placing a magnet on your head can temporarily turn a right-handed person into a left-hander. By positioning a powerful magnet on the left posterior parietal cortex—a region of the brain that deals with planning and working out the relationship between three-dimensional objects—researchers at the University of California, Berkeley, found that normally right-handed volunteers started to use their left hand more frequently for tasks such as picking up a pencil. This is because the magnet disrupted and confused the volunteers' brains.

R epic climb Three U.S. war veterans climbed 19,341-ft (5,895-m) Mount Kilimanjaro in Tanzania in 2010—despite having only one good leg between them. Amputees Dan Nevins, 37, of Jacksonville, Florida, who lost his legs in Iraq; Neil Duncan, 26, of Denver, Colorado, who lost both legs in a roadside bomb attack in Afghanistan; and Kirk Bauer, 62, of Ellicott City, Maryland, who lost a leg in Vietnam in 1969, made the climb on their prosthetic legs in just six days.

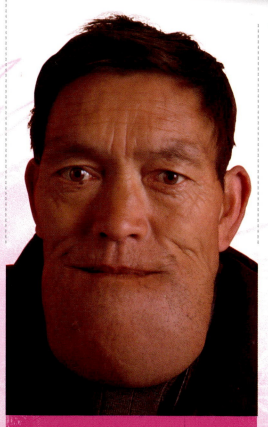

FACE BOOKED

In 2010, Chang Du from Lishuguo, China, went public with an offer to sell advertising space on his oversized chin. After a small pimple in his mouth swelled massively over a period of five years, Chang made the bizarre proposal in order to raise funds to reduce his chin back to normal size. He confirmed that an $8,000 offer would be enough to secure the space on his face.

R fridge raider Anna Ryan of Blue Springs, Missouri, put on 126 lb (57 kg) over several years—by eating food from her refrigerator while sleepwalking. She was puzzled why her weight ballooned to 266 lb (121 kg) despite adhering to a strict low-fat diet. However, when she awoke one morning to find cookies in her bed it emerged that, unbeknown to her, she had been getting up regularly in the night to eat cheese, chocolate and even meat.

R human heads When airport workers in Little Rock, Arkansas, noticed a package that was not labeled properly, they checked the contents and found a shipment of 60 human heads. Further investigation revealed the heads were on their way to a company in Fort Worth, Texas, to be used by neurosurgeons for the study of ear, nose and throat procedures.

R heroic landing In early 2010, Lt. Ian Fortune of Britain's Royal Air Force was shot between the eyes while piloting a helicopter in Afghanistan. He survived the incident and continued flying for another eight minutes before making a successful landing, saving all 20 people on board.

R full bladder After a 14-year-old boy in India was admitted to hospital complaining of pain and urinary problems, doctors were shocked to find a ¾-in-long (2-cm) fish in his bladder.

ℝ sucked hair After her car swerved off the road in Colorado, Cynthia Hoover survived for five days in the freezing wilderness of the Rocky Mountains by sucking water from her wet hair into her mouth. She was eventually found because she managed to crawl 450 yd (410 m)—despite having 11 broken ribs, a punctured lung and several broken vertebrae—to where she heard voices coming from a disused mine.

ℝ snowshoe beard David Traver of Anchorage, Alaska, was the winner of the 2009 World Beard and Moustache Championships with his 20½-in-long (52-cm) beard woven to resemble a snowshoe.

Ripley's Ask

What is the best thing about having such long hair?
My long locks are my pride and joy and my baby. They can be bundled and used as an extra pillow. I also bundle them behind my lower back when driving long distance, because they work better than a pillow for back support. They work as a great scarf in the winter when I visit cold states.

How do you keep your hair under control on a day-to-day basis?
For chores and running errands, I tie my locks in a wrap on my lower back, just like African women carry their babies. It secures my locks and allows me total freedom of movement, which is brilliant as I am very over-protective of my locks.

How often do you wash it, and how long does that take? For 20 years I washed my locks three times a week. Now I wash them only once a week, as per advice from a locks stylist. It takes about 30 minutes to wash them, about 40 minutes wrapped in a huge bath towel to absorb the water, and between 15 and 24 hours to totally dry.

Would you ever get your hair cut? Never is a strong word, but I will NEVER cut my locks. My locks are my baby... my crown... they hold 22 years of my sorrows and my joys, they're like another person... yet it's me... no, I will never cut my locks.

ℝ celebrity tattoos Steve Porter from Nottingham, England, has 12 autographed pictures of celebrities—including Alice Cooper, Anastacia and Ozzy Osbourne—inked onto his skin as tattoos. In total, he has more than 20 tattoos of actors and rock stars covering his body.

ℝ body bacteria There are as many as ten times the number of living bacteria and bugs in and on our bodies as there are human cells. Of the estimated 100 trillion microbes, the most densely populated areas of flesh are the belly button, the bottoms of the feet and between the fingers.

ℝ still singing After suffering a stroke, singer Ann Arscott of Birmingham, England, was left unable to speak—but she could still sing. She has aphasia, a condition caused by damage to the areas of the brain responsible for language. It impairs speech, but some people with it can still sing, as music activates a different part of the brain.

ℝ cat boy A boy in Dahua, China, has bright blue eyes that glow in the dark and enable him to see in the pitch black. Nong Youhui can read perfectly in complete darkness and also has good vision during the day. Medical experts think he was born with a rare condition called leukodermia, which has left his eyes with less protective pigment and made them more sensitive to light.

ℝ sneezed nail Prax Sanchez, 72, of Colorado Springs, Colorado, had an MRI scan for an ear problem, which dislodged a nail in his head that he then coughed up after the procedure. He had no idea the nail was there and it could have been decades old.

LONG LOCKS
Asha Mandela from Clermont, Florida, has hair that measures an incredible 19 ft 6 in (6 m), longer than a pickup truck. Asha has not cut her hair for an astonishing 22 years.

Ripley's Believe It or Not!® body

Q what knife? Julia Popova of Moscow, Russia, was attacked by a mugger in February 2010 but walked home not aware that she had been stabbed and that the knife was still impaled in her neck.

Q miss plastic A 2009 beauty contest in Budapest, Hungary, was open only to women who had undergone cosmetic surgery. "Miss Plastic" featured contestants who had enhanced their bodies with everything from new breasts and liposuction to hair transplants.

Q nasty shock In 2003, librarian Susanne Caro of Sante Fe, New Mexico, opened a 115-year-old medical book and found an envelope containing scabs from smallpox patients.

Q skeleton growth A person's skeleton continues to grow until around age 25, when the collarbone finally finishes developing.

Q strong boy Kyle Kane, a 12-year-old schoolboy from the West Midlands, England, lifted a 308-lb (140-kg) weight—more than twice his own body weight—at a junior bodybuilding event in 2010.

HUMAN SKELETON

Billed as the "Skeleton Dude" at Coney Island's Dreamland Circus in 1917, Eddie Masher of Brooklyn, New York, stood 5 ft 7 in (1.7 m) tall, but he declared he weighed just 38 lb (17 kg). Other records have put him at 48 lb (22 kg) or as much as 67 lb (30 kg), but even those weights were astonishingly light for an adult man. He was so skinny that tailors struggled to make a suit that would fit him. He died in 1962 at 70 years old—a good age for a skeleton!

Q secret bullet Vasily Simonov of Togliatti, Russia, has lived with a bullet in his lung for 70 years. As a child in 1941, he was playing with a rifle cartridge when he decided to take out the bullet and shove it up his nose. After trying in vain to remove it, he then breathed it in. He forgot all about it and the lodged bullet never caused him any problems, only coming to light during an MRI scan in 2009. Even then, doctors decided it was best to leave the bullet where it was.

Q body sale In 2010, anatomist Gunther von Hagens launched a mail-order service for his Plastinarium museum in the German town of Guben, selling human and animal body parts that had been preserved with a special plastic solution. Items for sale included a smoker's lung ($4,440), a chunk of human head ($2,000), a slice of a human hand ($228) and a cross-section of giraffe neck (price unspecified).

EDDIE MASHER, Skeleton Dude, Height 5 ft. 7 in. Weight 38 lbs.

BIG BABY

At age two, Fan Sijia of Yuncheng City, Shanxi Province, China, was 3 ft 7 in (1.1 m) tall and weighed 100 lb (45 kg)—about four times the average weight for a girl her age.

Q kept "dying" Motorcyclist Steven Nixon from Derbyshire, England, suffered a massive heart attack after being in collision with a car—but he pulled through even though he had technically "died" 28 times over the next few hours when his heart repeatedly stopped beating.

Q tall guy Sultan Kosen of Turkey stands 8 ft 1 in (2.5 m) tall. His hands measure 10¾ in (27.5 cm) and his feet 14⅓ in (36.5 cm). He lives with his parents, three brothers and a sister, all of whom are of normal height and normal size.

Q bionic bottom After suffering massive internal injuries in a motorcycle crash, a man from South Yorkshire, England, now presses a remote control to open his bowels and go to the toilet. Surgeons rebuilt his bottom by taking a muscle from above his knee, wrapping it around his sphincter, and then attaching electrodes to the nerves. The electrodes are operated by a handset that he carries in his pocket and switches to on or off to control his bowel movements.

constantly seasick Jane Houghton from Cheshire, England, went on a week-long Mediterranean cruise—and still feels permanently seasick more than nine years later. She suffers from the rare Mal de Debarquement Syndrome, which causes people to feel as though they are constantly bobbing about on a rough sea. She feels so nauseous and wobbly that she has even had to stop buying clothes with stripes or busy patterns because she is unable to focus to iron them.

chute terror Skydiver Paul Lewis survived after falling 3,000 ft (900 m) onto the roof of a hangar at Tilstock Airfield, Shropshire, England, in August 2009. His main parachute failed to open at 3,000 ft (900 m) and although his reserve chute opened at 2,000 ft (600 m), a problem caused him to spiral out of control from 1,000 ft (300 m) with the canopy only partially opened. Luckily, the parachute became snagged on the hangar roof, preventing him from plunging to the ground and almost certain death.

busy brain The number of neurons in your brain—100 billion—is about the same as the number of stars in the Galaxy.

Twisted Tiger

Double contortionists Hassani Mohammed (right) and Lazarus Mwangi of Cirque Mother Africa bend over backward to entertain the audience at a show in Hamilton, New Zealand.

matching horns A Chinese grandmother who grew a 2.4-in (6-cm) horn on the left side of her forehead in 2009 began to develop a similar growth on the right side of her forehead a year later. Zhang Ruifang from Linlou has cutaneous horns—growths made of keratin, the same substance that makes up fingernails. Most cutaneous horns are just a few millimeters long, but occasionally they can extend a number of inches from the skin.

weight loss In January 2010, former postman Paul Mason of Suffolk, England, weighed 980 lb (444.5 kg)—but then he instantly lost 294 lb (133.5 kg) after undergoing gastric bypass surgery. The operation involved having part of his stomach stapled off so that all the food he eats goes into a small pouch, vastly restricting the amount he can consume. At his heaviest he ate 20,000 calories a day—eight times the amount needed by an average man.

coal-powered bike Sylvester H. Roper of Roxbury, Massachusetts, built a steam-powered velocipede in the 1860s that drove like a motorcycle but was instead fueled by coal.

teenage toddler Although she is old enough to drive a car, Brooke Greenberg of Reisterstown, Maryland, weighs just 16 lb (7.2 kg), is 30 in (75 cm) tall and rides around in a stroller pushed by her mother. The teenager has the body and behavior of a tiny toddler, thought to be the result of a mutation in the genes that control her aging and development, and which has apparently left her frozen in time.

tooth test Scientists can determine the ages of people born after 1943 to within 18 months by examining the amount of radioactive carbon in their teeth, caused by above-ground nuclear weapons testing in the 1950s and 1960s.

body
Ripley's Believe It or Not!®

Major Mite

MAJOR MITE
AGE 20 YEARS
WEIGHT 20 POUNDS
HEIGHT 26 INCHES

▼ At only 28 in (71 cm) tall when fully grown, Major Mite was no bigger than the average toddler.

▲ Major Mite would travel with his normal-sized parents Frank and Helen Howerton. Frank entered Major Mite in local sideshows before he was snapped up by the Ringling Brothers for their traveling circus. Each of his four brothers grew to be 6 ft (1.8 m) tall.

Clarence C. "Major Mite" Howerton was born in February 1913, and was billed by the press in the 1930s as the smallest man in the world. He stood only 28 in (71 cm) tall and weighed just 20 lb (9 kg). *He was so small that he once traveled from New York to Chicago to find a tailor who would make a tuxedo for his diminutive size. He wore custom-made shoes just 2.5 in (6 cm) long.*

The Ringling Brothers and Barnum & Bailey Circus signed up Major Mite in 1923, when he was ten years old, and he starred in its sideshow for more than 25 years. As well as being a big draw on the sideshow circuit, Major Mite featured in several Our Gang comedy shorts and played a trumpet-playing munchkin in the 1939 film The Wizard of Oz.

After a life in showbusiness, he died in Oregon at the age of 62.

▲ The Ringling Brothers Circus was the biggest of its kind, featuring 800 performers and more than a thousand animals.

▼ Major Mite plays cards with 7-ft-8-in-tall (2.3-m) Jack Earle during downtime while performing for the Ringling Brothers Circus in the early 1930s.

▲ Tiny Major Mite being held aloft by his friend, giant Jack Earle.

• Clarence C. Howerton was not the only "Major Mite," although he was by far the most famous. A 33-in (84-cm) comedian who died in New York in 1900 also shared the name, as did other little people on the circus sideshow circuit.

• Major Mite became a mascot for the U.S. Marine Corps recruitment before retiring from the entertainment industry in 1948.

▲ Major Mite performed with many extreme individuals, such as 700-lb (318-kg) Ruth Pontico.

◀ Reports suggest that Major Mite had a rebellious streak, sometimes dressing in children's clothes and then shocking the public by smoking, shouting—or posing on a motorbike.

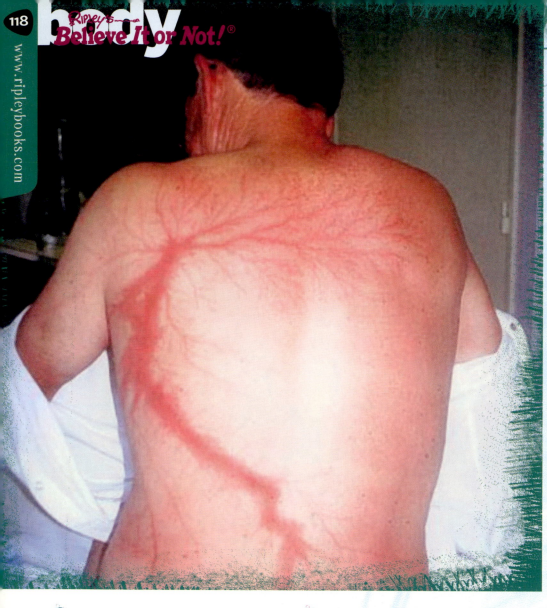

HEAVENLY STRIKE

This beautiful and unusual treelike pattern is the result of a lightning strike. The patient survived with no permanent injuries, and the red markings disappeared within two days. Known as a Lichtenberg Figure, or "lightning flower," the pattern on the skin is rarely seen and not fully understood. Experts believe that it may be caused by damage to small blood vessels along the path of the electric current, or bruising from shock waves in the air above the skin.

parasitic twin Eighteen-month-old Kang Mengru of Henan Province, China, had her dead twin removed from her stomach. Her parents were puzzled by her increasingly swollen stomach, which made her look pregnant, until medical scans revealed that she was carrying the parasitic fetus of her unborn twin in her belly. In such rare cases—affecting one in 500,000 births—one twin in the womb grows larger than the other and envelops its smaller sibling. The second fetus never fully develops, but continues to grow within the first baby, feeding off it like a parasite.

baby frozen Sixteen-week-old Finley Burton of County Durham, England, was put in a hospital "deep freeze" for four days to keep him alive when complications arose after heart surgery. His heart had started to beat alarmingly quickly, so his body was placed in a "cool bag," through which cold air was pumped to keep his temperature down. This slowed his metabolism, which in turn slowed his heart rate.

rare quads In December 2009, Lisa Kelly of Middlesbrough, England, gave birth to a set of quadruplets made up of two sets of identical twins—a ten-million-to-one chance!

vulture tonic In southern Africa, vultures' brains have become so popular as a traditional medicine that it has contributed to seven of the region's nine vulture species becoming endangered.

kangaroo care Having been told by doctors at a hospital in Sydney, Australia, that her premature baby Jamie had not survived the birth, Kate Ogg cuddled her lifeless son—born at 27 weeks and weighing just 2 lb (900 g)—next to her body and said her tearful goodbyes to him. Incredibly, after two hours of being hugged, touched and spoken to by his mother, baby Jamie began showing signs of life and was soon breathing normally and opening his eyes. The doctors called it a miracle but Kate put it down to "kangaroo care," a technique named after the way kangaroos hold their young in a pouch next to their bodies, allowing the mother to act as a human incubator and keep the baby warm.

knife horror Xiao Wei, a 16-year-old from Jilin, China, had a knife stabbed through his head that went in one side and out the other—but he survived after a two-hour operation to remove the blade.

big baby Muhammad Akbar Risuddin was born on September 21, 2009, in North Sumatra, Indonesia, at a weight of 19 lb 3 oz (8.7 kg)—more than twice the weight of an average baby.

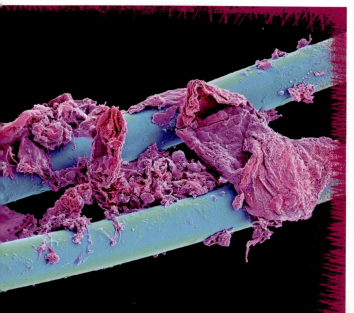

DENTAL DIRT

This is what your used dental floss looks like when magnified more than 500 times. Dental plaque, formed from bacteria and saliva, is clearly visible on the tiny floss fibers. Photographer Steve Gschmeissner from Bedford, England, used an electron microscope capable of magnifying objects more than 500,000 times to show everyday household items in a completely new light.

canadian citizen On December 31, 2008, a Ugandan woman gave birth on an airplane flying over Nova Scotia, Canada. Her newborn daughter was granted Canadian citizenship.

scaly growths Muhammad Yunusov from Kyrgyzstan was born with the rare skin condition *Granulomatous candidiasis*, which left his face and head covered in scaly barnacle-like growths. Cruelly dubbed "dragon boy," he never went out without wearing a mask to cover his face. After six years of torment, he was finally cured when a dermatologist got rid of the unsightly growths in just 17 days with a mixture of creams and medication.

star wars tattoos *Star Wars* fan Luke Kaye from Wiltshire, England, has undergone more than 100 hours of pain to cover his back, arms and legs with tattoos of over a dozen characters from all six *Star Wars* movies, including Luke Skywalker, C3PO and Darth Vader.

churchill's chompers A pair of gold-plated false teeth owned by former British Prime Minister Winston Churchill sold at auction for £15,000 in 2010. Without his dentures, Churchill would never have been able to make his rousing wartime speeches—in fact, they were so valuable to him that he carried a spare set at all times.

tiny tot A premature baby boy born at the University of Goettingen Hospital, Germany, in 2009 survived despite weighing less than 10 oz (283 g) at birth. The tiny tot weighed just 9.7 oz (275 g)—which is 75 grams below the weight doctors consider the minimum birth weight for a baby to survive.

human magnet Metal items such as coins, keys, safety pins and spanners can stick to the body of 50-year-old Brenda Allison from London, England, for up to 45 minutes without falling off. All through her life, her mysterious magnetic powers have set off car alarms, interrupted TV signals and blown out lightbulbs.

Beautiful Bite

To enhance their beauty, women in the Mentawai Islands of Indonesia have their teeth filed into sharp points. The unusual rite of passage, in which the teeth are chiseled into shape with no anesthetic, conforms to local opinions of beauty rather than any practical purpose. Observers have commented that Mentawai women seem to feel no pain during the process, and that they willingly undergo the ritual.

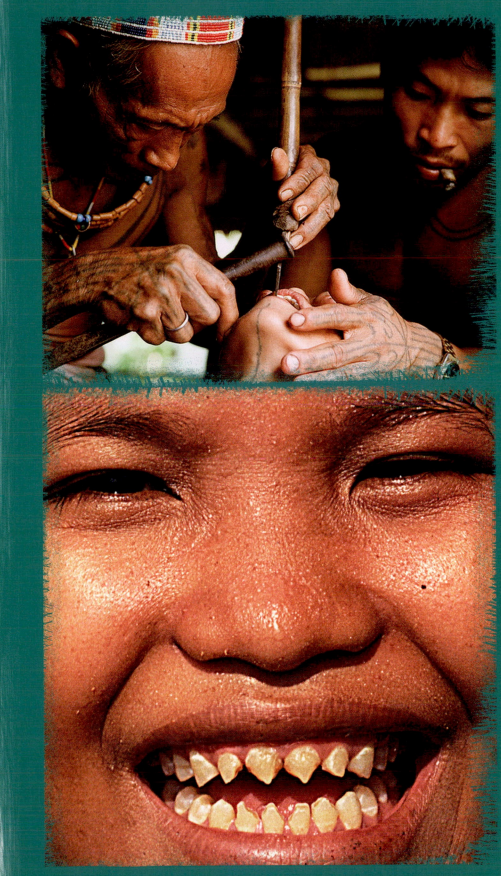

Ripley's—
Believe It or Not!®

RUSTY NAIL

A man had a rusty 4.7-in-long (12-cm) nail removed from his left kidney in Zhengzhou, Henan Province, China. The nail had been in Mr. Gao's body for 20 years following an accident at home. Although it had cut into his stomach and entered his body, he had sterilized the wound and it healed. In time, a membrane formed around the nail, preventing it penetrating deeper into his body.

glass eater Wang Xianjun of Sichuan Province, China, has eaten more than 1,500 lightbulbs. He started snacking on broken glass when he was 12 because it was "crispy and delicious," and now regularly eats a bulb for breakfast. He smashes the bulb and swallows it piece by piece while sipping from a glass of water. Although his bizarre diet has apparently not affected his health, it did cost him his marriage. He had kept his glass munching a secret from his wife, but when she caught him, she thought it was too weird and they separated.

blood camp The Indian political party Shiv Sena collected 24,200 bottles of blood in a single day at a blood donation camp in Goregaon.

impaled by tree A 13-in-long (33-cm) tree limb crashed through the windshield as Michelle Childers of Kamiah, Idaho, and her husband were driving down the road, impaling her through the neck. Amazingly, she survived.

titanic tumor Doctors in Buenos Aires, Argentina, removed an enormous tumor weighing 50 lb 11 oz (23 kg) from the womb of a 54-year-old woman in 2010. It had been growing inside her body for 18 months. She entered a hospital for the operation weighing 308 lb (140 kg), but after the removal of the tumor she was discharged weighing just 231 lb (105 kg).

saved by implants When a gunman opened fire with a semiautomatic assault rifle in a dentist's office in Beverly Hills, California, Lydia Carranza's life was saved by her size-D breast implants, which took the force of the blow and stopped bullet fragments from reaching her vital organs.

sticky situation Irmgard Holm, 70, of Phoenix, Arizona, sealed her eye shut after mistakenly using quick-drying glue instead of eye drops. She had confused the two products' similar-looking bottles. Doctors cut off the glue covering her eye and washed out the remainder to prevent serious damage.

MONSTER STONE

A kidney stone the size of a coconut was removed by surgeons in Hungary from the stomach of Sandor Sarkadi. Whereas even the largest kidney stones are seldom bigger than a golf ball, this one measured a whopping 6¾ in (17 cm) in diameter and weighed 2½ lb (1.1 kg).

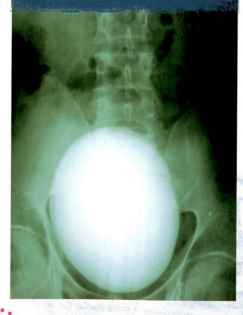

Kidney Hoard

In an operation that took four hours, doctors in Dhule, India, removed a staggering 172,155 kidney stones from the left kidney of 45-year-old Dhranraj Wadile in December 2009.

guardian angel Angel Alvarez survived despite being shot 23 times by New York City police officers during a disturbance in August 2010. Although he was shot in the arms, legs, abdomen and jaw, all the bullets somehow missed his vital organs.

self-amputation Jonathan Metz of West Hartford, Connecticut, saved his own life by partially sawing off his left arm after it had become trapped in his furnace boiler and started to turn gangrenous. Taking a blade from his toolbox, he began sawing through the arm to prevent the infection spreading to the rest of his body. To stem the flow of blood, he used first his shirt and then a telephone cord as a tourniquet. After more than two days —during which his only drink was rust-colored boiler water scooped into his mouth with a flip-flop he had been wearing— he was rescued and taken to hospital where doctors completed the amputation.

reading mystery On July 31, 2001, Canadian mystery writer Howard Engel awoke from a stroke and discovered he could no longer read—but could still write. He was diagnosed as having *alexia sine agraphia*, which meant that newspapers and even his own books appeared to be written in indecipherable oriental script.

supersized son At age three, Xiao Hao of Guangzhou, China, weighs a massive 140 lb (63.5 kg)—as much as an adult man. He dwarfs his mom and has been banned by some nurseries as a hazard to other children.

lucky bounce An 18-month-old boy escaped without a scratch after falling 80 ft (24.4m) from his seventh-floor apartment in Paris, France, bouncing off a café awning and into the arms of a passing doctor. The café was closed for the day and the awning was out only because a mechanism had jammed.

deadly device U.S. Army Private Channing Moss survived a direct body hit from an anti-vehicular rocket in Afghanistan. Luckily, the explosive head failed to detonate, but he was impaled by the rocket shaft.

on the run Former British Army soldier Mike Buss from Swindon, England, completed 517¼ mi (832.4 km) on a treadmill over seven grueling days. He ran the equivalent of nearly three marathons a day, sleeping for just two hours a day, and lost two toenails in the process.

Foreign Bodies

- SURGEONS IN CHINA FOUND A PIECE OF GRASS, 1 3/16 IN (3 CM) LONG, GROWING IN THE LUNG OF A TEN-MONTH-OLD BABY GIRL.

- AFTER SWALLOWING A BONE AT DINNER, A CALIFORNIAN BOY HAD IT STUCK IN HIS LUNG FOR THE NEXT 11 YEARS.

- A FRAGMENT OF A PLASTIC EATING UTENSIL WAS FOUND IN THE LEFT LUNG OF JOHN MANLEY FROM WILMINGTON, NORTH CAROLINA. HE HAD INHALED IT TWO YEARS EARLIER WHILE EATING AT A FAST-FOOD RESTAURANT.

- QIN YUAN FROM CHONGQING, CHINA, ACCIDENTALLY SWALLOWED HIS FALSE TEETH, WHICH WERE LATER FOUND LODGED IN ONE OF HIS LUNGS.

- SURGEONS IN INDIA REMOVED A TOOTHBRUSH FROM THE STOMACH OF ANIL KUMAR, WHO HAD ACCIDENTALLY SWALLOWED IT WHILE BRUSHING HIS TEETH IN FRONT OF THE TV.

- DEREK KIRCHEN FROM NORFOLK, ENGLAND, HAD A CASHEW NUT STUCK IN HIS LUNG FOR 18 MONTHS.

- A SMALL BRANCH OF WHITE CEDAR WAS FOUND IN THE LUNG OF A 61-YEAR-OLD JAPANESE WOMAN.

- CHRIS BROWN OF GLOUCESTERSHIRE, ENGLAND, COUGHED UP A 1-IN-LONG (2.5-CM) TWIG THAT HAD BEEN WEDGED IN HIS LUNG FOR 20 YEARS.

- A 62-YEAR-OLD FRENCHMAN SWALLOWED 350 COINS, AN ASSORTMENT OF NECKLACES AND SEVERAL NEEDLES. THE INGESTED MASS WEIGHED 12 LB 2 OZ (5.5 KG)—THE EQUIVALENT OF A BOWLING BALL—AND WAS SO HEAVY THAT IT HAD PUSHED THE MAN'S STOMACH BETWEEN HIS HIPS.

WEIRD INHALATION

After Artyom Sidorkin started coughing blood and complaining of chest pains, surgeons in Russia found a 2-in-long (5-cm) spruce tree inside his lung. He must have inhaled the piece of tree, which then got lodged in his lung, causing it to become seriously inflamed.

body

Ripley's
Believe It or Not!®

Accidental Discovery

X-rays were first observed in 1895 by German physicist Wilhelm Roentgen, who found them accidentally while experimenting with vacuum tubes. A form of electromagnetic radiation, they have gone on to become one of the most useful tools in medical history, employed for identifying everything from broken bones to accidentally swallowed toothbrushes.

chopstick removal A Chinese man had a chopstick removed from his stomach 28 years after swallowing it. Mr. Zhang had swallowed the chopstick in 1982, but thought it had been digested until he started suffering stomach pains. X-rays revealed that the remains of the chopstick were still inside him. Surgeons in Shanghai extricated it by making a small incision in his stomach.

▼ **FORK PAIN**
This patient had the misfortune to stand on a fork.

◄ **SAFETY PIN**
A safety pin lodged in the esophagus of a woman.

einstein scan An X-ray of Albert Einstein's skull fetched more than $35,000 at a 2010 auction in Beverly Hills, California. The genius scientist had the scan in 1945, ten years before his death at age 76.

botox cure A stroke victim who had been paralyzed for more than 20 years was able to walk again after being injected with Botox, a substance usually associated with smoothing wrinkles. Having been told by doctors that he would never regain his mobility, Russell McPhee of Victoria, Australia, was able to stand up and walk a few yards just a month after his first Botox injection.

chance discovery An X-ray of a 35-year-old woman from Para, Brazil, who complained of earache revealed that she had over 20 steel needles in her body. She had inserted the needles into herself as a child.

fatal pick In September 2008, a man from Manchester, England, died from a nosebleed caused by his aggressive nose picking.

horned man Jesse Thornhill of Tulsa, Oklahoma, has two devil horns on his head, created by surgically implanting Teflon lumps under the skin to stretch the scalp. The heavy-metal fan also boasts tattooed eyebrows, lengthened earlobes and implant earrings on his head.

echo location A blind English boy has learned to "see" again after adopting a technique used by dolphins and bats to detect where objects are. Jamie Aspland from Ashford, Kent, navigates his way around obstacles by means of echolocation, whereby he utters high-pitch clicks and then interprets the sound that rebounds off the surfaces.

tortoise woman For nearly 30 years, Sun Fengqin from Inner Mongolia carried a 55-lb (25-kg) tumor on her back, which resulted in her being nicknamed "Tortoise Woman." The tumor started as a yellow birthmark but grew so large that in the end she struggled to walk upright.

rubber man Vijay Sharma of Rajasthan, India, is so flexible that he can pass his body through a tennis racket, wind his arms around his back so that his hands grip each other at the front of his waist, wrap his legs over his head, and drink from bottles that he has gripped between his toes.

souvenir finger After losing part of his small finger, Matthew Tipler of Bend, Oregon, took the tip, encased it in clear plastic and made a keychain out of it.

▲ KEY LOCATION
This X-ray shows a key swallowed by a seven-year-old boy.

▼ SHARP REMINDER
Having penetrated a man's skin, a nail is lodged in the bones of his index and middle fingers.

▲ METAL MEAL
A variety of objects lodged in a patient's intestine, including a spoon and a blade.

bumpy landing In June 2009, window cleaner Alex Clay from Eau Claire, Wisconsin, fell six floors, bounced off a concrete first-floor roof and landed on the ground—surviving with nothing worse than a broken foot bone and a cut on his leg.

amnesia victim In 2009, a man later identified as Edward Lighthart walked out of a park in Seattle, Washington, with $600 in his sock but with no idea of who he was and how he got there—the victim of a rare form of dissociative amnesia.

too tall In 2010, at age 14, Elisany Silva from Belem, Brazil, already stood 6 ft 9½ in (2.07 m) tall—and was unable to go to school because she could not fit on the bus. She is believed to be suffering from gigantism, a condition in which the body produces excessive amounts of growth hormones.

facial transplant Thirty Spanish doctors at the Vall D'Hebron Hospital in Barcelona worked for 22 hours in March 2010 to perform a full facial transplant on a patient, which included skin, nerves, muscles, nose, lips, cheekbones, teeth and a jawbone. The recipient, a 31-year-old man, is eventually expected to regain up to 90 percent of his facial functions.

foot skills Born without arms, Ren Jiemei from Shandong Province, China, has learned to use her feet to eat, wash, comb her hair, draw pictures and cut paper. She is so skilled with her feet that when she uses them to thread a needle she is always successful on the first attempt—in fact, she is said to be the best embroiderer in her village. In her school days, she often topped the class despite having to write with her feet and use her mouth to turn book pages.

arm wrestler Joby Mathew from Kerala, India, may be only 3 ft 5 in (1.05 m) tall but he is a champion arm wrestler. Despite having severely underdeveloped legs, he is able to defeat able-bodied opponents who are twice his height. He can also jump up steps using only his hands and perform push-ups on just one hand.

first-aid app During the 65 hours that U.S. filmmaker Dan Woolley was trapped following the Haitian earthquake in January 2010, he used an iPhone first-aid application to treat his fractured leg and head wound.

skydiving champ Despite losing both his legs in a bomb explosion in Northern Ireland in 1992, former paratrooper Alistair Hodgson of Cumbria, England, is a freestyle skydiving champion and has made more than 5,000 jumps.

MINI MAN
At age 22, Wu Kang from Wuhan, China, wears the clothes of a nine-month-old toddler and stands just under 2 ft 3 in (68 cm) tall. Wu suffers from panhypopituitarism, which decreases the secretion of hormones, including growth hormones, produced by the pituitary gland in the brain.

body-building granny At age 73, grandmother Ernestine Shepherd of Baltimore, Maryland, gets up at 3 a.m. and spends her days running, lifting weights and working out. She runs 80 mi (130 km) a week—the equivalent of three marathons—bench-presses 150 lb (68 kg) and lifts 20-lb (9-kg) dumbbells.

heart stopped Joseph Tiralosi of Brooklyn, New York City, miraculously survived after his heart stopped beating for 45 minutes. The 56-year-old father had gone into sudden cardiac arrest inside the emergency room at New York-Presbyterian/Weill Cornell Medical Center, and it was nearly an hour before doctors succeeded in getting his heart going again. Usually if a person cannot be revived within six minutes, they die. Equally incredible, he came through the whole episode without suffering any form of brain damage.

poke-a-nut During a 2009 martial-arts demonstration in Malacca, Malaysia, Ho Eng Hui pierced four coconuts with his index finger in 31.8 seconds.

mass extraction Between the ages of seven and 12, Chelsea Keysaw of Kinnear, Wyoming, underwent three oral surgeries to remove a total of 13 extra permanent teeth and 15 baby teeth.

turtle boy Maimaiti Hali from Heping, China, was born with a hard, mutated growth covering most of his back, its shell-like appearance leading bullies to call him "Turtle Boy." The growth was removed from the eight-year-old's back in a two-hour operation in 2010 and replaced with skin grafts from his scalp and legs.

second face A baby born in China's Hunan Province has two faces. Kangkang was born in 2009 with a transverse facial cleft that extends nearly all the way up to his ears, making it look as if he is wearing a mask.

free flights Thirty-one-year-old Liew Siaw Hsia gave birth on an AirAsia flight over Malaysia in October 2009, and as a result the company granted her and her child free flights for life.

sandwich bag To keep the body temperature of a tiny premature baby warm, medics at Worcestershire Royal Hospital in England used the smallest insulating jacket they could find—a 6-in (15-cm) plastic sandwich bag from the hospital kitchens. The improvised insulator did the trick and saved the life of little Lexi Lacey who had been born 14 weeks early weighing just 14 oz (396 g) and had been given only a ten percent chance of survival.

making antivenom Snake antivenom is commonly produced by injecting horses with snake venom, then collecting the appropriate antibodies from their blood.

rope bed Gao Yang of Liaoning Province, China, can sleep on a single length of rope tied between two trees for up to seven hours at a time. He was taught special balancing skills at age 12 but it took him nearly a quarter of a century to master this feat by practicing on a 10-ft-high (3-m) rope in his local park every morning.

gold tattoo A business in Dubai offers temporary body tattoos made of real gold. The 24-carat gold-leaf tattoos are in demand for glitzy parties and weddings and can be bought for as little as $50. The company is also offering the tattoos in platinum.

•••••••••••••••• **BREATHE IN!** ••••••••••••••••
Steve McFarlane of South Jordan, Utah, can displace some of his internal organs to suck his stomach in with spectacular effect.

BEFORE

AFTER

Tattooed Mom

Bishop's daughter and mother-of-three Jinxi Boo, from Southern California, has almost her entire body covered in tattoos. She has a tattoo of a black-and-white dairy cow (because she's vegan), portraits of her family and her favorite musicians (Gwen Stefani, Björk, Cyndi Lauper and Meg White), plus a spectacular octopus tattoo across her throat and chest that took 26 hours to complete. A trip to Disneyland as a teenager inspired her love of tattoos, but she did not have her first design—a small cherry on her ankle—until she was 30.

Ripley's Believe It or Not!®

R nickel allergy Kim Taylor from Northamptonshire, England, is unable to touch hundreds of everyday items like keys, coins, zippers, scissors, door handles and saucepans because she is severely allergic to nickel. She takes her own wooden-handled cutlery to restaurants and has to cover everything nickel—even her eyeglasses, bra clasp and buttons—in nail varnish so that her skin doesn't come into contact with the metal.

R extra bones Dan Aziere of Danbury, Connecticut, suffers from multiple hereditary exostoses, a rare genetic disorder that causes extra bones to keep growing in his body. He estimates that he has about 50 excess bones—some as large as 4 in (10 cm) long—and since the age of five he has had more than a dozen operations to remove them.

R name jinx The parents of a boy who has failed to grow since being born on Dwarf Street claim the name has jinxed their child. Four-year-old Liu Chengrui from Wuhan, China, still weighs just 11 lb (5 kg) and stands only 2 ft (60 cm) tall.

R eye twitch Barbara Watkins of Halifax, England, suffers from a rare and bizarre condition that causes her to wink thousands of times a day. She has blepharospasm, an incurable condition that causes frequent muscle contractions around the eyes and affects just a handful of people in every million.

BEARDED LADY

When she suddenly started to grow facial hair in the 1920s, Mrs. Baker B. Twyman of Peoria, Illinois, supported her family by joining the circus as a bearded lady. She later had the surplus hair surgically removed.

R miracle boy Seventeen-month-old Jessiah Jackson of Leland, North Carolina, fell from a chair in July 2010 and a metal hook pierced his skull. It penetrated 2 in (5 cm) into his brain, but he survived.

R high life Husband and wife Wayne and Laurie Hallquist of Stockton, California, measure a combined height of 13 ft 4 in (4.07 m). He stands 6 ft 10 in (2.1 m) and she is 6 ft 6 in (1.97 m).

R hidden needle Doctors in China's Henan Province removed a needle from a man's brain that may have been there for 50 years. Following a seizure, Lin Yaohui, 51, was rushed to hospital where X-rays revealed the 2-in-long (5-cm) metal needle embedded in his skull. As an adult's skull is hard, surgeons believe the needle must have penetrated his head before he was 18 months old.

R sneezed bullet A man who was shot in the head during New Year's Eve celebrations in Naples, Italy, survived after sneezing the bullet out of his nose. The .22 calibre bullet went through the right side of Darco Sangermano's head, behind his eye socket, and lodged in his nasal passage. Bleeding heavily, he was rushed to a hospital but while waiting to be seen by doctors, he sneezed and the bullet flew out of his right nostril.

R tiny tot At 21 years old, Hatice Kocaman from Kadirli, Turkey, has the body mass of an eight-month-old baby. She suffers from a rare bone disease and stands just 28 in (70 cm) tall and weighs only 15 lb (6.8 kg).

TALL TEEN

At age 14, Brazilian teenager Elisany Silva towers over her sisters because she is already 6 ft 9 in (2.06 m) tall. She is so tall that she had to stop going to school because she could not fit on the bus. Medical experts believe she could be suffering from gigantism, a condition in which the body produces excessive amounts of growth hormones. If left untreated she could continue to grow up to 6 in (15 cm) more a year.

Dissecting Dad

To help teach anatomy to his students, Dr. Mahantesh Ramannavar dissected the body of his father, Dr. Basavanneppa Ramannavar, which had been embalmed for exactly two years. His father had specified in his will that his body should be donated to the university in Belgaum, India, where his son worked and that his son should perform the dissection, which was shown live on Indian TV.

turning the screw After an operation to remove a tumor left a gaping hole in his leg, 14-year-old Simeon Fairburn from Brisbane, Australia, saved the limb by turning surgical screws on a leg brace four times every day for over two years to stretch the bone by 1 ft (30 cm). He initially faced amputation, but after wearing the brace and undergoing 20 operations, he can once again dream of becoming a basketball player.

skewered neck Twelve-year-old Garret Mullikin from Houston, Texas, survived after a 9-in-long (23-cm) stick skewered his neck. Falling off a dirt bike, he hit the ground and the piece of tree branch, as thick as a broom handle, plunged into his neck and down into his chest, through his lung, past vital arteries and his heart. Doctors said that if the stick had been pulled out before he was rushed to hospital, he could have bled to death.

serial sleeper Claire Allen from Cambridge, England, falls asleep 100 times a day. Her condition—an extreme form of narcolepsy—causes her to fall into a trancelike state where she is unable to see or move. Each episode lasts between 30 seconds and five minutes and is triggered by emotions such as surprise and anger, and especially sufaces when she laughs.

worm's-eye view After John Matthews of Bellevue, Iowa, noticed two spots obscuring the vision in his left eye, doctors diagnosed the cause—a worm had got into his eye. The worm—thought to be either a hookworm or a raccoon roundworm—was then killed by medics who shot a laser into his left eyeball. "I could see it from behind," he said, "moving, trying to dodge the laser."

JOIN THE DOTS

Inspired by the idea of getting her birthmarks numbered, Colleen A.F. Venable from New York City has a connect-the-dots tattoo that creates the shape of a giraffe on her left leg.

R **nose leech** *Tyrannobdella rex*, a new species of leech with savage, sawlike teeth, was first discovered in the nose of a nine-year-old Peruvian girl. Named after the most ferocious dinosaur in history, the 2-in (5-cm) bloodsucker came to light after the girl, who regularly swam in tropical rivers and lakes, complained of feeling a sliding sensation in one of her nostrils.

R **latin tattoos** As a subject, Latin is ten times more popular in British schools than it was a decade ago. One theory for the ancient language's surge in popularity is that it is because celebrities such as Angelina Jolie, David Beckham and Colin Farrell have body tattoos with Latin inscriptions.

R **body piercing** In April 2010, Ed Bruns of Gillette, Wyoming, had more than 1,500 16-gauge needles inserted into his arms, back and legs by a body-piercing artist in less than 4½ hours.

R **tattoo proposal** When San Diego, California, tattoo artist Joe Wittenberg decided to propose to his girlfriend, he inked the words "Rachel, will you marry me?" on his own leg.

R **organs awry** Bethany Jordan from the West Midlands, England, was born with her internal organs in unexpected places in her body. Her heart is behind her lungs, her liver and stomach are on the opposite side of her body from normal and she has five tiny spleens instead of just one.

R **free leg** Needing a $60,000 bionic leg so that he could walk again, David Huckvale of Leicestershire, England, happened to go to his local pub on the same day as surgeon Alistair Gibson, who specializes in fitting the computer-controlled limbs. When the two got talking, Mr. Gibson mentioned he had a spare leg and could fit it for free!

R **hiccup cure** After hiccupping an estimated 20 million times over a period of three years, Chris Sands of Lincolnshire, England, finally stopped in 2009 following brain surgery. It is thought that a tumor on his brain stem had been pushing on nerves, causing him to hiccup every two seconds, 24 hours a day.

R **diamond tattoo** South African jeweler Yair Shimansky designed a temporary tattoo made of 612 diamonds and carrying a price tag of $924,000. It took more than eight hours to encrust the ornate floral design on the skin of a model using a special water-based adhesive.

R **rare phenomenon** A woman who had been pronounced dead hours earlier at a hospital in Cali, Colombia, following a series of unsuccessful resuscitation attempts suddenly started breathing again in a funeral home as workers began to apply formaldehyde to her body. Doctors later diagnosed her condition as a case of Lazarus Syndrome, an extremely rare phenomenon in which the body's circulation spontaneously restarts after failed resuscitations.

R **changing beard** Sameer Mehta, a businessman from Gujarat, India, makes weekly trips to the barber and has had more than 60 styles of short beard in the last four years. These have included a heart-shaped beard and another trimmed in the design of his country's flag.

R **rod removed** While playing on a construction site, 12-year-old Kalim Ali from Malegaon, India, was skewered by a rod 3 ft 4 in (1 m) long that pierced ten internal organs, including his rectum, small intestine, lungs and liver. Incredibly, the 0.6-in-thick (1.5-cm) pole didn't damage any major blood vessels, and surgeons successfully removed it after a three-hour operation.

R **26 digits** Heramb Ashok Kumthekar from Goa, India, has six fingers on each hand and seven toes on each foot, giving him a total of 26 digits. He is proud of his condition, called polydactylism, even though he has insufficient nerve endings to feel all his fingers and toes.

R **tall teen** At just 16 years old, schoolgirl Marvadene Anderson stood 6 ft 11 in (2.1 m) tall, making the New Jersey school basketball star 5 in (12.5 cm) taller than her idol, Michael Jordan. Height must run in the family because the Jamaican-born teenager's older sister, Kimberly, is 6 ft 4 in (1.9 m) tall.

R **bullet in head** After being shot at point-blank range by a German soldier in 1944, Ivan Nikulin of Chita, Russia, lived happily with a bullet lodged in his head for nearly 70 years.

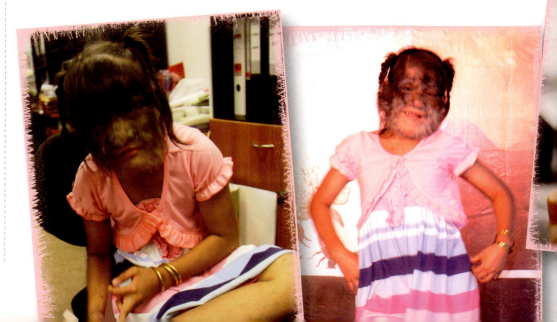

Furry Features

Supatra Sasuphan from Bangkok, Thailand, was born with Ambras Syndrome—or congenital hypertrichosis—a rare genetic disease that causes excessive hair growth on the face and other parts of the body. It affects one person in a billion, and there are fewer than 40 known cases in the world. There is no permanent cure for the condition, but nine-year-old Supatra doesn't let it affect her life and enjoys the same activities as her schoolfriends. She hopes eventually to become a teacher.

world

animals

sports

body

transport

feats

mysteries

food

arts

science

beyond belief

believe it!

Beatlemania

Art teacher Rebecca Bass and her students in Houston, Texas, won "Best of Show" at the 2010 Houston Art Car Festival with this dazzling vehicular tribute to the music of The Beatles. Each extravagant decoration is inspired by lyrics from Beatles songs. Ripley's soon snapped up the car, named *Lucy in the Sky with Diamonds*.

Ripley's—
EXHIBITS

124
125
126
127
128
129
130
131
132
133
134
135
136
137
138
139
140
141
142
143
144
145
146
147
148
149
150
151

THE LOST

Glacier Girl flying above Nevada in 2006. More than 80 percent of the new aircraft was built from original parts retrieved from deep beneath Greenland's ice and snow. In October 2002, before a crowd of 20,000 spectators, Glacier Girl took to the skies once again—60 years after her fateful crash in the Arctic. Now the plane can be seen at air shows across the U.S.A.

SQUADRON

A World-War-II fighter plane was rescued and restored to flying condition after spending 50 years buried beneath 268 ft (82 m) of solid snow and ice in Greenland.

The Lockheed P-38F Lightning, since nicknamed "Glacier Girl," was part of an eight-strong squadron making its way across the Atlantic to fight in Europe in June 1942. Bad weather forced the squadron to crash-land on a remote ice cap in Greenland. The crews were rescued after ten days on the ice, but the planes had to be sacrificed.

Later attempts to recover the aircraft proved unsuccessful because decades of snowstorms and shifting ice had carried them 2 mi (3.2 km) from their original location, and buried them so deep no one could find them. Then, in 1988, Glacier Girl was tracked down by a combination of magnetometers (to detect underground magnetic fields) and radar. A daring rescue and restoration project then swung into action.

To access the plane, hot water was passed down through long copper pipes to melt a 4-ft-wide (1.2-m) hole. Technicians rappelled down the hole for 20 minutes to reach the plane and used hot-water hoses to create a 50-ft-wide (15-m) chamber around it. Although the ice had crushed the canopy, the rest of the plane was intact. It took four months in 1992 to disassemble the plane and bring the parts to the surface, one piece at a time. The team, funded by businessman Roy Shoffner, had to sink five shafts to excavate a hole big enough for the last piece, the 17-ft-long (5.2-m), three-ton center section. The parts were taken to Middlesboro, Kentucky, for painstaking reconstruction.

R **all at sea** American sailor Reid Stowe returned to shore in June 2010 after spending more than three years at sea without touching dry land. He set off from New Jersey in his 70-ft (21-m) schooner *Anne* in April 2007 and docked in Manhattan at the end of a 1,152-day voyage, to be greeted by his girlfriend, who had joined him on part of the voyage, and their 23-month-old son, whom he had never seen before.

R **high security** The $400-million, 557-ft-long (170-m) yacht owned by Russian billionaire Roman Abramovich is equipped with a swimming pool, two helipads, a mini-submarine and a missile defense system.

R **highway party** Some 20,000 tables were set up along a 37-mile (60-km) section of a German autobahn between Dortmund and Duisberg for a street party with a difference. The high-speed road was closed to motorists and turned over to cyclists, skaters and picnickers in an event attended by more than three million people.

R **toilet car** Dave Hersch of Lakewood, Colorado, spent four years designing a twin-bowl motorized toilet capable of reaching speeds of 30 mph (48 km/h). His "toilet car" has a 6.5 horsepower motor, can seat two people and features six toilet rolls and a magazine rack.

R **yellow lines** Sally Baker left her Peugeot 206 on a street in Manchester, England, because the road had unrestricted parking—but when she returned she found the vehicle was facing the other way, had double yellow lines painted underneath and had a parking ticket on the windshield. In her absence, council workmen had hoisted her car into the air so that they could paint double yellow "no parking" lines beneath it.

R **homemade lamborghini** Truck driver Chen Jinmiao of Hunan Province, China, built a replica Lamborghini supercar—complete with the famous wing doors—for just $3,000. He downloaded the drawings from the Internet and bought materials from markets and bargain stores to construct a working car with a top speed of 50 mph (80 km/h)—compared to a real Lamborghini's 200 mph (320 km/h).

GatorBike

Jim Jablon from Florida has made a wild custom motorbike from a real-life alligator. Each year a number of wild alligators in the state are culled to control the population, and Jim decided to put one to good use. The reptilian chopper, named the GatorBike, took over a year to build, and features the full skull and skin of an alligator. Worth $80,000, the bike was created to raise funds for Jablon's wildlife rehabilitation park, which has its own rescued alligators alongside other animals, such as Arctic, the large albino Burmese python pictured above on the chopper.

Amphibious Bike In 2010, Lei Zhiqian of Hubei Province, China, rode an amphibious bicycle on a return trip across the 3,250-ft-wide (990-m) Hanjiang River in under 30 minutes. The bike, which is of normal design but has eight barrels for buoyancy and a propeller to push it forward in water, is the invention of Li Weiguo. Out of water the buoyancy barrels fold away so that it can be ridden like an ordinary bike.

bottle track Li Guiwen, a military driver from Beijing, China, gently steered a car along a track made up of two rows of upright bottles for more than 195 ft (60 m). His journey along the 1,798 bottles of beer took 8 minutes 28 seconds.

ship found In 2010, archeologists excavating the World Trade Center site in New York City discovered the remains of a wooden ship believed to have been buried there more than 200 years ago.

lucky leap During a traffic accident in August 2009, Carl Brewer of Canton, Ohio, saved himself by leaping from his motorcycle on to the back of a moving pickup truck.

persistent offender A Saudi-Arabian student racked up $97,000 in driving fines—the result of 400 traffic violations in Dubai over a period of less than two years.

HANG TIME

An Oklahoma driver escaped disaster after reversing his Mercedes sedan through the exterior wall of a parking garage—seven floors up! The driver's foot had become stuck on the gas pedal, but luckily the vehicle lodged itself halfway through the exterior wall. Falling debris damaged several cars, but no one was injured and the driver exited his vehicle safely.

BULLION BUGATTI

Made from solid 24-carat gold and platinum and featuring a large, flawless diamond on the front grille, the Bugatti Veyron Diamond must be the most expensive toy car ever made. It may be only toy-size, weighing 15 lb (7 kg) and measuring 10 in (25 cm) in length, but it costs a cool $2 million to buy—that's almost twice as expensive as a real, regular-size Bugatti Veyron! Jewelry designer Stuart Hughes from Liverpool, England, and Swiss model expert Robert Gulpen spent two months creating this intricate replica, which also features functional steering and a detailed engine.

transport

Believe It or Not!®

SPARKLING BLADES

War correspondent Michael Yon captured an unusual phenomenon while working in Afghanistan. When U.S. Air Force helicopters come into land, the dust in the air reacts with the spinning blades to create static electricity that throws out bright sparks around the chopper. Michael named this the Kopp-Etchells effect, after U.S. soldier Benjamin Kopp and British soldier Joseph Etchells, both of whom Yon knew and who died in the conflict.

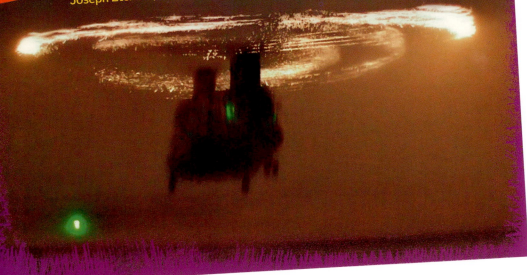

emergency landing Pilot Matt Conway was forced to make an emergency landing on a busy Atlanta, Georgia, highway after his plane experienced engine problems. He touched down on Interstate 85, a few miles from Peachtree DeKalb Airport, and skidded to a halt without hitting any cars. However, the plane did block four lanes, causing a long traffic jam until it was hauled away a few hours later.

flame thrower Fed up with car drivers cutting him off on the road, James Bond fan Colin Furze from Lincolnshire, England, designed the ultimate revenge—a gadget that fires 15-ft-long (4.5-m) flames out the back of his moped.

ejector scare A civilian passenger in a South African air force display plane accidentally activated the ejector seat while reaching for something to steady himself during a spectacular midair maneuver. The startled passenger instantly shot through the jet's Perspex canopy and was blasted 300 ft (90 m) into the sky by the rocket-powered emergency chair. He subsequently floated down to the ground on a parachute that opened automatically.

coal-powered bike Sylvester H. Roper of Roxbury, Massachusetts, built a steam-powered velocipede in the 1860s that drove like a motorcycle but was fueled by coal.

flying car A company from Massachusetts has devised a road car that can convert into an airplane in just 30 seconds. The Terrafugia Transition, which has four wheels, two folding wings, and a propeller at the rear, can reach speeds of 80 mph (130 km/h) on the ground and 115 mph (185 km/h) in the air. It can be stored in a conventional garage yet has a flight range of more than 490 mi (790 km).

personal potholes In an attempt to finance the repair of its crumbling roads, the village of Niederzimmern, Germany, put its many potholes up for sale in 2010. For $68, people could buy a hole in the road, and in return the authorities repaired it and put a personal message on top. TV channels and newspapers soon bought some of the potholes for advertising.

busy airport London's Heathrow Airport is six times the size of the country of Monaco and has three chaplains—Anglican, Catholic, Free Church—and representatives for the Jewish, Muslim, Hindu, Buddhist and Sikh faiths. Nearly 70 million passengers pass through each year, and 10 percent of Britain's perfume sales take place at the airport.

homemade sub In October 2009, Tao Xiangli, a farmer from Beijing, China, made a successful maiden voyage in his homemade submarine. Without any expert advice, he spent 18 months building the 4-ft-10-in-high (1.5-m), 21-ft-long (6.5-m), one-man, battery-powered sub from used scrap. The body is made out of five oil drums, the sonar is improvised from a stethoscope, and the periscope is an old camera. He tested the vessel by taking it down to the bottom of a local river and staying there for nearly five minutes.

JET BUS

It wouldn't take long to get to school in Paul Stender's jet-powered school bus. *School Time* is equipped with a massive Phantom jet-fighter engine with the power of more than 250 family automobiles, propelling the 35-ft (10.5-m) bus to speeds more than 350 mph (560 km/h). Turbine-crazy Paul has also built a 10,000-horsepower Dodge pickup that can reach 400 mph (645 km/h), and a jet-powered outhouse featured in *Ripley's Believe It or Not! Seeing is Believing.*

hypersonic flight Flying off the coast of southern California in May 2010, an unmanned X-51A Waverider aircraft flew for more than three minutes at Mach 5—that's five times the speed of sound and more than 3,800 mph (6,115 km/h).

police tractor To combat crime in rural areas of Lincolnshire, England, a farm tractor has been converted into a police vehicle, complete with a flashing blue light.

back to life A 1929 Austin 12/4 car that had been languishing idly in a garage in Lincolnshire, England, instantly roared into life in 2010 when its starter handle was turned for the first time in nearly 50 years. The car had been owned by Roger Bulled's late father, Leslie, who had last driven it in 1961.

helicopter rescue A Swiss van driver and his vehicle had to be rescued by helicopter after his GPS sent him up a remote mountain footpath near Bergun. Robert Ziegler found himself stranded on the narrow track, unable to go forward or turn around.

wrong nuts In May 2009, a car traveling down a Swiss highway lost all four of its wheels at the same time. The owner had used the wrong nuts to secure them.

lost torpedo The Taiwanese navy offered a reward of nearly $1,000 in 2010 after sailors aboard the submarine *Sea Dragon* lost a torpedo during a routine training exercise.

much traveled German police who stopped a double-decker Latvian tour bus in Berlin in 2010 found that it had 1.1 million mi (1.8 million km) on the clock—enough to go to the Moon and back twice.

barbie ban Forty-year-old Paul Hutton of Essex, England, was banned from the road after being caught drunk driving in a toy Barbie car that had a top speed of 4 mph (6 km/h). The electric car was designed for three-to-five-year-olds.

melon-coly motorists A busy motorway near Basel, Switzerland, was closed for two hours after a Spanish truck carrying melons lost its load and splattered fruit all over the road. Drivers in the 3-mi-long (5-km) traffic jam eased the pain of their delay by getting out of their cars and helping themselves to the melons.

Off the Rails

One of the most bizarre rail accidents in history occurred in 1895, when a steam locomotive thundered into the Montparnasse station in Paris, France, at full speed. The engine plowed through the platform and then the station wall, crashing into the street 30 ft (9 m) below and killing a pedestrian. The train had been 2 mi (3.2 km) from the station and traveling at 55 mph (90 km/h) when the driver realized that the brakes had failed. Despite the driver's best efforts, the locomotive hit the station at 35 mph (55 km/h). All those aboard escaped serious injury.

GREAT BALL OF FIRE

Pilot Captain Brian Bews parachuted to safety seconds before his $30-million CF-18 fighter jet crashed and exploded in a devastating ball of fire at Lethbridge County Airport, Alberta, Canada. Having completed his practice routine for the 2010 Alberta International Air Show, he was returning to land at the airport when the plane suddenly nose-dived on approach. Just 100 ft (30 m) from the ground, he managed to escape using the plane's rocket-powered ejector seat. Moments later, the plane smashed into the ground and was engulfed in smoke and flames, but Captain Bews survived with only minor injuries.

CHEATED DEATH

Stunt pilot Dino Moline cheated death by a split second by deploying his built-in parachute after a wing of his plane fell off at an air show in Santa Fe, Argentina. After performing a series of daring, acrobatic maneuvers, Moline was flying upside down when he felt an explosion and saw the shadow of the detached wing pass the cockpit. As the plane spiraled out of control, he instantly activated its parachute, which slowed the aircraft's descent and allowed it to float gently to the ground where it caught fire. Moline escaped with only one small injury—a burned foot.

GLIDER CRASH

Former racing-car driver Mike Newman escaped unharmed except for three broken vertebrae after the glider he was piloting crashed at high speed into the runway in front of 15,000 spectators at an air show in West Sussex, England. After performing his routine, he prepared to land but a malfunction caused the glider to plunge almost vertically to the ground, striking its wing first. The nose section crumpled around him and the cockpit burst open, leaving him dangerously exposed. He lay stunned amid the wreckage for a minute before managing to stumble out onto the runway.

PLANE SAILING

Is it a boat? Is it a plane? Actually, it's a bit of both—a plane–boat. Visitors to Fort Lauderdale, Florida, can charter Dave Drimmer's *Cosmic Muffin*, a boat recycled from movie-producer Howard Hughes' old Boeing B-307 airplane. The historic Stratoliner plane was rescued from landfill in 1969 by pilot Ken London, who bought it for $69 and spent four years removing the wings and converting it into a luxury boat. The cockpit of the original plane still houses the controls that pilot the boat.

When is a Stratoliner airplane not an airplane?

school flight When a ferry service was stopped in late 2009, the school children of Papa Westray in Scotland's Orkney Islands were forced to take a 96-second air flight to school each day.

horse-drawn hummer Jeremy Dean of New York City spent $15,000 on his Hummer H2 sport utility vehicle, and then turned it into a horse-drawn carriage.

warthog alert In November 2009, an Air Zimbabwe plane made an emergency stop after hitting a warthog on the runway in Harare, Zimbabwe.

mini motorbike Santosh Kumar of Mysore, India, built an electric motorcycle less than 18 in (45 cm) long and less than 1 ft (30 cm) tall, but capable of carrying a person.

cone fall Shortly after takeoff, a 20-lb (9-kg) engine tailcone, measuring 4 ft (1.2 m) long and 3 ft (90 cm) in diameter, plummeted thousands of feet from a Delta Air Lines jet and landed on the lawn of a home in Roosevelt, New York. None of the crew noticed that the part had fallen off, and the plane—a Boeing 777—was able to complete its journey from Kennedy Airport to Tokyo, Japan.

Monster Limo

The Midnight Rider, a giant tractor-trailer limo, is 70 ft (21 m) long, 13 ft 8 in (4.2 m) high, has 22 wheels, weighs about 50,560 lb (22,930 kg) and has room for 40 passengers. Owned by Pamela Bartholomew Machado from California, the monster vehicle, which costs $1,000 an hour to hire, boasts three lounges, a bar and a bathroom. To refuel it with a full tank of gas costs about $700 and a full oil change costs around $1,000.

Five decades later, when it's a boat...

... with steering controls in the cockpit.

sole owner Ninety-two-year-old Rachel Veitch of Orlando, Florida, bought her Mercury Comet Caliente new in 1964 and has since driven it nearly 600,000 mi (965,500 km).

wooden bicycles Max Samuelson of Cape May, New Jersey, builds functional bicycles out of wood, using as many as 120 pieces of wood in a single bike.

motorized unicycle In 2009, Japanese manufacturer Honda unveiled a motorized unicycle designed mainly for the country's aging population. It has a series of smaller, motor-controlled wheels inside the main wheel, so that to steer the 22-lb (10-kg) battery-powered device on a busy sidewalk all you have to do is perch on it and lean in the direction you want to go.

welcome tip Taxi driver Don Pratt from Cornwall, England, retired from work in 2010 after a grateful passenger left him a $375,000 tip in her will. Don had spent 20 years ferrying pensioner Mary Watson to and from her local shops.

electric bullet In August 2010, the Buckeye Bullet 2.5, an electric car designed by a team of students from Ohio State University, clocked an average speed of 307.7 mph (495.2 km/h) on Utah's Bonneville Salt Flats. The Bullet is powered by nearly 1,600 compact lithium-ion batteries, the kind that power laptops.

parking space An uncovered, outdoor parking space in Boston, Massachusetts, was sold for $300,000 in June 2009.

out to launch Having spent nearly 30 years building a boat in his mother's back garden in Hampshire, England, Owen Warboys finally launched the 40-ft-long (12-m) sloop in 2010. He got the 20-ton vessel out of the garden by hiring a crane that lifted it 40 ft (12 m) into the air over the house and onto a truck.

viking land boat Matt Norris of Austin, Texas, spent two years building a 45-ft-long (14-m) human-powered road vehicle in the style of a Viking longboat. Made of steel and corrugated plastic, it glides on trailer tires, has the axle of a golf cart and is propelled by its crew of 13 people who "row" a system of pulleys and cables.

close encounter A motorist in London, England, tried to avoid a fine for driving in a bus lane by claiming aliens had forced him into it.

extended journey Given permission to drive the family pickup truck to the end of the driveway to unload trash at their home in Damascus, Oregon, a 12-year-old boy kept going for nearly 100 mi (160 km) until he was stopped by police.

modern sailing To cut fuel costs by 20 percent and reduce greenhouse emissions, the 10,000-ton German cargo ship MV *Beluga Skysails* is partially powered by a huge kite. In a throwback to old sailing ships, the 433-ft-long (132-m) vessel is pulled by a computer-guided 1,720-sq-ft (160-sq-m) kite, which is tethered to a 49-ft-high (15-m) mast.

WHEELIE WIZARD

Tyler Shepard, the "Wheelie Wizard" of Middletown, Ohio, rides near-vertical wheelies on a Honda XR 50 motorbike without a front wheel. His wheelie shows include such incredible feats as riding his one-wheeled bike in a wheelie while blindfolded, and maintaining a wheelie for 1 hour 30 minutes nonstop during a parade.

FAKE PORSCHE

Austrian artist Hannes Langeder spent six months building a life-size Porsche sports car from plastic pipes, tape and cardboard. The aluminum-foil-covered Ferdinand GT3-RS has no engine, but is powered by a hidden bicycle, which is why it has handlebars instead of a steering wheel.

floating palace At 1,187 ft (362 m) long, the Finnish-built liner *Oasis of the Seas* is four times the length of a football field and, at 236 ft (72 m) high, it is taller than Nelson's Column in London. Over 3,300 mi (5,310 km) of electrical cabling and 150 mi (240 km) of pipework run through the ship, which took 8,000 man years to build (three years in actual time). Around 160,000 gal (600,000 l) of paint were used to decorate the luxury vessel, which boasts every conceivable facility, including basketball courts, ice rinks, a hospital, a landscaped park and a wedding chapel. Some 55 tons of ice are produced onboard every day to supply the ship's 37 bars and 20 cafés and restaurants, and no fewer than 50,000 pieces of cutlery are housed in the main dining room.

last orders Matthias Krankl of Maulburg, Germany, was banned from driving by police after converting a beer crate into a motorized mini quad bike.

bottle boat Four months after leaving San Francisco, California, the *Plastiki*, a 60-ft (18-m) catamaran built from 12,500 recycled plastic bottles, reached Sydney, Australia, in July 2010 at the end of an 9,550-mi (15,370-km) voyage across the Pacific Ocean. The boat's bottles were lashed to pontoons and held together with glue made from cashew nut husks and sugar cane. Even the sails were made from recycled plastic.

versatile vehicle Dave March of the Californian company WaterCar has created the Python, a $220,000 amphibious supercar that can reach speeds of 125 mph (200 km/h) on land and 60 mph (96 km/h)—faster than many speedboats—on water. All the driver has to do before entering the water is put the gears into neutral, engage the jet drive, then push a button to raise the wheels.

lucky escape A driving lesson on Good Luck Road, Lanham, Maryland, ended with a large family car crashing through the wall of a ground-floor apartment and finishing up on a bed where the homeowner had been lying just minutes earlier.

backward driver Indian taxi driver Harpreet Dev drives everywhere in reverse. His backward driving skills have become so famous in his hometown of Bhatinda that he has even been given a special government license allowing him to drive in reverse anywhere in the state of Punjab. His enthusiasm for driving backward at speeds of up to 50 mph (80 km/h) began one night in 2003 as he was returning home from a party. He discovered that, owing to a mechanical fault, only the reverse gear of his Fiat Padmini worked. He has since redesigned the car's gearbox so that it has four reverse gears and just one forward one.

super model Tony Nijhuis of East Sussex, England, has built a balsa wood and plywood model airplane that weighs more than 100 lb (45 kg) and, with a 20-ft (6-m) wingspan, is as wide as a house. The model is so large it is classed as a light aircraft and has to be licensed by the Civil Aviation Authority. He spent two years and £8,000 constructing the 1:7 scale version of a 1950s U.S. Air Force Boeing B-50 Superfortress bomber, which has four electric motors, 96 batteries and can reach a speed of 40 mph (64 km/h).

long leak The World-War-II ruin of the battleship U.S.S. *Arizona* is still leaking oil into the ocean nearly 70 years after it was sunk in Pearl Harbor, Hawaii.

ZIPPER BOAT

Japanese artist Yasuhiro Suzuki has designed a boat that looks like a zipper—and the wake it leaves behind it in the water makes it look like it's unzipping the ocean as it goes along.

Inflatable Weapons

Russian balloon manufacturer Rusbal has created a range of full-size inflatable weapons—including fighter planes and tanks (see above)—that look realistic to the enemy from as near as 330 ft (100 m). The country's defense department commissioned the models as decoys in order to protect real combat units from strikes.

Such inflatables are not a new invention. During World War II, the British army used blow-up rubber tanks as decoys. Designed to look just like a U.S. Sherman tank—and easily carried by four men—they were deployed before the Normandy Landings in 1944 in an attempt to deceive the German Army.

R **built to last** School caretaker Owen Hook of Cambridgeshire, England, has ridden the same bicycle for nearly 60 years. He bought the top-of-the-line three-speed Raleigh cycle in 1953 and still rides it half-a-mile to and from work every day.

R **maiden flight** After six years of design and construction, a Chinese cobbler, who left school with only a basic education, completed a maiden flight in his homemade airplane. Huang Jianjun of Hunan Province spent more than $15,000 on the project—and in June 2010 his plane soared to a height of over 1,640 ft (500 m) before landing successfully.

animals

sports

body

transport

feats

mysteries

food

arts

science

beyond belief

believe it!

world

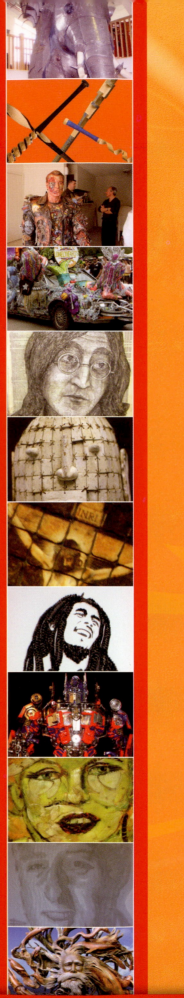

144
145
146
147
148
149
150
151
152
153
154
155
156
157
158
159
160
161
162
163
164
165
166
167
168
169
170
171

Dial - a - Portrait

Alex Queral's celebrity portraits, carved from whole phone books, jumped out of the pages of an earlier Ripley's Believe It or Not! book—*Enter If You Dare!* Ripley's now have several of his creations on display at a number of museums, including Marilyn Monroe, Jack Nicholson and, seen here, John Lennon.

Ripley's EXHIBITS

GREAT ESCAPES

At 32 years old, Akash Awasthi is already one of the most daring escapologists in India, risking life and limb to escape from a burning haystack, a locked box deep underwater and a coffin placed in the path of a speeding truck.

He has also ridden a motorbike through the packed city streets of Trivandrum, Kerala, while blindfolded. He is following in the footsteps of his father, Anand Awasthi, one of the most famous magicians in the country.

Akash is hoisted into the air by a 120-ft (37-m) crane.

THE GREAT FIRE ESCAPE

Akash's most dangerous feat is to escape from a giant burning haystack. First he is bound with 25 locks and a 25-ft-long (7.5-m) chain, and hoisted into the air on a 120-ft (37-m) crane.

Akash fights his way out of the burning haystack, which becomes an inferno within seconds.

UNDERWATER ESCAPE

Akash has twice taken on the famous underwater box escape. It was first performed by the legendary Harry Houdini in 1912 in New York, and he took 57 seconds to free himself. Akash's father also performed the stunt in 1970, taking 40 seconds to emerge. This escape is one of the most dangerous performed by escapologists. In 1983, Dean Gunnarson failed to escape from a coffin submerged in a Canadian river and stopped breathing before being resuscitated. In his first attempt at the underwater record in Hyderabad, Akash took just 15 seconds to reach the surface. His second attempt was in the harbor at Trivandrum. Handcuffed and chained, he was locked inside a box and lowered into water 150 ft (46 m) deep. Akash surfaced after only a few seconds. When the box was retrieved from the water, it was intact, with the chains and handcuffs still inside.

The box containing Akash, who has been bound with chains, is lowered into the water.

The fearless escapologist emerges from the locked box.

Akash emerges from the flames, unchained, moments before the haystack is completely engulfed. He is tended to by volunteers.

FAMOUS ESCAPES

1. Matt the Knife (U.S.A.) took just 11 seconds to free himself from handcuffs while underwater.

2. Dorothy Dietrich (U.S.A.) escaped from a straitjacket while suspended from a burning rope hundreds of feet in the air.

3. Dean Gunnarson (Canada) escaped from a straitjacket while hanging upside down from a trapeze 726 ft (221 m) above the gorge of the Hoover Dam.

4. David Merlini (Hungary) escaped from a shark-filled pool while in a straitjacket, weights and restraints.

5. Zdenek Bradac (Czech Republic) escaped from a pair of real police handcuffs in 1.6 seconds.

6. David Straitjacket (U.K.) escaped from a straitjacket while on stilts in 1 minute 38 seconds.

7. David Blaine (U.S.A.) took 15 minutes to free himself from shackles and a gyroscope that had been spinning him around 50 ft (15 m) above Times Square, New York, for 52 hours.

Ripley's Believe It or Not!®

Stilt Stunt

In 1891, Sylvain Dornon from Landes, France, walked from Paris to Moscow, Russia, on stilts! He completed the 1,830-mi (2,945-km) journey in 58 days, averaging more than 30 mi (50 km) each day. Earlier in the 19th century, stilts were a fairly common means of getting around marshy terrain in certain parts of France, especially among shepherds, but, by 1891, Dornon was considered very strange indeed.

spinning yo-yos At the 2010 London Toy Fair, Ben McPhee from Australia kept 16 yo-yos spinning simultaneously. He had yo-yos hanging off hooks, his fingers, and even his ears and teeth.

young climber At just five years old, Sail Chapman of East Yorkshire, England, achieved his ambition of scaling all 214 peaks listed in Alfred Wainwright's famous Lake District guidebooks. He began walking the Cumbrian hills with his family at the age of two and completed the Wainwright peaks when he reached the top of his namesake fell, Sale, which stands at 2,536 ft (773 m).

UNDERWATER JUGGLER
With a single breath, Merlin Cadogan from Devon, England, was able to juggle three objects underwater for 1 minute 20 seconds.

tough granny Pint-sized Sakinat Khanapiyeva, a 76-year-old grandmother from Dagestan, Russia, can tear through phone books, lift a 52-lb (23.5-kg) dumbbell while standing on a bed of nails, and break iron horseshoes. She first realized how strong she was at the age of ten when she moved a 660-lb (300-kg) box of grain—equal to the weight of four grown men.

NOSE-TO-NOSE
In March 2010, Robert Officer and John Milhiser from the Serious Lunch comedy group touched noses together for 10 hours 34 minutes, with no breaks or interruptions. Robert and John's record-breaking task included a trip on the New York subway and bathroom breaks together before appearing live on the Jimmy Fallon show.

wheelchair wheelie Nineteen-year-old Michael Miller of Ellington, Wisconsin, performed a 10-mi (16-km) wheelie in a wheelchair. Michael, who was born with spina bifida, completed 40 laps of a high-school track on two wheels in just under 4 hours. He performed his first wheelchair wheelie when he was just four years old.

text exchange Nick Andes and Doug Klinger, two friends from central Pennsylvania, exchanged a thumb-numbing 217,033 texts during March 2009. At the end of the month, Andes received an unexpected itemized bill for $26,000—for the 142,000 texts he had sent and the 75,000 he had received from Klinger.

happy hugger In Las Vegas, Nevada, on Valentine's weekend 2010, 51-year-old Jeff Ondash (a.k.a. Teddy McHuggin) of Canfield, Ohio, gave out 7,777 hugs in just 24 hours—the equivalent of more than five hugs a minute.

senior student Hazel Soares of San Leandro, California, received her college diploma in May 2010—at age 94! "It's taken me quite a long time because I've had a busy life," said the mother-of-six, who has more than 40 grandchildren and great-grandchildren.

tea potty Over a period of 25 years, Sue Blazye from Kent, England, has built up a collection of more than 6,000 teapots—and they take up so much room that she has converted her home (called Teapot Island) into a museum. Her favorite teapot is in the shape of Princess Diana's head, and was made when she got engaged to Prince Charles.

mayor moore Hilmar Moore has served as the mayor of Richmond, Texas, for more than 60 years. He was first appointed in 1949 and has been re-elected every two years since, although the last time he had an opponent was 1996.

bat breaker At the Riverwalk Stadium, Montgomery, Alabama—home of the Montgomery Biscuits Minor League baseball team—Steve Carrier broke 30 baseball bats over his leg in less than a minute. The 6-ft-4-in (1.9-m), 290-lb (131-kg) Carrier, from Dallas, Texas, also bends steel with his teeth.

Into the Skies

Aerial adventurer and qualified pilot Jonathan R. Trappe from North Carolina made history in May 2010 by traveling 76 mi (122 km) across the English Channel attached to a bunch of 55 helium balloons. Drifting from Ashford, England, toward France, Jonathan reached speeds of 35 mph (56 km/h) and heights of 7,000 ft (2,135 m). Three hours 22 minutes after taking off, and after a flight adjustment to avoid Belgium, he landed safely in a cabbage field near Dunkirk, France.

Ripley's Ask

Why did you first start balloon flying? I first became interested in balloon flight as a child—I wondered at a balloon, and how it floated upon the air. Then I thought "If I just get enough of these, couldn't I go into the sky?" As an adult, I left behind the idea that such a thing isn't possible and awakened a dream that had grown quiet.

What inspired you to cross the channel? The English Channel is a challenge that has called to aviators for generations. There is romance in flying over the famous White Cliffs of Dover and the Lighthouse at Dunkirk.

What was it like when you were in the sky? A quiet dream. I was 1,000 feet above the water and I could hear only the waves. When you're in the air, you move perfectly with the wind, not knowing where you'll land.

Was it a bumpy landing? The landing was smooth, but after the landing, as I worked to release the helium and take my balloons down, the winds kicked up!

What are your balloon ambitions? I would like to launch out of California, within sight of the ocean, and then fly inland, above the Sierra Nevada mountains, into the heart of America.

Ripley's Believe It or Not!

WALL OF DEATH

The crowd peers over the Wall of Death as the powerful motorbikes roll into the ring. The sound inside the track grows deafening as the motorbikes accelerate, tires rumbling. As they pick up speed, the bikes climb the steep, wooden walls until the riders flash inches past the faces in the audience.

Tubular tracks with steep walls, Walls of Death, or Motordromes, evolved in the early 20th century. Riders would start at the bottom of the circular track, increasing their speed and the angle, until they were racing at just over 55 mph (88 km/h) at right angles to the wooden wall. One slip could spell disaster—early Wall of Death riders had little or no safety equipment, often neglecting to wear helmets because the force of gravity would make it hard to keep their heads straight. Soon riders started to increase the risk, racing two or three abreast, crossing each other and even introducing motorcars. Optimum speed was essential. If the bikes went slower than 55 mph (88 km/h), they would drop off the wall; too much faster and the riders were in danger of blacking out as the centrifugal force could drain blood from the brain. Motordromes are now rare—few exist in North America and Europe, but they continue to draw big crowds in Asia.

Cookie Crum, still riding motorbikes and now living in Oregon, was one of the few female Motordrome riders. She first started to ride the Wall of Death in 1949, when only 17 years old, and toured the U.S.A. for eight years. Cookie also rode in what became known as "liondromes." To thrill the crowd even further, fully grown lions were let loose on the boards, the idea being that they would chase the rider around the ring. Incredibly, they were also trained to sit in vehicles as they tore round the Motordrome (see bottom right). ▼

Cookie, how did you start out riding on the wall of death? I can't remember when I didn't have a love for motorcycles. My mother used to say, "By the time you're 16 you won't even notice one going by." Well, here I am 79 years old and still riding—on the street—not the Wall of Death."

How hard was it to learn? I lived in Sarasota, Florida, where a boy named Kenny Kennedy taught me to ride. A few years later I saw an advertisement in the Sarasota newspaper for a female exhibition rider in a Motordrome. So I went for the interview and got the job! Learning to ride is different to how you would imagine. The instructor pushes you around the floor until you get over trying to "straighten up." Then you get one cylinder (the other one they have pulled the spark plug out of) until you can ride around the floor without putting your feet down. Then you get two cylinders and keep working up in stages till that wonderful day (six or eight weeks down the line) when you finally make it up to the straight wall!

Did you ever crash? Because my instructor was very slow and easy, I learned without an accident. Which is not to say I didn't "slide" off the wall a few times!

Were you ever frightened by the liondrome? I don't think I was ever "frightened" by the lion that was on the one show I played on. I do remember one thing about him, though. His cage was next to my stool out in front and almost every time the boys put him in it, he would stroll over to my side, lift his leg, and... you guessed it. Maybe he didn't like me?

What did it feel like to ride on the wall of death? I loved performing for the crowds, especially the children. I could walk inside, start my Indian motorcycle and take off up the wall like most people would open the door and go into a restaurant for a cup of coffee—that relaxed! Yet when I would go upstairs to watch one of the guys ride, I was as amazed as some of the crowd. I thought I couldn't possibly do that! To this day, all these years later, I still get the same feeling whenever I see a Motordrome. Which, by the way, there aren't too many of, so if you get the chance to see one—DO!"

▶ Stuntmen perform death-defying feats on motorbikes and in cars whizzing around the walls of "Wells of Death" at fairs across India. A modern twist on the original Walls of Death, these dromes attract large crowds wherever they spring up.

Ⓡ **everest landing** British skydivers Leo Dickinson and Ralph Mitchell and Indian Air Force officer Ramesh Tripathi successfully landed their parachutes at an altitude of 16,800 ft (5,120 m) on Mount Everest in September 2009. After jumping out of a helicopter at 20,500 ft (6,250 m), they had just five seconds of free fall in which to open their chutes. The trio had to home in on Gorak Shep—a narrow, sand-covered lakebed and the only safe landing spot for miles around. "It was pretty hairy," said 62-year-old Dickinson. "If you missed that or overshot it, you were either going to die or end up with something important broken."

Ⓡ **chopper leap** Defying potentially dangerous turbulence, U.S. daredevil motorcyclist Travis Pastrana successfully backflipped a dirt bike over a helicopter that was hovering off the ground in front of Australia's Sydney Harbour Bridge, clearing the revolving chopper blades by about 13 ft (4 m).

Ⓡ **paper round** Ted Ingram has been delivering newspapers in Dorset, England, for nearly 70 years. He started his job in 1942 and estimates that he has since delivered more than half a million papers.

Ⓡ **mass waltz** More than 1,500 couples—from children to pensioners—danced a waltz in the main square of Tuzla, Bosnia, in 2010. Organizers estimated that as many as 25,000 people danced in the surrounding streets, but the square had to be sealed off so that the couples had enough room to move.

Ⓡ **free haircuts** Working round the clock, a team of ten stylists from Pump Salon completed 618 free haircuts in 24 hours in Cincinnati, Ohio, in September 2010.

Ⓡ **old scout** Reg Hayes, 95, of Oxford, England, retired in 2010 after 87 years as a Boy Scout. He joined the 2nd Oxford Wolf Cub pack in 1923 and moved up to the SS Mary and John 2nd Oxford Scouts in 1930, where he stayed for the next 80 years.

Ⓡ **human wheelbarrow** In Helsinki, Finland, Adrian Rodrigues Buenrostro from Mexico and Sergiy Vetrogonov from Ukraine completed a 131-ft (40-m) human wheelbarrow race in just 17 seconds.

Ⓡ **car wash** Students from Bloomington High School South, Indiana, cleaned 1,207 cars in ten hours in a marathon car-wash.

STILL LIFE
S.C. Naganandaswamy of Karnataka, India, can float in 20 ft (6 m) of water for 22 hours continuously without moving any limbs.

Ⓡ **bulky wear** Croatia's Kruno Budiselic managed to wear 245 T-shirts—ranging in size from medium to extra large—at the same time. The extra clothing added around 150 lb (68 kg) to his overall weight.

Ⓡ **king gnome** Andy and Connie Kautza of Wausau, Wisconsin, built a concrete garden gnome that stands 15 ft (4.5 m) tall and weighs more than 3,500 lb (1,590 kg).

HUMAN SPARKLER
Dr. Peter Terren of Bunbury, Western Australia, shot more than 200,000 volts of electricity down his body to create a spectacular version of Rodin's *The Thinker*. He turned himself into a human sparkler for 15 seconds by using a homemade Tesla coil, which transforms a feed of domestic electricity into a supercharged bolt of power. He was saved from electrocution by wrapping his torso, arms and legs in builders' insulating foil—the electricity traveled through the foil and out to the earth from his foot. He also wore a tin-foil cap and a wire-mesh mask and taped steel wool to the bottom of his left shoe to create the shower of sparks from his foot.

backward running Germany's Achim Aretz ran 10,000 m backward in a time of 41 minutes 26 seconds at the third Retrorunning World Championships in Kapfenberg, Austria, on August 8, 2010.

beach towel A beach towel covering a whopping 24,110 sq ft (2,240 sq m) of beach was unveiled near Las Palmas on the Canary Islands. A team of 25 people spent 15 days making the towel, and more than 50 people were needed to roll it out on the beach.

heavy suit U.S. Air Force Staff Sergeant Owen Duff ran a mile (1.6 km) in 9 minutes 22 seconds at Kirkuk Regional Air Base, Iraq, in 2010 while wearing an 80-lb (36-kg) bomb suit.

wheelchair crossing Setting off from his home in Lynn, Massachusetts, in June 2010, Matt Eddy crossed the U.S.A. by wheelchair in just over four months. Matt has been confined to a wheelchair since the age of ten and suffers from Duchenne Muscular Dystrophy, as a result of which he is strong enough only to move two fingers and requires a ventilator to breathe. Traveling on the quieter back roads to reach his destination of Long Beach, California, he averaged at least 25 mi (40 km) a day.

Milk Man

New Yorker Ashrita Furman once walked more than 80 mi (130 km) around a track in Queens, New York, with a full milk bottle on his head.

Anthony Martin has been an escape artist for more than 30 years, during which time he has performed a number of truly death-defying stunts.

ANTHONY'S GREAT ESCAPES

• In 1984, Anthony escaped after being bound in 20 lb (9 kg) of chains secured with six padlocks and nailed inside a coffin. The coffin was tied twice at both ends with heavy rope, weighted with rocks and submerged in more than 6 ft (1.8 m) of water.

• After being chained hand and foot, tied with six sets of handcuffs and locked behind six prison doors, he escaped from the Waushara County Jail in Wautoma, Wisconsin, in only 4 minutes 45 seconds.

• Wearing two sets of handcuffs and chained to the inside of a locked freight box, he was pushed out of an airplane at 13,500 ft (4,115 m) in 1988. He escaped at 6,500 ft (1,980 m) and parachuted safely to the ground.

• In 1990, he freed himself from a padlocked chain while locked in a metal cage submerged in icy water in 1 minute 45 seconds.

• Bound with handcuffs, he leaped from an airplane at 11,000 ft (3,350 m) above Idaho's deadly Snake River Canyon and, with just 30 seconds to pick the lock and open the parachute, he successfully escaped in free fall and landed on the north rim.

• Handcuffed in a chain of 12 handcuffs that included a 20-lb (9-kg) ball and chain, Anthony was locked in a cell at the Porter County Jail, Indiana, in 2009. He overcame the handcuffs and three locked jail doors to walk free in 8 minutes 13 seconds.

But if you think these are amazing...

TURN THE PAGE...

LEAP OF FAITH

Escape artist and evangelist Anthony Martin performed a daring skydive from an airplane flying at 13,500 ft (4,115 m) over Illinois—wearing handcuffs that were locked to a chain around his neck and linked to leather cuffs fastened above each elbow.

To add to the stunt's death-defying nature, the safety device attached to his parachute that automatically deploys the chute at 700 ft (215 m) was turned off. Without this backup, he had just 45 seconds, while spinning to Earth at 180 mph (290 km/h), to free himself from the handcuffs and chains and to reach back to pull the release handle and activate the canopy.

Falling in a sitting-back position, Anthony seemed to struggle with the lock for about 25 seconds before working himself free and safely deploying the chute.

The 45-year-old from Sheboygan, Wisconsin, has been picking locks since he was a child and made his first authenticated escape at age 12, when he managed to work his way out of a regulation police straitjacket. He jokes that he comes from the "School of Hard Locks."

Since then he has broken out of a locked box thrown from an airplane, escaped from being buried alive beneath 2,000 lb (907 kg) of sand and freed himself from a heavily secured coffin submerged underwater. He has even requested permission to break out of Fort Knox—where most of the U.S. gold bullion reserves are stored—but the U.S. Government refused to allow the escape bid.

How did you first get into escapology?
I became interested in escapes as a result of becoming disappointed in magicians' tricks. Although I can appreciate the talent required to do tricks, I didn't want to fool people—I wanted to do something real. With the proper tools and training, locks can be legitimately compromised. My goal is to thrill, not deceive.

What was your first escape? It was around the age of six, with the help of my ten-year-old cousin. He used to padlock a chain around my wrists from which I would try to escape.

Which has been your most dangerous escape? Aerial escapes, whether in a box or not, are always the most dangerous. Once you leave the airplane there is no going back.

Have you ever thought during an escape that you weren't going to come out alive? There have been times in my career when I did not have 100 percent certainty that I was going to make it unscathed. However, I never thought I would fail and pay the ultimate price. If I believed that, I simply wouldn't do it.

What went through your mind when you jumped from the airplane? When I am "in the zone" and in the middle of an escape, I am thinking of nothing but the required tasks that must take place to succeed. Everything else is blocked out of my mind, yet I always seem to have an internal clock that knows how much time I have.

How difficult was it trying to focus on your hands while you were spinning in midair? The difficulty of a skydiving spin is that centrifugal force wants to take my eyes off the work I need to do. Sometimes in these situations I can alter the position of my legs and stop the spin, but that requires me to divide my attention (something I don't like to do).

How do you prepare for your escapes? When preparing for an escape, I practice with the specific type or model of restraint I expect to be facing. This process can take several weeks to several months depending on the complexity of the stunt.

How satisfying is it to break free from a seemingly impossible situation? The Great Escape strikes a cathartic cord in all of us. How many of us haven't been in a sticky situation we wish we could get out of?

fets

Ripley's Believe It or Not!®

WITH RINGLING BROS.'   *Millie Betra,* WORLD'S GREATEST SHOWS.

J. V. Brown,   THE SERPENT QUEEN.   *Milwaukee.*

PHOTOGRAPHER.

SERPENT QUEEN

While working for Ringling Bros. Circus in the 1880s, petite American Millie Betra, billed as the "Serpent Queen," regularly handled dozens of huge pythons that were almost twice her size, even wrapping many of the snakes around her body simultaneously.

R maggot transfer In May 2009, Charlie Bell of London, England, moved 37½ lb (17 kg) of live maggots from one container to another—in his mouth. He practiced at home with rice for months before finally replacing the grains with the "revolting" maggots.

R bike jump At Reno, Nevada, in 2009, U.S. motorcyclist Ryan Capes soared an astonishing 316 ft (96.3 m) through the air from one ramp to another.

R yoga queen At the age of 83, Bette Calman of Williamstown, Victoria, Australia, still teaches up to 11 yoga classes per week. She can perform headstands, "bridges" and, from lying on her front, raise her whole body off the ground, using only her arms.

R mighty pen Three men in Hyderabad, India, have created a pen that is not only mightier than a sword but is the size of a giraffe! The brass pen, which cost more than $5,000 to make, stands 16 ft (4.9 m) tall, 1 ft (30 cm) wide, weighs 88 lb (40 kg) and is embossed with Indian cultural illustrations.

R free-fall solution After jumping from an airplane at an altitude of 14,000 ft (4,300 m), Ludwig Fichte of Dresden, Germany, flew through the air while sitting in a rubber dinghy while solving a Rubik's Cube puzzle. It took him 31.5 seconds during a free-fall descent of 5,900 ft (1,800 m) to solve the cube, at which point he deployed his parachute.

KING BOARD

Californians Joe Ciaglia and Rob Dyrdek built a giant skateboard that measures 36 ft 7 in (11.15 m) long, 8 ft 8 in (2.6 m) wide, 3 ft 7 in (1.09 m) tall and weighs more than 3,600 lb (1,634 kg). It is 12 times larger than a standard board and is so big it is fitted with car tires and has to be transported on a flatbed truck.

Massachusetts stuntman Ses Carny, "the American Madman," entertains audiences by inserting two stainless-steel fishing hooks into his eyes. With the sharp hooks resting on the orbital bones at the base of the eyes, he then pulls down on the hooks to reveal what it looks like under his eyeballs!

top of the world Jordan Romero of Big Bear Lake, California, reached the summit of Mount Everest in May 2010—at the age of just 13. He climbed with his father and three Sherpa guides, and on getting to the peak of the world's highest mountain he telephoned his mother and said: "Mom, I'm calling you from the top of the world." Jordan has conquered many of the world's highest mountains, and climbed Africa's Mount Kilimanjaro when he was only ten.

limbo queen Shemika Charles from Buffalo, New York State, weighs 140 lb (63.5 kg) and stands 5 ft 9 in (1.75 m) tall, but can limbo under a bar just 8½ in (22 cm) off the ground—while carrying a tray with three fuel canisters in each hand.

happy meals Kelvin Baines of Devon, England, began his collection of McDonald's Happy Meal toys in the 1980s and he now has more than 7,500.

rubber bands Allison Coach, 11, from Chesterfield Township, Michigan, has created a rubber band chain that measures more than 1.3 mi (2.1 km) long. She keeps the chain, which consists of more than 22,000 rubber bands, wrapped around a wooden stand made by her grandfather.

clog dance More than 2,500 people in Pella, Iowa, took part in a mass clog dance in May 2010. To ease the discomfort of the wooden shoes they were wearing, many of the dancers put on extra-thick socks or stuffed their clogs with sponges.

blind speedster Turkish pop singer Metin Senturk drove a car at 182 mph (292.9 km/h)—even though he is blind. He drove a Ferrari F430 unaccompanied along the runway at Urfa airport, with a co-driver giving him instructions through an earpiece in his helmet from a car following behind.

giant clock The family clock-making firm Smith of Derby, England, built a huge mechanical clock 42 ft 8 in (13 m) in diameter with a minute hand 25 ft 7 in (7.8 m) long. The 11-ton clock took a year to design and build and was delivered to its final home—in Ganzhou, China—in 2010 for installation in the 371-ft-high (113-m) Harmony Tower.

cucumber man Frank Dimmock, 87, from Oxfordshire, England, grew a cucumber 41¼ in (104.8 cm) long in 2010. Known as the "Cucumber Man," he has been growing vegetables since before World War II when he became an apprentice to a gardener.

tower leap In May 2010, Algerian-born rollerblader Taig Khris leaped from the 131-ft-high (40-m) first floor of Paris's Eiffel Tower and landed safely onto a 98-ft-high (30-m) ramp.

Ripley's
Believe It or Not!®

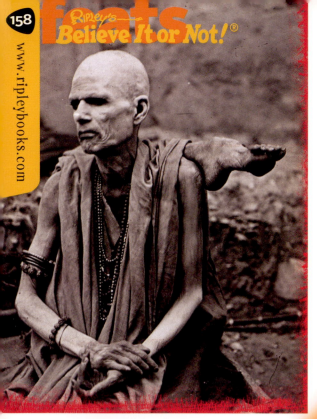

▼ HEAD IN THE SAND

Some Hindu sadhus—such as this gentleman photographed in the 1970s—will bury their heads in the ground for extended periods of time. In 1837, the English newspaper The Daily Telegraph reported that a famous Indian sadhu, Haridas, had survived being buried alive for an unbelievable 40 days without food or water. Witnesses claimed that when the casket in which he lay was opened, Haridas was revived within half an hour.

▲ FEET OF ENDURANCE

Robert Ripley photographed this Hindu sadhu in Calcutta, India, in 1923. As part of his religious devotion, the sadhu had contorted his body into this position for so long that his leg was permanently twisted behind his back, leaving his foot forever resting on his shoulder.

◄ HAND HELD HIGH

Many Hindu sadhus make a pilgrimage every four years to the Kumbh Mela festival at the Ganges River, India. In 2010, this man claimed to have held his right arm aloft, and not cut his nails, for more than 20 years.

NO SITTING ▲

This Hindu holy man from India remains standing for 24 hours a day. When he needs to sleep, he does it upright resting in a sling.

Extreme *Devotion*

These religious devotees are masters of mind over matter, performing totally unbelievable feats that require intense physical and mental discipline and endurance.

Sadhus, sometimes known as fakirs by people in the West, are largely Hindu mystics from India. Following an ancient practice of spiritual devotion, sadhus remove themselves from normal life and dedicate themselves to extreme physical feats, often for their entire lifetime. They often claim to be able to control pain using the power of thought, and some have demonstrated this by walking on razor-sharp blades, or piercing their flesh with metal pins. Some go for years without sitting down—or standing up.

◄ ON ALL FOURS

In 1936, Robert Ripley encountered a bizarre religious ascetic at the holy site of Bodh Gaya, India. He had assumed the shape of a monkey and taken to walking on all fours at all times.

◄ NAP ON NAILS

In 1907, English photographer Herbert Ponting took this picture of a sadhu in Varanasi, India He appears to be resting quite comfortably on a bed of nails.

shark incentive Spain's David Calvo solved two Rubik's Cube puzzles one-handed simultaneously in just 76 seconds while inside a tank with six sharks at the Terra Natura Park in Benidorm, Spain.

tightrope walk Chinese tightrope walker Adili Wuxor spent more than five hours a day for 60 days gingerly walking across a 1.3-in-thick (3.3-cm) steel wire strung across Beijing's Bird's Nest stadium at a height of more than 200 ft (60 m) above the ground. He walked about 12 mi (19 km) a day, so that he covered around 700 mi (1,130 km) in total.

gorilla run More than 1,000 people dressed in gorilla suits to take part in the 2009 Denver Gorilla Run, a 3½-mile (5.6-km) charity run/walk through the streets of the city to help mountain gorilla conservation.

poker session Professional poker player Phil Laak of Los Angeles, California, played poker for more than 115 hours from June 2 to June 7, 2010, at the Bellagio Hotel in Las Vegas, Nevada. He finished $6,766 up.

hang tough Strapped into special gravity boots and hanging upside down from a frame, Zdenek Bradac from the Czech Republic juggled three balls for 2 minutes 13 seconds, during which time he made 438 consecutive catches.

california wingwalk Traveling at speeds of 100 mph (160 km/h), often in the face of strong winds, Ashley Battles of Tulsa, Oklahoma, stood on the wing of a biplane for more than four hours in June 2010. Her wingwalk took place over San Francisco, California, giving her fabulous views of the Golden Gate Bridge and Alcatraz.

speedy mower Don Wales drove a lawn mower at a speed of more than 87 mph (140 km/h) at Pendine Sands in Wales, in May 2010. His grandfather, Sir Malcolm Campbell, broke the world land speed record, in a car, at the same venue in 1924.

stiletto sprinters Running along a 263-ft (80-m) course at Circular Quay in Sydney, New South Wales, Australia, a relay team comprising four women from Canberra—Brittney McGlone, Laura Juliff, Casey Hodges and Jessica Penny—completed the four legs in 1 minute 4 seconds—while wearing 3-in-high (7.5-cm) stiletto heels.

bathtub voyage Rob Dowling of Dublin, Ireland, sailed 500 mi (800 km) down the Amazon River in a motorized bathtub in 2006. The 5-ft-7-in (1.72-m) fiberglass tub was supported by six 36-gal (136-l) steel drums and propelled by a 15-horsepower motor. He had intended to sail from Iquitos in Peru to the Atlantic—2,465 mi (3,967 km)—but his journey ended after just over 500 mi (800 km) when Brazilian authorities told him he didn't have a licence for the bathtub!

Ice Bath

Wearing only swimming trunks, Jin Songhao and Chen Kecai immersed themselves in ice up to their necks for 120 minutes and 118 minutes, respectively, high up on Tianmen Mountain in China's Hunan Province in January 2011. Jin was even able to write Chinese calligraphy during his ordeal.

陈可财

长沙南湖医院
2011
天门山·传奇
冰冻活人挑战极限

长沙南湖医院
2011
天门山·传奇
冰冻活人挑战极限

金松浩

Head contortionist ▶ Martin Laurello discovered his unusual ability as a child and spent many years mastering his stunt of looking backward while walking forward, baffling scientists and amazing Odditorium audiences.

Grace McDaniels ▶ complained about her early billing as "the ugliest woman in the world," but nevertheless was a popular sideshow draw for many years, later becoming known by her preferred moniker, "The Mule-Faced Woman." After fielding several marriage proposals, she settled down and had a son, Elmer (pictured here), who later became her manager.

▲ Freda Pushnik from Pennsylvania was born with no arms or legs, but she was determined to master everyday tasks. Aged just ten years old, she wowed audiences at the 1933 World's Fair with her cheerful repartee and demonstrations of writing and sewing. Freda performed in Ripley's Odditoriums for six years, and went on to have a successful sideshow career before retiring from the stage in the 1950s.

Ripley's O

Habu Koller ▶ from Germany could lift over 100 lb (45 kg) using a hole in his tongue. According to his Ripley backstory, Habu reportedly received a split tongue as punishment in Asia after refusing to bear arms in World War I.

Professor A. L. Morrell, the "Jack-Knife King" was billed as the world's greatest whittler. Assisted by his wife, he wowed audiences with his astonishing exhibit of carved objects displayed in a variety of small-necked bottles. ▼

RUBBER SKIN
GIRL

SKIN STRETCHES
14 INCHES.
CAN BE PIERCED
IN ANY PLACE
WITHOUT PAIN
- OR DRAWING
BLOOD

AGNES SCHMIDT
HAMBURG
GERMANY

▲ Agnes Schmidt from Hamburg, Germany, was known as the "Rubber Skin Girl." Her skin stretched for 14 in (35 cm) and could be pierced in any place without pain or drawing blood.

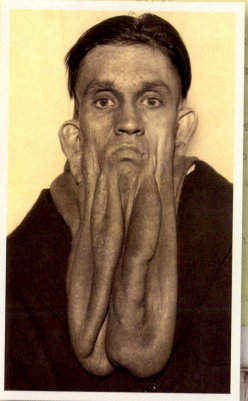

▲ Arthur Loos was known as the "Rubber-Skinned Man," because the skin of his neck would hang 18 in (45 cm) down onto his chest.

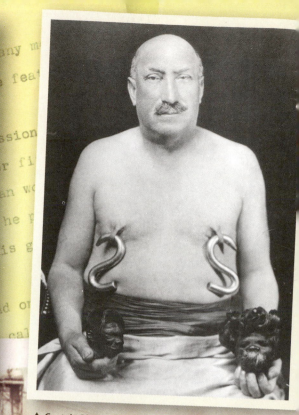

▲ Captain Ringman Mack—seen here holding two genuine shrunken heads—was a European strongman who could pull cars and suspend heavy weights with hooks through his nipples without any sign of pain. He had performed in sideshows since the early 20th century.

CHICAGO SKY LINE   FIELDS MUSEUM   SEARS-ROEBUCK BLDG.   SHEDD AQUARIUM   AVENUE OF FLAGS   HALL OF SCIENCE   DAIRY BLDG   GERMAN

12TH ST. BRIDGE   SOLDIER'S FIELD   LAMA TEMPLE   KAUFMANN

18TH ST. BRIDGE   GENERAL EXHIBIT

◀ With his unique ability to make his eyes pop out of his head, Leonard "Popeye" Perry from Richmond, Georgia, was an Odditorium sensation. He went on to work in other Ripley's Odditoriums for many years after the Chicago Fair.

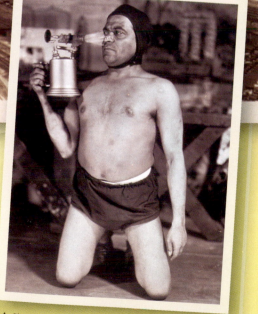

▲ Singlee, the "Fireproof Man," belonged to an Indian fire-worshipping sect. He said that fire was part of his religion and as long as he was faithful to his fire god, fire could not harm him.

▲ Known as the "Anatomical Wonder," A displace his entire abdomen, raising his in chest. Ladies in the audience were advised firm grip on [their] escort's arm" before h

Expands or

Displaces

Displaces

Chicago World's Fair

Between 1933 and 1934, about 48 million people visited the Chicago World's Fair—a showcase of thousands of exhibits including the latest scientific, architectural and transport innovations.

The Century of Progress Exposition, as the Fair was known, was held to commemorate Chicago's 100th anniversary and to illustrate the amazing technological developments that had taken place worldwide in that time. It was staged on an area of 427 acres (173 ha) along the shoreline of Lake Michigan, and opened on May 27, 1933. It closed on November 12, but had proved so popular that it was re-opened the following May, and ran until the end of October 1934.

Also appearing at the Fair was the first-ever Ripley's Odditorium, which was one of the most popular crowd-pullers, attracting over two million visitors. Show-business agent Clint Finney had been assigned by Robert Ripley to find the best performers to appear at this Odditorium, and Finney managed the show in 1933 and 1934 with C.C. Pyle. With their help, Ripley scoured the world for unusual performers, his "human rarities and oddities." Ripley's many international contacts also sent him photographs and telegrams suggesting possible people to include.

A CENTURY OF PROGRESS
CHICAGO 1933
INTERNATIONAL EXPOSITION
PAY ROLL No.

SERIAL No. **11303** 1933
IDENTIFICATION CARD
(NOT A PASS)
S. B. Ricketts 2
EMPLOYEE OF CONCESSIONAIRE
International Oddities, Inc.
AT A CENTURY OF PROGRESS
S. B. Ricketts
EMPLOYEE'S SIGNATURE
ACCEPTED SUBJECT TO CONDITIONS ON PASS
ISSUED BY
A CENTURY OF PROGRESS
Lenox R. Lohs
GENERAL MANAGER
FORM S. D. 44

NOTICE TO KULI ALI BEI, FAKIR CEKANAVICIUS AND OTHERS

People with peculiar characteristics or peculiar physical built (freaks), are wanted for worlds fair in Chicago, from June 1 to November 1, 1934. A certain firm will pay a round trip passage fare and living expenses such as meals, board etc. to all such exponents that will be demonstrated at the fair. The firm will cover all expenses and pay wages to guides who will accompany non English speaking exponents. It will also furnish all documentary ... for the entrance into the United ...

Official Post Card of
RIPLEY'S
"BELIEVE-IT-OR-NOT" ODDITORIUM
A CENTURY OF PROGRESS
CHICAGO, ILLS. 1933

The name & address on this card was written upside down and backwards and yet you can read this with ease. Now study the ... Just fill in the closed spaces, not the open ones.
WHATS 1/2 of 12, viz.: XII
CUT IN HALF VII

J. D. MORENO & CO., PRINTERS, CHICAGO, ILL.

POST CARD
CENTURY OF PROGRESS
CHICAGO 1933

Robert L. Ripley.
c/o New York American,
South Street,
New York City,
N.Y.

1933 U.S. POSTAGE
CHICAGO CENTURY OF PROGRESS

Postal Telegraph
THE INTERNATIONAL SYSTEM
Commercial Cables
Mackay
All America Cables
Radio

CLASS OF SERVICE DESIRED
DOMESTIC | FOREIGN
TELEGRAM | FULL RATE CABLE
...Y LETTER | DEFERRED CABLE
...HT MESSAGE | NIGHT CABLE
...T LETTER | WEEK-END CABLE LETTER
...RADIOGRAM | RADIOGRAM
...which check (one of two) is given desired, otherwise ... will be transmitted as a full rate telegram

RECEIVER'S NUMBER
CHECK
TIME FILED
STANDARD TIME

...the following message, subject to the terms on back hereof, which are hereby agreed to

New York Aug. 21, 1933

Captain Goic
Imperial Hotel Dubrovnik Jugu Slavia

Arrange to bring small man and father to America at once will pay all expenses and reasonable salaries Send their photos immediately

Riple...

Postal Telegraph
THE INTERNATIONAL SYSTEM
Commercial Cables
Mackay
All America Cables
Radio
TELEGRAMS

...INGTON AVE.
CHRYSLER BUILDING
VANDERBILT 1138-9

STANDARD TIME
INDICATED ON THIS MESSAGE

This is a full rate Telegram, Cablegram or Radiogram unless otherwise indicated by signal in the check in the address.
DL | DAY LETTER
NL | NIGHT MESSAGE
NL | NIGHT LETTER
LCO | DEFERRED CABLE
NLT | NIGHT CABLE LETTER
WLT | WEEK END CABLE LETTER
| RADIOGRAM

$12.00

NA119 54 WIRELESS COLLECT VIA MACKAYRADIO=N MANILA 1048A MAR 7 1934

DLT RIPLEY KINGSYN=
:NEWYORKNY (RIPLEY KINGS FEATURES SYNDICATE 235 EAST 45 ST)=

OBTAINABLE TWELVE MALE FEMALE PRIEST MAGNUNUS FIRE WALKERS ...ARITUALIST DAGGER CEREMONY PRECEDING WALK STOP OBTAINABLE UP ... SETS BONTOC IGOROT HEADHUNTERS ARMS WAR ... DANCES CORRECTLY EXECUTED ... LANGUAGE

Believe It or Not
ODDITORIUM

•FAIR FACTS•

- The electric lighting for the 1934 Fair came from 250,000 incandescent bulbs and totaled 30,000,000,000 candlepower—enough electricity to supply the needs of a town of 10,000 people.

- More than six million people rode in the Sky Ride elevators in the first 5½ months of the Fair.

- If all the steel cable in the Sky Ride had been stretched out in a single cable, it would have been more than 100 mi (160 km) long.

- The fountain at the 1934 Fair shot water 45 ft (14 m) into the air, pouring out 68,000 gal (260,000 l) a minute.

- A restaurant seating 3,500 people was a replica of the Old Heidelberg Inn, Germany.

- On October 26, 1933, the 776-ft-long (238-m) German airship *Graf Zeppelin* visited the Fair.

- The 1933 Fair employed 350 painters to create a "carnival of color" by using 25 different exterior colors and 36 interior colors of more than 25,000 gal (113,500 l) of paint to cover 10,500,000 sq ft (975,500 sq m) of surface area.

All the fun of the Fair

The Fair featured a multitude of dazzling exhibitions and displays that wowed audiences both by presenting cutting-edge technologies and by celebrating the diverse nature of the world in which they lived. Alongside exhibits demonstrating homes and cars of the future were re-creations of villages from over a dozen different countries—including England, France, Italy, Morocco, Belgium and Mexico—and newborn babies in incubators, which were a great scientific novelty at the time. Also on show was the ship belonging to Antarctic explorer Richard Byrd, and "Midget City," which was full of miniature houses inhabited by 60 "Lilliputians"—small people who included 18-year-old, 18.75-in-tall (46.8-cm) Margaret Ann Robinson, who weighed only 19 lb (8.6 kg).

star light The Fair was opened in spectacular style—when its lights were switched on with energy gathered from the rays of a distant star, Arcturus. With the aid of powerful telescopes, Arcturus' rays were focused on light-absorbent photoelectric cells in a number of astronomical observatories and then transformed into electrical energy, which was transmitted to Chicago. Arcturus was chosen because it was thought to be 40 light years away from Earth, and Chicago's previous World Fair had been 40 years earlier in 1893.

assembly line The central feature of the Fair's General Motors building was a complete automobile assembly plant, where 1,000 people at a time could watch cars being made from start to finish.

rainbow lights At night, the city and Lake Michigan were illuminated by an ever-changing rainbow provided by a color scintillator composed of 3-ft-wide (1-m) arc searchlights arranged in two banks of 12. The scintillator operators changed the color filters and the positions of the searchlight beams according to a prearranged schedule.

steel house Among the innovative exhibits at the Homes of Tomorrow Exposition was a fireproof house built from steel and baked iron enamel. After the Fair it was moved to Palos Heights, Illinois, where it remained until being demolished in 1992.

36A29

SKY RIDE, CHICAGO WORLD'S FAIR

3A-H8

HAVOLINE THERMOMETER *Century of Progress International Exposition* CHICAGO 1933

ROCKET TRAVEL
The most recognizable symbol of the Fair was the Sky Ride, an aerial tramway that visitors used to travel from one side of the Fair to the other. It had a span of 1,850 ft (564 m) and two towers 628 ft (191 m) tall. Visitors could travel to the top of the towers using high-speed elevators that ascended at a rate of 700 ft (213 m) per minute, and from the top, four different states were visible on a clear day. Suspended from the tramway 220 ft (67 m) above ground were rocket-shaped cars, each carrying 36 passengers across the Fair.

HIGH-RISE TEMPERATURE
Another principal landmark of the Fair was the 218-ft-high (67-m), 21-story thermometer that was sponsored by the motor oil manufacturer Havoline. The air temperature was shown by means of neon light tubes on the outside of the building.

Charles Romano, ▶ the "Rubber Arm Man," could twist and turn and throw his arms around in such a way that audiences were amazed that he could return his body to its normal shape and position.

J.T. Saylors from ▶ Georgia had never demonstrated his talent for jaw-dislocation and pulling funny faces professionally, despite offers from show people and motion picture companies, until he appeared at the Odditorium in Chicago.

dditorium

More than two million visitors flocked Odditorium to see sword-swallowers, and many other curiosities. The attrac that Ripley's founder, Robert Ripley, w other Odditoriums across the United S

PABST BLUE RIBBON CASINO
HOLLYWOOD CLUB
MAXWELL HOUSE COFFEE SHOP
STREETS OF PARIS
23RD ST. ENTRANCE
A. & P. CARNIVAL
BELGIAN
23RD S

Egyptian Hadji Ali could ▶ drink up to 50 glasses of water in quick succession and then return it all to a receptacle in a steady stream, turning himself into a "human fountain." He also swallowed a range of other items before regurgitating them in any order requested.

Sword-swallower ▶ Joseph Grendol had worked a season for the Ringling Circus before joining Ripley's Odditorium. He would swallow a 20-in (50-cm) bayonet attached to the butt of a rifle and then fire the gun while the bayonet was in his stomach!

▲ Kanichka, or "The Man with the Ostrich Stomach," swallowed billiard balls, goldfish, silver dollars, watches and doorknobs—and would then regurgitate them. As a finale, he would swallow electric lights, visible within his stomach when switched on. He was described as having an ostrich stomach because they swallow stones.

▲ Lydia McPherson of Los Angeles was billed as having the longest red hair in the world, which stretched 7 ft 5 in (2.3 m) in length.

to the Ripley's
fire-eaters, eye-poppers
tion proved so popular
ent on to open many
tates.

PANORAMA
OF
A CENTURY OF PROGESS EXPOSITION
CHICAGO · 1933

PANTHEON   ORIENTAL VILLAGE   THE MIDWAY   GETTYSBURG   CAMP WHISTLER   GENERAL MOTORS BLDG.   GOODYEAR FLYING FIELD   CHRYSLER MOTORS BLDG.   TRAVEL & TRANSPORT

VILLAGE

A seasoned ▶ performer known variously as the "Human Pincushion" or the "Painless Wonder," Leo Kongee would drive pins and nails into his face, and even had a button sewn onto his tongue, and seemingly felt no pain.

INTERNATIONAL
666 LAKE SHORE DRIVE
CHICAGO, ILLINOIS

May 8, 1934.

BELIEVE-IT-OR-NOT" EXHIBITION
ENTURY OF PROGRESS
NE 1. TO OCTOBER 31, 1934

RD NCT 29

RIDANCONSUL HARBIN (CHINA)
RRESPONDENCE WITH MARILYN REFERRED TO US FOR ATTENTION
NOT USE

Memo for Mr. Simpson:
            In regard to the Chinese man
you believe could be dressed in Korean religious co
and be a good attraction. are fr   feet tall wh
many giant   are fr   e this   erican
tower ove   le to   four
any goo
sul

Billy Cunningham
817 So. 4th St
Louisville Ky.

Ripley
Ripley
Believe It or Not Believe It or Not
ODDITORIUM

'S
" ODDITORIUM
OGRESS—1934
LLINOIS

CHICAGO

W. A. Cunningham
817-So.-4th St
Louisville Ky

At Chicago Exhibit of Believe-It-Or-Nots

Thousands of Americans who have followed the famous Believe-It-Or-Not Cartoons of Robert Ripley are seeing the actual Believe-It-Or-Nots housed in the palatial Ripley "Odditorium" at the Chicago Century of Progress. Included among the exhibits are (left) Singhlee, a Hindu who can grasp a red-hot metal bar and put it to his mouth; (below left) Albert Nelson and his one-man mechanical band of thirty instruments; and (below right) Blystone, the rice writer.

RIPLEY
BELIEVE IT OR NOT

HAITI.   "PINK MAN" FRO
            THIS IS GOOD,   DO
STORY ABOUT PILL.

CANT GET BORNEO BELLES
      "   "   CARVED FACE MEN
BUT TRY ALEKO E. LILIUS
      P.O. Box 3220 Manila.   Cable address
                                    AEOLUS
OBTAIN WILLIAM D'ANDREA
      88 - South Elm St
      Waterbury.
CAN PLACE

E L BLYSTONE
of ARDARA, Pa
WROTE 2871 LEGIBLE LETTERS
ON A SINGLE GRAIN OF RICE
PRIZE WINNER

lunge runner Jamasen Rodriguez of Modesto, California, is an expert in lunge running, where instead of running, the athlete lunges to his knees, alternating left and right with each step. In August 2010, he completed a lunge mile in just more than 25 minutes, taking 1,370 lunges.

human dominos Thousands of people in Ordos, Inner Mongolia, China, formed a human domino chain. Arranged in lines, the 10,267 participants slowly fell backward onto each other in sequence from a sitting position like a line of toppling dominos.

back handsprings At Valmeyer, Illinois, 13-year-old Chelsey Kipping did 32 consecutive back handsprings. She has been doing gymnastics since age four and practices for at least nine hours a week.

harley jump California stunt rider Seth Enslow jumped 183 ft 8 in (56 m) on a Harley-Davidson motorcycle near Australia's Sydney Harbour in March 2010. Three years earlier, the bike ace had performed a 200-ft (60-m) jump over a Convair 880 passenger jet airplane.

cat statues Winnie Ferring has a collection of more than 1,000 cat statues arranged on every available space inside and outside her home in Lansing, Iowa. She has been collecting them for more than 50 years, and each piece is numbered and documented.

africa trek French adventurers Alexandre and Sonia Poussin spent three years walking 8,700 mi (14,000 km) from Cape of Good Hope, South Africa, to Israel, living solely on the hospitality of people they met along the way.

trapeze veteran In his early seventies, Tony Steele still performed as a trapeze artist with the Gamma Phi Circus of Illinois State University, the oldest collegiate circus in the U.S.A.

karate kid Varsha Vinod from Alappuzha, India, became a karate black belt in May 2009—the highest grade in the martial art—at the age of just five. She has been training since she was two and already has more than 15 katas, or karate disciplines, to her name.

manhole museum Stefano Bottoni has collected manhole covers from across the world—including from Holland, Finland, Cuba, the Czech Republic, Austria and Romania—for exhibition at his International Manhole Museum in Farrara, Italy.

liberty walk French high-wire walker Didier Pasquette crossed a 150-ft-long (46-m) wire tied between two replicas of the Statue of Liberty on top of the 23-story Liberty Building in Buffalo, New York State, in September 2010. The feat took him about three minutes, and he stopped twice during his walk to wave to the crowds on the ground some 230 ft (70 m) below.

ball control Twenty-five-year-old schoolteacher Rohit Timilsina of Kathmandu, Nepal, managed to hold 21 standard tennis balls on the palm of his hand for more than 14 seconds in 2008. It took him three years of practice to achieve the feat.

Balancing Act

One man rode a bicycle 165 ft (50 m) along a tightrope suspended 26 ft (8 m) above a tiger enclosure while another hung below him on a ladder at China's Changzhou Yancheng Zoo in March 2010. The pair, who were part of a stunt that involved a three-year-old girl walking the rope behind them, narrowly avoided tragedy when one of the zoo's Siberian tigers leaped high off the ground and grabbed at the ladder, nearly causing the men to fall into the enclosure.

UNDERPANTS MAN

Gary Craig from Newcastle, England, also known as the Geordie Pantsman, took 25 minutes to clamber into an incredible 211 pairs of underpants in an unusual charity challenge in April 2010. Gary initially planned to wear 200 underpants, but an Australian rival had achieved this landmark only a few days before, so Gary was forced to set his sights higher and find bigger pairs of pants. This caused problems, as the smaller the underpants the greater the pressure, making it a painful physical challenge.

stamp collector Postman Alan Roy from Dorset, England, spent 70 years painstakingly peeling off two million stamps from envelopes. He soaked each envelope in water and then carefully removed the stamp with tweezers. His collection is so big it fills up 40 packing crates that stack as high as a house.

emerald hunter Jamie Hill of North Carolina has dug up nearly 18,000 carats of emeralds in his home state since 1998.

pi chart Using only a single standard desktop computer costing less than $3,000, French software engineer Fabrice Bellard calculated pi to nearly 2.7 trillion decimal places. The complex calculation took him 131 days.

beer house In Schleiden, Germany, Sven Goebel spent three months building a five-room apartment made entirely from 300,000 beer mats. It featured a table, chairs and a fireplace—all made of beer mats. After spending up to eight hours a day, seven days a week, on construction, he then had to knock down the finished building to prove that it had been held together only with static, not adhesive.

plane pull In Jilin, China, in 2010, martial-arts expert Dong Changsheng took less than a minute to pull a half-ton airplane for 16 ft (5 m)—by a rope hooked to his eyelids! He had previously pulled a car with his eyelids but this was his first attempt with a plane.

HOT HOOD

The Russian Extreme Games in Moscow were an opportunity for some of the most daring and crazy stuntmen in Russia to compete against each other in such dangerous events as riding BMX bikes with flaming tires, setting themselves on fire and riding on the hood of a vehicle as it crashed through an inferno.

Poker Face

Bai Deng from Shandong, China, can hurl a regular playing card so hard and with such accuracy that he can slice a cucumber in two. It's not as impossible as it might seem, given that in 2002 U.S. magician Rick Smith Jr. threw a playing card a distance of 216 ft 4 in (66 m) at over 90 mph (145 km/h).

human fly Jem Stansfield climbed the side of a 30-ft (9-m) wall of a school in Brighton, England, in 2010 using nothing more than suction from two vacuum cleaners. The 168-lb (76-kg) aeronautics graduate adapted the household appliances' motors into giant suckerpads, which were strong enough to support him and enabled him to cling to the wall.

flying lanterns More than 10,000 twinkling white paper lanterns were released simultaneously into the night sky from a beach in Jakarta, Indonesia, in December 2009. The flying lantern is a Chinese tradition. It is basically a paper bag containing a block of paraffin with a wick suspended by wire across the opening. When the wick is lit, the air inside is warmed like a hot-air balloon and the lantern lifts off into the sky.

rubber bands Eleven-year-old Allison Coach of Chesterfield Township, Michigan, created a chain of 22,140 rubber bands that stretched nearly 7,000 ft (2,130 m)—or 1.3 mi (2 km)—long.

champion plowgirl Thirteen-year-old schoolgirl Elly Deacon beat experienced farmers for first place in a plowing competition in Hertfordshire, England. Elly, who had driven a tractor for the first time only four days before the event, impressed judges with her straight and smooth plow marks on a 53,000-sq-ft (4,900-sq-m) patch of land, while at the wheel of the six-ton tractor.

turbo terry Terry Burrows from Essex, England, cleaned three windows, each measuring 45 sq in (290 sq cm), and wiped the sills in just 9.14 seconds during a 2009 window-cleaning competition in Blackpool, Lancashire. "Turbo Terry" actually finished the task in 8.14 seconds, but was handed a one-second time penalty for leaving two water marks on the glass.

rain dance More than 230 dancers took to the wet streets of Bath in Somerset, England, with umbrellas in May 2010 to perform a five-minute version of Gene Kelly's classic "Singin' in the Rain."

sand burial As part of the 2010 Clogherhead Prawn Festival in County Louth, Ireland, 524 people simultaneously buried themselves up to their necks on a sandy beach.

sports

body

transport

feats

mysteries

food

arts

science

beyond belief

believe it!

world

animals

164
165
166
167
168
169
170
171
172
173
174
175
176
177
178
179
180
181
182
183
184
185
186
187
188
189
190
191

Jade Burial Suit

One of Ripley's most valuable acquisitions is a jade burial suit—the head of which is seen here—from Han Dynasty China, dating back to 200BC. These were incredibly expensive to manufacture, and only a handful remain today. This suit is made from 2,000 pieces of "mottled jade," which does not have the deep green color of regular jade.

Ripley's
EXHIBITS

Ripley's Believe It or Not!® mysteries

raining birds More than 5,000 dead red-winged blackbirds rained from the sky over Beebe, Arkansas, on January 1, 2011, littering the streets with corpses. Three days later, another 500 birds—dead or dying—fell into the Louisiana Highway in Pointe Coupee Parish. Scientists say the birds, disturbed by New Year's Eve fireworks or a passing train, may have died after flying at night and crashing into trees, houses and power lines.

marfa lights For over a century, witnesses have been spooked by the Marfa Lights, a strange light phenomenon occurring around the Mitchell Flats, outside Marfa, Texas. Descriptions range from small dancing lights in the sky to a single, stationary bright light that changes color. In a failed attempt to solve the mystery, a former World-War-II pilot even chased the lights in an airplane.

tunguska explosion At 7.14 a.m. on June 30, 1908, a mysterious explosion took place in central Siberia that was 1,000 times more powerful than the atomic bombs dropped on Japanese cities of Hiroshima and Nagasaki in 1945. The Tunguska Explosion leveled a staggering 80 million trees over an area of 830 sq mi (2,150 sq m) and generated a huge shock wave that knocked people to the ground 37 mi (60 km) from the epicenter. Experts believe it could have been caused by a meteorite crashing into the Earth.

FLOATING HEADS

This may look like the disembodied head of Alfred Hitchcock floating in a field, but it is actually the eerie work of Spanish artist Ibon Mainar. Ibon uses ingenious projector techniques to beam images of famous people or objects, such as chandeliers and spooky cats' eyes, onto natural settings around his home in San Sebastián, Spain. He employs a car-mounted unit to project the images onto water, trees and mountainsides, and when viewed in real life the pictures have a strangely lifelike 3-D effect.

tunnel network Ten large holes and a network of tunnels—some big enough for a person to stand up in—suddenly appeared in the ground in the Krasnoyarsk region of Siberia in 2006. It is thought they were either the work of unknown animals or were somehow related to an earthquake that had hit the area in 2003.

ghost yacht A 40-ft-long (12-m) yacht, the *Kaz II*, was found drifting off the coast of Queensland, Australia, in 2007, with its engine running and a table laid for dinner but no sign of its three-man crew. The radio was working, the computers were running and the lifejackets were still on board, but there was no evidence of foul play and no bodies were ever found.

yellow deposit An unexplained greenish-yellow goo fell from the skies and splattered houses and streets in Snyder, New York State, on January 18, 2011. As temperatures dropped, homes were coated in yellow or green icicles.

taos hum For years, people in and around the town of Taos, New Mexico, have been able to hear a curious low-frequency noise known as the Taos Hum. Not audible to everyone, it has been described as sounding like a distant diesel engine, but its source has never been traced.

desert mummies Excavations at a 4,000-year-old graveyard in China's remote Taklimakan Desert uncovered around 200 mummies—but their D.N.A. showed they had partly European ancestry. The mummies also had European features, such as long noses, high cheekbones and reddish-blond hair.

SOMETHING IN THE GARDEN

Phyllis Bacon believes a fairy fluttered into her life and out again one evening in her garden in London, England. She wasn't even looking through the camera when she held it at arm's length and clicked the button to take a picture of her backyard. She spent months scouring the Internet for butterflies, beetles and moths that might match the image, but came up with nothing.

Real Fairies?

As reported in *Ripley's Believe It or Not! Enter If You Dare*, two cousins, Frances Griffiths and Elsie Wright, rocked the world in 1917 when they said they had photographed fairies in a leafy glen near Elsie's home in Cottingley, England. The five photographs were highly convincing and were published by Arthur Conan Doyle, author of the Sherlock Holmes novels, with an accompanying article. Many experts in photography and psychic research, who examined the pictures and questioned the girls, came to the conclusion that the images were genuine. It was only in the 1980s the girls admitted to faking the pictures with cardboard cutouts and hatpins. However, when Frances Griffiths' daughter appeared on the BBC TV show *The Antiques Roadshow* on January 4, 2009, with a camera given to her by Conan Doyle, she revealed that her mother claimed right up to her death that the fifth and final photograph, taken on a separate occasion and shown here, was genuine.

Ripley's Believe It or Not! mysteries

Ectoplasm

Communicating with the dead was a popular pursuit in the early 20th century, and mediums who went into a trancelike state were often seen to produce a peculiar white substance called ectoplasm from their mouth, ears, nose or navel. Participants at seances would then watch in amazement as the ectoplasm was apparently transformed into spiritual faces, fully functional arms and even entire bodies. It also appeared to give mediums the power to perform astonishing feats of telekinesis, such as raising tables and chairs without any physical contact. But was it all genuine or just an elaborate hoax?

GHOSTLY FACE

At a 1912 seance, ectoplasm from French medium Eva C. (Eva Carrière) formed into the shape of a man's head, which, according to an observer, then made bowing movements. Eva C. was renowned for being able to produce ectoplasm, but skeptics said it was nothing more than chewed paper or fabric that had been regurgitated. Once, after the flow of ectoplasm had been reabsorbed into her mouth, she was given a powerful emetic and when she failed to vomit, the doubters were satisfied that she had not swallowed anything to fake the ectoplasm.

RIPLEY RESEARCH

Ectoplasm is the supposed residue left by ghostly spirits. The term was first used in 1894 by French scientist Charles Richet to explain a third arm that seemed to grow from Italian medium Eusapia Palladino. Ectoplasm was described as having a rubbery texture with a smell of ozone. Touching it or exposing it to light was said to cause injury to mediums, which was why they insisted on conducting seances in the dark. Skeptics said this was simply to hide their deception and indeed many mediums were caught creating their own fake ectoplasm by using thin strips of muslin, egg white, soap or paper. However, other respected witnesses maintained that ectoplasm moved as if it were genuinely alive and could change its shape at will.

mockbeggar coffins In the early 20th century, a number of wooden coffins—containing the remains of men, women and children—were discovered buried in mud at Mockbeggar, Newfoundland, Canada. The wood was not local, leading to speculation that the deceased could have been French fishermen, but the French did not usually take their families when they went fishing in the area. To this day, their identities remain a mystery.

body glow In 1934, Anna Monaro, an asthma patient at a hospital in Pirano, Italy, produced a flickering glow of blue light from her chest for up to 10 seconds at a time while she was asleep. Observed by doctors, scientists and government officials, the phenomenon occurred a number of times each night until it suddenly stopped several weeks later. Physicians suggested the glow might have been caused by certain compounds in the woman's skin.

ringing rocks Ringing Rocks Park in Upper Black Eddy, Pennsylvania, is home to a field of boulders, which, when hit with a solid object such as a hammer, produce melodious bell-like tones.

fish deaths In December 2010, more than 80,000 drum fish were found dead along a 20-mile (32-km) stretch of the Arkansas River and 10,000 red drum fish were mysteriously washed up dead in Chesapeake Bay, Maryland.

MYSTIC CAT

Oscar the cat has correctly predicted the deaths of over 50 patients at the Steere House Nursing and Rehabilitation Center in Providence, Rhode Island, by curling up next to them some two hours before they die. For more than two years, he was present at every death in the home—except one when relatives asked him to leave the room. Nurses once placed Oscar on the bed of a patient they thought was close to death, but he immediately went to sit beside someone in another room. The cat's judgment proved better than that of the medics, because while the second patient died that evening, the first lived for two more days.

BEYOND DOUBT?

German physician Baron Albert von Schrenck-Notzing always imposed strict conditions to ensure that mediums could not fake ectoplasm. For this experiment, noted Polish medium Stanislawa P. was sewn into a special fraud-proof coat, but still appeared to create ectoplasm from her mouth.

HOLMES MYSTERY

While in a trance in Winnipeg, Canada, in 1929, Scottish medium Mary Marshall produced nasal ectoplasm at the center of which was a face that her spirit guide—Walter—claimed was that of Sherlock Holmes creator Sir Arthur Conan Doyle, himself a confirmed believer in spiritualism. The necklace worn by Mary in the photograph is an "apport"—an object that materialized during the seance, but was not there before or after the event.

plain of jars Hundreds of ancient stone jars, some weighing up to 6 tons, can be found scattered across several square miles in northern Laos. Their purpose remains a mystery, but they may have been used to house the bodies of dead people until decomposition, after which the remains would have been removed for burial or cremation.

crystal tears Between March and November 1996, a 12-year-old Lebanese girl, Hasnah Mohamed Meselmani, produced glass crystal tears from her eyes. She wept tiny crystals at an average rate of seven a day, and although they were razor-sharp, she felt no pain. Physicians were mystified by her condition, which stopped as suddenly as it had started.

bacterial rain Over a three-week period in August 1994, gelatinous blobs rained down over Oakville, Washington State, leaving animals dead and people with flu-like symptoms. The blobs contained human white blood cells and two types of bacteria, one of which is found in our digestive system, but no one knows where the blobs came from.

GRAVE VISITS

When ten-year-old Florence Irene Ford was buried after dying of yellow fever in 1871, her distraught mother Ellen had steps built down to the head of the casket and a glass window installed so that she could comfort her child during the thunderstorms that had always terrified her during her short life. On many nights, Ellen would ride up to the cemetery in Natchez, Mississippi, and go underground to sit with her dead daughter and read or sing to her.

In the early 1990s, a woman took her 13-year-old daughter to visit the Ford grave at night. After descending the steps, the woman suddenly emerged screaming with a strange green glow all over her. As she rolled on the grass the glow diminished until a cemetery worker was able to scoop it into his hands. He later said it felt like compressed air or a tennis ball. He then released it into the air where it went up, sparkled and disappeared.

mysteries

Ripley's Believe It or Not!®

WEE FOLK

Two tree pods shaped like fairies are kept in a glass box at the Wat Phrapangmuni Temple near Sing Buri, Thailand. According to popular belief, these *Naree Pons* (or pod people) appeared to the Buddha as beautiful women while he meditated in a secluded area. They then vanished and left behind a miniature humanoid pod form on a nearby tree.

advanced mechanism When the Antikythera Mechanism was recovered from a shipwreck near Crete in 1900, the writing on its case indicated that it was made around 80 BC—but an X-ray revealed a system of differential gears not known to have existed until 1575 AD. It is believed to be an ancient mechanical computer designed to calculate astronomical positions, but its sophistication is in fact comparable to a 19th-century Swiss clock.

stone balls In the Costa Rican jungle in the 1930s, workmen found over 300 man-made stone balls, many perfectly spherical and varying in size from as small as a tennis ball to huge boulders 8 ft (2.4 m) in diameter and weighing 15 tons. The stones date back at least 500 years, but nobody knows who made them and how such spherical precision was achieved.

flaming fireball A massive fireball lit up the sky over five U.S. states—Missouri, Iowa, Wisconsin, Illinois and Indiana—on the night of April 14, 2010. Puzzled scientists say it could have been a meteor, a chunk from an asteroid, or rocket debris.

milk miracle For several hours on September 21, 1995, Hindu religious statues all over the world drank milk. When a worshiper at a temple in New Delhi, India, offered a spoonful of milk to the trunk of a statue of the elephant-headed deity Ganesha, the liquid was seen to disappear. Soon Hindu temples in the U.K., Canada, Dubai and Nepal were reporting similar occurrences. Scientists were baffled by the phenomenon, which stopped before the end of the day when statues suddenly refused to accept milk.

unfinished city Having spent years constructing 30-ft-high (9-m) walls from perfectly hewn basalt, the inhabitants of the ancient city of Nan Madol, in the Micronesia region of the Pacific, mysteriously abandoned it, leaving some of the walls unfinished.

who goes hare! In 1971, a rabbit was shot by Jasper Barrett near his home in Jefferson, South Carolina. On being prepared for the pot by his wife and a friend, the outline in black of a woman's face was found on the skinned flesh of one foreleg. It was about an inch across and had a rosebud mouth, curly hair and long lashes. Within a week of the news breaking, 4,000 people had trekked to see the face and extra police were called in to control the crowds.

GHOSTLY VISION

When Kevin Horkin downloaded this photo and saw a pale young woman peering from a window on the first floor of Gwrych Castle in Abergele, he knew something spooky was afoot. The huge Welsh castle has been derelict since 1985 and the floor crumbled away years ago, so no one could possibly have been standing there. Countless sightings, orbs, cold spots and cases of objects moving have been recorded at Gwrych, said to be the most haunted building in Wales.

ghostly pleas Sightings of the ghosts of tormented slaves from the 1830s have been reported at Lalaurie House, New Orleans. Servants who begged the assistance of outsiders when the house was burning are seen running back inside, slamming doors, shouting repeatedly. Several people have seen ghostly faces of the dead peering from upper windows.

eerie face The image of a child's face dating back over 100 years was found burnt onto an old oven door at a restaurant in Saint John, New Brunswick, Canada, in the 1980s. A lady visitor to the property at 31 Leinster Street had gone into the cellar to inspect the original brick oven, but when the dirt was cleaned away the smiling face of a young girl became visible in the iron door. It is believed the family living there in the late 19th century had used the oven as a crematorium to dispose of their dead daughter. The image on the door was caused by carbons given off by the body during burning, the bright light of the fire having acted as a lens.

Burning Mystery

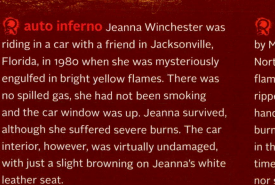

When 92-year-old Dr. John Irving Bentley was found in the bathroom of his home in Coudersport, Pennsylvania, in December 1966, all that remained of him was a pile of ashes and the lower half of his right leg. He is thought to have been a victim of spontaneous human combustion, a phenomenon where people suddenly burst into flames for no apparent reason. Although almost his entire body had been consumed by an intense heat, the fire was confined to a small area and, apart from a hole in the floor where he had been standing, the rest of the room was largely undamaged. The rubber tips on his walking frame were still intact and a nearby bathtub was hardly scorched.

ⓡ auto inferno Jeanna Winchester was riding in a car with a friend in Jacksonville, Florida, in 1980 when she was mysteriously engulfed in bright yellow flames. There was no spilled gas, she had not been smoking and the car window was up. Jeanna survived, although she suffered severe burns. The car interior, however, was virtually undamaged, with just a slight browning on Jeanna's white leather seat.

ⓡ charred remains In March 1997, the charred remains of 76-year-old John O'Connor were found in a chair some distance from the hearth of his living room in County Kerry, Ireland. Only his head, upper torso and feet remained unburned, yet there was little smoke damage to the room or the furniture.

ⓡ burning dress A dress being worn by Mrs. Charles Williamson of Bladenboro, North Carolina, unaccountably burst into flames in 1932. Her husband and daughter ripped off the blazing dress with their bare hands yet none of the three suffered any burns. Over the next four days, various items in the house suddenly caught fire, but each time the flames, which had neither smoke nor smell, simply vanished after the article had burned itself out.

ⓡ fatal fire Mrs. Olga Worth Stephens, 75, of Dallas, Texas, suddenly burst into flames while waiting in her parked car in 1964 and died before anyone could rescue her. The car was undamaged and firemen concluded that nothing in the vehicle could have started the fatal blaze.

ⓡ paper puzzle Anna Martin of West Philadelphia, Pennsylvania, was found incinerated at home in 1957, her body totally consumed by fire except for a piece of her torso and her shoes. The medical examiner estimated that temperatures must have reached at least 1,700°F (925°C)—far too hot for anything in the room to remain uncharred, yet newspapers lying just 2 ft (60 cm) away were found intact.

ⓡ vaporized flesh At Blackwood, Wales, in 1980, a man's body was found burned beyond recognition in his living room. The armchair that he was sitting in was hardly damaged—neither were some plastic objects nearby—but the fire was so intense that it left a coating of vaporized flesh on the ceiling.

FLORIDA MONSTER

Two boys playing on the beach near St. Augustine, Florida, in 1896 spotted the carcass of a huge creature half buried in the sand. It seemed to have a number of tentacles, some up to 30 ft (9 m) long, prompting the belief that it was some kind of giant octopus. However, a similar blob washed up in Chile in 2003 turned out to be a decomposing sperm whale. When some marine creatures decay, their form changes so much that they can look like unidentified sea monsters.

lake monster While fishing 900 ft (275 m) from shore on Russia's 770-sq-mi (1,990-sq-km) Lake Chany in 2010, a man saw his 59-year-old companion hook an unknown creature so powerful that it overturned his boat and dragged him beneath the surface to his death. At least 19 people have vanished on the lake since 2007. Most of the bodies have never been found, but some human corpses have been washed ashore with large bite marks on their bodies. Witnesses have described a snakelike beast with a long neck, a large fin and a huge tail.

baghdad battery An ancient clay vessel was an early example of a battery—even though batteries were not rediscovered for another 1,800 years. The 2,000-year-old Baghdad Battery contained a copper cylinder and an oxidized iron rod, both held in place by asphalt. When filled with an acid or alkaline liquid, it was capable of producing an electric charge.

metal spheres Over recent decades, miners in Klerksdorp, South Africa, have dug up hundreds of ancient metal spheres that look entirely man-made. However, they were found in Precambrian rock dating back 2.8 billion years—that's over 2.79 billion years before Neanderthal man! The mysterious spheres measure about 1 in (2.5 cm) in diameter and some are etched with three parallel grooves running around the middle.

unique stone The Mystery Stone of Lake Winnipesaukee, New Hampshire, has distinctive markings that make it unique. The egg-shaped stone—found encased in a lump of clay in 1872—has intricate man-made carvings and a hole bored through both ends, but its origins and purpose remain unknown and no matching stones have ever been discovered.

missing belt For reasons unknown, Jupiter loses or regains one of two belts every ten to 15 years. The planet usually has two dark bands in its atmosphere—one in its northern hemisphere and one in its southern hemisphere—but pictures taken by astronomers in April 2010 showed that the Southern Equatorial Belt had disappeared. The dark belts are clouds created from chemicals such as sulfur and phosphorus, which are blown into bands by 350-mph (560-km/h) winds.

scary site The Borley Rectory in England has been the site of a vast number of mysterious phenomena reported by resident reverends and their families since 1863. The appearance of a ghostly nun, wall writings, stone throwing, windows shattering, bells ringing, unexplained footsteps, a woman becoming locked in a room with no key, and spirit messages tapped out from the frame of a mirror are just some of the incidences said to have occurred. Mediums contacted two spirits there: a French nun murdered on the site and a man who said he would burn down the house. Burn it did—in 1939.

APE MAN

On an expedition to Venezuela in 1920, Swiss geologist François de Loys claimed to have stumbled across a 5-ft-tall (1.5-m), red-haired, tailless ape that walked upright like a human. He shot the animal and photographed it, using a long stick to prop up its head, but the corpse went missing before it could be examined. If genuine, it would have been the first ape ever discovered in the Americas, thereby rewriting the theory of primate evolution, but scientists decided that the photo was merely a common spider monkey whose tail was conveniently hidden or chopped off.

ⓡ RIPLEY RESEARCH

In early July 1947, an object described as a "flying disk" crashed near Roswell, New Mexico. The Roswell Army Air Force (RAAF) insisted the craft was a weather balloon, but speculation mounted that it was a U.F.O. A local rancher saw a shallow trench, several hundred feet long, gouged into the land and recovered metallic debris that turned liquid when dropped. Nurses said they saw small humanoid bodies being examined in a cordoned-off corner of the local hospital. A mortician at a Roswell funeral home revealed he had been asked to provide child-sized, hermetically sealed coffins. To this day no one knows whether the Roswell Incident was a cover-up or a flight of fancy.

Alien Autopsy

A display at the U.F.O. Museum at Roswell, New Mexico, re-creates the alleged autopsy of a dead alien killed when his spacecraft crashed in the area in 1947. The dummy extraterrestrial was originally made for the 1994 movie *Roswell*.

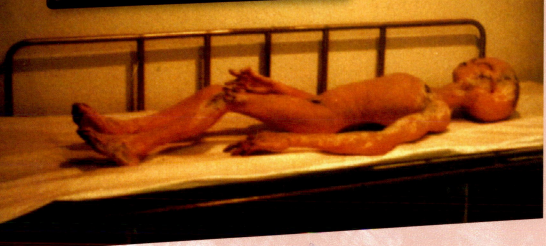

ⓡ fearsome forest Aokigahara Forest, Japan, at the foot of Mount Fuji, is reportedly haunted by strange beasts, monsters, ghosts and goblins. One popular myth states that the magnetic iron deposits underground cause compasses to malfunction and travelers to get lost in the forest. It is the world's third most popular suicide location.

ⓡ straight line Four ancient historical sites—Easter Island in the Pacific Ocean, the Nazca lines in southern Peru, the Inca city of Ollantaytambo, also in southern Peru, and the Great Pyramid of Giza, Egypt—are all exactly aligned along a straight line. Other world wonders that are within just one-tenth of a degree of this alignment include Persepolis, the capital of ancient Persia; Mohenjo Daro, the ancient capital of the Indus Valley; and the lost city of Petra in modern-day Jordan.

ⓡ ghost ship Carrying a shipment of coal, the *Carroll A. Deering* was found run aground off the coast of North Carolina on January 31, 1921—but its 11-man crew had vanished. There was no sign of the crew's belongings or the ship's navigating instruments, log or clock, yet evidence in the galley indicated that food was being prepared for the following day's meals.

ⓡ near miss Pilot David Hastings from Norwich, U.K., revealed a close encounter with a U.F.O. when flying over the Mojave Desert in the U.S.A. in 1987. He described how a mysterious black shape came at his plane head-on, then flashed overhead. Seconds later the object was moving at high speed at the plane's side. Hastings took photos and showed them to U.S. Navy officers, but they refused to comment.

ⓡ band of holes Nearly 7,000 man-made holes are located on a plain near Peru's Pisco Valley—but their origins and purpose remain unknown. The Band of Holes stretches for 1 mi (1.6 km) and some of the holes are up to 7 ft (2.1 m) deep.

ⓡ they're here! A 2010 April Fool's report in a Jordanian newspaper wreaked havoc in one town. Its front-page article described a U.F.O. landing near Jafr, 185 mi (300 km) from Amman. Residents panicked, keeping their children home from school; and Jafr's mayor even sent security forces in search of the aliens. He was at the point of emptying the town of its 13,000 residents when newspaper journalists came clean.

ⓡ aliens welcome Bob Tohak has believed in U.F.O.s since he was a kid. He is so eager to make contact with aliens that he has put a 42-ft-high (13-m) U.F.O. landing port on his property in Poland, Wisconsin. "I'm just hoping that something will show up," he says.

FIRE STARTER

A ghostly young girl was pictured in a building on fire in the town of Wem, England, in 1995. Many were convinced that the photograph captured the ghost of a girl that died after accidentally setting the same building alight in the 17th century. In 2010, after the photographer had died, it was suggested that the 1995 photograph was a fake. The ghostly girl in the fire had been copied from a 1922 Wem postcard, which was spotted in the local newspaper by an eagle-eyed reader.

ⓡ perfect fit The ancient site of Sacsayhuaman, Peru, features three huge stone walls built so expertly that it is impossible to insert a piece of paper between the different-shaped stones, some of which are 9 ft 10 in (3 m) high and weigh 200 tons.

body

transport

feats

mysteries

food

arts

science

beyond belief

believe it!

world

animals

sports

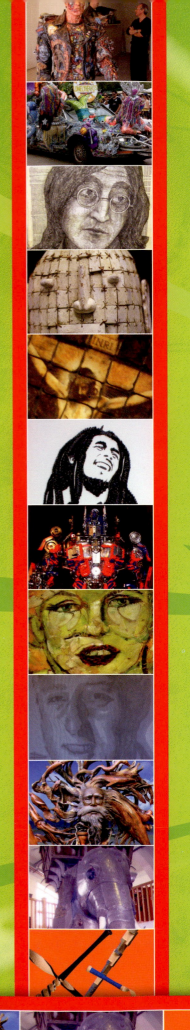

Toast Crucifixion

Ripley's have recently added their largest ever piece of toast art to their collection, depicting the Crucifixion. British artist Adam Sheldon first created the piece to hang in a church in Lincolnshire, England, but it is currently on display in the Ripley's museum in Branson, Missouri. The artwork was made using conventional toasters, blowtorches and scrapers, and 153 pieces of toast.

175
176
177
178
179
180
181
182
183
184
185
186
187
188
189
190
191
192
193
194
195
196
197
198
199
200
201
202

Ripley's EXHIBITS

FAST FOOD

RIPLEY RESEARCH

As you might imagine, the stomach of a competitive eater is not like that of the average person. Over time it is trained to expand way beyond regular stomach capacity in order to hold incredible amounts of food, and this is often achieved by drinking gallons of water. In 2007, doctors from the University of Pennsylvania studied the stomach of a speed eater alongside that of a regular person as they ate hot dogs. They discovered that the speed eater's stomach processed food far more slowly, expanding and expanding instead of contracting and digesting, so he never felt full. Eating athletes also need superhuman jaw strength to cope with the severe chewing required to win eating competitions. Both stretching the stomach and drinking large amounts of water are potentially very dangerous and should not be tried at home!

Patrick "Deep Dish" Bertoletti from Chicago is one of the world's most successful competitive eaters. In 2008, he became an official pizza-eating world champion, devouring 47 slices of 16-in (41-cm) deep dish in 10 minutes. Most people might not finish even half of one large pizza in that time.

Highlights of Patrick's career include finishing off more than 10 lb (4 .5 kg) of Key Lime Pie in 8 minutes and 275 pickled peppers in 10 minutes. These and many more appetite-busting achievements mean that Patrick is ranked in the top five eaters in the world by the sport's Major League Eating organization. In 2010, in Black Hawk, Colorado, Patrick swallowed 3 lb 11³/₄ oz (1.7 kg) of deep-fried bull's testicles in 10 minutes.

You don't need to be extremely heavy to be an eating champion; in fact many are in good shape. Culinary-school graduate Patrick weighs in at 190 lb (86 kg), relatively lightweight given his 6-ft-2-in (1.88-m) frame and the vast amounts that he consumes at eating competitions—regularly gulping down more than 10,000 calories in just a few minutes. Fittingly, Patrick works as a chef and hopes to open his own restaurant— serving regular-sized portions.

How did you start speed eating?
My first professional event involved me eating 5 lb (2.3 kg) of pizza in 15 minutes, but I have been doing it my entire life and I was genetically predisposed for speed eating.

What is your favorite speed-eating food? And do you have to like what you are speed eating to win? I love ice cream in contests, as I don't suffer any of the dreaded effects. If I am in eating shape and have a good day, I would eat shoe leather in a contest. I don't like oysters or pickled jalapenos, but I block that out and have records in both.

What is the worst thing to speed eat and why? Any type of sea oysters, raw, or rocky mountain oysters (bull testicles). The texture of both make speed eating quite difficult.

Do you do much training? And what is your diet like when you are not competing? I stay on a strict diet outside of contests because my appetite is truly insatiable. I have to keep my eating on lockdown because my appetite gets unleashed with a fury. I will eat a giant meal with a few gallons of water two days before as a final stretch, but my stomach has been trained so I don't need much extra training, perhaps a few practices for technique if I'm a little rusty.

Are there any downsides to speed eating? Heartburn and indigestion, but I keep the Pepto Bismol close. You have to be conscious of calories because it's very easy to gain weight if left unchecked when eating tens of thousands of calories.

Is it ever dangerous? All events have paramedics so there is little risk for healthy individuals at contests.

What are your tips for top speed eating? You can't train for speed eating; it's something you are born with.

What are your speed-eating ambitions? I would like to be the best eater in the world and to win the annual hot-dog contest, also to translate my eating fame into the opening of a gourmet diner in Chicago.

Patrick's Menu

Food	Amount	Time
Blueberry pie	9 lb (4 kg)	8 minutes
Slushie	22 fl oz (650 ml)	9 seconds
Hotdogs	55	10 minutes
Pizza (16 in/41 cm)	47 slices	10 minutes
Hamburgers	94	8 minutes
Chicken wings	227	30 minutes
Chili spaghetti	11.5 lb (5.2 kg)	10 minutes
Ribs	8.5 lb (3.85 kg)	12 minutes
Subs (8 in/20 cm)	14	10 minutes

THE HEAT

Headless Chickens

In parts of Asia, no part of the chicken goes to waste. In Bangkok, the capital of Thailand, barbecued chicken head kebabs are available to buy as fast food. Once cooked, the brain and soft tissue can be eaten. Roasted, boiled and deep-fried chicken heads are also popular.

slice of luck A restaurant in Hankou, China, selected from 15 applicants for the post of chef by asking the candidates to slice a melon on a woman's stomach. The successful candidate, Hu Gua, chopped up his melon in less than a minute without hurting the woman who was protected from the blade by just a thin sheet of plastic.

lime pie During the Key West, Florida, 2010 Conch Republic independence celebration, locals used 1,080 Key limes to prepare a 450-lb (204-kg), 7-ft-wide (2.1-m) Key lime pie.

taste test As a designer and tester with Fox's Biscuits, Simon Pope of West Yorkshire, England, is paid to eat more than 7,000 cookies a year.

margarine marge Restaurant owner Simon Smith of Staffordshire, England, celebrated the 20th birthday of *The Simpsons* by making a 4-ft-high (1.2-m) bust of his favorite character, Marge, out of margarine. He used 26 lb (12 kg) of special heat-resistant puff pastry margarine on the sculpture and achieved the shape by wrapping it around chicken wire.

chicken feast At the 2010 Canoefest in Brookville, Indiana, 1,654 lb (750 kg) of fried chicken was served up in a donated canoe. Up to 200 volunteers had cooked the 2,700 lb (1,225 kg) of raw meat.

cake tower Chef Gilles Stassart and architect Jean Bocabeille designed a cake for display in Paris, France, in July 2010 that was nearly 26 ft (7.8 m) tall—that's as high as a two-story house. The "Tower without Hunger" was made from 1,385 lb (628 kg) of flour, 1,120 lb (508 kg) of sugar, 350 eggs and 40 lb (18 kg) of butter. The towering cake was meant to last four days outdoors but sweltering temperatures made it soft and unstable and it had to be taken down after just 24 hours.

haute dog New York City restaurant Serendipity 3 introduced a $69 hot dog in 2010. The Haute Dog comes with white truffle oil, a salted pretzel bed, truffle butter, duck foie gras, Dijon mustard, Vidalia onions and ketchup.

locust topping When a plague of millions of locusts hit the town of Mildura, Victoria, Australia, in April 2010, pizza café owner Joe Carrazza put dozens of the dead insects on his pizzas as a topping.

placenta drink A new drink from Japanese health food manufacturer Nihon Sofuken tastes of peaches but contains 0.3 oz (10,000 mg) of pigs' placenta, a substance said to be able to restore youthful looks and help with dieting.

long fry John Benbenek of Buffalo, New York, was eating lunch at Taffy's Hot Dog Stand in 2010 when he found a 34-in-long (85-cm) French fry in his meal.

fiery sauce Eight teenagers in Augsburg, Germany, were treated in a hospital after a test of courage in which they drank chili sauce that was more than 200 times hotter than Tabasco. The sauce clocked 535,000 on the Scoville scale, which measures the hotness of sauce, compared to 2,500 for normal Tabasco sauce.

bridge picnic More than 6,000 people sat down to breakfast on Sydney's famous Harbour Bridge in October 2009 after it was closed to traffic and carpeted with grass for a giant picnic.

double yolks Fiona Exon from Cumbria, England, beat odds of more than a trillion to one when she discovered that all six eggs she had bought in a single carton from her local supermarket had double yolks.

bacon envelopes U.S. company J & D's, whose motto is "Everything should taste like bacon," have created "Mmmvelopes," envelopes that have a bacon flavor when you lick them.

chocolate landmark A team of Chinese confectioners built a 33-ft-long (10-m) replica of the Great Wall of China entirely out of chocolate. The wall was made of dark chocolate bricks held together by layers of white chocolate. It was unveiled at the 2010 World Chocolate Wonderland exhibition, which also featured 560 chocolate replicas of China's famous 2,200-year-old Terracotta Army.

giant pumpkin Christy Harp of Jackson Township, Ohio, took first place at the 2009 Ohio Valley Giant Pumpkin Growers' annual weigh-off with a pumpkin that weighed 1,725 lb (783 kg)—nearly ten times the weight of an average man. At one point her prizewinning pumpkin grew at a rate of 33 lb (15 kg) per day.

earthy taste Thuli Malindzi, 22, of Cape Town, South Africa, is addicted to eating soil and consumes a chunk every day. She has been eating earth for more than ten years and although she has tried to give up, she cannot resist hard lumps of clay, which she says taste like fudge.

salsa bowl During the 2010 Jacksonville Tomato Fest in Texas, a team of 20 volunteers made a 2,672-lb (1,212-kg) bowl of salsa.

1821 bun A hot cross bun baked on Good Friday, 1821, has been kept in a Lincolnshire, England, family for 190 years—and still shows no sign of mold. The fruity bun, which has the date March 1821 on its base, was made by Nancy Titman's great-great-great-grandfather, William Skinner, who owned a bakery in London. It was not eaten at the time and has been preserved in a box ever since, passed down through generations of the family as an unusual heirloom. The bun is now rock hard and the currants have disintegrated, but the shape of the cross is still visible.

PARTY BUG
Bug-eating parties are all the rage in Tokyo, Japan, where guests tuck into dishes such as grilled cockroaches, fried grasshoppers, cricket pie and this red moth larvae soup.

chocolate wall To mark the 20th anniversary of the fall of the Berlin Wall, French chocolate-maker Patrick Roger constructed a 49-ft-long (15-m) replica of the landmark in chocolate. Over three weeks in 2009, he used 1,980 lb (900 kg) of chocolate to build the wall, and even added graffiti and artwork to the surface by spraying it with cocoa butter mixed with food coloring.

scorpion snack Li Liuqun of Hunan Province, China, is addicted to eating live scorpions and estimates he has eaten more than 10,000 over the last 30 years. Stung by a huge scorpion one day, he angrily bit off its head and enjoyed the taste so much that he now eats up to 30 in a single sitting. Luckily, he appears immune to the venom, which can paralyze and even kill people.

curry favor Feeding curry to sheep could help save the planet by lowering methane emissions. The spices used in curry kill the "bad" bacteria in a sheep's gut, reducing the amount of methane produced by up to 40 percent.

CREATIVE CAKES
Debbie Goard of Oakland, California, has created hundreds of incredibly lifelike custom-made cakes in the shape of animals, foodstuffs and everyday objects. Her cake designs include dogs, a scorpion, a warthog, a burger, popcorn, spaghetti, sneakers, a Blackberry, a camera and a baby giraffe that was nearly 2 ft (60 cm) tall. Her life-sized Chihuahua cake was so realistic that restaurant patrons were concerned there was a dog on the table!

expensive bottle In London, England, in 2009, jeweler Donald Edge unveiled a gold, pearl and diamond-encrusted bottle of Chambord raspberry liqueur that was valued at over $2 million. The bottle featured 1,100 individual diamonds.

banana bonanza Banana peels make up more than half of the trash collected on Scotland's Ben Nevis mountain. During a September 2009 survey, more than 1,000 discarded banana skins were found on the summit plateau.

chocolate coin Chocolatiers Gary Mitchell, Jess Nolasco and Rita Craig, from Purdy's Chocolates, Vancouver, Canada, spent more than eight hours creating a 25-lb (11.3-kg) chocolate coin, measuring 24 in (60 cm) wide and 1½ in (4 cm) thick, and valued at $625.

fast food "Humble" Bob Shoudt from Royersford, Pennsylvania, won first prize of $2,500 for eating 7 lb 14½ oz (3.58 kg) of French fries in ten minutes at the Curley's Fries Eating Championship at Morey's Piers, Wildwood, New Jersey, in May 2010.

vintage cognac A French entrepreneur bought a bottle of Cognac dating back to 1788—the year before the French Revolution—for nearly $37,000 at a Paris wine auction in December 2009.

sushi roll In November 2009, hundreds of students at the University of California, Berkeley, assembled a 330-ft-long (100-m) sushi roll. They used 200 lb (90 kg) of rice, 180 lb (82 kg) of fish, 80 lb (36 kg) of avocado and 80 lb (36 kg) of cucumber. To cater for vegetarians, the final 15 ft (4.5 m) contained tofu instead of seafood.

moon beer In its thirst to create even better beer, the family-owned Brewery Caulier in Péruwelz, Belgium, has begun producing beer made by the light of a full moon. The full moon speeds up the fermentation process, shortening it from seven days to five, which adds extra punch to the beer, giving it a stronger flavor.

triple yolker Bob Harrop from Devon, England, beat odds of 25 million to one when he found a triple-yolk egg while preparing his breakfast. The former hotelier has fried more than 155,000 eggs over the years and has seen hundreds of double yolkers, but this was the first time he had ever come across an egg with three yolks.

FAT DRAGON

Japanese-born pastry chef Naoko Sukegawa created a sculpture of a dragon made from margarine. The dragon, built over a steel and mesh frame, stood 29 in (74 cm) high, weighed 35 lb (16 kg) and took four months to make.

super spud Amateur gardener Peter Glazebrook of Northampton, England, grew a potato that weighed 8 lb 4 oz (3.74 kg)—the weight of a newborn baby and 25 times more than the weight of an average potato. The supersized spud would make 66 bags of potato chips, 33 portions of fries, 80 roast potatoes or 44 portions of mash.

pizza chain A chain of 2,200 pizzas stretching 1,630 ft (496 m) was laid out in 14 rows at Bucharest, Romania, in 2009. The pizza chain required 1,320 lb (600 kg) of flour, 880 lb (400 kg) of mozzarella, 440 lb (200 kg) of tomato sauce, 4 gal (15 l) of olive oil and 6 lb 10 oz (3 kg) of yeast.

sundae lunch A London ice-cream parlor offered a new twist on the traditional British Sunday roast, with each course being a frozen dessert. The "Sundae Lunch," designed by Italian mixologist Roberto Lobrano, comprised a starter of fresh pea sorbet with mint, followed by a main course of beef bouillon and horseradish sorbet topped with a Yorkshire Pudding wafer. The final course was an apple-and-blackberry-crumble gelato.

status symbols Pineapples were status symbols in 17th-century Britain, and wealthy people would rent them by the day to place on their dinner table and impress their friends.

big dipper Students from Miami-Dade, Florida, filled a 13-gal (49-l) bucket with homemade guacamole. The guacamole weighed 4,114 lb (1,866 kg) and was made from 3,500 lb (1,588 kg) of avocados, 500 lb (227 kg) of tomatoes, 100 lb (45 kg) of mayonnaise and 500 limes.

lot of dough Using a secret 1950s sourdough recipe involving Somerset flour, Cotswolds spring water and Cornish sea salt, baker Tom Herbert from Gloucestershire, England, creates loaves of bread that cost over $30 each. Each 4½-lb (2-kg) hand-crafted shepherd loaf takes him two days to make from start to finish.

MICE LUNCH

While making sandwiches for his family in 2010, a father from Oxfordshire, England, found an unwelcome ingredient in the bread he had bought from a local supermarket—a dead mouse baked into the half-eaten loaf. To make matters worse, the unfortunate rodent was missing its tail, leading Stephen Forse to wonder whether his family had already eaten it.

YUCKY FOOD FACTS

• For every 3½ oz (100 g) of product, the U.S. Food and Drug Administration allows a certain amount of alien material before taking action. This includes up to three rodent hairs and 60 insect fragments in chocolate, five fly eggs and one maggot in tomato juice, and one rodent hair and 30 insect parts in peanut butter.

• In 2010, an English chef opened a tin of baked beans and discovered a dead rat inside. Tests showed that it had not eaten any beans.

• A family from Kentucky drank from a container of milk for three days before they noticed that a mouse had died inside it.

• In 2009, a Florida man found an entire mouse inside his can of cola after complaining that it tasted strange.

chocolate fashion At the 15th Paris Salon du Chocolat in Shanghai, China, chefs and clothes designers from across the world combined their talents to create dresses, jackets, shoes and handbags all made from chocolate.

edible plates To save on washing up after school dinners, catering boss Tiziano Vicentini from Milan, Italy, has devised a range of edible plates made from a kind of dough that is tough enough to last a lunchtime, but tasty enough to eat afterward.

Frog's Heart

Customers in Japan who order Frog Sashimi eat the still-beating heart of a freshly killed American bullfrog. The rest of the frog is eaten as a raw dish, with any leftovers, including the feet, turned into soup.

Ripley's Believe It or Not!®

food

R barter system In 2010, a bar owner on Estonia's Hiiumaa Island in the Baltic Sea revived the age-old barter system to allow customers to pay for drinks with goods. Tarvo Nomm agreed to sell beer in return for bundles of firewood and catches of fish to help the locals beat economic hardship.

R banana boxers Australian company AussieBum has unveiled a range of men's underwear made from bananas. The eco-friendly range incorporates 27 percent banana fiber, making the garments lightweight and absorbent without actually smelling of bananas.

R half-mile pizza In August 2010, chefs in Krakow, Poland, used 3.5 tons of flour to make a pizza measuring 3,280 ft (1,000 m) in length—that's more than half-a-mile long!

R chocolate shoes Confectioner Frances Cooley from Bristol, England, sells shoes and handbags made of chocolate. She has developed a line of individual, high-heeled shoes—including zebra-striped and polka-dot versions—which she makes by hand in her own kitchen. The largest shoe is 6¾ in (17 cm) long and made from two 3½-oz (100-g) bars of Belgian chocolate.

R $1,000 burger Joe El-Ajouz's restaurant in Sydney, New South Wales, Australia, has a burger on the menu that costs $1,000. It weighs 210 lb (95 kg), requires 178 lb (81 kg) of mince, 120 eggs, 120 cheese slices, 16 tomatoes, 4½ lb (2 kg) of lettuce, 46 lb (21 kg) of bread and 1.1 lb (500 g) of barbecue sauce. It takes over 12 hours to cook and serves more than 100 people.

R nacho tray At Northstar Church, Frisco, Texas, more than 300 volunteers built a 3,555-lb (1,613-kg), 48-ft-long (14.6-m) tray of nachos, loaded with 2,200 lb (998 kg) of yellow tortilla chips, 600 lb (272 kg) of nacho cheese, 250 lb (113 kg) of sour cream, 250 lb (113 kg) of jalapenos, 200 lb (90 kg) of shredded Cheddar cheese and 200 lb (90 kg) of sauce.

R soluble gum Scientists at Bristol University, England, have devised a nonstick chewing gum. Rev7 has the same taste and texture as normal gum, but it disintegrates over time and can be removed from shoes, hair and other surfaces with just soap and water.

SWEET SKULLS

Marina Malvada, an artist from Montreal, Canada, uses genuine human skulls—borrowed from a tribal art collector who specializes in collecting cannibal skulls—to cast life-sized skulls in chocolate. Each head is solid chocolate, takes four days to complete and is entirely edible, although weighing 5½ lb (2.5 kg) each, one is more than a mouthful.

R tea nation Britons drink 165 million cups of tea every day—around three cups a day for every adult and child. Although Great Britain accounts for less than 1 percent of the world's population, it is responsible for around 4 percent of its tea consumption.

R dogs' dinner An ice-cream van exclusively for dogs attended a 2010 pet festival in London, England. Created by a team of scientists, the canine-friendly, K99 ice cream comes in two flavors—Dog Eat Hog World, a gammon and chicken sorbet topped with a biscuit bone and served in a cone, and Canine Cookie Crunch, dog biscuits and ice cream topped with a biscuit bone.

R testicle cooking At the 2010 Testicle Cooking World Championship in Ozrem, Serbia, chefs produced dishes made from the testicles of animals including bulls, wild boar, horses, sharks, ostriches, kangaroos, donkeys, turkeys, goats, reindeer and elk.

R scott's butter Two blocks of New Zealand butter nearly a century old were found intact in 2009 in an Antarctic hut used by British explorer Robert Falcon Scott on his doomed 1910–12 expedition.

R humongous hummus Chefs in Beirut, Lebanon, prepared a massive plate of hummus weighing over two tons. They used 2,976 lb (1,350 kg) of mashed chickpeas, 106 gal (400 l) of lemon juice and 57 lb (26 kg) of salt to make the dish that weighed 4,532 lb (2,056 kg).

R exotic tea Made from older leaves, Puer tea is renowned in China for its exotic taste and healing properties, and is so coveted that just one third of an ounce (10 g) of century-old tea can sell for $10,000.

R double banana Having bought a bunch of bananas at a supermarket in Somerset, England, Cedric Hooper got home and found that one skin contained two bananas!

R burger candle Columbus, Ohio-based fast-food chain White Castle offered customers a new way to sniff its produce by introducing candles that smell like its oniony Slider hamburgers.

R mega meatball In 2009, Nonni's Italian Eatery in New Hampshire created a meatball that weighed a colossal 222 lb 8 oz (101 kg). The giant ball of mince took three days to cook.

R hot chocolate In 2009, scientists at Warwick University, England, unveiled an environmentally friendly racing car, built partly from vegetables and powered by chocolate. The bodywork of the WorldFirst car is made from plastic bottles and scraps from airplanes, the seat from flax and soy, and the steering wheel from the waste of juiced carrots. The car, which can reach speeds of 135 mph (217 km/h), uses plant-oil based lubricants and can run on biodiesel made from chocolate factory waste and stale wine.

® gigantic grill Jack Henriques, an engineer from Gloucestershire, England, has built a giant barbecue that can cook 1,000 sausages or grill 500 burgers at once. He spent three months welding together the steel grill, which weighs 2 tons and measures 16 ft (5 m) long, 6 ft 3 in (1.9 m) wide and 11½ ft (3.5 m) tall. The $15,000 barbecue, which requires 14 bags of coal to fill fully, is so big it can cook seven whole lambs, three whole pigs or two whole cows at the same time.

® curry boom In 1950, there were only six Indian restaurants in the whole of Britain, but by 2004 their number had grown to around 9,000.

SPOON FED
Surgeons in Rotterdam, the Netherlands, removed 78 different items of cutlery from the stomach of 52-year-old Margaret Daalmans after she had gone to the hospital complaining of stomach pains. X-rays showed she had swallowed dozens of forks and spoons as a result of her insatiable appetite for cutlery.

Bacon Kevin Bacon
J & D Foods in Seattle commissioned Pennsylvania artist Mike Lahue to create a sculpture of actor Kevin Bacon, from crispy bacon bits! The tasty Hollywood head took three months to complete, but unfortunately it is inedible owing to a protective lacquer coating. A bacon-obsessed food company from Seattle, J & D Foods produce bacon soda, "baconnaise" mayonnaise, bacon popcorn, envelopes that taste of bacon when you lick the seal and even bacon lip balm. Their company slogan is "Everything should taste like bacon."

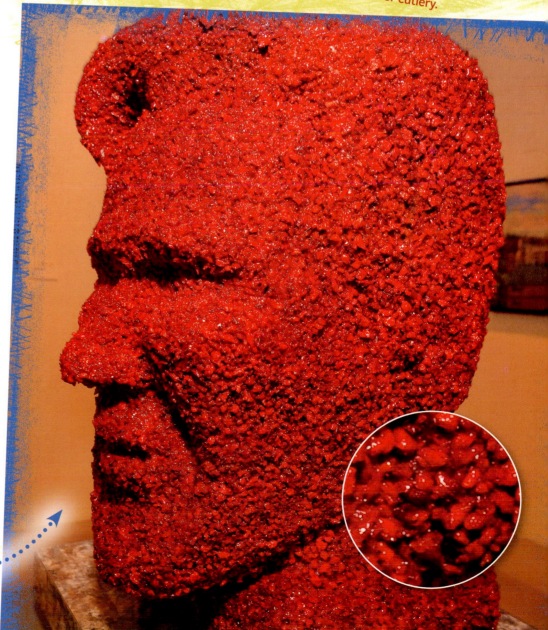

food
Believe It or Not!®

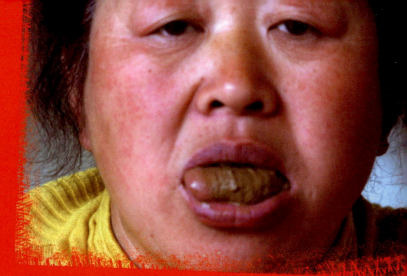

SHE'S CRACKED IT

Zhou Yuqin from Chongqing, China, says she has cured all her ailments by eating up to 50 eggshells every day for 13 years. She has even persuaded her children to copy her. When eggshells aren't enough to satisfy her appetite for the unusual, she also nibbles on sand and cullet (broken glass).

DIRT DISH

Fan Qianrong from China's Hebei Province has stayed healthy by eating soil and mud for more than 40 years. Millions of people around the world consume soil, a practice known as geophagy. Eating soil can supply useful minerals and fight nausea, indigestion and diarrhea.

Dig In!

Some people eat the strangest things—wood, glass, metal, clothing, stones, hair and even excrement. The Glore Psychiatric Museum in St. Joseph, Missouri, has a display of 1,446 unusual items swallowed by a patient and removed from her intestines and stomach—including 453 nails, 42 screws and assorted safety pins, spoons and salt and pepper shaker tops. She died during surgery from bleeding caused by her weird diet.

Prickly Eaters

THE CONSUMPTION OF ODD OBJECTS IS CALLED PICA. HERE ARE SOME EATING HABITS TO KICK:

- HYALOPHAGIA IS THE EATING OF GLASS. FRENCH ENTERTAINER MICHEL LOTITO ("MONSIEUR MANGETOUT") ATE GLASS, METAL, RUBBER, BICYCLES, SHOPPING CARTS, TV SETS AND EVEN A LIGHT AIRPLANE, WHICH TOOK HIM TWO YEARS TO DEVOUR.

- TRICHOPHAGIA IS THE EATING OF HAIR. SURGEONS IN CHICAGO RECENTLY REMOVED A 10-LB (4.5-KG) HAIRBALL FROM THE STOMACH OF AN 18-YEAR-OLD WOMAN.

- XYLOPHAGIA IS THE EATING OF WOOD. PEOPLE WITH THIS CONDITION OFTEN EAT PAPER, PENCILS AND TREE BARK.

- COPROPHAGIA IS THE EATING OF FECES. CENTURIES AGO, DOCTORS USED TO TASTE THEIR PATIENTS' EXCREMENT TO DIAGNOSE THEIR STATE OF HEALTH.

- UROPHAGIA IS THE DRINKING OF URINE. MARTIAL-ARTS FIGHTER LYOTO MACHIDA FROM BRAZIL DRINKS HIS OWN URINE EVERY MORNING AS PART OF HIS TRAINING ROUTINE. HE SAYS IT'S A FAMILY TRADITION, PASSED DOWN TO HIM FROM HIS FATHER.

- AUTOSARGOPHAGY IS THE DISORDER OF SELF-CANNIBALISM. IN 2007, CHILEAN ARTIST MARCO EVARISTTI HOSTED A DINNER PARTY FOR FRIENDS WHERE THE MAIN COURSE WAS PASTA TOPPED BY A MEATBALL MADE WITH THE ARTIST'S OWN FAT, REMOVED EARLIER IN THE YEAR BY LIPOSUCTION.

DIET OF BUGS

Mr. Zhu from Sichuan Province, China, has eaten live centipedes since he was a child. In just one month, he and his friends consumed over 3,000 bugs and worms.

Squirrel Ale

In 2010, a Scottish brewery packaged bottles of its new beer, "The End of History," inside the bodies of dead animals. BrewDog sold bottles of its strong, limited-edition Belgian ale—made with juniper berries and containing a staggering 55 percent alcohol—for $1,000 if housed inside a dead squirrel and $750 for bottles encased in a dead stoat. The limited edition of 12 dead animal bottles was hand-crafted by a Yorkshire taxidermist using creatures that had died of natural causes.

pub crawl Since 1984, Stuart Ashby of West Sussex, England, has drunk more than 8,500 pints of beer in over 17,000 British pubs, from Cornwall to the Shetland Islands, in the process traveling some 25,000 mi (40,000 km).

long lunch In September 2010, chefs in Italy served lunch on a table that was over a mile long. The 5,775-ft-long (1,760-m) spread was laid out for 2,700 diners and stretched from Bosco to nearby Borzano. The organizers' biggest problem was that it required a tablecloth 5,905 ft (1,800 m) long.

molto macaroni Chef John Folse cooked 2,469 lb (1,120 kg) of macaroni and cheese—enough for 6,500 servings—in New Orleans, Louisiana, in September 2010.

wee dram London-based designer James Gilpin has created whisky made from the high-sugar urine of elderly diabetic patients, including his own grandmother. Gilpin, who is himself diabetic, filters the urine by the same processes used to purify water, and in doing so removes the sugars, which are then used in fermentation. The drink, named Gilpin Family Whisky, is not for sale.

safe breakfast Scientists in the U.K. have developed a breakfast that won't make you sick if you go on a roller coaster shortly afterward. It consists of yogurt mixed with blueberries, grilled bacon in a wholemeal bun with tomato, served with a drink of celery and carrot juice with ginger. Staffordshire theme park Alton Towers were so confident in the product that they offered to refund anyone who was sick on a ride after eating the breakfast.

beers and spirits For more than nine months in 2009, a ghost apparently kept topping up drinkers' glasses at the Apsley House pub in Southsea, Hampshire, England. Landlady Janice McCormack complained that the specter was costing her a fortune because it was giving away her beer.

vegetable phobia Vicki Larrieux of Portsmouth, England, suffers from lachanophobia, a fear of vegetables. The only vegetables she can bear to eat, touch or see are potatoes. The sight of a carrot or a pea, not just on her plate but even on supermarket shelves, leaves her sweating and stricken with panic attacks.

giant cupcake Chefs in Boca Raton, Florida, unveiled a 1,500-lb (680-kg) chocolate cupcake. It stood 4½ ft (1.4 m) high, 6 ft (1.8 m) wide, and was topped with pink icing, handmade 5-in (12.5-cm) sprinkles and a cherry with a circumference of 12 in (30 cm). It was baked in an oven measuring 10 x 10 ft (3 x 3 m).

golden curry Restaurateurs Padma Prasad and Bhagat Saxena of Hyderabad, India, added finely ground flakes of gold and silver to create a chicken curry that costs $300 a serving.

ALTERNATIVE DINING

• IN SEVERAL COUNTRIES, DINNER IN THE SKY OFFERS A DINING TABLE SUSPENDED IN MIDAIR BY A CRANE 164 FT (50 M) ABOVE GROUND. IT SEATS 22 DINERS AND HAS FIVE STANDING STAFF.

• AN UNDERWATER RESTAURANT IN THE MALDIVES SEATS 14 PEOPLE AND IS LOCATED 15 FT (4.5 M) BELOW THE SURFACE OF THE INDIAN OCEAN.

• IN 2005, ADVENTURER BEAR GRYLLS, BALLOONIST DAVID HEMPLEMAN-ADAMS AND SKYDIVER ALAN VEAL STAGED A DINNER PARTY UNDER A HOT-AIR BALLOON AT AN ALTITUDE OF 25,000 FT (7,620 M).

• THE RESTAURANT AT THE CHACALTAYA SKI RESORT, CORDILLERA, BOLIVIA, IS 17,519 FT (5,340 M) ABOVE SEA LEVEL.

• TWENTY-TWO FLOORS BENEATH THE STREETS OF MOSCOW, RUSSIA, SITS A RESTAURANT BUILT IN WHAT WAS ONCE SOVIET LEADER JOSEF STALIN'S UNDERGROUND BUNKER.

• A CAFÉ IN ISTANBUL, TURKEY, IS LOCATED INSIDE A 1,500-YEAR-OLD UNDERGROUND BYZANTINE WATER CISTERN.

• THE FORTEZZA MEDICEA RESTAURANT NEAR PISA, ITALY, IS SITUATED INSIDE A PRISON WHERE THE WAITERS ARE ALL INMATES.

• IN 2007, 500 PEOPLE WEARING SCUBA-DIVING GEAR DINED UNDERWATER AT THE BOTTOM OF A SWIMMING POOL IN LONDON, ENGLAND.

SUPER SALAMI

A monster salami measuring 7 ft 3 in (2.2 m) long and weighing 143 lb (65 kg) went on show at the Agricultural Trading Exhibition in Anhui, China, in February 2010.

sausage drama A cleaner was taken to hospital in May 2010 after his head and shoulders were sucked into a sausage machine at a factory in Danvers, Massachusetts. The victim, who was not seriously hurt, was cleaning the inside of a cylinder that draws marinade into the meat, when the machine was accidentally switched on.

VOLCANO BARBECUE

When Iceland's Fimmvörðuháls volcano erupted in April 2010, Reykjavik chef Fridgeir Eiriksson cooked soup, flaming lobster, monkfish and shallots using the volcano's 390°F (200°C) lava as an oven. Two customers paid $1,000 to enjoy this special Champagne dinner on the bubbling volcano.

grass diet Fifty-year-old Li Sanju of Guangdong Province, China, has spent more than two years eating only leaves and grass. He says he enjoys his unusual diet but admits that he does smell strongly of grass.

full o bull The Cowtown Diner in Fort Worth, Texas, serves a chicken fried steak that weighs about 10 lb (4.5 kg) and packs 10,000 calories. The "Full O Bull," which comes complete with 6 lb (2.7 kg) of mashed potatoes and 10 slices of toast, normally costs $70—but if you can eat it solo, it's free!

jellyfish candy In response to an invasion of 6-ft-wide (1.8-m), 440-lb (200-kg) jellyfish, students at Obama Fisheries High School, Japan, harvested the creatures and turned them into caramel candies.

lion burger To mark the 2010 soccer World Cup in South Africa, a restaurant in Mesa, Arizona, added lion burgers to its menu. Cameron Selogie's Il Vinaio restaurant offered the burger (from farm-raised lion) at $21, served with spicy homemade chips and roast corn on the cob.

zebra pizza Alongside more familiar flavors, a pizza takeout store in Burnley, Lancashire, England, sells pizzas topped with the meat of zebras, crocodiles, kangaroos and buffalo. Owner Arash Fard sells around 20 of his exotic pizzas every week.

rich dish A 513-lb (233-kg) tuna sold for $177,000 at an auction in January 2010 in Tokyo's Tsukiji fish market. That works out to $345 a pound.

still bubbly In July 2010, divers exploring the wreck of a sailing vessel 180 ft (55 m) below the surface of the Baltic Sea off the coast of Finland discovered 30 bottles of champagne some 230 years old. As the bottles had been preserved in the ideal conditions of cold and darkness for so many years, experts said the champagne tasted remarkably good although it had lost some of its fizz.

long-life burger Wellness consultant Karen Hanrahan of Chicago, Illinois, has kept a burger for more than 14 years—without doing anything to preserve it—and it still looks as fresh as the day she bought it!

wrap artists In Lewisburg, Pennsylvania, cooks used 15 lb (6.8 kg) of bacon and 175 wraps held together with about 1,200 toothpicks to create a 102-ft-long (31-m) sandwich wrap.

tasty spider To raise funds for his school in Kent, England, headteacher Aydin Onac ate a baked Cambodian tarantula spider in front of a packed assembly. He said it tasted like burnt chicken.

deep-fried beer Texas chef Mark Zable has created a recipe for deep-fried beer. The beer is placed inside a pocket of salty, pretzel-like dough and dunked in oil at 375°F (190°C) for about 20 seconds. When customers take a bite, the hot beer mixes with the dough to give an alcoholic taste.

banana ketchup Made from mashed banana, sugar, vinegar and spices, banana ketchup is a popular Filipino condiment that is often colored red to resemble tomato ketchup. It was first produced during World War II when there was a shortage of tomato ketchup but an abundance of bananas.

Fast Grub
Eating insects is so popular in Thailand that the country even has its own insect fast food chain. Insects Inter has more than 30 outlets selling fried, crunchy grasshoppers, crickets, grubs and silkworms in $0.70 pots with ketchup or hot chili dips.

transport

feats

mysteries

food

arts

science

beyond belief

believe it!

world

animals

sports

body

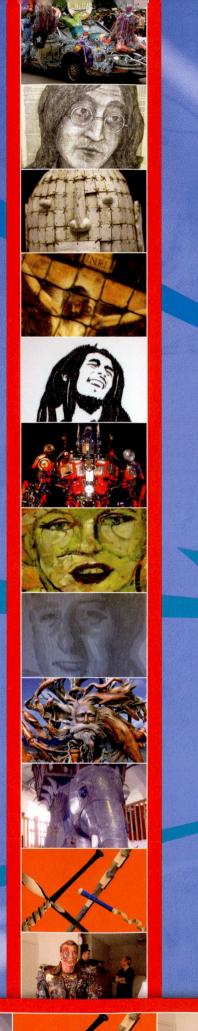

196
197
198
199
200
201
202
203
204
205
206
207
208
209
210
211
212
213
214
215
216
217
218
219
220
221
222
223

Cassette Stars

Ripley's has bought a number of Erika Simmons' recycled cassette-tape portraits, depicting Bob Marley (seen here), Michael Jackson, Debbie Harry and Kurt Cobain, among others. The Atlanta artist, featured in Ripley's Believe It or Not! *Enter If You Dare!*, has since become an internet sensation after her tape art inspired the video for the Bruno Mars hit "Just the Way You Are."

RIPLEY's EXHIBITS

Inflated Animals

Chinese artist Yang Maoyuan creates animal sculptures with a difference—he takes the skins of dead animals and inflates them to monstrous sizes, often dyeing them in lurid colors.

Beijing-based Yang travels to Hebei in northern China to buy horse, goat and sheep skins. He then stitches and processes the skins before blowing them up so that their bodies become bloated and round. He chooses animals from his Mongolian ancestry, making them larger than life to reflect his oldest dream symbols, and gives them a round shape that represents harmony in China. To make his sculptures even more grotesque, he gives some of the sheep two or three heads.

Yang's art has been a hit in galleries worldwide.

Yang's bright blue, three-headed, many-legged goat.

◀◀◀ After

Yang takes complete horse skins (right) and turns them into works of art that symbolize his philosophy and the nomadic traditions of his ancestors.

Before ▶▶▶

RIPLEY RESEARCH

Victor uses leaves from the maple-like Chinar tree, as they are particularly durable. The process takes around a month, involving as many as 60 individual steps. First he boils the leaf in water to soften it and remove any bacteria. Then he removes the layers of the leaf with a knife and needle, taking care to keep the delicate veins in place. Next he carefully cuts and sculpts the surface to create his chosen image. Then he brushes and shaves the leaf to make it appear transparent, coats it in an anti-aging treatment, dries it again, and finally waxes it before framing.

A NEW LEAF

Victor Liu collects dried old leaves from the streets around his home in Hebei Province, China, and very painstakingly carves into them beautiful images of subjects such as Barack Obama, Marilyn Monroe, the *Mona Lisa* and the Statue of Liberty.

new york bears Joshua Allen Harris placed inflatable polar bears made from discarded plastic bags above ventilation grates in the New York City subway so that the animals inflated and deflated with the passing of underground trains.

daily grind Instead of paint or ink, Bend, Oregon, artist Karen Eland creates replicas of famous artworks with coffee. Since her first espresso painting in 1998, she has completed more than 90 illustrations—many of which incorporate coffee drinking—including *Leonardo da Vinci's Mona Latte*, *Whistler's Mocha* and *Rodin's The Drinker*.

traveling bible A unique 1,500-page traveling Bible, written in 66 languages—one language for each book of the Old and New Testament—has toured more than 150 countries. The huge 15-lb (7-kg) book, which measures 18 x 12 in (45 x 30 cm), set off on its world tour from the Philippines in October 2008.

baseball mementos Mitch Poole, clubhouse manager with the Los Angeles Dodgers baseball team, turns milestones into mementos by painting significant game balls with details of the achievement. It is traditional for a clubhouse manager to retrieve the ball when an important hit, run, steal or win takes place, and for more than 20 years Mitch has decorated hundreds of balls. Using acrylic paint, he writes the player's name, opponent, accomplishment, date, box score and other information on the ball.

original nintendo In February 2010, a video-game collector paid $13,105 for an original Nintendo entertainment system and five game cartridges.

stage epic German producer Franz Abraham has created a stage version of the Roman epic *Ben-Hur* featuring 400 actors, 900 costumes, 50 scene designs, 46 horses, 120 doves, five chariots, two eagles and two vultures. The action takes place in a 26,000-sq-ft (2,415-sq-m) arena covered with 10 in (25 cm) of sand. The production uses 30 mi (48 km) of cable, 250 moving lights and 25 tons of sound equipment.

big business In Minneapolis, Minnesota, in 2009, entrepreneur Lief Larson presented a work contact with a giant business card that measured 60 x 34 in (150 x 85 cm).

CROCHET LIONS

English "crochetdermist" Shauna Richardson spent two years hand-crocheting three huge lions, each measuring 25 ft (7.5 m) long and 10 ft (3 m) high. She crocheted the skins in wool, accurately tracing the animals' muscular contours, over a polystyrene and steel framework. Shauna also crochets life-size pieces, which have included wild boars, bears and baboons.

tattooed pigs Belgian artist Wim Delvoye tattooed pigs with Louis Vuitton designer logos for an exhibit called *Art Farm*. He tattooed the LV logos on the animals when they were piglets and watched the designs increase in size as the pigs' bodies grew.

some yarn! Over the period of a week, Austin, Texas, artist Magda Sayeg covered a Mexico City bus from front to back with brightly colored knitted yarn. She has also knitted woolen coverings for trees, car antennas and signs in the U.S.A. as well as for the Louvre Museum in Paris.

typed portraits Keira Rathbone of Dorset, England, uses manual typewriters—some up to 70 years old—as her paintbrushes to create portraits of famous people, including Barack Obama, Marilyn Monroe and supermodel Kate Moss. After deciding which of her collection of 30 typewriters she wants to use, she turns the roller and selects different characters—numbers, letters and punctuation—to make the required shapes.

tan art James Titterton of London, England, endured a full body wax and eight sunbed sessions to have a fish, a cockerel and a ship's anchor bronzed onto his flesh. He masked off parts of his chest, arms and legs with vinyl stickers of the various images before having the outlines tanned on to his skin. Dressed in only underpants, he then exhibited his tanned artwork at a gallery in Sussex.

naked hug More than 5,000 people took off their clothes and embraced each other in the nude on the steps of Sydney Opera House, Australia, in March 2010 for a photo shoot by American artist Spencer Tunick.

$11 million book A copy of the book *Birds of America*, written and illustrated by Haitian-born John James Audubon in the early 19th century, was sold for more than $11 million in December 2010. Only 119 complete copies of the large-format book, which has foldout pages measuring 39½ x 29½ in (100 x 75 cm), are in existence, and all but 11 of those are in museums and libraries. To obtain such accurate likenesses of birds, Audubon stalked his subjects across the U.S.A. and shot them before hanging them from wires and painting them.

behind the smile Dr. Vito Franco of the University of Palermo, Sicily, Italy, believes the enigmatic smile on the face of Leonardo da Vinci's *Mona Lisa* was the result of very high levels of cholesterol. After studying the painting closely, the doctor says he can detect a build up of fatty acids around her left eye.

sound your horn! A giant, working vuvuzela horn 115 ft (35 m) long and 18 ft (5.5 m) in diameter was installed above a highway in Cape Town, South Africa, in 2010.

Living Dolls

When British artist Boo Ritson tells her subjects she wants to paint them, she means it literally. Boo covers her human volunteers in layers of water-based paint to create giant action figures, which she then photographs. She specializes in American symbols, which means that as well as painting subjects such as cheerleader and cowboy living dolls, she has also applied the technique to donuts.

Sticky Sculpture

When a popular adhesive tape company challenged people to come up with the best sculpture made entirely from sticky tape, they received some incredible entries. Artist Annie K. stuck together this giant jellyfish that appears to be floating in the air and ensnaring a bicycle in its tentacles. Some of the entries included an office desk made from 36 rolls of tape and a drum kit made from 48 rolls—that's over 7,770 ft (2,368 m), or enough tape to wrap round an aircraft carrier seven times.

Ⓡ **cardboard scream** Artist Mark Langan from Cleveland, Ohio, re-created Edvard Munch's haunting painting *The Scream* using discarded cardboard boxes. He spent 90 hours cutting up five old boxes with a craft knife and layering them to create a three-dimensional picture that measured 2.2 in (5.5 cm) deep. His cardboard creation sold for $2,500.

Ⓡ **noncontact instrument** The theremin is an electronic musical instrument that is played without any contact from the player! Named after Russian professor Léon Theremin, who invented it in 1919, it consists of two metal antennae that sense the position of the player's hands and send corresponding electric signals to a loudspeaker.

Ⓡ **microbial art** Dr. T. Ryan Gregory of the University of Guelph, Canada, is a pioneer of microbial art, where scientists design patterns by brushing fungi, deadly bacteria and dye around a petri dish. He creates images by using a small paintbrush and E. coli in liquid medium. These are then allowed to grow in a laboratory incubator, but the "living paint" soon dies, so the pictures are only temporary.

DEAD FLIES

Magnus Muhr collects dead flies from windows and lamps around his house in Sweden, places them on white paper, draws in legs and a crazy background, and then photographs them. The photos show the insects appearing to dance, sunbathe, dive, ride horses and perform acrobatic circus routines.

giant chair Furniture craftsman Radoslav Russev carved a wooden chair that was almost 15 ft (4.5 m) high and weighed more than 770 lb (350 kg). He made the oversized chair, which was placed in the main square of Razgrad, Bulgaria, from 70 cubic ft (2 cubic m) of pinewood.

leather portraits Welsh artist Mark Evans creates huge portraits of famous people—in leather. Using knives as his "brushes," he has scraped impressions of Muhammad Ali, Sir Winston Churchill and model Naomi Campbell into leather hides. He discovered his talent by accident after spilling blood on a new leather jacket. He tried to repair it with a palette knife but scratched too hard and ended up etching a portrait of Jimi Hendrix onto the back of the jacket.

cereal-ism With the help of 150 students, high-school teacher Doyle Geddes of Smithfield, Utah, used 2 tons of breakfast cereal to create a massive reproduction of Vincent van Gogh's painting *Starry Night* measuring 72 x 90 ft (22 x 27 m).

board game In 2009, board-game fanatic Luanga Nuwame created a 900-sq-ft (84-sq-m) wooden board game based on the city of Mississauga, Ontario, Canada... with real people as the pieces. He also built a huge dice with which to play it.

washington's fine New York Society Library says George Washington owes it $300,000 in library fines. Its ledgers show that the first U.S. President borrowed two books that were due to be returned on November 2, 1789, but are now more than 220 years overdue.

costly comic A copy of the 1938 edition of *Action Comics No. 1* sold in March 2010 for $1.5 million on an auction website. The issue, which features Superman's debut, originally sold for 10 cents.

french anthem Claude-Joseph Rouget de Lisle composed "The Marseillaise" in 1792 in return for a bottle of wine. The tune became the anthem of French Revolutionaries and was later adopted as the French national anthem. Ironically, Rouget de Lisle was a royalist who was thrown into prison during the Revolution and narrowly escaped being guillotined.

observation test To help improve their powers of deductive observation, a group of New York City police officers visited the Metropolitan Museum of Art to discuss with an expert what conclusions they could draw from the contents of pictures by the likes of Caravaggio and Guercino.

many parts Bollywood actress Priyanka Chopra played all 12 characters in the 2009 movie *What's Your Rashee?* Each character was one of the 12 zodiac signs.

serenading sharks Andy Brandy Casagrande IV, an American wildlife cinematographer, strummed a waterproof guitar and played a song underwater to sharks off the coast of Mexico—without a cage. He penned "The Great White Shark Song" to raise awareness of shark conservation and decided the best way to make his point was to don scuba gear and play his tune in shark-infested waters.

Kris Kuksi, a sculptor and painter from Kansas, creates macabre yet beautiful sculptures assembled from hundreds, sometimes thousands, of discarded toys, figurines and general trash. His work has been bought by celebrities and exhibited around the world.

Kris explains how Lies and Persuasion *came together:*

"My pieces are a collection of many different things. I started out by gathering miscellaneous figurines, small rocks, jewelry—anything I could incorporate. After I found some essential "supplies" that I felt were important for the individuality of the piece, I built a foundation, and everything after that is just assemblage. When it's all finished, the piece gets various coats of paint.

Lies and Persuasion has so many little things in it and, interesting enough, the skull forms in the piece are actually the same skull split in half. I'll buy anything, anywhere, if I feel it's needed for a piece. I'd say that the whole assemblage, that is, the creation itself—withholding the mental preparation and shopping— lasted about a month."

TURN THE PAGE...

Miscellaneous Mosaic

ILLUSION CONFUSION

There is a lot more to this portrait of legendary artist Salvador Dali than meets the eye. It is in fact a large three-dimensional illusion, consisting of a shark, a bull's head and a seal, among many other objects. These bizarre items appear to be randomly piled up but are actually meticulously placed to complete the image from just one perspective. Bernard Pras, the artist from Belgium, has been re-creating famous pictures out of junk for more than 30 years.

microscopic models Origami artist Mui-Ling Teh of Thornhill, Ontario, Canada, makes paper models so tiny—as small as 0.08 in (2 mm) long—that they look like a speck to the naked eye. She makes her microscopic models of objects such as birds, flowers and airplanes with scissors and tweezers. She first began to experiment with origami at age ten when she made small models out of candy wrappers.

auto robot A 33-ft-tall (10-m) version of Transformer Optimus Prime made from the bodies and tires of old cars and motorcycles was unveiled at Beijing's Green Dream Park in 2010. The Autobot sculpture weighed six tons and was assembled from five truckloads of recycled parts.

huge hammock Hansy Better Barraza, a professor at Rhode Island School of Design, created a 33-ft-long (10-m) hammock, covering an area of 264 sq ft (24.5 sq m) in Boston, Massachusetts, in 2010. The sculpture consisted of 4,278 ft (1,304 m)—that's nearly a mile—of "rope" made from recycled bottles woven over curved steel pipes.

beef bikini For the September 2010 cover shot of Japanese magazine *Vogue Hommes Japan*, U.S. singer Lady Gaga wore a bikini made of raw meat.

avid reader Nonagenarian Louise Brown from Dumfries and Galloway, Scotland, has borrowed 25,000 library books in her lifetime. She has read up to a dozen books a week since 1946 without incurring a single fine for late returns.

smelly issue Issue No. 23 of the German magazine *mono.kultur* was infused with 12 smells suggested by Norwegian scientist, artist and odor expert Sissel Tolaas. Using a technique called microencapsulation, the smells were printed into the pages of the magazine, with the reader rubbing the paper to release them.

human ashes Dutch artist Wieki Somers makes 3-D printed sculptures of common household appliances—including bathroom scales, a vacuum cleaner and a toaster—out of human ashes.

gallery blunder Polish experimental artist Leon Tarasewicz sued a gallery for $30,000 after it ripped up one of his paintings and threw it in a trash can in the mistaken belief that it was a large bunch of scrap paper used for getting excess paint off brushes. The 25-ft-high (7.6-m) exhibit had been on display in the gallery in Katowice, but staff thought that it had been left behind by decorators.

Tasty Shoes Israel's Kobi Levi has designed shoes in the shapes of bananas, cats, shopping baskets, dogs, rocking chairs—and one pair with a pink stiletto heel that makes it look as though the wearer has stepped in a piece of chewing gum.

GLASS HOLOGRAMS

Using special pencils, multiple layers of painted glass and between 14 and 30 glass panes, artist Xia Xiao Wan from Beijing, China, is able to transform ordinary 2-D glass into stunning 3-D holographic images.

fake porsche Austrian artist Hannes Langeder spent six months building a life-size Porsche sports car from plastic pipes and cardboard. The aluminum-foil covered Ferdinand GT3 RSX has no engine but is powered by a hidden bicycle, which is why it has handlebars instead of a steering wheel.

mosaic mural More than 130 artists and 500 children worked for three years to create a ceramic mosaic mural in Hanoi, Vietnam, that measures nearly 2½ mi (4 km) long. The brainchild of artist Nguyen Thu Thuy, the mosaic depicts images of Vietnam's history, life and culture.

whistle-stop tour German guitarist Vicente Patiz drove more than 600 mi (960 km) to give concerts in eight countries—Germany, Belgium, the Netherlands, France, Luxembourg, Switzerland, Lichtenstein and Austria—in just 24 hours.

bamboo dance More than 10,700 people assembled on March 12, 2010, to perform the Cheraw dance together in Aizawl, Mizoram, India. They spread out over an area of about 1¾ mi (3 km) to dance an eight-minute routine with bamboo sticks.

bargain buy A decade after buying 65 photographic plates at a garage sale in California for just $45, Rick Norsigian found that they could be the work of celebrated U.S. nature photographer Ansel Adams and therefore be worth around $200 million.

quick on the draw Singaporean artist Peter Zhou, aka Peter Draw, drew nearly 1,000 people nonstop, without food, for 24 hours.

Poo Shoes

British artist INSA created a pair of 10-in-high (25-cm) stiletto shoes with platforms made from elephant dung. He sourced the waste from the same family of elephants that provided the material for a famous series of elephant-dung collage paintings by Turner Prize-winning British artist Chris Ofili in the 1990s.

Roll the Dice Ari Krupnik, a software engineer from Silicon Valley, California, builds mosaics of famous people from hundreds of dice, achieving different shades of gray according to which face is up. He created a portrait of revolutionary leader Che Guevara from 400 dice and one of George Orwell, author of *Animal Farm*, from 1,925 dice. He has also made a 3-D image of actress Uma Thurman from hundreds of M&M's®.

pretty paddies Each year, the farmers of Inakadate Village, Aomori Prefecture, Japan, use different-colored varieties of rice to create works of art spanning entire rice paddies.

blind draft U.S. novelist Kent Haruf writes the first draft of each of his books blind! He takes off his glasses, pulls a stocking cap down over his eyes, and types his words in darkness.

rubik's replica Five artists in Toronto, Canada, spent two months making a replica of Leonardo da Vinci's *The Last Supper* measuring 8½ x 17 ft (2.6 x 5.2 m), using 4,050 Rubik's cubes.

poetry booth Starting in October 2009, an old-style telephone booth in Yellow Springs, Ohio, served as a stage for poetry readings, light shows and dance performances. People could walk into the booth, pick up the receiver and listen to a recorded reading of short poems or simply create their own experimental artworks.

vast violin In 2010, a dozen workers in Markneukirchen, Germany, created a playable violin that measured 13 ft 11 in (4.3 m) tall, 4½ ft (1.4 m) wide, and weighed more than 220 lb (100 kg).

gum-wrapper dress Elizabeth Rasmuson of Garner, Iowa, made her 2010 high-school prom dress out of hundreds of gum wrappers that she and her boyfriend, Jordan Weaver, had been collecting for six months. She also made him a matching vest out of blue-and-white gum wrappers.

in the dark London's Tate Modern gallery unveiled its latest giant installation in 2009—40 ft (12 m) of pitch darkness. It was created by Polish artist Miroslaw Balka who said that the darkness was a metaphor for life.

party poopers U.S. rock band Kings of Leon had to abandon a concert at the Verizon Amphitheater, St. Louis, Missouri, in July 2010 after they were bombarded with pigeon droppings. An infestation of birds in the rafters above the stage led to bassist Jared Followill being hit several times during the band's first two songs, including in the face.

lego plane LEGO™ enthusiast Ryan McNaught built a $5,500 replica of the world's biggest passenger plane—the Airbus A380—with more than 35,000 bricks. It took him more than eight months to build the model, which is 7 ft (2.1 m) long and 6 ft (1.8 m) wide, in the garage of his home in Melbourne, Victoria, Australia.

garbage pictures Richard Broom of Lincolnshire, England, spent hours photographing litter along Britain's roadsides and posting them on an Internet blog in an attempt to get the government to tidy up the country—but his photos, including discarded paper cups, old cans, a broken toilet and bottles of urine, proved so popular that they have turned into highly collectable art.

mini mansion Peter Riches of Hove, England, spent nearly 15 years creating an elaborately decorated doll house and sold it for $80,000—that's enough to buy a real home in some places. His miniature 23-room mansion boasted a music room with grand piano, a hand-crafted games room with snooker table, and a library with more than 1,000 individually bound books. He made the shell of the house from plaster and hand-etched 32,000 bricks on its walls. He cut the 5,000 roof tiles from cardboard. The finished house measured 4 ft (1.2 m) wide, 3 ft 3 in (1 m) high and 2 ft 7 in (80 cm) deep.

cloud graffiti U.S. pop artist Ron English created cloud graffiti in the skies above New York City in September 2009. He hired a skywriting plane and got it to spell the word "cloud" in puffy white dots several times over the city.

tiny tiger A Taiwanese artist has created a painted tiger sculpture that is smaller than a grain of rice. Chen Forng-shean spent three months carving the 0.04-in-high (1-mm) tiger from resin. He has also made delicate miniature sculptures from sand, dental floss, rice, ant heads and fly wings.

pinhead nativity In 2009, Italian craftsman Aldo Caliro sculpted a nativity scene—featuring hand-carved figures of the Virgin Mary, Joseph and an angel, plus a tiny baby Jesus in his crib—on the head of a pin! He painted the figures with a single paintbrush hair. He had previously carved nativity scenes on a lentil and a coffee bean.

chalk drawing *Head of a Muse*, a simple black chalk drawing on paper by Renaissance painter Raphael, sold at an auction in London, England, for $47.9 million in December 2009.

long story It will be nearly 1,000 years before the cover of the May 2009 issue of *Opium* magazine can be read in its entirety. It will take that long for the successive layers of ink to degrade—at the rate of one word per century—thereby revealing a nine-word tale created by U.S. conceptual artist Jonathan Keats.

precise worker U.S. bestselling horror writer Stephen King, originally from Portland, Maine, writes exactly ten pages (around 2,000 words) a day, whether he's in a creative mood or not.

coffee cups At the 2010 Rocks Aroma Festival in Sydney, Australia, a team of artists created a 21 x 18 ft (6.5 x 5.5 m) coffee mosaic of Marilyn Monroe. They formed the image by filling 5,200 cups of coffee with 180 gal (680 l) of milk and 205 gal (780 l) of coffee to varying levels.

enormous shirt A team of South-African tailors worked nonstop for three weeks to make a T-shirt bigger than the Statue of Liberty. About 6.5 million stitches held together the 208 x 140 ft (64 x 43 m) shirt, using over 22,965 ft (7,000 m) of fabric.

PENCIL TIPS

Dalton Ghetti of Bridgeport, Connecticut, has been creating miniature graphite masterpieces from the tips of pencils for more than 25 years, including a sculpture of Elvis wearing shades, carved from a single pencil tip. He uses three tools—a razor blade, a sewing needle and a sculpting knife—but no magnifying glass. He digs into the graphite with the needle, then scratches and creates lines, turning the pencil slowly in his hand. One piece—a pencil with interlinking chains—took him two-and-a-half years. He has made over 100 pencil-tip shapes in total, such as a saw, a screw, a key on a chain, a boot, a chair, a mini mailbox and all 26 letters of the alphabet.

Ripley's Believe It or Not!®

Gum Dog

Gareth Williams of the U.K. created this sculpture of a dog, which was exhibited at London's Royal College of Art in 2009, with hair clippings from his own head stuck together with pieces of used chewing gum.

same glass For more than 35 years on an almost daily basis, Peter Dreher of Wittnau, Germany, has painted a portrait of the same drinking glass in the same position in his studio. He has so far completed more than 4,000 paintings of the glass.

lego repairs German artist Jan Vormann travels the world fixing crumbling walls and monuments with LEGO®. Among areas he has brightened up with the toy bricks are the old quarter of Tel Aviv in Israel and New York's Bryant Park.

midnight knitter Under the cover of darkness in early 2010, an unknown person dubbed the "Midnight Knitter" draped tree branches and lampposts in West Cape May, New Jersey, with small, brightly colored woolen sweaters.

cool music Norwegian composer Terje Isungset has recorded several albums with instruments made entirely of ice, including percussion, horns and trumpets.

movie veteran Aachi Manorama, a veteran of India's Tamil film industry, has appeared in more than 1,500 movies and 1,000 stage performances.

early watch In 2009, art experts discovered a 450-year-old painting that featured an image of a watch. The portrait, painted by Italian Renaissance artist Maso da San Friano around 1560, shows Cosimo I de' Medici, Duke of Florence, holding a golden timepiece. Watches first appeared shortly after 1500, making this one of the oldest paintings to depict a true watch.

tower cozy Robyn Love of New York City crocheted a yarn cozy for a wooden water tower on Broadway. Over a period of three weeks, she and six assistants used 60 balls of yellow and black yarn to transform the tower into a huge yellow pencil, complete with point.

sitting in silence Over a period of nearly three months in 2010, Serbian performance artist Marina Abramović spent 700 hours simply sitting and staring across a table at members of the public at New York's Museum of Modern Art. She sat on a chair for seven hours a day, six days a week, for her installation *The Artist Is Present*. Around 1,400 people—including singer Björk and model Isabella Rossellini—sat opposite her and returned her silent gaze. Some managed an entire day; others lasted just a few minutes.

expensive doll A French doll designed by Paris artist Albert Marque in 1915 was sold at auction in Atlanta, Georgia, for $263,000 in 2009. Only 100 examples of the doll were ever made and each was individually costumed, in styles ranging from 18th-century French court to traditional Russian folklore.

hay castle In January 2010, visitors flocked to Rob Marshall's sheep farm in West Victoria, Australia, to see a castle measuring 100 x 20 ft (30 x 6 m) that he had built out of hundreds of bales of hay. The castle remained in situ for six weeks until Rob dismantled it and used the bales to feed his sheep.

tree sculpture Inspired by a silver birch tree, Swedish furniture chain IKEA created a huge tree sculpture made from white kitchen appliances—including a washing machine, a dishwasher and a microwave oven—that was erected outside London's Barbican Centre in 2010.

holiday snaps A series of 19th-century watercolor paintings of European beauty spots by an unknown female British holidaymaker was sold in London for more than $5,000 in 2010. The paintings of such picturesque locations as Bavaria, the Swiss Alps and the Belgian city of Bruges were made in journals as holiday snaps by the woman following vacations she took with her husband in 1850 and 1853.

Why did you start using your own blood for your paintings? I guess the easiest answer would be to prove to myself that I could. I have used every medium I could think of during the course of my artistic career, from oil paint, charcoal, graphite, automotive paints, inks, even coffee, so I think it was just to see if I could.

After my first one, I was so proud of my work and fascinated by the finish, even though my first one was somewhat clumsy in its execution, so I set off on my journey to perfect my blood work. And with each painting, I learned how to predict how it would handle on various surfaces, how it changes and how my blood itself varies depending on things like diet, hydration and so on.

How much blood do you use in a typical painting? This really depends on the image. As a guide, a 20 x 20 in (500 x 500 mm) painting will use between 1$\frac{1}{2}$ fl oz (40 ml) and 6$\frac{3}{4}$ fl oz (200 ml). It also depends on the tools I use—for example, airbrushed textures use a lot less than a paintbrush.

How much blood do you extract on a regular basis? Earlier on I was extracting up to twice per week. However, years of doing so has caused scar tissue in my vein walls so it is becoming increasingly painful to remove, so when we do, we take a lot, up to 1 pint (440 ml) at a time and then I store it in the refrigerator.

Is blood easy to use? How does it compare to regular ink? Not even close, it is by far the most difficult substance to use. It is not actually red—the cells within the plasma are—so essentially I'm painting with my body's tissue. These cells clog airbrushes, and don't give uniform coverage from a brush—once dry even the smallest amount of moisture will liquefy it again, so it's very easy to "burn" through what you have already painted. It has taken me a long time to master what I have, and I have almost completely given up all other mediums now because my blood painting has been deeply rewarding and proven very popular worldwide.

Blood Painter

Rev Mayers never runs out of the unique ink he uses for his paintings, because it's one hundred percent his own blood on the canvas. The extreme artist from Sydney, Australia, has the blood extracted from his arm using a syringe, just as a doctor would. He then applies the precious fluid with an airbrush or a standard paintbrush. More detail and depth becomes visible as the art ages. Rev estimates that he has so far used more than 12 pints of his own blood in his paintings, more than most adults have in their entire body.

Ripley's
Believe It or Not!®

BB-BALL GAGA

Sculptor and artist John O'Hearn of Gainesville, Florida, makes colorful mosaics from thousands of Airsoft BBs—the ¼-in (6-mm) plastic balls used in a BB gun. Among his designs are a portrait of Florida Gators quarterback Tim Tebow from 46,308 BBs, which measures 4 x 6 ft (1.2 x 1.8 m), and this larger-than-life mosaic of singer Lady Gaga that is 4 x 8 ft (1.2 x 2.4 m) and contains 61,509 BBs.

pothole scenes Urban artists Claudia Ficca and Davide Luciano from Montreal, Canada, travel North America transforming unsightly street potholes into works of art. They have been photographed in the guise of a woman washing her clothes in a pothole, a priest baptizing a baby in another, and a scuba diver taking a dip.

splendid sari A team of weavers in Chennai, India, spent 4,680 hours making a $100,000 sari, woven with precious metals and gems.

big monet At the 2010 Normandy Impressionist Festival, 1,250 fans of 19th-century French artist Claude Monet gathered in Rouen and held painted panels above their heads to create a giant, 6,460-sq-ft (600-sq-m) replica of his 1894 work *Rouen Cathedral at the End of the Day*. The result was captured by cameras perched 90 ft (27 m) above the city hall.

bone images Swiss-born artist and photographer Francois Robert, who is now based in the U.S.A., produces works of art from real human bones. He spent hours arranging bones into striking shapes for his photographic collection *Stop the Violence*, which featured bone images of a gun, a tank, a bomb, a grenade, a Kalashnikov rifle and a knife. He hit upon the idea after trading a wired-together human skeleton, found inside some school lockers he had bought, for a box of 206 human bones.

high horse Tony Dew from York, England, hand-carved a wooden rocking horse that stands 11 ft 10 in (3.6 m) high and 16 ft (4.9 m) long—more than twice the size of most real horses.

CART ART

Ptolemy Elrington trawls rivers and lakes near his studio in Brighton, England, for abandoned metal shopping carts and turns them into enchanting sculptures of animals, insects and birds. By breaking up the carts and welding them into the desired shapes, he has created such designs as a heron, a frog (with bulging eyes from the cart's wheels), a dragonfly with a 6-ft (1.8-m) wingspan, and this kingfisher eating a fish.

last suppers For his *Last Suppers* series, British artist James Reynolds re-created the final meals requested by American Death Row prisoners. He filled a succession of orange prison-issue trays with their genuine last meals, which included a single black olive; an onion, a packet of chewing gum and two bottles of coke; and six raw eggs.

dirt shirts Remembering how they always used to end up with manure on their clothes when they helped on the family farm as kids, Patti Froman Maine of Corry, Pennsylvania, and her brother Sonny Froman designed a range of T-shirts that are deliberately coated in the stuff. Their CowChipShirts don't smell and come in colors such as Udder Rose and Silage Brown.

gold painting Russian artist Elena Zolotaya created a 10-ft-wide (3-m) picture painted entirely with 14-carat gold.

DECORATIVE RECYCLING

Florida-based artists Alain Guerra and Neraldo de la Paz create stunning sculptures from discarded clothing. They drape old garments over a wire frame to form colorful designs including a rainbow, a snake, and a series of clothing trees that represent all four seasons of the year.

tall order For a wager, Norway's Ola Helland collected over one million giraffe pictures in 440 days. He was backpacking through South America when, as a keepsake to remember all the new friends he had met, he asked each to draw him a giraffe. When a friend bet him he couldn't collect a million, Ola set up a website and was soon deluged with giraffe pictures from 106 countries, including a giraffe made from a banana and another made out of bread.

new books Each year, in the U.S.A. alone, about 30 million trees are used to make paper to print new books.

turning heads After going bald in his twenties, Philip Levine of London, England, began using his scalp as a canvas for art. Every week, body painter Kat Sinclair transformed Philip's designs into a different piece of head art. He turned his head into a disco ball covered with 1,000 crystals, had it painted with flowers, cartoon characters and smiley faces, and even had acupuncture needles inserted into his scalp in the shape of a butterfly.

many hands At the 2010 Baltimore Book Festival in Maryland, 512 people contributed to a single piece of art. Local author K. Michael Crawford erected an easel with a blank canvas and invited passersby to add to the picture.

HELPING HAND

For his painting *The Hand With The Golden Ring*, Norwegian artist Morten Viskum said he used the hand of a human corpse as a paintbrush. He claims that he's been working with a severed hand as a brush for over a decade, and uses it to apply animal blood, acrylic paints and sometimes glitter to his canvases.

Morten Viskum, *The Hand With The Golden Ring II* : 2010.

arts

Ripley's Believe It or Not!®

comedy gig American comedian Bob Marley performed a 40-hour gig at the Comedy Connection in Portland, Maine, lasting 18 hours before having to repeat any jokes.

golden vuvuzela A Russian businessman bought an Austrian-made gold and diamond-encrusted vuvuzela horn for over $20,000. The plastic South African horns, sounded by soccer spectators at the 2010 World Cup, usually cost around $8 each.

embroidered map Textile artist Lucy Sparrow of Brighton, East Sussex, England, has embroidered a 97-sq-ft (9-sq-m) tapestry of the London Underground map. It took her 42 days to make the giant map, which is made up of 7,875 ft (2400 m) of thread and 142 buttons.

head banger Jim Bartek of Maple Heights, Ohio, listened to the album *Nostradamus* by heavy metal band Judas Priest once a day for 524 days in a row.

Paperback Titles On the bookshelves of his home in Wiltshire, England, Steve Hare has a collection of more than 15,000 Penguin paperbacks—including the first 2,000 titles published following their introduction in 1935. He has been collecting them for more than 45 years and has enough books to fill two trucks.

beach carving London, England, artist Everton Wright, aka Evewright, carved an outline of a 2,600-ft (800-m) artwork in the sand of a beach in Cumbria using a garden rototiller. A team of 20 horses and riders were then invited to walk along the outline to make the tracks deeper. The design took 18 months to plan, but lasted for only five hours until the tide came in and washed it all away.

long title When environmentalist Shripad Vaidya from Nagpur, India, released an anthology of eco-friendly poems in March 2010, the book's title consisted of no fewer than 355 words.

street strummers More than 850 ukulele players gathered in a London, England, street to play the Beach Boys' "Sloop John B" at the London Ukulele Festival in 2009.

cozy car Twenty grandmothers from Switzerland spent two months knitting nearly 70 lb (32 kg) of wool into a warm covering for a Smart car. The woolen car cover depicts a lace-up training shoe but exposes the car's wheels, giving it the appearance of a giant roller skate.

junk sculptures James Corbett of Ningi, Queensland, Australia, makes amazing sculptures out of old car parts that he picks up from junkyards. He's turned discarded spark plugs, exhaust pipes and radiators into such diverse artworks as a monkey, a yacht, a downhill skier, a kangaroo and, appropriately, a heavy metal guitarist.

RUBBER BEASTS

Artist Ji Yong-Ho from Seoul, South Korea, makes animal sculptures from old tires. Using the flexibility of the rubber to imitate skin and muscles, he has created powerful lions, dogs, rhinos and this 10-ft-long (3-m) shark, each work taking three months to make and selling for up to $75,000. To vary the skin texture, he uses different kinds of tread. For example, the neck and forehead of his rhinoceros are made from broad-treaded tractor tires layered beneath a rough outer skin of motorcycle tires.

Curioser Creation

Los Angeles art group LA Pop Art wrote out every word from the first 11 chapters of Lewis Carroll's novel, Alice In Wonderland, to create an illustration from the story. From a distance it appears to be solid color, but almost every inch of the artwork is formed from Lewis Carroll's own words, written clearly in felt-tip pens. The text was written upside down so that the artist didn't smudge the ink.

painting with wheels Ian Cook of Birmingham, England, created an artwork of a racing car 33 x 16½ ft (10 x 5 m)—painted with the wheels of remote-control cars, go-karts, a racing car, a sports car, a motorbike and a six-ton truck. He took a huge canvas, applied paint and then drove across it, creating the image with the different sizes and patterns of the tires. He said painting with the truck was particularly challenging because the back wheels were twice as wide as the front ones so it was difficult to see what he was doing.

guitar windmills Mimicking The Who guitarist Pete Townshend's windmill actions, Spencer Borbon of San Francisco whirled his arm around 79 times in 30 seconds at the 2009 San Francisco Treasure Island Music Festival.

tracker bob Bob "Tracker Bob" Hiemenz of Flora, Illinois, has a collection of more than 60,000 eight-track audio tapes. Since acquiring his first tapes in 1985, he has spent about $7,000 on his passion, which covers everyone from Abba to ZZ Top.

bard boost Performing William Shakespeare plays to cows can help boost milk production. After the Changeling Theatre Company entertained Friesian cows at a farm in Kent, England, with *The Merry Wives of Windsor*, milk yields increased by 4 percent.

finger portraits U.K.-based artist Kyle Lambert creates amazingly lifelike portraits of celebrities, including Jennifer Aniston and Beyoncé, using his fingers on an iPad.

Sore Jaw Ken Parsons sang karaoke for more than two days straight at a church in Moose Jaw, Saskatchewan, Canada, in 2010. He finally put down the microphone after singing popular songs for an incredible 55 hours 11 minutes 30 seconds.

sand sculpture A group of 30 artists took 75 days to create a 73-ft-tall (22-m) sand sculpture at the Zhoushan Sand Sculpture Festival in China. The sculpture depicted a Nigerian story of how a hummingbird managed to become king of all animals.

Tabletop Landscapes

New Jersey photographer and artist Matthew Albanese devises spectacular images of windswept tropical islands, tornadoes and volcanoes by building models from everyday items.

The azure sea in his tabletop D.I.Y. *Paradise* is actually melted sugar and tin foil, and the island is made from salt. He carefully arranged cotton wool over the scene to create clouds, and even the palm trees are not as they seem—the leaves are formed from feathers.

Matthew has also made convincing icebergs from sugar and waterfalls from salt, and re-created the surface of Mars with paprika, cinnamon, nutmeg and chili powder. His tornados are made from steel wool and he has created an impressive Aurora Borealis using a shower curtain, a corkboard and strobe lighting. His photographs of these homemade natural phenomena sell for over $900 each.

ⓡ ticket tower British artist Robert Bradford created scale models of three U.K. landmarks—St. Paul's Cathedral, Edinburgh Castle and Blackpool Tower—from a total of 115,000 used train tickets.

ⓡ moon scent Printers in Edinburgh, Scotland, have created a scratch 'n' sniff artwork that smells like the Moon. They developed it by talking to former NASA astronaut Charlie Duke, who was a member of the *Apollo 16* mission in 1972, and who described the Moon's surface as smelling like spent gunpowder.

ⓡ victory at last Using an original wooden beam from the H.M.S. *Victory*, sculptor Ian Brennan from Hampshire, England, spent 17 years carving a 47-in-long (1.2-m) model of Admiral Horatio Nelson's 18th-century flagship. The model, accurate to the last detail, contains 200 ft (60 m) of rope, 104 miniature guns and 37 sails.

ⓡ cow maze In a field near Berlin, Germany, workers cut corn and hemp into the shape of a giant cow. The maze depicted the bovine digestive system and was designed by the country's Federal Institute of Risk Assessment to promote healthy eating habits.

ⓡ screw mosaic Saimir Strati spent two weeks creating a mosaic of a U.S. banknote 8 ft (2.4 m) high and 16 ft 1 in (4.9 m) long from 300,000 industrial screws. The giant bill features a portrait of the ancient Greek poet Homer in the center.

ⓡ natural sculptures Peter Riedel, an artist and photographer from Toronto, Canada, spent five hours creating 42 temporary outdoor sculptures in the city's Humber River by balancing rocks and boulders on top of each other. He never uses glue in his works but arranges the rocks so that they don't fall.

still famous In the year following his death on June 25, 2009, Michael Jackson's estate earned one billion dollars.

same shot Except for the duration of World War II, Ria van Dijk had a photograph taken of herself at the same shooting gallery in Tilburg, the Netherlands, every year for 74 years. The first picture was taken in 1936 when she was 16.

poem boxing Japan hosts the National Poem Boxing Championships where contestants fight it out with words in three-minute rounds. The poets step into a boxing ring and read out verses on a wide range of subjects, hoping to secure a win. In the final round, the last two combatants still standing must improvise a poem incorporating a random word the judges tell them to use.

tiny bookw Hassan Abed Rabbo of Beirut, Lebanon, owns a handwritten, unabridged version of the Islamic holy book, the Quran, which is so tiny it can rest on the tip of his finger. The book, which dates back hundreds of years, contains 604 pages adorned in gold ink and measures just 0.95 x 0.75 in (2.4 x 1.9 cm).

young picasso A distinctive painting style of bold colors and disjointed Cubist forms led to ten-year-old Hamad Al Humaidhan from Bath, Somerset, England, being hailed as a young Picasso—even though he had never seen any of the Spanish master's work. The Kuwaiti-born youngster began painting at age seven, his first six pieces selling for $1,000 each. He closes his eyes, sees an image in his head and then transfers it to the canvas.

ardent fan Over a period of nearly 20 years, Ann Petty of Wiltshire, England, has traveled more than 60,000 mi (100,000 km) to see Irish singer Daniel O'Donnell perform—including trips to the U.S.A., New Zealand and Australia.

log pile Logger Ron Fahey began removing a stack of logs from the grounds of Mount Allison University, Sackville, Canada, only to be stopped by an official who told him he was dismantling a work of art. The woodpile sculpture, called *Deadwood Sleep* by Paul Griffin, had been in the grounds for three years.

one-armed d.j. In Johannesburg, South Africa, in 2010, dance D.J. Nkosinathi Maphumulo, who lost his left hand in an accident at age 13, spun records for 60 hours straight with just a short comfort break every four hours.

clogged streets More than 2,500 people gathered in Pella, Iowa, on May 8, 2010, to dance together in wooden shoes.

phone-book furniture Daniel Tosches of Pasco, Florida, creates furniture and sculptures from pages of the phone book.

APPLE KILLER

Together with photographer Paul Fairchild, San Francisco artist Michael Tompert staged an exhibition of butchered and mangled Apple products. Tompert has shot, burned, hammered and sawed his way through a range of merchandise and even ran over seven iPods with a diesel locomotive. His greatest challenge was an iPad, which survived a series of blows from a sledgehammer, before finally exploding after its insides were heated with a soldering torch. He says he's trying to make people think about their relationship with these highly popular items.

chocolate train In October 2010, London, England, food artist Carl Warner unveiled the *Chocolate Express*, a 6-ft (1.8-m) train sculpture made from chocolate, and running on chocolate tracks. It took ten days to build and also incorporated chocolate rolls, Wagon Wheels, Crunchie bars and Dime bars.

lord of the sticks Patrick Acton of Gladbrook, Iowa, spent three years building a replica of the *Lord of the Rings* city Minas Tirith from 420,000 matchsticks.

photographic memories Munish Bansal of Kent, England, has taken pictures of his children every day for 13 years. He has filled more than 600 albums with over 8,500 digital images of his daughter Suman, 12, and her 10-year-old brother, Jay, since the day they were born.

part art Artist Franco Recchia from Florence, Italy, constructs models of cityscapes from the discarded parts of old computers. He uses circuit boards, casings, processing chips and other computer components as his building blocks.

golden monopoly San Francisco jewelry designer Sidney Mobell has created a Monopoly set made with solid gold and jewels. The dice are encrusted with diamonds and these alone cost $10,000.

girl gucci At just ten years old, Cecilia Cassini of Encino, California, was already an accomplished fashion designer. After receiving a sewing machine for her sixth birthday, she has gone on to design children's clothes, and a number of celebrities have bought her designs for their kids.

toast portrait Laura Hadland from Leicester, England, created a portrait of her mother-in-law, Sandra Whitfield, from 9,852 slices of toast. Laura and 40 friends used nine toasters to brown the slices from 600 loaves of bread to varying degrees before arranging them to make a lifelike mosaic measuring 32 ft 8 in x 42 ft 3 in (10 x 13 m).

intrepid builder Using 250,000 pieces of LEGO®, Ed Diment took nine months to build a 22-ft-long (6.7-m) replica of the World-War-II aircraft carrier U.S.S. *Intrepid* in the conservatory of his home in Portsmouth, England. The finished model weighed more than 500 lb (227 kg).

porcelain seeds In 2010, London's Tate Modern gallery staged a work called *Sunflower Seeds* by Chinese artist Ai Weiwei. The piece consisted of more than 100 million individually handmade porcelain replicas of seeds.

party pooper With the help of local schoolchildren from Sichuan Province, China, sculptor Zhu Cheng made a replica of the famous *Venus de Milo* statue—from panda dung. The poop statue later sold for $45,000.

Plastic Fantastic

Sayaka Ganz creates amazing wildlife sculptures from items of discarded plastic found in garbage cans, charity shops or donated by friends—and her finished works sell for more than $12,000.

Sayaka, who was born in Japan but now lives in Fort Wayne, Indiana, has made models of a dog, an eagle, a horse, a cheetah and a fish, varying in length from 18 in (45 cm) to 8 ft (2.4 m) and incorporating plastic sunglasses, cutlery, baskets and cooking utensils. The biggest sculptures contain up to 500 pieces of junk and take nine months to make. She sorts all her plastic into 20 color groups in her basement and then ties the chosen items onto a wire frame to create each sculpture. Sayaka studies photographs showing her animal subjects from different angles so that she can perfect the lines of motion. She says, "I get great satisfaction from fitting these objects together to create a beautiful form that seems alive."

underground music Norwegian singer Unni Lovlid staged two sell-out 2010 concerts in a Victorian drain 20 ft (6 m) underground in Brighton, England. The sewer could accommodate 25 audience members wearing hard hats.

a klingon carol A Chicago, Illinois, theater staged a 2010 production of Charles Dickens' *A Christmas Carol*—entirely in Klingon. Written by Christopher O. Kidder and Sasha Walloch, the adaptation was performed in "tlhIngan Hol," the language of the Klingon race developed by linguist Marc Okrand for the 1984 movie *Star Trek III: The Search for Spock*.

spoon tree Students from Transworld University, Taiwan, made a 40-ft-tall (12-m) Christmas tree from 80,000 KFC plastic spoons.

pistol puzzle GarE Maxton, a machinist-artist from Michigan, U.S.A., created a 125-piece metal puzzle sculpture that can be assembled into a working, muzzle-loading pistol.

hidden treasure An old painting stuffed behind the sofa for nearly 30 years at the suburban home of Martin Kober in Buffalo, New York State, was identified in 2010 as being a lost 16th-century artwork by Michelangelo worth $300 million. The Kobers had hung *The Mike*—as they called it—on the wall until their children knocked it off with a stray tennis ball.

natural sculptures Peter Riedel, an artist and photographer from Toronto, Canada, spent five hours creating 42 temporary outdoor sculptures in the city's Humber River by balancing rocks and boulders on top of each other. He never uses glue in his works but arranges the rocks so that they don't fall.

wooden hats Chris Ramsey of Somerset, Kentucky, carves wearable hats and caps from single pieces of wood. Using a chainsaw, a lathe and cutting tools, it takes him about 40 hours to create a hat from a 120-lb (54-kg) block of hardwood.

blind photographer The photography art of Rosita McKenzie from Edinburgh, Scotland, was featured at the 2010 Edinburgh Art Festival—even though she has been completely blind since age 12. She homes in on people's personalities to capture the right shot and uses a digital camera on automatic setting to ensure all her pictures are in focus.

human jukebox Fredrik Hjelmqvist, owner of a hi-fi shop in Stockholm, Sweden, broadcast music from his stomach for more than three hours. He swallowed a 1.2-in-long (3-cm) plastic capsule containing a miniature battery-powered audio device and listened to tunes such as Gloria Gaynor's "I Will Survive" by using a stethoscope placed on his abdomen and connected to a sound amplifier.

third eye Wafaa Bilal, a professor at New York University, had a camera surgically implanted in the back of his head for an art project called *The Third I*. The digital camera captures his everyday activities—as "seen" from behind him—at one-minute intervals, 24 hours a day, with the images it took being transmitted to monitors at a museum in Qatar.

arts

Believe It or Not!®

MAN-MADE MONSTERS

Using only manmade materials, Californian artist Doug Higley makes monsters for showmen to display at flea markets and fairs across the world. He has created fake mummified and petrified creatures, bogus mermaids, shrunken heads, chupacabras, freaky jungle pygmies and atomic death worms. His work has been exhibited in 34 countries and one of his mermaids appeared at Buckingham Palace, London. He also once created 42 mermaids for a car-dealer promotion in the U.S.A. and Canada, whereby potential customers were invited to see the "strange creature" found in the trunk of a trade-in vehicle and take a test drive. The gimmick sold thousands of cars!

Water Dog Mermaid

Chupacabra

tentacle terror In 2008, artists Filthy Luker and Pedro Estrellas positioned huge inflatable green octopus tentacles through the windows of an unnamed building in France.

wooden chain Markley Noel of Hickory Corners, Michigan, carved a 480-ft-long (146-m) wooden chain from a single 25-ft-long (7.6-m) maple plank. The chain, which has 1,993 links, each 4 in (10 cm) long, took him seven years to make.

small portions Using acrylic paints and a magnifying glass, French artist Stephanie Kilgast creates miniature clay models of food in 1:12 scale. She painstakingly molds the clay with scalpels, blades, art knives and toothpicks, and has made more than 600 cakes, pastries, fruit and full meals, including a full English breakfast with baked beans, bacon, sausages and fried eggs.

phone dress A London fashion company has introduced the M-Dress, a little black dress that also serves as a mobile phone. The dress, which has a tiny antenna in its hem, allows wearers to make and receive calls by putting their SIM card under the label. To take a call, they raise their hand to their ear; to end it they let it fall to their side.

ancient shoe Archeologists in Armenia have found a leather shoe more than 5,500 years old. The shoe, which was stuffed with grass, was discovered in a mountain cave where it had been kept in excellent condition thanks to a thick layer of sheep excrement, which acted as a protective seal.

corn maze Bob Connors cut images of Stewie and Brian, two of the characters from the animated TV comedy *Family Guy*, into a seven-acre cornfield maze at his farm in Danvers, Massachusetts.

fashion ferrari A full-size replica of a Ferrari Formula-1 car was made out of $60,000 worth of designer clothing. Eight people worked for five hours at a store in London's Carnaby Street to turn 1,999 items of clothing—including 1,682 red T-shirts, 88 pairs of jeans, 64 pairs of shoes and 31 belts—into a 14-ft-long (4.3-m) model car. The wheels were made from water bottles, the wing mirror from sunglasses and the tires from black jeans.

human hoover
Artist Paul Hazelton of Kent, England, has made a model of a complete bedroom—including a TV, armchairs and a wardrobe—out of dust! Known as the "Human Hoover," he collects dust from furniture, pictures and window sills, and then transforms the bunches of tiny particles into 3-D sculptures by wetting, shaping and drying them. Some of his dust models—which also include a briefcase, a moth and a humanoid—are 20 in (50 cm) high.

hot lips
Makeup artist Rick DiCecca applied lipstick to over 300 women in one hour at Macy's Department Store, Chicago, Illinois.

lego ship
For nearly a week, 3,500 children used 513,000 LEGO® bricks to build a 25-ft-long (7.6-m) model of a container ship in Wilhelmshaven, Germany.

DISK PORTRAITS
British artist Nick Gentry uses old 3.5-in computer floppy disks as a canvas for his imaginative portraits. The features of each face are mapped into a grid, with each section the size of one disk. The disks are then arranged to create a collage before the outline of the head is partly drawn and painted over it. He sometimes also incorporates obsolete cassettes and V.C.R. tapes into his facial images.

Deep Drawings
Chilean artist Fredo creates mind-boggling 3-D pencil drawings that appear to rise out of the page. Despite its 3-D appearance, all his work is pencil on flat paper. At only 17 years old, Fredo is already exhibiting his work in Chile.

strand of beads
In October 2009, the city of Providence, Rhode Island, created a strand of red-and-white beads that measured 1,349 ft (411 m) long!

late returns
In 2009, a former student at Camelback High School, Phoenix, Arizona, returned two library books that had been checked out half a century earlier, and enclosed a $1,000 money order for the fines. The books had been taken out in 1959, but the borrower's family moved to another state and the books were mistakenly packed away.

toothpick city
Scott Weaver of Rohnert Park, California, spent thousands of hours during a 34-year period building a toothpick model of every major landmark in San Francisco, using a total of over 100,000 toothpicks. The construction, titled "Rolling Through the Bay," stands 9 ft (2.7 m) tall, 7 ft (2.1 m) wide and 2 ft (60 cm) deep. It has survived four house relocations, an earthquake, and Trooper—one of Weaver's four Great Danes—who once obliterated Fisherman's Wharf and about 100 hours' work with a careless wag of his tail.

monster mona A giant version of the *Mona Lisa* went on display in a shopping mall in Wrexham, Wales, in 2009—50 times bigger than Leonardo da Vinci's 16th-century original. It covered 2,600 sq ft (240 sq m) and was big enough to fit 22 buses inside. A total of 245 people worked on the project under artist Katy Webster, and it took 987 hours to create, using 23 gal (86 l) of paint.

wicker men In Cluj, Romania, a team of 16 craftsmen created a huge wicker basket that was large enough to hold one million loaves of homemade bread. It took nine days to make and measured 59 x 33 ft (18 x 10 m), and was 31 ft (9.5 m) tall.

celebrity pumpkins Gardener David Finkle carves impressive portraits of famous people—including Barack Obama, Michael Jackson and Simon Cowell—out of pumpkins that grow on his small farm at Chelmsford in Essex, England.

concert for dogs Australia's Sydney Opera House staged a concert for dogs in 2010. More than a thousand dogs turned up for the 20-minute Music For Dogs event, which was organized by U.S. musician Laurie Anderson and her rock-star husband Lou Reed. It featured a concerto of high-pitch whistles, whale calls, synthesizers and strings—some inaudible to human ears.

couscous city French-Algerian artist Kader Attia built a scale model of the ancient city of Ghardaia, Algeria, entirely out of cooked couscous.

dental display To entertain and relax his patients, dentist Ian Davis from London, England, has created a series of sculptures featuring miniature men scrubbing, cleaning and repairing teeth. The men can be seen digging out fillings with tiny pickaxes and polishing and scaling teeth with the help of scaffolding—and all the teeth he uses are taken from the casts of real patients' mouths.

dollar mosaics A Latvian artist creates mosaics made entirely out of U.S. dollar bills. Irina Truhanova sketches an outline of her subject before filling it in with snippets of the bills. Her creations include the Statue of Liberty, a Bentley car and Russian Prime Minister Vladimir Putin.

urban dancers As part of its 2009 "Bodies in Urban Spaces" project, Dance Umbrella, choreographed by Willi Dorner, placed its performers in unlikely locations around the center of London, England. Passersby stumbled across dancers squeezed between pillars, wrapped around lampposts, folded into a bicycle rack and clinging to a wall like Spider-Man.

typewriter art Cerebral-palsy sufferer Paul Smith (1921–2007) of Roseburg, Oregon, became a world-famous artist by creating masterpieces using manual typewriters. He achieved his amazing images by pressing the symbols at the tops of the number keys, and as his mastery of the typewriter grew, he developed techniques to create shadings, colors and textures that made his work resemble pencil or charcoal drawings. Over the years, he created hundreds of artworks—each one taking him up to three months—including landscapes, animals and portraits.

underwater gallery Diving enthusiasts in Lithuania have opened the country's first underwater picture gallery. Twenty large-format photographs by local artists were put on display beneath the surface of Lake Plateliai, and the organizers hope to expand the project to include sculptures, stained glass and watercolor paintings. The idea originated after a couple from a diving club put their wedding picture underwater so that they could enjoy it every time they dived.

roadkill hats Fashion designer James Faulkner of Edinburgh, Scotland, has created a range of hats from roadkill. Inspired by the idea of using a dead magpie he found by the roadside to complement a friend's black-and-white dress, he has developed a range of 36 animal hats, using the wings, feathers and fur of squashed pigeons, rabbits, foxes, pheasants and crows.

27-hour concert Gonzales, a Canadian musician, played a 27-hour concert in Paris, France, in 2009. His 300-song set ranged from Britney Spears to Beethoven.

ant invasion Dutch artist Henk Hofstra painted some 500 giant red ants over the town of Drachten for his work "Invasion of the Ants." The ants—each 10 x 6½ ft (3 x 2 m)—were created over three nights in May 2010 and were placed so that they appeared to be invading the De Lawei Theater, which was celebrating its 50th anniversary.

THE CANDY MAN

Mexico City artist Cristiam Ramos makes amazing candy portraits of celebrities. Instead of paint, he uses Gummi Bears, licorice, M&M's® and after-dinner mints as his artistic materials. His works include likenesses of Elvis and Michael Jackson from hundreds of M&M's®, and a portrait of Lady Gaga from gumdrops, M&M's® and yellow licorice.

Mini Me

Indonesian photographer Ari Mahardika has "cloned" himself dozens of times for a series of intricate montages. Using a self-timer to take photos of himself in different poses against a white background, he then shrinks the portraits into mini-me characters, positioning them so that it looks as though he is interacting with himself.

lost movie A lost Charlie Chaplin film valued at $60,000 was bought on eBay for $5.68 by a British collector in 2009. Morace Park of Essex, England, purchased the battered olive green film canister listed as "an old film" and was amazed to discover that the movie in question was *Zepped*, a 1916 Chaplin propaganda film poking fun at the zeppelin, the German instrument of terror during World War I. As recently as 2006, a movie expert stated that the seven-minute movie had almost certainly been lost forever.

junior drummer At just three years of age, Howard Wong's rock drumming has attracted nearly ten million hits on YouTube even though he can barely see over the top of his drum kit. Howard from Penang, Malaysia, first started playing at the age of 18 months and now performs regularly with his father's band.

bean mosaic A candy shop in Brighton, England, displayed a colorful mosaic of Queen Elizabeth II made from 10,000 jelly beans.

first exhibition When Leo Haines was born with cerebral palsy and a terminal condition affecting his lungs and heart, he was given only six months to live. However, in 2010 the five-year-old from Somerset, England, stunned doctors by opening his first art exhibition. He began painting alongside his grandmother and has since completed more than 40 works, which are said to be reminiscent of famous U.S. abstract artist Jackson Pollock.

feats

mysteries

food

arts

science

beyond belief

believe it!

world

animals

sports

body

transport

Life-size Transformers

Two 8-ft-tall (2.4-m) "Transformer" robot sculptures now stand in Ripley's museums in Orlando, Florida, and San Antonio, Texas. The heavy metal sculptures—each one weighing more than a ton—were built entirely from discarded car and bike parts in Bangkok, Thailand.

Ripley's EXHIBITS

215
216
217
218
219
220
221
222
223
224
225
226
227
228
229
230
231
232
233
234
235
236
237
238
239
240
241
242

Self Operation

While on a 1961 expedition in the frozen Antarctic, 27-year-old Soviet doctor Leonid Rogozov saved his own life by performing an operation on himself to remove his dangerously inflamed appendix.

Suffering from fever and a pain in his right lower belly, he quickly diagnosed appendicitis. However, he knew that no aid plane would be able to cope with the blizzards or reach such a remote spot in time to evacuate him, so, as the only doctor at the station, he set about conducting an auto-appendectomy on the night of April 30. He was assisted by an engineer and the station's meteorologist, who handed him the medical instruments and held a small mirror at his belly to help him see what he was doing.

After administering a local anesthetic of novocaine solution, Rogozov made a 4³/₄-in (12-cm) incision in his lower abdomen with a scalpel. Working without gloves and guiding himself mainly by touch from a semi-reclining position, he proceeded to remove the appendix before injecting antibiotic into the abdominal cavity and closing the wound. The self-operation took 1 hour 45 minutes, and saved his life. If he had left it another day his appendix would have burst. His stitches were taken out a week later and he made a complete recovery.

phone control The iDriver app enables motorists to drive a car using their cell phone. Devised by researchers from Berlin, Germany, the app has a steering wheel, separate buttons for accelerating and braking and is capable of directing a two-ton minivan.

first computer Unveiled in 1946 at the University of Pennsylvania, ENIAC (short for Electronic Numerical Integrator and Computer) was the world's first general-purpose computer. It weighed 30 tons and occupied an entire room. Yet its computing ability can be re-created today on a silicon chip smaller than your thumbnail.

anti-flu suit A Japanese menswear company has developed a suit that it claims protects the wearer from the deadly H1N1 strain of influenza. The $550 suit, produced by the Haruyama Trading Company, is coated with the chemical titanium dioxide—an ingredient of toothpaste and cosmetics—that reacts to light to break down and kill the virus on contact.

oh, crumbs! The Swiss-based Large Hadron Collider, the world's most powerful particle accelerator and probably the most complex machine ever built, was shut down in 2009 after a bird passing overhead dropped a piece of bread on a section of machinery, causing parts of the accelerator to overheat.

skiing robot A skiing robot that can navigate slalom courses has been developed by researchers at the Jozef Stefan Institute in Slovenia. The robot, which is about the size of an eight-year-old child and uses regular skis, has a pair of computer systems. One of them is attached to cameras to help plot the robot's course down the slope, the other is attached to gyroscopes and force sensors to keep it stable.

beige world After examining the amounts of light emitted by galaxies, scientists at NASA have concluded that the Universe is not really black at all—more a dull beige. They say that the shade is constantly changing and has become much less blue over the past ten billion years because redder stars are now more dominant.

large dish The Large Zenith Telescope at the University of British Columbia in Canada uses a mirror made from a spinning dish of liquid mercury nearly 20 ft (6.1 m) in diameter.

bell tribute On August 4, 1922—the day of the funeral of Alexander Graham Bell—all telephone services in the U.S.A. and Canada were shut down for one minute as a tribute to the inventor, who, in the 1870s, had invented the first workable telephone.

plasma knife To help stem the loss of blood from serious wounds, the U.S. military has been testing a plasma knife, with a blade consisting of heated, ionized gas, which can cut through flesh just as easily as a steel scalpel. The plasma knife seals off the damaged flesh, stopping the bleeding and protecting against infection.

stone-age surgery When archeologists in France unearthed the 7,000-year-old skeleton of a man, they were amazed to see that he had an amputated arm. The Stone Age surgery was probably performed using a sharpened flint stone, with painkilling plants acting as an anesthetic and an antiseptic herb such as sage being used to clean the wound.

rotten eggs As part of a safety campaign in 2010, Puget Sound Energy, a utility company in Washington State, added the stench of rotten eggs to its gas bills. Natural gas is odorless, but providers add a chemical with a sulfurlike aroma to the gas so that leaks can be detected.

BODY ART

Hong Kong radiologist Kai-Hung Fung has created stunning images of the human body that look like works of art. Dr. Fung scans the patient using a conventional computer topography (CT) scan, generally used for diagnosing brain and cardiac problems, before feeding the information into a computer and adding vivid color.

smells good

A view behind the human nose

bite size

Teeth captured from inside the mouth

say what?

Curves inside an ear

bullet blocker Colombian tailor Miguel Caballero runs a boutique in Mexico City where jackets and shirts are not stacked by size but by how well they will stop a bullet. He uses secret materials, the most expensive of which, called Black, is so light that it can be scrunched up like paper but will protect the wearer from a bullet fired at point-blank range.

speed of sound Sound travels 4.3 times faster in water than it does in air. When something vibrates, it causes molecules to bump into each other. As water molecules are closer together, the vibrations transfer faster between themselves.

frozen with heat Water can be frozen solid—by applying heat! Supercooled water, which can stay liquid down to −40°F (−40°C), will freeze as it is being heated, as long as the temperature also changes the electrical charge of the surface with which the water is in contact.

black hole Scientists at the Southeast University in Nanjing, China, have created a pocket-size black hole—an 8½-in-wide (21.5-cm) disk that absorbs all the electromagnetic radiation thrown at it. The metal disk has 60 concentric rings that affect the magnetic properties of passing light, bending the beams into the center of the disk and trapping them in a maze of etched grooves.

shrinking coins A powerful electromagnetic field can shrink a coin to half its diameter. The technique is known as high-velocity metal forming, a process which creates an invisible, pulsed magnetic field that batters the coin with a strong shock wave, forcing it to change its physical shape in the blink of an eye.

robot olympics At the 2010 International Robot Olympics held in Harbin, China, humanoid robots from 19 countries competed in 17 disciplines, including running, walking, boxing, kung fu and dancing. All robots had to be less than 2 ft (60 cm) tall and be built in human form with a head, two arms and two legs. The opening event, the 5-m (5-yd) sprint, was won in a time of 20 seconds.

ROBOTIC JELLYFISH

Scientists in Germany have developed a range of biologically inspired robotic jellyfish that can swim. The battery-powered jellyfish are propelled through the water by eight electrically driven tentacles, the construction of which is based on the anatomy of fish fins. With the help of sensors and control software, the jellyfish steer themselves and can communicate by means of 11 infrared light-emitting diodes, enabling them to work together as a team and to avoid bumping into each other.

Rat Supper

By using a special scanning technique, scientists Henrik Lauridsen and Kasper Hansen from Aarhus, Denmark, were able to take X-rays of a python digesting a rat. The rat can be seen gradually disappearing during the course of 132 hours—5½ days—after being swallowed by the snake.

iceman's relatives Nearly 20 years after discovering the mummified body of a 5,300-year-old man—known as Oetzi the iceman—in a melting Alpine glacier, scientists have extracted DNA from a bone in his pelvis with a view to tracking down his living descendants.

robot wedding A wedding that took place in a Tokyo, Japan, restaurant in May 2010 was conducted by a robot. Bride Satoko Inoue and groom Tomohiro Shibata were directed through the ceremony by I-Fairy, a 4-ft (1.2-m) robot, who wore a wreath of flowers and a set of wires that led to a human controller who was sitting at a nearby computer.

underground city A series of streets, houses and tombs belonging to an Egyptian city dating back more than 3,500 years has been located by radar. Austrian archeologists used radar imaging to show the outlines of Avaris, the ancient capital of the Hyksos people, beneath fields and modern buildings in the Nile Delta.

homemade reactor Mark Suppes, a 32-year-old web designer for fashion house Gucci, has built his own homemade nuclear fusion reactor on the third floor of a Brooklyn, New York City, warehouse. He took two years to build it, using $35,000 worth of parts he bought on eBay.

RIPLEY RESEARCH

A severely damaged hand can be temporarily grafted on to a healthy part of the patient's body—such as the leg—where the blood supply keeps it alive while the arm heals. The hand is later reattached to the arm using some skin and nerves from the leg. Doctors usually expect 70 percent of hand function to return in time and in this case hope that Ming Li will one day be strong enough to drive a car.

HEALING HAND

Surgeons in China saved a young girl's hand by grafting it on to her leg for three months. Nine-year-old Ming Li lost her left hand when she was run over by a tractor on her way to school in Zhengzhou, Henan Province. Her arm was too badly crushed to reattach the hand to her wrist so doctors grafted it on to her right calf instead, before transplanting it back on to her arm once it had healed.

toy parts Dr. William H. Sewell invented an artificial heart pump prototype with parts from an Erector set toy while at Yale Medical School.

strad beaten In a sound test conducted in Germany before an audience of 180 people, a violin made of wood that had been treated with fungus for nine months was judged better than a $2-million 1711 Stradivarius. Scientists say a fungal attack changes the cell structure of the wood, giving it a warmer, more rounded sound.

lost army Twin brothers Angelo and Alfredo Castiglioni believe they have found the remains of a 50,000-strong Persian army, said to have been drowned in the sands of the Sahara Desert 2,500 years ago. The Italian archeologists have discovered bronze weapons, a silver bracelet, an earring and hundreds of human bones that are thought to have belonged to the lost army of Persian King Cambyses II, whose men were reportedly buried in a terrible sandstorm in 525 BC.

INVISIBLE MAN

Scientists at Tokyo University have developed camouflage technology that makes people disappear. A coat made of a high-tech reflective material has a video camera placed in it, which sends film to a projector. This, in turn, bounces the moving image off the front of the coat, making the wearer appear transparent, even when the fabric is creased.

stench busters The city of Beijing, China, has installed 100 high-pressure deodorant guns, which can spray dozens of liters of fragrance per minute, to combat the stench from one of the city's many overflowing landfill sites. Beijing's 17 million people generate nearly 20,000 tons of waste every day—7,700 tons more than the capacity of municipal disposal plants.

magnetic lift Scientists have successfully levitated fruit, insects, frogs and mice by applying a repelling effect on the water molecules in their bodies with powerful magnets.

quake-proof bed Wang Wenxi from Shijiazhuang, China, has invented an earthquake-proof bed. When an earthquake strikes, a strong board automatically slides into place, protecting the person from falling debris. His secure bed has cupboards at both ends with water, canned food, a hammer and a megaphone to help the occupant survive for several days beneath rubble.

solar slug *Elysia chlorotica*, a green sea slug that lives along the Atlantic seaboard of the U.S.A., runs on solar power. Scientists at the University of Maine have discovered that it photosynthesizes using genes "stolen" from the algae it eats.

MAGIC GEL

"Aerogel" was created in 1931 by U.S. scientist Samuel Stephens Kistler following a bet with a colleague over who could replace the liquid in gel with a gas without causing shrinkage. Even though it is 99.8 percent air, the unique substance aerogel can withstand temperatures of up to 2,550°F (1,400°C) and is strong enough to support 2,000 times its own weight.

green

RIPLEY RESEARCH

Aerogel is derived from a silica gel, the liquid component of which is replaced with a gas to create an extremely low-density solid. It is 1,000 times less dense than glass, making it very lightweight. It has been used by NASA for thermal insulation of space suits and on the Mars Rover vehicle on its Stardust Mission to trap space dust. Whereas cosmic dust vaporizes on impact with solids and passes through gas, the nature of aerogel allows it to trap particles traveling at 1,350 mph (2,170 km/h) without damaging them.

Solar Detector

The Super-Kamiokande Detector is a gigantic cylindrical stainless steel tank, measuring 136 ft (41 m) high and 129 ft (39 m) in diameter, located more than half a mile underground in Japan. Holding 50,000 tons of water, it is lined with 11,146 ultra-sensitive light detectors and serves as a scientific observatory to monitor solar neutrinos—particles that are produced in the Sun by nuclear fusion. This will help us understand what goes on inside the Sun and how matter was created in the early Universe. The Detector is located underground to shield the experiments from cosmic rays and background radiation.

mysteries

food

arts

science

beyond belief

believe it!

world

animals

sports

body

transport

feats

225
226
227
228
229
230
231
232
233
234
235
236
237
238
239
240
241
242
243
244
245
246
247
248
249
250
251
252

Marilyn with wings

Mexican artist Enrique Ramos created this portrait of Hollywood icon Marilyn Monroe from hundreds of rainforest butterflies. Enrique has also created an image of United States' President John F. Kennedy in the same way. Both insect portraits are on display at the Ripley's Believe It or Not! museum in London, England.

Ripley's EXHIBITS

beyond belief
Ripley's Believe It or Not!®

Shocking Stories

ELEPHANT ELECTROCUTION

In an attempt to prove the dangers of Nikola Tesla's alternating current (AC) and the safety of his competing direct current (DC) for use in the home, Thomas Edison electrocuted an elephant in 1903. Topsy was an elephant with Forepaugh Circus at Coney Island's Luna Park, New York City, who had killed three men in three years, and her owners wanted her destroyed. Edison suggested electrocution, a method that had been used for human executions since 1890. Topsy was fed carrots containing potassium cyanide before a current of 6,600 volts was sent through her body, killing her in seconds. A crowd of 1,500 witnessed the event, which Edison also filmed.

MARY, THE HANGED ELEPHANT

Mary was a 5-ton Asian elephant who was hanged for her so-called crimes on September 12, 1916. Her story is a cautionary tale of circus abuse during the early 20th century. She had been prodded behind the ear by her trainer as she bent down to nibble on watermelon rind, so she grabbed him with her trunk and stamped on his head, killing him. Labeled a highly dangerous beast, the public demanded her death. She survived being shot with two dozen rounds, so it was decided to hang her. Mary was hanged by the neck the next day from an industrial crane in Erwin, Tennessee.

phone home A man has spent two years living in a cramped phone booth in Dalian City, Liaoning Province, China. He sleeps by curling up into a ball on top of cushions and hangs his spare clothes from the roof.

elephant collision Driving home from church in Enid, Oklahoma, a couple collided with an elephant that ran across the highway after escaping from a nearby circus. The elephant was unharmed apart from a broken tusk.

quiet companion Alan Derrick of Somerset, England, lived in a house with his friend's dead body hidden behind a sofa from 1998 to 2008.

paid piper Tourism bosses in Vienna, Austria, found a way to frighten off rats from the city's sewers—by playing the bagpipes. The Third Man tours, which walk the sewers made famous by Orson Welles' cult 1949 movie, were closed down when health chiefs ruled that the risk of rat bites was too great, but now they're back in business after hiring a bagpiper whose shrill sounds send the rodents running for cover.

dam coincidence J.G. Tierney drowned in 1922 while surveying the future site of the Hoover Dam. In 1935, his son Patrick became the last person to die in the dam's construction when he fell from an intake tower.

political clown A professional clown was elected to represent Sao Paulo in Congress after picking up 1.3 million votes in the 2010 Brazilian general elections. Tiririca (real name Francisco Oliveira) received the highest number of votes for any federal deputy across the country with his catchy TV slogans including: "What does a federal deputy do? I have no idea, but vote for me and I'll let you know."

traffic calming City transportation officials in Cambridge, Massachusetts, tried to calm drivers annoyed at receiving parking tickets by putting instructions on the reverse side about how to relax by bending the body into simple yoga positions.

fast food Perry Watkins of Buckinghamshire, England, has built a dining table that can travel at speeds of 130 mph (209 km/h). He took the chassis of a Reliant Scimitar sports car, fitted a 4-liter Land Rover Discovery engine boosted by nitrous oxide injection, and then added a table, six dining chairs and a fake meal. The driver sits under the roast chicken, the tax disc is stuck to a champagne bucket, the brake lights are built into rolled-up napkins and the exhaust fumes come out of two silver teapots.

ambulance stolen An Illinois man was arrested for stealing an ambulance in Mount Horeb, Wisconsin—with a patient and paramedics still inside it.

bottleneck mystery A 60-mi (96-km) traffic jam trapped thousands of vehicles on the Beijing–Tibet expressway for 11 days in August 2010—but then it completely disappeared overnight without any apparent explanation.

lost letters While on a 2010 field trip to the Alps, Freya Cowan, a geography student from the University of Dundee, Scotland, stumbled across a U.S.-bound mailbag from the *Malabar Princess*, an Air India plane that crashed near the summit of Mont Blanc while en route to London in 1950, killing all 40 passengers and eight crew on board. Some of the correspondence inside the mailbag was still in such good condition that she set about sending 75 letters and birthday cards on to their intended recipients 60 years late.

super sub Cyril Howarth from Lancashire, England, spent $75,000 on converting a 70-ft-long (21-m) canal narrow boat into a replica of a World-War-II German U-boat. Unlike other submarines, this vessel stays strictly on the surface.

Too Close for Comfort
Two people found themselves in an unbelievable predicament after being thrown from their motorcycle in Hubei Province, China, in 2010. They flew headfirst into the mouth of a drainpipe just 1 ft 8 in (50 cm) wide and were stuck fast. Fortunately, passersby saw their feet protruding from the polluted water pipe and notified firefighters, who dug the couple free in just ten minutes.

Ripley's Believe It or Not!® beyond belief

blamed vampire A Fruita, Colorado, woman who drove her car into a canal in June 2010 blamed the accident on a vampire. She said she was driving on a dirt road late at night, when she spotted a vampire in the middle of the road and hastily put the car in reverse. When troopers arrived, they found the woman's car in the canal but there was no sign of the vampire.

upside down Wang Xiaoyu, a barber from Changsha, Hunan Province, China, gives haircuts while standing on his head. A trained martial artist, he performs his headstands on a table to achieve the right height for cutting customers' hair.

leisurely stroll Paul Railton was fined $100 in 2010 for taking his dog for a walk while driving alongside in his car. He was spotted driving at low speed along a country lane in County Durham, England, holding his Lurcher's leash through the car window as the dog trotted next to him.

sailing in circles A nautical novice who thought he was sailing around the coast of Britain in a counterclockwise direction ended up circling a small island off Kent instead. He was rescued by a lifeboat after running out of fuel off the 8-mi-wide (13-km) Isle of Sheppey, whose shore he had been hugging day and night on the principle of keeping the land to his right. He had not realized that Sheppey was an island.

mayo misery A consignment of mayonnaise fell off the back of a truck in Hyogo, Japan, causing an eight-vehicle pileup as cars and motorcycles skidded wildly on the crushed sauce. The highway had to be closed for five hours.

google alert A ten-year-old girl who decided to act dead while playing in the street with her friends sparked panic among neighbors when her image was captured by Google Street View cameras. Azura Beebeejaun was pictured lying face down on the pavement outside her home in Worcester, England, prompting residents browsing their neighborhood online to fear they had stumbled across a murder scene.

wake up! An Australian mining company has invented a hat that wakes up sleepy truck drivers. The hi-tech SmartCap is fitted with brain monitoring sensors, and if the driver seems to be drifting off, the cap sends a message to a computer screen in the truck cab, which then flashes a warning.

Head Stand

Kris Sleeman of the Dallas extreme performance group Traumatic Stress Discipline appears to feel no pain. At the 2007 grand opening of the Ripley's Believe It or Not! Odditorium in San Antonio, Texas, he lay face down in a pile of freshly broken glass bottles, and then invited Ripley employee Viviana Ray to stand on his head. Kris's pain-defying feats also included having a concrete block on his chest shattered by a sledgehammer while lying on a bed of nails.

facebook phenomenon People across the world spend more than 700 billion minutes a month surfing through the website of Facebook, the Palo Alto, California-based social networking site. Since it was launched in 2004, more than 500 million people have joined Facebook—that's around eight percent of the world's population.

GUARDIAN ANGEL

Police in Fribourg, Switzerland, hired a roadside angel to stop motorists driving too fast. Dressed all in white, the angel, played by a bearded actor, stood at different locations and flapped his wings at speeding drivers.

concrete breaker Kung fu champion Chris Roper from Suffolk, England, can break a 26-in-thick (66-cm) block of concrete with his foot, 20 in (51 cm) with his elbow and 12 in (30 cm) with his bare hand.

strong hair In November 2009, Manjit Singh from Leicester, England, pulled a double-decker London bus 70 ft (21 m)—using only his hair. By attaching a clamp to his thick ponytail, he managed to pull the seven-ton bus through Battersea Park. The feat made up for his disappointment in 2007, when he had been unable to pull a similar bus with his ears.

versatile performer Yang Guanghe, from China's Guizhou Province, can perform more than 30 different stunts—including standing on lit lightbulbs, lifting buckets of water with his eyelids, using an electric drill on his nose, standing on upturned knives, pulling a car with his eyelids and inserting a live snake into one of his nostrils then pulling it out from his mouth.

subway pushers Human "pushers" are hired to work on Tokyo's subway system to help cram more people into the overcrowded train cars.

road hogs A section of road near Eureka, Missouri, is covered with asphalt made from recycled pig manure, courtesy of a nearby hog farm.

junior matador At age 12 and standing only 4 ft 10 in (1.5 m) tall, seventh-grader Michel Lagravere from Mérida, Mexico, is a seasoned bullfighter who has challenged more than 50 snorting, charging 500-lb (227-kg) beasts in Colombia, Peru and France, as well as in his native country. Known as "Michelito," he first stepped into the ring with a young bull when he was just four and a half years old.

strong stomach Julika Faciu from Piatra Neamt, Romania, allowed 50 motorbikes and a 3-ton jeep to ride over his stomach, one by one.

hoover fan As a teenager, James Brown from Nottinghamshire, England, had a collection of 50 vacuum cleaners—and his love for them has led to him opening Britain's first vacuum cleaner museum. He can identify different brands of vacuum cleaners in his collection simply by their sound.

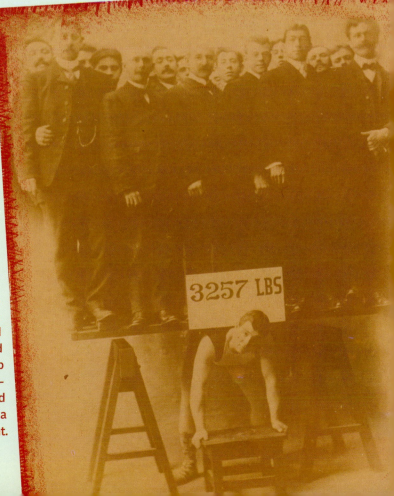

STRONG MAN

George Lavasseur, a strong man with Ringling Bros. Circus in the early 20th century, was able to bear a 17-man human pyramid on his back that weighed a total of 3,257 lb (1,477 kg). The Detroit-born performer could also carry the weight of a fully grown elephant.

3257 LBS

royal residence Janet and Philip Williams have turned their four-bedroom home in Woonona, New South Wales, Australia, into a royal museum, attracting thousands of visitors each year. They have more than 12,000 items of House of Windsor memorabilia, ranging from a life-size model of Queen Elizabeth II to a pair of Prince Charles and Princess Diana slippers. Even the toilet is decorated like a royal throne, complete with purple velvet trim.

$9,000 toothpick In December 2009, a toothpick that once belonged to British author Charles Dickens sold for $9,150 at an auction in New York City.

unwanted coins A stockpile of dollar coins worth more than $1.1 billion is languishing in storage because Americans prefer dollar bills. If stacked, the pile of coins would reach seven times higher than the altitude of the International Space Station.

cow suit Milkman Tony Fowler from Leicestershire, England, wore a black-and-white cow suit to receive his M.B.E. from Queen Elizabeth II at Buckingham Palace in June 2010. The Friesian outfit should have had a tail at the back, but Fowler's dog chewed it off.

same sneakers As part of a bet he made with his Spanish teacher, high-school freshman Ben Hedblom of Tampa, Florida, wore the same pair of sneakers every day for four years until he graduated—even though his toes eventually stuck out the front and he had to encase the shoes in plastic bags on rainy days.

pink lady Los Angeles actress Kitten Kay Sera has worn nothing but pink for over 25 years. "The Pink Lady," as she is known, even wears pink to funerals and once dumped a boyfriend because he was colorblind and therefore unable to appreciate the joy of pink. She dyes her Maltese dog, Kisses, in her favorite color using beetroot juice baths.

manure message To celebrate his wife Carole's 67th birthday, farmer Dick Kleis used a manure spreader to spell out HAP B DAY LUV U in a field visible from the living room of the couple's home in Zwingle, Iowa. It took him three hours and four loads of liquid manure to create the message—he was going to add a heart, too, but he ran out of manure.

bogus tycoon Echoing the real-life escapades of Frank Abagnale Jr. in the movie *Catch Me If You Can*, a 17-year-old boy from Yorkshire, England, posed as an aviation tycoon for six months. He tricked British companies into believing he was about to launch his own airline and that he had a fleet of jets. When the ruse was uncovered, the boy was found to be suffering from a form of autism, which enabled him to recall the exact detail of every airline's flight schedule.

renewed vows Margaret and John Beauvoisin of Hampshire, England, celebrated their diamond wedding anniversary in December 2008 by renewing their vows for the 60th time. The couple got married in 1948 and have renewed their vows every year since 1950, only missing out in 1949 because John was stationed in Bermuda with the Royal Navy.

doll house Bettina Dorfmann from Dusseldorf, Germany, owns more than 6,000 Barbie dolls—and some are worth up to $10,000. An entire room of her house is devoted to displaying 1,500 of them while another 3,000 Barbies from her collection are on show at exhibitions and museums around the world.

just the job Jason Sadler of Ponte Vedra Beach, Florida, earned more than $85,000 in 2009, promoting different businesses by wearing their T-shirts.

reptilian row A row over loud music between two South Carolina motel guests ended with one being accused of slapping the other in the face with the head of a 4-ft (1.2-m) python. The suspect was charged with assault and the weapon—the python—was handed over to his family for safe keeping.

jesus lives When a 50-year-old man was taken to a hospital with minor facial injuries after being hit by a car in Northampton, Massachusetts, in May 2010, he gave his name as Lord Jesus Christ. Police officers checked his I.D. and confirmed that it was indeed his legal name.

family success Father and son Brian and Jared Johnsrud of Marshfield, Wisconsin, both won cricket-spitting contests at the 2009 Central Wisconsin State Fair. Brian spat a thawed cricket 22 ft 8 in (6.9 m) to win the senior title and, minutes later, Jared spat his cricket 10 ft 5 in (3.2 m) to win the 9–11 age division.

DUST BUNNIES

These cuddly looking bunnies are actually composed of household detritus, including Christmas tree needles, discarded toddler toy parts, dryer lint, toenail clippings and human hair. Suzanne Proulx, from Erie, Pennsylvania, took 2½ years to collect enough dirt and dust to make 16 of her *Dust Bunnies*. Suzanne's first bunnies were a humorous comment on the dust and dirt that seemed to invade her house and multiply like wild rabbits. They are also about rebirth and renewal, taking what has been thrown away and creating something new.

sneaker line Collecting more than 10,500 sneakers sent in by readers, *National Geographic Kids* magazine unveiled a 1.65-mi (2.65-km) line of shoes, tied together by their laces, at Washington, D.C.

house of cards Without using glue or tape, Bryan Berg of Santa Fe, New Mexico, built a model of the Venetian Macao Resort-Hotel in Las Vegas from 218,792 playing cards. It took him 44 days and 4,051 decks of cards to complete the model that measured 33 x 10 ft (10 x 3 m) and weighed 600 lb (272 kg).

great shakes Dorena Young of Wallsburg, Utah, has a collection of more than 3,600 salt-and-pepper shakers. She has been collecting them for more than 60 years and has ones shaped like boats, cats, dogs, deer, vegetables, hats, lighthouses and sea horses. She even has a pair of J.F.K. and Jackie Onassis salt-and-pepper shakers.

packed court A total of 1,745 students played a single game of dodgeball on the University of California, Irvine, campus in September 2010.

daring plunge Amateur kayaker Christie Glissmeyer from Hood River, Oregon, paddled down the 82-ft-high (25.2-m) Metlako Falls at Eagle Creek, Oregon, in May 2010—a plunge that was nearly twice the height of any waterfall she had previously run.

hairy journey In 2007–08, German adventurer Christoph Rehage walked nearly 2,887 mi (4,646 km) across China from Beijing to Urumqi and took a picture of himself every day to document the growth of his beard.

Lint Leonardo

Laura Bell of Roscommon, Michigan, has made a replica of Leonardo da Vinci's painting *The Last Supper* out of laundry lint that measures 13 ft 8 in x 4 ft 4 in (4 x 1.3 m). She bought towels in the colors she wanted, laundering them separately to achieve the right shades. To obtain the amount of lint she needed to make the picture, she had to do about 800 hours of laundry and it then took her another 200 hours to re-create the famous Renaissance masterpiece.

Ripley's Believe It or Not!®
beyond belief

king charles Charles Wesley Mumbere worked as a nurses' aide for years in the U.S.A., but on October 19, 2009, he reclaimed his crown as head of the mountainous kingdom of Rwenzururu in Uganda, ruling over about 300,000 people.

skateboarding priest Reverend Zoltan Lendvai, a Hungarian Catholic priest, spreads the word of God from his skateboard. Father Lendvai, whose first skateboard incorporated the papal coat of arms, has become a YouTube hit with a video showing the 45-year-old, in full clerical dress, demonstrating his moves for youngsters outside his church in Redics. He believes his skateboarding prowess will encourage more young people to attend church.

rolling, rolling, rolling... Lotan Baba, the "Rolling Saint" of India, spreads his message of peace by rolling on the ground from town to town across the country. He rolls 6–8 mi (10–12 km) a day and estimates that over the years he has rolled about 18,650 mi (30,000 km). His enthusiasm for rolling may be partly explained by the fact that as penance he once spent seven years standing upright, in the same place.

vertical burials An Australian funeral home is saving space by burying people vertically. Melbourne company Upright Burials places each corpse in a biodegradable bag and then lowers the body feet first into a cylindrical hole about 30 in (75 cm) in diameter and 9½ ft (3 m) deep. Using this method, the company hopes to bury up to 40,000 bodies in a field outside the city.

debt unpaid Former British Prime Minister Winston Churchill (1874–1965) died owing 13 rupees to the Bangalore Club of Bangalore, India. The club has maintained the ledger showing that debt and displays it—but refuses to allow anyone to pay his tab.

idaho caveman Richard "Dugout Dick" Zimmerman (1916–2010) left his old life as a farmhand behind in 1947 and began digging out a series of caves near Salmon, Idaho. He cultivated a garden and lived without modern amenities for more than 60 years. Some of his caves were up to 60 ft (18.5 m) deep and were furnished with cast-off doors, car windows, old tires and other discarded items.

homemade plane In July 2010, 82-year-old Arnold Ebneter of Woodinville, Washington State, flew his homemade lightweight airplane, the E-1, nonstop from Everett, Washington State, to Fredericksburg, Virginia—a journey of 2,327 mi (3,746 km)—in 18 hours 27 minutes.

in a flap When Darren Cubberly's racing pigeon, Houdini, failed to arrive at the end of a 224-mi (360-km), six-hour race from the island of Guernsey to the West Midlands, England, he gave up hope of seeing the bird again. Then, five weeks later he received a call from Panama City—5,200 mi (8,370 km) away—to say that Houdini was there. It is thought she landed on a ship traveling to the area.

fire trim Italian-American hairdresser Pietro Santoro cuts hair using a naked flame at his barber shop in Washington, D.C. He says that cutting hair with fire gives it more body.

Dried Shark
A seafront store in Taiwan offers whole dried sharks for sale at a price of 6,500 Hong Kong dollars (U.S.$844) per 1 lb 5 oz (600 g). Shark fins are a popular delicacy in Chinese soup, while other parts of the shark are considered to have beneficial medicinal properties.

SKELETON STAFF

When the Post-Mortem Club held its annual breakfast in Chicago in 1934, the guest of honor was the skeleton of its late founder, Mr. J. M. McAdou of Florida, who had died the previous year. The club was an organization of naprapaths (practitioners of a manual medical technique similar to osteopathy) and had a rule that stated each member should leave them his skeleton so that it could attend future meetings... although probably not vote.

polar riddle When video footage showed a large, white beast lying on the shore, British TV presenter Naomi Lloyd excitedly told viewers that a polar bear from the Arctic had been washed up in Bude, Cornwall. It subsequently emerged that the animal was actually a cow that had been bleached white by seawater.

game proposal A New York City video-game fan proposed to his girlfriend with gold coins in a specially designed level of Super Mario World. Having persuaded her to play the game, he used a level-editing program called Lunar Magic to spell out "Lisa will you marry me?" on screen. He then recorded her delighted reaction in a video posted on YouTube.

resuscitating roadkill A 55-year-old man was arrested on a remote highway northeast of Pittsburgh, Pennsylvania, after he was seen performing mouth-to-mouth resuscitation on roadkill. Witnesses said the possum in question was not just playing dead, it had been deceased for some time.

slimy cure According to the African religion of *Ifa Orisha*, drinking the juices and mucus of Giant African snails can cure the sick.

dog driver A man was run over by his own dog in 2010 after it jumped into his pickup truck and accidentally knocked it into gear. Christopher Bishop of Webster, Florida, was lying under his truck checking for oil leaks and had the vehicle in neutral, the engine running and the driver's door open, when his bulldog, Tassey, leaped in and hit the gear stick into reverse, sending the vehicle rolling over his owner's body. Luckily, Christopher survived the incident without major injury.

Ripley's REVISITED

RIPLEY'S HERO

Daring Thai snake charmer Khum Chaibuddee, also known as the "King of Cobras," was honored as a Ripley's Ambassador by the *Ripley's Believe It or Not* museum in Pattaya, Thailand, in 2010. He celebrated by performing with his deadly cobras and even kissing them, his signature trick. In *Ripley's Believe It or Not! The Remarkable Revealed*, we reported that a fearless Khum had kissed 19 highly poisonous cobras one by one on the head without being bitten.

beyond belief

CAR COFFINS

Automobile fan Danny Mendez of Winchester, California, has designed a range of $1,500 fiberglass coffins in the shapes of classic cars. Each Cruisin' Casket features motorcycle headlights, alloy wheels from golf carts and extending side exhausts that serve as handles for pallbearers. In the absence of a death in the family, the coffins can also double as ice coolers.

snow palace To create a fairy-tale setting for his ultimately successful marriage proposal to Christi Lombardo in February 2010, Ryan Knotek built a snow castle near his home in Parma, Ohio. Using blocks of snow, he constructed a one-room, one-story palace topped with roof spires and furnished inside with a portable heater to keep the winter chill away.

favorite ride Vic Kleman of Knoxville, Pennsylvania, has ridden the Jack Rabbit roller coaster at Kennywood Park in West Mifflin near Pittsburgh more than 4,000 times since 1959. To celebrate the 90th birthday of the wooden ride, which has an 85-ft (26-m) double-dip drop, 78-year-old Vic went on it 90 times in one day in August 2010.

flamboyant funeral Flamboyant Hong-Kong lawyer Kai-bong Chau, 75, was buried in March 2010 with paper replicas of his gold and pink Rolls-Royce cars and a selection of his most colorful outfits. Paper models of cars, homes and money are traditionally burned at Chinese funerals to provide the dead with comfort and luxuries in the afterlife.

strange venue Jason and Rachael Storm decided to start their life together in 2008 by getting married at a place where it usually comes to an end—a funeral home in St. Joseph Township, Michigan, where the groom was a director.

blessed computers To attract bankers and financiers from the City of London to his church, the Rev. Canon David Parrott performed a service in which he blessed their cell phones and laptop computers.

wrong funeral After reading a death notice in her local paper in Merthyr Tydfil, Wales, stating that upholsterer Ron Jones had passed away, Margaret Griffiths sat through the funeral service for her old friend—only to discover later that she had got the wrong Ron Jones. The confusion arose because there were two men named Ron Jones of similar age in the town and both had worked as upholsterers.

young undertaker In September 2010, George Simnett set up his own funeral business in Leicestershire, England—at age 17.

CRAB DISPENSER

A food vending machine in Nanjing, China, sells live crabs. Designed by Shi Tuanjie, the machine offers live hairy crabs and accompanying bottles of vinegar. The crustaceans vary in price from $2 to $7, according to size. The crabs, a tasty delicacy in the region, are packed into plastic boxes and chilled to 40°F (5°C), leaving them sedated but still alive. An average of 200 crabs a day are sold, and customers are promised compensation of three live crabs should their purchase happen to be dead.

mobile chapel A 1942 firetruck owned by Rev. Darrell Best, of Shelbyville, Illinois, has been converted into a mobile wedding chapel called "Best Man." It has stained glass windows, an altar, two wooden pews and a fully working pipe organ.

bmw tomb Following his death at age 51, the family of motoring fanatic Steve Marsh of London, England, built him a tomb in the shape of a shiny black BMW, complete with personalized number plate "STEVE 1" and a parking ticket.

boxed art Vending machines in Germany sell miniature works of art in boxes for less than $3. About 100 refurbished machines, which once sold cigarettes or chewing gum, now sell tiny one-off sculptures, collages and paintings by professional artists.

saddle sore Riding 49cc mini-bikes that averaged just 20 mph (32 km/h), Ryan Galbraith and Chris Stinson traveled the 445 mi (716 km) from Denver, Colorado, to Sturgis, South Dakota, in 25 hours 29 minutes in 2009.

high fives Paralympic Alpine skiing silver medallist Josh Dueck of Vernon, Canada, high-fived 9,307 people in 24 hours in Vancouver in September 2010.

pole balance David Cain of Liberty Township, Ohio, can balance a 58-ft-long (17.7-m) fiberglass pole on his chin for more than 21 seconds. It took him two years to master the skill.

filthy rich Sixty-year-old Curt Degerman of Skellefteå, Sweden, ate from trash bins and collected cans for recycling for 40 years, but when he died it was discovered he was worth more than $1.4 million.

loop the loops Setting off at an altitude of 5,900 ft (1,800 m), Hungarian tandem paraglider Pál Takáts and his co-pilot Gábor Kézi performed 45 consecutive loop the loops on their descent over Lake Walenstadt, Switzerland.

wayward gps In 2009, a driver was fined after following the directions of his GPS up a narrow dirt track, unsuitable for cars, to the very edge of a 100-ft (30-m) cliff drop in West Yorkshire, England.

welded to flagpole On April 29, 2009, Alex Almy and Jesse Poe of Fruita Monument High School in Fruita, Colorado, spent 75 minutes welding a car around their school's flagpole as a year-end prank. They took off the passenger door and part of the roof to slide the Eagle hatchback into place before getting busy with welding tools. However, because the flagpole itself was undamaged and the boys agreed to remove the car, no one was punished.

Huge Hole

A 66-ft-wide (20-m) sinkhole opened up overnight in the yard of the Zhang family home in Leshan, China. Several fruit trees disappeared down the hole, which was more than 130 ft (40 m) deep and stopped less than 3 ft (1 m) from the house.

Ripley's Believe It or Not!®

beyond belief

human punchbag Xiao Lin, a fitness coach from Shenyang, China, rents himself out as a punchbag for stressed women who want to let off steam. The women pay $15 for a 30-minute session during which they can hit him as hard and as often as they like.

mother cat Peter Keonig, a Buddhist bank robber serving five years for armed robberies in Germany, had his request for his cat to be granted visiting rights to him in jail rejected by a court—despite his plea that the animal is the reincarnation of his mother.

bearly believable! A 2010 survey showed that more than one-third of British adults still take a childhood teddy bear to bed with them at night.

Upside-down House
A totally upside-down house opened as a tourist attraction in the grounds of a zoo in Gettorf, Germany, in 2010. Standing on a pointed roof and supported by steel beams in the attic, the 23-ft (7-m) house boasts an upside-down kitchen, as well as a completely inverted bathroom, living room and bedroom. Workers screwed 50 separate pieces into the "floor" (actually the ceiling), including beds, tables and a microwave oven. Needle and thread were used to keep bed linen in place.

cool customer A man walked into a restaurant in Warren, Michigan, with a 5-in (12.5-cm) knife sticking in his chest and calmly ordered a coffee. The 52-year-old, who had walked a mile to the restaurant after having been stabbed, did not complain of any pain and simply told staff that he was waiting for an ambulance to come to care for him. Following treatment in a hospital, the man was expected to make a full recovery.

dancing cop Dressed in police blues, white gloves and an officer's cap, Tony Lepore dances while directing the traffic at an intersection in Providence, Rhode Island. He began his dance routine in the 1980s through boredom and although he retired from the police department in 1988, he returns each year for two weeks to entertain passersby.

own juror William Woods was about to stand trial in Ottawa, Ontario, Canada, in 1999 on charges of dangerous driving, but the trial had to be postponed because Woods was summoned for jury duty—for his own case.

snake smuggler After customs officers in Kristiansand, Norway, discovered a tarantula in the bag of a ferry passenger who had traveled from Denmark, they decided to conduct a full body search. On investigation, they also found 14 royal pythons and ten albino leopard geckos taped to the man's torso and legs.

cash flow A 47-year-old Ukrainian man got his arm stuck in a public toilet in Chernigov for three hours after trying to retrieve $24 that he had dropped. With the man trapped up to his elbow, rescuers had to use hydraulic shears to cut him free. He emerged unharmed but $24 poorer, while the toilet itself was completely destroyed.

great survivor Frano Selak, a music teacher from Petrinja, Croatia, cheated death seven times, surviving three car accidents, two bus crashes, a train crash and even a plane crash—accidents that otherwise left 40 people dead. His run of good luck continued when he won $1,000,000 in a lottery. To give thanks for being the luckiest man alive, he gave away his winnings to family and friends.

subway hideaway A 13-year-old boy who thought he was in trouble at school spent 11 days hiding on the New York City subway in 2009. Francisco Hernandez Jr. hid on the D train he normally rides during his short commute from his Brooklyn home to school. He slept on trains and survived on junk food he bought from newsstands along the route.

surrounded city Although the city of Carter Lake is in Iowa, it is surrounded on three sides by the city of Omaha, Nebraska, and on the fourth by the Missouri River. It was formed by a flood that straightened the course of the Missouri and is the only city in Iowa that lies west of the river. It even gets its utility services from Nebraska.

HEAD FOR HEIGHTS
A six-year-old boy slipped through window bars of an eighth-floor apartment in Hubei Province, China, but ended up dangling by his ears 60 ft (18 m) above the ground after they got trapped in the bars because the rest of his head was too wide to pass through.

pillow talk In a special ceremony in March 2010, Korean Lee Jin-gyu married a large pillow adorned with a picture of female Japanese animated character, Fate Testarossa. He put the pillow in a wedding dress for the service, which was conducted before a priest. He takes the pillow everywhere—and when he and his pillow bride go to a restaurant, the pillow gets its own seat and its own meal.

cesspit hell A Chinese man was rescued in 2010 after spending two days stuck up to his neck in a toilet cesspit. The man had slipped while using an outhouse toilet in Wuyuan, Inner Mongolia, and had fallen into the pit below. Unsurprisingly, as soon as he was freed, he ran to a nearby pond to have a wash!

wonder well Chand Baori, a 100-ft-deep (30-m) stepped well in the village of Abhaneri, Rajasthan, India, was built more than a thousand years ago with 13 stories and 3,500 steps.

bike burial When Harry "The Horse" Flamburis, a Hells' Angels motorcycle club leader from Daly City, California, died, he was buried with his motorbike.

LIVELY LANDINGS ......

Is it a Bird?

Giant 300-ton Boeing 747s coming in to land at Princess Juliana Airport on the Caribbean island of Saint Martin fly just 60 ft (18.4 m) above the heads of vacationers on Maho Beach. They fly so low that they blow sand into the faces of plane spotters gathered below. The beach is right next to the runway, which, at 7,054 ft (2,170 m), is the shortest in the world to regularly accommodate 747s.

Over the autobahn
Leipzig Hall Airport, Germany

Low tide
Barra Airport, Scotland

Crossing the highway
Gibraltar Airport

Smoothed ice and snow

Ice runway in Antarctica

Page numbers in *italic* refer to illustrations

abdomen, breathing in a long way 124, *124, 163, 163*
Abdulleh, Safia (Som) 32
Abraham, Franz (Ger) 200
Abramović, Marina (Ser) 210
Abramovich, Roman (Rus) 134
accents
  bats with regional 67
  Foreign Accent Syndrome 110
Acton, Patrick (U.S.A.) 218
Adams, Ansel (U.S.A.) 207
adhesive tape, sculpture made of 202, *202*
Adili Wuxor (Chn) 160
aerogel 230, *230*
Afanasiev, Nick (U.S.A.) 105, *105*
Ahlgren, Anders (Swe) 89
Ai Weiwei (Chn) 218
airbeds, racing over waterfalls on 94, *94*
aircraft carrier, LEGO® replica of 218
airplanes
  babies born in 119, 124
  basketball shot made from 96
  boy pretends to be tycoon 238
  car converts to 136
  converted to boat 140, *140-1*
  crossing roads 245, *245*
  escapologist 153
  fly low over beach 245, *245*
  flying to school 140
  found under ice *132-3*, 133
  hits warthog on runway 140
  homemade 143, 240
  huge model 142
  hypersonic 137
  ice runway 245, *245*
  inflatable fighter planes 143, *143*
  land on beach 245, *245*
  lands on highway 136
  LEGO® replica of 208
  monkeys smuggled onto 60
  passenger accidentally ejects himself 136
  pilot saved by ejector seat 138, *138-9*
  pulling with eyelids 170
  tailcone falls off 140
  wing falls off 138, *138*
  wingwalking 160
airports
  size of Heathrow 136
  unusual runways 245, *245*
airship, at Chicago World's Fair 168
Al Humaidhan, Hamad (U.K.) 217
Albanese, Matthew (U.S.A.) 216, *216*
Alex, Vicki (U.K.) 108
Ali, Hadji (Egy) 165, *165*
Ali, Kalim (Ind) 128
Ali, Muhammad (U.S.A.) 203
aliens
  April Fool's hoax 181
  driver forced to drive in bus lane by 141
  landing port built for 181
  Roswell Incident 181, *181*
Allen, Claire (U.K.) 127
allergies 73, 126
alligators
  live in house 78
  lost at sea 63
  made into motorbike 134, *134-5*
Allison, Brenda (U.K.) 119
Almy, Alex (U.S.A.) 243
alphabet, very small 53
Alvarado, Requelme Abanto (Per) 108
Alvarez, Angel (U.S.A.) 121
Alvarez, Felipe (Col) 96, *96*
ambulance, stolen 235
Amorim, M. de (Bra) 94
Anderson, Laurie (U.S.A.) 222
Anderson, Marvadene (U.S.A.) 128
Andes, Nick (U.S.A.) 149
angel, to stop speeding 237, *237*
animal skins
  inflated 198, *198-9*
  beer bottles in 193, *193*
Aniston, Jennifer (U.S.A.) 215
Anne, Princess (U.K.) 91
Annie K. (U.S.A.) 202, *202*
Antarctic, very old butter found in 190

ants
  destroy electrical equipment 78
  exploding 63, *63*
  as living larders 62
  painful ritual 62
  paintings of 222
  portrait made with dead *58-9, 58-9*
  start fire 25
  Velcro-like claws 78
anvils, shot into air 94
Aparicio, Julio (Spa) 100, *100*
apartments
  security measures 42
  underground 44
ape, discovered in Venezuela 180, *180*
Apple products, exhibition of destroyed 217, *217*
appliances, tree sculpture from 210
aquarium, octopus floods 79
Aretz, Achim (Ger) 153
arm wrestling 123
arms
  armless and legless woman 164, *164*
  armless cyclist 106, *106*
  contortionist 165, *165*
  holding aloft continuously 158, *158*
  one-armed D.J. 217
  parasitic twin 108
  self-amputation 121
  stuck in toilet 244
  very long hair on 25
armies
  lost army found 230
  war-time deceptions 17, 143, *143*
Arscott, Ann (U.K.) 113
Ashby, Stuart (U.K.) 193
Aspaint, Philibert 51, *51*
asphalt
  lake of 50
  pig manure recycled into 237
Aspland, Jamie (U.K.) 122
asteroid, explodes in atmosphere 41
astronauts
  tears 50
  urine jettisoned from Space Shuttle 49
astronomy, giant neutrino detector 231, *231*
Atlantic Ocean, rowing across 94, 96
Attia, Kader (Alg) 222
audio tapes, large collection of 215
Audubon, John James (U.S.A.) 201
Awasthi, Akash *146-7, 146-7*
Aziere, Dan (U.S.A.) 126

Baba, Lotan (Ind) 240
babies
  bigger than mother 119, *119*
  born in airplane 119, 124
  enormous 107
  "frozen" after surgery 118
  kept warm with sandwich bag 124
  mummified 22, *22*
  premature baby survives after cuddling 118
  prenatal surgery 109
  significant numbers for 29
  sisters give birth at same time 16
  very big 118
  very tiny 119
  with tail 109
baboons
  in circus 70
  eat vineyard's grapes 66
  sells tickets for zoo 61
bacon
  bacon-flavored envelopes 186
  enormous sandwich wrap 195
  sculpted head 191, *191*
Bacon, Kevin (U.S.A.) 191, *191*
Bacon, Phyllis (U.K.) 174, *174*
Bacon, Tad and Karen (U.S.A.) 85
bacteria
  on dental floss 118, *118*
  in human body 113
  large colonies of 38
  microbial art 202
  music helps work faster 50
  in rain 177

bacteria (*cont.*)
  in toxic lake 52
bagpipes, frighten rats 234
Bai, Chouthi (Ind) 74
Bai Deng (Chn) 171, *171*
Baines, Kelvin (U.K.) 157
Bajpai, Radhakant (Ind) 25, *25*
baked beans, rat found in tin of 189
Baker, Sally (U.K.) 134
Baliker, Paul (U.S.A.) 35, *35*
Balka, Miroslaw (Pol) 208
balloons
  crossing English Channel under 149, *149*
  dinner party under hot-air balloon 194
  hydrogen hot-air balloons 17
balls
  ancient metal spheres found 180
  ancient stone balls found 178
  baseball mementos 200
  dog swallows 72, 79
  holding multiple tennis balls 169
  mosaic made of 212, *212*
bananas
  banana ketchup 195
  double banana in one skin 190
  peels found on mountain 188
  underwear made from 190
banknote mosaic, made from screws 216
Bansal, Munish (U.K.) 218
bar, bartering for drinks in 190
barbecue, giant 191
Barbie dolls, large collection of 238
Barnum & Bailey Circus 30, 31, 116
Barraza, Hansy Better (U.S.A.) 206
Barrett, Jasper (U.S.A.) 178
Bartek, Jim (U.S.A.) 214
Bartholomew, Pamela (U.S.A.) 140, *140*
base jumpers, leap from tallest building 46
baseball
  armless pitcher 110
  bat hits fan 98, *98*
  breaking bats over leg 149
  carved bats 87, *87*
  decorated balls as mementos 200
  foul balls 94
  injuries 99
  successful pitcher 93
  switch-hitting homers 96
basket, huge 222
basketball
  injuries 99
  multiple free throws 97
  one-handed player 96
  shot made from airplane 96
Bass, Rebecca (U.S.A.) 131, *131*
bathroom, image of Satan appears in 16
bathtub, motorized bathtub on Amazon 160
bats
  giant colony in cave 72
  orphans rescued 74, *74-5*
  regional accents 67
battery, very ancient found 180
Battles, Ashley (U.S.A.) 160
Bauer, Kirk (U.S.A.) 112
Baze, Russell (Can) 93
Beach Boys (U.S.A.) 214
beaches
  enormous beach towel 153
  giant artwork on 214
  mass burial on 171
beads, very long strand of 221
beards
  bearded women 29, *29*, 126, *126*
  documenting growth of 239
  multiple styles 128
  as sculpture 21, *21*
  very long 25
  woven to resemble snowshoe 113
bears
  abandoned cub adopted 82
  deterred by zucchini 75
  drives car 61
  lives with tiger and lion 66, *66*
  milk can stuck on head 66
  steals teddy bear 83
  walks into grocery store 60
  yoga routine 76
The Beatles (U.K.) 110
beauty contest, after cosmetic surgery 114
Beauvoisin, Margaret and John (U.K.) 238

beavers
  attacks fisherman 73
  huge dam 84
Beckham, David (U.K.) 128
bed, earthquake-proof 230
bedroom, dust model of 221
Beebeejaun, Azura (U.K.) 236
beer
  bottles in animal skins 193, *193*
  deep-fried 195
  drinking in many different pubs 193
  made by light of full moon 188
beer crates
  building made of 47, *47*
  motorized 142
beer mats, apartment made of 170
bees
  bee beard competition 72, *72*
  cure multiple sclerosis 110
  dog eats beehive 72
  drink human tears 85
  swarm on clothes line 84
beetles
  bifocal eyes 63
  infestation of stinkbugs 79
  very strong 64
Bell, Alexander Graham (U.K.) 227
Bell, Charlie (U.K.) 156
Bell, Laura (U.S.A.) *238-9*, 239
Bellard, Fabrice (Fra) 170
Belluso, Rose Ann (U.S.A.) 110
belly button fluff, teddy bears made of 108, *108*
Benbenek, John (U.S.A.) 186
Bentley, Dr. John Irving 179, *179*
Berendes, Henry Michael (U.S.A.) 29
Berg, Bryan (U.S.A.) 239
Berkowitz, Valerie (U.S.A.) 32
Berlin Wall, chocolate replica of 187
Bertoletti, Patrick "Deep Dish" *184-5, 184-5*
Best, Rev. Darrell (U.S.A.) 243
Betra, Millie (U.S.A.) 156, *156*
Bews, Captain Brian 138, *138-9*
Bible, world tour for 200
bicycles
  amphibious bicycle 135
  armless rider 106, *106*
  bicycle-powered Porsche 142, *142*, 207
  coal-powered 136
  cycling across U.S.A. 94
  cycling round world 92
  cycling up steps 93, *93*
  injuries on 99
  legless rider 106, *106*
  long journey on mini-bikes 243
  owner rides for 60 years 143
  prisoners' Tour de France 92
  riding on tightrope 169, *169*
  wooden 141
Bihain, Jörn (Bel) 47, *47*
Bikila, Adebe (Eth) 89
bikini, made of raw meat 206
Bilal, Wafaa (U.S.A.) 219
Bindra, Abhinav (Ind) 89
birds
  chicken/guinea fowl hybrid 72
  chicken kill fox 70
  chicken lays huge egg 80
  cockerel changes sex 64
  crane wears slippers 66
  crossbow bolt in head 77, *77*
  dead birds fall from sky 174
  dive through ice 74
  hawk attacks postman 76
  huge flock of starlings 41, *41*
  long migration 62
  mark on car 7, *7*
  mystery illness 62
  owl chick escapes lion 76
  parrot arrested 76
  pigeon arrested for spying 82
  pigeon droppings halt concert 208
  pigeon faster than broadband 77
  pigeon races to wrong destination 240
  rooster arrested 74
  stork's romantic attachment 83
  swans' fidelity to partners 62
  very old chicken 85
  very smelly 63
  very valuable book 201

Bishop, Christopher (U.S.A.) 241
Björk (Ice) 210
black holes
  gigantic 52
  man-made 228
bladder, fish found in 112
Blaine, David (U.S.A.) 147
Blanchard, Jean-Pierre (Fra) 17
Blayze, Sue (U.K.) 149
blind people
  abseiler 97
  catches huge fish 93
  drives car at speed 157
  photographer 219
  "seeing" with echolocation 122
  sprinter 97
  writes book in Morse Code 110
blindfolded, typing books 208
blood
  large number of donations 120
  painting with 211, *211*
  sweating 105, *105*
blowtorch, fire-eating with 19, *19*
Boa Sr. (Ind) 40
board game, with real people as pieces 203
boats and ships
  billionaire's yacht 134
  built in back garden 141
  canal boat converted into submarine 235
  catamaran built of plastic bottles 142
  crews disappear 174, 181
  giant liner 142
  human-powered Viking longboat road vehicle 141
  kite-powered cargo ship 141
  LEGO® replicas 218, 221
  long time at sea 134
  looks like zipper 142, *142*
  lost sailor circles island 236
  model of warship 216
  plane converted to 140, *140-1*
  ship found under World Trade Center 135
  shipwreck still leaking oil 142
  whale jumps onto yacht 80, *80-1*
  young round-the-world sailor 92
Bocabeille, Jean (Fra) 186
body painting 8, *8*, 12, *12-13*, 201, *201*, 213
body piercings, multiple 128
Böhling, Ivar (Fin) 89
Bolt, Usain (Jam) 67
Bond, Josh (U.S.A.) 39
bones
  chapel decorated with 50
  growing extra 126
  made into artworks 212
  muscles turn to 115
  stretching 127
  stuck in lung 121
  under Paris 51, *51*
bonobos, share food 75
Boo, Jinxi (U.S.A.) 125, *125*
books
  author writes ten pages a day 209
  huge number of library books borrowed 206
  large collection of paperbacks 214
  quantities of paper used for 213
  smallpox scabs found in 114
  tiny copy of Quran 217
  typing blindfolded 208
  very long title 214
  very overdue library books 203, 221
  very valuable 201
  written using Morse Code 110
Booth, David (U.K.) 20
boots, welly wanging contest 94
Borbon, Spencer (U.S.A.) 215
Botox, cures stroke victim 122
bottles
  beer bottles in dead animals 193, *193*
  car on track of upright bottles 135
  catamaran built of plastic bottles 142
  diamonds on liqueur bottle 188
  message in 20
  walking with milk bottle on head 153, *153*
bottom, bionic 114
Bottoni, Stefano (Ita) 169
bouncy castle, crossing lake on 15, *15*

Bowen, Eli (U.S.A.) 106, *106*
bowling
  centenarian player 94
  woman champion 93
boxing, poem boxing contest 217
Boy Scouts, elderly Scout retires 152
Boyle, Iain and Rachel (U.K.) 53
Bradac, Zdenek (Cze) 147, 160
Bradford, Robert (U.K.) 216
brain
  medicinal uses for vulture brains 118
  needle removed from 126
  number of neurons in 115
Brandt, Francois Antoine (Nld) 88
bread
  dead mouse found in 189, *189*
  shuts down particle accelerator 226
  very expensive loaves 188
breast implants, stop bullets 120
breathing in a long way 124, *124*, 163, *163*
Brennan, Ian (U.S.A.) 216
Brewer, Carl (U.S.A.) 135
Brick, Jacqueline (U.K.) 32
bridge, mass breakfast on 186
Broadbent, Betty (U.S.A.) 26–7, *27*
Broom, Richard (U.K.) 208
brothers, long-lost 14
Brown, Chris (U.K.) 121
Brown, James (U.K.) 237
Brown, Jeremy (U.S.A.) 110
Brown, Leven (U.K.) 96
Brown, Louise (U.K.) 206
Brown, Rupert and Emma (U.K.) 80
Bruin, Dick de (Nld) 24
Bruns, Ed (U.S.A.) 128
Budiselic, Kruno (Cro) 152
Buenrostro, Adrian Rodrigues (Mex) 152
bug-eating parties 187, *187*
Bulatovic, Zoran (Ser) 107
Bulled, Roger and Leslie (U.K.) 137
bullets
  breast implants stop 120
  bulletproof clothes 228
  found in body 108, 110
  in head 128
  in lung 114
  man survives multiple 121
  sneezed out of nose 126
bullfighting
  bullfighter quits job mid-fight 97
  matador gored 100, *100*
  very young matador 237
bulls, fire festival 94, *94*
burgers
  burger-scented candles 190
  enormous 190
  giant barbecue 191
  lion meat 195
  very old 195
burglars
  caught by webcam 24
  parrot scares off 72
  woman pretends to be dog 29
burial suit, jade 173, *173*
Burkhart, Melvin (U.S.A.) 19
Burrard-Lucas, Will and Matt (U.K.) 82
Burrows, Terry (U.K.) 171
Burton, Finley (U.K.) 118
buses
  covered with knitting 201
  jet-powered school bus 136, *136*
  pulling with hair 237
  very long distance traveled 137
business card, giant 200
Buss, Mike (U.K.) 121
Butera family (U.S.A.) 64
Butler, Lareece (S.A.) 107
butter, very old 190
Byrd, Richard (U.S.A.) 168

Caballero, Miguel (Col) 228
Cadogan, Merlin (U.K.) 148, *148*
café, in underground cistern 194
Cain, David (U.S.A.) 243
cakes
  realistic model of dog 187, *187*
  very tall 186
Caliro, Aldo (Ita) 209
Calloway, Denny (U.S.A.) 7, 7
Calman, Bette (Aus) 156
Calvo, David (Spa) 160
camel, falls into sinkhole 73
cameras
  diver loses 24

cameras (*cont.*)
  found in fishing net 29
  implanted in back of head 219
  octopus steals 85
camouflage, zebras 81
Campbell, Sir Malcolm (U.K.) 160
Campbell, Naomi (U.K.) 203
candles, burger-scented 190
candy portraits 222, *222*
Cañizares, Santiago (Spa) 92
Cannon, Peter (Aus) 24
canoe, chicken feast in 186
cans
  mouse found in cola 189
  rat found in baked beans 189
  stuck on cat's head 64
Capes, Ryan (U.S.A.) 156
Carbone, Giorgio (Ita) 38
Carny, Ses (U.S.A.) 157, *157*
Caro, Susanne (U.S.A.) 114
Carranza, Lydia (U.S.A.) 120
Carrazza, Joe (Aus) 186
Carrier, Steve (U.S.A.) 149
Carrière, Eva (Fra) 176, *176*
cars
  abandoned in sea 29, *29*
  amphibious supercar 142
  assembly line at Chicago World's Fair 168
  bear drives 61
  Beatles tribute 131, *131*
  bicycle-powered Porsche 142, *142*, 207
  blind man drives fast car 157
  BMW-shaped tomb 243
  burial with paper replicas of 242
  car-shaped coffins 242, *242*
  chocolate-powered 190
  collides with elephant 234
  converts to airplane 136
  dead man found in car in river 29
  dog sounds horn for help 74
  dog taken for walk by 236
  driver claims aliens forced him to drive in bus lane 141
  drives through garage wall 135, *135*
  driving with cell phone app 226
  drunk driver in toy car 137
  elephants wash 64
  expensive toy car 135, *135*
  guardian angel to stop speeding 237, *237*
  homemade supercar 134
  huge mileage 141
  Hummer converted to horse-drawn carriage 140
  kitten survives in engine 72
  knitted cover for 214
  learner crashes into apartment 142
  lion opens door 82, *82*
  loses all four wheels at once 137
  marathon car-wash 152
  mayonnaise causes highway crash 236
  no-parking lines painted under 134
  painting with remote-control cars 215
  pulling with eyelids 237
  replica made from clothes 220
  rolling over abdomen 123
  sculpture from old car parts 214
  speed record 160
  spontaneous human combustion in 179
  starts first time after long disuse 137
  on track of upright bottles 135
  Transformer made from 206
  vampire blamed for accident 236
  very fast electric car 141
  very valuable parking space 141
  Wall of Death 150–1, *150–1*
  welded around flagpole 243
carvings, whittling 164, *164*
Casagrange, Andy Brandy IV (U.S.A.) 203
Case, Rachel Betty (U.S.A.) 108, *108*
Cassini, Cecilia (U.S.A.) 218
Castiglioni, Angelo and Alfredo (Ita) 230
castles
  built of hay 210
  built of snow 242
  ghost photographed in *178*, 178
  new medieval castle built 54
catacombs, under Paris 51, *51*
caterpillars, invisible 70, *70*
cats
  bionic legs 77
  can stuck on head 64
  "cat" spelled out in fur 70
  dyed pink 77

cats (*cont.*)
  extra digits on paws 64, *64*
  four-eared kitten 74
  huge number in house 74
  kitten survives in car engine 72
  kitten survives in washing machine 75
  large collection of statues of 169
  long journey by 79
  marriage to 80
  mummified 23, *23*
  not allowed to visit prisoner 244
  predicts patients' deaths 176, *176*
  saves man from fire 62
  survives burial in rubble 60
  survives fall 70
  washing machines for 82
caves
  blind fish in 70
  huge number of bats in 72
  large colonies of bacteria 38
  living in 24, 50
  man digs 240
  under Paris 51, *51*
CDs, cremation ashes in 235
cell phones
  dress used as 220
  driving car with cell phone app 226
  in India 53
  iPhone first-aid app used in earthquake 123
  stolen one bought back by owner 17
  thief photographs himself with stolen cell phone 14
  unlucky number 28
  vicar blesses 242
centenarians
  non-existent 32
  plays bowling 94
  school pupil 24
centipedes, eating 192, *192*
cesspit, man rescued from 244
Chaibuddee, Khum (Tha) 241, *241*
chain, carved from wood 220
chair, enormous 203
Challis, Paul and Maria (U.K.) 32, *32*
chameleons
  new species found in snake's mouth 78
  very long tongues 72
champagne, found in shipwreck 195
Chang Du (Chn) 112, *112*
Chao Muhe (Chn) 20
chapels
  decorated with bones 50
  executive box decorated like Gothic chapel 97
  mobile wedding chapel 243
Chaplin, Charlie (U.S.A.) 223
Chapman, Sail (U.K.) 148
Charles, Prince of Wales 149, 238
Charles, Shemika (U.S.A.) 157
Chau, Kai-bong (Chn) 242
Chavez, Hugo (Ven) 20
cheetah, speed 67
Chen Forng-shean (Twn) 208
Chen Jinmiao (Chn) 134
Chen Kecai (Chn) 160, *160*
Chen Xinnian (Chn) 44
cherry stems, knotted with tongue 7, 7
chewing gum
  nonstick 190
  sculpture from 210, *210*
Chicago World's Fair 161–8, *161–8*
chicken
  chicken/guinea fowl hybrid 72
  cockerel changes sex 64
  feast in canoe 186
  kill fox 70
  lays huge egg 80
  rooster arrested 74
  very old 85
Childers, Michelle (U.S.A.) 120
chili sauce, extremely hot 186
chimpanzees
  make cutlery 61
  paintings by 67
  smoking and drinking problem 66
chin
  advertising space on 112, *112*
  balancing long pole on 243
chocolate
  chocolate-powered racing car 190
  clothes made of 189
  giant coin made of 188

chocolate (*cont.*)
  giant cupcake 193
  replica of Berlin Wall 187
  replica of Great Wall of China 187
  shoes and handbags 190
  skulls 190, *190*
  train sculpture 218
Chopra, Priyanka (Ind) 203
chopstick, in stomach 122
Chouinard, Jim and Maribel (U.S.A.) 24
christening gown, used by large family 29
Christmas-themed funeral 32
Christmas tree, made of plastic spoons 219
Chugg, Sami (U.K.) 110
church, family all marry in same 32
Churchill, Lady Randolph (U.S.A.) 27
Churchill, Sir Winston (U.K.)
  false teeth 119
  leather portrait of 203
  unpaid debt 240
Ciaglia, Joe (U.S.A.) 156, *156*
cigarette, exploding 110
cigarette packets, house decorated with 43, *43*
Clark, Tony (U.S.A.) 96
Clay, Alex (U.S.A.) 123
cliffs
  coffins hung over 44
  dog survives fall 80
  GPS takes driver to edge of 243
climbing
  frozen waterfall 95, *95*
  Olympic Games 90
  one-handed climber 108
  with vacuum cleaner suction 171
  young climber 148
Clinton, Bill (U.S.A.) 11, *11*
Clinton, Hillary (U.S.A.) 11
clocks
  enormous 43, 157
  large number in Pentagon 47
  wound by hand for 600 years 47
clog dance, mass 157, 217
clothes
  always wearing pink 238
  bulletproof 228
  cell-phone dress 220
  enormous T-shirt 209
  gum-wrapper prom dress 208
  invisibility coat 230, *230*
  made of chocolate 189
  manure-covered T-shirts 213
  promoting businesses with T-shirts 238
  replica car made from 220
  sculpture from discarded clothing 213, *213*
  very valuable sari 212
  wearing multiple T-shirts 152
  young designer 218
clouds
  Brocken Specter 54, *54*
  graffiti 208
  new type found 52
  snow prevented from falling on Moscow 48
  very high 49
clown, elected 235
Coach, Allison (U.S.A.) 157
coal-powered bike 136
cobras, kissing 241, *241*
Cockerill, Tim (U.K.) 18–19, *18–19*
cockroaches, population growth 62
coconuts
  octopuses live in 79
  piercing with finger 124
Coe, Robert and Sandra (U.S.A.) 72
coffins
  car-shaped 242, *242*
  escapologist gets out of 153
  glass window in 177, *177*
  groom goes to wedding in 32
  hung over cliffs 44
  JCB carries 32, *32*
  man comes back from dead in 32
  unidentified occupants 176
Cognac, very old bottle of 188
coins
  country's name mis-spelt on 14
  giant coin made of chocolate 188
  huge gold coin 24
  in stomach 121
  unwanted 238
Colón, David Morales (Pue) 28, *28*

Colón de Carbajal, Cristóbal (Spa) 91
colorblindness, zebra camouflage 81
Columbus, Christopher (Ita) 91
Colwill, Sarah (U.K.) 110
comas
  long-lasting 110
  waking from 108
combustion, spontaneous human 179, *179*
comedy gig, very long 214
comic, very valuable 203
computers
  ancient computer found 178
  first 226
  models of cities made from 218
  portraits on floppy disks 221, *221*
  vicar blesses 242
concrete, breaking with elbow 237
conjoined twins 105
Conley, Jamison (U.S.A.) 60
Connery, Sean (U.K.) 42
Connolly, James B. (U.S.A.) 89
Connors, Bob (U.S.A.) 220
Constantine, King of Greece 91
contortionists 115, *115*, 122, 158, *158*, 165, *165*
Conway, Matt (U.S.A.) 136
Cook, Ian (U.K.) 215
cookies, professional tester 186
Cool, Les (U.S.A.) 20, 20
Cooley, Frances (U.K.) 190
Corbett, James (Aus) 214
cosmetic surgery
  beauty contest for 114
  to look like Jessica Rabbit 110
Coubertin, Baron de (Fra) 88
cougar, dog saves owner from 61
couscous, model of city 222
Cowan, Freya (U.K.) 235
Cowell, Simon (U.K.) 222
cows
  jumps onto roof 60
  maze in shape of 216
  milkman receives honor wearing cow suit 238
  mistaken for polar bear 241
  prosthetic legs for 63
  rescued from apartment block 64
  Shakespeare plays to improve milk yields 215
  six-legged calf 79
  survives lightning strike 81, *81*
  woman breast-feeds calf 74
Cox, Vin (U.K.) 92
Crabbe, Buster (U.S.A.) 91
crabs
  long walk 75
  sold in dispenser 242, *242*
Craig, Gary (U.K.) 170, *170*
Craig, Rita (Can) 188
crane, dinner parties hanging from 194
crater, found in satellite picture 52
Crawford, K. Michael (U.S.A.) 213
cremation ashes
  in CDs 235
  sculpture from 206
  turned into works of art 33, *33*
cricket-spitting contest 238
crochet
  lions 200, *200*
  water tower cozy 210
crocodiles
  grabs elephant's trunk 82, *82*
  live in house 78
  piece of wood mistaken for 16
  in prison 79
  recognize own names 67
  rubbery fat 83
  tries to take fisherman's catch 97
Cromar, Angie (U.S.A.) 108
Crum, Cookie (U.S.A.) 150–1, *150*
Crucifixion, image made from toast 183, *183*
crystals, weeping 177
Csrefko, Andrea and Laszlo (Hun) 16
CT scans, as art 227, *227*
Cubberly, Darren (U.K.) 240
cucumbers
  cutting with playing card 171, *171*
  giant 157
Cui Jinxin (Chn) 60
cupcake, giant 193
curry
  boom in curry houses 191
  feeding to sheep 187

curry (cont.)
  gold and silver in 193
Curry, Raymond (U.S.A.) 110
curses, festival of 39
cutlery
  chimpanzees make 61
  swallowed 191, 191
cyclone, wind speed in 49
Cyparis, Louis Auguste (Mtq) 37

Daalmans, Margaret (Nld) 191, 191
Daisher, Miles (U.S.A.) 94
Dali, Salvador (Spa) 206
dams
  coincidental deaths 234
  giant beaver dam 84
  ibexes climb on face of 71, 71
  police guard 38
Dannecker, Alex (U.S.A.) 7, 7
darkness, as art installation 208
Das, Ramchandra (Ind) 54
Davis, Chelsea (U.S.A.) 101, 101
Davis, Geena (U.S.A.) 91
Davis, Ian (U.K.) 222
Davis, Ron (U.S.A.) 76
de Burgh, Frank and Emma (U.S.A.) 27, 27
de la Paz, Neralda (U.S.A.) 213, 213
Deacon, Elly (U.K.) 171
Dean, Jeremy (U.S.A.) 140
death
  body hidden behind sofa 234
  Brocken Specter 54, 54
  cat predicts patients' deaths 176, 176
  coincidental deaths on dam 234
  coming back from dead in coffin 32
  "Day of the Dead" festivals 39, 39
  dead man found in car in river 29
  dead man mistaken for Halloween
    dummy 14
  dead men elected 15, 25
  embalmed bodies kept in house 29
  embalmed body on motorcycle 28, 28
  image of child's face on oven door 178
  life-size cardboard cutout of dead man
    32, 32
  man goes to own funeral 14
  man keeps "dying" 114
  man killed by receiving cremation bill 28
  mediums communicate with 176–7,
    176–7
  mysterious jars 177
  painting with corpse's hand 213, 213
  vertical burials 240
  woman comforts dead daughter 177, 177
  woman starts breathing in funeral
    home 128
deer, lives in house 64
Degerman, Curt (Swe) 243
Delap, Beatrice (U.K.) 28
Delvoye, Wim (Bel) 201
DeNigris, Paul (U.S.A.) 32
dental floss, magnified appearance
  118, 118
dentures
  Churchill's 119
  in lungs 121
Depp, Johnny (U.S.A.) 28
Derrick, Alan (U.K.) 234
Dev, Harpreet (Ind) 142
Dew, Tony (U.K.) 212
Di Furia, Gaetano (U.K.) 32, 32
diamonds
  dog swallows 64
  expensive toy car 135, 135
  on liqueur bottle 188
  in tattoo 128
  vuvuzela horn 214
Diana, Princess of Wales 149, 238
dice, mosaics made of 208
DiCecca, Rick (U.S.A.) 221
Dickens, Charles (U.K.) 219, 238
Dickinson, Leo (U.K.) 152
Dietrich, Dorothy (U.S.A.) 147
Diment, Ed (U.K.) 218
Dimmock, Frank (U.K.) 157
dining table, very fast 235
Diogo, Paulo (Por) 99, 99
dissection, of father's body 127, 127
Dissmore, Perry (U.S.A.) 97
diving
  by horses 14, 14

diving (cont.)
  diver hits board 101, 101
  injuries 99
  scuba diving dog 64
D.J., one-armed 217
DNA, extracted from mummy 229
document, very old found 14
dodgeball, giant tournament 92
dogs
  allergies 73
  barbecue fork in head 64, 64
  bravery medal for 67
  burglar scared off by woman pretending
    to be 29
  chihuahuas attack police 74
  concert for 222
  disguised as wild animals 73, 73
  drives truck over owner 241
  dyed pink 238
  eats beehive 72
  eats golf balls 79
  eats owner's toe 77
  found on ice floe 64
  goes fishing 84
  ice-cream van for 190
  knows taxi routes 78
  large muscles 67, 67
  large vocabulary 78
  lights powered by poop 43
  long journey 62
  long-lost 66, 82
  magnets in stomach 79
  Mickey Mouse on fur 7, 7
  overgrown coat 76, 76–7
  paintings by 61
  parachute jumps 60
  pushes baby stroller 70
  Queen's corgis 80
  realistic cake model 187, 187
  rescued from storm drain 70
  saves owner from cougar 61
  saves owner from fire 84
  scuba diving 64
  shoots owner 64
  skateboarding 76
  sounds car horn for help 74
  survives being hit by train twice 64
  survives fall over cliff 80
  swallows ball 72
  swallows diamond 64
  swallows glass 75
  swollen tongue 77
  taken for walk by car 236
  two rows of teeth 67
  very tall 66
  very ugly 75, 75
  walks on back legs 80, 80
  washing machines for 82
  wedding for 72
  wind blows kennel away 79
  world tour 77
doll house, very valuable 208
dolls
  large collection of Barbie dolls 238
  very expensive 210
domino chain, human 169
Dong Changsheng (Chn) 170
Dore, Ahmed Muhamed (Som) 32
Dorfmann, Bettina (Ger) 238
Dorner, Willi (U.K.) 222
Dornon, Sylvain (Fra) 148, 148
Douglas, Eric Gordon (U.K.) 32
Douthett, Jerry (U.S.A.) 77
Dowling, Rob (Irl) 160
Doyle, Sir Arthur Conan (U.K.) 175, 177
Dreher, Peter (Ger) 210
dress, made from aluminum cans 7, 7
driftwood, sculptures made from
  35, 35
Drimmer, Dave (U.S.A.) 140, 140–1
drummer, very young 223
Dueck, Josh (Can) 243
Duff, Owen (U.S.A.) 153
Duke, Charlie (U.S.A.) 216
Dumont, Etienne (Swi) 111, 111
Dunbar, Dean (U.S.A.) 97
Duncan, Neil (U.S.A.) 112
Dunkley, Kez (U.K.) 93
Duschl, Gary (U.S.A.) 6, 6
Dwivedi, Twinkle (Ind) 105, 105
Dyrdek, Rob (U.S.A.) 156, 156

Earle, Jack (U.S.A.) 117, 117
Earnshaw, Charles (U.S.A.) 21, 21
ears
  four-eared kitten 74
  one-eared rabbit 74, 74
  save child from fall 244, 244
  very long earlobes 108
  very long hair in 25, 25
earthquakes
  earthquake-proof bed 230
  iPhone first-aid app used in 123
  makes river flow backwards 44
  moves city 40
  twists rail tracks 52, 52
Eastlack, Harry (U.S.A.) 115
eating strange objects 192
eBay, grandmother sold on 25
Ebneter, Arnold (U.S.A.) 240
echolocation, boy "sees" with 122
eclipses, solar 52
ectoplasm 176–7, 176–7
Eddy, Matt (U.S.A.) 153
Edge, Donald (U.K.) 188
Edison, Thomas (U.S.A.) 234
Edwards, Annette (U.K.) 110
eggs
  chicken lays huge 80
  eating eggshells 192, 192
  multiple double yolks 186
  smell of rotten eggs on gas bills 227
  tortoise eggs delivered by cesarean 80
  triple yolk 188
  in turtle fossil 80
Eiffel Tower, Paris
  rollerblader leaps from 157
  weight of 42
Einstein, Albert (Ger/U.S.A.) 122
Eiriksson, Fridgeir (Ice) 194, 194
El-Ajouz, Joe (Aus) 190
Eland, Karen (U.S.A.) 200
electricity
  at Chicago World's Fair 168
  long power outage 48
  shot through body 152, 152
elephants
  armor 57, 57
  car collides with 234
  crocodile grabs trunk 82, 82
  electrocuted 234, 234
  elephant-dung platform shoes 207, 207
  enormous 30–1, 31
  glass 44
  hanged 9, 234, 234
  plays with monitor lizard 21, 21
  secret language 82
  wash cars 64
Elizabeth II, Queen 238
  corgis 80
  jelly bean mosaic of 223
Elrington, Ptolemy (U.K.) 212, 212
Enslow, Seth (U.S.A.) 169
embroidery, map of London Underground
  214
Engel, Howard (Can) 121
English, Ron (U.S.A.) 208
Enslow, Seth (U.S.A.) 169
envelopes, bacon-flavored 186
escapologists 146–7, 146–7, 153, 154–5,
  154–5
Escobar, Andrés (Col) 96
Escobar, Pablo (Col) 16
Espin, Fernando (Ecu) 85
Esquivel, Martin (Mex) 67
Estrellas, Pedro (U.K.) 220
Etchells, Joseph (U.K.) 136
Eugenio, Michelle (U.S.A.) 14
Evans, Mark (U.K.) 203
Evans, Zach (U.K.) 50
Evaristti, Marco (Chl) 192
Everest, Mount
  parachuting onto 152
  young climber 157
Everingham, Luke (Aus) 43
Exon, Fiona (U.K.) 186
explosion, very powerful over Siberia 174
explosives, removed from scalp 105
eyebrows, very long hair 25
eyelids
  glued shut 120
  lifting weights with 237
  pulling airplane with 170

eyes
  beetle with bifocal eyes 63
  constant winking 126
  fishing hooks hanging under 157, 157
  frogs 78, 78
  popping out of head 163, 163
  reading in complete darkness 113
  sea urchins 72
  worm in 127
Eyser, George (U.S.A.) 89

face
  baby with two faces 124
  covered in hair 128–9, 129
  crying face in glacier 50, 50
  dislocating jaw 97, 165, 165–6
  hammering nails into 166, 166
  image of child on oven door 178
  image of Jesus Christ in satellite
    picture 50
  image of woman's face found on rabbit
    178
  transplant 123
  very ugly 164, 164–5
Facebook, time spent on 236
Faciu, Julika (Rom) 237
Fahey, Ron (Can) 217
Fairburn, Simeon (Aus) 127
Fairchild, Paul (U.S.A.) 217, 217
fairies
  photographs of 174, 174, 175, 175
  tree pods 178, 178
Falquerho, Yann (Fra) 50
Fan Qianrong (Chn) 192, 192
Fan Sijia (Chn) 114, 114
Fard, Arash (U.K.) 195
Farrell, Colin (Irl) 128
Faulkner, James (U.K.) 222
Fear, Liz (Aus) 75
feces, eating 192
feet
  armless people use 108, 123
  dog eats owner's toe 77
  extra toes 109, 109, 128
  footprints worn into floor 16, 16
  fork stuck in 122
  rotating 7, 7, 109
fence post, man speared with 110
Ferring, Winnie (U.S.A.) 169
festival, huge number of people at 44
Ficca, Claudia (Can) 212
Fichte, Ludwig (Ger) 156
Filthy Luker (U.K.) 220
Fine, Jay (U.S.A.) 40, 40
fingers
  amputated tip on keychain 122
  extra 128
  kept in freezer 110
  magnetic implants 107, 107
  man eats 107
  piercing coconuts with 124
  soccer player loses 99, 99
  very strong 110
Finkle, David (U.K.) 222
Finney, Clint (U.S.A.) 162
fire
  ants start 25
  blowtorch on face 163, 163
  bull with fiery horns 94, 94
  cat saves man 62
  cutting hair with 240
  dog saves owner 84
  enormous fireball 178
  escapologists 146, 146–7
  fiery crater in desert 45, 45
  fire-eating 18, 18
  firefighters' water freezes 55, 55
  ghost photographed in 181, 181
  man sleeps through house fire 16
  money burnt to keep child warm 16
  Olympic flame 91
  oxygen masks save tortoises 82
  river catches fire 44
  spontaneous human combustion 179,
    179
  stuntmen contest 170, 170
fireworks
  extreme festival 44, 44
  firecrackers thrown at man 44, 44
fish
  blind fish lives underground 70

fish (cont.)
  changes color 72
  climbing abilities 85
  eats turtle 70
  fall from sky 48
  found in bladder 112
  goldfish plays musical instruments 85
  hits kayaker 97
  hospital for 74
  huge number found dead 176
  long-lived goldfish 50
  look after manatees 70, 70
  regurgitating live fish 81
  thumb found inside 20
  in tunnels under Paris 51
fishing hooks, hanging under eyes 157, 157
Fitzpatrick, Noel (U.K.) 77
flagpole, car welded around 243
Flamburis, Harry "The Horse" (U.S.A.) 244
flies, dead flies as artwork 202, 202–3
floating, for long time 152, 152
floods, make gigantic lake 53
fog, catching in nets 41
Foggett, Shaun (U.K.) 78
Followill, Jared (U.S.A.) 208
Folse, John (U.S.A.) 193
food
  alien material in 189
  miniature clay models of 220
  prisoners' final meals re-created 213
  speed-eating 184–5, 184–5, 188
football
  injuries 99
  player insures hair 112
  footprints, scorched 105
Ford, Florence Irene (U.S.A.) 177, 177
forest, haunted 181
fork, in foot 122
Forman, Austin (Can) 61
Forse, Stephen (U.K.) 189, 189
Fortune, Lt. Ian (U.K.) 112
fossils
  of ancient spider 61
  eggs in fossil turtle 80
  giant limestone spikes 38
  squid ink 83
Foster, Mary Ann (U.S.A.) 44
Fowler, Tony (U.K.) 238
Franco, Dr. Vito (Ita) 201
Fredo (Chl) 221, 221
Freeman, Brian (Aus) 17
French fries
  speed-eating contest 188
  very long 186
frogs
  close road 78
  eaten by other creatures 85, 85
  eating still-beating hearts 189, 189
  eyes 78, 78
  long nose 73
  tadpoles with extra legs 79
  very tiny 77
Froman, Sonny (U.S.A.) 213
funeral home, wedding in 242
funerals
  ashes burnt in Viking ship 32
  Christmas-themed 32
  ice-cream van cortege 32
  JCB carries coffin 32, 32
  man goes to own 14
  motorbike hearses 32
  police tow body away 32
  telephone services shut down for 227
  tractors at 32
  very young undertaker 242
  for whale 79
  wives commit suttee 44
  of wrong person 242
Fung, Kai-Hung (Chn) 227, 227
fungi
  in dung 52
  microbial art 202
Furman, Ashrita (U.S.A.) 153, 153
furniture, phone book 217
Furze, Colin (U.K.) 136

Gabenhart, Darlene (U.S.A.) 7
Gadd, Will (Can) 95, 95
Gaga, Lady (U.S.A.) 206, 212, 212
Gage, Phineas (U.S.A.) 112, 112
Galbraith, Ryan (U.S.A.) 243

gall stones, multiple 108, *108*
gambler, mummified hand 15
Ganz, Sayaka (U.S.A.) 218, *218–19*
Gao, Mr. (Chn) 120, *120*
Gao Yang (Chn) 124
Gardner, Rulon (U.S.A.) 97
Garr, Susan (U.S.A.) 70
Gaynor, Gloria (U.S.A.) 219
Geary, Carl Robin Sr. (U.S.A.) 25
Geddes, Doyle (U.S.A.) 203
Gentry, Nick (U.K.) 221, *221*
Gettmann, Wolfgang (Ger) 63
Ghetti, Dalton (U.S.A.) 209
ghosts
  ectoplasm 176–7, *176–7*
  in forest 181
  green glow 177
  haunted house for sale 39
  photographs of 178, *178*, 181, *181*
  serves in pub 193
  of slaves 178
  spirits sold 28
  very haunted house 180
Gifford, Brad (U.K.) 107
Gilpin, James (U.K.) 193
Ginther, Joan (U.S.A.) 14
giraffes, collecting pictures of 213
glaciers
  crying face in 50, *50*
  man-made 54
gladiators, school for 47
Glazebrook, Peter (U.K.) 188
glider pilot, survives crash 139, *139*
Gliniecki, Al (U.S.A.) 7, *7*
Glissmeyer, Christie (U.S.A.) 239
gnome, giant 152
Gnuse, Julia (U.S.A.) 107, *107*
Goard, Debbie (U.S.A.) 187, *187*
goats
  clear weeds 78
  walks tightrope 81
Goebel, Sven (Ger) 170
gold
  in curry 193
  expensive toy car 135, *135*
  huge coin 24
  metal detector finds on first outing 20
  Monopoly set 218
  painting with 213
  tattoos 124
  vending machine for 47
  vuvuzela horn 214
goldfish
  longevity 70
  plays musical instruments 85
golf
  dog eats balls 79
  elderly player hits hole-in-one 92
  extreme golf 94
  insect loses match 93
  right-handed man plays with left hand 96
Goncalves, Ademir Jorge (Bra) 14
Gonzales (Can) 222
Goodall, Marion (U.K.) 25
Goosney, Stephen (Can) 14
Gorbunov, Sergei (Rus) 64
Gough, Fred (U.K.) 110
Gowen, Zach (U.S.A.) 93
graduate, elderly 149
graffiti, cloud 208
grandmothers
  huge number of descendants 16
  sold on eBay 25
Grant, John (U.K.) 72
Grant, Pauline (U.K.) 61
grapes, baboons eat vineyard's 66
grasshopper, pink 76, *76*
Great Wall of China, chocolate replica
  of 187
Greenberg, Brooke (U.S.A.) 115
Greenwood, Derek (U.K.) 32
Gregory, Barbara and Dennis (S.A.) 29
Gregory, Natasha (U.S.A.) 77
Gregory, Dr T. Ryan (Can) 202
Grendol, Joseph (U.S.A.) 165, *166*
Grey, Jimmy (U.S.A.) 42
Griffin, Paul (Can) 217
Griffiths, Frances (U.K.) 175, *175*
Griffiths, Margaret (U.K.) 242
Grylls, Bear (U.K.) 194
Grzebski, Jan (Pol) 110
Gschmeissner, Steve (U.K.) 118, *118*
guacamole, enormous bucket of 188
Guerra, Alain (U.S.A.) 213, *213*

Guevara, Che (Arg) 208
guinea fowl/chicken hybrid 72
guinea pigs, overrun apartment 84
guitarists
  multiple concerts in one day 207
  play to sharks 203
  whirling arm 215
Gulpen, Robert (Swi) 135
gum-boots, welly wanging contest 94
gum-wrappers, prom dress made of 208
Gunnarson, Dean (Can) 147
Gurjar, Badamsinh Juwansinh (Ind) 25
Guyot, Michel (Fra) 54
Guzy, Jozef (Pol) 32

Haase, Anna (Ger) 50
Hadland, Laura (U.K.) 218
Hagens, Gunther von (Ger) 114
hailstones, giant 40, 53
Haines, Leo (U.K.) 223
hair
  cutting with flame 240
  eating 192
  face covered in 128–9, *129*
  football player insures 112
  free haircuts 152
  long arm hair 25
  long eyebrow hair 25
  portraits on 104, *104*
  pulling bus with 237
  sculpture from 210, *210*
  upsidedown barber 236
  very long 25, 105, 113, *113*, 166, *166*
  very long ear hair 25, *25*
  very long leg hair 25
  very long mustache 25
  woman survives by sucking water
    from 113
Hairova, Ravila (Uzb) 79
Halder, Patit Paban (Ind) 74
Hallowes, Harry (U.K.) 47
Hallquist, Wayne and Laurie (U.S.A.) 126
hammock, enormous 206
hamsters, living in hotel as 50
handbags, chocolate 190
hands
  amputated fingertip on keychain 122
  breaking concrete with 237
  extra fingers 128
  finger kept in freezer 110
  grafted onto leg 229, *229*
  hairy transplants 108
  holding multiple tennis balls 169
  magnetic implants in fingers 107, *107*
  man eats finger 107
  mummified 15
  nail in 123
  one-handed basketball player 96
  one-handed climber 108
  painting with corpse's hand 213, *213*
  piercing coconuts with finger 124
  pulled off in tug-of-war 109
  soccer player loses finger 99, *99*
  very strong 110
handsprings, multiple back 169
Hanrahan, Karen (U.S.A.) 195
Hansen, Kasper (Den) 228–9, *229*
Hansen, Phil (U.S.A.) 11, *11*
Hare, Steve (U.K.) 214
hares, permanent pregnancy 75
Haridas (Ind) 158
Harp, Christy (U.S.A.) 187
Harrington, Les (U.K.) 42
Harrington, Padraig (Irl) 94
Harris, Joshua Allen (U.S.A.) 200
Harrop, Bob (U.K.) 188
Harsh, Navratan (Ind) 66, *66*
Hart, Colin (U.K.) 24
Hartel, Irmgard (Den) 89
Haruf, Kent (U.S.A.) 208
harvestmen 68, *68–9*
Hastings, David (U.K.) 181
Havel, Dan (U.S.A.) 43, *43*
hay, castle built of 210
Hay, Tran Van (Vnm) 25, 105
Hayes, Anato (U.S.A.) 163, *163*
Hayes, Chris (U.K.) 15, *15*
Hayes, Reg (U.K.) 152
Hazelton, Paul (U.K.) 221
head
  boy survives hook penetrating 126
  bullets in 108, 128
  burying in sand 158, *158*
  camera implanted in back of 219

head (*cont.*)
  hammering nail into 19, *19*
  horn implanted in 111, *111*, 122
  horns on forehead 115
  human heads found in air freight 112
  iron rod through 112, *112*
  knife stabbed right through 118
  live explosive removed from 105
  looking backwards 164, *164*
  missing from hanged man 110
  nail found in 113
  painting on 213
  preserved cryogenically 24
  two-headed snake 67
  walking with milk bottle on 153, *153*
heart
  artificial heart made with toys 230
  baby "frozen" after surgery 118
  man survives long time after stops
    beating 124
Hedblom, Ben (U.S.A.) 238
hedge, very long 190
hedgehog, no-parking lines painted over
  dead 16, *16*
Heinrichs, Ben (U.S.A.) 84
Helland, Ola (Nor) 213
Hempleman-Adams, David (U.K.) 194
Hendrix, Jimi (U.S.A.)
  leather portrait of 203
Henriques, Jack (U.K.) 191
Herbert, Tom (U.K.) 188
Hernandez, Christian (Mex) 97
Hernandez, Francisco Jr. (U.S.A.) 244
Hersch, Dave (U.S.A.) 134
Hiemenz, Bob "Tracker Bob" (U.S.A.) 215
Higley, Doug (U.S.A.) 220, *220*
Hildebrandt, Norah (U.S.A.) 26, 27, *27*
Hill, Jamie (U.S.A.) 170
Hinds, Lt. Sidney (U.S.A.) 90
Hindu sadhus 158–9, *158–9*
hippopotamus, pink 82
Hitchcock, Alfred (U.K.), image projected
  onto trees 174, *174*
Hitler, Adolf (Ger) 16, 91
Hjelmqvist, Fredrik (Swe) 219
Ho, Dr. Thienna (U.S.A.) 110
Ho Eng Hui (Mal) 124
Hodges, Casey (Aus) 160
Hodgson, Alistair (U.K.) 123
Hofstra, Henk (Nld) 222
Hoketsu, Hiroshi (Jap) 89
Holm, Irmgard (U.S.A.) 120
holograms 207, *207*
Hong Hong (Chn) 109
Hook, Owen (U.K.) 143
Hooper, Cedric (U.K.) 190
Hoover, Cynthia (U.S.A.) 113
Horkin, Kevin (U.K.) 178, *178*
horns
  on forehead 115
  implanted in head 111, *111*, 122
horses
  antivenom production 124
  enormous rocking horse 212
  high dives by 14, *14*
  Hummer converted to horse-drawn
    carriage 140
  Olympic Games 90
  riding injuries 99
  very intelligent 84
  very small 77
  veterinarian trapped under 83
hospital, for pet fish 74
Hostetler, Keri (U.S.A.) 70
Hot, Les (U.S.A.) 20, *20*
hot cross bun, very old 187
hot dog, very expensive 186
hot-water bottle, being blown up 7, *7*
Houghton, Jane (U.K.) 115
houses
  bulldozed to prevent bank repossessing
    43
  converted into 007 movie set 42
  covered in greenish goo 174
  cow jumps onto roof 60
  decorated with cigarette packets 43, *43*
  haunted 39, 178, 180

houses (*cont.*)
  hit by meteorites 48
  lava engulfs 37
  living in trees 39
  made of steel 168
  ram runs amok in 72
  rotating house 43
  as sculpture 43, *43*
  upside-down 244
  very narrow 53
  very small 47, *47*
Howard, Brierley (U.K.) 66
Howarth, Cyril (U.K.) 235
Howell, Gwen (U.K.) 76
Howerton, Clarence C. "Major Mite"
  (U.S.A.) 116–17, *116–17*
Hu Gua (Chn) 186
Hua Chi (Chn) 16, *16*
Huang, Victor (Nzl) 85
Huang Jianjun (Chn) 143
Huang Lijie (Chn) 82
Huang Yuyen (Twn) 80
Huckvale, David (U.K.) 128
Hughes, Howard (U.S.A.) 140, *140–1*
Hughes, Stuart (U.K.) 135
hugs, multiple 149
Hui Chung (Chn) 105
hummus, enormous plate of 190
hurricanes, tree survives 50
Hutton, Paul (U.K.) 137
hypnotizing rabbits 80

ibexes, climb dam face 71, *71*
ice
  birds dive through 74
  falls from sky 44
  firefighters' water freezes 55, *55*
  frozen waterfall 95, *95*
  giant hailstones 40, 53
  icicles kill people 49
  immersion in 160, *160*
  lake under 41
  lighthouse covered in 53, *53*
  man-made glaciers 54
  musical instruments made of 210
  planes land on 245, *245*
ice cream
  for dogs 190
  ice-cream vans at funeral 32
  whole meal of 188
ice hockey
  lucky escape for player 98, *98*
  match delayed for long time 92
igloo, built in yard 42
influenza, anti-flu suit 226
Ingram, Ted (U.K.) 152
Inoue, Satoko (Jap) 229
INSA (U.K.) 207
insects
  bug-eating parties 187, *187*
  eating 195, *195*
  mosquito-killing contest 80
Internet
  anti-leak document leaks 16
  pigeon faster than broadband 77
  time spent on Facebook 236
invisibility coat 230, *230*
iPad, portraits made on 215
Irwin, Steve (Aus) 64
Isner, John (U.S.A.) 96
isopods, giant 83, *83*
Isungset, Terje (Nor) 210
Ivanisevic, Goran (Cro) 92
Ivanov, Vyacheslav (Rus) 90

Jablon, Jim (U.S.A.) 134, *134–5*
Jackson, Brian (U.S.A.) 7, *7*
Jackson, Jessiah (U.S.A.) 126
Jackson, Michael (U.S.A.)
  candy portrait of 222, *222*
  income after death 217
  pumpkin portrait of 222
James, Cathy (Aus) 79
jaw, dislocating 97, 165, *165–6*
Jefferson, Thomas (U.S.A.), portrait on
  hair 104, *104*
Jeffries, John (U.S.A.) 17
jelly bean mosaic 223
jellyfish
  adhesive tape sculpture 202, *202*
  fisherman stung by 63
  robot 228
  turned into caramel candies 195
Jennings, Desiree (U.S.A.) 110

Jesus Christ
  face in satellite picture 50
  man named Lord Jesus Christ 238
  toast art 183, *183*
Ji Yong-Ho (Kor) 214, *214*
Jian Tianjin (Chn) 108
Jiang Juxiang (Chn) 28
Jin Songhao (Chn) 160, *160*
Jin Y. Hua (Chn) 104, *104*
Johnson, Larry (U.S.A.) 112
Johnson, Lyndon B. (U.S.A.), portrait on
  hair 104, *104*
Johnsrud, Brian and Jared (U.S.A.) 238
jokes, very long comedy gig 214
Jolie, Angeline (U.S.A.) 128
Jones, Rhiannon Elizabeth (U.K.) 29
Jones, Robert (U.K.) 47
Jones, Ron (U.K.) 242
Jones, Ron (U.S.A.) 110
Jordan, Bethany (U.K.) 128
judges, numbers of 53
juggling
  underwater 148, *148*
  upside down 160
Juliff, Laura (Aus) 160
Jupiter
  Great Red Spot shrinks 49
  loses belts 180

Kanaguri, Shizo (Jap) 90
Kane, Kyle (U.K.) 114
Kang Mengru (Chn) 118
Kangkang (Chn) 124
Kanichka 66, *166*
karaoke, nonstop 215
karate, young champion 169
Kato, Sogen (Jap) 32
Kautza, Andy and Connie (U.S.A.) 152
Kaye, Luke (U.S.A.) 119
Kazemi, Ali (Iran) 90
Keats, Jonathan (U.S.A.) 209
Kellas, John (U.K.) 72
Kelly, Lisa (U.K.) 118
Kendik, Alex (Can) 7, *7*
Kennedy, John F. (U.S.A.)
  portrait on hair 104, *104*
  salt-and-pepper shaker 239
Kenny, Gene (U.S.A.) 171
Keonig, Peter (Ger) 244
Kepner, Jeff (U.S.A.) 108
Kerr, Henry (U.K.) 32
ketchup, banana 195
Key lime pie, giant 186
Keysaw, Chelsea (U.S.A.) 124
Kézi, Gábor (Hun) 243
Khanapiyeva, Sakinat (Rus) 148
Khris, Taig (Alg) 157
Kidder, Christopher O. (U.S.A.) 219
kidneys
  giant stone removed from 120, *120*
  large number of stones removed from
    120, *120*
  nail removed from 120, *120*
Kilgast, Stephanie 220
killer whales, penguin escapes 62, *62*
King, Stephen (U.S.A.) 209
Kings of Leon (U.S.A.) 208
Kipping, Chelsey (U.S.A.) 169
Kirby, Dr. Richard (U.K.) 70, *70*
Kirchen, Derek (U.K.) 121
kissing cobras 241, *241*
Kistler, Samuel Stephens (U.S.A.) 230, *230*
kite-powered cargo ship 141
Klein, Roelof (Nld) 88
Kleis, Dick (U.S.A.) 238
Kleman, Vic (U.S.A.) 242
Klingon, performance of *A Christmas
  Carol* in 219
knives
  man orders coffee with knife stuck in
    chest 244
  in neck 114
  plasma knife 227
  stabbed right through head 118
  standing on 237
Knotek, Ryan (U.S.A.) 242
Kober, Martin (U.S.A.) 219
Kocaman, Hatice (Tur) 126
Kolodzinski, Jeff (U.S.A.) 92
Kongee, Leo (U.S.A.) 166, *166*
Kopp, Benjamin (U.S.A.) 110, 136
Kosen, Sultan (Tur) 114

Krankl, Matthias (Ger) 142
Krause, Fred (U.S.A.) 64
Krupnik, Ari (U.S.A.) 208
Kuksi, Kris (U.S.A.) 203, 203–5
Kulick, Kelly (U.S.A.) 93
Kulkarni, Deepa (U.S.A.) 110
Kumar, Anil (Ind) 121
Kumar, Santosh (Ind) 140
Kumthekar, Heramb Ashok (Ind) 128
Kurkul, Gennadi (U.K.) 72

LA Pop Art 215, 215
Laak, Phil (U.S.A.) 160
Lacey, Lexi (U.K.) 124
Lagravere, Michel (Mex) 237
Lahue, Mike (U.S.A.) 191
Laity, Bill (U.S.A.) 93, 93
Lajic, Radivoje (Bos) 48
Lambert, Kyle (U.K.) 215
landmines, rats hunt 28, 28
landscapes, model 216, 216
Langan, Mark (U.S.A.) 202
Langeder, Hannes (Aut) 142, 142, 207
Langseth, Hans (Nor) 25
lanterns, paper 171
Lapeyrouse, Tracy (U.K.) 76
LaPierre, Sandy (U.S.A.) 60
Larkin, Tommy (Can) 14
Larrieux, Vicki (U.K.) 193
Larson, Lief (U.S.A.) 200
LaRue, Josh (U.S.A.) 110
Latin tattoos 128
Laue, Kevin (U.S.A.) 96
laundry, Olympic Games 89
laundry lint, replica of The Last Supper 238–9, 239
Laurello, Martin (U.S.A.) 164, 164
Lauridsen, Henrik (Den) 228–9, 229
Lavasseur, George (U.S.A.) 237, 237
lawn mower, very fast 160
lead, gargling with molten 18, 19
Lee, Jin-gyu (Kor) 244
leeches
  found in girl's nose 128
  robber's blood found in 24
Lefson, Joanne (S.A.) 77
LeGendre, Robert (U.S.A.) 89
LEGO®
  mending monuments with 210
  replica of airplane 208
  ship replicas 218, 221
legs
  amputees climb mountain 112
  armless and legless woman 164, 164
  bent behind head 7, 7
  bionic legs for cat 77
  five-legged rat 60
  free bionic leg 128
  hand grafted onto 229, 229
  legless cyclist 106, 106
  man sews wound up himself 109
  one-legged wrestler 93
  prosthetic legs for cow 63
  self-amputation 108
  six-legged calf 79
  soccer player breaks 100, 100–1
  stretching bone 127
  tadpoles with extra legs 79
  two-legged lamb 60, 60
  two-legged pig 84, 84
  very long hair on 25
Lei Zhiqian (Chn) 135
lemurs, rub themselves with millipedes 78
Lendavi, Reverend Zoltan (Hun) 240
Lennon, John (U.K.),
  phone book portrait 145, 145
  toilet sold 25
Leonardo da Vinci (Ita)
  cholesterol levels of Mona Lisa 201
  coffee painting of Mona Lisa 200
  giant Mona Lisa 222
  laundry lint replica of The Last Supper 238–9, 239
  Rubik's cube version of The Last Supper 208
Leonardo, Jesus (U.S.A.) 93
Lepore, Tony (U.S.A.) 244
Levi, Kobi (Isr) 206
Levine, Philip (U.K.) 213
levitation, with magnets 230
Lewis, Jim (U.S.A.) 25

Lewis, Paul (U.K.) 115
Li Guiwen (Chn) 135
Li Liuqun (Chn) 187
Li Sanju (Chn) 195
Li Weiguo (Chn) 135
Libertiny, Tomas Gabzdil (Nld) 85, 85
libraries
  huge number of books borrowed 206
  very overdue books 203, 221
Liew Siaw Hsia (Mal) 124
Lighthart, Edward (U.S.A.) 123
lighthouses
  covered in ice 53, 53
  in lakes 53
lightning
  boy struck on Friday 13th 20
  cow survives 81, 81
  hits Hong Kong 41
  hotspot 49
  lucky escape 107
  patterns on skin 118, 118
  strikes Statue of Liberty 40, 40
lights
  at Chicago World's Fair 168
  luminous beams in sky 44
  Marfa Lights 174
  powered by dog poop 43
  produced from patient's chest 176
  rays from star switch on 168
limousine, tractor-trailer 140, 140
Lin, Mr (Chn) 84
Lin Su (Chn) 29, 29
Lin Yaohui (Chn) 126
Lincoln, Abraham (U.S.A.), assassination 110
lines, alignments on 181
Ling Wan (Chn) 42
lions
  burgers made from 195
  crochet 200, 200
  lives with tiger and bear 66, 66
  opens car door 82, 82
  owl chick escapes 76
  stolen from circus 14
  zebra camouflage and 81
liposuction, eating own fat 192
lipstick, mass application of 221
Liu, Victor (Chn) 200, 200
Liu Chengrui (Chn) 126
Liu Wei (Chn) 108
Lizardman 8, 8
lizards
  elephant plays with 21, 21
  lizard boy 66, 66
Lloyd, Naomi (U.K.) 241
Lobrano, Roberto (Ita) 188
lobster, blown up by World War II mine 20
locusts, as pizza topping 186
logs, sculpture mistaken for pile of 217
Lombardo, Christi (U.S.A.) 242
London, Ken (U.S.A.) 140, 140–1
London Underground, embroidered map of 214
Loos, Arthur (U.S.A.) 163, 163
Lopez, Felipe (U.S.A.) 96
Lopez, Heidi (U.S.A.) 16
Lorenc, Richard (U.S.A.) 29, 29
Lotito, Michel (Fra) 192
Love, Robyn (U.S.A.) 210
Lovlid, Unni (Nor) 219
Loys, François de (Swi) 180, 180
Luciano, Davide (Can) 212
luck, accident survivor wins lottery 244
lunch, on very long table 193
Lunden, Leon de (Bel) 90
lungs
  bone stuck in 121
  bullet in 114
  cashew nut in 121
  collapsible 62
  false teeth in 121
  grass found in 121
  pea plant growing in 110
  plastic eating utensil found in 121
  stolen 29
  twigs in 121, 121

Ma Xiuxian (Chn) 24
McAdou, J.M. (U.S.A.) 241, 241
macaroni, enormous meal of 193
McCarthy, Ellen (Irl) 107

McCartney, Macie (U.S.A.) 109
McCartney, Paul (U.S.A.) 110
McClure, Daryl (U.K.) 32
McCormack, Janice (U.K.) 193
McDaniels, Grace (U.S.A.) 164, 164–5
McFarlane, Steve (U.S.A.) 124, 124
McGlone, Brittney (Aus) 160
MacGregor, Helen (U.K.) 14
McHargue, Ozella (U.S.A.) 32
Machida, Lyoto (Bra) 192
Mack, Captain Ringman (U.S.A.) 163, 163
McKenzie, Rosita (U.K.) 219
McNaught, Ryan (Aus) 208
McPhee, Ben (Aus) 148
McPhee, Russell (Aus) 122
McPherson, Lydia (U.S.A.) 166, 166
McTindal, Russ (U.S.A.) 73
maggots, in mouth 156
Mahardika, Ari (Idn) 223, 223
Mahut, Nicolas (Fra) 96
mail
  hawk attacks postman 76
  lake deliveries 40
  long-lost 235
  very late delivery 17, 20
Maimaiti Hali (Chn) 124
Maine, Patti Froman (U.S.A.) 213
"Major Mite" (U.S.A.) 9, 9, 116–17, 116–17
Malarchuk, Clint (U.S.A.) 98, 98
Malindzi, Thuli (S.A.) 187
Malvada, Marina (Can) 190, 190
manatee, fish look after 70, 70
Mandela, Asha (U.S.A.) 113, 113
Mangrum, Lloyd (U.S.A.) 93
manholes, large collection of 169
Manley, John (U.S.A.) 121
Manorama, Aachi (Ind) 210
manure
  elephant-dung platform shoes 207, 207
  fungi in 52
  message spelt out in 238
  recycled into asphalt 237
  replica of Venus de Milo 218
  T-shirts covered in 213
map, embroidered 214
Maphumulo, Nkosinathi (S.A.) 217
marathons
  Olympic Games 88
  running with tumble-drier on back 93
March, Dave (U.S.A.) 142
Marfa Lights 174
margarine sculpture 186, 188, 188
Marley, Bob (Jam) 197, 197
Marque, Albert (Fra) 210
Mars, methane on 41
Marsh, Garry and Joan (U.K.) 70
Marsh, Steve (U.K.) 243
Marshall, Mary (U.K.) 177, 177
Marshall, Rob (Aus) 210
Martin, Anna (U.S.A.) 179
Martin, Anthony (U.S.A.) 153, 154–5, 154–5
Masala, Daniele (Ita) 90
Masher, Eddie (U.S.A.) 114, 114
Maso da San Friano (Ita) 210
Mason, Paul (U.K.) 115
matchsticks
  replica of Lord of the Rings city 218
Mathew, Joby (Ind) 123
Matt the Knife (U.S.A.) 147
Matthews, John (U.S.A.) 127
mattress, money hidden in 17
Maxton, GarE (U.S.A.) 219
May, Henrik (Ger) 96, 96
May, Sydney (U.S.A.) 60
Mayers, Rev (Aus) 211, 211
mayonnaise, causes highway crash 236
mazes
  cartoon characters in 220
  cow-shaped 216
Mazzotta, Matthew (U.S.A.) 43
meat, bikini made of raw 206
meatballs
  giant 190
  made with own fat 192
Medici, Cosimo I de' (Ita) 210
Mehta, Sameer (Ind) 128
melons
  close motorway 137
  slicing on woman's stomach 186
Mendez, Danny (U.S.A.) 242, 242
mercury, telescope mirror 227

Merlini, David (Hun) 147
mermaids, fake 220, 220
Meselmani, Hasnah Mohamed (Leb) 177
metal
  removed from stomach 108
  shrinking with magnets 228
metal detector, finds treasure on first outing 20
meteorites
  crater found in satellite picture 52
  explosion over Siberia 174
  hits truck 49
  multiple strikes on house 48
methane
  lake on moon 38
  lights powered by dog poop 43
  on Mars 41
Metz, Jonathan (U.S.A.) 121
Meyer, Allen (Can) 94
Meyer, Edward (Can) 9
Miao, Mrs (Chn) 108, 108
mice
  found in can of cola 189
  found in loaf of bread 189, 189
  found in milk container 189
Michelangelo (Ita), long-lost painting by 219
Mickelson, Phil (U.S.A.) 96
microbial art 202
migraine
  Chinese accent after 110
  unusual cure for 110
migration, by Arctic terns 62
Milhiser, John (U.S.A.) 148, 148
milk
  dead mouse found in 189
  milkman receives honor wearing cow suit 238
  Shakespeare plays to improve yields 215
  statues drink 178
millipedes, lemurs rub themselves with 78
mine, lobster blown up by 20
Ming Li (Chn) 229, 229
Mitchell, Gary (Can) 188
Mitchell, Ralph (U.K.) 152
Mitzscherlich, Uwe (Ger) 80
Mobell, Sidney (U.S.A.) 218
Mohammed, Hassani 115, 115
Moline, Dino (Arg) 138, 138
Monaro, Anna (Ita) 176
Monet, Claude (Fra), giant replica of painting 212
money
  burnt to alert rescuers 14
  burnt to keep child warm 16
  children find stolen 29
  coins in stomach 121
  dollar bill mosaics 222
  hidden in mattress 17
  hidden in shoe 15
Monforto, Steve (U.S.A.) 94
monk, mummified 22, 22
monkeys
  as guards 96
  smuggled onto plane 60
Monopoly set, gold 218
Monroe, Marilyn (U.S.A.)
  coffee mosaic of 209
  made from butterfly wings 233, 233
  portrait on leaf 200
  typed portrait of 201
Moon
  beer made by light of full moon 188
  giant pit on 44
  scratch 'n' sniff artwork 216
moons
  changing places 49
  methane lake on 38
Moore, Amanda (U.K.) 119, 119
Moore, Caroline (U.S.A.) 52
Moore, Hilmar (U.S.A.) 149
moped, with flamethrower 136
Morrell, Professor A.L. (U.S.A.) 164, 164
Morrison, Chris (U.K.) 79
Morse Code, blind man writes book in 110
mosaics
  coffee 209
  dice 208
  dollar bills 222
  huge mural 207

mosaics (cont.)
  jelly bean 223
  plastic balls 212, 212
  screws 216
mosquito-killing contest 80
Moss, Channing (U.S.A.) 121
Moss, Kate (U.K.) 201
motorcycles
  alligator made into 134, 134–5
  backflipping dirt bike over helicopter 152
  embalmed body on 28, 28
  as hearses 32
  long jump on 156, 169
  man buried with 244
  miniature 140
  ridden over stomach 237
  rider leaps to safety on truck 135
  riders trapped in drain 235, 235
  swan knocks rider off 81
  Wall of Death 150–1, 150–1
  without front wheel 141, 141
mountains
  amputees climb 112
  banana peels found on 188
  extreme golf 94
  highest unclimbed 49
  man digs tunnel through 54
  painted white 48
  school built on side of 52
  young climbers 148, 157
mouth
  lifting weights with 92, 92
  maggots in 156
movies
  house converted into 007 movie set 42
  lost Chaplin film 223
  stage version of Ben Hur 200
  12 parts for one actress 203
  veteran actor 210
Mozart, Wolfgang Amadeus (Aut) 50
Muhr, Magnus (Swe) 202
Mullane, Simon and Angie (U.K.) 42
Mullen, Dermot (U.K.) 77
Mullikin, Garret (U.S.A.) 127
Mumbere, Charles Wesley (Uga) 240
mummies 22–3, 22–3
  DNA extracted from 229
  European mummies found in China 174
  fake 220, 220
  mummified hand 15
Munch, Edvard (Nor) 202
Murchison, Lauren (U.S.A.) 90
Murdock, Karen 84
music
  broadcast from stomach 219
  concert for dogs 222
  concert in catacombs 51
  concerts in sewer 219
  fan travels long distance to concerts 217
  helps bacteria work faster 50
  listening to one album constantly 214
  pigeon droppings halt concert 208
  very long concert 222
musical instruments
  fungal treatment for violin 230
  goldfish plays 85
  made of ice 210
  played without touching 202
mustache, very long 25
Mwangi, Lazarus 115, 115

nachos, giant tray of 190
Nadiri, Sikeli (Fij) 105
Nagananddaswamy, S.C. (Ind) 152, 152
nails
  hammering into face 166, 166
  in hand 123
  in head 19, 19, 113
  lying on bed of 159, 159
  removed from kidney 120, 120
Nasheed, President (Mdv) 54
nativity scene, on head of a pin 209
neck, impaled on stick 127
needles
  in body 122
  removed from brain 126
Nelson, Admiral Horatio (U.K.) 216
Nero, Emperor 88
Netherland, Dan (U.S.A.) 110
Nevins, Dan (U.S.A.) 112
Newman, Lyn (U.K.) 72

Newman, Mike (U.K.) 139, 139
Niagara Falls, stopped 52, 52
Nijhuis, Tony (U.K.) 142
Nikulin, Ivan (Rus) 128
Nintendo, as collector's item 200
nipples, pulling weights with 163, 163
Nixon, Richard (U.S.A.), portrait on hair 104, 104
Nixon, Steven (U.K.) 114
Noel, Markley (U.S.A.) 220
Noel-Baker, Philip (U.K.) 91
Noemmer, Franz-Xaver 74, 74
Nolasco, Jess (Can) 188
Nong Youhui (Chn) 113
Norphel, Chewang (Ind) 54
Norris, Matt (U.S.A.) 141
Norsigian, Rick (U.S.A.) 207
nose
    bullet sneezed out of 126
    leech found in 128
    nosebleed causes death 122
    snakes in 237
    touching for long time 148, 148
    using electric drill on 237
nuclear reactor, homemade 229
nude people, mass hug 201
numbers
    baby's significant birthday 29
    lucky number in lottery 28
    memorizing 171
    unlucky cell phone number 28
Nurmi, Paavo (Fin) 89
nut, in lung 121
Nuwame, Luanga (Can) 203

Oatman, Olive (U.S.A.) 26, 26
Obama, Barack (U.S.A.)
    portrait of on leaf 200
    pumpkin portrait of 222
    typed portrait of 201
O'Connor, John (Irl) 179
octopuses
    floods aquarium 79
    huge tentacles through window 220
    live in coconut shells 79
    psychic abilities 79, 79
    steals camera 85
O'Donnell, Daniel (Irl) 217
Officer, Robert (U.S.A.) 148, 148
Ofili, Chris (U.K.) 207
Ogg, Kate (Aus) 118
O'Hearn, John (U.S.A.) 212, 212
oil wells, under school 48
Okrand, Marc (U.S.A.) 219
Oliver, Paul (Aus) 73
Olympic Games 88–91
Onac, Aydin (U.K.) 195
Onassis, Jackie (U.S.A.), salt-and-pepper shaker 239
Ondash, Jeff (U.S.A.) 149
orangutans
    takes photographs 60
    in tunnels under Paris 51
    zoo's animal escape drill 60, 60
organs
    organ donor 110
    pierced by rod 128
    in wrong places 128
origami, tiny models 206
Ortega, Daniel Roberto (U.S.A.) 33, 33
Orwell, George (U.K.) 208
otter, on kayaking trips 63
oven, image of child's face on door 178
owl chick, escapes lion 76

paintings
    of ants 222
    body painting 12, 12–13, 201, 201, 213
    by chimpanzee 67
    by dog 61
    by holidaymaker 210
    by whale 80
    coffee 200
    giant Mona Lisa 222
    giant replica of Monet painting 212
    on head 213
    help police improve powers of observation 203
    laundry lint replica of The Last Supper 238–9, 239
    many artists for 213
    microbial art 202
    Munch's The Scream re-created with cardboard boxes 202

paintings (cont.)
    portrait on hair 104, 104
    of same subject 210
    thrown away by mistake 206
    using blood 211, 211
    using typewriter 222
    using words from Alice in Wonderland 215, 215
    very early image of a watch 210
    very valuable painting found behind sofa 219
    very young artists 217, 223
    with corpse's hand 213, 213
    with gold 213
    with remote-control cars 215
Palladino, Eusapia (Ita) 176
pandas
    dog disguised as 73, 73
    dung replica of Venus de Milo 218
    genetic puzzle 72
paper
    eating 192
    quantities used for books 213
    tiny origami models 206
paragliding, looping the loop 243
Parfitt, George (U.K.) 29
Park, Morace (U.K.) 223
Parker, April (U.K.) 75
parking space, very valuable 141
parking tickets, relaxation instructions on 235
Parkinson family (U.S.A.) 83
parrots
    arrested 76
    mystery illness 62
    scares off burglars 72
Parrott, Rev. Canon David (U.K.) 242
Parsons, Ken (U.S.A.) 215
particle accelerator, bread shuts down 226
pasta, enormous meal of 193
Pastrana, Travis (U.S.A.) 152
Paswaan, Deepak (Ind) 108
Pattison, Jim Jr. (Can) 6, 6
Patiz, Vicente (Ger) 207
Patton, George S. (U.S.A.) 91
Pazos, Leslie (U.S.A.) 16
Pazos, Saby (U.S.A.) 16
Peabody, Harold (U.S.A.) 32
Peacock, Melissa (U.K.) 110
Pearce, Henry (Aus) 89
Peladi, Zsolt and Geza (Hun) 24
Pemberton, Wesley (U.S.A.) 25
Pemberton, Zoe (U.K.) 25
pen, enormous 156
pencils, carving tips 208–9, 209
Penfold, Sheila (U.K.) 93
penguin, escapes killer whales 62, 62
Pennington, Brad (U.S.A.) 97
Penny, Jessica (Aus) 160
Penrose, Cliff (U.K.) 80
performance art 210
Peric, Daniel (Ger) 123
Pericolo, Bridget and Angelo (U.S.A.) 14
Peterkin-Vertanesian, Brian (U.S.A.) 25
Petty, Ann (U.K.) 217
Pheidippides (Grc) 88
Philippoussis, Mark (Aus) 92
phone books
    furniture and sculpture from 217
    portraits from 145, 145
photographs
    blind photographer 219
    children photographed every day 218
    clones of photographer in 223, 223
    documenting growth of beard 239
    of fairies 174, 174, 175, 175
    of ghosts 178, 178, 181, 181
    of model landscapes 216, 216
    orangutan takes 60
    of roadside litter 208
    taken every year 217
    underwater gallery 222
    very valuable 207
pi, calculating 170
pigs
    enormous tusks 72
    invited to vote in election 61
    real piggy bank 24
    tattooed with designer logos 201
    on trampoline 76
    two-legged 84, 84
Pilâtre de Rozier, Jean-François (Fra) 17
pillow, marrying 244

pineapples, as status symbols 188
pistols, duelling at Olympic Games 90
pizza
    exotic meats 195
    giant 190
    huge chain of 188
    locust topping 186
placenta, in health drink 186
planets
    atmosphere of vaporized rock 49
    Jupiter loses belts 180
    Jupiter's Great Red Spot shrinks 49
    methane on Mars 41
    new ring found round Saturn 53
    solar eclipses 52
    very windy 48
plankton 70, 70
plants, toilet for treeshrews 62, 62
plasma knife 227
plastic bags, inflatable polar bears made from 200
plates, edible 189
playing cards
    cutting cucumber with 171, 171
    memorizing 171
    model of hotel 239
    throwing long distance 171
plowing competition, teenager wins 171
Podolsky, Dominik (Aut) 14
Poe, Jesse (U.S.A.) 243
poem boxing contest 217
poison, antivenom production 124
poker, very long session 160
Polamalu, Troy (U.S.A.) 112
polar bears
    cow mistaken for 241
    made from plastic bags 200
Poleykett, Scott (U.K.) 96
police
    chihuahuas attack 74
    dancing traffic cop 244
    guard dam 38
    improving powers of observation 203
    use tractor 137
    win lottery 20
Pollock, Jackson (U.S.A.) 223
Pondella, Christian (U.S.A.) 95, 95
Pontico, Ruth (U.S.A.) 117, 117
Ponting, Herbert (U.K.) 159, 159
Poole, Mitch (U.S.A.) 200
Pope, Simon (U.K.) 186
Popeyed Perry 163, 163
Popova, Julia (Rus) 114
population, boy/girl imbalance 53
Pordaeng, Loung (Tha) 22, 22
portraits
    burger grease 11, 11
    candy 222, 222
    carved pumpkins 222
    cassette tape 197, 197
    on floppy disks 221, 221
    on iPad 215
    leather 203
    made with dead ants 58–9, 58–9
    mosaic 208, 212, 212
    non-stop drawings 207
    portraits on hair 104, 104
    three-dimensional illusion 206, 206
    toast 183, 183, 218
    typed 201
postage stamps
    large collection of 170
    very valuable 16
postcards
    recipient pictured in 14
    very late delivery 20
postman, hawk attacks 76
potato, enormous 188
potholes
    for sale 136
    turned into artworks 212
Poussin, Alexandre and Sonia (Fra) 169
Powell, Ivor (U.K.) 96
Powell, Lewis (U.S.A.) 110
Pras, Bernard (Bel) 206
Prasad, Padma (Ind) 193
Pratt, Don (U.K.) 141
pregnancy
    prenatal surgery 109
    woman with two uteruses 108
Presley, Elvis (U.S.A.), candy portrait of 222, 222
Prichard, Richard (U.K.) 20

priest, skateboarding 240
prisoners
    cat not allowed to visit 244
    digs out of prison with spoon 20
    final meals re-created 213
    prisoners' Tour de France 92
    as school mascot 43
    typo keeps man behind bars 16
prisons
    dummy guard 24
    escapologist gets out of 153
    man caught in women's 29
    restaurant in 194
Proulx, Suzanne (U.S.A.) 239, 239
pubs
    drinking beer in many different 193
    ghost serves in 193
    moved up hill 47
    rabbit visits 78
    very isolated 38
Pugh, Lewis (U.K.) 107
Pullen, Ernest (U.S.A.) 17
pumpkins
    giant 187
    portraits carved in 222
punchbag, human 244
Purbrick, Hilaire (U.K.) 50
Pushnik, Freda (U.S.A.) 164, 164
Putin, Vladimir (Rus) 222
pythons
    as assault weapon 238
    fishermen catch 61
    lives in sewer 80
    moves into rabbit hutch 61
    "Serpent Queen" 156, 156
    trapped in washing machine 61
    tries to catch marsupial 61, 61
    X-rays of python digesting a rat 228–9, 229

Qin Yuan (Chn) 121
quadruplets 108, 118
Quran, tiny copy of 217

rabbits
    cleared from island 40
    dust bunnies 239, 239
    hypnotizing 80
    image of woman's face found on 178
    jumping contests 94
    one-eared 74, 74
    plays slot machines 78
Rabbo, Hassan Abed (Leb) 217
Railton, Paul (U.K.) 236
rain, bacteria in 177
Rains, Diane (U.S.A.) 85
Rak, Tomas (U.K.) 65, 65
Ramannavar, Dr Mahantesh (Ind) 127, 127
Ramlan (Idn) 108
Ramos, Cristiam (Mex) 222, 222
Ramos, Enrique (Mex) 107, 107, 233, 233
Ramsey, Chris (U.S.A.) 219
Raphael (Ita), valuable drawing by 209
Rasmuson, Elizabeth (U.S.A.) 208
Rasmuson, Svante (Swe) 90
Rathbone, Keira (U.S.A.) 201
rats
    bagpipes frighten 234
    cleared from islands 40, 47
    five-legged 60
    found in tin of baked beans 189
    hunt landmines 28, 28
    X-rays of python digesting 228–9, 229
Rawlinson, Jim (U.S.A.) 63
Ray, Viviana (U.S.A.) 236, 236
Reagan, Ronald (U.S.A.), portrait on hair 104, 104
Recchia, Franco (Ita) 218
Reed, Lou (U.S.A.) 222
regurgitating objects 81, 165, 165, 166, 166
Rehage, Christoph (Ger) 239
Rellecke, Horst (Ger) 44
Ren Jiemei (Chn) 123
restaurants
    at high altitude 194
    boom in curry houses 191
    huge 168
    image of child's face on oven door 178
    in prison 194
    in underground bunker 194
    underwater 194
Reynolds, James (U.K.) 213
rice paddies, as art works 208
Rich, Lucky Diamond 15, 15

Richardson, Orville (U.S.A.) 24
Richardson, Shauna (U.K.) 200, 200
Riches, Peter (U.K.) 208
Richet, Charles (Fra) 176
Riedel, Peter (Can) 216, 219
Ringling Brothers Circus 116–17
rings
    found in city dump 14
    soccer player loses finger 99, 99
Ripley, Robert (U.S.A.) 6, 6, 162
Ripley's museums
    list of 255
    South Korea 6, 6
Risuddin, Muhammad Akbar (Idn) 118
Ritson, Boo (U.K.) 201, 201
rivers
    catches fire 40
    crossed by amphibious bicycle 135
    flows backward after earthquake 44
    motorized bathtub on Amazon 160
    natural logjam 41
    swimming down 94
    turns red 54, 54
roadkill
    hats made of 222
    no-parking lines painted over 16, 16
    trying to resuscitate 241
robbers
    blood found in leech 24
    dressed as Darth Vader 20
    photographs himself with stolen cell phone 14
Robbins, Todd (U.S.A.) 110
Robert, François (Swi) 212
Robinson, Blake (U.S.A.) 20
Robinson, Margaret Ann (U.S.A.) 168
robots
    conducts wedding 229
    jellyfish 228
    Olympic Games for 228
    skiing 227
Rocca, Max (Arg) 52
rocket, soldier impaled on 121
rocking horse, enormous 212
rocks
    ringing 176
    as sculpture 216, 219
Rodin, Auguste (Fra)
    coffee version of The Thinker 200
    electrical version of The Thinker 152, 152
Rodriguez, Jamasen (U.S.A.) 169
Roentgen, Wilhelm (Ger) 122
Roger, Patrick (Fra) 187
Rogozov, Leonid (Rus) 226, 226
roller coasters
    multiple rides on 242
    non-sick breakfast to eat before 193
rolling, traveling by 240
Romano, Charles (U.S.A.) 165, 165
Romero, Jordan (U.S.A.) 157
rope, sleeping on 124
Roper, Chris (U.K.) 237
Roper, Sylvester H. (U.S.A.) 115, 136
Rossellini, Isabella (Ita) 210
Rouget de Lisle, Claude-Joseph (Fra) 203
rowing, across Atlantic Ocean 94, 96
Roy, Alan (U.K.) 170
royalty, house turned into museum of 238
rubber bands, very long chain of 157
Rubik's cube
    replica of The Last Supper 208
    skydiver solves 156
    solving in shark tank 160
Ruck, Dean (U.S.A.) 43, 43
running
    across deserts 94
    backward 153
    blind sprinter 97
    in bomb suit 153
    long run on treadmill 121
    lunge running 169
    in stilettos 160
    with tumble-drier on back 93
Russev, Radoslav (Bul) 203
Ryan, Anna (U.S.A.) 112

sadhus, Hindu 158–9, 158–9
Sadler, Jason (U.S.A.) 238
safety pin, in esophagus 122
Sakata, Harold (U.S.A.) 91
salamanders, giant 78
salami, enormous 194, 194
salsa, enormous bowl of 187
Samuelson, Max (U.S.A.) 141

San Francisco, toothpick model of 221
Sanchez, Prax (U.S.A.) 113
sand
  enormous sandstorm 48–9, 49
  giant artwork on beach 214
  giant sculpture 215
  skiing on 96, 96
Sands, Chris (U.K.) 128
Sangermano, Darco (Ita) 126
Santoro, Pietro (U.S.A.) 240
sari, very valuable 212
Sarkadi, Sandor (Hun) 120, 120
Sasuphan, Supatra (Tha) 128–9, 129
Satan, image of appears on bathroom
  tile 16
Saturn, new ring found round 53
Saurin, Victor (Fra) 89
sausage machine, man sucked into 194
sausages, giant barbecue 191
Saxena, Bhagat (Ind) 193
Sayeg, Magda (U.S.A.) 201
Saylors, J.T. 165, 165–6
Schauerman, Chris 80
Schmidt, Agnes (Ger) 163, 163
schools
  actor in pirate costume 28
  built on mountainside 52
  elderly pupil 24
  flying to 140
  oil wells under 48
  prisoner mascot 43
Schrenk-Notzing, Baron Albert von
  (Ger) 177
Schuyff, Peter (Nld) 87, 87
Schwartz, Yitta (U.S.A.) 16
Schwarzenegger, Arnold (U.S.A.) 103, 103
scorpions, eating live 187
Scott, Matthew 31
Scott, Robert Falcon (U.K.) 190
screws, mosaic made from 216
sculpture
  adhesive tape jellyfish 202, 202
  bacon head 191, 191
  beard as 21, 21
  chocolate train 218
  cremation ashes 206
  discarded clothing 213, 213
  driftwood 35, 35
  enormous hammock 206
  giant sand sculpture 215
  hair clippings and chewing gum 210,
    210
  houses as 43, 43
  inflated animal skins 198–9, 198–9
  junk plastic 218, 218–19
  margarine 186, 188, 188
  miniature clay models of food 220
  miniature tiger 208
  mistaken for log pile 217
  nativity scene on head of a pin 209
  old car parts 214
  old tires 214, 214
  pencil tips 208–9, 209
  phone book 217
  pistol puzzle 219
  rocks 216, 219
  shopping carts 212, 212
  teeth 222
  Terminator 103, 103
  Transformer made from cars 225, 225
  trash 203, 203–5
  tree sculpture from appliances 210
sea slug, uses solar power 230
sea urchins, vision 72
seals, collapsible lungs 62
seasickness, permanent 115
seeds, porcelain replicas 218
Selak, Frano (Cro) 244
Selogie, Cameron (U.S.A.) 195
Sena, Shiv (Ind) 120
Senturk, Metin (Tur) 157
Sepulveda, Lilian (U.S.A.) 16
Serra, Kitten Kay (U.S.A.) 238
sewage, music helps bacteria work
  faster 50
Sewell, Dr. William H. (U.S.A.) 230
sewers
  bagpipes frighten rats 234
  concerts in 219
  fat removed from 38
  python lives in 80

sharks
  beaten off with boogie board 107
  dried sharks for sale 240, 240
  guitar played to 203
  shark bites shark 79
  solving Rubik's cube in tank of 160
  surfer rides on 63
  swallows turtle 72
  woman escapes from 74
Sharma, Vijay (Ind) 122
Shaw, Justin (U.S.A.) 25
sheep
  burpless 75
  feeding curry to 187
  ram runs amok in house 72
  shrinking 60
  two-legged lamb 60, 60
Sheldon, Adam (U.K.) 183, 183
Shepard, Tyler (U.S.A.) 141, 141
Shepherd, Ernestine (U.S.A.) 124
Shi Tuanjie (Chn) 242, 242
Shibata, Tomohiro (Jap) 229
Shield, Arne (U.S.A.) 32
Shields, Kevin (U.K.) 108
Shimansky, Yair (S.A.) 128
shipwrecks
  ancient computer found in 178
  champagne found in 195
  still leaking oil 142
  watch found in 20
Sho Lau (Twn) 74
shoes
  bird wears slippers 66
  chocolate 190
  elephant-dung platforms 207, 207
  long line of sneakers 239
  money hidden in 15
  race in stilettos 160
  stolen 20
  unusual shapes 206
  very ancient 220
  wearing sneakers for four years 238
Shoffner, Roy (U.S.A.) 133
Shoppach, Kelly (U.S.A.) 98, 98
shopping carts, sculpture from 212, 212
Shoudt, "Humble" Bob (U.S.A.) 188
showers, singing in banned 20
Sibley, Dave (U.K.) 15, 15
sidewalks, heated 54
Sidorkin, Artyom (Rus) 121, 121
Silva, Elisany (Bra) 126, 126
Simmons, Erica (U.S.A.) 197, 197
Simnett, George (U.K.) 242
Simonov, Vasily (Rus) 114
Simpson, Sharon (U.K.) 54
Sinclair, Kat (U.K.) 213
Singapore, land reclamation 39
Singh, Frail Than (Ind) 28
Singh, Manjit (U.K.) 237
Singh, Sardar Pishora (Ind) 25
Singlee, the "Fireproof Man" 163, 163
sinkholes
  camel falls into 73
  opens up in yard 243, 243
  swallows factory 54
Sinnadurai, Nesan (U.S.A.) 97
Siwanowicz, Igor (Ger) 78, 78
skateboarding
  by dog 76
  by priest 240
  giant skateboard 156, 156
  injuries 99
skeletons
  chapel decorated with bones 50
  continuous growth 114
  guest of honor 241, 241
skiing
  robot 227
  on sand 96, 96
skin
  lightning patterns on 118, 118
  scaly growths on 119
  very stretchy 163, 163
Skinner, William (U.K.) 187
skulls
  chocolate 190, 190
  festival of 39, 39
  found in pond 40
  X-ray of Einstein's 122
skydiving
  by dogs 60

skydiving (cont.)
  escapologist 154–5, 154–5
  in kayak 94
  landing on Mount Everest 152
  legless champion 123
  parachute fails to open 115
  solving Rubik's cube 156
  surviving falls 107
Sleeman, Kris (U.S.A.) 236, 236
sleep
  hat to wake up sleepy drivers 236
  man sleeps through house fire 16
  narcolepsy 127
  sleeping on rope 124
  sleepwalker overeats 112
  standing man 158, 158
slot machines, rabbit plays 78
small people 124, 124, 128
  at Chicago World's Fair 168
  "Major Mite" 116–17, 116–17
  teenager 115
Smeathers, Gill (U.K.) 17
Smith, Paul (U.K.) 53
Smith, Paul (U.S.A.) 222
Smith, Reynolds Jr. (U.S.A.) 15
Smith, Rick Jr. (U.S.A.) 171
Smith, Simon (U.K.) 186
Smith, Tim (U.K.) 97
Smith family (U.K.) 157
smoking
  chimpanzee's problem 66
  exploding cigarette 110
  snake's habit 74
Smoltz, John (U.S.A.) 93
Smyth, Jason (Irl) 97
snails
  medicinal uses 241
  named after Steve Irwin 64
  speed 78
snakes
  antivenom 124
  fishermen catch python 61
  kissing cobras 241, 241
  new species of chameleon found in
    snake's mouth 78
  in nose 237
  python as assault weapon 238
  python lives in sewer 80
  python moves into rabbit hutch 61
  python trapped in washing machine 61
  python tries to catch marsupial 61, 61
  "Serpent Queen" 156, 156
  smoking habit 74
  smuggled onto ferry 244
  two-headed 67
  X-rays of python digesting a rat 228–9,
    229
snow
  castle built of 242
  debt paid with snowball 50
  in desert for first time 44
  heated sidewalks 54
  over whole U.S.A. 41
  prevented from falling on Moscow 48
  purple snow 54
  snowball kept in freezer 54
snowshoe, beard woven to resemble 113
Soares, Hazel (U.S.A.) 149
soccer
  elderly coach retires 96
  executive box decorated like Gothic
    chapel 97
  fan flies long distances 97
  goalkeeper dislocates jaw 97
  goalkeeper drops aftershave on foot
    92
  player breaks leg 100, 100–1
  player loses finger 99, 99
  soccer jersey tattoo 96, 96
  visiting every ground in England and
    Wales 96
softball, injuries 99
soil, eating 187, 192, 192
solar eclipses 52
solar power, sea slug uses 230
Somers, Wieki (Nld) 206
souls, sold online 28
sound, speed of 228
Space Shuttle, urine jettisoned from 49
Spak, Andres (Nor) 95, 95
Sparrow, Lucy (U.K.) 214

species, large number found in national
  park 49
speech, stroke damage 113
spiders
  as alien monsters 65, 65
  ancient fossil found 61
  barbed hairs 79
  eating 195
  enormous web 38, 38
  raid other spiders' webs 63
  smuggled onto ferry 244
  survival dance 63
  vegetarian 64
spitting, cricket-spitting contest 238
Spock, Dr Benjamin (U.S.A.) 91
spontaneous human combustion 179, 179
spoons
  Christmas tree made of 219
  prisoner digs out of prison with 20
sports
  most dangerous 99
  Olympic Games 88–91
  Olympic Games for robots 228
Spotz, Katie (U.S.A.) 94
Sprague, Erik (U.S.A.) 8, 8
Springer, Jim (U.S.A.) 25
spying, pigeon arrested for 82
squatter, awarded valuable piece of
  land 47
squid
  fossilized ink 83
  giant 70
  with human teeth 73, 73
Stadelbacher, Mary (U.S.A.) 61
Stanislawa P. (Pol) 177, 177
Stansfield, Jem (U.K.) 171
Star Wars
  bank robber dressed as Darth Vader 20
  tattoos 119
starfish, large numbers found on beach 49
stars
  huge star discovered 48
  rays from switch on fair lights 168
  supernova discovered 52
Stassart, Gilles (Fra) 186
statues
  drinking milk 178
  large collection of cat statues 169
  lightning strikes Statue of Liberty 40, 40
steak, huge 195
steam-powered bicycle 136
Steele, Tony (U.S.A.) 169
Stender, Paul (U.S.A.) 136, 136
Stephens, Olga Worth (U.S.A.) 179
Stepney, Alex (U.K.) 97
steps, cycling up 93, 93
Stevens, Jean (U.S.A.) 29
stilettos, race in 160
stilts, long walk on 148, 148
stinkbugs, infestation of 79
Stinson, Chris (U.S.A.) 243
stomach
  chopstick in 122
  coins swallowed 121
  cutlery removed from 191, 191
  hairball removed from 192
  magnets in dog's 79
  metal removed from 108
  music broadcast from 219
  parasitic twin removed from 118
  toothbrush removed from 121
stone, mysterious 180
store, bear walks into 60
stork, romantic attachment 83
Storm, Jason and Rachael (U.S.A.) 242
Stowe, Reid (U.S.A.) 134
Straitjacket, David (U.K.) 147
Strati, Saimir (U.S.A.) 216
stroke
  Botox cures 122
  singing after 113
  writing after 121
stroller, dog pushes 70
submarines
  canal boat converted into 235
  homemade 136
  loses torpedo 137
subway
  boy hides on 244
  pushing people onto 237
Sukegawa, Naoko (Jap) 188, 188

Sun
  eclipses 52
  giant neutrino detector 231, 231
  hydrogen content 52
Sun Fengqin (Mon) 122
sunbed, tanning artwork 201
Suppes, Mark (U.S.A.) 229
surfing
  Gaza Strip club 92
  marathon session 93, 93
surgery
  doctor operates on himself 226, 226
  plasma knife 227
  prenatal 109
  in Stone Age 227
Susanto, Andi (Idn) 110
sushi roll, giant 188
Sutcliffe, Dean (U.K.) 32
Suzuki, Yasuhiro (Jap) 142, 142
Sveden, Ron (U.S.A.) 110
swans
  fidelity to partners 62
  knocks rider off motorcycle 81
swimming
  across icy lake 107
  down river 94
  floating for long time 152, 152
  injuries 99
  obstacle race 90
  Olympic Games 88, 90
  underwater 90
swords, swallowing 165, 166
Szabo, Tibor (Can) 72, 72
Szymcakowi, Andrzej (Pol) 78

T-shirts
  covered in manure 213
  enormous 209
  promoting businesses 238
  wearing multiple 152
Tabary, Frederick (Fra) 50
tail, baby with 109
Takács, Károly (Hun) 89
Takáts, Pál (Hun) 243
tall people 114
  teenagers 126, 126, 128
  very tall thin man 114, 114
Tamas, Agnes (Hun) 79
tanks, inflatable 143, 143
tanning artwork 201
Tao Xiangli (Chn) 136
tape cassette art 197, 197
Tarasewicz, Leon (Pol) 206
Tarescu, Calin (Rom) 15
Tattersall, Mary (U.K.) 92
tattoos
  celebrity pictures 113
  celebrity signatures 110
  connect-the-dots 128, 128
  designer logos on pigs 201
  diamonds in 128
  entire body covered in 15, 15, 107, 107,
    111, 111, 125, 125
  gold 124
  Latin inscriptions 128
  marriage proposal on leg 128
  on mummy 22, 22
  over long period 110
  Route 66 110
  soccer jersey tattoo 96, 96
  Star Wars 119
  tattooed ladies 26–7, 26–7
taxis
  dog knows routes 78
  driven backward 142
  driver left legacy by grateful passenger
    141
Taylor, Kim (U.K.) 126
Taylor, Martin (U.K.) 100, 100–1
tea
  amount drunk in U.K. 190
  very expensive 190
  teapots, large collection of 149
tears
  astronauts 50
  bees drink 85
  weeping crystals 177
Tebow, Tim (U.S.A.) 212
teddy bears
  adults take to bed 244
  bear steals 83

teddy bears (*cont.*)
  made of belly button fluff 108, *108*
teeth
  Churchill's false teeth 119
  determining age from 115
  dog with two rows of 67
  false teeth in lung 121
  filed to sharp points 119, *119*
  mass extraction of 124
  miniature sculptures made with 222
Teh, Mui-Ling (Can) 206
telephone booths
  as entertainments center 208
  living in 234
telephones
  Alexander Graham Bell's funeral 227
  cell phones in India 53
  dress used as cell phone 220
  driving car with cell phone app 226
  iPhone first-aid app used in earthquake 123
  large number in Pentagon 47
  911 called after marriage refusal 29
  stolen cell phone bought back by owner 17
  thief photographs himself with stolen cell phone 14
  unlucky cell phone number 28
  vicar blesses cell phones 242
telescope, mercury mirror 227
temperature, salt water 41
tennis
  multiple double faults 94
  opponents bang heads 92
  played on train 92
  very long match 96
tents
  giant 42
  woman lives on traffic circle in 54
Terren, Dr. Peter (Aus) 152, *152*
testicles, cooking 190
text messages, huge number sent 149
Thavorn, Kamjai Khong (Tha) 16
Theodosius, Emperor 88
Theremin, Léon (Rus) 202
thermometer, giant 168, *168*
Thomas, Prena (U.S.A.) 54
Thompson, Don (U.K.) 90
Thornhill, Jesse (U.S.A.) 122
thumb, found inside fish 20
Thunberg, Nick (U.S.A.) 110
Thurman, Uma (U.S.A.) 208
Thuy, Nguyen Thu (Vnm) 207
tickets, models made from 216
Tierney, J.G. and Patrick (U.S.A.) 234
tigers
  dog disguised as 73, *73*
  lives with bear and lion 66, *66*
  miniature sculpture of 208
  tightrope walking over 169, *169*
tightrope walking
  at great heights 97, *97*
  by goat 81
  over long period 160
  over tiger enclosure 169, *169*
  on top of skyscraper 169
time zones, multiple in Russia 54
Timilsina, Rohit (Nep) 169
Tipler, Matthew (U.S.A.) 122
Tiralosi, Joseph (U.S.A.) 124
tires, animal sculptures 214, *214*
Tiririca (Bra) 235
Titman, Nancy (U.K.) 187
Titterton, James (U.K.) 201
toads, leather from 78, *78*
toast, portrait made of 218
toddlers, very large 114, *114*, 121
toe, run over by forklift 7, *7*
Tohak, Bob (U.S.A.) 181
toilets
  arm stuck in 244
  bionic bottom 114
  John Lennon's 25
  motorized 134
  plant toilet for treeshrews 62, *62*
  tour of in Berlin 50
Tolaas, Sissel (Nor) 206
tomb, BMW-shaped 243
Tompert, Michael (U.S.A.) 217, *217*
tongue
  blowtorch on 19, *19*
  chameleons 67
  dog with swollen tongue 77
  lifting weights with 164, *164*

tongue (*cont.*)
  very long 105, *105*
toothbrush, removed from stomach 121
toothpicks
  model of San Francisco 221
  very valuable 221
torpedo, submarine loses 137
tortoises
  cesarean birth for eggs 80
  extinct species re-created 80
  long-lost 66
  oxygen masks save 82
  tortoise in love with plastic tortoise 85
Tosches, Daniel (U.S.A.) 217
towel, enormous 153
tower, weight of 42
Townshend, Pete (U.K.) 215
tractor-trailer limo 140, *140*
tractors
  at funeral 32
  police use 137
Tracy, Craig (U.S.A.) 12, *12–13*
traffic circle, woman lives in tent on 54
traffic jam, enormous 235
traffic violations, multiple fines for 135
trains
  chocolate sculpture of 218
  dog survives being hit twice 64
  earthquake twists tracks 52, *52*
  hotel room for train lovers 43
  locomotive crashes out of station 137, *137*
  models made from tickets 216
  tennis played on 92
  toddler survives on track 105
trampolines
  injuries 99
  pig on 76
tramway, aerial 168, *168*
transplants
  face 123
  hand grafted onto leg 229, *229*
trapeze artist, elderly 169
Trappe, Jonathan R. (U.S.A.) 149, *149*
Traver, David (U.S.A.) 113
treadmill, long run on 121
trees
  adorned with knitting 210
  floating stump in lake 41
  flowers only once 49
  images projected onto 174, *174*
  living in 39
  quantities of paper used for books 213
  survives hurricanes 50
  tree pods 178, *178*
  very dense wood 44
  very smelly 41
  woman impaled on 120
Tripathi, Ramesh (Ind) 152
Tripp, Charles B. (U.S.A.) 106, *106*
trucks
  child drives long distance 141
  dog drives over owner 241
  hat to wake up sleepy drivers 236
  meteorite hits 49
Trueman, Chris (U.S.A.) 58–9, *58–9*
Truhanova, Irina (Lat) 222
Tsonga, Jo-Wilfried (Fra) 92
tug-of-war
  hand pulled off in 109
  Olympic Games 90
tumors
  on back 122, 124
  enormous 120
tuna, very expensive 195
Tunick, Spencer (U.S.A.) 201
tunnels
  man digs through mountain 54
  man rescued from collapsed 15
  network suddenly appears 174
  under Paris 51, *51*
  very long 50
turtles
  eaten by fish 70
  eggs in fossil 80
  shark swallows 72
tusks, enormous 72
twins
  huge family 108
  identical twins in set of quadruplets 118
  lead parallel lives 25
  marry twins 28
  parasitic 108, 118
  "snake babies" 105

Twitter, help for round-the-world traveler 53
Twyman, Mrs Baker B. (U.S.A.) 126, *126*
tycoon, boy pretends to be 238
typewriters, pictures made with 201, 222

U.F.O.s
  April Fool's hoax 181
  landing port built for 181
  pilot's close encounter with 181
  Roswell Incident 181, *181*
ukelele players, mass gathering 214
umbrellas, mass dance with 171
underground apartment 44
underwear
  made from bananas 190
  wearing multiple pairs of underpants 170, *170*
unicycles, motorized 141
Universe, color of 227
urine
  astronauts' 49
  drinking 192
  whisky made from 193
uteruses, woman with two 108

vacuum cleaners
  climbing wall using 171
  large collection of 237
Vaidya, Shripad (Ind) 214
vampire, blamed for car accident 236
van Dijk, Ria (Nld) 217
Van Gogh, Vincent (Nld) 203
Veal, Alan (U.K.) 194
vegetables, fear of 193
Veitch, Rachel (U.S.A.) 141
Venable, Colleen A.F. 128, *128*
vending machines
  for gold bars 47
  live crabs sold by 242, *242*
  selling artworks 243
Venus de Milo, panda-dung replica 218
Verdasco, Fernando (Spa) 92
Vetrogonov, Sergiy (Ukr) 152
Vicentini, Tiziano (Ita) 189
Victoria, Queen 31
video game, marriage proposal in 241
Viking ship burial 32
Viljanen, Jouni (Fin) 94
Vincent, Pat (U.K.) 32
vineyard, baboons eat all grapes 66
Vinod, Varsha (Ind) 169
Viola, Lady (U.S.A.) 26, *26*
violins
  enormous 208
  fungal treatment for wood 230
Viskum, Morten (Nor) 213, *213*
volcanoes
  constant eruptions 36, *36*, 37
  cooking on 194, *194*
  huge river of lava 37
  living close to 37
  mud volcano 44
  opens rift in desert 39
  power of 37
  rapid growth of 37
  Ring of Fire 52
  sole survivor of 37
  speed of lava 37
  speed of pyroclastic flows 53
  sunlight blocked by eruption 37
  toxic gases from 48
  underwater 37, 40
Vormann, Jan (Ger) 210
Voutsinas, Alex and Donna (U.S.A.) 20
vultures
  flies into helicopter 81
  medicinal uses for brains 118
vuvuzela horns
  giant 201
  gold and diamond 214

Wadile, Dhranraj (Ind) 120, *120*
Wainwright, Alfred (U.K.) 148
wakeboarding marathon 92
Wales, Don (U.K.) 160
walking
  on all fours 159, *159*
  hospitality for long-distance walkers 169
  rotating feet 109
Wall of Death 150–1, *150–1*
Wallace, Amanda Kay (U.S.A.) 7, *7*
Walloch, Sasha (U.S.A.) 219
walls, ancient 181

Wang Liping (Chn) 89
Wang Wenxi (Chn) 230
Wang Xianjun (Chn) 120
Wang Xiaoyu (Chn) 236
Wang Xihai (Chn) 84, *84*
Wangenheim, Konrad von (Ger) 89
Warboys, Owen (U.K.) 141
Ward, Lydia (Nzl) 107
Warner, Carl (U.K.) 218
warthog, plane hits 140
washing machines
  kitten survives in 75
  for pets 82
  python trapped in 61
Washington, George (U.S.A.), library fines 203
wasps
  giant nest 67
  woman survives multiple stings 62
waterfalls
  blind abseiler 97
  frozen 95, *95*
  Niagara Falls stopped 52, *52*
  paddling kayak over 239
  racing over on airbeds 94, *94*
Watkins, Barbara (U.K.) 126
Watkins, Jack (U.K.) 15, *15*
Watkins, Perry (U.K.) 235
Watson, Jessica (Aus) 92
Watson, Mary (U.K.) 141
Weaver, Jordan (U.S.A.) 208
Weaver, Scott (U.S.A.) 221
Webster, Katy (U.K.) 222
weddings
  dogs get married 72
  elderly couple 32
  family all marry in same church 32
  in funeral home 242
  groom arrives in coffin 32
  large age gap between couple 32
  marriage to cat 80
  marrying pillow 244
  mobile chapel 243
  robot conducts 229
  twins marry twins 28
  virtual bride 32
weights
  elderly body-builder 124
  lifting with eyelids 237
  lifting human pyramid 237, *237*
  lifting with mouth 92, *92*
  lifting with tongue 164, *164*
  pulling plane with eyelids 170
  pulling with hair 237
  pulling with nipples 163, *163*
  running in bomb suit 153
  running marathon with tumble-drier on back 93
  very small weightlifter 110
  very strong grandmother 148
  young weightlifter 114
Weissmuller, Johnny (U.S.A.) 91
well, very old 244
Welles, Orson (U.S.A.) 234
Werstler, Heidi Kay (U.S.A.) 20
whales
  friendship with 63, *63*
  funeral for 79
  jumps onto yacht 80, *80–1*
  paintings by 80
  strange monster found on beach 180, *180*
wheelbarrow, human 152
wheelchairs
  crossing U.S. in 153
  wheelies in 149
Wheeler, Vivian (U.S.A.) 29, *29*
whisky, made from urine 193
Whistler, J.A.M. (U.S.A.) 200
whistles, blown at litterbugs 43
White, Ron (U.S.A.) 171
Whitfield, Sandra (U.K.) 218
whittling 164, *164*
Williams, Andrew (U.K.) 62
Williams, Gareth (U.K.) 210
Williams, Janet and Philip (Aus) 238
Williamson, Mrs Charles (U.S.A.) 179
Willis, Tom (U.S.A.) 110
Winchester, Jeanna (U.S.A.) 179
windows, speed cleaning 171
winds
  blows dog and kennel away 79
  speed in cyclone 49
  very windy planet 48

Wiser, I.M. (U.S.A.) 20, *20*
Wiser, May B. (U.S.A.) 20, *20*
Wittenberg, Joe (U.S.A.) 128
wolverine, last in California 83
Wong, Howard (Mal) 223
wood
  bicycle made of 141
  chain carved from 220
  eating 192
  hats 219
Woodbury, Avie (Nzl) 28
Woods, William (Can) 244
Woodward, Irene (U.S.A.) 26, 27, *27*
Woolford, Geraint (U.K.) 20
Woolley, Dan (U.S.A.) 123
World War I, debt finally paid 16
World War II
  deceptions 17, 143, *143*
  lost battle site found 17
worms
  in eye 127
  very long intestinal 107
wrap, enormous sandwich 195
wrestling
  Olympic Games 88, 89
  one-legged wrestler 93
  very successful school 96
Wright, Elsie (U.K.) 175, *175*
Wright, Everton (U.K.) 214
Wright, Hayley and Matthew (U.K.) 70
writing, after stroke 121
Wu Kang (Chn) 124, *124*

X-rays
  of foreign bodies 122, *122–3*
  python digesting a rat 228–9, *229*
Xia Xiao Wan (Chn) 207
Xiao Hao (Chn) 121
Xiao Lin (Chn) 244
Xiao Qiang (Chn) 80
Xiao Wei (Chn) 118
Xie Quiping (Chn) 25

Yang Guanghe (Chn) 237
Yang Jian (Chn) 28
Yang Kang (Chn) 28
Yang Maoyuan (Chn) 198, *198–9*
Yang Shaofu (Chn) 85
yo-yos, spinning multiple 148
yoga
  bear's routine 76
  elderly teacher 156
  instructions on parking tickets 235
Yon, Michael (U.S.A.) 136, *136*
Young, Dorena (U.S.A.) 239
Yunusov, Muhammad (Kyr) 119

Zable, Mark (U.S.A.) 195
Zapata, Javier (Col) 93
zebras, camouflage 81
Zessin, Ellen (U.S.A.) 70
Zhang Lanxiang (Chn) 28
Zhang Ruifang (Chn) 115
Zhao Shuangzhan (Chn) 20
Zhou, Peter (Sgp) 207
Zhou Guanshun (Chn) 80
Zhou Yuqin (Chn) 192, *192*
Zhu, Mr. (Chn) 192, *192*
Zhu Cheng (Chn) 218
Zhu Xinping (Chn) 108
Ziegler, Robert (Swi) 137
Zimmerman, Richard "Dugout Dick" (U.S.A.) 240
zipper, boat looks like 142, *142*
Zolotaya, Elena (Rus) 213
zoos
  animal escape drill 60, *60*
  baboon sells tickets 61

Ripley's Believe It or Not!® acknowledgments

Page 9 (c) Getty Images; **12–13** Pictures courtesy of Craig Tracy; **14** (t) Getty Images; **15** (t) Honda Motor Europe Ltd, (l) Chin Boon Leng, (r) Reuters/Will Burgess; **16** (t/l, t/r) Reuters/Reinhard Krause, (b/l) Collect/PA Wire/Press Association Images; **17** Getty Images; **18-19** Alex Smith - www.as-images.com; **21** (t) Jagdeep Rajput/Solent, (b) Theo Stroomer/Demotix; **22** (l) EPA/Photoshot, (t/r) National Geographic/Getty Images; (b/r) Robyn Beck/AFP/Getty Images; **23** (t/l) SSPL via Getty Images, (t/r) Stephen L. Alvarez/National Geographic/Getty Images, (b) Jae C. Hong/AP/Press Association Images; **24** (t) The Cheeky/Rex Features, (b/l) wenn.com; **25** (b) Barcroft Media; **26** (t/r, t/l) Getty Images, (b) From the John and Mable Ringling Museum of Art Tibbals Digital Collection; **27** (c, t/r) Charles Eisenmann Collection/University of Syracuse, (b) Used with permission from Illinois State University's Special Collections, Milner Library; **28** (t) APOPO, (b/l) © EuroPics[CEN], (b/r) KeystoneUSA-ZUMA/Rex Features; **29** (t/l, t/r) © EuroPics[CEN]; **30** From the John and Mable Ringling Museum of Art Tibbals Digital Collection; **31** (b/r) Collection of the John and Mable Ringling Museum of Art Archives, (b/l, t/l, t/r) From the John and Mable Ringling Museum of Art Tibbals Digital Collection; **32** (l) Ross Parry Agency, (r) Caters News Agency; **33** Daniel Ortega; **36** (b) J.D. Griggs/US Geological Survey/Rex Features, (t) David Jordan/AP/Press Association Images; **37** (c/l) Ethel Davies/Robert Harding/Rex Features, (b/l, b/r) EPA/Photoshot; **38** (t) Donna Garde, TPWD, (b/r) John Terning, (b/l) Carl McCabe, **39** (t, b) Massimo Brega, The Lighthouse/Science Photo Library, **40** (t/l, t, r) Jay Fine/Caters News; **41** (b) Apex; **42** www.Freitag.ch; **43** (t) Photo by Havel Ruck Projects, "Inversion", 2005, (demolished), Dan Havel & Dean Ruck, Site-specific sculptural installation, Art League Houston, Houston, Texas, (b) Imagine China; **44** (t) Tsuzuki Minako, (b) Reuters; **45** Dmitry Dudin; **46** Bloomberg via Getty Images; **47** (t/l) Alain Van de Maele, (b) Tom Mackie/Photolibrary; **48–49** ChinaFotoPress/Photocome/Press Association Images; **50** Specialist Stock/Barcroft Media ltd; **51** Will Hunt; **52** (t) © Russ Glasson/Barcroft USA, (c) © Vladone/istockphoto.com, (b) Malcolm Teasdale/KiwiRail; **53** (l) Mark Duncan/AP/Press Association Images, (r) U.S. Coast Guard photo by Petty Officer 2nd Class Lauren Jorgensen; **54** (t/l, t/r) Solent News/Rex Features, (b) EPA/Photoshot; **55** © Hulton-Deutsch Collection/Corbis; **58–59** Chris Trueman/Alexander Salazar Gallery; **60** (b) © Europics [CEN], (t/l, t/c, t/r) Reuters/Michael Caronna; **61** (r) Wenn.com; **62** (t) ©Chi'en C. Lee, (b) R. Roscoe (photovolcanica.com); **63** (t) Barcroft Pacific, (b/r) Ann Moffett/Minden Pictures/FLPA; **64** (t/l, b/l) Tejnaksh Healthcare's Institute Of Urology, (b/r) Nicole Kane; **65** (t/l) Caters News, (sp) Tomas Rak/Solent News/Rex Features; **66** (b/l) www.noahs-ark.org, (b) Barcroft Media ltd; **67** (t) Stuart Isett/Anzenberger represented by: Eyevine; **68–69** Ingo Arndt/Nature Picture Library; **70** (t/l) Dr Richard Kirby/BNPS, (t/r) Conny Sandland/Rex Features, (b/l) Caters News; **71** Caters News; **72** (b/l) Tibo Szabo, Sue Lees, Photographer Michael Orescanin; **73** (b/l, b/r) China Foto Press/Barcroft Media ltd, (b/c) © Alex Potemkin/istockphoto.com, (t/r) Richard Young; **74** (t) Luke Marsden/Newspix/Rex Features, (b) Armin Weigel/DPA/Press Association Images; **75** Rossparry.co.uk/syndication/Doncaster Free Press; **76** (t) M & Y Agency Ltd/Rex Features; **77** (t) Jonathan Pow/Ross Parry Agency; **78** (t) www.toadfactory.com, (b/l) Igor Siwanowicz/Barcroft Media ltd; **79** Reuters/Wolfgang Rattay; **80** (t) Quirky China News/Rex Features, (b) James Dagmore/Polaris/Eyevine; **81** (b) James Dagmore/Polaris/Eyevine, (c) Chrissy Harris/APN; **82** (t) www.sell-my-photo.co.uk, (b) © Johann Opperman/solentnews.co.uk; **83** Image courtesy of Expedition to the Deep Slope 2006 Exploration, NOAA Vents Program; **84** Quirky China News/Rex Features; **85** (c) Luis Fernando Espin/Rex Features, (t) Karen Bacon/Solent News/Rex Features, (b) Michael Cenci/Solent News/Rex Features; **87** Peter Schuyff; **88–89** © dtimiraos/iStockphoto.com; **90–91** © -M-I-S-H-A-/ iStockphoto.com; **92** © Akintunde Akinleye/Reuters/Corbis; **93** (t) AP Photo/Luis Benavides; (c/l, b/l, b/r) Swell.com; **94** (l) Iain Ferguson, The Write Image, (r) © Wifredo Garcia Alvaro/epa/Corbis; **95** Christian Pondella/Caters News; **96** (t) AFP/Getty Images, (b) Henrik May/ski-namibia.com; **97** (b) Jeffrey Cunningham; **98** (t) Harry Scull Jr./AP/Press Association Images, (b) Ron Jenkins/Fort Worth Star-Telegram/Polaris; **99** Eric Lafargue /www.LPS.ch; **100** (b) Target Press/Barcroft Media ltd, (t) Stephen Pond/Empics Sport; **101** (t/l, t/r) Stephen Pond/Empics Sport, (b) Ryan Remiorz/AP/Press Association Images; **104** Sinopix/Rex Features; **105** (b/l, c) Nick Afanasiev, (t/r) Basit Umer/Barcroft Media ltd; **106** (t) Circus World Museum, Baraboo, Wisconsin; **107** (t) Dennis Van Tine/ABACA USA/Empics Entertainment, (b) Anders (The Piercing Guy) Allinger www.phatpiercings.com **108** (c) Chuck Nyce, (b) Quirky China News/Rex Features; **109** Reuters/China Daily China Daily Information Corp – CDIC; **110–111** Alan Humerose/Rezo.ch; **112** (t) Collection of Jack and Beverly Wilgus, (b) © Europics [CEN]; **113** Asha Mandela; **114** (t) Charles Eisenmann Collection/University of Syracuse, (b) Xinhua/Photoshot; **115** Christine Cornege/AP/Press Association Images; **117** (t/c) NY Daily News via Getty Images, (t/r) Getty Images; **118** (t) Image courtesy of the New England Journal of Medicine, (b) Steve Gschmeissner/Science Photo Library; **119** (t) Chad Grochowski (b) Bob Huberman; **120** (t) Quirky China News/Rex Features, (c/l, b/l) Tejnaksh Healthcare's Institute Of Urology, (b/r) EPA/Photoshot; **121** (b) Atlas Press/Eyevine; **122** (l) Science Photo Library, (r) Du Cane Medical Imaging ltd/Science Photo Library; **123** (l) Science Photo Library, (t/r) Scott Camazine/Science Photo Library, (b/r) Kaj R. Svensson/Science Photo Library; **124** (t) © Europics [CEN], (b/l, b/r) Pictures courtesy of Steve McFarlane; **125** Mario Rosenau/Bizarre archive/Dennis Publishing; **126** (t) Getty Images, (b) Reuters/Paulo Santos; **127** KPN India; **128** (t) Joey Miller; **132–133** Lou Sapienza/Polaris/Eyevine; **132** Philip Makanna/Polaris/Eyevine; **134** Barry Bland/Barcroft USA; **135** (b) Rex Features, (t) KPA/Zuma/Rex Features; **136** (t) Michael Yon, (b) Indy Boys Inc; **137** Roger Viollet/Getty Images; **138** (t) AP Photo, The Canadian Press, Lethbridge Herald, Ian Martens, (b) Gabriel Luque/Rex Features; **139** (t/l) AP Photo, The Canadian Press, Lethbridge Herald, Ian Martens, (t/r) Kurt Roy/Polaris/Eyevine, (b) Rob Yuill/Albanpix ltd/Rex Features; **140** (t) David Drimmer, (b) www.themidnightrider.com; **141** (t) David Drimmer, (b) Pictures courtesy of Tyler Shepard sponsored by Dreyer Honda of Indianapolis, IN; **142** (t/l) Hannes Langeder/Rex Features, (t/r) Manfred Lang/Rex Features, (b) Wenn.com; **143** (t) East News/Rex Features, (b) Roger-Viollet/Rex Features; **146–147** Akash Awasthi; **148** (b) Edmond Hawkins, (t) Getty Images; **149** (r) Nick Obank/Barcroft Media ltd; **150** Courtesy of Cookie Crum; **151** (t) Reuters/Amit Gupta, (c) Reuters/Fayaz Kabli, (b) Getty Images; **152** (t) Nagananda Swamy, (b/l, b/r) www.tesladownunder.com; **153** (r) anthonyescapes.com, (b) Dan Callister/Rex Features; **154–155** anthonyescapes.com; **156** (t) Charles Eisenmann Collection/University of Syracuse, (b) Californiaskateparks.com; **157** Jayna Sullivan Photography; **158** (t/r) Raghu Rai/Rex Features, (b) Rajesh Kumar Singh/AP/Press Association Images; **159** Herbert Ponting; **160** Qiu xiaofeng/AP/Press Association Images; **161** © Swim Ink 2, LLC/Corbis; **163–166** (dp) Library of Congress; **168** (l) © Rykoff Collection/Corbis, (r) © Blue Lantern Studio/Corbis; **169** Quirky China News/Rex Features; **170** (t) The Shields Gazette; **171** ChinaFotoPress/Photocome/Press Association Images; **174** (t) Ibon Mainar/Rex Features, (b) www.sell-my-photo.co.uk; **175** SSPL via Getty Images; **176** (t) Fortean Picture Library; **177** (t) Fortean Picture Library, (b) Courtesy of Donald Estes/Natchez Cemetery; **178** (t) Leon Shadeberg/Rex Features, (b) Courtesy of Caz Housey; **179** Fortean Picture Library; **180** (t) DeWitt Webb/www.cfz.org.uk, (b) Fortean Picture Library; **181** (t) Fortean Picture Library, (b) Tony O'Rahilly/Rex Features; **184–185** Zuma Press/Eyevine; **186** Paul Christoforou; **187** (t) Richard Jones/Sinopix/Rex Features, (b) Debbie Does Cakes/Rex Features, **188** Eddie Mitchell/Rex Features; **189** (t) INS News Agency Ltd./Rex Features, (b) Kevin Le; **190** Marina Malvada/Rex Features; **191** (b) Annie B. Brady, (t) © EuroPics[CEN]; **192** ChinaFotoPress/Photocome/Press Association Images; **193** David Branfield www.davebranfield.com; **194** (t) Wenn.com, (b) Kristjan Logason/Demotix; **195** AFP/Getty Images; **198–199** Yang Maoyuan; **200** (t) Victor Liu/Solent News/Rex Features, (b) Images courtesy of Shauna Richardson; **201** Caters News; **202** Solent News/Rex Features, **203** (t) Kris Kuksi; **202–203** (b) Geoffrey Robinson/Rex Features; **204–205** Kris Kuksi; **206** Bernard Pras; **207** (t) Xia Xiao Wan, (b) Insaland.com; **208–209** Solent News/Rex features; **210** Getty Images; **211** (sp) Dr Rev Bloodpainter; **212** © Mafaldita/istockphoto.com; **212** Drew Gardner/Eyevine; **213** (t/r) Images courtesy of Morten Viskum and VEGAS gallery, London, (t/l) Guerra de la Paz; **214** Ji Yong-Ho/Solent/Rex Features; **215** LA Pop Art www.lapopart.com; **216** (l) Matthew Albanese, (t/l, r) matthewalbanese.com/Solent News/Rex Features; **217** Michael Tompert/Paul Fairchild/Rex Features; **218** Solent News/Rex Features; **219** Solent News/Rex Features; **220** www.grindshow.com; **221** (t) Fredo, (b) Nick Gentry/Barcroft Media ltd; **223** Ari Mahardhika/Solent/Rex Features; **226** Pictures courtesy of Vladimir Rogozov; **227** Kai-Hung Fung/Barcroft Media ltd; **228–229** (t) Henrik Lauridsen, Kasper Hansen, Michael Pedersen and Tobias Wang; **228** (b) Focus/Eyevine; **229** (b) Quirky China News/Rex Features; **230** (t) Shizuo Kambayashi/AP/Press Association Images, (b) JPL/NASA; **231** Kamioka Observatory, ICRR (Institute for Cosmic Ray Research), The University of Tokyo; **234** © Illustrated London News Ltd/Mary Evans; **235** Quirky China News/Rex Features; **237** (t) © Europics [CEN], (b) Charles Eisenmann Collection/University of Syracuse; **239** www.suzanneproulx.com; **240** Claire Carter; **241** © Bettmann/Corbis; **242** (t/l) Andy Willsheer/Rex Features, (c, b) Reuters/Sean Yong; **243** Quirky China News/Rex Features; **244** Quirky China News/Rex Features; **245** (t) Fabi Fliervoet/Solent News/Rex Features, (c/l) Flughafen Leipzig/Halle GmbH/DPA/Press Association Images, (b/l) Cover/Getty Images, (c/r) James D. Morgan/Rex Features, (b/r) Getty Images

Key: t = top, b = bottom, c = center, l = left, r = right, sp = single page, dp = double page.
All other photos are from Ripley Entertainment Inc. Every attempt has been made to acknowledge correctly and contact copyright holders and we apologize in advance for any unintentional errors or omissions, which will be corrected in future editions.

Ripley's MUSEUMS

There are 31 Ripley's Believe It or Not! museums spread across the globe for you to visit, each packed full of weird and wonderful exhibits from the Ripley collection.

SOUTH KOREA

Atlantic City
NEW JERSEY

Bangalore
INDIA

Blackpool
ENGLAND

Branson
MISSOURI

Cavendish
CANADA

Copenhagen
DENMARK

Gatlinburg
TENNESSEE

Genting Highlands
MALAYSIA

Grand Prairie
TEXAS

Guadalajara
MEXICO

Hollywood
CALIFORNIA

Jackson Hole
WYOMING

Jeju Island
SOUTH KOREA

Key West
FLORIDA

London
ENGLAND

Mexico City
MEXICO

Veracruz
MEXICO

Myrtle Beach
SOUTH CAROLINA

New York City
NEW YORK

Newport
OREGON

Niagara Falls
CANADA

Ocean City
MARYLAND

Orlando
FLORIDA

Panama City Beach
FLORIDA

Pattaya
THAILAND

San Antonio
TEXAS

San Francisco
CALIFORNIA

St. Augustine
FLORIDA

Surfers Paradise
AUSTRALIA

Williamsburg
VIRGINIA

Wisconsin Dells
WISCONSIN

ANNUALS

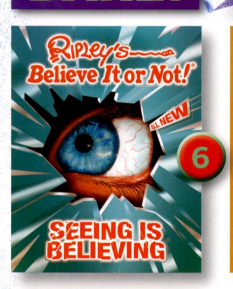
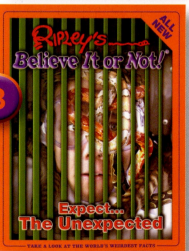
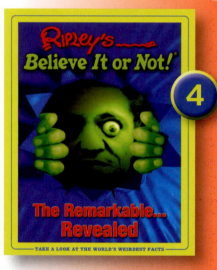
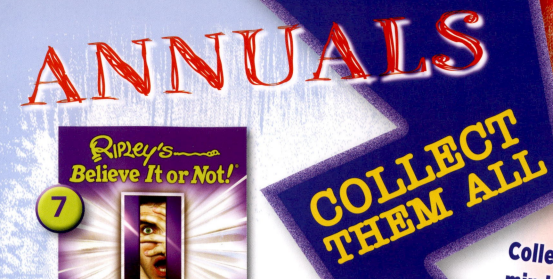

www.wadsworth.com

wadsworth.com is the World Wide Web site for Wadsworth Publishing Company and is your direct source to dozens of online resources.

At *wadsworth.com* you can find out about supplements, demonstration software, and student resources. You can also send e-mail to many of our authors and preview new publications and exciting new technologies.

wadsworth.com
Changing the way the world learns®

Introduction to Criminology

Brendan Maguire
WESTERN ILLINOIS UNIVERSITY

Polly F. Radosh
WESTERN ILLINOIS UNIVERSITY

West/Wadsworth

I T P® An International Thomson Publishing Company

Belmont, CA • Albany, NY • Boston • Cincinnati • Johannesburg • London • Madrid • Melbourne
Mexico City • New York • Pacific Grove, CA • Scottsdale, AZ • Singapore • Tokyo • Toronto

Criminal Justice Editor: Sabra Horne
Development Editor: Dan Alpert
Assistant Editor: Shannon Ryan
Editorial Assistant: Cherie Hackelberg
Marketing Manager: Christine Henry
Production Supervisor: Debby Kramer
Print Buyer: Karen Hunt
Permissions Editor: Susan Walters
Production: Johnstone Associates
Designer: Paul Uhl, Design Associates
Cover Designer: Laurie Anderson
Cover Image: The Blackboard, Conrad Marc-Relli. The Seattle Art Museum, Eugene Fuller Memorial Collection.
Photo, Title Page: Guy Marche, FPG International
Compositor: R&S Book Composition
Text Printer: World Color/Versailles
Cover Printer: Phoenix Color Corp.

Printed in the United States of America
1 2 3 4 5 6 7 8 9 10

For more information, contact Wadsworth Publishing Company, 10 Davis Drive, Belmont, CA 94002, or electronically at
http://www.wadsworth.com

International Thomson Publishing Europe
Berkshire House
168-173 High Holborn
London, WC1V 7AA, United Kingdom

Nelson ITP, Australia
102 Dodds Street
South Melbourne
Victoria 3205 Australia

Nelson Canada
1120 Birchmount Road
Scarborough, Ontario
Canada M1K 5G4

International Thomson Publishing South Africa
Building 18, Constantia Square
138 Sixteenth Road, P.O. Box 2459
Halfway House, 1685 South Africa

International Thomson Editores
Seneca, 53
Colonia Polanco
11560 México D.F. México

International Thomson Publishing Asia
60 Albert Street
#15-01 Albert Complex
Singapore 189969

International Thomson Publishing Japan
Hirakawa-cho Kyowa Building, 3F
2-2-1 Hirakawa-cho, Chiyoda-ku
Tokyo 102, Japan

Library of Congress Cataloging-in-Publication Data
Maguire, Brendan.
   Introduction to criminology/Brendan Maguire, Polly F. Radosh.
      p.   cm.
   Includes bibliographical references and index.
   ISBN 0-534-53784-7
   1. Criminology. I. Radosh, Polly. II. Title.
HV6025.M313 1999
364—dc21   98-43712

♻ *This book is printed on acid-free recycled paper.*

Brief Contents

part 1   **Crime and Criminal Justice 1**

  1   Introduction to Criminology 3

part 2   **The Nature and Extent of Crime 11**

  2   Images and Definitions of Crime 13

  3   Measures of Crime 29

  4   Myths and Facts About Crime 43

part 3   **Types of Crime 63**

  5   Violent Interpersonal Crimes 65

  6   Crimes of the Powerful 91

  7   Conventional Property Crime 113

  8   Public Order Crimes 133

part 4   **Theories of Crime 155**

    Your Personal Guide to Theory 156

  9   Crime as Individually Chosen Behavior 163

  10   Theories of the Driven Offender 183

  11   Micro Social Causes of Crime:
      Social Ecology and Differential Association 205

  12   Micro Social Causes of Crime:
      Labeling and Social Control 223

  13   Macro Social Causes of Crime:
      Strain, Marxist, and Feminist Theories 241

part 5   **The Criminal Justice System 261**

  14   Police 263

  15   Courts 285

  16   Corrections 313

  17   Patterns of Incarceration 331

part 6   **Conclusion 357**

  18   Current Themes in Criminology 359

name index   **369**

subject index   **372**

Contents

preface **xix**

part 1 *Crime and Criminal Justice* 1

1 Introduction to Criminology 3
The Scientific Study of Crime 4
Criminology and Alternative Perspectives 4
Aims and Limitations of Criminology 4
Debunking Crime Myths 4
Policy Proposals 5
Evaluation Research 5
Limitations of Criminology 6
Preview 7

part 2 *The Nature and Extent of Crime* 11

2 Images and Definitions of Crime 13
Popular Images of Crime and Criminals 14
Media Images 14
The "Crime Problem" 15
The "Typical Criminal" 16
Three Definitions of Crime 17
Legalistic Definition 17
Intention 17
Knowledge 18
Freedom 18
Labeling Definition 18
Harms-Based Definition 20
Sutherland's Statement of White-Collar Crime 20
Crime as Behavior That Violates Human Rights 20
Analogous Forms of Social Injury 21
Rating the Definitions 22
Models of Law Creation 23
Consensus Theory 23
Moral Entrepreneurship 23
Conflict Theory 24
Laws, Crime, and Actual Conditions 25
Summary 25

3 Measures of Crime   29

  History of Crime Reporting   30

  Sources of Crime Data   31

    Uniform Crime Reports (UCR)   31

      Part I of the UCR   31

      Part II of the UCR   32

      Crimes "Cleared" by Arrest   33

      Other Information in the UCR   33

      Criticisms of the UCR   34

      Crime Rates   35

    National Crime Victimization Survey (NCVS)   35

      Victimization Rates   35

      Criticisms of the NCVS   35

      Comparison of the NCVS and UCR Data   37

    Self-Report Surveys   37

      Benefits and Problems of Self-Report Research   38

    Other Sources of Crime Data   39

  Summary   40

4 Myths and Facts About Crime   43

  Myth 1: Crime Is Increasing   45

  Myth 2: Most Crime Is Violent   46

  Myth 3: Crime Occurs Mainly in the Lower Classes   47

  Myth 4: Crime Is Bad for Everyone   48

  Myth 5: Most Criminals Are Hard-Core and Strangers to the Victim   49

  Myth 6: Most Crimes Are Solved and Offenders Punished   51

  Myth 7: Most Criminals Who Go to Trial "Get Off"   52

    The Exclusionary Rule   52

  Myth 8: There Is No Relationship Between Guns and Violence   53

  Myth 9: Women Are Becoming "As Bad As" Men   54

  Myth 10: The Way to Remedy Crime Is To Get Tough   56

  Myth 11: Drugs Cause Crime   58

  Myth 12: Nothing Can Be Done To Reduce Crime   59

  Summary   60

part 3 **Types of Crime   63**

5 Violent Interpersonal Crimes   65

  Nature, Extent, and Costs   66

    Common Misperceptions About Violent Crime   66

    Patterns of Victimization   67

    Costs of Violent Crime   68

  Offenders and Victims   68

  Index Offenses   69

    Homicide   69

      Felony-Murder Doctrine   69

      Misdemeanor-Manslaughter Doctrine   69

      Trends in Murder Rates   70

      Demographic Patterns for Murder   70

    Rape   71

      Societal Stereotypes About Rape   72

      Changes in Legal Codes and Court Proceedings   73

        Reporting of Rape 74

        Male Victims of Rape 74

        False Reports 74

        Demographic Patterns for Rape 74

    Assault and Battery 74

        Patterns of Assault 75

        Hate Crimes 75

    Robbery 76

Offenses Within the Family 77

    Domestic Violence 77

        Research Controversy over Patterns of Victimization 77

        Domestic Violence as a Family Matter 77

        Danger to Victims of Domestic Violence 78

        Arrest Patterns 78

        The Battered Woman's Syndrome Defense 79

        Patterns of Abuse 80

    Child Abuse 80

        Intergenerational Patterns of Abuse 80

        Trends in Child Abuse 80

    Elder Abuse 81

Societal Issues 81

    Guns 82

        Guns and Crime 82

        Debate over Gun Control 83

    Media Violence 83

        Debate over Control of Media Violence 83

    Violence and Masculinity 85

Summary 85

6 Crimes of the Powerful 91

Definitions of Elite Crime 92

    White-Collar or Occupational Crime 92

    Corporate and Organizational Crime 92

    Governmental Crime 93

Nature, Extent, and Costs 94

    Double Standards of Justice 94

    Perils of White-Collar Crime 94

    Financial Costs 95

    Dangers 96

        The Pinto Case 96

        The Firestone Case 96

        Unsafe Working Conditions 96

        Misconceptions of Danger 96

    White-Collar Crime and Intent 97

        Profit vs. Harm 97

        Civil vs. Criminal Court 97

        Sentencing Trends 98

Offenders and Victims 98

    Power: Crime vs. Social Harm 98

    Offenders 99

        Gender and Elite Crime 99

    Victims 99

        Hidden Crime 99

Welfare for the Wealthy   100
    Government Support of the Wealthy   100
    Subsidies to the Wealthy   100
Crime and Deviance in High Places   100
  Corporate Deviance   101
  Corporate Dumping   102
    Third World Markets   103
  Environmental Racism   103
    Price Gouging   104
  Governmental Crime   105
    Assassination Attempts   105
    Experiments on U.S. Citizens   105
    Harassment of U.S. Citizens   105
    Contemporary Governmental Crime   106
Enforcement   107
  Progress in Enforcement   108
  Corporate Accountability   109
Summary   109

7 Conventional Property Crime   113
Definitions of Property Crime   114
Nature, Extent, and Costs   115
  Nature of Property Crime   115
  Extent of Property Crime   116
  Costs   116
Offenders and Victims   117
  Offenders   117
  Race and Property Crimes   118
  Gender and Property Crimes   118
  Age and Property Crimes   118
  Victims   119
Index Offenses   120
  Larceny-Theft   120
  Burglary   121
  Motor Vehicle Theft   122
  Arson   122
Non-Index Offenses   123
  Forgery, Fraud, and Embezzlement   124
  Computer Crime   125
Societal Issues   125
  Rationales for Class Distinctions   126
  Moral Values and Stealing   126
  Controlling Property Crime   128
Summary   129

8 Public Order Crimes   133
Defining Public Order Crimes   134
Standards of Morality   134
Nature, Extent, and Costs   135
Offenders and Victims   136
  Offenders   137
  Victims   138
Historical Patterns of Regulation   141
  Prohibition   141

Prostitution 142
Illegal Drugs 143
Gambling 144
Abortion 144
Pornography 144
Arguments About Decriminalization 146
Arguments To Decriminalize 146
Arguments for Maintaining Criminality 146
Organized Crime 147
Activities of Organized Crime 147
Gambling 149
Prostitution 149
Drug Trafficking 149
Organized Crime: Myth or Reality? 149
Summary 151

part 4 **Theories of Crime** 155

YOUR PERSONAL GUIDE TO THEORY 156
You Too Are a Theorist 156
Crime Theories Are Understandable 156
Ideal Components of a Good Theory 157
Plausibility 157
Real-Life Evidence 157
Falsifiability 157
What To Look For 158
Background 158
Core Propositions 158
Position on Agency (Responsibility) 158
Policy Implications 159
Critique 159
Final Caveats 159
No Theory Is Definitive 160
Understanding in Depth 160

9 **Crime as Individually Chosen Behavior** 163
Background 164
Intellectual Climate 164
Eighteenth-Century Criminal Justice 166
Core Propositions 168
Classical Criminology's Theory of Criminal Behavior 168
The Individual Is Self-Interested 168
The Individual Is Rational 168
Behavior Is Freely Chosen 168
Pleasure Seeking Often Results in Crime 169
Classical Criminology's Theory of Criminal Justice 170
Laws Shape Behavior 170
Punishment Should Be a Deterrent 170
Position on Agency (Responsibility) 172
The Individual Side of Agency 172
The Social/Structural Side of Agency 172
Policy Implications 172

Subsequent Developments   173
 Becker's Economic Model of Crime   173
 Gordon's Critique of Crime and Capitalism   174
 Deterrence Theory   175
 Rational Choice Theory   176
Critique   177
 Adequacy   177
 Comprehensive Nature   178
 Current Appeal   178
Summary 179

10   Theories of the Driven Offender   183
Background   184
 Positivism   184
 Evolutionary Thought   185
 Criminological Thought in the 19th Century   185
Core Propositions   186
 Rejection of Classical Criminology   187
 Scientific Study of Crime   187
 The Born Criminal   188
 Identification of Criminals   189
Position on Agency (Responsibility)   190
Policy Implications   190
Subsequent Developments   191
 Genetic Influences   191
  Body Type Theories   191
  Crime and Human Nature   192
  Adoption Studies   193
  XYY Theory   193
 Other Biological Factors Associated with Crime   194
  Autonomic Nervous System Deficiency   194
  Brain Dysfunctions   194
  Sex Hormones   194
  Dietary Conditions   195
Summary of Subsequent Biological Developments   196
Freudian Interpretations of Crime   197
  Personality Development   197
  The Unconscious   197
  Using Freudian Thought To Explain Crime   197
  Summary of Freudian Interpretations on Crime   199
 Low Self-Control   199
Critique   200
 Adequacy   200
 Comprehensive Nature   200
 Current Appeal   200
Summary   200

**11   Micro Social Causes of Crime:
Social Ecology and Differential Association   205**
Background   206
 The Chicago School   206
 The Search for Root Causes   208
  Discipline Building   208
  The Progressive Era   208

Core Propositions   208
    The Social Ecology Theory of Crime   208
        The City as a Natural Area   208
        The Concentric Zone Model   209
        Delinquency/Crime Varies by Zone   209
        Neither Individuals Nor Groups Are Criminogenic   210
    Differential Association Theory   211
        Criminal Behavior Is Learned   211
        Communication Within Intimate Personal Groups   212
        Techniques and Rationalizations   212
        Unfavorable Definition of the Legal Code   212
        Definitions Favorable to Law Violation   212
        Differential Association Varies   212
        Summary   213
Position on Agency (Responsibility)   213
Policy Implications   214
Subsequent Developments   214
    Routine Activities   214
    Differential Identification   215
Critique   216
    Adequacy   216
    Comprehensive Nature   216
    Current Appeal   218
Summary   219

**12 Micro Social Causes of Crime:
Labeling and Social Control   223**
Background   224
    Societal Changes   224
    Need for New Focus   224
    Sociological Theory   225
    Self-Report Studies   225
Core Propositions   225
    Core Propositions of Labeling Theory   225
        Etiology Left Unexplored   225
        No Act Inherently Criminal   226
        Behavior Becomes Criminal When So Labeled   226
        A Label Has Consequences   227
        Summary of Labeling Theory   228
    Core Propositions of Social Control Theory   228
        Powerful Inducements to Commit Crimes   228
        Most Individuals Are Constrained   229
        Summary of Social Control Theory   229
Position on Agency (Responsibility)   230
Policy Implications   231
Subsequent Developments   232
    Shaming   232
    Family Structure   232
    Low Self-Control   234
Critique   234
    Adequacy   234
    Comprehensive Nature   235
    Current Appeal   236
Summary   236

13 **Macro Social Causes of Crime:
Strain, Marxist, and Feminist Theories   241**

   Background   242

      Civil Rights Movement   242

      Anti-War Movement   242

      The "New" Sociology   243

   Core Propositions   244

      Merton's Strain Theory   244

         Cultural Goals and Social Structural Means   244

         Modes of Adaptation   244

         Crime Produced by Macro Social Forces   246

         Summary of Merton's Strain Theory   246

      Marxist Theory of Crime   246

         Capitalism Produces Crime   246

         Capitalist State Defines Crime, Controls Justice   247

         Ideology and False Consciousness Justify Existing Practices   248

         The Powerful Commit the Most Serious Crimes   248

         Social Justice Must Precede Criminal Justice   248

         Summary of Marxist Theory of Crime   249

      Feminist Theory of Crime   249

         Society Shaped by Patriarchal Relations   250

         Women Must Be Included   250

         Gender-Sensitive Explanations Required   250

         Unfair Treatment of Women in Justice System   251

         Summary of Feminist Theory of Crime   251

   Position on Agency (Responsibility)   251

   Policy Implications   252

   Subsequent Developments   255

      Extensions of Strain Theory   255

      Left Realism   255

      Peacemaking Criminology   256

      Postmodern Criminology   256

   Critique   256

      Adequacy   256

      Comprehensive Nature   257

      Current Appeal   257

   Summary   258

part 5   **The Criminal Justice System   261**

14 **Police   263**

   History of Policing   264

      Early English Society   264

      Colonial America   265

      The Professionalization of Policing: London's Constabulary   266

      American Police Expansion in Mid-Nineteenth Century   266

      Reforms of the 1930s to 1940s   267

   Costs   267

   Types of Police   268

      Federal Police   268

      State Law-Enforcement Agencies   268

      Local Police   269

Campus Police 269

Private Police 270

Current Issues and Trends 270

Functions of the Police 270

Police Recruitment 272

Community Policing 273

Women in Policing 275

Current Problems 276

Manning's "Mission Impossible" Thesis 276

Professionalism vs. Bureaucratization 277

Functional Awkwardness 277

Police Misconduct 277

Public Relations 279

Summary 280

15 Courts 285

Contemporary Issues Facing Courts 286

Cost 286

Types of Courts 287

Types of Law 287

Judicial Law 287

Administrative Law 287

Procedural Law 287

Constitutional Law 288

Civil Courts and Criminal Courts 289

Trial Courts and Appellate Courts 289

State Courts 290

Federal Courts 290

Issues and Trends 291

Judges 291

Qualifications of Judges 291

Judges' Salaries 291

Problems of Bias 291

Sentencing Strategies 294

Rehabilitation 294

Deterrence 294

Incapacitation 294

Retribution 294

Types of Sentences 295

Indeterminate Sentences 295

Determinate Sentencing 294

Mandatory Sentencing 296

Other Sentencing Trends 296

The Death Penalty 297

Appellate Review 299

Execution of Juveniles 299

Morality and the Death Penalty 299

Racial and Social Class Discrimination 300

Cost of Executions 301

Current Problems 302

Court Overload 302

Plea Bargaining 304

Other Contributing Factors   304
Frivolous Litigation   304
Prisoners' Lawsuits   305
Racial Disparity in Sentencing   305
Gender Disparity in Sentencing   306
The Muncy Act   306
Modern Gender Differentials   306
Summary   307

16   Corrections   313
Theories of Punishment   314
Retribution   314
Deterrence   314
Types of Deterrence   315
Conditions Under Which Deterrence Works   315
Rehabilitation   315
Incapacitation   316
Selective Incapacitation   316
History of Corrections   317
Punishments Before the Industrial Revolution   317
Punishment and Labor Demands   318
Decline in the Use of Torture   319
Nineteenth-Century American Punishments   319
The Pennsylvania System   320
The Auburn System   320
The Reformatory System   321
Twentieth-Century Punishments   321
Prison Industries   322
The Big House   323
The Modern Era   324
Professional Administration   325
Prison Litigation   325
The Shift to Custody and Control   325
Increases in Women's Corrections   326
Upward Trends in Incarceration   327
Summary   328

17   Patterns of Incarceration   331
Cost of Corrections   332
Monetary Costs   332
Social Costs   333
The Prison System   334
Prisons for Men   335
Prison Classification   336
Prison Culture   337
Gangs in Prison   338
Prison Violence   338
Prisons for Women   338
Incarcerated Mothers   340
Jails   340
Shock Incarceration or "Boot Camps"   341
Private Corrections   342
Co-Corrections   342

Community Corrections   344
    Community Corrections as an Alternative to Prison   344
    Costs of Community Corrections   346
Issues and Trends   346
  AIDS   346
  Tuberculosis   347
  Mental Illness   347
  Geriatric Issues   348
  Correctional Officers   349
    Salaries in Corrections   350
    Job Satisfaction Among Correctional Officers   350
    Women in Correctional Work   350
    Sexual Harassment of Inmates   351
  Overcrowding   352
    Overcrowding and Early Release   352
Summary   353

part 6   *Conclusion* 357

18 **Current Themes in Criminology**   359
Current Themes   360
  Theme 1 Crime Is Disproportionately a Male Enterprise   360
  Theme 2 Crime Crosscuts Class and Race   360
  Theme 3 Guilt Is an Insufficient Deterrent to Crime   361
  Theme 4 Many Types of Serious Wrongdoing Are Not Adequately Addressed   361
  Theme 5 Crime Is Individually Chosen and Structurally Determined   362
  Theme 6 Commitment to Ideology Can Handicap Crime Policy   362
    Definition of "Serious Crime"   362
    Ideological Gridlock   363
    Ideological Triage   363
  Theme 7 Results of Criminal Justice "Toughness" Are Unclear   364
  Theme 8 Future Crime Patterns in the United States   366

name index   *369*
subject index   *372*

List of Boxes
by Type and Chapter

GLOBAL VIEW

The Criminals of Milan, Italy, Go On Vacation (1)

Fear of Crime in Israel (2)

Crime Statistics in the Federal Republic of Germany (3)

The Swiss Approach to the Relationship Between Drugs and Crime (4)

Violent Crime in Sweden (5)

International Efforts to Stop Bribery (6)

Theft in Sweden and Germany (7)

Drug Trafficking from Columbia (8)

Chinese Organized Crime (8)

Iran's Criminal Justice System (9)

Categorizing Criminal Offenders in New Zealand and The People's
    Republic of China (10)

Singapore's Caning of Michael Fay (11)

Three C's: China, Crime, Control (12)

Socialism and Crime in Tanzania (13)

Women Police in South India (14)

Are the Poor Most Likely to Commit Homicide? (15)

French Criminal Procedure Required Secrecy Prior To the French
    Revolution of 1789 (16)

Punishment for Crime in Sweden (17)

Ideology and the Cuban Boat People (18)

HISTORICAL SNAPSHOT

Newspaper Coverage of Crime: One Day, One Newspaper, One Cen-
    tury Apart (2)

The M'Naghten Case (2)

Cesare Beccaria: Humanitarian Reformer and Reluctant Celebrity (9)

Jeremy Bentham: Voice of Utilitarianism (9)

Ten Significant Dates/Events in the Development of the American
    Police (14)

Nineteeth-Century Imprisonment of Women (16)

Big House Prisons and Violence (16)

LAW AND JUSTICE

Seat Belt Laws (2)

Developing and Implementing Anti-Stalking Laws (5)

Can Environmental Regulation Actually Promote More Environmental Crime? (6)

Pressures to Reform the CIA (6)

Stopping Motor Vehicle Theft Through Citizen Education (7)

Labels Can Make a Difference (12)

Responding to Corporate Crime (13)

Broken Windows, Computers, and Crime Control (14)

Primetime Television Police (14)

Race and Policing (14)

Key Players in the Criminal Trial Courtroom (15)

Sexism in the Courtroom (15)

Defense Attorneys in Death Penalty Cases Have Made National Headlines in Recent Years (15)

The Impact of "Three Strikes" Laws on the California State Prison System (17)

Types of Community Corrections Programs (17)

Race and Sex of Corrections Officers and Job Satisfaction (17)

CRIME IN AMERICA

Estimation of the Scope of Gang Crime from Law Enforcement Data (3)

Victims of Certain Offenses Are Often Blamed for Their Own Victimization (4)

Myths and Facts About Domestic Battery (5)

Myths and Facts About Rape (5)

Business Ethics and White-Collar Crime (6)

Is Marijuana Harmless? (8)

Danger in the Waste Industry (8)

Career Criminals (10)

"Wilding" in Central Park (11)

The Internet as a Crime Zone (11)

Hot Weather and Domestic Disputes (11)

Religion and Criminal Behavior (12)

Juvenile Violence and Demography (18)

READING BETWEEN THE LINES

There Are Many Reasons Why People Fail to Report Crime (3)

Some Crime Trends Differ from National Rates (4)

Statistical Trends Sometimes Hide Changes in Crime Categories (5)

Has Increased Use of Prisons Caused Property Crime to Decline? (7)

Criminals Are Not Always So Rational (9)

Should Adolescents Work? (12)

Preface

Everyone cares about crime. Not surprisingly, people have all sorts of ideas about crime and criminal justice. Some of these ideas are accurate, but many are misleading, incomplete, or just plain wrong. This is where criminology comes in. Criminology is the formal, systematic, and scientific study of crime. Criminologists have advanced numerous theories and findings about crime and criminal justice. In fact, criminology provides a useful storehouse of facts about crime. This book opens up that storehouse and we invite all students of crime to examine the contents. The chapters ahead present up-to-date information and statistical data on the nature and extent of crime, types of crime, theories of crime, and the American criminal justice system.

Organization

This book has four major substantive sections: the nature and extent of crime, types of crime, theories of crime, and the criminal justice system. Chapters 2 to 4 focus particularly on the nature and extent of crime in the United States. Chapter 2 offers an analysis of popular images and definitions of crime. Because crime is routinely defined in reference to the legal code, this chapter also discusses the leading models of law creation. Chapter 3 describes the various methods by which crime is measured and notes the strengths and weaknesses of each method. Chapter 4 rounds out this section by debunking twelve common beliefs (myths) about crime and criminal justice.

There are four chapters in the section on types of crime. Chapter 5 highlights violent interpersonal crimes, Chapter 6 examines crimes of the powerful, Chapter 7 addresses conventional property crime, and Chapter 8 considers public order crimes. Each of these chapters offers a detailed analysis of the specific type of crime under investigation. This includes a detailed discussion of the demographic characteristics (race, gender, and age) of the most frequent offenders and victims.

The section on criminological theory begins with an extended introduction, "Your Personal Guide to Theory,"

which is designed to help readers get the most out of the five theory chapters. Chapters 9 and 10 highlight individualistic causes of crime, while Chapters 11, 12, and 13 emphasize the social causes of crime. Each of the theory chapters follows a set format that includes background, core propositions, position on criminal responsibility, policy implications, subsequent developments, critique, and summary.

Finally, there are four chapters in the section on the criminal justice system. Chapter 14 focuses on the police, while Chapter 15 discusses the court system. Chapters 16 and 17 examine corrections. Theories of punishment and the history of corrections are the main topics of Chapter 16, and contemporary corrections and current patterns of incarceration are the primary subjects of Chapter 17.

Special Features

- **Accessible Writing Style.** This is an introduction to criminology text. Readers will not be expected to know sociological or criminological jargon. The book is written for a general audience.

- **Introductory Vignettes.** Many chapters open with a human interest account that relates directly to the content of the chapter. This helps students connect the readings to daily life.

- **Critical Thinking Theme.** A primary aim of this book is to prompt readers to think critically about crime and related topics. Frequently the chapters provide information and evidence that will challenge conventional beliefs. Moreover, students will be exposed to numerous debates within criminology. We hope that students will be actively engaged as they read, and that at the end of each chapter they have more answers about crime—and, perhaps, more questions!

- **Focus on Key Demographic Variables.** Crime is not a monolithic phenomenon in terms of commission or victimization. With regard to offenders and victims, there are four specific demographic variables that require systematic discussion: gender, race/ethnicity, age, and class. We offer a targeted analysis for each of these variables—particularly in the types-of-crime section.

- **Uniform Format.** As much as is practical, the chapters within a section will follow a consistent outline. For example, in the types-of-crime section, each of the chapters includes a discussion of the nature, extent, and costs of each type of crime; consideration of offenders and victims; and a breakdown of specific types of crime. Additionally, all five chapters in the theory section follow a set format (background, core propositions, position on criminal responsibility, policy implications, subsequent developments, critique, and summary).

- **Myths and Facts Chapter.** Commonsense and popular beliefs about crime, criminals, and criminal justice abound. Chapter 4 offers an explicit examination of twelve crime/criminal justice myths. Students will see that views gained from personal experiences and media representations frequently conflict with established scientific evidence.

- **Theory Section Introduction.** Preceding the theory chapters is a detailed introduction to theory in general and crime theorizing in particular. Many students initially find crime theories uninteresting or too abstract to understand. This introduction shows how theories are used in everyday life.

- **Agency (Criminal Responsibility) Issue.** Is action in society individually chosen or determined by social structure? In sociology this question is called the "agency" problem. Most theories of crime stress one side of the equation to the relative neglect of the other. Each of the theory chapters addresses this issue. Students want to know who or what is responsible for crime, and this approach to examining theories offers answers to this fundamental question.

- **Policy Implications.** Every chapter contains an implicit or explicit discussion of historical or current policies regarding crime or criminal justice. We specifically identify the policy implications of each of the major theories considered, and policy matters also receive particularly close attention in the criminal justice chapters.

- **Boxes.** There are 60 boxes highlighted throughout the book. Each of the boxes relates to one of five themes:

1. Global View boxes are offered in every chapter. A world perspective on crime and criminal justice has become increasingly relevant and these boxes address that concern (e.g., violent crime in Sweden in Chapter 5; Iran's criminal justice system in Chapter 9).

2. Historical Snapshot boxes feature noteworthy developments or patterns from the past (e.g., the case of Daniel McNaughtan, which laid the foundation for modern insanity defense standards in Chapter 2; historical imprisonment of women in Chapter 15).

3. Law and Justice boxes focus on policy matters (e.g., the surprising forces leading to the creation of state seat belt laws in Chapter 2; the impact of three-strike laws on California's prison system in Chapter 17).

4. Crime in America boxes draw attention to current crime issues in the United States (e.g., the scope of gang crime in Chapter 3; the Internet as a crime zone in Chapter 11).

5. Reading Between the Lines boxes are examples of critical thinking in criminology (e.g., has the increased use of prisons resulted in a reduction of property crime? in Chapter 7; do adolescents who work part-time jobs have lower rates of crime and delinquency? in Chapter 12). The insights of these boxes might surprise readers.

Pedagogical Aids

Each chapter begins with an outline and a list of key terms. At the conclusion of each chapter, readers will find a set of "critical thinking" questions and a list of suggested readings. As noted above, the text offers dozens of special focus boxes, and, of course, where relevant and useful, there are tables, figures, and charts. Wadsworth Publishing also makes available a full array of course supplements including an instructor's resource manual with test items, student study guide, video library, and a criminal justice web site that offers up-to-date information.

In Appreciation

We started this book at the invitation of Joseph Terry, formerly of West Publications. Joe, along with Sharon Adams Poore, also with West, were instrumental in guiding our early progress. Thank you, Joe and Sharon! We also appreciate the sound advice received from Francis Cullen and Richard Schaefer. Their insights and encouragement helped considerably. Carol Skiles, our department secretary, has worked tirelessly on numerous drafts. Carol helped us make deadlines that would otherwise have been unattainable. We also thank Jeff Radosh, Carol Rowland Maguire, and Georgie Ann Weatherby, who offered advice and support throughout.

Sabra Horne and Dan Alpert of Wadsworth have been crucial to the completion of this project. They inherited a rough project with potential and guided it to the finish. Along the way, Sabra and Dan made numerous suggestions that made the book more interesting and accessible to its readers.

No textbook comes to fruition without the careful review of experts in the field. The following people lent their suggestions and support, for which we are grateful:

Almore, Mary	University of Texas, Arlington
Austin, Timothy	Indiana University of Pennsylvania
Baird-Olson, Karren	Kansas State University
Ballard, John	Rochester Institute of Technology
Bannister, Shelly	Northern Illinois University
Bradel, Donald	Bemidji State University
Brinkley, Susan	University of Tampa
Chriswell, Elmer	Harrisburg Area Community College
DeLone, Miriam	University of Nebraska at Omaha
Donnelley, Patrick	University of Dayton
Donovan, Marjorie	Pittsburgh State University
Downing, Leo	North Georgia College
Early, Kevin	Oklahoma University
Einstadter, Werner	Eastern Michigan University
Garrett, Gerald	University of Massachusetts—Boston
Green, Gary	Columbus State Community College
Griset, Pamela	University of Central Florida
Harris, Kay	Temple University
Hayes, Curtis	Western New Mexico State University
Haynes, Peter	Arizona State University
Hinrichs, Donald	Gettysburg College
Hudson, James	Bob Jones University
Kessler, Raymond	Sul Ross State University
Lofquist, Bill	State University of New York at Genesee
Lundman, Richard	Ohio State University
Luxenburg, Joan	University of Central Oklahoma
Lyons, Philip	Sam Houston State University
Mantyh, Mark	University of Wisconsin, Milwaukee
Martin, Richard	Delaware County Community College
McConnell, Elizabeth	Valdosta State College
Mooso, Dale	San Antonio College
Perlstein, Gary	Portland State University
Perry, Barbara	University of Southern Maine
Pinder, Howard, Jr.	Delaware Tech Community College
Ren, Xin	California State University at Sacramento
Rise, Eric	University of Delaware
Russell, Gregory	Washington State University
Stine, George	Millersville University
Stoney, Tom	University of Wisconsin at Milwaukee
Talarico, Susette	University of Georgia
Thomas, Sally	California State University Long Beach
Thompson, Ken	Northern Michigan University
Thompson, Kevin	North Dakota State University
Tittle, Charles	Washington State University
Unnithan, Prabha	Colorado State University
Walker, Donald	Kent State University
Wright, Dean	Drake University
Zimmer, Lynn	City College of New York at Queens

Teaching a course on crime never gets old. After years of teaching criminology, it is clear to us that students typically have a keen interest in crime and criminal justice. This book responds to that interest by providing a scientifically informed examination of crime that offers up-to-date statistical data, theoretical insights, and policy research findings. The text does not provide any simple answers to crime questions, but each chapter offers insights intended to be eye-opening and provocative, and thus to prompt further interest in the study of crime.

Brendan Maguire
Polly F. Radosh

TO MY BROTHER

James L. Flannery

WHOSE LIFE WAS TRAGICALLY ENDED IN A RANDOM VIOLENT CRIME
DURING THE WRITING OF THIS BOOK.
P.F.R.

TO

Carol Rowland Maguire

B.K.M.

Crime and Criminal Justice

THE FOCUS OF THIS BOOK is on crime. Crime is a familiar topic, but one that is often misunderstood. We hope to correct many of those misunderstandings here. This book is designed to answer the essential questions about crime. For example: How is crime defined and measured? Is the crime rate increasing or decreasing? Are poor people most likely to commit crimes? What are the costs of white-collar crime? Are women as likely as men to commit crimes? How good are the police at solving crimes? What happens to convicted criminal offenders? These appear to be elementary questions about crime and criminal justice, and yet most people would be unable to answer them accurately. Using the most current data and the latest scientific evidence, we will provide the information required to answer these questions and dozens, maybe hundreds, of others.

A final thought before beginning. Crime is a complex phenomenon. As you read the chapters, we encourage you to think critically. In many cases, conventional wisdom about crime is utterly wrong. In some cases, there are no simple answers—and maybe no completely satisfactory answer at all. This is part of the learning process. By the time you finish the closing chapter you will have a good appreciation for what criminologists know, and do not know, about crime.

For updated information on theories of crime, consult the Wadsworth web site at http://www.wadsworth.com/cj.html

chapter 1

Introduction to Criminology

CHAPTER OUTLINE
THE SCIENTIFIC STUDY OF CRIME
CRIMINOLOGY AND ALTERNATIVE PERSPECTIVES
AIMS AND LIMITATIONS OF CRIMINOLOGY
   Debunking Crime Myths
   Policy Proposals
   Evaluation Research
   Limitations of Criminology
PREVIEW

KEY TERMS
criminology
debunking
evaluation research
Scared Straight
ideology
demographic factors

LESS THAN TWO HOURS after the start of 1998, two elderly Chicago residents learned that "Out with the old, in with the new" does not apply to crime. In separate incidents, a 72-year-old man and a 70-year old woman, both asleep in their own homes, were struck by stray bullets coming from the random gunfire of reckless New Year's celebrants.[1]

Luckily, neither victim was killed. Chicago had to wait until 4 A.M. for its first homicide of the year, a drive-by shooting.[2]

Because crime is so common, year after year, many Americans regard it as the most serious social problem facing the United States. Directly or indirectly, crime affects everyone in society. Crime results in thousands of deaths, millions of cases of physical injury or psychological damage, and, according to the National Institute of Justice, a financial cost of $500 billion annually.[3] Because crime is such a powerful, negative force in American society, people demand answers. Providing answers is the purpose of criminology. In his 1996 presidential address to the American Society of Criminology, Charles F. Wellford cited "controlling crime and achieving justice" as the historic goals of criminology.[4] Some criminologists might disagree with Wellford's view of criminology's mission, but there would almost certainly be a consensus that discovering the scientific "facts" of crime is the pre-eminent task of criminology.

The Scientific Study of Crime

Not all serious social problems lead to the formation of a special scientific discipline, but this is what happened in the case of crime. The practical significance of criminal behavior led to the development of **criminology**, the scientific study of crime. The term *criminology* derives from the Latin word *crimen,* which can be translated into "offense," and was coined by an anthropologist named Paul Topinard in 1889.[5] Even before that, however, researchers had begun to uncover facts and patterns concerning crime. Social scientists, particularly criminologists, use a variety of scientific methods to investigate criminal behavior and related topics. Because crime penetrates almost all areas of social life, the scope of these studies is virtually unlimited. To cite just a few examples, crime can be an issue for Americans when they decide on where to work, where to buy a house, where to shop, where to send their children to school, and even where to take a vacation (Box 1.1). As an important and pervasive phenomenon, crime has stimulated an immense volume of scientific studies; the following chapters grew out of this research literature.

Criminology and Alternative Perspectives

Views about crime are not always based on the work of professional criminologists. In fact, common sense, popular opinion, or personal experience often prevail over scientific facts. Individuals hold strong personal convictions about crime and criminal justice; unfortunately, these convictions are frequently incorrect. With this in mind, the serious student of crime must be willing to reject popular and personal beliefs when scientific evidence requires it.

Criminology is not common sense, nor is it guesswork. Rather, criminology is the scientific study of crime. Thus, criminologists offer the most valid and reliable information that is available on the subject of crime. In this book you will find numerous examples that demonstrate the advantages of criminology over common sense.

Aims and Limitations of Criminology

Criminology contributes to society in a variety of ways. Perhaps its three most important contributions are: (1) a knowledge base from which to debunk crime myths; (2) the advancement of policy recommendations; and (3) evaluation research.

Debunking Crime Myths

Sociologist Peter Berger states that the basic purpose of sociology is to document that "things are not what they seem."[6] According to Berger, the primary work of the sociologist is challenging, or **debunking**, ordinary common-sense beliefs and assumptions about life in society, and notions that fail to stand up to empirical testing need to be discarded. Criminology has a similar mission. Crimi-

BOX 1.1

The Criminals of Milan, Italy, Go on Vacation

When Americans plan their vacations they consider a variety of factors, including their prospects for personal safety and the likelihood of being victims of crime. Franklin Zimring, Adolfo Ceretti, and Luisa Broli are researchers who found a consistent pattern of crime rate reduction for non-contact theft, purse snatching, pickpocketing, robbery, and homicide for the month of August in Milan, Italy. Cities in the United States do not show a crime reduction for the month of August, or any other month for that matter. What accounts for the August decrease in crime in Milan? The researchers speculate that Milan criminals, like Milan residents in general, follow a strong cultural tradition of taking time off from work in August:

> Social processes unknown in American cities reduce criminal activity in Milan almost in half during the

vacation month of August. Since the opportunities to offend do not drop across the board, the general drop in offenses is probably the result of voluntary reduction in criminal activity by potential offenders. Crime takes a holiday in Milan during August apparently because criminals take a holiday.

This research highlights the distinctive influence of culture on crime patterns. The pattern found in Milan is not found in any American city. The focus on the vacation tendencies of criminals also illustrates how encompassing the field of criminology can be. Finally, this study "humanizes" criminals. We see that criminals are not necessarily so different from other members of society.

SOURCES: Franklin E. Zimring, Adolfo Ceretti, and Luisa Broli, "Crime Takes a Holiday in Milan," *Crime and Delinquency* 42 (1997): 269–78; Ibid., p. 277.

---

nologists provide *verifiable* knowledge about criminal behavior. When crime-related scientific evidence clashes with popular views about crime, the popular views must be rejected. To cite just one example, common sense tells us that having a job should serve as a deterrent to juvenile delinquency. Conventional thinking suggests that if adolescents are busy working, they will have little time—and reduced motivation—for delinquent behavior. But social scientific research shows that male adolescents with jobs demonstrate both weakened parental influence and less commitment to school, thereby increasing the likelihood of delinquency.[7]

Common sense and science do not always agree. With this in mind, Chapter 4 offers a detailed discussion of twelve commonly held beliefs about crime or criminal justice. In each case the popular view is mistaken or misleading. These cases underscore the fact that *the advancement of verifiable knowledge about crime is the first contribution of criminology.*

Policy Proposals

A second contribution of criminology is that criminologists influence, both directly and indirectly, how crime is conceptualized and addressed in society. An example of indirect influence is Edwin Sutherland's push to include white-collar crime as part of the generally recognized problem of crime. In 1939, Sutherland, president of the American Sociological Association at the time, gave a famous speech (later published as an article) in which he argued that

"white-collar crimes" are serious offenses and that the criminal justice system ought to enforce the laws against these crimes more vigorously.[8] It took decades, but public opinion and law enforcement agencies have gradually increased awareness of white-collar offenses. (It should be noted, however, that criminologists still have not settled on a definition of white-collar crime; indeed, there was a national workshop held on this very issue in the summer of 1996.)[9]

Today, criminologists routinely offer policy recommendations to prevent or reduce crime. To be sure, such recommendations are not always adopted by lawmakers or practitioners, and, even when implemented, the recommendations are not always successful. Nevertheless, the informed opinions and evaluations of criminologists have become an accepted part of society's response to crime. In fact, government agencies allocate millions of dollars annually to criminologists to conduct investigations that will lead to policy recommendations. Although crime experts might believe that the level of funding is insufficient, criminologists do have numerous opportunities to offer their practical advice.

Evaluation Research

A third contribution of criminology is that criminologists commonly conduct assessments of existing criminal justice system programs. **Evaluation research** provides evidence of program effectiveness. This information is used by policymakers who must decide whether to continue funding

Drafting and passing a crime bill is a political enterprise. Is it appropriate that politicians have more influence on crime legislation than do sociologists and criminologists?

particular programs. James Finckenauer's review of **Scared Straight** programs is a noteworthy example of evaluation research.[10] Scared Straight began with a group of inmates serving life sentences in New Jersey's Rahway prison. The lifers thought that a tour of Rahway penitentiary would scare juveniles into behaving themselves (going straight). Officials in the local juvenile justice system endorsed the idea and the tours began in 1976. It was believed that delinquent youth would be so scared that they would turn their lives around, and nondelinquent youth would be "inoculated" against a life of crime. Initially, the treatment was thought to be wildly successful and many jurisdictions throughout the country copied the program. Eventually, however, Finckenauer and other researchers found numerous drawbacks to the Scared Straight strategy. Most important, the empirical evidence simply did not show that adolescents who took the tours had a lower recidivism rate. If scaring adolescents has any effect, apparently it is short-lived. The program sounded too good to be true, and it was.

We have just considered three aims of criminology. Criminologists have been so successful in pursuing these objectives that the field itself has expanded greatly over the last few decades. Once merely a subdiscipline of sociology, criminology today is a program of study in its own right. In fact, the study of crime, law enforcement, and criminal justice has become one of the most popular majors at many colleges and universities. Before going further, however, it should be noted that criminology has certain limitations, and recognizing these limitations will enable you to more fully appreciate the chapters that follow.

Limitations of Criminology

While it is true that criminology provides the best available answers to questions about crime, no social science is perfect or all-knowing. One prominent criminologist, Don C. Gibbons, has gone further by charging that criminologists are too often guilty of imprecision and even sloppiness in their research and writing.[11] Readers of this book should be aware of three potential problem areas of criminological research: (1) errors in research, (2) disagreement among criminologists, and (3) unanswerable questions. First, criminologists occasionally make mistakes. Most research that has been published in a journal is scientifically accurate. This is because any paper published in a scientific journal has undergone a number of review stages. Experts scrutinize journal submissions before they are accepted for publication. Still, it is not unheard of for a published research article to contain errors in theoretical interpretation, methodological design, or statistical analysis.

"Scared Straight" programs began with the idea that adolescents could be deterred from crime if they toured a prison and saw for themselves the awful conditions behind prison walls.

Second, criminologists sometimes disagree with each other. Often, the basis for disagreement is **ideology,** that is, a set of ideas that are deeply felt but not scientifically testable. Consider the basic question, What is crime? Not all criminologists agree on a definition. Crime is variously defined as: (1) unlawful behavior, (2) behavior that is formally processed as criminal, or (3) socially harmful behavior. These definitions are not interchangeable. The fact that criminologists do not embrace a common definition of crime reveals, among other things, that criminology is not totally objective. Criminologists approach crime from varying ideological positions that affect their scholarly research. While it is very difficult to root out ideology completely, in this text we have presented research as objectively as possible.

Third, some criminological questions do have a definitive answer. For example, most people would like to know if there will be more, or less, crime in the future. Unfortunately, this provocative and important question cannot be answered with certainty. All scientists have trouble answering some questions. For example, physical scientists, like criminologists, have difficulty predicting the future. Only two decades ago environmental scientists reported to the media that the atmosphere was cooling and a new

ice age might be imminent.[12] Today, of course, most environmental scientists warn that there is a threat of global warming.[13] The point is, although we present numerous findings from the research literature, there are still some areas of investigation that remain elusive.

Underscoring the limitations of criminology is not meant to diminish the work of criminologists, but to indicate how complex and challenging this field is. As you read further, it will be useful to keep in mind the aims, the contributions, and the limitations of criminology.

Preview

The remainder of this book is organized into four main Parts entitled: The Nature and Extent of Crime; Types of Crime; Theories of Crime; and The Criminal Justice System.

Part II (Chapters 2, 3, and 4) addresses the most basic question, What is crime? There is no easy answer to the question of the nature of crime. Chapter 2 examines alternative and competing definitions of crime. Chapter 3 describes the methods used to measure crime. Each method has a set of strengths and shortcomings and each offers specific conclusions about particular forms of crime.

Crime is a problem that affects all people. It cuts across all distinctions of race, age, sex, and social class. Virtually all Americans have been touched by the problem of crime.

Chapter 4 contrasts popular beliefs concerning crime and criminal justice with scientific evidence, identifying and addressing twelve myths.

Another focus of the book, found in Part III, is on the major types of crime. Chapter 5 examines interpersonal violence (homicide, rape, domestic abuse); Chapter 6 focuses on the crimes of the powerful (corporate crime, government offenses); Chapter 7 considers conventional property crime (larceny, burglary); and Chapter 8 discusses public order offenses (drug crimes, prostitution, gambling). Special attention is given to such factors as the nature, extent, and cost of the crimes in question. In ad-

dition, each of these chapters describe the most typical offenders and victims for specific crimes. While the United States is often referred to as an equal opportunity society, the fact is that crime commission and victimization do not occur equally throughout society. As will be shown, they vary along with the **demographic factors** of social class, age, race, and gender. For example, statistics show that common crimes like robbery and burglary are disproportionately more likely to be committed by poor, young, minority males. In contrast, the most frequent perpetrators of corporate and political crimes tend to be affluent, older, white males. Moreover, while there are distinctive victimization rates within these four variables, the general pattern is that low-income members of society are the most common *victims* of crime. Class, race, age, and gender do make a difference, and the chapters in this section are sensitive to these variables.

Part IV focuses on the most influential theories of crime. Some students doubt their ability to understand "abstract" theories. The introduction to this section paves the way for a comfortable encounter. Chapter 9 looks at crime as individually chosen behavior. This perspective views the offender as rational, self-interested, and freely choosing to commit crime. Chapter 10 presents another individualistic view of crime, one that highlights the biological nature of the offender. Chapters 11 and 12 spotlight micro social causes of crime (*micro* refers to social forces in the immediate environment, like family and neighborhoods). Finally, Chapter 13 provides an examination of macro structural determinants of crime (*macro* refers to large-scale social influences like the national economy). Each of these chapters examines a particular theory's historical background, key propositions, logical strengths and shortcomings, and policy implications.

It is worth noting that many criminology texts cover theories of criminal behavior *before* discussing types of crime. Here the order is reversed, for two reasons. First, because Chapter 4 presents an extensive review of myths, we believe it is important to follow immediately with the actual facts of crime. In short, Chapter 4 will disabuse readers of many popular perceptions about crime, while Chapters 5 through 8 make possible a scientifically informed understanding of crime. Second, we assume you will be better able to assess theories if you are already familiar with the nature and extent of major types of crime. In short, the types-of-crime chapters provide a context for theories of criminal behavior.

The criminal justice system is the subject of Part V. The police (Chapter 14), courts (Chapter 15), and corrections (Chapters 16 and 17) are the three main components of the criminal justice system. Chapter 14 includes a consideration of the history of the police, the costs and types of law enforcement, the issues and trends in policing, and current police problems. Chapter 15 addresses the costs, trends, and problems, as well as the types of courts. Chapter 16, the first of two chapters that focus on corrections, presents and critiques the major theories of punishment and also offers a brief history of corrections. Chapter 17 discusses the costs of corrections and details specific correctional options for men and women, as well as current issues, trends, and problems. This will be of special interest to those contemplating a career in criminal justice.

Finally, Chapter 18 offers a brief summary of issue-oriented themes central to an understanding of crime and criminal justice in the United States. This concluding chapter highlights some of the most important findings and insights of criminology.

Critical Thinking Questions

1. How does criminology make a contribution to your everyday life?
2. Why is the study of crime not an exact science?
3. Do you think that criminologists will one day solve the problem of crime?

Suggested Readings

Don C. Gibbons, "An Apostle's Screed," *Crime & Delinquency* (October 1996): 610–22.

Jeff Ferrell, "Criminological *Verstehen:* Inside the Immediacy of Crime," *Justice Quarterly 14* (1997):1–23.

Jerome Skolnick, "What Not To do About Crime—The American Society of Criminology 1994 Presidential Address," *Criminology 33* (1995): 1–15.

Charles F. Wellword, "Controlling Crime and Achieving Justice—The American Society of Criminology 1996 Presidential Address," *Criminology 35* (1997): 1–11.

Notes

[1] Phat Chiem, "Three Are Killed, 3 Injured by New Year's Shootings," *Chicago Tribune,* 2 January 1998, 1–7.
[2] Ibid.
[3] Illinois Criminal Justice Information Authority, *The Compiler* (Chicago, Spring 1996) 19.
[4] Charles F. Wellword, "Controlling Crime and Achieving Justice—The American Society of Criminology 1996 Presidential Address," *Criminology 35* (1997) 1–11.
[5] Piers Beirne, *Inventing Criminology* (Albany: State University of New York Press, 1993).
[6] Peter Berger, *Invitation to Sociology* (New York: Anchor, 1963) 23.
[7] John Paul Wright, Francis T. Cullen, and Nicolas Williams, "Working While in School and Delinquent Involvement: Implications for Social Policy," *Crime and Delinquency 43* (1997) 203–221.
[8] Edwin Sutherland, "White-Collar Criminality," *American Sociological Review 5* (1940) 1–12.
[9] Reported in *ACJS Today* XV (1996) 31.
[10] James Finckenauer, *Scared Straight! and the Panacea Phenomenon* (Englewood Cliffs, NJ: Prentice-Hall, 1982).
[11] Don C. Gibbons, "An Apostle's Screed," *Crime and Delinquency 42* (1996) 610–22.
[12] Peter Gwynne, "The Cooling World," *Newsweek,* 28 April 1975, 64; "Another Ice Age?," *Time,* 24 June 1974, 86.
[13] Richard Kerr, "It's Official: First Glimmer of Greenhouse Warming Seen," *Science 270* (1995) 156; K. Hasselmann, "Are We Seeing Global Warming?" *Science 276* (1997) 914–15.

The Nature and Extent of Crime

IN CHAPTERS 2 THROUGH 4 WE explore the ways in which crime is defined, how it is measured, and common myths about patterns of crime in America. This section lays the foundation for interpreting many of the facts about crime that will be presented in later chapters, and you will also learn how to interpret information about crime from a variety of public sources.

Chapter 2 looks at the sources of a variety of crime definitions. Although many people may think that the definition of crime is self-evident (isn't it lawbreaking behavior?), definitions are actually much more complex and are subject to many interpretations. This chapter presents the primary means of defining crime, as well as the ways in which common misunderstandings of crime data are influenced by popular images and the media. For example, it is often difficult for people to believe that violent crime is less common in the United States than property crime. In this chapter we outline some of the popular images of crime and show how they distort our perceptions of actual crime patterns.

Chapter 3 explains how crime is measured. This is also more complex than most people realize. In this chapter you will see where crime data come from, how the data are used, and begin to understand both the assets and liabilities of common measures of crime.

Chapter 4 explores twelve common myths about crime in the United States. In this chapter you will examine issues that are often misinterpreted by the public. This chapter points out how false assumptions about crime are fostered by simplistic explanations or misinterpretations of crime data. Common perceptions about "rising crime rates," for example, may come from increased reporting of crime in the news media rather than real changes in patterns of offense. As you read the chapter, you may also begin to see additional myths not mentioned here that are often accepted in the media or by the public.

For updated information on crime statistics, consult the Wadsworth web site at http://www.wadsworth.com/cj.html

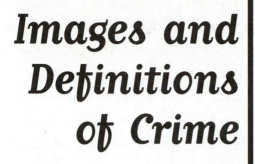

chapter 2

Images and Definitions of Crime

CHAPTER OUTLINE

POPULAR IMAGES OF CRIME AND CRIMINALS
   Media Images
   The "Crime Problem"
   The "Typical Criminal"
THREE DEFINITIONS OF CRIME
   Legalistic Definition
      Intention
      Knowledge
      Freedom
   Labeling Definition
   Harms-Based Definition
      Sutherland's Statement on White-Collar Crime
      Crime as Behavior That Violates Human Rights
      Analogous Forms of Social Injury
   Rating the Definitions
MODELS OF LAW CREATION
   Consensus Theory
   Moral Entrepreneurship
   Conflict Theory
   Laws, Crime, and Actual Conditions
SUMMARY

KEY TERMS

crime problem
problem of crime
typical criminal
carnival mirror image
legalistic definition of crime
mens rea
wild beast theory
M'Naghten rules
irresistible impulse test
felonies
misdemeanors
labeling definition of crime
white-collar crime
harms-based definition of crime
analogous forms of social injury
moral entrepreneurship

IN HIGH SCHOOL HE RECEIVED good grades, ran on the cross country team, and was voted by his classmates "most likely to be remembered."[1] Following high school, Andrew Cunanan lived the fast life, mostly as a high-class gigolo offering sexual companionship to affluent elderly men. After living on the edge for several years, his life began to unravel. He could not find satisfactory jobs and his personal relationships deteriorated to the point that in late April 1997 Cunanan used a claw hammer to bludgeon a close friend to death. Within a few days, he killed a former lover and two strangers who were unlucky enough to have cars that Cunanan wanted for his escape from police. Finally, on July 15 in Miami he murdered Gianni Versace, the rich and famous fashion designer. Cunanan's grisly crime spree, and the subsequent nationwide manhunt for him, stirred tremendous public interest. People became so frenzied during the manhunt that Cunanan was "seen" in over forty states. All of these supposed sightings were false, as Cunanan remained in the Miami area where he had killed Versace.

For more than a week, the Cunanan case was the top news story in the United States. Do cases such as these influence general perceptions about crime and criminals? This and related questions will be considered in the present chapter, which focuses on images and definitions of crime.

Few Americans answer survey questions about crime with a "don't know" response. Of course, not everyone in the United States is well-informed on the topic of criminal behavior, but most individuals have opinions about crime. Unfortunately, these views are often shaped by popular images. The most prominent and pervasive images of crime are those advanced by the news and entertainment media. Because these images have an extraordinary influence on crime policy in the United States, they serve as a good starting point for this chapter. Following a discussion of popular images, the chapter highlights three major definitions of crime and closes with an analysis of the relationship between law and crime.

Popular Images of Crime and Criminals

Most people's ideas about crime and criminals were not formed through personal experience. Generally, individuals develop attitudes about crime and criminals on the basis of accounts presented by the media. Because the media are a key source of information about crime, we will now consider the images of crime and criminals presented by news and entertainment organizations.

Media Images

Print and broadcast journalists are very selective in their coverage of crime stories. There is neither enough space in newspapers nor enough air time on television to cover all, or even most, criminal activities. In general, research has shown that *violent* crimes are most likely to gain the attention of the media.[2]

In addition to violence, researcher Bob Roshier identified three other factors as having the most influence on the selection of news media crime stories: (1) unusual circumstances, (2) dramatic elements, and (3) involvement of famous people.[3] Roshier's research is over two decades old, but his findings have been supported in subsequent studies.[4] It appears, then, that crime is not only a pressing social problem but it is also an activity used by newspaper editors and television news producers to help their businesses make money (Box 2.1). To this end, the news media often distort the actual pattern of crime by emphasizing violent and exceptional offenses. This results in the creation, dissemination, and perpetuation of crime stereotypes.

Research has shown consistently that television programming portrays crime and criminals in a highly stereotypical way.[5] Specifically, studies show that most television crime is violent, interpersonal, and motivated by individual pathology (greed, revenge, or mental unbalance). For example, one content analysis study of 46 hours of prime-time television crime and police programs found that 65

Newspaper Coverage of Crime: One Day, One Newspaper, One Century Apart

October 15, 1996, turned out to be a big day for crime news as reported in the *Chicago Tribune*. Four stories were highlighted:

Archer Daniels Midland Fined $100 Million
Teen Accused of Killing Father
Man Charged in Three Murders
Meeting at Bar Leads to Triple Killing

The front page reported that Archer Daniels Midland (ADM), a food products company, had been fined $100 million for price-fixing. (The fine broke the old record of $85 million.) Page 3 contained an account of a man charged with three murders. Page 7 presented two more crime stories; one concerned a teenager who killed his father, and a second focused on a triple killing.

We are not surprised to find crime stories prominent in big city news. After all, American society has become crime-ridden, hasn't it? Yet, if we were to go back one hundred years, we would find a similar pattern of reporting. Consider the stories covered by the *Chicago Tribune* on October 15, 1896:

Banker Absconds with $200,000
Woman Escapes Courtroom by Jumping Out Window
Two Women Arrested for Robbery
Three Bank Robbers Shot

These headlines indicate two things. First, crime was prevalent a century ago; the modern era is not unique in that respect. And, second, we find that a big-city newspaper, even one hundred years ago, focused considerable attention on criminal activities.

SOURCE: *Chicago Tribune,* October 15, 1996, and October 15, 1896.

---

percent of all crimes depicted were homicides or attempted homicides.[6] This same study concludes that television further misrepresents actual crime by virtually ignoring corporate and government crime. Clearly, neither television news nor television entertainment presents a complete and accurate portrayal of real crime.

Does it matter how television portrays crime? Are beliefs swayed or actions shaped by the routine depiction of violent crime? There are no conclusive answers to these questions, although many studies suggest that watching television has an effect on viewers. It has been shown that the media constitute a major source of information about crime for many people.[7] Moreover, several studies have documented that beliefs and reactions to crime are influenced by media presentations. Criminologist Jay Livingston argues that "people who watch a lot of television also picture the real world as being like the TV programs; that is, they overestimate levels of violent crime, killings by strangers, numbers of police officers, and their own risk of victimization."[8]

If television influences beliefs, does it also affect behavior? Numerous investigations have focused on the question of whether television violence promotes aggressive behavior in viewers.[9] With respect to this issue, a National Institute of Mental Health study stated flatly that findings show a causal relationship between televised violence and later aggressive behavior.[10]

Apparently, the depiction of violent crime does have some effect on viewers. To be sure, information and images coming from television are not accepted wholly, or uncritically. In fact, the "hypodermic-syringe" model of mass communications, which assumes that television content is directly injected into the brains of viewers, has been generally rejected.[11] Nevertheless, as noted above, research studies suggest that television does have an impact on viewer attitudes and behavior. To punctuate the seriousness of this issue, it should be noted that television is seen in over 98 percent of U.S. homes and that a set is turned on for almost seven hours a day.[12]

Because the media do help shape everyday views about crime, let us now consider two sociological analyses of the popular image of crime and criminals.

The "Crime Problem"

Criminologist Raymond Mickalowski distinguishes between what he calls the *crime problem* and the *problem of crime*.[13] These are alternative images of crime. The **crime problem** image refers to traditional and popular notions about crime in society; it focuses on murder, rape, robbery, and burglary. According to Michalowski, the "crime problem" is a recognized social phenomena about which there is a shared concern.[14] This shared concern often results in a marked fear of crime (Box 2.2).

Fear of Crime in Israel

Numerous studies have shown that fear of crime is high in the United States, especially among women, blacks, and residents of high-crime neighborhoods. Criminologists have also found that fear of crime is heightened by novel situations, darkness, and media reports of crime. But fear of crime is not unique to the United States; indeed, fear of crime has been documented in many other countries.

One particularly interesting international study was conducted in Israel. Researchers Gideon Fishman and Gustavo Mesch surveyed residents of Haifa, Israel's third largest city, and identified four distinct dimensions of fear of crime: concern for family members; fear of violence (for example, personal assault or rape); fear of property crime

(such as burglary); and fear of fraud. Fishman and Mesch found that one-third of Israelis report a fear of crime, whereas in the United States nearly one-half of the population is fearful.

While fear of crime in the United States varies by ethnicity, in Israel ethnicity is not a factor. In both nations there is a concern for family, although Americans are more concerned for children, while in Israel there is equal concern for all family members. Finally, as in the United States, fear of crime in Israel is highest for women, those who live in high-crime areas, and members of the lower socioeconomic classes.

SOURCES: Gideon Fishman and Gustavo Mesch, "Fear of Crime in Israel: A Multidimensional Approach," *Social Science Quarterly 77* (1996) 76–89; Keith Parker and Melvin Ray, "Fear of Crime: An Assessment of Related Factors," *Sociological Spectrum 10* (1990) 29–40; Mark Warr, "Dangerous Situations: Social Context and Fear of Victimization," *Social Forces 68* (1990) 891–907; Mark Warr, "Altruistic Fear of Victimization in Households," *Social Science Quarterly 73* (1992) 723–36.

The **problem of crime** is a more sophisticated and more inclusive image of crime. It embraces a concern for common crime, but it also includes an understanding that not all forms of socially harmful behavior are prohibited by law. Thus, this image of crime is based on an analysis of how behavior comes to be defined as criminal. While ordinary citizens, politicians, and criminal justice system employees generally have a view of crime in keeping with the "crime problem" image, sociologists and criminologists are more likely to adopt the "problem of crime" image.

The "Typical Criminal"

A second analysis of the popular image of crime is offered by Jeffrey Reiman, who characterizes the *typical criminal*.[15] The **typical criminal** is a stereotypical image that is produced by existing criminal justice practices, starting with the lawmaking process and including law enforcement, corrections, and even media coverage of crime and criminals. Reiman calls this the **carnival mirror image:** "The American criminal justice system functions as a mirror showing a distorted image of the dangers that threaten us—an image created more by the shape of the mirror than by the reality reflected."[16] Reiman argues that this mirror projects an image of a "typical criminal" as young, black, poor, urban, and male. Although this image is supported by arrest statistics and prison inmate data, it is a distortion of reality because *it represents only one dimension of crime in society.* Reiman explains that the harmful actions committed by the "typical criminal" have

been prioritized as the most threatening behavior in society. The criminal justice system is designed to combat the types of harmful behavior most likely to be engaged in by the "typical criminal," but other acts that might be more dangerous and harmful are either not defined as illegal or not thought of as especially threatening. These acts, such as unnecessary surgery or operating an unsafe work setting, "never become part of the reality reflected in the criminal justice mirror, although the danger they pose is at least as great and often greater than the danger posed by those [that] do!"[17] Hence, the "inescapable conclusion is that the criminal justice system does not simply *reflect* the reality of crime; it has a hand in *creating* the reality we see."[18]

Just as Americans have a mental image of the typical criminal, they also have a mental image of the typical crime. Reiman argues that the news and entertainment media, especially television, promote the view that most crime is one-on-one violence.[19] Reiman suggests that this depiction is misleading on two counts. First, many crimes, perhaps the most serious crimes, are not interpersonal. For example, when a pharmaceutical company knowingly sells an unsafe drug to the public, the wrongful behavior is not a one-on-one crime. Second, most crimes are not violent. Indeed, despite the media's emphasis on violent offenses, the typical crime is non-violent. For Reiman, then, the criminal justice system and the media project an image of crime that is incomplete and misleading.

It is important to appreciate the power of popular images of crime and criminals. These images influence how millions of Americans view crime. Sociologists and crimi-

The popular image of the "typical criminal" is a young, black, urban, male. This stereotype has many harmful consequences.

nologists, however, must go beyond popular images. To study criminal behavior scientifically it is necessary to consider formal definitions of crime. In the following section we will consider three distinctive definitions of crime that have had a significant influence on crime theory and crime research.

Three Definitions of Crime

The first step of sociology, according to pioneer sociologist Emile Durkheim, is to define the subject matter of investigation.[20] This is also a good starting point for criminology.

Legalistic Definition

The **legalistic definition of crime** states that crime is behavior that violates the law. This definition is not as simple and uncomplicated as it might appear to be. It is one thing to stipulate an abstract definition of crime, but quite another to define crime in the real world. In terms of practical interpretation, the legalistic definition of crime calls for an evaluation of behavior on the basis of intention, knowledge, and freedom to act.

Intention

Generally speaking, for an act to qualify as a crime under the legalistic definition, the actor must have had **mens rea** (a guilty mind, or evil intent). There are two issues to be considered. First, did the actor do exactly what was intended? Consider the fact that deer hunters occasionally shoot each other. Presumably, this is done by accident. In cases where there is no intention to kill another human being, the act is seldom prosecuted as a crime. On occasion, however, a misfiring hunter might be held partly accountable. On an October day in 1990, for example, Troy Moore killed a man he mistook for a turkey.[21] Moore was booked on a misdemeanor charge and faced a fine of up to $5000 and a ten-year revocation of his Pennsylvania hunting license.

Even in cases where it is clear that the actor intended the behavior, the law usually requires that prosecutors demonstrate that the actor had a guilty mind—that is, criminal intent. Consider the case of a farmer who takes old fencing from an abandoned military installation. The farmer intends to take the fencing, but does so in the belief that it is unwanted. Subsequently, the act comes to the attention of the government and the farmer is required to return the fencing. However, because the farmer had no criminal intent at the time of the act, a criminal prosecution is unlikely.

As a practical matter, *intent* is a particularly fuzzy area in jurisprudence. Any consideration of an actor's subjective state (the inner thoughts and motivations of a person at the time of an act) is bound to be fraught with difficulties. Science provides no sure method of identifying intention.

Knowledge

A second component of the legalistic definition of crime refers to whether the behavior in question was undertaken *knowingly.* Until about the year 1500, it was presumed that defendants were knowing agents, and only young children and individuals perceived to be mad were not prosecuted for their crimes.[22] From the sixteenth century to the middle of the nineteenth century, English jurisprudence embraced a number of tests for identifying whether offenders knew what they were doing at the time of the crime. One of these tests was the **wild beast theory,** which stipulated that for defendants to be acquitted on grounds of insanity it must be shown that they no more knew what they were doing than would a wild beast. Existing insanity criteria were challenged and eventually overturned by the famous M'Naghten case of 1843, which set new standards for judging sanity (Box 2.3).

The **M'Naghten rules** stated that a defendant is not guilty of a crime if, at the time of the act, mental illness prevents the actor from (1) knowing what he or she was doing, or (2) knowing that the act was wrong.[23] Even when intention and knowledge are accounted for, however, an act is not necessarily considered criminal by the legalistic definition. A third component must also be examined: freedom of action.

Freedom

In most Western legal systems there is a reluctance to pin responsibility on an individual who did not exercise free will. For instance, a person ordered at gunpoint to drive a getaway car for bank robbers would not be considered an accomplice in the robbery. Considerations of free will can be far more difficult to discern, however. What about individuals who are compelled to act by internal forces? These persons might know what they are doing but be unable to stop or control the behavior. With this in mind, several states use what is called the **irresistible impulse test.**[24] This test is relevant to defendants who have a mental disease that impairs self-control.

In the early 1950s, the American Law Institute offered the following definition of *responsibility:*

> **A person is not responsible for criminal conduct if at the time of such conduct as a result of mental disease or defect he lacks substantial capacity either to appreciate the criminality [wrongfulness] of his conduct or to conform his conduct to the requirement of the law.[25]**

This definition is called the *substantial capacity test* and it combines points made in the M'Naghten rules and the irresistible impulse test in that both knowledge ("appreciation") and freedom of choice in conduct are accounted for.

There is no universal legal criterion for judging a defendant insane. As of this writing, states are about evenly split in their adoption of the following standards: M'Naghten rules, irresistible impulse test, substantial capacity test, and guilty but mentally ill (GBMI) test. Current trends indicate that the latter standard, GBMI, might become predominant in future years.

In everyday life, including courtrooms, crime is defined as behavior that violates the law. Not all law violations are considered equal. The most serious violations of the law are called **felonies,** while minor violations are referred to as **misdemeanors.** Penalties for felony convictions are relatively severe (for example, long prison sentences). Those who are convicted of a misdemeanor are usually put on probation, fined, and/or incarcerated in a local jail for a period less than one year.

While the legalistic definition of crime is pre-eminent, it is problematic. Not all actions that violate the law are formally processed as criminal behavior. Partly, this is because the behavior does not meet the standards of intention, knowledge, and freedom, as discussed above. Also important, however, is that not all law violation is observed or processed. Because of the limitations of the legalistic definition, there is need for a supplemental definition. It is in this context that we now consider the *labeling definition of crime.*

Labeling Definition

Labeling theorists argue that no behavior is intrinsically criminal. It is a bold claim to say that no act is, in and of itself, criminal. Chapter 12 offers a detailed examination of the labeling position, but for now it is sufficient to note that the **labeling definition of crime** stipulates that crime is behavior defined as crime. A corollary is that the definition of crime rests with those who have the *power* to define it. According to the labeling perspective, the following are important variables in determining whether or not a specific behavior will ultimately be defined as criminal:

- Who commits the act

    After having several drinks at a bar, the president of a local bank becomes unruly and in the process smashes an expensive mirror.

    After having several drinks at a bar, you get rowdy and in the process smash an expensive mirror.

- Who observes the act

    Two adolescents out late at night observe a man breaking into an appliance store and then leaving with a television set.

The M'Naghten Case

It is generally conceded that the M'Naghten Case is the pre-eminent court case in the history of the insanity defense, but the historical account of the case is fraught with controversy and confusion. There are inconsistent accounts concerning how the verdict in the case was reached, the nature of the act in question, and the insanity standards that came out of this case.

Daniel McNaughtan was a political radical. As a young man, McNaughtan was active in various organizations that opposed existing Tory government practices. McNaughtan, a woodworker like his father, became increasingly upset with government policies that he believed disadvantaged the common worker as well as the owners of small businesses. Having engaged in numerous protests against the British government, McNaughtan began to feel "persecuted" by the Tories—Prime Minister Robert Peel in particular. The Tories did harass their political opponents; whether they actually did anything to McNaughtan personally is not known. In any event, McNaughtan was so opposed to the Tories that in 1843 he went to London and stalked a man he believed to be Robert Peel. Actually, he stalked—and subsequently fatally shot—Edward Drummond, Peel's private secretary. Drummond was approximately the same age and build as Peel and a person who traveled freqeuently in the prime minister's carriage.

McNaughtan's lawyers argued that before and during the act McNaughtan was harboring mental delusions. When the prosecution did not contest this claim, Justice Nicholas Tindal stopped the trial and virtually directed the jury to find the defendant not guilty by reason of insanity. This became the jury's verdict, and McNaughtan was taken to a mental institution where he stayed until his death 22 years later.

Now, let us clarify some key points. First, how was the verdict reached? Inexplicably, government prosecutors did not contest the defense claim that McNaughtan was mad. Moreover, in a rare move, the chief justice intervened in the actual court case. He stopped the trial and notified the jury, incorrectly, that it was the government's burden to establish that McNaughtan was sane at the time of the act. Further, he told the jury that if they found the defendant not guilty by reason of insanity McNaughtan

would be well taken care of. Clearly, the authorities favored the "not guilty by reason of insanity" verdict and did what they could to encourage the jury to return it.

Second, what was the nature of McNaughtan's act? Researcher Moran makes a strong argument for interpreting McNaughtan's act as a case of political assassination. There is clear evidence that McNaughtan and many others had bitter feelings toward Tory policies and that they held Robert Peel accountable. However, the description of McNaughtan as mad made it improbable that anyone would interpret the killing as politically motivated. McNaughtan the madman would never be thought of as a political martyr. It is a fact, however, that when he was arrested, McNaughtan had in his possession a huge deposit check. This large sum of money was used to obtain the services of the best attorneys available. How did this man of moderate means come to possess so much money? No one knows for sure. This fact supports the theory that McNaughtan was part of a political faction devoted to subversive political activities.

Third, what were the insanity standards to come out of this trial and how did they emerge? The court case ultimately resulted in the establishment of standards referred to as the M'Naghten Rules (for unknown reasons, historical legal documents consistently misspelled the man's name). These rules have two components: (1) Did the accused know what he or she was doing? and (2) Did the accused know that it was wrong? Although these criteria are traced to the McNaughtan trial, the M'Naghten Rules were established after the court case—indeed, had the M'Naghten Rules been in effect for Daniel McNaughtan, he would almost certainly *not* have been found insane. Instead, the rules were an outgrowth of a special session of the House of Lords. Immediately after McNaughtan was acquitted on the grounds of insanity, there was a general outcry that justice had not been done. Even members of royalty were concerned, thinking their lives might be endangered by this ruling. To deal with this matter, the House of Lords convened hearings to consider the insanity defense. Numerous legal experts were called to testify. The M'Naghten Rules are the product of these deliberations.

SOURCE: Richard Moran, "The Modern Foundation for the Insanity Defense: "The Cases of James Hadfield (1800) and Daniel McNaughtan (1843)," in *The Annals of the American Academy of Political and Social Science: The Insanity Defense,* ed. Richard Moran (Beverly Hills, CA: Sage, 1985) 31–42; Richard Moran, *Knowing Right from Wrong: The Insanity Defense of Daniel McNaughtan* (New York: Free Press, 1981); Richard Moran, "Awaiting the Crown's Pleasure: The Case of Daniel McNaughtan," *Criminology* 15 (1977) 7–26.

> *Two police officers out late at night observe a man break-*
> *ing into an appliance store and then leaving with a*
> *television set.*

- When the act occurs

  The Acme Company sells a product called "Nuhair" to
  prevent baldness.

  The Acme Company sells "Nuhair" after the government
  outlaws the product because it causes cancer.

- Who is the victim

  A homeless man is mugged.

  A wealthy man is mugged.

- Where the act takes place

  A person fires a rifle on a target range.

  A person fires a rifle in an apartment.

- Why the act occurs

  Mark shoots a man because the man has broken into his
  house and threatened to kill him.

  Mark shoots a man because the man told an insulting
  joke.

In the above examples, the first scenario describes behavior that is unlikely to be processed as a crime; in the second scenario, however, there is a high likelihood that the behavior will be treated as criminal. Labeling theorists argue two points concerning the designation of behavior as criminal. The first point is that the meaning of crime is relative. No behavior is always and everywhere criminal. The second point is that, when affluent and powerful individuals engage in behaviors some would consider criminal, they are far more likely to escape criminal prosecution than the poor and powerless. Whether the behavior in question is driving while intoxicated (DWI), shoplifting, rape, or a wide range of other offenses, the affluent are better able to defend themselves against the resources of the criminal justice system. An apt example is the O.J. Simpson double-murder case. Many people believe this case showed how a person of celebrity, wealth, and power was able to elude criminal conviction.

Harms-Based Definition

Some sociologists have found fault with both the legalistic and labeling definitions of crime. Indeed, there have been three specific proposals to define and treat harmful behavior as criminal activity. Each of the proposals merits elaboration.

Sutherland's Statement on White-Collar Crime

In his 1939 presidential address to the American Sociological Association, Sutherland sought to "reform" criminology by challenging the conventional working definition of crime.[26] Sutherland argued that the sociological study of crime focused almost exclusively on crimes committed by members of the lower class. According to Sutherland, this focus prevents consideration of **white-collar crime,** which is in many respects more harmful than conventional crime. Hence, white-collar violations of the law must be treated as crimes. Consider Sutherland's argument:

> **White-collar crime is real crime. It is not ordinarily called crime, and calling it by this name does not make it worse, just as refraining from calling it crime does not make it better than it otherwise would be. It is called crime here in order to bring it within the scope of criminology, which is justified because it is in violation of the criminal law. The crucial question in this analysis is the criterion of violation of the criminal law. Conviction in the criminal court, which is sometimes suggested as the criterion, is not adequate because a large proportion of those who commit crimes are not convicted in criminal courts.[27]**

Sutherland's position is not an objection to the legalistic definition of crime. He simply argues that an act in violation of the law should be regarded as a crime and addressed accordingly. In practical terms, however, this is not done. Most white-collar law infractions, if dealt with at all, are generally disposed of in civil courts. Sutherland describes the differential treatment in the following way:

> **The crimes of the lower class are handled by policemen, prosecutors, and judges, with penal sanctions in the form of fines, imprisonment, and death. The crimes of the upper class either result in no official action at all, or result in suits for damages in civil courts, or are handled by inspectors, and by administrative boards or commissions, with penal sanctions in the form of warnings, orders to cease and desist, occasionally the loss of a license, and only in extreme cases by fines or prison sentences.[28]**

The basis for Sutherland's position is that white-collar crimes have serious harmful effects. Furthermore, the harm is frequently visited on victims who have neither the organization nor the power to defend themselves. If any actions in society should be considered criminal, argues Sutherland, these should be. This idea has been expanded and refined in the two subsequent harms-based definitions that follow.

Crime as Behavior That Violates Human Rights

Three decades after Sutherland's landmark speech, Marxist criminologists Herman and Julia Schwendinger called for a definition of crime based not on legal statute but on the *historically determined rights of individuals*.[29] In ad-

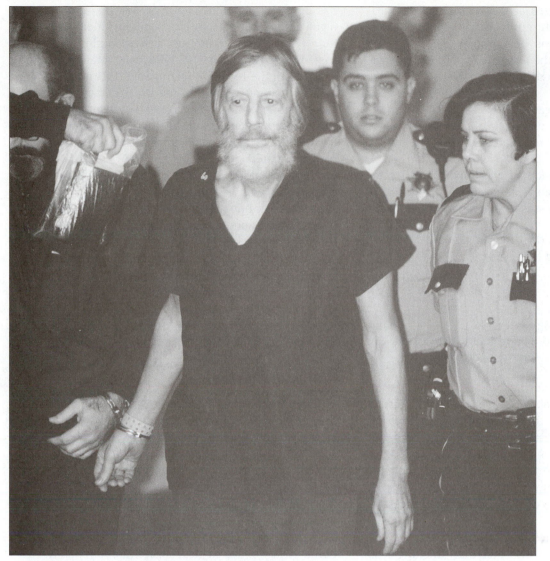

vancing this definition, these scholars make a moral assumption that has two components. First, they assume that human beings have a right to satisfy basic survival needs, and second, they assume that individuals have a right to live a life of dignity and enjoyment:

All persons must be guaranteed the fundamental prerequisites for well-being, including food, shelter, clothing, medical services, challenging work and recreational experiences, as well as security from predatory individuals or repressive and imperialistic social elites. These material requirements, basic services and enjoyable relationships are not to be regarded as rewards or privileges. They are rights![30]

Herman and Julia Schwendinger do not deny the harm caused by conventional crimes like rape and robbery. These offenses must be taken seriously but, accord-

ing to these authors, actions that violate basic human rights are even more fundamental and in fact frequently produce conventional crimes. For example, systematic economic exploitation can be expected to increase the incidence of crimes of theft. Thus, from this perspective, the war on crime should begin with a redefinition of criminal behavior so that all harmful actions are criminalized—particularly actions that infringe on human rights.

Analogous Forms of Social Injury
Criminologist Raymond Michalowski offers a third **harms-based definition of crime.** In his book, *Order, Law, and Crime,* Michalowski argues that a comprehensive examination of the relationship between law and social order calls for a consideration of illegal acts as well as "legally permissible acts or sets of conditions whose consequences are similar to those of illegal acts."[31] Michalowski is especially interested in placing the spotlight on legal behavior that results in social harm. He calls such acts **analogous**

forms of social injury. Even acts that are legal can produce suffering. With this in mind, Michalowski urges that all socially harmful actions be criminalized, ranked in terms of seriousness, and then assigned appropriate penalties.[32] He is most concerned with acts, legal or illegal, that result in:

- Violent or untimely death
- Illness or disease
- Deprivation of adequate food, clothing, shelter, or medical care
- Reduction or elimination of the opportunity for individuals to participate effectively in the political decision-making processes that affect their lives[33]

Although Michalowski does not provide a detailed list of such acts, the following five examples would probably be included:

- Tobacco advertising
- Corporate pollution
- Dangerous work settings
- Use of animals in product development research
- Corrupt or wasteful government spending

It is interesting to note that there are legal restrictions on all five of these activities. For example, tobacco companies are prevented from advertising cigarettes on television, environmental statutes regulate pollution levels, the Occupational Safety and Health Administration (OSHA) sets safety standards for workplaces, companies are not permitted to violate cruelty-to-animal codes, and there are laws prohibiting corrupt business practices by government.

Even with legal restrictions, however, these actions are commonplace. Despite the fact that smoking kills hundreds of thousands of people per year, tobacco companies continue to advertise their products (albeit not on television).[34] Although federal and state statutes set pollution levels, corporations continue to pollute, legally and illegally, the nation's water and air with what David Simon calls a "disregard for people and nature."[35] While employers are legally required to meet workplace safety standards, often they do not (or the standards are too lax to begin with), and the result is that 100,000 to 200,000 people die each year from work-related injuries or illnesses.[36] A few states have tough penalties for those who abuse animals, but many states do not.[37] In fact, the maximum penalty in several states is only a fine of one or two hundred dollars.[38] In general, current state laws, as well as the "unenforceable" national Animal Welfare Act, fail to prevent systematic torture of animals along many lines including product development research.[39] Finally, though there are laws prohibiting government corruption and waste, examples of each are common. Corrupt and wasteful government spending

has become so routine that *NBC Nightly News* regularly highlights extreme cases in a segment titled "The Fleecing of America." To cite just one example, NBC broadcasted a report on June 18, 1996, that detailed the waste involved in the federal government's $10 million annual outlay to kill off wildlife in the United States.[40] Environmentalists and others fail to see any useful purpose to this program except that it functions as a hidden subsidy to Western ranchers who are interested in having coyotes eliminated.

A harms-based definition of crime is flawed in at least one serious way: it tends to be excessively value-laden. What are basic human rights? It is unlikely that there would be a consensus on this question. Michalowski's "analogous social injury" might be even more difficult to define. Would abortion qualify as an analogous social injury? Further, in reference to an example cited earlier, farm subsidies could be considered "wasteful government spending" by some, and yet others might view the subsidies as appropriate. There are many such occasions where harm is in the "eyes of the beholder."

Rating the Definitions

All three definitions of crime are useful and yet all have drawbacks. The legalistic definition, which defines crime as law violation, is the conventional starting point for the criminal justice system as well as for academic criminology. In one sense, however, this definition predicts too much crime; not all lawbreaking is prosecuted as criminal behavior. The labeling definition corrects this shortcoming by stressing that only a small subset of all illegal behavior is formally prosecuted. Labeling theorists bring to attention a variety of sociological factors (predominantly, social class) that affect the chances of criminal prosecution. However, the labeling definition, like the legalistic definition, focuses on behavior that violates formal statutes. The harms-based definition offers a more comprehensive orientation. Defining crime as behavior that infringes on basic human rights, or behavior that produces harm, broadens the range of behavior considered criminal. The problem with this definition of crime, as seen earlier, is that it is too value-laden to allow for consensus.

Two conclusions can be drawn from our presentation of the three major definitions of crime. First, academic criminology uses all three definitions. While the legalistic definition is usually pre-eminent, the other definitions of crime are also important. Both the labeling definition and the harms-based definition have led to significant research in the field of criminology, and each definition is likely to have an increasing influence in the years ahead. Second, the common thread that links these three definitions is the *law*. Each crime definition is dependent, directly or indirectly, upon the law:

- The legalistic definition defines crime as a violation of law.
- The labeling definition stresses the importance of reactions to law violation.
- The harms-based definition of crime implicitly questions the law-making process by focusing on acts that may or may not violate the law.

Because each of these definitions has a crucial relationship to the law, we now turn to a brief consideration of the leading theoretical models of *law creation*.

Models of Law Creation

The sociology of law embraces a wide variety of views concerning the nature and function of law in society. One issue that has sparked considerable debate is the issue of how criminal laws are created. There are three prominent theories of law creation: (1) consensus, (2) moral entrepreneurship, and (3) conflict.

Consensus Theory

Emile Durkheim framed the early development of consensus theory in sociology. He argued that social life is characterized chiefly by order, integration, and smooth functioning.[41] According to Durkheim, the order of social life does not derive from individuals but from society: "Because the individual is not sufficient unto himself, it is from society that he receives everything necessary to him, . . ."[42] Laws are a vital component of the social core that individuals internalize through the socialization process. Laws ensure social harmony. Consider a traffic intersection. In the vast majority of cases, perhaps 999 times out of 1000, cars proceed smoothly through an intersection. Most of the time, if the light is green, motorists proceed, and if the traffic light is red, they stop. Consensus theorists argue that all of social life is like this. Members of society, acting like motorists, understand and follow the rules and laws of social life.

Sociologist George Ritzer states that consensus theories "see shared norms and values as fundamental to society. . . ."[43] Laws, then, are the formal expressions of these shared norms and values; they summarize what almost everyone in society already believes. Laws against murder and rape illustrate this. It is unlikely that people would object to these laws; they represent the collective sentiment of society. Hence, the consensus model of law creation states that formal legislation is driven by the needs and desires of the general public. This means that law violation (crime) is anti-social behavior and an outrage to the community at large.

Moral Entrepreneurship

The **moral entrepreneurship** theory of law creation states that laws are produced by groups in society that seek legal support for their values. In the consensus model it is assumed that laws represent the values held by everyone, while the moral entrepreneurship model assumes that laws represent particular values. Crime in the former case offends all members of society, whereas in the latter case crime offends only a segment of society.

A classic statement of the moral entrepreneurship theory is found in the book *Outsiders* by Howard S. Becker.[44] Here is Becker's basic thesis: "Rules are the products of someone's initiative and we can think of the people who exhibit such enterprise as *moral entrepreneurs* [Becker's italics]."[45] From this perspective, legislation is a means used to enforce someone's values. Those responsible for passing laws are moral crusaders: "The crusader is not only interested in seeing to it that other people do what he thinks right. He believes that if they do what is right it will be good for them."[46]

Moral entrepreneurs often seek to pass legislation as a solution to social problems. Throughout American history numerous laws have been enacted for this purpose. Often such laws are directed to control "problem" behavior related to religious convictions, sex, or use of drugs. An example of the latter is the legislation aimed at curbing alcohol use. Joseph Gusfield's examination of the Prohibition movement argues that efforts to prohibit the manufacture and sale of alcohol were spearheaded by rural, middle-class Protestants as a way of controlling urban, lower-class Catholic immigrants.[47] Another example of moral entrepreneurship in the area of alcohol use is the campaign against drunk driving. In his book, *Drunk Driving: An American Dilemma,* researcher James Jacobs shows how reformers have used, knowingly or not, invalid government data, dubious assumptions, and exaggerated claims to advance anti–drunk driving practices and laws.[48] Jacobs acknowledges that drunk driving is a serious problem in the United States but he cautions that it is "important not to exaggerate the potential effect that legal threats can have on drunk driving."[49] He argues that public education and treatment programs are likely to be more successful than laws in combating the drunk driving problem.

Do moral entrepreneurs make a positive or negative contribution to society? The answer is variable and depends upon the values of the person making the judgment. Today, some moral entrepreneurs are determined to enact legislation that would make abortion illegal. Whether that would be good or bad legislation hinges on your own view of a complex and controversial issue. However, before closing a discussion of moral entrepreneurship, it should be noted that moral entrepreneurs

Acting as moral entrepreneurs, anti-smoking groups have succeeded in changing public opinion about smoking. Recent legislation designed to discourage smoking is a product of this moral entrepreneurship.

have frequently led America in a progressive direction. Most Americans would probably approve of these examples of moral entrepreneurship: child labor legislation, civil rights laws, women's suffrage, and environmental safety statutes.

Conflict Theory

The conflict model of society argues that the creation and implementation of laws is an outgrowth of social struggle between classes or groups. According to conflict theory, the law is a tool used by the powerful in society to protect and further their interests. Decades ago, sociologist William Chambliss published a hallmark study documenting how ruling-class interests led to the creation and subsequent revision of vagrancy laws in England.[50] Chambliss notes that the first vagrancy statute was passed in 1349, shortly after the Black Death struck England. The plague decreased the labor force so significantly that feudal landowners, the ruling class at this time, were hard-pressed to secure enough serfs to work their estates. The first vagrancy statute made it illegal for anyone not gainfully employed to refuse a job offer. Moreover, begging was outlawed. The statute was formulated to help alleviate the problem (labor shortage) faced by the ruling class (feudal landowners).

Chambliss found that in 1530 the first vagrancy statute was revised in substantial form. At this time, merchants were emerging as a new, powerful class. Their concerns were far different from the concerns of the feudal landowners. In particular, the focal interest of merchants was the safe transportation of goods from one town to another. Highway robbery had become a serious threat to commercial trade. Thus, the vagrancy statute was revised to include heavy penalties for individuals unable to show how they made a living and individuals convicted, or even suspected, of fraud (for example, involvement in con games). These people were targeted because it was thought they were the ones most likely to be engaged in highway robberies.

Chambliss argues that the powerful feudal landowners of the fourteenth century created a vagrancy law to ameliorate the labor shortage problem that threatened their financial position, but that in the sixteenth century a different segment of the powerful class, merchants, revised the law to combat the problem of highway robbery. In both cases the powerful in society fashioned the criminal law for their own self-interest. Crime, from this per-

Seat Belt Laws

In 1984, United States Department of Transportation (DOT) Secretary Elizabeth Dole ordered automakers to equip at least 10 percent of their 1987 cars with air bags or automatic seat belts. By 1990, all cars would have to be so equipped. Dole added, however, that the order would be eliminated if a sufficient number of states passed mandatory-use seat belt laws. By "sufficient" Dole meant enough states to account for two-thirds of the nation's population.

The mandate issued by the transportation department set in motion a number of forces. First and foremost, the automakers began a vigorous campaign in support of state seat belt laws. Because of the added production expenses associated with this mandate, auto industry executives opposed the federal requirements announced by Dole. If enough highly populated states enacted appropriate legislation, the requirements could be avoided. Interestingly, most of the first states to pass seat belt laws were states with large populations. The automakers used various methods to sway lawmakers. For instance, General Motors announced that it would not build its huge Saturn plant in any state lacking a seat belt law. Further, in Illinois, the automakers funded an organization named "The Illinois Coalition for Safety Belt Use." This organization lobbied lawmakers and published literature in support of seat belt laws.

While the powerful auto industry had a financial interest in furthering seat belt legislation, other groups also campaigned for the legislation. Many individuals and groups argued for seat belt laws as a way of saving lives. For some, it was a moral crusade. Scores of government bureaucrats, research scientists, and political officeholders took an active part. Although exact estimates varied, all of these moral entrepreneurs agreed that seat belt laws would save numerous lives. In Illinois, both the governor and the state police superintendent stated that a mandatory-use seat belt law would save over 300 lives in its first year. Similar estimates were made by people in responsible positions all over the country. Many were personally convinced that this type of legislation was truly lifesaving.

The initial predictions were wrong. A comparison of law and non-law states for the years 1984 through 1993 shows that traffic fatality rates decreased as rapidly in non-law states as in law states. While seat belt legislation is positively associated with increased belt use, neither seat belt laws nor seat belt use are associated in any substantial way with traffic death rates. Seat belt legislation and seat belt use might be positively related to a reduction in serious injury rather than to death rates.

Today, forty-seven states have a seat belt law and the percentage of motorists who use seat belts has increased dramatically in recent years, up from about 15 percent in the mid-1980s to over 70 percent currently. The usefulness of seat belt laws remains a controversial issue, but what is clear is that the legislation was pushed forward by a disparate combination of groups and motives. The economically and politically powerful automakers apparently sought this legislation primarily for financial reasons. In addition, various other groups and individuals supported the legislation because they felt it was in the best interest of society. Thus, both the conflict and moral entrepreneurship models of law creation help explain the genesis of these laws.

SOURCES: Brendan Maguire, William R. Faulkner, and Richard A. Mathers, "Seat Belt Laws and Traffic Fatalities: A Research Update," *Social Science Journal 33* (1996) 321–33; Brendan Maguire, Rebecca Hinderliter, and William R. Faulkner, "The Illinois Seat Belt Law: A Sociology of Law Analysis," *Humanity & Society 14* (1990) 395–418; Brendan Maguire and William Faulkner, "Safety Belt Laws and Traffic Fatalities," *Journal of Applied Sociology 7* (1990) 49–61.

spective, is not necessarily a violation of the general will, but behavior seen as threatening or offensive to those in society who have economic and political power.

Laws, Crime, and Actual Conditions

There is empirical support for each of the three models of law creation. Some laws are passed to satisfy public opinion; other laws are the result of a specific group of "do-gooders" who feel that a law will further a moral agenda; still other laws are framed to protect and advance the interests of the powerful in society. Further, there are laws that reflect a mixture of two or three of these interests. For example, Box 2.4 discusses the mandatory use of seat belts in the United States. Segments of the ruling class and moral entrepreneurs combined to create seat belt laws. Finally, it is worth re-emphasizing that law is a concept relevant to all three major definitions of crime: legalistic, labeling, and harms-based.

Summary

Crime is an ordinary part of everyday life in the United States. Furthermore, crime is a topic that receives considerable attention from both the news and entertainment media. Popular images of crime influence attitudes and behavior. This chapter began with a discussion of popular images, showing that they are often contradicted by established facts. Next, three definitions of crime were highlighted: legalistic, labeling, and harms-based. The legalistic definition is a common starting point for criminologists. It states that crime is law violation. Labeling theorists have pointed out, however, that only some law-violating behavior is actually processed as crime. The labeling definition of crime stresses the social reaction to law violation. The third definition sees socially harmful behavior as criminal, whether or not the behavior violates legal statute. The final section of the chapter considered three prominent models of law creation and pointed out that theories of law formulation influence how crime is defined.

Critical Thinking Questions

1. How could the media improve its coverage of crime? Do newspapers and television handle crime stories in the same way? If there are important differences, what are they?

2. Do popular images of crime and criminals have negative consequences and, if so, what are they?

3. Describe the "carnival mirror image" of crime. Do you know people who have this image of crime? What are the negative consequences of this image?

4. Which model of law creation do you find most compelling? Which model would best explain drunk driving laws?

Suggested Readings

Mark Brown and Kenneth Polk, "Taking Fear of Crime Seriously: The Tasmanian Approach to Community Crime Prevention," *Crime and Delinquency 42* (1996) 398–420.

William Chambliss, "A Sociological Analysis of the Law of Vagrancy," *Social Problems12* (1964) 46–67.

Ted Chiricos, Michael Hogan, and Marc Gerts, "Racial Composition of Neighborhood and Fear of Crime," *Criminology 35* (1997) 107–131.

David Fabianic, "Television Dramas and Homicide Causation," *Journal of Criminal Justice 25* (1997) 195–203.

Richard Moran, "The Modern Foundation for the Insanity Defense: The Cases of James Hadfield (1800) and Daniel McNaughtan (1843)," in *The Annals of The American Academy of Political and Social Science: The Insanity Defense,* ed. Richard Moran (Beverly Hills, CA: Sage, 1985), 31–42.

Jeffrey Reiman, *The Rich Get Richer and the Poor Get Prison,* 6th ed. (New York: Macmillan, 1996) Ch. 2.

Surette, Ray, *Media, Crime and Criminal Justice,* 2nd ed. (Belmont, CA: Wadsworth, 1998).

Notes

[1] Evan Thomas et al., "Facing Death," *Newsweek,* 28 July 1997, 20–30.

[2] J.F. Sheley and C.D. Ashkins, "Crime, Crime News, and Crime Views," *Public Opinion Quarterly 45* (1981) 492–506.

[3] Bob Roshier, "The Selection of Crime News by the Press," in *The Manufacture of News,* eds. S. Cohen and J. Young (Beverly Hills, CA: Sage, 1973) 28–39.

[4] R. V. Ericson, P. M. Baranek, and J. B. Chan, *Visualizing Deviance: A Study of News Organization* (Toronto: University of Toronto Press, 1987); J. F. Sheley and C. D. Ashkins, "Crime, Crime News, and Crime Views," *Public Opinion Quarterly 45* (1981) 492–506.

[5] Brendan Maguire, "Image vs. Reality: An Analysis of Prime-Time Television Crime and Police Programs," *Crime and Justice 11* (1988) 165–88; Joseph Dominick, "Crime and Law Enforcement on Prime-Time Television," *Public Opinion Quarterly 37* (1973) 241–50; George Gerbner, "Violence in Television Drama: Trends and Symbolic Functions," in *Television and Social Behavior,* eds. George Comstock, John Murray and Eli Rubinstein (Rockville, MD: National Institute of Mental Health, 1972) 28ff.

[6] Maguire, "Image vs. Reality: An Analysis of Prime-Time Television Crime and Police Programs," 175–76.

[7] D. Graber, *Crime News and the Public* (New York: Praeger, 1980).

[8] Jay Livingston, *Criminology,* 2nd. ed. (Upper Saddle River, N.J.: Prentice-Hall, 1996) 35–36.

[9] R. Surette, *Media, Crime and Criminal Justice* (Pacific Grove, CA: Brooks/Cole, 1992).

[10] *Television and Behavior: Ten Years of Scientific Progress and Implications for the Eighties* (Rockville, MD: U.S. Department of Health and Human Services, 1982).

[11] Mark Warr, "Public Perceptions of Crime and Punishment," in *Criminology,* 2nd ed., ed. Joseph F. Sheley (Belmont, CA: Wadsworth, 1995), 15–31.

[12] *Newsweek,* "Tale of the Tube," 2 August 1993, 6.

[13] Raymond Michalowski, *Order, Law, and Crime* (New York: Random, 1985) 3–6.

[14] Ibid., 4.

[15] Jeffrey Reiman, *The Rich Get Richer and the Poor Get Prison,* 4th ed. (Boston: Allyn & Bacon, 1995) 52–56.

[16] Ibid., 51.

[17] Ibid., 55.

[18] Ibid.

[19] Ibid., 60.

[20] Emile Durkheim, *The Rules of Sociological Method,* tr. Sarah Soloway and John Mueller, ed., George Catlin (New York: Free Press, 1966 (1895)) 34.

[21] *Chicago Tribune,* "Man Mistaken as Turkey, Hunter Charged in Death," 1 November 1990, I:3.

[22] Nigel Walker, "The Insanity Defense Before 1800," in *The Annals of the American Academy of Political and Social Science: The Insanity Defense,* ed. Richard Moran (Beverly Hills: Sage, 1985) 25–30.

[23] *Daniel M'Naghten's Case,* 8 Eng. Rep. 718, 722-723 (1843), 10 C.F. 200, 210–211 (1843).

[24] Sanford Kadish and Monrad Paulsen, *Criminal Law and Its Processes* (Boston: Little, Brown, 1975) 215–16.

[25] American Law Institute, *Model Penal Code* 401 (1952).

[26] Edwin Sutherland, "White-Collar Criminality," *American Sociological Review 5* (1940) 1–12.

[27] Ibid., 5.

[28] Ibid., 8.

[29] Herman and Julia Schwendinger, "Defenders of Order or Guardians of Human Rights?" *Issues in Criminology 5* (1970) 123–57, 143.

[30] Ibid., 145.

[31] Michalowski, *Order, Law, and Crime,* 317.

[32] See Brendan Maguire, "The Applied Dimension of Radical Criminology: A Survey of Prominent Radical Criminologists," *Sociological Spectrum 8* (1988) 133ff.

[33] Michalowski, *Order, Law, and Crime,* 318.

[34] David Simon, *Elite Deviance,* 5th ed. (Boston: Allyn & Bacon, 1996) 136.

[35] Ibid., 154.

[36] Ibid., 39.

[37] *HSUS News,* Washington DC: The Humane Society of the United States, (1995)15; in Louisiana violators can be fined up to $25,000 and sentenced to ten years in prison, and in Oregon offenders can be fined up to $100,000.

[38] Ibid.

[39] Richard McLellan, "Animal Liberation: The Politics of the Possible," *Mainstream 27* (1996) 24–29.

[40] *NBC Nightly News,* "The Fleecing of America," 18 June 1996.

[41] Emile Durkheim, *The Division of Labor in Society* (New York: Macmillan, 1966 [1893]).

[42] Ibid., 228.

[43] George Ritzer, *Contemporary Sociological Theory,* 3rd ed. (New York: McGraw-Hill, 1992) 92.

[44] Howard S. Becker, *Outsiders: Studies in the Sociology of Deviance* (New York: Free Press, 1963).

[45] Ibid., 147.

[46] Ibid., 140.

[47] Joseph Gusfield, *Symbolic Crusade: Status Politics and the American Temperance Movement* (Urbana: University of Illinois Press, 1963).

[48] James Jacobs, *Drunk Driving: An American Dilemma* (Chicago: University of Chicago Press, 1989).

[49] Ibid., 105.

[50] William Chambliss, "A Sociological Analysis of the Law of Vagrancy," *Social Problems 12* (1964) 46–67.

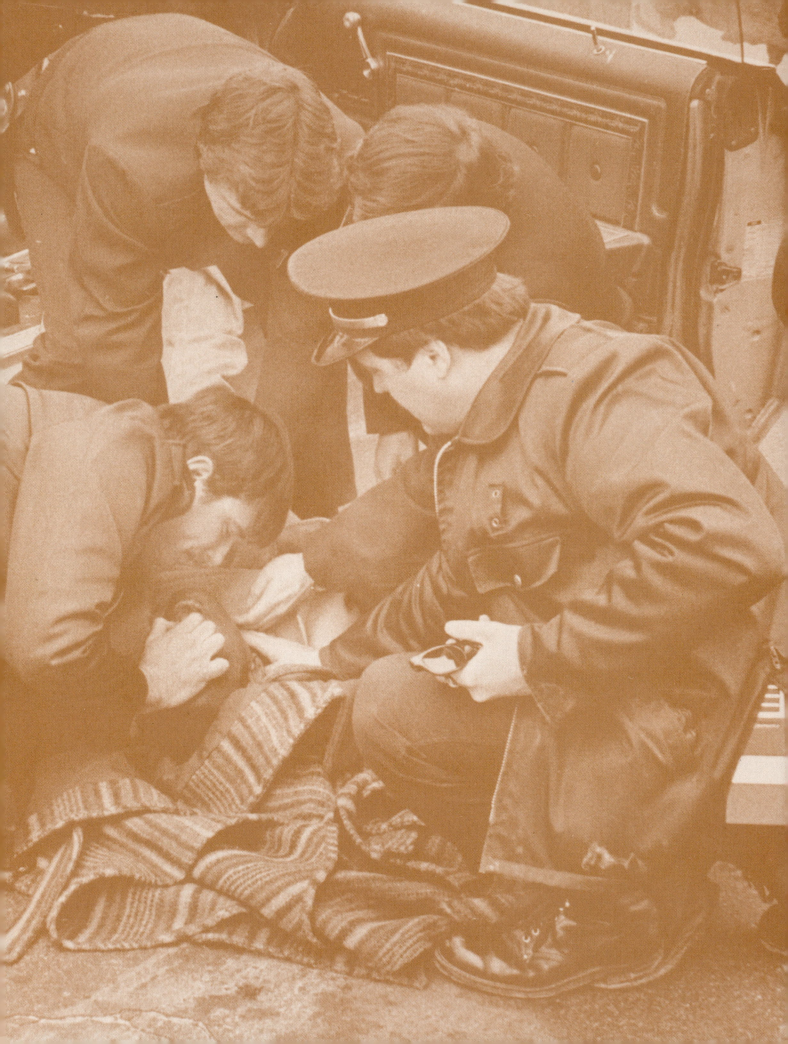

chapter 3

Measures of Crime

CHAPTER OUTLINE

HISTORY OF CRIME REPORTING
SOURCES OF CRIME DATA
    Uniform Crime Reports (UCR)
        Part I of the UCR
        Part II of the UCR
        Crimes "Cleared" by Arrest
        Other Information in the UCR
        Criticisms of the UCR
        Crime Rates
    National Crime Victimization Survey (NCVS)
        Victimization Rates
        Criticisms of the NCVS
        Comparison of the NCVS and UCR Data
    Self-Report Surveys
    Other Sources of Crime Data
        Benefits and Problems of Self-Report Research
SUMMARY

KEY TERMS

crime rates
Uniform Crime Reports (UCR)
National Crime Victimization Survey (NCVS)
index crimes
crime index
clearance rates
self report surveys
participant observation research

BETWEEN 1965 AND 1975 there was a 500 percent increase in homicides committed by women in England and Wales. Reports of the increase were shocking and led to much theorizing about the social problems created by a new breed of female offender.[1] Theorists related women's increased social opportunity to rising female crime. However, a problem of interpretation became apparent. In 1965 there was only one homicide committed by a woman in England and Wales; five homicides were committed by women in 1975. The use of percentages in this case distorted the reporting of crime trends because the low absolute number of homicides made any percentage increase appear great. A theory based upon a trend moving from one to five homicides would not provide much insight into patterns of crime. In other words, statistical information can distort reality if the information is used improperly or the wrong statistic is used for comparison. This chapter covers the various types of crime data and their uses, and it addresses the ways in which such data may be misused or misinterpreted.

Information about crime is readily available, but news, entertainment, and common folklore do not clearly reflect the true nature or extent of crime in America. In this chapter we will examine the means by which crime data are collected and reported. Then we will look at the interpretation (as well as some common *mis*interpretations) of crime statistics.

The casual observer might expect the measurement of crime to be fairly straightforward. A simple count of crimes, or categorization of criminals into various demographic groups, should give a reasonable assessment of crime trends. From such counts, researchers could ascertain the amount of crime in a given offense category and the characteristics of offenders. In reality, the collection of crime statistics is rather complicated. If we count offenses and measure trends over time, the problem of population changes may actually distort the picture of crime trends. In 1980, for example, there were 21,860 people reported to have been murdered in the United States and in 1994 there were reports to police of 23,310 murders.[2] A simple assessment of these facts would indicate that murder was a worse problem in 1994 than in 1980. The problem with this simple assessment is that it does not take into consideration the increase in population between 1980 and 1994. Actually, the homicide *rate,* or the number of murders per population, declined between 1980 and 1994, even though the absolute number of murders increased. Thus, **crime rates** are always expressed as a number per population.

Numerous political, legal, and social policy decisions are made on the basis of crime statistics. If either collection or interpretation of information about crime is flawed, then these decisions may be misguided. People who use information about crime without understanding the techniques of data collection easily misinterpret reports of crime. Policies or legal changes based upon the faulty assumption of increased homicide in the earlier example would be flawed; statistical analysis that takes population change into account actually indicates that the crime of homicide declined.

The point is that collection of crime statistics is more problematic than most people realize. In addition to the difficulties inherent in tracking crime over time, there are other problems, such as unreported or undetected crime, variations among states with regard to definitions of criminal offenses, political manipulations of crime data, and inconsistencies among government agencies in the methods by which crimes are counted and the data analyzed. This chapter explains the major sources of crime data and provides a foundation for your own future analysis of such data.

History of Crime Reporting

The first comprehensive crime statistics in the United States were collected in 1930 by the Bureau of Investigation, which is now called the Federal Bureau of Investigation (FBI). *Crime in the United States,* the first of the **Uniform Crime Reports (UCR),** was published in August 1930. The report contained information from 400 cities and included crime data on a population of about 20 million.[3] Contemporary reporting includes 16,000 jurisdictions and reports are calculated on a population base of 249 million.[4]

Before standardized reporting techniques were utilized for the 1930 UCR, most information about crime was local. National trends, changes in crime patterns over time, or interpretation of criminal activities were all inaccessible without a source of national data. Many early analysts of crime generalized from a small group of offenders to all criminals without sufficient knowledge of trends or variations in crime patterns. National reporting, coordinated by the FBI, not only increased knowledge about crime patterns but has also fostered more objective and consistent data collection in many areas of the criminal justice system.

Data supplied by the FBI in the UCR were the most commonly used sources of crime statistics until a new measure was introduced in 1972. In that year, the U.S. Bureau of the Census began collecting information from people who have been victims of crimes. The published results of the survey were called the National Crime Survey (NCS) until 1991, when it was renamed the **National Crime Victimization Survey (NCVS).** In 1994, this survey collected data from 120,000 people on the crimes they had experienced in the six months prior to their interview.[5]

The UCR and NCVS are not directly comparable because they measure different aspects of crime. The UCR records reports of crime with a focus on offenders, while the NCVS measures victimization trends. Both measures offer insight into crime trends, although each is subject to criticisms for its methods. While many criminologists prefer the NCVS because it is believed to be a more accurate measure of crime, data published in the UCR are more widely reported by news agencies and FBI statistics are frequently quoted in news stories or reports of crime.

The UCR and NCVS data are reported as *aggregates,* or complete categories of crime data. In the UCR, for example, all men arrested are compared to all women arrested. Aggregates are the foundation upon which *quantitative* statistics are computed. These statistics provide general information about crime patterns; they help with thorough analysis of the particular features of crime. From aggregate data in the UCR we learn, for example, that men account for about 80 percent and women account for about 20 percent of people arrested for crimes in the United States. Quantitative analysis does not reveal the reasons women are rarely arrested as compared to men. Further analysis of the differences in male and female arrest patterns would require more data than supplied by the UCR; nevertheless, these data help define the differences among groups so that researchers may investigate further.

Another new system of data collection was announced by the FBI in 1988. The National Incident-Based Reporting System (NIBRS) has been designed to provide a more comprehensive picture of related elements of crimes. Reports in the NIBRS system include data on drug or alcohol influence, weapons used, victim characteristics, location of the offense, and the relationship of the offender to the victim, among other crime-related factors. This system is expected to be in full use by the year 2000.

Sources of Crime Data

Uniform Crime Reports (UCR)

The primary source of data for the UCR is standardized reports of crimes submitted by local police departments to the FBI. These reports are compiled by the FBI and listed in the UCR under each crime category. The volume

Advanced scientific techniques make the study of crime a more accurate science than anyone could have imagined 100 years ago. Forensic evidence is increasingly more important in court cases.

of crime in each category is listed annually, as well as a rate of crime and the percentage change over the previous year and the past five years. The rate of crime is calculated as the number of crimes per 100,000 population. In 1996, for example, there were 7.4 murders for every 100,000 population in the United States.[6] This is lower than the murder rate in 1980, when there were 10.2 murders for every 100,000 population.

Part I of the UCR

The FBI collects data on eight crimes: murder or nonnegligent manslaughter, forcible rape, robbery, aggravated assault, burglary, larceny-theft, motor vehicle theft, and arson. The most recent addition to the list is the crime of arson, which was added in 1979. In addition, the UCR includes data on combined categories, such as hate crime, violent crime, property crime, and all crime. Hate crime was added as a category after legislation was passed by

There Are Many Reasons Why People Fail to Report Crime

Reported crime recorded in the FBI's Uniform Crime Reports (UCR) is only a fraction of all crime. For an offense to be recorded in the UCR it must be either reported to police or observed by police. Occasionally police intercept a crime in progress, but most of the offenses counted by the FBI result from citizen reports. If people do not report crime, the accuracy of the UCR as a measure of real crime trends is seriously undermined. Estimates of the amount of crime that is reported suggest that most crime is *not* reported to the police. According to the most recent National Crime Victimization Survey (NCVS), a little over one-third of all crimes recorded in the survey as victimizations were reported to police in 1994.[21] Violent crimes were more likely to be reported than property crimes, but all crime categories tracked by the NCVS showed less than 50 percent reported to the police.

Most people know they *should* report crime, but they do not—for a variety of reasons. The most common reasons people give for not reporting crime are:

1. *Some people don't believe that the police could or would do anything about the crime if it were reported.* People who live in high-crime neighborhoods often take the occurrence of crime for granted. They see crime in progress more often than they see intervention by police. People may believe the police are powerless against the volume of crime and that reporting it will not reduce or change the character of crime in their neighborhood. Others believe that the police are apathetic about crime in certain neighborhoods and that policing strategies are responsible for a failure to take crime seriously. They don't report because they don't believe the police will take the report seriously. If the crime is minor in nature, victims may think the police will not want to be bothered with reports or investigations. People who have experienced apathy or inaction on the part of the police after they reported previous crimes will be less likely to report subsequent victimizations.

2. *Some people fail to report to the police because they are afraid the offender will retaliate.* If the perpetrator of the crime was someone known to the victim, the offender threatened to do further harm if the crime was reported, or the victim believed the offender would return if the offense were reported, then victims may be unlikely to report to the police. While most crimes of rape are vastly undercounted, of those reported to NCVS investigators in 1994, two-thirds of victims knew their attacker. In nearly half of all violent victimizations tracked by the NCVS, the victim knew the offender.[22] If a victim has already been harmed by an offender, the fear of further harm may prevent reporting the offense.

3. *Often victims of crimes do not report to the police because they do not want to have to appear in court, fill*

Congress in 1990. It includes both violent and property crimes committed as an expression of bias or hatred against particular individuals or groups, who are hated because of their race, ethnicity, religion, disability, or sexual orientation. The violent crime category includes: murder, rape, robbery, and assault. Property crime categories include: burglary, larceny-theft, and motor vehicle theft. (The crime of arson will be included in property crime data eventually, but it has been treated as a separate category while data collection techniques are refined and improved. Many reporting agencies did not collect accurate or consistent data on arson in the first years after it was added to the UCR. As a result, the FBI has cautioned about probable flaws in arson data.) The eight listed crimes are generally called **index crimes** because they are included on the FBI index of serious crimes. The rates of crime calculated by the FBI for all crimes are called the **crime index**.

Part II of the UCR

In addition to index crimes, the FBI collects arrest data on **Part II offenses.** These are crimes that are generally believed to be less serious than index crimes. Rates are not calculated on Part II offenses, although the volume of arrests and the percentage change in the numbers of arrests from year to year and over five years are reported. Part II offenses include:

- Other assaults
- Forgery and counterfeiting
- Fraud
- Embezzlement
- Stolen property, buying, receiving, possessing
- Vandalism
- Weapons, carrying, possessing, etc.
- Prostitution and commercialized vice
- Sex offenses (except forcible rape and prostitution)
- Drug abuse violations
- Offenses against family and children
- Driving under the influence
- Liquor laws
- Drunkenness
- Disorderly conduct
- Vagrancy
- All other offenses (except traffic)
- Suspicion
- Curfew and loitering law violations
- Runaways

BOX 3.1

out forms, or talk about their victimization. Victims are often ashamed, embarrassed, demeaned, or humiliated by the crimes perpetrated against them. This is especially the case for rape, assault, domestic violence, and other crimes for which societal stereotypes of victim provocation are strong. Victims may know they did nothing to provoke the attack, but they believe others will judge their behavior as inappropriate. Victims may believe that time lost from work for court appearances to testify against the perpetrator is not worth the trouble. They often believe that they will have to invest too much time, expense, or personal emotional trauma to make a report worthwhile.

4. *Some victims do not want to see the perpetrator arrested or punished for the offense.* Victims of domestic violence, for example, may believe that reporting the offense will do too much harm to the perpetrator. They may want an end to their victimization, but they do not want the end achieved through the criminal justice system. They may wish that the perpetrator would get counseling or other help, which might be prevented by arrest for the charges against them. Some victims feel that the criminal justice system is too harsh and they may not report minor offenses because they do not want the perpetrator punished. Victims of petty crimes perpetrated by juveniles, for example, may dismiss the offenses as "child's play" rather than crime.

5. *With many crimes, there are no clear "victims" who would be likely to report to police, which means that such crimes are largely uncounted.* So-called victimless crimes, in which the participants of the crimes willingly engage in the illegal activity, are very difficult to count. When both a buyer and a seller of illegal drugs exchange money and drugs, for example, no one is likely to call police and report the offense. Similarly, prostitution, illegal gambling, sale of stolen property, and many other offenses fall within a range of illegal behaviors that are uncommonly reported to police. White-collar and corporate offenses are also unlikely to be reported. Victims may not realize they have been victimized or they may dismiss the victimization as a byproduct of business practices. White-collar and corporate offenses are as difficult to count as victimless crimes.

6. *Simple apathy often results in failure to report crime.* People may feel that it is too much trouble, too time-consuming, or otherwise inconvenient to report crime. Citizen apathy contributes to the volume of unreported crime.

Most arrests are in the Part II crime categories, although statistical tracking of these offenses is much less detailed than index crime categories. In 1996, for example, there were 15.2 million people arrested in all crime categories. About 2.8 million of these arrests involved one of the eight index crimes. In other words, over 80 percent of arrests were in non-index offenses categories in 1996.[7] Arrest patterns do not necessarily indicate crime trends, since not all people arrested actually committed the offense for which they were charged, and many crimes are committed that do not result in arrest of an offender (Box 3.1). Loose interpretation of these trends, however, indicates that the largest volume of crime in the United States falls among the relatively less serious Part II offense categories.

Crimes "Cleared" by Arrest

The FBI also collects data that compares the number of reports of crimes to the number of people arrested for crimes. If a reported crime results in the arrest of an offender, the crime is classified by the FBI as cleared. **Clearance rates** refer to the percentage of crimes cleared by arrest. While not all arrests of offenders result in prosecution or conviction, calculation of reports of crime compared to arrests for reported offenses reveal the crimes that are most likely to be "solved" by police. In general, violent crimes are more likely to be cleared than property crimes. Murder has the highest likelihood of clearance after report. In 1996, 67 percent of reported murders resulted in the arrest of an offender. Burglary and motor vehicle theft have the lowest clearance rates, with 14 percent cleared in 1996 in both offense categories.[8]

Other Information in the UCR

The UCR also contains data on regional crime trends, reports of crime in urban, suburban, and rural areas, and a breakdown of crime trends in the largest American cities, as well as many other details of crime trends. The information reported includes the time of day most crimes occur, the rates of crime in each month of the year, and many characteristics of particular index crimes: Did a burglary occurred in a locked or unlocked structure? Was a stolen vehicle returned to the owner? What was the monetary value of stolen property? These crime data include many details that significantly expand knowledge of index crime categories. Non-index, Part II crimes are reported with much less detail.

TABLE 3.1 | Uniform Crime Reports, Data on Police Officers, 1971–1996

	1971	1975	1980	1985	1991	1996
Percent female	1.4	2.1	5.0	6.8	9.0	10.1
Percent male	98.6	97.9	95.0	93.2	91.0	89.9
No. of officers feloniously killed on duty	178	129	104	78	69	55
Average no. of sworn officers per 1000 inhabitants	1.8	2.1	2.1	2.1	2.3	2.4

SOURCES: Federal Bureau of Investigation, *Crime in the United States, 1971* (Washington DC: U.S. Government Printing Office, 1972) 159, 160, 163; Federal Bureau of Investigation, *Crime in the United States, 1975* (Washington DC: U.S. Government Printing Office, 1976) 223, 225, 235; Federal Bureau of Investigation, *Crime in the United States, 1980* (Washington DC: U.S. Government Printing Office, 1981), 260, 338; Federal Bureau of Investigation, *Crime in the United States, 1985* (Washington DC: U.S. Government Printing Office, 1986) 243, 248; Federal Bureau of Investigation, *Crime in the United States, 1991* (Washington DC: U.S. Government Printing Office, 1982) 290; Federal Bureau of Investigation, *Crime in the United States, 1996* (Washington DC: U.S. Government Printing Office, 1997) 285, 290.

In addition to information about crime trends, the UCR also contains data on law enforcement agencies. Demographic information about police officers, regional variations in staffing trends, and changes over time in the hiring of law enforcement personnel are all found in the UCR.

Table 3.1 illustrates some of the demographic detail provided in the UCR on police officers in the United States. Comparison of the UCR over several years (Table 3.1) provides information about trends among police officers in the United States. This table shows that representation of women among the ranks of sworn police officers rose from 1.4 percent to 10.1 percent between 1971 and 1994. Given the slow increases presented in this table, it is unlikely that a large increase in the percentage of women officers will be evident in any given year. Table 3.1 also shows that the number of officers feloniously killed in the line of duty has decreased significantly from trends in the 1970s, while the number of officers per 1000 inhabitants has risen slowly in the 25 years represented by this table.

Criticisms of the UCR

The UCR provides valuable data on crime trends and a wide array of information on criminal justice activities, yet this report is subject to many criticisms. It is the most widely cited source of crime statistics, although many criminologists believe the NCVS is a more accurate reflection of crime trends. The criticisms of the UCR usually fall within three broad categories: (1) accuracy of the data, (2) exaggeration of crime trends, and (3) politically motivated reporting.

Those who question the accuracy of the UCR point out that changes in the technical aspects of reporting have led to increases in the accuracy of reporting, which gives the false impression of increases in crime. In the early 1980s, for example, UCR crime rates increased significantly. Whether crime actually increased is questionable. In the decade of the 1980s many police departments began computerized record keeping, which increased the accuracy of reporting. The UCR relies on reported crime; if *reports* increase, crime rates go up. Crime may actually decrease in a given period of time, but increased accuracy in reporting gives the false impression that crime increased. Most criminologists, and virtually all law enforcement agencies, recognize that the likelihood of police departments recording reported crime has drastically increased in the past two decades. When measurement of crime depends upon crimes reported, better reporting means more crime is recorded, which means that rates increase.

Do not underestimate the impact of technical changes in reporting. Methods of tabulating reported crime have been updated state by state in recent years. For example, Iowa updated in 1991, Kansas changed in 1993, and tabulation techniques in Illinois and Montana were altered in 1994. For the crime of rape, which researchers generally believe to be vastly underreported, national *estimates* of rape rates are calculated for the states. In 1994, the estimates previously published in 1993 for Minnesota and Nebraska were updated and revised, which altered the 1993 rates of rape for these states.[9] While each change in tabulation techniques is designed to improve the accuracy of the UCR, interpretation of crime data may be based on faulty assumptions (increase or decrease) that actually derive from technical changes.

While the use of reported crime as the primary measurement tool has the potential for exaggerating crime trends, critics point to another flaw in the method of recording reports of crime as a significant source of inflated rates. If two people are arrested for a single crime, the standard means of recording this is to count both arrests, rather than one crime. If, for example, a home is burglarized and two suspects are apprehended, the police would record two crimes of burglary, one for each suspect. Whether this is actually two crimes is a matter of debate. Only one home has been burglarized, but two individuals committed the crime. Recording of the crime as two burglaries tends to inflate the perception of the offense and to distort clearance rates. The practice of counting all suspects rather than one crime is especially problematic in calculating juvenile crime rates because juveniles are often arrested in groups.[10]

The final criticism of the UCR is that underlying political issues may affect reporting. Hiring practices, increases in equipment, and expansion of police roles in a given locale are commonly tied to perceived needs. If

TABLE 3.2 | FBI Crime Rates, 1995–1996

	NUMBER OF OFFENSES REPORTED	RATE PER 100,000 INHABITANTS
CRIME INDEX TOTAL		
1995	13,862,727	5,275.9
1996	13,473,614	5,078.9
Percent change	−2.8	−3.7
VIOLENT CRIME TOTAL		
1995	1,798,792	684.6
1996	1,682,278	634.1
Percent change	−6.5	−7.4
PROPERTY CRIME TOTAL[a]		
1995	12,063,935	4,591.3
1996	11,791,336	4,444.8
Percent change	−2.3	−3.2

[a]Arson is not included in the property crime totals or in the rates of property crime.

SOURCE: FBI, *Crime in the United States, 1996* (Washington DC: U.S. Government Printing Office, 1997) 5, 10, 35.

crime rates increase, the obvious solution is to deploy more police officers, to increase equipment, or to upgrade technical services. Critics contend that police have a vested interest in preserving high crime rates. Without crime, the need for all aspects of police work declines. Few people suggest that police actually alter reports, but many believe that policies (like the previously cited trend of reporting each suspect as a separate crime) may be integrated at many levels in implicit promotion of law enforcement as the solution to crime trends.

Crime Rates

Table 3.2 presents index crime rates in the largest categories for 1996. (Individual crimes will be discussed in subsequent chapters.) Recall that the FBI calculates the rate as the number of crimes per 100,000 population. Standardizing reported crime for the size of the population makes it possible to compare places with different populations. If the *volume* of crime were compared, rather than the *rate,* it would not be possible to compare sparsely populated regions with urban areas. Thus, the use of rates is a means of standardizing the comparison groups. In Table 3.2, the volume of crime reported in 1996 declined by just over 2.8 percent, but the rate of crime declined by 3.7 percent. In other words, the number of crimes declined while the population increased slightly. When the number of crimes is compared with the population increase, the rate of decline becomes even greater.

National Crime Victimization Survey (NCVS)

The NCVS is a measure of crime that uses interviews with household occupants who are 12 and older to determine the number and rate of personal and household offenses in a given year. Representatives from the Bureau of the Census interview each household participant at 6-month intervals. In 1994, approximately 120,000 residents of 56,000 households were interviewed about crimes they had experienced in the previous 6 months.[11] The data are compiled and analyzed by the Bureau of Justice Statistics.

The NCVS is second in size only to the U.S. Census as an ongoing household survey. Not all crimes are measured by the NCVS, but those most likely to be identified by survey participants are included in the general survey. Data include information about rape, robbery, assault, burglary, personal and household larceny, and motor vehicle theft. All respondents are asked to indicate whether they reported each crime to police. From this information measures of unreported crime are calculated. Data about victims of homicide are not included in the NCVS because murder victims cannot be interviewed. Commercial burglary and robbery were dropped from the survey in 1977 and victimless crimes (public drunkenness, prostitution, drug abuse) are not measured.[12]

A yearly report from the NCVS includes about 120 tables. Characteristics of victims, offenders, weapons use, degree of injury to victims, monetary losses from property crimes, costs of medical treatment in personal injuries, average amount of lost wages due to victimization, and reasons for reporting or failing to report crimes to the police are included in the many topics covered by the NCVS. Victimization trends that differ by age, race, sex, income, or region are detailed in the NCVS annual report.

Victimization Rates

The NCVS also calculates rates of victimization. Rates are based on the number of victimizations per 1000 population. UCR rates, which are based upon the number of crimes reported for every 100,000 population, are only roughly comparable to NCVS rates. Multiplying NCVS rates by a factor of 100 will provide a rough comparison of the number of crimes reported to police compared with the number of victimizations reported to NCVS interviewers. The NCVS cautions that only rough comparisons should be drawn. NCVS definitions are compatible with conventional usage of crime categories and with the definitions used by the FBI, but the populations from which the data are drawn are different. UCR data derives from reported crime. About 50 percent of crimes reported to the NCVS are not reported to police in any given year.[13]

Criticism of the NCVS

The NCVS is subject to much less criticism than the UCR because the interview strategies are similar to industry standards in any other scientific polling technique. Public opinion polls, Nielsen television ratings, and other surveys are similar in nature and technique. Most criticisms of the NCVS are similar to criticism of any other type of survey

BOX 3.2

Estimation of the Scope of Gang Crime from Law Enforcement Data

Specific types of crime that fall outside of traditional definitions of crime categories are often difficult to estimate. Assaults are calculated by both NCVS and UCR statistical measures, but determining the number of assaults perpetrated by gang members in gang-related activities may be difficult. While some people might argue that it doesn't really matter who commits an assault or whether the activity is gang-related, researchers use indices of gang crime to determine whether criminal activities of gangs are changing. The level of gang-related crime also influences a range of policy decisions and law enforcement strategies.

To estimate the magnitude and scope of gang-related crime, G. David Curry and colleagues took crime data from 122 municipalities with populations from 150,000 to 200,000, and data from 284 cities with populations from 25,000 to 150,000. The researchers sent letters to law enforcement agencies in those cities, inquiring about the existence of a gang crime problem in their jurisdictions. From those cities that tracked gang-crime activity, statistical profiles of the number of gangs, gang members, and gang-related crime were calculated. Findings were compared with previous studies to determine changes in gang-related crime over time.

The results of this research indicate that 88 percent of law enforcement agencies in the largest cities and 56 per-

cent in medium-sized cites reported problems with gang crime in 1994. Estimates of gang-related crime range from a conservative estimate of 437,066 to a "reasonable" estimate of 580,331 crimes. The conservative estimate reflects the *reported* gang-related crimes. Critics have charged that counting only those offenses that are known to have gang involvement underestimates the actual amount of gang-related crime, since not all jurisdictions count such crimes separately. The reasonable estimate includes estimates for cities that report a gang problem but do not calculate separate statistics for gang-related crimes.

The reasonable estimate of the number of gangs in American cities indicates that there are about 16,650 gangs. The greatest increase in gang-related crime is among cities with the smallest populations. The study further indicates that the gang problem in American cities has yielded increasingly higher levels of crime for several years.

While gang-related crime may seem to be self-evident from news reports or commonsense perceptions of gang problems, determining exact proportions of gang-related crime and changes over time is more problematic than a casual observer might assume. Research into this problem relies on reports from cities where gang-related crime is a problem, since standard statistical sources do not track crime of this type.

SOURCE: G. David Curry, Richard A. Ball, and Scott H. Decker, "Estimating the National Scope of Gang Crime from Law Enforcement Data, " *National Institute of Justice: Research in Brief* (Washington DC: U.S. Department of Justice, 1996).

research: respondents may lie to interviewers; some crimes may have been forgotten, exaggerated, or misrepresented; and use of a sample of households rather than all households may include a sampling error that would not be obvious to researchers.

The problem of potential sampling error is a perennial concern of all survey research. In theory, including households in the survey with either more or less than the average experience of crime could distort the picture presented by the NCVS. While these criticisms do represent potential problems, as would be the case with any other similar survey research, the use of 120,000 respondents reduces the likelihood of distortion that results from sampling error. The Bureau of the Census balances income, ethnic, regional, and other demographic characteristics of participants in the survey. Errors in the NCVS are no more likely than in political polls, public opinion surveys, or television viewing reports, all of which use similar

methods for data collection. People most likely to be excluded from the data are those who are homeless or transient, or who do not have telephones. Many researchers believe people in these circumstances are subject to higher-than-average crime victimization. If sampling error results in an undercount of victimization, the poor are the most likely to be excluded. Underrepresentation of the poor in most public polling, including the U.S. Census, has been a common criticism of survey research.

While criminologists have generally supported the use of the NCVS as an important source of crime data, one category of crime has been highly criticized as unreliable. Data on rape, as reported in both the UCR and the NCVS, are believed to be significantly underrepresentative of this crime. Because the UCR relies on reported crime, when victims do not report the offense the count is lower than the incidence of the crime. Similarly, the NCVS has been criticized because the questions about rape are ambiguous and often use archaic language to describe the crime. The victimization question asks respondents about "carnal knowledge through the use of force. . . ."[14] Victims may not understand the question, they may be reluctant to answer follow-up questions concerning the offense, or they may not understand that certain forms of coerced sexual behavior are criminal. Victims who may not know, for example, that rape by a husband is a crime would be unlikely to respond that they have been victims of this crime; indeed, rape by a husband is *not* a crime in all states. For a wide variety of reasons that will be discussed in Chapter 5, the victimization data on the crime of rape is believed to be significantly under-counted.

Comparison of NCVS and UCR Data

NCVS data tend to verify the rough trends presented by the UCR, but the increases in crime are less dramatically portrayed by the NCVS and the decreases tend to be more pronounced. In the early 1980s, the NCVS showed increases in crime that were similar to the increases presented by the UCR. The rates of victimization increased, in other words, when the FBI reported increases in UCR index offenses. The fact that the NCVS usually shows a less dramatic increase suggests either that some of the UCR reports of increase may be due to an increased flurry of reporting or that victimization is underreported to NCVS interviewers. Most researchers side with the representations of crime trends portrayed by the NCVS. Reports of crime are easily affected by media attention, technological adjustments in reporting, or other factors that are independent of true crime trends. Rough parallels between the two techniques indicate that both measures track crime trends, but there are significant differences between the two in exact measures of crime.

Table 3.3 illustrates NCVS tracking of the same crime categories identified in Table 3.2 from UCR data. Because the NCVS lags a couple of years behind the UCR, the data from the NCVS are one year different from the UCR data. As you can see from a comparison of Tables 3.2 and 3.3, both show overall declines in crime, but the rates are different. The NCVS showed an 8.8 percent decrease in the volume of violent crime, but a drop in the rate of 12.4 percent. The UCR decline in violent crime rates showed a 6.5 percent decrease during 1995–96. The NCVS showed no changed in the percentage of victims reporting violent crime to police in these years.[15] In general, the NCVS indicates that about 40 percent of violent crimes are reported to police. Police recording strategies, technical changes in data collection, or some other procedural change may account for differences in declines in violent crime portrayed by the two measures. Both measures have shown decline in violent crime in recent years, but there is variation in the amount of decline documented by each measure.

TABLE 3.3 | NCVS Crime Rates, 1994–1995

	NUMBER OF VICTIMIZATIONS EXPERIENCED	RATE PER 1000 INHABITANTS
ALL CRIMES TOTAL		
1994	43,362,000	Not calculated
1995	38,446,000	Not calculated
Percent change	–9.1	
VIOLENT CRIME TOTAL		
1994	11,350,000	50.8
1995	9,966,000	44.5
Percent change	–8.8	–12.4
PROPERTY CRIME TOTAL		
1994	31,012,000	307.6
1995	28,480,000	279.5
Percent change	–9.2	–9.1

SOURCE: Bruce M. Taylor, "Change in Criminal Victimization, 1994–95," *Bureau of Justice Statistics Bulletin* (Washington DC: U. S. Government Printing Office, 1997) 2.

Self-Report Surveys

In addition to government statistics, there are other techniques for the study of crime. **Self-report surveys** have been used for several decades as a means of determining levels of undetected crime. With this technique, respondents fill out an anonymous survey indicating whether they have committed any crimes listed on the survey. In 1947, James Wallerstein and Clement Wyle were among the first to use this method.[16] They asked over 1000 men and nearly 700 women whether they had committed any crimes on a list of 49 different offenses. Almost all respondents had committed an offense for which they could have been incarcerated for at least 1 year. Some had committed relatively minor offenses, but 64 percent of the men and 29 percent of the women had committed at least one felony. This survey has been criticized for a lack of sophistication in sampling and analysis, but the implications of the findings have been widely cited; that is, many more Americans engage in criminal behavior than appear in official statistics.

Most self-report research has concentrated on the study of juvenile offenders. Juvenile crime is by nature difficult to study because many offenders are warned and released without official action, and many juvenile offenses fall in petty or non-serious crime categories. F. Ivan Nye and James F. Short conducted one study of juvenile offenders in 1957.[17] They distributed 3000 surveys to high school students and over 300 surveys to youth incarcerated in juvenile correctional facilities. Among the findings of the research was that juvenile delinquency cuts across socioeconomic levels. Previous stereotypes that delinquents were most likely to come from lower-income families were broken by this research. While lower-class juveniles were more likely to be processed officially or punished as juvenile

Police rarely intercept a crime in progress. More commonly, they rely on citizens' reports of crime. Reports of crime to the police are the basis for crime data in the FBI's Uniform Crime Reports.

delinquents, the activities of upper-class juveniles also constituted serious delinquent behavior. Many other self-report studies followed Nye and Short's work.

Benefits and Problems of Self-Report Research

The appeal of this type of research is that it has the potential to expand knowledge provided by government statistics. Surveys of offenders may unmask sociocultural factors that help to explain crime. Respondents, for example, may be asked questions about family background, school experiences, employment history, or other potentially important factors that may influence criminal behavior. While UCR data provides aggregate (group) data about race, gender, or age of offenders, self-report studies break down these large demographic distinctions into more refined measures of criminal involvement.

The appeal of self-report data is great. Researchers are able to collect information about a wide array of personal or societal characteristics that would not be available from government statistics. The cost of such research, however, has become prohibitively expensive in recent years. Another problem with this type of research is that its data collection techniques are not standard-

ized. In contrast, government statistics may change over time as data collection techniques improve, but techniques are standardized for all parts of the country at any given moment. With the Department of Justice serving as the clearinghouse for statistical data, consistent methodologies are used from one study to the next and from one year to another. Most self-report research is conducted by researchers who are affiliated with a university or private foundation and overarching standardization is lacking.

A further problem with self-report data is that there is great potential for the generation of data based upon faulty reports by respondents. While the same may be said of any other type of survey research, this technique is especially prone to the potential of flawed data. People may be reluctant to admit to criminal behavior, even when they are assured anonymity. Most of the early evaluations of self-report research, however, found that respondents had been truthful in their responses about criminal involvement. John Clark and Larry Tifft, for example, told youths who had responded to a self-report survey in 1966 that a polygraph test would be used to verify their responses, and the researchers then allowed

Crime Statistics in the Federal Republic of Germany

As in the United States, crimes in the Federal Republic of Germany are divided into felonies and misdemeanors. The *Bundeskriminalamt,* or Police Crime Statistics, collect data on crimes known to the police. The statistics include data on the size of communities, use of firearms, and characteristics of suspects. For certain offenses, the amount of damage that resulted from the crime is calculated. Also for certain offenses, the age and sex of victims and prior relationships between victims and suspects are tracked. The Police Statistics include data on cleared cases and the age, sex, and place of residence of suspects. Offenses are tracked over time with crime rates, which include the number of offenses known to police per 100,000 inhabitants. According to the *Bundeskriminalamt,* the crime statistics are not completely accurate because not all crime is reported. As in the United States, some crimes are more likely to be reported than others.

In 1995, 57.7 percent of all crimes recorded in Germany were thefts. Of these, over 60 percent were committed under aggravated circumstances. Violent crime and drug offenses have risen sharply in recent years. Drug offenses, for example, increased by 19.7 percent in 1995.

At first glance it would seem that American crime statistics would be comparable to German statistics. There are many similarities in the means by which the statistics are maintained. For example, rates are calculated by the same formula, reported crimes are the basic unit of measure in both the United States and Germany, and crimes are divided into serious and less-serious categories. Differences in definition of crime categories, however, make direct comparison difficult. The FBI divides theft categories by the value of the stolen commodity. **Larceny** involves theft of something with little economic value. Other thefts are divided in the UCR by threat or use of violence (**robbery**) or whether the item stolen was a motor vehicle. In Germany theft is defined by whether violence was used, whether there was damage to property, or whether fraud was committed by the suspect. Even simple comparisons of rates of offense are problematic when the definitions of the crimes are different.

Similarly, overall crime rates between countries are not directly comparable. In the United States the crime rate is based on reported index offenses, which include only the eight crimes listed by the FBI in Part I crime statistics. In Germany the crime rate is based on 23 crimes, some of which would be comparable to FBI Part II offenses. Comparison of declines or increases in crime or changes in crime patterns between the two countries should be interpreted cautiously. In general, comparison of crime patterns of different countries is very difficult because laws vary from country to country and definitions of crime reflect cultural and societal patterns that are highly variable among countries.

SOURCE: Bundeskriminalamt, *Polizeiliche Kriminalstatistik* (Wiesbaden, Federal Republic of Germany, 1994).

---

the respondents to change answers on the survey. Only a few actually indicated that they should change some responses.[18]

In other research, the veracity of respondents has been questioned. Elliot Currie found in 1993, for example, that respondents were less likely to admit drug involvement than other prior criminal activity. In this study, arrestees were asked to complete questionnaires about drug use. The survey was followed by a urine test to determine whether respondents tested positive for drugs. Only about half of those who tested positive had reported drug use on the survey. The likelihood of reporting their drug use was lowest among those who had used drugs with the highest criminal penalties.[19] This research illustrates that the potential of misinformation is an important concern in self-report studies.

Other Sources of Crime Data

In addition to the sources of crime data previously cited, information is generated by several other means. The Department of Justice publishes regular reports on a wide variety of crime-related topics. For example, data on correctional populations, court statistics, state and federal justice employees, and sentencing are compiled by the Bureau of Justice Statistics. Highly specific types of crime data (crimes committed by military personnel or illegal aliens, or death penalty statistics) are published in regular special bulletins from the Bureau of Justice Statistics. One very large volume of crime data that compiles summaries from all government statistics is published annually by the Department of Justice as the *Sourcebook of Criminal Justice Statistics.*

All states compile and publish crime statistics as well as analysis of state programs for crime prevention, sentencing strategies, trends in corrections, or special crime problems, among other issues. In Illinois, for example, the Illinois Criminal Justice Information Authority publishes quarterly reports about crime and corrections in the state. Their publication, *The Compiler,* is published by a state agency for the purpose of disseminating information about criminal justice in the state.

Numerous criminal justice policies and police procedures are built upon crime statistics. Police look for crime among certain groups or in particular neighborhoods on the basis of information provided by crime statistics.

Many specialized services also publish crime data. Domestic violence shelters, rape crisis programs, shelters for the homeless, private and public drug treatment facilities, and juvenile shelters often compile both victimization data and criminal history data, which is sometimes published as aggregate data.

Participant observation research, in which the researcher joins a group for the purpose of studying the activities of the group, also provides insider information about the intricacies of certain types of criminal justice or crime activities. Researchers interested in police strategies for crime prevention might ride in a squad car to observe officer behavior, or those interested in gang activities might hang out where gang members are likely to congregate. One of the most famous participant observation studies was William Whyte's *Street Corner Society,* which was published in 1955.[20] In this study, field observers observed a Boston street gang while remaining in the background of the gang and without involving themselves in ongoing gang activities. Data collected by participant observation techniques provide *qualitative* information (intensive study without statistical analysis) about crime, criminals, or the criminal justice system.

In addition to these sources, many private research groups collect crime data. The National Opinion Research Center, the Gallup Poll, and many social science research services include crime questions on their national surveys. The data derived from national polls is often combined with crime data from government sources to expand understanding of crime. The Gallup Poll might ask respondents to indicate whether they favor having a greater share of public funds directed to crime fighting programs or education. The poll results could direct attention either toward or away from crime fighting programs supported by politicians. National survey questions about drug use or attitudes about drugs are often combined with crime statistics in research on the proposed relationship between drugs and crime.

Summary

Collection and interpretation of crime data is much more problematic than most people realize. Many crime statistics may be interpreted in a variety of ways, and uninformed interpretations often lead to inaccurate representation of crime data. Simple assessments are often inaccurate because crime data are never simple. News reports of FBI data that indicate "declines" or "increases" in crime, for example, should be interpreted cautiously. When UCR data indicate crime has "decreased" or "increased," there is no assurance that *rates* have actually changed in one direction or another. Rather, the UCR "decreases" or "increases" measure changes in *reports* of crime.

Many factors other than fluctuations in actual crime may account for changes in UCR data. Increases in police personnel often lead to increases in the reporting of crime because more personnel are available to handle the workload of reporting. If the UCR is interpreted as a measure of crime, rather than *reports* of crime, the logical solution would be to reduce the number of police officers as a crime fighting measure. If more police are associated with increases in UCR crimes, then the logical solution to crime would be to reduce police personnel. If the UCR is interpreted as reports of crime, rather than actual crime, the implications are quite different. More police means better reporting, which means more crime reports are included in the UCR.

While other measures of crime are not as prone to misinterpretation as the FBI statistics, the likelihood of misuse or misinterpretation is still a potential problem with most crime data. Virtually all crime statistics may be misused if the means of data collection are not understood by the users of the statistics. Sometimes crime data are intentionally distorted for political purposes. Often statistics are selectively reported to give the impression that crime trends have shifted. As you study further, you will become aware of the many alternative responses that may be derived from a single crime "fact." You will begin to see a complex picture of crime rather than the simple solutions often proposed by politicians.

In this chapter we have examined the most commonly used measures of crime in the United States. In subsequent chapters we will examine the ways in which these measures are used, and misused, in the study of crime.

Critical Thinking Questions

1. Which measure of crime would you choose as the most accurate source of crime data? Why did you choose this measure, and what is wrong with the other methods of collecting crime data that you did not choose?
2. Which crimes would you add to the FBI list of index crimes? Why?
3. Explain why it is difficult to measure certain crimes, such as rape or domestic violence. Are there other crimes, not listed in the chapter, that are difficult to measure?

4. If you were trying to develop a recommendation for punishment of drunk drivers, what crime statistics would you use to support your policy recommendation? What information, in addition to crime statistics, would be useful for the development of such a public policy?

Suggested Readings

Elliot Currie, *Reckoning: Drugs, the Cities, and the American Future* (New York: Hill and Wang, 1993).

Steven R. Donziger, ed., *The Real War on Crime: The Report of the National Criminal Justice Commission* (New York: Harper Perennial, 1996).

Notes

[1] Carol Smart "The New Female Offender: Reality of Myth?" in *The Criminal Justice System and Women*, ed. Barbara Raffel Price and Natalie J. Sokoloff (New York: Clark Boardman, 1982) 109.

[2] Kathleen Maguire and Ann L. Pastore, *Sourcebook of Criminal Justice Statistics* (Washington DC: U.S. Government Printing Office, 1996) 338–39; Federal Bureau of Investigation (FBI), *Crime in The United States* (Washington DC: U.S. Government Printing Office, 1995) 58.

[3] FBI, *Crime in The United States*, iii.

[4] Ibid. About 96 percent of the population is represented by the UCR reporting program.

[5] Craig Perkins and Patsy Klaus,"Criminal Victimization 1994," *Bureau of Justice Statistics Bulletin* (Washington DC: U.S. Government Printing Office, 1996) 8.

[6] FBI, *Crime in the United States* (Washington DC: U.S. Government Printing Office, 1997) 13.

[7] Ibid., 214.

[8] Ibid., 38, 42, 52. In addition, police "clear" some crimes after the conviction of an offender, even if he or she has not been convicted of a particular crime. In the case of the Atlanta serial murderer, for example, Wayne Williams was convicted of only two murders, but the police cleared twenty-seven from their files.

[9] FBI, *Crime in The United States*, 377.

[10] Steven R. Donziger, ed., *The Real War on Crime: The Report of the National Criminal Justice Commission* (New York: Harper, 1996) 4.

[11] Perkins and Klaus, "Criminal Victimization 1994," 8.

[12] Lisa D. Bastian and Marshall M. DeBerry, Jr., "Criminal Victimization in the United State, 1992," *U.S. Department of Justice Bureau of Justice Statistics* (Washington DC: U.S. Government Printing Office, 1994) iii, 1.

[13] Ibid., iii.

[14] Mary P. Koss, "The Measurement of Rape Victimization in Crime Surveys," *Criminal Justice and Behavior 23* (1996) 1, 57.

[15] Perkins and Klaus, "Criminal Victimization 1994," 3.

[16] James Wallerstein and Clement Wyle, "Our Law-Abiding Law-Breakers." *Federal Probation 25* (1947) 107–118.

[17] F. Ivan Nye and James F. Short, Jr., "Scaling Delinquent Behavior," *American Sociological Review 22* (1957) 326–31.

[18] John P. Clark and Larry L. Tifft, "Polygraphy and Interview Validation of Self-Reported Deviant Behavior," *American Sociological Review 31* (1966) 516–23.

[19] Elliot Currie, *Reckoning: Drugs, the Cities, and the American Future* (New York: Hill and Wang, 1993).

[20] William Whyte, *Street Corner Society* (Chicago: University of Chicago Press, 1955).

[21] Ibid., 1.

[22] Ibid., 7.

chapter 4

Myths and Facts About Crime

CHAPTER OUTLINE
MYTH 1: CRIME IS INCREASING
MYTH 2: MOST CRIME IS VIOLENT
MYTH 3: CRIME OCCURS MAINLY IN THE LOWER CLASSES
MYTH 4: CRIME IS BAD FOR EVERYONE
MYTH 5: MOST CRIMINALS ARE HARD-CORE AND STRANGERS
    TO THE VICTIM
MYTH 6: MOST CRIMES ARE SOLVED AND OFFENDERS PUNISHED
MYTH 7: MOST CRIMINALS WHO GO TO TRIAL "GET OFF"
    The Exclusionary Rule
MYTH 8: THERE IS NO RELATIONSHIP BETWEEN GUNS AND VIOLENCE
MYTH 9: WOMEN ARE BECOMING "AS BAD AS" MEN
MYTH 10: THE WAY TO REMEDY CRIME IS TO GET TOUGH
MYTH 11: DRUGS CAUSE CRIME
MYTH 12: NOTHING CAN BE DONE TO REDUCE CRIME
SUMMARY

KEY TERMS

rate of crime
volume of crime
acquittal
dismissal
hung jury
exclusionary rule
search warrant
good faith efforts of police
get-tough policies
recidivists
truth in sentencing laws
minimum mandatory sentences

MOST PEOPLE ARE AWARE of the pervasive nature of crime in modern American society. Television dramas and news reports contribute to commonly held perceptions about American crime. Reports of new forms of criminal activity, as well as daily examples of violent crimes from virtually all segments of society, seem to indicate escalating problems and a tendency toward more dangerous types of antisocial behavior. In reality, the portrayal of crime, both in news reporting and entertainment, distorts the typical patterns of American crime. Television crime shows, for example, often develop the story line of a drama around a murder. While the unfolding of the plot engages viewers in unraveling the mystery, the repeated use of murder as the basis of fictitious crime stories gives the impression that homicide cases are routine police duties. Actually, homicide is the least frequently committed violent crime in America.

In this chapter we will review some common myths about crime in the United States. Many of the stereotypes people hold about crime do not match reality. We will discuss only the most prevalent misperceptions here, although there are many others that could be examined. After reading this chapter you may become skeptical of simplified explanations of crime, thus sparking your own discovery of additional myths.

In recent years several books have been published that specifically address many common myths about crime and criminal justice in America.[1] While each book has a unique approach to explaining real patterns, there are several common themes. First, many myths about crime originate from the differential reporting of crime by news media. While murders, assaults, carjackings, and other violent offenses are newsworthy because of their sensational nature, media focus on these crimes gives the false impression that they are the most serious and prevalent crimes in the United States. Few people believe that the news media consciously distort the image of crime. Rather, the reporters' own curiosity about highly unusual events and the pressures to attract and maintain an audience often direct attention to the sensational while ordinary events are ignored. It is the nature of "news" that ordinary events are less interesting than extraordinary events. Thus, much greater media attention is devoted to violent crime than common property crime. The effect is the widely accepted belief that violent crime is rising, when in fact news coverage of violence is actually rising faster than violent crime rates.

A second common theme of the recent books exploring the myths about crime is that many of the designations of "danger" that are applied to crime are related as much to political values as to the inherent nature of the behavior. No one seriously disputes the danger of violent crime, but the penalties for many crimes are weighted to reflect underlying political values. In his book *The Rich Get Richer and the Poor Get Prison*, Jeffrey Reiman discusses the differences between murders and industrial tragedies as an example of this differential weighting. When willful behavior perpetrated by one individual against another results in death, the act is called murder. Yet, according to Reiman, when willful illegal behavior of corporations results in deaths of workers, the result is termed an accident or a tragedy.[2] The underlying difference in perception of these events reflects the motivations behind the offenses and the social status of the offenders. Individuals who perpetrate murder do so with the intent of harming or killing victims. Corporations who neglect worker safety or knowingly put workers in danger do so with the intent of increasing profits, even if "accidents" happen in the process. The difference in official response to the two acts reflects political values as well as the inherent seriousness of the behaviors. The books noted earlier explore the divergent values that underly many designations of crime. Drug crime, in particular, has been a myth-laden designation.

A third theme that runs through many recent explorations of crime myths is the effect of false perceptions about crime on the development of criminal justice policy. The U.S. criminal justice system has outstripped all expectations; a higher proportion of the population is imprisoned in the United States than in any other country in the world. Among the many crime myths is the belief that rising rates of crime justify increased incarceration of offenders and the building of new prisons. Actually, the rate of crime has not increased proportional to rising rates of incarceration. Current criminal justice policy, which calls for combating crime through more and longer prison sentences and reduced use of alternative sentences, does not reflect changing crime patterns. Other factors motivate criminal justice policies. Recent theorists blame various social trends for the accelerated use of prisons, but increased crime is not among them. We begin our discussion of crime myths with one of the most widely believed ideas about crime in America.

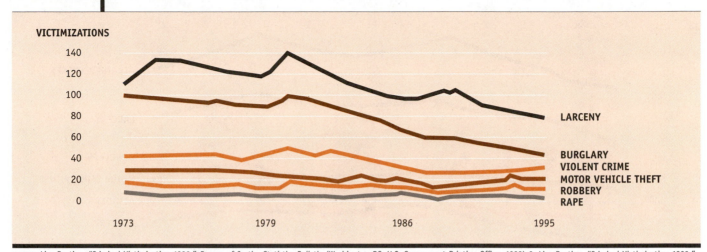

VICTIMIZATIONS

LARCENY

BURGLARY
VIOLENT CRIME
MOTOR VEHICLE THEFT
ROBBERY
RAPE

1973   1979   1986   1995

SOURCE: Lisa Bastian, "Criminal Victimization 1992," *Bureau of Justice Statistics Bulletin* (Washington DC: U.S. Government Printing Office, 1993) 2; Lisa Bastian, "Criminal Victimization 1993," *Bureau of Justice Statistics Bulletin* (Washington DC: U.S. Government Printing Office, 1995) 2; Bruce Taylor, "Changes in Criminal Victimization, 1994–95," *Bureau of Justice Statistics Bulletin* (Washington DC: U.S. Government Printing Office, 1997) 2.

Myth 1: Crime Is Increasing

The problem of crime sparks considerable political debate over the way convicted offenders should be punished. Changes in sentencing strategies (see Chapters 15, 16) have increased the amount of time offenders are incarcerated, which has contributed to overcrowding in prisons. Current crises of overcrowding have prompted many people to assume that a shortage of cell space is related to rising crime rates. General impressions of rising rates of crime are prevalent, but data on crime trends indicate that official rates of crime have declined or remained stable since the early 1980s.

As discussed in Chapter 3, the most commonly used measures of crime in the United States are the National Crime Victimization Survey (NCVS) and the Uniform Crime Reports (UCR). The NCVS tracks crime trends from reports of victimization collected by the National Institute of Justice (NIJ), and the UCR is a compilation of data collected by the Federal Bureau of Investigation (FBI) from crimes reported to police. Both types of crime statistics indicate declines in some crime rates and stable trends in others since the early 1980s, although the UCR pattern of decline is more erratic than that indicated by the NCVS data.

Accurate interpretation of crime data is dependent upon the use of rates of crime, as opposed to the volume of crime. The **rate of crime** is standardized to control for population fluctuations, while the **volume of crime** is the number of crimes in a given time. In 1981, for example, there were 19,009 household crimes reported in the NCVS. In 1992, there were 14,817 NCVS household crimes reported, which represented a 22 percent decline in the *vol-*

ume of household crimes between 1981 and 1992. When the rates of household crime for 1981 and 1992 are compared, however, the decline is significantly greater because the population increased over the decade. The rate of household crimes in 1981 was 226.0 per 1000 persons; by 1992 this rate had declined to 152.0, which represents a 33 percent decline in household crimes.[3] Those who interpret increases in crime from the volume of crime reported may distort the impact of actual changes. Increases will occur as the population expands, but the more accurate question to be addressed is whether crime is increasing *faster* than population increases. For the most part, the volume of crime in the 1990s is close to that of the 1970s, but the rate of crime has generally declined.

Crime rates did peak in the early 1980s, with another smaller peak in 1990. In other words, there was an increase in the rate of crime in the first few years of the decade of the 1980s and another less dramatic peak in 1990 that indicated higher crime than in the late 1970s or currently. Other than these peaks, crime trends have been stable or declining. Current rates are roughly comparable to rates in the 1970s. Figure 4.1 shows the decline from NCVS data and Figure 4.2 indicates the UCR rate changes.

The fact that rates of crime have declined in recent years is difficult for people to understand because publicity about crime is high and contemporary political rhetoric suggests that crime is a more serious threat to most Americans than it was in earlier generations. While overall trends indicate that these assumptions are false, certain facts about modern crime patterns do warrant concern. In spite of general declines in crime, the rates *are* up among the youngest offenders. That is, crime

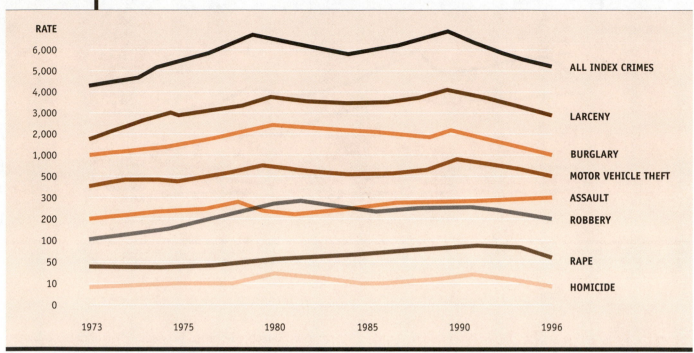

SOURCE: Kathleen Maguire and Ann L. Pastore, *Sourcebook of Criminal Justice Statistics* (Washington DC: U.S. Government Printing Office, 1995) 305; Federal Bureau of Investigation, *Crime in the United States* (Washington DC: U.S. Government Printing Office, 1995) 4, 5, 10, 12, 23, 26, 31, 38; Federal Bureau of Investigation, *Crime in the United States* (Washington DC: U.S. Government Printing Office, 1997) 4, 5, 10, 12, 23, 26, 31, 38.

rates indicate that offenders between the ages of 16 and 19 have the highest rates of violent offenses, and that these rates have been rising since the late 1980s.[4] Rates of violent crime among the youngest offenders have not altered the general downward crime trends, but they may show some influence in future trends if crime continues to rise among this group.

Myth 2: Most Crime Is Violent

The frequency with which violent crime is reported often gives the public the impression that this is the most common type of crime in the United States. Graphic violence in entertainment further exacerbates the common perception that these crimes pervade American culture. In reality, violent offenses are less common than either property offenses or non-index "victimless" crimes (public drunkenness, prostitution, drug abuse). The violent crime with the most frightening outcome, homicide, is the least frequently committed index offense traced by the FBI. Table 4.1 presents, from the UCR data of 1996, the rates of violent crime compared with property crime and the total index rates.

The most common types of criminal offenses in the United States are property crimes. The lowest-level prop-

TABLE 4.1 | Uniform Crime Reports: Violent Crime, 1996 (rate per 100,000 population)

CRIME	VOLUME	RATE	FREQUENCY OF OCCURRENCE
Murder	19,645	7.4	1 every 27 minutes
Rape	95,769	36.1	1 every 6 minutes
Robbery	537,050	202.4	1 every 59 seconds
Assault	1,029,814	388.2	1 every 31 seconds
Total violent crime	1,682,278	634.1	1 every 19 seconds
Property total	11,791,336	4,444.8	1 every 3 seconds
All index total	13,473,614	5,078.9	1 every 2 seconds

SOURCE: Federal Bureau of Investigation, *Crime in America* (Washington DC: U.S. Government Printing Office, 1995) 4, 5, 10, 13, 23, 26, 31, 35.

erty offense, larceny, is the single most common offense category. The FBI calculates that one reported larceny occurs about every 4 seconds, although the NCVS estimates that only 25 percent of larceny crimes are actually reported to the police.[5] Figure 4.3 illustrates the relationship of violent crime to the overall volume of crime from 1973 through 1993.

While violent crime may not be as prevalent as other types of crimes in the United States, the consequences for victims of such offenses are often severe and long-lasting; thus, the relative infrequency of such crimes should not

FIGURE 4.3 | Victimization Trends, 1973–1995

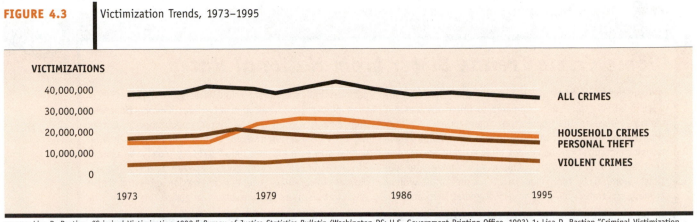

SOURCE: Lisa D. Bastian, "Criminal Victimization 1992," *Bureau of Justice Statistics Bulletin* (Washington DC: U.S. Government Printing Office, 1993) 1; Lisa D. Bastian,"Criminal Victimization 1993," *Bureau of Justice Statistics Bulletin* (Washington DC: U.S. Government Printing Office, 1995) 1; Bruce M. Taylor, "Changes in Criminal Victimization, 1994–95," *Bureau of Justice Statistics Bulletin* (Washington DC: U.S. Government Printing Office, 1995), 2.

imply that violent crime is an insignificant fact of modern life. The often-random, uncontrollable, "senseless" violence that is all too common in many large urban areas is a serious threat to social stability (Box 4.1).

Myth 3: Crime Occurs Mainly in the Lower Classes

Both the UCR and the NCVS collect information on crimes that are frequently reported to the police. Many observers believe that these are the most prevalent crimes in America because (1) the most comprehensive crime statistics are drawn from these data, (2) these statistics are commonly reported to the public, and (3) the crimes listed in the UCR and NCVS appear in virtually all reports on crime trends. These crime statistics generally reflect crime trends among the lower classes; that is, most arrests and convictions for index crimes are among people with relatively low incomes. Most of the people in prison have been incarcerated for index offenses.[6] In a recent survey of prison inmates, about 70 percent had incomes below the government poverty level before being incarcerated for their current offense.[7] These facts lead to the common assumption that crime is a problem of the lower classes.

There are at least two fallacies in this assumption. First, the FBI designation of index offenses is an abbreviated list of all crimes, and it is *specifically designed* to measure crimes that are committed almost exclusively by individuals in the lower socioeconomic levels. Second, the assumption that index crime is the most serious crime facing American society grows out of the attention devoted to this short list of crimes, while other serious crime is downplayed or ignored.

The designation of index offenses as the most serious crime is tied to widely dispersed values about the danger

of particular activities. For most people it is easier to see the specific danger posed by an individual who assaults another individual than to see the nonspecific dangers posed by unsafe products, for example. The danger of assault is immediate and violent, and both offender and victim are clearly identifiable. When a manufacturer knowingly markets an unsafe product, the danger is dispersed to a wider range of (unseen) victims and the harm is potential as opposed to certain. Many people may be hurt by a dangerous consumer product, but the potential danger may be delayed, which diffuses the perception of harm. American crime statistics focus on individual pathology, or crimes perpetrated by individuals, more often than crimes perpetrated by corporations or government because individual crimes are easier to count and categorize. The conceptual framework for understanding an assault is easily grasped (Theodore Kaczynski), but determining the chain of responsibility in corporate crime is problematic (R.J. Reynolds). The focus on individual crime is, in part, a reflection of the ease with which such behavior is classified as crime.

Several theorists over the last three decades have also pointed out that designations of crime are made by people with the most power and influence in American society.[8] From this perspective, designating crimes committed by the lower classes as the most serious is a direct result of the fact the those who make and interpret the laws are members of the upper classes. They are not likely to see or define crime committed by people like themselves as serious. Designations of criminals as *other,* or people not like yourself, is part of justifying your own behavior as harmless, in other words. Lawmakers who acknowledge the harm inherent in the marketing of an unsafe product are more likely to interpret the wrongful behavior as a "bad business decision" rather than a pathological act of recklessness, because it is easy for them to identify with the motivations of business (to sacrifice safety for increased

Some Crime Trends Differ from National Rates

Even though general trends indicate that violent crime is relatively rare when compared to other offenses, for certain groups in the population violent crime is higher than other groups. African Americans, for example, have rates of victimization for violent offenses that are 25 percent higher than European Americans. Women are four times more likely than men to be victims of a violent crime perpetrated by a relative.[68] General victimization patterns indicate violent crime is less often perpetrated than property offenses, but rates are disproportionately high among certain groups in the population. Still, the highest victimization rates for violent crimes (rates among people who earn incomes below $7500 annually, or among African Americans, or for people between 12 and 15 years old) are lower than general victimization rates for property offenses in all demographic categories.

profit). Theorists who identify this perspective suggest that, if the lower classes were in a position to determine the seriousness of crime, they would probably focus on crimes committed by members of the upper classes.

The problem of defining crime as a lower-class phenomenon is not only a matter of definition. The fact is that crime permeates all social classes, as well as all demographic designations. In fact, there is considerable evidence to suggest that crime in the upper classes is a more serious social problem than the index crimes counted by the FBI. In the area of property crime, for example, economic losses from index offenses are estimated at about $10 billion annually. Economic losses from crimes perpetrated by members of the upper classes, usually called *white-collar* or *corporate crime,* are estimated at $200 billion annually.[9]

Myth 4: Crime Is Bad for Everyone

Virtually anyone would acknowledge that crime hurts society. Individual victims of crime may suffer a lifetime of insecurity, fear, and anxiety, being forever cautious about lifestyle and relationships. Crime causes social upheaval. It is an immense financial drain on society as institutions are expanded to handle offenders and their punishment. Yes, social harm is a corollary to crime—but, are there any *benefits* to crime?

Over a century ago two theorists postulated some of the benefits of crime to society. Emile Durkheim pointed out in his famous work, *The Rules of Sociological Method,* that crime is an "ingredient of all healthy societies."[10] Crime establishes boundaries of acceptable behavior in all societies, according to Durkheim. It also unites people against a common foe and produces solidarity among those who are charged with its control. In other words, crime makes people more aware of their common inter-

ests and helps to define appropriate, moral, or lawful behavior. While crime may seem to be undesirable, it actually produces a healthy unity among social groups that organize efforts to curb the illegal activities of a small minority in any society, according to Durkheim.

A second perspective on the benefits of crime was articulated by Karl Marx:

> **. . . the criminal comes in as one of those natural "counterweights" which bring about a correct balance and opens up a whole perspective of "useful" occupations . . . [crime] produces the whole of the police and of criminal justice, constables, judges, hangmen, juries, . . . and all these different lines of business which form equally many categories of the human spirit, create new needs and new ways of satisfying them. Torture alone has given rise to the most ingenious mechanical inventions, and employed many honorable craftsmen in the production of its instruments.[11]**

Marx intended to poke fun at the justice system with this statement, but his point has modern implications. Crime benefits society by contributing to the economy. In 1992, for example, justice employees at all levels of government earned $4.8 billion in salaries.[12] In the same year, 1.8 million people were employed in police, judicial, legal, and correctional occupations in the United States.[13] In addition to employment and earnings, many industries have benefited from the expansion of the criminal justice system in recent years. Each time a new prison is constructed, a courtroom is renovated, or police equipment is upgraded, the economy directly benefits from the infusion of justice dollars into the trades, architectural industries, or equipment manufacturers. While crime is regrettable for its social expenses, the prison construction industry is booming. Crime, in other words, may produce incidental benefits to society by promoting economic

BOX 4.2

Victims of Certain Offenses Are Often Blamed for Their Own Victimization

Who was responsible for the offense? Victims of sexual harassment, domestic violence, and rape are often believed to have "provoked" the perpetrator. In this stereotypical thinking, something about the victim (manner of dress, for example) turned the offender into an uncontrolled perpetrator. This **stereotyping** sees the victim as bearing some responsibility for the offender's actions:

- "If she had not been so attractive, he would not have suggested that she have sex in exchange for an office promotion."
- "If she had not nagged him so much, he would not have beaten her."
- "If she had not worn such a revealing dress, he would not have raped her."

Questions about what the victim was wearing, why she was out late at night, whether she had "flirted" with her boss prior to allegations of sexual harassment, or whether she had previously had sex with the perpetrator of a rape, all suggest that the victim must have signaled the perpetrator to proceed with the crime. The common misperception is that she must have done *something* to provoke him.

Some crimes do involve victim provocation. Often the victim of an assault has "thrown the first punch." Similarly, murder victims may have instigated a confrontation that resulted in their own murder. The problem with many cultural stereotypes, however, is that they represent underlying assumptions about *appropriate* behavior. Women should not go out late at night; they should not dress "provocatively"; and they should expect "advances" if they are physically attractive. Men who are out late at night, skimpily dressed, or particularly attractive are not similarly stereotyped. By this yardstick, it becomes clear

that while going out late may be unwise or naive, it is not an invitation to sexual assault.

Under most legal designations of crime, offenders bear responsibility for their own actions. Perpetrators of burglary are not exonerated from the crime because the house was just too nice to pass up. Similarly, motor vehicle thefts are not justifiable because the stolen car was so enticing. Yet, when the victim was a woman and sex was involved or implied in the crime, there is a tendency to see the perpetrator as less responsible for his own actions. The criminal justice system is not immune to these stereotypes. In recent years significant criticism has focused upon the courts and police for failing to protect women against physical violence and for failing to take seriously crimes perpetrated against women. High recidivism among perpetrators of crimes targeted against women reflects in part the failure of the criminal justice system to prosecute such crimes vigorously.

While most of the stereotypes of crimes involving sex focus on women, some stereotypes cause difficulty for male victims of sexual assault. The cultural assumption is that homosexual rape is the chief sex crime perpetrated against male victims. Rarely are males perceived as victims of predatory sex crimes perpetrated by females and, even when such crimes occur, the implication is that males are not true victims. A common stereotype is that men cannot be raped by women.

Stereotypes are difficult to challenge and often persist unquestioned. Recent attention to stereotypes has highlighted some inequitable social and legal practices. Common perceptions about the nature of shared responsibility are questioned as people become more aware of the values that underlie such biased thinking.

---

growth through industries and occupations that serve the criminal justice system.

Myth 5: Most Criminals Are Hard-Core and Strangers to the Victim

Stereotypes of crime frequently give the impression that crime strikes people who happen to be in the wrong place at the wrong time. In other words, if victims had traveled a different route, avoided particularly dangerous parts of the city, or otherwise stayed out of the path of an of-

fender, they would not have been victimized. There are two implications in these stereotypes. On the one hand, the behavior of the victim is perceived as contributing to the crime because of some misjudgment, error, or lack of insight. While it is easy to judge the behavior of a victim after the fact, such an analysis is an unfair "blame the victim" approach to crime (Box 4.2). Errors and misjudgments are unfortunate, but crime is the responsibility of the offender, not the victim. Offenders are legally culpable for their behavior, but victims are not legally responsible for errors in judgment about where or when to go to particular places.

On the other hand, the stereotype that the victims would not have been hurt if they had avoided some

Dramatic increases in the number of inmates incarcerated in the United States since 1980 have spurred many states to build new prisons.

crime-prone area implies that crime is nearly inevitable there and that someone unknown to the victim is *likely* to attack. Stereotypes of crime often place the source of crime in particular places, perpetrated by definable "types" of people. Certain parts of major cities are nationally known as "dangerous" places to be avoided by all who live elsewhere.

Undoubtedly, levels of urban crime are unfathomable to some non-urban Americans, but the stereotype that crime is perpetrated by certain types of offenders who prey upon innocent strangers is flawed. Such crimes occur, but they represent a smaller portion of all crimes than is commonly believed. Most offenders are not hard-core, socially rejected people who wait for innocent people to cross their paths. In fact, victims of violent crimes often know their attackers. Stranger-perpetrated violent crimes are much less common than those committed by a friend or relative, for certain types of crimes.[14] About half of all violent crimes are perpetrated by someone known to the victim; for some crimes the victim has much more to fear from friends and relatives than from strangers.[15] While percentages vary slightly annually, for about a decade certain patterns have been evident in

victim-offender relationships. In about half of all assaults, 70 percent of sexual assaults, 78 percent of completed rapes, and nearly 30 percent of robberies in which there is some injury to the victim, the perpetrator is someone known to the victim.[16]

Many crimes for which no consistent rates are calculated are believed to be committed almost exclusively by someone known to the victim. Crimes such as child abuse, domestic battery, elder abuse, and sexual harassment, for example, are most commonly committed by a person who knows and cares for the victim or someone with whom the victim has daily contact. The frequency with which such offenses occur suggests that common perceptions of crime as perpetrated by hard-core criminal strangers is in error. Some may dismiss the fact that domestic violence is as serious as a stranger-perpetrated robbery, but over 80 percent of robberies by strangers involved no injury to victims in 1994, while virtually all cases of domestic battery involve an assault on the victim.[17]

The likelihood that perpetrators will be known to the victims of crime varies with a wide variety of circumstances and types of crimes. Violent crimes, for example, have a higher likelihood of a prior victim-offender relationship than property crimes. And, men are more likely than women to be victims of violent crimes perpetrated by strangers.[18] Yet, for many crimes and for most women, elders, or children who are victims of crime, the most likely perpetrator is someone whom the victim knows.

Myth 6: Most Crimes Are Solved and Offenders Punished

In mystery novels or television crime shows the entertainment lies in the unfolding of evidence that ultimately leads to apprehension of a criminal offender. In real life, police rarely have the time or resources for long or elaborate investigations of crime. Many serious crimes have required police attention over a number of years, but these cases are rare by comparison to the daily barrage of crimes that are reported to the police and never solved. In the case of the so-called unabomber, Theodore Kaczynski, who sent package bombs through the U.S. Postal Service to targeted victims for almost two decades, the FBI and many local police departments traced leads and evidence for 18 years before a suspect was finally apprehended. More mundane cases fail to attract national efforts and, frequently, no suspect is ever arrested.

The FBI tracks the proportion of crimes reported to police compared to arrests made for reported crimes. The comparisons are called clearance rates, or **crimes cleared.** If police arrest a suspect for a particular offense, the crime is considered to be cleared, even though arrest does not necessarily mean conviction. The percentages of crimes cleared in 1996 are presented in Table 4.2. As the table shows, violent crimes are more likely to be cleared than property offenses.

Arrested offenders in crimes reported to police are, of course, a small subset of all offenders. Many crimes are never reported and may be known only to the victim. According to NCVS estimates, only about 36 percent of all crimes are reported to police.[19] Some crimes, such as motor vehicle theft, have a relatively high likelihood of report, while other crimes, such as larceny theft, are rarely reported to police. In 1994, 78 percent of stolen vehicles were reported, but only 27 percent of minor thefts were reported.[20] Larceny-theft is not reported in about 75 percent of cases, and the police clear only 20 percent of reported crimes of larceny-theft.[21] In other words, low-level theft is vastly underreported and suspects are rarely arrested.

In addition to low-level reporting of a variety of crimes, the likelihood of conviction or punishment is low for most crimes. Table 4.3 illustrates the decline in the number of offenders who appear in each stage of the criminal justice system. In all crimes tracked by either the NCVS or the UCR, there is a vast difference between the number of victimizations or reports to police and the number of people who are actually sentenced for offenses. While the numbers are not directly comparable across columns in Table 4.3 (because people who have

TABLE 4.2 | Percentage of Crimes Cleared by Arrest, 1996

CRIME	PERCENTAGE CLEARED
Murder	67%
Aggravated assault	58
Forcible rape	50
Robbery	27
Burglary	14
Larceny-theft	20
Motor vehicle theft	14

SOURCE: Federal Bureau Of Investigation, *Crime in the United States* (Washington DC: U.S. Government Printing Office, 1997) 22, 24, 29, 34, 42, 48, 52.

TABLE 4.3 | Index Crimes, 1993

CRIME	NCVS REPORT OF VICTIMIZATION	UCR REPORTS TO POLICE	ARRESTS	CONVICTIONS	NEW COURT COMMITMENTS
Murder	a	24,530	17,922	12,548	9,700
Rape	160,380	106,010	30,540	21,655	7,875[b]
Robbery	1,291020	659,870	146,507	51,878	33,100
Assault	9,071,790	1,135,100	237,599	58,959	25,100
Residential burglary	5,984,000	2,834,800	318,672[c]	114,630[c]	44,500[c]
Motor vehicle theft	1,960,540	1,563,100	162,696	19,332	8,400
Larceny-theft	24,237,780	7,820,900	1,162,120	119,000	9,800

[a]The NCVS does not collect data on murder.
[b]Includes both state and federal
[c]Includes all burglary, not just residential

SOURCES: Allen J. Beck and Darrell K. Gilliard, "Prisoners in 1994," *Bureau of Justice Statistics Bulletin* (Washington DC: U.S. Government Printing Office, 1995) 13; Federal Bureau of Investigation, *Crime in the United States* (Washington DC: U.S. Government Printing Office, 1995) 225; Kathleen Maguire and Ann L. Pastore, *Sourcebook of Criminal Justice Statistics* (Washington DC: U.S. Government Printing Office, 1995) 230, 455, 485.

committed offenses in one year may not be arrested, tried, convicted, or sentenced in the same year), the trends through the system do indicate that only a small portion of offenses are actually punished with incarceration. The gap between NCVS reports in the first column of Table 4.3 and new court commitments in the last column is much wider than could be explained by such factors as court continuances or delayed sentencing.

Most people believe that police are more devoted to fighting crime and apprehending suspected offenders than they are to any other activity. This common belief is at odds with the facts of daily police work, which is often clogged with paperwork and routine duties. Reported crime is unlikely to be investigated if police personnel are overworked, resources are strained, there is doubt about the report, or more serious crimes draw the attention of law enforcement officials. Stereotypes of police, attorneys, and the judiciary suggest that solving crime is the first priority of the criminal justice system. Actually, preserving the peace and safety of communities through exercise of routine duties takes precedence.

Myth 7: Most Criminals Who Go to Trial "Get Off"

In a democratic system of justice, proof of guilt is, of course, a vital part of the legal apparatus used to punish offenders. If evidence against the accused is not sufficient for conviction, witnesses fail to testify, or improper procedures were used at any stage before or during trial, the U.S. Constitution prohibits the government from depriving the suspect of liberty. In plain language, this means the government is charged with the *precise* exercise of legal duties and the criminal justice system is prevented from punishing people on the intuition of those who simply know or believe that the suspect is guilty. Solid evidence, which has been collected by carefully articulated methods, is required for conviction.

Many Americans believe that guilty offenders are routinely released back into society after a harmless mistake in some aspect of apprehension, trial, or conviction led to dismissal of a serious case. This belief is often summarized with a description of legal decisions not to prosecute or convict as a "loophole" or a "technicality." The implication is that the rules of evidence are too rigid and impossible for police to follow if they want to get a conviction for a given offense. While it is true that most people who are arrested are not brought to trial, only cases in which there is significant evidence are actually routed through the trial stage. Arrest does not mean guilt in a democracy that requires proof for conviction. Over 60 percent of felony defendants brought to trial are con-

victed. Of those who are not convicted, about 30 percent of cases involve an **acquittal**, which means there was not enough evidence against the accused to convict, or **dismissal,** which means that the case is insufficient for prosecution or there was not enough evidence that the accused was involved in the crime. Another 7 percent of cases include those where there was no conviction for a reason other than acquittal or dismissal, such as a mistrial, or a **hung jury,** which means the jurors could not agree on either conviction or acquittal.[22]

The Exclusionary Rule

One of the primary reasons people believe criminals "get off," or are not punished on the basis of a "technicality," is that many assume the **exclusionary rule** prevents the admission of incriminating evidence in a large number of trials. While this rule has been subject to a wide variety of court interpretations, basically it means that improperly obtained evidence cannot be used against the accused in trial. The exclusionary rule draws its support from the Fourth Amendment to the Constitution, which protects Americans from unreasonable searches and requires the use of a **search warrant,** a legal document signed by a judge or magistrate with jurisdiction in the area that describes the nature of the search and the articles to be seized by police.

The purpose of the exclusionary rule is to protect citizens from unlawful searches and to force law enforcement officials to conduct their searches within the dictates of reasonable procedures. If police know that evidence collected improperly cannot be used to support a case against the accused, they are more likely to follow carefully articulated procedures in the collection of evidence. If *any* evidence were admissible in court (whether police had a search warrant or not, tortured the suspect, or fabricated the evidence) there would be nothing to prevent tyrannical or totalitarian exercise of police power. The spirit of the exclusionary rule is protection, both of the accused and of society, from unwieldy police power.

The problem with the protections embodied in this rule is that excluding all improperly obtained evidence sometimes has the effect of also excluding evidence in which some harmless error in procedure is responsible for freeing a suspect. If the search warrant, for example, contained a typographical error and designated the place to be searched as 125 Elm *Street,* when the suspect actually lived at 125 Elm *Lane,* the evidence collected in the search could be thrown out in a literal interpretation of the exclusionary rule. In this hypothetical case, the police went to the correct address, but the search warrant contained an address that had been typed incorrectly. Recent Supreme Court interpretations in two cases, *United States*

All of the research on domestic violence indicates that it is serious, extremely dangerous to victims, and likely to escalate over time. Abusers rarely stop beating their victims without legal or therapeutic interventions.

v. Leon and *Massachusetts v. Shepperd,* have eliminated this literalist interpretation.[23] Under these rulings **good faith efforts of police** officers to collect evidence with proper procedure, but which involves some minor error, may now be admitted into evidence against the accused. If the police believed they were following proper procedure, but used a search warrant that included errors, for example, the evidence may be used in court under these rulings. Critics contend that such rulings give opportunity for police abuse of power and undergird shoddy police work. Supporters believe that human errors by police should not be used to force the release of guilty offenders who cannot be convicted without the improperly obtained evidence.

This debate focuses on a very small number of cases in which an offender is released because the police, or other criminal justice employees, made a technical error in the formulation of the case against the accused. Contrary to news items that highlight such events, release of offenders on a "technicality" occurs in less than 1 percent of cases.[24] Only in cases of "victimless crimes" or moral offenses (for example, drug crimes or illegal gambling, which are notoriously difficult to prove because the of-

fender willingly engages in the offense and no victim complains about the crime) are the exclusionary rule violations more common than 1 percent of cases. Estimates are that about 3 percent of drug cases involve exclusionary rule violations.[25] In fact, most cases that go to trial result in conviction of the offender.

Myth 8: There Is No Relationship Between Guns and Violence

Many Americans hold the preservation of the second amendment to the Constitution, which affirms the right to bear arms, as one of the most important constitutional issues of our day. This issue is symbolic of freedom and democracy for many, who believe that citizens deprived of arms may be hostage to the whim of government. The fact that the American Revolution was fought by a small band of rebel colonists who used arms against the British symbolizes for many the importance of citizen action against tyranny. Others believe that the right to bear arms is one of the most important means of self-defense in a nation where crime threatens basic freedoms. Armed criminals call for defensive armaments by private citizens, according to this perspective.

From both perspectives, private citizens who lose their right to bear arms are at a disadvantage. Either they are threatened by the tyranny of government or by the danger of armed criminals. To lose the right to bear arms is to lose the right to defend yourself against the tyranny of government or the predatory nature of crime. Both perspectives represent ideological views. The reality of gun use in the United States is that weapons are less likely to be used either for defense against the tyranny of government or in self-defense than they are in the commission of a crime. Americans may affirm the right to bear arms in the abstract, but 78 percent favor at least minimal controls over the sale of guns.[26]

Guns are used in a wide array of violent acts in American society. Murder by firearm is the leading cause of death among African American males between the ages of 15 and 19.[27] The number of homicide deaths from firearms has tripled in the last 30 years, even though the homicide rate has varied only a few points in the last half-century.[28] In other words, guns have become the weapon of choice for homicide. It has been estimated that if firearms were eliminated the homicide rate would drop by two-thirds.[29] Critics contend that the purported decline in the homicide rate from elimination of firearms is exaggerated because many perpetrators of murder would find another means of killing their victims. While there may be disagreement over the impact of a gun ban on homicide rates, the relationship of guns to lethal violence in the United States is less in dispute. The annual number of deaths from firearms is, currently, the highest that it has been in this century.[30]

In 1996, 68 percent of murders were committed with guns.[31] About 30 percent of all crimes reported to the FBI involve the use of a gun.[32] A high proportion of crime in which firearms are used involve stolen weapons. The FBI has received annual reports of an average of 274,000 stolen guns since 1985.[33]

In addition to crimes committed with guns, nearly 3000 people were killed accidentally with firearms, and guns were used in over 37,000 suicides in one study that covered the years 1990 and 1991.[34] The relationship of guns to violence is clear, but there is considerable debate about what should be done to curtail violence. This issue is discussed more fully in Chapter 5, but the primary debate revolves around whether the problem rests with the availability of guns or with the people who use them. Proponents of gun control contend that limiting the accessibility of guns would reduce the likelihood that they could be used for lethal purposes. Of particular concern to gun control proponents are cheap, small, easily concealed hand-guns, which are readily available both through legitimate sales and illegal means, and which are used in 86 percent of gun-related crimes.[35] Opponents to gun control point out that *people* kill other people and that guns are merely a vehicle for accomplishing the crime. Illegal weapons are readily available; reducing the availability of legal guns unfairly impacts law-abiding citizens, they contend. Opponents argue that gun control hinders self-protection and gives criminals an unfair advantage over victims.

Both sides of the debate offer important points toward understanding the complexity of this problem. Another issue, however, may ultimately provide more insight into the advisability of gun control. Other attempts to ban substances or services that have been widely available to Americans have created "underground," or illegal, markets to meet consumer demand. In each case, the banning of some commodity or service has increased illicit markets and accelerated demand for the illegal substance. During Prohibition, for example, the manufacture, distribution, and consumption of alcohol was not halted; rather, an illegal market supplied consumers, at great profit to distributors. Most analysts believe that modern networks of organized crime were born out of Prohibition. Similarly, the banning of narcotics increased sales and instigated a new market for illegal trafficking. Prostitution and gambling bans have taken similar routes. In other words, banning guns would probably be less effective than regulating them. When highly desired commodities are outlawed, illicit markets generally develop.

Myth 9: Women Are Becoming "As Bad As" Men

Crime theorists have been saying for over one hundred years that increases in opportunity for women in American society will cause women's crime to increase. The presumption has been that women's involvement with home and family restrains female crime. From this perspective, if women move into the realm of men's activities, the "masculinizing" effect of altered social roles will cause them to commit more crimes. Theorists have said, for example:

> *In 1907*: It is probable that as women come more into line with men in their occupations, in their struggles for existence, in their independence and the like . . . [they] exhibit similar signs of degeneracy and an equal tendency to criminality.[36]

> *In 1929*: It is possible, of course, that the comparative emancipation of women, her greater participation in commercial and political affairs and the tendency towards greater sexual freedom may be playing their part in bringing about [increases in the numbers of female prisoners].[37]

FIGURE 4.4 | Sentenced Male and Female Prisoners in State and Federal Prisons 1925–1995

PRISONERS

1,000,000	MALE
800,000	
600,000	
400,000	
200,000	
100,000	FEMALE
50,000	
40,000	
30,000	
20,000	
10,000	
0	

1925   1940   1960   1980   1995

SOURCE: Kathleen Maguire and Ann L. Pastore, *Sourcebook of Criminal Justice Statistics, 1995* (Washington DC: U.S. Government Printing Office, 1996) 538–39; Darrell K. Gilliard and Allen J. Beck, *Prison and Jail Inmates, 1995* (Washington DC: U.S. Government Printing Office, 1996) 5.

In 1975: **The forces behind equal employment opportunity [and] women's liberation movements . . . have been causing and reflecting a steady erosion of the social and psychological differences which have traditionally separated men and women. It would be natural to expect parallel developments in female criminality. . . . as the position of women approximates the position of men, so does the frequency and type of their criminal activities."[38]**

There are several problems with the assumption that increased opportunity for women means more crime among women. First, the fact is that almost all crime is committed by men. This is true cross culturally and historically. Women's crime is generally estimated at about 10 percent of men's *recorded* crime, and women constitute only about 6 percent of the prison population.[39] In addition to recorded crime (that which is statistically tracked), men have a virtual monopoly over business, governmental, environmental, or global endangerment crimes.[40] These crimes are much less frequently reported, prosecuted, or punished, which means that they are vastly underrecorded. Women are very rarely reported to be involved in any of these crimes by comparison to men. Even if women's crime suddenly begins to escalate beyond all previous measures, it would take many decades for women to reach the level of men in all crime categories.

A second problem with the assumption that female and male crime patterns are merging because men and women have more-equal opportunities than in previous generations is that women's crime tends to be circumscribed to a few offense categories. Women are most likely to be involved in low-level property offenses or drug crime. They are rarely perpetrators of violent crimes, by comparison to men. If increased economic and social participation causes women to behave more like men, those women who have benefited most significantly from greater social equity should commit the most crimes. Actually, the reverse is true. Almost all women who commit crimes are lower-class and poor, and about 80 percent are primary providers for dependent children.[41] Women who commit crimes are, generally, outside of the cultural shifts that have increased economic opportunity for middle- and upper-class women. It is not women doctors and lawyers who are writing bad checks, cheating on welfare, or shoplifting, which are typical female offenses; rather, these crimes are commonly committed by poor women who have insufficient incomes to support their children.

A third problem with this premise is that increases in women's crime have actually paralleled increases among men, even though the rates of offense are much lower for women than men. Reports that women's crime has "doubled," "tripled," or "escalated" should be interpreted cautiously. The originally low levels of women's crime make any report of percentage increases seem large. Figure 4.4 illustrates the increase in men's and women's incarceration from 1925 to 1995.

Not all offenders are incarcerated, which may lead some to argue that women's crime is "underrecorded" because women are likely to be involved in the lowest category of offenses, which also has the lowest likelihood of incarceration. While it is true that many women who commit low-level property offenses are not incarcerated, the same is true for men. And, even though women are most likely to be involved in low-level property crime, this category is still dominated by men. In other words, more men than women commit even the lowest levels of crime. FBI arrest statistics, for example, illustrate that even among the most likely female offenses (forgery, fraud, embezzlement) about 60 percent of arrests for these crimes are men.[42] Men constitute 86 percent of arrests for violent crime, 73 percent of property crime arrests, and 77 percent of total index crime arrests.

Myth 10: The Way to Remedy Crime Is to Get Tough

Many people believe that "tough" punishments will stop crime. The underlying assumption is that rational people will try to avoid painful experiences. If punishments for crime are "tough," then potential offenders will be deterred from committing offenses and those who have been punished once will refrain from any future offenses. Current **"get tough" policies** have targeted several areas of punishment. They have, for example, focused on sentencing. Longer sentences for **recidivists,** or repeat offenders, **truth in sentencing laws** that do not allow for early release from prison for good behavior, and "three strikes and you're out" standards that require life sentences for third-time felons are among the most common "tough" sentencing options implemented in recent years. Further get-tough measures have included **minimum mandatory sentences,** or required minimum sentences, for certain crimes and reduction in the use of sentencing alternatives such as drug rehabilitation programs. The effect of these policies has been that offenders spend longer periods of time in prison and that virtually all states have built new prisons to accommodate their larger prison population. In theory, the ideals of "tough" policies should work to lower crime rates. There are several flaws in current get-tough policies, however.

The first problem with the get-tough policies is that they are based upon a faulty premise. People who support these policies believe that the crime rate is rising and that a tougher response to crime will halt the increase. As demonstrated by Figures 4.1 and 4.2, the crime rate has remained consistent, with the exception of a few peaks and declines, for the last 25 years. The measures of crime indicated by the NCVS, which are believed by criminologists to be a more accurate measure of crime than the UCR, show declines in crime. Tougher penalties will not curb "rising" crime because the crime rate is not rising.

A second problem with these current approaches is that, in spite of a decade of tough criminal justice policies, the crime rate has not changed significantly. The prison population has tripled since 1980, but the crime rate remains comparable to that of the 1970s. Over 1 million people are incarcerated in American prisons and jails, but the crime rate reflects no significant change. An expanded criminal justice system now costs American taxpayers over $100 billion annually but the crime rate remains stable.[43]

A third problem with the get-tough approach is that many blanket policies, such as the "three strikes and you're out" standard, are actually very expensive, often inappropriate to the circumstances of the crime, and have a negligible impact on overall crime trends. This standard says that third-time felons should be sentenced to life in prison. The rationale is that offenders who have not learned to mend their ways after two felony convictions should not be released to victimize society after a third conviction. In some cases, especially those involving dangerous or violent offenders, a third felony conviction *should* signal most officials that the offender is not to be trusted in society. The problem lies in the use of a blanket penalty for all third-time felons. Many offenders who commit a third offense are not dangerous to society and their life imprisonment will cost taxpayers millions of dollars. In the case of Michael Garcia, who shoplifted a package of meat priced at $5.62 from a grocery store, the 25-years to life-in-prison sentence that derives from the "three strikes" legislation in California is not proportionate to his crime and will cost taxpayers disproportionate to the danger he poses to society. In this case, the offender was temporarily out of work, his mother's Social Security check was late, and he stole three chuck steaks— one for himself, one for his mother, and one for his retarded brother. His two prior offenses had also been small monetary crimes with no physical injury.[44] While few people would argue that Garcia's crime should go unpunished, most would advocate less than 25 years to life for his offense. If this case was exceptional, the argument for third-time offenders to receive life sentences would still stand. Unfortunately, Garcia's case is more routine than the type of offenders these laws are intended to incarcerate: third-time, dangerous, antisocial offenders. One study of California three-strikes cases found that 70 percent of second and third offenses involved non-serious, nondangerous crimes. In Los Angeles County, only 4 percent of third-felony convictions involved murder, rape, kidnapping, or carjacking in 1994.[45]

Most crime in the United States is motivated by economic factors. About 80 percent of index offenses are property crimes, and most low-level non-index crimes are

The Swiss Approach to the Relationship Between Drugs and Crime

A Swiss study that covered the years 1992 to 1995 sheds new light on the relationship between drugs and crime and suggests an innovative approach to solving social problems associated with drug use. While the assumption that drugs cause crime is widespread, hard data linking the two phenomena is not easily obtained. Martin Killias and Ambros Uchtenhagen reviewed data from the Zurich Police showing the proportion of cleared crimes committed by drug addicts to obtain cash to buy drugs. They found that drug addiction did explain crime rates in Zurich and that a rise in the crime rate was associated with the spread of drug use among youth in Switzerland. The link, however, was not clearly *causal*.

Further research into the background characteristics of offenders found that drug use was "in most cases preceded by all sorts of minor offenses, such as theft and minor forms of violence over several years. Drug use [was] rarely the first deviant activity in the life course." Delinquency preceded drug use in nearly all cases. Rather than a drugs-cause-crime relationship, Killias and Uchtenhagen found *delinquency* precedes, and perhaps causes, drug use, which leads to further crime to support drug addiction. Prevention, in other words, should start prior to the drug addiction problem and focus on delinquency.

One solution to the drug-crime link in Switzerland has been the "harm reduction" approach. This highly controversial program is designed to reduce harm through modification of environmental or situational factors. There is no attempt to change the offender. In other words, the goal is not to break the addiction but to meet the needs of the addict so there is no need to commit crimes to buy illegal drugs. Under this program addicts are given prescriptions for the drug to which they are addicted.

This approach is highly controversial because it accepts the offenders' drug dependency and does not require that they change through drug treatment or punishment. Many people believe that drug addiction represents a moral failing and that the state should not offer opportunities to obtain illegal substances. The program, however, has pragmatic merits. The occurrence of several property offenses, such as burglary, vehicle theft, and robbery have been reduced substantially since the inception of this program. Although the program has been successful on a number of levels, one crime, mugging, has not been reduced. Also, heroin addicts appear to reduce offending patterns better than cocaine addicts. The Swiss are cautiously optimistic that the prescription program will become even more successful as it is modified and improved.

SOURCE: Martin Killias and Ambros Uchtenhagen, "Does Medical Heroin Prescription Reduce Delinquency Among Drug Addicts? On the Evaluation of the Swiss Heroin Prescription Project and its Methodology," *Studies on Crime and Crime Prevention* 5 (1996) 245–56.

---

also more likely to involve property or economic factors than personal injury. If the goal of the criminal justice system is to decrease crime, the most appropriate response is to attack the source, rather than the outcome. Tough punishments attack the outcome; early intervention strategies strike at the source of crime. Steven Donziger, Director of the National Criminal Justice Commission, says:

Those who wish to prevent crime before it occurs cannot ignore the fact that the majority of people filling our prisons come from impoverished backgrounds and lack a formal education. Research shows that children from low-income families who are placed in early childhood development programs such as Head Start have lower rates of crime and higher rates of marriage than those who are not in the program. We need to recognize that investing money in early childhood development produces a safer and healthier society over the long run. Unfortunately, the

United States is the wealthiest nation on earth but has the highest child poverty rates of any industrialized country.[46]

Not all crime is related to poverty, but most index offenders are poor, underemployed, or undereducated. Economic pressures, hopelessness, frustration, and anger permeate high-crime areas and are generally believed to be related to crime causation.[47] Punishment may be justified as a rational response to crime, but tough punishments since 1980 have not solved U.S. social problems and the crime rate has been largely unaffected. The prison population has soared beyond any modern or historical levels, but the crime rate has not changed. In other words, tough punishments have not reduced crime because they do not attack the social problems that cause crime. While some may argue that the crime rate would be even higher without the threat of harsh punishments, data from other countries indicate that tough punishments tend to push the crime rate up rather than to deter

"Drug busts" or the apprehension of offenders who sell illegal drugs has become a common component of urban life.

crime. One study of juvenile offenders in Western Europe found that the strongest deterrents to crime were fears of negative reactions from parents and society. Punishment was not mentioned by any respondents as a factor that restrained them from criminal behavior.[48]

Comparative research that tracks the effects of both get-tough and alternative sentencing approaches is rare in the United States, but data from Germany indicate that youthful offenders between the ages of 18 and 25 have the highest recidivism when the punishment is the most severe.[49] Several research studies have documented different aspects of the effect of sentencing on the subsequent success of offenders. Prison sentences, for example, show higher rates of recidivism than alternative sentences such as community service, probation, or fines, regardless of the seriousness of the offense. Young offenders sent to prison are more likely to become involved in crime again than those who have been sentenced to alternative programs. This is true, regardless of the crime, in Germany. Similar research in Germany found that offenders sentenced by punishment-oriented judges have a recidivism

rate that is 21 percent higher than those sentenced by judges who advocate holistic approaches to sentencing that involve community groups, social workers, churches, and educators. The seriousness of the crime is less important to the offender's likelihood of recidivism than the amount of community support provided by the criminal justice system, according to these studies of crime. In Germany, the result of these studies has been a decline in the use of prison and an increase in community involvement with alternative sentencing programs.[50]

Myth 11: Drugs Cause Crime

One of the issues most central to contemporary drug enforcement policies is that drugs cause crime. Several studies articulating a relationship between drugs and crime have further reinforced the belief that the relationship is causal. A study by James Inciardi, for example, found higher crime rates among narcotics users than among non-users.[51] Drug testing requirements in many industries, in government occupations, and among airplane pilots and train engineers further the stereotype that use of drugs causes crime and social harm. In 1991, which is the last year for which data are available, 79.6 percent of state prison inmates had a prior history of drug use, which also suggests a drugs and crime connection.[52]

These data seem to indicate a causal relationship between drugs and crime, although the link is not as definitive as most people believe. The fact that nearly 80 percent of prison inmates had used drugs prior to incarceration, for example, does not mean that drug use *caused* their crime. When asked whether they were using drugs at the time of their offense, only 30 percent responded affirmatively, and only 17 percent reported that they had committed their crime to obtain money for drugs.[53] According to data from the National Household Survey on Drug Abuse, 34 percent of Americans surveyed have used marijuana and over 11 percent have used cocaine. In other words, several million people who use or have used illegal drugs do not commit crimes. A few thousand people commit crimes that are related to drug use. If drugs caused crime, several million more people should have committed drug-related offenses, according to patterns of American usage.

While illegal drug use is a serious problem that should not be dismissed, the legal drugs of alcohol and nicotine probably pose more serious threats to Americans than those related to illegal drug use. In 1994, for example, 16,589 people were killed in alcohol-related motor vehicle crashes.[54] In the same year 23,310 people were killed in homicides.[55] There were, in other words, almost as many people killed by drunk drivers as were murdered in 1994. Over 320,000 people die from tobacco-related causes annually, compared to under 4000 drug-related deaths.[56]

Addiction to either legal or illegal drugs is, of course, harmful to individuals and to society. Many social problems are related to abuse of illegal drugs. People who are addicted are often unable to work and sometimes support expensive drug habits through crime. In such cases it is not the drug that causes the crime; rather, addiction to a substance that cannot be obtained legally and which is expensive induces addicts to commit crimes to pay for drugs. Drug abuse causes addiction, which causes crime. It is the addiction and the illegal status of drugs that induce law violation, not the drug *per se*. Some theorists have argued that drug *laws* cause more crime than drugs.[57] Illegal markets inflate prices, increase illegal networks of exchange, and create an underworld market of demand and supply. More crime results from the market, sale, and distribution of illegal drugs than is actually sparked by drug use. Highly competitive and profitable illegal markets foster corruption, violence, and turf wars among drug entrepreneurs. It is the illegal status of drugs that promotes this type of drug crime.

Myth 12: Nothing Can Be Done to Reduce Crime

Since 1968, six major crime bills have been passed by Congress and signed by the President.[58] All have used federal crime policies to direct official responses to crime. Most of these bills have shaped crime policies within the states by requiring adoption of certain policies before the states can qualify for federal money for crime programs. In 1994, for example, the federal crime bill specified that states could receive part of the $9.7 billion budgeted for prison construction only if they required that inmates serve 85 percent of their prison sentences before parole. In effect, this policy doubled the sentences of many offenders and increased the number of prisoners incarcerated in U.S. prisons.[59] While the policy may or may not be a good means of reducing crime, the point is that the federal government directed the policies of the states through allocation of federal money. Similar get-tough approaches have been instigated by all other federal crime bills since 1968, so that national crime policies are now reflected in most states.[60]

The positive outcome of national crime policies is that greater consistency is achieved in criminal justice procedures and policies. A negative aspect of national policies is that alternatives to federal get-tough measures are discouraged or unfunded. While it is possible that the national get-tough approach is the best answer to modern crime problems, innovation that might provide alternatives to the punishment approach is discouraged by funding mandates.

Criminologists and other social scientists have been saying for over 30 years that the place to stop crime is in the community. Punishing crime after it has occurred may be just, but research has demonstrated for three decades that punishment does not prevent crime.[61] Rather, investment in neighborhoods, communities, housing, job training, and education all provide more hope for crime control than current get-tough policies.[62] As Samuel Walker and colleagues have pointed out, disintegration of communities and failure to support families in the face of rapid social change have contributed more than any other factors to modern crime problems. Crime can be reduced by addressing the social problems that cause crime. Walker says:

> ... the cities have continued to lose hundreds of thousands of manufacturing jobs. Chicago lost more than 320,000 manufacturing jobs between 1967 and 1987; Philadelphia more than 160,000; New York City more than 500,000. These jobs, which traditionally facilitated entry of the poor into the labor force and provided decent wages

that could support a family, have been replaced by highly technical service sector jobs, for which the poor are not qualified, or low-paid, dead-end fast food jobs, or no jobs at all."[63]

Victor Kappeler and his colleagues point to similar social problems that could be addressed in pursuit of crime reduction:

The preponderance of the evidence is clear: economic inequality, poverty, unemployment and underemployment and relative deprivation are stimulants to crime in American society. They are also the most neglected and masked aspects of crime control policy. . . .it should be amply clear that our priorities are in the wrong place and our punitive response to [crime] is a social disaster.[64]

As the National Criminal Justice Commission has pointed out, if Americans want to get serious about reducing crime, we must look to nations similar to our own that have successful policies. The Commission points out:

Our rate of incarceration is 555 per 100,000 citizens; our homicide rate is about 9 per 100,000 (that means each year 9 out of every 100,000 citizens are killed by homicide). In Canada, the incarceration rate is 116 per 100,000 citizens and the homicide rate is 2.2 per 100,000. In Australia, the rate of incarceration is 91 per 100,000 citizens and the rate of homicide is 1.9. Most countries in Europe have the same general numbers.[65]

The crucial question is, of course, what do these countries do differently from us? First, they have highly developed social networks to protect children from poverty. Second, they have severe restrictions on the availability of firearms. Third, they have much shorter prison sentences for non-violent crimes, and a much greater emphasis on rehabilitation of offenders in prison.[66] Whether or not these policies are appropriate for criminal justice changes in the United States, they represent successful approaches to crime that distinguish other countries from the United States.

Among the steps the National Criminal Justice Commission recommends for crime reduction in the United States are:

- Adopt a three-year moratorium on new prison construction until a systematic assessment of prison needs can be completed. Replace prison sanctions with alternative programs that are less expensive and often more effective at reducing crime.

- Replace the war on drugs with a policy of harm reduction where the police work with public health and other professionals to stem substance use. Substance abuse should be treated as a public health challenge rather than a criminal justice problem.
- Criminal justice spending must be cost-effective, so it does not drain resources from other civic activities. Require a fiscal impact statement before major changes are made to crime policy.
- All levels of government should create crime prevention councils to develop a coordinated anti-crime strategy. These councils should be created at the city, county, state, and national levels. They should include representatives from the community, law enforcement, prosecutors, social service professionals, public health specialists, child welfare officials, crime victims, and representatives of other government agencies concerned with crime prevention.
- In order to reduce street crime, the nation must commit itself to reducing poverty by investing in children, youth, families, and communities.
- Shift crime policy from an agenda of "war" to an agenda of "peace."[67]

While it is doubtful that crime could be eradicated by a shift from punishment to community-building strategies, it is probable that the shift would reduce crime. These approaches are associated with lower crime in Europe. Current get-tough policies have been largely ineffective in reducing crime rates. Many crime theorists have called for a shift to preventive strategies and away from punitive policies that address only crime and fail to see its association with contemporary social problems.

Summary

In this chapter we have examined some of the most persistent myths about crime in American society. There are other myths that were not reviewed here but will be introduced in subsequent chapters. The purpose of this chapter is to stimulate thinking about the complexity of the crime problem and to begin questioning commonly held beliefs about it. Questioning, skepticism, and attention to alternative explanations will help you to formulate your own perspectives about crime. There are often no absolute facts about crime; rather, there are interpretations of crime statistics that vary with the viewpoint of the observer. Liberals see crime one way; conservatives see it another way. Crime policy is created within a social and political arena that reflects the points of view of those who formulate policies. These points of view and policies are subject to change as politics or social trends change. As you progress through this text you will begin to notice other issues and trends that (1) are often misinterpreted by the public, or (2) are subject to various interpretations.

Critical Thinking Questions

1. Why are most crimes committed by men? If the pattern of women's involvement in crime is consistent cross culturally, what causes the pattern?

2. Should there be limits on the sale or ownership of guns? Are there any firearms that simply should not be available to private citizens? Why, or why not?

3. Do you favor a moratorium on prison construction? Why, or why not?

4. If a victim of a crime engages in irresponsible behavior before the crime occurs (such as leaving keys in a car, traveling into "bad" neighborhoods, or leaving a house unlocked while away), does the victim bear any responsibility for the crime?

Suggested Readings

Steven R. Donziger, ed., *The Real War on Crime: The Report of the National Criminal Justice Commission* (New York: Harper Perennial, 1996).

John Hagan, *Crime and Disrepute* (Thousand Oaks, CA: Pine Forge, 1994).

Victor E. Kappeler, Mark Blumber, Gary W. Potter, *The Mythology of Crime and Criminal Justice,* 2nd ed. (Prospect Heights, IL: Waveland, 1996).

Jeffrey Reiman, *The Rich Get Richer and the Poor Get Prison: Ideology, Crime, and Criminal Justice,* 4th ed. (Boston: Allyn & Bacon, 1995).

Samual Walker, *Sense and Nonsense About Crime and Drugs: A Policy Guide,* 3rd ed. (Belmont, CA: Wadsworth, 1994).

Notes

[1] Marcus Felson, *Crime and Everyday Life: Insights and Implications for Society* (Thousand Oaks, CA: Pine Forge, 1994); John Hagan, *Crime and Disrepute* (Thousand Oaks, CA: Pine Forge, 1994); Victor E. Kappeler, Mark Blumber, and Gary W. Potter, *The Mythology of Crime and Criminal Justice,* 2nd ed. (Prospect Heights, IL: Waveland, 1996); Steven F. Messner and Richard Rosenfeld, *Crime and the American Dream* (Belmont, CA: Wadsworth, 1994); Jeffrey Reiman, *The Rich Get Richer and the Poor Get Prison: Ideology, Crime, and Criminal Justice,* 4th ed. (Boston: Allyn & Bacon, 1995); Samuel Walker, *Sense and Nonsense about Crime and Drugs: A Policy Guide,* 3rd ed. (Belmont, CA: Wadsworth, 1994).

[2] Reiman, *The Rich Get Richer and the Poor Get Prison: Ideology, Crime, and Criminal Justice,* 4th ed., 50–51.

[3] Lisa D. Bastian, "Criminal Victimization 1992," *Bureau of Justice Statistics Bulletin* (Washington DC: U.S. Government Printing Office, 1993) 2, 4.

[4] U.S. Department of Justice, "Violent Crime," *Bureau of Justice Statistics Selected Findings* (Washington DC: U.S. Government Printing Office, 1994) 2.

[5] Federal Bureau of Investigation, *Crime in America* (Washington DC: U.S. Government Printing Office, 1995) 4; Lisa Bastian, "Criminal Victimization 1993," *Bureau of Justice Statistics Bulletin* (Washington DC: U.S. Government Printing Office, 1995) 5.

[6] Kathleen Maguire and Ann L. Pastore, *Sourcebook of Criminal Justice Statistics* (Washington DC: U.S. Government Printing Office, 1995) 538.

[7] Allen Beck et al., "Survey of State Prison Inmates, 1991" (Washington DC: U.S. Government Printing Office, 1993) 3.

[8] See, for example, Richard Quinney, *The Social Reality of Crime* (Boston: Little, Brown, 1970); William Chambliss and Robert Seidman, *Law, Order and Power* (Reading, MA: Addison-Wesley, 1971); William Chambliss, "A Sociological Analysis of the Law of Vagrancy," *Social Problems* 12 (1964) 67–77.

[9] Messner and Rosenfeld, *Crime and the American Dream,* 31; Jay S. Albanese, *White Collar Crime in America* (Englewood Cliffs, NJ: Prentice Hall, 1995) 85.

[10] Emile Durkheim, *The Rules of Sociological Method* (Glencoe: Free Press, 1958) 67.

[11] Karl Marx, *Theories of Surplus Value,* Vol. 1 (Moscow: Foreign Language Publishing House [no date]) 375–76.

[12] Maguire and Pastore, *Sourcebook of Criminal Justice Statistics,* 26.

[13] Ibid., 33.

[14] Ibid.

[15] See, for example, Maguire and Pastore, *Sourcebook of Criminal Justice Statistics,* 25.

[16] Ibid.

[17] Jan M. Chaiken, "Criminal Victimization in the United States, 1994," *Bureau of Justice Statistics* (Washington DC: U.S. Government Printing Office, 1997) 70.

[18] Lisa D. Bastian and Marshall M. DeBerry, Jr., "Criminal Victimization in the United States, 1992," *Bureau of Justice Statistics* (Washington DC: U.S. Government Printing Office, 1994) 57.

[19] This percentage varies from year to year, but remains roughly around one-third. In 1993, for example, 35 percent of crimes were reported by Bastian (1995) 5; Chaiken (1997) reports 36 percent, 84.

[20] Chaiken, "Criminal Victimization in the United States, 1994," 84.

[21] Ibid.; FBI *Crime in America,* 207.

[22] Maguire and Pastore, *Sourcebook of Criminal Justice Statistics,* 497.

[23] *United States v. Leon* (1984) 104 S. Ct. 3405; *Massachusetts v. Shepperd* (1984) 104 S. Ct. 2424.

[24] James J. Fyfe, "Enforcement Workshop," *Criminal Law Bulletin* 19 (1983) 253–60; Craig Uchida and Timothy Bynum, "Search Warrants, Motions to Suppress and 'Lost Cases': The Effects of the Exclusionary Rule in Seven Jurisdictions," *Journal of Criminal Law and Criminology* 81 (1991) 1034–66; see also U.S. Department of Justice, *The Effects of the Exclusionary Rule: A Study in California* (Washington DC: U.S. Government Printing Office, 1982).

[25] Ibid.

[26] Maguire and Pastore, *Sourcebook of Criminal Justice Statistics,* 193.

[27] F. Landis Mackellar and Machiko Yanagishita, "Homicide in the United States: Who's at Risk?" *Population Trends and Public Policy* 21 (1995) 8.

[28] Ibid., 8, 10.

[29] Ibid., 9.

[30] Ibid.

[31] Federal Bureau of Investigation, *Crime in America* (Washington DC: U.S. Government Printing Office, 1997) 18.

[32] Kathleen Maguire and Ann L. Pastore, *Sourcebook of Criminal Justice Statistics, 1995* (Washington DC: U.S. Government Printing Office, 1996) 337; Marianne W. Zawitz, "Guns Used in Crime," *Bureau of Justice Statistics* (Washington DC: U.S. Government Printing Office, 1995) 1.

[33] Ibid., 3.

[34] Maguire and Pastore, *Sourcebook of Criminal Justice Statistics, 1996,* 379.

[35] Zawitz, "Guns Used in Crime," 2.

[36] Vernon Harris, "The Female Prisoner," *Nineteenth Century and After* 61 (1907) 780–97.

[37] City of New York Department of Corrections, *Annual Report* (1929) 13–14.

[38] Freda Adler, *Sisters in Crime: The Rise of the New Female Criminal* (New York: McGraw-Hill, 1975) 251.

[39] Tracy L. Snell, "Women in Prison," *Bureau of Justice Statistics Special Report* (Washington DC: U.S. Government Printing Office, 1994); Kathleen Daly, *Gender, Crime, and Punishment* (New Haven, CT: Yale University Press, 1994).

[40] See David R. Simon and D. Stanley Eitzen, *Elite Deviance,* 4th ed. (Boston: Allyn & Bacon, 1993).

[41] Phyllis Jo Baunach, "Critical Problems of Women in Prison," in *The Changing Roles of Women in the Criminal Justice System,* 2nd ed., ed. Imogene L. Moyer (Prospect Heights, IL: Waveland, 1992) 99–111.

[42] FBI (1995), 234. Contrary to popular belief, these crimes are usually rather petty in nature. Forgery is likely to involve credit card or check theft. Embezzlement often is very minimal in nature. A trusted secretary or clerk skims a few hundred dollars from a petty cash fund, for example.

[43] Steven R. Donziger, ed., *The Real War on Crime: The Report of the National Criminal Justice Commission* (New York: Harper Perennial, 1996) 1.

[44] Example taken from Ibid., 20.

[45] Ibid.

46 Ibid., 27.
47 Ibid.
48 Jeremy Travis, "Alternative Sanction in Germany: An Overview of Germany's Sentencing Practices," *National Institute of Justice Research Preview* (Washington DC: U.S. Government Printing Office, 1996) 1.
49 Ibid., 1.
50 Ibid., 1, 2.
51 James Inciardi, *The War On Drugs II: The Continuing Epic of Heroine, Cocaine, Crack, Crime, AIDS, and Public Policy* (Mountain View CA: Mayfield, 1992).
52 Tracy L. Snell, "Correctional Populations in the United States, 1991," *Bureau of Justice Statistics* (Washington DC: U.S. Government Printing Office, 1993) 35.
53 Ibid.
54 Maguire and Pastore, *Sourcebook of Criminal Justice Statistics, 1995*, 303.
55 Ibid., 324.
56 Kappeler et al., *The Mythology of Crime and Criminal Justice*, 2nd ed., 170.
57 Ibid., 174.
58 Donziger, *The Real War on Crime: The Report of the National Criminal Justice Commission*, 13.
59 Ibid., 14.
60 Ibid., 13–14.
61 See Donziger, *The Real War on Crime: The Report of the National Criminal Justice Commission*; Reiman, *The Rich Get Richer and the Poor Get Prison: Ideology, Crime, and Criminal Justice*, 4th ed.; Kappeler et al., *The Mythology of Crime and Criminal Justice*, 2nd ed.; Messner and Rosenfeld, *Crime and the American Dream*.
62 Walker, *Sense and Nonsense About Crime and Drugs: A Policy Guide*, 3rd ed., 290; Kappeler et al., *The Mythology of Crime and Criminal Justice*, 2nd ed., 342–43; Reiman, *The Rich Get Richer and the Poor Get Prison: Ideology, Crime, and Criminal Justice*, 4th ed., 182.
63 Walker, *Sense and Nonsense about Crime and Drugs: A Policy Guide*, 3rd ed., 290.
64 Kappeler et al., *The Mythology of Crime and Criminal Justice*, 2nd ed., 343.
65 Donziger, *The Real War on Crime: The Report of the National Criminal Justice Commission*, 196.
66 Ibid.
67 Ibid., 199–219.
68 Ibid., 4, 6.

part 3

Types of Crime

IN CHAPTERS 5 THROUGH 8 WE explore the common themes of crime in the United States as well as significant trends in certain specific crimes. Each chapter highlights the nature, extent, and costs of one type of crime, its offenders and victims, and the societal issues it raises. All chapters focus on the most recent crime patterns and explain current trends as they relate to overall crime patterns of the late twentieth century.

Chapter 5, "Violent Interpersonal Crimes," presents not only the index offenses that everyone recognizes as violent (murder, rape, robbery) but also violent crimes that are commonly categorized as "social problems." Domestic violence, child abuse, and elder abuse are serious crimes that often have deadly consequences for their victims but do not usually receive the same attention as index offenses. Throughout the chapter there are challenges to common perceptions about the nature of violent crime in the United States. The chapter also presents common patterns of offense and victimization.

Chapter 6, "Crimes of the Powerful," contrasts the cost of crimes committed by people in elite social positions with "ordinary" crime. This chapter challenges the common belief that elite crime is less serious than "real" crime. In fact, it is often more expensive, more dangerous, and more threatening to the nation than the index offenses most people fear. Part of the problem in evaluating crimes committed by the powerful is that the threat imposed by an offender robbing a store clerk at gunpoint, for example, is perceived to be more dangerous than, say, a potentially unsafe consumer product. This chapter challenges many of our common perceptions about danger.

Everyday crimes of theft are presented in Chapter 7, "Conventional Property Crime." This chapter reviews information from government statistics and other research on the most commonly committed property offenses. From this chapter you will learn that theft is very common in the United States. Most Americans have been victims of theft, and the majority of people have committed a theft crime at some time in their lives! Crimes of theft are so common that Americans no longer notice anti-theft devices; surveillance cameras are omnipresent and alarms sound without turning a head. Crimes of theft affect the daily lives of all Americans.

Chapter 8, "Public Order Crimes," explores the complex problems inherent in the regulation of morality. The public order crimes arise from moral questions, but often regulation of these crimes results in other kinds of crime. Corruption and organized crime are two problems directly related to enforcement of public order laws. Organized crime became a significant force in the United States during Prohibition, the first major American attempt to regulate morality. Since the repeal of Prohibition, organized crime has expanded into other crime categories and, indeed, many legitimate businesses. Similarly, corruption occurs because enforcement of public order crimes is exceptionally difficult and profits to be made by law violators are enormous. Opposing values about the regulation of morality through law are discussed in this chapter.

As you read through Part 3, look for common threads that run through all the chapters and try to conceptualize solutions to some of the complex social, political, and moral issues raised here. There are no clear answers to some of these questions, but alternatives are possible.

For updated information on types of crime, consult the Wadsworth web site at http://www.wadsworth.com/cj.html

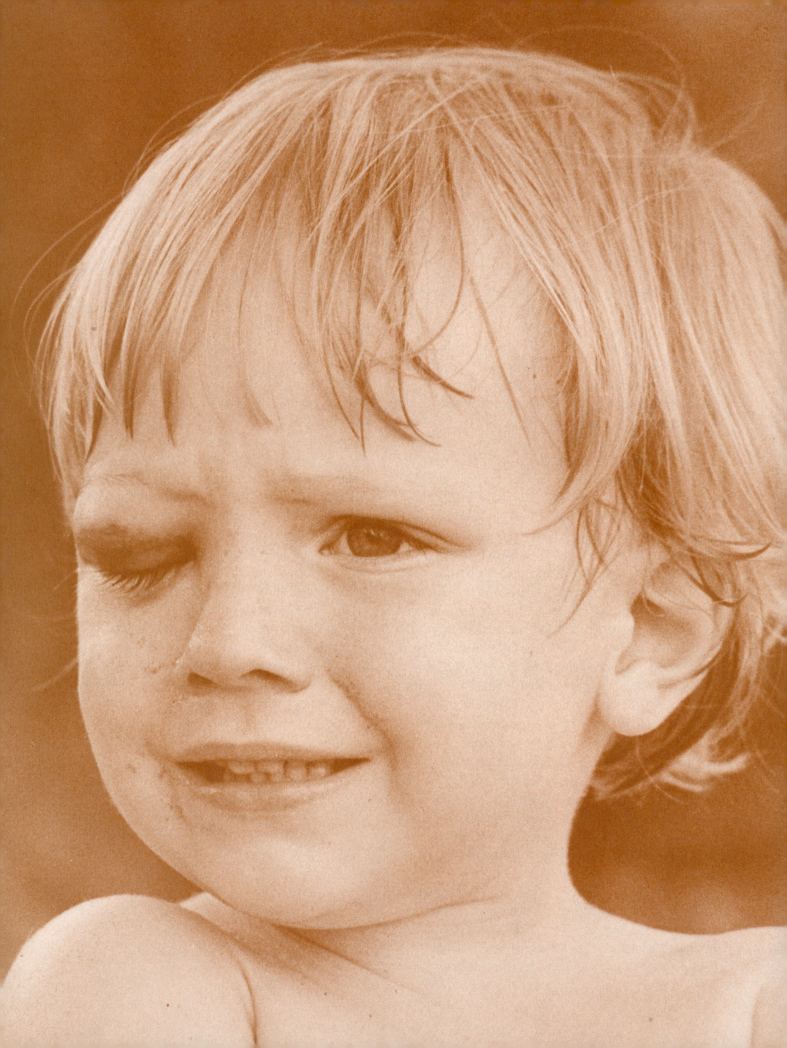

chapter 5

Violent Interpersonal Crimes

CHAPTER OUTLINE

NATURE, EXTENT, AND COSTS
    Common Misperceptions About Violent Crime
    Patterns of Victimization
    Costs of Violent Crime
OFFENDERS AND VICTIMS
INDEX OFFENSES
    Homicide
        Felony-Murder Doctrine
        Misdemeanor-Manslaughter Doctrine
        Trends in Murder Rates
        Demographic Patterns for Murder
    Rape
        Societal Stereotypes About Rape
        Changes in Legal Codes and Court Proceedings
        Reporting of Rape
        Male Victims of Rape
        False Reports
        Demographic Patterns for Rape
    Assault and Battery
        Patterns of Assault
        Hate Crimes
    Robbery
OFFENSES WITHIN THE FAMILY
    Domestic Violence
        Research Controversy over Patterns of Victimization
        Domestic Violence as a Family Matter
        Danger to Victims of Domestic Violence
        Arrest Patterns
        The Battered Woman's Syndrome Defense
        Patterns of Abuse
    Child Abuse
        Intergenerational Patterns of Abuse
        Trends in Child Abuse
    Elder Abuse
SOCIETAL ISSUES
    Guns
        Guns and Crime
        Debate over Gun Control
    Media Violence
        Debate over Control of Media Violence
    Violence and Masculinity
SUMMARY

KEY TERMS

rates of crime
rates of victimization
murder
mens rea
criminal intent
felony-murder doctrine
misdemeanor-manslaughter doctrine
criminal sexual assault
"real rape"
date rape/acquaintance rape
unfounded rape
simple assault
aggravated assault
battered woman syndrome defense
elder abuse

ON DECEMBER 31, 1995, headlines in the *Chicago Tribune* read: ONLY 800 SLAIN—IT'S A GOOD YEAR. Murders in Chicago in 1995 were down to 810 for the year, compared to 923 in 1994.[1] In all, violent crime dropped by 5 percent between 1994 and 1995, and it dropped another 6.5 percent between 1995 and 1996. Was this a reason for optimism in Chicago? Not exactly. More people were murdered in Chicago and New York in either 1995 or 1996 than have been killed in all of the *combined* years of conflict in Northern Ireland since 1972.

Worry about the threat of lethal violence pervades American culture because danger seems ubiquitous. Yet, murder is actually the most rarely committed violent crime. As you read further in this chapter, you will become aware of common patterns of violence in the United States and of common misinterpretations of trends in violent crime.

When most Americans think about violent interpersonal crimes, they imagine the index offense categories of homicide, rape, robbery, and aggravated assault. Millions of people are victims of these crimes each year. Yet, other crimes also threaten personal safety and may actually pose a more pervasive threat to the lives of ordinary Americans than the short list of index offenses. Domestic violence and child abuse are believed to be the most frequently committed crimes in the United States—as well as the most underreported crimes. Similarly, elder abuse appears to be a growing phenomenon, and one that is grossly underreported. Underlying these crimes are contemporary explosions in both the technology and availability of weapons with which to accomplish violent crime. The availability of guns, the relationship of guns and drugs to violence, and a proliferation of violent entertainment media are all hotly debated social and political issues that bear a direct relationship to perceptions of danger, as well as to the actual occurrence of violent crime in the United States today.

The cost of violent crimes is impossible to estimate because of low reporting, inconsistencies in recording procedures, and an inability to measure the cost of intangibles (such as chronic terror in a victim's life). While accurate cost estimates are not possible, violence does "cost" Americans in a variety of ways. There are direct costs of prosecution and punishment, time lost in work-related activities, expenses associated with medical care, and psychological problems inherent in both implied threats and physical attack. These crimes take an enormous toll on the lives of victims. Similarly, the cultural patterns that give rise to such behavior create a climate of acceptance, ensuring that these crimes will follow us into the twenty-first century.

Nature, Extent, and Costs

Crimes in which there is a physical threat to the victim create fear in the minds of most Americans, causing many people to make lifestyle choices designed to reduce their exposure to crime. Attention of the news media to the most horrible crimes heightens the fear that violent crime is rising rapidly and may soon pose a personal threat to everyone.

The risk of victimization is certainly serious, as is the level of fear endemic to the lives of many Americans. Gallup polls have indicated for more than 20 years that Americans believe crime is increasing, especially in their own neighborhoods.[2] Perceptions of danger persist, even during periods of declining crime.[3] Fear of crime has led to harsher penalties for those convicted and to increased rates of incarceration in both federal and state prisons. Still, many misconceptions persist about the nature and frequency of the threat of personal violence.

Common Misperceptions About Violent Crime

A common misperception about violent personal crime is that these crimes are usually perpetrated by strangers. Actually, for some crimes the perpetrator is likely to be known by the victim. This is especially true for women. For violent crimes reported in the National Crime Victimization Survey (NCVS) in 1994, 62 percent of violent crimes against women and 37 percent against men were committed by someone known to the victim.[4] Among the elderly of both sexes, completed violent crimes are perpetrated by someone known to the victim in about 14 percent of cases.[5]

For women, rape and assault are most likely to be perpetrated by someone the victim knows. Among men, assault is also commonly associated with a prior victim-offender relationship.[6] And, among the elderly, assault has the highest likelihood of a prior relationship between the victim and the offender; 42 percent of assaults reported in the 1994 NCVS were perpetrated by someone whom the victim knew.[7]

According to official measures, the likelihood of reporting violent offenses is considerably lower than the

TABLE 5.1 | Volume and Victimization Rates per 1000 Persons Age 12 and Over by Type of Crime and Sex of Victims, 1996

TYPE OF CRIME	VOLUME	RATE BOTH SEXES	MALE	FEMALE
All violent crime	10.9 million	50.8	59.6	42.5
Rape	32,700	0.8	0.0	1.5
Robbery	1.3 million	6.1	8.1	4.1
Assault	9.1 million	42.1	51.3	34.7

SOURCE: Kathleen Maguire and Ann L. Pastore, *Sourcebook of Criminal Justice Statistics, 1996* (Washington DC: U.S. Government Printing Office, 1997) 232.

likelihood of property crimes. The fact that so many victims know their attackers is one reason for low reporting. In such cases, victims may fear retaliation; they may see the crime as an isolated incident and may not want to cause the offender undue harm by reporting; or they may believe that authorities will do nothing about the crime, given the nature of the relationship between themselves and the offender.

Another common misperception about victims of violent crime is that wealthy people are more common targets of criminals. Actually, the lower one's income, the higher the rate of victimization.[8] In fact, in 1994 the rate of victimization in violent personal crimes committed on people of low income was double the rate for people with annual incomes over $75,000. Generally, African Americans have higher rates of victimization at all income levels among both men and women. For example, in 1994 the rate of victimization for violent personal crimes among blacks with incomes of less than $7500 was 68.2 per 1000 people. For blacks with incomes over $75,000, the rate was 42.5 per 1000 people.[9]

Patterns of Victimization

People who live in rural areas have lower rates of victimization than people who live in urban areas.[10] Urban neighborhoods with the lowest average incomes have very high rates of victimization for both violent personal crimes and property offenses. Theorists have suggested possible causal factors in this pattern, including the population density of neighborhoods, economic frustration, and the disintegration of family or other primary-group structures.

Offical reports show that a small portion of American households actually experienced a violent interpersonal crime in 1994.[11] Table 5.1 lists the number of victimizations reported in the 1994 NCVS for violent crime. While millions of crimes may seem like a large number of victimizations, the reported incidence of all violent victimizations was 10 percent lower than those recorded in 1981, which was the peak year for violent victimizations. And, the total number of households in which there was

TABLE 5.2 | Comparison of Victimization Rates per 1000 Population for Violent Crime, 1973 to 1992

YEAR	ALL PERSONAL CRIMES	TOTAL VIOLENT	RAPE	ROBBERY	ASSAULT
1973	123.6	32.6	1.0	6.7	24.9
1975	128.9	32.8	0.9	6.8	25.2
1981	120.5	35.3	1.0	7.4	27.0
1985	99.4	30.0	0.7	5.1	24.2
1987	98.0	29.3	0.8	5.3	23.3
1989	97.8	29.1	0.7	5.4	23.0
1990	93.4	29.6	0.6	5.7	23.3
1991	95.3	32.2	0.7	5.9	25.5
1992	91.2	32.1	0.7	5.9	25.5

SOURCE: U.S. Department of Justice, *Criminal Victimizations in the United States* (1994) 6.

a violent victimization other than homicide was the lowest since 1975.[12]

More important than absolute numbers of specific crimes are the **rates of crime,** which are standardized per population for comparison over time, even when populations increase or decrease. Table 5.1 also gives the NCVS **rates of victimization** for 1994 crimes of violence. In this table, the rate that seems most incongruous to perceptions of crime is the rate for rape. The rates are calculated per 1000 population, which means that both men and women are calculated in the rate, even though this crime is experienced almost exclusively by women. Critics have held that the rate for rape should be calculated as X per 1000 women and X per 1000 men. In a 1993 revision of the NCVS, more sexual offenses were added to the categories of victimization, but the calculation methods for sex offenses were not changed. Murder is excluded from the victimization rates because calculations depend upon respondents being asked about their own experiences with particular crimes.

In general, trends in NCVS data for violent interpersonal crime have shown decline for over a decade. Table 5.2 illustrates the rate changes for selected years since 1973.[13] Data from the NCVS for the years 1993 through 1995 have been released, but they could not be used in

Statistical Trends Sometimes Hide Changes in Crime Categories

The general downward trend in violent victimization may be somewhat misleading. For some groups, and for some crimes, victimization is on the rise. Among African Americans, for example, 1994 represented the highest recorded incidence of violent crime since the NCVS began collecting data in 1972. Similarly, people between the ages of 12 and 24 had the highest-ever recorded rates of victimization for that age group in 1994. The overall rate has fallen, in part because the age structure of the population has changed. The rates of violent interpersonal victimization of the elderly have always been low by comparison to the rest of the population. As the percentage of people who are elderly continues to increase, the number of young people, who occupy a position in the population that experiences high victimization, has continued to decrease. Thus, the rate of victimization may indicate decline in general patterns of violent interpersonal crime, but among those groups where the crimes are most frequently perpetrated, the rates are increasing. The rates are down, in part because the crime-prone age cohort, both in terms of perpetration and victimization, is down.

In addition, the official rates of victimization measure only a fraction of violent interpersonal crime. Domestic violence, for example, is not cohort-specific, but cross-cuts all age, race and socioeconomic distinctions. This crime is vastly underreported, and thus may or may not effect the overall downward trend in violent interpersonal crime. Similarly, if domestic violence perpetrations were included in the calculations of prior victim-offender relationships, the percentage of women who know their attackers would undoubtedly rise above the official 62 percent cited by the 1994 NCVS.

SOURCE: Kathleen Maguire and Ann L. Pastore, *Sourcebook of Criminal Justice Statistics, 1995* (Washington DC: U.S. Government Printing Office) 232; Lisa D. Bastian and Marshal M. DeBerry, Jr., *Criminal Victimization in the United States, 1992* (Washington, D.C.: U.S. Government Printing Office, 1994) 56.

Table 5.2 because the method by which data are collected by NCVS interviewers has changed (Box 5.1). The Department of Justice recommends that comparisons from 1993 onward not be made to earlier data. Trends from 1993 through 1995 indicate the pattern of continued decline, according to the Department of Justice reports.[14]

Costs of Violent Crime

The costs of violent personal crime, as previously stated, are impossible to estimate accurately. Overall, we know that expenditures by all levels of government for justice activities such as law enforcement, courts, defense, and correctional activities were about $94 billion in 1992, which is the last year for which figures have been calculated.[15] And, we know that justice expenditures in 1992 had risen over 160 percent since 1982.[16] Of those people who could calculate financial loss from a violent personal crime in 1992, 41 percent estimated costs to themselves of over $100, but these estimates include only losses due to theft or damage to property.[17] Victims of violent crime suffer many additional expenses. The direct expenses of medical care, time lost from work to attend court proceedings, and continued medical expenses cost victims $1.4 billion in 1992.[18] Loss of self-esteem, personal insecurities, and anxiety are additional, non-measurable expenses of violent personal crimes.[19]

Offenders and Victims

The victimization rates, as indicated by NCVS data, show overall decline in recent years even though rates are up in some demographic categories. The Uniform Crime Reports (UCR) data compiled by the FBI also show decline in rates of reported violent crime. Overall violent crime rates were down by 6.5 percent from 1995 to 1996.[20] The two rates are not directly comparable and the UCR generally shows less dramatic shifts in crime trends than the NCVS (see Chapter 2). Differences in the means by which crime data are calculated may account for variations in crime trends as reported by the two sources. The UCR is based upon crimes *reported to the police* and the NCVS counts reports of *victimization*. In addition, the NCVS data is calculated as X per 1,000 and the UCR is based upon X per 100,000 population. (Thus, to compare the UCR to the NCVS rates, the decimal point on the UCR rates should be moved two digits to the left.) In addition, the NCVS data accounts for considerably more crime than is reported in the UCR because of a high degree of non-reporting among many crimes. The UCR data on violent interpersonal crime is reported in Table 5.3.

Victimization rates show decline, indicating the number of people who experience crime has declined, and reported crime has also shown decrease, according to the FBI.[21] Because the range of violent interpersonal crimes

TABLE 5.3 | Uniform Crime Reports Rate per 100,000 of Violent Crime, 1992 to 1996

YEAR	ALL OFFENSES TOTAL	VIOLENT TOTAL	MURDER	RAPE	AGGRAVATED ROBBERY	ASSAULT
1992	5660	757	9.3	43	264	442
1996	5079	634	7.4	36	202	388
Percent decline	9%	8%	8%	8%	16%	6%

SOURCE: Federal Bureau of Investigation, *Crime in the United States* (Washington DC: U.S. Government Printing Office, 1993) 5–12; Federal Bureau of Investigation, *Crime in the United States, 1996* (Washington DC: U.S. Government Printing Office, 1997) 5, 10, 13, 23, 26, 31.

cross-cuts many categories of crime and includes both index offenses and non-index offenses, patterns of victimization and perpetration are not completely dependable indications of trends in this crime category. Some of these crimes are commonly perpetrated by one group of people upon another group, while others in this category appear to be random acts, where factors such as age, race, or socioeconomic indicators are irrelevant to either the offender or the victim. The easiest distinctions among types of interpersonal violence are between index offenses and non-index offenses. Statistical data on index offenses are carefully calculated by government bureaus, but non-index interpersonal violence is often merely estimated because of the low incidence of reporting. Official statistics indicate that the most common victims of violent crimes are young black men, with a rate of victimization of 113 per 1000 population. Similarly, elderly white women have the lowest rates of victimization at a rate of 3 per 1000 population.[22]

Index Offenses

Homicide

The commonsense definition of *homicide* suggests death perpetrated by an aggressor whose intent was to harm or kill the victim. This is actually quite similar to the official definitions of **murder** as recognized by each of the states. The important distinction in this definition is the word *intent*—in law known as **mens rea**, which translates from the Latin as *guilty mind*. Americans have carried over the British distinction between the death of another caused by willful actions (**criminal intent**) and the unintended death of another caused by accident. Consequently, the most common distinctions are between murder and manslaughter. Even within these categories, there is a difference between those individuals who cause their victims great suffering and those who intended only bodily harm but murdered "accidentally." There is also a distinction between those who cause a death while committing another felony and those who cause a death while committing a misdemeanor. All of these distinctions imply a

difference in moral decisionmaking that has been translated into differential penalties.

If the person who commits a murder does so without intent to cause death, for example, most people would argue that punishment should be less severe than for a person who planned and executed a murder deliberately. If another crime is involved, the offender may be punished for murder or manslaughter, depending upon the seriousness of the additional crime.

Felony-Murder Doctrine

If, for example, a landlord intended to commit the crime of arson by burning down a rental property while the renters were on vacation, the crime would be a felony. If the same arsonist, in an attempt to defraud an insurance company and unaware that the renters had not left for vacation, were to burn down the home while the renters slept there, the crime would be defined differently. The "intended" crimes, arson and fraud, did not include the loss of life of the tenants, but such a loss occurred. In most jurisdictions, the offender would be liable for the highest murder distinction under what is called the **felony-murder doctrine;** if a death occurs in the process of committing another felony, the perpetrator is liable for murder.

Misdemeanor-Manslaughter Doctrine

Similarly, if an individual commits a misdemeanor that unintentionally causes the death of another, the individual is liable for the lesser distinction of manslaughter in most jurisdictions. A driver, for example, is speeding when a small child runs between two parked cars. The driver, who is unable to brake in time to avoid the accident, kills the child. In this case, the offender would be liable for a lesser degree of murder, or manslaughter. This is called the **misdemeanor-manslaughter doctrine.** The offender would be punished less severely than the person who caused the death in the arson murder because the speeding violation was a misdemeanor. The punishment applied to the murderer is theoretically related to the seriousness of the offender's intent to cause harm. If a person intends to commit a felony and causes the death of another, that is morally (and therefore legally) more serious

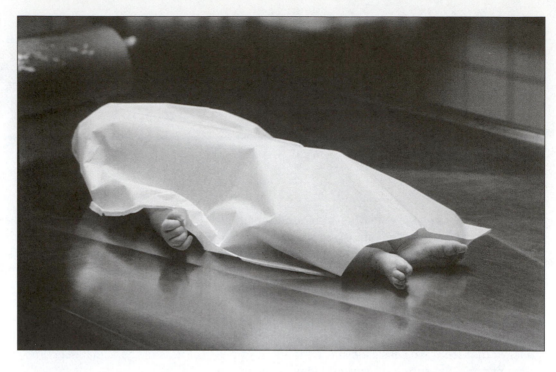

Reports of child abuse have increased considerably since the 1980s. Whether abuse is increasing or reports are up is debatable. Consequences for victims are often deadly, regardless of the prevalence of the problem.

than intending to commit a misdemeanor and causing a death.

Trends in Murder Rates

Murder rates in the United States increased from the mid-1980s until the early 1990s and then began to decline. As Table 5.4 indicates, the homicide rate in the United States had dropped to a relatively low level of 5.1 murders for every 100,000 people in the United States in 1960; the rate climbed through the 1970s, then peaked in 1980 at 10.2, which was the highest level in this century. Since 1980 the rate has fluctuated and is currently at 7.4 per 100,000 population.

One of the most striking features of current murder trends is the pattern of firearm use associated with the crime. In 1996, 67.8 percent of murders were committed with a gun.[23] Fifty-six percent of these firearms were handguns.[24] The Population Research Bureau estimates that if handguns were eliminated, and no other weapon was substituted for a murder, the homicide rate would drop by 57 percent.[25] Whether these murders would be committed by some other means is a matter of debate. Gun control is a very hotly debated political issue. The United States has the highest incidence of the use of firearms for murder weapons in the industrialized world.[26] Table 5.5 indicates the homicide rates for selected countries in 1994.

Demographic Patterns for Murder

In the United States, black men between the ages of 15 and 44 are the most likely to be murdered, comprising

TABLE 5.4 | Homicide Rate per 100,000 Population, 1900 to 1996

YEAR	RATE	YEAR	RATE
1900	1.5	1970	7.9
1910	4.0	1975	9.6
1920	7.1	1980	10.2
1930	8.7	1985	7.9
1940	6.1	1990	9.4
1950	5.8	1992	9.3
1960	5.1	1994	9.4
1965	5.1	1996	7.4

SOURCES: Kathleen Maguire and Ann L. Pastore, *Source Book of Criminal Justice Statistics, 1993* (Washington DC: U.S. Government Printing Office, 1994) 352; Federal Bureau of Investigation, *Crime in the United States* (Washington DC: U.S. Government Printing Office, 1994); Federal Bureau of Investigation, *Crime in the United States* (Washington DC: U.S. Government Printing Office, 1997) 13.

TABLE 5.5 | Homicide Rates per 100,000 Population, 1994

COUNTRY	HOMICIDE RATE
United States	9.4
Mexico	7.3
Norway	7.0
Canada	5.6
Costa Rica	5.3
Australia	4.4
Germany	3.9
United Kingdom	2.3
Japan	1.0

SOURCE: *Software Toolworks World Atlas*, 1995.

TABLE 5.6 | Percent of Arrests by Demographic Categories, 1996[a]

CRIME	PERCENT OF ARRESTS				
	MALES	FEMALES	WHITES	BLACKS	UNDER 18
Total all crimes	75.5	24.5	62.0	35.3	30.8
Total violent	84.9	15.1	54.6	43.2	18.7
Murder	89.7	10.3	42.8	54.9	15.0
Rape	98.8	1.2	56.1	41.6	17.0
Robbery	90.3	9.7	39.8	58.2	32.1
Aggravated assault	82.1	17.9	59.6	38.1	14.7

[a]Percents should be read in categories, not across the table.

SOURCE: Federal Bureau of Investigation, *Crime in the United States, 1996* (Washington DC: U.S. Government Printing Office, 1997) 230, 231, 232.

nearly half of all homicide victims. In fact, in the mid-1990s, homicide was the leading cause of death for black men *and* black women between the ages of 15 and 24, and the fourth leading cause of death for blacks of all ages[27]; homicide was the tenth leading cause of death for all Americans.[28]

In 1996, 50 percent of murder victims knew their assailants.[29] About 31 percent of murders resulted from arguments and 19 percent occurred in the process of another felony such as robbery or arson.[30] Of offenders for whom sex, age, and race were known, 90 percent were male; 86 percent were 18 years old or older, 52 percent were black, and 45 percent were white.[31]

In almost all murders of men the offender was also a man, and 90 percent of women were murdered by men. In other words, most people who murder are men. The arrest patterns for murder have changed considerably since 1970. As indicated by Table 5.6, over 90 percent of arrests for the crime are men, but the ages of the perpetrator have shifted.[32] The likelihood that a very young man would be arrested for this crime was much greater in the 1990s than in the 1970s, and the likelihood of arrest of men over the age of 65 has decreased.

In 1992, which is the last year for which statistics are available, 4.1 percent of new court-mandated commitments to prison for the crime of murder were women and about 10 percent of all people incarcerated for murder were women.[33] Women who commit murder are much more likely than men to have been long-term victims of physical, sexual, or emotional abuse by their victim. Of the 38,109 women incarcerated in state prisons for all crimes in 1991 (the last year for which data are available), 43 percent reported that they had been victims of physical or sexual abuse prior to their incarceration.[34] This is a strikingly high number when compared to the responses of incarcerated men. Of the 662,367 men incarcerated in state prisons at that time, only 5 percent reported any physical or sexual abuse prior to incarceration.[35] While

men may be more reluctant to report such experiences, this finding is consistent with the current research literature on this topic, which stresses that women are more likely to murder out of desperation or frustration.

Women who murder often commit the crime after enduring years of brutality from their victim.[36] Still, this phenomenon is rare by comparison to the crime of murder as perpetrated by men. Women are more likely *victims* than perpetrators of murder. In 1996, 30 percent of women murder victims were slain by husbands or boyfriends, while 3 percent of male murder victims were killed by wives or girlfriends.[37] In family murders, 70 percent of the victims are female; in non-family murders the most typical victim is a male.[38]

Rape

The crime of rape is believed to be one of the most underreported crimes in the United States today. Traditionally, the definition of rape has included forced sexual intercourse perpetrated by a male upon a female against her will. Most states revised their statutes in the 1980s to include a variety of sexual acts perpetrated against people of all ages by either men or women. Old definitions required female victims, physical force, sexual intercourse including ejaculation, and resistance on the part of the victim. A wider range of behaviors, such as "indecent sex acts," or the use of objects to cause harm to the victim in a sexual way, are now included in most states' laws. Such revised statues are called **criminal sexual assault** laws and they have largely replaced older statutes that more narrowly defined criminal behaviors.

While the intent of these new laws has been to increase the range of behaviors specifically prohibited by rape statutes, researchers disagree on interpreting reports of sexual assault under these new laws. The laws have expanded definitions of sexual assault to include behaviors beyond forced sexual penetration, but researchers in this

Violent Crime in Sweden

In Sweden, as in the United States, victimization surveys conducted by the government are used to determine the number and the rate of victimization of violent crimes. Each year, between 5 and 6 percent of all adults have been victimized by what they perceive as violence or threats of violence. For about 2 percent of the adult population, the violence produces visible injury or bodily harm. Between 10 and 15 percent of the population report that they have modified their lifestyle slightly to avoid victimization. About 5 percent of violent incidents in Sweden result in medical attention to the victim.

Almost half of violent crime in Sweden occurs at home or at work. As in the United States, young people are subject to the greatest risk of violence. People between the ages of 16 and 24 report the highest victimization, while people over the age of 64 rarely report encounters with violence or threats of violence. Single mothers of young children also report higher-than-average victimization in their homes.

In 1992, there were 174 murders, 1700 rapes, 6200 robberies, and 3700 assaults reported in Sweden. While fear of crime in Sweden is high, the occurrence of crime is low by comparison to the United States. In 1992 in the United States, there were 23,760 murders, 109,060 rapes, 672,480 robberies, and 1.1 million assaults known to police. Differences in absolute numbers may be deceiving, however. Sweden has a much smaller population than the United States. With the crime of assault (one of the most common violent crimes in Sweden), for example, in 1992 the rate of assault was 5 per 1000 inhabitants. In 1992 in the United States, the rate was 25.5.

About 5 percent of households in the United States reported they had experienced violent crime in 1992, and the percentage was comparable in Sweden. Percentages of the population who experience violence are not greatly different in the United States and Sweden, but violence is much more likely to lead to serious injury or death in the United States. In Sweden, a verbal threat of violence is considered to be a serious violent crime. The amount of violence reported by Swedish citizens is vastly lower than that of the United States if the threat of violence is removed from the comparison, and nearly 60 percent of violent victimizations in Sweden are *threats* of violence. As with other international analyses, direct comparison is problematic because of variations in definition. In the United States threats of violence are not included in violent crime categories. If, for comparison purposes, the threat of violence is removed from the Swedish violent crime category, the overall level of violent crime in Sweden would be about 60 percent lower than in the United States.

SOURCES: Kathleen Maguire and Ann L. Pastore, *Sourcebook of Criminal Justice Statistics, 1995* (Washington DC: U.S. Government Printing Office, 1996) 324; Jan Carling, *Crime and Law in Sweden* (Stockholm: Statistics Sweden, 1994) 10–17.

---

area have often failed to separate by seriousness the offenses committed under sexual assault laws. There is a difference, for example, between grabbing the genitals of the victim and forced sexual penetration, just as there is a difference between simple and aggravated assault. Many studies have combined all types of sexual assault, which is why some estimates are significantly higher than others as to the frequency of this crime.

Societal Stereotypes About Rape

In addition to problems of definition, there are many stereotypes about appropriate female behavior that influence whether victims will report the crime of rape. Researchers and victim advocates have contended for decades that victims are harmed first by the perpetrator and second by the system of justice that focuses great attention on the behavior, attributes, and demeanor of the victim. Susan Estrich, professor of law and political science at the University of Southern California, who was herself a victim of rape, says that the system of justice defines **"real rape"** as sex forced by a stranger, who uses a weapon and threatens to kill, injure, or otherwise maim the victim if she refuses to submit.[39] Under such circumstances judges, prosecutors, and the public all treat the attack as a serious crime. According to Estrich, the crime of rape is less clearly understood if the situation is "non-traditional" (for instance, when there has been a prior relationship between the offender and the victim).

The crime of rape is one of the few crimes in which the victim has had to prove, traditionally, absolute innocence in the crime. Prior sexual experiences, the clothing of the victim, flirtatious behavior on the part of the victim, or the independent lifestyle of the victim have all been accepted, both by cultural definitions and legal response, as factors that would mitigate the guilt of the offender.[40] The application of legal standards to this crime has been historically unique because of emphasis on the intent of the *victim* in influencing the intent of the offender. Victims have had to prove that their motivations for dressing stylishly, going out late at night, or drinking alcohol were not intended to be sexual enticements.

Underlying these assumptions about the behavior of the victim as an "enticement" to the offender is the myth

BOX 5.3

Myths and Facts About Rape

Myth	Fact
When a woman has had a prior relationship with a man, it is not rape if he forces her to have sex. Rather, it is a disagreement about when to have sex.	Prior relationships are not a factor in determining whether a crime has occurred. When a woman has sex with a man she does not permanently revoke her right to say no to future sex.
Women who do not fight back in a rape actually enjoy it and say no to tease men.	Many rape victims are afraid that the attacker will become more violent if they resist. They cooperate out of fear. No woman enjoys a sexual assault of any kind.
Some women deserve to be raped. They dress or behave in ways that are enticing to men. They tease or flirt with men because they enjoy the attention. Such women get what they ask for.	Some women may flirt or tease because they want to have a good time, or because they are looking for a sex partner. Looking for sex is not an invitation to rape. Sex involves intimacy and consent. Rape is a crime of aggression and domination. There is no consent from the victim in a rape. A woman does not deserve to be raped because of what she is wearing any more than a man deserves to be mugged if he wears expensive clothes.
Women who go out alone late at night, drink too much, or otherwise show a lack of respect for themselves or for social norms about appropriate female behavior should expect to be raped.	Suggesting that women should not go out late at night or that they should monitor their drinking to avoid rape implies that women should live secluded lives if they want to be safe from sexual assault. A woman who behaves in such a way may violate social norms, but her behavior is legal. Rape is a felony.
Married women cannot be victims of rape. When a couple marries, the wife agrees to have sex with her husband. He has a right to force her if she will not cooperate.	Many people believe that rape in marriage is just a disagreement about the timing of sex. Research indicates, however, that marital rape is often exceptionally brutal and that it is frequently a pattern in domestic abuse. When a woman signs her marriage license she does not give up all rights to her own body for the rest of her life. Rape in marriage is not a crime in all states, however. In some states men do have the right to rape their wives; in some states this is true even when the couple is legally separated.

that suggests men have uncontrollable sexual urges when faced with alluring female sexuality. Many researchers and writers have pointed out that such an assumption both insults men and misplaces blame on women.[41] Further, many critics (including Susan Brownmiller, author of the well-known book *Against Our Will: Men, Women, and Rape*) argue that rape is a crime of domination, aggression, and power, and has little to do with sex.[42]

Changes in Legal Codes and Court Proceedings

Within the last decade, most legal codes have been changed to protect the victim from questions regarding her prior sexual experiences during the trial of accused rape offenders. For many decades, defendants were pro-tected from admission of evidence of past rape convic-tions in their trials, while victims could be questioned about their sexual experiences before the rape, either with the accused perpetrator or with others. The tradi-tional defense of those accused of rape was to suggest that the victim was immoral.

Most states, and federal law, now prohibit the use of a victims' earlier experiences as evidence in the trial. In addition, many police departments and hospitals train staff in evidence-collecting techniques as well as in sensi-tive, nonthreatening techniques for questioning victims. Still, many victims complain of abuse by police depart-ments, insinuated blame by hospital staff, and a general-ized doubt of their credibility.[43] Victims commonly state that they would never have reported the crime if they had realized how they would be treated.

Reporting of Rape

The reporting of the crime of rape is notoriously low. According to NCVS data, the most common reason women give for not reporting is that they believe the police would do nothing. In addition, women often choose not to report because they fear reprisals by the perpetrator, they are embarrassed, or they do not think they will be believed. The NCVS estimates that only about half of all cases of rape are reported to the police, although other researchers suggest the percentage of reported rapes falls somewhere between one-tenth and one-third of the actual number. Still others contend that risk of rape is much lower than most research indicates, with between a 2 and 6 percent lifetime risk of victimization.[44] There is controversy among researchers about how rape should be counted. Broadened offense categories that include unwanted sexual touching, among other acts, may actually contribute to inflated estimates of the frequency with which this crime occurs. One study by Mary Koss reported that about 27 percent of female college students had been victims of rape or attempted rape at least twice between the ages of 14 and 21.[45] These findings have been criticized because very broad definitions of rape were used. The importance of Koss' research, however, goes beyond debates about the number of rapes committed each year. According to Koss, deviant sexual assault is much more common than official statistics indicate.[46]

According to the 1994 NCVS, two-thirds of rape or sexual assault victims knew their assailants. This type of sexual assault is usually called **date rape** or **acquaintance rape**. The likelihood that victims will report the crime is much lower when they know or have dated the offender. Almost two-thirds of victims of completed rapes do not report the crime to police.[47] Statistical information is, therefore, incomplete because of the small percentage of cases reported; collected information is likely to be about stranger rape. NCVS data indicate that victims are more likely to use self-defense if the offender is known to the victim than if the offender is a stranger. Also, strangers are more likely to use a weapon than are acquaintances of the victim.[48] About half of women who try to protect themselves believe that their actions helped the situation.[49] About half of rapes occur in or near victims' homes.[50]

Male Victims of Rape

One component of rape about which little is known is the rape of men. Women are rarely charged with the crime of rape, but that does not mean it does not occur. Men, who also believe societal stereotypes, may be very reluctant to report the crime. When women are charged with this crime they are often prosecuted as an *accomplice,* or someone who aided in the crime of another. Men raped by men, which is believed to be very common in prisons, is also rarely reported.[51]

False Reports

False reports of rape are a further problem in the study of rape. While any crime may be falsely reported (for example, theft of a motor vehicle may be falsely reported to cover an unreported accident), prosecution of rape is confounded by suspicion of false reports. This is especially the case when a prior relationship existed between the victim and the offender. The FBI noted that 8 percent of reports to law enforcement agencies were found to be false or baseless in 1996. The percentage of false reports of rape is higher than for other index offense categories, which average 2 percent of reports found to be false.[52] Police commonly classify false reports into a category called **unfounded rape,** which includes not only those crimes in which there is clearly no evidence of rape but also those that would be nearly impossible to prosecute. When victims were too drunk to recall attributes of attackers, victims are mentally retarded or impaired, victims have prior prostitution arrests or any of a series of other attributes that make their reports less believable, the report may designated to the unfounded category, even if police believe a rape occurred.

Demographic Patterns for Rape

Table 5.6 illustrated arrest patterns for rape among various demographic groups. Of those individuals incarcerated in state prisons in the United States, 3.7 percent of offenders, or 33,800 men, had been sentenced to prison with rape as their primary or most serious offense in 1994.[53] A larger number of inmates, 54,300, were incarcerated for other sexual assault. In 1992, the average sentence of inmates in state prisons for rape was just over 12 years (8.25 years for other sexual assault), although offenders were released after serving an average of 4.9 (2 years for other sexual assault).[54] In prison, men incarcerated for sex offenses are sometimes housed in separate facilities. In 1995, twenty-four states and the Federal Bureau of Prisons had separate housing or a treatment program for sex offenders.[55] The most common treatment programs available include group counseling and the use of drugs (Depo-Provera, for example) to reduce sex drive.

Assault and Battery

Assault and battery crimes are actually separate categories, although people tend to link them. Assault refers to the *attempt* to injure another and battery is the actual injury. Some behaviors that do not actually injure are included, such as spitting in someone's face or fondling a person against his or her will. These actions imply threat

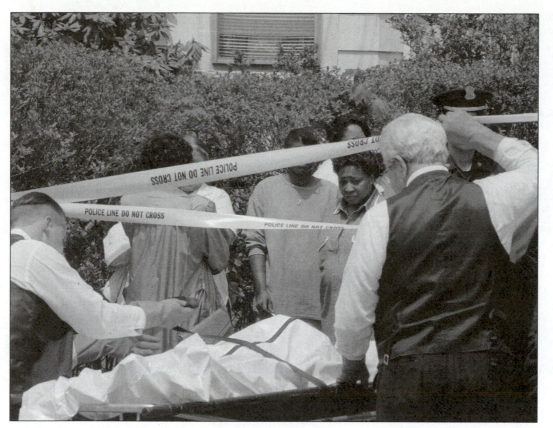

rather than physical injury. All jurisdictions distinguish between **simple assault** or battery and **aggravated assault** or battery. The difference rests in the degree of threat or injury. For example, use of a weapon, in most cases, would imply an *aggravated* charge.

Patterns of Assault

According to NCVS data, in 1994 there were 6.6 million assaults, or a rate of about 31 assaults for every 1000 persons 12 years of age or older in the United States. The rate has fluctuated around 25 since 1973.[56] About half of all assaults were reported to police in 1994. The likelihood of reporting was greater if the assault was aggravated, or if injury resulted from the crime.[57] African American men are the most likely victims of assault, followed by white men, black women, and white women. The highest victimization occurs among people 12 to 24 years of age. People over the age of 65 are rarely victims of assault by comparison to young people.[58] Elderly people often fear assault, as well as other violent crimes, and they take great precautions to avoid victimization, but the actual likelihood of assault is statistically very low for people in this age group.

While the rate of victimization for either simple or aggravated assault has changed very little in the last two decades, the arrest rate for aggravated assault has increased considerably. In 1972, the rate of arrest was 97 per 100,000 population; in 1994, the rate was 216.6 per 100,000 population.[59] A number of factors may explain the increased attention to this crime. First, most cases of assault involve both victims and perpetrators under the age of 25. Public fear of the threat of violence perpetrated by young people has heightened enforcement. Also, laws permitting formal intervention into crimes of violence or the threat of violence by young people have changed in the last two decades. That is, most states have lowered the age of majority for crimes of violence, which allows arrest and punishment of youthful offenders. Since most assault crimes are committed by young people, the arrest rates have increased as the laws have changed. Table 5.6 showed patterns of arrest for various groups.

Second, increased public awareness of the threat of violence, particularly in urban areas, has instigated widespread demand for police intervention. Third, the common use of guns for protection increases the volatile nature of assault. Arrest is a likely precaution to prevent further violence, especially among young people. The fact that homicide is the leading cause of death among young black men and women, especially, implies that preventive arrest in cases of assault may actually lessen the likelihood of murder.[60]

Hate Crimes

Hate crimes encompass one of the newest variations of assault. These are crimes that arise from stereotyped hatred

Robberies that involve weapons, extreme danger, and injury to victims are rare. It appears that the robbery depicted in this picture was completed in only a few seconds.

on the part of the offender. The victim is targeted not because of a disagreement or some identifiable rift between the victim and the perpetrator, but solely because the victim possesses characteristics the offender finds distasteful. Hate crimes are targeted against people on the basis of the victims' race or ethnicity, religion, sexual orientation, or gender. While hate crimes can involve vandalism, theft, arson, rape, murder, or other crimes, the most common expression of hatred is assault upon the victim. In 1996, there were 10,702 hate crimes reported to police, which was three times the number reported in 1991.[61] Simple assault, aggravated assault, and intimidation constituted 90 percent of these crimes.[62]

Robbery

The FBI classification of violent crimes includes robbery, although many people think of robbery as a property crime. Some criminologists refer to this offense as a "violent property crime." Robbery involves theft of money or property through the threat or use of violence. The threat of violence (as well as the display of violence) underlies the inclusion of this crime among other violent offenses. By comparison to either property offenses or other violent offenses (like assault), robbery is a crime that occurs with relatively less frequency. In 1994, the arrest rate for robbery was 71 per 100,000 population,

roughly equivalent to the rate for 1972.[63] Unlike many other index offenses, arrests for the crime of robbery have remained fairly consistent for two decades. In 1994, there were 544,618 crimes of robbery known to the police, although the NCVS put the number for 1994 at a higher level, indicating 1.3 million cases of victimization for this crime.[64] Almost 50 percent of robberies involve a loss to the victim of over $100 in money or goods, although blacks report higher losses than whites from robbery. Most robberies are completed without injury to the victim, yet whites are proportionately more likely to escape injury in a robbery than African Americans. Hospital treatment was necessary in less than 8 percent of reports of victimization.[65] In 1992, 94 percent of those convicted of robbery in state courts were men and 6 percent were women. Robbery comprised 6 percent of all convictions, and the average sentence imposed by state courts for this crime was 7.3 years in prison.[66] Table 5.6 showed the patterns of arrest for robbery among various groups in 1996.

Victimization is evenly distributed among all age groups under 30, but sharply reduced after age 30. The rate of victimization among people over the age of 65 is the lowest victimization category, with an average of 1.4 people in 1000 reporting victimization of robbery in 1994. The rate of victimization for men is double the rate of victimization for women.[67]

Offenses Within the Family

Offenses particularly targeted against family members could, technically, be subsumed under index offense categories. These offenses involve assaults, rape, murder, and other crimes that fall within the FBI guidelines for index offense categories. There is something distinct about these offenses, however, that deserves special attention. Ideally, families are supposed to love and support their members, and the thought of intentional brutality, terror, or psychological harm inflicted within a family is the antithesis of our common understanding. Unfortunately, our idealized views of family life are not always a reflection of reality. Family crimes are common, serious, and dangerous.

There is some evidence to suggest that the incidence of crimes within the family is increasing. Discerning the patterns of increase is another matter. Because these crimes occur in the privacy of homes, families often hide such offenses out of embarrassment or fear, and there is often an attempt to protect the offender as a means of holding the family together. Statistics regarding crimes against family members are notoriously unreliable. Most experts agree that violence within the family is increasing, although it is possible that increasing public and official awareness of these crimes leads to faulty assumptions. Whether the incidence is increasing or not, the fact remains that these crimes are strikingly common in the United States.

Domestic Violence

This crime has been called domestic violence, spousal abuse, wife beating, or domestic battery. The most common pattern is that a male in a relationship beats, abuses, rapes, or tortures his female counterpart. The reverse pattern does occur (a wife or girlfriend abuses or batters her husband or boyfriend) but such crimes appear to be much less frequent. NCVS data indicate that women experience about 90 percent of violence perpetrated by an intimate.[68]

Most recent research suggests that this crime is common, vastly underreported, largely misunderstood by the public, cross-cuts all social classes and ethnic distinctions, and that the violence tends to escalate over time.[69] One woman in four is likely to experience domestic battery during her lifetime.[70] If a woman is murdered, the perpetrator is more likely to be her husband or boyfriend than any other possible victim/offender configuration.[71] Nine out of every 10 female murder victims are killed by men.[72] Wives who kill their husbands generally do so after years of abuse or brutality.[73]

Research Controversy over Patterns of Victimization

A frequently cited 1988 research study by Gelles and Straus found that men and women report comparable amounts of violence perpetrated by their partners.[74] Many people have interpreted this research to indicate that violence is *equally* perpetrated by both men and women. However, the Gelles and Straus study has been criticized on several counts. First, it failed to take into account the seriousness of the abuse (a slap as opposed to a broken arm). Women may engage in violence against their partners, but the violence perpetrated by men is much more likely to cause serious injury.[75] The second major flaw in the research of Gelles and Straus is that they considered neither the intent of the violence nor the instigator of the violence. Whether the violence is in self-defense or an aggressive attack is an important distinction. Most research on this topic indicates a gender disparity in perpetration of the crime. That is, men constitute over 95 percent of offenders and women are most commonly their victims.[76] Hospital emergency room records tend to support the research, in that women are much more likely than men to sustain serious injury that requires medical attention.[77]

Some violence perpetrated by women may be hidden by the fact that men are reluctant to admit they have been beaten by their female partner. A variety of sources do indicate that violence is predominantly perpetrated by men against women, even if there is some degree of underreporting by male victims.

Domestic Violence as a Family Matter

For many years the problem of domestic abuse was not considered to be serious, nor a matter that required the attention of the criminal justice system. The battery was perceived as a component of marital relations, a private affair between the parties involved, or simply "a family matter." Victims of battery were often questioned by police, prosecutors, or judges about what they had done to bring about the abuse. Implicit in this approach to the problem is a belief that the behavior of the perpetrator is dependent upon some aspect of the victims' behavior, demeanor, or attitude.[78] "He wouldn't have hit her if she hadn't . . ." has been a traditional means of exonerating the perpetrator. This approach is similar to that taken with rape victims. As previously discussed, "blaming the victim" is not common with other crimes.

Similarly, the long-term nature of abusive relationships is often overlooked when women are murdered by their abusers or when victims of domestic battery kill their abusers. In interviews with the jury after the O.J. Simpson trial, juror Brenda Moran commented that pursuing the spousal abuse component of Simpson's behavior toward Nicole Brown Simpson was "a waste of time."[79] Such sentiments have been expressed in a variety of contexts, illustrating a widespread societal dismissal of the problem of domestic abuse.

In the past, the typical means of dealing with cases that required medical attention, counseling, or police or

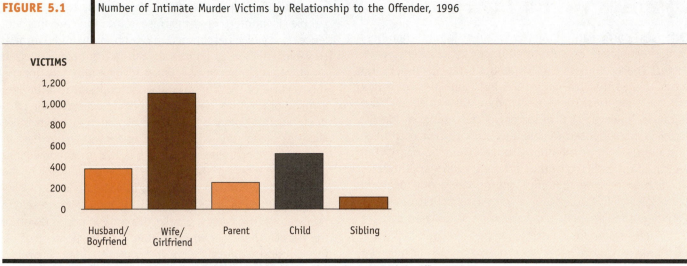

SOURCE: Federal Bureau of Investigation, *Crime in the United States, 1996* (Washington DC: U.S. Government Printing Office, 1997) 17.

judicial intervention was to counsel the parties to forgive and forget. Wives were often counseled to be "better" wives to their husbands, and Bible verses admonishing women to be meek, obedient, or humble were quoted to the victim.[80] Over the last two decades, however, academic writing, important court cases, activism by feminists, and media attention to the problem of domestic battery have all contributed to a more enlightened understanding of this social problem as a criminal activity involving both a perpetrator and a victim. The old myths about domestic battery are less acceptable to the public than in previous generations. Box 5.4 contrasts some common myths and actual facts about domestic battery.

Danger to Victims of Domestic Violence

In general, women who are violently victimized are twice as likely to be seriously injured if the perpetrator is an intimate, and they are more likely to need medical care if the attacker was a relative as opposed to a stranger.[81] For the years 1971–91, two-thirds of all reported violent victimizations against women were committed by someone known to the victim.[82] This, of course, implies that those most dangerous to women are people they know. If a woman is killed, the most likely perpetrator is a family member.[83] Most cases of murder of women occur after years of abuse by their partners; this is true for all age categories, across ethnic and racial lines, and throughout all social classes.[84] FBI data indicate that 1103 women were killed by husbands or boyfriends and 369 men were killed by wives or girlfriends in 1996.[85] Even in situations where both partners are violent, women are more likely than men to be seriously injured, or to be killed.[86]

Women often fight back against abuse; they are not passive victims. According to NCVS data, women attempt to fight back, reason with their attackers, or use physical force as self-defense in about 80 percent of cases.[87] Domestic battery is most often fatal for the victim after escalating incidents of violence become repeatedly more serious.[88] Figure 5.1 shows the pattern of intimate murder victims for 1996, with wives and girlfriends at the highest frequency. This pattern is consistent with the literature on domestic violence that indicates women abused by male partners are the most common female murder victims.

Arrest Patterns

Because of the extraordinary danger to the victims of domestic violence, several states now require police officers to arrest suspects with probable cause, even without the victim's consent. Research indicates, however, that officers still use considerable discretion about whether to make an arrest. Arrests are less likely in violent domestic crimes involving family members than in crimes involving strangers.[89] Many researchers believe the new laws requiring arrest are the best solution to recidivism among perpetrators of domestic battery. Forty states now have some form of mandatory arrest or reporting of domestic violence cases.[90] Early research on the effectiveness of mandatory arrest laws was encouraging. A now-famous Minneapolis study of mandatory arrest found a greatly reduced incidence of the crime when perpetrators were arrested.[91] Subsequent studies have been less encouraging, however. It appears that mandatory arrest is significantly associated with lowering domestic battery if the perpetrator is married and employed, where subsequent arrest may cause hardship.[92] A study published in 1997 by Robert Davis and Bruce Taylor indicated that neither arrest nor treatment of offenders has actually produced a reduction in domestic violence, although active intervention strategies have increased citizens' confidence in the ability of the police to handle domestic violence situations.[93]

Myths and Facts About Domestic Battery

Myth	Fact
If she would behave differently he would not abuse her.	Her demeanor or behavior cannot control his behavior. He is responsible for his own actions.
Women who stay with batterers must get something out of the relationship—perhaps they secretly like to be battered.	No one likes to be battered. Women stay with batterers because they are afraid that he will get worse if they leave, he has threatened to kill the children or other relatives, or they have no resources for escape. The threat of violence in the past has become real danger; they are afraid that he will kill them or someone they love if they try to escape.
If she really wanted to get out she would find a way to escape. People who stay in a violent relationship have no one to blame but themselves.	Many women in these circumstances have been psychologically belittled, humiliated, and blamed for years. They often believe that they are inept, stupid, incompetent, and unemployable. Their self-esteem is so low that they suffer from what has been termed "learned helplessness."
If she really didn't want to be battered she would fight back or leave.	After years of abuse many women accept their status and believe that fighting back will only make matters worse. They do not feel they have any control over themselves, the situation, or the batterer.
If she behaves appropriately and concedes to his demands and desires he will stop beating her.	All the research on this topic suggests that the problem seldom corrects as a result of anything the victim does or does not do. In fact, the research confirms that the violence tends to worsen over time. If she does not leave, it is, statistically, very likely that he will eventually kill her.
When the police are called, the victim often fails to press charges or later drops the charges. If she was serious about stopping the abuse, she would follow through with charges against the abuser.	Most experts agree that it is an unfair responsibility for the victim to be the one who presses charges. She may fear for her safety or that of her children if she follows through; or she may be worried about loss of income if he is jailed and can't work; or she may want him to get help, not punishment. The current trend is to take the responsibility for pressing charges away from the victim and to place it onto the police or states' attorneys, as is commonly the case with most other crimes. Many states have moved to "mandatory reporting" laws which means that state law mandates reporting of domestic violence situations.

The Battered Woman Syndrome Defense

In all states, there is some degree of admissible legal defense for use in cases where victims of domestic violence who have been chronically brutalized kill their partners. This defense, **battered woman syndrome defense,** has been used to defend women who do not fit the usual self-defense requirement of immediate threat of danger. In many cases, battered women believe there is no escape from the battery aside from murder of their partner. Many women have tried every legitimate avenue, such as restraining orders, orders of protection, divorce, or relocation, and they are still unable to escape the abuse. Under such circumstances, they feel trapped, and may ultimately kill their spouses. Defenders of such cases may use the battered woman syndrome defense, developed on the basis of research by Lenore Walker.[94] The use of this legal defense of battered women who commit violent crimes against their batterers received increased attention with the passage of the 1994 Violent Crime Control and Law Enforcement Act, which required the attorney general and the secretary of the Department of Health and Human Services to transmit to Congress reports on the extent to which this syndrome has been considered in criminal trials. Expert testimony on battering and its effects is admissible, or has been admitted as evidence, in all fifty states and the District of Columbia. Nearly 70 percent of states have found expert testimony about the battered woman syndrome to be relevant to self-defense claims or the state of mind of the defendant at the time of her charged crime.[95]

Patterns of Abuse

While victims of domestic abuse are common in all ethnic, racial, class, and educational categories, the likelihood of victimization increases with certain characteristics of both perpetrators and victims. Younger women with less education and lower incomes are more likely to be victims of domestic battery than older women or women with higher education and higher incomes.[96] Men are more likely to batter their partners if they were abused as children. Other factors associated with the propensity for men to abuse their partners include problems with anger control, difficulty in communicating, and rigid stereotypes of male and female roles. Alcohol abuse and low income have also been associated with offenders in research studies.[97]

Child Abuse

In Western culture it has been traditionally accepted practice to discipline children physically. Literature and advice manuals dating back to the sixteenth century recommend corporal (physical) punishment as a means of shaping character and controlling mischief.[98] Public attitudes toward "cruelty" to children did not change significantly until the latter part of the nineteenth century, when advice books began to recommend "limited" use of corporal punishment.[99] Historical records recount common punishments with whips, horsewhips, switches, rods, fists, razor strops, belts, hair brushes, and harness whips, as well as locking children in closets, boxes, and other confined places or depriving children of food.[100] It was not until the early twentieth century that many of these practices were challenged. The history of childhood discipline includes many practices that would be considered abusive today. How common these discipline practices were is not clear, although two-thirds of childrearing books recommended such punishments in the early nineteenth century. By the

late nineteenth century, advice books recommended use of a "hair brush" or "mother's slipper," rather than whips or confinement, indicating that the severity of punishment moderated during the nineteenth century.[101]

Discipline of children has undergone dramatic change during the twentieth century. What was once considered beneficial to children's development falls within the realm of abuse or neglect under contemporary standards. Similarly, parental behavior that was once considered a reasonable response to inappropriate child behavior has been criminalized as cruel and unlawful. Standards have changed and societal expectations are more humane, but, for many of the behaviors, long-time patterns have persisted in American society. While people may generally disapprove, behaviors described in the sixteenth century still occur today.

Intergenerational Patterns of Abuse

Contemporary professionals in child care and treatment fields, such as physicians, educators, and psychologists, have been extolling the societal dangers of child abuse for over 30 years.[102] Researchers in this field note the relationship between the abusive treatment of children and abusive behavior of adults who were themselves abused as children.[103] The relationship is not causal, in that most people who were abused as children do not grow up to abuse their own children or spouses. However, abusers carry the characteristic of childhood abuse much more frequently than people who do not abuse. Thus, experience of childhood abuse does not *always* cause adults to be abusers, but it is a contributing factor among many abusers.[104]

Trends in Child Abuse

How commonly child abuse actually occurs is a matter of debate. Measurement of child abuse is complicated for at least three reasons. First, many individuals who were abused as children may repress the experience and not report it in victimization studies. Second, criminal offenders may falsely claim that they were abused as children, hoping the claim will mitigate their present situation. Third, recent research shows that interviewers sometimes elicit erroneous claims of abuse from very young children by leading the child's imagination with the questions asked. From the data available, some researchers have actually found a decline in the incidence of abuse, even though public knowledge of child abuse events and official reports of abuse have increased in recent years.[105] Other researchers have found that reported cases of abuse are a valid sample of all cases.[106] National data collected in accordance with the 1974 Child Abuse Prevention and Treatment Act indicate that reports of abuse increased 15 percent between 1990 and 1995 and that 1995 reports were 49 percent higher than in 1986.[107] Overall, the rate of substantiated victims of child abuse was about 15 out of every 1000 children in 1995.[108]

Surveys suggest that 75 percent of the American public believe that abuse is increasing, although 85 percent of people aged 18 to 29 say they were not abused as children.[109] Certain types of childhood abuse are more prevalent among particular groups in the population. Approximately 35 percent of adult women report that they were raped or sexually abused as children, although most experts believe this grossly underrepresents the actual numbers.[110] Girls are about 8 times more likely to be victims of childhood sexual abuse than boys.[111]

Almost 20 percent of inmates serving time in state prisons have committed a violent crime against a child.[112] Over half of the violent crimes were committed against children under the age of 12. Seventy percent of offenders who committed a crime against a child raped or sexually assaulted the victim.[113] Seventy percent of offenders who perpetrate violent crimes against children are white; they are generally older than offenders who commit crimes against adults; and 97 percent of offenders who commit violent crimes against children are men.[114]

Child abuse is a crime with long-term personal consequences for the victims, as well as societal effects that include higher rates of violence perpetrated by adults who grew up in abusive homes. The scars people carry from child abuse tend to persist for a lifetime. Child abuse cross-cuts socioeconomic, religious, ethnic, racial, and gender distinctions, and it affects millions of children annually.

Elder Abuse

During the 1980s, attention to child abuse and spousal abuse uncovered other types of family violence. The term **elder abuse** was coined to describe physical, psychological, and financial mistreatment of elderly people. Not all of such mistreatment is criminal, but 37 states have enacted laws to require mandatory reporting of incidents of abuse or neglect of elderly persons.[115]

Patterns of elder abuse are exceptionally difficult to uncover because it has only recently been identified as a specific crime. According to available research, the majority of victims are elderly women. While the pattern of family violence in this crime fits other types of victimization of family members, in that a very high percentage of victims are female, it is also the case that elderly women outnumber elderly men because women live longer than men.[116] Unlike other crimes of family violence, however, a high percentage of *offenders* are women, who are more likely to be caretakers of elderly parents. Adult male children also commit elder abuse crimes, although national data illuminating the rates are scarce. As with other types of family violence, a pattern of abuse appears to cross-cut generations. Pillmer and Finkelhor found that some adult abusers of elderly

parents were themselves abused as children and learned violence toward intimates in childhood.[117] The abuser of an elder may be retaliating for experiences of abuse when the adult abuser was a child; some elder abuse is the result of frustration incited by the responsibilities of care for the elderly; and some abuse reflects the powerlessness of abusers who are still dependent upon the elderly parent for financial support.[118] Steinmetz points out the need for national data related to both offender patterns and victimization.[119] Much of the available information has been obtained from small, non-random samples of official police or social service agency reports. Unreported abuse, or that which does not draw the attention of outside observers, is unknown and therefore unrecorded. Nursing home or other institutional abuse generally draws official attention only when the situation is exceptional. Routine indignities, disrespect, and minor law violations are commonly overlooked. Most research to date is inconclusive regarding characteristics of offenders, demographic patterns of abuse, or rates of victimization of elders.

Societal Issues

Interpersonal violence is pervasive in American society. Many people make lifestyle choices, decisions about where to live, or occupational choices based on fear of violence. Contemporary violence often appears to be random, frequent, and uncontrollable. Gang violence, drive-by shootings, serial killings, kidnappings of children, shootings of co-workers or strangers in public places, and domestic terrorism appear from news media accounts to be on the increase, and they often involve "senseless" violence (that is, violence occurs not for some utilitarian end, such as in the commission of a robbery, but simply for the sake of violence itself). The random nature of such violence increases the level of fear pervading the entire culture. It is not possible to review the literature of all types of interpersonal violence in this chapter, but some current explanations of the prevalence and fear of violence are pertinent.

Popular theories abound regarding the origins of violence in contemporary America. A commonsense approach to this problem suggests that if we could just eliminate the components of our culture that foster violence we would be a more peaceful society. For example, proponents of gun control argue that regulating availability of lethal weapons would reduce the use of guns for criminal purposes. Similarly, critics of violence in the entertainment media claim that reducing exposure to violent images would reduce people's violent inclinations. In this section, we will examine some of the societal trends that have been blamed for the patterns of violence, as well as some of the criticisms of these perspectives.

TABLE 5.7 | Attitudes Toward Gun Control

YEAR	POLICE PERMIT TO PURCHASE A GUN		REGISTRATION OF HANDGUNS		BAN OF HANDGUNS EXCEPT FOR POLICE	
	OPPOSED	FAVOR	OPPOSED	FAVOR	OPPOSED	FAVOR
1982	26%	72%	30%	66%	58%	39%
1990	20	79	17	81	55	41
1993	17	81	18	81	54	42

SOURCE: Kathleen Maguire and Ann L. Pastore, *Sourcebook of Criminal Justice Statistics* (Washington DC: U.S. Government Printing Office, 1994) 204, 207.

Guns

One of the problems in measuring the relationship between guns and crime is that researchers have difficulty ascertaining the number of guns currently owned by Americans. There are two ways of calculating the number of firearms possessed by private persons. One is to take reports of guns manufactured in the United States, subtract those exported for sale to other countries, and add guns imported into this country. Given that most guns last about 40 years before corrosion, loss, theft, or confiscation cause them to be dropped from ownership, the cumulative total of production, less exports, plus imports, should provide a fairly accurate estimate of the number of guns owned in the United States.[120] With this method of calculation, the number of guns owned by Americans is estimated to be between 200 and 400 million, or at least one gun for every American (with some people owning none and other people owning several).[121]

The second method of discovering the number of guns owned is to ask about ownership in a national survey. This type of data has estimated for several decades that guns are owned in nearly 50 percent of American households.[122] The problem, according to Gary Kleck and others who have studied this issue, is that there is an enormous difference in estimates of gun ownership between the two methods. The manufacture/import/export data show vastly more guns owned than the survey data. It is possible that survey respondents failed to report some guns because they did not understand the question. If they are asked about guns in their household, for example, they may not report guns in their place of business, vehicle, garage, or other places where they may keep a gun. It is also possible that the manufacture/import/export data more closely estimates gun ownership because a large portion of guns are owned by young people, transients, or criminals, who are unlikely to be surveyed regarding gun ownership.[123]

The Bureau of Alcohol, Tobacco, and Firearms (ATF) estimates that between 1899 and 1993 about 223 million guns became available in the United State, including over 79 million rifles, 77 million handguns, and 66 million shotguns.[124] Even by the smallest estimates of ownership, more firearms are owned by private citizens in the United States than in any other country in the world. The closest competitor for ownership is Switzerland, where one-third of households have guns as a result of military service requirements.[125]

Guns and Crime

Ownership does not necessarily mean that the gun will be used for illicit purposes. Most crime is not committed with a gun. Gun control proponents suggest that it is the proliferation of handguns that is most problematic for America. When guns are used in crime, handguns are the most frequently used type of firearm. In 1994, the ATF received over 85,000 requests from law enforcement agencies for traces of guns used in crime; 75 percent of those traced by the ATF in 1994 were handguns.[126] Increases in handgun ownership have surpassed increases in other types of gun ownership since the 1960s. Estimates of handgun ownership are around 65 million, although stolen guns are the most likely guns of any type to be used in crime.[127] Thefts of guns, the majority of which are handguns, increased by more than 200 percent between 1968 and 1994. About 300,000 guns were stolen in 1994.[128]

Seventy percent of Americans think that handgun availability contributes to violence in America.[129] Similarly, most Americans believe there should be some restriction on the ownership or sale of guns. Table 5.7 illustrates some of the attitudes regarding gun control in the United States.

While most people are opposed to a complete ban on handguns, the majority of Americans favor some regulations or restrictions. Eighty-five percent of Americans polled in 1993 favored banning the sale of guns to people under age 18. Eighty-eight percent of those polled favored a seven-day waiting period; and 69 percent favored a complete ban on assault rifles in 1993.[130] Since the Brady Handgun Violence Prevention Act of 1994 went into effect, the Department of Justice estimates that each month about 6600 purchases of firearms have been prevented by the required background checks of potential gun buyers. Over 70 percent of rejected purchasers were convicted or indicted felons.[131] Whether those rejected for purchase ultimately obtained stolen or otherwise illegal weapons is not known. Portions of the Brady Bill were struck down by the Supreme Court in 1997, but the direct result of these changes has yet to be studied.

Debate over Gun Control

Opponents to gun control of any type point out that restrictions are most likely to affect the law-abiding people who use guns for protection. According to this view, criminals hide ownership and would not be affected by registration laws or ownership restrictions. If most violence with guns was perpetrated by "criminals" this would, of course, be a legitimate criticism of any attempts to restrict. Private ownership for protection has increased in recent years, especially for handguns.[132] It has been estimated that guns are used for self-protection as often as 2.1 to 2.5 million times annually.[133]

Opponents to gun control often cite constitutional protections, the negative effects of governmental intrusion into the private lives of ordinary citizens, and the necessity of firearms for self-defense. Considerable research indicates that guns can be an effective deterrent to some crime.[134] At least one research study has found that when guns are used for protection against those attempting robbery the attempt is more likely to be thwarted than if a gun is not used.[135] Opponents also point out that many items (knives, clotheslines) could be used for lethal purposes, but no one proposes banning such items, and they see controls as leaving law-abiding people unarmed and disadvantaged against heavily armed criminals.

Proponents usually cite the low crime rates, lack of lethal violence, and urban safety in those countries with the greatest firearm restrictions. In 1990–91, there were 34,493 homicide deaths from firearms, but 37,211 suicides and 2857 accidental firearm deaths.[136] In 1992, there were 37,776 firearm-related deaths and 99,025 nonfatal firearm-related injuries in the United States.[137] While the debate rages, with both sides representing important issues, the fact remains that firearms were used in 75,472 deaths and they were instrumental in 582,000 violent crimes in the United States in 1993.[138]

Media Violence

About 98 percent of American households own at least one television set. In typical households the television is turned on almost 8 hours each day. Research over the last five decades indicates that primetime television is replete with depiction of violent behaviors.[139] For example, in 46 hours of primetime crime and police programs, Brendan Maguire identified depictions of 113 criminal offenders. Of

this total, 97 (86 percent) committed acts of violence—with homicide (48), interrupted homicides (15), and shoot-outs (10) appearing most frequently.

For at least 30 years, psychologists, sociologists, educators, and the surgeon general of the United States have indicated through an exceptionally wide range of research studies that exposure to violent media images increases the expression of aggression in children.[140] Early research focused upon short-term aggression, such as whether viewing of Saturday morning cartoons or other violent television programming would increase immediate aggression in play.[141] Later, the concern became the long-term effects of violence. In 1972, the surgeon general of the United States released a report warning that a growing volume of research supporting the idea that exposure to television violence did have a long-term, adverse affect on childhood development, with subsequently increased societal violence as the net result.[142] Currently, research focuses upon violence in children's programming and gratuitous violence in other areas of media attention. Exposure to media violence may have real-life consequences with regard to the way people treat one another or solve personal problems.[143]

The research generally shows that exposure to media violence increases tolerance for aggression in real life. Children are especially susceptible to media violence. They are often desensitized to violence and, over time, tend to see few or no negative consequences for behaving in violent ways similar to those viewed in media. Children's perceptions of the nature of violence become distorted by media illustrations, especially when the fictitious victim of a lethal attack reappears in another program. Violent images punctuated by advertisements for toys, candy, and breakfast cereals nullify the shock value of violence and make it appear to be harmless, normal, and acceptable. Many research studies have affirmed that media violence reduces children's inhibitions against behaving violently, increases children's acceptance of violence as a means of solving problems, and demonstrates techniques and ideas for violent interaction.[144]

Debate over Control of Media Violence

There is little debate about the nature of the relationship between media violence and subsequent societal violence. Rather, the questions center around how best to address the relationship, or how definitively the relationship should be interpreted. Not all people who watch rape, assault, or murder in entertainment media are incited to commit these crimes. And, the slapstick aggression of comedians such as *Abbott and Costello* or *The Three Stooges* does not necessarily lead to more hitting, bickering, or fighting among children who view such entertainment. The relationship between media violence and societal violence is a subtle force that influences some more than others. It is

Developing and Implementing Anti-Stalking Laws

Stalking is a crime that has been defined recently through combined state and federal efforts to develop legal codes to curtail the behavior. Definitions of the crime are variable by state, but a few common elements have surfaced. *Stalking* is generally defined as "willful, malicious, and repeated following and harassing of another person." Several states list specific prohibited behaviors; many states prohibit unwanted, repeated communications from the stalker; and seven states include surveillance in the description of stalking behavior. Illinois has a category of "aggravated stalking," which includes restraint, confinement, or bodily harm to the victim of stalking. Texas requires that the stalking behavior continue after the victim has reported the conduct to law enforcement for the accused stalker to be charged with the crime.

The problem of stalking captured widespread national attention after actress Rebecca Schaeffer was murdered by a stalker in 1989 and comedian David Letterman was persistently harassed by a fan. California enacted the first anti-stalking legislation in 1990. Currently, 48 states and the District of Columbia have anti-stalking laws.

Developing the anti-stalking laws was difficult because stalking is different from other criminal behavior. It involves a series of acts, each of which may be legal in isolation from the series. Taken collectively, the acts cause the victim fear, injury, or death. Sending flowers or gifts, for example, would not be illegal under most circumstances. If the stalker continually harasses, calls, follows, or threatens the victim in conjunction with the gifts, the act of sending the gifts is part of the stalking behavior. Developing legal codes to cover acts that would normally be legal, such as sending gifts, proved to be a challenge

to the states as the anti-stalking laws were enacted. Congress appropriated funds for the U.S. Bureau of Justice Assistance (BJA) to hold a series of seminars on the development of anti-stalking laws in 1993. Nearly all states developed their anti-stalking laws in conjunction with the model anti-stalking codes recommended by the BJA. While some laws have been subsequently challenged in appellate courts, most have been upheld.

Among the difficult challenges facing lawmakers in the initial formulation of these laws was developing model codes that addressed the behavior of the stalker, rather than the motivation for stalking. Stalking varies greatly from case to case. One stalker may seek to win the affections of the victim through repeated calls, letters, and gifts. The actions toward the victim become threatening when the stalker persists after being rejected. Another stalker may be angry with the victim for some real or imagined injury. Pursuit of the victim is motivated by a desire to get even or scare the victim. Other stalkers may pursue the victim because of psychological disorders or mental illness. Stalkers engage in their behavior out of anger, jealousy, obsession, revenge, to establish contact, or to control the victim.

An important component of the BJA seminars was a recommendation that state laws include an evaluation-and-treatment component in their response to the perpetrator. Convicted stalkers who are punished, without treatment, are unlikely to address their own behavior or the mental condition that caused their behavior. The BJA stressed that stalkers who are confined or imprisoned without treatment may become more violent toward the victim once they are released.

SOURCE: Bureau of Justice Assistance, *Regional Seminar Series on Developing and Implementing Antistalking Codes* (Washington DC: U.S. Government Printing Office, 1996) 1–15.

not a direct causal relationship; all people who view violence do not imitate what they see.

Rather, graphic depictions of violence tend to reduce the shock of violence in real life. Violence appears to be a normal component of social life and a common means of addressing interpersonal conflict. Children who view violence for entertainment may internalize the use of violence to express anger, or make a point as a facet of normal interaction. The internalized understanding of violence as an appropriate response to discord, combined with daily examples of widespread societal violence and a ready supply of media examples for imitation, may instigate violent behavior in undefinable ways. Media violence is not directly causal in most cases, but it does contribute

to the climate of violence pervading American society. Real-life tragedies have sometimes become an extension of the fictional ones.

Film versions of real-life events also redefine the tragic as entertainment. For example, in the film *The Accused,* which was released in 1988, Jodie Foster played a rape victim. The film told the story of a real-life gang rape that occurred in New Bedford, Massachusetts. When the film was shown in theaters, young men reportedly hooted, cheered, and clapped during the rape scene.[145] While such behavior might be considered merely crude by some, it illustrates a generalized convergence of real violence and entertainment on the part of those watching the film.

While 92 percent of Americans surveyed in 1996 thought that television and movie violence contributes to violent crime, there is less agreement about how to reduce public exposure to violent entertainment media.[146] A variety of proposals have been suggested by citizen action groups, government commissions, religious leaders, and the concerned public. Suggestions include:

- Bans on violent programming during times when children are watching
- The recently enacted TV industry rating system
- Boycotts of products that advertise during violent programming
- Citizen boycotts of films with graphic violence
- Educational programs aimed at countering the affects of violent media or at educating parents about monitoring television viewing of their children
- Electronic blocking devices used to interrupt the cable signal during violent programming

While these suggestions are reassuring, in that they seem to reflect public concern and may result in more wholesome entertainment options, they tap only a limited avenue of violent expression. In other words, entertainment options mirror our societal acceptance of violence as legitimate, justifiable, or utilitarian.

Violence and Masculinity

American history is fraught with incidents of violence that served to establish American prominence as a world leader. Many of the values that underlie the use of violence as a means to an end are fundamentally linked to traditional ideas of masculinity and male social roles. Not all men hold these values, and the values are not limited to men; but, the predominant expression of violence as a means of solving problems is a pattern most consistently illustrated by the activities of men. Many women also believe violence is a legitimate means of solving problems under certain circumstances, although the use of violence is more likely to be expressed by men according to virtually all measures of violent crime.

Violence in the United States is not a new phenomenon. Brutality, terrorism, rape, murder, and assault have been perpetrated upon entire groups of people (African American slaves, Native Americans). Similarly, violence for entertainment has been an American cultural pattern for many generations. Boxing, baiting of animals, public executions, and public whippings or mutilations are social events that have drawn, and in some cases continue to draw, thousands of spectators. Research on the societal impact of these events indicates that there are real-life adverse effects to the public exhibition of aggression. David Phillips, for example, found an increase in homicide rates for several days after each highly publicized boxing match.[147]

The use of violence to solve problems, or for entertainment, is not limited to men, but most crimes of interpersonal violence are committed predominantly by men. Women are rare offenders in violent interpersonal crimes by comparison to men. The rate of incarceration for men with sentences of more than one year for all crimes is 753 per 100,000 population, compared to 45 women incarcerated for more than one year per 100,000 population.[148] Some violent crimes are committed almost exclusively by men against women, such as sexual abuse of children, rape, and domestic battery. There are no comparable reverse relationships, where women are the primary perpetrators of interpersonal violence against men. It is unlikely that crimes of interpersonal violence will begin to decline until some of the larger issues related to violence in general are addressed.

Summary

The rate of violent interpersonal crime as reported in the NCVS has declined over time. The UCR data also indicate declining violent crime. Declining crime rates may be deceiving, however. For certain groups in the population the rates have risen drastically, notably among young men under the age of 25. The overall rate has remained stable because there is an increased number of people in the older demographic categories who have a low likelihood of either perpetration or victimization in any violent interpersonal crime.

Arrests for assault have increased over the last two decades. Part of the increase, as indicated by official measures, is due to changes in the age of majority for many violent interpersonal crimes in all states. Assault is among those crimes that most clearly reflect changes in attitudes toward illegal behavior committed by young people. Some people believe that lowering the age at which people are accountable for violent crimes is a realistic approach to the problem of violent crime perpetrated by teenagers. Others believe that traditional protections of children who engage in such behavior should remain intact. Many people believe that focus on punishment, without attention to the societal causes of rising rates of violence among young people, is doomed to failure.

Changes in other types of violent interpersonal crime are not as easily measured as the index offense categories. Child abuse, domestic violence, and abuse of the elderly are generally cited as escalating problems, but the indications of increase are clouded by the likelihood of underreporting. Discerning between actual increases in the occurrence of the behavior and increased tendencies to report the crimes is a problem that has perplexed researchers for decades.

Regardless of the fluctuations in reports, violent crimes are very common. Most women who are murdered are killed by a relative, and most victims of childhood sexual abuse are girls. Most violent crime is committed by men, and entire categories of offenses are targeted almost exclusively at women. Victims of rape, domestic battery, and childhood sexual abuse are targeted because they are women. For most other crimes, the target of the offense is chosen because of proximity, convenience, low risk of detection, or other factors associated with the technical aspects of crime commission. With violent interpersonal crimes against women, these factors are important, but the fact that the victim is a woman is an overriding concern of the perpetrator. This makes violent interpersonal crime against women an especially difficult social problem. Gender-role stereotypes, attitudes toward women as a group, and underlying assumptions about the worth of women interface with the legal issues associated with these crimes.

When all of the statistical, demographic, and legal issues are held constant, it must be acknowledged that the use of violence to address conflict is an underlying social fact in American society. Social patterns that promote violence as an acceptable recourse for solving problems will have to be addressed if there is any hope for reducing the current levels of violent interpersonal crime in America.

Critical Thinking Questions

1. Why do you think murder occurs more commonly in the United States than in any other industrialized nation?

2. Even though there is not a causal link in intergenerational abuse (not all abused children grow up to be abusers), there does appear to be an association between childhood victimization and adult perpetration of interpersonal abuse. What do you think causes this pattern?

3. Robbery is classified as a violent crime, even though physical injury is relatively rare in the commission of this crime and the object of the crime is material gain. What role should the threat of violence play in our understanding of violent crime? Do you think robbery should be classified as a property crime or a violent crime? Why, or why not?

4. Violent crime is declining in the United States, but violence perpetrated by youth is increasing. What do you think could be done to curtail violence by youthful offenders?

Suggested Readings

Susan Brownmiller, *Against Our Will: Men, Women and Rape* (New York: Simon & Schuster, 1975).

Marcus Felson, *Crime and Everyday Life: Insights and Implications for Society* (Thousand Oaks, CA: Pine Forge Press, 1994).

Gary Kleck, *Point Blank* (New York: Aldine De Gruyter, 1991).

Steven F. Messner and Richard Rosenfeld, *Crime and the American Dream* (Belmont, CA: Wadsworth, 1994).

Amye Warren and Lucy McGough, "Research on Children's Suggestibility," *Criminal Justice and Behavior 23* (1996):269–303.

Notes

[1] Andere Martin, "Only 800 Slain—It's a Good Year," *Chicago Tribune* (31 December 1995) 2-9.

[2] Gallup polls, as reported in the *Sourcebook of Criminal Justice Statistics, 1993*, 182–85; Kathleen Maguire and Ann L. Pastore, *Sourcebook of Criminal Justice Statistics, 1993* (Washington, D.C.: U.S. Department of Justice, Bureau of Justice Statistics, 1994).

[3] Michael R. Rand, "Crime and the Nation's Households, 1992" (Washington D.C.: U.S. Department of Justice, Bureau of Justice Statistics, 1993).

[4] Diane Craven, "Female Victims of Violent Crime," *Bureau of Justice Statistics Selected Findings* (Washington DC: U.S. Government Printing Office, 1996) 2; Jan M. Chaiken, "Criminal Victimization in the United States, 1994," *Bureau of Justice Statistics* (Washington DC: U.S. Government Printing Office, 1997) 31; Diane Craven, "Sex Differences in Violent Victimization, 1994," *Bureau of Justice Statistics Special Report* (Washington DC: U.S. Government Printing Office) 1.

[5] Lisa D. Bastian and Marshal M. DeBerry, Jr., "Criminal Victimizations in the United States, 1992" (Washington, D.C.: U.S. Department of Justice, Bureau of Justice Statistics, 1994) 56.

[6] Ibid.

[7] Chaiken, "Criminal Victimization in the United States, 1994," 31.

[8] Ibid., 19.

[9] Ibid., 20

[10] Ibid., 40.

[11] Craig Perkins and Patsy Klaus, "Criminal Victimization 1994," *Bureau of Justice Statistics Bulletin* (Washington DC: U.S. Government Printing Office, 1996) 2–3.

[12] U.S. Department of Justice, "Violent Crime" (Washington, DC: Bureau of Justice Statistics Selected Findings, 1994).

[13] Although not all rates for 1995 have been released, the rate of violent crime shows decline. U.S. Department of Justice, *Social Statistics Briefing Room* (World Wide Web, White House Statistics, Released 30 May 1997).

[14] Maguire and Pastore, *Sourcebook of Criminal Justice Statistics,1995*, 232; Lisa D. Bastian and Marshal M. DeBerry, Jr., "Criminal Victimization in the United States, 1992" (Washington, D.C.: U.S. Department of Justice, Bureau of Justice Statistics, 1994) 56.

[15] Sue A. Lindgren, *Justice Expenditure and Employment Extracts, 1992: Data from the Annual General Finance and Employment Surveys* (Washington DC: U.S. Government Printing Office, front cover, 1997).

[16] Ibid., 1.

[17] Kathleen Maguire and Ann L. Pastore, *Sourcebook of Criminal Justice Statistics,1993* (Washington, D.C.: U.S. Department of Justice, 1994) 256.

[18] U.S. Department of Justice, "Violent Crime," 3.

[19] Ibid.

[20] Federal Bureau of Investigation (1997), *Crime in the United States, 1996* (Washington DC: U.S. Government Printing Office 1997) 10.

[21] Rate changes in the FBI data should be interpreted cautiously, however. Often increases in police personnel, changes in policing strategies, or new technical equipment lead to better reporting, which misleads many people into thinking crime has changed, whereas the ability to report or record crime has changed more than actual incidents of crime. Uniform Crime Report data should be used in conjunction with NCVS data because the UCR is subject to many flaws in interpretation. The NCVS also is problematic, in that large numbers of crimes are underreported, but the data from the NCVS is more extensive and detailed than the UCR.

[22] Craig Perkins and Patsy Klaus, "Criminal Victimization 1994," 3.

[23] Federal Bureau of Investigation (1997), *Crime in the United States,1996*, 22.

[24] Ibid; Maguire and Pastore, *Sourcebook of Criminal Justice Statistics,1995*, 337.

[25] F. Landis Mackellar and Machiko Yanagishita, *Homicide in the United States: Who's at Risk?* (Washington, DC: Population Reference Bureau, Inc., 1995).

[26] Ibid.

[27] Ibid.

[28] Ibid.

29 Federal Bureau of Investigation, *Crime in the United States* (Washington DC: U.S. Government Printing Office, 1997) 10.

30 Ibid.

31 Ibid.

32 Ibid.

33 Maguire and Pastore, *Sourcebook of Criminal Justice Statistics, 1995,* 568; Tracy Snell, *Women in Prison,* Bureau of Justice Statistics Special Report, (Washington, D.C.: U.S. Department of Justice, 1994) 5.

34 Tracy Snell, "Women in Prison," 5.

35 Ibid.

36 See, for example, Pauline Bart and Eileen Geil Moran, *Violence Against Women: The Bloody Footprints* (Newbury Park, CA.: Sage, 1993).

37 Federal Bureau of Investigation, *Crime in the United States, 1996,* 17.

38 Marianne W. Zawitz, "Violence Between Intimates," *Bureau of Justice Statistics Selected Findings* (Washington DC: U.S. Government Printing Office, 1994) 3.

39 Susan Estrich, "Rape," in *Feminist Jurisprudence,* ed. Patricia Smith (New York: Oxford, 1993).

40 For a comprehensive examination of the legal and cultural response to the crime of rape, see Susan Brownmiller, *Against Our Will: Men, Women and Rape* (New York: Simon & Schuster, 1975).

41 See Brownmiller, *Against Our Will: Men, Women and Rape;* Bart and Moran, *Violence Against Women: The Bloody Footprints;* and Diana Russell, *The Politics of Rape* (New York: Stein & Day, 1975).

42 Brownmiller, *Against Our Will: Men, Women and Rape.*

43 See Bart and Moran, *Violence Against Women:The Bloody Footprints.*

44 Ronet Bachman, "Violence Against Women," A National Crime Victimization Survey Report (Washington DC: U.S. Government Printing Office, 1994) 13; Maguire and Pastore, *Sourcebook of Criminal Justice Statistics, 1993,* 252; Mary P. Koss, "Hidden Rape: Sexual Aggression and Victimization in a National Sample of Students in Higher Education," in *Rape and Society: Readings on the Problem of Sexual Assault,* ed. Patricia Searles and Ronald J. Berger (Boulder: Westview, 1995). See also Bart and Moran, *Violence Against Women: The Bloody Footprints.*

45 Koss, "Hidden Rape: Sexual Aggression and Victimization in a National Sample of Students in Higher Education."

46 Henry J. Kaiser Family Foundation, "Was it Rape? An Examination of Sexual Assault Statistics," 10.

47 Craig Perkins and Patsy Klaus, "Criminal Victimization, 1994," *Bureau of Justice Statistics Bulletin* (Washington DC: U.S. Government Printing Office, 1996) 1.

48 Maguire and Pastore, *Sourcebook of Criminal Justice Statistics, 1995,* 239.

49 Ibid., 241.

50 Ibid., 237.

51 Daniel Lockwood, *Prison Sexual Violence* (New York: Elsevier, 1980) 21.

52 FBI, *Crime in the United States,1996* (Washington DC: U.S. Government Printing Office, 1997) 24.

53 Jodi M. Brown et al., *Correctional Populations in the United States, 1994* (Washington DC: U.S. Government Printing Office, 1996) 11.

54 Maguire and Pastore, *Sourcebook of Criminal Justice Statistics,1995,* 570, 573.

55 Ibid., 578–79.

56 Perkins and Klaus, "Criminal Victimization, 1994," 1; Maguire and Pastore, *Sourcebook of Criminal Justice Statistics, 1993,* 246–47.

57 Ibid; Maguire and Pastore, *Sourcebook of Criminal Justice Statistics, 1995,* 232.

58 Ibid.

59 Ibid., 396.

60 Mackellar and Yanagishita, *Homicide in the United States: Who's at Risk?*

61 Ibid., 349.

62 Ibid; FBI, *Crime in the United States, 1996,* 230–32.

63 Ibid., 395.

64 Ibid., 367; Perkins and Klaus, "Criminal Victimization 1994," 1.

65 Ibid., 256, Lisa D. Bastian and Marshall M. DeBerry, *Criminal Victimization in the United States, 1992* (Washington, D.C.: U.S. Department of Justice, 1994).

66 Maguire and Pastore, *Sourcebook of Criminal Justice Statistics, 1995,* 498–99, 408, 403.

67 Ibid., 232.

68 Zawitz, "Violence Between Intimates," 2.

69 See Kathleen Waits, "The Criminal Justice System's Response to Battering: Understanding the Problem, Forging the Solutions," in *Feminist Jurisprudence,* ed. Patricia Smith (New York: Oxford, 1994).

70 Ibid., 189.

71 Dawson and Langan, "Murder in Families," *Special Report from the Bureau of Justice Statistics* (Washington, D.C.: U.S. Department of Justice, 1994).

72 Diane Craven, "Female Victims of Violent Crime," *Bureau of Justice Statistics, Selected Findings* (Washington DC: U.S. Government Printing Office, 1996) 2.

73 Angela A. Browne, *Battered Women Who Kill* (New York: Free Press, 1987).

74 Richard J. Gelles and Murray A. Straus, *Intimate Violence* (New York: Simon & Schuster 1988).

75 Bachman, "Violence Against Women," 5; Eve Buzawa, Thomas L. Austin, and Carl G. Buzawa, "Responding to Crimes of Violence Against Women: Gender Differences versus Organizational Imperatives," *Crime and Delinquency 41* (1995) 443–66.

76 See Bart and Moran, *Violence Against Women: The Bloody Footprints.*

77 S. McLeer and R. Anwar, "A Study of Battered Women Presenting in an Emergency Department," *American Journal of Public Health 79* (1989) 65–66.

78 See Bart and Moran, *Violence Against Women:The Bloody Footprints,* for discussion of these issues in more detail.

79 "Why Batterers So Often Go Free," *Newsweek,* 16 October 1995, 61–62.

80 See Dorie Klein, "Violence Against Women: Some Considerations Regarding Its Causes and Its Elimination," *Crime and Delinquency 27* (1981) 64–80; Del Martin, "Battered Women: Society's Problem," in *The Criminal Justice System and Women,* ed. Barbara Raffel Price and Natalie J. Sokoloff (New York: Clark Boardman, 1982).

81 Bachman, "Violence Against Women," 1.

82 Ibid.

83 Ibid.

84 Ibid., see also Browne, *Battered Women Who Kill;* Martin, "Battered Women: Society's Problem."

85 FBI, *Crime in the United States, 1996,* 19.

86 Zawitz, "Violence Between Intimates." For a review of the literature that discusses this problem see Demie Kurz, "Social Science Perspectives on Wife Abuse: Current Debates and Future Directions," in *Violence Against Women: The Bloody Footprints,* ed. Pauline Bart and Eileen Morgan (Newbury Park, CA: Sage, 1993).

87 Zawitz, "Violence Between Intimates."

88 Loretta J. Stalans and Arthur J. Lurigio, "Responding to Domestic Violence Against Women," *Crime and Delinquency 41* (1995) 387–98.

89 Ibid. See also Buzawa et al., "Responding to Crimes of Violence Against Women: Gender Differences versus Organizational Imperatives."

90 Sylvia Mignon and William M. Holmes, "Police Response to Mandatory Arrest Laws," *Crime and Delinquency 41* (1995) 430–42.

91 Buzawa et al., "Responding to Crimes of Violence Against Women: Gender Differences versus Organizational Imperatives."

92 Ibid.

93 Robert C. Davis and Bruce G. Taylor, "A Pro-Active Response to Family Violence: The Results of a Randomized Experiment," *Criminology 35* (1997) 307–333.

94 Lenore Walker, *The Battered Woman Syndrome* (New York: Springer, 1984).

95 Malcolm Gordon and Mary A. Dutton, "The Validity and Use of Evidence Concerning Battering and Its Effects on Criminal Trials. Overview and Highlights of the Report," National Institute of Justice, CD-ROM Current Issues Source-File. Record: GO 17-35, pp. 5–13.

96 Zawitz, "Violence Between Intimates."

97 Stalans and Lurigio, "Responding to Domestic Violence Against Women."

98 Elizabeth Pleck, *Domestic Tyranny* (New York: Oxford, 1987).

99 Ibid.

100 Ibid.; see especially Appendix A.

101 Ibid., 41.

102 Stephen J. Pfohl, "The Discovery of Child Abuse," *Social Problems 24* (1977) 310–23.

103 Cathy Spatz Windom, "The Cycle of Violence," *Science 244* (1989) 160–66; Cathy S. Windom, "Victims of Childhood Sexual Abuse—Later Criminal Consequences," National Institute of Justice, CD-Rom Current Issues SourceFile. Record G017-21, 1995, pp. 1–8.

104 Ibid.

105 Richard Gelles and Murray Straus, "Is Violence Toward Children Increasing? A Comparison of 1975 and 1985 National Survey Rates" (Durham, NH: Family Violence Research Program, 1985).

106 Leo C. Downing and Jack E. Bynum, "Substantiated Reports of Child Abuse and Neglect," *Free Inquiry in Creative Sociology 10* (1982) 197, 201–206.

107 Chin-Tung Lung, "Current Trends in Child Abuse Reporting and Fatalities: The Results of the 1995 Annual Fifty State Survey," National Committee to Prevent Child Abuse, CD-ROM Current Issues SourceFile. Record (1996): A137-10.

108 Ibid.

109 Maguire and Pastore, *Sourcebook of Criminal Justice Statistics, 1993,* 216, 278.

110 Meda Chesney-Lind and Randall G. Shelden, *Girls, Delinquency and Juvenile Justice* (Pacific Grove, CA: Brooks/Cole, 1992) 26–27.

111 Ibid.

112 Lawrence A. Greenfeld, "Child Victimizers: Violent Offenders and Their Victims," *Bureau of Justice Statistics Executive Summary* (Washington DC: U.S. Government Printing Office, 1996) 1.

113 Ibid.

114 Ibid.

115 Claire M. Renzetti and Daniel J. Curran, *Women and Men in Society,* 3rd ed. (Boston: Allyn & Bacon, 1995).

[116] Ibid.; see also Older Women's League, "The Facts About Violence Against Mid-Life and Older Women," Current Issues SourceFile. Record: A020-2, pp. 1–2.

[117] Pillemer and Finkelhor (1988), as reported in Renzetti and Curran (1995), 250.

[118] Ibid.

[119] Suzanne K. Steinmetz (1994), as reported in Renzetti and Curran (1995), 250.

[120] Gary Kleck, *Point Blank* (New York: Aldine De Gruyter, 1991).

[121] Ibid., 18.

[122] Ibid.; Maguire and Pastore, *Sourcebook of Criminal Justice Statistics, 1993,* 203; William Bankston, Carol Y. Thompson, Quentin A.L. Jenkins, and Craig Forsyth, "The Influence of Fear of Crime, Gender, and Southern Culture on Carrying Firearms for Protection," *Sociological Quarterly 31* (1990) 287–305.

[123] Kleck (1991) 19.

[124] Marianne W. Zawitz, "Guns Used in Crime," *U.S. Department of Justice Statistics Selected Findings* (Washington DC: U.S. Government Printing Office, 1995).

[125] Martin Killias, "Gun Ownership and Violent Crime: The Swiss Experience in International Perspective," *Security Journal 1* (1990) 169–74.

[126] Zawitz, "Guns Used in Crime," 1.

[127] Ibid.; Kelck (1991) 18.

[128] Zawitz, "Guns Used in Crime," 3.

[129] Maguire and Pastore, *Sourcebook of Criminal Justice Statistics, 1993,* 176.

[130] Ibid., 208.

[131] Don Manson, "Presale Firearm Checks," *Bureau of Justice Statistics Bulletin* (Washington DC: U.S. Government Printing Office, 1997) 1.

[132] Bankston et al., 1990.

[133] Gary Kleck and Marc Gertz, "Armed Resistance to Crime: The Prevalence and Nature of Self-Defense with a Gun," *The Journal of Criminal Law and Criminology 86* (1995) 150–87.

[134] Kleck, 1991; Gary Kleck and Marc Gertz, "Armed Resistance to Crime: The Prevalence and Nature of Self-Defense with a Gun," *Journal of Criminal Law and Criminology 86* (1995) 150–89.

[135] Gary Kleck and Miriam DeLone, "Victim Resistance and Offender Weapon Effects in Robbery," *Journal of Quantitative Criminology 9* (1993) 55–81.

[136] Maguire and Pastore, *Sourcebook of Criminal Justice Statistics, 1993,* 379.

[137] Maguire and Pastore, *Sourcebook of Criminal Justice Statistics, 1995,* 366.

[138] Ibid.; Federal Bureau of Investigation, *Crime in the United States, 1993* (Washington DC: U.S. Government Printing Office, 1994).

[139] See James Garofalo, "Crime and the Mass Media: A Selective Review of Research, " *Journal of Research in Crime and Delinquency 18* (1981) 319–50; George Gerbner, "Violence in Television Drama: Trends and Symbolic Functions," in *Television and Social Behavior,* Vol 1, ed. G.A. Comstock and F.A. Rubinstein (1972) 28–187; Brendan Maguire, "Image vs. Reality: An Analysis of Prime-Time Television and Police Programs," *Crime and Justice 11* (1988) 165–88.

[140] For a summary of the literature, see Fred Molitor and Kenneth William Hirsch, "Children's Toleration of Real-Life Aggression After Exposure to Media Violence: A Replication of Drabman and Thomas Studies," *Child Study Journal 24* (1994) 191–207.

[141] Albert Bandura and R.H. Walters, *Social Learning and Personality Development* (New York: Holt, Rinehart and Winston, 1963).

[142] Surgeon General's Scientific Advisory Committee on Television and Social Behavior, "Television and Growing Up: The Impact of Televised Violence," (Washington, D.C.: U.S. Government Printing Office, 1972).

[143] See Molitor et al., "Children's Toleration of Real-Life Aggression After Exposure to Media Violence: A Replication of Drabman and Thomas Studies"; Garland F. White, Janet Katz, and Kathryn E. Scarborough, "The Impact of Professional Football Games upon Violent Assault on Women," *Violence and Victims 7* (1992) 157–71; Nancy Theberge, "A Feminist Analysis of Responses to Sports Violence: Media Coverage of the 1987 World Junior Hockey Championship," *Sociology of Sport Journal 6* (1989) 247–56.

[144] See Molitor et al., "Children's Toleration of Real-Life Aggression After Exposure to Media Violence: A Replication of Drabman and Thomas Studies."

[145] Susan Faludi, *Backlash: The Undeclared War Against American Women* (New York: Anchor, 1991) 139.

[146] Maguire and Pastore, *Sourcebook of Criminal Justice Statistics,1995,* 222.

[147] David P. Phillips, "The Impact of Mass Media Violence on U.S. Homicides," *American Sociological Review 48* (1983) 560–68.

[148] Maguire and Pastore, *Sourcebook of Criminal Justice Statistics, 1995,* 556.

chapter 6

Crimes of the Powerful

KEY TERMS

street crime
social harm
social structure
white-collar crime
occupational crime
corporate crime
organizational crime
governmental crime
criminal intent
welfare for the wealthy
elite deviance
corporate deviance
corporate dumping
environmental racism
whistleblowers

CHAPTER OUTLINE

DEFINITIONS OF ELITE CRIME
   White-Collar or Occupational Crime
   Corporate and Organizational Crime
   Governmental Crime
NATURE, EXTENT, AND COSTS
   Double Standards of Justice
   Perils of White-Collar Crime
   Financial Costs
   Dangers
   White-Collar Crime and Intent
OFFENDERS AND VICTIMS
   Power: Crime vs. Social Harm
   Offenders: Gender and Elite Crime
   Victims: Hidden Crime
   Welfare for the Wealthy
CRIME AND DEVIANCE IN HIGH PLACES
   Corporate Deviance
   Corporate Dumping
   Environmental Racism
   Governmental Crime
ENFORCEMENT
   Progress in Enforcement
   Corporate Accountability
SUMMARY

IT IS NOT SURPRISING that our images of crime tend to focus on the Federal Bureau of Investigation's (FBI) index offenses, often called **street crime.** Index offenses are the most common themes of crime stories. They are, indeed, dangerous and all too common. Yet, focus on these crimes may distort the reality of crime.

Many criminologists believe crime committed by people in respectable positions costs Americans more than all of the index and other street offenses *combined* in any given year.[1]

Crimes of the powerful are common and expensive to Americans, but there are many methodological problems in determining the nature and extent of elite crime. Collecting crime data of this type is hindered by the fact that many of these crimes are concealed by their powerful perpetrators.

Traditional inquiry into crime uses law violation as the primary means of defining crime. Many criminologists who study elite crime use a critical perspective. This means the study of this type of crime goes beyond law violation to include social harm, or that behavior which may be legal but harms others. Underlying questions about social structure, or the position of people in the economic hierarchy, are also included in the study of crime when a critical perspective is used.

Definitions of Elite Crime

While fear of index offenses or street crime is high for most people, risk of victimization for crimes committed by those in elite social positions is also a very real threat. Such crime is commonly called *white-collar crime, occupational crime, corporate crime, organizational crime,* or *governmental crime.* There are distinctions among these categories, although many people use the terms interchangeably.

As noted in Chapter 1, it was Edwin Sutherland who in 1939 first drew the attention of sociologists to the problem of white-collar crime when he delivered his presidential address to the American Sociological Society. He used *white-collar crime* to refer to crime committed by ordinary business people and professionals in the course of their occupations. Sutherland, in his subsequent book *White-Collar Crime,* pointed out that the failure to collect statistics on white-collar offenses results from common misunderstandings about the facts of crime. While index offenses were serious, according to Sutherland there was a whole area of crime that went largely undetected and unaddressed.[2] Sutherland's analysis of white-collar crime weakened many previous theories that proposed poverty as the cause of crime. If crime resulted from a lack of economic opportunity, then why would employed, responsible, well-to-do business people engage in criminal activities?

White-Collar or Occupational Crime

White-collar implies a person employed in an occupation of high respect. The term **white-collar crime** originally referred to crimes committed by men who wore white shirts to work, as opposed to workingclass men, who wore blue shirts. While styles have changed, the terms still roughly distinguish between those who dress as professionals and workingclass employees, who are expected to dress casually or wear a uniform.[3] Many crimes committed by people in the course of their jobs are committed by individuals employed in blue-collar occupations. Auto mechanics who misrepresent repairs, cashiers who steal from the till, or electricians who overcharge customers would be included in occupational crime categories even though they are not employed in white-collar occupations. Thus, the term **occupational crime** includes the category of crimes committed in the normal course of employment, but does not exclusively refer to people employed in white-collar occupations. Occupational crime is an extension of the concept of white-collar crime.

Corporate and Organizational Crime

The term *corporate crime* clarifies even more precisely the nature of crime by powerful people. White-collar or occupational crime refers to crimes committed by people in the course of their occupations; **corporate crime** refers to crime committed by corporations, or groups of people, acting in the interests of a corporation. The distinction is between those people who engage in law violations for personal gain and those who are interested in furthering the goals or profits of the corporation.

Organizational crime refers to crime committed by people in a variety of organizations to further the goals of

Between 1942 and 1953 Hooker Chemical Company dumped 20,000 tons of toxic chemicals into a site at Love Canal, New York. They subsequently sold the land to developers who built homes and schools over the site.

the group to which they belong. In these cases, the organization itself is the offender. Goals and policies of the organization motivate the crime, rather than individual crime by members of the group. The typical perpetrators of such crimes are those who belong to organizations with strongly articulated beliefs about particular issues or businesses with interests that are more easily served through illegal means than through legal channels. Companies that engage in consumer fraud for the benefit of the company, rather than for the benefit of particular people in the company, would be candidates for this category of elite crime. Anti-abortion demonstrators who violate federal laws regulating protests outside abortion clinics do so for reasons that are grounded in their beliefs about the organization to which they belong. Laws prohibiting their actions are secondary to what they consider higher principles. Extremist political groups have engaged in organizational crimes against the American government, the people of the United States, or particular demographic groups. Such crimes range from acts of civil disobedience

to murder. There is considerable overlap between organizational crime and other categories of crimes of the powerful. In this chapter, the category of organizational crimes is subsumed under other categories, such as governmental crime and corporate illegalities.

Governmental Crime

Governmental crime includes crimes committed by the government to further the interests of political or bureaucratic leaders in office. Governmental agencies such as the Central Intelligence Agency (CIA) or the FBI have been known to violate both federal and state laws to further the interests of the government (or their *interpretation* of the best interests of the nation) within the course of their routine operations. Thousands of people have died as the result of covert activities by governmental agencies and administrative offices. This lawbreaking behavior has often been dismissed by individual political leaders as patriotism that should be above the law.[4]

Nature, Extent, and Costs

Ascertaining the parameters or patterns of crimes committed by people in elite positions is a formidable task. With other offense categories, the easiest way of measuring any particular crime is to check official reports (FBI data) and compare reported crime with self-report data (NCVS data). In this way, the researcher can compare crimes reported to the police with rates of victimization. While there are many flaws in this technique, in that many crimes are underreported in both measures and not all categories of crime are carefully tracked, such measures provide estimates of both perpetration and victimization. There are currently no index categories to cover elite crime. Most information on these offenses is gathered from newspaper reports of companies prosecuted, from individuals who have been convicted, or from court records.[5]

Double Standards of Justice

Many crime researchers believe that a double standard in criminal justice distinguishes crimes by powerful members of society from crimes committed by the powerless. Crimes of the powerful are rarely discovered, prosecuted, or punished. Groups of people, like companies, corporations, or the U.S. government, are rarely charged with crimes compared to other offenders.

Even if wrongdoing is established and a company is, for example, found guilty of collusion in pricing, fraud, false advertising, or overcharging, the case is typically handled in civil court with no criminal penalty applicable. Civil penalties are usually monetary (a fine), small by comparison to the benefit of the wrongdoing to the company, often tax-deductible, and have little deterrent effect on the likelihood of subsequent re-offense.[6] Criminal penalties in cases of crimes committed by the powerful are exceedingly rare and there is generally no prison sentence handed down.[7]

In the famous electrical price-fixing case of the 1950s, for example, where General Electric (GE), Westinghouse, and twenty-nine other companies were found guilty of conspiring to fix prices, rig bids, and divide markets on electrical equipment valued at $1.75 billion annually, penalties were light by comparison to the benefits of the illegal activities. Prices of electrical equipment were grossly inflated as a result of the conspiracy. The vice president of GE, who was a forty-year veteran of the company, was fined $2000 and received a thirty-day jail sentence. Seven GE executives were jailed for 30 days, and twenty-four executives received suspended jail sentences (no time actually served). One executive commented "Sure, collusion was illegal, but it wasn't unethical." At the time, this was the biggest criminal case ever prosecuted in the history of the Sherman Anti-Trust Act, with forty-five defendants included in the indictment.[8]

Detection of crimes by powerful individuals is rare, in part because few enforcement efforts are directed toward these crimes. For many years, these crimes have been assumed to be non-violent, relatively harmless, rare, and not seriously threatening to the health, safety, or security of most Americans. Many people in the criminal justice system, as well as the general public, have presumed that resources should be spent on better detection, enforcement, prosecution, and punishment of "real" crime.

White-collar, corporate, and governmental offenders are generally middle- and upper-class people who bear a striking resemblance to attorneys and judges with regard to their income, lifestyle, education, civic and club memberships, demeanor, and other measures of social status. Ordinary stereotypes of "criminals" do not include lifestyle or personal characteristics that merge with those of judges and attorneys, which creates a chasm of "us versus them" in ordinary treatment of criminal offenders. The psychological dissonance created by elite crime has been met, for the most part, with a denial of real harm done by upper-class offenders. White-collar suspects are seldom arrested by uniformed police officers, held in local jails, or sent to prison, regardless of the costs of their crime or the endangerment or deaths that resulted from their actions. These offenders are generally respectable members of their communities and continue to be afforded the dignity and respect accorded to others of their social status.

Perils of White-Collar Crime

Research in white-collar crime indicates that common stereotypes of harmlessness may be misplaced. These crimes are serious, dangerous, and expensive; in many cases they have jeopardized the safety of millions of Americans over a long period of time. Many industrial workers have been "accidentally" maimed or killed because of unsafe working conditions that were in direct violation of state and federal law. Companies have knowingly endangered the lives of millions of Americans through pollution of the environment and degradation of the ecosystem, in direct violation of laws prohibiting their actions. Products have been manufactured, marketed, and maintained on the market even when the manufacturers knew the products could cause injury or death. Profit motivations have caused professionals in medicine, law, and science, among others, to falsify information, accept kickbacks, mislead consumers, clients, or patients, and perform unnecessary services for personal enrichment. Even the United States government has knowingly violated civil and criminal laws and constitutional prohibitions in furtherance of political ideologies or profits for lawmakers. All of these crimes are serious and dangerous, but most have gone unacknowledged or unpunished. Many theorists believe that violation of the law and covert illegal practices are the *modus operandi* of most businesses, corporations, and a large segment of the U.S. government.[9]

Financial Costs

Determining the cost of crimes by the powerful is as difficult as discerning the extent of such crimes. Several individual cases of white-collar price-fixing, consumer fraud, and corporate tax evasion have cost Americans collectively more than all of the index property offenses combined in any given year. Some cases of white-collar or corporate crime cost consumers more than the combined costs of index property offenses *for several centuries*. The savings-and-loan scandal of the 1980s, for example, is expected to cost American taxpayers $1.4 trillion when final expenses are tallied. This is "more money than American street criminals steal in 4000 years."[10] Tables 6.1 and 6.2 illustrate some of the distortions in common perceptions of the cost of crime. Single incidents of property crime are expensive to victims, threatening to personal safety, and all too common. Yet the loss to victims is minimal compared to losses to victims of crimes perpetrated by powerful people in respectable positions.

Each of the white-collar losses in the tables are single cases, as with single cases of index offenses. Those cases that last several years, or that involve multiple corporations in collusion, are much more expensive than the ones cited. For example, the savings-and-loan fraud cases are ongoing. Over 7000 cases were scheduled for investigation, although the FBI highlights only 100 per year. The total losses of $1.4 trillion are merely estimated, because it will take many years to complete the investigations and prosecutions. Similarly, the Bank of Credit and Commerce International (BCCI) scandal has an estimated price tag of $5 to $15 billion.[11] According to the National Insurance Crime Bureau, fraudulent insurance claims cost all Americans up to $50 billion in increased insurance rates, higher taxes, and inflated prices for consumer goods and services.[12]

Monopolist price distortions, many of which are criminal, are believed to cost consumers about $87 billion every year.[13] Estimates of between $174 and $231 billion are added to the costs of goods and services for Americans annually as a result of corporate crime.[14] The most conservative estimates of the costs of white-collar and corporate crime suggest that average costs to Americans are at least 20 times greater than all index property offenses combined. Economic losses from street crimes are about $10 billion annually, while losses from white-collar crime are estimated at $200 billion each year.[15] Costs of white-collar and corporate crime are double the $93.7 billion spent on all federal, state, and local criminal justice activities in 1992 (the last year for which figures are available).[16]

For the most part, Americans are still more fearful of street criminals, regardless of the expense incurred by white-collar or corporate offenders. A robbery at gunpoint is perceived to be more threatening than what is often dismissed as paper shuffling or manipulation of bookkeeping

TABLE 6.1 Average Losses in Single Cases of Specific Crimes, 1991

SINGLE CASES OF SPECIFIC CRIMES	AVERAGE LOSSES
Robbery	$ 817
Burglary	1,246
Motor vehicle theft	4,983
Larceny-theft	478

SOURCE: FBI, *Crime in the United States* (Washington DC: U.S. Government Printing Office, 1992) 27, 39, 44, 50.

TABLE 6.2 Average Losses in Single Cases of White-Collar Crime, 1991

SINGLE CASES OF WHITE-COLLAR CRIME	AVERAGE LOSSES
Bechtel and Westinghouse—Illegal manipulation of construction funds and cleanup of subsequent environmental disaster. Costs totaled:	$200 billion
American defense industry companies illegally sold Iraq weapons in 1991 *during* the Gulf war. Profits totaled:	$52.8 billion
Don Dixon fined for using call girls, paid with depositors money, to help decisionmaking at staff meetings. Dixon also received three consecutive five-year prison terms. Fine totaled:	$611,000
Mario Renda convicted of skimming money from failed savings and loans and defrauding Federal Deposit Insurance Corporation. He received a two-year sentence. Profit totaled:	$16 million

SOURCE: David R. Simon and D. Stanley Eitzen, *Elite Deviance*, 4th ed. (Boston: Allyn & Bacon, 1993).

records. Thus, the perceptions of danger are influenced not only by small estimates of monetary loss per individual victim but also by the threat of personal danger. If Americans pay higher taxes to bail out the savings-and-loan industry, or the national debt is impacted by the costs, these are abstract expenses that do not touch people with the same terror that accompanies home invasion, burglary, or robbery. Yet the cost of street crime pales by comparision to the white-collar crime of many businesses, corporations, and governmental bodies.

Dangers

Sociologist David Simon, who has published extensively on the topic of crimes by the elite, estimates that at least 5 times as many people die from illnesses and injuries related to their jobs than are murdered by all index offenders in a given year. A report from the National Commission on Product Safety concludes that 20 million Americans are injured annually in the home by faulty consumer products. This number includes 110,000 people who are permanently disabled and 30,000 who are killed. Safety, protection of consumers, and attention to the legal duty to market safe products are often secondary to profit and market competition.[17] Many famous cases punctuate the real-life tragedies associated with corporate crime.

The Pinto Case

Among the most renowned cases was that of the Ford Pinto. In this case, the Ford Motor Company knew about a design flaw in the car that could cause it to explode if hit in a rear-end collision. The company made a carefully calculated decision to disregard the safety issue and pay any costs of litigation in the event than anyone was killed as a result of the design defect. Ford executives calculated the costs and benefits of retooling the manufacturing process to make the car safer and then estimated costs of litigation if they did not correct the problem. The Ford people determined that the cost of correcting the design flaw would be $11 per car, for a total expenditure of $137 million. Litigation was estimated at $200,000 per death, $67,000 per injury, and $700 per vehicle. Ford believed that 180 deaths, plus 180 injuries and 2100 burned vehicles, represented a reasonable forecast of losses from the 1.5 million Pintos to be built. Total losses from deaths, injuries, and burned vehicles would cost the company an estimated $49.5 million. Ford opted for the cheaper route and decided not to correct the flaw or change the manufacturing process. In 1978, the Department of Transportation ordered a recall of Pintos manufactured between 1971 and 1976. In the same year, a California jury awarded $127.8 million to a teenage driver who had been badly burned when his Pinto was hit from the rear by a car driving 35 miles per hour.[18]

The Firestone Case

In a similar celebrated case the Firestone company knew that their Firestone 500 radial tires were seriously flawed. The 500s showed a consistently high rate of sudden blowouts caused by "separation failure," where the tread separated from the steel-belted inner layer. They continued to manufacture the tires and spent $28 million annually to advertise them. By 1978, they had manufactured 23.5 million Firestone 500 tires and there were 11 million in use. The Highway Traffic Safety Administration began investigation in 1976 and pressured Firestone to issue a voluntary recall, but the company refused. Instead, they dumped the remaining stock of tires on the market and sold them for clearance prices. Firestone 500 tires caused thousands of accidents, hundreds of injuries, and 34 known fatalities. The company was fined $50,000 in 1980 for selling a defective product.[19]

Unsafe Working Conditions

Dangers in the workplace, preventable accidents, unnecessary exposure to risk, and failure to implement safety changes take the lives of thousands of workers annually. Companies complain that worker safety precautions cost too much. Owners of mills, mines, and factories fail to protect the safety of their workers because the costs would reduce production profits.[20] Companies often fail to inform workers about the dangers inherent in the workplace, or diminish the importance of safety study findings. On-the-job accidents annually cause 3.3 million injuries requiring hospital treatment, and exposure to toxic chemicals in the work environment is responsible for at least 100,000 deaths and 390,000 new occupationally caused diseases each year.[21] Exposure to synthetic chemicals, dust, asbestos, nuclear radiation, metal particulates, vinyl chloride, chemical compounds, and other toxins shortens the lives of many workers, and exposure often could be reduced with minimal precautions. About 2 million people are injured on the job each year because of dangerous working conditions that violate requirements.[22]

Misconceptions of Danger

"It is estimated that about 140,000 people die each year from air pollution alone, most of which is the result of a violation of governmental regulations by corporations."[23] Thousands more are sickened by unsafe or polluted groundwater, agricultural chemicals in foods and water, or contaminated food—all within the boundaries of "normal business practice" by corporate producers, and most in violation of existing state, federal, or local laws restricting or regulating the unsafe practices.

When the dangers posed by corporate crime are compared to the dangers of index offenses, many criminologists believe the corporate offenders are more threatening to the lives and safety of ordinary Americans. The

Many workplace precautions that could improve worker safety are avoided as too costly to make the efforts worthwhile. The consequence is that thousands of workers are injured and killed on the job each year.

multiple millions of victims of corporate illegal behavior far outnumber the 1 million reports of assault, 537,050 robbery reports, or 19,645 murders known to the police in 1996.[24] More people are killed annually through corporate negligence, the marketing of unsafe products, or blatant violations of law than are murdered by index offenders in 10 years.

White-Collar Crime and Intent

One of the most difficult problems in defining white-collar and corporate offenses is the issue of intent. With index murderers, the seriousness of **criminal intent** is defined by whether the offender caused the victim great suffering, whether the offense was accidental, and whether the offense occurred in the course of commission of another crime, such as an unplanned murder that occurs in the process of a robbery. The variations in the level of intent of the offender are differentiated by issues such as crime planning, infliction of suffering, and other illegal behavior. The law, in this case, reflects a moral distinction in the character of the offenders' actions toward the victim.

Profit vs. Harm

With white-collar and corporate offenders, the issue of intent is often clouded in two ways. First, most corporate and white-collar offenders do not intend to harm anyone. Their purpose in putting an unsafe consumer item on the market, for example, is to make money, not harm consumers. While their failure to manufacture a safe product may harm many people, any harm that occurs is "accidental." Their real goal is to make money. Thus, the issue of harm is muddled by the intent of the offender. Knowing something *could* cause harm and actually *planning* to harm another are two different issues. Even in cases of willful violation of the law, which employers know will harm workers employed in an unsafe work environment, the intent is still to save money, not hurt anyone. The Environmental Protection Agency estimates that 90 percent of the 88 billion pounds of toxic waste produced annually by American companies is disposed of illegally.[25] Companies that illegally dump toxic wastes intend to cut costs; the net result is groundwater contamination, increased exposure to toxins, higher rates of cancer, and many other health problems. Companies do not intend to cause harm; it happens as a result of their real intentions to save money.

Civil vs. Criminal Court

The second problem with the issue of intent is that cases of illegal behavior on the part of corporate or white-collar offenders are generally not handled by criminal courts. Civil courts handle most cases, implying a less-serious degree of wrongful behavior than the index crimes that are prosecuted in criminal courts. Penalties for white-collar offenders are light by comparison to those for index offenders. The most common penalty applied is a fine, often representing only a token gesture—one that makes recidivism worthwhile. Sentences to prison are rare and are generally completed in less than 2 years if they are served at all. The average amount of time served for larceny-theft is 2 years in prison, compared to an average of 7 months served for violation of environmental protection laws.[26] The light penalties applied to white-collar and corporate offenders reflect a double standard in American justice that is widely criticized from many quarters. Ralph Nader writes:

> **The double standard—one for crime in the streets and one for crime in the suites—is well known. A man in Kentucky was sentenced to 10 years in jail in 1983 for stealing a pizza. . . . Dozens of corporations have been caught illegally dumping toxic wastes. Yet, only small fines followed. . . . The [FBI] has its updated list of the 10 most wanted criminals, but has no high-visibility listing for the most wanton corporate recidivists.[27]**

Sentencing Trends

General trends in sentencing indicate that penalties are lightest for those who steal the largest sums of money or who endanger the largest number of people. A person who steals a wallet is more likely to be sentenced to prison than a person who sells fraudulent real estate development options and makes millions of dollars on the illegal activity. Similarly, a single offender who commits murder, armed robbery, or assault is likely to receive a harsher penalty than those who are responsible for multiple injuries or deaths through the marketing of unsafe tires, pharmaceuticals, cars, toys, baby clothes, or other consumer items, or who endanger millions through environmental pollution.

Offenders and Victims

Numerous studies of index crimes have highlighted poverty as an underlying factor associated with many individual crimes. Not all index crime is related to the social structural position of offenders, but the issue of economic opportunity has been a recurring theme in many of the theories of crime and delinquency throughout the twentieth century.[28] In other words, social structural opportunities are associated with patterns of crime among all segments of society. In the study of elite crime, law violation is as important as it is to any of the index crime

categories, but social structural position *dictates the pattern of crime*. William Chambliss, Richard Quinney, Austin Turk, and others, argue that the hierarchical arrangement of social classes influences goals, values, and cultural traditions in each social class.[29] Crime reflects these standards. Each group in the social structure tries to maximize its own position through legitimizing the goals, values, and norms of the group. The reality of crime, as articulated by Quinney, is such that elite members of society are in a position to foster their values as legitimate social power.[30]

Power: Crime vs. Social Harm

From the perspective of those who follow Quinney's ideas, definitions of crime reflect the interests of those who have the power to have their views made law. From this view, it is not accidental that our society focuses on index offenses as the most serious and socially harmful crimes, rather than focusing on the crimes of the powerful. Focus on index crimes is an outgrowth of the social structural distinctions that give power to the elite. The reality of crime, from this perspective, is distorted by the powerful to deflect attention from their activities and refocus it upon lower-class offenders, whose crime is portrayed as direct harm perpetrated in face-to-face encounters.[31]

Many people see both the poor and criminals (index offenders) as lazy, immoral, and greedy. Political rhetoric often implies inherent shiftlessness among the lower classes, while the upper classes are portrayed as honest business people. President Reagan, for example, saw regulation of worker safety through the Occupational Health and Safety Administration (OSHA) as an infringement upon the profits of corporations. He said,

> **I believe that in a variety of ways, through environmental controls, through such things as OSHA, the government is trying to minimize the ownership of private property in this country.[32]**

This view, and the belief that lower-class crime grows out of rebellion against the rules of free enterprise, is problematic. Not all of the reprehensible behavior of powerful members of society is criminal; much of it is a reflection of inequitable social arrangements that disproportionately advantage the powerful as social agents who have the ability to have their interests protected at the expense of people with little social power. Crime, according to this view, is an outgrowth of arrogance, a sense of entitlement, and greed that characterizes powerful people who believe their interests should be protected because of their elite social position.

From the perspective of a social harm definition, the concept of crime is broadened; it includes not only behaviors that violate the law but also social harm perpetrated by a system that encourages powerful people to pursue their own interests at the expense of the less powerful. Law violation, from this perspective, is not the only component of crime. It also includes behavior that harms others through greed, personal enrichment, and pursuit of power by the economic elite. Many social and political policies protect the interests of the powerful and permit social harm to remain unchecked.

Offenders

Characteristics of powerful offenders coincide with characteristics of all elite groups in the American social hierarchy. Considerable attention by sociologists has been devoted to delineating interrelationships among officials of government, the wealthy elite, corporate boards of directors in key industries, and veiled connections among elite banking and financial institutions. The activities, education, social life, and economic opportunities of the wealthiest Americans are closed, tightly organized to maintain the elite status of members, and designed to protect wealth among the wealthy.[33] Offenders are not significantly different from any other members of the economic elite. They are employed in businesses and occupations that are essential to the American economy, and their activities, lifestyles, income, and personal characteristics are equivalent to others in their social class.

Gender and Elite Crime

The one distinguishing characteristic of crimes by the powerful is that almost all of these crimes are perpetrated by men. Crimes of the powerful, by definition, are perpetrated by people with high social positions. Women, who do not commonly hold such elite positions, are rare offenders. Leona Helmsley is among the more famous women convicted of elite crime in recent years. In 1991, she was convicted of tax fraud after illegally billing personal expenses to her company and evading $1.7 million in taxes. She was sentenced to 4 years in prison, ordered to pay $2 million in restitution, and assessed a $7 million fine. In another case, Jeanne Lawson pleaded guilty in 1992 to cashing her father's railroad pension checks for 24 years after he had died.[34]

Some recent theorists, including Jay Albanese, have claimed that women's representation in crimes of the powerful is increasing. He cites the percentage change in the number of women arrested for such crimes as fraud and embezzlement from 1970 to 1990 as examples of this increase. The data compiled from the UCR cited by Albanese show that 25 percent of arrests for embezzlement and 27 percent of fraud arrests were women in 1970, compared to 41 percent of embezzlement and 44 percent of fraud arrests in 1990.[35] From the numbers presented,

increased arrests of women for these crimes represents a significant change over the 20 years cited. Others, such as Darrell Steffensmeir and Cathy Streifel, have pointed out that increases among women in white-collar crime categories should be interpreted cautiously. Most arrests of women for fraud involve petty welfare theft (failing to report additional income to welfare authorities), misuse of credit cards, or bad checks (writing checks with insufficient funds). Similarly, embezzlement by women is characterized more by small-time theft from office petty cash than lucrative elite embezzlement.[36] The vast majority of crimes of the powerful continue to remain in the domain of wealthy white men.

Victims

Victims of these crimes may never know they have been victimized; thus, reports of white-collar crime are very low. If, for example, consumers are overcharged for breakfast cereal, new gym shoes, or toothpaste, they may be unaware of the overcharge. Similarly, if food manufacturers conspired to fix prices on cereals to keep costs artificially inflated for the mutual benefit of all companies, consumers would be unaware of the inflated cost of the cereal. Even if consumers know that they pay too much for a commodity, it is hardly worth their interest to try to recover the loss or to draw attention to the wrongdoing. An overcharge on breakfast cereal would cost the individual consumer only a few cents per box, for example, but it could be worth multiple millions of dollars to the company.

Many white-collar crimes are committed without the knowledge of direct victims, or victimization of specific individuals is so minimal as to be inconsequential. This is true for a wide range of crimes, including price fixing, pollution of the environment, consumer fraud, and many governmental crimes. Even if consumers know that they have been victims of price fixing, it is unlikely that report of victimization would result in any official action taken against the offender. Index offenses are much more likely to receive the attention of criminal justice officials than crimes committed by the powerful. There are many flaws in the current system and large numbers of offenders are never caught, not punished when they are caught, or punished with minor penalties. The criminal justice system is much more successful in responding to index crime than crimes of the powerful.[37] Breakfast cereal price-fixers, for example, are rarely apprehended by the police, prosecuted in the courts, or incarcerated.

Hidden Crime

Companies that engage in illegal activities are adept at hiding their activities. They have large staffs of attorneys and consumer "liaisons" to buffer accusations of wrongdoing; the illegal activities may be dispersed over a wide geographic area or a long period of time, or both; and laws regulating consumer complaint vary from one state to another. If breakfast cereal costs too much, who is at fault? The board of directors of the company, the president of the company, lower-level company managers, competitive markets, the local grocer who marked the price on the box, or a host of other parties could be responsible for the overcharge. Responsibility in corporations is difficult to discern and easily passed from one person or department to another. Victims are often unaware of the facts of their victimization, or they lack the power to stop offenders.

Welfare for the Wealthy

In the United States, the most widely recognized form of welfare is that which supplies the poor with life necessities, such as housing, food, a small income allotment, help with medical expenses, and other assistance (usually temporary). Such assistance to the poor has been widely criticized in recent years as a "free lunch," implying that the helping hand of government should not be extended to those who are physically able to work. Welfare changes have recently specified limits on the amount of help extended to the poor. Freezing the welfare payments of unmarried mothers who have subsequent children while on welfare has become a symbol of welfare reform and a catalyst for further cuts into the services provided to poor families.

Many Americans believe that the majority of welfare benefits are paid to the poor, who siphon tax dollars from "hard-working Americans," and who refuse to work even when they are able. Many people believe that the poor would rather take government handouts than work, and that the government contributes to their laziness by providing the handouts in the first place. Actually, both assumptions are suspect.

Government Support of the Wealthy

In the United States, those who receive the greatest government benefits are those with the highest incomes. Such benefits are not commonly referred to as "welfare," although many theorists in this field have begun to adopt this term (or sometimes, "wealthfare") as a means of drawing attention to the high level of support provided by the U.S. government to the wealthiest segment of society. Benefits to the wealthy include a wide range of corporate and individual tax breaks that have significantly lowered the amount of taxes paid by the highest income earners over the last two decades.[38] Thousands of U.S. corporations currently pay no income tax. One-third of tax revenues came from corporations just two decades ago. Currently less than 8 percent of tax revenue is received from corporations.[39]

Subsidies to the Wealthy

In addition to tax breaks for the rich, government monies filtered into specific industries, individuals, and corporations engage in a host of legal practices, such as the establishment of private foundations, institutes, and grants that are used to hide assets or to avoid capital gains taxes. Many industries receive not only government contracts (such as defense industries) but also subsidies to support their businesses. Most of the $20 billion in agricultural subsidies, for example, is not distributed to struggling family farmers. Rather, most is paid to corporate farmers to limit their production or to buy surplus production. A high percentage of farm subsidies is paid to tobacco farmers.[40] Other subsidies include such items as $6.4 million to a ski resort in Idaho, $13 million for repairs to a privately owned dam in South Carolina, $3.1 million to convert a ferry boat into a crab restaurant in Baltimore, $33 million to pump sand onto privately owned beaches in Miami, and special subsidies to beekeepers that have resulted in 110 million pounds of honey stored at a government expense of $1 billion while the U.S. annually imports 110 million pounds of honey from other countries.[41]

The list of subsidies to the wealthy is too lengthy for discussion here. The point is that welfare for the wealthy implies greater worth attributed to the activities and interests of the wealthy, which contributes to arrogance among the elite with regard to both elite deviance and elite crime. Members of the elite engage in routine, lucrative, often dangerous crimes that not only threaten lives of ordinary citizens but that also undercut some of the most essential precepts of democratic government. Companies, individuals, and the U.S. government engage in routine illegal activities with virtual impunity from prosecution or punishment (Box 6.1).

Crimes and Deviance in High Places

Recent researchers in the study of crimes of the powerful distinguish between *crimes* by the elite and what is referred to as **elite deviance**.[42] Many activities of economically elite groups are legal but still cause social harm. Some activities that violate basic tenets of fairness, judicial consistency, or moral responsibility are actually legal. Tax loopholes, for example, that allow corporations to pay no taxes, or wealthy individuals to pay minimal tax, while the heaviest tax burden is left to the poor, are legal. Many people would argue that it is unfair for poor people to pay a higher proportion of their income in taxes than rich people, but rich people are just as likely to contend that the government already takes

Can Environmental Regulation Actually Promote More Environmental Crime?

According to the U.S. Department of Justice, criminal prosecution of environmental offenders is one of the most important strategies for combating environmental crime. The Department of Justice believes that prosecution of offenders is an effective way of punishing environmental crime and deterring others from similar behavior. The American public supports this view. In public opinion surveys, environmental crime has been designated one of the most serious forms of criminal wrongdoing—often indicated as more serious than traditional crimes such as burglary or bank robbery. In one such public opinion survey, 84 percent of Americans stated that damaging the environment is a serious crime, and 75 percent believed that corporate officials should be held personally responsible for such crimes.

Laws regulating activities that affect the environment have become increasingly more complex and stringent over the last 20 years. Laws regulating the disposal of hazardous waste, transportation or disposal of toxic substances, and pollution of air or water are designed to protect the environment, but compliance with the laws is often very expensive for businesses and corporations. Increases in regulation have contributed to more incidents of environmental violations, according to the Department of Justice.

Because compliance with the new statutes is expensive, pressures on businesses to avoid the costs, even through law violation, are often enormous. The Department of Justice reports that "midnight dumping," or randomly dumping hazardous materials along roadsides or in vacant lots, is a serious problem. Just as serious, however, is an increasingly common business trend of consciously and systematically violating environmental laws to save money or increase profit margins.

A second common trend among a large number of firms is the use of "dummy corporations" to shield their illegal activities. According to the Department of Justice, many environmental defense attorneys are former prosecutors who know the laws and are adept at using procedural techniques for shielding their clients. The use of dummy corporations may deflect attention away from the central company onto the dummy, which will eventually be written off as a business loss if the corporation is convicted of environmental crime.

Prosecution of environmental crime is expensive and it often takes many years to complete a single case. According to the Department of Justice, the new environmental laws are the best avenue for controlling environmental crime, but the laws also promote more creative means of circumventing regulations among corporations or businesses that find compliance to be contrary to business interests.

SOURCE: Theodore M. Hammett and Joel Epstein, "Prosecuting Environmental Crime: Los Angeles County," *National Institute of Justice Program Focus* (Washington DC: U.S. Government Printing Office, 1993) 2–3.

---

too much, so they should be entitled to avoid taxes in any legal way possible.

Traditional definitions of crime that highlight law violation are often broadened by criminologists who focus on socially harmful behavior. Pharmaceutical companies that overcharge AIDS patients for the only medicines that effectively treat AIDS may set prices within the boundaries of the law, but their exploitation of AIDS patients for corporate profit would be judged immoral by most people. Such was the case when Lypho Med, Inc. was granted the exclusive right by the Food and Drug Administration (FDA) to produce and sell the antibiotic pentamidine for treatment of AIDS. The company increased the price of the drug for a 3-week supply from $500 to $2000. Similarly, pharmacies in New York City charged between $900 and $3384 for a month's supply of AZT as a treatment of AIDS, when the wholesale cost was $752.[43] From the perspective of the pharmaceutical companies, the higher

prices are justifiable in a free-market economy or may be justified as a means of recouping costs of research.

The distinctions between law and morality are merged in these cases to include a wider category—deviance. In this case, **elite deviance** refers not only to those activities that are criminal in the lawbreaking sense but also to behavior that causes social harm. In other words, many people would agree that such behavior *should* be criminal, even if it technically falls within the realm of legal behavior.

Corporate Deviance

A wide range of behaviors falls within the realm of deviance, even if the corporate activities are legal. Overcharges for goods and services and manufacture of products that are legal but clearly harmful to all humans (cigarettes) are among the many activities of corporations

TV evangelist Jim Bakker was convicted of defrauding followers of $3.7 million. He sold "lifetime partnerships" in his religious retreat and diverted money he solicited for the ministry to personal luxuries.

that fall on the borderline between legal behavior and immoral behavior. Price gouging, or overcharging consumers for necessary goods, as in the example of AIDS medication, may be illegal under certain conditions in some states, but is more likely to fall within the realm of immoral behavior. Many pharmaceutical companies, for example, make both the brand-name and generic versions of drugs marketed by the company. The pills are dispensed from the same machines and include identical ingredients, but they are dyed different colors. Mylan Pharmaceutical Company, for example, produces three colors of erythromycin tablets. The pink ones are generic and sell for $6.20; the yellow are marketed to Smith-Kline and sell for $9.20; and the orange are called Bristamycin and sell under the company name for $14.00. All three are identical.[44]

Legal, yet morally questionable, behavior pervades many professions. Members of the U.S. Congress often accept expensive trips, vacations, tennis and golf workshops in Caribbean resorts, and gifts such as televisions, cars, and boats, from lobbyists who "educate" members and their aides during the trips and excursions.[45] This activity is legal. It is not considered bribery.

Corporate Dumping

Among the practices deemed most unethical by researchers in this field is the practice of **corporate dumping.** This is the common business tactic of exporting to other countries goods that have been banned as unsafe for American consumers, goods that have never been approved as safe for use in the United States, or goods that are known to cause harm and for which American market demand has declined.

While regulation of American consumer industries does not always protect people from hazardous products manufactured by American-owned companies, the review processes, approval of new products by specific commissions, and ordered recalls of hazardous items attempt to insulate people from the most dangerous products. When an item is recalled from the market, the manufacturer is no longer allowed to sell the product to American consumers without modification and reapproval. Hazardous chemicals, birth control devices, pharmaceuticals, infant clothing, toys, and appliances are among the many goods that have been recalled from the consumer market in the United States. When faced with recall of the dangerous item, the manufacturer suffers loss of profit from the sale of the item. If the manufacturer is able to locate a new market for the product, profit is protected.

Third World Markets

The most common route for dangerous items banned for sale or use in the United States is to market the product in Third World, or developing, countries. Chemicals such as the pesticide DDT, which has been illegal in the United States for over two decades, are sent to countries with less stringent controls on agricultural chemicals. Ironically, produce grown in countries to which dangerous agricultural chemicals are exported is often imported into the United States for sale to U.S. consumers.[46] Importation of agriculture products is subject to only cursory examination because the time involved in chemical tests would result in spoilage of the products.

Among other pesticides banned in the United States and exported to developing nations, DCBP, which is believed to be a carcinogen and has been linked to 800 cases of sterility among plantation workers in Latin America, is a blacklisted product that is sold only outside of the United States. About one-quarter of American pesticide production includes products banned in the United States and sold exclusively to other countries. This amounts to about 150 million pounds of banned pesticides, worth $800 million, which are exported overseas annually.[47]

In similar cases, 450,000 infant pacifiers and 120,000 teething rings that did not meet safety standards were banned for sale in the United States because they were linked to choking deaths in babies. The remaining supplies were exported to developing countries. When the synthetic male hormone Wistrol was found to stunt the growth of American children, the remaining supplies were sent to Brazil, where it was promoted as an appetite stimulant for children. After the anti-diarrhea medicine Lomotil was found to be fatal in animals at just slightly over the recommended doses, the product was sent to Sudan in packages claiming that it could be used for children as young as 12 months. After the Consumer Product Safety Commission forced infant sleepwear treated with the chemical Tris off of the domestic markets, the remaining supply of several million Tris-treated infant garments was shipped overseas. Tris was a fire retardent that was believed to cause cancer in children who wear garments treated with the chemical.[48]

The United States government often works with corporations in the distribution to other countries of products illegal in the United States. For example, after the Dalkon Shield intrauterine birth control device (IUD) was banned in the United States because it causes uterine infections, blood poisoning, spontaneous abortion in pregnant women, and perforations of the uterus, the Agency for International Development (AID) purchased hundreds of cartons of unsterilized Dalkon Shields for distribution in Third World countries. AID bought the IUDs at a 48 percent discount because they were not sterile, and the devices were sent to 42 nations, largely in the Third World.[49]

Developing nations are among the most preferred sites for the dumping of toxic waste produced in the developed nations. Sixty percent of toxic waste dumping overseas originates in the United States. American companies often pay a dumping stipend to the host company that is more than the entire gross national product (GNP) of the country in a given year, thus creating a ready demand for receipt of the toxic waste. Turkey, Haiti, the Philippines, and Nigeria have been common sites for dumping of waste materials that can cause cancer and birth defects, and have been found to be radioactive in some sites. Much of this dumping is legal, although there have been several scandals involving fraud, mismanagement, and corruption in the actual dumping of the toxic waste.[50]

The tobacco industry, which must contend with stiff advertising restrictions in the United States, and which is required to label all products with consumer warnings about the increased risk of cancer and heart disease among users of the products, is not subject to similar restrictions in most Third World countries. Thus, marketing strategies to addict very young consumers to nicotine are employed with little or no restrictions in most countries.[51] Children and teenagers who become addicted to tobacco products are generally lifetime consumers. Thus, advertising the youthful, healthful, glamorous, and vigorous image associated with tobacco use, combined with distribution of free cigarettes to young people, are common tactics used by American tobacco companies to promote their products to the youngest citizens of developing nations. Tobacco farmers are among the largest recipients of U.S. agricultural subsidies, thus providing support for an industry whose financial success is built upon the ability of the industry to promote addiction to a drug that ensures early death in virtually all of its consumers.[52] While the promotion of tobacco products is legal, the manipulation of additives in the products to promote addiction in users is currently under review by the Food and Drug Administration with a view to requiring its regulation as a dangerous drug.[53]

Environmental Racism

Among the newest and most controversial charges of corporate deviance is what has been termed **environmental racism**. This refers to the practice of locating in poor

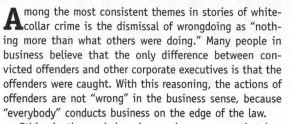

Business Ethics and White-Collar Crime

Among the most consistent themes in stories of white-collar crime is the dismissal of wrongdoing as "nothing more than what others were doing." Many people in business believe that the only difference between convicted offenders and other corporate executives is that the offenders were caught. With this reasoning, the actions of offenders are not "wrong" in the business sense, because "everybody" conducts business on the edge of the law.

Ethics in the workplace is a serious concern that has drawn the attention of lawmakers as well as companies vulnerable to charges of white-collar crime. The 1991 Federal Sentencing Guidelines provide that heavy fines may be levied against companies convicted of white-collar crime if they cannot prove that they have taken steps to avoid illegal business practices. Ethics training programs are the most common avenue used by companies to avoid the fines and to train employees in legal business ethics.

Companies may reduce fines by 60 percent if they have an effective ethics program in place.

The need for ethics training is widely acknowledged by researchers and businesses. A recent study of more than 4000 business employees found that about one-third of respondents felt they had been pressured to violate company policies to achieve business objectives. The respondents also reported that they had viewed various forms of misconduct in their business during the past year. For example, 56 percent of respondents witnessed lying to supervisors. Forty-one percent said they had seen lying on reports or falsifying records. Thirty-five percent witnessed stealing and theft on the job, and 35 percent viewed sexual harassment of co-workers. Thirty-one percent saw alcohol or drug abuse on the job, and 31 percent witnessed conflicts of interest between company employees and business interests.

SOURCE: Julie Amparan, "As Ethics Crisis Grows, Businesses Take Action," *Arizona Republic 24* (November 1996) D1.

---

neighborhoods (predominantly, African American or Native American) toxic dumps, landfills, garbage dumps, and factories that produce offensive odors, air pollution, or contamination of surrounding land and water. Whether the location of the dump or factory is legal, chances are that the site has been chosen because of the neighborhood. Industries that emit high levels of pollution are not located in, or near, expensive neighborhoods. Poor people living with contamination suffer high rates of specific cancers, respiratory problems, birth defects, miscarriages, emphysema, and other health problems. The industries that locate in poor neighborhoods contend that the sites were chosen, not out of a conspiracy to hurt the poor, but because of lower costs there. Sometimes poor neighborhoods grow up around factories or toxic areas because land prices are affordable.

Social structural factors limiting both people's ability to escape from exposure to toxins in the neighborhood and their access to health care make the problem of environmental racism especially complex. The Environmental Protection Agency has responded with regionally based plans to try to curtail the trend toward location of lead-paint pollution, urban smog, and toxic waste sites in poor and minority areas, although significant change has not yet begun to emerge.[54]

The issue of environmental racism is beginning to attract national attention. The National Association for the Advancement of Colored People (NAACP), for example,

highlighted environmental racism in its 1994 annual convention in Chicago.[55] In a rare move by local government, Maryland's Prince George's County Council approved emergency legislation that helped an inner-city neighborhood keep out further industrial development in 1995.[56] Residents of low-income neighborhoods who fight against environmental degradation are beginning to be heard. Aurora Castillo, who is the 81-year-old founder of Mothers of East Lost Angeles won the $75,000 Goldman Environmental Prize for protecting her neighborhood from toxic waste.[57] Similarly, Hazel Johnson has attracted national attention for her personal crusade against air pollution and other toxins that especially affect people in public housing areas close to industries.[58]

Price Gouging

Conditions of the environment are not the only problems of the poor in low-income neighborhoods, however. Price gouging is a recurrent problem. The cost of doing business in poor neighborhoods is often higher because of high crime, high insurance rates, and increased risk of default in credit obligations. As a consequence, food stores, jewelry stores, liquor stores, and many neighborhood businesses charge customers higher prices. While some increase is justifiable, given the greater cost to businesses, prices are often disproportionate to risk. *Price gouging* (exorbitantly higher prices) by merchants, banks, finance companies, landlords, and others is common in poor neighborhoods.[59]

Governmental Crime

Because of political connections and interrelationships among various levels of government, crime by agents of the government is often hidden for decades before it becomes public knowledge. The impact of the events in which crime played a part is generally less by the time the illegal activities come to light, thus lessening the political ramifications of the illegal behavior. Responsibility for illegal actions is often passed among agencies and employees of the government without clearly acknowledging any responsible party. It is, therefore, difficult to ascertain clear patterns or prevalence of crime by governmental officials in the name of national or political interests.

Assassination Attempts

Among the most famous cases of governmental crime are attempts to interfere with the activities of prominent public and international figures. Evidence from Senate investigating committees has shown, for example, that the CIA has been involved in over 900 surreptitious manipulations of foreign governments and attempts to assassinate legitimate leaders of foreign countries since the founding of the agency in 1947.[60] Between 1960 and 1965, the CIA initiated at least eight plots to assassinate Fidel Castro, the president of Cuba. In these cases, the CIA conspired with organized crime to deliver poisoned cigars and a poisoned pen, to contaminate the inside of Castro's wet suit with a fungus, and to place an explosive device in a seashell near his skin-diving equipment. None of these plans were actually executed, but the use of the CIA to hatch plots to overthrow legitimate governments of foreign countries is legendary.[61] The CIA has also been implicated in assassinations of the dictator of the Dominican Republic, Rafael Trujillo, South Vietnam's President Ngo Dinh Diem, and President Allende and General Rene Schneider, both of Chile.[62]

Experiments on U.S. Citizens

The CIA has also conducted experiments on U.S. citizens without the subjects' knowledge. Among the more-famous experiments was the CIA's study of the effects of LSD (lysergic acid diethylamide) on human behavior. The study was conducted under the code name MKULTRA and experiments were carried out from 1953 to 1964. In one experiment, LSD was dropped into the drink of an unsuspecting subject in a public place. The subject, Dr. Frank Olson, began to exhibit signs of acute paranoia almost immediately after ingesting the drink. He was taken to a hotel room, where he jumped to his death from a tenth story window. In spite of Dr. Olson's death, the CIA continued experimenting with LSD among subjects who were not informed of their participation. Dr. Olson's family was not told the truth about his death for over 20 years.[63] In simi-

lar cases, the CIA hired prostitutes to slip drugs to their customers, who were then observed through two-way mirrors. Other subjects were chosen at random in bars or off the street, with no prior screening or medical evaluation, for CIA experimentation with the effects of drugs on human behavior. Terminally ill patients have also been used by the CIA for experimentation on the effects of "knockout drugs"; again, the subjects were not informed of their participation in the experiments.[64]

In similar cases, federal agencies conducted radiation experiments on human subjects from the mid-1940s through the 1970s without informing the subjects about the nature of the experiments. Between 1963 and 1971, x-rays were applied to the testes of 131 inmates in Oregon and Washington state prisons. Between 1953 and 1957, twelve patients with terminal brain tumors in Massachusetts were injected with uranium. The Atomic Energy Commission deliberately released radioactive iodine into Idaho ground water seven times between 1963 and 1965. Between 1949 and 1969, people living in U.S. cities were subject to 239 open-air bacterial tests by the U.S. Army. In these tests, the Army studied the spread of bacteria by wind to determine the magnitude of spread for eventual use in biological warfare. In one of these experiments, San Francisco was sprayed with the poisonous bacterium *Serratia*, which causes potentially fatal *Serratia* pneumonia.[65]

One of the longest-running experiments on unwitting U.S. citizens was conducted by the U.S. Public Health Service from 1932 until 1972, when the Associated Press publicized the story. This was the Tuskegee (Alabama) experiment, where 400 African American men with syphilis were withheld treatment so that the U.S. Public Health Service could observe the effects of the disease over time. The men were told they had "bad blood," and were monitored on a yearly basis for progress of the disease. Their wives were also not treated and their children who were born with congenital syphilis were not treated.[66] In 1997, President Clinton made a public apology to the victims of the Tuskegee experiment.

Harassment of U.S. Citizens

CONTELPRO, which lasted 30 years, was a program orchestrated by the FBI to disrupt, harass, and discredit groups or individuals the FBI deemed "un-American."[67] Groups and individuals targeted by the FBI for harassment included the American Civil Liberties Union, anti-Vietnam war activists, black militant groups, the NAACP, Dr. Martin Luther King, Jr., Malcolm X, Robert F. Kennedy, actress Jane Fonda, and many newspaper reporters, journalists, and college professors.

The harassment of Martin Luther King, Jr., by the FBI used virtually every intelligence-gathering device available at the time to gather evidence that could discredit him or his colleagues. For example, the FBI routinely called in

Cigarette advertising that targets youth or implies that cool, sophisticated people smoke has been highly criticized as a factor that promotes addiction. Consequently, many American cities have banned cigarette ads on billboards. Such ads are legal in many nations.

false fire alarms to places where he was scheduled to speak. Just before he received the Nobel Peace Prize in 1964, the FBI sent Dr. King a tape recording made from electronic surveillance of his bedroom. The accompanying note suggested that Dr. King should commit suicide before the tapes were released to the public. After Dr. King's famous "I Have A Dream" speech, in which he urged that all people should be judged by the content of their character, not the color of their skin, the FBI designated Dr. King as "the most dangerous and effective Negro leader in the country."[68] Immediately after Dr. King was named by *Time* magazine their Man of the Year, the FBI determined that he should be "destroyed," because he was a potential "messiah" who could "unify and electrify" the "black nationalist movement."[69] In 1997, the King family called for a reopening of the 1968 assassination of Dr. Martin Luther King, Jr., because they believe that government agents had something to do with the assassination. To date, no evidence has been found to support that allegation.

Contemporary Governmental Crime

The misuse of the CIA, the FBI, and various other governmental agencies for illegal political purposes is not isolated in the distant past. The Iran Contra affair, in which President Ronald Reagan approved the trading of 2000 TOW missiles and more than 200 spare parts for Hawk missiles to Iran in exchange for American hostages held in Lebanon, included in the team of conspirators then–CIA director William Casey, presidential advisors Robert McFarlane and John Poindexter, and Colonel Oliver North. The funds generated from sale of the guns to Iran were channeled into military aid to the Contras of Nicaragua, in violation of specific congressional limits. Colonel North directed secret operations from the White House and subsequently lied to Congress about it. The debate over responsibility for the illegal activities of high government officials in this affair has not yet ended. In 1995, a federal court ruled that former president George Bush should be reimbursed $272,352 for legal expenses during the investigation of his role in the Iran Contra dealings.[70] Similarly,

International Efforts to Stop Bribery

In 1996, new global initiatives against bribery were announced by the World Bank and the International Monetary Fund (IMF). In the past they had opposed anti-corruption efforts as too political. Wealthy nations had also opposed efforts to limit corruption because they believed that such restrictions would put their industries at a disadvantage.

The new guidelines have been adopted because the costs of political corruption to developing nations have been too great to ignore. Corruption also distorts public spending, increases the costs of doing business in foreign countries, and may deter foreign investment. According to the new guidelines, evidence of corruption would result in cancellation of World Bank support for investment or business interests for the offending company.

The United States outlawed payment of bribes to public officials in 1977, but until 1996 only the United States and Sweden had such laws. Among other measures adopted to end corruption was a resolution from the Paris-based Organization of Economic Cooperation and Development (OECD), which ended tax deductibility for bribes in their 27 member states. Since this action by the OECD, Britain, Nor-

way, Canada, and Australia have announced plans to enforce their own new laws against bribery. France and Germany have argued that political party officials and heads of state-owned corporations should be excluded from the new anti-bribery laws.

Throughout the world, national campaigns to curb corruption have led to significant changes. In 1996, a 6-month anti-corruption effort led to the arrest of 981 people and the dismissal of two Cabinet ministers in South Korea. In Argentina, the anti-corruption crusade led to an overhaul of the judicial system. More than 50 government officials in Nicaragua were under investigation for corruption in 1996, and Mexican investigators linked family members of former President Carlos Salinas y Gortari to illegal payoffs. There were similar efforts in Italy, Belgium, and France when evidence in Swiss bank accounts led to charges of corruption among government officials.

While new laws and financial pressures from the global economy have begun to draw attention to problems of corruption, the issue is far from settled. Investigations are underway in many countries.

SOURCE: Gail Russell Chaddock, "Ethics in Business Dealings Urged by World Leaders," *Christian Science Monitor 20* (November 1996) 1.

---

the District of Columbia Bar was petitioned in 1995 to reinstate Elliot Abrams, who was convicted and later pardoned for his role in the Iran Contra scandal.[71]

The involvement of the U.S. Government, or agents of the government, in illegal and anti-democratic activities in pursuit of political goals is seen by many as an abuse of the power of government. Crimes committed by officials of government in the name of government are exceptionally difficult to uncover. As with many other crimes committed by elite citizens, these offenders face little or no punishment.

Enforcement

Enforcement of laws against corporate illegal behavior were weakened considerably in the 1980s. Believing that federal regulatory agencies stultified economic growth, President Reagan used two tactics for reducing the power of these agencies. First, in a strategy not employed by his predecessors, he sharply cut the budgets of agencies charged with enforcement, which made implementation of regulations more difficult than under previous presidents.[72] The Consumer Product Safety Commission's bud-

get was decreased by 30 percent, the number of OSHA inspectors was cut to a few hundred (to monitor the 4 million workplaces under their jurisdiction), and the Federal Trade Commission's enforcement powers and personnel were slashed until their enforcement capabilities were seriously undermined. The Reagan administration canceled, as unnecessary interference, the requirement that pharmaceutical manufacturers list possible risks of medications they marketed. In addition, safety requirements in many industries, including auto manufacturing, were reduced.[73] There is currently considerable political rhetoric that calls for curtailment of the Environmental Protection Agency and OSHA.

The second tactic used by the Reagan administration was to appoint people sympathetic to the views of business as administrators of the regulatory agencies. Administrators appointed by President Reagan were generally opposed to the objectives of the agencies for which they worked. This served to undermine the effective regulation of unethical business activities and increased blatant violations of the law.[74]

Many observers believe that the savings-and-loan (S&L) crisis of the 1980s was promulgated by the changes in S&L regulations that made it easier for industry investors to

Pressures to Reform the CIA

With the end to the Cold War, many have suggested that the need for U.S. intelligence services has declined. The CIA contends that the world still holds many dangers and that the activities of the organization should not be downsized. At the least, critics favor more accountability in the activities of the agency. Abuse of authority is still a problem in the CIA, despite several decades of criticism of the means by which the agency has gathered information. In 1996, the Intelligence Oversight Board (IOB) found numerous violations of U.S. law in the agency's operations. The CIA was accused in the *Report on the Guatemala Review* of selectively withholding information, manipulating journalists and lawyers in order to uncover documents, and blatantly disregarding proper procedures. The CIA was also accused of withholding information from Congress, misleading organizations within the government intelligence community, and condoning intimidation as a means of obtaining crucial information.

Proposals for the future of the CIA call for a "leaner" organization, with more clearly articulated goals. The efforts of the CIA should be long-term analysis, according to the Council on Hemispheric Affairs. The CIA should gauge international political trends, monitor nuclear arms sales, and aid in efforts to stop terrorism, drug trafficking, and multinational corporate espionage.

SOURCE: Council on Hemispheric Affairs, "Washington Report on the Hemisphere," CD-ROM 16, 1, 7. Current Issues SourceFile. Record: A315-2.

---

engage in a host of financial tricks. Many people got rich when safeguards were relaxed and little or no collateral was required for investment. Executives of failing S&Ls sold shares of the businesses to each other many times over, sometimes on the same day, to generate profits on paper, with no real exchange of money and some fictitious loses and gains. One Arizona businessman, James Fall, received $1.5 billion in government subsidies to buy fifteen failed S&Ls, while putting up only $1000 of his own money. Another investor, Robert Bass, put up $550 million for American Savings and Loan and received ownership of a $30 billion business and $2.5 billion in cash.[75]

Ineffective regulatory agencies have made enforcement of the weak laws prohibiting unethical business practices a formidable task. For example, a 1992 study by the General Accounting Office (GAO) assessed the top 100 theft and fraud cases in the S&L scandal that were referred to the Department of Justice. Total losses in these cases were almost $600 million, with 219 indictments, 145 convictions, court-ordered restitution of $79 million, and $4.5 million in fines. At the time of the study, $349,810 in restitution and just over $15,000 in fines had been collected, or less than 0.5 percent of the fines and restitution ordered by the courts in these cases.[76]

Progress in Enforcement

In spite of weak regulatory laws through the 1980s and the apparent double standard in application of the principles of law enforcement against powerful criminal offenders, some recent progress has been made. In 1991, BCCI was fined $200 million in financial penalties by a federal court. And, in 1994, twelve top executives from BCCI who were instrumental in the collapse of the investment house were convicted of fraud and mismanagement. They were sentenced to prison terms of 14 years and ordered to pay $9.13 billion to the government of Abu Dhabi.[77] In 1991, Exxon Corporation agreed to pay $1 billion in fines and damages for the Exxon *Valdez* oil spill. Both the numbers of indictments and the amounts of fines have increased over the last few years. In 1985, the Environmental Protection Agency referred 40 cases of environmental crime to the Department of Justice. In 1989, there were 100 indictments, with $12.7 million in fines. In 1995, 256 cases were referred. There were thousands of white-collar offenders prosecuted in the S&L scandal, which has not yet ended.[78] Federal sentencing guidelines that took effect in 1991 hold potential for more stringent enforcement of laws against crime by elites.[79] Early feedback from the application of the 1991 federal guidelines has indicated that the reach of the law is more limited than predicted, however. Prosecutors have not yet begun to press for full application of the guidelines.[80]

In 1994 Morris English, who headed the real estate investment company Wellington Group, and whose actions were cited as responsible for one suicide and $30 million in losses to the company, was sentenced to 18 years in prison. This was the harshest sentence ever imposed in Los Angeles for a white-collar crime.[81] Still, patterns persist of more lenient treatment for white-collar and corporate offenders, and most such offenders receive little or no punishment.[82] **Whistleblowers,** or those who turn in white-collar or corporate offenders, are often ostracized, fired, forced to quit, or harassed by those who have the most to lose in the event that the company or individual is sanctioned. Legislation to protect whistleblowing is a means of encouraging responsible action by those who are aware of illegal or unethical business practices, and it protects from retaliation against those who report misconduct. Legislation in this area is just beginning to emerge as an effective enforcement tool.[83]

Guilty verdicts, and the application of sanctions against elite offenders, does appear to have some effect on recidivism. Changing penalties from misdemeanors to felonies, and risks of formal sanction and penalties, are predicted to hold promise for deterrence of elite crime.[84] Some argue, however, that the law is not always the most effective means of reducing either corporate crime or the social harm done by corporations. As John Braithwaite has pointed out in his extensive study of bribery by pharmaceutical companies, the use of criminal law to address such problems is a clumsy, costly, and scattered device for reform. He sees pressure from regulatory agencies, professional pressure within the industry, and consumer activism as more promising mechanisms for nurturing industry self-regulation. When media attention, whistleblowing within companies, and consumer skepticism foster distrust of the industry, corporations are more likely to support internal changes to avoid external pressures. Braithwaite argues that criminal law should provide a backup threat if other pressures toward self-regulation fail.[85]

Corporate Accountability

Some progress in fostering accountability among key corporate executives is evident. For example, it was common business practice throughout the 1980s and into the 1990s for chief executive officers (CEOs) of large corporations to earn multiple million dollar salaries with annual bonuses of over $1 million, lucrative stock options allowing purchase of unlimited stock at prices far below market value, and numerous other company benefits. Such perks were awarded even when companies lost earnings, laid off employees, or reduced employee salaries. In 1991, General Dynamics (GD), for example, laid off 30 percent of its workers because of company losses but gave $7.6 million in bonuses to the company's top 25 executives.[86] Stock options and company bonuses among the top 50 U.S. corporations in 1992 ranged from a few hundred thousand dollars up to $42 million (PepsiCo) for the top company executives.[87] None of these economic benefits were in any way criminal. Rather, the siphoning of company funds to pay top executives lucrative salaries and benefits, even when companies falter, was criticized be-

cause it fostered arrogance, elitism, and lack of personal responsibility.

Many theorists have charged that a sense of entitlement and arrogance has always characterized the economic elite, and this has led to unethical, criminal, and disdainful business policies as the *modus operandi* of American corporations.[88] Now, a 1994 change in tax law links CEO salaries to company performance and the company cannot deduct compensation exceeding $1 million unless the salaries are tied to earnings or other measures of performance.[89] As a consequence, 1995 reports of 1994 salaries indicated that declines in bonuses paid to top executives ranged from a few hundred thousand dollars to as much as several million dollars. For example, among New York Wall Street firms in 1994, the top 100 earners were compensated at levels 35 percent below what they were paid in 1993. The aggregate of these top New York executives experienced a drop in pay to $389.7 million from $567.1 million in 1993. Long-term pay (deferred compensation such as stock options) was cut in half to $150.9 million.[90] While such cuts may seem insignificant to ordinary Americans, they are symbolic of a trend toward greater accountability.

In spite of these changes, however, salaries of company executives are many times higher than the average company employee, who is also subject to considerably greater occupational risk than the highest-paid executive officer. Even with the tax law changes, base salaries for most executives rose considerably in 1994. (The base salary is the amount the executive is entitled to be paid regardless of company performance.) A survey of 350 companies by the *Wall Street Journal* indicated that CEO base salaries rose 11.4 percent in 1994, compared to a 2 to 4 percent gain among other company workers.[91]

Summary

Many common perceptions about the dangers of crime to individual victims are challenged by a study of crimes of the powerful. This chapter highlighted numerous types of white-collar, corporate, and governmental crimes. A sample of elite crime and an examination of elite deviance were provided to illustrate issues of cost and danger of crimes by the powerful, in comparison to costs and dangers posed by index offenders highlighted in other chapters in this book. The thrust of the chapter is that common perceptions of danger are often influenced by the proximity of the offender to the victim, rather than long-term risks. Most people are more concerned about protecting ordinary citizens from the dangers of muggers, rapists, and murderers than they are about stopping environmental crime perpetrated by industries that has the potential of endangering millions of people or even threatening the survival of the planet. Global endangerment perpetrated by the environmental practices of large corporations is an abstract problem that seems too far removed from most people's lives to merit real concern. A mugger attacking people in a local neighborhood appears to most people to pose a more imminent threat. Both are serious problems. The most notorious serial killers count their victims in single digits over their lifetime careers. Single incidents of corporate illegalities, such as the manufacture and marketing of the Firestone 500 tires or the defective Ford Pinto, and the U.S. Army experimentation with biological warfare, killed dozens of people. Likewise, loss of property in single cases of index crimes usually fall within the range of a few hundred to a few thousand dollars. Single cases of corporate fraud have cost consumers many billions of dollars, and in the case of the S&L scandal, the costs are over $1 trillion. While the threat to personal safety, financial loss, and infringement upon the physical and emotional integrity of victims of index offenses should never be underestimated, crimes of the elite also pose serious danger to ordinary Americans.

The ubiquitous nature of these white-collar offenses make them appear unstoppable, yet some progress has been made in recent years. Attempts have been made to crack down on offenders and to reduce some of the economic control of the elite. The facts that some recent offenders have been sentenced to prison, that fines in some cases have been more than token penalties, and that there has been an increasing interest, both among the public and in the criminal justice system, in curtailing the abuse of political and economic power suggests that more attention will be addressed to these problems in the future.

Whether crime by the economically powerful will be reduced due to the trend toward greater accountability is impossible to estimate. Most predictions suggest that accountability is among the hopeful signs of reform, although many others suggest that reform is impossible without redefinition of the ethics of business competition.[92]

Critical Thinking Questions

1. What do you think the penalties should be for crimes such as corporate dumping or governmental crime? How should these penalties differ from those applied to individual white-collar offenders, such as those who commit tax evasion?

2. If the standard way of doing business in a given company is illegal, but all parties involved know what the policies are and accept the business conditions, is there anything wrong with continuing to do business illegally?

3. Most of the emphasis in this chapter has been on crimes by those with social power, but occupational crime is also committed by blue-collar workers. How do these crimes differ from crimes of the powerful, and how are they the same?

4. Most of the material presented in this chapter has drawn on the critical perspective. Are there other ways of explaining crimes of the powerful? How might the perspective used in this chapter be biased?

Suggested Readings

James W. Coleman, *The Criminal Elite: The Sociology of White-Collar Crime,* 3rd ed. (New York: St. Martin's, 1994).

Francis T. Cullen, William J. Maakestad, and Gary Cavender, *Corporate Crime Under Attack: The Ford Pinto Case and Beyond* (Cincinnati: Anderson, 1987).

Gary S. Green, *Occupational Crime,* 2nd ed. (Chicago: Nelson Hall, 1997).

David R. Simon (1996) *Elite Deviance,* 5th ed. (Boston: Allyn & Bacon, 1996).

Edwin H. Sutherland, *White-Collar Crime* (New York: Holt, Rinehart & Winston, 1949).

Notes

[1] David R. Simon and D. Stanley Eitzen, *Elite Deviance,* 4th ed. (Boston: Allyn & Bacon, 1993); Gary S. Green, Occupational Crime, 2nd ed. (Chicago: Nelson Hall, 1997).

[2] Edwin H. Sutherland, *White-Collar Crime* (New York: Holt, Rinehart & Winston, 1949).

[3] A third classification refers to *pink-collar* occupations, or jobs that are performed primarily by women, such as secretary, librarian, teacher, or nurse.

[4] See Simon and Eitzen, *Elite Deviance,* 4th ed.; M. David Ermann and Richard J. Lundman, eds., *Corporate and Governmental Deviance: Problems of Organizational Behavior in Contemporary Society,* 4th ed. (New York: Oxford, 1992).

[5] David R. Simon and Stanley L. Swart, "The FBI Focuses on White Collar Crime: Promises and Pitfalls," *Crime and Delinquency 30* (1984): 109.

[6] James W. Coleman, *The Criminal Elite: The Sociology of White-Collar Crime,* 3rd ed. (New York: St. Martin's, 1994).

[7] Francis T. Cullen, William J. Maakestad, and Gary Cavender, *Corporate Crime Under Attack: The Ford Pinto Case and Beyond* (Cincinnati: Anderson, 1987).

[8] Richard Austin Smith, "The Incredible Electrical Conspiracy Case," *Fortune 63,* (1961):132–37, 170–80; David R. Simon and D. Stanley Eitzen, *Elite Deviance,* 3rd ed. (Boston: Allyn & Bacon, 1990) 97.

[9] See Simon and Eitzen, *Elite Deviance,* 4th ed., for discussion.

[10] Ibid., 2.

[11] Ibid., 53–55.

[12] Kathy Scruggs, "Ripoffs Can Add up to $50 Billion to Public's Tab," *Atlanta Constitution,* 13 June 1994, B4.

[13] Ibid., 19.

[14] Ibid., 40.

[15] Steven F. Messner and Richard Rosenfeld, *Crime and the American Dream* (Belmont, CA: Wadsworth, 1994) 31; Jay S. Albanese, *White Collar Crime in America* (Englewood Cliffs, NJ: Prentice-Hall, 1995) 85.

[16] Sue A. Lindgren, "Justice Expenditure and Employment, 1990" (Washington, DC: U.S. Government Printing Office, 1992); Kathleen Maguire and Ann L. Pastore, *Sourcebook of Criminal Justice Statistics* (Washington DC: U.S. Government Printing Office, 1996) 4.

[17] David R. Simon, *Elite Deviance,* 5th ed. (Boston: Allyn & Bacon, 1996).

[18] Simon and Eitzen, *Elite Deviance,* 4th ed., 123–24.

[19] Ibid., 146–47.

[20] Ibid., 139–40.

[21] Ibid., 140.

22 Victor E. Kappeler, Mark Blumberg, and Gary W. Potter, *The Mythology of Crime and Criminal Justice* (Prospect Heights, IL: Waveland, 1993), 104.

23 Ibid., 104.

24 Federal Bureau of Investigation, *Crime in the United States* (Washington, D.C.: U.S. Government Printing Office, 1997) 13, 26, 31.

25 James Coleman, *The Criminal Elite*, 2nd ed. (New York: St. Martin's Press, 1989).

26 Maguire and Pastore, *Sourcebook of Criminal Justice Statistics*, 562, 651.

27 Ralph Nader, "America's Crime Without Criminals." *New York Times*, 19 May 1985, F3, as quoted in Kappeler et al., 1993, 117–18.

28 See Chapters 11, 12, and 13 of this volume.

29 William J. Chambliss, "A Sociological Analysis of the Law of Vagrancy," *Social Problems 12* (1964) 67–77; Richard Quinney, *The Social Reality of Crime* (New York: Little, Brown, 1970). Austin Turk, *Criminality and Legal Order* (Chicago: Rand McNally, 1972).

30 Quinney, *The Social Reality of Crime*.

31 Ibid.

32 Ibid, 81.

33 For discussion of these concepts, see G. William Domhoff, *The Powers That Be: Processes of Ruling Class Domination in America* (New York: Vintage, 1978); C. Wright Mills, *The Power Elite* (New York: Oxford University Press, 1956).

34 Albanese, *White Collar Crime in America*, 34–35.

35 Ibid., 154.

36 Darrell Steffensmeir and Cathy Streifel, "Trends in Female Crime, 1960–1990," in *Female Criminality: The State of the Art*, ed. Concetta C. Culliver (New York: Garland, 1993) 63–101.

37 See Samuel Walker, *Sense and Nonsense About Crime and Drugs: A Policy Guide*, 3rd ed. (Belmont, CA: Wadsworth, 1994); see pages 45–48 for an excellent analysis of loopholes as a myth of criminal justice policy in America.

38 Simon and Eitzen, *Elite Deviance*, 4th ed., 61.

39 Ibid.

40 Simon and Eitzen, *Elite Deviance*, 4th ed., 64; Brown and Pizer, *Living Hungry in America*, 237.

41 David R. Simon, *Elite Deviance*, 5th ed. (Boston: Allyn & Bacon, 1996) 67.

42 See, for example, Simon and Eitzen, *Elite Deviance*, 4th ed.; Frances T. Cullen, William J. Maakestad, and Gray Cavender, *Corporate Crime Under Attack: The Ford Pinto Case and Beyond;* James W.Coleman, *The Sociology of White Collar Crime* (New York: St. Martin's Press, 1989).

43 Whether such increases are legitimate efforts to recoup costs of research or fund future research has been questioned by critics and by AIDS activists, who contend that these increases are an unfair and immoral exploitation of AIDS victims. Simon and Eitzen, *Elite Deviance*, 4th ed., 106.

44 Ibid., 108.

45 *Dateline NBC*, 18 October 1995.

46 Simon and Eitzen, *Elite Deviance*, 4th ed., 193.

47 Ibid., 191.

48 Ibid., as cited from Mark Dowie, "The Corporate Crime of the Century," *Mother Jones 9* (November, 1979) 24–25.

49 Simon and Eitzen, *Elite Deviance*, 4th ed., p. 1993, from Barbara Ehenreich et al., "The Charge: Genocide; The Accused: The U.S. Government," *Mother Jones 9* (November, 1979) 28.

50 Simon and Eitzen, *Elite Deviance*, 4th ed., 193.

51 Ibid., 139.

52 Ibid., 134.

53 National Public Radio, *All Things Considered*, 18 October 1995.

54 Usha Lee McFarling, "EPA Target Minority Areas," *Boston Globe*, 9 May 1994, 13.

55 Byron P. White, "NAACP Takes Civil Rights into '90s," *Chicago Tribune*, 10 July 1994, 1-1.

56 Robert E. Pierre and Terry M. Neal, "P.G. Council Sides with Residents Against Crematory," *Washington Post*, 10 May 1995, D1.

57 Michael Quintanilla, "The Earth Mother," *Los Angeles Times*, 24 April 1995, E2.

58 Heather M. Little (1995) "Toxic Shock," *Chicago Tribune*, 15 January 1995, 6-3.

59 Simon and Eitzen, *Elite Deviance*, 4th ed., 104.

60 Ibid., 271.

61 Ibid., 271; Charles H. McCaghy and Stephen A. Cernkovich, *Crime in American Society*, 2d ed. (New York: Macmillan, 1987) 405.

62 Simon and Eitzen, *Elite Deviance*, 4th ed., 271.

63 McCaghy and Cernkovich, 1987, 406.

64 Simon and Eitzen, *Elite Deviance*, 4th ed., 269–70.

65 Ibid., 268–69.

66 Ibid., 268.

67 William J. Chambliss, "State-Organized Crime": The American Society of Criminology 1988 Presidential Address, *Criminology 27* (1988):183–208.

68 McCaghy and Cernkovich, 1987, 409.

69 U.S. Senate, Final Report of the Select Committee to Study Governmental Operations with Respect to Intelligence Activities, "Dr. Martin Luther King, Jr., Case Study," in *Intelligence Activities and Rights Of Americans: Book III* (Washington DC: U.S. Government Printing Office) 107–198, cited in Simon and Eitzen, 1993; and McCaghy, 1987.

70 *The New York Times*, "U.S. to Pay Bush $272,352 for Inquiry Cost," 10 June 1995, A9.

71 Saundra Torry, "DC Bar Seeks Reinstatement of Abrams Penalty," *Washington Post*, 24 July 1995, A12.

72 Coleman, *The Criminal Elite: The Sociology of White-Collar Crime*, 3rd ed.

73 Kappeler et al., *The Mythology of Crime and Criminal Justice*, 112–13.

74 Coleman, *The Criminal Elite:The Sociology of White-Collar Crime*, 3rd ed., 150.

75 Simon and Eitzen, *Elite Deviance*, 4th ed., 50–52; Maguire and Pastore, *Sourcebook of Criminal Justice Statistics*, 533.

76 Coleman, *The Criminal Elite:The Sociology of White-Collar Crime*, 3rd ed., 150.

77 *Wall Street Journal*, "Twelve Ex-Officials of BCCI Convicted, Sentenced for Fraud," 15 June 1994, A14.

78 Kitty Calavita and Henry N. Pontell, "The State and White Collar Crime: Saving the Savings and Loans," *Law and Society Review 28* (1994): 297–324.

79 Ibid.

80 Saul Pilchen, "When Organizations Commit Crimes: Sentencing under the Federal 'Organization Guidelines,'" *Judicature 78* (1995): 202–206.

81 Richard Greer, "18-Year Term in Fraud Case." *New York Times*, 16 June 1994, G3.

82 Robert Tillman and Henry N. Pontell, "Is Justice 'Collar-Blind'?: Punishing Medicaid Provider Fraud," *Criminology 30* (1992): 547–74.

83 Terance D. Miethe and Joyce Rothschild, "Whistleblowing and the Control of Organizational Misconduct," *Sociological Inquiry 64* (1994): 322–47.

84 Sally S. Simpson, "Deterring Corporate Crime," *Criminology 30* (1992): 347–75.

85 John Braithwaite, "Transnational Regulation of the Pharmaceutical Industry," *The Annals 525* (1993).

86 Simon, *Elite Deviance*, 5th ed., 57.

87 Ibid., 58-59.

88 See Coleman, *The Criminal Elite: The Sociology of White-Collar Crime*, 3rd ed.; Simon, *Elite Deviance*, 5th ed.

89 Eric Greenberg, "Tax Law Axes CEO Salaries," *Crains New York Business*, 19 July 1995, 11:25.

90 Ibid.

91 Stephen Keating, "Executive Pay: Stock-Based Compensation Catches On," *Denver Post*, 4 June 1995, G1.

92 Simon, *Elite Deviance*, 5th ed., 337.

chapter *7*

Conventional Property Crime

CHAPTER OUTLINE
DEFINITIONS OF PROPERTY CRIME
NATURE, EXTENT, AND COSTS
   Nature of Property Crime
   Extent of Property Crime
   Costs
OFFENDERS AND VICTIMS
   Offenders
   Race and Property Crimes
   Gender and Property Crimes
   Age and Property Crimes
   Victims
INDEX OFFENSES
   Larceny-Theft
   Burglary
   Motor Vehicle Theft
   Arson
NON-INDEX OFFENSES
   Forgery, Fraud and Embezzlement
   Computer Crime
SOCIETAL ISSUES
   Rationales for Class Distinctions
   Moral Values and Stealing
   Controlling Property Crime
SUMMARY

KEY TERMS
shoplifting
opportunistic crimes
career criminals
professional criminals
fence
burglary
larceny
motor vehicle theft
arson
hackers
ethic of justice
ethic of care

ON APRIL 19, 1997, TWO BROTHERS, James and Sanford Williams, were arrested in Morris County, New Jersey with a carload of stolen merchandise. They were accused of more than 150 office building break-ins in which a sledgehammer was used to smash through the exterior walls of buildings to get inside.[1] While their crime may seem to many to be characteristic of a new breed of criminals who no longer use stealth or concealment to commit burglary, it is not actually typical. Rather, the vast majority of property crimes are petty, often committed by amateurs, and usually do not involve sledgehammer-style destruction of property.

Definitions of Property Crime

The category of property crime includes those crimes that would most commonly be categorized as theft in ordinary language. In this chapter we examine conventional property crimes, but there are many new areas of property crime just beginning to attract the attention of criminal justice researchers. These newer forms of property crime will soon be recognized.

In 1996, there were 11.8 million property crimes reported to the Federal Bureau of Investigation (FBI) by state and local police agencies.[2] These reported offenses included only those crimes listed in the FBI index crime categories and did not account for unreported crimes, difficult-to-detect offenses such as employee theft, computer crime, credit card theft, or numerous other crimes that are either not included in index offense categories or are seldom reported. Recall that the FBI carefully counts only reported burglary, larceny-theft, motor vehicle theft, and arson each year. The reported 11.8 million property crimes represent only these four categories.

Property crime is a pervasive American phenomenon. Most people in the United States have been victims of property crime, and the majority have also committed property crimes at some point in their lives. For many juveniles **shoplifting,** or theft from stores, has become a thrilling pasttime. A high percentage of employed people have stolen office supplies, tools, merchandise, or money from their place of employment. Many people steal towels, dishes, bedding, and even appliances from hotels and restaurants where they have stayed or dined. Many such crimes are **opportunistic crimes**, illegal actions that occur solely because the opportunity is available and the risk of detection is low. Theorist Jack Katz, for example, argues that material objects are enticing and that people get a "sneaky thrill" from stealing.[3] People who engage in such crimes do not consider themselves to be criminal and they may never commit serious crimes.

By contrast, **career criminals,** or **professional criminals,** commit crime as their primary means of economic support. Career criminals are skilled in the techniques for accomplishing their crimes, they have contacts with whom they may **fence,** or market, the property they have stolen, and they are committed to continued criminal activity. Career criminals commit crime as a business activity, and they improve their skills as they practice the craft of stealing. Most people have engaged in opportunistic crime at some time in their lives. A relatively small number of people are committed to crime as a professional life work.

The fact that nearly everyone in the United States has some direct experience with property crime, either as victim or perpetrator, attests to a high tolerance for theft as a cultural phenomenon. Americans are accustomed to video surveillance in stores, electronic detection devices attached to library books, inspection of packages by staff in stores and museums, and the presence of chains connecting park benches or picnic tables to trees or cement slabs. The fact that these devices to control, detect, or prevent property crime are daily components of life in America is unquestioned by most people.

People know that they must take precautions to prevent the loss of things they value. If they forget to bolt a door, bring the lawn furniture in before dark, lock up a bicycle, or otherwise fail to secure things they own, they tend to place partial blame on themselves for the theft. A high percentage of property crime is unreported, in part because people believe they have a responsibility to take precautions to prevent theft. The 11.8 million reported property crimes account for only a portion of the property that is maliciously destroyed or stolen annually. People fail to report property crimes because they believe their own carelessness may have made the theft easier for the perpetrator, or they believe that the value of the property was insufficient to bother police about, or they don't believe the police would be able to do anything about the crime if they did report it. Property crime is such a normal component of daily life that many people expect that items will be stolen under certain conditions.

Many individuals see nothing wrong with taking things that belong to others, following the rationale that victims are foolish, naive, or even stupid if they failed to secure the object of the theft. Children see parents steal in this manner, co-workers protect one another in employee theft, and many people rationalize their behavior on the belief that items are insured, the owner must not have cared about the item if it was available for theft, or the value of such an item is so low that no one will care about the loss. Occasional criminals commit millions of property crimes in this manner every year. Professional criminals, who make stealing a career, increase the vulnerability to theft that is a cultural fact of life for Americans.

In this chapter, we will examine the property crimes that are tracked by the FBI in the Uniform Crime Reports (UCR) as well as the reports of victimization calculated in the National Crime Victimization Survey (NCVS). In addition, we will address two new forms of property crime, credit card theft and computer crime. The economic impact of these crimes, as well as their effect on societal standards of behavior and class differences in victimization rates, will also be addressed.

Nature, Extent, and Costs

As discussed earlier, the FBI began collecting data on property crime in 1930, although the techniques for data collection have changed considerably in the past several decades. The current definitions of each crime have been simplified from earlier versions to increase consistency in reporting. According to the FBI,

property crime includes the offenses of burglary, larceny-theft, motor vehicle theft and arson. The object of the theft-type offenses is the taking of money or property, but there is no force or threat of force against the victims. Arson is included since it involves the destruction of property; its victims may be subjected to force.[4]

Each of the property crimes is defined specifically by the FBI to differentiate degrees of crime against property and the type of damage done by the offender. **Burglary,** for example, includes unlawful entry of a structure to commit a felony or theft. **Larceny** is simple theft. Crimes of shoplifting, purse snatching, pickpocketing, theft from vehicles, and other types of stealing are included in this category. **Motor vehicle theft** could be subsumed under the category of larceny, but the FBI distinguishes this type of theft from other property offenses. **Arson** involves the unlawful burning of any structure, but the category does not include fires that originate from "unknown" or "suspicious" forces. This newest category of crime was added to the FBI index offenses in 1979.

Nature of Property Crime

Data from the NCVS indicate that about one-third of all property crimes are reported to the police. Stolen motor vehicles have the highest prevalence of report to the police because insurance companies commonly require a police report to accompany claims for reimbursement. As a consequence, 78 percent of stolen motor vehicles were reported to the police in 1994. Property crimes with the lowest incidence of police report include larceny-theft of items or money valued at less than $50.[5] For obvious reasons, people generally believe the police can or will do nothing about larceny-theft of items with low economic value. Only about 12 percent of these crimes are reported, even though larceny-theft of less than $50 represents 40 percent of all property crime. In other words, a large proportion of property crime is low-level and rarely reported to police.

The NCVS estimated there were over 31 million property crimes in 1994, compared to over 12 million reported to the FBI in the same year.[6] (The NCVS data usually lags behind FBI data by about two years because the NCVS includes a lot of detailed information that takes years to calculate.) The rate of victimization calculated by the NCVS is 307.6 per 1000 persons aged 12 and older in the population.[7] This rate is almost seven times higher than the FBI rate of reported property offenses for 1994. The discrepancy between the two estimates results from the means by which each government agency collects data. The FBI counts crimes reported to the police and publishes the data in the UCR, thus excluding all unreported crimes. The NCVS interviews 100,000 people in 50,000 households annually and asks them about criminal victimizations in the past year.

According to the NCVS, 34 percent of property crimes were reported to the police in 1994. These percentages of reported crimes have been consistent for several years.[8] In all cases, property crimes have lower clearance rates, or a lower likelihood that a suspect will be arrested, than violent offenses. In 1996, 19 percent of property offenses were reported by the FBI as cleared by arrest compared to 47 percent of violent offenses. In some cases, victims may not discover that items are missing or that property has been burglarized until long after the crime was committed. The secrecy inherent in most property crimes makes detection difficult, and the frequency with which all types of property crimes are committed means that police resources are generally inadequate for systematic pursuit of offenders. Approximately 2 million people were arrested for property crimes in 1996, which accounted for 13 percent of all arrests.[9]

The southern states have the highest rates of property crime, followed by the western, midwestern, and northeastern states. Forty percent of all property crimes were reported in the southern states in 1996. Urban and metropolitan areas have higher rates of property crime than rural areas. Cities with populations over 250,000 have the highest reports of property crime. Reports of property crime declined for five consecutive years prior to 1996 and they were 9 percent lower than in 1992.[10] The NCVS has documented the same downward trend in property offenses.

Has Increased Use of Prisons Caused Property Crime to Decline?

Declines in crime have been evident for over a decade. This is true by both NCVS measures and FBI reports of crime to police. Some people charge that these slow declines in the rate of crime are attributable to higher rates of arrest and increased rates of incarceration. Get-tough policies hold that crime would be lower if more people were locked in prisons and sentences were longer. The assumption behind these policies is that crime is reduced by punishment. Incarceration prevents offenders from repeating their crimes, and punishment deters them from future offenses, according to this perspective. People who support get-tough policies presume that FBI and NCVS crime rates are falling because punishments in the 1990s are tougher than they were in the 1980s.

There were over 1 million people in jail or prison in the United States in 1996. Supporters of get-tough policies cite the size of the prison population as the reason for recent declines in crime rates. While it is true that offenders in prison are deterred from crime, at least for the duration of their sentences, the likelihood is negligible that the 1 million people incarcerated would have a significant effect on the 42.3 million crimes reported through the NCVS in the United States annually. Rather, these slight declines in the crime rate should be interpreted cautiously. In the early 1990s, the rates of theft, for example, had declined 23 percent from the rates of the early 1980s. But high unemployment in the early 1980s, the economic recession of that era, or other factors, may explain the increase during that period. Rates of victimization in the early 1990s were comparable to rates in the early 1970s. Current declines may be interpreted more accurately as a return to consistent rates of crime from unusually high crime in the early 1980s.

SOURCE: Christopher Mumola and Allen J. Beck, "Prisoners in 1996," *Bureau of Justice Statistics Bulletin* (Washington DC: U.S. Government Printing Office, 1997) 1.

Extent of Property Crime

The downward trend of all crime, including property crime, is not isolated to the 1990s. Crime has risen and then declined during other decades (Box 7.1). Figure 4.3 shows that property crimes, including "household crimes," constitute the largest category calculated by the NCVS; three-quarters of all victimizations studied by the NCVS in 1994 were in the property crime categories.[11] Eighty-seven percent of the crimes reported to police between 1993 and 1996 were property offenses.[12] More property crimes are reported in the United States than any other type of crime.

While recent declines in crime rates are encouraging—and researchers are beginning to interpret the high crime of the early 1980s as an anomaly rather than a trend—the daily prevalence of crime is a disturbing facet of American culture. Even though property crime has declined in the 1990s, it is still a common phenomenon. Everyone residing in the United States lives with daily reminders to take precautions against loss from theft. Fences, locks, lights, electronic barriers, security devices, surveillance cameras, and private security systems are all designed to protect Americans from crime and to detect perpetrators. Property crime extends into each individual's life in countless intrusions as well as in higher costs for virtually every item and service. Property crimes are so common and such a prevalent cultural force that most people fail to notice the mundane effects of crime on their lives. The FBI estimates there are 4445 property crimes for every 100,000 people in the United States. Over the course of a year, a reported property crime occurs once every 3 seconds.[13]

Costs

While the rate of property crime has been dropping, the dollar value of stolen property has been increasing. The FBI estimates that the value of stolen property in 1996 was over $15 billion. This was an increase from the estimated $14.8 billion in 1993, even though the number of reported property crimes declined during these years.[14] Table 7.1 indicates FBI estimates of the average loss to vic-

TABLE 7. 1 | Average Dollar Costs for Property Crimes

PROPERTY CRIME	AVERAGE DOLLAR COSTS
Arson	$10,280
Burglary	1,332
Larceny	532
Motor vehicle theft	5,372

SOURCE: Federal Bureau of Investigation, *Crime in the United States* (Washington DC: U.S. Government Printing Office, 1997) 39, 44, 50, 55.

Stopping Motor Vehicle Theft Through Citizen Education

As part of a campaign to reduce motor vehicle theft in Illinois, Governor Jim Edgar declared the week of October 13–20, 1997, as "Park Smart Awareness Week." The governor noted that vehicle theft in Illinois costs consumers and insurance companies nearly $1 million per day. The "Park Smart Awareness Week" was part of an ongoing campaign in Illinois to reduce the number of car thefts in the state. Other activities included a booth at the state fair dedicated to citizen education about ways of avoiding vehicle theft, a demonstration at the state fair on how professional car thieves strip a car, and direct mail campaigns to educate the public about the crime of motor vehicle theft. Vehicle thefts declined 22 percent between 1991 and 1997 in Illinois, in part as a result of the campaign to prevent motor vehicle theft through citizen awareness.

Tips to avoid vehicle theft include commonsense reminders to encourage motorists to lock their cars, roll up windows, use anti-theft devices, and remove valuables from sight. The primary goal of the campaign is to educate the public about ways to protect against theft.

Citizen education programs are controversial, however. The fact that the campaign focuses on victims, rather than offenders, cuts into an old debate. Should the responsibility for crime fall on the shoulders of the victim, who must avoid contact with the offender, or should crime control efforts focus on stopping the illegal actions of offenders? While most people acknowledge that crime is best stopped at its source—the offender—the practical means of preventing crime often falls to potential victims. Preventing victimization through use of commonsense steps to avoid crime appears to be a harmless and useful technique for cutting crime.

Such techniques do tend to frame the ways in which people think about crime, however. Focus on characteristics or behavior of the victims, rather than on offenders, directs attention away from the source of crime. Certainly, commonsense avoidance of crime is important, but it should not be substituted for attention to the real source of crime, according to critics of citizen action campaigns. In other words, reminders to citizens to lock their vehicles should not be substituted for investigation of the techniques of vehicle theft, the market for stolen vehicles, or the career patterns of motor vehicle theft offenders.

SOURCE: Gerard Ramker, "Governor Proclaims Oct. 13–20 State 'Park Smart Week'," *The Compiler,* Illinois Criminal Justice Information Authority, Fall (1997) 19.

---

tims of each of these property crimes. The estimated costs of property crime released by the FBI indicate that loss of property has a significant impact on the economic security of many Americans. Yet, monetary losses are minimal compared to the *social* costs of property crime. The non-measurable effects of social distance among people who fear one another and shun social experiences because of crime have irreparably altered American culture. Widespread victimization in many sectors of American society, particularly in urban areas, increases feelings of vulnerability, fosters an unwillingness to trust others, and fractures social connections among diverse groups in the population. Stereotypes of property offenders as lower-class minority men who ruthlessly victimize those who are weaker have widened racial chasms in recent years. Many of the stereotypes of property offenders are not accurate, but the cultural rifts created by the stereotypes have real consequences in American society. The effects of widespread property crime cost Americans more in personal and societal security than any of the economic indicators can measure (Box 7.2).

Offenders and Victims

All Americans have been touched by the effects of property crime. Offenders perpetrate their crimes in all social classes, among all racial and ethnic categories, and among all ages and both sexes. Property crime is pervasive, although some groups have higher victimization than others. Lower-class people are much more likely to be arrested for property crimes than upper-class people, although stealing is prevalent among all social classes.

Offenders

In recent years, the rates of arrest of property offenders have increased moderately; there were 5 percent more arrests in 1996 than in 1992.[15] Most people arrested for property crimes are men, although arrests of women have gone up faster than arrests of men since 1987. The largest increase in arrests of women has been in the area of motor vehicle theft. Arrests of men for this crime decreased 1.9 percent between 1987 and 1996, while

	TOTAL	MEN	WOMEN	UNDER AGE 18	OVER AGE 18	BLACK	WHITE	NATIVE AMERICAN
Burglary	264,193	234,208	29,985	91,129	156,288	78,473	179,063	2,853
Larceny-theft	1,096,488	726,006	370,482	341,092	670,707	351,993	709,109	13,707
Motor vehicle	132,023	114,125	17,898	52,359	73,319	53,022	74,618	1,579
Arson	13,755	11,703	2,052	7,285	6,038	3,297	10,175	132
All property crime	1,506,459	1,086,042	420,417	492,415	906,352	486,785	972,965	18,271

SOURCE: Federal Bureau of Investigation, *Crime in the United States* (Washington DC: U.S. Government Printing Office, 1997) 222, 231–32.

women arrested for motor vehicle theft increased by 43 percent between 1987 and 1996.[16]

Among property offenses, the largest volume of arrests are for the crime of larceny-theft. This is true among all ages and races, and for both sexes. There were nearly 1 million arrests for larceny-theft in 1996. Table 7.2 illustrates the number of arrests for property offenses among various demographic categories in 1996.

Race and Property Crimes

In general, the people most likely to be arrested for property offenses are white men, although for several years African American men have accounted for about one-third of arrests in the property crime area. In 1992 (the last year for which comparable figures have been calculated), 32 percent of persons arrested for property offenses were African American, although 54 percent of new commitments to prison for property crimes were black. This difference between arrest and incarceration indicates that whites are more likely to be arrested for property offenses, but blacks are more likely to be sent to prison.[17]

Several research studies have indicated that blacks are arrested on weaker evidence than whites, which accounts for the higher conviction rate among whites.[18] Black suspects are likely to be arrested on the basis of scant evidence, which results in dismissal of their cases; and whites are more likely to be arrested on evidence that is sufficient for conviction.

The fact that more whites are arrested and convicted, but that more blacks are sent to prison, points to discrimination in the application of sanctions against black offenders, at least in the area of property offenses. Some writers, such as William Wilbanks, deny that discrimination is the cause of the disparity between arrest and incarceration.[19] Wilbanks argues that there is little evidence that discrimination in sentencing, rather than patterns of offense, explain differences between blacks and whites in incarceration trends. He suggests blacks commit more property offenses, therefore they are sent to prison more

often. Wilbanks' analysis lacks credibility on several counts, but is questionable primarily because his assumptions are unprovable. Several research studies suggests that discrimination against blacks in the application of sanctions for property offenses is significant.[20]

Motor vehicle theft constitutes the largest share of African American arrests. In 1996, 40 percent of people arrested for this crime category were black. This is almost 4 times the number of arrests that should be expected, given the proportion of African Americans in the general population. Blacks constituted close to one-third of those who were arrested for larceny-theft and burglary, but only 24 percent of those arrested for arson.[21]

Gender and Property Crimes

High male arrest rates cross-cut all of the property offense categories, with larceny-theft as the largest single category. Women arrested for larceny-theft constituted 34 percent of arrests in this category in 1996. This share of arrests among women is significantly higher than for other property offense categories, where women consistently account for less than 15 percent of arrests. The pattern of women's arrests for low-level property offenses as the most significant area of women's crime has been characteristic of gender differences in offense categories for decades.[22] Women are rarely involved in other crimes by comparison to men.

Age and Property Crimes

Most people arrested for property crimes are under 25 years of age. While arrest reports are not always the best indicators of patterns of offense, since a large percentage of crime is not reported and arrest does not constitute conviction, the implications from arrest statistics appear to be accurate. The indication that young people are disproportionately involved in property crime is supported by other research sources.[23] Table 7.3 shows the percent of arrests in each age category in 1996.

Victims

According to the NCVS, households headed by African Americans are most highly victimized for all types of property crime. Black households are more likely to be burglarized, and members of black families are more likely to be victims of larceny-theft and motor vehicle theft, than members of other minority groups, or whites. That is, African American households are more likely to experience property crime than white households, even when income, location of residence, and home ownership are taken into account.[24]

Generally, as household income increases, the likelihood of victimization from property crime decreases. In other words, poor people are more likely to be victims of property crimes than wealthy people. Among low-income households, the rate of burglary in African American households is double the rate of burglary among white households. Burglary is also higher in central city areas than in suburban or rural areas.[25]

Contrary to popular belief, victimization for crimes of theft decreases with age. The people with the lowest rates of victimization for property offense categories are those who are over 65 years of age. The highest victimization is among those aged 20 to 24. After age 24, victimization drops significantly in each age category calculated by the NCVS. Much of the high incidence of property crime victimization among young people is attributable to the fact that likely offenders are also young. People generally associate with others of a similar age. Older people are rare offenders, and thus potential older victims are not likely to be in frequent contact with offenders. Young people are both frequent offenders and frequent victims. People under the age of 25, in particular, are likely to increase the potential of victimization through their association with offenders in their own age group.

Men have higher victimization than women in the property offense categories. This is especially true for African American men, who have the highest general victimization of any group among all property crimes. The rates of victimization are highest for black men, followed by white men, white women, and black women.[26] As with other groups in the population, rates of victimization of property offenses for both men and women decline as income increases. Table 7.4 illustrates some of the patterns in victimization according to the NCVS.

Trends in victimization for all property crimes tracked by the NCVS indicate that rates are significantly lower than they were in the decade of the 1980s. All property crimes, except for motor vehicle theft, have declined steadily for over a decade. While the UCR also shows significant decline, the downward trend is not as sharp as indicated by the NCVS because both reporting and arrest have increased in recent years. The NCVS, for example, illustrates a 32 percent decline in property offenses from 1981 through 1992, but an 8 percent increase in the number of property crimes reported to police.[27] Because the FBI records *reported* crime, the declines illustrated by the UCR are not as dramatic as the declines documented by the NCVS. Both sources indicate decline in rates of property

TABLE 7.3	Percent Distribution of Arrests for Property Crimes by Age, 1996

	PERCENT DISTRIBUTION			
CRIME	UNDER 15	UNDER 18	UNDER 21	UNDER 25
Burglary	14.0	37.0	53.6	64.2
Larceny-theft	14.2	33.8	47.2	57.0
Motor vehicle	11.0	41.5	59.0	70.0
Arson	35.5	53.1	62.3	69.6
All property crime	14.0	35.2	49.5	59.5

SOURCE: Federal Bureau of Investigation, *Crime in the United States* (Washington DC: U.S. Government Printing Office, 1997) 230.

TABLE 7.4	Property Crime Victimization Rates per 1000 Population by Region and Demographic Variables, 1994

	ALL PROPERTY	HOUSEHOLD BURGLARY	MOTOR VEHICLE THEFT	ALL THEFT
All demographic groups	307.6	54.4	9.0	235.8
Urban areas	376.4	69.4	29.3	277.7
Suburban areas	296.5	46.5	15.6	234.3
Rural areas	246.4	49.6	6.9	189.9
Blacks	341.3	70.8	26.6	243.8
Hispanics	425.5	71.0	39.9	314.5
Whites	302.0	51.7	15.6	234.6
People 65 and older	124.9	32.1	3.8	86.4
People age 20–34	380.6	66.8	23.9	289.8
Income over $75,000	356.6	40.9	17.7	297.9
Income below $7500	295.7	78.7	13.9	203.2

SOURCE: Tina Dorsey and Jayne Robinson, "Criminal Victimization 1994," *Bureau of Justice Statistics* (Washington DC: U.S. Government Printing Office, 1997) 21–56.

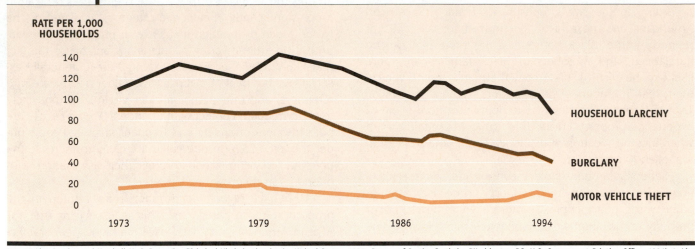

RATE PER 1,000 HOUSEHOLDS

HOUSEHOLD LARCENY
BURGLARY
MOTOR VEHICLE THEFT

SOURCE: Lisa Bastian and Marshall M. DeBerry, Jr., "Criminal Victimization in the United States, 1992, *Bureau of Justice Statistics* (Washington DC: U.S. Government Printing Office, 1994) 4; Lisa Bastian, "Criminal Victimization 1993," *Bureau of Justice Statistics* (Washington DC: U.S. Government Printing Office, 1995) 2; Tina Dorsey and Jayne Robinson, "Criminal Victimization 1994," *Bureau of Justice Statistics* (Washington DC: U.S. Government Printing Office, 1997).

crime, but the UCR shows a more moderate decline than the NCVS because more people reported crime to police. Figure 7.1 shows the rates of victimization of property crimes recorded by the NCVS between 1973 and 1994.

Property Crime: Index Offenses

Downward trends in rates of property crime are an encouraging feature of crime trends in the 1990s. Whether the significant declines illustrated by the NCVS or the more moderate declines reported in the UCR are used, the consistent finding is that rates of crime have fallen from the 1980s and now resemble rates of the early 1970s. Downward trends should not be accepted too optimistically, however. The volume of property crime in the United States is strikingly high, even though the rate of crime has returned to the consistent levels of the early 1970s. Focus on the upward or downward trend in crime can obscure an important issue: crime in the United States is a common, daily occurrence that affects the life of virtually every American. Interestingly, property crimes are most often reported to the FBI during August and least often reported during February. Higher rates of property offenses are recorded in the southern states than in any other region of the country. Whether reporting is higher in the South because the prevalence of crime is higher or because people are more inclined to report crime is unknown.

In this section, the particular features of each of the property crimes are examined from profiles established by the FBI in the UCR. Table 7.5 summarizes the rates of property crime as reported to the FBI and the percentage

TABLE 7.5 | FBI Calculated Rates of Crime per 100,000 Population and NCVS Estimates of Percent Reported to Police, 1980, 1994

CRIME	FBI RATE		NCVS ESTIMATED PERCENT REPORTED	
	1980	1994	1980	1994
Burglary	1,684	1,042	48%	51%
Larceny	3,167	3,025	25%	27%
Motor vehicle	502	591	60%	78%

SOURCES: Lisa Bastian and Marshall M. DeBerry, Jr., "Criminal Victimization in the United States, 1992," Bureau of Justice Statistics (Washington DC: U.S. Government Printing Office, 1994) 7; Federal Bureau of Investigation, *Crime in the United States* (Washington DC: U.S. Government Printing Office, 1995) 35, 38, 43, 49; Lisa Bastian, "Criminal Victimization 1993," *Bureau of Justice Statistics* (Washington DC: U.S. Government Printing Office, 1995) 5; Tina Dorsey and Jayne Robinson, "Criminal Victimization 1994," *Bureau of Justice Statistics* (Washington DC: U.S. Government Printing Office, 1997) vii.

of crimes estimated, as reported by the NCVS for the peak year of 1980 and the most recent year for which both FBI and NCVS data are comparable, which is 1994. Arson is excluded from this table because the NCVS does not calculate victimization for this crime, and because this category was added to the FBI index offenses in 1979. Early reports of arson were incomplete, which makes comparison over time problematic.

Larceny-Theft

The FBI data and the reports of victimization in the NCVS coincide in the presentation of larceny-theft as the property crime with the highest volume of offenses. Over one million people were arrested and charged with larceny-theft in 1996.[28] Other property offenses are prevalent and have serious economic and social consequences, but theft is a pervasive American problem.

Over half of all reported index crime and two-thirds of the property crime reported is in the larceny-theft category in any given year, which affirms that this crime is exceptionally common.[29] The most active area of larceny-theft, according to the FBI (which admittedly counts only a small proportion of these crimes) is in the area of theft of motor vehicle parts, accessories, or contents. Thirty-six percent of larceny-thefts in 1996 involved theft of a part or the contents of a motor vehicle. Shoplifting accounts for about 15 percent of reported larceny-theft. In proportion to other crimes of larceny-theft, purse snatching and pickpocketing occur relatively rarely, with each constituting less than 1 percent of larceny-thefts, but average losses to victims are higher than might be expected. The average loss in a purse snatching is $296 and the average loss in a pickpocketing incident is $320.[30]

Nationally, the costs of reported larceny-theft totaled over $4 billion in 1996, even though the amount stolen per incident was small by comparison to losses among other property crime categories. The average value of property stolen per incident was just over $500 in 1996.[31] Since only a small percentage of larceny-theft is reported, and the lower the value of the stolen item the lower the likelihood of reporting, estimates of average values per incident should be interpreted cautiously.

The clearance rate, or the number of arrests per reported incident of larceny-theft, is 21 percent. In general, incidents of larceny-theft are more likely to result in an arrest in small towns and rural areas. Large cities rarely clear these offenses. Arrest statistics indicate that the people most often arrested for this type of crime are young white men under the age of 18. While this crime is primarily perpetrated by men, it is also one of the few crimes in which women are often arrested. About one-third of arrests for larceny-theft are women, which is a distinction to this category, given women's overall low involvement in most property offenses. Several authors have pointed out that declines in the economic security of many poor women during the feminization of poverty of the 1980s have pushed upward the low-level property offenses among women.[32] Larceny-theft is among the crimes most characteristically associated with women's crime in the index categories. In the United States a reported larceny-theft occurs once every 4 seconds.[33]

Burglary

Reports of burglary declined significantly during the 1990s. The rate of reported burglary dropped 29 percent between 1987 and 1996. Nationally, reported burglaries in 1996 had a total value of $3.3 billion in losses.[34] Burglaries of homes suffer an average dollar loss that is less than the dollar loss of nonresidential burglaries, such as warehouses or businesses. About two-thirds of reported burglaries involve forced entry; and, in about one-third

Most Americans don't think twice about the many precautions that must be taken to avoid crime. Property crime is so pervasive in American culture that virtually everyone takes such precautions.

of these crimes, the offender(s) entered the structure through an unlocked door or window, or they used a key hidden under the doormat. Residential burglaries occur more often during the day and nonresidential burglaries occur more often after dark. Two out of three burglaries are residential.[35]

The likelihood that the crime of burglary will be cleared with an arrest is relatively low. Only 14 percent of burglaries reported to the FBI resulted in an arrest of a suspect in 1996. The larger and more urban the area of the crime, the lower the likelihood of arrest. Small towns

Two-thirds of burglaries involve forced entry. In one-third, the crime is committed without force, such as with a key hidden under the doormat, or through an unlocked door or window.

and rural areas have clearance rates that are about double the rates of large metropolitan areas. The characteristics of offenders may account for some of the differences in rates of arrest between urban and rural areas. Those arrested for burglary in urban areas are usually over age 18 and those in rural areas are commonly under 18. Perhaps the younger, less experienced offenders in rural areas have fewer burglary skills. In general, most people arrested for this crime are young white men under the age of 25. Over two-thirds of arrested offenders fit this demographic category. In the United States a reported burglary occurs about once every 13 seconds.[36]

Motor Vehicle Theft

In 1996, over 1.4 million cases of motor vehicle theft were reported to the FBI. While the overall rate was 526 per 100,000 people in 1996, this is primarily a big-city problem. The rate of motor vehicle theft is 1223 per 100,000 in cities with populations of a quarter of a million people or more. In rural areas, the rate is only 126 per 100,000 population. Nationwide, one out of every 147 registered motor vehicles was stolen in 1996. Motor vehicle theft accounts for about 13 percent of all property crime. The reported incidents of this crime cost Americans $7.5 billion in 1996.[37]

About 78 percent of motor vehicle thefts involve automobiles. Sixteen percent of stolen vehicles are trucks or buses, and the remaining 6 percent of vehicles include snowmobiles, boats, motorcycles, and other vehicles. National clearance rates are fairly low, with arrests of suspects in only about 14 percent of motor vehicle thefts, but the recovery rate of stolen vehicles is higher than for any other property crime. More than 68 percent of vehicles stolen in 1996 were recovered, which implies that many stolen motor vehicles are used temporarily for joyriding or for the commission of another crime and then are abandoned. Vehicles that are not recovered have often been "chopped," or cut into pieces to be sold as auto parts.[38]

People under the age of 18 accounted for 42 percent of the arrests for motor vehicle theft in 1996. Most people who are arrested are young white men. Sixty percent of arrestees are under 21 years of age, 86 percent are men, and 57 percent are white. In the United States, a reported motor vehicle theft occurs once every 23 seconds.

Arson

Because arson is the crime category that has been added to the index list most recently, the collection of data on this crime is the most incomplete of all crimes calculated by the FBI. Only cases of arson that include full police reports are calculated in the FBI data. Incomplete reports, which constitute a sizable number of reports annually according to the FBI, and fires of "unknown" or "suspicious" origins are not included in yearly totals. Both the volume of arson cases and the rates of arson per population have increased in recent years, but the FBI cautions that these increases should not be interpreted as more crime because of inconsistencies in reporting.[39] Rather than an indication of trends, the data supplied by the FBI are used to provide a profile of case characteristics.

Throughout the late 1990s church arsons have occurred in many parts of the country. Some, but not all, of the arsons have been racially motivated. Most have not been solved.

This crime category is often assumed to imply the burning of buildings. Actually, the burning of other property, such as personal belongings of victims or motor vehicles, is also included in the crime of arson. Buildings ("structures") account for about half of all cases of arson. The average monetary amount lost in the malicious burning of a structure in 1996 was $17,892. Nationwide, the average loss in all cases of arson was $10,280 in 1996. The FBI does not calculate a national estimate of all losses because reporting to date is considered sporadic and incomplete.

The overall rate of arson is 44 reported incidents of this crime per 100,000 population. Rural areas have lower rates of arson than urban areas. Most cleared cases of arson involve young people. Fifty-three percent of those arrested for the crime in 1996 were under the age of 18; 70 percent were under the age of 25. Eighty-five percent of those arrested were male, and three-quarters were white in 1996. In general, arrests have increased in recent years, reported offenses have increased, and the value of property burned has increased. Because there is no comparable victimization report data, such as that collected by the

NCVS, no one knows whether the crime is increasing or reporting is on the rise.[40]

Non-Index Offenses

Information supplied by the FBI with regard to the index property crime categories provides opportunity for the study of trends or patterns among these offenses. The fact that information is limited to crimes reported, however, presents a troubling dilemma for researchers, who cannot make definitive statements about crime trends without complementary data. A further problem with the UCR is that the index list of property offenses is limited to four common crimes. Many other property crimes plague Americans, ranging over many types of theft or property destruction. Arrests for other types of property crimes, such as embezzlement, are included in Part II offenses recorded in the UCR, but further elaboration of reporting patterns, or changes in reported offenses over time, are not calculated. Table 7.6 reports the arrests for non-index property offenses recorded by the FBI in 1996 and the

TABLE 7.6 | Arrests of Males and Females: 1996, and Percent Change Since 1987

OFFENSE CHARGED	MALES	PERCENT CHANGE SINCE 1987	FEMALES	PERCENT CHANGE SINCE 1987
Forgery and counterfeiting	51,372	+28.7	28,105	+33.5
Fraud	168,385	+32.1	116,746	+18.5
Embezzlement	5,633	+5.2	4,619	+38.8
Stolen property: buying, receiving, possessing	84,867	−2.2	14,435	+26.4
Vandalism	182,709	+13.9	29,336	+52.6

SOURCE: Federal Bureau of Investigation, *Crime in the United States* (Washington DC: U.S. Government Printing Office, 1997) 219.

percentage of change from 1987. Arrests increased in most categories between 1987 and 1996, but it is not clear whether increased arrests mean that crime is increasing, crime detection has improved, or there is now a greater tendency to arrest suspects for these crimes.

Some arrests and convictions in these categories include white-collar offenders who bilk large sums of money from their employers or the public through embezzlement or fraud. Many cases of fraud, theft of property, embezzlement, or forgery are not lucrative and are not connected with high-level economic crime by the wealthy. Employee theft is a matter of grave concern to most American businesses, but the level of theft in any single case is usually quite small. Theft of small amounts of money by clerks or office personnel from a petty cash fund, money skimmed from the till by cashiers, and thefts of merchandise, tools, or supplies by all types of employees generally are insignificant losses to businesses on an individual basis—but collectively they cost employers billions of dollars annually (Box 7.3). Such cases fit the typical pattern for crimes of embezzlement, fraud, and forgery. Estimates of employee theft range from $40 billion to over $100 billion in losses to American businesses each year.[41]

Forgery, Fraud, and Embezzlement

Most people arrested for forgery, fraud, or embezzlement are men, but a surprisingly large number of women are also arrested each year. Forty-one percent of arrests in these crime categories in 1996 were women.[42] Almost two-thirds of those arrested were white and about one-third were African American.[43]

Gender Issues

Darrell Steffensmeier and Cathy Streifel explain the relatively high representation of women in these crime categories by reference to several modern American phenomena. First, the feminization of poverty has induced many women to supplement insufficient incomes with petty property crime. As is typical with most of women's crime, offenses are concentrated in the least serious category of each crime designation. Women engage in petty offenses such as larceny, fraud, and embezzlement because opportunities for theft arise, risk appears low to individual offenders, and economic pressures to supplement their incomes are significant. The growing number of poor women who are primary caretakers of dependent children has significantly affected the prevalence of petty property offenses committed by women. Many of these women turn to crime to supplement the money they earn from low-paying jobs or receive as welfare benefits.

Second, increased efficiency in the detection of fraud offenders has fostered increases in arrest and prosecution. Computer-based recordkeeping and security surveillance have made detection and proof of involvement more likely. And third, the growth of a credit-based economy in the United States has both increased the likelihood poor women will rely on credit for daily needs and increased the temptation to supplement income with fraudulent use of credit. The writing of bad checks, credit card fraud, and fraudulent use of welfare services all fall within the categories of fraud, forgery, and embezzlement. Such crimes have been typical of women's offending patterns for several decades, but they increased significantly as women's poverty increased during the 1980s.[44]

While men's involvement in these crime categories has been consistently greater than women's, the share of arrests for fraud, forgery, and embezzlement that include women has steadily increased for more than a decade. Steffensmeier and Streiffel maintain that opportunities for other types of theft have drawn men away from these crimes in favor of more lucrative property crime. Theft of bicycles and theft from parked cars, for example, expanded rapidly among men during the 1980s. Arrests among males for fraud, forgery, and embezzlement have remained high primarily because detection is easier and more efficient with contemporary computer checks and surveillance technology.[45]

Detection Trends

Private businesses, and many state governments, have actively pursued techniques for detection of fraud, forgery, and embezzlement crimes. Many companies, for example, maintain anonymous hotlines for reporting of com-

Theft in Sweden and Germany

As in the United States, property crime constitutes a disproportionately large share of crime in both Sweden and Germany. Over half of reported crimes are thefts in both countries. In the United States, theft is classified according to the circumstances of the theft and the type of article stolen. American classifications, for example, designate whether a structure was broken into for the purpose of theft (burglary), whether the value of the article stolen was small (larceny), or whether the item taken was a motor vehicle. In both Sweden and Germany, the most important classification of the crime indicates whether the offender threatened the victim. Aggravated theft involves use of a weapon or threat to accomplish the theft. In Sweden, the most common type of theft is something stolen from inside a car, and theft of a bicycle, moped, motorcycle, or parts of vehicles. Motor vehicle theft is more rare than theft of the contents of a car. In Germany, aggravated theft, or threat to complete a theft, is the most common property crime. About one-third of all crimes in Germany are aggravated thefts. Another one-quarter of crimes are thefts without aggravated circumstances. A common problem of theft in Sweden involves break-ins of summer cottages. Crime classification in Sweden includes a special category for such break-ins.

Cultural differences between the United States and either Sweden or Germany help to explain the differences in the way crimes of theft are classified in these countries. Americans are very concerned with the monetary value of stolen property, which is reflected in the FBI classification of property crimes. In either Sweden or Germany, the use of violence or the threat of violence is a more important consideration than the value of the stolen item. Thus, crime tracking in both countries emphasizes the use of force rather than the monetary value of stolen items. Crime statistics in either Germany or Sweden do not estimate value or monetary losses to victims. American crime statistics from either the FBI or the NCVS indicate detailed analysis of monetary losses from all crime categories.

SOURCES: Bundeskriminalamt, 1996. *PKS Berichtsjahr 1994.* Wiesbaden: Bundeskriminalamt; Jan Carling (1994) *Crime and Law in Sweden.* Stockholm: Statistics Sweden.

pany embezzlers. Discovery of employee theft through reports by other employees has risen 40 percent among some such businesses.[46] The problem is exceptionally common. Even companies that provide assistance to other businesses in preventing employee theft and fraud, such as Arthur Andersen & Co., have been victimized by serious employee embezzlement.[47]

Computerized detection of theft has been increasing rapidly in recent years.[48] In Westchester County, New York, a state-of-the-art electronic fingerprinting program was initiated in July 1995 as a pilot program in an antifraud campaign aimed at apprehending welfare cheats.[49] Most states have initiated or increased requirements that healthy welfare recipients work for all or part of their government stipend. These programs are also aimed at curtailing fraudulent theft of welfare.[50]

Computer Crime

The corollary to use of computers for a very wide variety of personal, business, government, and economic activities has been widespread abuse of this technology. While a high percentage of computer crime is perpetrated by white-collar thieves, there is also a large share of petty embezzlement by employees through computerized manipulation of records. Computer crime is, generally, attributable to two sources: hackers, or internal staff or contract workers authorized to access computer records. **Hackers** are skilled computer amateurs who enter the computer security system and vandalize hardware or software by implanting a computer virus to alter or damage the functioning of the computer, or who manipulate internal computer files for their own benefit. Authorized staff or contractors may steal through manipulation of records or may do malicious damage to computerized files. By most accounts, computer crime is accomplished primarily by authorized users rather than external hackers.[51] According to Knogo North America, Inc., which manufactures computer security systems, theft in the computer industry is perpetrated 20 percent by outsiders and 80 percent by employees or authorized computer operators.[52] Computer companies lost more than $8 billion in 1994 to armed robberies and employee theft of computer chips; and computer crime is among the most threatening offenses facing many businesses.[53] Some experts rank computer security as a more significant concern than physical security issues.[54]

Societal Issues

In the United States, cultural emphasis on possessions as a measure of personal worth places enormous pressure on Americans to accumulate material possessions. Consumer advertising creates desire for consumption and images of deprivation among those without the resources to purchase more or better consumer products. Personal measurements of happiness, satisfaction, or success often focus upon ownership of property or financial security as the most important indicators of accomplishment.

Power, in addition to accomplishment, is measured in material terms in the United States. Common terms such as *buying power, consumer power, economic power,* and *the power of money,* all signal the importance of material accumulation as symbols of American success. Pressures to increase material possessions and accumulate property are felt by people within all economic and social divisions. With strong cultural prescriptions for accumulation, the temptation is overwhelming for many people to engage in crime as a means of acquiring property when legitimate alternatives are closed or limited. Even among people who are financially secure, such as corporate executives, politicians, or wealthy professionals, cultural pressures to drive income or possessions still higher motivate even the financially secure to engage in tax evasion, consumer fraud, or illegal business transactions. Crimes committed to increase property accumulations pervade all social classes, in part because American cultural forces place material success above adherence to laws that prohibit financial enhancement at the expense of others. The focus in this chapter is on conventional property crime, rather than the white-collar or corporate crime that was discussed in Chapter 6, but many of the pressures to steal are the same, regardless of the offender's social class.

Crimes committed to enhance material accumulation by upper-class offenders, such as business executives, politicians, and professionals, are generally not classified as property crimes. Stealing by members of the upper classes is rarely calculated with arrest statistics or incarceration rates, even though their theft may constitute a more significant economic threat than conventional property offenses. Crimes counted as conventional property offenses are committed almost exclusively by members of the lower classes.

Rationales for Class Distinctions in Property Crime

Part of the rationale for distinction in the crimes of theft committed by members of the upper and lower classes is traceable to the characteristics of the offenses. While business crime is serious, costly, and prevalent, it is much more difficult to detect than conventional theft. It is easier to calculate the number of stolen bicycles or motor vehicles, for example, than to determine the value of theft through violation of banking regulations or insider (stock) trading.

Another part of the rationale for focus upon conventional property offenses is the individualized threat inherent in such crimes. While violation of banking regulations may financially harm large numbers of people, the threat is often perceived as indirect. No single person is seriously injured by such crimes, in most cases. Conventional property crimes are categorically directed toward theft from individual victims. The FBI counts the individual cases of burglary, larceny, motor vehicle theft, and arson, as well as the arrests for non-index property offenses such as fraud, forgery and embezzlement. Each case is an individual theft. Violation of banking regulations, overpricing of consumer items, and a host of other white-collar or corporate crimes may affect individuals, but the impact on each victim is small and the intentions of the perpetrators are unfocused. The individualized threat inherent in conventional property crime makes such crimes *appear* to be more dangerous than the largely indirect threat characteristic of other types of theft.

An additional rationale for the dominant focus upon conventional property crimes is related to the characteristics of the offenders. Most people who are arrested, convicted, and incarcerated for crimes of theft are poor, a disproportionate number are members of racial or ethnic minorities, and most live in inner-city areas. There has been a strong tendency among most Americans to disconnect perpetrators of conventional property crimes from dominant white middle-class values and lifestyles. An "us versus them" dismissal of property offenders pervades most people's understanding of contemporary crime patterns. Many believe that urban decay, moral decline, and cultural differences explain high rates of property crime, especially in urban neighborhoods. The question of moral values, in particular, has been a matter of debate among theorists for many years. As you will see in Chapter 12, family structure, socialization, and the development of moral values have been core issues among theorists trying to discern differences between those who commit crimes and those who do not.

Moral Values and Stealing

In American culture there a host of moral values that orient people, but cultural emphasis on material success pervades the entire society. Cultural values that stress the importance of "conquering the unknown" and using individual ingenuity to "beat the odds" foster a strong ideal of individual achievement as the means of overcoming adversity. The ability of individual entrepreneurs to achieve material success through perseverance and ingenuity pervades folklore and the popularized values about material accumulation and the American dream. "Rugged individualism" conjures the image of achievement of social rewards through personal commitment to overcoming obstacles to success. Several books, such as the best-seller *Habits of the Heart: Individualism and Commitment in American Life* by Robert Bellah and colleagues, or *Crime and the American Dream* by Steven Messner and Richard Rosenfeld, have illustrated the far-reaching implications of American cultural values that place material success as the primary measurement of self-worth.[55] Messner and Rosenfeld, for example, sum up the association between individual achievement and measures of success and their implications for crime:

> . . . [T]he dominant value patterns of American culture, specifically its achievement orientation, its competitive individualism, its universalism in goal orientations and evaluative standards—when harnessed to the preeminent goal of monetary success—crystallize into the distinctive cultural ethos of the American Dream. The American Dream, in turn, encourages members of society to pursue ends [limited only by considerations of technical expediency]. This open, widespread, competitive, and anomic quest for success provides a cultural environment highly conducive to criminal behavior.[56]

When presented with an abstract moral problem about stealing, most people agree that it is wrong to take things that belong to others under most conditions. Stealing is wrong unless certain conditions prevail, such as threat of starvation, personal danger, or the enhancement of some higher good such as a cure for disease. Stealing is wrong, they believe, but some human needs make the wrongful behavior justifiable.

Some Stealing Is "Right"

The fact that exceptions to the general rule that "stealing is wrong" are easily identifiable indicates that reasons for violation of moral standards are accessible. Some moral standards override other moral standards. Stealing is wrong—but theft to prevent death from starvation would be justifiable. In this case, the higher moral principle of preventing death supersedes the usual social rule that dictates the wrongfulness of stealing. In American society, certain higher principles prevail over all others, according to Messner and Rosenfeld, and as articulated more than a half century ago by Robert K. Merton.[57] The American requirements for success, material accumulation, and personal security as measured by financial stability override the moral standard that stealing is wrong.

Guilt feelings about property offenses are easily mediated for those people who steal on the basis of their hierarchical ordering of moral principles. Certainly it is wrong to take what belongs to others, but overriding cultural requirements that dictate measurement of self-worth on the basis of material success incite many people to order their moral principles in such a way that illegal access to some of the American Dream is prioritized over the usual rule that stealing is wrong. Some of America's most beloved political leaders have "cut a few corners," or "cheated a little"

to "get ahead," which helps to softens the internal guilt of individuals who also cut a few corners in their efforts to achieve success. Respected national figures such as Richard Nixon, whose popularity remained high even after he resigned in disgrace from the presidency, or former President Ronald Reagan, who repeatedly lied to the American public and was also implicated in the illegal selling of arms to Iran, have been embraced by the American public in the belief that their intentions were honorable even if their actions were morally wrong.[58] Personal moral schemes that re-prioritize the inherent wrongfulness of particular acts contribute to the pervasive nature of property offenses in America. Certainly stealing is wrong, but stealing of tools or supplies from employers, shoplifting, or burglary may all be justified by the overarching cultural value that "getting ahead" requires ingenuity and creativity.

Problems with Moral Arguments

While focus on morality may offer some insight into the pervasive nature of property crime in America, there are problems with this analysis. If the overarching American emphasis on material accumulation causes many people to adjust their moral priorities in such a way that crime becomes personally excusable as a means of achieving success, why are most property crimes committed by men? The American dream is not gender-specific. Thus, if goals of achievement and self-worth, as exemplified by material success, induce people to commit common property crimes in order to obtain money or goods, why do so few women engage in such offenses? Women, who by all accounts have less access to valuable social rewards and whose social placement slipped considerably lower than men's during the feminization of poverty of the 1980s, should have higher rates of property crime than men by such an analysis. Table 7.7 illustrates the gender differences in total arrests for 1996.

TABLE 7.7 | Total Arrests for Property Offenses, Distribution by Sex, 1996

OFFENSE CHARGED	PERCENT MALE	PERCENT FEMALE
INDEX PROPERTY CRIME TOTAL	72.1	27.9
Burglary	88.7	11.3
Larceny-theft	66.2	33.8
Motor vehicle theft	86.4	13.6
Arson	85.1	14.9
NON-INDEX PROPERTY OFFENSE ARRESTS		
Forgery/counterfeiting	64.6	35.4
Fraud	58.3	41.7
Embezzlement	55.3	44.7
Stolen property (buying, selling, possessing)	85.4	14.6
Vandalism	86.2	13.8

SOURCE: Federal Bureau of Investigation, *Crime in the United States* (Washington DC: U.S. Government Printing Office, 1997) 231.

The problem of explaining property crime in terms of moral and cultural values may be confounded by gendered variations in the development of moral systems. Psychologist Carol Gilligan, for example, has argued that men and women are oriented by different moral voices.[59] She suggests men are more likely to be motivated by an **ethic of justice,** which includes ideals of power, social status, getting even, competition, and authority. Women, according to Gilligan, are oriented by an **ethic of care,** which requires attention to the needs of others, peaceful resolution of conflict, and responsibility. Women's relatively low involvement in property crime may be a function of moral priorities that set the ethic of care above the values of economic success. Recent pressures of poverty may account for the rise in women's involvement in some property offense categories.

Perhaps the pressure to achieve American ideals of material accumulation explains the rise in women's property offenses over the last decade, but this perspective does not explain why women's offenses remain relatively low in the face of increased alienation from the sources of economic success. Women's involvement in property crimes has increased only in the lowest offense categories: larceny-theft, forgery (primarily bad check writing), fraud (usually welfare fraud), and embezzlement (generally petty cash).

Controlling Property Crime

Numerous defensive mechanisms for preventing property offenses have been initiated in recent years. The home security business is booming. In many communities, housing divisions have become walled communities with security guards, fences, and electronic detection devices. New policing strategies have been adopted, both for curtailing offenses and apprehending offenders. Consulting firms that specialize in security and crime prevention have proliferated in many parts of the country.[60] State-of-the-art digital technology is designed not only for efficiency of operation but also for protection against fraudulent use. Video surveillance of business and financial transactions in all types of settings is commonplace. All of these strategies are aimed at controlling crime or apprehending offenders.

Some strategists have acknowledged the interconnections among various types of offenses. In Florida, for example, property crime has been reduced by pouring more police resources into enforcement of drug laws. Arrests of drug offenders have significantly reduced property crime because a high proportion of property offenses are committed to raise cash for the support of drug habits.[61] Prevention of offenses with such strategies cuts to the motivations of offenders.

Conservative and Liberal Strategies
Controlling property crime generally falls into one of two camps: conservative or liberal. Conservatives usually favor punishment of offenders. Recent "wars" on crime are a prime example of the conservative approach. With such strategies, neighborhoods are "cleaned up" by removing criminals, who are apprehended, convicted, sentenced, and incarcerated. Long sentences are favored by conservatives as a get-tough answer to the crime problem.

Liberals usually focus upon the social conditions that give rise to crime. Poverty, joblessness, racism, and disadvantaged access to societal opportunities such as education are commonly targeted as the underlying causes of crime. Reducing crime, from this perspective, means enhancing the opportunities of those who have had little access to the ideals of the American Dream. With less poverty, more education, and better access to jobs, crime should be reduced.

While both strategies have had some limited success, neither fully addresses the underlying forces of crime in American society. For conservatives, the problem is "bad" people; for liberals, the problem is "bad" social conditions. Neither orientation addresses the underlying cultural values that make theft, getting ahead by any means, ruthless competition, and material accumulation the quintessential American values. Moral values not only designate right and wrong but also dictate the activities that are an acceptable means of achieving personal goals. For some, theft is never legitimate. For others, it is the only means of acquiring money or goods. And for still others, there is some middle ground that allows them to engage in some crime (stealing supplies from an employer) but never other crimes (burglary). Underlying cultural values cross-cut social classes. Eliminating poverty will not stop property crime because these offenses are not limited to people who are poor. Locking away "bad" people is impractical, given the predominance of property crimes in all social classes and across all social strata of American society.

Alternative Strategies
The most effective strategies for reducing the prevalence of property crime are among the most difficult to implement because they involve long-term attention to social institutions. Messner and Rosenfeld suggest,

> **... initiatives such as the provision of family leave, job sharing for husbands and wives, flexible work schedules, employer-provided child care, and a host of other "pro-family" economic policies should help to alter the balance between economic demands ... and obligations and opportunities. ...**[62]

Social reorganization, according to Messner and Rosenfeld, that returns traditional emphases to family, education, occupational placement, and community responsibility—rather than current emphasis on individual self-promotion—will reduce crime as the means of achieving money or goods as the measure of self-worth. Crime results from an exaggerated emphasis on monetary success. When cultural change redefines worth in terms of human connections and reduces monetary success to a proportionate goal rather than the most important goal, cultural restraint will tame materialistic pressures, according to Messner and Rosenfeld.[63] Such reform cuts to the heart of American values and is not likely to be undertaken without debate. Yet, fluctuation between conservative and liberal policies has solved little. Models of successful pro-family, pro-community social supports are available from many countries that have much lower crime rates than the United States. Highly industrialized and highly stratified countries such as Japan, Canada, Sweden, and Germany provide models for success in social reorganization.

Summary

Property crime is a pervasive American phenomenon. It is the largest designated area of crime, according to FBI reports. Both NCVS and FBI data indicate that virtually every American has been touched by the effects of property crime, either as a perpetrator of such offenses or as a victim. A reported property crime occurs in the United States every 3 seconds, but by all accounts reported offenses are only a small proportion of all property crimes. All Americans live with the threat of theft or damage to property and virtually everyone in American society takes precautions at some time to prevent or curtail the threat of theft. Americans live with daily reminders that anything not secured could be lost to theft at any time.

Why theft and damage to property is so common in America is a matter of debate. Many people believe that important cultural emphases on accumulation of private property and the measurement of self-worth in terms of material success exert societal pressures upon people to do almost anything, including violation of moral standards against stealing, to "get ahead." The pressure to accumulate is a strong force that drives many people to cheat and steal if other means of advancement seem to be too slow or inefficient for achieving success goals. Likewise, people who are disadvantaged by poverty, insufficient education, or other barriers to achievement, commit property crimes as a means of acquiring some of the money or goods that are symbolic of success.

The pressure to have money and goods is so great in American society that most people have either cheated or stolen, or they know someone else who has engaged in these activities to get ahead. Americans feel immense pressure to have money and goods, which also exerts pressure to acquire these outside of legitimate channels through crime.

Curtailing property crime through prevention or punishment strategies does stop some crime, but little real change occurs. More promising, yet more difficult strategies, focus upon family, community, and human connections as the redirected orientation for measures of success. Removing some economic pressures upon families through day care, job sharing, medical insurance, paid leave from jobs for family needs, as are provided in all European nations, would have the dual benefit of relieving economic pressures and directing attention to human relationships through strengthening of families and promotion of community responsibility. Political pressures to reduce funding for core community programs makes such a reorganization unlikely for now. Nevertheless, going beyond liberal or conservative positions to emphasize support for strong family and community ties will likely have the greatest long-term impact on controlling property crime.

Critical Thinking Questions

1. What are the most important distinctions between theft committed by people of different social classes? Is there a differences between larceny-theft on the street and larceny-theft by an employee on the job?
2. What penalties should apply to people who commit property crimes that are different from the penalties that apply to people who commit violent offenses?
3. What effect do you think the common, everyday preventions of property crime (security cameras in stores, electronic devices on university library books, or security chains on park benches) have on American life and culture?
4. Why do you think stealing is more common in the United States than in many other countries?

Suggested Readings

Robert N. Bellah, Richard Madsen, William M. Sullivan, Ann Swidler, and Steven M. Tipton, *Habits of the Heart: Individualism and Commitment in American Life* (New York: Harper Torchbooks, 1985).

Marcus Felson, *Crime and Everyday Life* (Thousand Oaks CA: Pine Forge, 1994).

Harry King, *Box Man: A Professional Thief's Journey, As Told To and Edited by Bill Chambliss* (New York: Harper Torchbooks, 1972).

Steven F. Messner and Richard Rosenfeld, *Crime and the American Dream* (Belmont, CA: Wadsworth, 1994).

Notes

[1] "Around the Nation," *Law Enforcement News, XXIII:* 467, 15 May 1997, 2.

[2] Federal Bureau of Investigation, *Crime in the United States* (Washington DC: U.S. Government Printing Office, 1997) 35.

[3] Jack Katz, *Seductions of Crime: Moral and Sensual Attractions in Doing Evil* (New York: Basic Books, 1988).

[4] Federal Bureau of Investigation, *Crime in The United States* (Washington DC: U.S. Government Printing Office, 1996) 35.

[5] Tina Dorsey and Jayne Robinson, "Criminal Victimization 1994," *Bureau of Justice Statistics* (Washington DC: U.S. Government Printing Office, 1997) v, vii.

[6] Ibid., vi.

[7] Ibid.

[8] Ibid., vii.

[9] FBI, *Crime in the United States* (1997) 36.

[10] Ibid, 36.

[11] Dorsey and Robinson, "Criminal Victimization 1994," vi.

[12] FBI, *Crime in the United States* (1997) 8.

[13] Ibid., 4, 35.

[14] Ibid., 36

[15] Ibid., 213.

[16] Ibid., 219.

[17] Kathleen Maguire and Ann L. Pastore, *Sourcebook of Criminal Justice Statistics, 1994* (Washington DC: U.S. Government Printing Office, 1995) 551; Kathleen Maguire and Ann L. Pastore, *Sourcebook of Criminal Justice Statistics, 1993* (Washington DC: U.S. Government Printing Office, 1994) 433.

[18] Victor E. Kappeler, Mark Blumberg, and Gary W. Potter,*The Mythology of Crime and Criminal Justice,* 2nd ed. (Prospect Heights, IL: Waveland, 1996) 242.

[19] William Wilbanks, *The Myth of a Racist Criminal Justice System* (Monterey CA: Brooks/Cole, 1987) 128.

[20] For a good discussion of this issue and summaries of several research studies, see Kappeler et al., *The Mythology of Crime and Criminal Justice,* 241–43.

[21] FBI, *Crime in the United States* (1997) 232.

[22] For discussion, see Alida V. Merlo and Joycelyn M. Pollock, *Women, Law, and Social Control* (Boston: Allyn & Bacon, 1995).

[23] See U.S. Department of Justice, *Felony Defendants in Large Urban Counties, 1992* (Washington DC: U.S. Government Printing Office, 1995) 2.

[24] Lisa Bastian and Marshall M.DeBerry, Jr., *Criminal Victimization in the United States, 1992* (Washington DC: U.S. Government Printing Office, 1994) 20.

[25] Ibid.

[26] Ibid., 25.

[27] Ibid., 6–7.

[28] FBI, *Crime in the United States* (1997) 221; Bastian (1994) 2.

[29] FBI, *Crime in the United States* (1997), *Crime in the United States,* 44.

[30] Ibid.

[31] Ibid.

[32] See, for example: Susan Faludi, *Backlash: The Undeclared War Against American Women* (New York: Anchor, 1991); Darrell Steffensmeier and Cathy Streifel, "Trends in Female Crime, 1960–1990," in *Female Criminality: The State of the Art,* ed. Concetta C. Culliver (New York: Garland, 1993) 63–103; Martin Milkman and Sarah Tinkler, "Female Criminality: An Economic Perspective," in *Female Criminality: The State of the Art,* ed. Concetta C. Culliver (New York: Garland, 1993) 291–304.

[33] FBI, *Crime in the United States* (1997), 4.

[34] FBI, *Crime in the United States* (1997), 39, 40.

[35] Ibid., 39.

[36] Ibid., 4, 42.

[37] Ibid., 50.

[38] Ibid.

[39] Ibid., 55.

[40] Ibid., 55, 56.

[41] Mark Lipman and W.R. McGraw, "Employee Theft: A $40 Billion Industry," *Annals of the American Academy of Political and Social Science 498* (1988) 51–59; James M. Lukawitz and Paul John Steinbart, "Investor Reaction to Disclosures of Employee Fraud," *Journal of Managerial Issues* 7 (1995) 358–67.

[42] FBI, *Crime in the United States* (1997) 231.

[43] Ibid., 232.

[44] Steffensmeier and Streifel,"Trends in Female Crime, 1960–1990," 90–91.

[45] Ibid.

[46] Phil Britt, "Hotlines Help Apprehend Thieves," *Savings and Community Banker 3* (1994) 45.

[47] Matt O'Connor, "Accounting Firm Victim of Embezzling," *Chicago Tribune,* 23 June 1995, C3.

[48] Deborah Branscum, "Desperately Seeking Security," *Macworld 11:10* (1994) 181–82.

[49] Elsa Brenner, "Shield Against Welfare Cheats," *New York Times,* 30 July 1995, WC6.

[50] Joyce Purnick, "Cheating the Reformers: Ins and Outs of Welfare," *New York Times,* 6 April 1995, B3.

[51] *USA Today,* "Computer Crime Usually an Inside Job," 25 October 1995, B1.

[52] Anne R. Carey and Bryant Web, "USA Snapshots: Tech Theft Often Inside Job," *USA Today,* 24 October 1995, A1.

[53] Ron Trujillo, "Computer Chips 'Better than Gold' to Thieves," *USA Today,* 20 September 1995, B1; Britt, "Hotlines Help Apprehend Thieves."

[54] Britt, "Hotlines Help Apprehend Thieves."

[55] Robert N. Bellah, Richard Madsen, William M. Sullivan, Ann Swidler, and Steven M. Tipton, *Habits of the Heart: Individualism and Commitment in American Life* (New York: Perennial Library, 1985); Steven F. Messner and Richard Rosenfeld, *Crime and the American Dream* (Belmont, CA: Wadsworth, 1994). See also: John Hagan, *Crime and Disrepute* (Thousand Oaks, CA: Pine Forge, 1994), especially Chapter 3.

[56] Messner and Rosenfeld, *Crime and the American Dream,* 71.

[57] Robert K. Merton (1938) "Social Structure and Anomie," *American Sociological Review 3* (1938) 672–82.

[58] For discussion, see Messner and Rosenfeld, *Crime and the American Dream,* 67–68.

[59] Carol Gilligan, *In A Different Voice: Psychological Theory and Women's Development* (Cambridge, MA: Harvard University, 1982).

[60] Tim Sewell, "Job Security Has a Special Meaning for Safety Firm," *Memphis Business Journal,* 20 March 1995, Issue 46, 1-23.

[61] David L. Sollars, Bruce L. Benson, and David W. Rasmussen, "Drug Enforcement and the Deterrence of Property Crime Among Local Jurisdictions," *Public Finance Quarterly 22* (1994) 22–45.

[62] Messner and Rosenfeld, *Crime and the American Dream,* 103.

[63] Ibid., 109–111.

chapter 8

Public Order Crimes

CHAPTER OUTLINE

DEFINING PUBLIC ORDER CRIMES
STANDARDS OF MORALITY
NATURE, EXTENT, AND COSTS
OFFENDERS AND VICTIMS
    Offenders
    Victims
HISTORICAL PATTERNS OF REGULATION
    Prohibition
    Prostitution
    Illegal Drugs
    Gambling
    Abortion
    Pornography
ARGUMENTS ABOUT DECRIMINALIZATION
    Arguments to Decriminalize
    Arguments for Maintaining Criminality
ORGANIZED CRIME
    Activities of Organized Crime
    Gambling
    Prostitution
    Drug Trafficking
    Organized Crime: Myth or Reality?
SUMMARY

KEY TERMS

public order crimes
moral offenses
vice
victimless crimes
complainant
organized crime
eradication
interdiction
pandering
street level drug enforcement
syndicate
bookie

MANY RESEARCHERS BELIEVE that public order crimes receive too much attention from law enforcement. The crimes in this category are often, but not always, petty offenses that involve only the offender or the offender and another consenting adult. Other researchers believe that the only effective way of establishing a moral

Defining Public Order Crimes

In most cases, crime implies some clearly definable wrong. In both the legal use of the word and in common understandings of what crime means, the act of crime implies that there is both a perpetrator and a victim of the wrongful behavior. With public order crimes, this general rule does not always apply. **Public order crimes** refer to those crimes in which no clear victim is readily identifiable. This category of crime includes many cases in which the only injured party is the offender. In other words, the offender engages in some self-destructive behavior, such as drug use, that is illegal. These crimes are also called **moral offenses,** or **vice,** indicating that the designation of the behavior as illegal is a reflection of societal moral standards. Many of these crimes are also called **victimless crimes**, which implies that no one was harmed. Such crimes are consensual, rather than coercive.

There are many types of public order crimes, and great debate continues over whether these behaviors should be regulated by law or whether they should be private decisions made by consenting adults. Those who favor legal regulation of these behaviors believe that some activities are too important to the preservation of moral standards to be left to individual decisionmakers. Opponents, who favor legalization of most of the behaviors, point out that adults have the right to engage in many self-destructive behaviors (smoking, drinking to excess), and that it should not be the role of government to choose which private behaviors are legal and which are not. The debate is complex and has many interesting historical twists. This chapter will present the arguments for and against the regulation of morality, along with a discussion of the most common public order crimes.

Standards of Morality

Definitions of public order crimes tend to change over time as moral standards change. Behavior that was once criminal may become so common that the criminal designation is lifted; or, the prevailing moral values that underlie the legal designations change, which results in legalization of the behavior. For example, Margaret Sanger, who in 1916 founded the first birth control clinic in New York City, was jailed for violation of public morals. She was accused of distributing obscene materials.[1] The distribution of materials related to birth control is no longer considered to be obscene. The moral standards related to birth control information have changed, and legal restrictions on the distribution of birth control information have been decriminalized.

Among the most common public order crimes currently cited in the literature are gambling, sexual offenses, drug use, abortion, and obscenity. All of these crimes are influenced by personal choices to engage in behaviors that lack full societal approval, but that attract sizeable numbers of participants. Gambling, for example, is legally available in all states through church-sponsored raffles, state lotteries, local bingo games, and in many states organized betting on sports and even casinos are legal. Americans legally bet an estimated $394 billion annually.[2] New techniques for gambling have been prolific for over two decades, with riverboat gambling, casino games, Indian reservation gambling, and lotteries toping the list of legal varieties. An emerging trend in gambling is television call-in betting. A Pittsburgh-based cable television channel, for example, handles bets for viewers of TV games via an 800 call-in number.[3]

The legal opportunities to gamble are only slightly different from the illegal varieties. The same is true for most of these crimes. Attitudes toward public order crimes have been variable over time and subject to many societal pressures about moral standards. Unfortunately, there is no national standard of morality that applies to all people and is consistent over time. Moral standards are highly individual and closely tied to religious beliefs, ethnicity, and societal trends. Regulation of private behavior through law is, therefore, exceptionally difficult. The law cannot reflect the moral standards of all people; thus, it is often adjusted according to pressures imposed by vocal groups that support particular principles or standards of behavior.

For many people, the package of public order crimes represents a mixed group. Not all people believe that each of these activities represent immoral conduct. A person may be opposed to buying or selling sex, but finds nothing wrong with buying a weekly lottery ticket. Moral standards vary with individuals, vary over time, and fluctuate with political influences. As a result, many activities that are, stricly speaking, illegal are actually commonplace. The law in these cases does not reflect morality, but rather tries to impose moral standards. In other words, while the behaviors may be common, the law is used to tell people that they should not engage in such actions.

Enforcement of public order crimes is notoriously problematic. Because the laws are not based on clear definitions of harm done, the actions of the offenders often appear to be harmless self-indulgence. Police find enforcement exceptionally difficult because there is often no clear perpetrator. If, for example, both parties to an act of prostitution willingly exchange money and sexual services and their behavior is private, enforcement is rare. Most public order crimes are committed in privacy, the harm is minimal, and typical enforcement strategies are inapplicable. The temptations to accept bribes in exchange for non-enforcement, to use illegal detection strategies, or to enforce the law selectively have contributed to police corruption, especially when pressures for enforcement escalate. As a consequence, enforcement of public order crimes is fraught with abuse and inequity.

Nature, Extent, and Costs

Because of the private nature of many of these crimes, discerning clear patterns of offense is difficult. Arrest rates provide some insight into prevalence, but these crimes are notoriously underdetected. Also, numbers of arrests often reflect current community pressures rather than actual incidence of the behavior. Overworked police are likely to ignore public order crimes unless citizens, churches, or local community leaders press for enforcement. When public order crimes spill into conventional crime, then police are more likely to pursue them vigorously. For example, if neighborhood property crimes are linked to drug addicts, police action to clean up a neighborhood is likely.

The fact that public order crimes occur does not mean the law will be invoked against offenders. Official records of arrest are vague indicators of patterns of offense. Detection for some crimes is minimal, and in other cases arrest is sporadic. Federal Bureau of Investigation (FBI) data on public order offenses is collected in Part II of the Uniform Crime Reports.

Volume, rates of arrest for 1996, and percentage of change from 1987 are presented in Table 8.1. For some of the crimes listed, the offenses are clearly personal and exclusively associated with the behavior of the individual offender. For other crimes, potential victims could be injured as a result of some action related to the offender's illegal behavior. With driving while under the influence

TABLE 8.1 | Number and Rate per 100,000 Population of Arrests for Public Order Crimes, 1996, and Percent Change 1987–96

OFFENSE	TOTAL	RATE	PERCENT CHANGE
Prostitution	81,036	42.7	−10.3
Drug abuse	1,128,647	594.3	+57.5
Gambling	16,984	8.9	−18.0
Driving under the influence	1,013,932	533.9	−20.2
Liquor laws	491,176	258.6	+12.0
Drunkenness	522,896	275.3	−20.3
Disorderly conduct	626,918	330.1	+15.4
Vagrancy	21,735	11.4	−34.0

SOURCE: Federal Bureau of Investigation, *Crime in the United States, 1996* (Washington DC: U.S. Government Printing Office, 1997) 15, 18.

(DWI), or drunk driving, for example, the offender's behavior is not limited to self-destruction but could also cause serious injury or death to others. This is generally an exception to most categories of public order crimes. In most cases victims are identified, not in the legal sense, but as innocent parties who must put up with the behavior of the perpetrator. The spouse of a person who solicits the services of prostitutes may be an emotional victim, but has no clear connection to the offense.

Some of the offenses that were listed in Table 8.1 show decline in arrests since 1987, and others indicate increase. Decline or increase in arrests does not necessarily indicate changes in the occurrence of the behavior. Rates of arrest often change due to factors independent of the prevalence of these crimes. Police may ignore public order crimes if other more pressing law-enforcement issues draw their energies elsewhere. Also, if law-enforcement personnel are cut, enforcement of these crimes generally declines. Public pressure to address these crimes, as is current with drug offenses, will cause an increase in arrest rates.

Public order crimes are generally counted by arrest statistics rather than reports to police. Arrest data are used because there are few reports to the police to be recorded. Index offenses are often reported because (1) police reports are needed for insurance reimbursement, (2) injured parties expect police investigation of the offense, (3) the crime scene provides clues for police investigation, (4) police assistance is needed at the time the crime is discovered—and for a variety of other reasons. With public order crimes there is usually no **complainant;** that is, there is no injured party to call the police and report a crime. The crime is a private violation of the law, which only becomes part of UCR data if police discover the crime and record the arrest.

The UCR data on public order crimes reflect police trends in enforcement rather than actual prevalence of

TABLE 8.2 | Percent of Arrests for Public Order Crimes by Race, Gender, and Age, 1996

OFFENSE	RACE		GENDER		AGE	
	WHITE	BLACK	MALE	FEMALE	UNDER 15	UNDER 25
Prostitution	59.0%	38.3%	40.0%	60.0%	.2%	21.1%
Drug abuse	60.4	38.4	83.3	16.7	2.4	45.4
Gambling	45.4	50.6	86.2	13.8	1.7	39.5
Driving under the influence	86.7	10.4	85.2	14.8	—	22.5
Liquor laws	80.9	16.0	80.5	19.5	2.5	69.4
Drunkenness	81.1	16.2	87.9	12.1	.5	23.5
Disorderly conduct	62.4	35.7	78.9	21.1	8.6	54.1
Vagrancy	54.3	43.4	79.9	20.1	2.9	40.4

SOURCE: Federal Bureau of Investigation, *Crime in the United States, 1996* (Washington DC: U.S. Government Printing Office, 1997) 230–32.

the behavior. If arrests go up or down in a given year, the numbers are more likely to reflect the level of police resources devoted to arrests than actual changes in offense patterns. Nevertheless, arrest data are generally used to describe these offenses, in the absence of any other indicators of trends. Table 8.2 illustrates the percentage of arrests by race, gender, and age categories.

The UCR data on public order crimes provides an abbreviated list of offenses that fall under this category of crime; these data fail to illustrate the subtle distinctions in categories of these offenses. For example, DWI, liquor law violations, and drunkenness categories provide information about how many people are arrested, but little insight into alcohol abuse as a social or medical problem. Arrests are a mere snapshot of a much larger picture of societal problems with alcohol abuse.

It is difficult to discern the extent of public order crimes because of the secrecy inherent in many of these crimes. Moreover, many of the vices, or public order crimes, are facilitated through the efforts of organized crime. The term **organized crime** refers to syndicated crime organizations—highly organized, secretive bureaucracies that are run like legitimate businesses, except that many of the activities of the organization are illegal. Organized crime thrives because of the high demand among Americans for goods and services that are illegal. Organized crime became a force in the United States during Prohibition, when alcohol was illegal yet highly demanded.

Tracking public order crimes committed by organized crime is problematic for obvious reasons. Many have argued that organized crime flourishes simply because Americans demand the services provided. According to this argument, there would be no need for organized crime if the behaviors in question were legally available. Organized crime bridges the gap between the demand for particular activities of vice and the illegal status of these highly demanded goods or services.

Offenders and Victims

Analyses of public order crimes are fraught with controversy as to whether these behaviors should be crimes and whether offenders are, in fact, criminal. One of the most consistent criticisms of this category of crimes is that labeling the activities as "crime" encourages disrespect for the law. People who commit public order crimes are often ordinary citizens. The fact that they pursue opportunities to engage in vice while maintaining otherwise respectable social positions can be seen as evidence of deception and disdain for the law. Offenders are often middle-class, employed, committed to home and family, and stereotypically "normal." Criticism of the criminal status of these behaviors emphasizes the fact that legal prohibitions do not stop people from engaging in these activities.

People who favor maintaining the criminal status of these activities contend that the law *does* restrict people from committing offenses that are morally reprehensible. They believe that counting those who violate the law is not the way to determine whether the law works; those who uphold the moral principles dictated by these laws should be counted. Law-abiding people outnumber offenders, thus indicating the success of the laws in fostering stronger morality, according to this perspective. Proponents also point out that not all offenders of public order crimes are respectable middle-class people, and that vice crimes are both perpetrated and consumed by people who lack moral control.

The debate is complicated and controversial, but the offenses are common. Laws have failed to keep people from engaging in these behaviors, and the demand for opportunities to commit these crimes keeps organized crime in business.[4] In the view of many, the illegality of these behaviors actually *encourages* law violation because the prohibited status of the activity makes it alluring to violate moral principles and act outside of the law.[5]

Offenders

Official statistics on offenders of public order crimes are highly unreliable, for the reasons cited. Arrest statistics, as indicated by Table 8.2, suggest that most offenders are young white men. Young black men are also disproportionately represented by arrest statistics. Both white and black women are arrested less often for FBI-reported public order crimes than men of either race. The arrest statistics are misleading, however.

Gender

Prostitution, for example, is the one crime that shows higher arrests for women than for men. The ratio of arrests is approximately 6 women for every 4 men arrested. Buying and selling sex are equally illegal in all states that prohibit prostitution, yet women are disproportionately arrested.[6] There are many more men who buy sex than women who sell sex, and the arrest statistics that disproportionately target the sellers grossly underestimate the actual parameters of the offense. In addition, many of the men who are arrested are prostitutes, which suggests that the number of customers arrested for soliciting prostitutes is disproportionately low.

While it is not possible to give an accurate picture of offenders from arrest statistics, most researchers in this field believe that the primary offenders of public order crimes are men. This is especially true with vice crimes involving sex. Exchange of money for sex, illegal acts of homosexuality (which are still criminalized in some states), purchase, use, and production of pornography, and acts of indecency are primarily perpetrated by men. While women may engage in illegal sex acts, such as selling sex or prohibited acts of homosexuality, men are more active on all levels of sexuality than women.[7] A higher percentage of men are exclusively homosexual than women; and men have a wider range of socially acceptable opportunities for expression of sexual preferences.[8] Increased freedom of sexual expression for women in recent decades has opened opportunities previously closed to women, but men continue to outnumber women in all measures of legal and illegal sexual activity.[9]

Traditional condemnation of women's overt sexuality, or the "double standard," may account for the lower incidence of offenses among women. Professor of psychiatry Jennifer James points out that women who sell sex are categorically treated as lower class, regardless of family background, income, education, or other measures of social status. Men who buy sex do not experience a similar decline in social status because of the purchase. The exchange is equally illegal from either the buyer's or the seller's perspective, but social disapproval is greater for the seller.[10]

Race

Offenders of other public order crimes are differentiated by race as well. African American men are proportionately more likely to be arrested for drug offenses, even though they are less likely to be users of illicit drugs than whites. Samuel Walker, a noted researcher on the common myths about drugs and crime, points out that African Americans account for only about 14 percent of all users.[11] "In the federal system and some states, the penalties for possession of crack cocaine, which is favored by non-whites, are higher than for powdered cocaine, which is more heavily used by whites."[12] African American and Hispanic offenders account for 90 percent of arrests for crack. The penalties for offenders caught with 50 to 150 grams of powder cocaine, who are generally white, earn an average prison sentence of 18 months. For an equal amount of crack, which is favored by blacks, the average sentence is 10 years.[13] Most drug enforcement efforts are directed toward minority, inner-city neighborhoods, rather than suburban, largely white, communities. Similarly, arrests for gambling are more likely to focus upon illegal numbers games in inner cities than insider trading on Wall Street, even though a few recent cases have drawn attention to the high-stakes gambling in business crime.[14]

Drug Offenders

The public order offense that draws the greatest attention from criminal justice authorities, legislators, and the American public is drug crime. Offenders in this category are commonly lower-class sellers, rather than middle- and upper-class consumers. For obvious reasons, enforcement is targeted at the most visible, easy to apprehend, street sellers in inner-city neighborhoods. Official federal policy on drug enforcement has hinged upon three basic policies: **eradication,** or eliminating the supply of illegal drugs, **interdiction,** or stopping illegal drugs from entering the boundaries of the United States, and **street level drug enforcement.** It is the final strategy, street level enforcement, that has led to high increases in arrest of drug offenders.[15]

While incarceration of other types of offenders has shown percentage declines in recent years, imprisonment for drug offenses has increased sharply. Combined federal and state prisoners who are incarcerated for violent offenses declined 12 percent between 1980 and 1993; and incarceration for property offenses declined 8 percent for the same years. Overall incarceration for drug offenses in both federal and state corrections increased from 8 percent in 1980 to 26 percent in 1993. Most of the increase in incarceration of drug offenders is in federal prisons. Sixty percent of federal prisoners were drug offenders in 1993 compared to 25 percent in 1980.[16]

TABLE 8.3 | Summary of Current American Drug Trends

TYPE OF DRUG	USE TRENDS	PRIMARY USERS	COST
Heroin	High purity has made it possible to inhale, which is the newest trend. This drug has traditionally been injected directly into veins of users.	Young, white affluent users inhale. Inner city poor inject.	$5–25 per 2/10 gram bag.
Cocaine	Crack users are beginning to make their own supplies, thus reducing street dealing. Use seems to be declining in some areas—users are switching to other drugs.	Minority populations primarily use crack. Whites in their 20s and 30s use powdered cocaine, called HCI.	Crack—$5–10 per bag or vial. HCI—$60–100.
Marijuana	Availability is high in all areas. Use seems to be increasing. This is the most commonly used drug in the United States.	Use cross-cuts all racial, gender, and age boundaries in all parts of the country. Highest use is people under 20.	Joints and small bags sell for about $10. Ounce costs $90–100.
EMERGING DRUGS			
Methamphetamine	This is called "workingman's cocaine." It is less adulterated than cocaine and the effects last longer. Supplies come from Mexico and Canada.	Increase in use is highest in white working-class users.	$60–80/gram.
Rohypnol	Also called "flunitrazapam." It is benzodiazepine, produced by the Hoffman-LaRoche company for treatment of sleep disorders. Sedative effects are increased with alcohol consumption.	Primary users are young adults, especially on college campuses. Long-term use leads to dependence.	Cost not reported.

SOURCE: Executive Office of the President, Office of National Drug Control Policy, Lee P. Brown, Director (Summer 1995), "Pulse Check: National Trends in Drug Abuse." Rockville, MD: Drugs and Crime Clearinghouse.

As a group, drug offenders are generally young, have low socioeconomic status, and are disproportionately black. Although women of all ethnic and racial groups are rare offenders by comparison to men (6 percent of the prison population is women), women who are incarcerated for drug offenses are most often African American.[17]

Societal Trends and Sale of Drugs

Increased selling of illicit drugs and, to a lesser extent, the sale of other vices in inner-city neighborhoods is traceable to several societal trends in recent years. First, the gap between rich and poor has been increasing since about 1980.[18] Poverty motivates many non-users to sell illegal drugs to supplement inadequate resources.[19] Second, the national trend among American manufacturers to move manufacturing to developing countries has reduced the number of legitimate occupations for many working- and lower-class people.[20] Selling illegal drugs provides income in the absence of legitimate work opportunities. Third, the income generated from illegal drugs is generally much higher than that for other occupations in the service economy (fast-food restaurant employees, store clerks, cleaners), which have largely replaced manufacturing jobs of prior generations. Fourth, pockets of ghetto poverty have increased since 1980, substantially decreasing opportunities for minority youth in particular, as urban schools, housing, recreational facilities, businesses, and community organizations have deteriorated significantly.[21] Both the use and sale of illegal drugs have lessened the pain of poverty in such conditions. Commonly used illicit drugs are described in Table 8.3.

Victims

Identifying victims of public order crimes is more problematic than for other offense categories. The problem, as noted earlier, is that some of the crimes are committed by the offender alone, or in intimacy with another person who is a willing participant; and the absence of a complainant makes detection unlikely. Offenders of these crimes may have committed acts prohibited by law, but generally there is no direct harm. Victims are often defined loosely in the law as "society," or "community moral standards," or "the people."

These crimes actually represent socially reprehensible behavior that is only criminal if the gambling opportunity, for example, is illegal. Other people may be hurt by the offender's behavior (the family of a person who loses a paycheck through illegal gambling) but the harm done is indirect. Irresponsibility, lack of restraint, and bad judgment are character flaws that could apply to people who gamble legally. The families of people who gamble illegally are not victims of crime, but emotional or economic victims of irresponsibility. The family has no legal standing in a judgment against the offender. The crime is against the law that prohibits illegal gambling; it is not a crime against the gambler's family.

Victims are undefined with many public order crimes. Others, such as drunk driving, show clear potential of victimization. There were 16,589 alcohol-related motor vehicle accidents in 1994; these were 41 percent of all car crashes.[22] Drug offenses have also been linked conceptually with drunk driving as offenses where clear harm to others is probable. With illegal drug offenses, however, there are many misunderstandings of the harm done to victims.

Drug Crime and Victimization

People addicted to drugs often commit other crimes to support their drug habits. The crimes are related to the expense of illegal drugs, which are inflated as the market availability fluctuates, or as risk in distribution increases. The high cost of illegal drugs prompts many addicts to support drug habits through crime.[23] Drug use is rarely associated with causes of crime in the traditional sense; in other words, "drug-crazed addicts" do not attack people, as popular folklore sometimes implies. Rather, the crimes associated with drug use are influenced more by the costs of illegal substances and the lack of resources available to the addict. The legal drug, alcohol, has been causally associated with a wide variety of predatory crimes such as rape, murder, assault, and domestic battery.[24] Alcohol causes more crime than illegal drugs, but drugs are associated with more secondary crime caused by the high costs of supporting addiction. Many proponents of the legalization of drugs have pointed out that decriminalization would bring the costs in line with other legal drugs, such as tobacco and alcohol, thus reducing the secondary crimes committed to support expensive addictions.[25] Opponents counter that legalization would make addiction more common.

A second misunderstanding of victims of drug use relates to dangers of use. There are, of course, serious health consequences to illicit drug use, but many researchers believe the dangers have been exaggerated as federal funding of several drug wars has increased. Many more people become addicted to the legal drug, nicotine, each year than all of the illegal drugs combined. There are more deaths related to alcohol and tobacco consumption annually than all of the illegal drugs in a given year. There are, annually, about 7500 deaths from all illegal drugs combined.[26] Most of these deaths result from the use of adulterated drugs produced through clandestine operations that are not subject to regulation or certification, rather than from use or misuse of the drugs themselves.[27] There are about 400,000 tobacco-related deaths each year.[28]

Corruption and Drug Crime

One frequently noted "victim" of the drug war is democratic process and respect for law. Drug laws are inherently difficult to enforce because the illegal networks for manufacture, import, sale, and distribution are intricate and highly lucrative. Enormous profits are available for entrepreneurs in the drug trade and for organized crime. Temptations to take bribes, join in the trafficking, or otherwise profit from the network of distribution foster considerable corruption. Piers Beirne and James Messerschmidt report that police corruption is rampant in the drug trade. They describe, for example, cases in rural Georgia where sheriffs have accepted bribes of $50,000 to allow drug smugglers to land planes in their counties. In another case cited, a member of the Justice Department's Organized Crime Strike Force provided drug dealers with the names of government informants in return for $210,000. An FBI agent accumulated $850,000 in money and real estate for curtailing cocaine sales by drug dealers, but he sold cocaine himself. In another case, a customs agent was paid $50,000 per car load of marijuana that he allowed to pass into the United States from Mexico without inspection.[29]

Corruption has been so lucrative for participants that some jurisdictions offer rewards of property and money seized from drug dealers to law-enforcement agents as an incentive to maintain their allegiance to the legal side of the drug war. Helper, Utah, for example, provides police officers with a cut of the cash or property they seize in drug cases. Critics charge that financial payoffs to agents and officers from government sources will lead to just as much corruption and abuse of power as illegal drug sales themselves.[30]

The most notorious corruption of democratic process has been the use of the Central Intelligence Agency (CIA) in drug trafficking. The CIA has fostered money-laundering campaigns for drug syndicates in the Caribbean, Laos (during the Vietnam war), Australia, Mexico, and Panama. Several of the world's largest opium merchants have been on the CIA's payroll, and the CIA has conspired with organized crime in many drug schemes with political outcomes.[31]

Drug offenses involve clear harm to victims, but often the damage is not as would be expected; that is, the harm is not to the user who becomes hopelessly addicted through the efforts of unscrupulous "pushers" hawking drugs on street corners or in schoolyards, as popular myth implies. Of the 20 million cocaine users, for example, about 3 percent are problem cocaine abusers.[32] Victims of AIDS who contract the disease through sharing drug needles are of more concern; about one-quarter of AIDS victims contract the disease through some activity connected with the use of illicit drugs.[33] The true victims of illicit drug crimes are the American taxpayers, who must support the expansion of the criminal justice apparatus to accommodate increased incarceration for offenders, and American democracy, which has been abused through corruption in the war on drugs (Box 8.1).

Drug Trafficking From Colombia

Colombia ranks behind Peru and Bolivia as the world's third largest producer of coca, the parent plant of cocaine. Much of the coca grown in Peru and Bolivia, however, is transported to Colombia for processing in conversion laboratories. Colombia-based international drug trafficking organizations export more cocaine to the United States and Europe than any other country in the world. In recent years, Colombian drug organizations have increased their involvement in the cultivation of opium poppies for heroin production, and Colombia is an important supplier of marijuana.

Cocaine. The most important drug trafficking organizations in Colombia are the Cali and Medellin drug mafias, although there are numerous smaller organizations. Together, these drug organizations supply most of the cocaine consumed worldwide. Traffickers use private aircraft to drop bales of cocaine in the waters off the Bahamas, Puerto Rico, and other Caribbean islands for retrieval by boat, and on clandestine airstrips throughout Central America and Mexico. Most cocaine is smuggled into the United States by boat. The most common ports of entry into the United States are Houston, Los Angeles, New York City, and Miami. In western Europe the cocaine enters through Amsterdam, Barcelona, and Hamburg.

Heroin. Colombian drug traffickers have only recently become important suppliers of heroin. American demand for heroin is increasing, which has fostered increased cultivation of opium poppies in Colombia. The country has a good climate for cultivation of opium poppies. The crop matures in 90 to 140 days and it is possible for growers to harvest three crops per year. Current supplies of heroin exported from Colombia are low by comparison to other world sources, but crop cultivation is on the increase. Most heroin from Colombia arrives in the United States on commercial airlines. Couriers conceal the processed heroin in personal items such as shoes, luggage, and clothing. The most common method of concealment is ingestion of small amounts in balloons for later retrieval.

Marijuana. Cannabis, the parent plant of marijuana, had been widely cultivated in Colombia prior to the 1990s, but some of the crop has been replaced by coca, which is more profitable. Recently, there has been a resurgence of interest in cannabis that has been fueled by high demand in the United States. During the 1980s, Colombia was the major supplier of marijuana in the United States but it slipped to second (behind Mexico) in the 1990s. Most marijuana is trafficked by independent organizations not affiliated with the Cali or Medellin drug cartels. Colombian marijuana is smuggled by boat through the Caribbean. Some is channeled through Mexico for transportation over the border. The United States is the primary consumer of Colombian marijuana, but some is exported to Europe.

SOURCE: U.S. Department of Justice Drug Enforcement Administration, "Colombia: Status in International Drug Trafficking." Current Issues SourceFile, 1995. Record: G078-1.

Pornography and Victimization

Among the other public order crimes in which ideas about the victim have been largely misunderstood is the pandering of pornography. Traditional views of the immoral use of pornography have highlighted the male consumers of pornographic materials as the victims. This view has focused upon male users of pornography who become "addicted" to sex, and in particular to pornographic depictions of sex. Some theorists believe that the women who participate in the making of pornography should be seen as victims of pornography. In addition, some women have become real-life victims of men who act out the fantasies inspired by pornographic depictions.

Whether the production, distribution, or **pandering** of pornography (solicitation of women or girls for production of pornography) is illegal depends upon "community standards" (whether the community tolerates the sale of explicit sexual materials), the age of the participants in the acts of sex depicted, whether the U.S. Postal Service is used to distribute certain types of pornography, and local zoning laws. The focus, in other words, is on regulation of degrees of distribution, not the legality of pornography itself. The U.S. Supreme Court ruled in *Miller v. California* (1973) that state laws banning pornography must define obscenity according to the standards in communities where obscenity trials take place.[34] The problem with this, according to Catherine MacKinnon, a widely known anti-pornography activist, is the relativity in the standard. If a community has a high tolerance for terrorist treatment of women, then such pornographic treatment is protected speech. MacKinnon calls for absolute, rather than relativistic, intolerance for any type of hate speech. This requires disengaging the concepts of morality and obscenity from pornography so that the human rights issues may be examined.[35] To do so would redefine the victims of pornography as women and children who experience sexualized assaults by male consumers of pornography.

This issue is far from settled. Current trends include restricting or controlling the sale of pornography to particular zoned areas. The Supreme Court ruled, in the case of *Young v. American Mini Theaters* (1976) that the state has a right to restrict the places where pornography may be viewed.[36] The heaviest control over the pornography industry is in the area of child pornography, or "kiddy porn." Exploitation of children to make this type of pornography, as well as the implicit encouragement of consumers of kiddy porn to exploit children sexually, has been judged to be damaging to children by the U.S. Supreme Court in *New York v. Ferber* (1982).[37] In addition, the traditional "community standards" doctrine has been refined somewhat to include behavior that would be found to lack social value by a "reasonable person." In the case of *Pope v. Illinois* (1987), the U.S. Supreme Court still could not define obscenity, but allowed for reasonable judgments that reflect common standards of social value.[38] In many ways, resolution of the issue has not progressed much beyond Justice Potter Stewart's statement in 1964 regarding his definition of obscenity, when he said, "I know it when I see it."[39]

Historical Patterns of Regulation

Law and morality are linked in any society; law reflects moral standards. Laws against murder, for example, reflect underlying values about the worth of all people. Likewise, laws that prohibit stealing are a reflection of the values that protect the integrity of private ownership. Social order exists because there are discernible threads of a continuous moral fabric that unite all members of a society. There is consensus about the importance of most of the laws that govern social order. While there may be disagreements regarding particular issues of interpretation, enforcement, or punishment, general agreement about rules of social order pervade every society.

The problems associated with public order crimes arise, not from the morality that undergirds social order, but with the regulation of private morality. The purpose of such laws is to improve the private morality of individuals.[40] Laws that prohibit stealing or harm to others are clearly defensible for promotion of the common good. Laws prohibiting private consensual sexual behavior are not so easily defensible. It is the area of private behavior that has proven historically vexatious.

Prohibition

Efforts to enact legislation that would prohibit the availability of alcohol began in the early nineteenth century and fostered considerable interest in enforcing sobriety, or abstinence from alcohol, as a national standard. Most reformers were middle-class white women who saw "demon alcohol" as the downfall of the family, the ruin of men, a source of financial insecurity, and a symbol of degeneracy and moral decline. By the early twentieth century, progress was evident toward a constitutional amendment prohibiting the sale or use of alcohol. The Women's Christian Temperance Union (WCTU) and the Anti-Saloon

After a 6-year campaign by federal prosecutors, Mafia boss John Gotti was convicted of murder and racketeering in 1992.

from 13.3 per 100,000 in 1910 to 7.2 per 100,000 in 1930.[42] Yet most historians have deemed the period of Prohibition as a dismal failure.[43] When government began to intrude into the private lives of ordinary citizens through regulation of alcohol, many law-abiding citizens with deep commitment to the sanctity of government were disillusioned. Violations of the eighteenth amendment were widespread among ordinary Americans. In addition, an organized network of suppliers and distributors who worked outside of the law, and whose livelihood was dependent upon law violation, satisfied the market demand for the illegal products.

Organized crime had been a minor influence in most urban communities before Prohibition. Many urban immigrant groups used the network of organized crime as a vehicle for assimilation. Irish, Jewish, English, Australian, and Chinese street gangs protected illegal enterprises in urban neighborhoods as each wave of immigration brought a new group into the cities.[44] When Prohibition was enacted, Italians were the newest immigrant group to offer protection in urban neighborhoods, and Prohibition launched Italian Americans into organized crime like no previous group. The demand for alcohol was great, and networks of *bootleggers,* or illegal producers of alcohol, had to be connected with the distributors who supplied consumers. Profits from alcohol fostered the growth of organized crime in the 1920s. Without Prohibition, organized crime would probably have remained an insignificant crime element in urban neighborhoods. The advent of Prohibition, however, propelled loosely organized groups into national syndicated networks that delivered illegal goods and services for profit. The highly organized, tightly controlled networks of crime that developed out of Prohibition survived even after the repeal of the nineteenth amendment in 1933. When alcohol became legal again, organized crime simply switched to other highly demanded services that were legally prohibited.

Prostitution

Reformers in the early nineteenth century called for the elimination of prostitution, but little real action toward eradication was evident until the early part of the twentieth century. As with alcohol, prostitution was seen as a symbol of immoral forces that were perceived to be a threat to the family and a source of degeneracy in men. Prostitution was a fairly open and accessible occupation for women who found few economic opportunities outside the traditional family throughout the nineteenth and into the early twentieth centuries. Between 1900 and 1918, the moral evils of prostitution were elevated politically to the status of "internal domestic enemy," and reform campaigns similar to those waged against alcohol were launched against the red-light districts.[45] These de-

Most "red light" districts were closed in the United States by 1918. Other forms of prostitution, such as "streetwalkers," or prostitutes who sell sex on street corners, replaced the older forms of prostitution.

League were formidable political forces in the early twentieth century. The temperance movement, with its goal of improving morals and promoting industrious, reliable citizens, was a serious political force by 1913. Its advocates promoted law as the most potent force that could conscript people into moral reform.[41]

The eighteenth amendment to the Constitution was passed into law in 1919. This amendment, which was supported by the Volstead Act, made the manufacture, sale, or transportation of alcohol illegal. The law remained in effect for 14 years, until it was repealed in 1933.

During the period of Prohibition alcohol consumption did decline. Deaths from cirrhosis of the liver declined

scriptively named areas were specifically designated as places where houses of prostitution (brothels, whorehouses) were located. Most early efforts to clean up prostitution focused on regulation. Many cities required periodic health checks of prostitutes or regulated their trade to the red-light districts exclusively. The social purity crusades of the early twentieth century proposed that closing red-light districts would force prostitutes out of business and thereby eliminate the moral menace of prostitution.[46]

Laws regulating prostitution began to tighten by 1910, when the Mann Act prohibited the transportation of women across state lines for "immoral purposes."[47] In 1916, the American Social Hygiene Association published a list of 47 cities that had closed their red-light districts, and the campaign against vice districts became national.[48]

Closing the red-light districts was the supposed solution to prostitution because most people believed it could not flourish outside of specified places of business. By 1918, most vice districts throughout the country had been closed, but prostitution was not eradicated. Brothels and whorehouses, which offered relative safety for prostitutes, were illegal in most cities and were replaced by new types of prostitution, including *streetwalkers,* who sold sex on street corners, *call girls,* who sold sex by appointment, *b-girls* who sold sex from bars, and *massage parlors,* which were set up as fronts for prostitution. Thus relative safety and the open sale of sex was replaced by much riskier forms of prostitution as the profession was forced underground. Regulation and hygiene checks for disease nearly disappeared. Most important, the subversion of regulated forms of prostitution opened opportunities for illegal regulation by criminal entrepreneurs. After 1918, organized crime regulated the supply of prostitution for American consumers who could not buy sex openly. During the 1920s and 1930s, syndicated vice rings organized prostitution into highly lucrative businesses in most cities.[49]

Illegal Drugs

The use of recreational drugs has deep roots in many civilizations. The ancient Greeks, Persians, Hindus, Arabs, and Chinese all refer to marijuana use in their writings. The Incas used coca leaves as a stimulant for several centuries before Francisco Pizarro discovered their empire in 1531. And, drug use in the United States is traceable to the colonies *before* the American Revolution, and was known in several Native American tribes.[50]

The use of opium products, and later morphine, was common in nineteenth-century America. Opium was a typical ingredient in home remedies such as cough syrups, elixirs, or pain pills, also called *patent medicines.* Respectable middle-class people frequented "opium dens" to smoke opium or marijuana (primarily *hashish,* or the resin of marijuana) in urban areas in the late nineteenth cen-

tury. Extracts from the coca leaf (the parent plant of cocaine) were included in the original recipe of Coca-Cola. Sigmund Freud was a regular user of cocaine and promoted it as a treatment for fatigue, depression, and indigestion. In 1900, heroin was promoted as a cough suppressant and a treatment for lung diseases.[51]

Laws Regulating Drugs

By the turn of the twentieth century, concern over the number of people addicted to patent medicines began to creep into public discussion. Use of patent medicines to uplift mood and improve outlook were among the vices that came to be seen as morally ruinous in the early part of the twentieth century. With the 1906 publication of Upton Sinclair's *The Jungle,* which exposed the unsanitary conditions of meat packing industries, public attention was drawn to the necessity for regulating industries that produced, promoted, and sold food and medicines to American consumers. The Pure Food and Drug Act, which prohibited the interstate transportation of adulterated or mislabeled food or drugs, was passed in 1906. The new law required, among other things, that labels on medicine list the proportion of each ingredient in the preparation. Marketing of addictive drugs in patent medicines was problematic after the new legislation passed. While the medicines themselves were not outlawed, companies were required to reveal their ingredients. The new legislation had the added effect of discouraging consumers from purchasing the medicines because of a generalized moral judgment about the use of addictive narcotics.[52]

In 1914 a new law, the Harrison Act, was passed that required all people who imported, manufactured, produced, compounded, sold, or dispensed cocaine and opiate drugs to register with the Treasury Department and to keep records of the transactions. This was a recordkeeping and tax law that did not actually outlaw any substances, but aimed to restrict the prescription and administration of narcotics to the realm of physicians by imposing high taxes on all other distributors. However, the U.S. Supreme Court, in *Webb v. U.S.* (1919) and *U.S. v. Behrman* (1922), held that even physician prescription of narcotic drugs to addicts was no longer legal in the United States. As a result, narcotics use was pushed underground and an illegal network developed that marketed drugs to addicts.[53]

Through the 1920s and 1930s, the number of people addicted to narcotics began to decline significantly.[54] The Federal Bureau of Narcotics, which was the enforcement arm of the Treasury Department for narcotics control, was beginning to lose power in the advent of declining addiction and the underground status of narcotics use in the United States. But, beginning with the appointment of Harry J. Anslinger as head of the Bureau of Narcotics in 1930, a new menace was identified and publicized: marijuana.[55] This drug, which had actually been widely grown in herb gardens as a medicinal herb, for bird seed, and was also found as a roadside weed, redirected the earlier emphasis on narcotics addiction and fostered new ground for investigation, thus renewing the importance of the agency.

The Federal Bureau of Narcotics publicized the purported dangers of marijuana use and fostered general fear of a drug that was used by a relatively small number of people. Despite the fact that marijuana had been used for medicinal purposes for thousands of years, it was now described as a moral menace that would corrupt youth, cause urban decline, and lead directly or indirectly to suicides, venereal disease, rape, insanity, and mass murder.[56] The Marijuana Tax Act, passed in 1937, classified marijuana with narcotics. Deliveries of marijuana and narcotics were now taken over by organized crime.

Gambling

While there were some prohibitions against gambling in Colonial America, legalized gambling has been a fairly common American tradition for hundreds of years.[57] After the Civil War, some southern states used lotteries as a means of raising money for Reconstruction, although public opinion was negative and the lotteries were abandoned.[58] In the late nineteenth century, concern over the morality of gambling was expressed by various religious groups who believed that gambling was sinful. The basic aim of gambling, to get something for nothing, was offensive to some interpreters of Christianity who see material success as a reward for hard work and perseverance and not properly the result of chance.

Opposition to gambling in the early twentieth century came largely from churches, which portrayed participation in gambling activities as evidence of weak moral character. Ironically, churches have opposed gambling as immoral while depending upon raffles, bingo games, and other types of gambling for financial support. National campaigns against gambling have never drawn the attention commanded by alcohol, prostitution, and narcotics. Yet, gambling was intertwined with the supply of alcohol during Prohibition. Many illegal liquor establishments also provided opportunities for gambling. When Prohibition ended in 1933, organized crime took over the supply of large-scale illegal opportunities for gambling in most urban areas.

Abortion

Both contraception and abortion were legally available in the United States until the mid-nineteenth century. Various types of contraception, as well as abortion, have been practiced for thousands of years. Historically, women in all cultures have had primary responsibility for devising mechanisms to prevent or eliminate pregnancies; thus, women have led the social movements to legalize family planning methods. Men, by contrast, have been the primary proponents of laws regulating women's reproductive decisions.

By 1850, most methods of contraception, along with abortion, were illegal in the United States.[59] While this issue is often included in discussions of moral offenses, the decisions about restrictions of women's access to abortion and contraception have been political. Abortion was criminalized at the same time the medical profession began to professionalize.

Before formation of the American Medical Association (AMA) in 1848, the medical profession was a loosely organized, largely social group with few professional standards. As physicians began to upgrade their status, they eliminated competition through campaigns that discredited lay practitioners, who were providing services that overlapped those of the medical profession.[60] Among those targeted for elimination were midwives, who provided most abortion services (in addition to delivery of about half of all babies born in the United States as late as 1900).[61] When abortion was criminalized, it eliminated a portion of midwifery practice, which was instrumental in the elimination of traditional midwifery.

Some researchers have attributed other political motivations to the criminalization of abortion. Luker, for example, stresses that the use of midwives for abortion services was most common among middle- and upper-class white women in the first half of the nineteenth century.[62] But the Civil War, and the subsequent demise of slavery, as well as high immigration in the late nineteenth century, threatened the primacy of social position among middle- and upper-class white, native-born Americans. Criminalization of abortion and contraception thus forced increased childbearing among those women who had most frequently attempted to limit family size with the help of midwives. Contraception was partly legalized (according to state law, and exclusively for married couples) in most states in the 1920s and 1930s, but abortion was not legalized until 1973. While early motivations for criminalization may have been political, current controversy centers around issues of morality. Contemporary social movements to re-criminalize abortion generally focus upon moral and religious beliefs about when a life becomes truly human.

Pornography

Controversy over pornography is more recent than any of the previously discussed public order crimes. Displays of nudity, either in art form (erotica) or in real life (public indecency), have been regulated throughout U.S. history, but they had been a rather minor social concern until the latter half of the twentieth century. The first federal law prohibiting the importation of indecent and obscene prints, paintings, lithographs, and transparencies was the Tariff Act of 1842.[63] Obscene literature was barred from the mails in 1865, and the purity crusades of the early 1900s highlighted the evils of obscenity, along with drugs, alcohol, gambling, and prostitution.[64]

It was not until after modern printing, film, and other visual technologies made mass production possible that the issue of pornography became a significant social concern, however. With the publication of the first issue of *Playboy* magazine in 1950, concern over mass marketing of sexually explicit materials became a controversial issue.[65] Opponents were primarily religious or moralist organizations who found offensive the issues of explicit sexuality in commercially available magazines. They believed pornography was about sex and sex outside marriage was evil; therefore, pornography was evil.[66]

Modern feminist opposition to pornography was first articulated by Kate Millet in her book *Sexual Politics,* which was published in 1969.[67] In her book, Millet articulated issues of male dominance, female subjugation, and objectification of women as inherent to pornography. According to Millet's analysis, expressions of male hostility toward women had been sexualized by pornography and had become increasingly more sadistic as women began to enter occupations and opportunities traditionally reserved for men. As other authors focused upon the political implications of the anti-woman component of modern pornography, a feminist critique emerged in the 1970s.[68] With the release in 1975 of the film *Snuff* (a pornographic film that showed the sexual assault, murder, and dismemberment of a woman), feminists began to draw parallels between the rising rates of real-life violence against women and increasingly realistic and sadistic portrayals of sexualized violence against women.

Feminist authors claimed that women's rejection of male control and male domination was the root cause of increased fantasy violence against women in pornography. Men who felt displaced by women's increased independence were creating images of hatred, contempt, exploitation, and terrorism to reassert fantasy control over women. According to many observers, these fantasy displays inspire real-life violence.[69]

Presidential Commissions on Pornography

Two presidential commissions have been convened to determine the extent of social harm caused by pornography. The first commission, which released *The Report of the Commission on Obscenity and Pornography* in 1970, concluded that control of pornography represented unwarranted interference from government into the private lives of citizens.[70] They said that pornography was at worst "harmless," and at best a "means of increasing

marital openness."[71] Criticism of the report was so widespread that the commission was reconvened in 1985 and published a second report in 1986. The second report published conclusions directly opposite those of the 1970 report. It said that violent pornography was directly linked to increased violence against women, rising rates of rape, sexual exploitation of children, and domestic battery.[72]

The discrepancies between the two reports are largely attributable to the different methods used by the two commissions. The first commission did not review violent ("hard core") pornography because it considered such materials too obscene to be commonly viewed. Their primary method of study was the use of attitude surveys in which they asked people's opinions about pornography. The second commission actually examined pornographic materials and reviewed the academic literature and experimental studies on the effects of exposure to anti-social stimuli on human behavior. Their findings were that violent pornography increases real-life violence against women and children. They found a link between the imagery of rape, terror, violence, and degradation and an increase in sexual assaults against women and children. The commission called for a national campaign against pornography.[73]

The second commission has also been significantly criticized. The commission was stacked politically with people who had already indicated public opposition to pornography. Critics contend that members of the commission had made up their minds about the issues before the commission was even convened, which means they could not have produced an objective analysis. In addition, members of the commission employed coercive tactics to make their points, such as threatening convenience-store owners with public exposure of the fact that they sold "smut" if they did not voluntarily remove pornographic magazines from their shelves.[74] While the commission has been roundly criticized by many who fear the constitutional effects of any restrictions, many of the conclusions published in their report have been endorsed.[75]

Since publication of the 1986 findings, violent pornography has become increasingly more graphic. In addition, fantasy violence against women has become evident in rock music videos, popular rap music, computer games, and made-for-television movies. Sexualized violence against women is currently a common theme in mainstream entertainment media.[76] As the violent pornography and mainstream images of violence against women have become increasingly more graphic, so-called soft porn (sexually explicit materials that are generally not violent) has shown a decreasing tendency to degrade women or to include cartoons with violent images.[77] Such soft porn falls closer to the range of traditional erotica. Future issues and court cases will likely involve the electronic media and the use of electronic information systems to convey pornographic images or to solicit sex from on-line computer users.

The Arguments About Decriminalization

Public order crimes represent a wide variety of behaviors that cause varying degrees of social harm. They are not clearly delineated social wrongs for all people at all times. Many people favor decriminalizing some public order crimes, or recriminalizing others that have been legalized, such as abortion. The behaviors that fall into this category are widely divergent, yet uniformly connected to private decisions about morality. To say that all such behaviors should be criminal or that all should be legal is too simplistic for most people. These activities involve a wide variety of moral considerations that are often influenced by religious belief or by fears of social upheaval. Whether the government has the right or the responsibility to enforce laws prohibiting private behavior is a central issue in the debate over classifying these activities as crime.

Arguments to Decriminalize

Those people who favor decriminalization, or legalization, of all or some of the behaviors that fall within the realm of public order crimes contend that it is not the proper function of government to regulate morality. They argue that government should be concerned with the common good, or the activities of society as a whole, not with the individual private activities of citizens. The ineffectiveness of government in regulating morality demonstrates that laws do not deter people from committing these crimes; in fact, the ineffectiveness of law in stopping these behaviors actually encourages disdain for the law. With certain crimes, such as illegal drug offenses, the law-enforcement branch of government has colluded with criminal forces and corrupted the democratic process.

Not only are the laws ineffective but they are also unenforceable. The volume of illegal behavior that falls under the category of public order crimes is so great that true enforcement would require a police state to address the behaviors completely. Public support for extension of the criminal justice system into such complete control of the private lives of ordinary citizens is lacking and the financial commitment to accomplish such an aim would drain national resources. Current attempts to fine or jail some offenders do not deter the majority of people from engaging in these activities; and to increase police action to eradicate the activities would require a public expenditure that is not seen to be worth the effort. With the cur-

rent war on drugs we have already witnessed the most massive increase in criminal justice expenditures ever in the history of the human race, and we have not even scratched the surface of the problem. To direct added resources to other public order crimes without any evidence that past efforts have eradicated these behaviors is irresponsible, according to this perspective.

Proponents of legalization further argue that there is no evidence that removing the criminal status of these offenses will increase their occurrence. In countries that do not enforce drug prohibitions on a large scale, use is significantly lower than in the United States, and abuse is rare.[78] Drug use is already widespread and accessible to anyone who wants to participate. The example of Prohibition should have taught us that attempts to regulate private morality are doomed to failure. Organized crime flourishes because government tries to regulate private behavior. If government would stay out of the lives of private citizens, there would be no reason for organized crime to exist.

In addition, proponents of legalization believe that people should have a right to live as they want so long as they do not harm others (Box 8.2). This principle of individual freedom is one of the most fundamental ideals upon which this country was founded. To interfere with this principle is to alter the values upon which the Constitution is based.

Arguments for Maintaining Criminality

People who believe that public order crimes should not be legalized believe that the morality of individuals affects the viability of the nation, and therefore it is the proper function of government to legislate morality through law. Without laws prohibiting these offenses, the prevalence of the behaviors would cause the downfall of the nation. Law actually leads the morality of the people, rather than people leading the morality of law. If the United States is to be a strong nation, its laws must reflect strong moral character. Laws prohibiting public order crimes enforce standards that promote a strong national character.

If the laws do not serve as a deterrent to the behaviors they prohibit, the fault is not with the laws. Rather, the problem is that the laws are not uniformly and consistently enforced. If law enforcement strictly addressed these offenses, people would begin to curtail their behavior. Currently, people know that the likelihood of arrest, prosecution, or punishment for these offenses decreases with each step of the process. If we, as a nation, want to eradicate the behaviors prohibited by public order offenses, we should begin serious, consistent efforts to arrest, prosecute, and punish all offenders. Strict enforcement would serve as a current deterrent and ultimately reduce the need for future enforcement as Americans reform their behavior.

BOX 8.2

Is Marijuana Harmless?

For many years, proponents of legalization of marijuana have argued that it is a non-addictive substance with fewer harmful side effects than the legal drugs of alcohol and nicotine. Recent research published in the journal *Science* prompts some closer examination, however. Two studies have shown that the effects of marijuana on the human brain are similar to the effects produced by other highly addictive drugs, such as cocaine, heroin, alcohol, and nicotine. Researchers in these studies have concluded that marijuana produces brain reactions in the same way that the more potent drugs produce addiction.

One study, conducted in Spain, found that the symptoms of emotional stress triggered by withdrawal from mar-

ijuana are traced to the same brain chemical that causes anxiety produced by withdrawal from opium, alcohol, or cocaine. The other study, which was conducted in Italy, found that tetrahydrocannibinol (THC), which is the active chemical in marijuana that produces the "high," causes the same brain chemical reaction that leads to dependence on nicotine and heroin. The casual use of marijuana may not be as harmless as many people have assumed. Further research into brain chemical and biochemical reactions may verify dependence as an outcome of marijuana use, which has been assumed by many opponents to drug legalization.

SOURCE: *Chronicle of Higher Education Daily Report,* 27 June 1997, http://chronicle.com.

The argument that the laws are unenforceable is hollow. No law is fully enforceable, yet people generally agree that laws should remain in place. Murder and theft laws do no prevent all cases of murder and theft, but few people would advocate elimination of these laws. Rather than legalizing these behaviors, it is preferable to allocate more resources to enforcement. The problem is not with the laws, but with the application of the laws.

Those who favor maintaining the criminal status of public order offenses argue that elimination of these crimes or even modification of the laws would result in dramatic increases in the prohibited behaviors. If marijuana were legalized, for example, proponents of maintaining the criminal status of public order offenses believe that the use of marijuana would increase, which could lead to increased use of other recreational drugs, which would lead to moral decline. Abortion is a prime example of the problems inherent in legalization. Since 1973, when abortion was legalized, millions of women have terminated their pregnancies through abortion. People who hold this perspective believe that if this behavior was still illegal, women would have no access to abortion services.

According to people who believe that the criminal status of public order crimes is appropriate, the health and wealth of the nation is dependent upon the strength of its laws. To modify or eliminate criminal penalties for public order offenses will lead to moral decline, decadence, and the destruction of the nation. All public order offenses are violations of the principles of Christianity, which are the fundamental precepts upon which this nation was founded. Our Founders were Christians and the values rep-

resented by the U.S. Constitution reflect Christian moral principles. To eliminate the criminal penalties for these offenses is contrary to the intentions of our Founders.

Organized Crime

Organized crime in the United States involves intricately organized organizations that provide highly demanded commodities to Americans, while circumventing legitimate market structures and law. Organized crime has also been called the *syndicate,* the *confederation,* the *Mafia, La Cosa Nostra,* the *Black Hand,* or *The Mob.* All terms refer to organizations that supply Americans with commodities and services outside of the law, although many organized crime groups operate legal businesses that overlap with their illegal activities. Most Americans are familiar with the concept of organized crime and stereotype all syndicated crime operations as organized by the Mafia. This stereotype is somewhat misleading, although some syndicated crime operations have power and influence comparable to the stereotypes of the Mafia.[79]

Activities of Organized Crime

There are, actually, many varieties of organized crime. Very large, syndicated organizations run by crime "families" that oversee operations in entire regions of the country are the most commonly noted type of organized crime. There are, however, thousands of smaller, independently organized, crime groups in American cities.[80] During the

BOX 8.3

Danger in the Waste Industry

Organized crime is involved in many legitimate businesses. An overriding concern within these businesses is to monopolize the market and to cut out competitors. In the waste disposal business, consumers pay up to 50 percent higher rates for mob-run garbage disposal than for disposal not linked to organized crime. As indicated by the following examples, the influence of organized crime is not only expensive, it is highly dangerous.

- In 1993, two Long Island garbage haulers who gave information to investigators about organized crime in the waste disposal business were murdered. The Lucchese crime family was implicated.

- In New York City, the Gambino crime family and the Lucchese and Genovese families were linked to a scheme to sell contaminated waste oil as fuel oil for commercial and public buildings, schools, and hospitals. The front company, Noble Oil Co., collected used oil from service stations and industries in several states. Instead of treating it, they mixed it with other oil and sold it as new. The used oil contained heavy metals and pollutants.

- In 1993, the head of the Association of Trade Waste Removers of Greater New York was indicted on racketeering charges. Prosecutors charged that he was a captain in the Gambino family and that he used force and threats to divide up waste collection routes.

- In 1995, 17 individuals and 26 companies in the New York City area, including the best-known private waste haulers, were indicted for criminal conspiracy. Ties between waste haulers and organized crime are not limited to the United States. Many nations report similar connections.

- In 1995 a senior officer from the Moscow police said that 50 tons of radioactive sludge stored in rusty, leaky barrels had been found in a factory outside of Moscow. Some of the barrels carried a label that indicated they had originated from an American recycling firm and that the contents were radioactive and carcinogenic. Organized crime was believed to be involved in the transportation and storage of the waste.

- The "garbage mafia" was involved in the dumping of over 400 tons of old pesticide and industrial waste in and around Sibiu, Romania in 1993.

- Thousands of barrels of toxic waste were transported from Italy to Lebanon during the 1980s. The "toxic waste mafia" were implicated in the illegal disposal.

- Italy has a serious problem with illegal disposal of toxic waste, particularly around Naples. Mafia-linked businessmen have been arrested, and several large waste disposal companies with links to the camorra (the Neapolitan mafia) have been linked to the crimes. According to government officials, half of the industrial waste produced in Italy each year is disposed of illegally by organized crime groups.

SOURCE: Internet: http//: www.css.com. Original sources: *New York Times,* 16 September 1995; 13 April, 7 October 1993; 28 May 1993; *Reuter Literary Report,* 4 April 1993; *Reuters,* 19 June 1995; *IL MONDO,* 26 April 1993, P71.

1980s, many urban street gangs began to syndicate their activities and offer the services of organized crime. Such groups often specialize—with one group operating gambling operations, another running prostitution through dating services, and another supplying drugs to street dealers, for example.[81] Coexistence among groups that provide wide varieties of differing services is common in large urban areas.

A high proportion of the business of organized crime is providing Americans with access to the vices described as public order crimes in this chapter. They are, however, also heavily involved in labor unions, politics, Wall Street financial institutions, and many legitimate businesses such as restaurants, race horses, food industries, waste disposal, transportation, and the garment industry—to name just a few of their business interests (Box 8.3). Criminal enterprises of organized crime take in an annual income of about $100 billion, with a loss in tax dollars of about $6.5 billion.[82] This is a conservative estimate of only the criminal activities of organized crime; covert connections to legitimate businesses make true estimates of income impossible. The criminal activities of organized crime are run like any other business except that they deal in illegal products or services. They sell their products or services to consumers for profit, as do legitimate businesses.[83] Organized crime employs attorneys, accountants, managers, clerical staff, and other personnel, just as would be found in any highly organized business. The business is hierarchically organized with chief executives, mid-level managers, and lower-level employees. The work of organized crime is secretive by nature, and includes access to profound wealth, power, and influence. And, or course, the income is tax-free.

Organized crime activities may resemble legitimate businesses in many ways, but the tactics employed to achieve business goals are conspiratorial and coercive.

Moreover, crime syndicates are likely to use physical intimidation, violence, and corruption to further their interests. Economic gain through monopoly is the ultimate business goal of organized crime.[84] Crime syndicates have taken over supplying most of the prohibited vices in the United States since the Volstead Act ushered in Prohibition in 1919. While some gambling, prostitution, drug, or other vice opportunities are provided by private entrepreneurs, most of these activities are coordinated through organized crime, which reaps huge profits from the illegal status of these activities.[85]

Gambling

For many years, gambling was the most lucrative division of organized crime, but, as states began to legalize many types of gambling in the 1970s, emphasis was redirected to the import and sale of drugs.[86] Still, gambling is an important illegal enterprise for organized crime. Typical gambling operations include numbers games. In these games, an individual chooses an arbitrary number, such as a birthdate, and places a bet with a **bookie** (numbers agent) who works for the crime syndicate. The bet is that the number will appear in the next state lottery drawing, or in the number of bets placed at a race track on a specific day, or in the Dow Jones total for a certain day, or some other arbitrary posting of numbers. Bets are very small, usually 50 cents to two dollars, and the odds are high, but the payoff is exceptionally lucrative if the bettor wins.

Other enterprises include illegal casinos, traveling card or dice games, illegal bets on racing or sports events, or high-stakes wagering in legitimate gambling houses that exceeds house limits. Illegal gambling is often identical to legal gambling, except for the reports of winnings and the organization of the gambling enterprise.

Prostitution

Syndicated crime regulates all types of prostitution except the streetwalker—the prostitute who sells sex from street corners. Prostitution rings are run undercover through bars, massage parlors, computer-selected dating services, magazine advertisements, call-girl or dating services, photo studios, and secretarial services. The benefits for prostitutes affiliated with such services are protection from police attention and screening of clients. For clients, the dangers of extortion and intimidation accompany the usual problems of exposure to disease that are inherent in sexual encounters with individuals who have had multiple sex partners.[87]

Drug Trafficking

Currently, the highest income for organized crime is derived from the drug trade. Americans spend over $49 billion on illegal drugs annually, which implies high profits for the main supplier—organized crime.[88] The trafficking of illegal drugs is managed like any other import and distribution business. While organized crime has been loosely involved in the drug trade for several decades, serious involvement is a relatively recent phenomena. Profits from drug sales are enormous. Because of the inherent secrecy of their activities, evidence of the influence of organized crime over the international drug cartels is sketchy, but experts believe their involvement is substantial. Increased risk of prosecution under current drug war policies may be an inducement for a shift to other activities, however. Counterfeiting of credit cards, transportation tickets, or computer software, and banking fraud are "safer" activities.[89]

Organized Crime: Myth or Reality?

There are several theorists who do not believe that organized crime exists as a highly interconnected, bureaucratic organization with national and international contacts, as popular folklore holds. Dwight Smith and Joseph Albini, for example, independently concluded over two decades ago that much of what Americans, including law enforcement and government officials, believe about organized crime is a myth.[90] Both conceded that there are crime organizations, but believed these are loosely organized systems of patronage and reciprocity, rather than highly integrated bureaucracies. In such loose organizations, people with "contacts" do favors for others, who return favors at a future date. The interconnections develop because of friendships, contacts, and criminal opportunities, rather than allegiance to a higher crime organization. More recently, sociologist Allan Block argued in 1983 that organizations that do exist are loosely organized groups that mirror the wider American social structure.[91] Philip Jenkins and Gary Potter found almost no evidence of a strong Mafia hold on the crime organizations of Philadelphia in their study published in 1987.[92]

Others, such as sociologist Donald R. Cressey, who served as a consultant to the President's Commission on Law Enforcement and Administration of Justice in 1966, found the evidence overwhelming for organized crime. Cressey, who was initially skeptical of the existence of such highly organized crime syndicates, concluded that there were at that time at least 24 "families," tightly knit organizations with strong ethnic ties, that coordinated national crime syndicates.[93] Much of the evidence supporting national conspiracy theories, however, has come from informants who testified before government commissions regarding their knowledge and activities in organized crime activities. These testimonies, combined with court records and a few field studies, have comprised the bulk of evidence supporting the large conspiratorial crime bureaucracy theories.[94]

Most cocaine is smuggled into the United States by boat. Traffickers drop bales from an airplane and they are retrieved by boat for delivery into the United States.

Government Commissions on Organized Crime

The first governmental commission, the Senate Special Committee to Investigate Organized Crime in Interstate Commerce, also called the Kefauver Committee in honor of the chair of the committee, was convened in 1950. This committee found that national crime cartels cooperated in joint crime activities. They reported political bribery, murder of enemies, and international connections to be the nucleus of a highly powerful crime organization known as the Mafia.[95] In 1963, a second committee, the McClellan Committee, or the Senate Subcommittee on Investigations, found organized crime to be heavily involved in labor union racketeering. The principle witness before the hearings, a low-level member of a New York crime family, Joseph Valachi, disclosed information about nationally syndicated crime networks and narcotics trafficking. This testimony, combined with electronic surveillance of gangster activities, and the 1967 *Report of the President's Commission on Law Enforcement and Administration*

of Justice, which included further disclosures and testimony, convinced the government and most Americans that a highly organized, powerful network does exist.[96]

Prosecution of Organized Crime

Several important cases prosecuted under the Racketeer Influence and Corrupt Organization Act of 1970 (RICO) have illustrated the far-reaching power of organized crime. Information gained through prosecution under RICO of preeminent crime families (such as the Lucchese, Genovese, and Bonnano families in New York in 1985) has further verified the government version of organized crime and crime conspiracies. Under RICO, a person convicted of racketeering is subject to 20 years in prison, a $25,000 fine, and profits from the illegal business enterprise are forfeited to the U.S. government. Further penalties of forfeiture are included in the Comprehensive Drug Prevention and Control Act of 1970, the Comprehensive Crime Control Act of 1984, the Money Laundering Act of

Chinese Organized Crime

Chinese crime groups are global in organization and they are widely diversified in their crime activities. Some global crime activity is limited to a single product, such as narcotics trafficking, but Chinese groups provide a wide range of services. The most commonly identified activities of Chinese transnational organized crime are:

- Drug production—primarily the smuggling and distribution of heroin and methamphetamine. Estimated annual earnings are over $200 billion.
- Alien smuggling—usually to the United States, but also to Japan and Europe. Estimated annually earnings over $3.2 billion.
- Weapons smuggling—distribution from Russian and Chinese military stores and Burmese narco insurgents to Southeast Asia, Japan, North and South America. Estimated annual earnings over $3 billion.
- Theft and smuggling of consumer goods—luxury cars, yachts, and consumer goods from United States, Europe, and Hong Kong are diverted into China. Estimated annual earnings over $10 billion.
- Counterfeiting—currency, credit cards, access devices, trade marked goods, and documents are produced for sale in United States and Europe. Annual earnings estimated at $100 billion; $200 billion losses in intellectual property rights.
- Theft of high-technology items—advanced computer chips, chip manufacturing equipment, industrial

processes, and technology are stolen from North America and Europe to be used and copied in China, Taiwan, Hong Kong, Thailand, and Malaysia. No cost estimates available.

- Illegal manipulation of commodities and stock markets—principally Southeast Asian and Chinese markets. Annual estimated earnings of $2 billion but growing rapidly.
- Smuggling, piracy, and theft of agricultural commodities (agri-crime)—sugar, rice, wheat, and corn are stolen from world markets and diverted to China and the Philippines. Annual earnings estimated at $2 billion and growing.

Chinese crime groups are not coordinated from single hierarchical structures, as is the case in Russia and (often) in the United States. Chinese groups are transitory, decentralized, and highly specialized. Legitimate entrepreneurs are often involved in Chinese organized crime activities that are present in all countries in the world. People who run legitimate business often derive substantial additional income from crime activities coordinated by Chinese crime specialists. Chinese organized crime is an emerging trend and one that will have a substantial impact on global markets.

SOURCE: Willard H. Myers, "Statement on Current Trends in Transnational Chinese Enterprise Crime." Testimony presented to the Subcommittee on Crime of the House Committee on the Judiciary, 104th Congress, Second Session, Washington, DC, January 25, 1996.

1986, and the Anti-Drug Abuse Act of 1986.[97] In 1991, U.S. attorneys handled 3055 cases of racketeering and extortion (compared to 1631 in 1982).[98]

Whether increased prosecution of organized crime under RICO and other racketeering laws will have any affect on the power of the syndicates is doubtful. They exist because they supply Americans with services and commodities that are highly demanded but not available through other means. As long as the demand is high and the economic rewards are sufficient to balance the risks, criminal entrepreneurs will continue to provide these services (Box 8.4).

Summary

With all of the public order crimes discussed in this chapter, underlying issues of morality are at the core of the legal prohibitions of the behaviors. The crucial question for

each of these crimes is whether the government should prohibit the behaviors, or whether the decisions should be private and protected. Some decisions to engage is self-destructive behaviors are left to the individual, such as those involving tobacco or alcohol, but others are regulated by government. Critics contend that the government should not have the right to decide which moral activities are legal and which are not. Morality changes over time and it is not the role of government to legislate the private consensual behavior of individual citizens.

Others contend that the central role of government should be to legislate right and wrong for the good of the nation. Personal decadence would be ruinous for the nation if government did not prevent people from engaging in immoral activities through the sanctions of law. Others point out that the allure of these activities is their illegal status. If we were to legalize the behaviors, they would be less enticing. For example, alcohol abuse among teenage drinkers is higher in the United States than in countries that do not legislate a legal age for alcohol consumption because in the United States it is a forbidden commodity that symbolizes adulthood. Without the allure of a forbidden activity, initiation to drinking would be gradual, as a normal part of growing up. This pattern is typical in European countries.

Similar arguments could be made for any of the vices described in this chapter. People tend to see them either as so reprehensible that they should be forbidden by government, or as relatively harmless activities that have been blown out of proportion to their actual danger by the attention of the criminal justice apparatus. Regardless of personal views on these crimes, the fact remains that prohibitions of these behaviors are the major force behind a wide variety of related criminal activities. Police corruption and political abuse of power are closely tied to the relative unenforceability of these crimes. The enormous profits to be made through supply of these goods and services to American consumers fuels the fires of organized crime. The activities are exceptionally common, often expensive because they are illegal, and subject to no quality controls or regulations, which increases consumer risk of disease or danger, especially with illicit drug use or prostitution.

Guilt over involvement in these crimes is often mediated by private moral values that override the issues of law. Illegal gambling may be justified in the eyes of the gambler by knowledge that state lotteries offer gambling opportunities that are only slightly variant from the illegal opportunities. Men who seek sex from prostitutes may rationalize their behavior in terms of personal choices about private matters. Guilt is most likely to involve emotional responses from friends or relatives if the crimes become known, rather than serious remorse for law violation. Participants in public order crimes know that their behavior is illegal, but rationalize their rights or desires on a number of levels that either mediate feelings of guilt or disavow any real wrongdoing.

As long as Americans continue to demand access to these activities, the supply will abound. Legal prohibitions have done little to eradicate any of these vices since Prohibition. It is possible that government enforcement through the crime control efforts enacted into law over the last 25 years will begin to curb the behaviors in question, but such an outcome is not likely. Many of the activities associated with public order crimes are thousands of years old. Law or increases in law enforcement will probably not eradicate these offenses.

Critical Thinking Questions

1. Do you favor the legalization of moral crimes? Why, or why not? Are there some that should be legalized but others that should not? Why, or why not?

2. Should the "war on drugs" attack the problem from the source or the demand side of drugs? That is, should drug enforcement be targeted at the supply of drugs or consumer demand for illegal drugs?

3. What effect do you think legalization of vice crimes would have on organized crime? Would they go out of business or just find other activities?

4. Should more law enforcement resources be directed into the enforcement of victimless crimes? Why, or why not?

Suggested Readings

Jay Albanese, *Organized Crime in America,* 2nd ed. (Cincinnati: Anderson, 1989).

Joseph R. Gusfield, *Symbolic Crusade: Status Politics and the American Temperance Movement* (Chicago: University of Illinois Press, 1963).

James A. Inciardi, *The War On Drugs II: The Continuing Epic of Heroin, Cocaine, Crack, Crime, AIDS, and Public Policy* (Mountain View CA: Mayfield, 1992).

Kristin Luker, *Abortion and the Politics of Motherhood* (Berkeley: University of California, 1984).

Ruth Rosen, *The Lost Sisterhood: Prostitution in America, 1900–1918* (Baltimore: Johns Hopkins University Press, 1982).

Samuel Walker, *Sense and Nonsense About Crime and Drugs: A Policy Guide,* 3rd ed. (Belmont CA: Wadsworth, 1994).

Notes

[1] Grolier, Inc., *The New Grolier Multimedia Encyclopedia* (Cupertino, CA: Apple Computer, Inc., 1993).

[2] Neil Milbert, "Gambling Network to Bring Winner Home," *Chicago Tribune,* 5 October 1994, 4-1.

[3] Ibid.; Samuel Walker, *Sense and Nonsense About Crime and Drugs: A Policy Guide,* 3rd ed. (Belmont, California: Wadsworth, 1994).

[4] Ibid, 265.

[5] Ibid.

[6] Jennifer James, "The Prostitute as Victim," in *The Criminal Justice System and Women: Women Offenders, Victims, Workers,* ed. Barbara Raffel Price and Natalie J. Sokoloff (New York: Clark Boardman, 1982) 291–315.

[7] Claire M. Renzetti and Daniel J. Curran, *Women, Men and Society,* 3rd ed. (Boston: Allyn & Bacon, 1995) 189.

[8] Ibid., 188–92.

[9] Ibid.

[10] James, "The Prostitute as Victim," 291–315.

[11] Samuel Walker, *Sense and Nonsense About Crime and Drugs: A Policy Guide,* 3rd ed., 254.

[12] Ibid., 254–55.

[13] Marc Mauer and Tracy Huling, "Young Black Americans and the Criminal Justice System: Five Years Later," *Sentencing Project.* Current Issues SourceFile, Record, 1995: R019-6; *Chicago Tribune,* "The Elusive Logic of Drug Sentences," 30 March 1995, 1–12. See also: Alfred Blumstein, "Racial Disproportionality of U.S. Prison Populations Revisited," *University of Colorado Law Review* (1993): Vol. 64.

[14] Charles H. McCaghy and Stephen A. Cernkovich, *Crime in American Society* (New York: Macmillan, 1987) 436.

[15] Victor E. Kappeler, Mark Blumberg, and Gary W. Potter, *The Mythology of Crime and Criminal Justice* (Prospect Heights, IL: Waveland, 1993) 159–60.

[16] Allen J. Beck and Darrell K. Gilliard, "Prisoners in 1994," *Bureau of Justice Statistics Bulletin* (U.S. Washington DC: U.S. Government Printing Office, 1995).

[17] Ibid.

[18] John Hagan, *Crime and Disrepute* (Thousand Oaks, CA: Pine Forge Press, 1994) 63.

[19] Ibid., 78.

[20] Ibid., 65–66.

[21] William Julius Wilson, "Studying Inner-City Social Dislocations: The Challenge of Public Agenda Research," *American Sociological Review 56* (1991): 1–14.

[22] Kathleen Maguire and Ann L. Pastore, *Sourcebook of Criminal Justice Statistics, 1995* (Washington DC: U.S. Government Printing Office, 1996) 303.

[23] Kappeler et al., *The Mythology of Crime and Criminal Justice,* 158.

[24] Ibid.

[25] Ibid.

[26] U.S. Department of Justice, "Drugs and Crime Facts, 1994," Office Of Justice Programs (Washington DC: U.S. Government Printing Office, 1995) 31.

[27] Kappeler et al., *The Mythology of Crime and Criminal Justice,* 154–55.

[28] Ibid.

[29] Piers Beirne and James Messerschmidt, *Criminology* (New York: Harcourt Brace Jovanovich, 1991), as cited in Kappeler et al., 163.

[30] Associated Press, "Utah Cops to get a Cut of Property From Drug Busts," 1 February 1995, cited from the *Chicago Tribune.*

[31] Kappeler et al., *The Mythology of Crime and Criminal Justice,* 164.

[32] Ibid., 155.

[33] Ibid.

[34] 413 U.S. 15, 1973.

[35] Catherine A. MacKinnon, "Pornography: Not a Moral Issue," in *Radical Voices: A Decade of Feminist Resistance from Women's Studies International Forum,* ed. Renate D. Klein and Deborah Lynn Steinberg (New York: Pergamon, 1989) 163.

[36] *Young v. American Mini Theaters,* 427 U.S. 50, 1976.

[37] *New York v. Ferber,* 50 L.W. 5077, 1982.

[38] *Pope v. Illinois,* 107 S.Ct. 1918, 1987.

[39] MacKinnon, "Pornography: Not a Moral Issue," 146.

[40] Joseph R. Gusfield, *Symbolic Crusade: Status Politics and the American Temperance Movement* (Chicago: University of Illinois Press, 1963).

[41] Ibid., 109.

[42] Walker, *Sense and Nonsense About Crime and Drugs: A Policy Guide,* 3rd ed., 263.

[43] See Gusfield, *Symbolic Crusade: Status Politics and the American Temperance Movement,* for example.

[44] Charles H. McCaghy and Stephen A. Cernkovich, *Crime in American Society,* 2nd ed. (New York: Macmillan, 1987) 272.

[45] Ruth Rosen, *The Lost Sisterhood: Prostitution in America, 1900–1918* (Baltimore: Johns Hopkins University Press, 1982) 1.

[46] Ibid., 15–17.

[47] Ibid., 19.

[48] Ibid., 30.

[49] Ibid., 33.

[50] James A. Inciardi, *The War On Drugs II: The Continuing Epic of Heroin, Cocaine, Crack, Crime, AIDS, and Public Policy* (Mountain View CA: Mayfield, 1992) 1–2.

[51] Ibid., 6–11.

[52] Ibid., 15.

[53] Ibid., 15–16.

[54] Ibid., 17.

[55] Ibid., 22; Howard S. Becker, *Outsiders: Studies in the Sociology of Deviance* (New York: Macmillan, 1963); Edwin M. Schur, "Drug Addiction in America and England," Commentary 30 (1960) 241–48.

[56] Becker, *Outsiders: Studies in the Sociology of Deviance,* 141–43; Inciardi, *The War On Drugs II: The Continuing Epic of Heroin, Cocaine, Crack, Crime, AIDS, and Public Policy,* 22–24.

[57] Virgil W. Peterson, "Obstacles to Enforcement of Gambling Law," *Annals of the American Academy of Political and Social Science* 269 (1950) 15.

[58] Ibid., 15.

[59] Renzetti and Curran, *Women, Men and Society,* 3rd ed., 193.

[60] Polly F. Radosh, "Midwives in the United States: Past and Present," *Population Research and Policy Review 5* (1986): 129–45.

[61] Ibid.

[62] Kristin Luker, *Abortion and the Politics of Motherhood* (Berkeley: University of California, 1984).

[63] Charles H. McCaghy and Stephen A. Cernkovich, *Crime in American Society,* 2d ed., 463.

[64] Ibid., 463–64.

[65] Barbara Ehrenreich, *The Hearts of Men: American Dreams and the Flight from Commitment* (Garden City, NY, 1983) 42.

[66] Irene Diamond, "Pornography and Repression: A Reconsideration," in *The Criminal Justice System and Women,* ed. Barbara Raffel Price and Natalie J. Sokoloff (New York: Clark Boardman, 1982), 335–51.

[67] Kate Millet, *Sexual Politics* (New York: Doubleday, 1969).

[68] Brownmiller, *Against Our Will: Men, Women and Rape* (New York: Simon & Schuster, 1975); Robin Morgan, *Going Too Far* (New York: Random House, 1977); Andrea Dworkin, *Woman Hating* (New York: Dutton, 1974).

[69] See Brownmiller, *Against Our Will: Men, Women and Rape;* Dworkin, *Woman Hating;* MacKinnon, "Pornography: Not a Moral Issue."

[70] McCaghy and Cernkovich, *Crime in American Society,* 2nd ed., 464.

[71] Diamond, "Pornography and Repression: A Reconsideration," 341.

[72] McCaghy and Cernkovich, *Crime in American Society,* 2nd ed., p. 465.

[73] Ibid.

[74] Beirne and Messerschmidt, *Criminology,* 159–61; McGaghy and Cernkovich, *Crime in American Society,* 2nd ed., 464.

[75] See MacKinnon, "Pornography: Not a Moral Issue," for discussion.

[76] For an excellent discussion of this topic, see Susan Faludi, *Backlash: The Undeclared War Against American Women* (New York: Anchor, 1991).

[77] Joseph Scott and Steven Cuvelier, "Violence in *Playboy* Magazine: A Longitudinal Analysis," *Archives of Sexual Behavior 16* (1987): 279–88.

[78] Stephen Chapman, "The Flip Side: There Is No 'Disaster' When the Sale and Prossession of Cannabis Is Sanctioned by the Law," *Chicago Tribune* (9 November 1995) 1–13.

[79] Denny F. Pace, *Concepts of Vice, Narcotics, and Organized Crime,* 3rd ed. (Englewood Cliffs, NJ: Prentice-Hall, 1991) 12–14.

[80] Ibid., 18.

[81] Ibid., 14.

[82] Ibid.; McCaghy and Cernkovich, *Crime in American Society,* 2nd ed., 280.

[83] Ibid., 21.

[84] Task Force on Organized Crime, *Organized Crime* (Washington, DC: U.S. Government Printing Office, 1976).

[85] Pace, *Concepts of Vice, Narcotics, and Organized Crime,* 3rd ed., 47.

[86] Ibid., 9.

[87] Pace, *Concepts of Vice, Narcotics, and Organized Crime,* 3rd ed., 74–90.

[88] William Rhodes, "What America's Users Spend on Illegal Drugs, 1988–1993: Executive Summary," (Washington, DC: U.S. Government Printing Office, 1995) 4.

[89] Jay Albanese, *Organized Crime in America,* 2nd ed. (Cincinnati: Anderson, 1989) 67–68.

[90] Dwight C. Smith, Jr., *The Mafia Mystique* (New York: Basic Books, 1975); Joseph L. Albini, *The American Mafia: Genesis of A Legend* (New York: Appleton-Century-Crofts, 1971).

[91] Alan Block, *East Side/West Side* (New Brunswick, NJ: Transaction Books, 1983).

[92] Philip Jenkins and Gary Potter, "The Politics and Mythology of Organized Crime: A Philadelphia Case Study," *Journal of Criminal Justice* 15 (1987) 473–84.

[93] Donald R. Cressey, *Theft of the Nation* (New York: Harper & Row, 1969).

[94] See, for example, Francis A.J. Ianni, *Black Mafia: Ethnic Succession in Organized Crime* (New York: Simon & Schuster, 1974).

[95] William Howard Moore, *The Kefauver Committee and the Politics of Crime: 1950–1952* (Columbia, MO: University of Missouri Press, 1974).

[96] The President's Commission on Law Enforcement and Administration of Justice, *Task Force Report: Organized Crime* (Washington DC: U.S. Government Printing Office, 1967) 6–8.

[97] Bureau of Justice Statistics, *Report to the Nation on Crime and Justice,* 2nd ed. (Washington DC: National Institute of Justice, 1988) 93.

[98] Maguire and Pastore, *Sourcebook of Criminal Justice Statistics, 1995,* 486.

part 4

Theories of Crime

IN CERTAIN RESPECTS, CHAPTERS 9 through 13 are the core chapters of the book. They examine the most prominent theoretical explanations of criminal behavior. These theories can be complex and complicated, especially for those who have never encountered them before, but they are invaluable because they offer tentative answers to why people commit crimes. This is the most essential question for criminologists to explore. Unfortunately, it is also the most difficult question to answer definitively.

At this time, there is no theory to explain all forms of crime. Instead, crime theorists have advanced an array of competing theories to explain criminal behavior. This section contains five chapters that present and critique distinctive theories. Some of these theories emphasize the individualistic basis of behavior—for example, biological drives, genetics, or psychological factors. Many other theories center attention on social forces. A person's neighborhood is an example of a social force that is limited in scope. Other social forces, like poverty, might apply to an entire society. In either case, the force or influence is social. Thus, the chapters in this section will present and critique individualistic (personal) and social explanations of criminal behavior.

A personal guide precedes the five theory chapters. This guide describes the ideal components of theories in general, and also foreshadows the organization of each of the theory chapters. A careful reading of this guide will give you a better appreciation and understanding of the theories to follow.

For updated information on theories of crime, consult the Wadsworth web site at http://www.wadsworth.com/cj.html

Your Personal Guide to Theory

Professors know that the word *theory* often raises the anxiety level of college students. Years ago, a sociology student told one of us "Theory is what dead people thought." That student was alluding to the fact that many major theories originated with people who lived long ago. Sociologists, for example, still use and debate the ideas of Emile Durkheim, Max Weber, and Karl Marx, the classic figures in the development of sociology. Durkheim, Weber, and Marx have all been dead for a long time, but they advanced complex and sophisticated explanations of society and social behavior that have endured because they were full of insight. As we shall see, theories have much more to do with living people than dead people.

You Too Are a Theorist

There are at least two reasons that theories need not be feared. The first is that *we are all theorists*. People constantly construct their own theories. Suppose you notice that your biology exam scores are better than your scores for psychology, yet your class attendance and exam preparation is roughly the same for each course. The only difference you can identify is that your biology exams come before lunch, while your psychology exams are scheduled afterward. From this, you theorize that eating lunch exerts an adverse influence on your ability to score well on exams. Perhaps lunch makes you sleepy. You could test your explanation (or theory) by skipping lunch before psychology exams to see if your performance improves. If you continue to do poorly in psychology, you will have to consider other possible explanations.

Crime Theories Are Understandable

The second reason for relinquishing any lingering fear of theories is that theoretical explanations range from complicated to extremely simple. If all theories were as difficult to grasp as Albert Einstein's theory of relativity, it would not be surprising that people tried to avoid them.

However, this is not the case. Your theory that linked eating lunch with poor exam performance was not complicated at all. Many, if not most, of the theories we use in daily life are just as simple. The crime theories that will be presented and critiqued in the following group of chapters are not as simple as yours, but then they are not as difficult as Einstein's theory, either.

Here is an example of a theory related to the study of crime. Criminologists have established that there is a relationship between age and crime.[1] Arrest data indicate that participation in conventional crime peaks in late adolescence. Why does criminal behavior decline as individuals get older? Criminologists are still investigating, but numerous theoretical explanations have been proposed. For example, as individuals age, (1) self-control increases; (2) peer pressure decreases; (3) social controls become stronger—that is, family and employment commitments intensify and individuals face tougher criminal penalites for unlawful behavior; or (4) physical skills (running, fighting) diminish. Although these different theoretical explanations may be difficult to measure, they are readily understandable.

As you read the theory chapters, keep in mind that each crime theory can be reduced to its core ideas. It is not always advisable to simplify theories this much because significant detail may be lost; nevertheless, you can feel easier knowing that all of the theories can be reduced to core propositions understandable to virtually anyone. Now let us look at the components of a theory.

Ideal Components of a Good Theory

Long ago Max Weber, one of the founding figures of academic sociology, introduced the concept of "ideal type." An ideal type is an embodiment of the characteristic features of a phenomenon. An ideal type lecture, for example, would be totally accurate, flawlessly delivered, well organized, highly informative, and inspiring. Perhaps obviously, an ideal type is unlikely to be completely realized in the real world! Consider Weber's own statement on the matter: ". . . it is probably seldom if ever that a real phenomenon can be found which corresponds exactly to one of these ideally constructed pure types."[2] An **ideal type,** then, is an analytical construct designed to enhance understanding of a phenomenon. With this in mind, let us look briefly at certain ideal characteristics of a good theory. They include plausibility, real-life (empirical) evidence, falsifiability, and predictability.

Plausibility

A theory needs to be, first of all, a plausible explanation of the relationship between two or more facts. For example, a theory that poverty is the product of helium-filled balloons would not be considered plausible. The major crime theories to be examined in this section all satisfy the plausibility test; there would be no point in focusing on explanations of criminal behavior that do not make sense.

Real-Life Evidence

A second factor used to gauge the adequacy of a theory is the degree of real-life (empirical or experiential) support the theory enjoys. One of the most famous of all sociological theories is Emile Durkheim's theory of suicide.[3] Durkheim argued that the act of suicide, seemingly an individualistic act, is influenced greatly by social factors. Specifically, he advanced the theory that individuals who had strong social bonds were least likely to kill themselves. For example, a married person with a spouse and children might be expected to feel more of an obligation to stay alive than a single person with no direct responsibility for others. This is a plausible account, but Durkheim's theory also had supporting empirical evidence, which is an added advantage for any theory. Indeed, Durkheim found that, in real life, suicide rates were higher for single people than married people.

Falsifiability

Religion and science are frequently set against each other. Religious statements, it has been said, cannot be confirmed, whereas scientific statements can be proven. A better way to describe the difference between religion and science is to think of religion as based on belief, while science is based on skepticism. Contrary to popular opinion, the mission of science is *not* to discover truth. As philosopher of science Karl Popper has argued, the claims of science can never be proven, they can only be refuted.[4] Scientists seek to produce explanations that are precise enough to allow for testing, and the essence of scientific testing is the effort to *dis*confirm. Only after researchers have failed many times to disconfirm a proposed explanation do scientists accept a theory, and even then acceptance is conditional. It is crucial to understand that *no amount of research or testing can ever establish that a scientific hypothesis is true,* only that scientists have been unable to disconfirm it. Consider this hypothesis: Every day that the temperature rises above 100 degrees in Chicago, a Chicago police officer will be murdered. This may be a bizarre hypothesis, but it is testable; attempts can be made to disconfirm it. Only one day with a high temperature of over 100 degrees without a police officer's murder would falsify it. On the other hand, consider a hypothesis that the Devil causes divorce. Scientific inquiry is presently unable to falsify this hypothesis. There is no electronic gadgetry to detect the presence of the Devil; moreover, if we asked divorcing spouses whether the Devil made them do it, their answers could not be accepted as definitive. So we see that theories need to lend themselves to tests of scientific falsification.

Predictability

Scientists seek valid explanations of the physical world, the natural world, and the social world. For example, a physicist may seek to understand the behavior of atoms and a biologist may attempt to understand the behavior of lizards, while a criminologist is chiefly interested in the social behavior of humans. All scientists, however, value most highly those explanations that have predictive power. The best criminological theories will not only offer a compelling account of past and present behavior but will also provide sound predictions for future behavior. Because humans act on the basis of free will, unlike atoms or lizards, predicting behavior in society is especially problematic. By anticipating future behavior, a good theory of crime will suggest fairly specific policy implications that can be used to develop helpful programs and sanctions.

What to Look for

The five chapters in this section of the book describe, discuss, and critique the most prominent theoretical explanations of crime. Chapter 9 features those theories that attribute criminal behavior to individuals, where the criminal is seen as a person who rationally chooses to commit crime. Chapter 10 also focuses on theories that view crime as a problem with individuals, but these theories view individuals as internally flawed, biologically or psychologically, rather than free and knowing actors; forces inherent in the individual, but out of personal control, produce criminal behavior. In Chapters 11 and 12, attention shifts away from individuals to social phenomena. These chapters offer theories that stress micro social forces as the primary causes of criminal behavior. **Micro social forces** include social phenomena such as family, friends, neighborhoods, and schools. Whereas micro sociology refers to aspects of a person's immediate social environment, **macro social forces** have to do with social phenomena that are societywide (the school a person attends is a micro force, while education nationally is a macro force). There are points of interaction between micro and macro levels, but there are also important distinctions. In Chapter 13, emphasis rests on the macro social forces underlying crime. Theories that advance macro explanations of criminal behavior generally focus most on society's economic and political structure (including the criminal justice system), with some attention devoted to cultural themes as a whole.

Each of the theory chapters has a distinctive focus, but all are uniform in format. Chapters 9 through 13 have five common sections: background, core propositions, position on agency (responsibility), policy implications, and a critique.

Background

Magicians appear able to produce rabbits out of thin air. It is sometimes thought that a theory of crime is similar to that rabbit, the product of a criminologist who happened to have unique imagination and insight. Although the theory appears to come from the head of the theorist, this is never the complete picture. Respected theorists may possess individual genius, but their theories are always influenced by their social and intellectual environment. In the theory chapters, therefore, we present a context for the theory by identifying environmental influences of the time.

Core Propositions

Theories can be incredibly complex and detailed. Almost always, however, their essence can be reduced to a few core propositions. Several decades ago C. Wright Mills, a sociologist, put this idea to the test when he reduced to four paragraphs the 555 pages of theorizing in Talcott Parsons' *The Social System*.[5] At the time, Parsons was the most prominent sociologist in the world, but many felt Mills' had been essentially accurate. Mills argued that any book could be reduced to a few representative paragraphs without losing its essence. While Mills may have exaggerated a bit, his general argument is well taken and may be extended to theories as well as books. No matter how elaborate a crime theory may be in its full form, we can reduce it to core propositions. In the five chapters that follow, the essential points of a theory will be emphasized; they will often be expressed in the theorists' own words. This last is important. No presentation of a theory should stray too far from its original expression.

Position on Agency (Responsibility)

For at least three centuries, crime has been recognized as a serious social problem. The study of crime has generated many theories, yet our theoretical understanding of crime is far from satisfactory. A primary reason for this has been the lack of success in dealing with the **problem of agency** (responsibility), which asks the following question: Individuals act, but to what extent do they act as free agents?

This issue, the question of agency, has long been a central concern of sociological theory. It is an even more acute problem for criminology, since responsibility for action is the paramount consideration in the study of crime. Nevertheless, even in sociology (and certainly outside of it, as in psychology, biology), existing theories tend to explain criminal behavior as a product of either individual or environmental factors; hence, one side of the equation is emphasized to the relative exclusion of the other. This will no longer do. The general public, and those in government, are demanding more compelling explanations of the causes of crime.

So each theory must be evaluated in terms of its answer to the agency question. Every crime theory in the chapters that follow has a position with regard to agency. As we shall see, currently the most scientifically favored theories of criminal behavior emphasize social/structural causes. Yet, criminal justice policies are based fundamentally on the concept of individual responsibility for behavior. Given this state of affairs, the theories are not totally convincing and the policies are not totally effective. An appreciation for this discrepancy between theory and practice will yield valuable insights about the problem of crime and criminal justice in the United States.

Policy Implications

Theories can be wonderfully interesting. They can captivate the imagination. Oliver Stone's fanciful film about the assassination of John F. Kennedy led to the production of a movie, *Kennedy,* which attracted considerable interest. This movie was based on the theory of former New Orleans District Attorney Jim Garrison. Garrison's theory suggested that the Kennedy assassination was carried out by the Mafia in coordination with the Central Intelligence Agency (CIA), perhaps with the assistance of Vice President Lyndon Johnson. Of course, Garrison's theory had little or no supporting evidence; nevertheless, interest in the theory made the film a success.

While Garrison's conspiracy theory of the JFK assassination focuses on one crime and obviously makes no claim to be a general theory of crime, it has a certain relevance for us here. First, it shows that theories can be inherently interesting. However, from the point of view of criminology, the Garrison theory is seriously flawed. As suggested earlier, in the scientific world theories are successful only if there is supporting empirical evidence. Furthermore, a theory of crime should contain policy implications. If a theory presents a convincing insight into why people commit crimes, then policy implications will follow. Few students of crime are content to consider theories in the abstract without reference to practical applications. In the chapters ahead, a special effort will be made to answer this question: If the theory is correct, then what specific policies or programs should be instituted in society? Thus we unite theorizing, an abstract enterprise, with policymaking, a practical enterprise. A major aim of the theory chapters is to ensure that the discussion of crime theories relates to everyday life.

Critique

Critique (evaluation) has become a staple feature of American society. To cite just three examples, movie critics evaluate films, political pundits evaluate presiden-

tial speeches, and former professional athletes evaluate sport competitions. Critique is not a bad thing; in fact, with regard to crime theories it can be an especially useful learning device. Accordingly, each of the theory chapters includes a critique section wherein the theoretical perspective is evaluated as to adequacy, comprehensiveness, and usefulness. **Theoretical adequacy** refers to a theory's plausibility, empirical support, falsifiability, and predictability. For now, enough has been said about these factors, but a few comments are appropriate as to the comprehensive nature and current appeal of theories.

Not all crime theories are comprehensive explanations of criminal behavior. Some do not even seek to be. But comprehensiveness is an important consideration when evaluating a theory. First, for a theory of crime to be considered comprehensive it must explain all crime— for example, that of the rich, the poor, and those in between. More than a few crime theories attempt only (or mainly) to explain crimes committed by lower-class members of society; these theories are not comprehensive. Second, comprehensive theories aim to explain violent crimes as well as property crimes. Again, not all theories focus on both forms of criminal behavior. When this is the case, the theories are not comprehensive in the sense referred to here.

It is important to note that there is nothing wrong with a narrowly focused theory—even if the theory explains only one type of crime. For example, Donald Cressey's theory of embezzlement, although advanced over 40 years ago, continues to be cited as a useful theoretical explanation.[6] Most of the theories we will examine, however, are generally thought to be comprehensive theories.

Finally, as part of the critique of each theory, attention will be paid to the issue of current appeal. Most theories eventually die, or are at least modified (for example, newtonian physics prevailed for centuries, but ultimately gave way to einsteinian physics[7]). Similarly, with regard to crime theories, it may be said that some are far more current than others. Moreover, several of the major theories of crime have been updated. Still others now seem antiquated, their basic propositions having been rendered inapplicable by changes in society. Clearly, it is of some importance to highlight which theories have current applicability.

Final Caveats

Caveats are warnings: "You have five minutes to complete your exam," "Do not drink the water," "Bridge icy when wet." We are issuing three caveats to the readers of the theory chapters. They concern so-called causal relationships, the nondefinitive nature of crime theories, and the best intellectual approach to understanding crime theories.

Causal Relationships

More than two centuries ago, David Hume (1711–1776) argued that "cause" can never be observed.[8] This remarkable contention has obvious implications for science, inasmuch as scientific inquiry has generally sought to discover causal laws. It should be noted from the outset, however, that scientists have been unable to offer a compelling refutation to Hume's disturbing insight. Let us look at the argument before examining the theories of crime that follow; the theories, after all, address causal relationships.

Begin by supposing that "A causes B," where A equals an intravenous injection of pentothal and B equals an unconscious state. In most cases, humans undergoing surgery will become unconscious about 30 seconds after being injected with pentothal.[9] Still, even in this example, all we can say is that A and B appear to be constantly conjoined, with B always following A. Cause itself remains out of view. Now, before drawing the conclusion that this is just intellectual nitpicking, consider the example of two grandfather clocks striking the hour, one slightly after the other, for months on end. Clearly, the grandfather clocks are independent—that the one clock strikes the hour does not *cause* the other clock to do so, and yet the two clocks strike the hour in unvarying succession. So we can see that, even in objective cases, cause itself cannot always be readily identified. The concept of cause is even more problematic when applied to human behavior.

In 1982, the federal government released the results of a comprehensive study of the effects of television violence on behavior. This study stated flatly: "Recent research confirms the earlier findings of a causal relationship between televised violence and later aggressive behavior."[10] Putting aside the fact that not all researchers agree that television violence induces actual violence, the government's conclusion is still misleading in a technical sense: No one has detected any cause operating between watching television and subsequent violent behavior. Moreover, it could be that other factors—school experiences, peer group relationships, or family abuse—may exert a prior or intervening influence. In any event, social scientists may speak with confidence about correlations between two variables (poverty and crime, for example), but when they speak of a causal connection (poverty *causes* crime), they are on shaky ground. Indeed, many social scientists believe that the "*complexity of human actions defeats causal analysis.*"[11] The vast array of social forces, added to human will, make it extremely difficult to identify precisely what has influenced a person to act in a certain way.

Despite what has just been said, we should not abandon the attempt at causal theorizing altogether. While direct causal relationships cannot be verified in the physical or social world, a "soft" form of causal reasoning can be employed. That is, it is possible to focus on relationships between variables for which there are *highly probable outcomes.* High probability does not equal cause, but it often comes close enough to be considered cause-like. We must simply be careful not to overstate causal relationships in the theories that follow. To do so would lead to a naive understanding of what the theories actually suggest.

No Theory Is Definitive

In criminology courses, it is common for a professor to discuss a number of sociological theories of crime. Students typically want to know which of the theories is "the right one." Regretfully, professors must reply that there is no one "right" theory of crime. Chapters 11, 12, and 13 present several sociological theories of crime, and readers are advised to note the special strengths and weaknesses of each. A particular theory may explain one form of crime but not another, which may be better explained by a different theory. Each of the sociological theories here offers a worthwhile, distinctive insight into criminal behavior, but each of these theories has certain deficiencies. You need to choose wisely.

It is not even true that sociology offers the only useful scientific explanation of crime. While we are convinced that sociological theories offer the most authoritative and compelling explanations of criminal behavior, we do not claim that other scientific disciplines have nothing to offer. Psychologists and biologists, for example, have proposed explanations of crime (some of which are discussed in this text) that offer suggestive, if not entirely persuasive, evidence for explaining certain types of criminal behavior.

No one should be dismayed because there is no single definitive theory of criminal behavior. Crime in society is a very complex phenomenon for which there is no obvious, comprehensive theoretical explanation available. As indicated earlier, we need to evaluate the merits and shortcomings of each theory. Taken collectively, these theories can begin to provide an encompassing account of crime.

Understanding in Depth

Theories of criminal behavior are relevant to many courses in sociology and criminal justice. It is possible, if not probable, that you will have previously encountered the crime theories that follow. If so, use this as an advantage, not a disadvantage. Earlier exposure should be viewed as a first step toward understanding, not a final step from which no further insight can be gained. Those tempted to think they already fully understand the theories should be forewarned—it is very unlikely to be so.

You see, it is not sufficient to simply go over and over a theory. You need to understand it from the inside. Some years ago, Clint Eastwood starred in a film called

Firefox. Eastwood portrayed a pilot whose mission was to infiltrate a Russian military installation where a technologically advanced fighter jet had been built. With inside help, the Eastwood character was to steal the prototype plane and fly it to the United States. Before takeoff, one of the scientists working on the top-secret project (and covertly helping the Americans steal the plane) advised the pilot to operate the controls by *thinking in Russian;* the scientist warned against translating from Russian to English, which would take too much time and might not work. Much the same can be said with regard to understanding these crime theories. Look at the internal logic of each theory. Each theory has an essential logical framework, those key propositions that define it. To fully appreciate what a theory has to offer, it is imperative to do more than merely memorize names and propositions (although this is important). Instead, you need to interpret real-life actions and events from the internal perspective of each theory. When you have arrived at this type of understanding, the theories will leave a lasting impression and be a source of significant insight and relevance. Scientific theories are not always easy to grasp, but if you keep the points of this introduction in mind, the important insights that follow should be readily accessible.

Notes

[1] See Charles R. Tittle, "Two Empirical Regularities (Maybe) in Search of an Explanation: Commenting on the Age/Crime Debate," *Criminology* 26 (1988) 75–85; Charles R. Tittle and David Ward, "The Interaction of Age with Correlates and Causes of Crime," *Journal of Quantitative Criminology* 9 (1993) 3–53; Daniel Nagin and Kenneth Land, "Age, Criminal Careers, and Population Heterogeneity: Specification and Estimation of a Nonparametric, Mixed Poisson Model," *Criminology* 29 (1993) 163–89.

[2] Max Weber, *Economy and Society,* ed. Guenther Roth and Claus Wittich (Los Angeles: University of California Press, 1968) 20.

[3] Emile Durkheim, *Suicide,* tr. John A. Spaulding and George Simpson (New York: Free Press, 1951 [orig. pub. 1897]).

[4] Karl Popper, *Conjectures and Refutations* (New York: Harper Torchbooks, 1968).

[5] C. Wright Mills, *The Sociological Imagination* (New York: Oxford University Press, 1959); Talcott Parsons, *The Social System* (New York: Free Press, 1951).

[6] Donald Cressey, *Other People's Money: A Study in the Social Psychology of Embezzlement* (Belmont, CA: Wadsworth, 1971 [orig. pub. 1953]).

[7] D.C. Phillips, *Philosophy, Science, and Social Inquiry* (New York: Pergamon Press, 1987) 16.

[8] David Hume, *Treatise of Human Nature* (Buffalo, NY: Prometheus, 1992 [orig. pub. 1739]).

[9] Joan Luckmann and Karen Creason Sorenson, *Medical-Surgery Nursing,* 3rd. ed. (Phiadelphia: W.B. Saunders, 1987) 284.

[10] *Television and Behavior: Ten Years of Scientific Progress and Implications for the Eighties,* Vol. I (Rockville, MD: U.S. Department of Health and Human Services, 1982).

[11] Keith Dixon, *Sociological Theory: Pretense and Possibility* (London: Routledge & Kegan Paul Ltd., 1973) 27.

chapter *9*

Crime as Individually Chosen Behavior

CHAPTER OUTLINE
BACKGROUND
    Intellectual Climate
    Eighteenth-Century Criminal Justice
CORE PROPOSITIONS
    Classical Criminology's Theory of Criminal Behavior
        The Individual Is Self-Interested
        The Individual Is Rational
        Behavior Is Freely Chosen
        Pleasure Seeking Often Results in Crime
    Classical Criminology's Theory of Criminal Justice
        Laws Shape Behavior
        Punishment Should Be a Deterrent
POSITION ON AGENCY (RESPONSIBILITY)
    The Individual Side of Agency
    The Social/Structural Side of Agency
POLICY IMPLICATIONS
SUBSEQUENT DEVELOPMENTS
    Becker's Economic Model of Crime
    Gordon's Critique of Crime and Capitalism
    Deterrence Theory
    Rational Choice Theory
CRITIQUE
    Adequacy
    Comprehensive Nature
    Current Appeal
SUMMARY

KEY TERMS

classical criminology
reasoning actor
purposeful actors
free agents
utilitarian principle
social contract theory
greatest happiness principle
proportionate punishment
felicity calculus
agency
specific deterrence
general deterrence
recidivism rate
choice structuring
Three Rs
crime displacement

"BECAUSE THAT'S WHERE THE MONEY IS." Willie Sutton, the famous bank robber, may be best remembered for offering this reply to the question "Willie, why do you rob banks?" The fact is, the exchange never took place.[1] Nevertheless, the comment attributed to Sutton remains popular today as a catchy way of stating the obvious (for example, medical students are cited "Sutton's Law" as an admonition always to look first at the obvious when making a diagnosis). So why *did* Sutton rob banks? In his own words:

> Because I enjoyed it. I loved it. I was more alive when I was inside a bank, robbing it, than at any time in my life. I enjoyed every thing about it so much that one or two weeks later I'd be out looking for the next job.[2]

Because Sutton continued to rob banks long after he was financially well off, we must conclude that he chose this behavior—he was not pressured into it by circumstances. Moreover, it is clear that Sutton's behavior was self-interested. Finally, his approach to robbing banks was highly calculative and rational: "In robbing a bank I always planned the job carefully, leaving nothing to chance."[3]

Willie Sutton, bank robber, can be seen as a paradigm for the present chapter. Sutton's criminal behavior was freely chosen, self-interested, and rational. As we shall see, these are the cornerstone principles of classical criminology.

Background

The first scholarly explanation of crime can be traced to the 1700s, when the classical school of criminology took shape. **Classical criminology** is most often associated with two men. Cesare Beccaria (1738–1794) was an Italian intellectual with expertise in economics and mathematics (Box 9.1), and Jeremy Bentham (1748–1832) was a British philosopher, legal expert, and reformer (Box 9.2). Beccaria wrote very little. His principle work was the book *On Crimes and Punishments,* which may be the most acclaimed publication in the history of criminology. It is a short book—an essay really—but it has had an enormous influence on the development of most Western legal systems. It caused such a stir, in fact, that it was placed on the Roman Catholic Church's Index of Condemned Works from 1766 until 1962, when the Index was abolished.[4] At the age of 12, Bentham was already a student at Oxford University. Unlike Beccaria, he was a prolific writer with hugely ambitious scholarly and political plans. His most extravagant career goal was to supervise the overhaul of the existing system of law in such a way as to remedy all social and political problems.[5]

Beccaria and Bentham, it should be emphasized, were specifically interested in reforming the law and criminal justice practices. Their writings on proposed reforms, however, are built upon a theory of criminal behavior. Before considering either their legal reforms or their theories of crime, we need to examine the intellectual climate of the time. Both men were influenced by Enlightenment writers.

Intellectual Climate

Though Beccaria and Bentham expressed an interest in crime and criminal justice, neither was known as a criminologist. Just like the founding figures of sociology (Durkheim, Marx, and Weber), Beccaria and Bentham had wide-ranging areas of expertise that included philosophy, economics, history, sociology, and the law. Beccaria thought of this as an unqualified virtue: "Never will a man be great and illustrious in his science if he confines himself to that science and neglects others that have with it connections and analogies."[6] Our purpose is not to praise Beccaria and Bentham as encyclopedic scholars, but to show that they were well aware of the broad intellectual climate in which they lived. As we shall see, their theories were shaped in large measure by the ideas of the Enlightenment.

From the early seventeenth century to the beginning of the nineteenth century, Europe underwent a cultural and intellectual revolution known as the Enlightenment. Some of the most famous Enlightenment writers were Montesquieu (1689–1755), Voltaire (1694–1778), Locke (1632–1704), and Rousseau (1712–1778). These intellectuals challenged the rule of both the monarchy and the church. In particular, they rejected the religious precept that stressed the basic sinfulness and fallibility of "man,"

Cesare Beccaria: Humanitarian Reformer and Reluctant Celebrity

Cesare Beccaria was born in Milan in 1738. His parents were members of the aristocratic class and, like other aristocrats in Milan, they were Roman Catholics. Young Cesare was sent to a private school run by Jesuits. He did so exceptionally well in mathematics that the other schoolchildren called him "Newtoncino," meaning "little Newton."

At the age of 20, Beccaria received his doctor's degree in law. Two years later he fell in love with Teresa Blasco, 16-year-old daughter of an army colonel. Cesare's father was totally against the romance and threatened to disinherit his son if he married Teresa. Beccaria vacillated for several months, unable either to displease his father or turn away from his bride-to-be. At one point Cesare beseeched his father "in the name of Jesus Christ to stop putting obstacles to this marriage." Though his father did not relent, Cesare nevertheless chose to marry Teresa. As vowed, his father withdrew financial support and so the young couple lived in poverty. After about a year, Pietro Verri, a close friend of Cesare's, devised a ruse to win the father's approval of Teresa. Out for a walk one day, Cesare rushed Teresa into his parents' home, claiming that his bride had fallen suddenly ill. Cesare's parents came to her aid and, following a tremendous show of appreciation by Teresa, Cesare's father finally warmed to his daughter-in-law.

The Verri brothers, Pietro and Alessandro, urged Beccaria to study and write about penal reform; Pietro supplied the idea and Alessandro, as a high-ranking prison administrator, offered Beccaria firsthand observations of penal practices. In 1764 at the age of 26, Beccaria published his famous essay *On Crimes and Punishments*. Fearing that the work might provoke a negative reaction from government or church officials, Beccaria published the book anonymously. After it became clear that the government approved of the book, Beccaria claimed authorship. He was an instant celebrity, recognized by secular leaders and intellectuals all over the world as a first-rate writer and a legal reformer without peer. The Catholic Church was not so favorably disposed. In fact, a Vallombrosian monk accused Beccaria of being "an enemy of Christianity, a wicked man and a poor philosopher."

On Crimes and Punishments has had an enormous impact on all Western legal systems. Within 18 months of its publication, the book was reprinted in several editions and translations. As indicated above, Beccaria became famous almost overnight once he acknowledged authorship. Even the intellectual elite of Paris summoned Beccaria. Begrudgingly, and only at the insistence of Pietro Verri, Beccaria journeyed to Paris. The trip to Paris distressed Beccaria, as did his stay there. He missed Teresa and counted down the days until he would return to Milan. He became so depressed that he lied about his health, claiming to be ill when he was not and using this as an excuse to reduce the length of his visit from 6 months to 2 months. Despite his melancholy, he was generally well received by the great intellectuals of Paris. He returned to Milan and lived off sinecures (paid public offices having little responsibility) until his death in 1794. Never again, however, did he write anything of real importance.

SOURCES: Marcello Maestro, *Cesare Beccaria and the Origins of Penal Reform* (Philadelphia: Temple University Press, 1973); Henry Paolucci, "Translators Introduction" to Cesare Beccaria, *On Crimes and Punishments* (Indianapolis: Bobbs-Merrill, 1963) ix–xxiii.

---

preferring to advance the notion of the inherent worth and great potential of "man."[7] For these scholars, the individual, as a reasoning creature, replaced tradition and superstition as the measure of all things. In three key respects, the Enlightenment view of the individual had a huge influence on the development of classical criminology. It would not be an exaggeration to say that these three points form the basis from which classical criminology emerges.

The first point is that the individual is described as a **reasoning actor.** Faith in God had its place in guiding church affairs, argued Locke, but secular activities should be governed by reason. The social world is accessible to reason, and reason is a faculty of the individual, "that faculty whereby man is supposed to be distinguished from beasts and wherein it is evident he much surpasses them."[8] The second point of continuity between the Enlightenment and classical criminology is that individuals are viewed as **purposeful actors.** Rousseau agrees with Locke that human beings reason, but goes on to say that human action is directed by two principles that are prior to reason: the pursuit of one's own well-being and self-preservation, and the repugnance for suffering.[9] Individuals use reason, then, to attain their needs and wants and to avoid pain and suffering. The third point of congruence is that Enlightenment thinkers characterized individuals as **free agents,** that is, as human actors capable of choosing how to behave in society. Social institutions may

Jeremy Bentham: Voice of Utilitarianism

Jeremy Bentham was born in 1748. His father was a London lawyer who prospered in real estate. Jeremy's mother died when the boy was only 10 years old and his childhood could not be described as other than grim, shaped as it was to the expectations and demands of his taskmaster father. Though shy socially, Bentham was intellectually precocious, studying Latin at the age of 3, and entering Oxford as a 12-year-old. He went on to study law, although never in the course of his life did he argue a case in court.

As a young adult, Bentham proved himself to be a prolific writer. His most extended work at this point of his life concerned punishment and legal theory. He read Beccaria's *On Crimes and Punishments* and was greatly impressed. In particular, Bentham sought to embrace and advance Beccaria's notion that legislators ought to promote the greatest happiness in society. For Bentham, this came to be known as the principle of utility, and this principle alone was able to "afford the only true solution that could be given to every question of right and wrong."

During the middle part of his life, Bentham studied and wrote about public finance policies, the burdensome poor in society, and prison architecture. Regarding the latter topic, Bentham introduced the Panopticon, a prison constructed on a circular plan so that there was a central observation point from which prison officials could monitor the behavior of all inmates. Bentham invested a considerable amount of time and money in an effort to see his Panopticon adopted (he sought to build and manage the structure personally). After persistent lobbying, Parliament agreed to sponsor the plan and government agencies purchased land on which to build this new type of penitentiary. Soon enough, however, wealthy owners of estates near the proposed prison site forced a halt to the proposal. Bentham's dream was dashed and he never forgot how monied interests interrupted a project in the public service.

Earlier in life, a different sort of plan, but one no less dear to Bentham's heart, was similarly dashed—this time by his father. In his middle twenties, Bentham wished to wed Mary Dunkley, an orphaned daughter of an Essex surgeon. At the time, however, Bentham was financially dependent upon his father, who firmly opposed the marriage. Unlike Beccaria, who had faced a similar dilemma, Bentham acquiesced to his father's wishes. Several years later, in 1781 at the age of 43, Bentham met a friend's niece, 13-year-old Caroline Fox. Bentham fell in love with Caroline and, after a long absence, in 1805 Bentham proposed marriage to Caroline—but she declined. Over 30 years later, at nearly 80 years of age, Bentham wrote to Caroline and informed her that since their last meeting not a single day had passed without him thinking of her.

No doubt, Bentham had regrets about how his life was lived. In a letter written to his brother, Samuel Bentham, he noted that Samuel had enjoyed many exciting moments while he had "been but vegetating." Moreover, Bentham was stung by the fact that governments did not act on his proposals, despite his overtures to several world leaders, including President James Madison of the United States. The later years of his life, however, were generally favorable. He was in good health, jogging and playing badminton well into his seventies. Moreover, he was financially secure. He had his father's inheritance and a Parliament-voted settlement to compensate for the government's default on his Panopticon scheme. Also, his thoughts on penal reform were well known nationally and internationally. Less well known were his progressive thoughts on civil rights and animal rights.

Though Bentham eventually had his detractors (for example, Karl Marx referred to him as "a genius in the way of bourgeois stupidity"), the fact is that his utilitarian school of thought remains a powerful influence today. As if in anticipation that his ideas would live on, Bentham arranged to have his body preserved as well. His mummified body, dressed in original clothes and topped with a wax head (the skull is placed between his feet) is encased in a glass box in University College in London.

SOURCES: John Dinwiddy, *Bentham* (New York: Oxford, 1989); M. P. Mack, *Jeremy Bentham: An Odyssey of Ideas* (New York: Columbia University Press, 1963); *An Introduction to the Principles of Morals and Legislation*, ed. J.H. Burns and H.L.A. Hart (London: University of London Press, 1970) 283; *Collected Works of Jeremy Bentham: Correspondence of Jeremy Bentham, Vol. 2* (98–101) and *Vol. 3* (158–63), ed. J. H. Barns (London: University of London Press, 1971).

---

influence humans, even corrupt them, but ultimately behavior is freely chosen: ". . . each man is born free and his own master, . . ."[10]

Enlightenment philosophers viewed individuals as rational, self-interested, and free. This orientation was adopted by Beccaria and Bentham and forms the basis for their theory of behavior (including criminal behavior) in society. But what about their concern for criminal jus-

tice practices, which was more pressing than anything else? On this point they were influenced by the social and criminal justice conditions of the time.

Eighteenth-Century Criminal Justice

Social life in Europe during the eighteenth century was often unpleasant. Most people were poor, uneducated, roughhewn, and vulnerable to illness. The lowness of life was matched by existing criminal justice practices, which can be characterized as inconsistent, unfair, corrupt, and brutal.[11] The laws were ambiguous and poorly publicized. Moreover, when a criminal wrong was committed, it was not at all clear what would happen next. The victim or the victim's family might exact vengeance. The "watchman," a person with legal authority, may or may not make an arrest. (He might be afraid of the offender, or susceptible to a bribe.) Will and Ariel Durant, esteemed chroniclers of history and philosophy, sum up the uncertainties of arrest and prosecution in eighteenth-century London:

Even if the watchman was not terrified by the violence of the robbers, he could be bribed; so could the constable to whom he reported; so could the magistrate to whom the constable brought a criminal."[12]

While the guilty were not always arrested or prosecuted, innocent people often were—such were the vagaries of the justice system. Guilty or innocent, when individuals were taken into custody they were subject to a wide range of physical attack, from simple whippings to the most diabolical forms of torture and punishment. Bear in mind that the accused was *not* presumed innocent; it was not until 1820 when presumption of innocence became standard policy in England.[13]

Lacking an assumption of innocence, the authorities felt that it was their right, indeed their duty, to use whatever means available to extract information and confessions and/or to punish. Will and Ariel Durant provide a trenchant statement describing the brutality of punishments in eighteenth-century England:

By a law repealed in 1790 a woman convicted of treason, or of murdering her husband, was to be burned alive, but custom allowed her to be strangled before burning. Men guilty of treason were cut down from the gallows while still alive; their bowels were extracted and burned before their faces; they were then beheaded and quartered. Gallows were raised in every district of London, and on many of them the corpses were left for the nourishment of birds.[14]

Practices were similarly frightful in other countries, although each country (even each region of a country) had its own peculiar methods of applying torture and punishment.[15] In Bologna those accused of crimes might be starved, injected with water, vinegar, or oil, have hot eggs placed under their armpits, find lighted candles tied to their fingers so that the fingers would be consumed with the wax, or have their feet layered with salt water and then be subject to goats licking their feet, a particularly

painful form of torture. In France, favored practices included tying the suspected offender to an iron chair and then pushing the chair closer and closer to a burning furnace, squeezing the thumbs of the accused in a screw, and putting high boots on the person in custody and then pouring boiling water into the boots with the effect that the water would eat away at the flesh and dissolve the bones. No judicial cruelty was more horrible than *quartering*. This practice, found in many countries, dictated that each of the four limbs (arms and legs) be individually attached by rope and then fastened to four bars, each of which was harnessed to a horse. For hours, the horses were made to give short jerks, resulting in agonizing dislocations. Eventually, the horses pulled away completely, severing the tendons and ligaments of the accused totally so that the limbs popped out in all directions. The trunk, which often still showed signs of life, was then burned to ashes.[16]

Not all capital offenders were subject to these frightful punishments; however, over one hundred offenses called for the death penalty. Among the list of capital crimes were these: housebreaking, maiming or stealing cattle, cutting down trees in a park, sending threatening letters, shooting a rabbit, counterfeiting, forgery, and sodomy.[17]

In addition to the above, an accused person had to worry about the actions of the prosecutor, and especially the judge. Neither prosecutors nor judges were constrained by concern for a defendant's rights; for all practical purposes there were none. Moreover, since there were no appeals, a judge could conduct the proceedings in whatever manner he chose, including making all decisions in secret. Judges dominated, and had considerable discretionary power; they could assure a positive outcome for the defendant, and often did if the defendant had wealth, or they could turn the outcome the other way.[18]

Finally, convicted defendants who survived any torture that might take place before or after the trial could look forward to deportation or imprisonment, the former being much preferred. Prisons were filthy, which meant that germs and disease were rife. A new inmate would be put in irons, given a bed of straw and a pound of bread per day. However, an inmate with money, or at least a family who would provide funds, could bribe guards and the warden in order to improve the circumstances of confinement. Such inmates could pay for much better food and accommodations, and be granted wider liberties, including extended visits by relatives and friends (for example, a wife might stay over). An inmate with enough money might even be able to buy holiday release time out of the prison. For the poor, which meant most inmates, none of this was possible.[19]

Beccaria and Bentham were not ignorant of the leading ideas and social practices of their time. Quite the contrary. As we shall presently see, their writings on the law, crime, and criminal justice have direct connections to Enlightenment thinking and eighteenth-century criminal justice policies and procedures. We turn now to a consideration of the essential propositions of classical criminology.

Core Propositions

Beccaria and Bentham did not collaborate on any publications, yet their theories of human behavior and their thoughts on reform are exceptionally compatible. Partly this is so because Bentham was familiar with Beccaria's views and much influenced by them, as he acknowledged on more than one occasion. Indeed, their arguments are so congruent that most crime scholars have linked the two with just one school of thought: classical criminology. Although Beccaria and Bentham were mainly interested in reforming criminal justice practices, they could not have proposed comprehensive reforms without first having a theory of criminal behavior. To prevent or control crime and deal effectively with offenders, it is necessary to have an understanding of why crime takes place.

Their most important and influential ideas grow out of four key points, which summarize the theory of behavior identified with both Beccaria and Bentham:
1. All individuals seek to maximize self-interests.
2. Rational calculation is used to achieve aims.
3. Behavior is freely chosen.
4. The tendency to seek pleasure often results in crime.

Classical Criminology's Theory of Criminal Behavior

According to Beccaria and Bentham, crime is seen as self-interested, rational, and freely chosen behavior. This is a theory of crime that places the spotlight on the individual offender. Forget about notions of people being forced into a life of crime; the fact is, claim classical criminologists, individuals choose crime. As we will see, the points that constitute the classical theory of crime are close reflections of the Enlightenment ideas discussed earlier.

The Individual Is Self-Interested

For Beccaria, action in society is shaped by the pursuit of pleasure and the avoidance of pain. Beccaria considered this an axiomatic principle of human behavior: ". . . pleasure and pain are the motives of sensible beings."[20] Bentham could not agree more. Individuals are always and everywhere motivated to seek pleasure and avoid pain. This was, for Bentham, the most fundamental tendency of human behavior and it has been referred to as the **utilitarian principle** (see Box 9.1). Bentham assumed that all humans are directed by a sort of internal programming based on this principle:

Nature has placed mankind under the governance of two sovereign masters, *pain* and *pleasure*. It is for them alone to point out what we ought to do, as well as to determine what we shall do. . . . They govern us in all we do, in all we say, in all we think. . . .[21]

Of course, pleasure and pain are just abstract concepts that have no force until individuals define their content. That is, each person must decide what is pleasurable and what is painful. For his part, Bentham offered an extensively detailed inventory of possible pleasures and pains.[22] He identified fourteen categories of simple pleasures and twelve categories of simple pains, with each of these categories broken down into many more subcategories (for example, there is a pleasure of the sense that contains a pleasure of the ear that contains a pleasure of hearing a bird chirp). Whatever meaning pleasure or pain have for an individual—and each person has great latitude in deciding—the crucial point is that humans attempt to maximize pleasure and minimize pain.

The Individual Is Rational

For Beccaria, the faculty of reason explains how society was formed in the first place. As a foundational point of his general social philosophy, Beccaria accepted the **social contract theory** of society (see Box 9.2), which alleges that individuals, in order to escape the danger and uncertainty of living in the wild (the natural state of life Hobbes had referred to as "short, nasty, and brutish"), organized themselves into a collectivity.[23] Just as ancient individuals were rational enough to see that forming a central government was to their benefit, contemporary humans are able to calculate the negative consequences of crime. The individual then, is presumed to be a rational actor. A person rationally determines what is in his or her best interest and then acts accordingly.

Bentham was equally vigorous in advancing the proposition that behavior is the product of rational thought. He stated that everyone is a rational actor: "Men calculate, some with less exactness, indeed, some with more, but all men calculate. I would not say that even a madman does not calculate."[24] The argument here is that all behavior, even behavior that is madness, is rationally devised. A sniper who shoots passing motorists at random, for example, may be expected to calculate rationally the most favorable vantage point from which to shoot, as well as the most effective weapon to accomplish the deed.

Behavior Is Freely Chosen

The idea that individuals are able to direct their own behavior was generally taken for granted by Beccaria. He accepted the philosophical argument that society begins at

the point when individuals recognize that it is in their self-interest to agree to a social contract. But this agreement entails a tradeoff. In return for the protections society offers, individuals must concede some of their personal liberties (not eating fruit from someone else's tree, for example). In Beccaria's words, a lawful society is "a just recompense to men for their sacrifice of that universal liberty of action over all things, which is the property of every sensible being, limited only by its own powers"[25]

Classical criminology conceptualizes behavior as freely chosen. Because of this, the classical criminologists have frequently been criticized for attributing too much freedom to individual behavior. Clearly, Beccaria and Bentham embraced the view that human will propels behavior, at least up to a point. Of course, no amount of will power can enable a man to become pregnant, or to fly. In addition to such obvious exceptions and limitations, Beccaria assumed that some amount of freedom is conceded to society in fulfillment of the social contract. Neither did Bentham hold such a naive notion as to think that individuals are totally free. In choosing a course of action, Bentham argued, individuals necessarily respond to environmental circumstances: "Take any act whatsoever, there is nothing in the nature of things that excludes any imaginable object from being a circumstance to it."[26] What this means is that virtually anything in a person's physical or social environment, "an indefinite multitude of circumstances" may influence behavior.[27] People choose how to behave, but their choices are not made in a vacuum.

Seeking Pleasure Often Results in Crime

Classical criminology accepts the presupposition that pursuing one's own interest is a basic behavioral predisposition. However, as individuals seek to maximize their gratifications, it will often be the case that others may be harmed in the process. This point is so obvious that it demands little amplification. Nonetheless, Bentham provided this example: Acting on the desire to have bread for nothing, a man steals bread from a bakery.[28] The assertion, though, is much broader and involves more than just instrumental gains. It is true, from the classical perspective, that individuals seek to further their *instrumental* desires (bread, a jacket, a car, etc.), but they also seek to

TABLE 9.1 | Classical Criminology's Criminal Justice Reforms

LAWS SHAPE BEHAVIOR
- Legislators must apply the greatest happiness principle in the formulation of laws.
- Laws must be clearly stated and well publicized.
- Laws must contain a punishment provision.

PUNISHMENT SHOULD DETER
- Proportionate sentences must be calculated by a felicity calculus.
- Punishment must be certain, not necessarily severe.
- Trials must be speedy, public, and fair.

gratify their *expressive* desires (status, romance, etc.). In either case, the satisfaction of personal wants can impinge on the desires and rights of others, thus resulting in the commission of a crime.

Classical Criminology's Theory of Criminal Justice

Theorizing about human behavior was not the foremost concern of Beccaria and Bentham; they were more interested in trying to reform the criminal justice system. Yet, two overarching themes characterize their reform proposals. The first is that laws shape behavior, and the second is that punishments should deter crime (Table 9.1). Each of these themes warrants discussion.

Laws Shape Behavior

According to Beccaria, laws form the foundation of society:

Laws are the conditions under which independent and isolated men united to form a society. Weary of living in a continual state of war, and of enjoying a liberty rendered useless by the uncertainty of preserving it, they sacrificed a part so that they might enjoy the rest of it in peace and safety.

From the viewpoint of classical criminology, laws not only keep people in check, they form the core of all social relations. For Bentham, the law is everything: "It is the tie that holds society together."[29] Given the overall significance of the laws, the process of lawmaking takes on paramount importance. Here, the classical criminologists argue, lawmakers must be guided by the **greatest happiness principle.** Beccaria asserted that, throughout history, laws have been accidental creations or "a mere tool of the passions of some."[30] What is required is a "dispassionate student of human nature" (the legislator) who will form the laws based on the viewpoint of the "greatest happiness shared by the greatest number."[31] It is known that

Bentham read Beccaria's account of the greatest happiness principle and was very much impressed with it—so much so that he emphasized it in his own work and made the doctrine even more famous. Said Bentham: "The business of government is to promote the happiness of the society, . . ."[32] It accomplishes this through lawmaking. The general object of the laws "is to augment the total happiness of the community. . . ."[33]

Once the legislator has determined what social relations would best promote the greatest happiness in society, a law must be fashioned to insure that result. If laws are to be effective, they must be clearly stated. Laws that are obscure in meaning create mischief. On the other hand, if laws are written plainly enough so that their meaning is readily understandable, and if the laws are accessible to the general public (Beccaria here notes the usefulness of the printing press), then they will be highly effective in regulating behavior: "When the number of those who can understand the sacred code of laws and hold it in their hands increases, the frequency of crimes will be found to decrease, . . ."[34]

There is more. The laws should not only specify clearly what behavior is disallowed in society but they should also contain a provision that states the penalties for violations. This, Beccaria argued, would guarantee crime reduction, "for undoubtedly ignorance and uncertainty of punishments add much. . . ."[35]

Punishment Should Be a Deterrent

The classical criminologists approached the topic of punishment with caution. Beccaria argued that there is only one justification of punishment and that is deterrence: "For a punishment to attain its end, the evil which it inflicts has only to exceed the advantage derivable from the crime; . . . All beyond this is superfluous and for that reason tyrannical."[36] Bentham was equally adamant about the limitations of punishment: "But all punishment is mischief: all punishment in itself is evil. Upon the principle of utility, if it ought at all to be admitted, it ought only to be admitted in as far as it promises to exclude some greater evil."[37] Bentham cited four situations in which no punishment should be inflicted: when punishment is groundless (there was no crime); when punishment is ineffective as a deterrent; when punishment is excessively expensive; and when punishment is needless. Beccaria and Bentham were of the opinion that forms of punishment had gotten out of hand. Punishment had become excessive both in terms of frequency and harshness.

As noted earlier, the classical theorists argued that deterrence is the sole justification for punishment. If punishments are to be effective deterrents, they must be just and certain. Punishments that are excessively cruel (Beccaria noted the example of invoking capital punishment for killing a pheasant[38]) inspire general disrespect for the law. Moreover, severe punishments for minor offenses will incline the offender to commit further crimes to avoid detection (for example, a bank robber will be tempted to kill all witnesses if there is no added punishment for murder). In Beccaria's words: "For a punishment to be just it should consist of only such gradations of intensity as suffice to deter men from committing crimes."[39] This is the principle of **proportionate punishment.** Serious crimes require serious punishments, while minor crimes demand minor punishments.

At this point an important question is likely to surface: How can a society be assured of having proportionate punishments? Beccaria's answer was that the legislator must use "the calculation of probabilities."[40] Bentham contended that lawmakers must adopt the greatest happiness principle as a practical guide for legislation. The legislator, perhaps with the assistance of philosophers such as Bentham, will calculate impartially all human actions in terms of pleasure and pain. Those actions that produce more pleasure than pain to society are promoted by a system of rewards, while acts that produce more pain than pleasure are discouraged by a system of punishments. In practical terms, the legislator's capacity for "creative legislation" is based on a **felicity calculus,** a coding of all forms and variations of behavior into units of pleasures and pains.[41] The pleasure associated with a crime must be outweighed by the pain attached to the crime's punishment.[42] In developing the felicity calculus, the legislator must account for an "indefinite multitude of circumstances." Although this is an ambitious project, it is not, in Bentham's view, beyond the scope of enlightened legislation.

Punishments need to be proportionate, but that alone does not guarantee effectiveness. To be effective, punishments must also be certain. The certainty of punishment, Beccaria stated, will always make a greater impression than the harshness of punishment.[43] Moreover, Becarria argued that the certainty of punishment works as a deterrent even when the punishment is moderate. Hence, in the classical school of jurisprudence certainty always outweighs harshness as a consideration.

Finally, classical criminology urges that judicial proceedings be speedy, public, and fair. Beccaria apparently embraced an elementary theory of human psychology based on conditioning. Crime and punishment need to be linked, the "one as the cause, the other as the necessary inevitable effect."[44] Long delay between crime and punishment weakens the psychological association that a person may form. With this in mind, the workings of the criminal justice system should be expeditious: "The trial itself should be completed in the briefest possible time."[45]

Trials should also be public and fair. This means that secret testimony should be disallowed. An accused person has the right to face and attempt to defeat those who

Beccaria and Bentham criticized the criminal justice practices of their day for being brutal, corrupt, and inefficient.

bring accusations. Furthermore, judges should make their rulings in public, and their rulings should apply narrowly only to decisions of guilt or innocence. Judges should not be allowed to set punishments. In determining sentences, judges are too easily corrupted, and defendants with power and wealth are likely to receive more lenient punishments than are defendants who are without money and influence.

We have just completed an extended discussion of the core propositions of classical criminology, both its theory of crime and its program for criminal justice reform. Keeping the main points in mind, we turn now to a consideration of how classical criminology addresses the problem of **agency** (responsibility).

Position on Agency (Responsibility)

All major theories of crime provide an explicit or implicit answer to agency considerations. The question of agency asks who or what is responsible for behavior. More specifically, crime theories tend to argue either that something internal to the individual produces crime, or that the cause of criminal behavior lies in factors or forces external to the actor; some theories attempt to integrate both internal and external dimensions. One thing is certain: No question in criminological theory is more important than the question of agency, and the answer to the agency question becomes a nucleus for each theory. As we shall see, classical criminology's position with regard to agency leans heavily on the side of internal factors.

The Individual Side of Agency

In the United States, each state has its own precise definition of sanity, which it applies to criminal offenders. There is considerable overlap, however, between the states, as well as with the federal system of law. In general, a defendant is presumed sane if (a) he knew what he was doing; (b) he knew that it was wrong; and (c) he was not harboring under any kind of longstanding mental defect. If we amend this latter point to read, "not harboring under any kind of longstanding mental defect *or social force*," then we have a usable formula for estimating individual agency, the topic we are currently examining.

Let us see how classical criminology would answer these three questions. First, clearly Beccaria and Bentham conceptualized the criminal as a rational actor. For proof of this, call to mind Beccaria's statement that "each person calculates the inconveniences of crime" and Bentham's assertion that "all men calculate, even madmen." Classical criminology also assumes that criminals know their actions are wrong. Here, however, there is one caveat. Only when the laws are well-written and accessible to the population can people be expected to understand the wrongfulness of particular actions. Finally, Beccaria and Bentham consistently promoted the idea that individuals act on the basis of free will (they are free *agents*). Though humans act to maximize their interests, as those interests are self-defined in terms of seeking pleasure and avoiding pain, this is viewed neither as a force beyond individual control nor as a defect. What emerges out of classical criminology, then, is a strong theory of the individual holding that the offender is a knowing agent who understands the consequences of personal behavior, and is not acting under the influence of any recognizable or unrecognizable internal or external force. Of all the major theoretical explanations of crime, classical criminology provides the strongest theory of the individual. In this theory, crime is behavior that is authored by an offender who is rational, self-interested, and free.

The Social Structural Side of Agency

Sociology is committed to the idea that social phenomena shape behavior in society. Social phenomena linked to crime would include family life, economic opportunities, neighborhood norms, racism, and group contacts, to name just a few. Beccaria and Bentham gave little attention to most such factors. For them, there was only one compellingly important social structural influence on action: the law. They recognized that laws have the potential to shape human behavior, and held that enlightened legislation could direct behavior along positive lines, while at the same time restricting behavior likely to have a negative impact on society.

Beccaria and Bentham thought that enlightened legislators could influence behavior, but ultimately they felt that agency rests with individuals. Behavior, including criminal behavior, is the result of knowing, purposeful agents who are free to choose.

Policy Implications

If the classical theory of crime is essentially correct, what could society do to prevent and control criminal behavior? In other words, what are the policy implications that emerge from the theory? Because the classical theorists were primarily interested in legal reform, their policy proposals were stated explicitly. We have already discussed many of these points, but a few merit further consideration. First, legislators should enact laws that are clear and simple. Second, the laws should promote the common good. This requires that the legislators be "enlightened." Neither Beccaria nor Bentham thought that legislators were typically enlightened; in fact, they tended to assume just the opposite. A glimmer of this low view of legislators may be seen in a letter Bentham wrote to his brother. The letter addressed the legal consequences of divorce, something which Bentham thought his brother should be concerned about. Bentham wrote: "Take notice that the foolish nincompoops called Legislators have not made provision for a tenth part of the varieties that may take place with relation to such an affair."[46] The "foolish nincompoops" would need help in creating legislation to properly govern society. Accordingly, Bentham was always ready to share with lawmakers his own ideas on utilitarian governance. Beccaria felt similarly. He too thought that philosophers, as disinterested experts, would have to assist legislators: "Philosophers acquire needs and interests unknown to ordinary men, . . . they also acquire the habit of loving truth for its own sake."[47]

That sentences should be fixed in advance is a third policy implication of classical criminology. Indeterminate sentencing should be avoided because it reduces the certainty of society's response to crime. Fixed sentences, on the other hand, allow individuals to calculate beforehand the consequences of their actions. Fixed sentences also restrict the discretionary power of judges. According to classical criminology, judges must be restrained. This is the case for numerous reasons, not the least of which is that judicial discretion reduces the predictability of criminal justice.

In addition to certain punishment, the classicists also argued for proportionate punishment, a fourth policy implication. Harsh offenses must be met with harsh punishments, while minor offenses should result in minor punishments. The justification for any punishment is deterrence. Excessively severe punishments will tempt an offender to commit additional crimes in order to avoid detection or capture and also undermine the sense of legitimacy and respect citizens have for the justice system. Punishments that are too lenient will only encourage further crime. Only proportionate punishment deters.

A fifth policy implication of classical criminology is that defendants should be guaranteed a speedy and public trial. Not just coincidentally, the first part of the Sixth Amendment to the United States Constitution explicitly affirms this: "In all criminal prosecutions, the accused shall enjoy the right to a speedy and public trial, . . ."[48] Present conditions in the criminal justice system, however, do not allow for prompt trials. Defendants may go months or even years awaiting trial. What is more, many defendants are kept in jail while waiting for their trial appearance: "In 1990, there were 403,019 adult jail inmates, of whom 207,358 were unconvicted."[49] Those parties involved in civil lawsuits are even less likely to receive a speedy trial. The Illinois Civil Justice League, an organization that seeks civil justice reform, complains that, in Chicago, 6 years is "the average number of years that a trial is delayed following the date of the incident."[50]

Laws should avoid that area of social behavior governed by emotions or, at any rate, types of behavior not motivated primarily by reason (remember, "all men calculate"). This, then, is the sixth policy implication of classical criminology and Bentham explained the point as follows:

> **With what chance of success, for example, would a legislator go about to extirpate drunkenness and fornication, by dint of legal punishment? Not all the tortures which ingenuity could invent would compass it: and, before he had made any progress worth regarding, such a mass of evil**

> **would be produced by the punishment, as would exceed, a thousand-fold, the utmost possible mischief of the offense.[51]**

A legislator should never overstretch the reach of law. To do so would be to promote law violation, and this in turn would encourage a general disrespect for the legal system. No doubt, Bentham would have been dismayed by passage of the Volstead Act, which enforced a ban on the production and sale of alcoholic beverages. As Bentham might have guessed, Prohibition legislation was eventually repealed. One can only conjecture what Bentham would say about the "war on drugs."

A seventh, and for our immediate purposes, final policy implication of classical criminology is the assertion that individuals are accountable for their behavior. The notion that individuals are responsible for their own actions is no longer universally accepted. To some extent at least, American society presently allows individuals to deflect personal responsibility for behavior by claiming victimhood.[52] Victimization is defined by a wide variety of categorical statuses, the most prominent of which are based on racial/ethnic heritage, gender, sexual behavior preference, age, income level, body fat, physical ability, and the urge to gamble. The idea that human actors could be overcome by any of these "conditions" does not resonate with classical criminology and its view of the individual as a rational, purposeful, free agent.

Subsequent Developments

Classical criminology provided the first systematic and scholarly theory of crime, but many other major theories followed. These other formulations were highly critical of the ideas advanced by Beccaria and Bentham. Beginning in the 1960s, however, and extending through the present, the classical position on crime has been revived. We will now consider four versions of this revival: Gary Becker's economic model of crime, David Gordon's critique of crime in capitalist society, deterrence theory, and rational choice theory.

Becker's Economic Model of Crime

In what has been referred to as a seminal article, Gary Becker in 1968 sought to disinter the classical theory of crime by forwarding an economic analysis of criminal behavior.[53] Becker states his objective as follows:

> **Lest the reader be repelled by the apparent novelty of an "economic" framework for illegal behavior, let him recall that two important contributors to criminology during the eighteenth and**

nineteenth centuries, Beccaria and Bentham, explicitly applied an economic calculus. Unfortunately, such an approach has lost favor during the last hundred years, and my efforts can be viewed as a resurrection, modernization, and thereby I hope improvement on these much earlier pioneering studies.[54]

According to Becker, sociological theories of crime that highlight various social phenomena such as neighborhoods, friends and colleagues, family attachment, and subcultural norms, are all special (specific) theories. These special theories can be "dispensed with," claims Becker, by applying an economic framework to the study of crime.[55] The author supplies a complex and extensive quantitative analysis of criminal behavior and its relationship to punishments and legislation. For present purposes, however, the main argument advanced by Becker is that, independent of any and all social forces that may influence behavior, human actors ultimately do a cost/benefit analysis of their actions in society. The analysis of criminal behavior is thus subsumed under a more general theory of behavior: all things being equal, individuals will pursue those behaviors that hold the greatest promise for gratification and/or the least probability of personal cost. Similar to assertions made by Beccaria and Bentham centuries ago, Becker portrays the criminal offender as a rational actor. This does not mean, he hastens to add, that his model assumes "perfect knowledge, lightning-fast calculation, or any of the other caricatures of economic theory."[56] It does mean, however, that the criminal offender is a knowing agent, not someone so overwhelmed by internal or external forces as to lose a personal sense of reason.

Gordon's Critique of Crime and Capitalism

In the early 1970s, David Gordon argued for a reconsideration of mainstream criminological theory.[57] He specifically rejected both conservative and liberal conceptions of the criminal offender. Although conservatives and liberals disagree on most of the key issues concerning crime, stated Gordon, they do share the assumption that criminals are irrational individuals, conservatives tending to blame internal causes for the irrationality while liberals accent social sources. According to Gordon, it is a fundamental error to view criminals as irrational: "Many kinds of crime represent perfectly rational responses to the conditions of competition and inequality fostered in capitalism; . . ."[58] Examples of rational illegal behavior are white-collar crime, organized crime, and what he refers to as *ghetto crime*.

Early in the twentieth century a Dutch criminologist, Willem Bonger, made "corporate profits" the cornerstone around which he constructed a general theory of crime in capitalist society.[59] Gordon's focus is not quite so expansive. He argues, first of all, that white-collar criminals (corporations and their executives, for example) have much to gain from illegal actions. Indeed, in previous chapters we have emphasized the enormous financial benefits of white-collar crime. It is no surprise, then, that repeated studies of white-collar crime have shown corporations to be frequent and serious law violators.[60] Despite a high level of lawbreaking, however, corporations and their white-collar employees are infrequently punished—and rarely punished severely. Referring to the findings of a comprehensive study, James W. Coleman, an expert on white-collar crime, states that "corporate fines seldom even equaled the amount of profit made from the illegal actions. . . ."[61] Coleman adds that not just corporations "get off," but so do the executives in charge. Hence, business white-collar criminals have little to fear personally from law enforcement authorities. The same applies to white-collar criminal offenders who have a professional affiliation. States Coleman: "Physicians, lawyers, and other professional groups generally have succeeded in keeping the criminal offenses of their members out of the criminal justice system."[62]

White-collar criminals have much to gain from crime and little worry about being caught, convicted, or sentenced to prison. Faced with this set of circumstances, it seems clear that white-collar criminals are acting rationally when they violate the law.

Many of the same arguments that applied to white-collar criminals also hold true for organized crime offenders. These law violators supply goods and services (narcotics, gambling, prostitution) that are illegal but in high demand. The profits involved in the illegal drug market alone are staggering, estimates ranging in the billions of dollars annually. Illegal gambling too is big business. It has been suggested that 25 percent of all gambling is illegal.[63] The dollar value of legal gambling is estimated to be about $400 billion annually, thus making the illegal gambling total approximately $125 billion yearly.[64] Without question, there are substantial financial gains available to organized crime offenders. Just as clearly, the chances for criminal apprehension and prosecution are not necessarily high. Even though the United States' "war on drugs" has led to dramatic increases in drug offense arrests and convictions,[65] organized crime offenders still have relatively little to fear from the criminal justice system. After all, in some situations the "fix" is in—police and/or prosecutors are part of the organized crime team. Once again, Gordon argues, it is perfectly rational to follow a course of action that derives from a cost/benefit analysis, as do many organized crime activities.

Gordon's final example of rational crime is ghetto crime. Here, attention is centered on the options of a

In the early 1990s Michael Milken served about two years in prison and paid over $1 billion in fines and restitution for securities-law violations.

young inner-city resident. Typically, such an individual lacks the kind of marketable skills that might lead to a rewarding and gratifying job. Which is more desirable, to be a dishwasher or a mugger? A dishwasher may expect to work long and boring hours for low pay and little status. On the other hand, a mugger could work short and exciting hours for (probably) more pay and higher esteem. Given the choices, is the mugger acting irrationally? Gordon's answer is no.

In each of the three major types of lawbreaking highlighted by Gordon, it appears to be the case that the offender is a rational actor. In all cases, the benefits of the crime outweigh, in theory at least, the potential costs.

Deterrence Theory

A third reformulation of classical criminology is the body of thought known as *deterrence theory*.[66] Jack Gibbs, one of the most prominent proponents of the deterrence doctrine, argues that the ideas of this perspective can be reduced to the following proposition: "The rate for a particular type of crime varies inversely with the celerity,

certainty, and severity of punishments of that type of crime."[67] Deterrence may be conceptualized as specific or general. **Specific deterrence** refers to any correctional response that deters a particular individual from engaging in future criminal behavior, while **general deterrence** refers to discouraging the general population from future criminal acts. Like their predecessors, Beccaria and Bentham, contemporary deterrence theorists are most concerned with criminal justice policy. Broadly stated, the deterrence doctrine suggests that punishment will be an effective deterrent if it is certain, appropriately severe, and swift (laboratory research suggests that certainty and severity may be more important than swiftness).[68] It is commonly thought that a prison sentence will specifically deter an individual from committing more criminal offenses. Indeed, if individuals are incarcerated, they will not perpetrate crimes on the outside. But most inmates are eventually released from prison, and it is at this point that effectiveness of specific deterrence is measured by something called the **recidivism rate** (the likelihood of the individual being rearrested). The results are not promising. Consistent with other studies, Joan Petersilia and her colleagues found that 72 percent of released prison inmates were rearrested within 2 years of their discharge.[69] Using prison statistics and official police data to estimate the overall effects of imprisonment on the crime rate, David Greenberg offered the general conclusion that "there is no compelling evidence that imprisonment substantially increases (or decreases) the likelihood of subsequent criminal involvement."[70] Why is specific deterrence so unsuccessful? Conservatives might explain this by arguing that the punishments are not severe enough, while liberals would be likely to lay the blame on the fact that prison rehabilitation programs have been scrapped. In any case, specific deterrence is highly effective only so long as offenders remain incapacitated.

Most of the research on deterrence theory has dealt with general deterrence rather than specific deterrence and has tended to focus on the certainty and severity of punishments. A typical form of deterrence research has been to identify a relationship between arrests and prison admissions (certainty), and/or length of prison sentence (severity), and the crime rate. Charles Tittle examined the relationship between these variables for index crimes and found that states with higher certainty of punishment had lower crime rates, but that severity of punishment was a factor only for homicide.[71] In examining cities and counties in Florida, Tittle and Alan Rowe have also argued that a "tip point" of certainty is necessary for general deterrence to be effective.[72] These researchers found that a 30 percent tip point of certainty was required "before there is a noticeable change in volume of crime."[73] This means that the perceived likelihood of punishment must at least be at the 30 percent level for punishment to be an effective deterrent.

There is more to be said about the alleged relationship between certainty of punishment and crime commission, however. First, it could be that the causal relationship is just the opposite of what most deterrence researchers allege (namely, that certainty of punishment results in low crime rates). Instead, a low crime rate may *increase* the certainty of punishment; that is, where the crime rate is low, the resources of the criminal justice system will not be overburdened and this will increase the probability of offender arrest and prosecution. On the other hand, where there is "system overload," the police and courts will be less able to respond with high certainty to crime commission.[74]

A second difficulty with conventional thinking on deterrence is that other variables may be even more important than certainty of punishment. In the Tittle and Rowe study noted earlier, the researchers identified several control variables, including sex, age, race and socioeconomic status. Perhaps the most important finding from their research was that socioeconomic status had the most effect on criminal offending: "The lower the socioeconomic status, the higher the crime rate, regardless of certainty of arrest."[75] Nonetheless, the authors conclude that deterrence theory has much to contribute to our understanding of crime. Whereas most crime theories highlight some motivating reason to commit a crime, deterrence theory can embrace all of the motivating reasons and pair them with the other side—reasons for not committing an offense. In short, deterrence theory can help to explain negative cases. For example, if poverty motivates people to steal, we should expect poor people to become thieves. Deterrence theory would explain that most poor people are deterred from stealing by the perceived threat of penalties. Despite the various shortcomings of deterrence theory, it is likely to remain an active area of inquiry in criminology.

Rational Choice Theory

A fourth and most recent restatement of classical criminology is *rational choice theory*. This formulation has important but subtle differences with both classical criminology and deterrence theory. Unlike classical criminology, rational choice theory identifies a **choice structuring** process that is specific to both offenders and offenses. Derek Cornish and Ronald Clarke, perhaps the two most prominent exponents of rational choice theory, developed the concept of choice-structuring properties.[76] In essence, this concept refers to the **Three Rs:** risks, rewards, and requisites. What are the perceived risks involved in committing a particular offense? What are the rewards likely to be realized? And, what skills or resources are required to perform the criminal act successfully? Beccaria and Bentham had spoken more generically about offenders and offenses; rational choice theory emphasizes that the risks, rewards, and requisites will vary from offender to offender, from offense to offense, and from initial involvement to continued involvement to possible desistance.

Rational choice theory also differs from deterrence theory in that the latter tends to stress the perceived risks attending a criminal offense, while the former seeks to account for both risks (probability of being caught, imprisonment) and rewards (financial gain, prestige, enjoyment). Deterrence theory suggests that the greater the risk, in certainty and severity of negative sanctions, the less likely an individual will be to commit an offense. In fact, this is the core proposition of deterrence theory. Piliavin and associates have argued, however, that the perceived reward component of behavior has been generally neglected by deterrence theory. A satisfactory rational choice model accounts for perceived returns from criminal behavior as well as the probable risks and costs of the act.

Another advance made by rational choice theory is its handling of **crime displacement,** a concept suggesting that the prevention of a particular crime will result in the criminal activity's being displaced to other targets, locations, or types of crime. For example, community residents and the police may patrol a neighborhood so effec-

Criminals Are Not Always So Rational

The classical theory of crime describes criminal offenders as rational and calculative actors. This view is challenged by Daniel Butler, Leland Gregory, and Alan Ray in their book *America's Dumbest Criminals*. Here are just three of the one hundred accounts reported by Butler and his associates. First is the case of a robbery suspect who was picked up by the police as someone fitting the general description of the offender. The police told the man that they were taking the suspect back to the scene of the crime so that the victim could make an identification. Once they arrived, the suspect blurted out: "Yeah, that's her—that's the woman I robbed."

A second case concerns a man arrested for cashing a stolen check. Police accused the man of forging the name on the front of the check. When the man denied it ("Nah, you've got the wrong man"), the police explained that he had used his *real* name when he endorsed the check. Not only that, he provided the teller with his real driver's license and current address.

Finally, in a third case, a Savannah, Georgia, uniformed police officer knocked on the door of a known drug house and stated that he wanted to buy a bag of dope. The person answering the door said "But, you're a cop." The officer replied "So, why can't I buy some dope?" A minute later the man sold the officer the dope, after which he was promptly arrested.

Cases such as these do not disprove the general thrust of classical criminology. At the same time, they indicate that rational calculation is sometimes in the eye of the beholder. In other words, proponents of the classical theory of crime tend to exaggerate the calculative powers of criminal offenders.

SOURCE: Daniel Butler, Leland Gregory, and Alan Ray, *America's Dumbest Criminals* (Thorndike, MA: Thorndike Press, 1995).

tively that illegal drug business is forced elsewhere. The crime has been displaced. Many other forms of crime, however, may be eliminated, not merely displaced. Increased airport security, to cite another example, appears to have minimized airplane hijackings. What is more, there is no evidence that individuals have turned to train or bus hijackings in lieu of airplanes. Clearly, of all the subsequent developments of classical criminology, rational choice theory provides the greatest specification with regard to crime and criminals.

Critique

Adequacy

Classical criminology provides an explanation of crime that is partly plausible. The internal logic of the theory is consistent, and it has a practical plausibility as well. There are problems, however. In particular, the key concepts of rationality, self-interest, and freedom are overstretched. Many offenders do not behave rationally, at least not in a conventional sense (Box 9.3). Nor do all offenders act on the basis of material gain. For example, sociologist Jack Katz describes various crimes wherein the offender is stimulated by moral posturing, existential validation, and excitement—not rationality or material self-interest.[77] Moreover, the classical view of free will ignores the ordinary constraints and limitations faced by individuals. Theoretical freedom is one thing; freedom in everyday life is something else. This point leads directly to classical crim-

inology's inadequate theory of social structure. Arguing that the legal code is the only, or even the main, social influence on human action invites criticism. There are many other social structural forces that restrict or direct behavior in society.

Empirical support for the theory is also less than compelling. Strictly speaking, Beccaria and Bentham were philosophers rather than researchers. Moreover, subsequent developments in this school of thought have not enjoyed a great deal of empirical confirmation. Deterrence theory and rational choice theory now receive the most attention, but research findings are mixed at best. Consider Ronald Akers' evaluation:

> **In fact, some of the studies purporting to find evidence favoring rational choice theory actually test models that are indistinguishable from other supposedly non-rational choice theories.[78]**

Deterrence theory fares no better. Research shows that the individuals are often deterred from crime by informal factors such as family attachment, self-concept, and conscience, not necessarily legal sanctions, which are the favorite focus of deterrence theory.[79] These informal factors are addressed more specifically in other theories of crime.

Is the classical theory of crime falsifiable and predictable? The answer to the former is a qualified yes, and to the latter, not very. Survey research may be used to determine what offenders were thinking just before committing their crimes. Findings of such research indicate that a high percentage of felons report drug or alcohol use prior to crime commission. Data from Bureau of Justice Statistics surveys show that 31 percent of 1991 prison inmates admitted that they were under the influence of an illegal drug at the time of their offense.[80] Of course, the inmates may be lying, but 1991 crime victimization studies indicated that 33 percent of violent crime victims believed their assailants were under the influence of drugs or alcohol at the time of the crime.[81] Findings such as these run contrary to classical theory. In any event, within limitations, falsifiability is possible. Unfortunately, the predictability of crime from the classical perspective is not impressive. For example, as the certainty and severity of punishment is increased for crime, classical theory would predict corresponding reductions for the crime rate. Over the last two decades in the United States, there has been an enormous increase in law enforcement and punishment, but the crime rate has not decreased proportionally. This is specifically the case with regard to drug offenses, the target of so many additional criminal justice efforts.

In summary, the classical approach to crime is plausible and falsifiable, but lacking in significant empirical support and not very predictive of future crime commission. It is, however, as we shall presently see, fairly comprehensive and current.

Comprehensive Nature

Any theory of crime that seeks to be comprehensive in scope must account for a wide variety of offenses as well as the gender and social class standing of offenders. In this respect, classical criminology surpasses many other theories of criminal behavior. To begin with, it is generally accepted that classical theory offers a fairly persuasive explanation for crimes against property. Stealing offenses, almost by definition, include the promise of financial gain to the offender, and calculation and planning is usually called for. The classical explanation of interpersonal violence, however, is not as convincing. Some violent acts do result in financial gain (robbery), but many others do not (rape). Moreover, while some killings are planned, most emerge spontaneously out of an emotionally charged situation. Classical theory is least able to explain expressionistic crimes, that is, offenses wherein the only reward is emotional satisfaction (e.g., adolescents smashing the principal's car window). Although, even here, it is well to remember Bentham's declaration that calculation is a part of any crime: "Even a madman calculates."

Classical criminology portrays the criminal offender as rational and self-interested. This would indeed seem to apply for most criminals, whether men or women and regardless of class position. Although longstanding stereotypes describe men as more rational than women, the fact is women criminal offenders are even more disproportionately "rational" in their criminal activities than men. For example, men are much more likely to engage in expressionistic and violent behavior than women. On the other hand, indicators such as the fact that absent fathers are considerably more prevalent than absent mothers would suggest that men may be more self-interested than women. In the final analysis, classical criminologists would argue with some justification that when men or women violate the law, the behavior is likely to be rational and motivated by self-interest of some kind.

This leaves social class to be considered. Once again the argument is that the classical explanation is able to transcend differences. The classicists argue that most of the crimes of all social classes can be interpreted as calculative and self interested. For example, the mugger, the embezzler, and the price-fixer are all engaged in a stealing offense that is fundamentally self-interested. What is more, at least a minimal amount of rational deliberation is to be expected for each of these class-based stealing offenses.

In sum, with the exception of impulsive and expressionistic crime, it is difficult to think of any significant type of crime, or variable related to criminal offending, that could not be at least partly explained by classical criminology. The classical theory of crime is characterized by a breadth of coverage unequaled by many other crime theories.

Current Appeal

The classical theory of crime is well over two hundred years old, Beccaria having laid the foundation for this perspective in 1764, but the theory remains current. Since the late 1970s, there has been a sweeping trend away from flexible, open-ended criminal sentences and toward fixed punishments. Much as Beccaria and Bentham urged, judicial discretion has been curtailed. Moreover, public sentiment, backed or pushed by politicians, has adopted a sober attitude toward crime and criminals. This appears to be in response to a general belief that criminals are being dealt with too leniently. In 1983, Ronald Reagan provided a succinct summary of this point of view when he said that the "criminal element now calculates that crime really does pay."[82] Even liberals have gotten into the spirit, as *Newsweek* editor Howard Fineman reported:

> **Heavy spending on new prisons, "three strikes and you're out" sentencing laws, "deadbeat dad" statutes, "boot camps" for youthful offenders, "two years and you're out" welfare reform, denying welfare benefits to unwed mothers, police sweeps through housing projects, even local caning and curfew ordinances—all are ideas being supported by Democrats.[83]**

Iran's Criminal Justice System

Some societies have turned away from the Western model of criminal justice, and others have never adopted it to begin with. The Islamic Revolution in 1978–79 placed Iran in the former category. Having won the cultural and political battle, the Ayatollah Khomeini instituted fundamental change in Iranian society. For instance, Islamic fundamentalists established a system of justice starkly opposed to the classical practices that generally prevail in the United States and Europe. There are at least three points of sharp difference. First, whereas classical crimininoligists argued that laws should be made by secular authorities (legislators), in Iran, religious officials are the ultimate source of law. In Iran, God's law, as stated in the holy Quran and interpreted by religious leaders, defines both crime and punishment. A second Iranian rejection of classical theory has to do with the main purpose of punishment. Beccaria and Bentham stated that deterrence is the pre-eminent justification of punishment. In Iran, however, punishment has two primary aims: deterrence and compensation. Iranian justice stipulates that families are victims. Hence, in a murder case, as well as many other crime situations, "blood money," or compensation, is an integral aspect of correctional policy. Finally, Western legal systems have tried to adopt the classical position of proportionate punishment. Generally, this results in incarceration, probation, fines, or community service, to mention a few possibilities. This list would typically not include corporal punishment. But, in Iran, corporal punishment is common: public floggings and mutilations occur regularly. When a thief has his hands cut off (this procedure has been described as the most frequent type of punishment in Iran), it is said to offer a vivid lesson to all others who might be tempted to steal.

There is one point of agreement between the two cultural traditions—in both cases judges are viewed with skepticism. Classical theory sought to make judges the underlings of legislators, whereas in Iranian justice the judges must answer to clerics, the religious leaders. In sum, while classical criminology has had a huge impact on the development of Western legal systems, its emphasis on secular authority makes it an alien approach in countries where religious fundamentalism is in power.

SOURCE: Nader Entessar, "Criminal Law and the Legal System in Iran," in *Criminology: A Cross-Cultural Perpective,* ed. Robert Heiner (New York: West, 1996) 163–71.

All of these measures are based on the assumption that offenders know what they are doing and that they freely choose to commit crime. To counter crime, punishments must be certain and proportionate, just as the classical criminologists urged. While there are problems and flaws with the classical theory of crime, it continues to have a powerful voice in academic criminology, the criminal justice system, and general public sentiment. However, not all nations embrace the classical view of criminal justice (Box 9.4).

Summary

This chapter has described and discussed the classical theory of crime. The two most prominent advocates of classical criminology, Cesare Beccaria and Jeremy Bentham, sought to reform the criminal justice practices of their time. In so doing, they set forth, at least implicitly, a theory of crime. Following the Enlightenment theory of general social behavior, they contended that criminal offenders, like all other individuals in society, were rational, self-interested, and free. From the classical viewpoint, the criminal justice system, working on behalf of society, must convince would-be offenders that crime does not pay. Hence, criminal punishments must be certain and severe enough to discourage individuals from committing crimes.

Classical criminology has not successfully resolved the problem of agency. Beccaria and Bentham advanced a too-strong theory of the individual and an incomplete view of social structure. Crime is not just a product of individual initiative, nor does the formal legal code account for all social structural influence on behavior. Despite its failure with regard to the problem of agency, classical criminology advanced a number of worthwhile policy proposals: clear laws, enlightened legislation, fixed sentences, proportionate punishments, the guarantee of a speedy and public trial, caution against the overuse of the law to shape private behavior, and the notion that individuals are accountable for their behavior.

This chapter has also identified four contemporary reformulations of the classical theory. These consist of Becker's economic analysis of crime, Gordon's argument that crime is a rational response to capitalist conditions, deterrence theory, and the rational choice perspective. Finally, we have seen that classical criminology's theory of crime is somewhat plausible, fairly comprehensive, and very current.

Critical Thinking Questions

1. If you had to explain the five main points of classical criminology to someone who knew nothing about sociology or criminology, what would you say?

2. If Beccaria and Bentham were alive today, what would they think of American criminal justice?

3. What political party in the United States would be most likely to endorse the principles of classical criminology?

4. What is the single greatest insight of the classical theory of crime? What is the single greatest weakness of this theory?

5. Do you have a family member or a friend who was victimized by a crime within the last few years? If so, consider whether or not classical criminology offers a good explanation for that criminal offense.

6. What are the major policy implications of classical criminology? Explain why you would or would not support these policies.

Suggested Readings

Cesare Beccaria, *On Crimes and Punishments*, tr. Henry Paolucci (New York: Bobbs-Merrill, 1963 [orig. pub. 1764]).

Piers Beirne, "Inventing Criminology: The 'Science of Man' in Cesare Beccaria's *Dei Delitti e Delle Pene* (1764)," *Criminology 29* (1991) 777–820.

Derek Cornish and Ronald Clarke, "Understanding Crime Displacement: An Application of Rational Choice Theory," *Criminology 25* (1987) 933–47.

Elio Monachesi, "Cesare Beccaria," *Journal of Criminal Law, Criminology, and Police Science* 46 (1955) 439–49.

Notes

[1] Willie Sutton, *Where the Money Was* (New York: Viking Press, 1976) 120.

[2] Ibid.

[3] Ibid., 28.

[4] Elio Monachesi, "Cesare Beccaria 1738–1794," in *Pioneers in Criminology*, ed. Hermann Mannheim (Montclair, NJ: Patterson Smith, 1972) 36–50.

[5] Mary Peter Mack, *Jeremy Bentham: An Odyssey of Ideas* (New York: Columbia, 1963), 4–10.

[6] Quoted in Marcello Maestro, *Cesare Beccaria and the Origins of Penal Reform* (Philadelphia: Temple University Press, 1973) 82–83.

[7] The Enlightenment thinkers are routinely thought of as great liberators, and in many respects they were. However, they were also sexist. When they put forth the view that men were rational and capable of self-governance they were indeed speaking of men—not women. Rousseau, for example, had this to say about women: "From this diversity arises the first assignable difference in the moral relations of the two sexes. One ought to be active and strong, the other passive and weak. . . . Thus the whole education of women ought to relate to men. To please men, to be useful to them, to make herself loved and honored by them, to raise them when young, to care for them when grown, to counsel them, to console them, to make their lives agreeable and sweet—these are the duties of women at all times, and they ought to be taught from childhood" (Jean Jacques Rousseau, *Emile, or On Education*. Introduced and tr. Allan Bloom (New York: Basic Books, 1979) 358, 365 [originally published in 1762]). The distinction here between "man" and "individual" is deeper than just semantics. Many of the ideas propounded by Enlightenment writers have been accepted,

formally and informally, by modern societies. Today, however, the attributes accorded to men by eighteenth-century thinkers would be extended to women. Thus, the text discussion henceforth will refer to individuals, not just men, as was so often meant by these historical figures.

[8] John Locke, *An Essay Concerning Human Understanding* (Oxford: Clarendon University Press, 1894) 436.

[9] Jean Jacques Rousseau, *The Essential Rousseau*, tr. Lowell Bair (New York: Mentor, 1974) 140.

[10] Ibid., 88.

[11] Coleman Phillipson, *Three Criminal Law Reformers: Beccaria, Bentham, Romily* (Montclair, NJ: Patterson Smith, 1970). See also Harry Elmer Barnes, *The Story of Punishment*, 2nd ed. (Montclair, NJ: Patterson Smith, 1972 [orig. pub. 1930]).

[12] Will and Ariel Durant, *The Story of Civilization, Part IX: The Age of Voltaire* (New York: Simon & Schuster, 1965) 71.

[13] J. M. Beattie, *Crime and the Courts in England, 1660–1800* (Princeton, NJ: Princeton University Press, 1986) 341.

[14] Will and Ariel Durant, *The Story of Civilization, Part IX: The Age of Voltaire*, 69.

[15] Paul Lacroix, *France in the Middle Ages* (New York: Frederick Ungar, 1963), 407–433.

[16] Ibid., 420–22.

[17] Will and Ariel Durant, *The Story of Civilization, Part IX: The Age of Voltaire*, 73.

[18] J. M. Beattie, *Crime and the Courts in England, 1660–1800*, 340–52.

[19] Ibid.

[20] Cesare Beccaria, *On Crimes and Punishments*, tr. Henry Paolucci (Indianapolis: Bobbs-Merrill, 1963 [orig. pub. 1764]).

[21] Jeremy Bentham, *An Introduction to the Principles of Morals and Legislation*, Vol. I (London: Pickering, 1823).

[22] Ibid., 55–71.

[23] Elio Monachesi, "Cesare Beccaria 1738–1794," 39–43. See also Bertrand Russell, *A History of Western Philosophy* (New York: Simon & Schuster, 1945), 629–37.

[24] Jeremy Bentham, *The Works of Jeremy Bentham*, ed. John Bowring (Edinburg: Tait, 1843) 90–91.

[25] Cesare Beccaria, *On Crimes and Punishments*, 1963, 67.

[26] Bentham, *An Introduction to the Principles of Morals and Legislation*, 128.

[27] Ibid., 132.

[28] Jeremy Bentham, *An Introduction to the Principles of Morals and Legislation*, ed. J.H. Burns and H.L.A. Hart (London: Athlone Press, 1970 [orig. pub. 1823]).

[29] Quoted in Mack, *Jeremy Bentham: An Odyssey of Ideas*, 78.

[30] Beccaria, *On Crimes and Punishments*, 1963, 8.

[31] Ibid.

[32] Bentham, *An Introduction to the Principles of Morals and Legislation*, 74.

[33] Ibid., 158.

[34] Beccaria, *On Crimes and Punishments*, 17.

[35] Ibid.

[36] Beccaria, *On Crimes and Punishments*, 43.

[37] Bentham, *An Introduction to the Principles of Morals and Legislation*, 158.

[38] Beccaria, *On Crimes and Punishments*, 63.

[39] Ibid., 47–48.

[40] Ibid., 63.

[41] Bentham, *An Introduction to the Principles of Morals and Legislation*, 11.

[42] Jeremy Bentham, *An Introduction to the Principles of Morals and Legislation*, Vol. I (London: Pickering, 1823) 30–31.

[43] Ibid., 58.

[44] Beccaria, *On Crimes and Punishments*, 56.

[45] Ibid.

[46] *Collected Works of Jeremy Bentham: Correspondence of Jeremy Bentham*, Vol. 3, ed. J. H. Barns (London: University of London Press, 1971) 162.

[47] Cesare Beccaria, *On Crimes and Punishments*, 97.

[48] Quoted in *The Citizen's Handbook*, compiled by T.J. Stiles (New York: Berkley Books, 1993) 64.

[49] Jeffrey Reiman, *The Rich Get Richer and the Poor Get Prison*, 4th ed. (Boston: Allyn & Bacon,1995) 114–15.

[50] "How Big a Problem Is Lawsuit Abuse in Illinois," flyer sent by Illinois Citizens Against Lawsuit Abuse, Chicago, Illinois, December 1994.

[51] Bentham, *An Introduction to the Principles of Morals and Legislation*, 290.

[52] Charles Sykes, *A Nation of Victims* (New York: St. Martin's Press, 1992).

[53] Gary Becker, "Crime and Punishment: An Economic Approach," *Journal of Political Economy 78* (1968) 189–217.

[54] Ibid., 209.

[55] Ibid., 170.

[56] Ibid., 176.

[57] David Gordon, "Capitalism, Class and Crime in America," *Crime and Delinquency 19* (1973)163–86; "Class and the Economics of Crime," *The Review of Radical Political Economics 3* (1971) 51–72.

58 Gordon, "Capitalism, Class and Crime in America," 163.

59 Willem Bonger, *Criminality and Economic Conditions* (Bloomington: Indiana University Press, 1969 [orig. pub. 1916]).

60 See especially Edwin Sutherland, "White Collar Criminality," *American Sociological Review 5* (1940) 1–12; "Is White Collar Crime 'Crime'?" *American Sociological Review* 10 (1945) 132–39; and Marshall Clinard and Peter Yeager, *Corporate Crime* (New York: Free Press, 1980).

61 James W. Coleman, *The Criminal Elite: The Sociology of White Collar Crime,* 2nd ed. (New York: St. Martin's Press,1989) 154–55.

62 Ibid., 154.

63 Diana Church, Mark Siegel and Nancy Jacobs, *Gambling: Crime or Recreation?* (Wylie, TX: Information Aids, Inc., 1988) 19.

64 Neil Milbert, "Gambling Network Hopes to Bring a Winner Home," *Chicago Tribune,* 5 October 1994, 4-1.

65 Patrick Langan and Helen Graziadei, "Felony Sentences in State Courts, 1992," *Bureau of Justice Statistics Bulletin* (Washington D.C.: U.S. Department of Justice) 8.

66 See in particular John Andenaes, *Punishment and Deterrence* (Ann Arbor: University of Michigan Press, 1974); Jack Gibbs, *Crime, Punishment and Deterrence* (New York: Elsevier, 1975); and Franklin Zimring and Gordon Hawkins, *Deterrence* (Chicago: University of Chicago Press, 1973).

67 Jack Gibbs, *Crime, Punishment, and Deterrence,* 5.

68 Alfred Miranne and Louis Gray, "Deterrence: A Laboratory Experiment," *Deviant Behavior 8* (1987) 191–203.

69 Joan Petersilia, Susan Turner, James Kahan, and Joyce Peterson, *Prison versus Probation in California: Implications for Crime and Offender Recidivism* (Santa Monica: Rand Corporation, 1986).

70 David Greenberg, "The Incapacitative Effects of Imprisonment: Some Estimates," *Law and Society Review 9* (1975) 558.

71 Charles Tittle, "Crime Rates and Legal Sanctions," *Social Problems 16* (1969) 408–423.

72 Charles Tittle and Alan Rowe, "Certainty of Arrest and Crime Rates: A Further Test of the Deterrence Hypothesis," *Social Forces 52* (1974) 455–62.

73 Ibid., 458.

74 Marvin Krohn, "Control and Deterrence Theories of Criminality," in *Criminology: A Contemporary Handbook,* 2nd ed., ed. Joseph F. Sheley (Belmont, CA: Wadsworth, 1995) 329–47.

75 Ibid., 461.

76 Derek Cornish and Ronald Clarke, "Understanding Crime Displacement: An Application of Rational Choice Theory," *Criminology 25* (1987) 933–47.

77 Jack Katz, *Seductions of Crime* (New York: Basic, 1988).

78 Ronald Akers, *Criminological Theories: Introduction and Evaluation* (Los Angeles: Roxbury, 1994) 60.

79 Ibid., 56.

80 *Drugs and Crime Facts, 1993* (Washington D.C.: U.S. Department of Justice, 1994) 4.

81 Ibid.

82 Quoted in *The New York Times,* 19 April 1983, 1, 15-1.

83 Howard Fineman, "The Virtuecrats," *Newsweek,* 13 June 1994, 36.

chapter 10

Theories of the Driven Offender

CHAPTER OUTLINE

BACKGROUND
  Positivism
  Evolutionary Thought
  Criminological Thought in the Nineteenth Century
CORE PROPOSITIONS
  Rejection of Classical Criminology
  Scientific Study of Crime
  The Born Criminal
  Identification of Criminals
POSITION ON AGENCY (RESPONSIBILITY)
POLICY IMPLICATIONS
SUBSEQUENT DEVELOPMENTS
  Genetic Influences
    Body Type Theories
    Crime and Human Nature
    Adoption Studies
    XYY Research
  Other Biological Factors Associated with Crime
    Autonomic Nervous System Deficiency
    Brain Dysfunctions
    Sex Hormones
    Dietary Conditions
  Summary of Subsequent Biological Developments
  Freudian Interpretations of Crime
    Personality Development
    The Unconscious
    Using Freudian Thought to Explain Crime
    Summary of Freudian Interpretations on Crime
  Low Self-Control
CRITIQUE
  Adequacy
  Comprehensive Nature
  Current Appeal
SUMMARY

KEY TERMS

scientific method
positivists
phrenology
cartography
transmitted behavior
early positivism
naturalistic definition of crime
agency
atavist
born criminal
physical stigmata
forms of elimination
ectomorph
endomorph
mesomorph
XYY Theory
autonomic nervous system (ANS)
premenstrual syndrome (PMS)
hypoglycemia
id, ego, superego
identification
repression
low self-control

IN 1990, JOHN WAYNE GACY was convicted of murdering 33 boys and young men. Fourteen years later, on May 11, 1994, he was executed at Stateville Correctional Center in Illinois. The very next day, the University of Chicago Medical Center announced that the Gacy family had consented to their performing a neuropathological post-mortem exam on Gacy's brain.[1] Such examinations have never yielded positive evidence linking brain structure or function to criminal behavior. Nevertheless, some researchers believe that brain analysis is the key to discovering the biological basis of crime.

This is not ancient history—1994 is not that long ago. And yet this approach to seeking an answer to criminal behavior is very old. Cesare Lombroso, referred to by some as the father of criminology, did hundreds, if not thousands, of post-mortems. Lombroso, and the other theorists presented in this chapter, all felt that behavior is a reflection of forces inside the individual; hence, the criminologist must examine the individual offender. As you read this chapter, consider whether you think that a microscopic analysis of John Wayne Gacy's brain is a promising way in which to learn more about crime.

Background

While the classical theory of crime describes the criminal offender as a person in control, as one who chooses to commit crime, the theories highlighted in this chapter arrive at just the opposite conclusion—that an offender is driven to commit crimes by individualistic forces beyond personal control. These theorists explain criminal behavior as the predicted outcome of *internal flaws* within the individual. Most often, the internal flaws are associated with a biological or psychological irregularity. Historically, the two most pivotal figures identified with this theoretical approach are Cesare Lombroso (1835–1909) and Sigmund Freud (1856–1939). Both Lombroso and Freud found trouble inside the individual. While Lombroso advanced a biological theory of crime, Freud offered an account of antisocial behavior based on psychic structure. Although it may seem odd to link Lombroso and Freud, the fact is that each viewed human actors as "driven." Hence, from this point of view, behavior in society is determined for the individual and not the product of individual will.

Chapter 9 noted two great influences on the work of the criminal justice reformers, Beccaria and Bentham: (1) The brutal and ineffective criminal justice practices of their time, and (2) Enlightenment philosophy. But that was the eighteenth century. Beccaria and Bentham died before Lombroso and Freud were born. In addition to living in a different era than the classical criminologists, Lombroso and Freud were men of science and medicine rather than judicial reformers or philosophers. Hence, the forces which shaped their thinking were far different from those that made an impression on Beccaria and Bentham. In particular, three sources of intellectual influence require elaboration: positivism, evolutionary theory, and the existing criminological literature.

Positivism

The **scientific method** is a way of studying phenomena by using objective observation and measurement. The scientific method enabled Copernicus (1473–1543), Bacon (1561–1626), Galileo (1564–1642), and Newton (1642–1727) to totally transform the basic tenets of astronomy and physics. Science provided a more positive (that is, *certain*) understanding of the physical world. Subsequently, Charles Darwin (1809–1882) applied the scientific method to the study of the natural world, and his theory of evolution challenged the traditional and prevailing views of human nature and biology. Finally, in this vein, Auguste Comte (1798–1857) sought to apply the scientific method to social life. Comte was not nearly as successful as the others mentioned, but he came to be regarded as the "father of positivism," as well, it may be added, as the "father of sociology." According to Comte, knowledge has evolved through stages. That is, explanations of the physical and social world evolve through the centuries from religious, to philosophical, to (currently) positivist or scientific.[2] A scientific understanding, he argues, provides positive (certain) knowledge. Indeed, certain or sure knowledge is what Lombroso and Freud sought. By focusing attention on the individual, they sought to discover positive knowledge about human behavior. In this sense, then, Lombroso and Freud have each been identified as **positivists.**[3]

Evolutionary Thought

Charles Darwin and Karl Marx have been referred to as *the* scientist and *the* sociologist, respectively.[4] What was common between them was that each offered an evolutionary model of development—biological development from Darwin, and social development from Marx. Darwin argued that forms of plant and animal life change gradually over time and that, while some species die out, others emerge in the "natural selection" process.[5] In his *Descent of Man,* published in 1871, Darwin provided evidence that humans, like other animals, were products of this process.[6] What was true for gnats was no less true for humans. What is more, Darwin suggested that, while all humans descended from ape-like ancestors, we could speak of uneven evolution; some humans might be more or less evolved than others. As we shall see shortly, Lombroso and his followers made much of this idea that the criminal must be less evolved than other human beings.

Marx sought to advance a comprehensive theory of social relations. For him, the most fundamental insight was that the evolution of material conditions determines human social life.[7] Human history unfolds not by accident, nor through the efforts of great men, but as a result of changes in the economic structure of society. As the following passage highlights, Marx viewed the individual as subordinate to the flow and evolution of historical materialism:

> **Upon the different forms of property, upon the social conditions of existence, rises an entire superstructure of distinct and peculiarly formed sentiments, illusions, modes of thought and views of life. . . . The single individual, who derives them through tradition and upbringing, may imagine that they form the real motives and the starting point of his activity.[8]**

This reference to Marx's thought contains two particularly relevant points. First, the individual is not seen as a determining agent. Lombroso adopts a similar viewpoint with respect to criminal offenders. Contrary to what the classical theorists propounded, this approach assumes that individuals do *not* choose to commit crimes. Second, Marx suggests that there is a real world and a world that is only imagined. Individuals may "imagine that they form" their own motives, but really, argues Marx, motives are socially given. Freud too, it will be seen, rejected the notion that human actors are routinely aware (consciously) of their true motives.

Criminological Thought in the 19th Century

Those who formulated the nineteenth-century theories of the "driven" offender were at least minimally influenced by several existing theoretical approaches to crime, including classical criminology, phrenology, the cartographic school, and explanations resting on biological or social transmission of criminal tendencies. Virtually every proposition of the previously discussed classical theory was rejected by Lombroso and his associates. In this sense, positivism emerged almost as an anti-theory. The connection between classicism and positivism will be revisited later, but it will be useful now to discuss the other three schools of thought.

Phrenology research is frequently viewed as the immediate predecessor of Lombroso's positivism. Franz Joseph Gall (1758–1828), a physician, is considered the founder of phrenology. Gall studied the physical makeup of the brain and speculated on how the brain affected personality and behavior.[9] In short, Gall argued that the human brain has three major regions, each having a specific location in the cranium and each having a distinctive function that was said to correspond roughly to intellectual, moral, and base (animalistic) faculties. Destructive and violent behavior was associated with the base faculties. For most individuals, it was thought, base tendencies would be held in check by the intellectual and moral faculties. Interestingly, Gall hypothesized that proper examination of the exterior of the skull could reveal something about the inner workings of the brain. For instance, an irregular indentation of the skull could be taken as a sign of pathological brain functioning. Hence, according to this approach, criminal offenders could be identified on the basis of physical characteristics.

For the first half of the nineteenth century, in Europe and the United States, phrenology was widely acclaimed as a scientific perspective having considerable potential.[10] By mid-century, however, phrenology came to be viewed as unscientific—in part because charlatans began to "read" heads just as fortunetellers read palms.[11] Nevertheless, phrenology's commitment to detailed physical examination and measurement of the human body became a cornerstone of Lombroso's criminology.

The cartographic school of criminology, characterized by its emphasis on social statistics, dates back to the 1830s. **Cartography** is generally identified with the pioneer work of the French government statistician A.M. Guerry (1802–1866) and the Belgium statistician Adolphe Quetelet (1796–1874). Guerry and Quetelet used government-collected data on crime to make informed observations about the rates and causes of criminal behavior. Specifically, Guerry constructed "ecological maps," which showed the differing rates of personal and property crimes for various regions within France.[12] Guerry argued that disparate crime rates could be explained with reference to the distinctive social conditions of each region.

Unlike Guerry, with his emphasis on regional differences, Quetelet focused on the year-to-year similarities in national crime statistics.[13] Quetelet highlighted the

Enrico Ferri was opposed to the jury system. He thought that ordinary people had neither the training nor disposition to capably decide court cases.

constancy and immutability of social life, at the societal level. For example, the age and sex composition of a nation's population is relatively stable over time. Unchanging social factors such as these, he argued, would make for highly consistent crime rates year after year.

Guerry, Quetelet, and others working in this tradition elevated data to the level of scientific facts. It was the cartographers' methodology, with its focus on exact tabulation and classification, that most impressed the early positivists.

Finally, by the time Lombroso and Freud had developed their theories of human behavior, there were numerous published accounts that explained crime as **transmitted behavior.** Issac Ray, for example, centered attention on deficient mental faculties.[14] Cerebral disease, he argued, whether present at birth or developmental, could lead to moral insanity, which in turn might result in the commission of horrible crimes.[15] Richard Dugdale (1841–1883) applied the notion of the biological transmission of criminal traits in his famous report on the Jukes family.[16] Dugdale traced a host of individual problems of degeneracy, including participation in crime, through several generations of the ancestral Jukes family. Dugdale's research led to a spate

of similar family studies, all of which concluded that crime was a product of "biologically inherited depravity."[17]

The nineteenth century was characterized by fundamental social and intellectual changes. Agriculture was giving way to industrialization and rural society was becoming displaced by urbanization. Science was also ascendant. Use of the scientific method had already yielded compelling explanations of physical and natural phenomena, and now researchers sought to use science to provide insight into human behavior and suggest solutions to social problems, including crime.

Core Propositions of Early Positivism

There are three historical figures most closely identified with early positivism, or as it is sometimes called, the Italian school of criminology: Cesare Lombroso, Enrico Ferri (1856–1929, not to be confused with Enrico Fermi, the nuclear physicist), and Raffaele Garofalo (1852–1934). Lombroso was a medical doctor, while Ferri and Garofalo

TABLE 10.1 | Classicism versus Positivism

	CLASSICAL SCHOOL	EARLY POSITIVISM
Background:	Enlightenment philosophy	Scientific method
Focus:	Crime and criminal justice	Criminal offender
Goal:	Criminal laws	Scientific law
Crime def.:	Legal definition	Natural definition
Agency issue:	Free will	Determinism
Sentencing:	Fixed	Flexible

were lawyers, and yet each became in his own way a criminologist. They shared a common orientation to the study of crime, one advanced in basic form by Lombroso, and one that has come to be known as early positivism. The core ideas of **early positivism** include the following: rejection of classical criminology, adoption of the scientific method in the study of crime, the importance of the born criminal (the "atavist"), and the ability of trained experts to identify and classify criminal offenders.

Rejection of Classical Criminology

In virtually every respect, classicism and early positivism are opposed. As Table 10.1 highlights, the early positivists disagreed with all of the main points of classical criminology. Perhaps most fundamental, Lombroso, Ferri, and Garofalo saw themselves as scientists, not philosophers. Rather than engage in abstract speculation (something they accused Beccaria and Bentham of doing), the positivists were in search of certain, empirical knowledge about crime and criminals. Accordingly, the positivists centered attention on criminal offenders. They assumed that the key to understanding crime commission was necessarily tied to an understanding of those who committed criminal behavior.

Another major point of departure between classicism and positivism is that the former sought to produce effective criminal laws, while the latter sought to discover the scientific laws governing human behavior. Because Lombroso, Ferri, and Garofalo embraced what they regarded as the scientific model, they were unable to accept the legalistic definition of crime, which states that crime is behavior that violates the law. This definition of crime, although suitable for Beccaria and Bentham, was too relativistic for a scientific framework committed to the study of universals. Laws vary in content from culture to culture—and even within a culture. Hence, a definition of crime based on law violation will not work as the starting point of a research process designed to yield scientific laws. Science, the positivists believed, must deal with universals (conditions or facts that occur everywhere). Just as the scientific laws governing the causes of a thunderstorm

do not vary from country to country, neither should the scientific laws governing the causes of criminal behavior vary.

The problem of defining crime was not just a subtle theoretical issue for the positivists. Rather, it was seen as an issue posing serious practical considerations. Garofalo attempted to resolve the problem by advancing what he called a **naturalistic definition of crime.** Natural crime, Garofalo argues, "exists in human society independently of the circumstances and exigencies of a given epoch or the particular views of the law-maker."[18] In essence then, natural crimes consist of behaviors that cause suffering (a violation of the human sense of pity) or violate property rights (a violation of the human sense of probity).[19] Garofalo's proposed solution is less than compelling because pity and probity are themselves culturally relative. The positivists never resolved this issue satisfactorily.

On two further points there was sharp division between classicism and positivism. The first of these two remaining points has to do with the **agency** (responsibility) issue. While Beccaria and Bentham embraced the view that individuals were *free agents* responsible for their actions, the positivists rejected the free will doctrine as fantasy. Lombroso and his followers generally conceptualized human behavior as determined by internal biological/genetic forces.

A final point of disagreement between the two schools of criminological thought reflects their views regarding sentencing options. The classicists recommended fixed sentences while the positivists argued that sentences should be indeterminate, that is, tailored to the specific characteristics of each offender.

Scientific Study of Crime

As was noted earlier, by the nineteenth century, science had made revolutionary gains in understanding the physical and natural worlds. The positivists believed that science could yield similar results with respect to the social world. The scientific study of crime, they argued, must be grounded in empirical investigation. It was their contention that criminal offenders should be examined and observations recorded before any truly reliable conclusions about the nature of crime could be advanced. Indeed, Lombroso has frequently been referred to as "the father of scientific criminology."[20] This title was bestowed because of his effort to construct a theory of crime based on observable and recorded facts rather than speculation.

While modern criminologists would not object to the idea of basing criminology on facts, most would find fault with the manner in which Lombroso gathered and interpreted crime facts. For Lombroso, the most important facts were those that emerged from minute and precise anatomical measurements. Lombroso personally performed such investigations on hundreds of skulls and skeletons and also relied on similar examinations conducted by like-minded researchers. In *The Female Offender,* authored by Lombroso and William Ferrero, readers are supplied with statistics on body weight and height, span of arms, average height of body seated, length of limbs, length of hands, length and width of feet, cranial capacity, cranial circumference, and antero-posterior diameter.[21] For the early positivists these are the type of facts used to produce scientific statements about crime and criminals.

The direct study of the criminal offender through clinical observation and measurement was advanced by the positivists as the ideal method for crime analysis. Consider Ferri's assessment of the positivist approach to studying crime, as contrasted with the methods used by the classicists:

> **It is clear that the classical criminologists would oppose this new scientific movement, were it only through the force of inertia. Accustomed as they are to build abstract theories with the aid of pure logic and without other tools than paper, pen, ink, and the volumes of their predecessors, . . .[22]**

This statement indicates that Ferri defined the positivist study of crime as scientific, and that he felt this approach made positivism superior to classicism.

The Born Criminal

Unlike the classical thinkers, the positivists argued that criminals were fundamentally different from non-criminals. Most importantly, criminal offenders were said to be physiologically and anatomically distinct from "normal" individuals. Lombroso reported that he came to this conclusion all at once:

> **Suddenly, one morning, on a gloomy day in December, I found in the skull of a brigand a very long series of atavistic abnormalities . . . analogous to those that are found in inferior vertebrates. At the sight of these strange abnormalities—as an extensive plain is lit up by a glowing horizon—I realized that the problem of the nature and generation of criminals was resolved for me.[23]**

Lombroso wrote of this incident in the mid-1860s and then repeated details of the episode in his opening address at the Sixth Congress of Criminal Anthropology held in Turin in 1906.[24] The special insight that Lombroso accepts as the answer to the question of crime causation is that most serious crime is a product of atavism. The **atavist** is a biological throwback, a creature who belongs properly to an earlier evolutionary time period. Hence, the criminal offender is likely to be a person who is underdeveloped biologically, as indicated by peculiar physical characteristics. Because the atavist has not evolved to the same extent as others in society, it would be unrealistic to expect civilized and socially acceptable behavior from such a creature.

The claim that most, or certainly a high proportion of all criminals, were born in this way to a life of crime, was roundly criticized in academic circles. Perhaps not just coincidentally, over a period of many years Lombroso qualified his atavistic thesis. Most important, he reduced his estimate of the percentage of offenders who fall into the atavistic type. Ultimately, Lombroso argued that about one-third of all criminals fit into this category.[25] Lombroso further qualified his theory of atavistic crime by noting that atavism is not the sole explanation for congenital (biological) criminality. In other words, the **born criminal,** a term coined by Ferri, need not be an atavist (a degenerative disease unrelated to atavism could be present). Finally, Lombroso admitted that crime has many causes. Indeed, the first sentence of the 1912 edition of *Crime: Its Causes and Remedies* begins with this phrase: "Every crime has its origin in a multiplicity of causes. . . ."[26]

Despite all of the qualifications by Lombroso and his immediate followers concerning the atavistic and general biological basis of crime, the born-criminal category retained a prominent place in early positivism. For example, in his five-fold criminal offender classification scheme, Ferri includes the born-criminal type and describes it in this way:

> **. . . there are men born for crime whose anti-human conduct is the inevitable effect of an indefinite series of hereditary influences which accumulate in the course of generations. This is proven by the success which has attended in ordinary language my expression, the *born-criminal*.[27]**

Ferri, like Lombroso, attempted to moderate, with rhetoric at least, his emphasis on the biological nature of crime. For example, he offered this admonition: "Let us repeat once more that in our opinion crime is not an exclusively biological phenomenon. . . ."[28] Despite all of the qualifying statements, however, it is clear that early positivism was most closely associated with a biological theory of crime. Born criminals, as conceptualized by Lombroso and Ferri, were thought to commit a high percentage of all crimes in society. In part this was because the atavist was "refractory to all treatment, even to the most affectionate care begun at the very cradle, . . ."[29] If the born criminal could not be rehabilitated, could he be identified? This is the next issue to be considered.

Categorizing Criminal Offenders in New Zealand and the People's Republic of China

The early positivists felt that the best way of protecting society from the harms associated with crime was to identify criminals. To this end, they offered various systems for categorizing offenders. This still happens today. New Zealand's Criminal Justice Amendment Act of 1993 created two categories of offenders: ordinary and serious/dangerous. This legislation represents a rejection of the notion that criminal behavior falls on a continuum. Instead, New Zealand lawmakers assume that the criminal justice system can identify criminal offenders who are truly dangerous. Offenders are categorized on the basis of the nature of their present offense. For example, offenses including murder, sexual violation, and shooting a police officer automatically place offenders in the dangerous category. These individuals receive the most serious sentences; they are most likely to be incarcerated, and they tend to receive the longest periods of incarceration. As criminologist Mark Brown found, however, there are problems with New Zealand's policy. Brown studied 613 New Zealand criminal offenders and found that "dangerous" criminals were no more likely than "ordinary" criminals to be reconvicted after release from prison. This casts doubt on the proposition that it is possible in a practical sense to identify the offenders who pose the most danger to society.

The People's Republic of China (PRC) also attempts formally to identify "dangerous" offenders. In the PRC there are two concepts of dangerousness. The first applies to offenders who have committed a crime perceived as dangerous to society. This category includes any act that endangers the state or undermines the socialist revolution. Following Mao Zedong's teachings, these offenders are viewed as "enemies of the people." The second type of dangerous offender is a criminal who has a perceived propensity to reoffend. This is individual dangerousness. Such a person is said to have a basic antisocial character. In China, these two types of dangerous offenders are most likely to be sent to prisons or labor camps. Because of the closed nature of the PRC, there has been no objective policy evaluation of the disposition of dangerous criminals. However, this does represent another current attempt to categorize offenders. Indeed, the practical task of offender categorization advocated by positivists over a century ago is evidenced in most nations throughout the world, including, as seen here, New Zealand and China.

SOURCES: Mark Brown, "Serious Offending and the Management of Public Risk in New Zealand," *British Journal of Criminology 36* (1996) 18–36; Edward Epstein and Simon Hing-Yan Wong, "The Concept of 'Dangerousness' in the People's Republic of China and Its Impact on the Treatment of Prisoners," *British Journal of Criminology 36* (1996) 472–97.

Identification of Criminals

The early positivists emphasized the use of offender typologies (Box 10.1). Classification, they reasoned, was a tremendously important method in the natural sciences, and it could be similarly important for social scientific study. Lombroso's classification scheme of offenders identified four criminal types: epileptic, insane, born, and occasional.[30] Ferri put forth a similar typology, although his contained five criminal types: insane, born, habitual, passionate, and occasional.[31] The insane criminal is a person who is so incapacitated by a psychiatric pathology that there is virtually no understanding of behavior in society. The born criminal acts on the basis of a biologically given flaw. Unlike the insane criminal, this offender can be rational and calculative, but cannot distinguish between good and evil. The habitual criminal is an individual who begins committing crimes as a youth. The adolescent is dealt with either too harshly (put in the penitentiary with hardened adult criminals) or too leniently (and therefore emboldened). The criminal by passion is an offender who is overcome by emotions of the moment and situation, and is unlikely to commit further criminal offenses. Finally, the occasional criminal type represents a grab-bag category, including those offenders who do not fit anywhere else. Ferri estimated that the insane and passionate offenders make up about 5 to 10 percent of all criminals, while the born and habitual offenders account for approximately 40 to 50 percent of all criminals[32] (Box 10.2).

For the early positivists the identification of criminals could be an even more explicit process than categorization; that is, they thought that on-sight identification was possible. Lombroso believed that criminal offenders, particularly the born-criminal type, could be identified on the basis of **physical stigmata.** Examples of the physical markings of specific types of offenders are paraphrased thus:

> . . . *thieves* have mobile hands and face; small, mobile, restless, frequently oblique eyes; thick and closely set eye-brows; flat or twisted nose; thin beard; hair frequently thin; . . . *rapists* often

have brilliant eyes, delicate faces, and tumid lips and eyelids; as a rule they are of delicate structure and sometimes hunchbacked . . . *homicide offenders* have cold, glassy eyes, . . . the jaws are strong, the cheekbones large, the hair curly, dark, and abundant; the beard is frequently thin, the canine teeth well developed. . . .[33]

Ferri also emphasized that criminals had physical markings. This was true in particular, he argued, for the born murderer: "We know how to distinguish the born-murderer from the rest of criminals by bodily characteristics, . . . To me, initiated as I am in the positive method, this fact of itself has more value than a hundred volumes of our adversaries' reasonings; . . ."[34]

The notion that criminals can be identified *on sight* is vividly conveyed in a statement by Ferri (a statement that may be one of the greatest boasts in the history of criminology):

I shall always remember how, as I studied seven hundred soldiers man by man in comparison with seven hundred delinquents one day, there came before me and the doctor who was present at these examinations, a soldier obviously of the type of the born-criminal, with enormous jaws, extremely developed temples, a pale and earthy skin, and a cold and ferocious physiognomy. Well knowing that persons who had been convicted of serious offenses were not admitted to the army, yet I hazarded the remark to the major that this man must be a murderer. In reply to indirect questioning, the soldier told me a few minutes later that he had served fifteen years in prison for a murder committed in his childhood. The major looked at me in astonishment and I said to myself: "I wish that the critics who have never studied a living criminal might be here in hiding to make their reasonings and say that criminal anthropology has no foundation."[35]

Ferri and the other early positivists wished to reduce the understanding of crime to simple, direct, and objective measures. The early positivists were committed to advancing a "scientific" explanation of crime. They thought that the identification of criminals in terms of physical stigmata was consistent with that purpose. Despite their intentions, however, most critics have found the methods of early positivism to be fundamentally flawed. In particular, the positivists have been criticized for not using control groups in any rigorous way. Indeed, for this and other reasons, Lindesmith and Levin described Lombroso's methods as "notoriously slipshod."[36]

Position on Agency (Responsibility)

Classical criminology holds that all individuals are free agents. According to this view, crime is purposefully chosen behavior. For the positivists, though, criminal behavior was seen as produced by a multiplicity of factors, none of which has to do with individual agency. Although most remembered for his emphasis on biological causes of crime, Lombroso also noted numerous other causes such as temperature, geology, barbarism, population congestion, alcoholism, hashish, illiteracy, religion, prisons, and associations.[37] Similarly, Ferri argued that various anthropological, physical, and social factors produced crime, while "the pretended free will is a purely subjective illusion."[38] The positivist position on agency is aptly summed up by Garofalo with this comment: "When we undertake to ascertain whether a man is really responsible for what he does, we always end by discovering that he is not."[39]

Policy Implications

Lombroso, Ferri, and Garofalo each advanced specific criminal justice policy proposals. Lombroso held that punishment served the dual purpose of protecting society and improving the offender.[40] This meant that correctional policy had to be individually structured to the particular problems and needs of the offender. Just as medical science does not prescribe the same treatment for all sick people, correctional treatment must also be individualized. This theory of corrections, however, applied only to offenders who were not of the born-criminal classification. Lombroso argues that it "would be a mistake to imagine that measures which have been shown to be effective with other criminals could be successfully applied to born criminals; for these are, for the most part, refractory to all treatment, . . ."[41]

Criminologists have typically emphasized Ferri's focus on the biological causes of crime, but he also stipulated that there were many social causes of criminal behavior. Ferri thought that these social causes could be mitigated and was an advocate for numerous preventive measures. Vold repeats some of these measures: "Free trade, abolition of monopolies, inexpensive workmen's dwellings, public savings banks, better street lighting, birth control, freedom of marriage and divorce, recreation, . . ."[42]

Finally, Ferri was adamantly opposed to the jury system of jurisprudence. First of all, no twelve individuals can "really represent the popular conscience, which, in fact, often protests against and revolts from their decisions."[43] Moreover, jury members too often let emotions, for compassion or vengeance, influence the decisions they make. Perhaps most important, jurors are not trained for the job. The jury system "imposes on one individual functions very different and distinct from those which he habitually pursues."[44]

Garofalo was even more concerned than Lombroso or Ferri with the practical aspects of criminal justice. As his starting point, Garofalo embraced a particular interpretation of the darwinian notion of "adaptation."[45] Darwin's famous theory of biological evolution centered around the idea that species had to adapt to environmental demands or else perish. Garofalo argued that criminal offenders were individuals who could not or would not adapt to the demands of civil society. Accordingly, society must eliminate those who cannot or will not adapt. The **forms of elimination** constitute Garofalo's special contribution to corrections. For offenders with a permanent abnormality, *total elimination* (the death penalty) was called for. *Partial elimination* (for example, imprisonment) could be used for offenders who were temporarily uncontrollable. Finally, for those individuals who have committed a crime because of extenuating and exceptional circumstances, *enforced reparation* would be the preferred punishment. Garofalo concluded that the implementation of these specific correctional guidelines would satisfy the public's desire for punishment, serve as a crime deterrent, and upgrade the genetic quality of the population.[46] Garofalo may have been pleased with his recommendations, but overall his program was not well received.

Subsequent Developments

Many researchers have sought to extend or refine the ideas of early positivism. What follows is a brief summary of several of the most prominent developments in this tradition.

Genetic Influences

Body Type Theories

At one point in his career, Lombroso offered to recant his theories of criminal behavior if a team of unbiased researchers would examine 100 born criminals, 100 persons with criminal tendencies, and 100 normal individuals and conclude that there were no significant physical and behavioral differences between the groups.[47] In 1901, Charles Goring (1870–1919), a medical officer at a prison in England, accepted Lombroso's challenge and began a research project in which he studied thousands of criminals and thousands of noncriminals (not the three groups of 100 as specified by Lombroso). Goring's investigations led him to reject Lombroso's general theory of the relationship between physical stigmata and criminal behavior. Nevertheless, Goring concluded that criminals are physically inferior to normal individuals in the sense that criminals tend to be shorter and weigh less than noncriminals.[48]

Just as Goring found fault with Lombroso's work, Goring himself was criticized. E.A. Hooton (1887–1954), a Harvard anthropologist, reexamined Goring's research and also studied over 17,000 individuals in his own project.[49] Vold has summarized the general findings of Hooton's research as follows:

[T]all thin men tend to commit forgery and fraud, undersized men are thieves and burglars; short heavy persons commit assault, rape, and other sex crimes; whereas men of "mediocre" physique flounder around among crimes (as in everything else) with no specialty.[50]

Hooten's contentions were not compelling. His sample of criminals (prison inmates) identified individuals in terms of the offense for which they were presently incarcerated. Just because a person was last arrested for robbery does not mean that he has never raped. But body type theory was not dead. A German psychiatrist, Ernst Kretschmer (1888–1964), identified three major types of body build: thin, heavy, and muscular. William Sheldon (1898–1977), an American physician and psychologist, expanded on Kretschmer's model by developing a theory which fused physiology and personality.[51] Sheldon argued that thin individuals (**ectomorphs**) tended to be fatigued and withdrawn, while heavy-set persons (**endomorphs**) typically have a relaxed and comfortable disposition. People having a muscular and athletic physique (**mesomorphs**), however, are routinely active and aggressive; these are the individuals most likely to commit crimes.

Sheldon's hypothesis that mesomorphs are most likely to commit crime was tested extensively by Sheldon and Eleanor Glueck. In the 1930s, the Gluecks compared 500 persistent juvenile delinquents with 500 nondelinquents. Photographs were used to categorize the subjects with regard to predominant body type. By this method, it was found that 60 percent of the delinquents were mesomorphs but only 31 percent of the nondelinquents fit the mesomorphic classification.[52] Further, the Gluecks found that mesomorphic youth were more likely to have personality traits (aggressiveness, insensitivity, and emotional instability) consistent with crime commission (Box 10.2).

Even if one were to concede that a disproportionately high percentage of adult criminals and juvenile delinquents fit the mesomorphic physique classification, there are fundamental shortcomings to body type crime theory. First, the process of social selection may be more important than body type. That is, the criminal justice system

Career Criminals

In a sense, the main mission of early positivism was to identify the "career" criminal, the flawed person who would be likely to commit crimes throughout an entire lifetime. The positivists believed that scientific methods would enable them to identify such individuals and, once identified, the criminal justice system could isolate them from general society. Even today there are many, including politicians, who suggest that a small percentage of offenders commit a high percentage of all crimes. In part, this view derives from social scientific research. In the 1930s and 1940s, Sheldon and Eleanor Glueck sought to plot the career involvement in illegal activities of their youthful subjects. Subsequently, Marvin Wolfgang and his associates conducted a longitudinal study (one that covers many years) on 10,000 boys born in Philadelphia in 1945. The researchers found that less than 7 percent of the sample (the chronic offenders) committed 57 percent of the all the crimes attributed to the 10,000 boys. Today, however, the concept of "career criminal" has generated considerable controversy. Some criminologists contend that there are particular individuals who are especially predisposed to commit crimes throughout their lifetimes. The reason for this could be faulty genes, undersocialization, having been labeled negatively, living in poverty, or an assortment of other possibilities. Other criminologists argue that there is insufficient empirical support for identifying specific individuals as, invariably, criminal. Factors affecting frequency of law violation must be linked to distinct periods of *onset, persistence,* and *termination.* Rather than just looking for a career criminal, Daniel Nagin and Kenneth Land suggest four categories of offenders: innocents, adolescent-limited offenders, low-rate chronic offenders, and high-rate chronic offenders.

Perhaps one day criminologists will be able to confirm that a small percentage of street criminals commit most street crime, and that a small percentage of white-collar criminals commit most white-collar crime. Much more research is required, however, before definitive statements can be made about career criminals.

SOURCES: Kenneth Land and Daniel Nagin, "Micro-Models of Criminal Careers: A Synthesis of the Criminal Careers and Life Course Approaches via Semi-Parametric Mixed Poisson Regression," *Journal of Quantitative Criminology 12* (1996) 163–91; David Greenberg, "Modeling Criminal Careers," *Criminology 29* (1991) 17–46; Alfred Blumstein, Jacqueline Cohen, and David Farrington, "Criminal Career Research: Its Value for Criminology," *Criminology 26* (1988) 1–35; Michael Gottfredson and Travis Hirschi, "Science, Public Policy, and the Career Paradigm," *Criminology 26* (1988) 37–55; Charles Tittle, "Two Empirical Regularities (Maybe) in Search of an Explanation: Commentary on the Age/Crime Debate," *Criminology 26* (1988) 75–85; Marvin Wolfgang, Robert Figlio, and Thorstein Sellin, *Delinquency in a Birth Cohort* (Chicago: University of Chicago Press, 1972); Sheldon and Eleanor Glueck, *Juvenile Delinquents Grown Up* (New York: Commonwealth Fund, 1940).

may react differently to an adolescent who is tall and muscular than to an adolescent who is small in stature. School authorities, police officers, as well as those working in the juvenile justice system, might perceive the larger adolescent as more dangerous and thus more deserving of a harsher disposition. A second problem with body type theories is that they are conspicuously unsuccessful in explaining white-collar crimes. Nowhere in the criminological literature is there an established explanation of how body type is associated with corporate fraud, tax evasion, political corruption, or other crimes of this sort.

Crime and Human Nature

The biological approach to the study of human behavior was given a boost in the mid-1970s when Pierre van den Berghe published an influential article in which he argued that sociology ought to "bring back the beast."[53] What Van Den Berghe meant is that sociological theory should not dismiss the biological nature of human actors. A year later, Edward O. Wilson, a Harvard zoologist, published a controversial book titled *Sociobiology: The New Synthe-sis.*[54] This book served as a clarion call for social and behavioral scientists to integrate biological and genetic factors into their social theories of human behavior. Shortly thereafter, C. Ray Jeffery, as well as Sarnoff Mednick and Jan Volavka, advocated an inclusion of biological analyses into the study of criminal behavior.[55]

Despite the developments just noted, it was not until 1985, with the publication of *Crime and Human Nature,* that a significant number of mainstream criminologists took a serious look at the biological explanation of crime.[56] The authors, James Q. Wilson and Richard Herrnstein, argued that "individuals differ at birth in the degree to which they are at risk for criminality."[57] Wilson and Herrnstein, a political scientist and experimental psychologist respectively, did not dismiss social environmental factors in crime causation, but they clearly underscored the primary importance of the individual's biological makeup.

Crime and Human Nature provoked strong reactions, both positive and negative. What is apparent, however, is that the book has fundamental limitations. Most important is the fact that Wilson and Hernnstein operationally define crime as murder, rape, and common theft.[58] While these crimes are important, they are only a part of the complete list of serious crimes.

In 1994, Hernnstein and Charles Murray published *The Bell Curve: Intelligence and Class Structure in American Life*, a bestselling but controversial book.[59] The main argument of this book is that low IQ is associated with a myriad of social problems, including crime. Recently, Francis Cullen and associates reviewed the data and methods upon which Hernnstein and Murray drew their conclusions.[60] The Cullen team offered this general assessment: "By portraying offenders as driven into crime predominantly by cognitive disadvantage, Hernnstein and Murray mask the reality that stronger risk factors not only exist but also are amenable to effective correctional intervention."[61] The debate over the influence of IQ on behavior is unsettled, but the contention that native intelligence is related to crime has a long history and is likely to generate research for some time.

In an interview to *U.S. News & World Report,* James Q. Wilson made the following observation: "Studies of twins and adopted youngsters are the best evidence of the genetic basis for the precursors of criminality."[62] In fact, scientists have long sought to determine the relative importance of genetic makeup versus social environment in the behavior of humans (nature versus nurture). Twins separated at birth provide special insight into the genetic basis of behavior. There are two types of twins: identical or fraternal. Identical (monozygotic) twins are created when a fertilized egg splits into two eggs and produces two genetically identical individuals who share 100 percent of their chromosomes. Fraternal (dizygotic) twins are created when two eggs are fertilized at the same time; these twins share 50 percent of their chromosomes. Thus, if genes determine behavior, identical twins reared apart should have closer behavioral tendencies than fraternal twins reared apart. Of course, conventional ethics would never permit the separation of twins at birth for experimental purposes, but there have been studies of twins who, for a variety of reasons, were separated at birth and reared apart.[63] For example, James Shields, a British sociologist, examined 44 identical twins who were brought up separately, and found striking similarities in mannerisms, interests, occupations, sexual behavior, drinking and smoking habits, as well as emotional states.[64]

Karl Christiansen went beyond the identification of general parallels in behavior by focusing attention on crime involvement. Christiansen studied 3586 twin pairs born in one area of Denmark and found that identical twins were three times as likely as fraternal twins to have a matching criminal record.[65] If one identical twin had a criminal conviction, the other twin also had a conviction in 35 percent of the cases; with fraternal twins the con- gruence rate was only 12 percent. These rates are consistent with what one might expect if genes are influential. However, the Christiansen study did not include separated twins. It is possible that identical twins may share a more similar social environment than fraternal twins and that the social environment rather than genetics might be determinate. The research findings from studies of twins are interesting, but far from conclusive.

Adoption Studies

Findings from adoption research also provide some tentative support for the proposition that there is a relationship between genetics and crime. The largest crime-focused adoption project was based on an analysis of over 14,000 male and female adoptions in Denmark between 1924 and 1947.[66] The major findings of this research lend support for the role of both genetics and social environment. Adopted boys who had a biological father with a criminal record were more likely to be convicted of a crime than boys who had noncriminal biological fathers. This is an argument for genetic influence. The study also showed, however, that most adopted boys, even those whose biological fathers had been convicted of a crime, did not have a criminal record. This underscores the power of social factors.

Adoption studies, including the one just cited, frequently offer suggestive evidence in support of the genetic theory of crime. The support is never strong, however, and certainly not conclusive. In fact, methodological problems (for example, defining criminal behavior only in terms of having a police record) dictate a cautious approach to this research.

XYY Theory

Most human beings are born with 23 pairs of chromosomes, one of which determines sex. The female sex chromosome is called an X chromosome and the male sex chromosome is called a Y chromosome. Females typically have an XX sex chromosome constitution, while the male norm is XY.[67] Some males are born with an extra X chromosome (Klinefelter's syndrome), while other males possess an extra Y chromosome. Most research has focused on XYY men, leading to the **XYY theory.** Numerous studies have suggested that a disproportionately high percentage of male prison inmates are XYY type, that XYY men tend to be more aggressive and violent than XY men, and that XYY men tend to be taller and more muscular than XY men.[68]

In the 1970s, results from XYY research were widely reported by the mass media. Many people believed that scientists had finally found the cause of serious crime. The theory was even applied (falsely) to Richard Speck, the 1968 murderer of eight Chicago nursing students. More important, a few states passed laws to establish screening programs to identify boys with the XYY config-uration and, in Boston, a hospital began screening new-born male infants.[69]

Subsequent research has identified a number of prob-lems with XYY research. First, prison inmates, the most frequent subjects of XYY investigation, are not necessarily representative of the criminal population. White-collar criminals, for example, are underrepresented in prison populations. Second, even if there is a greater percentage of XYY males in prison than in the general population (a controversial proposition at best), it may be that their prison sentence has more to do with social perception than behavior. If XYY males are unusually large physically, as is argued, then judges and juries may regard these men as particularly dangerous. Third, current research does not support the contention that XYY men are more aggressive or violent than XY men.[70] Lastly, by most ac-counts, XYY males make up a small percentage of males, either in prison or out of prison—one estimate is 0.15 percent of the general male population.[71] Thus, even if the XYY theory were scientifically compelling, which it is not, it would still not qualify as a robust, comprehensive explanation of criminal behavior.

Other Biological Factors Associated with Crime

Autonomic Nervous System Deficiency

In everyday life, individuals are subjected to an almost in-finite array of sense stimuli organized around five sys-tems: visual, auditory, taste, olfactory, and tactile. Sensory input is translated into a biochemical code that is trans-mitted to the brain. Though common sense suggests that humans see with their eyes, it is really the brain that sees, for it is the brain that must process the informational light stimulus conducted by the eye.[72] Responding to external stimuli, then, is fundamentally a brain function. More specifically, it is a function of special cells called neurons that make up the **autonomic nervous system** (ANS). Hans Eysenck, a British psychologist, developed a theory of crime based on the sensitivity of the ANS.[73] He argued that some individuals are comparatively insensitive to ex-ternal stimuli, whether the stimuli be bright lights, loud music, parental decisions, or teacher demands. Such indi-viduals are less adept at identifying and responding to or-dinary cues in the social environment. This means that they are not as likely to become successfully socialized. More specifically, it means that they may have an under-developed *conscience* (set of internalized social norms).

Sociologists have long held that some deviants and criminals are inadequately socialized. What is original with Eysenck's formulation is the idea that undersocialization is fundamentally a physiological (biological) process. Al-

though Eysenck's hypothesis is provocative, it has not yet been supported sufficiently by empirical evidence.

Brain Dysfunctions

On August 1, 1966, Charles Whitman took a rifle to the top of a tower at the University of Texas and shot at indi-viduals on the ground. He killed fourteen people and wounded many others. It was subsequently determined that Whitman had a malignant brain tumor. This was a shocking illustration of how pathological brain activity can result in horrible and violent behavior. As might be ex-pected, this incident inspired a renewed interest in the re-lationship between the workings of the brain and the manifestation of criminal activity.

Essentially, the brain governs motor, sensory, and emotional activities. The outer layer of the brain, the cor-tex, processes incoming sensory information and controls outgoing motor activity. The cortex is divided into two hemispheres, left and right. Left hemisphere activity spe-cializes in language and memory functions, while the right hemisphere directs spatial and tactile functions.[74] The effects of hemispheric dysfunctions in information processing have been indicated by cognitive, clinical, and experimental measures. In turn, these hemispheric dys-functions have been linked statistically to behavioral prob-lems ranging from dyslexia to juvenile delinquency.[75] Moreover, electrophysiological tests have even shown that it is left-hemisphere dysfunction specifically that tends to be associated with violent criminal behavior.[76]

In a frequently cited study of brain waves, 335 violent delinquents were divided into two groups: delinquents who were repeatedly violent and delinquents who had committed a single violent act. Of the repeatedly violent delinquents, 65 percent had abnormal electroencephalo-gram (EEG) recordings, while only 24 percent of the sec-ond group had irregular EEG recordings.[77]

Research on the association between the brain and behavior, specifically criminal behavior, is ongoing. As study findings build, it may be possible to develop a more integrated and convincing explanation of how brain dys-functions lead to criminal behavior.

Sex Hormones

A considerable amount of animal research has docu-mented an association between sex hormones and ag-gressive, violent behavior. The most generalized conclu-sion from this research is that a high level of male sex hormones (testosterone) is positively associated with a high level of aggressive behavior. This is said to be the case across species and even when the animal injected with testosterone is female.[78] The relationship between testosterone and human behavior, however, is inconclu-sive. While many researchers have concluded that there is an association between testosterone level and violent sex-

ual behavior, the exact relationship has not been determined.[79] Is violence a product of a high testosterone level, or does violent behavior cause the testosterone level to elevate? This chicken-or-egg phenomenon is endemic to much of the research on the relationship between hormones and behavior.

Present research on hormonal influence has centered increasingly on women. Specifically, many investigators have studied the effects of the onset of the menstrual cycle, **premenstrual syndrome** (**PMS**). It is known, for example, that estrogen and progesterone levels climb until the 4 days immediately preceding menses, when there is a sharp decline in both hormone levels.[80] The connection between PMS and female crime received considerable attention with the publication of research by Katharina Dalton, who found that English women had higher rates of crime and traffic accidents before and during menstruation.[81] In her most famous study, Dalton interviewed 156 women inmates whose crime had been committed within the previous 28 days. After obtaining information on their menstrual cycles, she calculated that 49 percent of the women were either in the premenstrual phase (4 days prior to onset) or were menstruating at the time of

the crime. This is much higher than the expected statistical probability of 29 percent (8 days out of 28).

How many women suffer significant ill effects of PMS? Estimates range from 5 percent to 40 percent.[82] Typical symptoms of PMS include irritability, lethargy, and mood swings. While a number of studies have found an association between PMS and high crime participation, it is not clear what is causing what.[83] Put simply, does the menstrual cycle trigger criminal behavior or does the trauma associated with apprehension for a crime trigger the menstrual cycle? There is strong evidence in support of the latter.[84] Therefore, the burden of proof rests with those who would argue that PMS contributes to female criminality. Despite the relative lack of evidence for the PMS hypothesis, it has enjoyed considerable popularity.

Dietary Conditions

Medical science in the late twentieth century has shown an increasing appreciation for the importance of diet. There is some research suggesting a link between dietary condition and social behavior. Specifically, there are at least a few studies that claim to find an association between low blood

Most arrestees are male. Early positivism suggested that women criminals were genetically unlike most women.

sugar level (**hypoglycemia**) and criminal behavior as well as low cholesterol and criminal behavior.[85]

Hypoglycemia is an interesting example of the biological approach to criminal behavior. Low blood sugar levels have been associated with "poor neuro-muscular coordination, weakness, palpitations, sweating, lightheadedness, . . . feelings of fatigue, malaise, 'uptight feelings,' irritability, and a host of other symptoms."[86] Despite there being no definitive evidence explaining how low blood sugar level ignites criminal behavior, on occasion hypoglycemia has been favorably received as a legal defense. In 1979, for instance, Dan White, a San Francisco city supervisor (see chapter opener photo), assassinated the Mayor of San Francisco soon after consuming forty Twinkies.[87] White was given a reduced sentence on the grounds that the large dose of sugar from the Twinkies used up his insulin supply, without which his blood sugar level became too low, resulting in a decreased supply of glucose (blood sugar) to the brain. After serving 5 years in prison, White was released. Shortly thereafter he committed suicide. Research on the possible association between dietary abnormalities and crime continues.

Summary of Subsequent Biological Developments

By the year 2050, it may be possible to analyze, control, and predict human behavior on the basis of genetic coding. Molecular biologists, computer experts, and engineers have already begun a monumental 15-year project to translate and map the human genome—"the complete set of instructions for making a human being."[88] These instructions, written on DNA threads that are more than 5 feet long but only 50 trillionths of an inch across, are found in the nucleus of each of the human body's 100 trillion cells (except red blood cells, which have no nucleus).[89] The genome project, which has an estimated $3 billion cost, has scientists excited about the prospect of understanding, once and for all, the biological nature of human behavior.

In his edited work, *Taboos in Criminology*, criminologist Edward Sagarin observes:

In criminology, it appears that a number of views . . . have become increasingly delicate and sensitive, as if all those who espouse them were

inherently evil, or at least stupidly insensitive to the consequences of their research. . . . In the studies of crime, the examples of unpopular orientations are many. Foremost is the link of crime to the factors of genes, biology, race, ethnicity, and religion.[90]

Sagarin's observation has some merit. There is no denying that the climate of "political correctness" has had an influence on science and research. That said, it remains the case that to date no comprehensive, compelling biological theory of crime has yet been advanced.

Freudian Interpretations of Crime

Freudian theory is not a development in the tradition of Lombrosian criminology. However, Freud's explanation of behavior did stress the importance of internal, individualistic factors. Specifically, Freud's theory rests on the notion that *instincts* propel human action.[91] Like early positivism, Freudian thought conceptualizes the human actor as driven. The free-choice model of action, as embraced by the classical theorists, is rejected directly by Freud's commitment to psychic determinism.[92] Freud's contention is that the inner workings of one's personality are the motor force of human behavior. It is difficult to show how this contention can be relevant to an understanding of crime, because Freud never developed a specific theory of criminal behavior, offering instead a general theoretical model of behavior. Hence, applications of Freudian thought to the study of crime must be, by necessity, extensions from what Freud actually wrote. Our analysis begins with his view of personality.

Personality Development

According to Freud, personality is divided into id, ego, and superego.[93] The **id** is the original system. Present at birth, the id is a reservoir of instinctive drives that operate at the unconscious level. The two most important instincts are sex (Eros) and aggression or destruction (Thanatos). The id desires and seeks immediate gratification; it operates on the pleasure principle. The id is neither aware of nor concerned with external reality. It is essentially amoral.

The **ego** is a secondary system, developing 6 to 8 months after birth, and it operates on the reality principle. The ego has an appreciation for the external world. In large measure, the ego develops because of the conflict that arises as the id comes into contact with the real world. Freud described the relationship between the id and ego by suggesting the following comparison:

One might compare the relation of the ego to the id with that between a rider and his horse. The horse provides the locomotive energy, and the

rider has the prerogative of determining the goal and of guiding the movements of his powerful mount towards it. But all too often in the relations between the ego and the id we find a picture of the less ideal situation in which the rider is obliged to guide his horse in the direction in which it itself wants to go.[94]

The **superego** is the third system of personality and, like the ego, it emerges after birth and develops as a person matures. By the time the child is 3 to 5 years old, the superego has begun to build up a collection of internalized societal expectations that functions as a conscience and operates on the normative principal. It is the superego that produces feelings of guilt.

Personality, then, consists of internal processes associated with the id, ego, and superego that are frequently working at cross-purposes. Hence, if we could see into a psyche, we would observe intense conflict.

The Unconscious

Freud argues that the battles waged by the id, ego, and superego are directly consequential in determining behavior and yet these conflicts commonly take place at the unconscious level. Individuals have little or no conscious awareness of what is going on. According to Freud, it is the unconscious that most frequently motivates and directs behavior.

How does the unconscious shape behavior? Imagine a man who agrees to be hypnotized. While under hypnosis the man receives an hypnotic suggestion to "go outside and bark like a dog." The man does as he was instructed and, if asked why he is doing this, the man may respond in a number of ways ("I don't know," "I'm just fooling around," "It's a gag"), but he will not report the real reason underlying his behavior—that he was acting in response to an hypnotic suggestion. Similarly, Freud contends, we all have a tendency to do things for reasons not understood at the conscious level. The actual reasons reside at the unconscious level. When we are asked about such behavior we offer after-the-fact explanations. We rationalize our actions in terms that seek to be convincing to ourselves and others. The idea that human beings are often directed by unconscious drives is now a basic axiom of all the behavioral sciences; it may be the greatest contribution of Freudian thought.

Using Freudian Thought to Explain Crime

As suggested earlier, Freud paid little attention to crime. While his collected works total twenty-four volumes, there are few references to crime and criminals.[95] Therefore, at least to a certain degree, Freudian-based explanations of criminal behavior must be extrapolations. Below are three such examples.

Viennese physician Sigmund Freud (1856–1939) invented psychoanalysis and argued that humans act on the basis of impulses and urges.

1. *Imbalance between id, ego, and superego.* Because the id is concerned only with self-gratification and is amoral, it must be held in check by the ego. A strong ego will successfully repress id impulses or channel them to a socially acceptable outlet (a process Freud called *sublimation*). Clearly, if the id is too strong, or the ego is too weak, crime may result.

The role of the superego is also key. If the superego is weak, the individual will not be deterred by social pressure. There will not be a sufficient commitment to social rules of order and no compelling set of guilt feelings to restrain the wants of the id. Individuals with a weak superego may commit acts that most members of society might describe as horrific. But crime may also result from an overpowering superego. This can occur in one of two ways. First, a too-strong superego is so inflexible and strict that it may produce excessive feelings of guilt. The guilt feelings become so intense that the individual desires punishment. Consequently, this is the type of criminal offender who will unconsciously leave obvious clues to

wrongful actions in an effort to be caught and punished. The second way in which an overdeveloped superego may stimulate criminal behavior is to be socialized into a life of crime. If the social environment tolerates or encourages criminal attitudes and behaviors, a person may become a criminal by simply adapting to group norms.[96]

2. *Criminal identification.* **Identification** is one psychological, and largely unconscious, way of responding to frustration and anxiety. In Freudian thought, the most discussed example is sexual identification, which takes place between a baby boy and his father. (The Freudian view of the sexual identification of young girls, which has been strongly criticized, is even more complex, but it is not necessary to treat here.) Freud argues that by the age of 2 or 3, the boy wishes to displace the father as the mother's sexual partner. Freud wrote: "While he is still a small child, a son will already begin to develop a special affection for his mother, whom he regards as belonging to him; he begins to feel his father as a rival who disputes his sole possession."[97] When the boy sees female geni-

talia, however, feelings of jealousy begin to subside. Sight of the clitoris suggests to the boy that girls have been castrated and he fears that the same thing may happen to him if he competes with the father. Indeed, recognizing that the father is too strong to defeat, and fearing castration, the boy "chooses" identification over rivalry. Presumably, the boy identifies with the father, sensing that he will eventually attain the same kind of sexual privileges that the father now enjoys. If identification does not occur as discussed, repressed conflict may ignite problem behavior (including criminal behavior) later in life.[98]

Psychologists have expanded Freud's view of identification.[99] It is possible to conceptualize identification as a process that responds to frustration and anxiety not based on sex. Adolescents, for example, are frustrated by numerous individuals, events, and situations. When a teenager responds to family and school frustration by identifying with an older adolescent who is involved in a street gang, participation in criminal behavior may result. On the other hand, when a teenager identifies with an older adolescent who is active in church activities, school sports, and has a part-time job, law-abiding behavior may result. In this sense, identification can be a crime inducement or a crime deterrent.

3. *Repression.* **Repression** is a process that offers individuals protection from sensations and feelings that would be upsetting or even debilitating. Freud offers the following metaphor to explain the process:

> **Let us therefore compare the system of the unconscious to a large entrance hall, in which mental impulses jostle one another like separate individuals. Adjoining this entrance hall there is a second, narrower, room—a kind of drawing-room—in which consciousness too resides. But on the threshold between the two rooms a watchman performs his function: he examines the different mental impulses, acts as a censor, and will not admit them into the drawing-room if they displease him.[100]**

Freud's view is that it is a part of the human condition to repress certain experiences. For instance, a person who has been in a serious automobile accident might repress the memory of the experience. In fact, until the painful memories of the accident are repressed sufficiently, the person may be unable to drive or even ride in an automobile. Clearly, repression can serve a beneficial purpose.

Repression may also have negative consequences. First of all, people can learn from their painful experiences, providing they do not repress them. The youngster who burns her finger on an oven ought not repress that sensation altogether; if she does, she may get burned

again. Second, in certain cases, if too much is repressed there is a threat of internal explosion. For example, one might argue that a rapist is a person who has repressed a surplus of bad feelings toward women. According to this framework, the built-up tension of these negative feelings may eventually cause the rapist to snap psychologically as he strikes out against a woman victim who is symbolic of the women he hates. Hence, repression is a necessary defense mechanism but, in a Freudian sense, an overdose of repression may lead to criminal behavior.

Summary of Freudian Interpretations of Crime

Freud advanced a number of ideas, and his views have evoked strong reactions, both favorable and unfavorable. While his writings are voluminous and complex, we have only touched on a few basic notions in an attempt to apply some of his insights to an analysis of crime behavior.

Perhaps the two most common criticisms of Freudian theory refer to his methodology and his view of human agency. With regard to methods, many of his suppositions cannot be tested against empirical reality.[101] Freud was a clinician concerned with the experiences of his patients; he was not a social researcher committed to testing his theories on a representative sample of the population. In fact, Freudian theory is generally incapable of being tested (that is, falsified), a shortcoming for any theory.

A long line of scholars have also challenged Freud's model of the individual. Freud has often been accused of an excessive reliance on biological factors.[102] The individual is conceptualized as a creature controlled by instincts that operate at the unconscious level. In his system there is virtually no room for conscious, individual agency. Rather, actors are seen as predetermined to act in ways consistent with the demands of the psyche. The internal battles waged by the id, ego, and superego propel and direct the actor, often toward the commission of criminal behavior. In short, as Fromm and others have charged, Freud has likened humans too much to other animals.[103]

Low Self-Control

In *A General Theory of Crime,* Michael Gottfredson and Travis Hirschi argue that crime is caused by a lack of self-control.[104] Self-control accounts for "the differential tendency of people to avoid criminal acts whatever the circumstances in which they find themselves."[105] **Low self-control,** or lack of self-control, is said to predispose individuals of all ages to commit crimes. The inability to control oneself successfully is linked to childhood experiences that portend of lifelong propensity for committing illegal acts. While the Gottfredson/Hirshi theory is not typically associated with criminological positivism, the idea that there is one factor (low self-control) differentiating criminals from non-criminals is certainly in keeping with the positivist tradition. This influential theoretical development will be discussed further in Chapter 12, but for now it should be noted that there is at least some empirical support for the theory.[106]

Critique

This chapter has highlighted theories that view crime as caused by internal, individual forces. A general critique of this overall perspective is now in order.

Adequacy

Biological and psychoanalytical theories tend to portray the criminal offender as driven to commit crimes. Crime is not chosen behavior, but behavior forced upon an individual who is incapable of resisting law violation. For most people in American society, the idea that criminals are forced to commit their acts probably does not ring true. Indeed, ever since Lombroso first popularized the notion that internal factors cause crime, this school of thought has had problems of credibility. Lombroso and his followers have been roundly criticized for the view that atavists, or born criminals, commit most crimes in society. In fact, the proposition that physiological or anatomical traits determine human behavior has never been accepted by the scientific community. In fairness, however, most modern sociobiological approaches do not advocate extreme positions. They argue that both genetics and social environment influence human behavior.[107] Such formulations have more credibility than the extreme positions taken by early positivists.

The Freudian explanation of behavior, which accents the internal forces of personality rather than physical traits, has also had a large number of critics. Like biological approaches, it also has failed to gain general scientific endorsement—in part, no doubt, because so many of Freud's contentions do not lend themselves to scientific testing.

Comprehensive Nature

A truly comprehensive explanation of criminal behavior explains crimes of violence as well as stealing offenses and crimes that cut across class boundaries. For the most part, the early positivists defined the crime problem in terms of interpersonal violence and lower-class stealing. White-collar crimes, to say nothing of corporate crime or crimes committed by government officials, were beyond their scope. Even today, those who conduct research within the biological perspective on crime generally take the same narrow focus. Genes are said to be related to physically aggressive behavior. There has been no effort, however, to explain the criminally fraudulent actions of white-collar criminals in terms of genetic constitution. Freudian theory seeks to be more comprehensive, but specific explanations in this tradition are so dependent upon inner states and psychic elements that mainstream science remains skeptical.

Current Appeal

Despite the serious problems noted above, both positivist criminology and the Freudian view on crime enjoy a certain level of current popularity. Scientific discoveries in the area of genetic research have become almost routine. Indeed, a wide range of behavioral tendencies have been associated with specific genes. Some think that it is only a matter of time until "crime genes" are identified. Even the Freudian view of behavior, with its emphasis on "inner turmoil," has a receptive audience, particularly as American culture appears to embrace the notion that much behavior is "addicted." At the same time, many social scientists and politicians seek to combat the notion that individuals should be considered helpless in the face of biological or psychological forces.

Summary

This chapter has focused attention on theories that highlight the importance of internal, individualistic sources of crime. Early positivism was the first and major exemplar of this criminological school of thought. The early positivists, Lombroso, Ferri, and Garofalo, rejected the classical theory of crime, especially the view that individuals freely choose to commit crime. Lombroso and his associates sought to apply the scientific method to the study of crime in order to make possible the positive identification of criminals. Central to the positivist perspective is the idea that many, if not most, criminals are born with a biological predisposition to commit criminal behavior. Contemporary researchers have attempted to expand on the insights of early positivism and many of these formulations were discussed.

In addition to positivist thought, this chapter examined the Freudian analysis of behavior. The internal forces that captured the attention of positivist criminologists are biological in nature, but the Freudian view of crime underscores the influence of both biological and psychological factors. The most crucial component of this theory is the contention that the unconscious directs individuals to behave as they do, including behavior which violates the law. Like positivist criminology, however, the Freudian explanation of crime is controversial. Although the biological and psychological perspectives speak to important aspects of crime causation and have great potential for discovering useful insights about criminal behavior, at this point no biological or psychoanalytical theory of crime enjoys wide approval within mainstream criminology.

Critical Thinking Questions

1. What does *positivism* mean in criminology? Is positivist criminology a contradiction in terms?
2. Lombroso and Freud offered distinctive theories of behavior. Describe the major similarities and differences in their thoughts.
3. How can biological and social explanations of crime be merged?
4. What are some specific policy implications of biological theories of crime?
5. Who is most responsible for crime, the individual offender or the social environment?

Suggested Readings

Lee Ellis and Anthony Walsh, "Gene Based Evolutionary Theories in Criminology," *Criminology 35* (1997) 229–76.

David Dixon, "On the Criminal Mind: An Imaginary Lecture by Sigmund Freud," *International Journal of Offender Therapy and Comparative Criminology 30* (1986) 101–109.

Diana Fishbein, "Biological Perspectives in Criminology," *Criminology 28* (1990) 27–72.

Alfred Lindesmith and Yale Levin, "The Lombrosian Myth in Criminology," *American Journal of Sociology 42* (1937) 653–71.

Randy Martin, Robert Mutchnick, and W. Timothy Austin, "Chapter 4: Sigmund Freud," in *Criminological Thought: Pioneers Past and Present* (New York: Macmillan, 1990) 67–92.

Marvin Wolfgang, "Cesare Lombroso," in *Pioneers in Criminology*, 2d ed., ed. Hermann Mannheim (Montclair, NJ: Patterson Smith,1972) 232–89.

Notes

1 William Mullen, "Gacy Brain Is Set for U. of C. Exam," *Chicago Tribune*, 12 May 1994, 1–3.
2 Quoted in Lewis Coser, *Masters of Sociological Thought*, 2nd ed. (New York: Harcourt Brace Jovanovich, 1977) 7.
3 George Vold, *Theoretical Criminology*, 2nd ed., rev. Thomas Bernard (New York: Oxford University Press, 1979).
4 Jacques Barzun, *Darwin, Marx, Wagner*, 2nd ed. (New York: Anchor, 1958) 1.
5 Charles Darwin, *The Origin of Species*, intro. Charles Mickner (New York: Random House, 1993).
6 Charles Darwin, *The Descent of Man* (Norwood, PN: Telegraph Books, 1986).
7 Coser, *Masters of Sociological Thought*, 44.
8 Karl Marx, *The Eighteenth Brumaire of Louis Bonaparte* (New York: International, 1975 [orig. pub. 1852]).
9 L. Savitz, S.H. Turner, and T. Dickman, "The Origin of Scientific Criminology: Franz Joseph Gall as the First Criminologist," in *Theory in Criminology*, ed. R. F. Meier (Beverly Hills, CA: Sage, 1977) 41–56.
10 Daniel Curran and Claire Renzetti, *Theories of Crime* (Boston: Allyn & Bacon, 1994) 41.
11 Ibid., 41–42.
12 Alfred Lindesmith and Yale Levin, "The Lombrosian Myth in Criminology," *American Journal of Sociology 42* (1937) 653–71; Richard Quinney and John Wildeman, *The Problem of Crime*, 2nd ed.(New York: Harper & Row, 1977) 43.
13 Vold, *Theoretical Criminology*, 39.
14 Issac Ray, *A Treatise on the Medical Jurisprudence of Insanity* (C.C. Little & J. Brown, 1838; reprinted by Harvard University Press, Cambridge, 1962).
15 Gennaro Vito and Ronald Holmes, *Criminology* (Belmont, CA: Wadsworth, 1994) 121.
16 Richard Dugdale, *The Jukes* (New York: Putnam, 1877).
17 Vold, *Theoretical Criminology*, 78.
18 Quoted in Francis Allen, "Raffaele Garofalo," in *Pioneers in Criminology*, 2nd ed., ed. Hermann Mannheim (Montclair, NJ: Patterson Smith, 1972) 318–40.
19 Ibid.
20 Lindesmith and Levin, "The Lombrosian Myth in Criminology."
21 Caesar Lombroso and William Ferrero, *The Female Offender* (Littleton, CO: Fred Rothman & Co., 1980 [orig. pub. 1895]).
22 Enrico Ferri, *Criminal Sociology* (New York: Agathon, 1967 [orig. pub. 1881]) 37.
23 Quoted in Leon Radzinowicz, *Ideology and Crime* (New York: Columbia University Press, 1966) 29.
24 Marvin Wolfgang, "Cesare Lombroso," in *Pioneers in Criminology*, ed. Hermann Mannheim (Montclair, NJ: Patterson Smith, 1972) 248.
25 Cesare Lombroso, *Crime: Its Causes and Remedies*, tr. Henry Horton (Boston: Little, Brown, 1912) 365.
26 Ibid., 2.
27 Ferri, *Criminal Sociology*, 145.
28 Ibid., 115.
29 Lombroso, *Crime: Its Causes and Remedies*, 432.
30 Wolfgang, "Cesare Lombroso," 252.
31 Ferri, *Criminal Sociology*, 138–60.
32 Ibid., 160.
33 Quoted in Wolfgang, "Cesare Lombroso," 251.
34 Ferri, *Criminal Sociology*, 60.
35 Ibid.
36 Lindesmith and Levin, "The Lombrosian Myth in Criminology," 664.
37 Lombroso, *Crime: Its Causes and Remedies*.
38 Ferri, *Criminal Sociology*, 38.
39 Quoted in Allen, *Pioneers in Criminology*, 332.
40 Lombroso, *Criminal Sociology*.
41 Quoted in Wolfgang, "Cesare Lombroso," 278.
42 Quoted in Vold, *Theoretical Criminology*, 42.
43 Ferri, *Criminal Sociology*, 485.
44 Ibid., 494.
45 Raffaele Garafalo, *Criminology* (Montclair: Patterson Smith, 1968 [orig. pub. 1914]).
46 Vold, *Theoretical Criminology*, 45–46.
47 Ibid, 58.
48 Charles Goring, *The English Convict: A Statistical Study* (His Majesty's Stationery Office, London, 1913; reprinted by Patterson Smith, Montclair, 1972) 200.
49 E.A. Hooton, *The American Criminal: An Anthropological Study* (Cambridge: Harvard University Press, 1939).
50 Vold, *Theoretical Criminology*, 63.
51 William Sheldon, *Varieties of Delinquent Youth* (New York: Harper & Brothers, 1949).
52 See Sheldon and Eleanor Glueck, *Physique and Delinquency* (New York: Harper, 1956); and *Unraveling Juvenile Delinquency* (Cambridge: Harvard University Press, 1950).
53 Pierre Van Den Berghe, "Bringing Beasts Back In: Toward a Biosocial Theory of Aggression," *American Sociological Review 39* (1974) 777-88.
54 Edmund O. Wilson, *Sociobiology: The New Synthesis* (Cambridge: Harvard University Press, 1975).
55 C. Ray Jeffery, "Biology and Crime: The New Neo-Lombrosians," in *Biology and Crime*, ed. C. Ray Jeffery (Beverly Hills: Sage, 1979) 7–18; Sarnoff Mednick and Jan Volavka, "Biology and Crime," in *Crime and Justice: An Annual Review of Research*, Vol. 2, ed. Norval Morris and Michael Tonry (Chicago: University of Chicago Press, 1980), 85-158.
56 James Q. Wilson and Richard Herrnstein, *Crime and Human Nature* (New York: Simon & Schuster, 1985).
57 Ibid., 70.
58 Ibid., 22.
59 Richard Herrnstein and Charles Murray, *The Bell Curve: Intelligence and Class Structure in American Life* (New York: Free Press, 1994).
60 Francis T. Cullen, Paul Gendreau, G. Roger Jarjoura, and John Paul Wright, "Crime and the Bell Curve: Lessons from Intelligent Criminology," *Crime and Delinquency 43* (1997) 387–411.

61 Ibid., 406.

62 Ibid., 54.

63 See, for example, Lawrence Taylor, *Born To Crimes: The Genetic Causes of Criminal Behavior* (London: Greenwood, 1984) 35–49.

64 James Shields, *Monozygotic Twins* (London: Oxford University Press, 1962).

65 Karl Christiansen, "A Preliminary Study of Criminality Among Twins," in *Biosocial Bases of Criminal Behavior*, ed. Sarnoff Mednick and Karl Christiansen (New York: Gardner, 1977) 89–108.

66 Sarnoff Mednick, William Gabrielli, and Barry Hutchings, "Genetic Influences in Criminal Behavior: Evidence from an Adoption Court, " *Science* 224 (1984) 891–94.

67 Lee Ellis, "Genetics and Criminal Behavior," *Criminology* 20 (1982) 43–67.

68 Janet Katz and William Chambliss, "Biology and Crime," in *Criminology*, 2nd ed., ed. Joseph Sheley (Belmont, CA: Wadsworth, 1995) 275–303; Freda Adler, Gerhard O.W. Mueller, and William Laufer, *Criminology* (New York: McGraw-Hill, 1991) 93; P. Jacobs et al., "Aggressive Behavior, Mental Subnormality and the XYY Male," *Nature 208* (1965) 1351–52.

69 Ibid., 287–88.

70 A. Theilgaard, "Aggression and the XYY Personality," *International Journal of Law and Psychiatry 6* (1983) 413–21.

71 Ibid., 287.

72 C. Ray Jeffery, *Criminology: An Interdisciplinary Approach* (Englewood Cliffs, NJ: Prentice-Hall, 1990)193–94.

73 Hans Eysenck, *Crime and Personality* (Boston: Houghton Miffin, 1964).

74 Jeffery, *Criminology: An Interdisciplinary Approach,* 366.

75 W. Buikhuisen, "Cerebral Dysfuntions and Persistent Juvenile Delinquency," in *The Causes of Crime: New Biological Approaches,* ed. Sarnoff Mednick, Terrie Moffitt, and Susan Stack (New York: Cambridge University Press, 1987) 168–84.

76 Israel Nachshon and Deborah Denno, "Violent Behavior and Cerebral Hemisphere Function," in *The Causes of Crime: New Biological Approaches,* ed. Sarnoff Mednick, Terrie Moffitt, and Susan Stack (New York: Cambridge University Press, 1987) 185–217.

77 D. Williams, "Neural Factors Related to Habitual Aggression—Consideration of Differences Between Habitual Aggressives and Others Who Have Committed Crimes of Violence," *Brain 92* (1969) 503–520.

78 Katherine and Kermit Hoyenga, *Motivational Explanations of Behavior* (Monterey, CA: Brooks/Cole, 1984) 291–92.

79 R. Prentky, "The Neurochemistry of Sexual Aggression," in *Aggression and Dangerousness,* ed. D. Farrington and J. Gunn (New York: Wiley, 1985) 7–56.

80 Joan Luckmann and Karen Creason Sorensen, 3rd ed., *Medical-Surgical Nursing* (Philadelphia: WB Saunders, 1987) 1678, 1747.

81 Katharina Dalton, *The Premenstrual Syndrome* (Springfield, IL: Charles C Thomas, 1971).

82 Susan Lark, *Premenstrual Syndrome Self-Help Book* (Los Angeles, CA: Forman, 1984) 19; C. Ray Jeffery, 1990, 381.

83 K. Dalton, "Menstruation and Crime," *British Medical Journal 2* (1986) 1752–53; Ruth Masters and Cliff Roberson, *Inside Criminology* (Englewood Cliffs, NJ: Prentice-Hall, 1990) 250.

84 J. Horney, "Menstrual Cycles and Criminal Responsibility," *Law and Human Behavior 2* (1978) 25–36.

85 Matti Virkkunen, "Metabolic Dysfunctions Among Habitually Violent Offenders: Reactive Hypoglycemia and Cholesterol Levels," in *The Causes of Crime: New Biological Approaches,* ed. Sarnoff Mednick, Terrie Moffitt, and Susan Stack (New York: Cambridge University Press, 1987) 292–311.

86 Helen Guthrie, *Introductory Nutrition,* 5th ed. (St. Louis: CV Mosby, 1983) 24.

87 Freda Adler, Gerhard O.W. Mueller, and William Laufer, *Criminology* (New York: McGraw-Hill, 1991), 98.

88 Leon Jaroff, "The Gene Hunt," *Time,* 20 March 1989, 62.

89 Ibid., 62–67.

90 Edward Sagarin, "Taboo Subjects and Taboo Viewpoints in Criminology," in *Taboo in Criminology,* ed. Edward Sagarin (Beverly Hills, CA: Sage, 1980) 8–9.

91 A. Bandura, *Aggression: A Social Learning Analysis* (Englewood Cliffs, NJ: Prentice-Hall, 1973); L. Wrightsman and K. Deaux, *Social Psychology in the 90s,* 6th ed. (Monterey, CA: Brooks/Cole, 1993).

92 Randy Martin, Robert Mutchnick, and W. Timothy Austin, *Criminological Thought: Pioneers Past and Present* (New York: Macmillan,1990) 71; Walter Mischel, *Introduction to Personality,* 2nd. ed. (New York: Holt, Rinehart and Winston, 1976) 350–51.

93 Sigmund Freud, *Introductory Lectures on Psycho-*Analysis, tr. and intro. James Strachey (New York: Norton, 1966 [orig. pub. 1917]) 12.

94 Sigmund Freud, *New Introductory Lectures on Psycho-Analsysis,* tr. W.J.H. Sprott (New York: Norton, 1933) 108.

95 Martin, Mutchnick, and Austin, *Criminological Thought: Pioneers Past and Present,* 77.

96 August Aichhorn, *Wayward Youth* (New York: Viking, 1935).

97 Freud, *Introductory Lectures on Psycho-Analysis,* 256.

98 Martin, Mutchnick, and Austin, *Criminological Thought: Pioneers Past and Present,* 79.

99 Erik Erikson, *Identity and the Life Cycle* (New York: Norton, 1980).

100 Freud, *Introductory Lectures on Psycho-Analysis,* 365–66.

101 Martin, Mutchnick, and Austin, *Criminological Thought: Pioneers Past and Present,* 84.

102 Ibid., 86.

103 Erich Fromm, *Escape from Freedom* (New York: Aron Books, 1941).

104 Michael Gottfredson and Travis Hirschi, *A General Theory of Crime* (Palo Alto, CA: Stanford University Press, 1990).

105 Ibid., 87.

106 See John Gibbs and Dennis Giever, "Self-Control and Its Manifestations Among University Students: An Empirical Test of Gottfredson and Hirschi's General Theory," *Justice Quarterly 12* (1995):231–55; Bruce Arneklev, Harold Grasmick, and Charles Tittle, "Low Self-Control and Imprudent Behavior," *Journal of Quantitative Criminology 9* (1993) 225–47; Harold Grasmick, Charles Tittle, and Robert Bursik Jr., "Testing the Core Empirical Implications of Gottfredson and Hirschi's General Theory of Crime," *Journal of Research in Crime and Delinquency 30* (1993) 5–29.

107 Diana Fishbein, "Biological Perspectives in Criminology," *Criminology 28* (1990) 27–72.

chapter 11

Micro Social Causes of Crime: Social Ecology and Differential Association

CHAPTER OUTLINE

BACKGROUND
  The Chicago School
  The Search For Root Causes
    Discipline Building
    The Progressive Era
CORE PROPOSITIONS
  The Social Ecology Theory of Crime
    The City as a Natural Area
    The Concentric Zone Model
    Delinquency/Crime Varies by Zone
    Neither Individuals Nor Groups Are Criminogenic
    Summary
  Differential Association Theory
    Criminal Behavior Is Learned
    Communication Within Intimate Personal Groups
    Techniques and Rationalizations
    Unfavorable Definition of the Legal Code
    Excess of Definitions Favorable to Law Violation
    Differential Association Varies
    Summary
POSITION ON AGENCY (RESPONSIBILITY)
POLICY IMPLICATIONS
SUBSEQUENT DEVELOPMENTS
  Routine Activities
  Differential Identification
CRITIQUE
  Adequacy
  Comprehensive Nature
  Current Appeal
SUMMARY

KEY TERMS

micro social forces
social ecology
differential association
natural area
concentric zone model
social disorganization
direct instruction
operant conditioning
imitation
cognitive social learning
techniques and rationalizations
unfavorable definition of the legal code
routine activities
motivated offenders/suitable targets/absence of guardians
differential identification
identity maintenance
subculture of violence
techniques of neutralization

IN LATE OCTOBER 1991, three Milwaukee teenagers were on the street, looking for trouble.[1] As they walked along, they stopped several people at gunpoint, robbing them of clothing, jewelry, and footwear. One young woman resisted. Brenda Adams refused to surrender the new leather coat she had recently received as a birthday present. So 17-year-old Felicia Morgan shot and killed Adams. In her trial, Morgan's lawyer claimed that "urban psychosis" was responsible for the killing. The lawyer argued that Felicia grew up in a violent inner-city home and neighborhood, and that this killing was an inevitable outgrowth of her experience. The urban psychosis defense failed in court, but it illustrates the importance often attached to family and neighborhood influence. Is crime produced by micro social forces such as family, friends, and neighborhood? This is the main question of the present chapter.

Background

Neither classical criminology nor early positivism was able to resolve the problem of crime. Classical theory advanced the view that crime is behavior committed by rational, self-interested, and freely choosing individuals. Positivist criminology turned the classical position completely around. For the most part, positivists held that crime is behavior produced by internal forces beyond the control of human actors. The theoretical study of crime had reached an impasse. This is the point of entry for American academic sociology, which seeks to explain crime as the product of social environmental forces. As we shall presently see, American sociologists were quick to reject the free agency view promoted by classicists as well as the biological determinism advanced by positivists. Instead, the first American sociological theories of crime emphasized the importance of **micro social forces.** In sociological terms, *micro* refers to social phenomena within an individual's immediate social environment (family, church, and school are micro social forces). Early micro theories of crime were a product of the development of academic sociology in the United States and the search by early American sociologists for root causes of social problems.

The Chicago School

By all accounts, the sociology department at the University of Chicago spearheaded the development of sociology in the United States.[2] The university itself was chartered in 1891, with John D. Rockefeller as its founding benefactor. William Harper, the university's first president, used Rockefeller's money to hire 120 top faculty members (nine of whom were former university presidents) for the school's opening in 1892.[3] Harper's intention was to make the University of Chicago the premier research institution in the United States. Harper entered college at age 10, received his Ph.D. from Yale University before his

nineteenth birthday, and he had lofty expectations for this new university.

The president of Colby College in Maine, Albion Small, was invited by Harper to start the history department at the university. Instead, Small requested that he be put in charge of establishing a sociology department. This request was granted, and Small's department rapidly dominated the field. The department's focus on empirical research and social problem solving shaped the development of academic sociology in the United States.

President Harper required his faculty to conduct research. He argued that "it is only the man who has made investigation who may teach others to investigate."[4] It should also be noted that the prominent philosopher and educator, John Dewey, was at the University of Chicago from 1894 to 1904. His presence there insured that philosophical pragmatism influenced all of the social sciences at the university.[5] Dewey's pronouncements about education became especially famous. He embraced the view of the philosopher Charles Peirce that the meaning of an idea can only be seen in its consequences.[6] Theorizing in the abstract would not do; ideas must be tested empirically. As sociology department chair, Albion Small felt similarly. Small believed that the goal of sociology was to provide objective and scientific insights about the social world. To do so, it must necessarily be grounded in empirical study.[7]

Robert E. Park was another central figure in Small's sociology department from 1914 to 1933.[8] Park had been an undergraduate student of Dewey's at the University of Michigan in the 1880s, and then was a newspaper reporter and editor for about a dozen years before returning to academia. It was Park who coined the term *human ecology* and it was Park who particularly insisted that sociology graduate students immerse themselves in the real world.[9] Park found little value in abstract theory; he believed that theory had to emerge from an analysis of actual conditions. Park's influence was huge. From 1925 to 1926 he was president of the American Sociological Society (the name was later changed to American Sociological

John D. Rockefeller frequently gave dimes to the "less fortunate." Rockefeller was also the founding benefactor of the University of Chicago, where early American sociology flourished.

Association) and eight of his former students eventually became president of this national association.[10] One of his former students was Clifford Shaw, whose theories we will examine shortly.

Early sociologists at the University of Chicago were not interested in empirical research for its own sake. Rather, they were committed to the identification, examination, and resolution of social problems—particularly the problems of the city of Chicago. There were several reasons for this. First, as far back as the 1880s, college sociology courses were introduced in lieu of moral philosophy courses.[11] In other words, sociology initially secured a presence in academia by taking a moral-philosophical, social reformist point of view. Those students interested in social reform and philanthropy expected that sociology courses would offer useful insight and guidance.[12]

A second factor that linked Chicago School sociology to a social-problems orientation was Small's conviction that sociology had an ethical obligation to improve society. He felt that sociological inquiry must take place in the real world and that the fruits of such inquiry should be used to make a better society. Finally, through the early decades of the twentieth century, the Chicago sociology department employed many adjunct professors who had positions in social agencies. On many occasions, academicians collaborated with practitioners, another factor which promoted a concern for practical social problems.

The theories and research findings published by those affiliated with the Chicago school defined the field of early American sociology. In 1905, Small helped found the American Sociological Society, and for many years this organization was dominated by University of Chicago sociologists.[13] It was also in 1905 that the Chicago department started the first American sociology journal, *The American Journal of Sociology*. With Small as the editor, the *AJS* was the preeminent journal for at least three decades. The Chicago school of sociology was also the national leader in terms of prestige rankings of departments and number of doctorates awarded.[14] Hence, it should come as no surprise that the first major American theories of crime were developed by sociologists affiliated with the University of Chicago.

The Search for Root Causes

Discipline Building
Identifying causal relationships was central to defining the purpose and boundaries of sociology as a new discipline. The French pioneer sociologist, Emile Durkheim (1858–1917), sought to establish sociology as a distinct and worthwhile science. Durkheim argued that "sociological explanation consists exclusively in establishing relations of causality, that it is a matter of connecting a phenomenon to its cause, or rather a cause to its effects."[15] Durkheim further argued that "the determining cause of a social fact should be sought among the social facts preceding it and not among the states of the individual consciousness."[16] Moreover, it was his position that theory comes after investigation.[17]

In developing academic sociology in the United States, Chicago School sociologists embraced the points advanced by Durkheim. Like Durkheim, they sought to establish causal connections, they stressed the importance of social factors in explaining behavior, and they held that theory emerged from empirical investigation. In this way, they sought to justify this new field of study. Sociology, in order to be considered a science, needed to identify causal relationships; in order to be considered a *distinct* science of behavior, it had to emphasize social—not biological or psychological—phenomena; and in order to be considered worthwhile, it had to be relevant to practical social problems, which demanded context-generated and empirically based theories.

The Progressive Era
The search for root causes was not just a product of discipline building. The Progressive Era (1890–1910), a social, political, and intellectual movement, exerted an influence as well. Progressives thought that society could be made better. All that was required was enlightened and uncorrupted government action. Science—even social science, it was thought—could lead the way. Consider the statement submitted in 1880 by the editor of *The Popular Science Monthly*: "Social phenomena may be analyzed and classified, and reduced to general expressions or principles, like other phenomena of Nature. . . ."[18] Hence, sociologists

could make a contribution by identifying the most pressing problems of social life, examining these problems, and then suggesting a resolution. This is precisely what was attempted at the University of Chicago where research was to get to the bottom of social problems in the city of Chicago. This meant that ultimate or root causes must be uncovered.

Core Propositions

Each of the theories examined in this chapter views criminal behavior as resulting from social phenomena operating at the micro level (a person's immediate social environment). The first theory, **social ecology,** centers attention on the criminal offender's neighborhood. The second theory, **differential association,** stresses the importance of the offender's family, friends, and associates.

The Social Ecology Theory of Crime

Clifford Shaw and Henry McKay were researchers with Chicago's Institute for Juvenile Research. Shaw and McKay are most often cited as the chief architects of the social ecology model of crime. Although neither Shaw nor McKay were on the faculty at the University of Chicago, they were associated with members of the sociology department, and they were particularly influenced by Robert Park and Ernest Burgess. Below are the key features of their theoretical perspective.

The City as a Natural Area
The tendency to view social phenomena as if they were biological entities is as old as sociology itself. August Comte, the putative father of sociology, spoke frequently of society as if it were a biological organism (the family was likened to an organism's heart, while highways were thought of as blood vessels). In addition to the Comtean tradition, another incentive for early twentieth-century sociologists to think of society as if it were a living phenomenon was based on Charles Darwin's theory of evolution, which was gaining popularity at the time. Even social scientists had begun to embrace Darwinian theory, perhaps thinking that it would make their disciplines appear more scientific. This, then, was the intellectual context that produced ecological studies of society and social life.

Social ecologists argued that there were important parallels between plant and animal life on the one hand and human social life on the other. All living creatures are part of an ecological system. Moreover, the city, as a human habitat, could reasonably be viewed as a **natural area,** as was outlined by Robert Park and Ernest Burgess.[19] In other words, just as biologists might examine a forest and its life forms, so could sociologists examine the life forms of the city. Shaw and McKay took this as a basic point of departure. In viewing the city as a natural area requiring investigation, they accepted two fundamental propositions of ecological analysis: (1) that city life is characterized by certain universal processes; and (2) that non-random variations develop among areas of the city.

The two most important processes of city life are invasion and succession. Invasion and succession occur when industry encroaches on residential areas. Human groups, argued Shaw and McKay, also engage in invasion and succession. For example, when an immigrant population first comes to the United States, there is a tendency to settle in the center of the city where rental rates are lowest. After some years, this ethnic group becomes financially established and departs for another residential location just as a new ethnic immigrant group arrives (invades and succeeds).

As to the variations between city areas, Shaw and McKay researched a broad range of variables, including but not limited to (a) predominant use of area, for example, industrial or residential, (b) ethnic origin of the area's population, (c) truancy, delinquency, and crime rates, (d) disease and mortality rates, as well as (e) differences in standards and cultural values.[20] The findings of their investigations will be discussed shortly, but we now address a second component of the Shaw and McKay method of analysis. In addition to taking a social ecological perspective, Shaw and McKay used the **concentric zone model** of city development.

The Concentric Zone Model

Burgess advanced the thesis that American cities develop in the form of concentric zones.[21] He argued that the city, as a natural area, consisted of five zones:

- Zone I, the central business district
- Zone II, a zone in transition (from residential to industrial)
- Zone III, the zone of workingmen's homes (blue-collar homes)
- Zone IV, the residential zone (middle- and upper-class homes)
- Zone V, the commuter zone (suburbs)

These zones grow in circular form and encroach upon one another. The first zone makes up the city's interior and consists mainly of professional offices, retail stores, financial institutions, hotels, theaters, and some apartments. The second zone is characterized by physical deterioration caused by industrial encroachment. There are some small-business ventures in this zone, such as pawn shops, as well as residential units of the economically disadvantaged. The outer three zones are all residential areas, with the highest priced housing in the two outer zones—far removed from the poorer residential neighbor-

TABLE 11.1	Delinquency Rates by Zone per Hundred Male Adolescents Aged 10–16[59]

ZONE	DELINQUENCY RATE
Zone 1	9.8 per 100
Zone 2	6.7 per 100
Zone 3	4.5 per 100
Zone 4	2.5 per 100
Zone 5	1.8 per 100

hoods as well as from the noise and pollution of factories. Now it is time to consider the important differences found by Shaw and McKay among these areas (zones).

Delinquency/Crime Varies by Zone

As described by Park and Burgess, the five zones of city life have distinctive forms of social, and even physical, organization. Assuming that these differences might account for variations in social-pathological behavior, Shaw and McKay collected empirical data on crime and delinquency rates. Their two most important findings were as follows: (a) delinquency rates are highest toward the center of the city and lowest toward the exterior of the city; and (b) in certain areas of the city (areas characterized by social disorganization), delinquent and criminal behavior is tolerated, if not encouraged.

Using official statistics from juvenile court proceedings over a period of several decades, Shaw and McKay calculated rates of delinquency for each zone. What they found was that delinquency rates for interior zones were considerably higher than the delinquency rates for exterior zones. See Table 11.1 for the pattern of delinquency rates for male adolescents 10 to 16 years of age, based on the juvenile court records from 1927 to 1933.

Shaw and McKay explained the disparate rates by arguing that areas of the city had distinctive social qualities (Box 11.1). Specifically, the areas characterized by **social disorganization** were the areas with the highest delinquency and crime rates. Delinquency rates do not *just happen* to vary by area (zone); Shaw and McKay argued that certain areas promote delinquent and criminal behavior, while other areas inhibit such behavior. High delinquency and crime areas are typified by "social confusion and disorganization."[22] After all, these areas feature "physical deterioration, decreasing population, and the disintegration of the conventional neighborhood culture and organization.[23]

It is instructive to note that the authors use the word *neighborhood*. This is a key concept. Neighborhoods have physical boundaries as well as cultural tradition. Shaw and McKay contended that certain neighborhoods have an opportunity structure conducive to the commission of crime and delinquency.[24] For instance, joining a gang is easiest

Singapore's Caning of Michael Fay

Shaw and McKay argued that some sections of a city are so socially disorganized that crime and delinquency are encouraged. Other sections are highly ordered, and have such a fixed tradition of right and wrong, that crime and delinquency are rare. The island city-state of Singapore in Southeast Asia is an example of an entire urban area that enjoys a low crime rate. In fact, Singapore is often referred to as the "safest city on earth." Deviant behavior is very uncommon, and not tolerated. Even spitting and chewing gum is outlawed, and violators are subject to fines in the hundreds of dollars. It is no exaggeration to say that all neighborhoods in Singapore are rigidly controlled socially. In 1994, Singapore's social organization came to the attention of the world through the Michael Fay case.

Michael Fay, 18-year-old son of an affluent CEO from Dayton, Ohio (photo on page 222), admitted to Singapore authorities that, using eggs and spray paint, he had ruined the appearance of two cars. For this offense, Fay was sentenced to 4 months in prison, fined $2200, and told that he would be caned—six lashes from a rattan cane (this was subsequently reduced to four lashes). Caning is a common punishment in Singapore. The subject is stripped, bound by the hands and ankles, and strapped to a wooden trestle while his buttocks are whipped. The procedure typically splits the skin, draws blood, and leaves lifelong scars. If the subject passes out from the pain, a doctor is present to revive the individual so that the punishment can be completed.

Many Americans were outraged by this punishment. They thought that it was too brutal. Many other Americans approved of this response to criminal behavior and wished that American society could be organized along similar lines. Lee Kuan Yew, Singapore's political leader for nearly thirty years, believes that the Singapore model of social organization is preferable to what is found in the United States. Yew contends that in Singapore the primary goal is a well-ordered society, while in the United States the emphasis is on individual freedom. These are two very different orientations to social life.

Shaw and McKay stressed the differences found between different areas within a metropolitan area. Singapore provides an example of an entire urban community having a fixed social tradition where conformity is strictly enforced. It also illustrates a sharp international difference in social organization and culture.

SOURCES: Michael Elliott, "The Caning Debate: Should America Be More Like Singapore?" *Newsweek*, 18 April 1994, 18–22; Melissa Roberts, "Justice in Six Lashes," *Newsweek*, 11 April 1994, 40; Philip Shenon, "Singapore, The Tiger Whose Teeth Are Not Universally Scorned," *New York Times*, 10 April 1994, IV-5; Fareed Zakaria, "Order and Liberty, East and West," *New York Times*, 11 April 1994, A19.

in the inner zones because the gangs are most prevalent in these areas. Furthermore, the inner zones have numerous abandoned or condemned buildings that can be used as gang headquarters and a ready storage area for stolen goods. In addition to there being more opportunities for crime and delinquency in these inner zones, there are fewer legitimate opportunities (appropriate employment, for example). In general, Shaw and McKay saw some neighborhoods (zones) as socially blessed, while others were described at the opposite extreme.

Perhaps the most important aspect of social disorganization is the moral atmosphere of an area. It was presumed that exterior zones had a fixed tradition of right and wrong, whereas the interior zones lacked this feature of social life. Regardless of who the inhabitants of Zone I or Zone II might be at any particular time, Shaw and McKay argued that these zones were characterized by conflicting moral standards:

. . . in the areas of low rates of delinquents there is more or less uniformity, consistency, and universality of conventional values and attitudes

with respect to child care, conformity to law, and related matters; . . . (whereas in the high-rate areas systems of competing and conflicting moral values have developed).[25]

Hence, social disorganization promotes delinquency and crime. This is the heart of the Shaw and McKay theory. As we shall now see, *areas* are pathological, but not individuals or groups.

Neither Individuals Nor Groups Are Criminogenic

People who engage in delinquency or crime are *normal;* such individuals have no biological or psychological disorders and neither the delinquent nor the criminal offender is a born miscreant. Rejecting both Lombrosian and Freudian explanations, Shaw and McKay contended that offenders do not differ from law-abiding people in regard to "intelligence, physical condition, and personality traits."[26] Nor does a particular ethnic group have a predisposition for social pathology. Rather, the answer to delinquency and crime is rooted to social disorganization, which is itself linked to particular areas. How else, Shaw and McKay asked, can it be that a certain zone retains a high delinquency rate even while the ethnic composition of the zone changes drastically? For example, Germans, Irish, and Scandinavians made up 85 percent of the population of the high-rate zones in 1884, but by 1930 the ethnic constitution of these zones had altered to the extent that 75 percent of the population was of Italian, Polish, or Slavic ethnic origin.[27] Moreover, when ethnic composition is held constant, the pattern still remains. That is, Poles living in Zone II, for instance, will show consistently higher rates of delinquency than Poles living in Zone IV. Therefore, it appears not to be the individuals, nor their customs or ethnic heritage, that generates pathological social behavior. Rather, it is the zone itself.

Summary

The social ecology theory developed by Shaw and McKay is recognized as American sociology's first systematic explanation of crime. This theory of crime emerged from data showing that interior sections of urban areas had persistently high crime and delinquency rates while exterior sections had low rates. Shaw and McKay contend that high crime rate areas are socially disorganized. Hence, some city areas, or neighborhoods, are criminogenic—they tolerate and even encourage crime commission. It should be noted here that the primary focus of the social ecology theory is on conventional "street" crime.

Differential Association Theory

Edwin Sutherland (1883–1950) has been referred to as "the most important criminologist of the twentieth century."[28] Among Sutherland's accomplishments is his differential association theory of crime. This theory was hinted at in 1934, first formalized in 1939, and completed in 1947.[29] Differential association theory can be seen as a corrected extension of the social ecological perspective.[30] Though Shaw and McKay argued that the delinquent or criminal lived in a world that was socially unlike "respectable" society, they never fully developed the point. They were generally satisfied to identify an ecological factor (neighborhood social disorganization) as the leading cause of delinquency and crime. Sutherland's differential association theory went further by explaining with more precision how a person becomes a criminal. His explanation is based on the assumption that all behavior, including criminal behavior, is learned. Specifically, crime is seen as the outcome of social contacts and relationships. Sutherland and his collaborator in later years, Donald Cressey, phrased the argument in the following way:

When persons become criminal, they do so because of contacts with criminal patterns and also because of isolation from anticriminal patterns.

Any person inevitably assimilates the surrounding culture unless other patterns are in conflict; . . .[31]

The basic idea that people learn criminal behavior from others spawned a well-developed and influential theory. The essence of the theory can be captured in the following:

- Criminal behavior is learned through communication occurring within intimate personal groups.
- The learning of criminal behavior includes techniques and rationalizations.
- These rationalizations derive from the group's unfavorable definition of the legal code.
- Hence, a person becomes delinquent (criminal) when there is an excess of definitions favorable to law violation.
- Finally, differential association varies by frequency, duration, priority, and intensity.

Criminal Behavior Is Learned

Sutherland argued that the individual offender is not flawed in any fundamental way. Crime is not the product of faulty genes or a troubled psyche, nor is crime typically the result of a person losing control. Further, criminal behavior cannot be explained as an attempt to satisfy basic human needs. If that were the case, then poor people would be expected to steal far more often than they do. Rather, criminal behavior is like all other behavior—it is learned. Just as people learn to drive a car, learn to play football, or learn how to shingle a roof, they learn to behave criminally.

Sutherland did not offer a detailed description of how learning takes place, but there are at least four major ways in which humans learn criminal behavior. The first is **direct instruction**. When one person tells another the best way to disable an alarm system, that is an example of direct instruction. When an adult says to an adolescent that the laws are "passed by the rich and mighty and they don't have to be followed," that too is an example of direct instruction.

A second way in which an individual learns is through a process called **operant conditioning**. B.F. Skinner popularized this method.[32] In his research, Skinner noted that a pigeon will quickly "learn" to press down on a bar if food appears each time it happens. Using such methods, Skinner even taught pigeons to play table tennis! In terms of human action, the central principle of operant conditioning is that a person's environment encourages or discourages certain behavior through a system of rewards and punishments.[33] The tendency is for individuals to learn those behaviors that produce positive consequences. The investment broker who has repeatedly engaged in insider trading and made millions of dollars doing so has learned a criminal behavior pattern through positive reinforcement.

A third form of learning takes place through **imitation.** Gabriel Tarde, a nineteenth-century social philosopher, argued that criminal behavior was learned by imitating others. Tarde believed that individuals are most likely to imitate those who are near at hand and those who are thought of as superior.[34] Furthermore, if the role model's behavior is rewarded, then a person is more likely to imitate the behavior.[35] Thus, it should not be surprising that inner-city adolescents seek to join a gang whose members are conspicuously successful in making money by selling drugs.

Finally, **cognitive social learning** is a process by which "a person begins to form a mental representation for the situation, the required behavior, and the expected outcome."[36] A rookie police officer who observes veteran officers accepting bribes may quickly learn the prevailing definition of the situation and also surmise the likely consequences of the behavior (for example, if the rookie objects to the bribe-taking, he or she may be ostracized by the other officers).

Of the different methods by which people learn to commit crime, imitation and cognitive social learning probably come closest to what Sutherland had in mind when he emphasized the importance of learning.

Communication Within Intimate Personal Groups

Sutherland argued that the most important social context for learning criminal behavior is the primary group. Sociologists draw a distinction between primary groups and secondary groups. The former is generally characterized by emotionally close, face-to-face contact, while interaction in the latter type of group tends to be emotionally neutral, brief, and short-lived. According to Sutherland, primary groups provide the most significant and influential learning experiences. Hence, individuals are most likely to learn criminal behavior within intimate personal groups such as the family and peer group.

Techniques and Rationalizations

Learning criminal behavior includes learning **techniques and rationalizations.** Technique refers to the step-by-step process by which a crime is committed effectively. For example, how does a burglar open a safe without triggering an alarm system? Or, how does a politician ask a lobbyist to exchange money for a vote without being accused of extortion and corruption? Although some techniques of crime commission may originate with the individual, Sutherland held that most are learned in interaction with others.

In addition to learning techniques, criminal offenders also learn rationalizations, that is, moral justifications. For example, employees may steal from the company they

work for and justify the behavior on the grounds that the company makes huge profits and yet refuses to pay satisfactory employee salaries. Rationalizations are extremely important. In Donald Cressey's classic study of embezzlers, for example, no cases of embezzlement occurred until a rationalization ("just borrowing company funds") was in place.[37]

Unfavorable Definition of the Legal Code

According to Sutherland, rationalizations for criminal acts do not typically originate with individuals. Generally, rationalizations derive from the attitudes held by members of the offender's primary group. Most important, if a person spends a considerable amount of quality time with a certain group of people who express an **unfavorable definition of the legal code,** that alone may provide the person with sufficient rationalization to commit crimes. It is a fairly obvious point. If individuals think that the laws are unfair and illegitimate, then they are not likely to feel morally bound to them. This is basically what is meant by sociologists who use the expression "definition of the situation." If social conditions are defined as real, they become real in their consequences. (Many years ago, consumers began hoarding toilet paper because they took seriously Johnny Carson's comment that the nation's supply of toilet paper was nearly exhausted; the talk-show host was joking.)

Excess of Definitions Favorable to Law Violation

When a person is surrounded by intimates who favor law violation, pressure will build to think and behave accordingly (Box 11.2). Individuals tend to assimilate the surrounding culture, patterning their behavior to fit the social environment. Of course, much behavior is neutral with regard to crime—for example, when *significant others* (family members, close friends, work associates) encourage individuals to play tennis, take a bath, or rake leaves. The point is that significant others may encourage criminal behavior; rather than playing tennis, the individual may be influenced to rob a convenience store. When the surrounding social environment provides an excess of definitions favorable to law violation, it is virtually assured that crime will result. This is the cornerstone of differential association theory. Note that it represents the flip side of the previous point concerning rationalizations. Negative attitudes toward the legal code predispose one, morally, to violate the laws and an excess of positive attitudes toward breaking the laws is the final push toward crime. In this regard, bear in mind that "excess" of definitions refers to social weight in terms of significance and intimacy, not sheer volume.

Differential Association Varies

Differential association may vary in terms of frequency, duration, priority, and intensity. *Frequency* refers to how

BOX 11.2

"Wilding" in Central Park

What follows is an extreme example of differential association and its relationship to criminal conduct. It seems clear that the adolescents involved in these crimes shared a definition of the situation. Set in the proper context, crime can become expected, if not normative, behavior.

On the evening of April 19, 1984, a roving band of teenagers embarked on a 75-minute rampage of Central Park, assaulting at least nine people. The most seriously injured victim was a 28-year-old woman jogger. This victim, an investment banker, was struck with a metal pipe, punched in the face, repeatedly raped, and eventually left for dead. She was found 4 hours later and, despite two serious skull fractures and brain damage, she has survived. One of the attackers explained that the group had simply decided to go "wilding"—to be totally unrestrained even to the point of being violent and savage. Several adolescents, ages 14 to 17, were charged as adults with rape, assault, and attempted murder.

SOURCES: "Going 'Wilding': Terror in Central Park," *Newsweek*, 1 May 1989, 27; George Hackett and Peter McKillop, "Opinions, But No Solutions," *Newsweek*, 15 May 1989, 40.

---

often the criminal contacts are made: daily, weekly, monthly, yearly? All things being equal, the more frequent the contacts, the more influence they will have. The second variable, *duration*, has to do with the length of the contacts once they are initiated. Criminal contacts that last hours at a time, rather than minutes or even seconds, as in a greeting, are likely to be more influential. *Priority* is the third variable. Here the basic idea is that early childhood experiences will probably be most critical. The individual is thought to be most impressionable early in life. Finally, *intensity* refers to how significant certain contacts are for the individual. Usually, contacts with family members and close personal friends are the most intense relationships a person has. It is when these contacts support criminal behavior that the individual is most likely to become an offender.

Summary

For decades, differential association theory has been one of the dominant perspectives within criminology. The two most fundamental claims of the theory are that criminal behavior is learned and that the learning usually occurs among family members, close friends, or work associates. Finally, Sutherland intended for his theory to be a comprehensive explanation of virtually all forms of crime.

Position on Agency (Responsibility)

The theories presented in this chapter highlight a micro social influence on behavior. Social ecology theory stresses the importance of the neighborhood, while dif-

TABLE 11.2	Socially Determined Crime		
THEORY	KEY MICRO SOCIAL FORCE	IMAGE OF INDIVIDUAL	RESULT
Social ecology	Neighborhood	Sponge	Crime
Differential association	Intimate group	Follower	Crime

ferential association theory centers attention on the people with whom a person interacts. In either case, an aspect of the person's micro social environment determines behavior (Table 11.2).

Most sociologists would agree that a person's environment, physical as well as social, exerts some influence on behavior, but Shaw and McKay went too far in their social ecology explanation of crime. At least one critic has stated that the social ecology model rests on an unmitigated determinism.[38] This theory seems to suggest that the process of crime and delinquency causation is similar to contracting an airborne disease. If an individual happens to reside in a "contaminated" area, it is almost certain that the person will get caught up in delinquent and criminal activities. Such behavior is seen, not as a product of rational decision making or free choice, but as the inevitable consequence of ecological forces. Hence, the offender is never depicted as a knowing or purposeful agent, but as a human sponge, who "soaks up" the values and norms of the neighborhood. Social ecology does not resolve the problem of agency—it just does away with the agent.

Sutherland's differential association theory has also been criticized for being overly deterministic.[39] The theory has been challenged because it devalues free will and human purpose.[40] Sociologist David Matza has summarized this criticism as follows:

> **Partly obsessed by the idea of ecology, Sutherland nearly made his subject a captive of the milieu: Like a tree or a fox, the subject was a creature of affiliational circumstance, except that what Sutherland's milieu provided was meaning and definition of the situation. Sutherland's subject was a creature, but he was half a man.[41]**

At one point, even Sutherland recognized that the theory contained no provision for individual action. In his review of the various criticisms of differential association theory, Sutherland conceded that the omission of personal traits was such a grave shortcoming that the entire hypothesis would have to be radically changed.[42] Nevertheless, despite many modifications, the perspective never has been able to provide a compelling theory of individual agency. Instead, the individual is described as a follower, a person who uncritically accepts and mimics the attitudes and actions of relatives and close friends and colleagues. Like social ecology theory, this is an explanation of criminal behavior that suggests crime is caught like a disease—only with differential association theory, crime is acquired through personal contact.

Policy Implications

Social ecology and differential association theories of crime each suggest specific policy implications. Social ecology pinpoints the neighborhood as the source of crime; that is, certain areas are identified as criminogenic. Responding to this conclusion, conservatives and liberals have offered distinctive policy proposals. Conservatives most often argue for an increase in the number of police in neighborhoods having a high crime rate. They also advocate stiffer criminal sentences for offenders. Liberals take an opposite approach. Rather than cracking down on criminal behavior, they tend to favor policies directed to the underlying causes of crime. For example, liberals typically urge that more money be spent on job creation and educational opportunities in high-crime areas.

Because differential association theory is so comprehensive in scope, it is difficult to identify specific policy proposals. Nevertheless, there are three policy suggestions that appear to be consistent with the theory. First, there must be programs in place to help reduce the membership and participation in criminal gangs. If crime is behavior learned in the context of intimate groups such as gangs, then society must do what it can to weaken such groups. Second, if crime is behavior learned from television (not something considered at the time Sutherland developed the theory), then the content of television shows must be more carefully scrutinized, if not censored. And, third, if negative definitions of the legal code are a crucial part of the etiology of crime, then reforms in society must be instituted that will alter such definitions. This requires that measures be taken to advance *social* justice. If individuals do not perceive society as just, then negative definitions of the legal code will persist.

There can be little doubt that micro social phenomena influence the crime rate. The social ecology model and differential association theory make powerful arguments to that effect. Moreover, each of the theories suggests some practical policy measures to reduce crime. Nonetheless, in the present social and political climate, there is a preference for policies geared toward individuals, not social phenomena.

Subsequent Developments

In the past several decades, theorists have refined and extended the two micro social theories presented in this chapter. Two subsequent developments are examined next.

Routine Activities

Shaw and McKay argued that inner-city social areas generate crime. Subsequent researchers have attempted to upgrade this argument in two respects. First, they have sought to identify with more precision the social dynamics that actually promote crime. Second, they have tried to formulate a model that applies to all social areas, not just inner-city areas.

Criminologists Lawrence Cohen and Marcus Felson specified the ecological processes associated with crime and broadened the scope of analysis to include virtually any social area. Cohen and Felson advanced the thesis that crime is an outgrowth of the **routine activities** of social life, especially activities centered around home, work, and recreation. They cite three specific components to crime: motivated offenders, suitable targets, and an absence of guardians.[43] Regarding the first point, these researchers assume that there will always be some members of society motivated to commit crimes. In effect, therefore, **motivated offenders** are taken as a given (critics of the theory see this as a major shortcoming). The second point is that crime is more likely where there is an abundance of **suitable targets.** Houses, apartments, convenience stores, boats, and even a lone pedestrian could all be considered targets. Highly populated areas contain an extraordinary number and variety of targets. The **absence of capable guardians** is a third factor in explaining the occurrence of crime. Settings not protected by police,

The Internet as a Crime Zone

Much has been written about the positive uses of the Internet. Recently, however, attention has focused on potential dangers. Usually the dangers have involved issues of pornography, financial fraud, and invasion of privacy. The Eddie Werner case opens up a new area of concern: murder.

In 1996, 15-year-old Sam Manzie visited an on-line chat room named "boyz." Here he met Stephen Simmons, a 42-year-old convicted pedophile. The two began an affair, meeting in motel rooms. Eventually, Manzie told his therapist about the relationship, and the therapist informed the police. With the assistance of the boy, the police set a trap for Simmons and he was subsequently arrested. Manzie became so distraught over his role in the set-up that his parents requested that he be institutionalized. A judge denied this request and Manzie's psycholog-

ical state deteriorated further. Shortly thereafter, 11-year-old Eddie Werner came calling. Eddie was going door-to-door trying to sell wrapping paper for a school fundraising project. He went to the Manzie home when Sam was home alone. A police investigation concluded that Sam sexually assaulted the younger boy and then strangled him and stuffed his body in a suitcase.

The Internet did not cause Eddie's murder, but it did provide an opportunity for Manzie and Simmons to meet, and that meeting resulted in an illegal sexual relationship. The Internet introduced a "suitable target" to a "motivated offender." It is doubtful that the theorists who developed the routine activities model ever envisioned anything like the Internet, but it fits within the theory. The Internet expands the range of targets and is often characterized as lacking supervision or guardianship.

SOURCE: Steven Levy, "Did the Net Kill Eddie?" *Newsweek*, 13 October 1997, 63.

---

family members, or neighbors make especially inviting target areas (Box 11.3).

Routine activities theory provides an interesting interpretation of rising crime rates over the last several decades.[44] Technology has played a key role by increasing the number of targets and decreasing the number of guardians. Consider just three examples of modern technology: microwave ovens, videocassette recorders, and telephone answering machines. These products not only add to the list of choice items to be stolen, but they enable, even encourage, guardians to leave their homes and apartments unattended.

Social ecology theory focused mostly on crimes committed in inner cities by poor people. Routine activities theory is broader. For example, Felson identifies four types of crime: *exploitative* (robbery, rape); *mutualistic* (gambling, selling or buying illegal drugs); *competitive* (fighting); and *individualistic* (suicide).[45] All of these crimes can be explained by a convergence in space and time of offenders, targets, and guardians. Moreover, the theory applies to corporate crime and other crimes of the powerful as well as traditional street crime. Upper-class criminals, like all criminals, identify targets and take notice of guardians.

In conclusion, routine activities theory is an interesting and insightful extension of the social ecology model. Criminal victimization and perpetration is presented as part of the ordinary rhythm of everyday life in society (Box 11.4). Regrettably, this theory does not explain why

some individuals, and not others, are motivated to commit crimes in the first place.

Differential Identification

Over the years, there have been many alterations to Sutherland's differential association theory. One of the most notable reformulations is Daniel Glaser's differential identification model.[46] Glaser argues that there is a tendency for individuals to adopt role models, identify with those role models, and then behave in ways corresponding to the values and norms of the role models. Occasionally, criminal offenders serve as role models for others. Thus, **differential identification theory** holds that "a person pursues criminal behavior to the extent that he identifies himself with real or imaginary persons from whose perspective his criminal behavior seems acceptable."[47]

Closely tied to Glaser's formulation is the **identity maintenance** research of Walter Reckless and Simon Dinitz.[48] As part of a longitudinal study concerning the relationship between sense of identity and delinquent behavior, Reckless and Dinitz asked teachers to identify sixth-grade boys who were most and least likely to commit delinquent behavior. Follow-up research showed that the boys generally shared the perceptions of the teachers. Moreover, the adolescents who had a "bad boy" self-image were far more likely to get into trouble with the law. This suggests that delinquent behavior is self-perceived by

Hot Weather and Domestic Disputes

It has long been hypothesized that hot weather promotes crime while cold weather discourages it. The underlying assumption of this hypothesis is that weather conditions affect the routine activities that precipitate crime. Criminologist James L. LeBeau addressed one aspect of this issue by examining the number of domestic-dispute police calls to see if time of day or night and the temperature/humidity index were associated with domestic disturbances. LeBeau found that in 1996 the Charlotte, North Carolina, police received 288,814 calls. Of this total, 20,841 (7.2 percent) pertained to domestic abuse. The highest numbers of domestic calls occurred at night (peaking at 10 P.M.), on weekends, and when the temperature and humidity were especially high.

When the weather is excessively uncomfortable, individuals may alter their routine activities. Patterns of sleeping, working, and recreation might change. Even normal interaction may be strained. Indeed, one of LeBeau's conclusions is "As discomfort increases, so do domestic disputes."

Routine activities theory usually explains crime as an outgrowth of patterned social relations. As we have just seen, however, systematic deviation from routine activities can also result in crime.

SOURCE: James L. LeBeau, "The Oscillation of Police Calls to Domestic Disputes with Time and the Temperature/Humidity Index," *Journal of Crime and Justice 27* (1994) 149–61.

those with a negative sense of self as consistent with personal identity.

Glaser's model has drawn praise for two reasons. First, his theory explains how individuals may be influenced by someone outside of an intimate personal group setting, which is something not provided by Sutherland's scheme. Second, differential identification "allows for human choice, . . ."[49] Once a person establishes an image of self, the individual will choose behavior that reinforces the image. Research on identity maintenance provides tentative evidence for this hypothesis.

Critique

Adequacy

The social ecology perspective presents a generally plausible account of crime. Certain neighborhoods may generate more crime than others. To use the terminology of routine activities theory, some areas have more accessible "targets" and fewer "guardians." It is also the case that these same areas may offer fewer opportunities to succeed in legitimate ways. Empirical research has found that this constellation of factors produces high rates of street crime in the inner city. In fact, contemporary researchers have looked more closely (than did Shaw and McKay) at how factors such as political and economic deprivation influence the social ecology of areas.[50] The emphasis on areas should not be taken to the extreme, however. It is certainly not the case that crime exists only in some areas. Many of the costliest forms of crime—costly in terms of financial loss *and* bodily harm—do not originate on inner city streets but in corporate boardrooms, which may be located almost anywhere. Moreover, even in high crime rate neighborhoods, many residents do not engage in crime, while many individuals who live in low crime rate neighborhoods do commit criminal behavior. Location is only one variable in explaining crime.

Differential association also provides a plausible explanation of crime. First, it is clear that most social behavior is learned. Second, it is well established in the social and behavioral sciences that individuals are influenced greatly by the attitudes and behavior of intimates. These are the cornerstone principles upon which differential association theory is built.

Differential association theory is impressive in many respects, but the theory does have shortcomings. First, it does not explain why a person has certain associations. Where do the associations originate and why do they persist? A second unanswered question has to do with why some groups, rather than others, hold unfavorable attitudes toward the law. Perhaps economic disadvantages stimulate such attitudes but, if so, economic factors should be highlighted in the theory. Finally, a third weakness of the theory is that it is nearly untestable.[51] This is because the terms of the theory are inherently vague and do not lend themselves to precise operational definitions.

Comprehensive Nature

In its original form, social ecology was not a comprehensive theory. Shaw and McKay focused nearly all their attention on explaining crime in the inner city. Outlying urban areas drew relatively little attention and rural areas were ignored. They were seeking an explanation of crime

"Everybody deserves a chance" is a particularly common and relevant policy recommendation for inner-city areas.

in the city, which they interpreted as lower-class street crime (essentially, those now identified as index crimes). The criminal offenses committed by members of the middle and upper classes—crimes such as employee theft, fraud, and corporate crimes—were largely outside the purview of their investigation.

It is important to note that the routine activities reformulation of the social ecology model is a much more comprehensive explanation of crime. The emphasis on suitable targets and absence of guardians applies across class, race, and gender. It applies to inner-city crime as well as crime in suburban and rural areas, and it applies to crimes of property as well as violent offenses. What it does not do, however, is explain the basic motivation for committing crime. For example, why does the presence of targets and absence of guardians induce one person to commit crime and yet not have the same effect on another person?

In his 1939 presidential address to the American Sociological Association, Sutherland criticized conventional theories of crime (for example, the social ecology model) for focusing exclusively on lower-class crime.[52] Sutherland felt strongly that a crime theory should explain all forms

of crimes and all types of criminal offenders. It should, first of all, explain crime across class boundaries. Indeed, differential association does this. Street crime can often be linked to participation in urban gangs that typically have a negative attitude toward society, the law, and the police, while defining law violation and violent behavior in positive terms. When a person joins a gang, it is expected that the prevailing attitudes of gang members will eventually entice the person to engage in criminal activity.

At the other extreme, upper-class price-fixing is linked to criminal corporate executives. Rarely are corporate offenses the result of individual action. Almost always, this behavior is a product of collective decisionmaking, with at least several high-ranking executives possessing knowledge of the activities. In short, offenders of any class are influenced by the criminal attitudes and behaviors of the groups to which they belong.

Differential association theory also explains both stealing and violence. The explanations for stealing offenses such as robbery, burglary, and price-fixing all lend themselves to a differential association interpretation. These crimes are frequently group activities and the techniques and rationalizations for such offenses generally

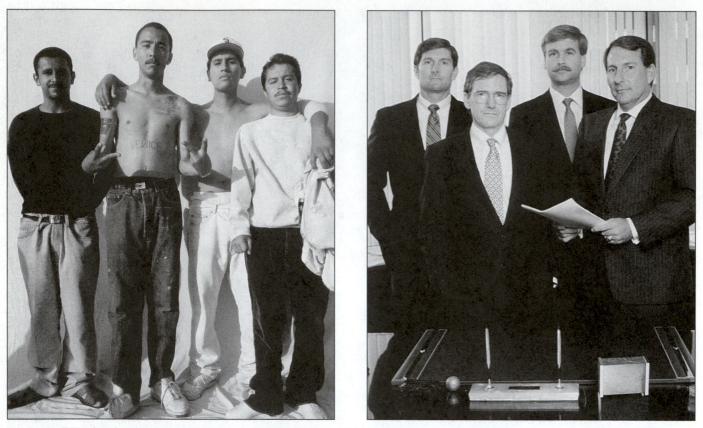
Two "gangs." Despite what popular stereotypes suggest, young gangs are not always criminal, and white-collar gangs are not always law-abiding.

originate in the intimate personal groups described by Sutherland. What about violent offenses and crimes of passion? Here, too, it is arguable that offenders may have learned to commit these offenses. Consider a "typical" homicide case, a killing that results from an emotionally charged argument. Here is a vivid account of an incident that took place between neighbors:

> **A witness said the victim had complained to the suspect about talking too loud in front of his apartment. The victim then drew a gun, pointed it at the suspect's head, and pulled the trigger three times, without the gun going off. The suspect ran toward the project across the street, and the victim fired one shot at him. The suspect then came back with a shotgun, fired through the victim's door, and fled the scene.[53]**

Perhaps it is possible to interpret such examples as related to childhood learning experiences. For instance, when a third-grade boy is shoved to the ground by another third-grade boy, it is likely that the shoved boy will retaliate, because not retaliating might invite ridicule or further attacks. Fighting back is a child's response, which, given certain circumstances, may be reasonable if not totally "proper." The problem is that some adults have retained child-specific responses to aggressive behavior. Hence, it may be possible to interpret some cases of emotional crimes and crimes of violence as learned behavior.

Clearly, one reason differential association theory has been popular for several decades is that it offers a comprehensive explanation of crime. In this regard, the theory is set apart from most other accounts of crime.

Current Appeal

Many sociologists and criminologists view the social ecology theory of crime as current and plausible. This is particularly true with regard to (for example) the routine activities approach, which offers a revision of the original model. The basic idea that neighborhoods produce crime is so popular that it has been tried as a legal defense (recall the beginning of this chapter).

In their book *The Subculture of Violence,* Marvin Wolfgang and Franco Ferracuti argued that individuals living in areas characterized by violence are more likely to acquire "favorable attitudes toward . . . the use of violence."[54] This **subculture of violence** formulation has a close affiliation with social ecology theory and it continues to be a popular approach. For example, a $32 million study of neighborhood violence and crime is now underway in Chicago.[55] Funds for this 8-year study come from both public and private sources. The directors of the project are Albert Reiss, a sociologist at Yale University, and Felton Earls, professor of child psychiatry at Harvard's School of Public Health. According to Earls: "We're not going to get very far lowering the crime rates in the United States until we learn to attend to the properties of neighborhood social organizations."[56]

Differential association also remains a popular theory of crime. This perspective is credited with two fundamental advances in the theoretical analysis of crime: (1) crime is learned behavior; and (2) individuals are greatly influenced by the attitudes and actions of intimates. Included in the second point is the idea that moral rationalizations for behavior are also learned. Considerable research has been undertaken on this issue, the most famous of which is the work by Gresham Sykes and David Matza.[57] Sykes and Matza argue that **techniques of neutralization** (blaming the victim, denial of injury) are used to assuage guilt feelings that accompany wrongdoing. Various techniques such as these help to excuse criminal behavior. Hence, learning these techniques promotes participation in crime.[58]

Differential association is still used to explain crimes committed by street gangs as well as by corporations. The fact that sociologists and criminologists continue to refine and update the theory shows that its essential framework remains useful as an explanatory model.

Summary

This chapter has examined two powerful theories of crime. Each of the theories emphasizes a particular micro social force as the primary explanation of criminal behavior. The social ecology model stresses the importance of the neighborhood as a criminogenic force. Individuals who reside in a neighborhood that is characterized by social disorganization and a tradition for tolerating (or even encouraging) criminal behavior are likely to bend to the ways of the community. In this formulation, the individual offender is viewed as a captive of the social environment.

Differential association theory suggests that the techniques and rationalizations of crime are learned from significant others. For the most part, individuals learn crime from family members, friends, or colleagues. This theory applies to all types of crimes and all types of offenders. The individual offender is seen as following the lead of a criminogenic group.

Critical Thinking Questions

1. Is it possible to explain urban/rural crime differences by using the social ecology model?
2. Can you think of examples of crime that are *not* learned behavior patterns?

3. If Sutherland were alive today, would he be likely to incorporate watching television as a central feature of his theory? Or, would he continue to emphasize the primacy of family, friends, and colleagues?
4. How would a conservative politician evaluate social ecology theory and differential association theory? How would a liberal politician perceive these theories?

Suggested Readings

Robert J. Bursik, Jr. and Harold G. Grasmick, *Neighborhoods and Crime: The Dimensions of Effective Community Control* (New York: Lexington Books, 1993).

Ross Matsueda, "The Current State of Differential Association Theory," *Crime & Delinquency* 34 (1988) 277–306.

Bill McCarty, "The Attitudes and Actions of Others: Tutelage and Sutherland's Theory of Differential Association," *British Journal of Criminology* 36 (1996) 135–47.

Clifford Shaw and Henry McKay, *Juvenile Delinquency and Urban Areas* (Chicago: University of Chicago Press, 1972 [orig. pub. 1942]).

Edwin Sutherland, "Development of the Theory," in *The Sutherland Papers,* ed. Albert Cohen (Bloomington, IN: Indiana University Press, 1942) 13–30.

Notes

[1] Rogers Worthington, "Jury Rejects 'Urban Psychosis' as Defense," *Chicago Tribune,* 5 November 1992, 1–4.

[2] Martin Bulmer, *The Chicago School of Sociology* (Chicago: University of Chicago Press, 1985) xiii; Dennis Smith, *The Chicago School* (New York: St. Martin's Press, 1988) 2.

[3] Paul Westmeyer, *A History of American Higher Education* (Springfield, IL: Thomas, 1985), 93.

[4] Ibid., 1985, 15.

[5] Bulmer, *The Chicago School of Sociology,* 30.

[6] Will Durant, 1974 (1953), *The Story of Philosophy* (New York: Pocket, 1974 [1953]) 512.

[7] Ibid., 34–35.

[8] Randy Martin, Robert Mutchnick, and W. Timothy Austin, *Criminological Thought: Pioneers Past and Present* (New York: Macmillan, 1990) 97.

[9] Ellsworth Faris, "Robert E. Park 1864–1944" (an obituary) *American Sociological Review 9* (1944) 322–25.

[10] Randy Martin et al., *Criminological Thought: Pioneers Past and Present,* 111.

[11] Stephen Turner and Jonathan Turner, *The Impossible Science* (London: Sage, 1990) 22–23.

[12] Ibid., 24.

[13] Roscoe Hinkle, *Developments in American Sociological Theory 1915–1950* (Albany, NY: State University of New York Press, 1994), 14.

[14] Ibid., 14.

[15] Emile Durkheim, *The Rules of Sociological Method* (New York: Free Press, 1966 [1885]) 125.

[16] Durkheim, *The Rules of Sociological Method,* 110.

[17] Durkheim, *The Rules of Sociological Method,* 25.

[18] Quoted in Turner and Turner, *The Impossible Science,* 11.

[19] Robert Park and E. W. Burgess, *The City* (Chicago: University of Chicago Press, 1925).

[20] Clifford Shaw and Henry McKay, *Juvenile Delinquency and Urban Areas* (Chicago: University of Chicago Press, 1972 [1942]) 17.

[21] Ernest Burgess, *The Urban Community* (Chicago: University of Chicago Press, 1926).

[22] Clifford Shaw, *The Natural History of a Delinquent Career* (Chicago: University of Chicago Press, 1931) 15.

[23] Clifford Shaw, Henry McKay, Frederick Zorbaugh, and Leonard Cottrell, *Delinquency Areas: A Study of the Geographic Distribution of School Truants, Juvenile Delinquents and Adult Criminals in Chicago* (Chicago: University of Chicago Press, 1929).

[24] Clifford Shaw, Henry McKay, and James McDonald, *Brothers in Crime* (Chicago: University of Chicago Press, 1938) 355–56.

[25] Shaw and McKay, *Juvenile Delinquency and Urban Areas,* 170.

[26] Shaw, McKay, and McDonald, *Brothers in Crime,* 350.

[27] Shaw and McKay, *Juvenile Delinquency and Urban Areas,* 156–57.

[28] Ronald Akers, *Criminological Theories* (Los Angeles: Roxbury, 1994) 91.

[29] Martin, Mutchnick, and Austin, *Criminological Thought: Pioneers Past and Present,* 155–56.

[30] See Edwin Sutherland, *Criminology,* 3rd ed., and *Criminology,* 4th ed. (Philadelphia: Lippincott, 1939ff); "Development of the Theory," in *The Sutherland Papers,* ed. Albert Cohen (Bloomington, IN: Indiana University Press, 1942), 13–30.

[31] Edwin Sutherland and Donald Cressey, *Criminology,* 9th ed. (Philadelphia: Lippincott, 1974).

[32] B. F. Skinner, *Science and Human Behavior* (New York: Macmillan, 1953).

[33] Barbara Newman and Philip Newman, *Development Through Life: A Psychosocial Approach,* 6th ed. (New York: Brooks/Cole, 1995) 110.

[34] Piers Beirne, "Between Classicism and Positivism: Crime and Punishment in the Writing of Gabriel Tarde," *Criminology* 25 (1987) 785–819.

[35] A. Bandura and R. H. Walters, *Social Learning and Personality Development* (New York: Holt, Rinehart & Winston, 1963).

[36] Newman and Newman, *Development Through Life: A Psychosocial Approach,* 113.

[37] Donald Cressey, *Other People's Money* (Belmont, CA: Wadsworth, 1971).

[38] Christen Jonassen, "A Reevaluation and Critique of the Logic and Some Methods of Shaw and McKay," *American Sociological Review* 14 (1949) 608–617, 614.

[39] Richard Korn and Lloyd McCorkle, *Criminology and Penology* (New York: Holt, Rinehart and Winston, 1959) 298–301; Sheldon Glueck, "Theory and Fact in Criminology: A Criticism of Differential Association," *British Journal of Delinquency* 7 (1956) 92–109.

[40] Robert Caldwell, *Criminology,* 2d ed. (New York: Ronald Press, 1965) 212–13; Ian Taylor, Paul Walton, and Jock Young, *The New Criminology* (London: Routledge and Kegan-Paul, 1974) 129.

[41] David Matza, *Becoming Deviant* (New York: Prentice-Hall, 1969) 107.

[42] Edwin Sutherland, "Development of the Theory," in *The Sutherland Papers,* ed. Albert Cohen (Bloomington, IN: Indiana University Press, 1942) 13–30, 25.

[43] Lawrence Cohen and Marcus Felson, "Social Change and Crime Rate Trends: A Routine Activity Approach," *American Sociological Review* 44 (1979) 588–608.

[44] Ibid., 600–604.

[45] Marcus Felson, "Routine Activities and Crime Prevention in the Developing Metropolis," *Criminology* 25 (1987) 911–31.

[46] Daniel Glaser, "Criminality Theory and Behavioral Images," *American Journal of Sociology* 61 (1956) 433–44.

[47] Ibid., 440.

[48] Walter Reckless and Simon Dinitz, *The Prevention of Juvenile Delinquency: An Experiment* (Columbus: Ohio State University Press, 1972).

[49] Taylor, Walton, and Young, *The New Criminology,* 129.

[50] Robert Bursik Jr. and Harold Grasmick, *Neighborhoods and Crime: The Dimensions of Effective Community Control* (New York: Lexington Books, 1993).

[51] Sheldon Glueck, "Theory and Fact in Criminology: A Criticism of Differential Association."

[52] Edwin Sutherland, "White-Collar Criminality," *American Sociological Review* 5 (1940) 1–12.

[53] Quoted in Robert Bonn, *Criminology* (New York: McGraw-Hill, 1984) 189.

[54] Marvin Wolfgang and Franco Ferracuti, *The Subculture of Violence: Toward an Integrated Theory in Criminology* (Beverly Hills: Sage 1982) 314.

[55] Charles Storch, "Going to the Roots of Violence," *Chicago Tribune,* 24 February 1994, 1-1.

[56] Ibid., 1-6.

[57] Gresham Sykes and David Matza, "Techniques of Neutralization: A Theory of Delinquency," *American Sociological Review* 22 (1957) 664–73.

[58] Ibid., 667.

[59] Cited in Shaw and McKay, *Juvenile Delinquency and Urban Areas,* 69.

chapter 12

Micro Social Causes of Crime: Labeling and Social Control

KEY TERMS

social reaction
tagged
etiology
primary and secondary deviation
self-fulfilling prophecy
looking-glass self
amoral
internal and external controls
social bond
attachment
commitment
involvement
belief
reactor
menace
diversion
deinstitutionalization
reintegrative and disintegrative shaming
low self-control

CHAPTER OUTLINE

BACKGROUND
  Societal Changes
  Need for New Focus
  Sociological Theory
  Self-Report Studies
CORE PROPOSITIONS
  Core Propositions of Labeling Theory
    Etiology Left Unexplored
    No Act Inherently Criminal
    Behavior Becomes Criminal When So Labeled
    A Label Has Consequences
    Summary of Labeling Theory
  Core Propositions of Social Control Theory
    Powerful Inducements to Commit Crimes
    Most Individuals Are Constrained
    Summary of Social Control Theory
POSITION ON AGENCY (RESPONSIBILITY)
POLICY IMPLICATIONS
SUBSEQUENT DEVELOPMENTS
  Shaming
  Family Structure
  Low Self-Control
CRITIQUE
  Adequacy
  Comprehensive Nature
  Current Appeal
SUMMARY

AT AGE 14, NUSHAWN WILLIAMS dropped out of school. Seven years later he was in jail for selling crack. Worse, he admitted to having unprotected sex with as many as 75 young women *after* learning that he was HIV-positive.[1] "We would have been much better off if he'd died," said his mother, Denise Williams.[2] Nushawn's cousin, however, blamed the women: "The parents of them girls shoulda taught them to keep their legs closed, or use condoms."[3] Further, the cousin said of Nushawn, "We stand by him till we die—that's our family."[4]

Could Nushawn's family background help explain his behavior, especially his reckless disregard for the health of his women lovers? Neighbors claim that Nushawn grew up in a dysfunctional family, and they allege that both Nushawn's mother and grandmother used and sold drugs. Moreover, it was reported that his mother Denise prostituted herself and her daughter to obtain money for drugs. These facts, if true, would be of special interest to social control theorists, who emphasize the importance of parenting and family relations. Control theorists believe that poor parenting can be, and often is, a source of crime.

What else could account for Nushawn's actions? Maybe his antisocial behavior was caused by the way people treated him. Nushawn was a learning-disabled student and perhaps he had been labeled negatively, even called stupid. It is possible that Nushawn was identified by teachers and others as a failure and trouble maker. Labeling theory, another theory discussed in this chapter, suggests that negative labels can have dire consequences, including involvement in crime.

This chapter discusses labeling theory and social control theory. As you consider the propositions and insights of these two theories, think of Nushawn Williams and ask yourself if either or both of these theories provide an explanation for his behavior.

Background

As noted in Chapter 11, early American sociologists were seeking to establish sociology as an academic discipline, and many of them thought this could be accomplished by identifying the root causes of social problems. This belief was the impetus for both the social ecology model and differential association theory. By the middle of the twentieth century, however, both the conditions of society and the priorities of sociology had changed.

Societal Changes

Through the first half of the twentieth century, Americans experienced two world wars and an economic depression. The 1950s, however, ushered in a new era. Peace and unprecedented economic success characterized social life for a growing middle class. In fact, conventional wisdom suggested that all American institutions were thriving: not only was the economy on an upswing but also family life was stable, schools were expanding, and organized religion was strong. Despite this overall pattern, as the 1950s turned into the 1960s it became increasingly apparent that the underprivileged in society, particularly African Americans, were not sharing in this social improvement. The underprivileged were victims of unequal and unfair treatment that extended to the area of crime and criminal justice. At this time, sociologists and criminologists began in earnest to study the relationship of class and race to crime and law enforcement. As will be seen, this was especially true for researchers affiliated with labeling theory.

Need For New Focus

Emerging theories typically offer a new focus. Social ecology and differential association stressed social sources of criminal behavior. While these theories provided significant insights, there remained many unanswered questions about crime as a social *process*. Hence, labeling theorists shifted the focus from the offender's behavior to the **social reaction** to behavior. Social control theorists did something similar. They argued that an explanation of criminal behavior must be preceded by an understanding of conforming behavior. If conformity can be understood, then deviance and crime can be explained. Thus, control theorists also shifted the focus away from criminal behavior.

Sociological Theory

At mid-century, structural functionalism was the dominant theoretical perspective in sociology.[5] Structural functionalism highlights the agreement and order in society. In so doing, it describes individuals as extremely socialized. Members of society are depicted as thinking and behaving only in ways that are socially acceptable. Thus, society is the crucial unit of analysis and consideration of individuals is secondary; structural functionalism stipulates that society shapes individuals.

Although structural functionalism became the preeminent theoretical perspective in sociology, interpretive sociology provided a competing vision, one which stressed the importance of the individual. Interpretive sociology, including most prominently symbolic interactionism and ethnomethodology, argues that individuals constitute society. According to symbolic interactionism, individuals provide the meanings necessary to social life and ethnomethodology describes individuals as active negotiators and creators of definitions of social reality.

The insights of symbolic interactionism and ethnomethodology were taken seriously by theorists working in the area of crime and deviance studies, at least some of whom felt that structural functionalism did not adequately account for individual initiative or deviant behavior. Labeling theorists argued that reactions to behavior cannot always be anticipated. Individuals decide for themselves how to respond. Social control theorists argued that the process that guarantees individual conformity is more problematic than structural functionalists allow.

Self-Report Studies

Austin Porterfield investigated hidden delinquency in the 1940s by asking several hundred college students to "self-report" if they had ever committed delinquent acts.[6] All of the students admitted that they had participated in delinquent behavior, but few students reported any encounters with legal authorities. Throughout the 1950s and 1960s, the self-report measure of delinquency and crime became increasingly popular. According to two criminologists, it became the "dominant form of criminological evidence."[7] That claim may or may not be justified, but it is certainly the case that self-report studies offered clear evidence that many, if not most, law violators escaped the attention of law-enforcement authorities.

The main conclusion of self-report studies, namely, that lawbreaking is widespread, provided a point of departure for both labeling and social control theorists. Labeling theorists argued that self-report findings confirmed the fact that only some offenders are formally processed by the legal system. Hence, they believe, it is imperative to understand the process that defines some offenders as criminals, while other offenders escape stigmatization. Control theorists also had a reaction to the self-report evidence. They agreed with labeling theorists that these measures showed law violation to be common. Given this, a detailed explanation of conformity was required. A better understanding of conformity might provide, indirectly, for an improved understanding of crime.

Core Propositions

In this section of the chapter we will consider the core propositions of labeling theory and social control theory. Labeling theory highlights the significance of the social reaction to behavior while social control theory focuses on social constraints—that is, ways in which individuals are kept in check.

Core Propositions of Labeling Theory

Although no single theorist is credited with establishing the labeling perspective, Frank Tannenbaum is generally seen as a significant forerunner. In 1938, Tannenbaum suggested that juveniles who come to the attention of the authorities are **tagged**. For Tannenbaum, the tag had important consequences:

> **The process of making the criminal, therefore, is a process of tagging, defining, identifying, segregating, describing, emphasizing, making conscious and self-conscious; it becomes a way of stimulating, suggesting, emphasizing, and evoking the very traits that are complained of.[8]**

Tannenbaum's insight was expanded in the 1950s and early 1960s by Edwin Lemert, Kai Erikson, John Kitsuse, and Howard S. Becker. Although it may not have been their intention to establish a theory (for instance, Becker argued that the labeling formulation was simply a "way of looking at human activity"[9]), the points of convergence among these four sociologists form the structure of a theoretical perspective. These shared points will now be examined.

Etiology Left Unexplored

The first shared proposition among Lemert, Erikson, Kitsuse, and Becker is that sociologists should not attempt to

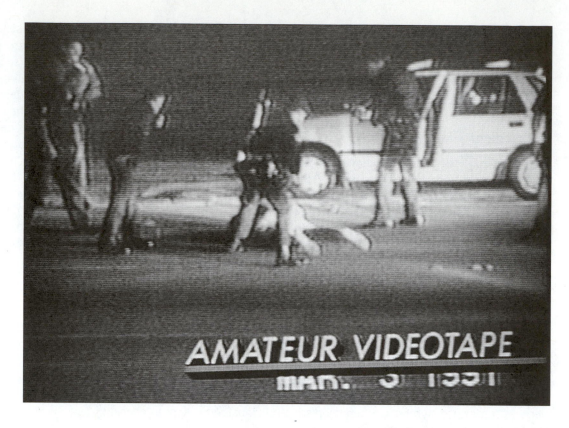

An illegal act is not always processed as a crime. According to labeling theory, much depends on who observes the act.

AMATEUR VIDEOTAPE
MAR. 3, 1991

determine the **etiology** (original cause) of deviance or crime. That question should be bracketed (that is, left unexplored). This is so because "first causes" are many and varied.[10] In short, the argument is that social action is too complex to be understood in its entirety. While it is virtually impossible for sociology to determine why individuals originally deviate (**primary deviation**), it is possible to explain why people continue to deviate (**secondary deviation**).

Lemert argued that secondary deviation "is pragmatically more pertinent for sociology"[11] than primary deviation. Kitsuse was even more adamant: "I propose to shift the focus of theory and research from the forms of deviant behavior to the *processes by which* persons come to be defined as deviant by others."[12] Clearly, labeling is relatively unconcerned about why individuals commit their first crime.

No Act Inherently Criminal

The second point of consensus among the labeling theorists highlighted here is that behavior is not the determining factor in deciding what is or is not deviant, or criminal. In short, the action is not as important as the reaction.

Erikson stated this position explicitly: "Deviance is not a property *inherent* in certain forms of behavior; . . ."[13]

In Lemert's view: ". . . it is a fallacy to designate forms of behavior as criminal if in effect they are not symbolized and treated as such by members of the society in which they occur."[14] Because deviance is not a quality of the act, the reaction to behavior is the crucial component

to understanding crime. An act, any act, becomes criminal only if and when it is defined as such by society.

Behavior Becomes Criminal When So Labeled

The four principle architects of modern labeling theory contended that the determining agents of crime are not offenders but those in society who have the power to define the meaning of social action:

LEMERT: ". . . sociopathic behavior is deviation which is *effectively* disapproved."[15]

KITSUSE: "The data suggest that the critical feature of the deviant-defining process is not the behavior of individuals who are defined as deviant, but rather the interpretations others make of their behaviors, . . ."[16]

ERIKSON: Deviance "is a property *conferred upon* (behavior) forms by the audiences which directly or indirectly witness them."[17]

BECKER: Deviance is "a consequence of the application by others of rules and sanctions to an 'offender' . . . [Hence] *social groups create deviance by making the rules whose infraction constitutes deviance,* and by applying those rules to particular people and labeling them as outsiders."[18]

According to labeling theory, there is no certain relationship between an act and the reaction that follows it.

Labels Can Make a Difference

Members of the Los Angeles Lakers basketball team wear Nike-supplied uniforms. Because star player Shaquille O'Neal has a contract with Reebok, however, he tapes over the Nike swoosh. Companies take their labels seriously. So do many consumers when it comes to buying cars, appliances, electronic equipment, and so on. Sociologists and criminologists also take labels seriously. For example, many years ago sociologist William Chambliss studied two groups of male adolescents and found that school authorities and police officers reacted differently to the two sets of boys based on their being labeled *good* or *bad*. Eight white upper-middle-class high school boys made up one group observed by Chambliss. These boys, referred to by Chambliss as *the saints*, were active in school affairs and earned good grades. They also consistently participated in illegal drinking, petty theft, and vandalism. Despite their delinquent behavior, they never had serious run-ins with the police. This was not the case with *the roughnecks*, the second group of boys. The roughnecks, a group of six white lower-class boys, did poorly in school and were constantly in trouble with teachers and the police. Each group of boys engaged in an equal amount of delinquency, but only the roughnecks, who were labeled *bad boys* by school and community authorities, got into official trouble.

Speaking more generally, labeling theorists have observed that individuals identified with labels that have negative connotations ("poor," "minority group," "drug addict," "homosexual") are discriminated against in American society. One of the areas of disadvantage is said to be the criminal justice system. According to labeling theory, poor people and minority group members are at a disadvantage at every stage of the criminal justice system. Is justice blind? If so, why are our prisons disproportionately filled with the poor and members of minority groups? Labeling theorists would say that the labeling process is part of the answer.

SOURCES: William Chambliss, "The Saints and Roughnecks," *Society 11* (1973) 24–31; Joe Knowles, "Hit & Run," *Chicago Tribune,* 17 October 1997, 4-1.

Whether an act is eventually labeled "criminal" depends on a variety of factors. First, *who commits* the act is important. In general, the labeling theorists argue that members of the middle and upper classes are more likely to "get away" with the same type of behavior that often results in the arrest of lower-class individuals (drunk and disorderly behavior, for example). Second, *who observes* the act can be crucial. It makes a difference whether the person who observes a motorist speeding through a red light is a mail carrier or a police officer. Third, *when* an act occurs is significant. When a teenager walks down a street at 2 A.M., the police may take the adolescent into custody for curfew violation. If the same person walks down the same street at 2 P.M., there is no infraction. A fourth factor refers to the *victim*. For example, if a bank president is beaten up, the police are likely to respond quickly; however, if a homeless person is beaten up, the police may respond with less enthusiasm. In general, labeling theory predicts that the criminal justice system is more likely to respond positively to victims who have economic and political power than to victims who are poor and have no political clout. Fifth, *where* an act takes place is often decisive. Firing a rifle on a shooting range would probably be acceptable behavior, but firing a rifle in a church is likely to be regarded as inappropriate.

Labeling theorists offer even more qualifying conditions, but their point should now be clear: the act is not as important as the reaction.

A Label Has Consequences

When society reacts to behavior by conferring a negative label on an actor ("crazy," "criminal," "deviant"), the label has consequences for the future:

> **LEMERT:** "[Older sociology] tended to rest heavily upon the idea that deviance leads to social control. I have come to believe that the reverse idea, i.e., social control leads to deviance, is equally tenable and the potentially richer premise for studying deviance in modern society."[19]

> **KITSUSE:** "Individuals who are publicly identified as homosexuals are frequently denied the social, economic, and legal rights of 'normal' males."[20]

> **ERIKSON:** Labeling ceremonies have an "almost irreversible effect on moving (the deviant) out of his normal position in society."[21]

> **BECKER:** "One of the most crucial steps in the process of building a stable pattern of deviant behavior is likely to be the experience of being caught and publicly labeled as a deviant."[22] [This] "produces a self-fulfilling prophecy."[23]

These statements underscore that a label has power of its own, frequently becoming a lasting force in an individual's life (Box 12.1). The labeling process is said to affect both the individual who is labeled and those with whom the individual interacts. In terms of the actor's own sense of self, the label may serve as a **self-fulfilling prophecy.** That is, a person is characterized in a certain way and then begins to exhibit the traits that were said to exist. This is consistent with Cooley's well-known concept of the **looking-glass self,** which suggests that an individual will develop a self-identity that corresponds to the perceptions of others.[24] In short, other people serve as "mirrors" for self-reflection.

A label also influences how others will perceive and treat the individual. David Rosenhan's study illustrates this point.[25] Over a 3-year period, eight "normal" individuals voluntarily committed themselves to a variety of mental hospitals. Once admitted into an institution, however, the volunteers had great difficulty convincing the hospital staff that they were completely sane. This led Rosenhan to conclude that:

> **Once a person is designated abnormal, all of his other behaviors and characteristics are colored by that label. Indeed, that label is so powerful that many of the pseudopatients' normal behaviors were overlooked entirely or misinterpreted profoundly.[26]**

This is a key point for the labeling theorists. They make no attempt to explain why a person first commits crime, but they argue that, once a crime is committed, for whatever reason, and the offender is stigmatized negatively, then the force of the label encourages subsequent criminal behavior (secondary deviation). For example, a former robber who is released from prison might find that employers in his home community know of his previous crime and do not trust him. If that is the case, it makes obtaining a job very difficult. Without employment, the person is more likely to commit further criminal offenses, perhaps another robbery.

Summary of Labeling Theory
Lemert, Kitsuse, Erikson, and Becker are the primary authors of modern labeling theory. Their writings suggest four foundational points:

1. In most cases the original cause of crime cannot be known.
2. No behavior is intrinsically criminal.
3. Behavior becomes criminal when it is labeled as such.
4. Once a label is conferred on a person, the label has significant consequences for future behavior.

As shall be noted later in the chapter, the theoretical insights of this perspective have led to important policy changes in the juvenile and criminal justice systems.

Core Propositions of Social Control Theory

Why do most people, most of the time, obey the laws? This is the question social control theorists attempt to answer. They are more interested in explaining conformity than in explaining deviance and crime. This alone makes social control theory unique. All of the theories previously examined focus on the criminal, not the conformist. A compelling account of conforming behavior, however, may also shed light, indirectly, on nonconforming behavior such as crime. Hence, the social control explanation of behavior can be evaluated as a theory of crime.

Social control theories of crime tend to advance two general propositions: (1) there are powerful inducements to commit crimes; and (2) most individuals are constrained from crime commission. Hence, to a certain extent, proposition two negates proposition one. Let us look more closely at these propositions.

Powerful Inducements to Commit Crimes
One of the founding figures of sociology, Emile Durkheim, said long ago that the "only power which can serve to moderate individual egotism is the power of the group; . . ."[27] Twentieth-century social control theorists agree that, if left to their own devices, individuals are likely to violate social norms. F. Ivan Nye, for example, linked wrongful behavior to the tendency of individuals to gratify internal needs and drives.[28] Nye embraced a Freudian view of human nature that pits individual wishes against societal constraints. In Nye's formulation, the id (pleasure orientation) is always a powerful factor in accounting for motives to act.

Walter Reckless, another social control theorist, took a different point of departure. Reckless focused on the interface between the individual and social environment. According to Reckless, there are always social environmental "pushes" and "pulls" toward lawbreaking.[29] Unemployment is an example of a push to crime. A person who commits a mugging following an unsuccessful search for a job may be said to have been pushed to crime. Selling illegal drugs or participating in price-fixing could be explained in terms of pulls to crime. Crimes which are perceived as exceptionally appealing and rewarding qualify as examples in which individuals have been pulled to crime commission.

Travis Hirschi is perhaps the most prominent contemporary social control theorist. The starting point of his theory is the supposition that human beings are **amoral.**[30] It is important to note that an amoral orientation is neither moral nor immoral. Knowing the difference between "right and wrong" and choosing the right course of action is behaving morally; knowing the difference between right and wrong and choosing the wrong course of action is behaving immorally. *Amorality* describes a lack of concern for the right or wrong consequences of behavior. Hirschi argues that this is how humans are oriented to the social world. Individuals are naturally disposed to act in ways that satisfy their interests, without concern for the moral aspects of action.

Amorality is the original state for humans. A hungry baby, for example, will cry out in the middle of the night without regard for sleeping parents who must go to work in the morning. Research indicates, however, that most individuals develop morally—that is, they progress from their original amoral state and become moral creatures.[31] Despite evidence to the contrary, Hirschi stands by his amorality thesis; this is a rather unusual position for a sociologist to take, given that almost all sociological theories assume a moral human nature. Indeed, Hirschi has been charged with making assumptions "that most twentieth-century theorists had long since discarded."[32] Nevertheless, Hirschi, like Reckless and Nye before him, has stipulated individual self-interest as a source of criminal behavior.

The social control theorists specify a wide range of social-environmental pushes and pulls to commit crime. Individuals are described as amoral in their orientation to behavior and driven to satisfy urges. Given these assumptions, shouldn't the crime rate be much higher than it is? It would seem so, but the social control theorists argue that crime does not rage out of control for one reason: because individuals are constrained.

Most Individuals Are Constrained

According to Nye, the id propels behavior, but society "effectively forbids the satisfaction of some goals and prescribes laborious routes involving lengthy postponement to others."[33] Individuals acquiesce to societal dictates only as long as social control is exerted. Social controls may be **internal** (conscience) or **external** (police supervision). If controls weaken, crime is likely to result. Internal (inner) and external (outer) controls keep individuals in check.

Reckless offered a similar account. The behavioral urges resulting from pushes and pulls toward crime, he argued, may be "contained" by inner and outer controls. While controls remain strong, individuals will be dissuaded from committing crimes.

Hirschi's model is more elaborate. Postulating that people are naturally inclined to do as they please without regard for moral considerations, Hirschi seeks to explain why people so often conform.[34] His answer is that most individuals are bonded to society.[35] The bond of the individual to society provides a check on behavior. The **social bond** consists of attachment, commitment, involvement, and belief.[36] **Attachment** to others, such as parents, a spouse, or children, works as an internal control. Some

people may choose not to get involved in a criminal activity because of potential embarrassment to significant others. Moreover, parents may be deterred from crime because, if caught, they would be unable to care for their dependent children. For Hirschi, attachment is the flip side of Sutherland's notion of differential association (friends, relatives, or colleagues that draw a person to crime).

Commitment to rules (norms) serves as another control on behavior. Simply put, a person who is committed to society's norms is not as likely to commit crime. Again, this is the flip side of differential association, which highlights the fact that offenders perceive the legal code in negative terms. Interestingly, commitment to rules might be due to the internalization of society's normative structure or it might be that violation of the norms is perceived as too risky (the police are nearby).

A third component of the social bond is **involvement.** Here the argument is that people who participate fully in legitimate activities have little time left over to commit crime. Moreover, involvement in socially approved activities (a job) can also provide a person with enough money to purchase desired products and services. There is no need to steal (Box 12.2).

Finally, **belief** in the value system of society mitigates against crime commission. Why would individuals commit acts that are opposed to their fundamental beliefs? Indeed, Hirschi argues, people are unlikely to behave in such a fashion. It should be noted that "commitment to rules" is not synonymous with "belief in the value system." It is possible to have commitment without belief. Parents who do not believe in formal education may nevertheless ensure that their children attend school regularly. It is also possible to display "belief" without "commitment." An example is a motorist who believes in highway safety rules as a general proposition but nevertheless drives through red lights in order to save time.

Taken as a whole, the social bond provides an answer to why crime is or is not committed. Those individuals who are not bonded to society are most likely to commit crime, while "bonded" persons are constrained from crime (Box 12.3).

Summary of Social Control Theory

Social control theorists seek to explain why most people conform to the rules of social life. These theorists assume that the motivations for criminal behavior are many and varied. All things being equal, most people, most of the time, are disposed to commit crimes. But, all things are not equal. Generally, individuals are deterred from crime by internal and external restraints. Hence, in most instances, conformity is assured by a system of social controls on behavior.

Should Adolescents Work?

Common sense, as well as social control theory, suggests that part-time work is healthy for adolescents. Parents typically think that a job will build character and a sense of responsibility. Many parents also believe that working children will help with family finances (if only because parents will not have to provide an allowance). Moreover, a job requires time and energy—time and energy that will not be taken up by gang activity or crime involvement. High schoolers who work will have spending money to pay for such things as clothes, stereo equipment, concert tickets, automobile insurance, and so on. Having their own money, teenagers will not resort to stealing. While this thinking is plausible, is it correct?

Social scientific research suggests problems with this interpretation. John Wright and his colleagues used a national sample to study the effects of having a job on delinquency for high school students. Surprisingly, the researchers found that "work intensity" (the number of hours worked) was "positively and significantly" related to delinquency for male adolescents. It appears that the independence obtained from part-time work can lessen commitment to school and family, which in turn can increase the risks for criminal offending. Thus, for some high-school-age children, working outside the home presents more risks than benefits.

SOURCE: John Paul Wright, Francis T. Cullen, and Nicolas Williams, "Working While in School and Delinquent Involvement: Implications for Social Policy," *Crime & Delinquency 43* (1997) 203–221.

Position on Agency (Responsibility)

Both labeling and social control theorists highlight a specific social influence on behavior: the labeling perspective emphasizes the forcefulness of social stigmatization, and social control theory focuses on phenomena such as family ties and police supervision. In each case, some aspect of the person's micro social environment determines behavior (Table 12.1).

Individuals act, but their actions count for little until they are labeled. This is a dictum of labeling theory. The labeling theorists argue that the audience is far more important than the actor.[37] What this means is that behavior has no firmly established social meaning, that actors are incapable of anticipating how others will respond to their actions. According to Lemert, norms are beyond the grasp of most individuals. Norms are: ". . . recognized retrospectively . . . few people, unless they are professional social scientists, are conscious of the standards of behavior in their culture."[38] The average person acts, waits to see how others respond, and then reacts to the response. For example, when a behavior results in a negative response,

the actor is likely to be branded with a pejorative and harmful label ("deviant," "criminal"). In such cases, it is expected that the actor will react to the branding by shaping future behavior so that it conforms to the negative label. In labeling theory, the individual is a **reactor** and when crime occurs, it is simply a reaction by the offender to the label of "criminal."

Many sociologists have objected to this account of individual agency as too weak and an altogether inadequate picture of men and women in society.[39] Quadagno and Antonio, for example, have rejected this view by contending that individuals are not passive, but actively fight the labels that others attempt to place on them.[40] In their study of a group of people labeled mentally ill, the authors found that patients resort to a number of strategies to shake off the label. Numerous studies of crime suggest the same conclusion. The argument that murder, rape, shoplifting, embezzlement, price-fixing, safety code violation, and scores of other criminal acts are committed by individuals acting on the basis of a negative label lacks plausibility and empirical support.

In summary, the labeling explanation of crime provides yet another theory of social determinism. Labeling theory's view of the individual is too weak and its view of social structure (the audience) is too strong. Individuals are more than docile reactors.

Social control theorists describe the individual actor as impulsive, self-interested, and amoral. The individual is portrayed as a *menace,* as someone virtually always inclined to commit crime. It is as if the actor is on a treadmill, continuously in motion, constantly and favorably disposed to engage in criminal behavior. Because of restraints, how-

TABLE 12.1 | Socially Determined Crime/Conformity

THEORY	KEY MICRO SOCIAL FORCE	IMAGE OF INDIVIDUAL	RESULT
Labeling	Branding	Reactor	Crime
Social control	Bonding	Menace	Conformity

BOX 12.3

Religion and Criminal Behavior

Several years ago, one of us asked the chaplain of an Illinois maximum security prison to comment on the effectiveness of rehabilitation. His reply: "The only hope is if an inmate finds Jesus." Social control theorists would never make such a restrictive statement, but they have long held that participation in religion, as a major social institution, works as a crime deterrent. In exploring the link between religion and crime, however, researchers have found mixed results.

In their landmark study, "Hellfire and Delinquency," Travis Hirshi and Rodney Stark surprised even themselves when they found that religiously inclined adolescents are as likely to engage in delinquent behavior as adolescents who do not have strong religious beliefs. Subsequently, Stark and his associates found that personal religiosity tends to be a crime deterrent only if the individual lives in a *community* that is itself characterized by a strong religious orientation. It appears that religion is an influential variable as a social phenomenon, but not necessarily as a psychological phenomenon.

More recently, T. David Evans and his colleagues found that participation in religious activities is a deterrent to a broad range of criminal acts. The Evans study found that religion "matters" for adult crime, even independent of social context—although the authors acknowledge that engaging in religious activities (church attendance, for example) presupposes reinforcing relationships with fellow believers.

Much remains to be done in this area. Researchers need to draw distinctions between subjects (adults and adolescents, men and women), types of crimes (illegal drug use, robbery, price-fixing), and types of religious variables (church attendance, religious beliefs). At this point, however, and in line with social control theory, the general conclusion is that religion does serve as a crime deterrent.

SOURCES: T. David Evans, Francis Cullen, R. Gregory Dunaway, and Velmer Burton, Jr., "Religion and Crime Reexamined: The Impact of Religion, Secular Controls, and Social Ecology on Adult Criminality," *Criminology 33* (1995) 195–234; Travis Hirschi and Rodney Stark, "Hellfire and Delinquency," *Social Problems 17* (1969) 202–213; Rodney Stark, Lori Kent, and Daniel Doyle, "Religion and Delinquency: The Ecology of a 'Lost' Relationship," *Journal of Research in Crime and Delinquency 19* (1982) 4–24.

---

ever, the person rarely moves forward. This notion that the human actor is a menace, a persistent threat to society, is not new. In a religious context, it is the idea that men and women are inherently sinful and must be restrained by divine grace. In sociology, for the control theorists, it means that the actor's criminal tendencies must be restrained by social controls, most importantly the social bond. Bonded people will be deterred from criminal behavior, but those who are not bonded are likely to commit crimes. Thus, like the three micro social theories previously discussed, social control theory is deterministic. Behavior is described as the outcome of a social process, the bonding process. This strong theory of social structural influence emphasizes how individuals are held in check.

Policy Implications

Labeling theory had a profound impact on juvenile and criminal justice policy from the 1950s through the early 1970s. During these years especially, policymakers and practitioners appreciated the argument that negative labels may induce criminal behavior. Diversion and deinstitutionalization are two prominent examples of this influence. **Diversion** is the practice of steering juveniles, and to a lesser extent adults, away from the formal justice systems to minimize the chances of explicit labeling. **Deinstitutionalization** has one of two meanings: shutting down state institutions and placing individuals in community-based corrections, or using institutional settings as a last resort and only for the most serious offenders. The sole example of the former occurred in the early 1970s, when Jerome Miller closed down all the juvenile training schools in the state of Massachusetts.[41] Generally, deinstitutionalization has meant that only repeat or dangerous offenders should be placed in a state institution. At least in theory, both the juvenile and criminal justice systems continue to practice this form.

The get-tough spirit characterizing criminal justice over the past 15 to 20 years has hindered efforts to divert and deinstitutionalize. What is more, recent proposals to "shame" offenders with negative labels indicate that traditional labeling theory has lost influence in applied settings. In fact, the new policy implications are directly opposed to the old insights. Forcing individual offenders to identify themselves in terms of former crimes (mailboxes labeled *convicted child molester*, drunk drivers displaying special auto tags, and corporate offenders compelled to advertise earlier misconduct) is representative of new policy proposals.

Finally, control theory suggests that internal and external controls should be strengthened. Family attachment is an example of an internal control. Control theorists advocate programs that promote family unity and stability. In addition, control theorists argue for increased funding plus support for external controls such as the police and courts. Here the policy implication favors increasing the number of police officers and instituting mandatory and longer prison sentences for criminal offenses. Interestingly, these policy recommendations, while theoretically consistent, are sometimes mutually exclusive in practice. For example, Robert Sampson, a sociologist who has done extensive research on the relationship between family disruption and crime, speaks to this issue with reference to African Americans: "Simply put, by locking up an ever-increasing proportion of blacks, we risk further disruption of black families via imbalanced sex ratios."[42]

Subsequent Developments

Recent research has extended the insights of the two micro social theories presented in this chapter. Three developments are now examined.

Shaming

Australian sociologist John Braithwaite has applied principles of labeling theory to the problem of corporate crime.[43] The key concept in Braithwaite's model is *shaming,* which is defined as social disapproval. Of course, traditional labeling theory suggests that when wrongful behavior is followed by the application of a negative label, the label is likely to produce further wrongful behavior. Hence, a corporation that has been publicly shamed for its criminal activities should be expected to engage in even more criminal behavior. Braithwaite has a different view. He maintains that "societies with low crime rates are those that shame potently and judiciously."[44] The author cites Japan as a country that uses shaming, and notes that Japan is the only industrialized country that has experienced a downward trend in its crime rate since World War II.

Braithwaite distinguishes between reintegrative and disintegrative shaming. **Reintegrative shaming** focuses on bringing the offender back into the community. It includes an overt denunciation of the wrongful behavior accompanied by an acceptance of the offender as a member of the community. **Disintegrative shaming** uses sharp-edged stigmatization to separate the offender from the community. While reintegrative shaming yields positive results, disintegrative shaming, the phenomenon on which labeling theorists have concentrated, usually has detrimental consequences.

Braithwaite's theory of shaming stems in part from his participation in an empirical study undertaken with Brent Fisse. Fisse and Braithwaite conducted an extensive investigation of the consequences of adverse publicity on large organizations.[45] The researchers found that adverse publicity had relatively little direct financial consequence, but there were significant nonfinancial costs to the firms and their employees including a tarnished corporate image, loss of prestige in the community, a decline in employee morale, and an increase in unpleasant experiences (for example, having to respond to hostile questions from the media, and distraction from normal duties). Importantly, Braithwaite and Fisse found that in many cases, as a result of adverse publicity, companies initiated organizational reforms in order to avoid similar situations in the future. This is the positive side of the shaming process.

The application of negative labels for the purpose of shaming has been advocated for a wide variety of offenders ranging from rapists and child molesters to swindlers and corporations. It is likely to be an increasingly popular criminal justice practice.

Family Structure

In the 1960s, Daniel Patrick Moynihan, then an aide to President Lyndon Johnson and now a U.S. Senator, wrote a famous report on black family life.[46] Moynihan concluded that the high black illegitimacy rate and the large number of female heads of households in the black population indicated that black family structure was disintegrating. Family decay was offered as an explanation for why so many blacks were caught up in a "tangle of pathology" (for example, disproportionately high delinquency and crime rates). The report was roundly criticized and Moynihan was even labeled a racist. Decades have passed and now Moynihan's focus on family decay indicators is widely applied by conservatives and liberals to black *and* white families. For example, the final report of the bipartisan National Commission on Children (1991), chaired by Senator John D. Rockefeller, noted increasing patterns of illegitimacy and single-parent families, and concluded: "Observers from many quarters worry that these changes have had largely deleterious effects on family life and have caused a dramatic decline in the quality of life for many American children."[47]

Traditional social control theory suggests that strong family attachment enables children to resist the allure of criminal behavior. But do research findings support this contention? Is family structure associated with crime and, if so, what are the crucial variables? Recent research suggests tentative answers to these questions. To begin with, Nan Marie Astone and Sara McLanahan argue that it is now established that children raised in single-parent families are at a disadvantage when compared with children

Criminal offenders are labeled by the criminal justice system and even sometimes by the general public.

raised in two-parent families: "Researchers have been relatively successful in 'accounting for' the disadvantages associated with living in a single-parent family."[48]

Single parents are faced with financial, emotional, and task overload. Lower family income, decreased parental involvement and supervision, and increased residential mobility are all associated with single-parent families.[49] The results for children in single-parent families include higher rates of school failure, higher rates of involvement in delinquency and crime, and more emotional and behavioral problems in general.[50] While income level itself accounts for some of these problems, the negative consequences of single parenting are present even after controlling for income, race, and education.[51]

Robert Sampson has shown that communities with a high proportion of broken homes are likely to have high crime rates.[52] Sampson states that family structure "is one of the strongest, if not the strongest predictor of variations in urban violence across cities in the United States."[53] This holds for both black and white violence. Regarding black family disruption specifically, Sampson argues that black adult male joblessness results in an increase of female-headed households in black communities, and that this family disruption increases the rates of violent crime, especially for juveniles.[54] A general conclusion of Sampson's study of 171 cities with a population greater than 100,000 states this:

> **Independent of the major candidates supplied by prior criminological theory (e.g., income, region, size, density, age and race composition), black family disruption has the largest effects on black juvenile robbery and homicide.[55]**

For Sampson, the real importance of family disruption is the fact that one-parent families invariably change the social dynamics of a community. There are fewer parents available for supervision of their own and other children and low levels of community involvement (sports, Scouts, schools). The end result is that informal controls are weakened and delinquency and crime become more prevalent.[56]

Family structure research is highly controversial. Most studies examine single-parent families, and because most

of these families are female-headed and a high proportion are black, researchers are wary of charges of sexism, racism, or "blaming the victim."[57] Nonetheless, there is a growing body of research suggesting that family patterns such as those just discussed do promote delinquency and crime. Until large-scale longitudinal data is available, however, the findings should be regarded as tentative rather than conclusive. Furthermore, virtually all of the research has explored the relationship between family structure and violent or conventional crime. While this is an important consideration, it omits entirely a concern for white-collar crimes. For example, it is rarely suggested that children who grow up in one-parent families are more likely to become corporate criminals as adults.

Low Self-Control

Finally, Michael Gottfredson and Travis Hirschi have narrowed the focus of control theory with the publication of their book *A General Theory of Crime.*[58] This book has been described as "contentious, stimulating, and provocative."[59] The main thesis is that crime is caused by a **low self-control.** Self-control accounts for "the differential tendency of people to avoid criminal acts whatever the circumstances in which they find themselves."[60] This is said to be the crucial determinate for all crimes and for all age groups. Clearly, as the title of their book suggests, Gottfredson and Hirschi seek to advance a comprehensive theory of crime.

What accounts for low self-control? According to Gottfredson and Hirschi, it is linked to the failure of children to be properly socialized and is especially the product of ineffective parenting. Parents who are not closely attached to their children and do not provide careful supervision are not likely to punish acts that reveal a lack of self-control. This promotes a lack of self-control in children. Such children (and, subsequently, adults) are likely to be "impulsive, insensitive, physical (as opposed to verbal), risk taking, short-sighted, and nonverbal."[61]

The low self-control theory has stimulated considerable research. Several studies provide empirical support for the theory,[62] while other investigations have found mixed results or data inconsistent with the theory.[63] More research is necessary, especially that which would overcome what some theorists believe is a fundamental conceptual problem—namely, that crime and lack of social control are concepts so closely linked that it is difficult to distinguish one from the other.

Critique

Adequacy

As a general theory of behavior, the labeling model has intuitive plausibility; moreover, there is considerable empirical evidence to support it. But, as a theory of criminal behavior, it is not as compelling. For example, it is obvious that a great deal of crime is not in keeping with what the labeling theorists call "secondary deviation." That is, most criminal behavior cannot be explained as behavior undertaken because of a negative label. For instance, it would be very difficult to explain the crimes of the powerful from this point of view. Moreover, while the labeling theorists are correct in emphasizing the importance of the reaction to behavior, the point is often overstated. It is plausible to say that the social reaction to behavior is often a key factor in labeling an act as criminal; but, to say that no behavior is inherently criminal is sociologically misleading because society is based on shared meanings and expectations. In fact, research shows that there is a consensus among people regarding the perception of wrongful behavior.[64] Perhaps the best way to assess labeling theory on this point is to say that it is plausible as a partial theory of crime in society.

The adequacy of labeling theory has been challenged on two further points. First, labeling theory provides no explanation for why a person first commits crime. This is a rather conspicuous omission and yet in keeping with labeling theory's inattention to either the actor or action itself. Instead, social reaction is focused upon almost exclusively. This is a "backward" view of behavior, as Ronald Akers points out, because "behavior precedes and creates the label more than the label creates the behavior."[65] Second, and perhaps most damning of all, labeling theory's most fundamental claims have not been confirmed by empirical research.[66]

Finally, control theory appears to be highly plausible. The notion that many people would commit crimes except that they are held back by some internal or external constraint resonates with common sense. And, indeed, there is empirical support for the theory.[67] To cite just one example, in their examination of high-school dropouts, Leslie Samuelson and associates found that crime-prone dropouts had weak social controls in comparison with dropouts who did not commit crimes.[68] It appears that the adolescents with weaker social controls have more free time, are more often bored, and are more likely to interact with deviant peers.

Despite the supportive evidence found in some studies, when social control theory is scrutinized more carefully, difficulties appear. First, the assumptions about human nature are very problematic. For example, are humans really amoral? Even more important, how does control theory explain the fact that bonded people commit crimes? Most middle- and upper-class criminals fit the social control definition of "bonded," and yet they violated the law. Furthermore, the empirical research that supports the theory tends to be based on too narrow a definition of crime (that is, on street crime).

It may be that contemporary versions of control theory, in particular the Gottfredson-Hirschi model, will prove

more fruitful. At this point, however, a definitive judgment about the overall adequacy of social control theory should be postponed until further theoretical and empirical work is completed.

Comprehensive Nature

Labeling theory does not provide a comprehensive explanation of crime. In fact, there are many gaps in it. In the first place, this formulation purposely excludes from consideration the initial act of crime. Labeling theory deals only with behavior that occurs after a person is branded with a negative label. Second, like social ecology, the labeling approach focuses particularly on members of the lower class. Little attention is directed to middle- and upper-class crime, for the obvious reason that these offenders are seldom stigmatized negatively. This reflects a fundamental proposition of the perspective that states that the powerful in society confer labels on the powerless—not the other way around. This presents a difficulty, however, in that the theory is ill-equipped to explain any of the wide range of criminal activities committed by the powerful. Once again it may be said that the labeling perspective is useful as a partial explanation. Unfortunately, it does not qualify as a comprehensive theory.

Social control theorists seek to provide a comprehensive explanation of crime. This theory is not restricted to a particular type of crime or a particular type of offender. There are theoretical and empirical problems with this effort, however. First, at the most general level, any crime can be explained in terms of an uncontrolled offender. Rapists, muggers, embezzlers, tax evaders, shoplifters, drunk drivers, and swindlers all fit this characterization in one way or another. But at this point, the theory becomes tautological (circular reasoning), that is, x (lack of control) leads to y (crime) where y is defined in terms of x. An example of a tautology would be to define singers in terms of their ability to carry a tune and then measure the relationship between singing and carrying a tune. Theoretically, the control model makes intuitive sense because there seems to be a close correspondence between criminal behavior and an offender who has not been controlled, but on closer inspection it appears that one variable is used to define the other.

The empirical problem with this formulation is that many people who are bonded to society, and therefore presumably controlled, still commit crimes. Of course, the control theorist can always say that it just *appeared* as if the individual was bonded when that was not really the case after all. That kind of after-the-fact analysis is not compelling. In sum, control theory offers an explanation of crime that is comprehensive but not altogether satisfactory.

Three C's: China, Crime, Control

Can you imagine living your whole life in the same town? For decades, that was exactly the situation in China. Beginning with the Communist takeover in 1949, the people of China were generally not allowed to change their residence. In particular, it was exceedingly difficult for rural residents to obtain jobs in a city, nor were they eligible for government subsidies for housing, food, and fuel that city residents were entitled to. While this system surely suppressed individual freedom, it did create stable communities that were characterized by low crime rates.

China's rigid patterns of social control changed dramatically with the economic reforms of the early 1980s. At that time, China began to permit the establishment of capitalistic enterprises. These market-driven businesses required a more mobile work force. This led, invariably, to a huge rural to urban migration—an estimated 80 million peasants moved to various urban areas.

What effect did this migration have on city crime rates? Researchers Yingyi Situ and Weizheng Liu investigated this question, and according to official crime data the *transient* population accounts for the large majority of urban crime. Situ and Liu argue that the relaxation of longstanding social controls is responsible for the increase in urban crime. Coming to the same conclusion, the Chinese government has re-imposed a set of strict formal controls. City migrants must now obtain a residency permit from the city police, a work permit from the municipal bureau of labor, and a rent permit from the city housing office. Before migrating, transients must secure an approval document from their home town government. Among other things, this document guarantees that the transient has no criminal record.

Once again, as in decades past, formal social controls have been instituted as a deterrent to crime. If social control theory is correct, these formal actions will lower the crime rate. In the next few years, researchers will test this prediction.

SOURCE: Yingyi Situ and Weizheng Liu, "Transient Population, Crime, and Solution: The Chinese Experience," *International Journal of Offender Therapy and Comparative Criminology* 40 (1996) 293–99.

Current Appeal

After at least three decades of prominence, labeling theory has lost some of its appeal. Although many of the insights of this perspective have been embraced as conventional wisdom in the behavioral sciences, as a theory of crime its influence has declined. One important reason for this is that the labeling explanation for *crime* has not been supported by convincing empirical evidence.[69] In fact, many research findings contradict some of the core features of the theory. Despite its decline in scientific circles, labeling theory has been embraced by the general public. Labeling is accepted as a counterpart concept to victimization. Images of victimization are strong in contemporary society, and are frequently identified with stigmatization. Virtually everyone in society is saddled with some kind of negative label and this, it is said, results in victimization. The processes highlighted so effectively and persuasively by labeling theorists decades ago are now used to explain a plethora of real and imagined experiences.

Finally, social control theory has considerable current appeal (Box 12.4). The idea that individuals, or at least some individuals, need to be controlled is almost taken as a given in current social and political thought. Accordingly, criminal justice policies at both the state and federal level reflect this orientation. Moreover, current research often examines either the effects of various forms of policing as an external control on behavior or the effects of family structure as an internal control on behavior. This type of research will continue as long as legislators and other policymakers favor the social control model.

Summary

This chapter has examined two prominent theories of crime. Each of the theories emphasizes a particular micro social force as the primary explanation of criminal behavior. Labeling theorists advance the notion that the social reaction to behavior is more significant than the behavior. They argue that behavior carries with it so many contingent elements (when and where it takes place, who commits the act, who observes the act) that it alone can never be the standard that defines crime. In general, labeling theory suggests that members of the lower class are most likely to be labeled and that this stigmatization may result in future criminal behavior. The individual offender is seen as a victim of a negative label.

Finally, social control theorists offer an explanation for conforming behavior. If conformity is explained, then the theory can be turned around to explain nonconforming (criminal) behavior. Control theory stipulates that individuals are predisposed to commit crimes and therefore must be restrained. Generally, a variety of internal and external controls combine to assure conformity. Crime occurs when the controls are absent or too weak. The individual offender is a menace who, by definition, has not been held in check by conventional controls.

Critical Thinking Questions

1. Would you prefer to live in a society with strict social controls? Why or why not?
2. Do you think strong social controls reduce crime? Would caning (whipping) reduce juvenile crime? Michael Fay, caned in Singapore for his wrongdoing, is pictured at this chapter's opener.
3. Doesn't everyone carry some positive and negative labels? How much crime, if any, is the product of people having a negative label?
4. Evaluate the strengths and weaknesses of labeling theory and social control theory. Which is the best theory?

Suggested Readings

Howard Becker, *Outsiders: Studies in the Sociology of Deviance,* 2nd ed. (New York: Free Press, 1973).

David Camp and Chan Hellman, "Chaos and the Withering Family: Explaining American Criminality," *Humanity & Society 21* (1997) 190–98.

John Gibbs and Dennis Giever, "Self-Control and Its Manifestations Among University Students: An Empirical Test of Gottfredson and Hirschi's General Theory," *Justice Quarterly 12* (1995) 231–55.

Michael Gottfredson and Travis Hirschi, *A General Theory of Crime* (Palo Alto: Stanford University Press, 1990).

John Paul Wright, Francis T. Cullen, and Nicolas Williams, "Working While in School and Delinquent Involvement: Implications for Social Policy," *Crime & Delinquency 43* (1997) 203–221.

Notes

[1] Joseph Perkins, "HIV—As a Lethal Weapon," *San Diego Union-Tribune,* 7 November 1997, B-5.
[2] Quoted in T. Trent Gegax, "The Aids Predator," *Newsweek,* 10 November 1997, 53–59.
[3] Ibid.
[4] Ibid.
[5] George Ritzer, *Contemporary Sociological Theory,* 3rd ed. (New York: McGraw-Hill, 1992) 93.
[6] Austin Porterfield, "Delinquency and Its Outcome in Court and College," *American Journal of Sociology 49* (1943) 199–208.
[7] Franklin Williams III and Marilyn McShane, *Criminological Theory,* 2nd ed. (Englewood Cliffs, NJ: Prentice-Hall, 1994) 183.
[8] Frank Tannenbaum, *Crime and the Community* (New York: Columbia University Press, 1938) 19–20.
[9] Howard S. Becker, *Outsiders: Studies in the Sociology of Deviance,* 2nd ed. (New York: Free Press, 1973) 181.
[10] Edwin Lemert, *Social Pathology: A Systematic Approach to the Theory of Sociopathic Behavior* (New York: McGraw-Hill, 1951) 17, and *Human Deviance, Social Problems and Social Control* (New York: Prentice-Hall, 1967) 75.
[11] Lemert, *Human Deviance, Social Problems and Social Control,* 18.
[12] John Kitsuse, "Societal Reaction to Deviant Behavior: Problems of Theory and Method," *Social Problems 9* (1962) 247–56, 248.
[13] Erikson, "Notes on the Sociology of Deviance," 309.
[14] Lemert, *Social Pathology: A Systematic Approach to the Theory of Sociopathic Behavior,* 284.
[15] Lemert, *Social Pathology: A Systematic Approach to the Theory of Sociopathic Behavior,* 23.
[16] Kitsuse, "Societal Reaction to Deviant Behavior: Problems of Theory and Method," 255.
[17] Erikson, "Notes on the Sociology of Deviance," 308.
[18] Becker, *Outsiders: Studies in the Sociology of Deviance,* 9.
[19] Lemert, *Human Deviance, Social Problems and Social Control,* v.
[20] Kitsuse, "Societal Reaction to Deviant Behavior: Problems of Theory and Method," 249.
[21] Erikson, "Notes on the Sociology of Deviance," 311.
[22] Becker, *Outsiders: Studies in the Sociology of Deviance,* 31.
[23] Ibid., 34.
[24] Charles Horton Cooley, *Human Nature and the Social Order* (New York: Scribner, 1922).
[25] David Rosenhan, "On Being Sane in Insane Places," *Science 179* (1973) 250–58.
[26] Ibid, 254.
[27] Emile Durkheim, *The Elementary Forms of the Religious Life* (New York: Free Press, 1965) 405.
[28] F. Ivan Nye, *Family Relationships and Delinquent Behavior* (New York: Wiley, 1958).
[29] Walter Reckless, *The Crime Problem,* 5th ed. (New York: Appleton-Century-Crofts, 1973); "A New Theory of Delinquency and Crime," *Federal Probation 25* (1961) 42–46.
[30] Travis Hirschi, *Causes of Delinquency* (Berkeley, CA: University of California Press, 1969) 10–13.
[31] Lawrence Kohlberg, *The Development of Sociomoral Knowledge* (New York: Praeger, 1980).
[32] LaMar Empey, *American Delinquency* (Boston: Dorsey, 1982) 266.
[33] Nye, *Family Relationships and Delinquent Behavior,* 4.
[34] Hirschi, *Causes of Delinquency,* 10.
[35] Ibid., 16.
[36] Ibid., 16–27.
[37] Erikson, "Notes on the Sociology of Deviance," 308; John Hepburn, "The Role of the Audience in Deviant Behavior and Deviant Identity," *Sociology and Social Research 59* (1975) 387–405.
[38] Lemert, *Social Pathology: A Systematic Approach to the Theory of Sociopathic Behavior,* 31.
[39] Joseph Scimecca, "Labelling Theory and Personal Construct Theory: Toward the Measurement of Individual Variation," *Journal of Criminal Law and Criminology 68* (1977) 652–59; Jill Quadagno and Robert Antonio, "Labelling Theory as a Oversocialized Conception of Man: The Case of Mental Illness," *Sociology and Social Research 60* (1975) 33–45; Joseph Rogers and M.D. Buffalo, "Fighting Back: Nine Modes of Adaptation to a Deviant Label," *Social Problems 22* (1974) 101–113; Paul Schervish, "The Labelling Perspective: Its Bias and Potential in the Study of Political Deviance," *The American Sociologist 6* (1973) 47–57.
[40] Quadagno and Antonio, "Labelling Theory as a Oversocialized Conception of Man: The Case of Mental Illness."
[41] Clemens Bartollas, *Juvenile Delinquency,* 2nd ed. (New York: Macmillan, 1990) 425.
[42] Robert Sampson, "Unemployment and Imbalanced Sex Ratios: Race-Specific Consequences for Family Structure and Crime," in *The Decline in Marriage Among African-Americans,* ed. M. Belinda Tucker and C. Mitchell-Kermanpp (New York: Russell Sage, 1995) 229–54, 251.
[43] John Braithwaite, *Crime, Shame, and Integration* (Cambridge: Cambridge University Press, 1989).
[44] Ibid., 1.
[45] Brent Fisse and John Braithwaite, *The Impact of Publicity on Corporate Offenders* (Albany: State University of New York Press 1985).
[46] Daniel P. Moynihan, *The Negro Family: A Case for National Action* (Washington DC: U.S. Government Printing Office, 1965).
[47] Quoted in David Popenoe, "American Family Decline, 1960–1990: A Review and Appraisal," *Journal of Marriage and the Family 55* (1993) 527–55, 539.

48 Nan Marie Astone and Sara McLanahan, "Family Structure, Residential Mobility, and School Dropout: A Research Note," *Demography 31* (1994) 575–84, 576.

49 Ibid.

50 James Q. Wilson, "The Family-Values Debate," *Commentary,* April 24–31, 1993, 27.

51 Ibid., 27; Sara McLanahan, "The Reproduction of Poverty," *American Journal of Sociology 90* (1985) 873–901; Elizabeth Thomson, Thomas Hanson, and Sara McLanahan, "Family Structure and Child Well-Being: Economic Resources vs. Parental Behaviors," *Social Forces 73* (1994) 221–42.

52 Robert Sampson, "Crime in Cities: The Effects of Formal and Informal Social Control," in *Communities and Crime,* ed. Albert Reiss, Jr. and Michael Tonry (Chicago: University of Chicago Press, 1986) 271–311.

53 Ibid., 249.

54 Robert Sampson, "Urban Black Violence: The Effect of Male Joblessness and Family Disruption," *American Journal of Sociology 93* (1987) 348–82.

55 Ibid., 376.

56 Robert Sampson and W. Byron Groves, "Community Structure and Crime: Testing Social-Disorganization Theory," *American Journal of Sociology 94* (1989) 774–802.

57 Sampson, "Unemployment and Imbalanced Sex Ratios: Race-Specific Consequences for Family Structure and Crime," 229.

58 Michael Gottfredson and Travis Hirschi, *A General Theory of Crime* (Palo Alto, CA: Stanford University Press, 1990).

59 Gresham Sykes and Francis T. Cullen, *Criminology,* 2nd ed. (New York: Harcourt Brace Jovanovich, 1992) 309.

60 Gottfredson and Hirschi, *A General Theory of Crime,* 87.

61 Ibid., 90.

62 Harold Grasmick, Charles Tittle, and Robert Bursik, Jr., "Testing the Core Empirical Implications of Gottfredson and Hirshi's General Theory of Crime," *Journal of Research in Crime and Delinquency 30* (1993) 5–29; John Gibbs and Dennis Giever, "Self-Control and its Manifestations Among University Students: An Empirical Test of Gottfredson and Hirschi's General Theory," *Justice Quarterly 12* (1995) 231–55.

63 Bruce Arneklev, Harold Grasmick, and Charles Tittle, "Low Self-Control and Imprudent Behavior," *Journal of Quantitative Criminology 9* (1993) 225–47; Raymond Paternoster and Robert Brame, "Multiple Routes to Delinquency? A Test of Developmental and General Theories of Crime," *Criminology 35* (1997) 49–84.

64 Michael O'Connell and Anthony Whelan, "Taking Wrongs Seriously: Public Perception of Crime Seriousness," *British Journal of Criminology 36* (1996) 299–318.

65 Ronald Akers, *Criminological Theories,* 2nd ed. (Los Angeles: Roxbury, 1997), 111–38.

66 Ibid., 106.

67 Ibid., 92–95.

68 Leslie Samuelson, Timothy Hartnagel, and Jarvey Krahn, "Crime and Social Control Among High School Dropouts," *Journal of Crime and Justice 28* (1995) 129–65.

69 Ronald Akers, *Criminological Theories,* 110.

POLICE DEPARTMENT
954280
2993 0652

chapter *13*

Macro Social Causes of Crime: Strain, Marxist, and Feminist Theories

KEY TERMS

anomie
success goals
conformity
innovation
ritualism
rebellion
retreatism
egoistic personality
crimes of control
crimes of economic domination
crimes of government
predatory crimes
personal crimes
crimes of resistance
instrumentalist theory
structuralist theory
ideology
false consciousness
patriarchal culture
liberal feminist criminology
Marxist feminist criminology
radical feminist criminology
socialist feminist criminology
double failures
negative social relations
negative and positive peace
postmodernism

CHAPTER OUTLINE

BACKGROUND
  Civil Rights Movement
  Anti-War Movement
  The "New" Sociology
CORE PROPOSITIONS
  Merton's Strain Theory
    Cultural Goals and Social Structural Means
    Modes of Adaptation
    Crime Produced by Macro Social Forces
    Summary of Merton's Strain Theory
  Marxist Theory of Crime
    Capitalism Produces Crime
    Capitalist State Defines Crime, Controls Justice
    Ideology and False Consciousness Justify Existing Practices
    The Powerful Commit the Most Serious Crimes
    Social Justice Must Precede Criminal Justice
    Summary of Marxist Theory of Crime
  Feminist Theory of Crime
    Society Shaped by Patriarchal Relations
    Women Must Be Included
    Gender-Sensitive Explanations Required
    Unfair Treatment of Women in Justice System
    Summary of Feminist Theory of Crime
POSITION ON AGENCY (RESPONSIBILITY)
POLICY IMPLICATIONS
SUBSEQUENT DEVELOPMENTS
  Extensions of Strain Theory
  Left Realism
  Peacemaking Criminology
  Postmodern Criminology
CRITIQUE
  Adequacy
  Comprehensive Nature
  Current Appeal
SUMMARY

IN 1997, AMERICANS WERE OUTRAGED, shocked—and amused—at Marv Albert's bizarre sex case. Testimony in a Virginia courtroom described the sportscaster as a man who liked to wear women's underwear and preferred to have sex with a woman and a man at the same time.[1] More serious, Albert was formally charged with forced sodomy and assault and battery (for biting a woman's back). Ultimately, Albert pleaded guilty to the latter charge and the sodomy charge was dropped.

Followers of this story may have concluded that Albert's actions were a product of a psychological disorder. Why else would a man enjoy biting a woman's back? But two macro-level sociological theories of crime could apply. For example, the Marxist theory of crime suggests that under capitalism, individuals lose their sensitivities—that is, people start to treat others as objects to exploit. Perhaps this is what Albert was doing. A second school of thought, feminist criminology, might also be relevant. According to this perspective, most crime, especially crimes men commit against women, are produced by patriarchal social relations. Hence, Albert's biting of women could be a manifestation of male supremacy.

This chapter features three macro-level theories of crime. The Marv Albert case illustrates how difficult it can be for a macro theory to explain a seemingly individualistic act. As you read the chapter, consider how well the theories explain broad patterns of criminal behavior, as well as the specific actions of individuals.

Background

Sociologist Amitai Etzioni argues that American society in the 1950s was ordered on the basis of a fixed ethical structure with clear values and norms.[2] This ethical code was dismantled in the 1960s because it was overtly authoritarian and discriminatory. The driving force behind the social revolution of the 1960s was the belief that the main problems of social life, and their solutions, lay at the *macro* level. Evidence for this can be seen in the civil rights movement, the anti-war movement, and the shifting focus of the sociological imagination.

Civil Rights Movement

In 1962, the University of Mississippi was forced to admit James Meredith, the first black student in the history of the school. The next year, Martin Luther King, Jr., led a famous march on Washington, D.C., in which he argued that blacks live on an "island of poverty" in a country with vast wealth. Subsequent passage of the 1964 Civil Rights Act prohibited discrimination in public accommodations and facilities on the basis of race, color, creed, national origin, and gender. Even with this legislation, however, progress was slow. As King said, "privileged groups seldom give up their privileges voluntarily."[3] Because of

continued discrimination, there were numerous race riots in the 1960s, including over 300 between 1965 and 1968.[4]

Throughout the 1960s, it became increasingly obvious that racism was not fundamentally a *micro,* or local, phenomenon. It was a societal problem, and as such, it demanded a society-wide solution. This same analysis applied with respect to sexism. By the 1960s, there was a growing recognition that many rights, privileges, and opportunities available to men were denied to women. Women were held back not just by individuals but by the patriarchal structure of society. In 1963 Betty Friedan, known by many as the founder of the women's liberation movement, published *The Feminine Mystique,* which offered a critical analysis of the confining role of "housewife."[5] Perhaps most important was the issue of widespread economic discrimination against women. Hence, the feminist movement of the 1960s campaigned most vigorously for equal opportunities in jobs and education.[6]

Finally, in 1969, at a tavern called the Stonewall Inn in Greenwich Village, a group of men protested recent police arrests of homosexuals. These men came out of the "closet" and insisted on their civil rights. This marked the emergence of the gay rights movement.[7] Not only was American society identified as racist and sexist but it was now also viewed as homophobic. For decades, sociologists and criminologists had sought the cause of social problems in the micro environment. Civil rights concerns required a broader perspective.

Anti-War Movement

Most historians note that American involvement in the civil war between North and South Vietnam began in the early 1960s, when the United States dispatched a few

Social protests were common in the 1960s. Protests challenged existing conditions in society; similarly, at about the same time, many sociologists and criminologists began to challenge mainline criminological theory.

thousand troops to Southeast Asia as "advisors." This quiet beginning escalated rapidly and fiercely. By 1968, there were more than 500,000 American troops in Vietnam. Continued escalation of the war resulted in a strong anti-war movement. This movement reached a high point at the 1968 Democratic National Convention in Chicago, where anti-war protesters clashed with local police. Further protests erupted in the months and years ahead. In 1970, Ohio National Guardsmen killed four Kent State students during one such protest. Americans were sharply divided over U.S. involvement in the Vietnam war, but one thing was certain: this was no micro concern. As students of society, sociologists saw once again that the key social dynamics in the 1960s were at the macro level.

The "New" Sociology

As was noted in Chapter 12, academic sociology in the 1950s was dominated by the functionalist perspective, which viewed social life as essentially harmonious. In 1959, sociologist C. Wright Mills published *The Sociological Imagination.*[8] This book was highly critical of the prevailing theories and methods of sociology. Indeed, Mills' career was based on seeing the "other" side of society, the side that the functionalists chose not to stress. Where

functionalists saw consensus, Mills saw conflict. When functionalists highlighted equality, Mills emphasized inequality. Following Mills' death in 1962, Irving Louis Horowitz published *The New Sociology,* a volume of essays in honor of Mills.[9] This "new" sociology, as Horowitz labeled it, was based on a *critical* and *macro* level analysis. Consider how Horowitz framed the task:

> **Sociology has an obligation, first and foremost, to reflect upon the problems dealt with at the level they occur, and to provide the information and theory for social solutions to human problems. . . . The master problems for a modern sociology—the multiplication of social forms of capitalism and socialism, the social costs and benefits of economic development, the new nationalism and the rise of polycentric doctrines of socialism, the relation of racial competition to democratic norms, the connection between industrial life and anomic responses, the problems of world population and human health, and, above all, the question of world conflict and conflict resolution—these are large-scale problems. . . . The new turn in sociology is thus an examination of large-scale problems.[10]**

Not all sociologists embraced this call for a new sociology. Many refused to adopt a critical stance and many continued to investigate micro social issues. Nonetheless, the new sociology attracted powerful adherents, and academic sociology was significantly reshaped. This was especially true for studies of crime.

Core Propositions

Merton's Strain Theory

Emile Durkheim introduced the term *anomie,* by which he meant a social condition in which norms (rules of conduct) are absent or unclear. Anomie inevitably produces strain as individuals try to identify appropriate norms. On an individual level, anomie is often experienced on a first date, or a first job interview. Behavioral expectations are not entirely clear and this produces anxiety. Durkheim, however, was most concerned about the structural dimensions of anomie, the fact that anomie can be a fundamental feature of an entire society. In 1893, he published *The Division of Labor in Society,* in which he argued that social relations in simple, traditional societies are ordered on the basis of interpersonal pressure to conform.[11] In simple societies, most people think and behave similarly and everyone is able to recognize and understand the prevailing norms. But Durkheim argued that industrialization and urbanization transformed society so thoroughly that traditional norms were destroyed. Without clear norms, he asserted, behavior is deregulated.

In a famous article published in 1938, American sociologist Robert Merton extended Durkheim's notion of anomie.[12] In this article titled "Social Structure and Anomie," Merton attempted to lay the foundation for a macro-level explanation of deviant behavior. Merton agreed with Durkheim that anomie was produced by social structure at the most general level, but he altered the meaning of anomie. Rather than viewing anomie as a condition of normlessness, Merton defined **anomie** as a discrepant relationship between culturally induced goals and social structural means. Merton specifically argued that culture and social structure are rarely in complete harmony. It is the dissociation between cultural goals and socially available means to pursue the goals that is the actual cause of deviance. Hence, anomie (strain) is the product of the basic organization of society itself. Many individuals who commit deviant or criminal behavior are simply responding to this strain. Let us now examine in detail the core propositions of Merton's formulation.

Cultural Goals and Social Structural Means

In any society there is a cluster of commonly shared cultural goals. Every society has **success goals,** which are identified explicitly and implicitly. In American society, success goals are typically defined in terms of social power and material wealth. Economic success is perhaps the most universal goal in American culture. It is not that everyone sets out to become a millionaire, but virtually all members of American society wish to have some measure of financial success. The value of having money cuts across class, race, gender, and age categories. This is part of the "American Dream."

A society not only has common goals but also socially approved means for obtaining the goals. In the United States, the conventional pathway to economic success is defined in terms of hard work and perseverance, particularly in the areas of education and occupation. This is the ideal pattern but, as Merton notes, many are unable to follow it. Indeed, millions of Americans seek economic success but fail to achieve it because of macro-level barriers to success. Those who lack the opportunity or ability to gain educational credentials fail to find employment or are forced to take jobs with low wages. The American Dream is not attainable for everyone.

Modes of Adaptation

All members of society must *adapt* to their own configuration of goals and means. Unfortunately, in American society there is a pronounced discrepancy between success goals and approved means. This produces strain in two ways. First, in the United States there is a strong cultural emphasis on "hitting it big." Those individuals who become wealthy, famous, and powerful tend to be most idealized. Included here are professional athletes, rock stars, movie actors, people in high political office, CEOs (chief executive officers) of large corporations, doctors, and lawyers. Only a small percentage of the population achieves this level of success, which means that most members of society must cope with feelings of being left out or left behind. This creates strain.

Second, and more significant, is the strain that accompanies the failure to obtain even a modest level of success in society. Merton's emphasis here is on the lower class. Not everyone can become president of the United States, a famous athlete, or a movie star, but it is expected that everyone should attain middle-class standards of economic success. In American culture, the goal of economic success is seen as legitimate, and inability to achieve the goal produces personal frustration. What is more, personal frustration is exacerbated by an egalitarian ideology that assumes all Americans can and should be economically successful. The ideology suggests that commitment and hard work will surely result in success. Thus, failure is often interpreted as a product of insufficient effort. As frustration and strain build, individuals adapt to their predicament in one of the following ways: conformity, innovation, ritualism, retreatism, or rebellion.

In Merton's scheme, are militia members conformists or rebels?

Conformity occurs when individuals embrace both the goals and means of the dominant society. Success goals are sought through socially approved channels. Conformists may still feel strain because success may take many years to achieve, but they choose to play by the rules of society. This ordinarily includes graduating from school and working at a job. Conformists account for little crime. After all, they are doing what the social order encourages. Happily, according to Merton, conformity "is the most common and widely diffused" mode of adaptation.[13]

Innovation occurs when the goals are accepted but legitimate means are unavailable or rejected. People who innovate achieve economic success through a variety of illegal enterprises. This adaptation results in a considerable amount of crime, particularly property offenses committed by members of the lower class.

The individual who places more importance on means than goals engages in **ritualism.** The ritualist is so completely committed to proper procedures and rules that overarching goals are obscured. A non-economic example is the ambulance driver who refuses to exceed the speed limit when taking a critically ill patient to the hospital. This driver is not breaking a law, but the goal of saving the life of the patient is compromised. By definition, ritualists do not commit crimes.

Retreatism accounts for certain crimes. Merton refers to retreatists as "*in* the society but not *of* it."[14] Individuals who retreat from society accept neither the goals nor the means of the dominant culture. Included in this category are "vagrants, vagabonds, tramps, chronic drunkards, and drug addicts."[15]

The final mode of adaptation is **rebellion.** Like the retreatist, the rebel rejects the dominant goals and means but, unlike the retreatist, the rebel seeks to establish alternative goals and means. A political revolutionary who bombs a government building and a religious zealot who bombs an abortion clinic are each engaged in rebellion. In contemporary American society there appears to be a proliferation of so-called militia—anti-government groups. The individuals involved could be considered rebels. Rebels occasionally resort to violent means and, when they do so, they violate the law.

Crime Produced by Macro Social Forces

In his 1938 article, Merton noted the tendency to attribute nonconformity to biological drives or psychological disorders. These explanations are variations of an Original Sin dogma where the individual is to blame.[16] Merton sought to advance an interpretation more in keeping with what he called "socially derived sin."[17] He argued "that certain phases of social structure generate the circumstances in which infringement of social codes constitutes a 'normal' response."[18] Before this article appeared, social ecology and differential association theory had already emphasized the social causes of crime, but neither of these perspectives took a macro focus. Merton's theory directed attention to two macro elements of the social environment: dominant culture goals and socially approved means for achieving them. Crime emerges as a social adaptation to the *discontinuity* between universal goals and means.

Summary of Merton's Strain Theory

Merton's explanation of deviance and crime is one of the most enduring theoretical formulations in sociology. Simply put, Merton suggests that a discrepancy between expectations and realizations promotes personal strain and frustration, which often results in criminal behavior. Success goals in American culture are defined overwhelmingly in terms of economic achievement. Further, popular ideology stipulates that in America anyone who makes an honest effort will succeed. Hence, failure is blamed on personal shortcomings. This creates considerable strain and frustration to which individuals respond in a number of ways, not least of which is criminal conduct. Innovation, retreatism, and rebellion are three modes of adaptation that can include criminal activity.

Marxist Theory of Crime

Between 1969 and 1971, criminological theory took a new turn, and a systematic conflict theory of crime was advanced.[19] According to this view, conflict is the natural order of relations in society; the crucial factor as regards crime is definitional, not behavioral, that is, criminality "is a definition applied by those in power";[20] and the criminal justice system, as an apparatus of the state, enables the powerful in society to bestow criminal definitions on those who threaten the status quo.

In the United States, conflict criminology served as a bridge to a more extreme theoretical perspective that was variously described as "new," "critical," "radical," or "Marxist" criminology (the term applied here). Though Karl Marx wrote little about crime and criminals, his ideas have been influential in the formulation of a macro-level explanation of crime. The following five propositions provide a summary of the Marxist account of crime.

Capitalism Produces Crime

In 1905, Willem Bonger published *Criminality and Economic Conditions.*[21] In his book, Bonger argued that the profit motive of capitalism generates an **egoistic personality** structure wherein individuals look out only for themselves. Crime is an inevitable outcome. More recently, Robert Bohm concluded that "the fundamental basis of most crime in the United States is the relentless quest for surplus value and capital."[22] As noted in Chapter 9 of this book, David Gordon explained crime as a "rational response to the conditions of competition and inequality fostered by capitalism; . . ."[23] But it is Richard Quinney who has offered the most detailed and prominent explanation of the relationship between capitalism and crime. Quinney argued in 1977 that crime is either directly or indirectly produced by the capitalist state and political economy.[24]

Crimes of control, crimes of economic domination, and crimes of government are all *directly* produced by the capitalist order. **Crimes of control** include all of the felonies and misdemeanors committed by law-enforcement agencies, ranging from local police brutality to illegal monitoring of citizens by the Central Intelligence Agency (CIA). In seeking to preserve the established order, the state often oversteps its legal authority.

For the most part, **crimes of economic domination** are offenses committed by large corporations. Price-fixing, false advertising, and illegal pollution are examples. Even acts committed by corporations that are technically legal (profitable companies terminating employees, for example) might be considered crimes of economic domination because of the social harm they cause. Significantly, the activities of organized crime are also included in this category. Marxist criminologists tend to explain organized crime with reference to the illegal ventures of "upright" local elites;[25] the illegal application of principles of capitalist production;[26] enterprises that provide a means of support for groups who might otherwise be a burden on the state;[27] or as behavior entirely dependent on the capitalist ruling class.[28]

Third, **crimes of government** include deceiving, cheating, or harming the public. Various investigations have discovered that American military services occasionally pay exorbitant prices for ordinary items (including $200 for a hammer). When the results of such investigations are publicized, many people might be inclined to dismiss the information as an example of government waste or foolishness. In fact, however, it may signal corruption between high-ranking members of the military and defense contractors.

Quinney further argues that there are crimes generated indirectly by capitalism. **Predatory crimes** consist of offenses such as robbery and burglary. These crimes are prompted by the dire economic conditions of poverty and unemployment that are necessary features of a capitalistic system. Under capitalism, to keep the wages of labor-

Responding to Corporate Crime

Many would agree that corporate crime is a major problem in American society, and yet there is no consensus on how to respond to it. A former president of the United States advanced an interesting metaphor. He compared corporate crime to reckless driving. The president stated that, just as society ought to punish the reckless driver, not the passengers or the automobile, so too should society punish the guilty executives, not the stockholders or the company. What president used this metaphor? Was it Richard Nixon, Jimmy Carter, or Ronald Reagan? Actually, it was Woodrow Wilson, in the early part of this century. Clearly, corporate crime has been a part of the American scene for a long time.

This is no surprise to Marxist criminologists, who argue that corporate crime is a regular and inevitable accompaniment to a capitalist economy. According to these criminologists, one explanation of the persistence of corporate crime is the tepid criminal justice response to these types of criminal behavior. Under existing practices, they argue, companies that violate the law are not punished harshly enough to discourage future illegal behavior. It appears that, even to this date, Wilson's admonition not to punish stockholders or companies has been followed in general.

SOURCE: Richard Hofstadter, *The American Political Tradition* (New York: Vantage, 1973) 323–24.

ers depressed there must always be a reserve pool of unemployed workers who could replace current workers in the event of a strike. In such conditions, Quinney held, the poor and unemployed will occasionally resort to stealing as a way to "get by."

Personal crimes such as murder, assault, and rape are also linked to capitalist conditions. These are horrible acts committed by people who have been dehumanized by the harsh conditions of capitalism. Having been exploited by the system and alienated from friends and work, these individuals are so emotionally and spiritually brutalized that they have lost their sensitivity for basic human values. These offenders have been treated as objects and they treat their victims in like fashion.

Finally, there are **crimes of resistance.** These are the criminal offenses committed against employers and the government. Wrecking company property, performing careless work, and releasing secret information are examples of crimes that weaken the existing order. These acts are either conscious or unconscious reactions to exploitation.

All Marxist criminologists link crime to capitalist conditions. Quinney's conceptual framework suggests how a wide variety of crime categories are produced by capitalism.

Capitalist State Defines Crime, Controls Justice

Quinney argues that in a capitalist society the state (government) emerges "to protect and promote the interests of the dominant class, the class that owns and controls the means of production."[29] This is called an **instrumentalist theory** of capitalist rule because the state is conceptualized as a mere instrument that is used by the most powerful members of society. More specifically, Quinney asserts that the "state exists as a device for controlling the exploited class, the class that labors, for the benefit of the ruling class."[30] Hence, those who adopt an instrumentalist interpretation contend that members of the upper class create laws that protect their interests and at the same time target the unwanted behavior of all other members of society. For example, in the United States index crimes are considered the most serious criminal offenses and yet robbery, burglary, and larceny are not nearly as costly as non-index offenses like price-fixing and false advertising. Defining as most serious those offenses more likely to be committed by the poor is a great advantage for the wealthy. Furthermore, the criminal justice system is run to the advantage of the powerful. In his book, *The Rich Get Richer and the Poor Get Prison,* Jeffrey Reiman argues that the poor are at a disadvantage at every stage of the criminal justice system including suspicion, arrest, prosecution, conviction, sentencing, and parole.[31]

Other Marxist criminologists have embraced a **structuralist theory** of state control. According to structuralists, public policies are not the result of ruling class conspiracies; capitalists do not directly control the state. Quite the contrary, the state functions independently—sometimes in ways that disadvantage individual corporations (laws against false advertising or corporate collusion). This view emphasizes the power of the system itself rather than the people who, at any one time, constitute the system. The fundamental principle, according to the structuralists, is that the state promotes the long-term best interest of the capitalist order (Box 13.1).

An example of structuralism is offered by crime theorist Raymond Michalowski, who notes that social relations are "shaped by the interaction of a variety of factors that together can be called the mode of production."[32] Another structuralist, Stephen Spitzer, argues that the capitalist system inevitably produces problem populations referred to as "social dynamite" (thieves, vagrants, drug addicts).[33] These groups are identified, monitored, and restrained by the capitalist state. According to criminologists Theodore Chiricos and Miriam Delone, there is "empirically plausible" evidence to conclude that, when there is a labor surplus, forms of criminal punishment become more harsh.[34] They base this conclusion on an analysis of forty-four empirical studies. The evidence suggests that, as a higher proportion of the population becomes unemployed, penal sanctions become more severe as a means of deterring these individuals from law violation.

The distinction between instrumentalist and structuralist views of the state is important. The former focuses on individuals, while the latter highlights the system. It is a little like explaining the excellence of Notre Dame football either by the players presently on the roster or the program itself. Because Notre Dame football has literally outlived many star players (and coaches), some would suggest it must be the program itself that is most significant. Structuralists offer a similar argument in reference to the capitalist state; it outlives individual capitalists.

In general, both instrumentalists and structuralists agree that crime definitions and criminal justice practices regulate the behavior of those who are most likely to threaten the capitalist order: the poor. Accordingly, Marxist criminologists advance a more inclusive definition of crime than is presently adopted by the legal system. Herman and Julia Schwendinger, for instance, argue that crime ought to be defined in terms of violations of "historically determined rights of individuals." This requires that *all* socially injurious acts be considered criminal.

Ideology and False Consciousness Justify Existing Practices
If the legal code benefits the minority and hinders the majority, why is it generally seen as legitimate and binding? Furthermore, if capitalist criminal justice is as bad as Marxist criminologists allege, why is there so little protest? Marx addressed these issues even more broadly when he explained how ideology helps preserve capitalist society as a whole. For Marx, an **ideology** is a set of ideas that distorts reality in an effort to defend the status quo. The prevailing ideology of capitalism hides, or at least clouds, the injustices of capitalist society. The ills of capitalist society are blamed on individuals, not the system itself.

Although most people accept the dominant ideology, thinking that the ideas are their own, Marx argued that "sentiments, illusions, modes of thought, and views of life" are themselves fabricated by the capitalist system.[35]

This means that the "single individual, who derives them through tradition and upbringing, may imagine that they form the real motives and the starting point of his activity."[36] But this is a mistaken view. Individuals who believe that capitalist social relations are fair, and that anyone can succeed in life, suffer from **false consciousness.** Marx stated that the "ruling ideas of each age have ever been the ideas of its ruling class."[37]

Contemporary Marxist criminologists agree. Reiman, for example, classifies members of capitalist society as "have-plenties," "have-littles," and "have-nots."[38] Because "have-plenties" are so few in number, they must convince the vast majority that the social order is fair and reasonable. In short, "the system requires an effective ideology to fool enough of the people enough of the time."[39]

The Powerful Commit the Most Serious Crimes
In the mid-1970s, Tony Platt and his associates at the Center for Research on Criminal Justice in Berkeley, California, placed a spotlight on "the crimes of the powerful." In one publication they argued explicitly that "the most dangerous criminals sit in corporate and government offices."[40] About one decade later, Michalowski offered a similar appraisal: "Taken together, the crimes of capital constitute the single greatest source of untimely death, injury, illness, and economic loss faced by American citizens."[41] Reiman has recently echoed these sentiments:

The workplace, the medical profession, the air we breathe, and the poverty we refuse to rectify lead to far more human suffering, far more death and disability, and take far more dollars from our pockets than the murders, aggravated assaults, and thefts reported annually by the FBI.[42]

Marxist criminologists argue that the evidence is on their side. The most injurious and costly crimes in American society, they contend, are offenses such as corporate collusion, making unsafe consumer products, maintaining unsafe work settings, and the many and varied professional and organized illegal activities—all acts committed by the powerful in society.

Social Justice Must Precede Criminal Justice
Marxist criminology links "the study of crime with the larger pursuit of social justice. . . ."[43] Marxist criminologists agree that the capitalist mode of production generates socially harmful behavior, some of which is presently labeled criminal. To prevent or reduce conventional criminal behavior requires a restructuring of society so that basic inequities can be eliminated. *Social* justice must be obtained before *criminal* justice can be secured. Marxist criminologist T. R. Young urges that the criminal justice system be replaced with a "comprehensive social justice

system."[44] Crime will be far less pronounced in societies where "community, prosocial behavior and social justice take precedence over profit, private accumulation, and affluent life styles."[45] Only after the basic organizing principles of social life have been altered will criminal justice be possible.

Summary of Marxist Theory of Crime

Marxist criminology explains crime as a product of capitalist social relations. The powerful in society (capitalists) determine what behaviors are defined as criminal and otherwise control the workings of the criminal justice system. The Marxist theory of crime further suggests that most crimes committed by the powerless are in response to societal exploitation and repression.

Feminist Theory of Crime

There is no overall consensus on what constitutes feminist theory.[46] Despite this, Gaye Tuchman has advanced a "common-denominator" definition of feminist theory: "The term *feminist theory* is an invention of the academic branch of the middle and late twentieth-century feminist movement. It refers to generating systematic ideas that define women's place in society and culture, including the depiction of women. . . ."[47] This definition can at least be used as a guidepost in identifying feminist theory.

Just as there is no one feminist theory, there is "no single, unified feminist criminology."[48] There are several theoretical versions of feminist criminology, four of which are particularly significant: liberal, Marxist, radical, and socialist. **Liberal feminist criminology** focuses on gender inequalities. Liberal feminists do not believe that gender discrimination is systemic or inevitable.[49] Women and men can change society to make it egalitarian. In their comprehensive statement on feminist criminology, Kathleen Daly and Meda Chesney-Lind classify the scholarly work of criminologists Rita Simon and Freda Adler as fitting in the liberal tradition.[50] In her book *Women and Crime,* published in 1975, Simon argued that the low rate of female crime could be explained historically in terms of limited opportunities for women.[51] For example, if women are unable to obtain jobs involving financial trust, they will not have an opportunity to embezzle funds. Hence, Simon's assessment predicts a higher rate of female property crime as job opportunities increase. In a similar vein, Freda Adler's book *Sisters in Crime: The Rise of the New Female Offender,* also published in 1975, argued that the women's movement had resulted in women becoming more "masculine" and therefore committing more crimes.[52] These claims have sparked considerable controversy.

Marxist feminist criminology differs fundamentally from the liberal approach. Marxist feminists typically trace the source of gender inequality to capitalist relations. Capitalism exploits any number of minority groups, women being one such group. An example of a Marxist feminist approach is the work of Julia and Herman Schwendinger, who have explained male violence, particularly rape, from this perspective.[53] The Schwendingers argue that male violence is a product of class relations and the economic mode of production. Polly Radosh has outlined a more encompassing Marxist feminist theory of female crime in which she explains: (1) the means by which women are defined as criminals; (2) the class status of women criminals; and (3) the overall system of social control over women.[54] Like the Schwendingers, Radosh emphasizes the influence of capitalist class relations and the mode of production.

Radical feminist criminology points to *patriarchy* (society designed for the benefit of men) as the root cause of all forms of inequality and socially harmful behavior. Among other issues, this perspective focuses on violence against women.[55] For example, Susan Griffin, in her classic article on the relationship of male dominance in society to aggression against women, described rape as an "All-American crime."[56] Griffin argues that patriarchal society teaches and rewards violent behavior in men. For Griffin, rape is an act of violence endemic to patriarchal culture. Another radical feminist, Susan Brownmiller, analyzed rape, but offered a different conclusion.[57] Brownmiller contended that inherent *biological* differences between men and women promote the ideology of rape through patriarchy. Men's greater average size and strength has extended beyond mere differences between the sexes to the standard upon which domination of men over women is based. Rape is a mechanism by which "*all men* keep *all women* in a state of fear."[58] In a further distinction of types of radical feminist criminology, cultural feminists, such as Catherine MacKinnon, point out the cultural benefits of femininity and the detrimental effects of masculinity on social order.[59] Women's greater lawfulness, involvement in nurturing tasks, and near absence from either socially approved violent behavior or criminal violence is juxtaposed against characteristics of masculinity. Men have a near monopoly on violent behavior, whether the behavior is socially acceptable, as in sports, or unacceptable, as in criminal activities. Men's affinity for violence, coupled with a traditional disdain for nurturing roles, promotes cultural dominion over women and denigration of the worth of women's pursuits, according to this version of radical feminism.[60]

Socialist feminist criminology prioritizes both class and gender relations as crucial factors in explaining crime. James Messerschmidt's book *Capitalism, Patriarchy, and Crime* is an example of this perspective.[61] In this work, Messerschmidt argues that exploitation of the powerless is endemic to both patriarchy and capitalism. The interaction of gender and class creates positions of power and powerlessness that result in "different types and degrees of criminality and varying opportunities for engaging in them."[62]

Though specific versions of feminist criminology diverge in terms of theoretical focus and methodological strategies, there are four points (core propositions) over which there is general agreement.

Society Shaped by Patriarchal Relations

There is disagreement within feminist criminology about whether gender is one of several influential factors in society or whether it is the single most important force in society. Nevertheless, all variants of feminist criminology agree that in the United States men have benefits and opportunities unavailable to women. These gender advantages reflect, and affect, the ways in which a person thinks and behaves. Because gender is an overarching variable, that is, a master status, it necessarily has an impact on crime. Indeed, James Messerschmidt calls gender "the strongest predictor of criminal involvement."[63]

Women Must Be Included

Women have generally been a missing factor in criminological theory. Messerschmidt refers to this omission as "gender-blind criminology."[64] He argues that all of the traditional crime theories, including anomie, social control, and labeling, as well as Marxist theory, fail to account for women. In the rare instances when women's criminal behavior is addressed, the explanations have centered attention on women's alleged "want of passion," "undeveloped intelligence," "diminished courage," "natural deceit," and "immorality."[65] Radosh offers this summary of the treatment of women in crime theory: "The subliminal message has been that because men commit most crime, then there must be something atypical about women who commit crimes."[66]

Because existing theories of crime are almost always theories of male crime, the question arises as to whether the theories apply to women. Daly and Chesney-Lind call this the "generalizability" question in criminology, and their answer is "yes and no."[67] On the one hand, women are a part of the same society as men and so will be influenced by many of the same forces. For instance, the economy influences both men and women. On the other hand, there are certain social forces that exert a differential influence on men and women. Criminal gangs, for example, may be more likely to explain male crime participation than female crime participation. In any event, Daly and Chesney-Lind believe that the generalizability question should be "bracketed" (overlooked) and that criminologists ought to "plunge more deeply into the social worlds of girls and women."[68] This strategy would also help overcome another shortcoming in criminological research: the tendency to overlook "key differences among female populations."[69] Like men, women are not a monolithic category. This means that key variables such as age, race, and class must also be examined.

Gender-Sensitive Explanations Required

Criminological research has determined conclusively that men are far more likely than women to commit crime. While traditional crime theories might explain male criminal behavior, they do not explain female criminal behavior—or the lack of it. Why is it that women commit only a small fraction of total crimes? And why are women nearly exempt from certain offenses such as acts of global endangerment, lucrative occupational crimes associated with fraud and theft in the business world, and sex-related crimes?[70]

A number of answers have been advanced. First is the biological explanation. Is there something biologically distinctive about women that makes them less inclined to commit crime? Some radical feminists have suggested that inherent "femaleness" does explain why women are less likely to engage in crime.[71] However, in their extensive review of the literature regarding the connection between crime and biology, Janet Katz and William Chambliss did not identify any credible research establishing a link between biology and a female predisposition to refrain from crime or a male tendency to commit crime.[72]

The socialization process offers a second possible explanation for the low rate of female participation in crime. Psychologist Shirley Weitz argues that differential treatment and differential identification are primarily responsible for gender role socialization.[73] Here, the basic idea is that girls and boys are socialized differentially. Girls are socialized to be nurturing, emotional, and submissive, while boys are socialized to be aggressive, calculating, and dominant. Through the years, many sociologists have explained the low crime rate of girls and women as the end result of the socialization process. For example, Talcott Parsons, the most prominent sociologist of his generation, wrote that "girls are more apt to be relatively docile, to conform in general according to adult expectations to be 'good.'"[74] Differential socialization offers an intriguing explanation for women's minimal participation, but it does not explain why only a small percentage of men commit serious crimes. If socialization were causally linked to crime, the rates of male offense would actually be much higher than current patterns indicate. It is true that most crimes are committed by men, but most men do not engage in serious crime. The impact of socialization may be one of several confounding factors that fosters the development of criminal patterns in some and inhibits the likelihood of crime in others. Rather than being a causal variable associated with crime, socialization is more likely to contribute to a combination of factors that may cause crime in some people. The linkage between socialization patterns and crime requires further analysis.

A third explanation of women's low involvement in crime centers attention on mothering. A number of scholars have noted the importance of "maternal thinking" and the caring and rearing of children. Sara Ruddick suggests that the daily practices of mothering necessarily entail attention to conflict resolution, compromise, and social acceptability.[75] As Nancy Chodorow and others have argued, the decisive factor is not the biological distinction of being female, but the ongoing activities involved in raising children.[76] The practice of mothering promotes caring for others, attention to the needs of children, and mature coping with daily stress. Men can and do involve themselves in these activities, but the fact is that women are far more likely than men to be immersed in parenting activities and to develop values that affirm peaceful coexistence with others as a daily life activity. The qualities necessary to mothering, such as peaceful resolution of conflict, patience, and deprivation of self for the benefit of others, promote values that are contrary to the commission of crime. As a result, women's values, goals, and life activities are directed away from crime. Men, who rarely adopt these nurturing values, do not face the same conflicts between the promotion of nurturance and the denigration and exploitation of others inherent in crime.

Cultural constraint is a fourth explanation of women's low participation in crime. The behavior of girls and women is much more likely to be monitored than is the behavior of boys and men. Moreover, many opportunities extended to men in the areas of politics, religion, education, and employment have been traditionally withheld from women. This reduced structural opportunity has effectively closed the path to many forms of crime (political crime, price-fixing). Further, because women have been closely scrutinized and controlled throughout their lives, crime participation has been a risky proposition; therefore, the female crime rate remained low for generations. One notable problem with this explanation is that, as opportunities for women have opened in recent decades, the female crime rate has not gone up dramatically. In fact, the increases in female crime have been consistently in the area of lower-class property theft and drug crime, not the areas predicted by this explanation.

None of these four explanations is satisfactory on its own. The real answer to why women commit so few crimes is perhaps a selective composite of all four explanations. At this point more research is needed before this important question can be answered convincingly.

Unfair Treatment of Women in Justice System

Otto Pollak argued that women offenders are treated more leniently at every stage of the criminal justice system. He stated that lenient treatment of women by police officers and judges reflected an ethic of "chivalry."[77] The research literature on this issue is sharply divided. Some studies have found that women offenders are treated more leniently, while other investigations have found that women receive harsher penalties than men for the same offense.[78] It is probably the case that evidence for the chivalry factor varies by type of offense and stage within the criminal justice system. In the final analysis, however, it is unlikely that any major institution in a patriarchal society works to the specific advantage of women. Feminist criminologists call for further research that "addresses how gender relations structure decisions in the legal process, rather than whether men and women are treated 'the same' in a statistical sense."[79]

Summary of Feminist Theory of Crime

Feminist crime theories have developed in response to the inadequate accounts of female crime found in conventional theories. Conventional theories either ignore women entirely or treat them in a stereotypical fashion. Although there is no unified feminist theory of crime, there is general agreement by feminist theorists on a few core propositions, most important of which is that patriarchal relations affect behavior in society, including criminal behavior.

Position on Agency (Responsibility)

All of the theories of crime examined in previous chapters located the source of criminal behavior in individual actors or micro social phenomena. None of these theories was able successfully to integrate a strong theory of the individual actor with a strong theory of social structural influence. We will now see if macro social crime theories are better able to explain the human agency dimension of criminal behavior.

Merton's strain theory, as originally stated (1938), suggested that crime can be regarded as an individually chosen adaptation to a social structural dissociation between goals and means. Merton certainly appears to describe individuals as free and purposeful agents. In fact, some sociologists thought that Merton had gone too far by describing individuals almost like "isolated atoms."[80]

Merton, too, was apparently dissatisfied with the perceived individualistic bias. He admitted that such criticism, when applied to the 1938 essay, was justified.[81] By 1957, Merton had begun to emphasize that "these deviant ways of achieving the goals occur within social systems."[82] The implication is that Merton reconsidered his position. In fact, in the 1957 version of the theory, the focus of the response to macro structural conditions shifts *away from* the individual: "The underlying premise here is that class strata are not only differentially subject to anomie but are differentially subject to one or another type of response to it."[83]

Had individual agency been vanquished? At least one prominent theorist, Edwin Lemert, argued that Merton did not go far enough. Lemert still objected to Merton's depiction of the individual as a free agent. Humans, Lemert stated, should be seen as "hostages of groups, not free agents."[84] But others have taken the opposite position, claiming that Merton's revised theory neglects the individual.[85] So which is it? Consider Marshall Clinard's assessment. He states that the adaptations played out by individuals are in no sense reflective of human capability or freedom: "None of these adaptations, as Merton points out, is deliberately selected by the individual or is utilitarian, . . ."[86] Clinard's interpretation of Merton's shift away from the individual side of action is generally accurate. It is clear that strain theory, as Merton eventually formulated it, depicts the individual as a pressured, frustrated, and generally uncalculating actor. This does not qualify as a sufficiently strong theory of individual agency.

Marxist criminology pairs a strong theory of the individual with a strong theory of social structural influence. This perspective holds that capitalist social relations produce crime. The capitalist state shapes the set of behavioral possibilities, opportunities, and limitations that confront individuals, and the dominant ideology of capitalist society predisposes how people interpret their perceived options. This is a vigorous interpretation of macro social structural influence on behavior.

The other side of agency concerns the actor. Here too, by advancing a strong theory of the individual, Marxist criminology provides a compelling account. Marx's writings contain an implicit model of the actor that portrays the individual as a purposeful and self-aware agent.[87] According to Marx, the individual's "life activity is the product of will and consciousness."[88] The human agent shapes reality and is not "overdetermined" by ideas or material conditions.[89] Marx argues that just as individuals produce cloth and linen, so do they also produce their social relations.[90]

Despite his persistent efforts to reveal the oppressive nature of capitalist social structure, Marx did not depict humans as pawns or vessels of circumstance. Instead, Marx argued that individuals are capable of "changing history." Marxist criminologists take a similar point of view. They specifically reject mainstream criminology's description of the individual (offender) as passive, incompetent, and/or irrational. Quinney was one of the first to reject the mainstream view. In 1965, Quinney called for a complementary conceptualization of the individual:

The deterministic, oversocialized conception of man must be balanced by the facts of man's reason, creativity, freedom of action, autonomy, consciousness, and potential—facts which require an alternative, not necessarily mutually exclusive, but complementary conception of man.[91]

Several years later, Quinney provides a more elaborate view of the criminal actor when he argues that crimes *evolve* "from unconscious reactions to exploitation, to conscious acts of survival within the capitalist system, to politically conscious acts of rebellion."[92]

In the final analysis, Marxist criminology explains crime as the purposeful activity of human agents within the context of a repressive social structure. Both sides of the equation are given their due: A strong theory of the individual is paired with a strong theory of social structural influence.

It is difficult to describe the feminist theory of agency because there are so many diverse examples of feminist thought. Most feminist accounts are based on the notion that patriarchal social relations shape behavior in society. Some versions of radical feminist crime theory present a deterministic view of action, particularly for males. The mere fact of being male predisposes a person to act in a certain way (for example, violently). Mark Liddle calls this a "model of male agency which is at best one-dimensional."[93] Other theorists have noted that an exaggerated focus on patriarchal structures results in a conceptualization of *all* men as villains and agents of patriarchy.[94] Ironically, other versions of feminist criminology favor the other extreme where action in society, at least behavior undertaken by men, is viewed as the result of intrinsic maleness. Here, committing violence against women, for example, is in the nature of the human male. Hence, whether the focus is on patriarchal structure or masculinity, certain versions of feminist criminology advance a deterministic view of action.

Any macro theory of social structural influence is challenged to incorporate individual agency. Because of the tendency to rely on hard distinctions between men and women, most feminist formulations have difficulty doing this. Only when men and women are viewed as purposeful agents (not *men* agents or *women* agents) acting in the context of constraints and opportunities set by patriarchal structures, can both sides of agency be addressed adequately.

Policy Implications

The essential argument of Merton's strain theory is that individuals become frustrated because of the incongruity among aspirations, expectations, and realizations. There are numerous interpretations of this scenario, but the problem is most commonly defined in economic terms. In short, the argument is that people experience strain when they do not attain the material goals that they want and expect. This generates frustration that often results in criminal behavior. Strain theory proponents have offered a number of policy recommendations, three of which will now be discussed.

Socialism and Crime in Tanzania

Marxist criminologists contend that capitalistic systems promote high rates of crime, while much lower crime rates are expected in socialistic societies. Does socialism actually result in less crime? With this question in mind, researcher John A. Arthur used the Republic of Tanzania as a test case. Even though official crime data in Tanzania (and most other developing countries) must be approached with caution, Arthur assumed that some insight could be gained from examining the relationship between Tanzania's socialist practices and its crime rates.

Tanzania is located on the eastern coast of Africa. The nation became independent from Britain in 1961 and, after a few years, adopted a socialist economy. Banks, major raw materials, and important consumer goods were nationalized. Private property, the essential feature of capitalism, has little standing in Tanzania.

Official crime data show that, under socialism, there have been increases in homicides, major thefts, and minor

thefts. In response to high rates of crime, the Tanzania government has relied on increasingly harsher penalties—even making flogging mandatory for numerous offenses. None of this has worked. Economic conditions remain dire, and the crime rate has not abated. In fact, Dar es Salaam, the Tanzanian capital, was the site of one of the most horrific crimes of 1998: the bombing of the U.S. Embassy on August 7, which killed scores of people and wounded thousands.

Despite what has been said, it is not correct to conclude that socialism is the major cause of crime in Tanzania. Neighboring countries such as Kenya, Zambia, and Malawi also have high crime rates and these nations are pro-capitalistic in orientation and practice. Nevertheless, Tanzania offers an empirical example in opposition to the projection of Marxist criminology that socialism produces low crime rates.

SOURCE: John A. Arthur, "Crime and Penal Policy in the Socialist African Republic of Tanzania," *International Journal of Offender Therapy and Comparative Criminology* 40 (1996) 157–73; Michael Elliott, "Terror Times Two," *Newsweek,* 17 August 1998, 22–28.

Because strain theory addresses a macro-level problem, the proper policy proposals should be aimed at macro-level social structure.[95] Hence, a liberal resolution to the problem identified in strain theory calls for an increase in structural opportunities.[96] Here it is argued that an increase in educational and job opportunities will elevate realizations. This will produce a greater symmetry between what people aspire to and expect, and what they actually achieve. Lower-class stealing, for example, can be reduced by offering more and better job opportunities to members of the lower class.

Another liberal policy response to the strain problem highlights rehabilitation. As a correctional philosophy, rehabilitation seeks to change an offender's "character, attitudes, or behavior patterns."[97] One way this can be achieved is to increase an offender's marketable skills. For many years liberals have advocated academic and vocational training in prison for this very reason.

There are also conservative policy implications consistent with the insights of strain theory. Specifically, instead of elevating realizations, aspirations and expectations can be lowered. In fact, a main thrust of rehabilitation has been to "counsel" offenders to adopt more modest and realistic life expectations. This is another way in which the gap between expectations and realizations can be narrowed. On a more macro level, politicians and other public figures could "mount a campaign to tell everyone that the American Dream is over."[98] That might reduce expec-

tations, but it seems unlikely that politicians would ever present such a gloomy message to the public.

Marxist criminology has often been criticized for its seeming inability to provide specific solutions to the problem of crime.[99] There is some validity to this criticism, inasmuch as Marxist criminologists have typically argued for a complete overhaul of society. For example, Raymond Michalowski states that "any resolution to the contemporary problems of crime will necessitate *some* form of transition to *some* form of socialism."[100] Michalowski also states that crime prevention can be bolstered by reducing inequality in the broadest sense (Box 13.2). This includes defining as criminal the harmful behavior of the powerful and then prosecuting such offenders. Reducing the crimes of the poor requires actions that assure full employment and increase the minimum wage.[101] Robert Bohm adds that Marxist criminologists need to work for "the repeal of inequitable laws and for the passage of equitable ones."[102] Finally, a third Marxist criminologist, T.R. Young, offers this view:

The fact is that most people who engage in crime and antisocial behavior cease such behavior as they become integrated into work, family, friendship and community roles. Putting people in prosocial roles early on in life may be a better way to deal with crime than punishment. However, the larger social factors which promote crime must

Marxist criminology embraces a harms-based definition of crime. From this perspective, smoke pollution, whether technically legal or not, could be considered criminal.

be transformed or else no justice system, criminal, civil, medical or prosocial will work.[103]

Patricia Smith has argued that the one "irreducible" issue that unites all feminist perspectives is the opposition to patriarchy.[104] In fighting patriarchy, however, feminists are not of one mind. Liberal feminism seeks solutions to a myriad of social problems, including but not limited to the "feminization of poverty," domestic abuse, sexual harassment, and insufficient child care options. This branch of feminism advocates passage of equal opportunity legislation to guarantee gender equality in the workplace and before the law. It is thought that such reforms would eliminate some of the negative effects of gender discrimination and, in the process, decrease the number of violent crimes against women and reduce the number of lower-class property offenses committed by women.

Another liberal feminist policy proposal has been advanced by psychologist June Stephenson, who argues that men ought to pay a special tax, that is, a "user" fee to subsidize expenses associated with the criminal justice system.[105] Stephenson maintains that crime suspects, criminal offenders, and prison inmates are most likely to be male. Because police officers, probation and parole workers, public defenders, prosecuting attorneys, judges, correctional officers, and other functionaries of the criminal justice system attend mostly to men, it should be men who pay the bill. For various reasons, it is unlikely that this proposal will ever be implemented.

Some of the policy implications that flow from liberal feminism have clarity and practical appeal. Radical feminists, however, view the liberal feminist agenda as limited in scope. The radicals seek a more comprehensive dismantling of patriarchal structures. From their point of view, "dabbling" with social reforms is insufficient. For example, cultural feminist Catherine MacKinnon argues for an entirely new jurisprudence.[106]

To some extent, there is a lack of clarity in radical feminist policy proposals. Part of the ambiguity is due to theoretical difficulties. Messerschmidt identifies three fundamental theoretical errors of radical feminist criminology: (1) treating all men as identical; (2) equating heterosexuality with the violent control of women by men; and (3) viewing male sexuality as "uncontrollable and preordained" and female sexuality as "nurturant and serene."[107] Until radical feminists working in the area of criminology can resolve these problems, no unified radical feminist policy program is likely to be forthcoming.

Subsequent Developments

The three macro theories discussed in this chapter have inspired numerous extensions and reformulations. Four areas of subsequent theoretical work will now be highlighted.

Extensions of Strain Theory

Since its inception, Merton's strain theory has had an enormous influence on crime theory, and it has stimulated a number of subsequent theoretical developments. The first important modification of the original model was Albert Cohen's subcultural theory of delinquency.[108] A main thrust of Merton's theory suggested that members of the lower class resort to crime and deviance in adapting to structural *economic* strain. Cohen advanced the idea that adolescents also adapt to strain. However, for adolescents, particularly lower-class boys, the strain derives from *status-frustration*. Cohen explained the development of delinquent subcultures (gangs) as a reaction to this problem. All adolescents crave esteem, he argued, but lower-class males, unlike other adolescents, were particularly ill-equipped to succeed in middle-class school environments. Not succeeding academically or socially at school, these boys are often attracted to gangs. According to Cohen, the adolescent cannot "go it alone."[109] The gang subculture is a collective response to this strain.

Sociologists Richard Cloward and Lloyd Ohlin extended strain theory in yet another way.[110] Like Merton and Cohen before them, Cloward and Ohlin conceptualize crime and deviance as a collective subcultural phenomenon, not an individual action: "We exclude from our purview acts of delinquency that are committed by isolated individuals, or by members of groups in which delinquent acts are not prescribed."[111] Unlike Merton and Cohen, these authors note that illegitimate means are problematic. Merton assumed that, in the quest for financial success, illegitimate innovation was readily available, and Cohen assumed that teenagers could always join a delinquent gang for status attainment. But Cloward and Ohlin argue that illegitimate means are themselves scarce. For example, it is not certain that an adolescent will be accepted into a delinquent gang. Hence, some individuals might become **double failures.**

The most noteworthy recent development in strain theory is Robert Agnew's general strain theory (GST).[112] Agnew argues that strain is caused by a wide variety of factors. He notes that individuals must reconcile *aspirations* (ideal goals), *expectations* (goals perceived as realistic) and *achievements*. Strain is produced when aspirations exceed expectations or when expectations exceed achievements. The most strain occurs in the latter case. Strain is specifically caused by three manifestations of **negative social relations:** (1) strain is produced when others prevent or threaten to prevent the achievement of goals, as in being fired from a job; (2) strain is produced with the actual or threatened removal of valued possessions, as in a house foreclosure; and (3) strain occurs when a negative stimuli is introduced or threatened to be introduced, as in a prison sentence. These negative relations engender emotions such as fear, depression, frustration, and hostility, which themselves "create pressure for corrective action, and crime is one possible response."[113]

Agnew summarizes GST in this way: "At heart, the GST is very simple. It argues that if we treat people badly, they may get mad and engage in crime."[114] It should be noted, however, that crime is not an inevitable response to the strain highlighted by Agnew. Individuals respond differently based on numerous personal factors including intelligence, self-esteem, coping skills, problem-solving skills, and temperament.

GST is significant because it broadens strain theory. However, empirical testing of the theory has provided mixed results. Moreover, Agnew's theory has been described as "heavily psychological in character."[115] For these reasons, GST is unlikely to be the final strain theory formulation.

Left Realism

When Marxist criminology first emerged, proponents stressed that capitalism is a criminogenic system and that lower-class criminals must be understood in context. This occasionally resulted in exaggerated claims regarding the "evil nature" of capitalism and the "good nature" of street criminals. Left realists are comfortable with the basic theoretical structure of Marxist criminology, but they are uncomfortable with unfounded or exaggerated empirical claims. They specifically reject the claim that capitalist economic conditions produce *all* crime and the notion that muggers, rapists, and murderers are political criminals. Instead, left realists seek to "take crime seriously" and "take crime control seriously."[116] Roger Matthews argues that this means in particular that crime "has a negative effect upon the cohesion and the quality of life of communities—urban communities in particular. It impacts disproportionately upon the powerless. . . ."[117]

According to sociologists Martin Schwartz and Walter DeKeseredy, left realist criminology is particularly concerned with the harmful effects of crime on the lower class.[118] Marxist criminologists, they argue, have focused almost entirely on the crimes of the powerful, to the near exclusion of street crime. Left realists want a balanced orientation to crime and they advocate realistic criminal justice measures. Thinking that Marxist policy proposals are unlikely to be adopted, left realists support humane criminal justice policies that have a reasonable chance of implementation (community policing, community corrections). In short, left realism is idealistic in theory, but practical in terms of policy orientation.

Peacemaking Criminology

Harold Pepinsky ties peacemaking criminology to three traditions of thought: religious, feminist, and critical.[119] In describing the core components of peacemaking criminology, Richard Quinney offers several "elementary observations," which can be summarized and paraphrased in the following four points:

1. **Human existence is characterized by suffering.**
2. **The source of suffering lies within each of us.**
3. **Through love and compassion, beyond the ego-centric self, we can end suffering.**
4. **Crime is ended only when suffering ends; peace is obtained through love and compassion which enable understanding, service and justice.**[120]

Quinney's program has much in common with Buddhist thought. The Buddha's "Four Noble Truths" are: (1) life is suffering; (2) the cause of suffering is individual desire; (3) the cure for suffering lies in defeating ego-centric cravings; and (4) treatment of human misery lies in accepting the eightfold path that enables a person to overcome delusion, craving, and hostility.[121] As Pepinsky states, Quinney does not endorse Buddhism, he is simply "talking about Buddhist insight into universal human experience."[122]

Quinney also distinguishes between **negative peace** and **positive peace.** The present criminal justice system seeks a negative peace because it is a peace based on force, whereas a positive peace is founded on minimizing or eliminating exploitative social conditions such as poverty, inequality, racism, and alienation.[123] Quinney states: "There can be no peace—no positive peace—without social justice. Without social justice and without peace (personal and social) there is crime."[124]

As a philosophical orientation, many criminologists find value in peacemaking criminology. Although most of the champions of this perspective have come out of a Marxist tradition, peacemaking criminology represents a view of life that is centuries old and, to some extent, cuts across ideological barriers. For example, Francis Cullen's call for a "social support paradigm" represents a "main-

stream" criminology proposal that has much in common with the peacemaking perspective.[125] As a scientific enterprise, however, peacemaking criminology is less impressive. Further, the proponents of this perspective have "little to say about *how* the grandscale changes they propose might be achieved."[126] Despite these difficulties, many feel that peacemaking criminology makes so much intuitive sense that it is likely to become more popular and influential in the future.

Postmodern Criminology

Postmodernism has been called "one of the most important multidisciplinary intellectual developments in recent years."[127] Although postmodern thought has appeared in many disciplines, including criminology, it has no precise or unified meaning.[128] This qualification notwithstanding, most postmodernists agree on three basic points: (1) rejection of all overarching explanatory systems; (2) rejection of the idea that definite and sure knowledge is possible; and (3) rejection of the assumption that knowledge claims are value-neutral.[129]

General explanations characterize much of criminological thought. Classical theory, positivism, and Marxism are three examples. Postmodern criminology rejects all "totalizing" theories. Crime is seen as too diverse to be explained by any one theory. Postmodern criminology also rejects the notion that the scientific method is the *only* pathway to understanding crime. Instead, it is argued that science does not merit privileged status as an all-encompassing explanatory system; it is just one of many possible and legitimate methods of understanding in social life. Criminologist T.R. Young puts it this way: "It is not that modern science and its project is to be rejected; only that it is to reserve its claims to those very simple, natural and social systems which behave linearly and predictably."[130] Finally, postmodern criminologists view knowledge claims as more closely linked to power than truth.[131] This is a recognition that what society "knows" about crime is a product of the socially and politically dominant mode of discourse.

Postmodern criminology is just beginning to take shape. Postmodernists argue that the explanations of crime advanced by modern science are theoretical fabrications that do not necessarily account for actual behavior. This perspective is still very much a work in progress.

Critique

Adequacy

The strain theory of crime is plausible. When Merton advanced his formulation in 1938, it was greeted as a tremendous theoretical advancement. Here, finally, was a macro-level sociological explanation of deviance and crime. Strain theory has remained popular ever since. Recently, dissatisfaction with financial status (strain) has been found to be positively associated with both income-generating crime and drug use.[132] Over the years, however, empirical support for the theory has been mixed.[133] For example, while most versions of strain theory predict that those with fewer opportunities (members of the lower class) will have higher rates of crime and delinquency, research findings on this issue have been contradictory. Police statistics have supported the strain theory prediction, whereas self-report studies tend to find little difference in crime rates between classes.[134] Agnew's general strain theory may prove more promising, but it has yet to be tested extensively.

The Marxist theory of crime provides an account of crime that is unique, powerful, and controversial. Most sociological theories of crime identify a specific social entity as criminogenic (families, gangs, neighborhoods). Marxist theory indicts capitalist society as a whole. There is considerable support for the theoretical contention that capitalist structures produce crime. Many mainstream criminologists accept Marxist claims that laws tend to favor the powerful in society; that crime is defined in ways that disadvantage the poor; that most prison inmates come from the lower class; and that corporations commit the most harmful crimes in society. At the same time, there is little support within academic criminology for claims suggesting that street criminals are political rebels, that prisons serve no useful purpose, and that crime will cease when capitalism is abolished; these too are positions advanced by Marxist criminologists at one time or another.

The Marxist explanation of crime has been widely criticized as "passionate political diatribe" rather than scientific theory.[135] Many further contend that Marxist criminology has not garnered sufficient empirical support for its propositions.[136] These challenges are legitimate. However, all theories of crime are vulnerable, to one degree or another, to the same objections. Despite some glaring shortcomings, Marxist criminology has made fundamental contributions to our current understanding of crime and criminal justice.

Feminist theories of crime also have general plausibility. True, some feminist accounts are mutually exclusive, and a few radical feminist theories have been discredited or dismissed (for example, the theory that all violence against women is linked to heterosexuality[137]). Nonetheless, the basic feminist argument that patriarchy affects all aspects of crime is tenable. Just how patriarchal structures encourage or discourage crime commission remains a topic for empirical research. Particular patterns of male and female crime must be linked by empirical evidence to specific forms of patriarchal structure. As noted by criminologist Ronald Akers, this has yet to be done:

"Feminist theory is still in formation, and the paucity of direct tests of its hypothesis have not yet provided a clear evaluation of its empirical validity."[138] Nevertheless, research on this perspective holds great potential. It is likely that in the next decade researchers will conduct many empirical tests of the feminist perspective on crime.

Comprehensive Nature

Most strain theory formulations do not provide a comprehensive explanation of crime. Rather, it is clearly the case that strain theories focus on members of the lower class, minorities, and males. In Merton's original account, adult lower-class males are conceptualized as the most likely victims of social structural strain, for they are the ones who experience the greatest gap between expectations and realizations. The theory is ill-equipped to explain middle- and upper-class crime, not to mention female crime. Recent revisions of the strain perspective have broadened the scope of the theory, but it remains, fundamentally, a theory explaining the behavior of lower-class males.

A strong suit of Marxist criminology is that it presents a comprehensive explanation of crime. Both crimes of the upper class and crimes of the lower class are explained with reference to capitalist structures. In each case, criminal activities are viewed as reasonable adaptations to structural realities. There is also an effort by Marxist criminologists to explain crimes against property and crimes against person. Stealing is stimulated because of basic economic inequalities, and murder, rape, and assault are linked to the brutalizing and dehumanizing conditions of capitalism. Even age and race are accounted for; Marxist criminologists argue that juveniles and minorities have high rates of criminal justice system involvement because they are regarded as "problem populations."[139] Finally, unlike most mainstream theories of crime, Marxist criminology has offered explanations of female involvement in crime.[140]

Although there is no unified feminist theory of crime, much has been written about male violence—particularly male violence against women. There have also been numerous theoretical attempts to explain various forms of female involvement in crime. Currently, there is a need for further research exploring the relationship between crime and variables such as class, race, and age. Feminist formulations do not yet offer a comprehensive explanation of crime.

Current Appeal

Strain theory has been a very popular theory of deviance and crime for many decades. It is likely that the theory will continue to be revised and applied to a wider variety of social contexts. The fact that strain theory holds out the promise of integrating macro-level structural forces and individual decisionmaking is a strength that few theoretical perspectives enjoy. For it to truly endure, however, strain theorists will have to find a convincing way of expanding the theory to incorporate female offenders and members of the upper class who commit crimes.

Marxist criminologists have often been at odds with mainstream criminology. Consider, for example, opinions expressed by T.R. Young:

> **American criminology is a disgrace to the good name of social science . . . It has all the critical and theoretical elegance of a school for morticians. . . . It is a pathetic apology for the status quo and a disreputable discipline on the take from the state. It should be banned from all respectable universities or at least placed on probation until it gets its theoretical house in decent repair.**[141]

Young held these views in the mid-1980s, and at that time many criminologists might have felt similarly. Whether Marxist-oriented criminologists still feel this way is an open question. Because of criminologists such as Young, mainstream criminology is different today; it has embraced many of the insights advanced by proponents of the Marxist perspective. Nevertheless, the appeal of Marxist criminology may have peaked.[142] Applied criminologists have never been attracted to Marxist thought, and now many former proponents have embraced alternative perspectives such as feminist criminology and peacemaking criminology. International developments, particularly the collapse of nearly all communistic societies, combined with the ascendancy of conservative ideology in the United States, have weakened the position of Marxist theory in all academic disciplines, including criminology.

Crime theorist Don Gibbons states that feminist criminology has already "made significant contributions to the field of criminology, and will continue to flourish in the future."[143] In their book *Theories of Crime,* Daniel Curran and Claire Renzetti predict that feminist criminology "will undoubtedly play a major role in mapping the future direction of the discipline."[144] Feminist research has corrected the most glaring flaw of traditional criminological theory—the omission of women. Feminist theory devotes attention to women offenders and women victims. Also spotlighted by feminist theory is the enduring influence of gender relations and patriarchal structures. It is probable that these issues will become even more prominent topics of research in the years ahead.

Summary

In this chapter we have examined three important macro level theories of crime. Merton's strain theory links deviance and crime to macro structure inequalities. Marxist criminology argues that capitalist structures are responsible for virtually all crime in society. And, finally, feminist perspectives on crime highlight gender as a key component of crime perpetration and crime victimization.

This chapter concludes the theory section of the book. At this point it should be apparent that no single theory is definitive. All of the theories have strengths and shortcomings. We can be sure that theorizing will continue to be a pre-eminent enterprise within criminology. Without sound theory, there is little that criminologists or policymakers can say or do about crime.

Critical Thinking Questions

1. Are poor people more likely to commit crimes? Consider how strain theorists and Marxist criminologists would respond to this question.
2. What are the major claims of feminist criminology? How could these be proven?
3. What are the strengths and weaknesses of macro theories of crime?
4. Do you think that peacemaking criminology will one day become the dominant theoretical perspective in the field? Why or why not?

Suggested Readings

Robert Agnew, Francis T. Cullen, Velmer S. Burton Jr., T. David Evans, and R. Gregory Dunaway, "A New Test of Classic Strain Theory," *Justice Quarterly 13* (1996) 681–704.

Kathleen Daly and Meda Chesney-Lind, "Feminism and Criminology," *Justice Quarterly 5* (1988) 497–538.

David Friedrichs, "Peacemaking Criminology and the Punitive Conundrum: A New Foundation for Social Control in the Twenty-First Century," in *Punishment: Social Control and Coercion,* ed. Christine Sistare (New York: Peter Lang, 1996) 29–54.

Robert Merton, "Social Structure and Anomie," *American Sociological Review 3* (1938) 672–82.

Richard Quinney, *Class, State, and Crime* (New York: Longman, 1977).

Notes

[1] Matthew Cooper, "Marv Goes to the Showers," *Newsweek,* 6 October 1997, 40.
[2] Amitai Etzioni, *The Spirit of Community* (New York: Crown, 1993).
[3] Martin Luther King, Jr., *Why We Can't Wait* (New York: American Library, 1964) 80.
[4] Barbara Salert and John Sprague, *The Dynamics of Riots* (Ann Arbor, MI: The University Consortium for Political and Social Research, 1980).
[5] Betty Friedan, *The Feminine Mystique* (New York: Norton, 1963).
[6] Janet Chafetz and Anthony Dworkin, *Female Revolt: Women's Movements in World and Historical Perspective* (New York: Rowman & Allanheld, 1986).
[7] Beth Rubin, *Shifts in the Social Contract: Understanding Change in American Society* (Thousand Oaks, CA: Pine Forge, 1996) 102.

8 C. Wright Mills, *The Sociological Imagination* (London: Oxford University Press, 1959).

9 Irving Louis Horowitz, *The New Sociology* (London: Oxford University Press, 1964).

10 Ibid., 21, 23.

11 Emile Durkheim, *The Division of Labor in Society*, tr. George Simpson (New York: Free Press, 1965 [orig. pub. 1893]).

12 Robert Merton, "Social Structure and Anomie," *American Sociological Review 3* (1938) 672–82.

13 Ibid., 677.

14 Ibid.

15 Ibid.

16 Ibid., 672.

17 Ibid.

18 Ibid.

19 Austin Turk, *Criminality and Legal Order* (Chicago: Rand McNally, 1970); Richard Quinney, *The Social Reality of Crime* (Boston: Little, Brown, 1970); William Chambliss and Robert Seidman, *Law, Order and Power* (Reading, MA: Addison-Wesley, 1971).

20 Turk, *Criminality and Legal Order*, 10.

21 Willem Bonger, *Criminality and Economic Conditions* (Boston: Little, Brown, 1916 [orig. pub. 1905]).

22 Robert Bohm, "Beyond Employment: Toward a Radical Solution to the Problem," *Crime and Social Justice 21, 22* (1982) 213–22, 220.

23 David Gordon, "Capitalism, Class and Crime in America," *Crime and Delinquency 19* (1973) 163–86, 163.

24 Richard Quinney, *Class, State and Crime* (New York: Longman, 1977).

25 William Chambliss, *On The Take: From Petty Crooks to Presidents* (Bloomington, IN: Indiana University Press, 1988).

26 T.R. Young, "Crime and Capitalism," in *The Sociology of Human Rights: A Prospectus*, ed. T.R. Young (Livermore, CO: The Red Feather Institute, 1980), 1–15.

27 Stephen Spitzer, "Toward a Marxist Theory of Deviance," *Social Problems 22* (1975) 638–51.

28 Frank Pearce, *Crimes of the Powerful* (London: Pluto Press, 1976).

29 Richard Quinney, *Class, State and Crime*, 44–45.

30 Ibid., 45.

31 Jeffrey Reiman, *The Rich Get Richer and the Poor Get Prison*, 4th ed. (Needham Heights, MA: Allyn & Bacon, 1995), 101.

32 Raymond Michalowski, *Order, Law, and Crime* (New York: Random House, 1985) 21.

33 Stephen Spitzer, "Toward a Marxist Theory of Deviance."

34 Theodore Chiricos and Miriam Delone, "Labor Surplus and Punishment: A Review and Assessment of Theory and Evidence," *Social Problems 39* (1992) 421–46.

35 Karl Marx, *The 18th Brumaire of Louis Bonaparte* (London: International, 1975 [orig. pub. 1852]) 47.

36 Ibid.

37 Karl Marx and Frederick Engels, *The Communist Manifesto* (New York: Appleton-Century-Crofts, 1955 [orig. pub. 1848]) 30.

38 Jeffrey Reiman, *The Rich Get Richer and the Poor Get Prison*, 168–71.

39 Ibid., 171.

40 Susie Bernstein et al., *The Iron Fist and the Velvet Glove*, 2nd ed. (Berkeley, CA: Center for Research on Criminal Justice, 1977).

41 Raymond Michalowski, *Order, Law, and Crime*, 396.

42 Jeffrey Reiman, *The Rich Get Richer and the Poor Get Prison*, 89.

43 Barry Krisberg, *Crime and Privilege* (Englewood Cliffs, NJ: Prentice-Hall, 1975) 2.

44 T.R. Young, "Social Justice vs. Criminal Justice," in *Transforming Sociology Series*, ed. T.R. Young (Livermore, CO: Red Feather Institute, 1984) 1–16.

45 Ibid., 13.

46 Ronald Akers, *Criminological Theories: Introduction and Evaluation* (Los Angeles: Roxbury, 1994) 175; Kathleen Daly and Meda Chesney-Lind, "Feminism and Criminology," *Justice Quarterly 5* (1988) 136–68; Frank Williams III and Marilyn McShane, *Criminological Theory*, 2nd ed. (Englewood Cliffs, NJ: Prentice-Hall, 1994) 235.

47 Gaye Tuchman, "Feminist Theory," in *Encyclopedia of Sociology*, ed. Edgar Borgatta and Marie Borgatta (New York: Macmillan, 1992) 695–704, 695.

48 Kathleen Daly and Meda Chesney-Lind, "Feminism and Criminology," *Justice Quarterly 5* (1988) 497–538, 501; Sally Simpson, "Feminist Theory, Crime, and Justice," *Criminology 27* (1989) 605–631, 606; Daniel Curran and Claire Renzetti, *Theories of Crime* (Boston: Allyn & Bacon, 1994) 271.

49 Sally Simpson, "Feminist Theory, Crime, and Justice," 607.

50 Kathleen Daly and Meda Chesney-Lind, "Feminism and Criminology," 507.

51 Rita Simon, *Women and Crime* (Lexington, MA: DC Heath, 1975).

52 Freda Adler, *Sisters in Crime: The Rise of the New Female Offender* (New York: McGraw-Hill, 1975).

53 Julia and Herman Schwendinger, *Rape and Inequality* (Beverly Hills: Sage, 1983).

54 Polly Radosh, "Women and Crime in the United States: A Marxian Explanation," *Sociological Spectrum 10* (1990) 105–131.

55 James Messerschmidt, *Masculinities and Crimes: Critique and Reconceptualization of Theory* (Lanham, MD: Rowman & Littlefield, 1993) 31.

56 Susan Griffin, "Rape: The All-American Crime," *Ramparts 10* (1971) 26–35.

57 Susan Brownmiller, *Against Our Will: Men, Women and Rape* (New York: Simon & Schuster, 1975).

58 Ibid., 15.

59 James Messerschmidt, *Masculinities and Crimes: Critique and Reconceptualization of Theory*, 39.

60 Catherine MacKinnon, *Toward a Feminist Theory of the State* (Cambridge, MA: Harvard University Press, 1989) 131, 172–74.

61 James Messerschmidt, *Capitalism, Patriarchy, and Crime: Toward a Socialist Feminist Criminology* (Totowa, NJ: Rowman and Littlefield, 1986).

62 James Messerschmidt, *Masculinities and Crimes: Critique and Reconceptualization of Theory*, 56.

63 Ibid., 29.

64 Ibid., 2.

65 Ibid., 6–9.

66 Polly Radosh, "Women and Crime in the United States: A Marxian Explanation," 108.

67 Daly and Chesney-Lind, "Feminism and Criminology," 514.

68 Ibid., 519.

69 Sally Simpson, "Caste, Class, and Violent Crime: Explaining Difference In Female Offending," *Criminology 29* (1991) 115–35, 115.

70 Polly Radosh, "Social Character, Cultural Forces, and the Importance of Love: Erich Fromm's Theories Applied to Patterns of Crime." Paper presented at the meeting of the American Society of Criminology, Boston, November, 1995, p. 14.

71 James Messerschmidt, *Masculinities and Crimes: Critique and Reconceptualization of Theory*, 39.

72 Janet Katz and William Chambliss, "Biology and Crime," in *Criminology: A Contemporary Handbook*, ed. Joseph Sheley (Belmont, CA: Wadsworth, 1995), 275–303.

73 Shirley Weitz, *Sex Roles: Biological, Psychological, and Social Foundations* (New York: Oxford University Press, 1977) 60–110.

74 Talcott Parsons, "Age and Sex in the Social Structure of the United States," *American Sociological Review 7* (1942) 604–616, 605.

75 Sara Ruddick, *Maternal Thinking: Toward a Politics of Peace* (Boston: Beacon, 1989).

76 Nancy Chodorow, *Reproduction of Mothering: Psychoanalysis and the Sociology of Gender* (Berkeley: University of California Press, 1978).

77 Otto Pollack, *The Criminality of Women* (Philadelphia: University of Pennsylvania Press, 1961).

78 See, for example, Gail Armstrong, "Females Under the Law: 'Protected' but Unequal," in *The Criminal Justice System and Women: Women Offenders, Victims, Workers*, ed. Barbara Raffel Price and Natalie J. Sokoloff (New York: Clark Boardmann, 1982) 61–76; Kathleen Daly, *Gender, Crime, and Punishment* (New Haven: Yale University Press, 1994); Candace Kruttschnitt and Donald E. Green, "The Sex-Sanctioning Issue: Is It History?" *American Sociological Review 49* (1984) 541–51.

79 Kathleen Daly and Meda Chesney-Lind, "Feminism and Criminology," 525.

80 Albert Cohen, "The Sociology of the Deviant Act: Anomie Theory and Beyond," *American Sociological Review 30* (1965) 5–14, 6.

81 Robert Merton, "Anomie, Anomia, and Social Interactions: Contexts of Deviant Behavior," in *Anomie and Deviant Behavior*, ed. Marshall Clinard (Glencoe, IL: Free Press, 1964) 213–42, 231.

82 Ibid.

83 Robert Merton, *Social Theory and Social Structure* (Glencoe, IL: Free Press, 1957) 163.

84 Edwin Lemert, "Social Structure, Social Control, and Deviation," in *Anomie and Deviant Behavior*, ed. Marshall Clinard (Glencoe, IL: Free Press, 1964), 57–97, 68–70.

85 Hermann Mannheim, *Comparative Criminology* (Boston: Houghton Mifflin, 1967) 504; Michael Phillipson, *Understanding Crime and Delinquency* (Chicago: Aldine, 1974) 150–51.

86 Marshall Clinard, *Anomie and Deviant Behavior* (New York: Free Press, 1964) 16.

87 See Joseph O'Malley, "History and Man's 'Nature' in Marx," *The Review of Politics 28* (1966) 508–527.

88 Karl Marx, *Early Writings*, tr. and ed. Tom Bottomore (New York: McGraw-Hill, 1964 [orig. pub. 1843–44]) 127.

89 Schlomo Avineri, *The Social and Political Thought of Karl Marx* (London: Cambridge University Press, 1976) 66–75.

[90] Karl Marx, *The Poverty of Philosophy* (New York: International, 1975 [orig. pub. 1847]) 109.

[91] Richard Quinney, "A Conception of Man and Society for Sociology," *The Sociological Quarterly 6* (1965) 119–27, 124.

[92] Richard Quinney, *Class, State and Crime*, 59.

[93] Mark Liddle, "Feminist Contributions to an Understanding of Violence Against Women—Three Steps Forward, Two Steps Back," *Canadian Review of Sociology and Anthropology 26* (1989) 759–75, 762.

[94] Tim Carrigan, Bob Connell, and John Lee, "Hard and Heavy: Toward a New Sociology of Masculinity," in *Beyond Patriarchy: Essays by Men on Pleasure, Power and Change*, ed. Michael Kaufman (New York: Oxford, 1987) 139–92.

[95] Frank Williams III and Marilyn McShane, *Criminological Theory*, 98.

[96] J. Robert Lilly, Francis Cullen, and Richard Ball, *Criminological Theory: Context and Consequences* (Newbury Park, CA: Sage, 1989) 78–80.

[97] Clemens Bartollas, *Juvenile Delinquency*, 2nd ed. (New York: Macmillan, 1990) 351.

[98] Frank Williams III and Marilyn McShane, *Criminological Theory*, 98.

[99] John Conklin, *Criminology* (New York: Macmillan, 1986) 460; Brendan Maguire, "The Applied Dimension of Radical Criminology: A Survey of Prominent Radical Criminologists," *Sociological Spectrum 8* (1988) 133–51.

[100] Raymond Michalowski, "Crime Control in the 1980s: A Progressive Agenda," *Crime and Social Justice*, (Summer 1983) 13–23, 13.

[101] Ibid.

[102] Robert Bohm, "Criminology's Proper Role—A Rejoinder," *The Criminologist 10* (1985) 4–8, 4.

[103] T.R. Young, "Social Justice vs. Criminal Justice," 12.

[104] Patricia Smith, *Feminist Jurisprudence*, 9.

[105] June Stephenson, *Men Are Not Cost Effective* (New York: HarperCollins, 1995).

[106] Catherine MacKinnon, "Toward Feminist Jurisprudence," in *Feminist Jurisprudence*, ed. Patricia Smith (New York: Oxford University Press, 1993), 610–19, 611.

[107] James Messerschmidt, *Masculinities and Crimes: Critique and Reconceptualization of Theory*, 45–50.

[108] Albert Cohen, *Delinquent Boys* (New York: Free Press, 1995).

[109] Ibid., 157.

[110] Richard Cloward and Lloyd Ohlin, *Delinquency and Opportunity* (New York: Free Press, 1960).

[111] Ibid., 33.

[112] Robert Agnew, "Foundation for a General Strain Theory of Crime and Delinquency," *Criminology 30* (1992) 47–87.

[113] Robert Agnew, "Strain and Subcultural Theories of Criminality," in *Criminology*, ed. Joseph Sheley (Belmont, CA: Wadsworth, 1995) 305–327, 314.

[114] Ibid., 315.

[115] Don Gibbons, *Talking About Crime and Criminals* (Englewood Cliffs, NJ: Prentice-Hall, 1994), 112.

[116] See Jock Young and Roger Matthews, eds., *Rethinking Criminology: The Realist Debate* (Newbury Park, CA: Sage, 1992); John Lea and Jock Young, *What Is To Be Done About Law and Order?* (New York: Penguin, 1984); John Lea and Jock Young, "A Realistic Approach to Law and Order," in *The Political Economy of Crime: Readings for a Critical Criminology*, ed. Brian MacLean (Englewood Cliffs, NJ: Prentice-Hall, 1986) 358–64; Roger Matthews, "Taking Realist Criminology Seriously," *Contemporary Crisis 11* (1987) 371–401.

[117] Roger Mattthews, "Taking Realist Criminology Seriously," 373.

[118] Martin Schwartz and Walter DeKeseredy, "Left Realist Criminology: Strengths, Weaknesses and the Feminist Critique," *Crime, Law and Social Change 15* (1991) 51–72.

[119] Harold Pepinsky, "Peacemaking in Criminology and Criminal Justice," in *Criminology as Peacemaking*, ed. Harold Pepinsky and Richard Quinney (Bloomington, IN: Indiana University Press, 1991) 299–327, 299.

[120] Richard Quinney, "The Way of Peace," in *Criminology as Peacemaking*, ed. Harold Pepinsky and Richard Quinney (Bloomington, IN: Indiana University Press, 1991), 3–13, 3–4.

[121] See Huston Smith, *The Religions of Man* (New York: Harper & Row, 1965), 109–123.

[122] Harold Pepinsky, "Peacemaking in Criminology and Criminal Justice," 303.

[123] Richard Quinney, "Socialist Humanism and Critical/Peacemaking Criminology: The Continuing Project." Paper presented at the annual meeting of the American Society of Criminology, Boston, November 1995.

[124] Richard Quinney, "Socialist Humanism and Critical/Peacemaking Criminology: The Continuing Project," 6–7.

[125] Francis Cullen, "Social Support As an Organizing Concept for Criminology: Presidential Address to the Academy of Criminal Justice Sciences," *Justice Quarterly 11* (1994) 527–59.

[126] Don Gibbons, *Talking About Crime and Criminals*, 172.

[127] George Ritzer, *Contemporary Sociological Theory*, 3rd ed. (New York: McGraw-Hill, 1992) 493.

[128] Douglas Kellner, "The Postmodern Turn: Positions, Problems, and Prospects," in *Frontiers of Social Theory: The New Synthesis*, ed. George Ritzer (New York: Columbia University Press, 1990) 255–86, 257.

[129] Pauline Rosenau, *Postmodernism and the Social Sciences* (Princeton: Princeton University Press, 1992).

[130] T. R. Young, "Chaos Theory and Human Agency: Humanist Sociology in a Postmodern Era," *Humanity & Society 16* (1992) 441–60, 443.

[131] Ibid., 445.

[132] Robert Agnew, Francis T. Cullen, Velmer S. Burton Jr., T. David Evans, and R. Gregory Dunaway, "A New Test of Classic Strain Theory," *Justice Quarterly 13* (1996) 681–704.

[133] Robert Agnew, "Strain and Subcultural Theories of Criminality," 315.

[134] Ronald Akers, *Criminological Theories: Introduction and Evaluation*, 150–51.

[135] Mary Marzotto, Tony Platt, and Annika Snare, "A Reply to Turk," *Crime and Social Justice* (Fall-Winter 1975) 43–45, 43.

[136] Ronald Akers, *Criminological Theories: Introduction and Evaluation*, 36–39.

[137] See James Messerschmidt, *Masculinities and Crimes: Critique and Reconceptualization of Theory*, 43.

[138] Ronald Akers, *Criminological Theories: Introduction and Evaluation*, 178.

[139] Steven Spitzer, "Towards a Marxian Theory of Deviance," *Social Problems 22* (1975) 638–51.

[140] See Polly Radosh, "Women and Crime in the United States: A Marxian Explanation."

[141] T.R. Young, "Social Justice vs. Criminal Justice," 4, 12, 13.

[142] Don Gibbons, *Talking About Crime and Criminals*, 41.

[143] Ibid., 168.

[144] Daniel Curran and Claire Renzetti, *Theories of Crime*, 277.

part 5

The Criminal Justice System

CHAPTERS 14 THROUGH 17 present an introduction to the criminal justice system. The primary focus of this section is on the police, courts, and corrections, as they respond to crime in the United States. The themes that recurred throughout this text—race, gender, age, and social class—are all evident in the criminal justice system. Each of the following chapters reviews important historical information about the components of the criminal justice system, along with their costs, issues, trends, and current problems.

Chapter 14 presents the various types of policing in the United States today. Contemporary changes in the functions of the police are juxtaposed against their historical roles. The chapter examines emerging trends, such as community policing, that are designed to meet the demands of modern society.

Chapter 15 reviews the many layers of courts in the United States. It presents types of law, distinctions among courts, sentencing issues, and contemporary problems. It examines the current tendency to use the courts to solve social problems, a phenomenon unique to the United States. Issues that are often addressed through public agencies in other countries, such as drug addiction, are mediated through the U.S. courts. This can have the effect of criminalizing behavior that might be better dealt with in other ways. As you read through the chapter, look for issues you think might be more appropriately dealt with in other than legal ways.

Both Chapters 16 and 17 examine the U.S. system of corrections. They trace the historical development of philosophies of punishment, sentencing strategies, and modern trends in corrections. Many of the trends in modern corrections are related to an expansion of incarceration; modern use of prisons has grown beyond all historical or cross-cultural comparison. The impact of growth in prisons is discussed from several perspectives.

For updated information on the criminal justice system, consult the Wadsworth web site at http://www.wadsworth.com/cj.html

Police

CHAPTER OUTLINE

HISTORY OF POLICING
  Early English Society
  Colonial America
  The Professionalization of Policing: London's Constabulary
  American Police Expansion in Mid-Nineteenth Century
  Reforms of the 1930s to 1940s
COSTS
TYPES OF POLICE
  Federal Police
  State Law-Enforcement Agencies
  Local Police
  Campus Police
  Private Police
CURRENT ISSUES AND TRENDS
  Functions of the Police
  Police Recruitment
  Community Policing
  Women in Policing
CURRENT PROBLEMS
  Manning's "Mission Impossible" Thesis
  Professionalism vs. Bureaucratization
  Functional Awkwardness
  Police Misconduct
  Public Relations
SUMMARY

KEY TERMS

frankpledge system
hue and cry
shire reeve
constable
watch/ward system
dangerous class
professional standards
highway patrol
state police
sworn officers
municipal police
county police
proprietary security
contractual services
bureaucratic and clerical duties
patrol
community service
order keeping
broken windows
law enforcement
community involvement
beat integrity
assignments and situations
mission impossible
police corruption
shakedown/bribery/shopping
police brutality
deadly force
exclusionary rule
Miranda warning

ABOUT 9 P.M. ON SEPTEMBER 26, 1997, 18-year-old Jeremiah Mearday left his home to walk to the drug-store for medicine.[1] He had just suffered an allergic reaction to eating shrimp-fried rice. On his way to the store, he picked up three friends. As the four young black men walked along, a police car suddenly pulled up and two officers charged out of the car, one with his gun drawn. Seconds later, a police officer used his flashlight to crack Mearday's jaw. Mearday ended up so badly beaten that his father did not recognize him. What happened? Mearday claims that he was the victim of an unprovoked police attack. The police say that there was an arrest warrant for one of Mearday's friends and that Mearday tried to obstruct them from taking the person into custody.

Mearday's case is one of about 3000 complaints leveled each year against the Chicago Police Department for use of excessive force. Such cases are incredibly difficult to resolve, but they certainly demonstrate the strain between the public and police. There has always been tension between citizens and police, especially when the citizens are minority-group members. Community relations is just one of many issues addressed in the present chapter. As you read about the police, their history, their job functions, and the problems they confront, shift your perspective back and forth between citizen and police officer. This is a way of seeing what is involved in the policing of society.

History of Policing

The police are one of the most powerful occupational groups in society. This was not always so. In the earliest human societies there were no police; people simply banded together to enforce kinship-based rules.[2] As society evolved, however, state power emerged, and with it came formal police systems.[3] By 1829, with the creation of the London Constabulary, policing became not just formalized but professionalized. The social developments that accounted for the shift from no police to a professional police force are instructive.

Early English Society

Before the Norman Conquest of England in 1066, and for several centuries thereafter, "policing" was a collective enterprise. Police historian T.A. Critchley describes this system of communal responsibility as follows: "If any member of the group committed a crime, the others had to produce him for trial; if they failed to do so they could be fined or called upon to make compensation. . . ."[4] After the Norman Invasion, the **frankpledge system** was formalized. Basically, this meant that each male over age 12 was pledged to and for all other members of the community. Communal responsibility extended to both the detection and apprehension of wrongdoers. Everyone was duty-bound to sound an alert whenever they observed wrongful behavior. Anyone noticing a person stealing a

horse, for instance, was obliged to literally cry out and alert others (the **hue and cry**). Men of the community would then pursue the offender.

The chief law-enforcement officer at this time was the **shire reeve,** or sheriff. This person, appointed by the king, was responsible for keeping the peace in the shire (county). The shire reeve supervised and controlled the activities within the towns of his shire by holding court and, when necessary, organizing and leading a *posse comitatus* (Latin for "power of the county") made up of able-bodied men in the shire.[5] Frequently, in acquiring power and wealth, the shire reeve abused the people under his jurisdiction. Hence, the despicable behavior of the Sheriff of Nottingham, made famous by Robin Hood stories, is grounded more in fact than fiction.[6]

By the end of the twelfth century, the feudal manor emerged as the most significant social-political unit and each feudal estate had a manorial court. Manorial courts elected various officers including the **constable,** a person charged with assisting the lord in monitoring and regulating communal activities.[7] The constable, as the executive agent of the manor, was responsible for the workings of the frankpledge system and the hue and cry. He also submitted periodic reports to the manorial court.

The hue and cry, the constable, and the shire reeve all had one thing in common: they constituted aspects of a *reactive* system. As societies became more complex, and particularly as cities emerged, the inadequacies of a reactive system of policing became apparent. Thus, in the

Ten Significant Events in the Development of the American Police

1631 Boston initiates the first night watch in America.

1801 Boston hires a permanent night watch and pays the men a "generous" fifty cents per night.

1844 New York City combines the day and night force to form the first consolidated police department.

1845 Texas joins the United States, and its Rangers become the first state police, although the force is mainly a border patrol.

1870 U.S. Department of Justice is established.

1893 Chicago policeman's widow, Mrs. Marie Owens, becomes the first female "patrolman" in the United States.

1897 Wichita elects Sam Jones as town marshal, the first African American marshal in the United States.

1961 In the *Mapp v. Ohio* case, the U.S. Supreme Court advanced the "exclusionary rule," which held that illegally obtained evidence was not admissible in court.

1966 In *Miranda v. Arizona,* the U.S. Supreme Court mandated that the police must inform those they arrest of their legal rights.

1969 Law Enforcement Assistance Administration (LEAA) goes into effect, providing millions of dollars for police hardware and training.

SOURCES: William Bopp and Donald Schultz, *A Short History of American Law Enforcement* (Springfield, IL: Charles C Thomas, 1972).

thirteenth century, with passage of the Statute of Winchester (1285), the **watch/ward system** was created.[8] This system was designed to prevent wrongdoing, not just react to it. The watch/ward measure required that the names of all men living in a city be placed on a roster. The roster of names was controlled by the constable (no longer just a manorial agent), who would see to it that the men served regular rotations as watchmen. The watchmen were stationed at city gates and in wards within the city during hours of darkness. The night watch arrested individuals who tried to enter or leave the city during the night as well as anyone who created a disturbance or was suspected of wrongdoing. In the morning, arrestees were turned over to the constable.

Colonial America

With respect to law enforcement, as well as many other social institutions, American colonists were great imitators of the English. In Colonial America, the primary law-enforcement officials were the sheriff, the constable, and the night watch.[9] The sheriff was the most powerful law-enforcement officer because he controlled the civil and criminal matters of the county. In Colonial times, the United States was overwhelmingly rural—so counties, not cities, held most of the population and wealth (Box 14.1). Appointed by the governor of the colony, the sheriff was responsible for investigating crimes, making arrests, serv-ing subpoenas, conducting elections, and collecting various taxes. Sheriffs did not receive a salary, but were compensated by payment of fees for their services, which sometimes proved quite lucrative.[10]

The constable and night watch were the main law-enforcement agents in Colonial towns and cities. The first constable on record was Joshua Pratt of Plymouth Colony (1634).[11] Pratt and subsequent constables carried out a broad range of duties, including keeping the peace, meting out punishments, surveying land, and directing the night watch.[12] The night watch protected the city from crime and fires during hours of darkness. Originally, service on the night watch was a rotating duty of all the men in the community.

Colonial law enforcement left much to be desired. The constable and sheriff carried out various civic duties, but they did little to prevent crime or preserve social order. The night watch was little better. Over the years it became common for affluent men to pay others, often drunks and petty criminals, to take their watch rotations. The result was that night watches were increasingly lazy, incompetent, and corrupt. By the 1830s, it became apparent that the Colonial system of policing was inadequate. Police historian Samuel Walker offers this assessment:

The quality of service provided by the sheriff, the constable, and the watch was extremely poor. Very quickly, inefficiency, corruption, and political

The early London police (bobbies) were charged with preventing crime, even though they carried no guns.

interference emerged as American traditions. There was never a golden age of efficiency and integrity in American law enforcement.[13]

The Professionalization of Policing: London's Constabulary

In 1829, at the urging of British Prime Minister Robert Peel, Parliament passed the London Metropolitan Police Act, which created a full-time day and night police patrol force.[14] The London police, called *bobbies* because of Robert Peel's founding role, began with a force of 1000 men chosen from 12,000 initial applicants.[15] Twelve principles were formulated by Peel that served to guide the organization and operation of the London police. These principles are paraphrased below:

- The police must be organized along military lines.
- The police must be under government control.
- The absence of crime will best prove the efficiency of the police.
- The distribution of crime news is essential.
- Police will be deployed by time and strength.
- Police are to keep perfect command of temper.
- Good appearance commands respect.
- Securing and training proper persons is the key to efficiency.
- Public security demands that every police officer have a number.
- Police headquarters should be centrally located for accessibility.
- Police should be hired on a probationary basis.
- Police record keeping is necessary.[16]

The London model of policing advanced a number of innovations, but two are preeminent. First, Peel insisted that London police officers be hired and promoted with regard to professional qualifications rather than political patronage.[17] Second, the London police were directed to *prevent* crime (note the third principle above). This was no idle directive, for police effectiveness was evaluated on the basis of their crime control mission. In the earliest instructions to the London police, this was made clear: "It should be understood, at the outset, that the principal object to be attained is the 'Prevention of Crime,' . . . The absence of crime will be considered the best proof of the complete efficiency of the Police."

American Police Expansion in Mid-Nineteenth Century

While crime control was the major reason for establishing the London police, many have argued that social upheaval, not crime, led to police expansion and reorganization in the United States. According to various criminologists, the leading factors explaining the emergence of the new, professionalized American police were "urban disorder,"[18] "fear of civil disorder,"[19] "urban mob violence,"[20] and "riots and disorders."[21] What was the cause of the social disorder and upheaval? Walker argues that it was urbanization, industrialization, and immigration.[22] Indeed, many feared these forces would destroy the "American way of life." They believed some type of institutional control was desperately needed; specifically, American cities needed police forces that were organized, efficient, professional, and proactive.

Not all police researchers agree that social disorder, or the threat of it, was responsible for development of the professionalized police in the United States. Some scholars contend that the perceived presence of a **dangerous class** was most significant.[23] According to this view, in each historical city a particular group of people, often an ethnic group such as the Irish or blacks, was identified as a threat to society. The police, as agents of the dominant class, were directed to control the dangerous or powerless class. Focusing principally on Buffalo, Milwaukee, Chicago, Pittsburgh, Cleveland, and Detroit, Sidney Harring concluded that the police in these cities developed as an instrument of class rule.[24] In his study of the historical police in Savannah, Atlanta, and St. Louis, Brendan Maguire found further evidence for the class-control orientation to policing.[25] Maguire argues that nineteenth-century arrest data for these three cities suggest a class bias in law enforcement, with members of the lower class showing the highest rates of arrest. Researcher H. Kenneth Bechtel found that the historical development of the *state* police followed a similar pattern, that is, those in power shaped the early state police forces.[26] Perhaps the most succinct summary of this line of thinking is R.J. Lundman's statement: ". . . elites used their influence to create police who would protect and promote their vested interests."[27]

In reality, it is probable that crime, social disorder, and the threat posed by a perceived "dangerous" class all combined to hasten the formation of a new and expanded police presence. Clearly, crime was an issue of some importance. This view is supported by two prominent police historians, Roger Lane and James Richardson, who chronicled the development of the police in Boston and New York City, respectively.[28] Both Lane and Richardson cite increasing crime and disorder as a motivating force for expanding the police. Historian Erik Monkkonen also argues that police development was tied to crime, disorder, and concern about the dangerous class that included "criminals, paupers, and tramps."[29] More specifically, Monkkonen argues that the main thrust of policing gradually shifted from keeping order to crime control. His research shows that big-city arrest rates for public offenses such as drunkenness and disturbing the peace declined between 1860 and 1920.[30] In summary, the nineteenth-century police sought to control crime, social disorder, and a category of people designated as dangerous.

Reforms of the 1930s to 1940s

Organizational reforms and technological innovations changed the nature of American policing in the 1930s and 1940s. First, in contrast to the famous London model of policing, American police had traditionally been linked to local political machines.[31] This pattern was so pronounced in the nineteenth century that researcher Robert Fogelson referred to the police as "adjuncts of the machine."[32] Local politicians often had control over police hirings, salaries, and duties. This type of political power was anathema to national police leaders such as August Vollmer, police chief of Berkeley, California, and O. W. Wil-

son, Wichita, Kansas, police chief. These men attempted to replace political cronyism with **professional standards.** Vollmer hired college graduates, developed entrance tests, established a police training school, and sought to make crime fighting a scientific enterprise.[33] In capsule form, here is Vollmer's reform plan:

> **. . . raise the educational and intellectual standard of our police departments, elevate the position of the policeman to that of a profession, eliminate politics entirely from the force, and secure the people's confidence, sympathy, respect, and cooperation.**[34]

A second police reform had to do with establishing crime fighting as the preeminent police function. In part this was prompted by the emergence of the Uniform Crime Reports (UCR). The publication of yearly crime statistics meant that the police would be evaluated on the basis of crime rate trends. In order to appear effective, the police had to make sure crime rates did not soar. This required extensive crime control activities on the part of the police. Furthermore, leaders such as Vollmer and Wilson viewed crime fighting as the singular professional duty of the police. Wilson was so committed to crime fighting that he agreed to a substantial salary reduction (that was never restored) to help pay for squad car radio systems.[35]

Technological innovations led to a third set of reforms. In the 1930s and 1940s, squad cars, radio systems, and telephones began to have a profound impact on the nature of policing. Squad cars enabled the police to cover more territory. Before the widespread use of automobiles, police spent most of their patrol time on "Main Street." Police cars meant rapid transportation and this allowed the police to patrol outlying areas. Of course, putting officers into cars had the effect of taking the police off the street, away from people and their everyday concerns, but this was compensated by the increasing accessibility of telephones. Citizens began to use the telephone to call the police for a variety of services. It was easy and effective. While the use of squad cars reduced the number of officers walking beats, cars, telephones, and radios had the effect of putting the police anywhere quickly. Often, the police were called to citizens' homes and apartments, and that meant police now had more intimate, face-to-face contact with ordinary citizens than ever before.

Costs

The financial cost of law enforcement in the United States is difficult to estimate with precision. While financial figures exist at local and state levels, aggregate national data are less common. Further, the available cost calculations are dated; there is considerable lag time before expenditures are published and disseminated. Despite these problems, it is possible to offer some rough cost estimates. Government data show that the total justice system expenditures for 1992 were approximately $94 billion. This includes money spent at the federal, state, and local levels for police ($41 billion), corrections ($31 billion), and the judicial system ($21 billion).[36] The police category is the costliest component of the entire justice system, and most of the bill for law enforcement is borne at the local level. In fact, counties and municipalities pay 72 percent of the cost of policing in the United States.[37]

Spending $41 billion a year on the police is a substantial financial commitment. What does this huge sum of money buy? Simply put, it pays for almost 1 million law-enforcement employees—68,825 federal officers and 841,099 state and local police personnel.[38] These officers engage in a wide variety of duties and perform numerous services.

The total financial cost of policing society can be seen as staggering. Americans might wonder why it is necessary to spend so much on the police. There is another way of assessing the cost, however. For example, if the price of policing is calculated on a per capita basis, we find that police protection costs about $136 dollars for every man, woman, and child in the United States.[39] Of course, this figure varies by state. People living in Alaska, California, and New York pay more than $190 per capita per year, while individuals living in Arkansas, Indiana, Kansas, Mississippi, South Dakota, and West Virginia pay less than $80 per year for their police. In any event, if individuals were asked whether it was worth $136 (the national average) a year to them to have a local police force, many would probably answer yes.

It should also be noted that police protection costs far less than many other governmental programs and services. For example, Americans spend more than twelve times as much on national defense, more than six times as much on federal-debt interest payments, and more than four times as much on public welfare.[40] What is more, compared to other components of the justice system (the judiciary and corrections), police costs have shown the slowest increase in expenditures.[41]

Types of Police

Federal Police

The oldest federal police force is the United States Coast Guard (USCG), and the most famous federal police force is the Federal Bureau of Investigation (FBI). The USCG was created in 1790, when Congress authorized funds to build ten boats for a "Revenue Cutter Service."[42] At this time, Alexander Hamilton, secretary of the U.S. Treasury Department, argued that goods were being smuggled into the country to avoid paying taxes set by the Tariff Act of 1789. The early Coast Guard patrolled the waters off ports stretching from New England to Georgia in order to ensure that ships paid import tariffs and tonnage dues.[43] Hence, the first federal police in the United States was an ocean patrol. Currently, one of the most publicized functions of the USCG is the interdiction of drugs.

The FBI is by far the most prominent federal police force. This agency was established at the urging of President Theodore Roosevelt in 1908 as the Bureau of Investigations. Roosevelt thought that a special investigative agency was needed to combat government corruption and corporate violations of the Antitrust Act.[44] Unfortunately, the Bureau of Investigations proved to be inefficient and corrupt itself. In 1924, a young government attorney named J. Edgar Hoover was appointed to clean up the Bureau. Hoover remained as director until his death in 1972, by which time the agency had been renamed (in 1935) the Federal Bureau of Investigation. By the 1970s, however, it was discovered that under Hoover the FBI had itself engaged in a wide variety of illegal activities including wiretaps and burglaries.[45] Things were unraveling so fast that at the time of Hoover's death, an admirer said "I think his passing was a godsend, a godsend for him, for the country, for his reputation, and for the Bureau."[46]

Through the years, the FBI has been both a crime-fighting and intelligence-gathering agency. Today the FBI has slightly over 10,000 full-time officers licensed to carry firearms and make arrests.[47] The agency currently has three principle functions. First, it investigates all federal law violations, notably espionage, sabotage, treason, murder of federal officers, mail fraud, bank robberies, kidnappings, interstate transportation of stolen vehicles and property, and civil rights violations. Second, the FBI houses a sophisticated crime laboratory and a vast fingerprint file, both of which aid investigations by state and local police. Third, the FBI processes and publishes annual crime data for the United States.

In addition to the USCG and the FBI, there are some fifty other federal law-enforcement agencies. Table 14.1 provides a listing of the sixteen federal agencies that have 500 or more full-time officers with authority to carry firearms and make arrests.

State Law-Enforcement Agencies

Individual states vary considerably in how they enforce state laws, but they generally operate one of the following state law-enforcement agencies:

1. **Highway patrol,** defined as a state agency with "uniformed field patrol [providing] police services restricted to or concentrated on traffic, vehicle, and highway-related activities;"[48]

TABLE 14.1 | Federal Agencies Employing 500 or More Full-Time Officers with Authority to Carry Firearms and Make Arrests, June 1996

AGENCY	NUMBER OF OFFICERS
Immigration and Naturalization Service	12,403
Federal Bureau of Prisons	11,329
Federal Bureau of Investigation	10,389
U.S. Customs Service	9,749
Internal Revenue Service	3,784
U.S. Postal Inspection Service	3,576
U.S. Secret Service	3,185
Drug Enforcement Administration	2,946
Administrative Office of the U.S. Courts	2,777
U.S. Marshals Service	2,650
National Park Service	2,148
Bureau of Alcohol, Tobacco and Firearms	1,869
U.S. Capitol Police	1,031
U.S. Fish and Wildlife Service	869
GSA-Federal Protective Service	643
U.S. Forest Service	619

SOURCE: Brian Reaves, *Federal Law Enforcement Officers, 1996* (Washington, DC: U.S. Department of Justice, 1997) 2.

2. **State police,** defined as "uniformed field patrol responsible for general police services."[49]

More than twenty states have a state police and over twenty states have a highway patrol. Hawaii has neither type of state-wide law-enforcement agency.

Politics is thought to be the decisive factor in explaining the preference for a highway patrol rather than a state police. States in which county sheriffs enjoy substantial political power tend to have a highway patrol, while other states are more likely to have a state police. The difference is that the highway patrol has very focused authority, while the state police has a fuller range of police powers. Interestingly, the first state police, the Texas Rangers, had a narrowly defined job function; it served in the mid-1800s as a Texas/Mexico border patrol.

As of June 1996, there were 83,742 full-time state police employees, of which 54,587 were **sworn officers** (those having full arrest powers) and 29,155 were civilian workers.[50] Typically these law-enforcement personnel regulate traffic, help trace stolen vehicles, assist with crowd control, and aid county and municipal police in a variety of ways.

Local Police

There are 18,769 local law-enforcement agencies.[51] Local police can be categorized as municipal or county. The **municipal police** are the largest and most important sector of policing in the United States. By itself, New York City has 43,976 law-enforcement employees, including 36,813 sworn police officers.[52] Other major American cities employ large forces as well. City police engage in a wide variety of duties and activities, notably crime patrol, crime investigation, traffic control, and crowd control. The police in urban areas tend to be highly specialized. For example, some officers work only on homicide cases, while other police officers might be assigned to a vice squad that enforces laws against drug dealing, gambling, and prostitution. Still other officers might be on traffic detail.

Throughout American history, the municipal police have been intertwined with local politics. In the most blatant cases, local political machines did the hiring and firing of police officers. Today, the municipal police are typically controlled by a popularly elected city mayor. In terms of organization, city police departments are framed around a military command structure with ranks of ascending authority from patrol officer to sergeant to lieutenant to captain to inspector to chief. The police chief answers to the mayor directly and the city council indirectly.

County police (that is, the sheriff's office) are responsible for policing outside of municipal jurisdictions, whether huge cities or little towns. Unlike the municipal police chief, who must answer to the mayor, the sheriff generally answers only to the electorate; in all but two states the sheriff is elected by county voters. The sheriff is the top law-enforcement official in the county, an officer of the court duty-bound to serve warrants and subpoenas, and a corrections officer who maintains a county jail. Historically, especially in the South and West, the position of sheriff has had considerable political power.

Although most police officers serve urban areas, most law-enforcement agencies are rural. Virtually every little town or village has a police department, although in many cases the department might consist of just one person. Rural police officers work under limitations in that the officer-to-citizen ratio is very high, the geographic area is expansive, and the tax base is often too low to support adequate resources and personnel.[53] Despite these difficulties, rural police officers are expected to perform a wide variety of job duties; indeed, rural citizens tend to expect their police to accept a "do-everything" job description.[54] Evidence suggests that city residents also evaluate all police functions as important, although "breaking up gangs" and "drug busts" are seen as most significant in urban areas.[55]

Campus Police

It is generally thought that the first campus police force was established at Yale University in 1894, when rioting broke out between Yale students and the city police.[56] Throughout the first half of the twentieth century, however, campus police were little more than night watchmen charged with protecting university property. It was not until the 1960s that most universities felt the need to have a professionalized police presence. This was brought on by campus unrest over the Vietnam war and a marked increase in crimes such as thefts, assaults, rapes, and drug-related offenses.[57] Today, crime is a major concern on university campuses. It has recently been estimated that one of every three students will be the victim of a campus crime.[58]

A series of lawsuits have sensitized universities to their responsibility for taking appropriate steps to secure a safe environment on campus.[59] To provide a safer environment, universities have expanded programs such as foot patrols, escort services, and dorm alarms.[60] Moreover, in 1992 Congress passed the Crime Awareness and Campus Security Act, which mandated that universities inform current and prospective employees and students about the incidence of campus crime. Hence, campus police are responsible for compiling and providing crime statistics (although it is not required that these data be reported for inclusion in the FBI's yearly national report). Findings suggest that universities have very high rates of property crime but low rates of violent crime.[61] In his study of the two largest universities from each state, researcher Max Bromley found that 98 percent of all reported campus crimes were property offenses.[62]

The most current data available show that there are more than 20,000 full-time university or college law-enforcement employees in the United States.[63] Of this total, slightly over half are sworn officers, with the remainder being civilian employees. Universities vary considerably in how many officers they employ: for example, the University of Florida has 86 officers, while the University of Nebraska at Lincoln has only 24 officers.[64]

Private Police

Allan Pinkerton, Chicago's first police detective, established the Pinkerton Detective Agency in 1850.[65] This agency is considered the first systematic private police group in the United States. The early Pinkertons specialized in apprehending train robbers for railroad companies and protecting company property during labor disputes. In the 1960s and 1970s, with the explosion of crime rates, private policing grew rapidly. Today, private policing tends to take one of two forms: proprietary security or contractual services.[66] **Proprietary security** is defined in terms of an organization's hiring its own employees as guards and investigators, whereas under **contractual services** guards and investigators are provided by private security companies such as the Pinkerton Agency. It has been estimated that there are 1.5 million private police working in the United States at an annual cost of about $52 billion.[67] If these estimates are accurate, it indicates that the number of private police and the budgets for private policing far outstrip comparable figures for the public police. It is worth noting, however, that many public police officers work off-duty hours in private security jobs.

Current Issues and Trends

Functions of the Police

What are the primary functions of the police? This question appears easy to answer, and yet the research literature on policing reveals little agreement. In 1973, The National Advisory Commission of Criminal Justice Standards and Goals concluded that the police have as many as twelve distinct job functions.[68] Some criminologists, however, argue that the police have just one pre-eminent function. For example, Steve Cox and John Wade suggest that the main function of the police is to provide services.[69] Arriving at a different conclusion, Clinton Terry contends that the fundamental purpose of the police is to prevent crime.[70] Offering another view, Geoffrey Alpert and Roger Dunham submit that the patrol function is most important.[71] Finally, Anthony Platt and his associates claim that the "class control function is always the most essential function that the police serve in a capitalist society . . ."[72]

Despite the differences outlined above, it is possible to identify five job functions that command the time and resources of most police departments. These functions are:

- Bureaucratic and clerical duties
- Patrol
- Community service
- Keeping order
- Law enforcement

Little attention is given to the **bureaucratic and clerical duties** of police officers, although these are increasingly important job tasks. Included are such activities as writing reports, discussing criminal cases with prosecutors, and testifying in court. Recording and testifying requires that police officers communicate effectively in both oral and written discourse. With regard to filing reports, the police must record *incident* data (what, where, when); *person* data (who); *property* data (what); and then write a *narrative* (why, how).[73] In the last few years, many police agencies have shifted to phone-in reports or pen-based computerized reporting.[74]

Developing technology makes it even more desirable that police recruits have adequate formal training and education. The accuracy and precision of a police report can be a crucial factor in gaining a criminal conviction. As was made famous in the O.J. Simpson murder trial, police errors in investigation and recording can be influential factors in the jury's consideration of evidence. Though these bureaucratic duties are significant, there is some evidence that police officers do not enjoy these activities as much as other job-related assignments.[75]

Patrol has always been a staple activity of the professionalized police in the United States. Designed to deter

Broken Windows, Computers, and Crime Control

In recent years, crime has declined substantially, particularly in urban areas. For example, the murder rate decreased over 50 percent between 1990 and 1996 in both New York City and Houston. Los Angeles and New Orleans, to cite just two other large cities, have also experienced huge reductions in crime. What accounts for this? Many believe that a change in police tactics is part of the answer. First, the police in these cities have become more focused on the general presentation of the community. The article, "Broken Windows: Police and Neighborhood Safety," has had an influence. This article, written by James Q. Wilson and George Kelling, makes the case that the police must attend to the small things that happen in a community—for example, panhandling and "broken windows." By dealing with minor problems, a signal is sent to potential drug dealers, robbers, and murderers that no

transgressions are tolerated. A second change in police strategy has to do with computers. In New York City and New Orleans, police have used computers to analyze block-by-block data so that crime "hot zones" can be identified and flooded with police officers.

In addition to these two new police strategies, it can be said that policing overall has become more aggressive. Proponents rejoice in the fact that crime is going down. Critics contend, however, that, in their zeal to reduce the crime rate, officers have increasingly crossed the line in committing acts of harassment and brutality. As Kelling himself has acknowledged, "there is enormous potential for abuse." Despite this possibility, it is likely that aggressive policing will persist so long as the crime rate continues to drop.

SOURCES: Daniel Pedersen, "'Go Get the Scumbags,'" *Newsweek*, 20 October 1997, 32; Larry Reibstein, "NYPD Black and Blue," *Newsweek*, 2 June 1997, 67–68; James Q. Wilson and George Kelling, "Broken Windows: Police and Neighborhood Safety," *Atlantic Monthly 249* (1982) 29–38.

crime, patrol is by automobile, horse, bicycle, or foot. Historically, foot patrol was dominant. Foot patrol requires that a police officer walk through a particular area, or *beat*. By the middle decades of the twentieth century, motor patrol began to displace foot patrol. While the advantage of foot patrol is that officers are able to establish a personal rapport with community members, the motor patrol enables police officers to cover a large geographic area. This is an important consideration that explains why motor patrol is still common. Nevertheless, with an increasing emphasis on community policing, a topic we will consider shortly, there is movement back to foot patrol.

Patrol can be exciting, boring, and dangerous—all in one shift. Patrol work entails a variety of tasks, including such things as breaking up fights, assisting senior citizens, chasing suspected criminal offenders, giving place and location directions, picking up garbage, making security checks, and applying first aid.[76]

Community service includes such duties as providing direction and information to those who ask for help; assisting motorists; speaking publicly, particularly in schools; rescuing animals; offering referrals to social service agencies; and locating missing persons. It also includes a range of social work activities. Historically, *women* police officers have had particularly high involvement in these assignments.[77] Unlike other police functions, which often create hostile feelings between the police and those with whom they interact, community service activities are almost to-

tally positive in nature. While citizens appreciate these job duties, the police do not always have a high regard for what they feel is social work. Nevertheless, studies have shown that both urban and rural police spend more time doing these tasks than crime control activities.[78]

The **order keeping** function of police work is vital to society. It includes such disparate activities as resolving neighborhood disputes, controlling crowds, regulating traffic, and monitoring the behavior of adolescents. To appreciate how important the order keeping function is, imagine driving away from a professional sports event without police traffic regulation.

Speaking more generally, maintaining order requires that the police do "little things." In a widely cited article titled "Broken Windows: Police and Neighborhood Safety," James Q. Wilson and George Kelling argue that the police must ensure that the quality of life in a neighborhood does not deteriorate.[79] **Broken windows** is a metaphor for community decay (Box 14.2). Kelling contends that increasing numbers of drunks, vagrants, emotionally disturbed persons, panhandlers, and dangerous youth on the street inspire both a disregard for the law and public fear.[80] Symbolically, *broken windows* sends a message that no one cares. To overcome this perception, disregard for the law, and public fear, the police must secure neighborhood order and civility. Many researchers argue that the restoration of order and civility will produce more cooperative relationships between community members.

Primetime Television Police

The television police have been popular for decades. Various types of primetime programs feature police officers and policing. In general, these shows depict the police in stereotypical terms. Traditionally, most television police have been portrayed as exceptionally bright, courageous, and virtuous. Examples are Joe Friday of *Dragnet*, Steve McGarrett of *Hawaii Five-O*, and Lieutenant Columbo of *Columbo*. At the other extreme, some detective programs depict the police as stupid, inflexible, and even corrupt. In these shows the brilliant figure is the detective. In nearly all of the crime/police programs, police work is equated with crime fighting.

This distorted image of the police and what they do has negative consequences. First, this might cause some citizens to expect too much of the real police. Unlike their television counterparts, the real police are not masterminds who always solve the crimes that they investigate. Second, some citizens might evaluate the actual police on the basis of negative depictions. These people might suspect the real police of being lazy, stupid, and corrupt. Furthermore, research reveals that real police do not appreciate the way they are depicted on television. Despite these negative consequences, things will probably not change—primetime programs are likely to favor entertainment value over a regard for accuracy.

SOURCE: Brendan Maguire, "Television Police," in *The Encyclopedia of Police Science*, ed. William G. Bailey (Hamden, CT: Garland, 1995) 758–61.

The **law enforcement** or crime control function of policing includes crime prevention, offender apprehension, and serving as a team member of the criminal justice system. Clearly, this job function receives the most media publicity. First, the news media, when reporting on police work, are most likely to focus on criminal cases such as the investigation of a rape or a sting operation involving the sale of drugs. Occasionally, a news program will film police officers directing traffic or speaking in schools, but such features are relatively uncommon. Second, there is a long line of research showing that the entertainment media also overwhelmingly portray the law-enforcement function of policing.[81] In primetime crime and police programs, the police are routinely showcased as crime fighters rather than service providers[82] (Box 14.3).

Although the media devotes considerable attention to the law-enforcement function of policing, studies of police time allocation have shown that this is misleading. Researchers have measured police time allocation in three major ways: personal monitoring of police work, asking officers to estimate the time spent in various job duties, and recording telephone calls to police stations. In virtually all cases, it is shown that the police do not spend a majority of work time in the law-enforcement function. Indeed, many studies reveal that both urban and rural police spend only 10 to 20 percent of their time on actual law enforcement.[83]

Police Recruitment

Historically, police recruits had only to be male, white, and properly sized. Today, recruitment is far more challenging. Probably many individuals dismiss policing as a possible career because of the supposed *danger* of police work. Actually, several other occupations have a higher job fatality rate than policing. For example, the chance of being killed on the job is much higher in areas such as agriculture, construction, and mining.[84] Nevertheless, police work carries a psychological danger not present in other occupations. Although a farmer has a greater chance of being killed at work than a police officer, farmers do not typically wonder if "the tractor is going to get me today," whereas, police officers carry with them the thought that "some nut may shoot me today just because I am a cop." Without question, fear of on-the-job death or injury reduces the potential pool of police applicants.

A second recruitment concern is *diversity*. In recent decades, police recruitment has emphasized the need to increase the number of women and minority police officers. As we will see shortly, women are underrepresented in police work.

Minority representation must be examined on a city-by-city basis. Virtually every major city in the United States has increased its hiring of black and Hispanic police officers, but some cities have a better record than others. Table 14.2 highlights three cities with a relatively good record of hiring blacks and three cities with a relatively poor record on this issue.

Between 1983 and 1992, all of the cities identified in Table 14.2 increased their percentage of black police officers. A 1.0 "index" percentage indicates that a city has a representation of black police officers equal to the proportion of black city residents. Interestingly, Los Angeles, which has a reputation for police discrimination against

TABLE 14.2

Percent of Black Police Officers by City and Year, and Index of Black Representation per Local Population Base

CITY	1983	1992	1992 INDEX
Los Angeles	9.4%	14.1%	1.00%
Seattle	4.1	8.5	0.84
Atlanta	45.8	54.6	0.81
Chicago	20.1	24.9	0.64
Milwaukee	11.6	14.4	0.47
Minneapolis	2.9	5.5	0.42

SOURCE: Kathleen Maguire and Ann Pastore, *Sourcebook of Criminal Justice Statistics, 1994* (Washington, DC: U.S. Government Printing Office, 1994) 49.

blacks, has the second highest index score of the fifty largest cities in the United States (only Honolulu, with a 1 percent black population base, has a better record).[85]

The record of hiring Hispanic police officers should also be looked at by individual city. For example, Los Angeles, which has a good record of hiring blacks, has a less impressive record of hiring Hispanics. Although Los Angeles employed 1787 Hispanic police in 1992 (22.3 percent of the department), its index score was only 0.56.[86] On the other hand, in 1992, 34.2 percent of the Albuquerque, New Mexico, police force was Hispanic. That figure represented an index score of 0.99. Because there is so much variability from city to city, it is difficult to discern meaningful overall patterns. It does appear, however, that the hiring of Hispanic police officers lags behind the hiring of black police officers. This might be related to the fact that Hispanics have little political power, either nationally or within communities. Demographers project that within three decades Hispanics will become the largest minority ethnic group in the United States. This would indicate that efforts to increase the number of Hispanic police will continue for some time.

A third recruitment issue has to do with *qualifications*. When police departments decided to hire more women and minorities, they also attempted to increase their professional stature. The modern police do not want to be hounded by negative stereotypes that portray officers as trigger-happy, lazy, stupid, and out-of-shape. In this regard, law-enforcement agencies seek psychologically well-adjusted, industrious, intelligent and educated employees who are in good physical condition. In making hiring decisions, police departments routinely use a psychological screening test, cognitive exams, and a physical agility test. The implementation of these selection criteria has become so problematic, however, that they have inspired a spate of lawsuits.

Robin Inwald and Dennis Kenney argue that psychological tests "can be cost-effective and are able to provide objective data that can aid in identifying personality characteristics and/or disorders of applicants."[87] But many researchers do not share this positive appraisal of psychological testing. Donald Walker, for example, has challenged the validity of the testing instruments, submitting that there is no psychological test that can accurately predict police misconduct.[88] Another criticism of psychological testing is that it is necessarily invasive of personal attitudes and emotions. Because of this, tests have been challenged in court as an infringement upon privacy rights.

Cognitive exams and physical tests have traditionally put minority-group members and women at a disadvantage. Such testing has prompted a number of lawsuits by minorities and women, who argue that they are protected under Title VII of the Civil Rights Act of 1964, which prohibits employment tests that discriminate against minorities and women and which was made applicable to public organizations in 1972.[89] Although court rulings in such cases have been uneven, overall it has been held that tests must show demonstrable and legitimate job-relatedness in order to be acceptable. For example, it would not be legitimate to ask police applicants to dead-lift 200 pounds because that type of test does not reflect an ordinary or necessary police assignment and would likely discriminate against women applicants. On the other hand, requiring a candidate to pull a dummy a certain distance within a set time probably would be an acceptable test of physical strength.[90]

In addition to stricter testing, there has been a push for hiring more college-educated police officers. By all accounts this has had several positive consequences. Research has shown that police officers who are college graduates tend to communicate more clearly with the public, write better reports, receive fewer citizen complaints, show more initiative, behave in a more professional manner, show more sensitivity to racial and ethnic groups, and have fewer disciplinary problems.[91]

Community Policing

Throughout the United States there is an unmistakable trend toward community policing. Indeed, community policing has been described as "the prevailing model of law enforcement in the United States."[92] Despite this popularity, there is no general consensus as to what community policing actually entails. Community policing is variously defined as "team policing," "foot patrol," "neighborhood policing," or "problem-oriented policing." More generally, Kevin Morison, coordinator of special projects for the Chicago Police Department, has defined the two most essential aspects of community policing as beat integrity and community involvement.[93] **Beat integrity** assures that officers work the same beat and shift week after week. This means that police are neither dispatched outside their home community nor subject to shift rotations. This allows community members to get used to the

A goal of most police departments is to increase the race and gender diversity of its personnel.

same officer being in the same place continually. It is hoped that such familiarity inspires trust and confidence. The community involvement dimension of policing requires that officers record chronic problems, make themselves aware of available resources to treat the problems, and meet regularly with community residents, leaders, and elected officials to develop specific strategies to combat the social problems of the area and reduce the community's crime rate.

The current popularity of community policing can be attributed to at least three things. First, the concern pointed to in the broken-windows article mentioned earlier has been instrumental in changing attitudes about what is the most important police job function.[94] Wilson and Kelling, the authors of this article, argue that communities characterized by physical decay invite social disorder. One way of deterring acts such as breaking windows, shooting out street lights, or writing graffiti is to make the police a more visible part of the community.

Strained relations between the police and community members, particularly in ethnic neighborhoods, is a second impetus for community policing. If the police are viewed as interlopers, coming into neighborhoods only to

make arrests, they are likely to be mistrusted and even despised. To foster positive ties between the police and community members, officers must be perceived as having a stake in the community. Continuous and predictable interactions between police and shopkeepers, residents, and local officials can encourage close and positive ties. In fact, research suggests an inverse relationship between feelings of job strain and attitudes supportive of community policing: Officers with positive attitudes toward community police work have lower rates of job frustration.[95]

Third, most police work takes place within a particular community. Whether one is talking about police **assignments** (patrol, traffic direction) or **situations** (intercepting crimes in progress, responding to accidents), the fact is that both assignments and situations are community-based.[96] It follows that the organizational structure of the police should be defined in terms of the community. Emphasizing good citizenship within a community enhances police-resident relations and may actually promote citizen patrols that work in cooperation with their local police.[97]

Community policing is currently popular. While some see community policing as a return to an earlier time, others view this form of police organization as a new development. Old or new, community policing appears to be the wave of the future. Gene Stephens, police futurist, argues that the twenty-first century police will be community-concerned healers of conflict. The "war model" of policing will be replaced by a "peace model."[98]

Women in Policing

In tracing the history of women in American policing, three names stand out: Mary Owens, Lola Baldwin, and Alice Stebbins Wells. In 1893, the Chicago Police Department appointed Mary Owens, the widow of a police officer, to the position of "policeman."[99] Although Owens had full arrest powers, she mainly assisted other officers in cases involving women and children. In 1905, the city of Portland, Oregon, granted police powers to a social worker named Lola Baldwin.[100] It was expected that Baldwin would help preserve order during the Lewis and Clark Exposition. Not until 1910, however, was the first police-*woman* hired. This was Alice Stebbins Wells, who joined the Los Angeles Police Department.[101] Wells actually lobbied for her appointment, arguing that the city police department needed an officer to work with the women and children who came into contact with the police. For sev-

eral years, speaking in cities throughout the country, Wells campaigned for the hiring of women officers. By 1915, twenty-five cities had policewomen.[102]

Historically, women represented only a tiny proportion of police in the United States; for all practical purposes, police work was considered the domain of white males. Are women now as likely as men to be employed by law-enforcement agencies?

Table 14.3 indicates that there are still significant gender differences in law-enforcement employment. Two conclusions can be drawn from this data. First, the data show that women make up less than 10 percent of America's

TABLE 14.3	Full-Time Law Enforcement Employees as of October 31, 1993		
	TOTAL POLICE EMPLOYEES	SWORN OFFICERS	CIVILIAN EMPLOYEES
Total number	813,536	586,756	226,780
Percent male	75.7%	90.2%	38%
Percent female	24.3%	9.8%	62%

SOURCE: Kathleen Maguire and Ann Pastore, *Sourcebook of Criminal Justice Statistics, 1996* (Washington, DC: U.S. Government Printing Office, 1996) 54.

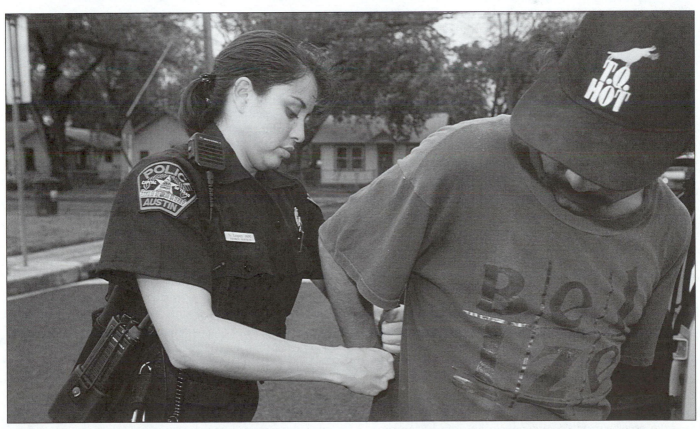

Research shows that women police officers are highly effective in the performance of their duties, and yet many continue to face discrimination on the job.

sworn police officers (officers with full arrest powers). In 1973, women accounted for 1.7 percent of sworn officers; in 1983, the figure increased to 5.1 percent, and, by 1993, women constituted 9.4 percent of sworn officers.[103] Although the percentage of women sworn officers increased over fivefold between 1973 and 1993, the absolute numbers are comparatively small. Some observers interpret this to mean that women still face barriers to employment in police work (Box 14.4).

Second, Table 14.3 reveals that most women working in law enforcement are civilian employees. This has a number of important implications, not least of which is that women law enforcement personnel are paid less than men. Department of Justice statisticians Brian Reaves and Pheny Smith report that median expenditures for officers far outdistance the median expenditures for civilian employees.[104] This holds true for county police, municipal police and state police.

Recalling her first appearance at Los Angeles police headquarters in 1910, Alice Stebbins Wells is reported to have said "they neither wanted me nor knew what to do with me."[105] Despite the fact that the 1972 Equal Employment Opportunity Act granted women equal access to all aspects of police work, today's women police officers might respond similarly to Wells. Even though there is considerable empirical evidence documenting the effectiveness of women officers, many male patrol officers and police supervisors continue to view women officers as emotionally unstable and physically unfit.[106] As more and more studies show that women are as capable as men in the full range of police activities, attitudes may change. Police researcher Mary Cuadrado believes that ex-

isting perceptions might change with "increased recruitment of women, gender sensitivity training provided at the academies, and a higher level of education."[107]

Current Problems

There are many problems associated with the police in the United States today. Some of these problems are the result of actions taken by police officers, but the most important and persistent problems are social structural in nature.

Manning's "Mission Impossible" Thesis

Sociologist Peter Manning notes that there are certain perennial problems found in all human societies and each of these problems gives rise to a specialized occupational group.[108] One example is sickness. In the United States, the medical profession, defined principally by medical doctors, has emerged to deal with sickness. Medical doctors have been successful in staking out the treatment of "sickness" as the core feature of their occupational mandate. A similar analysis is applicable to police work. Social disorder and crime are perennial problems and the "profession" of policing developed as a response to these problems. Today, the police occupation mandate is usually defined in terms of providing social services, keeping order, and enforcing the law. Manning argues that even if law enforcement were the only job function that the police had to accomplish, it would be a **mission impossible.**

Law enforcement entails at least these three objectives: crime prevention, crime detection, and offender apprehension. In all cases, states Manning, the police fail miserably. By their own admission, the police are unable to prevent all crime. The police have no (or limited) control over commonly identified sources of crime such as unemployment, faulty socialization, racism, and so on. When a crime does occur, the police are often unaware of it. Generally, the police must rely on victims or witnesses to report crime but, as shown in Chapter 3, victim studies reveal that many, if not most, crimes are not reported to the police. Finally, when a crime occurs and the police find out about it, they must apprehend the offender. By their own official recordings, the police admit that the chances of criminal apprehension are slim. For example, of all robberies that the police investigate, police will make an arrest in about one-fourth of all cases. For some other serious offenses, the chances of arrest are even smaller.

Beginning in 1829 with the establishment of the London Constabulary, the modern professionalized police identified crime control as a pre-eminent task of policing. The police have defined their occupational mandate and, what is more, they have been successful in convincing political leaders and the public that they are responsible for crime prevention. Unfortunately, according to Manning, they can never achieve this mission. Although the police do what they can to portray a positive image, the fact is that their occupational mandate is too broad and too ambitious. The failure of policing is structural; it is not the result of lazy, stupid, or corrupt officers.

Professionalism vs. Bureaucratization

The modern police seek to be viewed as professionals but they are also employees of bureaucratic organizations. On the one hand, police are professionals in that they have special expertise based on training and work experiences. As professionals, police should be allowed to make decisions on the basis of individual discretion. On the other hand, they are governed by written rules and regulations. In an age of lawsuit frenzy, the police must be careful to always "go by the book." This, then, is the dilemma faced by the police: How can officers exercise personal judgment and at the same time follow rigid written guidelines? There is no satisfactory answer. Clearly, police work is highly contextual and variable. It is impossible to anticipate every decision that a police officer will be asked to make on the job. Nonetheless, when the police make snap decisions, they must be prepared to justify their actions as consistent with procedural guidelines.

Functional Awkwardness

As noted earlier in this chapter, the police have many job functions. Occasionally, the demands of one job function are at cross purposes with the requirements of another job function. For example, enforcing the law is sometimes at odds with keeping order. In the 1970s and 1980s, Carbondale, Illinois (home of Southern Illinois University) was the site of an annual Halloween celebration that attracted tens of thousands of visitors. The partying in the downtown streets was very intense and examples of law violation were almost routine. However, the police did not attempt to arrest every law violator; such actions might well have led to widespread social disorder, including rioting. Instead, the police responded to only the most serious and blatant examples of law violation, and in so doing they were able to maintain social order.

When the police enforce the law, they sometimes displease community members. This is another example of functional awkwardness. Imagine a small-town poker game going on at 2 A.M. in a golf clubhouse. The patrol officer notes that the clubhouse is open past the 1 A.M. curfew. On entering the clubhouse, he also notices that there is cash on the table where card players are gambling—another law violation. The police officer arrests no one, nor does he order the clubhouse closed or the gambling stopped. Why is the officer so tolerant? The most compelling reason is that the poker players include the county's prosecuting attorney, the president of the local bank, the CEO of the town's biggest company, the superintendent of schools, and one or two other powerful members of the community. One of the authors of this book saw this scene repeat itself many times for several years. Patrol officers never intervened and no one questioned their judgment, but the officers themselves must have noted the functional awkwardness of their job duties.

Police Misconduct

Discussion of twentieth-century police misconduct in the United States brings to mind the Wickersham Commission, the Knapp Commission, and the Rodney King case. In 1929, United States Attorney General George Wickersham headed a committee investigating criminal justice system practices. Findings of this investigation were published two years later in a fourteen-volume set that included two books devoted especially to the police. The Wickersham Commission specifically condemned various types of police misconduct, including common use of the *third degree,* described as a "flagrant violation of the law by the officers of the law."[109]

In the early 1970s, police detective Frank Serpico was instrumental in initiating a comprehensive review of police misconduct in New York City that became known as the Knapp Commission. The Knapp Commission uncovered "widespread" police corruption. Its report noted that over half of New York City's police officers were involved in extensive and common payoffs or gratuities from gambling and narcotics violators, underworld figures, or business owners. The report categorized the implicated officers as *grass eaters* or *meat eaters:* the former passively accepted small gratuities, while the latter aggressively sought substantial payoffs.[110]

In March of 1991, American television viewers watched a home video of several Los Angeles police officers brutally beating an African American named Rodney King. King suffered multiple injuries from having been clubbed or kicked 56 times in 81 seconds.[111] The officers charged with the assault were acquitted after the first trial, prompting rioting in the Los Angeles area. Although the officers were subsequently found guilty and King was awarded over $1 million in damages, the case focused national attention on the issue of police brutality.

Police misconduct is a broad term. Perhaps the two most pervasive and significant forms of misconduct are corruption and police brutality. Herman Goldstein has defined **police corruption** as "acts involving the misuse of authority by a police officer in a manner designed to produce personal gain for himself or for others."[112] This definition embraces a wide range of activities. There is, first of all, the matter of *gratuities,* a practice wherein an owner or manager of a commercial establishment offers a police officer free service or discounts. Accepting gratuities is a common practice in police work, and merchants may be more than pleased to exchange a meal or theater ticket for congenial police relations—and perhaps a little extra patrol coverage.

A second, and more serious, form of corruption occurs when an officer initiates payments or services from businesses. Rather than a friendly gratuity, this type of transaction becomes outright extortion, or what is called a **shakedown.**

Officers who engage in shakedowns are also more likely to accept bribes from law violators. **Bribery** represents a third dimension of police corruption. Motorists, drug dealers, contractors, bar owners, and many others may be willing to buy police nonenforcement of the law. Bribery can be in the form of a one-shot transaction or a monthly payment, something known in New York City slang as "on the pad."[113]

A fourth type of corruption is theft. Occasionally police officers will find a store door unlocked while doing security checks at night. After reporting this, and while waiting for the proprietor or manager to arrive, the officer might take (steal) items such as candy, cigars, or a camera. Usually this illegal **shopping** does not amount to a great loss. A more costly form of shopping occurs when the police arrive at the scene of a burglary and remove expensive items for their personal use. In such cases, the police assume that what they have taken will appear on the list of missing items and that insurance will cover the loss.

A fifth type of corruption is poor job performance. Officers who ignore their occupational duties or perform their duties in a careless or incomplete manner, are also engaged in corruption. Police who intentionally avoid work assignments receive pay for work not rendered.

Researchers have offered alternative explanations of police corruption.[114] First is the "rotten-apple" model, which states that some individual officers are personally corrupt. The solution here is to weed out the offending individuals. Second is the theory that corruption is systemic—that it is driven by an organizational structure. According to this view, corruption is produced by structural features of the workplace. This perspective suggests that police corruption can be fought successfully only by implementing major changes in policing and society itself (for example, legalizing drugs would likely reduce payoffs to vice police).

Police brutality is a controversial issue in American policing. The publicity sparked by the Rodney King incident has placed the spotlight on police departments across the country.[115] Racial and ethnic minorities have been particularly concerned with police brutality.[116] However, despite strong public interest, it is difficult to measure.[117] First, complaints must be filed at the station where the officer works. For the person filing a complaint, this is awkward at best. Second, the police "code of silence" can inhibit investigation. Third, law-enforcement agencies often have incomplete records on such cases. Finally, distinguishing between the use of necessary force and police brutality can be problematic. Every day, police encounter situations where they must establish control and make an arrest. How much force is required to make an arrest? The answer is necessarily situational. Use of **deadly force** is another matter; universal restrictions can be applied. For example, in 1985 the U.S. Supreme Court ruled that police cannot use deadly force against an "unarmed or nondangerous" fleeing felon.[118] Perhaps as a result of media scrutiny, public outrage, the threat of lawsuits, and new training, the use of deadly force has dropped significantly over the last few decades.[119]

Police work is governed by a set of legal procedures. One of the rulings set by the Supreme Court to deter police misconduct is the **exclusionary rule.** In 1914, the Court ordered that federal trial courts not consider any evidence illegally obtained; in 1961, the Court held that this standard must apply to state trial courts as well.[120] The exclusionary rule has come under serious and sustained attack by those who argue that the ruling enables too many guilty defendants to escape conviction on "technicalities." In *Massachusetts v. Sheppard* (1984) the Court issued a compromise interpretation: that evidence obtained *in good faith* could be legally admitted into state criminal trials.[121] This Supreme Court decision was based on a murder case where the police officer made a clerical error by using the wrong form to obtain the search warrant. The Court ruled that the exclusionary rule should not "deter objectively reasonable law-enforcement activity."[122]

Whether to admit such evidence into trial proceedings is up to the states (some states do, some do not).

A second famous procedural rule is the **Miranda warning.** In 1966, the Supreme Court ordered that police inform suspects that they have the following rights under law:

- Right to remain silent
- Any statement made by the suspect can and will be used against him or her in court
- Right to consult an attorney and have an attorney present during police interrogation
- If suspect cannot afford an attorney, one will be appointed[123]

The exclusionary rule and the Miranda warning, along with many other procedural restrictions, help to deter police misconduct. Police officers may still seize evidence improperly or make illegitimate arrests, but procedural safeguards make it more difficult.

Public Relations

The news media often present the police in an unfavorable light. Stories about "increases" in crime suggest to people that the police are not doing an effective job. Moreover, when the media focus directly on the police, it is often in connection with cases of police brutality or corruption. Given this type of public attention, it would not be surprising to find that Americans hold a low opinion of police. However, 58 percent of those who responded to a 1995 national poll stated that they had "a great deal" or "quite a lot" of confidence in the police.[124] (The same cannot be said for the criminal justice system, where only 19 percent of respondents reported "a great deal" or "quite a lot" of confidence.[125]) In addition, police receive higher scores for honesty and ethics than do bankers, journalists, contractors, real estate agents, members of Congress, and many other professions.[126] What is more, positive attitudes toward the police are higher now than they were 15 to 20 years ago.[127]

This is a pretty picture of how the public regards the police, but it is not a complete one. Importantly, white and black Americans differ significantly in their attitudes toward the police. Sixty-three percent of whites have "a great deal" or "quite a lot" of confidence in the police, while only 26 percent of blacks report such an attitude.[128] Four factors help explain why blacks have less positive feelings toward the police (only about one-third of blacks actually have negative attitudes). First, racial discrimination in police employment produces unfavorable attitudes among black residents. If there are few black officers patrolling predominantly black neighborhoods, residents might perceive this as evidence of white racism, resulting in negative attitudes toward the police. Second, police re-

searcher Donald Walker argues that black officers, unlike their white counterparts, hold values that correspond to the values of black residents.[129] To the extent that white police officers are oriented to a different, and perhaps competing, value system, black residents may feel resentment toward the police. Third, underpolicing of black communities is a source of concern for black residents. Often, these are areas where crime rates are high and police attention is most needed. Police inattention, real or perceived, can result in negative views toward the police. Fourth, black community members would be likely to personalize cases of police discrimination and brutality against blacks (Box 14.5). Such incidents strike most Americans as outrageous, but for blacks they would be especially relevant.

Despite the problems described, if communities hire more minority officers, shift additional resources to community policing, and more vigorously prosecute cases of police discrimination and brutality, relations between the police and black citizens can improve. As an illustration of the last point, recall the Jeremiah Mearday case discussed at the beginning of this chapter. Mearday was severely injured by the police and blamed it on police brutality, whereas the officers claimed the beating was the result of justifiable police action. Just 25 days after the incident occurred, Chicago Police Superintendent Matt Rodriguez suspended the officers in question and called for their firing (a decision left to a police oversight board).[130] Most investigations of this type take months or even years to complete, and rarely do they result in police officer firings (in Chicago, in 1996, out of 3,200 complaints of this nature, less than two dozen led to police firings[131]).

Other steps taken by the police to foster improved relations with community members include, but are not limited to, the formation of police/community athletic teams, police/youth discussion groups, police-sponsored college scholarship programs, police/community summer camps, DARE (Drug Abuse Resistance Education),[132] and cultural diversity training courses for the police (shown to be more effective for new hires than veteran officers).[133] Programs such as these may result in more positive images of the police and, just as important, may lead police to form more positive images of community members. Finally, actions taken to enhance the general living conditions of a neighborhood are likely to result in more satisfaction with the police. Recent research has found that the "primary indicator of attitudes toward the police is how people feel about where they live."[134] Paul Jesilow and his associates found that satisfaction with one's area of residence is more significant in determining attitudes toward the police than ethnicity, age, education, or gender. Hence, the importance of quality of life indicators cannot be overstated.

Race and Policing

In 1995, Pittsburgh businessman Jonny Gammage died at the hands of five police officers. The police stopped Gamage at 1:45 A.M. for "erratic driving." Following the stop, an argument and scuffle broke out. Eventually, Gammage was pinned to the ground, and his neck was pressed down by a metal club. Within minutes, Gammage died from suffocation.

There is more to the story: Gammage was an African American and the five police officers were white. Will Thompkins, vice president of the Pittsburgh Urban League, was quoted as follows: "When you combine an African American male, a non–African American police officer, and a traffic stop, what that adds up to is a beating or a death."

While there is no research to support Thompkins' extreme claim, studies do show that African Americans are more likely to have negative attitudes toward the police. For example, Chicago construction worker Joe Moore states: "As a black man in Chicago, I'm afraid of the po-lice . . . We see them as the enemy." Are such views based on actual police brutality or police harassment? Or is it just a matter of perceptions? There are no conclusive answers to these questions yet, but researchers Jack Levin and Alexander Thomas have recently suggested that perceptions can be an important factor. Levin and Thomas showed respondents a videotape of police officers arresting a black suspect (the arrest was staged, but textbook police procedures were used and respondents thought they were viewing an actual arrest). Findings show that both black and white respondents were more likely to see police violence and illegality when both arresting officers were perceived as white.

It would be risky to assume that these perceptions have no grounding in actual police encounters. In perceptions of being hassled, racial differences are so extreme that the issues of police harassment and police brutality merit further examination.

SOURCES: Sandra Lee Browning, Francis T. Cullen, Liqun Cao, Renee Kopache, and Thomas J. Stevenson, "Race and Getting Hassled by the Police: A Research Note," *Police Studies 17* (1994) 1–11; Joseph Kirby, "NAACP Takes on Police Issues," *Chicago Tribune,* 16 July 1997, 1–5; Stephanie Banchero and Flynn McRoberts, "Forces Collided to Highlight Cop-Abuse Charges," *Chicago Tribune,* 13 October 1997, 1–1, 1–6.

Summary

This chapter traced the historical development of the police from old English systems through American Colonial times to the present. It addressed the costs and various types of police organizations, including federal, state, local, campus, and private police systems. The chapter highlighted functions of the police, police recruitment, community policing, and women in policing as the most important current issues in policing. Finally, the chapter offered an assessment of the following chronic problems experienced by most police departments: the impossible mission of police work, the tension between professional and bureaucratic requirements, functional awkwardness, police misconduct, and public relations.

Critical Thinking Questions

1. Could society get along without the police? What would happen in your community if there were no police officers?
2. Do you think that there should be separate women police units? What would be the advantages and disadvantages of such units?
3. Rank the relative importance of the major police job functions.
4. What historical event has had the greatest influence on the development of the modern police?

Suggested Readings

Victor Kappeler, ed., *The Police & Society* (Prospect Heights, IL: Waveland, 1995).

Vincent Webb and Charles Katz, "Citizen Ratings of the Importance of Community Policing Activities," *Policing: An International Journal of Police Strategies & Management 20* (1997) 7–23.

James Q. Wilson and George Kelling, "Broken Windows: Police and Neighborhood Safety," *Atlantic Monthly 249* (1982) 29–38.

Notes

[1] Stephanie Banchero and Flynn McRoberts, "Forces Collided to Highlight Cop-Abuse Charges," *Chicago Tribune,* 13 October 1997, 1–1, 1–6; WGN Nightly News, 21 October 1997.
[2] Cyril Robinson and Richard Scaglion with J. Michael Olivero, *Police in Contradiction: The Evolution of the Police Function in Society* (Westport, CT: Greenwood Press, 1994) 6.
[3] Raymond Michalowski, *Order, Law, and Crime* (New York: Random House, 1985) 170.

4 T.A. Critchley, *A History of Police in England and Wales* (Montclair, NJ: Patterson Smith, 1972) 2.

5 H.R. Loyn, *The Governance of Anglo-Saxon England, 500–1087* (Stanford: Stanford University Press, 1984) 137, 196.

6 William G. Bailey, "Sheriff," in *The Encyclopedia of Police Science,* 2nd ed., ed. William G. Bailey (New York: Garland, 1995) 713–15, 714.

7 Critchley, *A History of Police in England and Wales,* 5.

8 Ibid., 6.

9 Samuel Walker, *The Police in America* (New York: McGraw-Hill, 1983) 4.

10 Ibid.

11 National Constables Association, "The Constable," in *The Encyclopedia of Police Science,* ed. William G. Bailey (New York: Garland, 1995) 114–15, 114.

12 Ibid.

13 Walker, *The Police in America,* 5.

14 Wilbur Miller, *Cops and Bobbies* (Chicago: University of Chicago Press, 1977) 2.

15 Robert Pursley, *Introduction to Criminal Justice* (Encino, CA: Glencoe Press, 1977).

16 George Kirkham and Laurin Wollan, Jr., *Introduction to Law Enforcement* (New York: Harper & Row, 1980) 29.

17 Walker, *The Police in America,* 17.

18 Robert *Bonn, Criminology (New York: McGraw-Hill, 1984)* 394.

19 Raymond Michalowski, *Order, Law, and Crime* (New York: Random House, 1985) 173.

20 Larry Siegel, *Criminology* (St. Paul: West, 1983) 441.

21 Walker, *The Police in America,* 6.

22 Ibid., 6.

23 Michalowski, *Order, Law, and Crime;* Richard Quinney, *Criminology,* 2nd ed. (Boston: Little, Brown, 1979); Alan Silver, "The Demand for Order in Civil Society: A Review of Some Theories in the History of Urban Crime, Police and Riot," in *The Police: Six Sociological Essays,* ed. David Bardua (New York: Wiley, 1967) 1–24.

24 Sidney Harring, *Policing a Class Society: The Experience of American Cities, 1865–1915* (New Brunswick, NJ: Rutgers University Press, 1983).

25 Brendan Maguire, "The Police in the 1800s: A Three City Analysis," *Journal of Crime and Justice 13* (1990) 103–132.

26 H. Kenneth Bechtel, *State Police in the United States: A Socio-Historical Analysis* (Westport, CT: Greenwood, 1995).

27 R.J. Lundman, *Police and Policing: An Introduction* (New York: Holt, Rinehart and Winston, 1980) 15.

28 Roger Lane, *Policing the City: Boston, 1822–1885* (Cambridge: Harvard University Press, 1967); James Richardson, *The New York Police: Colonial Times to 1900* (New York: Oxford University Press, 1970).

29 Erik Monkkonen, *The Dangerous Class: Crime and Poverty in Columbus, Ohio, 1860–1885* (Cambridge: Harvard University Press, 1975) 4.

30 Erik Monkkonen, *Police in Urban America, 1860–1920* (New York: Cambridge University Press, 1981).

31 George Kelling and Mark Moore, "The Evolving Strategy of Policing," in *The Police & Society,* ed. Victor Kappeler (Prospect Heights, IL: Waveland, 1995) 3–27, 5.

32 Robert Fogelson, *Big-City Police* (Cambridge: Harvard University Press, 1977).

33 Nathan Douthit, "August Vollmer, Berkeley's First Chief of Police, and the Emergence of Police Professionalism," *California Historical Quarterly 54* (1975) 101–124.

34 Quoted in Gene Carte and Elaine Carte, *Police Reform in the United States* (Berkeley, CA: University of California Press, 1975) 34.

35 William Bopp, *O. W. Wilson and the Search for a Police Profession* (London: Kennikat, 1975) 48.

36 Kathleen Maguire and Ann Pastore, *Bureau of Justice Statistics Sourcebook of Criminal Justice Statistics, 1994* (Washington, DC: Government Printing Office, 1995) 3.

37 Ibid., 5.

38 Ibid., 45, 61.

39 Ibid., 11.

40 Sue Lindgren, "Justice Expenditure and Employment, 1990," *Bureau of Justice Statistics Bulletin* (Washington DC: U.S. Department of Justice, 1992).

41 Maguire and Pastore, *Bureau of Justice Statistics Sourcebook of Criminal Justice Statistics, 1994,* 3.

42 Malcolm Willoughby, *The U.S. Coast Guard in World War II* (Annapolis, MD: U.S. Naval Institute, 1957) 3.

43 Ibid.

44 Don Whitehead, *The FBI Story* (New York: Random, 1956) 17.

45 Samuel Walker, *Popular Justice* (New York: Oxford University Press, 1980) 238.

46 Quoted in Sanford Unger, *FBI* (Boston: Little, Brown, 1976) 38.

47 Brian Reaves, *Federal Law Enforcement Officers, 1996* (Washington, DC: U.S. Department of Justice, 1997) 2.

48 Maguire and Pastore, *Bureau of Justice Statistics Sourcebook of Criminal Justice Statistics, 1994,* 63.

49 Ibid.

50 Brian Reaves and Andrew Goldberg, *Census of State and Local Law Enforcement Agencies, 1996* (Washington, DC: U.S. Department of Justice, 1998) 11.

51 Ibid., 1.

52 Ibid., 6.

53 Scott Decker and Steven Ward, "Rural Law Enforcement," in *The Encyclopedia of Police Science,* 2nd ed., ed. William Bailey (New York: Garland, 1995) 698–700.

54 Brendan Maguire, William Faulkner, Richard Mathers, Carol Rowland, and John F. Wozniak, "Rural Police Job Functions," *Police Studies 14* (1991) 180–87.

55 Vincent Webb and Charles Katz, "Citizen Ratings of the Importance of Community Policing Activities," *Policing: An International Journal of Police Strategies & Management 20* (1997) 7–23.

56 John Powell, *Campus Security and Law Enforcement* (Boston: Butterworth, 1981).

57 Ibid., 9.

58 A. Mathews, "The Campus Crime War," *The New York Times Magazine 7* (1993) 38–47.

59 Max Bromley, "Comparing Campus and City Crime Rates: A Descriptive Study," *American Journal of Police XIV* (1995) 131–48.

60 J. Castelli, "Campus Crime 101," *The New York Times Education Life 6* (1990) 1.

61 "Rates of Campus Crime," *Society 31* (1994) 2–3.

62 Ibid., 136.

63 Kathleen Maguire and Ann Pastore, *Sourcebook of Criminal Justice Statistics Bulletin, 1996* (Washington, DC: Government Printing Office, 1997) 47.

64 Federal Bureau of Investigation, *Crime in the United States, 1996* (Washington, DC: U.S. Government Printing Office, 1997) 366–67.

65 William Bopp and Donald Schultz, *A Short History of American Law Enforcement* (Springfield, IL: Charles C Thomas, 1972) 55.

66 Larry Siegel, *Criminology,* 5th ed. (St. Paul: West, 1995) 498.

67 Sue Titus Reid, *Crime and Criminology* (New York: Harcourt, Brace, 1994) 507.

68 National Advisory Commission on Criminal Justice Standards and Goals, *Police* (Washington, DC: U.S. Government Printing Office, 1973).

69 Stephen Cox and John Wade, *The Criminal Justice Network: An Introduction* (Dubuque, IA: Wm. Brown, 1985) 97.

70 Clinton Terry III, *Policing Society* (New York: Wiley, 1985), 82.

71 Geoffrey Alpert and Roger Dunham, *Policing Urban America,* Prospect, IL: Waveland, 1988) 21.

72 Anthony Platt et al., *The Iron Fist and the Velvet Glove: An Analysis of the U.S. Police* (San Francisco: Crime and Social Justice Associates, 1982).

73 John Coumoundouros, "Computerized Report Entry Systems," *Police Chief 62* (1995) 50–52.

74 Ibid.

75 Maguire et al., "Rural Police Job Functions."

76 John Van Maanen, "The Asshole," in *The Police and Society,* ed. Victor Kappeler (Prospect Heights, IL: Waveland, 1995) 307–328, 311.

77 Gary Perlstein, "Certain Characteristics of Policewomen," *Police 16* (1972) 45–46.

78 Maguire et al., "Rural Police Job Functions"; John Webster, "Police Task and Time Study," *Journal of Criminal Law, Criminology, and Police Science 61* (1970) 94–100.

79 James Q. Wilson and George Kelling, "Broken Windows: Police and Neighborhood Safety," *Atlantic Monthly 249* (1982) 29–38.

80 George Kelling, "Acquiring a Taste for Order," *Crime and Delinquency 33* (1987) 90–102.

81 Brendan Maguire, "Image vs. Reality: An Analysis of Prime-Time Television Crime and Police Programs," *Crime and Justice XI* (1988) 165–88; Joseph Dominick, "Crime and Law Enforcement on Prime-Time Television," *Public Opinion Quarterly 37* (1973) 241–50; Dallas Smythe, "Reality as Presented by TV," *Public Opinion Quarterly 18* (1954) 143–56.

82 Brendan Maguire, "Television Police," in *The Encyclopedia of Police Science,* 2nd ed., ed. William G. Bailey (New York: Garland, 1995) 758–61.

83 James Q. Wilson, *Varieties of Police Behavior: The Management of Law and Order in Eight Communities* (Cambridge, MA: Harvard University Press, 1968); Maguire et al., "Rural Police Job Functions."

84 *USA TODAY,* "Job-Related Deaths," 6 September 1991, I-A; *Chicago Tribune,* "Remembering Workers Killed, Injured on the Job," 29 April 1994, 3–1, 3–2.

85 Ibid.

86 Ibid., 50.

87 Robin Inwald and Dennis Jay Kenney, "Psychological Testing of Police Candidates," in *Police and Policing,* ed. Dennis Jay Kenney (New York: Praeger, 1989) 34–42.

88 Donald Walker, "The Relationship Between Social Research and Public Policy: The Case of Police Selections Processes," *American Journal of Police 5* (1986) 1–22.

[89] Joan Pynes, "Police Officer Selection Procedures: Speculation on the Future," *American Journal of Police 13* (1994) 103–124.

[90] Susan Martin, "Women in Policing: The Eighties and Beyond," in *Police and Policing,* ed. Dennis Jay Kenney (New York: Praeger, 1989) 3–16, 8.

[91] David Carter, Allen Sapp, and Darrel Stephens, *The State of Police Education: Policy Direction for the 21st Century* (Washington, DC: Police Execcutive Research Forum, 1989); Chris Eskridge, "College and the Police: A Review of the Issues," in *Police and Policing,* ed. Dennis Jay Kenney (New York: Praeger, 1989) 17–25, 20.

[92] Gail Dantzker et al., "Preparing Police Officers for Community Policing: An Evaluation of Training for Chicago's Alternative Policing Strategy," *Police Studies XVIII* (1995) 45–69, 46.

[93] Kevin Morison, "The Chicago Alternative Policing Strategy," *The Compiler* (Fall 1993), 4–7.

[94] Wilson and Kelling, "Broken Windows: Police and Neighborhood Safety."

[95] Donald Yates and Vijayan Pillai, "Attitudes Toward Community Policing: A Causal Analysis," *The Social Science Journal 33* (1996) 193–209.

[96] David Bayley, *Patterns of Policing: A Comparative International Analysis* (New Bruswick, NJ: Rutgers University Press, 1985).

[97] R. Dean Wright, "Community Response to Crime: Two Middle-Class Anti-Crime Patrols," *Journal of Criminal Justice 13* (1985) 227–41.

[98] Gene Stephens, "The Future of Policing: From a War Model to a Peace Model," in *The Past, Present, and Future of American Criminal Justice,* ed. Brendan Maguire and Polly Radosh (New York: General Hall, 1996).

[99] Dorothy Moses Schulz, "From Policewoman to Police Officer: An Unfinished Revolution," *Police Studies: The International Review of Police Development 16* (1993) 90–98, 90.

[100] Ibid.

[101] Ibid.

[102] Ibid.

[103] Source: Uniform Crime Reports relevant to each year.

[104] Reaves and Smith, *Law Enforcement Management and Administrative Statistics, 1993: Data for Individual State and Local Agencies with 100 or More Officers,* x.

[105] Quoted in Schulz, "From Policewoman to Police Officer: An Unfinished Revolution."

[106] Peter Block and Deborah Anderson, *Policewomen on Patrol: Final Report* (Washington, DC: Police Foundation, 1974); Leslie Kay Lord, "A Comparison of Male and Female Peace Officers' Stereotypic Perceptions of Women and Women Peace Officers," *Journal of Police Science and Administration 14* (1986) 83–97.

[107] Mary Cuadrado, "Female Police Officers: Gender Bias and Professionalism," *American Journal of Police XIV* (1995) 149–65, 163.

[108] Peter Manning, "The Police: Mandate, Strategies, and Appearances," in *The Police & Society,* ed. Victor Kappeler (Prospect Heights, IL: Waveland, 1995) 97–125.

[109] National Committee on Law Observance and Enforcement, *Report on Lawlessness in Law Enforcement, No. 11* (Washington, DC: U.S. Government Printing Office, 1931) 5.

[110] Knapp Commission, *Report on Police Corruption* (New York: Braziller, 1973) 4.

[111] Richard Lacayo, "Anatomy of an Acquittal," *Newsweek,* 11 May 1992, 30–32.

[112] Herman Goldstein, *Police Corruption: A Perspective on Its Nature and Control* (Washington, DC: Police Foundation, 1975) 3.

[113] Walker, *The Police in America,* 176.

[114] Walker, *The Police in America,* 178–79.

[115] Robert Barry and Clyde Cronkhite, "Back to Basics: Managing Law Enforcement to Avoid Excessive Use of Force," *Sheriff 44* (1992) 10–13.

[116] Darlene Ricker, "Behind the Silence," *ABA Journal 77* (1991) 45–48.

[117] Christopher Daskalos, "Current Issues in Policing," in *The Past, Present, and Future of American Criminal Justice,* ed. Brendan Maguire and Polly Radosh (New York: General Hall, forthcoming).

[118] *Tennessee v. Garner;* 1985, 105 S.Ct. 1694.

[119] William Geller and Michael Scott, "Deadly Force: What We Know," in *Thinking About Police,* ed. Carl Klockars and Stephen Mastrofski (New York: McGraw-Hill, 1991) 446–77.

[120] *Weeks v. United States,* 1914, 232 U.S. 383; *Mapp v. Ohio,* 1961, 367 U.S. 643.

[121] *Massachusetts v. Sheppard,* 1984, 468 U.S. 981.

[122] Ibid.

[123] *Miranda v. Arizona,* 1966, 384 U.S. 436.

[124] As reported in Maguire and Pastore, *Bureau of Justice Statistics Sourcebook of Criminal Justice Statistics, 1994,* 147.

[125] Ibid., 146.

[126] Ibid., 150.

[127] Ibid., 151.

[128] Ibid., 147.

[129] Donald Walker, "Black Police Values and the Black Community," *Police Studies 5* (1983) 20–28.

[130] Steve Mills, "Firing Urged for 2 Cops Linked to Beating Case," *Chicago Tribune,* 22 October 1997, 1–1–14; WGN TV Evening News, 21 October 1997.

[131] Ibid.

[132] Freda Adler, Gerhard O.W. Mueller, and William Laufer, *Criminal Justice* (New York: McGraw-Hill, 1994) 173–74.

[133] Larry Gould, "Can an Old Dog Be Taught New Tricks?" *Police: An International Journal of Police Strategies & Management 20* (1997) 339–56.

[134] Paul Jesilow, J'ona Meyer, and Nazi Namazzi, "Public Attitudes Toward the Police," *American Journal of Police XIV* (1995) 67–89, 85.

chapter **15**

Courts

KEY TERMS

legislative law
judicial law
precedent
stare decisis
administrative law
procedural law
procedural error
constitutional law
common law
civil courts
torts
criminal courts
trial courts
appellate courts
federal courts
state courts
courts with limited jurisdiction
U.S. circuit courts
U.S. district courts
U.S. Supreme Court
original jurisdiction
remanded
sentencing disparity
Missouri Plan
deterrence
incapacitation
selective incapacitation
retribution
indeterminate sentencing
administrative sentencing
determinate sentencing
suspended sentence
split sentence
good time
plea bargaining
presumptive sentencing
mandatory sentencing
capital offenses
protective statutes

CHAPTER OUTLINE

CONTEMPORARY ISSUES FACING COURTS
  Cost
TYPES OF COURTS
  Types of Law
    Judicial Law
    Administrative Law
    Procedural Law
    Constitutional Law
  Civil Courts and Criminal Courts
  Trial Courts and Appellate Courts
  State Courts
  Federal Courts
ISSUES AND TRENDS
  Judges
    Qualifications of Judges
    Judges' Salaries
    Problems of Bias
  Sentencing Strategies
    Rehabilitation
    Deterrence
    Incapacitation
    Retribution
  Types of Sentences
    Indeterminate Sentences
    Determinate Sentencing
    Mandatory Sentencing
    Other Sentencing Trends
  The Death Penalty
    Appellate Review
    Execution of Juveniles
    Morality and the Death Penalty
    Racial and Social Class Discrimination
    Cost of Executions
CURRENT PROBLEMS
  Court Overload
    Plea Bargaining
    Other Contributing Factors
  Frivolous Litigation
    Prisoners' Lawsuits
  Racial Disparity in Sentencing
  Gender Disparity in Sentencing
    The Muncy Act
    Modern Gender Differentials
SUMMARY

IN THE UNITED STATES, basic principles of fairness and constitutional protections are symbolized by the courts. More than any other institution, the judicial system is trusted as the guardian of impartiality and justice and

Contemporary Issues Facing Courts

Historically, in American law there has been an overriding concern with preserving the rights of the accused. Constitutional protections of suspects from self-incrimination, torture, or illegal searches, for example, were designed to prevent abuse of power that could have replicated the English abuse of power to which American Colonists were subject before the American Revolution. The emphasis on protection of the accused was an important innovation in American law in the late eighteenth century.

Contemporary trends have been to lessen the impact of many of the protections of the accused in an effort to increase the likelihood of conviction. Controversy centers around protection of suspects' rights juxtaposed against protection of victims' rights. Many of the principles of protection have been mediated by fear of crime in the United States today. Expediency in addressing issues of crime has often seemed more important than preserving the principles of protection.

Among the most significant issues facing modern courts is the financial cost associated with all components of justice. Unfortunately, accessibility to "justice" today varies with the income or social status of defendants; in other words, wealthy and powerful people are better able to protect themselves and their interests. Many theorists have pointed to inherent unfairness in such a system. Critics of American justice, such as Jeffrey Reiman, have charged that a two-tiered system of justice assures that wealthy people benefit while poor people are punished.[1] Such a charge is a serious indictment of American justice, given the principles of protection defined in the Constitution to check the power of the state against the accused.

Whether a two-tiered system of justice exists is not seriously debated. Most people acknowledge that the positive impact of wealth and the negative impact of poverty is a fault of the American system. Actually, the American judicial process is multi-tiered rather than two-tiered. Many factors affect justice aside from social status or the particular facts of a case. This chapter examines the basic features of the judicial system. Demographic characteristics such as race, gender, and social status are included as components of the multi-tiered nature of justice.

Among the most important concerns currently facing all aspects of criminal justice are the rising costs of each phase of the system. As with other components of the criminal justice system, the costs for prosecution, defense, and the provision of court services (pre-sentence investigation, court supervision after conviction) have skyrocketed in recent years.

Cost

All government expenditures increased during the 1980s as American social problems worsened. For example, welfare costs increased with an increase in the number of people living below official poverty levels. Along with government subsidies to farmers, tax cuts to the wealthy, and increased federal subsidies to many businesses and industries, increases in justice expenditures and corrections budgets were also characteristic of the 1980s. Local governments spent almost half of their justice dollars on judicial and legal activities in 1992, which is the last year for which figures are available.[2] State governments spent almost one-third of justice dollars on judicial and legal activities. And, the federal government spent one-fifth of justice dollars on judicial and legal activities in 1992. The remaining justice expenditures were divided among federal, state, and local police and corrections activities.[3]

Expenditures for all levels of judicial and legal activities increased steadily between 1982 and 1992. Federal judicial and legal activities increased most drastically, with a 430 percent increase in expenditures during these years.[4] In all branches of government there were nearly 38,000 people employed as judges, court recorders, bailiffs, and other justice personnel in the United States in 1992.[5] Federal, state and local governments spent just under $21 billion on judicial and legal costs in 1992, a 170 percent increase from the $8.6 billion spent in 1982.[6] The courts expended $9.3 billion in 1990, while prosecution and legal services cost $5.5 billion. Over $1.7 billion was spent on public defense of indigent clients who could not afford a private attorney in 1990.[7] With all this, the justice and legal expenses were much lower than expenses for police protection or corrections, which siphoned the largest share of justice dollars nationally; over two-thirds of justice dollars were directed to police and corrections out of the $93.7 billion justice budget in 1992.[8]

Types of Courts

There are many features of American law that appear complicated or frightening to most Americans. The courts, with their volumes of legal jargon, confuse ordinary citizens, who are often intimidated by perceptions of a foreboding legal system. Actually, there are a few basic terms and ideas that permeate all of the types of courts. Given some basic knowledge, most people can understand the workings of the court system. Most important is to distinguish among five basic types of law: legislative law, judicial law, administrative law, procedural law, and constitutional law.

Types of Law

Legislative Law

Legislative law refers to laws passed by state or federal legislators. State legislatures, or the United States Congress, pass laws that govern particular people, places, or activities within the boundaries of a particular state or the entire nation, respectively. People who live under the laws of the United States and a particular state are required to adhere to the stipulations or prohibitions outlined in the laws passed by their representatives, both at the state and federal level.

Judicial Law

Judicial law is judge-made law. This type of law refers to a legal ruling made by a judge in a particular case. Often the ruling is an interpretation of the way in which state or federal law should be applied in an individual case (Box 15.1). Once the judge's ruling on a particular issue has been made, people are subject to that interpretation until the ruling is overturned by a higher court or until it is reinterpreted in a future case. Judges' rulings on particular points of law often become legal **precedent,** the body of law to which similar future cases can refer for an interpretation of a particular issue in question. This legal principle is called *stare decisis,* which means that judges' rulings hold as the standard for similar cases.

Administrative Law

Administrative law refers to the rules or laws made by various administrative offices either at the state or federal level. Agencies of the government are charged with making rules governing the activities of people subject to the jurisdiction of the agency. The Food and Drug Administration (FDA), for example, is an agency that makes rules for labeling food or medicine, approves new drugs as either prescription or non-prescription, and oversees procedures for research on new food substances or drugs. Pharmaceutical companies are subject to many intricate rules and

In this scene prospective jurors await the call to court. American courts are characterized by delays at all levels. People involved in court cases spend many hours waiting.

guidelines that were developed by the FDA. Administrative law is among the largest bodies of law in the United States.

Procedural Law

Procedural law is often called "the law's law." This is the body of laws that outlines the procedures by which other laws are carried out. Procedural law in the courtroom governs the way juries are selected, the types of evidence that may be admitted, the types of questions witnesses may be asked, and the order in which the case is presented. Procedural law delineates highly specific methods

Key Players in the Criminal Trial Courtroom

Judges

Judges preside over court proceedings. Their duties include: presiding over all pre-trial proceedings involving the accused offender, or defendant; review of motions or official requests made by courtroom attorneys; issuing of orders to any members of the courtroom staff, including juries, witnesses, court recorders, bailiffs, attorneys, and others; deciding issues of law or procedure within the trial; and supervision of plea bargaining, sentencing, or other official actions taken by the court. The actions, or decisions, of the judge are final and may only be reversed if an appellate judge finds some portion of the trial or a decision by the trial judge to be in error. The judge is the final authority in the courtroom.

Prosecutors

The prosecutor in a criminal trial represents the interests of the people. This means that the government *of the people* brings charges against the accused. In either a state or federal trial the actions against the defendant are handled by the prosecutor on behalf of the interests of the state or federal government. In plain language this means that the prosecutor is charged with proving that the accused offender violated the law. Prosecutors may be called the states' attorney, the district attorney, the attorney for the people, or any other similar designation—all refer to the person charged with prosecution of the case against the defendant.

Defense Attorneys

The Sixth Amendment to the Constitution guarantees those accused of crimes the right to counsel. Defense attorneys represent the defendant in the trial. They are there to see that defendants' legal rights are protected at every stage of the criminal justice process. Those defendants who can afford to hire their own attorneys choose who will represent them. These attorneys are usually called "privately retained counsel." Occasionally, defendants will represent themselves in their own trials. Most commonly, court-appointed counsel is provided in cases where the accused offender cannot afford to hire an attorney.

Each state has an established procedure for appointing attorneys to those defendants who cannot afford to hire their own counsel. In some states, "public defenders" are permanently appointed attorneys who defend poor clients. Funding may be through state or local budgets, but the attorneys are salaried employees whose sole job is defense of clients who cannot afford their own attorneys. In other states, judges appoint defense attorneys from private practice as they are needed. These are usually called "assigned counsel" or "court-appointed counsel." Attorneys, in this system, are paid case by case. In a few states, a contract system is used. In this case, the state has ongoing contracts with private law firms, legal aid societies, or the state bar association to provide attorneys for defense of poor clients.

Juries

Juries are made up of private citizens who are selected by the defense and prosecution to decide whether the offender should be convicted or acquitted in the trial. Juries commonly include twelve people but the number may be lower, depending on state law. A few alternates are also included in the selected panel in case a juror becomes ill or is disqualified for some reason.

The process of selection of the jury is called *voir dire*. Both the prosecution and the defense want people on the jury whom they believe will see or understand the issues better from their point of view. While the goal is justice, most people recognize that there are sympathetic trends that may help one side or the other. A white supremacist, for example, would not be considered an appropriate juror by the defense attorney of a minority defendant. The defense attorney, in this case, would use a *peremptory challenge* to exclude the juror. Prosecutors and defense attorney are each given a certain number of peremptory challenges during the selection process. They use them to exclude people they believe would be unfavorable to their side. In addition, prosecutors and defense attorneys use "challenges for cause" to exclude jurors who would have a conflict of interest in the case (for example, a relative of the defendant).

for carrying out most other types of law. When people say that a **procedural error** has occurred, they mean that a procedural law has been violated. If members of a particular minority group were intentionally excluded from jury selection in a court case, for example, this procedural error may become the foundation of a subsequent decision to re-try the case. Procedures for implementation of all types of law are intricate and must be followed precisely.

Constitutional Law

Constitutional law is the highest body of law; it is laid down by the United States Constitution. The application of constitutional principles is subject to interpretation by various federal court judges. But the highest court to hear arguments based upon the rule of constitutional law is the United States Supreme Court. Constitutional law is the overarching law to which all other rules and law are subject, so all laws in the United States are expected to fall under the general rule of law specified in the Constitution. If a state has a law that conflicts with basic constitutional requirements, then the state must change its law. Many protections of private citizens, as well as restrictions on the various activities of government, are specified in the Constitution, which makes it a common source of litigation with regards to the rights, privileges, and opportunities of ordinary citizens.

American courts are based upon **common law** traditions. That is, the implementation of law in the courts follows the British model of rule by tradition or law based on precedent. Rulings in prior cases become the foundation for argument of present cases. The use of common law traditions, or precedent, makes law dependable over time and fairly predictable for the future. While precedents may occasionally be overturned in the present, the usual reliance on past rulings assures a high level of consistency in the application of American law.

Civil Courts and Criminal Courts

In the United States, different types of law are interpreted in different types of courts. While there are many divisions among the courts, a primary distinction is between *civil* and *criminal* courts. **Civil courts** hear cases related to private matters. Divorce cases or inheritance issues, for example, are heard in civil courts. Civil courts also decide **tort** cases, in which an individual or group sues for compensation after an injury or death that resulted from some action or negligence on the part of a party who should have been responsible for preventing the injury or damage. Many cases of corporate crime are heard in civil courts.

Criminal courts hear cases considered serious enough to involve threat to all society in addition to a specific injury. Thus, the state prosecutes the accused offender in criminal cases because the actions seriously endanger social order. Serious crimes are further divided into misdemeanors and felonies to differentiate least serious from most serious offenses. The total number of adults convicted of felonies in the United States increased almost 60 percent between 1986 and 1990.[9] Conviction rates fell slightly from 1992 to 1994, but it is too early to tell whether this represents a trend.[10] Drug trafficking convictions are the most active area of criminal conviction, with an increase of 111 percent between 1986 and 1990.[11] In 1994, about one-third of offenders sentenced to state or federal prison had been convicted of a drug crime.[12]

Trial Courts and Appellate Courts

Some courts hear only cases involving factual issues and others hear only cases involving procedural law. Courts that hear and decide facts are called **trial courts.** Those that hear and decide issues related to procedural law are called **appellate courts.** Trial courts generally are the first court to hear and decide a case. During the trial, evidence, witnesses, and expert testimony are used to persuade the judge or the jury either to **convict** (find the defendant guilty), or to **acquit** (decide the evidence against the defendant is not sufficient for conviction). Trial courts are thus concerned with the facts of the cases, to determine whether the accused should be convicted or acquitted.

While trial courts are concerned with fair procedure, the role of appellate courts is to decide whether the law has been applied fairly and within the standards established under procedural law. In an appellate case, the facts of the original trial are not at issue; the concern is with the legal procedures that led to the outcome of the original trial. When a defendant convicted in a trial court files an appeal with an appellate court, the basis of the appeal must be purely legal; the facts of the case, such as guilt or innocence, are not argued. Rather, the procedures of the case are examined to determine whether an error occurred in the trial that might have affected the outcome of the case. For example, if an illegally obtained confession had been admitted into evidence, the appeal would argue that the outcome of the case was altered by the admission of the illegal confession. If the defendant were to win the appeal, the defendant would be entitled to a new trial that excludes the illegally obtained confession from evidence.

In addition to distinctions between trial and appellate courts, there are other types of distinctions. The United States is generally characterized as a dual-court system. Laws passed by Congress for the entire United States, or laws related the U.S. Constitution, fall under the **federal court** system. Laws passed by state legislatures, or ones pertaining to a state constitution, are represented in **state courts.** While it may seem unwieldy to some observers that a country as large as the United States would have fifty different state court systems, there is actually considerable similarity among the state courts. In recent years, the federal court system has expanded jurisdiction into areas that have traditionally been handled exclusively by the states. Enforcement of drug laws, for example, has become an important federal issue in the last decade. Involvement of the federal courts in areas that have been traditionally handled by the states has led to much criticism of the expanded role of government, and may be one of the factors related to increased rates of incarceration at the federal level. Regardless of the controversies over jurisdiction or expansion of federal judicial powers, two legal systems operate in the United States. One system is implemented by state courts and the other is within the domain of the federal courts.

The majority of judges in the United States are white men. However, more women and minorities have been appointed to the federal judiciary during the Bush and Clinton presidencies than at any previous time.

State Courts

As noted, state courts hear cases that pertain to state law. All states have at least two levels of courts and many have multiple levels. In addition, all states have specialized courts that hear cases related to specific issues (traffic court, family court, juvenile court, small claims court). The highly specialized courts are called **courts with limited jurisdiction.** The term *jurisdiction* refers to the authority of the court to hear and decide cases. A court with limited jurisdiction is one that is limited to cases of a specific legal nature. Traffic courts try cases related exclusively to issues surrounding traffic or motor vehicle problems (speeding, unregistered autos). Traffic courts could not decide cases involving murder or child custody.

State courts process the bulk of all criminal cases in the United States. In 1994, state courts handled nearly 900,000 felony convictions of adults.[13] General trends in state courts indicate increased likelihood of conviction in recent years, but a slight decline in the number of cases since 1992.[14] Drug crime represents the largest single category of felony cases heard in state courts.

Federal Courts

As previously stated, federal courts hear and decide cases related to federal law or constitutional issues. The federal system is three-tiered. That is, the federal court system is comprised of trial courts, called **U.S. district courts,** and two levels of appellate courts. **U.S. circuit courts** are appellate courts and the court of last resort or the highest appellate court is the **U.S. Supreme Court.** The federal system also has courts of limited jurisdiction, such as military courts, patent courts, or immigration courts. The U.S. Supreme Court is basically an appellate court, but it does have **original jurisdiction** (it is the first court to hear a case) on a limited number of issues, including some matters involving Congress or the presidency. Generally, the U.S. Supreme Court serves as an appellate court for matters involving federal rights, interpretation of the U.S. Constitution, and state court decisions that affect either federal rights or U.S. constitutional rights.

In 1994, there were 48,678 defendants convicted in U.S. district courts.[15] In the same year, 42,983 appeals were filed in U.S. courts of appeal, including the circuit courts.[16] The U.S. Supreme Court heard arguments presented in 94 cases out of the 8100 cases on the court docket for 1994.[17] Most of the cases filed with the Supreme Court are reviewed without oral argument, are refused by the court, are **remanded** (sent back to a lower court), or reinstate the lower court appellate decision. The Supreme Court hears oral arguments on only a few cases each year.

Issues and Trends

Throughout American history, the courts have been responsive to prevailing social values. Some people believe that the courts, especially the Supreme Court, lead American ideals of justice and equity. Others think the courts merely reflect a mirror image of prevailing sentiment. Regardless of the direction of the relationship between the courts and society, there has been considerable change in the operation of American courts in recent decades.

Judges were criticized throughout the 1970s for failing to provide consistency in sentencing and for maintaining an "Old Boy" network of exclusion. The problem of inconsistency in sentencing, or **sentencing disparity,** was an especially troubling concern. In 1977, Senator Edward Kennedy called the problem of sentencing disparity a "national scandal."[18] Throughout the 1980s, sweeping sentencing reforms weakened the amount of discretion judges had over sentencing decisions. Similarly, the hold on the Old Boy network has been challenged with the appointment of two women to the Supreme Court and by appointments of more women to the federal judiciary under the Bush and Clinton presidencies than had ever before served on the federal courts.

Judges

In the United States, judges are selected by several methods. In twenty-two states and the District of Columbia, a nominating commission—a nonpartisan group of lawyers and private citizens—actively recruits, screens, and nominates prospective judges to the governor of each state, who appoints judges from those nominated. Once appointed, judges in these states serve from 6 to 12 years, and then their names are placed unopposed on an election ballot, with a "yes/no" question to voters, who indicate whether they are to be retained. This method is often called the **Missouri Plan,** after the first state to adopt the procedure of non-partisan selection followed by electorate approval. The remaining twenty-eight states have various methods of selection that include partisan elections, non-partisan elections, legislative appointments, and appointments by governors.[19] Federal judges are appointed by the president and confirmed by the Senate, although recommendations are usually channeled through the attorney general, who consults with the American Bar Association. Members of Congress are also influential in the nomination of federal judges. Unlike state judges, who are appointed or elected for a specific term, federal judges are appointed for life. An Act of Congress and formal impeachment proceedings are required for removal of federal judges.[20]

Qualifications of Judges

Qualifications for judges are variable by state. Critics of the judiciary often point out that judges have little formal education in issues that routinely face the courts. That is, judges often have no real knowledge of the social sciences, which could help them to understand social problems that underlie reported crime in the United States. Demographic characteristics of judges appointed since the early 1960s, for example, indicates that the majority of federal judges have been educated in Ivy League or private colleges, which has led many critics to charge that judges are simply out of touch with the economic realities faced by defendants in their courtrooms.[21] Many judges have had no formal training in issues related to performance of their duties before they begin their term on the bench, although in recent years some states have provided orientation training for new judges and continuing education courses for judges already on the bench. In many states, lower-court judges are not required to be attorneys, nor to have graduated from college.[22] Federal judges *are* required to be attorneys, and experience is one of the criteria used in selection standards.

Judges' Salaries

In most states, judges earn above-average salaries, although they are considerably lower than the income judges could earn in private law practice. Salaries range from a national average of almost $86,000 for trial judges to nearly $96,000 for the highest appellate judges in 1996.[23] The highest salaries are paid to judges in California and New Jersey; the lowest salaries are paid in North Dakota and South Dakota. In the federal system, average salaries range from over $133,000 for trial court judges to $164,000 for the highest appellate court judges.[24]

Problems of Bias

While the issue of sentencing disparity has been an important concern in the criminal justice system, in recent years other controversies have been equally important. Judges, in general, have been accused of sexism, racism, and social class bias. Perceptions of the judiciary as a bastion of privileged white males who are out of touch with the economic realities of the 1990s are based upon several research studies that have documented significant bias. In the mid-1990s, for example, forty states, two federal circuits, Puerto Rico, and the District of Columbia

TABLE 15.1 | Percentage Characteristics of Presidential Appointments to Federal Judgeships

	PRESIDENT JOHNSON (1963–68)	PRESIDENT NIXON (1969–74)	PRESIDENT FORD (1974–76)	PRESIDENT CARTER (1977–80)	PRESIDENT REAGAN (1981–84)	PRESIDENT REAGAN (1985–88)	PRESIDENT BUSH (1989–92)	PRESIDENT CLINTON (1993–)
U.S. DISTRICT COURTS								
Sex								
Male	98.4%	99.1	98.1	85.6	90.7	92.5	80.4	68.2
Female	.6	.6	1.9	14.4	9.3	7.4	19.6	31.8
Race								
White	93.4	95.5	88.5	78.7	93.0	91.9	89.2	64.5
Black	4.1	3.4	5.8	13.9	.8	3.1	6.8	25.2
Hispanic	2.4	.1	1.9	6.9	5.4	4.3	4.0	8.4
Asian	0.0	0.0	3.9	.5	.8	.6	0.0	.9
Qualifications[a]								
Exceptional	48.4	45.3	46.1	50.9	50.4	57.1	57.4	60.7
Qualified	49.2	54.8	53.8	47.5	49.6	42.9	42.6	36.4
Not qualified	2.5	0.0	0.0	.5	0.0	0.0	0.0	2.8
U.S. COURTS OF APPEALS								
Sex								
Male	97.5	100.0	100.0	78.6	96.8	93.6	81.1	72.2
Female	2.5	0.0	0.0	16.1	3.2	6.4	18.9	27.8
Race								
White	95.0	97.8	100.0	78.6	93.5	100.0	89.2	72.2
Black	5.0	0.0	0.0	16.1	3.2	0.0	5.4	16.7
Hispanic	0.0	0.0	0.0	3.6	3.2	0.0	10.8	11.1
Asian	0.0	2.2	0.0	1.8	0.0	0.0	0.0	0.0
Qualifications[a]								
Exceptional	75.0	73.3	56.3	75.0	64.5	55.3	64.9	83.3
Qualified	20.0	26.7	33.3	25.0	35.5	44.7	35.1	16.7
Not qualified	2.5	0.0	8.3	0.0	0.0	0.0	0.0	0.0

[a]American Bar Association rates qualifications as "exceptionally well qualified, qualified, not qualified."

SOURCE: Kathleen Maguire and Ann L. Pastore, *Sourcebook of Criminal Justice Statistics* (Washington DC: U.S. Government Printing Office, 1995) 68–69.

all had commissions or task forces to study gender bias in their courts. Twenty five task force reports documenting significant gender bias had been published by the mid-1990s, and seventeen more task forces established for the investigation of racial and ethnic bias had been commissioned.[25]

Most judges are white men who bring to the bench many of the stereotypes about gender roles and racial issues that are characteristic of other men with similar education and background characteristics. The lifetime appointment of federal judges or reappointment of state judges through unopposed election assures that a high percentage of judges are older men, many of whom have not kept abreast of changing social trends. The "ivory tower" characterization of judges often fits the profile of men in this profession, whose values and ideals were formed at a time when women stayed at home to rear children, divorce was relatively rare, and men were the primary supporters of their families. The fact is that 4 out of 5 judges in the United States are men.[26] Whether the low representation of women in the profession significantly affects judicial decisions is controversial. Both the Bush and Clinton administrations have been sensitive to

the overrepresentation of white men in this occupation. As a result, appointments of women and minorities to federal judgeships occurred more frequently during these two presidential terms than at any other time in American history. Table 15.1 illustrates the demographic trends in presidential appointments to federal judgeships at both the trial (U.S. district courts) and appellate court levels under recent presidents.

Sexism in the courtroom has been evidenced for decades by biased treatment of women prosecutors, defense attorneys, witnesses, and defendants. Underlying beliefs about women's roles in society, the homemaking responsibilities of women, and the sexualization of all women have become evident at virtually every level of the judiciary. Some of the gender-bias task forces have found, for example, a tendency in most states to "punish" women who ask too many questions, who report sexual abuse of their children, or whose lifestyles are nontraditional. Fathers who seek custody are awarded primary custody in 70 percent of cases, regardless of other factors including spousal violence by the husband seeking custody or his prior conviction for child molestation.[27] This problem is thematic throughout the United States.

292   THE CRIMINAL JUSTICE SYSTEM

Sexism in the Courtroom

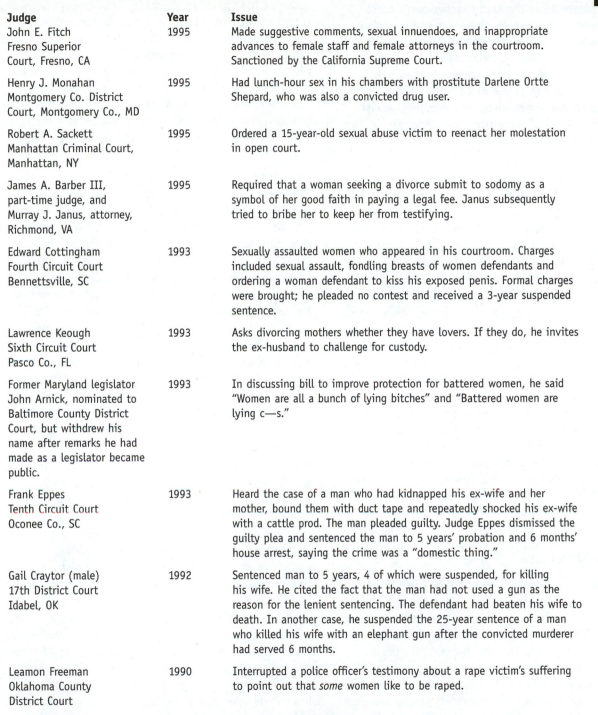

Judge	Year	Issue
John E. Fitch Fresno Superior Court, Fresno, CA	1995	Made suggestive comments, sexual innuendoes, and inappropriate advances to female staff and female attorneys in the courtroom. Sanctioned by the California Supreme Court.
Henry J. Monahan Montgomery Co. District Court, Montgomery Co., MD	1995	Had lunch-hour sex in his chambers with prostitute Darlene Ortte Shepard, who was also a convicted drug user.
Robert A. Sackett Manhattan Criminal Court, Manhattan, NY	1995	Ordered a 15-year-old sexual abuse victim to reenact her molestation in open court.
James A. Barber III, part-time judge, and Murray J. Janus, attorney, Richmond, VA	1995	Required that a woman seeking a divorce submit to sodomy as a symbol of her good faith in paying a legal fee. Janus subsequently tried to bribe her to keep her from testifying.
Edward Cottingham Fourth Circuit Court Bennettsville, SC	1993	Sexually assaulted women who appeared in his courtroom. Charges included sexual assault, fondling breasts of women defendants and ordering a woman defendant to kiss his exposed penis. Formal charges were brought; he pleaded no contest and received a 3-year suspended sentence.
Lawrence Keough Sixth Circuit Court Pasco Co., FL	1993	Asks divorcing mothers whether they have lovers. If they do, he invites the ex-husband to challenge for custody.
Former Maryland legislator John Arnick, nominated to Baltimore County District Court, but withdrew his name after remarks he had made as a legislator became public.	1993	In discussing bill to improve protection for battered women, he said "Women are all a bunch of lying bitches" and "Battered women are lying c—s."
Frank Eppes Tenth Circuit Court Oconee Co., SC	1993	Heard the case of a man who had kidnapped his ex-wife and her mother, bound them with duct tape and repeatedly shocked his ex-wife with a cattle prod. The man pleaded guilty. Judge Eppes dismissed the guilty plea and sentenced the man to 5 years' probation and 6 months' house arrest, saying the crime was a "domestic thing."
Gail Craytor (male) 17th District Court Idabel, OK	1992	Sentenced man to 5 years, 4 of which were suspended, for killing his wife. He cited the fact that the man had not used a gun as the reason for the lenient sentencing. The defendant had beaten his wife to death. In another case, he suspended the 25-year sentence of a man who killed his wife with an elephant gun after the convicted murderer had served 6 months.
Leamon Freeman Oklahoma County District Court	1990	Interrupted a police officer's testimony about a rape victim's suffering to point out that *some* women like to be raped.

SOURCES: Brian Mooar, "Prosecutor Details Sex Allegations Against Maryland Judge," *Washington Post,* 30 November 1995, C-1; *Washington Post,* "Top Lawyer, Partner Indicted in Richmond," 9 May 1995, B-5; David Kocieniewski, "Judge Orders Victim, 15, to Re-Enact Sexual Abuse in Court," *New York Times,* 14 October 1995, A-21; Brian Mooar, "Bid to Buy Prostitute's Silence Alleged," *Washington Post,* 23 September 1995, B-1; Maura Dolan, "High Court Censures Fresno Judge for Sexual Harassment," *Los Angeles Times,* 10 February 1995, A-3; National Organization For Women (NOW) Legal Defense and Education Fund's National Judicial Education Program to Promote Equality of Women and Men in the Courts, directed by Lynn Hecht Schafran.

Lynn Hecht Schafran, a researcher for the National Organization of Women (NOW) legal defense project, sums up the treatment of women in the courtroom:

> **Most fundamental is the fact that women's credibility is often devalued on the basis of sex rather than substance. Women are not believed simply because they are women. Women in the courts, particularly women lawyers, are sometimes subjected to demeaning forms of address, comments on their physical appearance, and clothing, sexist remarks and "jokes," unwanted touching, and verbal and physical sexual harassment.[28]**

Just because the judiciary is composed predominantly of white males from privileged backgrounds certainly does *not* always suggest bias. The problem is lack of representation across the spectrum of American diversity. In other words, judges (like the rest of us) often lack knowledge, sensitivity, or awareness of issues and lifestyles that exist outside of their own repertoire of experience. Representation among the judiciary of diverse racial and ethnic groups, as well as women, could enhance the effectiveness of judicial decisionmaking at all levels.

While gender bias in the courtroom has been widely cited in recent years, it is not the only problem associated with a nearly all-white, all-male judiciary. Racial bias is also a significant problem. Significant evidence of sentencing disparity has been available for several decades. Inconsistencies in sentencing, among other factors, have contributed to the national trend to reduce the power of judges in sentencing decisions. All states have converted at least part of sentencing to the domain of state legislators, who decide the length of sentence for each crime through mandates in the law.

Sentencing Strategies

Chapter 16 provides a detailed discussion of the philosophies that underlie sentencing strategies in the United States, but we will present a brief overview of the strategies here as well. There are four basic objectives of sentences imposed in American courts: rehabilitation, deterrence, incapacitation, or retribution. Through most of the twentieth century, rehabilitation and deterrence have been the dominant strategies. Currently, trends are toward incapacitation and retribution as increasingly important goals of sentencing.

Rehabilitation

Strategies promoting rehabilitation are aimed at reforming the offender. The ideals of **rehabilitation** stress that people commit crimes because some deficiency in their character, economic status, or social background caused them to engage in crime. If the problem can be "cured," the offender will refrain from further criminal behavior. If, for example, an offender commits property crimes because of having no marketable skills, being unemployed, or being without financial resources, the solution to is to train the person in job skills. Future crime will be unnecessary if the person secures a job. Rehabilitation strategists highlight a myriad of social, personal, and economic problems related to crime. From the perspective of rehabilitation proponents, sentences that retrain convicted offenders in socially acceptable activities can both reduce crime and humanely redirect offenders.

Deterrence

Sentences with the goal of **deterrence** are used to serve as an example to all others who may be contemplating similar criminal activities. Deterrence strategies presume that rational people, having experienced the negative repercussions of crime, will refrain from illegal activities to avoid similar punishments. There are two types of deterrence: general and specific. **General deterrence** uses the offender as *an example for society.* Under this philosophical approach to sentencing, *anyone* should be deterred. **Specific deterrence** is an attempt to prevent the *individual* offender from reoffending through the *pain* of the punishment. Under this strategy, the offender will not commit subsequent crime if the punishment for the current offense is significantly painful.

Incapacitation

The use of prison sentences to incapacitate offenders is, currently, one of the most important strategies in the American criminal justice system. **Incapacitation** presumes that offenders who are imprisoned are prevented from further offenses for the duration of the prison term. If the prison term is lengthy, the incapacitating benefit of the sentence is great. A variation of this strategy, **selective incapacitation,** is the practice of sentencing particular offenders to longer prison terms than would be average. Repeat offenders, dangerous or violent offenders, and many drug offenders have been awarded longer prison sentences, not on the characteristics of their current offense but on the basis of their offense history. As discussed in Chapter 16, this practice is controversial, but the goal is to incapacitate offenders whose behavior is especially reprehensible.

Retribution

The strategy of **retribution** is based upon the belief that offenders *deserve* to be punished because their behavior is socially abhorrent. The sentence is not imposed to reform the offender or to prevent other offenses. Under this strategy, offenders receive sentences exclusively because they deserve to be punished. The death penalty is a retributive sentence. While many proponents of the death penalty may hope that others are deterred by the sentence, the primary motivation for sentencing offenders to death is to express social outrage.

Types of Sentences

There are basically four types of sentencing strategies in the United States. They are: indeterminate, determinate, presumptive, and mandatory sentences.

Indeterminate Sentences

Indeterminate sentences arise from laws that provide both a minimum and a maximum amount of time the convicted offender could serve for a particular crime, but the exact length of the sentence is not specified in the law. Judges and prison authorities have great discretion with the use of indeterminate sentences. For example, if the range of sentencing possibilities for a particular offense specifies not less than 10 years but not more than 25 years, the judge is able to award a sentence somewhere between 10 and 25 years. Some indeterminate sentences that were established under rehabilitation ideologies in the 1960s and 1970s left the decision for the length of the sentence up to correctional administrators. These were called **administrative sentences.** The convicted offender, under administrative sentencing, would be released from prison after showing evidence of rehabilitation. In such cases, the offender might be sentenced for a term of not less than 10 years but not more than 25 years. If the offender showed sufficient evidence of reform after 10 years that person could become eligible for **parole,** or supervised early release from prison under administrative sentencing guidelines.

Some indeterminate sentencing has been applied with very broad discretion by judges or correctional administrators. If the crime carried a sentencing option of a prison term ranging from 1 day to life, the judge, prison administrator, or state parole board would decide, within that very broad range, when the offender would be released. State law determines whether the judge or the prison authorities would make the final decision. In states where the judge set the length of the sentence, due-process protections and the right to appellate review were an automatic component of sentencing. If correctional authorities or a parole board determined when offenders should be released, no due-process protections or right-to-appeal decisions regarding release were required.

The prevalence of sentencing disparity under indeterminate sentencing strategies led all states to begin reform of sentencing laws in the 1970s. The problem was that some offenders received lenient sentences, such as probation or a short prison term, while others received lengthy prison sentences for the same offense. Non-legal criteria, such as race, socioeconomic status, and gender, were found to be more relevant to sentencing than the offense in some studies.[29]

Determinate Sentencing

Under **determinate sentencing,** the legislature specifies a fixed sentence for each offense, which can be raised or lowered with aggravating or mitigating circumstances. If, for example, the usual penalty for rape is 10 years, but in a particular case the offender used a weapon, the sentence might be increased because of the greater threat and trauma to the victim. Likewise, mitigating factors such as extreme passion at the moment of the offense might lessen the required sentence. If a man shoots a neighbor whom he has caught molesting his daughter, the fit of anger brought about by the pain caused to his daughter might mitigate, or lessen, the sentence ordinarily imposed for murder.

Under ordinary circumstances, determinate sentencing fixes a specific sentence for each offense. These sentences are often called *flat sentences,* or *definite sentences.* Under determinate sentencing, particular circumstances of the offense may be considered and judges have several options at the time of sentencing. They may, for example, *suspend* a sentence, eliminating the requirement that the offender must actually serve the sentence. They may also *split* sentences, such as imposing a period of incarceration followed by a lengthy period of supervision, or *probation.* In most cases determinate sentences may not be changed by parole boards or other review commissions once they are imposed. The only exception is state-sponsored **good-time** policies, which allow for early release from prison after offenders have served a specified amount of their sentence without trouble to prison authorities.

Between 1976 and 1984, ten states enacted determinate sentencing laws and eliminated paroled release from prison.[30] All other states have undertaken sentencing changes to reduce judicial discretion or lessen the breadth of indeterminate options. Initial analysis of sentencing changes suggested that the shift to determinate sentencing had caused subsequent increases in the prison population. But Thomas Marvell and Carlisle Moody have found that it is not the sentencing strategy that has increased the size of the prison population.[31] Other factors, such as the increased likelihood of using prison instead of alternative sentencing options, or the use of **plea bargaining,** which is a guilty plea by the defendant in exchange for a favor from the prosecutor (for example, the dropping of some charges against the defendant), are responsible for the increase in the prison population. Marvell and Moody have found no association between determinate sentences and a reduction in the crime rates.

There are variations in the determinate sentencing models. One type of determinate sentencing, **presumptive sentencing,** requires judges to impose a particular sentence within a range of possible sentencing options that have been determined by the legislature. The sentences available to the judge are highly specific and allow for only very limited discretionary options on the part of the judge. Under presumptive sentencing guidelines, the law may specify narrow conditions under which the judge is allowed to deviate from required sentences. Prior felony convictions, or violence directed toward the victim, might be circumstances that would justify a harsher sentence. In this case, the judge sentences the offender to a penalty that is harsher than the usual sentence imposed for the offense on the basis of the circumstances relating to the particular crime. Deviation from the required sentence is rare and must be justified in writing by the sentencing judge under presumptive sentencing guidelines.

Mandatory Sentencing

Under **mandatory sentencing,** the judge is required by law to impose a specified sentence after conviction of an offender. State legislatures or the U.S. Congress determine the length of sentence for particular offenses. The judge has no discretion in the type or length of sentence to be imposed under this sentencing requirement. Often sentencing tables are used that place the offenses along one axis of the table and prior convictions or other aggravating factors along the other axis. The judge, for example, finds the offense along the y-axis, counts the number of prior convictions along the x-axis and joins the two on a grid, which specifies the sentence. Many mandatory sentencing requirements have been adopted by state legislatures in an effort to reduce or eliminate sentencing disparity. Under mandatory sentencing, like offenders should be given like sentences, since the judge has no power to deviate from the mandated sentence.

Theoretically, mandatory sentencing should eliminate disparity that results from judges' attitudes toward particular demographic groups. In reality, however, discretion at other stages of the criminal justice system still influences gender and racial differences in punishment. Prosecutors and the police still have wide discretion in decisions regarding who is charged or prosecuted. Research on this issue indicates that prosecutors, for example, levy heavier and more numerous charges against non-whites than against whites. Some studies have found that sentences under mandatory guidelines have become even more discriminatory than under previous sentencing models where significant judicial discretion was allowed. This is especially true for non-white offenders.[32]

At the federal level, the Sentencing Reform Act of 1984, which took effect November 1, 1987, shifted federal sentencing to mandatory sentences. Judges maintain very limited options in sentencing offenders under the new guidelines, and most sentences are mandatory. Drug offenses have been especially targeted under the federal guidelines. Federal sentences are to be served in full, with minimal allowances for good behavior. Change to mandatory sentences at the federal level has meant that offenders convicted in federal courts are more likely to go to prison, and they serve longer sentences since the Sentencing Reform Act went into effect. Prior to the act, for example, 50 percent of convicted offenders in 1982 were sentenced to prison. Sixty-five percent of offenders convicted in Federal District Courts were incarcerated in 1992. Similarly, in 1982 the average length of sentence for all federal offenders was 48 months in prison, and in 1992 the average federal prison sentence for all offenses was 62 months.[33] The increased use of prison as the predominant sentence, and the longer average sentences at the federal level, have led to extraordinary increases in the size of the federal prison population. The number of inmates held in federal prisons increased 240 percent between 1980 and 1993, partly as a result of mandatory sentencing.[34]

Other Sentencing Trends

Regardless of which type of sentencing predominates in any state, various sentencing options are available in all states and in the federal system. Chapter 17 presents a detailed description of many sentencing options imposed by American courts. While prison may be the most commonly assumed sentence, other options are often used. *Probation,* or the supervised release of offenders who are believed to be unlikely to commit subsequent offenses and who show potential of reform through supervision, has been widely used in the United States for over one hundred years. The use of probation has been strongly criticized in recent years because it was the leading penalty in many states during the 1970s and because many people believed that it was not harsh enough to have a deterrent impact on the offender. The movement toward harsher penalties and mandatory prison terms has caused a decrease in the use of probation in the last decade. Table 15.2 illustrates the types of sentences imposed by state courts in 1994. Generally, sentences to jail involve a penalty of 1 year or less, while sentences to prison include sentences longer than 1 year.

The length of sentences imposed in American courts is also controversial. Many people believe that convicted offenders should serve long prison sentences, both as a deterrent to future offenses and as a matter of retribution. The average length of sentences imposed both in state and federal courts has increased in recent years. With a

MOST SERIOUS[a] CONVICTION	OFFENSE TOTAL	INCARCERATION			PROBATION
		TOTAL	PRISON	JAIL	
ALL OFFENSES	100%	71%	45%	26%	29%
VIOLENT OFFENSES	100	82	62	20	18
Murder	100	97	95	2	3
Rape	100	88	71	17	12
Robbery	100	88	77	11	12
Aggravated assault	100	75	48	27	25
PROPERTY OFFENSES	100	68	42	26	32
Burglary	100	75	53	22	25
Larceny	100	66	38	28	34
Fraud	100	60	32	28	40
DRUG OFFENSES	100	69	42	27	31
Possession	100	66	34	32	34
Trafficking	100	71	48	23	29
WEAPONS	100	69	42	27	31
OTHER OFFENSES[b]	100	66	36	30	34

[a] For persons with a combination of sentences, the most severe sentence designation is used. The death penalty is included in percent sentenced to prison.
[b] Includes non violent offenses such as receiving stolen property or vandalism.

SOURCE: Patrick A. Langan and Jodi M. Brown, "Felony Sentences in State Courts, 1994," *Bureau of Justice Statistics* (Washington DC: U.S. Government Printing Office, 1997) 2.

reduction in the use of probation and other alternative sentences, the size of the prison population has increased greatly. Americans incarcerate more people, and a higher percentage of the population, than any other country in the world. Ramifications of the increase in the size of the prison population are discussed in Chapter 17. Table 15.3 presents the average length of sentences imposed for particular crimes in state courts.

Most offenders do not serve their entire imposed sentence. All states reduce the sentence proportionate to the amount of good time served by the offender. While the issue of early release from prison is politically controversial, good time is built into the sentencing strategies. Judges, state sentencing commissions, and prosecutors all understand that the imposed sentence is greater than the amount of time to be served. The public often feels that the disjuncture between the imposed sentence and the amount of time served represents a reduction in the punishment effect of the sentence. Actually, the good-time policy is a very effective means of prison control. Prisoners who know they will be released before the specified length of their sentence are more likely to behave in prison, rather than risk loss of good time. With judges, legislators, and prosecutors all knowledgeable about good-time policies, only the public believes an offender was released before the sentence was served. Judges who impose a 6-year sentence, for example, are fully aware that the offender will probably serve about 3 years. Political rhetoric that calls for "truth in sentencing" is aimed primarily at the public, which is not as well-informed about the meaning of sentences as those who work within the criminal justice system.

The Death Penalty

The death penalty is the sentence that is among the most controversial and least used in the United States. This sentence is imposed in cases where the offender has committed an especially *heinous* (horrifying) murder and is sentenced to die as a punishment. The definitions of **capital offenses,** or crimes in which the death penalty may be applied, are variable by state. The U.S. Supreme Court has specified a narrow range of circumstances where the death penalty may be used as a sentencing option. In 1976, the Court handed down several rulings that clarified the restrictions that must apply when an offender is sentenced to death. The Court ruled that if a jurisdiction has the death penalty it cannot be mandatory; aggravating and mitigating factors must be weighed; and the circumstances of the crime, the character of the defendant, and the defendant's prior record must be considered.[35] Since 1976, numerous rulings have further delineated the procedures by which the penalty of death may be applied and the means by which offenders may be executed. In 1993 alone, there were nine cases heard by the U.S. Supreme Court on death penalty issues.

Among the most controversial rulings of the Supreme Court was that involving a defendant, Leonel Herrera, in

TABLE 15.3 Mean Length of Felony Sentences Imposed by State Courts by Offense and Type of Sentence, 1992 (mean maximum sentence length in years)[a]

MOST SERIOUS CONVICTION OFFENSE	INCARCERATION			PROBATION
	TOTAL	PRISON	JAIL	
ALL OFFENSES	4.1 yr	5.9 yr	0.5 yr	3.3 yr
VIOLENT OFFENSES	7.7	9.8	0.5	3.7
Murder	21.8	22.4	0.6	4.9
Rape	11.1	13.2	0.6	5.0
Robbery	8.7	9.7	0.7	4.2
Aggravated assault	4.5	6.6	0.5	3.5
Other violent	3.9	5.8	0.5	3.6
PROPERTY OFFENSES	3.2	4.7	0.5	3.5
Burglary	4.2	5.7	0.7	3.9
Larceny	2.4	3.7	0.5	3.3
Fraud	2.7	4.2	0.4	3.4
DRUG OFFENSES	3.3	5.1	0.5	3.2
Possession	2.3	4.1	0.3	3.1
Trafficking	4.0	5.5	0.7	3.3
Weapons	2.8	3.9	0.4	2.7
OTHER OFFENSES[b]	2.6	3.4	0.4	2.7

[a] mean sentences do not include death or life in prison
[b] includes non-violent offenses such as receiving stolen property

SOURCE: Patrick A. Langan and Jodi M. Brown, "Felony Sentences in State Courts, 1994," *Bureau of Justice Statistics* (Washington DC: U.S. Government Printing Office, 1997) 4.

TABLE 15.4 Executions and Death Penalty Prisoners, 1995

EXECUTIONS DURING 1994		NUMBER OF PRISONERS UNDER DEATH SENTENCE	
Texas	19	California	420
Missouri	6	Texas	404
Illinois	5	Florida	362
Virginia	5	Pennsylvania	196
Florida	3	Ohio	155
Oklahoma	3	Illinois	154
Alabama	2	Alabama	143
Arkansas	2	N. Carolina	139
Georgia	2	Oklahoma	129
N. Carolina	2	Arizona	117
Pennsylvania	2	Georgia	98
Arizona	1	Tennessee	96
Delaware	1	Missouri	92
Louisiana	1	22 other jurisdictions	549
Montana	1		
S. Carolina	1		
TOTAL	56	TOTAL	3054

SOURCE: Tracy L. Snell, "Capital Punishment 1995," *Bureau of Justice Statistics Bulletin* (Washington DC: U.S. Government Printing Office, 1996) 1.

TABLE 15.5 Jurisdictions Without a Death Penalty, 1995

Alaska	Minnesota
District of Columbia	North Dakota
Hawaii	Rhode Island
Iowa	Vermont
Maine	West Virginia
Massachusetts	Wisconsin
Michigan	

SOURCE: Tracy L. Snell, "Capital Punishment 1995," *Bureau of Justice Statistics* (Washington DC: U.S. Government Printing Office, 1996) 1.

1993. In this case, the Court ruled that evidence of innocence was irrelevant to the application of the death penalty. Herrera, whose lawyers tried to introduce new evidence in his case after his appeals process had been exhausted, was denied a federal hearing by the U.S. Supreme Court in January 1993. The Court ruled that Herrera had been given a fair trial; whether he was innocent when convicted was irrelevant. The Constitution does not prohibit executions of innocent people, but it does require that defendants be tried fairly.[36] Herrera was executed in Texas in May 1993.

Thirty-seven states and the federal government have statutes that permit the use of the death penalty for specified offenses. Each state defines the crimes eligible for the death penalty. All thirty-seven states specify murder, complicated by a variety of circumstances: the rape of a child, the commission of another felony, murder of a police officer or firefighter, or murder by bomb or explosive. The federal government offers the longest list of specific crimes of murder for which the death penalty may be applied. There are forty-three federal capital offenses.[37]

The number of people executed each year has been increasing annually since 1976. Between 1967 and 1976, the execution of people sentenced to death was halted while the Supreme Court examined the constitutionality of this sentencing option. In 1977, Gary Gilmore was the first person executed (in Utah) after the Supreme Court reinstated the death penalty. Between 1977 and the end of 1995, 313 people were executed. There have been 4172 executions in the United States between 1930 and 1995. Most executions, both currently and historically, have been carried out in Southern states.[38]

At year end in 1995, there were 3054 prisoners under sentence of death in thirty-four states and the federal prison system. All death-row inmates had committed murder. A total of 310 new death-row prisoners were received by the states during 1995. One percent of death-row prisoners are women.[39] Table 15.4 illustrates the distribution of executions and the number of death-row inmates by state at the end of 1995. The jurisdictions that did not have a death penalty in 1995, which represents the most current Department of Justice listing, are presented in Table 15.5.

Appellate Review

In 1995, the average length of time executed prisoners had been on death row was 11 years and 2 months.[40] The time between sentencing and execution has been increasing for two decades. In 1972, all prisoners on death row were removed from death penalty status when the Supreme court invalidated existing death penalty laws. Since 1972, all death penalty states have rewritten their capital offense laws. As each of the death penalty laws has been challenged by appeal, the length of time sentenced offenders await execution has increased.[41] The appeals process is automatic in all death penalty states except Arkansas; it is lengthy; and appellate review significantly increases the cost of each execution. Without the appeals process, the likelihood of inappropriate use of the death penalty or the execution of innocent people would be considerably increased. Between 1973 and 1995, for example, 1911 death sentences or convictions were overturned by appellate courts.[42] Without appellate review, execution is quicker but the likelihood of error is increased. Recent trends suggest that appellate review—and numerous court rulings that have refined procedure and application of death sentences over the last two decades—may have resulted in more assured sentences than were characteristic of this penalty ten years ago. In 1985, for example, thirty-seven convictions with death sentences were overturned by appellate courts; no convictions in either 1994 or 1995 were overturned by appellate courts.[43]

Execution of Juveniles

Twelve states authorize capital punishment for offenders aged 16 or under, with Arkansas and Virginia stipulating the youngest approved age as 14. Arkansas sentenced a 17-year-old offender to death in 1996.[44] Eight states do not specify a minimum age of eligibility.[45] As recently as 1983, a person as young as 10 years of age could be sentenced to death in North Dakota.[46] In 1995, the youngest death penalty offender was 18 and the oldest was 80.[47]

There are three important issues that underlie the use of the death penalty in the United States. They are: (1) the morality of capital punishment; (2) racial and social class inequities that have been associated with the application of the death penalty; and (3) the high economic costs of executions.

Morality and the Death Penalty

The issue of morality involves questions over whether death is a moral requirement for justice or whether it is prohibited by higher moral principles. Those who favor the death penalty generally argue either that the offender deserves to die because of the seriousness of the offense (retribution), or that the offender should die as a signal to all others and thus as a prevention of future similar offenses (deterrence). Those who oppose the death penalty believe that state-sanctioned killing is no more appropriate than individual acts of homicide.

Those who defend the death penalty on the grounds that retribution is morally mandated by certain offenses focus upon the justice of death for offenders who have committed especially horrifying murders. In other words, some people *deserve* to die as a punishment for their offense. This is sometimes called the "just deserts" model for use of capital punishment. The Supreme Court affirmed in *Gregg v. Georgia* that the imposition of retributive pain and suffering on defendants is constitutional as long as the punishment is proportionate to the crime.[48] Execution for drug addiction, for example, is disproportionately harsh, according to the Supreme Court, but death for the crime of murder is within the realm of retributive punishments, with the provision of certain safeguards against arbitrary application of death sentences.

Those who oppose the death penalty point out that it is inconsistently applied. Some offenders who commit horrible murders are sentenced to death, while others are sentenced to life in prison. Opponents to the death penalty believe that the morality argument is diluted by the inconsistent application of death sentences.

An alternative angle of the morality argument for the death penalty focuses upon the deterrent effect of capital punishment. However, there is controversy over whether death sentences are a deterrent to murder. There are approximately 25,000 homicides every year, about 300 new death sentences annually, and less than sixty executions in the highest recorded year in the modern era. Thus, the likelihood is minimal that any single offender (out of the potential 25,000 in a given year) will be sentenced to death and executed. Current murderers have a less than 0.01 percent chance of receiving the sentence of death after conviction.[49] With an average delay of about 10 years between sentencing and execution, the impact of the death sentence is further diluted as a consequence for murder.

Proponents of the deterrence argument point out, however, that even though the likelihood of a death sentence in any particular case is low, it is still possible that the threat of death may deter some potential offenders. It is possible that people are fearful of the death penalty, no matter how low the likelihood that it will be applied in any single case. The problem of deterrence is especially murky because research on deterrence is difficult to design. It is easier to count those who have not been deterred than those who have refrained from crime because of the threat of punishment. For obvious reasons, it is difficult to locate or study the motivations of people who could have committed the crime of homicide but did not. The problem is further complicated by the fact that people refrain from murder for a wide variety of reasons, only one of which may be fear of punishment. Underlying motivations for *not* committing a murder may include moral issues, religious beliefs, or humanistic values, as well as the possible fear of the death penalty. Studying offenders who have not been deterred is much easier than ascertaining the deterrent effect of a seldom-used punishment. For this reason, research on the deterrent effect of capital punishment is complicated and methodologically very difficult.

Most research in this area has focused upon a variety of issues that might indicate a decline in homicide as an effect of capital punishment. Some studies have compared homicide rates in the United States to other developed nations. Since the United States is the only Western nation to retain the death penalty, the deterrence argument would predict that the homicide rate should be lowest in the United States. Actually, the rate of homicide is higher in the United States than in any other developed Western nation. Research by Thorsten Sellin compared murder rates in states with and without the death penalty. The deterrence prediction would suggest that death penalty states should have lower homicide rates than non–death penalty states. However, Sellin found the opposite effect. Non–death penalty states actually had murder rates comparable to, and sometimes lower than, those with the death penalty. In this research, the death penalty was found to have no deterrent effect on the murder rates in states that used capital punishment.[50]

The most recent direction of research has focused upon correlations between publicity surrounding executions and subsequent changes in the homicide rate. If the death penalty deters potential murderers, research suggests that the effect should be strongest in the aftermath of highly publicized executions. Findings have been mixed, with a few studies indicating a slight decline in homicide rates correlated with publicity and other studies indicating no measurable effect in the rate of homicide after executions.[51] Most analysts believe that if the death penalty deters murder, the effect is very slight.[52]

Racial and Social Class Discrimination

The second major issue that orients discussion of the death penalty is the problem of racial and social class discrimination in the use of capital punishment. Historically, many more black than white offenders have been executed, which has led to charges of racism in the application of death sentences. Between 1930 and 1993, for example, over 2000 black offenders and under 1900 white offenders were executed in the United States. The disproportionality is especially evident with the crime of rape. Between 1930 and 1965, the death penalty for rape was applied to 405 black offenders and 48 white offenders.[53] Because of increased attention to racial bias in the use of capital punishment since the 1972 *Furman v. Georgia* case

(which specifically prohibited death sentences applied on the basis of arbitrary racial criteria), discrimination has become more subtle.[54] While there is a disproportionately high representation of African Americans under sentence of death, there are currently more white death-row prisoners than black. In 1995, 42 percent of death-row inmates were black and 57 percent were white.[55]

The disproportionality in racial distributions of death sentences is not as much linked to the race of the offender as to the race of the victim. Offenders who kill white victims are more likely to be sentenced to death than offenders who kill black victims.[56] Since 1977, over 85 percent of those who have been executed in the United States have killed white victims, even though about half of all people murdered are black.[57] The issue of the race of the victim has been explored as a measurement of discrimination in death sentences since the U.S. Supreme Court heard the case of *McKlesky v. Kemp* (1985), in which the research of David Baldus was presented to the Court as a justification for vacating the sentence of McKlesky and invalidating the Georgia death penalty statute under which he had been sentenced. Baldus and his colleagues found, in their study of 11,000 Georgia murder convictions between 1973 and 1980, that a defendant was 11 times more likely to get the death penalty if the victim was white than if the victim was black. If the offender was black and the victim was white, the chances of getting the death penalty were 22 times greater than if the victim was black. Whites who killed black victims did not receive the death penalty in Georgia.[58] The U.S. Supreme Court did not rule in favor of McKlesky. Although Baldus' data on racial discrimination has been widely accepted by social scientists, McKlesky's attorneys had not demonstrated that McKlesky was the victim of discrimination in sentencing. In other words, patterns of discrimination are relevant only when a defendant can demonstrate the application of discriminatory policies in his case.

Among the more serious problems in death penalty cases is the fact that nearly all defendants who are sentenced to death are too poor to hire attorneys who can adequately defend them. Most offenders sentenced to death have been represented by court-appointed counsel. Court-appointed attorneys are often the lowest paid, most overworked lawyers in American courts. Young, inexperienced lawyers, or those who do not have the skills or initiative to practice law in other settings, are often appointed by the court to represent poor clients. In Texas, for example, the average payment to court-appointed attorneys for death penalty cases is $40,000. From this fee, attorneys pay for lab tests, expert witnesses, and their own services. Privately retained defense attorneys in death penalty cases begin fee schedules in the hundreds of thousands of dollars[59] (Box 15.3). Temptations to limit

Defense Attorneys in Death Penalty Cases Have Made National Headlines in Recent Years

The competence of legal counsel can be a factor that significantly undermines offenders' cases. Among the more notorious cases of incompetent defense attorneys have been those who have slept through testimony during the trials of their clients or attorneys who have been too drunk in court to offer objections during trials of death penalty clients.

In the trial of Bill Garrison, who was convicted in 1988 for the murder of a convenience-store clerk in Texas, the court-appointed attorney did not show up in court for jury selection because he was in the drunk tank of the county jail after arrest for driving with an 0.27 blood alcohol count (0.10 is the legal limit in most states). Witnesses said he staggered into court during the trial. In another Texas case, Calvin Burdine was sentenced to death and his death sentence has been upheld, even though three jurors and the court clerk testified that his attorney slept during his trial.

One court-appointed attorney in Texas, Ron Mock, runs a bar in Harris County and handles death penalty cases as they arise. Twelve cases he has represented have resulted in death sentences for his clients. Three of the defendants have been executed. Harris County, Texas, sent fifteen murder defendants to death row in 1994. All had court-appointed attorneys. Another fifteen defendants in 1994 would have been eligible for the death penalty, based on characteristics of their crimes, but did not receive a death sentence. All of these defendants were represented by private counsel.

Eddie Lee Ross, an African American defendant from Georgia, was sentenced to death after his defense attorney, who was 81 years old and had been the grand wizard of the local Ku Klux Klan for fifty years, called him a "nigger" before the presiding judge and fell asleep during the trial. Ross' death sentence was eventually overturned by the Georgia Supreme Court after the Georgia State Bar threatened to disbar his attorney because of senility. When the presiding judge in this case, Judge Clarence Peeler, was questioned about the defense attorney's affiliation with a white supremacist group, the judge said "The fact that he was in the Ku Klux Klan did not trouble me. I believed that he could try a case and he could do it well."

SOURCES: *ABC* (American Broadcasting Company) *World News Tonight,* 21 November 1994, "Attorneys for Death Row Inmates." Transcript provided by Research Publications International; CNN, 25 June 1995; ABC, 21 November 1994.

the defense of clients to enhance their own payment may be overwhelming for some court-appointed attorneys under this system (Box 15.4).

Cost of Executions

The final controversy associated with the use of the death penalty in the United States is the high cost of executions. Many people believe that it is cheaper to execute offenders who have committed horrible offenses than to keep them in prison for life. Supporters of the death penalty often point out that the state should not have to pay the expense of imprisonment for offenders who have committed such heinous crimes that they will never be released. Actually, it is much more expensive to execute offenders than to keep them alive for life in prison. In Harris County, Texas, which is called the death penalty capital of the United States, the cost of death penalty cases is calculated at $2 million per case. Taxpayers have begun to question the justification for increased capital indictments because no deterrent effect of the heavy use of the death penalty has been seen. In fact, the murder rate in Harris County has *increased* along with the trend toward greater

use of the death penalty.[60] In general, Texas averages an expenditure of $2.3 million per case from jury selection to lethal injection. Florida averages $3.2 million per case, which is six times more that the average expenditure for conventional murder trials. California estimates that the death penalty option adds $1.2 million to the cost of each murder trial. California has reported that taxpayer savings would be approximately $90 million annually if the death penalty were abolished. New Jersey estimates the cost of executing offenders at $7.3 million per case.[61]

Costs of the death penalty are high because murder trials in which a death sentence is an option are usually longer, appellate review is expensive and usually takes many years to complete, and death-row confinement (which includes higher security than average prison custody) is expensive to maintain. Reducing costs through elimination or reduction in appellate review is an option that few legal scholars support because of the potential danger of arbitrary death sentences. When error is uncovered, it is usually at the appellate stage.

Popular support for increased use of the death penalty remains high, in spite of these problems. Public opinion

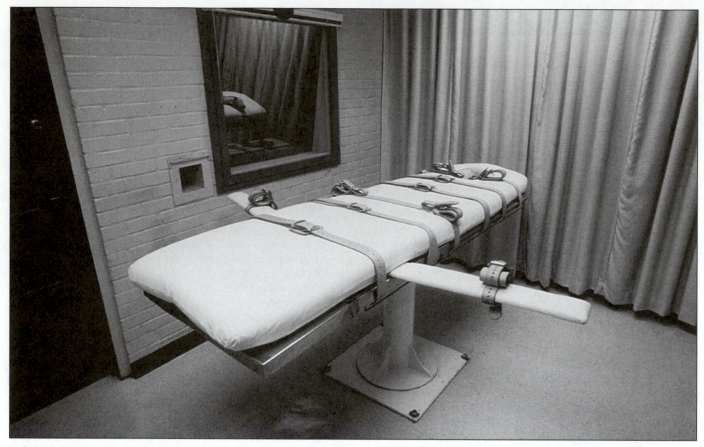

Lethal injection has become the preferred method in most states for execution of those who have been sentenced to death.

polls indicate that 77 percent of the American public supported the death penalty in 1995.[62] In 1966, only 42 percent of Americans favored capital punishment, which indicates significantly increased support for the use of the death penalty over the last three decades.[63] While support for capital punishment is generally strong, the highest support is expressed by people with the lowest educational attainment. Whites express stronger support than blacks; people under age 30 express stronger support than people over 30; and men are more likely to favor the death penalty than women. The highest support for use of capital punishment is measured by political affiliation; Republicans are significantly more likely to support the death penalty than Democrats or Independents.[64]

Current Problems

The American court system is highly complex and there is considerable variation among jurisdictions on how cases are routed through the judicial system. Many problems in judicial processing clog American courts, and constitutional protections that prevent the abuse of judicial power mandate procedural standards in virtually all types of courts.

Americans believe that courts are too lenient with criminals and that punishments should be more harsh. In 1994, public opinion polls indicated that 85 percent of Americans believed that sentences imposed by American courts are not harsh enough.[65] There is considerable dissatisfaction with American courts and there has been a significant decline in the confidence Americans place in the judicial system over the last two decades.

Court Overload

In 1994, there were 911,842 felony convictions in state and federal courts in the United States.[66] Cases handled by juvenile courts added another 1.5 million court cases annually.[67] The volume of convictions in U.S. courts has increased significantly since the early 1980s. Increases are most significant among drug offenses. Among offenders convicted in U.S. district courts in 1994, for example, 41 percent of total cases were drug offenses.[68] In state courts, about one-third of offenders were convicted of drug offenses, one-third were convicted of property offenses, 18 percent were convicted of violent offenses, and the remaining offenders were convicted of other miscellaneous offenses in 1994.[69]

Are the Poor Most Likely to Commit Homicide?

Anthropological data, as well as studies of American homicide, show that most offenders in the modern era are lower class. Data from Denmark, England, Finland, Italy, Mexico, South Africa, Sri Lanka, and the United States indicate, overwhelmingly, that the majority of homicides and other assaultive crimes are committed by people in the lowest social classes. In Australia and New South Wales, 0.5 percent of homicide offenders are professionals or managers. In the United States, less than 1 percent of homicides are committed by upper-class offenders.

Historical and anthropological studies suggest that this pattern is a recent development in the history of this crime. In simpler societies, in many earlier social systems, and throughout American history, homicide was committed by people of all social levels. Murder has been, historically, a means by which people handle their conflicts. Most murders involve some prior relationship between the victim and the offender. Common cross-cultural patterns indicate that people who murder commit the crime to settle a conflict. While a growing number of opportunistic and predatory murders occur each year, and workplace death or injury is commonly perpetrated by elite offenders, these crimes represent a special category of homicide. The majority of interpersonal homicides are committed by lower-class offenders.

In addition, the crime of homicide is most commonly perpetrated by people with little education, and disproportionately by members of racial and ethnic minorities; this is true cross culturally. In Australia, Aborigines are nine times more likely to commit homicide than non-Aborigines. In Canada, Native people make up 3 percent of the population, but 19 percent of homicide suspects. Turkish minority immigrants to Germany have a homicide rate that is 3.5 times higher than native Germans. In Sweden, immigrants from foreign countries make up 5 percent of the population, but 29 percent of convicted homicide offenders. In the United States, African Americans are about 5 times more likely to be arrested for homicide than whites. The contemporary pattern of homicide concentrated among low-status people is one of the most consistent findings in the criminological literature.

If the social class character of the crime of murder is a recent development in human history, what has caused the shift? Research by Mark Cooney, who draws on the theories of Donald Black, proposes that this cross-cultural shift is related to the availability of alternative, legal means for settling conflicts. Upper-class people in most cultures use the courts and the legal system to settle their differences. While some of the propensity to use the courts may be related to greater access, Cooney points out that legal officials are also members of the upper classes.

Low-status people in most societies express hostility, frustration, suspicion, and unsatisfactory outcomes in their interface with the legal system. Cooney points out that low-status people "are clearly patrolled, monitored, stopped, questioned, arrested, convicted, and sentenced much more frequently than those above them in status hierarchy." Low-status groups often believe that the legal system is biased against them and that they cannot win if they pursue a legal solution to their problems. As a consequence, low-status people often believe that the law is unavailable to them for dispute settlement; homicide sometimes fills the void.

For upper-class people, the law is a means of refining social standards and arbitrating differences. Lower-status people often interpret the law as repressive, inaccessible, and distant, avoiding interaction with all aspects of the legal system because it is often interpreted as an alien force that will make matters worse. As a consequence, according to Cooney, *lethal conflict among the lower classes is a function of the unavailability of law for dispute settlement.*

SOURCE: Mark Cooney, "The Decline of Elite Homicide," *Criminology 35* (1997) 381–407.

Millions of cases are routed through state and federal courts every year. Budgetary increases for court services and attendant criminal justice activities have increased dramatically since the early 1970s. For example, court expenses increased 58 percent, prosecution and legal services increased 152 percent, and public defense expenditures increased 259 percent between 1971 and 1990.[70] In 1992, the last year for which data are available, about 80 percent of defendants in criminal trials used public defenders or court-appointed counsel for legal representation.[71] In 1979, state and local governments spent about $350 million to provide legal representation to those accused of crimes who were too poor to hire their own counsel. In 1990, state and local governments spent $1.3 billion for public defense.[72] The economic pressures of such costs foster policies to curtail expenses or to route cases through the judicial system more quickly. The most commonly used mechanism for speeding up the disposition of criminal cases is *plea bargaining,* or negotiation between the defense and the prosecution for a guilty plea. In 1994, which is the last year for which statistics are available, 89 percent of felony convictions in state courts were the result of plea bargaining. In other words, felony convictions where defendants were actually tried for the offense represented 11 percent of cases.[73]

Plea Bargaining

The U.S. Supreme Court has upheld plea bargaining as a necessary means of reducing court overload since 1971, although the practice remains controversial.[74] While there are many variations to the process, in most cases the defendant agrees to plead guilty in exchange for leniency in sentencing, a reduction in the charges, or the promise that some charges will be dropped. Among the common criticisms of this practice are that some innocent people are wrongly convicted and many guilty people are not punished. Defendants who are fearful of the judicial system, for example, may feel pressure to plead guilty even if they have not committed a crime. They may believe that the evidence is too convincing, or fear that the outcome of a trial might be worse than a guilty plea, and they plead guilty out of fear. Similarly, defendants who are guilty of crimes may be able to negotiate a lower penalty, a reduction in charges, or possibly probation, in exchange for a guilty plea. Punishment in such cases would probably be more severe if a trial resulted in conviction of the original charge. While such cases undoubtedly occur, it is common practice for prosecutors to file extraneous or more serious charges against the accused than would actually withstand a trial. This practice gives prosecuting attorneys disposable charges with which to bargain.

Critics of plea bargaining point out that negotiations of pleas represents a misuse of the Sixth Amendment to the Constitution, which entitles defendants to the right to counsel. Most defendants represented by public defenders or court-appointed attorneys do not have sufficient time with their attorneys to consider all options before pleas are entered. The pressure to bargain cases rather than take them to trial may circumvent defendants' constitutional right to trial.

Supporters point out that long court delays, current overcrowding of court dockets, and considerable economic strain on justice dollars make plea bargaining the only practical solution to the volume of cases in contemporary courts. The purpose of trial is for the establishment of facts in any particular case. If facts are not in dispute, a plea bargain is an efficient means of dealing with the defendant's criminal conduct. Elimination of plea bargaining would further drain justice dollars and exacerbate court overload, from this perspective.

There have been some limited attempts to curtail plea bargaining. Alaska, between 1975 and 1980, required a moratorium (temporary ban) on plea bargaining. During the ban, trials and convictions increased but court delays actually decreased. The ban illustrated that many delays in the processing of criminal cases result from the plea bar-

gaining system, rather than from the volume of cases.[75] Other attempts to eliminate plea bargaining have not been as successful. In El Paso, Texas, during the 1980s, local judges attempted a ban on plea bargaining but found that negotiations continued in covert meetings between defense and prosecuting attorneys despite the ban.[76] Most analyses of the practice predict that court delays will be increased with any attempts to reduce or eliminate the practice of plea bargaining.

Other Contributing Factors

Court overload is attributable to many factors, including a propensity to prosecute a large volume of cases that might be handled outside of the courts in other countries. Americans have long been criticized for a tendency to "criminalize" activities that are considered to be private matters elsewhere. In 1994, for example, as many people were arrested for prostitution, sexual indecency, drug abuse, gambling, liquor law violations, and drunkenness as were arrested for all index offenses.[77] While not all arrests, either for moral offenses or for serious crime, actually make it to trial, Americans tend to enforce crimes that offend public morals at levels comparable to serious crimes that endanger public security. Common "wrongful" behavior is treated as criminal behavior. This, among other factors, affects court overload in modern American courts.

Frivolous Litigation

Many people hold the view that courts are plagued with frivolous lawsuits. While such cases do arise, the time and expense involved in litigation ensure that such actions are not common among ordinary people. The assumption of widespread misuse of the courts has been influenced by sensational cases spotlighted by the media. Actually, there does not appear to be consistent or credible evidence to suggest that frivolous litigation is a common problem in American courts.

Among the widespread misperceptions of misuse of the courts is the belief that product liability and malpractice cases have risen disproportionately to other types of civil litigation. Current political rhetoric calls for limitations in monetary awards to the **plaintiff,** or the party who brings suit in a civil case, especially in product liability cases. Many people believe that consumers who are injured either by faulty products or by their own misuse of products sue manufacturers, which results in court overload and high monetary awards for successful litigants. Actually, product liability cases account for less than 2 percent of civil cases in state courts. Punitive damages are awarded to plaintiffs in jury trials in only about 6 percent of cases, and the average award is about $52,000.[78] Million-dollar awards are actually very rare. In the relatively small number of cases in which a monetary award is assessed, an amount of $1 million or more is awarded in less than 4 percent of cases.[79]

The case that has symbolized the widespread belief that plaintiffs commonly prevail in frivolous lawsuits is that of 81-year-old Stella Liebeck, who sued the McDonald's restaurant chain in 1994 after she received third-degree burns from spilled coffee she had purchased at a McDonald's in Albuquerque, New Mexico. In this case, the plaintiff was awarded $2.9 million in a jury trial.[80] Lawmakers, insurance companies, and corporations that market consumer products have used the case to signify the rampant misuse of the courts by consumers who could prevent injury with commonsense use of products. Actually, the facts of this case are often distorted. First, the $2.9 million award was reduced to $640,000, which has been rarely reported in the news. Second, McDonald's coffee was sold at a temperature that was 20 degrees hotter than the industry standard. They had received over 700 complaints of coffee burns over a 10-year-period preceding the injury of Stella Liebeck. Third, the case was actually quite unusual, which is why it made headlines. Other cases of burns from hot foods in restaurants have found liability in the restaurants, but have failed to produce monetary awards for plaintiffs. In the case of Alecia Wallace, who sued Wendy's restaurants when she was blistered by burns from hot chili, the company was found to have been negligent, but no monetary award was made. Similarly, a Starbuck's hot-coffee suit in 1995 and another hot-coffee case from Burger King in Franklin County, Ohio, in 1989 did not result in monetary awards.[81] The McDonald's hot-coffee case is not typical of product liability lawsuits; it is exceptional, which is why it made headlines.

Similarly, proposals for limitation of medical malpractice cases have been used to illustrate problems of overuse of the courts to settle issues that should not clog the judicial system. The problem of medical malpractice cases is also a distorted issue. Less than 3 percent of civil cases involve medical malpractice issues.[82] Over half of civil cases involve complaints of sellers of goods or services who seek to break a contract. Over 94 percent of civil contract cases involve businesses, hospitals, or government agencies who sue individuals or other businesses.[83]

Prisoners' Lawsuits

Another area of concern with regard to frivolous lawsuits is the number of lawsuits filed by prisoners. In 1995, for example, there were 63,550 petitions filed by prisoners in federal and state prisons.[84] Many of these cases were frivolous and involved mundane elements of prison life, such as the type of peanut butter served to inmates. These cases are not likely to be heard by the courts; they are dismissed long before trial. Critics contend that such misuse of prison law libraries and waste of court resources for review of these cases indicates that prisoners should not be entitled to use the courts.[85] However, many important cases regarding the conditions of prison life, as well as constitutional interpretations, have been decided in the last three decades on the basis of litigation brought by prisoners.

One of the most famous of these cases was brought by a Florida inmate in 1963. Clarence A. Gideon was convicted of breaking and entering a poolroom to commit a misdemeanor in 1962. He was convicted without legal counsel because Florida provided court-appointed attorneys only for defendants accused of capital crimes. He was sentenced to five years in prison. Gideon's case was appealed to the U.S Supreme Court, which ruled that indigent (poor) defendants who do not have the resources to hire an attorney shall have one appointed by the court.[86] This is one of the most important cases to be decided in modern judicial history. If prisoners were prohibited from use of the courts, Gideon's case and several hundred other important cases regarding prisoners' rights, decided since Gideon, would not have been heard.

The current trend is to try to curb the tendency for prisoners to pass time by contriving frivolous lawsuits. In Missouri in 1995, for example, a law was passed that applies punitive sanctions to prisoners who file lawsuits later deemed frivolous. The U.S. Supreme Court, in a 1995 ruling, verified that it was within states' rights to make it more difficult for prisoners to file lawsuits. The Court ruled that prisoner lawsuits should be limited to cases that impose "atypical and significant hardship to the inmate."[87]

Frivolous lawsuits are, indeed, annoying and a drain on court resources. They should not be considered normative in the American courts system, however. News media accounts of silly cases or grandiose awards in frivolous cases contribute to misperceptions of normal patterns. Multiple million-dollar awards for spilled coffee are unusual and dramatic, which is what makes them newsworthy.

Racial Disparity in Sentencing

Whether racial characteristics influence sentencing is much more difficult to measure than most people believe. The issue involves not only the sentence imposed after criminal conviction but also pre-sentencing decisions, such as whether to arrest or file charges against a suspect, which charges will be levied, and access of the accused to legal services, jury selection, and trial evidence. All of these factors, as well as many other issues, may be influenced by racial criteria that are not central to sentencing, but influence the likelihood of whether particular defendants are tried or convicted. Jeffrey Sobal and Donald Hinrichs, for example, found that people with particular demographic characteristics were unlikely to appear on rosters of potential jurors in Pennsylvania. Among groups likely to be excluded were the elderly, blacks, the unemployed, and women.[88] Such exclusions may be unfair. Racial disparities, in other words, are more subtle and difficult to measure than mere differences in sentencing.

Black defendants are more likely to be represented by court-assigned counsel than white defendants.[89] This is true for all types of offenses in both state and federal courts. Public defenders and court-appointed attorneys are notoriously overworked and underpaid throughout the United States. By itself, the preponderance of court-assigned attorneys in defense of African Americans indicates patterned differentials in judicial representation by most measures.

Sentences of black offenders are not significantly different from sentences of white offenders.[90] Sentencing differentials seem to be related more to factors that occur prior to conviction, such as the charges filed or representation by private vs. court-appointed counsel. Some researchers, such as William Wilbanks, who measure disparity on the basis of sentencing outcome, have claimed that sentencing disparity is a myth.[91] Other analyses, as we have seen, cite death penalty research that targets the race of the victim as more important than that of the offender in death sentencing. This model provides insight into the subtle effect of race that is not obvious from analysis of sentences of black and white offenders.

Other Sources of Racial Disparity in Sentencing

Sentences that are mandated by the law should, in theory, eliminate racial disparity that is based upon overt discrimination. Even though required sentences prevent the use of racial criteria in the application of penalties for criminal behavior, crimes that are common to minority communities have harsher required penalties than those characteristic of white communities. In the case of drug sales, for example, sale of powder cocaine under federal sentencing standards has an average sentence of 18 months in prison. As previously discussed in Chapter 8, about 75 percent of those convicted of simple possession of powder cocaine receive no prison term at all. The average sentence for crack cocaine offenders is 10 years. About 90 percent of all crack offenders are black or Hispanic; 3 out of 5 powder offenders are white.[92] Sentencing of cocaine offenders may not reflect racial disparity at the sentencing stage, but differential weighting of the criminal activities of minority offenders and those of white offenders is apparent from the mandated sentences. Sentences may not be applied with the intent of discrimination, but the effect of longer mandated sentences for crimes committed by minority offenders is evident in racial proportions in prisons.

Much of the change in the weighting of crimes has occurred since 1980, when political reforms initiated attention to particular types of offenders and enforcement efforts began to target crimes committed by distinct groups in the population. In 1980, 39 percent of new admissions to state prisons were black; at year-end 1993, two-thirds of all sentenced prison inmates were black, Asian, Native American, or Hispanic. The rate of incarceration of African American men increased from 1111 per 100,000 population in 1980 to 3250 per 100,000 in 1996.[93] Differential sentencing can account for only a small influence over the shift in the demographic character of prisons. Most of the change is attributable to subtle strategies that target certain types of offenders while offering greater leniency in others. The average sentence for black male offenders was about 1 year longer than the average sentence for white male offenders among new court commitments in 1992, but current standards that require consideration of prior offenses may explain that difference.[94] The greater racial disparity is evident in the rates of incarceration rather than the length of the sentence.

Gender Disparity in Sentencing

Most people believe that women are treated more leniently in sentencing because chivalry, or a protective bias in sentencing, has caused judges to apply more lenient sentences to women than they would apply to men convicted of identical crimes. Historically, the reverse has been true. In the early part of the twentieth century, many states passed laws requiring longer sentences for women. These laws were called **protective statutes,** and they were based upon the belief that most crime is committed by men. Lawmakers, and the public, believed that only the most depraved, evil women committed crime. Thus, longer average sentences were applied to "protect" society from the depravity of women criminals and to teach women offenders that criminal activities result in harsh penalties.

The Muncy Act
Many laws were modeled after the Muncy Act of Pennsylvania, which was passed in 1913. The law said:

> **All delinquent women are sexually immoral and breed feeble-minded bastards; prolonged confinement deters delinquency and impedes sexual immorality; the conclusion to be drawn from this reasoning is that women should be given indefinite sentences.[95]**

The Muncy Act required that women offenders in Pennsylvania who were convicted of a crime punishable for more than 1 year should be sent to the Muncy State Industrial Home for Women. All women sentenced to Muncy were required to serve a minimum of 3 years, even if the statutory maximum for the offense was less than 3 years. The law further required that all women should be sentenced to the maximum penalty under the law, while the standard formula for sentencing men was half the maximum. Women, under the Muncy Act, were not eligible for minimum penalties, but convicted male offenders could receive a minimum penalty. In Pennsylvania, women offenders served sentences that were commonly double or triple the time men served for the same offense. Thirteen states had similar legislative mandates to apply longer sentences to women offenders.[96]

The Muncy Act was not challenged until 1968. Since Muncy was overturned, other states have eliminated sentencing requirements that mandated longer sentences for women. Elimination of required longer sentences did not eliminate sentencing disparity, however. Women had longer average sentences than men into the 1980s.[97]

Modern Gender Differentials

Some researchers have proposed that the longer average sentences imposed upon women in modern courts reflect underlying "chivalry," which assures that women offenders who do not present a serious social threat are selected out early in the criminal justice system. That is, women who are not dangerous are unlikely to be prosecuted, thus the longer average sentences may reflect the greater seriousness of offenses by those women who are convicted of crimes. Sociologists Candace Kruttschnitt and Donald Green have confirmed that some "chivalry" does influence pre-trial release of female defendants, but found the disparity is primarily motivated by the nondangerous nature of the crimes. They also found the effect of differential release at the pre-trial stage to be related to the race, demeanor, and social class of the accused offender. White middle-class women who were respectful to police officers were most likely to benefit from differential treatment.[98]

At the sentencing stage, the longer average sentences do not appear to be related to greater dangerousness, or lengthy criminal histories among women offenders. Rather, underlying values about appropriate female behavior seem to have influenced sentencing of women offenders until recently. Current trends toward mandatory sentencing, which require consideration of prior offenses and characteristics of the current offense, have tended to reduce the average sentences of women offenders. That is, women offenders are less likely than men to have had prior convictions, to use violence in the perpetration of their current crime, or to have had prior violent convictions. These factors, which are commonly considered in contemporary sentencing requirements, are used to mandate longer sentences for repeat offenders. With few prior criminal experiences and relatively infrequent violent crime, average sentences for women offenders are less

| **TABLE 15.6** | Sentences in Years—1986 and 1992 |

CRIME	1986		1992	
	AVERAGE FEMALES	AVERAGE MALES	AVERAGE FEMALES	AVERAGE MALES
Homicide	16.6	16.3	25.0	36.1
Rape	12.2	11.9	10.0	10.0
Robbery	7.5	12.7	4.5	6.0
Assault	5.6	3.6	4.0	4.0
Burglary	4.7	3.4	3.0	4.0
Larceny-theft	4.3	2.7	2.0	2.0
Motor vehicle	2.8	3.5	2.0	3.0
Arson	7.2	2.0	5.0	5.0
Fraud	4.3	2.7	3.0	3.0
Stolen property	3.6	3.1	2.5	3.0
Drug offenses	4.5	5.2	2.6	3.3
Possession	4.6	3.4	2.4	3.0
Weapons	4.4	3.7	2.2	3.0
Average	6.4	5.7	5.2	6.6

SOURCES: Kathleen Maguire and Ann L. Pastore, *Sourcebook of Criminal Justice Statistics* (Washington DC: U.S. Government Printing Office, 1995) 555; Lawrence A. Greenfeld and Stephanie Minor-Harper, "Women in Prison," *Bureau of Justice Statistics Special Report* (Washington DC: U.S. Government Printing Office, 1991).

likely to be longer than men's sentences under mandatory sentencing guidelines. Table 15.6 illustrates changes in gender differences in sentences in recent years.

The less serious criminal histories of women offenders probably account for the shorter average sentences under current sentencing practices. In 1991, for example, 66 percent of women inmates had fewer than three prior sentences either as juveniles or adults, while 55 percent of men had fewer than three prior sentences. In 1986, the differential was similar, when 69 percent of women had fewer than three prior sentences, but 54 percent of men had been sentenced less than three times prior to their current sentence. In 1986, many states still used judicial sentencing models that allowed for subjective judicial discretion, and the Sentencing Reform Act had not yet been implemented at the federal level. Sentencing changes have tended to lessen judicial discretion and have reduced the longer average sentences applied to female offenders. Standards that take criminal history into account mandate shorter sentences for less serious offenders and longer sentences for recidivists. On this basis, men's sentences are currently longer than women's.

Summary

This chapter set forth the basic organization of the courts and some characteristics of the American judicial system. It presented issues of contemporary concern, and ones that are often misinterpreted, in order to clarify trends and myths about American courts. Many of the issues discussed in this chapter are symptomatic of long-term American social problems.

It is an unfortunate artifact of American culture that social problems are often addressed by those institutions least able to mediate the issues effectively. Many of the issues discussed in this chapter fall under the vast umbrella of the courts, but effective remedies are probably out of the scope of the judicial system. Problems of racism, sexism, poverty, and contemporary patterns of drug use are handled by the courts, but these are enduring threads in the fabric of American society that surface in the courts as symptoms of wider social issues. The courts become involved only when snags or tears in the fabric draw attention to specific problems.

It is not within the scope of the judicial system to "fix" racism, for example. The fact that the death penalty has been applied with racial bias is rarely disputed by either side of the debate over capital punishment, yet attention is usually directed to whether racism was evident in a particular case, rather than toward the whole system of capital punishment. Opponents of capital punishment would like to see an end to executions, in part because of the systematic nature of racism. Proponents of capital punishment argue that the entire system should not be abolished because individual cases are flawed. As with most criticism of American courts and judicial practice, both sides of the issue present valid points.

In nearly any dispute settled in the courts, the problem is deeper than the individual issue at hand. The courts handle facts and legal disputes, but patterns of offense are rarely altered by individual cases. The prevailing problems of drug abuse, for example, are addressed as violations of the law and punished according to current sentencing standards. The courts cannot address the social problems of poverty or unemployment that may prompt illegal sales, nor can they address the personal nature of choices to engage in drug use. These problems are beyond the scope of the courts.

Still, Americans hope for judicial answers. Tougher laws, longer sentences, higher conviction rates, and more prisons are proposed as the perennial answers to crime. Crime patterns and solutions to crime are tied to cultural problems that persist despite the criminal justice system. Courts and the judiciary are encumbered by their own challenges to maintain a system that accomplishes their prescribed duties with impartiality. Symptoms of inequity that signal a tear in the fabric of American democracy may surface in the courts, but solutions to social problems are more likely to emerge from the culture itself.

Critical Thinking Questions

1. Do you think that the fact that most judges in the United States are white men has any effect on the outcome in American courts? Why or why not?

2. If the death penalty is actually applied with racial bias, as many theorists believe, is that a sufficient justification for eliminating it? Why or why not?

3. Should states limit prisoners' access to the courts in order to curtail the number of frivolous lawsuits filed by inmates? Why or why not?

4. Most legal analysts believe that plea bargaining is an efficient means of dealing with the volume of cases that come before American courts. Critics contend that it promotes unfairness. Argue both sides of this issue. What are the arguments for and against plea bargaining?

Suggested Readings

David Baldus, Charles Pulaski, and George Woodworth, "Comparative Review of Death Sentences: An Empirical Study of the Georgia Experience," *Journal of Criminal Law and Criminology 74* (1983) 661–78.

Anthony Lewis, *Gideon's Trumpet* (New York: Random House, 1964).

Doris M. Provine, *Judging Credentials: Nonlawyer Judges and the Politics of Professionalism* (Chicago: University of Chicago Press, 1986).

Gerry Spence, *With Justice for None* (New York: Penguin, 1989).

Notes

[1] Jeffrey Reiman, *The Rich Get Richer and the Poor Get Prison: Ideology, Crime and Criminal Justice* (Boston: Allyn & Bacon, 1995).

[2] Expenditures for justice activities, which include police, courts, and corrections, lag behind statistics in most other areas of the criminal justice system. Most figures are released three or more years after the year they describe. The figures for 1992, for example, were released in 1995 and re-released in 1997.

[3] Kathleen Maguire and Ann L. Pastore, *Sourcebook of Criminal Justice Statistics,1995* (Washington DC: U.S. Government Printing Office, 1996) 5.

[4] Ibid., 3.

[5] Ibid., 33.

[6] Ibid., 3.

[7] Sue A. Lindgren, "Justice Expenditures and Employment, 1990," *Bureau of Justice Statistics Bulletin* (Washington DC: U.S. Government Printing Office, 1992) 3.

[8] Maguire and Pastore, *Sourcebook of Criminal Justice Statistics, 1995,* 4.

[9] Patrick A. Langan and Jan Chaiken, "Felony Sentences in the United States 1990," *Bureau of Justice Statistics Bulletin* (Washington DC: U.S. Government Printing Office, 1994) 2. Note that comparative sentencing data that includes both federal and state sentencing trends lags several years behind current years. Data for 1990 was released in late 1994.

[10] Patrick Langan and Jodi M. Brown, "Felony Sentences in State Courts, 1994," *Bureau of Justice Statistics Bulletin* (Washington DC: U. S. Government Printing Office, 1997) 7.

[11] Ibid., 2.

[12] Langan and Brown, "Felony Sentences in State Courts, 1994," 2; Jan Chaiken, "Compendium of Federal Justice Statistics, 1993," *Bureau of Justice Statistics* (Washington DC: U.S. Government Printing Office, 1996)13. Federal statistics are for 1993.

[13] Langan and Brown, "Felony Sentences in State Courts, 1994," 2.

[14] Ibid., 7.

[15] Maguire and Pastore, *Sourcebook of Criminal Justice Statistics, 1995,* 468.

[16] Ibid., 519.

[17] Ibid., 520–21.

[18] Edward M. Kennedy, "Justice in Sentencing," *New York Times,* 29 July 1977, 21.

[19] Maguire and Pastore, *Sourcebook of Criminal Justice Statistics, 1995,* 79.

20 For an excellent discussion of this issue see: Sharon Schmickle and Tom Hamburger, "The Secretive World of Judicial Discipline," *Minneapolis Star Tribune,* 25 June 1995, A-1.

21 Ibid., 68–69. See also Martha A. Myers, "Social Background and the Sentencing Behavior of Judges," *Criminology* 26 (1988) 649–75.

22 See Doris M. Provine, *Judging Credentials: Nonlawyer Judges and the Politics of Professionalism* (Chicago: University of Chicago Press, 1986).

23 Maguire and Pastore, *Sourcebook of Criminal Justice Statistics, 1995,* 72.

24 Ibid.

25 Lynn Hecht Schafran, "Overwhelming Evidence: Gender Bias in the Courts," in *The Criminal Justice System and Women: Offenders, Victims, and Workers,* 2nd ed., ed. Barbara Raffel Price and Natalie J. Sokoloff (New York: McGraw-Hill, 1995) 332–42.

26 Ibid., 333.

27 Schafran, "Overwhelming Evidence: Gender Bias in the Courts," 335.

28 Ibid., 337.

29 See, for example, Candace Kruttschnitt and Donald E. Green, "The Sex-Sanctioning Issue: Is It History?" *American Sociological Review* 49 (1984) 541–51; Robert D. Peterson and John Hagan, "Changing Conceptions of Race: Towards an Account of Anomalous Findings in Sentencing Research," *American Sociological Review* 49 (1984) 56–70.

30 Thomas B. Barvell and Carlisle E. Moody, "Determinate Sentencing and Abolishing Parole: The Long-Term Impacts on Prisons," *Criminology 34* (1996) 107–128. The ten states that eliminated indeterminate sentencing were: California, Colorado, Connecticut, Illinois, Indiana, Maine, Minnesota, New Mexico, North Carolina, and Washington. Some form of parole has been reinstated in several states.

31 Ibid.

32 Edward A. Adams, "State Commission Finds Racism in Courts: 70 Suggestions Proposed to Eliminate 2-Tiered System." *New York Law Journal 5* (June 1991) 1; Douglas C. McDonald, Kenneth E. Carlson, and ABT Associates, Inc., "Federal Sentencing in Transition, 1986–90," *Bureau of Justice Statistics Bulletin* (Washington DC: U.S. Government Printing Office, 1992).

33 Maguire and Pastore, *Sourcebook of Criminal Justice Statistics, 1995,* 454–55, 457.

34 Allen J. Beck and Darrell K. Gilliard, "Prisoners in 1994," *Bureau of Justice Statistics Bulletin* (Washington DC: U.S. Government Printing Office, 1995) 2.

35 *Roberts v. Louisiana,* 428 U.S. 325 (1976); *Woodson v. North Carolina,* 428 U.S. 280 (1976); *Proffit v. Florida,* 428 U.S. 242 (1976); *Jurek v. Texas,* 429 U.S. 262 (1976); *Gregg v. Georgia,* 428 U.S. 153 (1976).

36 In this case, Texas has a law that requires that newly discovered evidence be presented within 60 days of the original trial. The Supreme Court ruled the Texas law is fair. If new evidence is uncovered after the 60-day requirement, the defendant is not entitled to a new trial, even if the evidence proves innocence. James Stephan and Peter Brien, "Capital Punishment 1993," *Bureau of Justice Statistics Bulletin* (Washington DC: U.S. Government Printing Office, 1994); David G. Savage, "Court To Decide If New Data Can Stay Executions," *Los Angeles Times,* 23 February 1992, A-1; Jordan Steiker, "Can They Execute the Innocent? Probably." *New York Times,* 11 March 1992, A-23.

37 Tracy L. Snell, "Capital Punishment 1995," *Bureau of Justice Statistics Bulletin* (Washington DC: U.S. Government Printing Office, 1996) 4, 11–12.

38 Ibid., 11.

39 Snell "Capital Punishment 1995," 1.

40 Ibid.

41 For discussion, see Mimi Cantwell, "Capital Punishment 1983," *Bureau of Justice Statistics* (Washington DC: U.S. Government Printing Office, 1984) 3.

42 Snell "Capital Punishment 1995," 15; Stephan and Brien, "Capital Punishment 1993," 9; Lawrence A. Greenfeld and James J. Stephan, "Capital Punishment 1992," *Bureau of Justice Statistics* (Washington DC: U.S. Government Printing Office, 1993) 7.

43 Snell, "Capital Punishment 1995," 13.

44 Damond Sanford, "Boy, 17, Gets Death Penalty in Arkansas; Jury Finds Age To Be No Mitigating Factor," *New York Times,* 11 January 1996, A-11.

45 Snell, "Capital Punishment 1995," 6.

46 Cantwell, "Capital Punishment 1983," 5.

47 Snell, "Capital Punishment 1995," 8.

48 *Gregg v. Georgia* (1976) 428 U.S. 153, 170.

49 Percent calculated from the number of homicides and the number of death sentences in 1993. Data derived from Stephan and Brien (1994) and Federal Bureau of Investigation, *Crime in the United States* (Washington DC: U.S. Government Printing Office, 1995) 107.

50 Thorsten Sellin, *The Death Penalty* (Beverly Hills: Sage, 1980). Some critics of this research have charged that if the death penalty actually causes an increase in homicide, then the rates should have been lower when executions were halted between 1966 and 1977. Actually, the rate was a little lower at that time and has gone up since executions have resumed. The average homicide rate between 1966 and 1976 was 8.1 per 100,000. In the 10 years after the death penalty was reinstated, the average rate was 9.4 per 100,000.

51 Studies indicating no relationships between publicity about executions and homicide include: William C. Bailey and Ruth D. Peterson, "Murder and Capital Punishment: A Monthly Time Series Analysis of Execution Publicity," *American Sociological Review 54* (1989) 722–43; William C. Bailey, "Murder, Capital Punishment, and Television: Execution Publicity and Homicide Rates," *American Sociological Review* 55 (1990) 628–33. Studies indicating a slight decline in homicide after executions include Steven Stack, "Publicized Executions and Homicide, 1950–1980," *American Sociological Review* 52 (1987) 532–40; David J. Phillips, "The Deterrent Effect of Capital Punishment: New Evidence on an Old Controversy," *American Journal of Sociology* 86 (1980) 139–48.

52 There was one other important deterrence study, conducted by Issac Ehrlich, that found significant deterrence associated with the death penalty, but researchers who have tried to reproduce Ehrlich's findings have been unsuccessful. Most theorists therefore discount the findings of Ehrlich. See Issac Ehrlich, "The Deterrent Effect of Capital Punishment: A Matter of Life and Death," *American Economic Review 65* (1975) 414; William J. Bowers and Glenn Pierce, "Deterrence or Brutalization: What Is the Effect of Execution?" *Crime and Delinquency 26* (1980) 453–84; Richard M. McCahey, "Dr. Ehrlich's Magic Bullet: Economic Theory, Econometrics, and the Death Penalty," *Crime and Delinquency 26* (1980); Brian Forst, "Capital Punishment and Deterrence: Conflicting Evidence," *Journal of Criminal Law and Criminology 74* (1983).

53 Maguire and Pastore, *Sourcebook of Criminal Justice Statistics, 1995,* 598.

54 *Furman v. Georgia* (1972) 408 U.S. 238.

55 Snell "Capital Punishment 1995," 8.

56 Erik Eckholm, "Studies Find Death Penalty Tied to Race of the Victims," *New York Times,* 24 February 1995, B-1.

57 Ibid.

58 David Baldus, Charles Pulaski, and George Woodworth, "Comparative Review of Death Sentences: An Empirical Study of the Georgia Experience," *Journal of Criminal Law and Criminology 74* (1983) 661–78; *McKlesky v. Kemp,* 478 U.S. 109 (1985).

59 CNN (Cable News Network), 25 June 1995, CNN Specials: "By Penalty of Death, Part 3—Lethal Lawyers." Transcript provided by Primary Source Media.

60 NPR (National Public Radio), 28 September 1994, All Things Considered, "Capital Punishment Part Three," Transcript provided by Research Publications International.

61 Ibid.; Victor E. Kappeler, Mark Blumberg, Gary W. Potter, *The Mythology of Crime and Criminal Justice,* 2nd ed. (Prospect Heights, IL: Waveland, 1996) 320.

62 Maguire and Pastore, *Sourcebook of Criminal Justice Statistics, 1995,* 181.

63 Ibid.

64 Ibid.

65 Ibid., 175.

66 Langan and Brown, "Felony Sentences in State Courts, 1994", 1.

67 Patricia McFall Torbet, "Juvenile Probation: The Workhorse of the Juvenile Justice System," *Juvenile Justice Bulletin* (Washington DC: U.S. Government Printing Office, 1996), 1.

68 Langan and Brown, "Felony Sentences in State Courts, 1994," 3.

69 Ibid., 3.

70 Lindgren, "Justice Expenditures and Employment, 1990," 4.

71 Steven K. Smith and Carol J. DeFrances, "Indigent Defense," *Bureau of Justice Statistics Selected Findings* (Washington DC: U.S. Government Printing Office, 1996), 1.

72 Ibid., 2.

73 Langan and Brown, "Felony Sentences in State Courts, 1994," 7.

74 *Santobello v. New York* (1971), 404 U.S. 257, 260–61.

75 Michael Rubinstein, "Alaska Bans Plea Bargaining," *Bureau of Justice Statistics Bulletin* (Washington DC: U.S. Government Printing Office, 1980).

76 Robert Weninger, "The Abolition of Plea Bargaining: A Case Study of El Paso County, Texas," *UCLA Law Review 35* (1987) 265–313.

77 FBI, *Crime in the United States* (Washington DC: U.S. Government Printing Office, 1995) 221.

78 Smith and DeFrances, "Indigent Defense," 2; Carol J. De Frances et al., "Civil Jury Cases and Verdicts in Large Counties," *Bureau of Justice Statistics Special Report* (Washington DC: U.S. Government Printing Office, 1995) 1, 4.

79 Ibid.

80 Anthony Marshall, "Costly Cup of Coffee Stirs Legal Question," *Hotel and Motel Management 210* (1995) 12, 13; Eric Schine, "McDonald's Hot Coffee Gets Her Cool Cash," *Business Week,* 5 September 1994, 38.

81 Angela King, "Starbucks Faces Hot-Coffee Lawsuit," *USA Today,* 25 January 1995, B-2; Dan Crawford, "Study Debunks Perception of High Jury Verdict Awards," *Business First-Columbus 12,* 15 January 1996, 1-1.

82 Ibid.

83 Ibid.

84 Maguire and Pastore, *Sourcebook of Criminal Justice Statistics, 1995,* 517.

85 See, for example, Dennis Vacco, Del Papa, Sue Frankie, Pamela Carter, and Christine Gregoire, "Free the Courts from Frivolous Prisoner Suits," *New York Times*, 3 March 1995, A-26.

86 *Gideon v. Wainwright* (1963) 372 U.S. 335. See also Anthony Lewis, *Gideon's Trumpet* (New York: Random House, 1964).

87 Laurle Shaper Walters, "State Rewrite Laws to Weed Out Suits for Cruel and Unusual Jello," *Christian Science Monitor*, 16 October 1995, 3-1; Linda Greenhouse, "High Court, Changing Recent Course, Makes It Harder for Prisoners to Sue," *New York Times*, 20 June 1995, B-7.

88 Jeffrey Sobal and Donald W. Hinrichs, "Bias Against Marginal Individuals in Jury Wheel Selection," *Journal of Criminal Justice 14* (1986) 71–89.

89 Smith and DeFrances, "Indigent Defense," 3.

90 Allen Beck et al., "Survey of State Prison Inmates, 1991," *Bureau of Justice Statistics* (Washington DC: U.S. Government Printing Office, 1993) 7.

91 William Wilbanks, *The Myth of a Racist Criminal Justice System* (Monterey, CA: Brooks/Cole, 1987).

92 Marc Mauer and Tracy Huling, "Young Black Americans and the Criminal Justice System: Five Years Later," Current Issues SourceFile Record: R019-6, 1995, 1–36; see also *Chicago Tribune*, "The Elusive Logic of Drug Sentences," (1995) 1-12.

93 Christopher Mumola and Allen J. Beck, "Correctional Populations in the United States, 1996," *Bureau of Justice Statistics Report* (Washington DC: U.S. Government Printing Office, 1997) 3, 5, 9; Michael Tonry, *Malign Neglect: Race, Crime, and Punishment in America* (New York: Oxford University Press, 1995) 4.

94 Maguire and Pastore, *Sourcebook of Criminal Justice Statistics, 1995*, 555.

95 *Commonwealth v. Daniels*, 210 Pa. Super. 156, 232 A.2d 247, as quoted in Gail Armstrong, "Females Under the Law—'Protected' but Unequal," *Crime and Delinquency* (1967) 109–120.

96 The thirteen states were: Alabama, Arkansas, California, Indiana, Iowa, Maine, Massachusetts, Minnesota, New Jersey, New York, Ohio, Pennsylvania, Wisconsin. See Armstrong (1977).

97 Lawrence A. Greenfeld and Stephanie Minor-Harper, "Women in Prison," *Bureau of Justice Statistics Special Report* (Washington DC: U.S. Government Printing Office, 1991) 4.

98 Candace Kruttschnitt and Donald E. Green, "The Sex-Sanctioning Issue: Is It History?" *American Sociological Review 49* (1984): 541–51.

chapter 16

Corriections

CHAPTER OUTLINE
THEORIES OF PUNISHMENT
   Retribution
   Deterrence
      Types of Deterrence
      Conditions Under Which Deterrence Works
   Rehabilitation
   Incapacitation
      Selective Incapacitation
HISTORY OF CORRECTIONS
   Punishments Before the Industrial Revolution
      Punishment and Labor Demands
      Decline in the Use of Torture
   Nineteenth-Century American Punishments
      The Pennsylvania System
      The Auburn System
      The Reformatory System
   Twentieth-Century Punishments
      Prison Industries
      The Big House
THE MODERN ERA
   Professional Administration
   Prison Litigation
   The Shift to Custody and Control
      Increases in Women's Corrections
   Upward Trends in Incarceration
SUMMARY

KEY TERMS

retribution
just deserts
deterrence
probation
indeterminate sentencing
incapacitation
Pennsylvania System
Walnut Street Jail
Auburn System
reformatory system
Elmira Reformatory
Big House
mechanical solidarity
organic solidarity
repressive law
restitutive law

THE APPLICATION OF CORRECTIONAL POLICIES has changed significantly throughout American history and it is currently in transition as the criminal justice system adjusts to a large influx of offenders. A higher percentage of the U.S. population is incarcerated than any other country in the world.[1] This is a costly enterprise and one that is subject to wide criticism, both within the United States and throughout the world. Choices for correctional responses to crime are tied to political ideology and fluctuate with changing American values. This chapter presents the theories of punishment as well as a general history of corrections. It also takes a look at many of the problems that face American corrections in the dawn of the twenty-first century.

Theories of Punishment

Commonsense judgments about why people are punished generally emphasize that (a) wrongful behavior deserves punishment; (b) punishment provides an example to others who might consider such actions; (c) punishment will teach the offender a lesson; and (d) punishing the offender protects society. While these judgments may arise from common sense, each is grounded in theory. Many of these ideas about punishment have surfaced, declined in popularity, and then re-surfaced. The trends in punishment and corrections vary with economic and political conditions, fear of crime, and cultural patterns. The most common rationales for correctional policies include retribution, deterrence, rehabilitation, and incapacitation. Each philosophy of punishment implies a different reason for sanctioning offenders' behavior.

Retribution

Retributive punishments are applied to offenders because they deserve to be punished. With **retribution,** the purpose of sanctioning the offender's behavior is to respond to the crime by treating offenders in a way comparable to their own wrongful action. The biblical "eye for an eye" represents a retributive punishment.

Clearly this is one of the oldest rationales for punishment, and it is based on the belief that crime disrupts social balance. To punish a person who has committed a crime is to restore order. The great social philosopher Immanuel Kant argued that imposition of punishment for wrongful behavior restores the moral balance in the universe that is upset by the offender's actions.[2] Underlying this philosophy is a belief that people who cause harm should suffer in proportion to the damage done. This is sometimes called the **just deserts** philosophy of punishment, implying that offenders get what they deserve.

Some have argued that the philosophy of retribution is nothing more than state-sanctioned revenge. Punishing offenders because they should suffer for their wrongful actions is different from private revenge only in that the agent of punishment is the state, from this perspective. Actually, there are differences between revenge and retribution. Most important, retribution is backed by law, and

punishments are applied within the restrictions of law. Punishments under law fall within a range of possibilities that prevent excessive revenge by private citizens. Thus, law prevents true revenge.

If, for example, a man is convicted of sexually molesting a child, retributive punishment applies a sentence that inflicts suffering on the offender but does not exact revenge. True revenge would involve sexually molesting the offender's child. This would inflict pain on an innocent person. Instead of revenge, the state specifies particular punishments that would likely include deprivation of liberty (through imprisonment) in this case.

A second important distinction between retribution and revenge is that retribution restricts the authority of punishing agents. Revenge could easily involve excessive punishment as a reflection of the outrage of the victim or of society. Retributive punishments, which are grounded in law, prevent excessive punishment. A person cannot be executed for shoplifting, for example, no matter how outrageous the actions of the offender may seem to the victim.

Deterrence

With the philosophy of **deterrence,** punishment is imposed on the offender to prevent future offenses. This philosophy is based upon the belief that the offender will remember the pain of the punishment and will not want to risk a second offense.

For deterrence to work, several conditions must be met. First, the punishment must be appropriate. According to Cesare Beccaria (see Chapter 9), if the punishment is too severe or too lenient, no deterrent effect will be achieved. If offenders were executed for shoplifting, the severity of the punishment would be too great for people to believe it could actually happen to them; thus, the deterrent effect of severe punishments is negligible. Likewise, if the punishment for shoplifting is a letter of reprimand from a judge, the punishment is so light that shoplifters might be encouraged; in this case, the crime might be worth the effort because the punishment would not be painful.

The second condition for deterrence to work is that the punishment must be swift. If there is a long period of time between the crime, conviction, and ultimate punishment, the offender will not be able to identify the offense with the punishment, or the crime will seem worthwhile because the sanctions were imposed at a time greatly removed from the original offense.

The third criteria is that the punishment must be sure. If not all people are punished for the offense, or the punishments are light for some and severe for others, the offender is likely to believe that punishment can be avoided or that a light sentence will be imposed. One of the precepts of classical criminology, as discussed in Chapter 9, is that punishment must be inescapable if deterrence is to work. Inherent in the nature of crime is the offenders' belief that they will escape detection because of their particular criminal skills. It follows, naturally, that optimism about punishment is likely if there is variability in the application of sanctions. If punishments for crime are uniformly applied to all convicted, the likelihood of deterrence is greater.

Types of Deterrence

There are two types of deterrence: general deterrence and specific or individual deterrence. With *general deterrence,* the offender is punished to serve as an example to all others who may be contemplating a similar offense. The lesson for all other citizens is that they should refrain from criminal behavior or they too will suffer as the offender is suffering. People are punished, in other words, to serve as an example to others.

Specific or *individual deterrence* refers to punishment of the offender to prevent him or her from re-offending. Presumably the memory of the punishment will prevent the offender from any further criminal activities. In the case of specific deterrence, it is especially important to apply the appropriate sanction for this type of punishment to work. A punishment that is too lenient will be viewed as worth the risk of crime.

Conditions Under Which Deterrence Works

While many people believe that the philosophy of deterrence works to prevent crime because no rational person would want to repeat a punishment such as imprisonment, there are some problems with the concept. In the United States, punishments are not always sure, swift, or consistent (appropriate). First, there is great disparity in punishments among various offenders. White-collar offenders generally receive only token sentences, or no punishment at all. Lower-class offenders convicted of individual property crimes such as burglary or motor vehicle theft commonly receive longer sentences, and they are confined under harsher conditions than upper-class offenders. Lower-class offenders are prosecuted under criminal law, while white-collar and corporate offenders are typically prosecuted in civil courts. Thus, the application of punishment varies by social class membership. Punishment also varies by race and gender.

Second, people who commit crimes generally do not intend to get caught. Their motivations may be economic, personal, or thrill-seeking. The offender may believe that the skills, knowledge, or experience brought to the crime will prevent detection. Only a fraction of those who commit crimes in the United States are prosecuted, convicted, and sentenced. The pattern of "getting away with it" may be more widely recognized among criminals than most people realize.

Third, there is great variability in the types of punishments used in the United States. Offenders are not sure what punishments apply to their cases, the penalties are variable by state or between state and federal court systems, and in many states the individual discretion of judges may increase variability. Even in states with mandatory penalties, prosecutors use discretion in the charges that are filed. Offenders often believe the myth that large numbers of criminals are set free because of technical flaws in arrest or prosecution.[3] Punishments are rarely swift in the American judicial system. Cases are clogged in overcrowded courts and often take months or years to go through the system. Recent sentencing trends have increased the severity of sentences to levels that are often beyond the comprehension of offenders.[4] Long sentences for some offenders, while others get probation or no punishment at all, increases the perception of great inconsistency in the system.

A fourth problem with deterrence philosophies of punishment is verifying that they work. The most significant problem in studying deterrence is that the subject of study is a group of people who were *not* deterred—that is, the offenders. People who refrain from crime may do so because they are fearful of punishment, but it is just as likely that moral values, religious beliefs, faith in law or government, or fear of social embarrassment are just as effective in preventing people from committing crime. We know that fear of punishment is not an effective means of preventing offenders from committing crimes, but does it work for others who are law-abiding?

Rehabilitation

With this philosophy of punishment, the focus is on treating offenders' problems so that future offenses will be prevented. The focus is upon identifying either internal or external forces upon individuals that cause them to engage in crime. Rehabilitation theorists generally highlight factors intrinsic to the offender such as mental illness, insufficient education, or lack of marketable skills, that may be addressed with rehabilitation.

Rehabilitation theorists often imply a medical model of pathology caused by "ills" that are "curable" with the right rehabilitation strategy. The solution to crime is the discovery of predominant social pathologies and the employment of appropriate techniques for treatment of offenders.

The use of probation and indeterminate sentencing are both based upon rehabilitation models. Probation strategies presume that giving offenders a second chance, coupled with guidance and supervision, will help them redirect energies to more law-abiding activities. Indeterminate sentencing, which is now rarely used in the United States, was based upon the assumption that the offender should be incarcerated for only as long as necessary for reform. No judge, probation officer, correctional official, or other authority can predict the length of time it will take a given offender to reform. Under the philosophy of rehabilitation, indeterminate sentences should be imposed with latitude for release as soon as the offender shows evidence of rehabilitation. The punishment, in other words, should be tailored to individual offenders.

The problem with this model is that a prisoner's ability to prove that rehabilitation has occurred is hampered by the prison environment. It may be nearly impossible to convince authorities of a change of heart. Also, good intentions in the controlled prison environment are often corrupted by real-life challenges after release. A person may be "rehabilitated" to prison authorities, but unable to maintain commitment to the same good intentions after release. In addition, some people are adept at convincing authorities of reform, but real rehabilitation has not taken place. In other words, hinging release on change in the offender is problematic for the offender, for prison authorities, and for society.

Various rehabilitation strategies have been used for over a hundred years. The appeal of reform peaks and declines with correctional officials and lawmakers as new methods of rehabilitation are tried and fail. Currently, most rehabilitation strategies are unpopular. Whether the problem is with the strategies employed or with the philosophy of rehabilitation is not clear. Some theorists, such as Jeffrey Reiman, suggest that no rehabilitation strategy will ever work unless significant adjustments to social structural inequalities alleviate the economic problems that motivate most lower-class crime, as well as the economic advantages that make upper-class crime worthwhile.[5] Others claim that rehabilitation is doomed to failure because external forces, such as prison authorities or opportunities for self-improvement, cannot change offenders. Rehabilitation must come from within the offender, and most criminals are not motivated to reform.

Incapacitation

The use of incapacitation strategies is as old as punishment itself. Most techniques of **incapacitation** have been aimed at making it impossible for offenders to re-offend, historically. The hands of a thief would be cut off or the individual would be branded with an insignia indicating a symbol for the crime committed. These punishments have ancient historical precedent, and they are still used in some parts of the world.

In the United States, the primary means of incapacitating offenders is through incarceration. This punishment strategy presumes the offender is prevented from committing further crime, at least for the duration of the prison term. Many theorists believe that prison terms should be longer for all criminals because locking offenders away from society lowers crime rates by preventing criminals from committing subsequent offenses.[6] Theorists who hold this view advocate building more prisons to house more offenders, especially those who have proven their antisocial tendencies by committing repeat offenses. According to some, criminals should be incarcerated for life if they have re-offended multiple times.[7] The current "three strikes and you're out" political rhetoric is an example of this thinking.[8]

The problem with this approach is that most criminals have relatively short careers. It may make intuitive sense to remove repeat offenders from society permanently, but the massive prison building projects necessary to hold offenders who may spend 40 or 50 years in prison will significantly drain already-strained public resources. If the threats to society from offenders with multiple convictions were truly dangerous, prison expansion would be worth the expenditure. However, several researchers have questioned the purported danger of such individuals. Kyle Kercher, for example, suggests that offenders' likelihood of re-offense declines significantly after age 30 and tapers off to about a 2 percent chance of re-offense by age 50.[9] Similarly, sociologists Michael Gottfredson and Travis Hirschi point out that offense histories peak in the late teens and early twenties, and then decline as individuals age.[10]

The strategy to incarcerate offenders for life after repeat offenses is actually a retributive punishment rather than a means of protecting society, as political rhetoric often implies. "Three strikes and you're out" rings more resonantly in the retributive argument, with the implication that offenders deserve the punishment because of their offenses. Incapacitation may be a smoke screen for retribution in this case. Release of middle-aged or elderly offenders would very rarely be a danger to society. If the goal of incarceration is truly incapacitation, a more cost-effective strategy would be to incarcerate young offenders until they reach age 30, rather than to set the length of incarceration by offense history. With this policy, incarceration would be for "criminal life," rather than "natural life."

Selective Incapacitation

Another variation of the incapacitation rationale is **selective incapacitation.** This idea is based upon the research of Peter Greenwood, Allan Abrahamese, and others, who suggest that a small proportion of all offenders who

Most early American punishments focused upon punishment of the body, such as torture, or public humiliation. This dunking stool would have accomplished both goals of punishment.

chronically re-offend should be incarcerated for longer periods of time.[11] Greenwood and Abrahamese found in their study of 2000 inmates in three states that selective incarceration of chronic offenders with common background characteristics, such as poor employment history, prior offenses, or drug use, could reduce the robbery rates by 15 percent.[12] There are problems, though. Identification of chronic offenders is problematic without national connections among regional data sources or the opening of juvenile court records. Possible false identification of offenders who are not likely to re-offend may result in unjustifiably long prison terms for some. Failure to identify problem offenders who may not meet statistical criteria could result in release of seriously dangerous people. Other researchers have found that doubling the prison population between 1973 and 1983 reduced the number of robberies and burglaries by only 6 to 9 percent.[13] Some researchers, such as Lee Bowker, believe that increasing the length of sentence actually increases the likelihood of further criminal offenses after release.[14] The expense of selective incapacitation is enormous and the ethical considerations of incarcerating some longer than others for the same offense because of the *potential* of re-offense have not been adequately addressed.

History of Corrections

Punishment in Western civilization has undergone significant change as economic and political developments have spawned revisions in treatment of offenders. The economic and cultural changes spurred by the Industrial Revolution (about 1776 to 1830) caused extensive changes in punishment strategies. Development of modern prisons and articulation of punishment theory are directly traceable to sociocultural and economic changes that resulted from the Industrial Revolution and the subsequent development of capitalism.

Punishments Before the Industrial Revolution

Among the earliest recorded punishments, banishment and forced labor or slavery were among the most commonly cited means of addressing criminal behavior.[15] Criminals were *banished,* or exiled, to foreign lands, either for a specified period of time or for life. In ancient Greece, even inanimate objects could be tried and banished. A rock that had been used in the death of a human might be tried, found guilty, and thrown over the border into a neighboring state.[16] Conscription into state military service, sale into

French Criminal Procedure Before the Revolution of 1789

Among the most important precepts of American constitutional law are the requirements that procedures be open, accessible to all parties involved, and that those accused of crimes will not only have the right to hear charges against them but will also be able to confront their accusers. These protections of the rights of those accused of crimes are embodied in the Bill of Rights, the first ten amendments to the Constitution. They were added to the Constitution because they represented deviation from common procedure in France and most other European countries at the time.

In France, all criminal procedures prior to sentencing of the convicted offender were secret. Not even the accused knew the charges or the evidence that were brought before the court. Knowledge about the proceedings was a privilege reserved for the prosecution. An edict published in 1498 required that all preliminary investigations of suspects of any crime be carried out in secrecy. An ordinance of 1670 confirmed more specifically that defendants should never have access to any documents related to the case against them, that they should not be informed about the identity of their accusers, that evidence and witnesses in the case should be kept secret from the defendant, and that defendants should not be provided with lawyers to help with their cases. The judge could accept anonymous statements about the accused as proof of guilt, and all information was kept secret until the time of sentencing. At this time, the convicted offender heard all charges, the evidence of his guilt, and the sentence.

Even though the proceedings were secret, there was concern that they be fair. In the eighteenth century there were distinctions between true, direct, and legitimate proof, which would involve the use of evidence and witnesses, and indirect or artificial proof, which meant that there was an arguably good case against the accused. There was a distinction between "full proof" and "semi-full proof," which, for example, meant the difference between eye witnesses and suspicious behavior by the suspect. Penalties were greater for "full proof" convictions than for "semi-full proof" convictions.

In France, torture was a common punishment after conviction, but it was also used to obtain "proof" of offenders' guilt before conviction. Among the most serious forms of evidence used against those accused of crimes were confessions, which were often obtained by torture of the accused. The American Constitution prohibits forced confession through the Fifth Amendment in the Bill of Rights. This was an important American issue because it was commonly used in other parts of the world in the late eighteenth century.

source: Michel Foucault, *Discipline and Punish: The Birth of the Prison* (New York: Vintage, 1979) 35–36.

---

slavery, or forced labor for state projects were also common punishments in both the Greek and Roman empires.

Many punishments in ancient Greece and Rome were private matters. Roman or Greek husbands who caught their wives in adultery could kill them without penalty. (Wives who caught their husbands were obliged to look the other way, however, which implies the double standard in sexual prerogative characteristic of all ages and most cultures.[17]) In medieval England, most crimes were punished with monetary compensation to the victims (Box 16.1). Even crimes that are now seen as serious threats against public safety because of the personal injury inflicted by the perpetrator of the crime (rape, assault) were punished with monetary penalties. Rape, for example, was a *property* crime; the victim of a rape was owned by her father, husband, or a male relative. The perpetrator of the rape was obliged to reimburse the owner of the despoiled property. The father of the raped woman would be paid a monetary sum that depended upon her worth and the damage done. If she had been a virgin, she was worth more. If she was married and pregnant, her husband would receive greater compensation than if she had not been pregnant.[18]

Punishment and Labor Demands

After the Protestant Reformation (1517) punishments became more severe, and social class distinctions in the application of sanctions were striking. The calvinist doctrine that wealth signifies favor from God instigated judgments of the poor as inherently lacking in motivation, industry, or inclination to work.[19] Laws prohibiting idleness, such as the English Vagrancy Law of 1530 and the Poor Laws of 1572 and 1601, prescribed physical punishments and gaol (jail) for petty offenders, vagbonds, petty thieves, prostitutes, beggars, and the poor who refused to work.[20] King Henry VIII of England, who reigned from 1509 to 1547, had 72,000 thieves and vagabonds (vagrants) executed.[21]

High demand for labor to support the expanding wealth of a small upper class further instigated harsh penalties for relatively minor offenses in the sixteenth and seventeenth centuries. Maximum wages made it unlawful to pay workers more than stated limits and prohibited collective bargaining. Labor conditions were horrible and included forced labor of poor families held in workhouses.[22] Such a system virtually assured that the rich would become wealthier through the labor of the poor. Noted philosopher and sociologist Michel Foucault has proposed that the torturous, barbaric punishments characteristic of the sixteenth, seventeenth, and eighteenth centuries served to maintain the compliance of the poor and working class with this system of exploitation.[23] Minor law violations, such as petty property crimes, were punishable by torture and death because they challenged control over labor and economic distribution and they threatened rebellion, according to this perspective.

Douglas Hay further documents the increasing severity of punishments designed to protect the property of the wealthy in the seventeenth and eighteenth centuries. Forced entry into factories, destruction of linen or the tools used to make linen, forgery of bank notes to rob merchants, or theft of food were all capital crimes in the eighteenth century. Hay argues that the severity of sanctions increased to protect the wealth generated by emerging commercial and industrial enterprises. Punishments were applied to the poor and lower classes who challenged the rights of the propertied classes to amass greater wealth. Even minor infractions, such as "malicious damage" (vandalism), were punishable by death.[24]

Regardless of the motivations for torturous sanctions, punishments prior to the writings of Cesare Beccaria and Jeremy Bentham (see Chapter 9), focused upon the body of the offender. Punishments for stealing a rabbit or a loaf of bread commonly included burning at the stake; drawing and quartering (a team of horses attached to arms and legs to be pulled in opposite directions until all limbs were severed); amputation of fingers, toes, hands, or other body parts, which were then burned in front of the offender; and drowning. Iron rings along the retaining walls of the River Thames in London still reveal the places where people convicted of crimes were restrained as the tide rolled in and drowned them. In 1760, there were 160 capital crimes, or crimes in which the death penalty was applied. By 1819, there were 223 crimes that required the penalty of death.[25]

Decline in the Use of Torture

Torture declined after the French Revolution (1789) and greater sobriety in punishments was evident by the early nineteenth century. The hanging machine, which was invented in England and first used in 1760, provided for a quicker, less tortured death. The machine allowed the condemned to be hanged by falling through a trap door, rather than strangling slowly on the end of a hoisted rope. The guillotine was first used in 1792. This machine severed the head of the convicted offender by dropping a blade from a height.[26] Both inventions, combined with the concurrent tendency to shroud the face of the prisoner during execution, marked a turn away from torture in favor of swift, sober executions. As the writings of Beccaria and Bentham drew international attention to the barbaric nature of many types of corporal punishment and the liberal use of capital punishment, the severity of punishment techniques began to wane.

The greater humanitarianism promoted by Enlightenment philosophers, combined with the influential works of Beccaria and Bentham, were only part of the reason for the change in punishment strategies, however. The use of forced servitude and convict labor became a formidable source of free labor both in England and in the new American states. The work force was expanded by creating a supply of conscripted laborers, which kept wages down and provided emerging industry (and the state) with a labor source.

As the Industrial Revolution transformed the means of economic production in the early nineteenth century, punishment shifted away from emphasis on the body and physical suffering. Deprivations of liberty through imprisonment, enforced silence, and isolation from society replaced many of the earlier physical punishments that had caused great pain and suffering. Punishment was transformed in the early nineteenth century to focus the suffering toward the inner soul of the offender.[27] This shift toward the inner person, which left the physical body able for eventual return to society, was aimed at reforming the offender for re-entry into the work force. Many Colonial American and early nineteenth-century punishments focused upon the utility of work for reform and payment of penance to society. Indentured servitude from England was common until the American Revolution. With this punishment, the offender was sent to the American Colonies to work for a contractor who paid a sum to the courts of England in exchange for the work of the convict. The indentured servant was bound to servitude for a specified period of time and then freed. After 1776, England continued to dump convicts in other British colonies such as Australia and New Zealand. Slaves imported from Africa replaced the use of indentured servants in the United States.

Nineteenth-Century American Punishments

After the Industrial Revolution with its subsequent increase in urban populations, crime rates rose significantly in both England and the United States.[28] The gap between the rich and the poor was greatly increased by the onset of industrial production in the early nineteenth century. The U.S. Constitution, which was guided by Enlightenment principles of humanitarianism and utilitarianism, prohibited excessive ("cruel and unusual") punishments through the Eighth Amendment. Innovative techniques of punishment emerged simultaneous with the development of American democracy and the Industrial Revolution. Emphasis shifted away from torture, mutilation, and public scorn, and began to focus upon individual liberty. Deprivation of liberty through imprisonment became the preferred punishment in the nineteenth century.

Prisons existed before the development of the American prison system, but they were loosely organized and rarely used by comparison to other punishments; there were only a few prisons located in all of Western Europe. When the great prison reformer, John Howard, began his work in 1773, he found all prisons in England to be unhygienic, old, overrun with vermin, and many contained underground chambers filled with instruments of torture.[29] Workhouses and houses of corrections were more commonly used than prisons. These were institutions where indigent men, women, and children who had committed petty crimes were conscripted to work for the duration of their sentences. They were commonly used throughout England, Germany, Holland, and to a lesser extent, in other European countries.[30] The use of hulks (broken down, old war ships moored in rivers and harbors) was a notoriously unsanitary means of confining prisoners in England. Most prisoners died from disease before completing their sentence under these conditions.[31]

These models of inhumane confinement, combined with the emergence of humanitarian punishment philosophies that recommended penalties proportionate to the crimes committed, as proposed by Bentham, spurred the development of two distinct styles of imprisonment in the United States. The ideas of reform through the inculcation of Christian virtue, which was supposed to ensure that offenders would eventually be released back to the labor force as productive citizens, was central to both systems. Underlying beliefs about the ability of punishment to both reform and deter oriented the development of both prison systems. The American penitentiary system is based upon the belief that punishment is beneficial to the offender and prevents the corrupt from spreading their evil ways to others.[32] Evidence of this underlying philosophy is apparent in both early prison systems. Otherwise, there were important distinctions. The nineteenth-century American efforts to create prison environments that were both humane and efficient fostered the models upon which other countries have built.

The Pennsylvania System

The first of the two American systems was the **Pennsylvania System,** which began in 1790 when Pennsylvania converted an old jail on Walnut Street in Philadelphia into a state prison, often called the Walnut Street Jail.[33] The jail was remodeled for implementation of a punishment

philosophy that had first been articulated by Benjamin Franklin and Benjamin Rush. In the Walnut Street Jail, prisoners were housed in individual cells, separated by sex and offense (whether convicted or awaiting trial), and expected to work 8- to 10-hour days. Religious instruction was an important component of the system. Work was performed in inmates' individual cells and silence was enforced throughout the day. Prisoners were allowed to talk for a short time in the evening. Guards did not use weapons and corporal punishment was not permitted.[34]

By 1800, problems with the Walnut Street Jail were significant. Insufficient work meant many prisoners sat in idleness. Escapes became problematic when correctional personnel were not added to keep up with inmate increases. Some changes were instituted. Uniforms for prisoners were color-coded to indicate first, second, or third offenders. Corporal punishment, primarily in the form of whippings, was re-introduced, and isolation of recalcitrant prisoners in solitary confinement was used for discipline. When it became obvious that inmates needed some exercise, gardening programs were initiated. These failed, however, because prisoners were poorly skilled and prison officials were poor managers. The prison operated at a loss and was deemed a failure by 1820. However, the failures in the operation of the Walnut Street Jail provided important insight for the full development of the Pennsylvania Prison System in the next few years.[35]

In 1826, the second Pennsylvania prison was opened in Pittsburgh. It was called the Western Penitentiary. Another prison was opened in 1829 in Philadelphia and named Cherry Hill because it was located in a cherry orchard; this prison was also called the Eastern Penitentiary. Cherry Hill was the first large-scale prison to use solitary confinement at all times, with work provided in individual cells. The architectural design, completed by John Haviland, was extraordinarily innovative for the time. It consisted of seven wings connected to a central hub and to one another by passages. Each prisoner had a single cell with an outside exercise yard. Prisoners were blindfolded when taken into the prison and not allowed to communicate with other prisoners once inside. Prisoners remained in their cells even for religious services. The chaplain spoke from the central rotunda in the hub of the prison. The Pennsylvania model, both the architectural design and the punishment strategy, became the basis for most prisons in Europe, South America, and (later) Asia.[36]

The Auburn System

While many other countries adopted the plan of the Pennsylvania System, the **Auburn System** became the model for most prisons in the United States. New York State built two prisons concurrent with the development of the Pennsylvania System. The first opened in Newgate in 1797 and the second opened in Auburn in 1817. The

TABLE 16.1 | Comparison of Pennsylvania and Auburn Systems

	PENNSYLVANIA	AUBURN
Architecture	Designed like a wheel with a hub and seven spokes.	Fortress with tiers of cells around a central core.
Work	Individual cells in isolation.	Congregate, with enforced silence.
Discipline	No corporal punishment.	Corporal punishment was central to control.
Religion	Inmates were to memorize Bible verses.	Bible was central to reform.
Economic support	Self-supporting.	Self-supporting. Emphasis on profits, not work training.
Goals of prison programs	Communion with God; conversion of the human spirit; virtue and integrity.	Alteration of habit. Prison teaches useful skills that prisoners can use to find gainful employment and avoid crime.

SOURCE: Robert Johnson, *Hard Time: Understanding and Reforming the Prison*, 2nd ed. (Belmont, CA: Wadsworth, 1996).

Newgate prison featured congregate work during the day and several prisoners housed together in cells at night. Discipline was a problem, however, and a new plan first tried at Auburn was adopted. The Auburn System required congregate work during the day, individual cells at night, and enforced silence at all times. This became known as the *silent system*. Prisoners ate front to back, they were to stand with arms folded and eyes cast downward, and they walked in lock step with eyes down. Absolutely no communication, not even eye contact, was permitted. Prisoners sat in private booths for religious services and outside communication was strictly controlled. No newspapers were permitted and letters were strictly monitored. In 1821, permanent solitary confinement was instituted for dangerous prisoners by the warden, Captain Elam Lynds, who believed that reform could not occur unless the spirit of the prisoner was broken. The isolation of solitary confinement led to mental illness and some deaths.[37]

The architecture of the Auburn System was a fortress-style building with a hollow core. Tiers of cells surrounded the core. Both operation and construction of Auburn-style prisons were more economical than the Pennsylvania System[38] (Table 16.1).

The Reformatory System

A third style of imprisonment emerged in the latter third of the nineteenth century. The **reformatory system** developed from the correctional style established at the **Elmira Reformatory** in Elmira, New York, in 1876. In this system, which was primarily designed for young offenders, the treatment rationale abandoned old ideas of punishment and focused upon reforming offenders. The architecture of Elmira resembled Auburn but, under the direction of prison reformer Enoch C. Wines, the prison emphasized rehabilitation. Educational programs, vocational training, classification of offenders according to conduct and achievement, and opportunities for early re-lease through parole characterized this new model. Indeterminate sentences allowed for early release of offenders who showed evidence of reform. The system of parole established at Elmira became the model upon which all other parole programs were based for the next hundred years.[39]

While the emphasis at Elmira on self-respect and personal improvement were praiseworthy ideals, the system eventually failed. Heavy reliance on local teachers, lawyers, and university professors from Elmira College for instruction at the institution could not be maintained over a long period of time. The emphasis on rehabilitation of offenders did survive beyond the immediate problems of the institution. Many prisons built in the early twentieth century were called reformatories and offered at least some opportunities for rehabilitation. However, subsequent reformatories have been criticized for offering vocational training that suited the needs of the institution or the state rather than the needs of offenders (Box 16.2). Reform at Elmira was based on improvement of offenders' potential for post-release success.[40] Many twentieth-century reformatories have been organized around the premise that punishment aids reform.

Twentieth-Century Corrections

Two opposing points of view prevailed in correctional strategies in the early twentieth century. The Progressive Era (1890–1920) was generally characterized by enthusiasm for social reform through creation of humane, educated, and morally committed citizens. Progressive influence on prisons advocated training, religion, vocational programs, and education. All were aimed at rehabilitating offenders. Women's prisons, in particular, were targets of Progressive reformers. Programs designed to teach women to behave appropriately to their sex, or to be "ladies," were instituted in all women's prisons in the early twentieth century.[41]

Nineteenth-Century Imprisonment of Women

In the early nineteenth century there were many prison reforms that significantly improved the conditions under which men were incarcerated. Improvements such as classification systems that separated dangerous offenders from others, new prison buildings that reduced overcrowding, and reduced use of corporal punishment of offenders represented nineteenth-century trends in men's corrections. None of these trends were characteristic of women's incarceration, however.

Overcrowding, harsh conditions of confinement, and sexual abuse by guards and male prisoners were common conditions of women's incarceration throughout most of the nineteenth century. Separate facilities for women were not established until the end of the century. Most incarcerated women were held in a small section of men's prisons. In Auburn, New York, for example, in the 1820s there were no separate cells for the 20 to 30 women who were confined there at any given time. Some had sentences as long as 14 years, but all were confined in a single room in the attic of the prison. The windows were sealed shut to prevent the women from communicating outside of the room. In 1826, prisoner Rachel Welch became pregnant while in solitary confinement; she was flogged by a prison officer and died shortly after giving birth. A grand jury investigated the flogging, but was unconcerned with the pregnancy or with the conditions under which other women were held in Auburn.

In 1859, a newspaper in Michigan reported that women's confinement was "hot and putrid," and that prisoners dwelled in a state of "pandemonium." Accounts of virtually all confinement of women prisoners include mention of illegitimate births. In Indiana, sexual exploitation of women prisoners was systematic. An administrator of the Indiana state prison operated a prostitution service for male guards, using the forced labor of women inmates. In the 1870s in Illinois, 22 female inmates were held on the fifth floor of the warden's house, which was called the "chicken coop." They sat in a row of chairs all day every day mending male prisoners' clothes. They were allowed out for a stroll in the yard once a year.

Most prison reformers avoided the issue of women's incarceration until the late nineteenth century because women who had committed crimes were considered to be too depraved to be reformed. That is, women were believed to be, by nature, more virtuous and moral than men. For women to commit crimes meant that they had "fallen" from a higher level of virtue than was characteristic of men. Women criminals were believed to be the "personification of evil," and thus too far gone for redemption.

Conditions of women's confinement began to improve as the reformatory movement gained support around the turn of the twentieth century. Attitudes about women also changed and women criminals in the twentieth century were more likely to be viewed as weak, uneducated, or easily led by men. Early twentieth-century women's corrections focused upon teaching women criminals to be "ladies."

source: Estelle B. Freedman, *Their Sisters' Keeper: Women's Prison Reform in America, 1830–1930* (Ann Arbor, MI: University of Michigan Press, 1984) 17–19.

The other prevailing point of view, which was predominantly held by prison administrators and state officials, was that prisoners both needed and deserved harsh discipline, rigid rules, and militaristic style management. Overt corporal punishment declined, but private beatings, severe dietary restrictions, and the use of solitary confinement prevailed into the 1930s. New prisons built at Attica, New York, in 1931 and Stateville, Illinois, in 1925, as well as others built in Western states during the same period, were characterized by the rigid, discipline-oriented, custody-focused style of the Auburn System. The reformatory philosophy was more commonly applied to women's prisons or juvenile institutions.[42]

From the end of the Progressive Era until the 1950s, little public attention was focused on prisons. Disturbances such as riots were relatively rare; the incarceration rate was low during the Great Depression and World War II, and the prison system was stable. The rate of incarceration increased from a low of 79 per 100,000 population in 1925 to 109 per 100,000 in 1950, but intervening years were characterized by fluctuations, rather than steady increase.[43]

Prison Industries

Among the most important developments in prisons during the 1920s and 1930s was the decline in prison industries. Because of complaints of unfair advantage from private industry, prisons began to decrease their emphasis on industrial production in the 1930s. The problem was that prisons could produce goods at a much lower price than private industry because of the free labor provided by prisoners. Sale of prison-made goods undercut market competition. The Hawes-Cooper Act of 1929 and the Ashurst-Summers Act of 1935 restricted the transportation and sale of prison-made goods. After 1935, goods such as

Big House Prisons and Violence

Modern prisons are characterized by a high degree of violence. While staff-perpetrated violence is problematic in modern prisons and the courts have restricted techniques of control in several courts cases, most of the violence in modern prisons is inmate-driven. Inmates attack fellow inmates within a culture of violence that rules prisons. In Big House prisons, which were characteristic of American corrections from the turn of the twentieth century until the 1960s, inmate-perpetrated violence was rare.

Big House prisons were institutions of total control. Rigid discipline that enforced silence, punctuality, absolute obedience to all prison rules, regular work, lock-step marching between daily activities, and strict, coercive conformity was common in Big House prisons. Violence in these prisons was used as a means of control over inmates. Inmates exhibited self-control as a means of avoiding the brutality of prison authorities. These prisons were orderly, efficient, clean, predictable, and highly stable. Ideas of rehabilitation from the 1930s until the 1960s focused on discipline as the most effective means of reforming inner character among prisoners. Prisoners who learned self-control in the Big House would have a better chance of long-term success because discipline,

rigid structure, and suppression of self built character. Inmates who did not conform to prison authority did "hard time." That is, they were subject to the coercive authority of prison officials who had few restrictions and wide discretion in their means of enforcing prison rules. Recalcitrant inmates could spend years in solitary confinement. Obedience to authority prevailed among inmates.

While many observers have classified this era of prison management as heartless, brutal, or repressive, many others have pointed to the efficiency and security of such management. Exploitation and corruption were common in Big House prisons, as they are in modern prisons. Inmate informers were used by prison authorities to maintain control, reciprocal relationships developed between inmates and staff; and contraband flowed into and out of the prison through staff corruption as it does today. The most notable difference between Big House prisons and modern corrections was the higher degree of internal safety in the earlier model. Corporal punishment and brutality were used, but daily danger among those who minded their own business and followed the rules was less common than in modern prisons.

SOURCE: Robert Johnson, *Hard Time: Understanding and Reforming the Prison* (Belmont, CA: Wadsworth, 1996) 134–41.

soap, brooms, shoes, furniture, flags, and other products manufactured in prisons were sold to other state agencies, but they were not openly marketed. Leasing of prisoners in chain gangs to private contractors in lumber, road construction, and agricultural industries also ceased during the 1930s. Public sentiment was negative because cheap labor supplied through lease of prisoners unfairly hindered the employment of destitute men during the Great Depression. The labor of convicts chained together in public work details was also too close to patterns of slavery, which many people could still remember. Public disfavor was responsible for the elimination of chain-gang convict labor.

The Big House

An American prison, during the first half of the twentieth century, was referred to as the **Big House.**[44] This term implies that the penitentiary was a tightly controlled institution with a high degree of regimentation and strict discipline. There were few prison disturbances during the period from 1900 to 1950. Discipline, exercise of authority through force, and rigid routine characterized American

corrections during this period. Correctional officers wielded nearly total power over prisoners and the authority of the warden was unchallenged. Part of the punishment, according to Robert Johnson, a noted author and theorist of the development of the modern prison, was the loss of physical security that resulted from the experience of imprisonment. The Big House controlled prisoners with often-brutal authority, frequently reflecting the early nineteenth-century Auburn philosophy that the spirit of the prisoner had to be broken for reform to take place.[45]

Wardens of Big House prisons had virtually complete control over the techniques of discipline in the first half of the twentieth century (Box 16.3). While prisoners had the legal right to bring suit against the state regarding conditions of their confinement, there was virtually no willingness of courts to hear such cases. The authority of the warden to decide issues of custody and control within prisons was unquestioned. In one of the classic analyses of penitentiary history, *Stateville: The Penitentiary in Mass Society,* author James Jacobs describes the authority of Warden Ragen, who governed the toughest prison in the nation from 1936 to 1961:

Ronald Ward waits on death row. Black inmates disproportionately await death sentences, but race of victims is actually more important in death penalty cases. Those who kill white victims are more likely to receive the death penalty than those who kill black victims.

Joe Ragen's thirty-year rule of Stateville was based upon the patriarchal authority that he achieved. In the vocabulary of both employees and inmates, "he ran it." The "Old Boss" devoted his life to perfecting the world's most orderly prison regime. He exercised personal control over every detail, no matter how insignificant. He tolerated challenges neither by inmates nor by employees nor by outside interest groups. He cultivated an image which made him seem invincible to his subordinates as well as to the prisoners.

In the course of thirty years he transformed Stateville into an efficient paramilitary organization famous and infamous throughout the world. . . . Ragen fired a guard for brutality at Menard, but many informants also insist that he often turned his back on beatings at Stateville. He would castigate guards for referring to inmates as "sons-of-bitches" but he would do so himself in the next breath. While many of the inmates may have seethed with bitterness, an equal number preferred doing time at Stateville because "you knew where you stood."[46]

In the early 1950s, the character of American prisons began to change. Increasing agitation over brutal conditions of confinement, inadequate medical care, and spoiled food spurred twenty-five riots in 1952 and 1953, which resulted in many injuries and loss of property.[47] Ideas of rehabilitation were beginning to creep back into correctional strategies and inmates began to demand opportunities for participation in educational and treatment programs. Civil rights issues outside of prisons began to foster awareness of racial injustices inside.[48]

The Modern Era

During the 1960s, the philosophy of rehabilitation was reintroduced into American prisons more completely than in any previous era. Many changes in the organization of prisons, in inmate culture, and in strategies of corrections fostered prolific redesign of both the ideals of corrections and the rudimentary management of prisons in the 1960s. Treatment-oriented programs reflected the genre of the times and fostered renewed hope that rehabilitation was a realistic goal of corrections.

Professional Administration

Two specific changes closed the door on the old Big House strategy of control and ushered in modern prisons. First, the preference for professional administrators of prisons, rather than gubernatorial appointments of political patronage, became common practice in the 1960s. That is, wardens (prison superintendents) were recruited from professional ranks on the basis of experience, knowledge, expertise, and performance criteria. In all prior history of American corrections, professional qualifications for the position of warden were largely irrelevant. Wardens were picked at the discretion of governors. The increased attention toward professional training, experience, and articulation of goals and ideals of treatment changed the ways in which all correctional staff were viewed both by prisoners and by the public. Professional administration raised expectations of rehabilitation.[49]

Prison Litigation

The second important change in corrections that began in the late 1960s was the use of litigation by prisoners to solve problems of prison life. Courts, by longstanding tradition, had had a "hands off" policy toward prisoners. As late as 1950, a federal court ruled that it had no concern with internal discipline in prisons in any of the states.[50] For one hundred years prior to this decision, the few court cases regarding prisoners involved the constitutionality of confinement, or *habeas corpus*, not the conditions of confinement. In 1969, the U.S. Supreme Court invalidated a Tennessee prison regulation that prohibited interaction among inmates in the preparation of legal cases.[51] This opened the door to further litigation, and there has been an exponential increase in the cases filed in the subsequent decades.

The use of courts to address problems of prison life is important for a variety of reasons. First, it has reduced the control of prison staff over inmates' lives through judicial scrutiny of the conditions of prison life. Second, courts have reintroduced rationality into prison governance. Rules must be reasonable, within the confines of the goals of the institution, and not arbitrary restrictions for convenience. Third, many of the cases brought before the courts in the last three decades have instigated positive reforms. They have, for example, limited brutality by staff, improved medical care, addressed constitutional issues such as religion and freedom of speech, and otherwise clarified the authority of the state. And fourth, they have given legitimacy to inmate protest against the authority of the state. This final point is among the most important changes because it increases the accountability of prison authorities, who must monitor their own personnel more cautiously.[52]

TABLE 16.2 | Petitions Filed in U.S. District Courts by State and Federal Prisoners

YEAR	PETITIONS BY FEDERAL PRISONERS	PETITIONS BY STATE PRISONERS	TOTAL
1977	4,691	14,846	19,537
1980	3,713	19,574	23,287
1983	4,354	26,421	30,775
1986	4,432	29,333	33,765
1989	5,577	35,904	41,481
1992	6,997	41,426	48,423
1993	8,456	44,995	53,451
1994	7,700	50,240	57,940
1995	8,951	54,599	63,550*

*Increases in this table should be reviewed within the context of increases in corrections. The prison population increased by half a million inmates during the years presented.

SOURCES: Kathleen Maguire and Ann L. Pastore, *Sourcebook of Criminal Justice Statistics, 1995* (Washington DC: U.S. Government Printing Office, 1996) 499; Kathleen Maguire and Ann L. Pastore, *Sourcebook of Criminal Justice Statistics, 1995* (Washington DC: U.S. Government Printing Office, 1996) 517.

The use of the courts by prisoners is a matter of current concern because of the large number of cases filed annually. Unfortunately, many frivolous lawsuits are filed—on topics as trivial as the color of an inmate's shoelaces or the type of peanut butter available in the prison cafeteria. Most of the frivolous cases are dismissed before they reach court, but critics contend that prisoners should not have the right to use the courts if they abuse the privilege with such minor problems. Actually, use of the courts is a constitutionally guaranteed right, not a privilege. To reduce access for minor claims, unfortunately, would reduce access for legitimate claims, which should be heard. Important issues such as visitation, privacy, brutality by staff, and provision of adequate health care have been settled in the courts in recent years. Prisoners, of course, have no monopoly over frivolous lawsuits. The proliferation of televised court proceedings in recent years has drawn attention to the fact that Americans are an exceptionally litigious society. Suits over the color of roses on a wedding cake or the length of a haircut are representative of frivolous lawsuits filed in contemporary courts.

Nevertheless, the cost of review of inmate lawsuits is enormous. There are over 50,000 inmate lawsuits each year at a cost of $50 million. In Indiana alone, there were 1700 lawsuits which took ten full-time lawyers to examine, at a cost of $1 million.[53] Table 16.2 illustrates the increase in petitions filed by prisoners in recent years.

The Shift to Custody and Control

During the 1970s, disenchantment with rehabilitation strategies was coupled with a call for a return to custody and control as the primary purpose of prisons. High

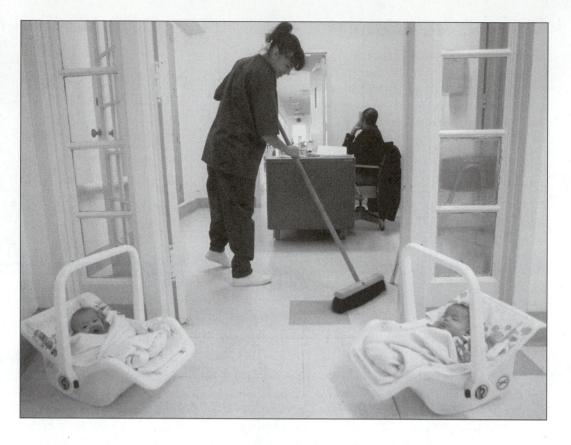

Women inmates who are pregnant at the time of incarceration present a special problem for prison management. A few prisons allow mothers to keep their infants with them until the babies are a year or two old.

recidivism, increased attention to the costs of rehabilitation programs, and disillusionment with the ideals of rehabilitation instigated calls for "law and order" and punishment.[54] By the end of the 1970s, most rehabilitation programs had been eliminated or severely curtailed.

The 1980s initiated the era of overcrowding. The prison population more than doubled between 1980 and 1990, which brought the greatest increase in prison population in any decade in U.S. history. The massive increases in inmate populations and return to custody and control as the *modus operandi* of U.S. prisons turned American corrections into what Johnson has called "warehouses of social rejects." [55] Changes in sentencing strategies in the 1980s, more than any other factor, caused the explosion in the prison population. Crime rates remained stable, or declined in some areas, but prison populations skyrocketed to unprecedented heights.[56] Longer sentences and mandatory sentences, an increased use of incarceration rather than other sentencing alternatives, and a general fervor for punishment all conspired to drive the rates of incarceration to unprecedented levels.

The 1990s has been a repeat of the 1980s. The United States in the late 1990s has a higher incarceration rate than any other country in the world, and sentences are among the longest in the world.[57] The trend through the 1990s has been to increase the pain of imprisonment with a return to punishment as the primary ideal of corrections. Particular groups in the population, such as minority men, have been especially impacted by the acceleration in corrections. Declines in social programs, employment training, and the use of foreign labor in developing countries for low-level manufacturing jobs previously available in the United States, have all contributed to increased hopelessness among all poor, but especially among minority youth, and have indirectly increased prison populations through the 1990s.[58]

Increases in Women's Corrections

Among the significant changes in corrections in the 1980s and 1990s has been the increase in women's corrections. Women constitute the fastest-growing demographic group in the prison population.[59] While this may seem alarming, women's incarceration rates started at a point so much lower than men's that it is not likely that women will come close to equaling male incarceration in the next century. Nevertheless, the increase in women's incarceration is a matter of concern, and it is often cited as the most rapidly changing demographic category in corrections. Table 16.3 illustrates the changes in corrections since the U.S. Department of Justice began calculating rates of incarceration in 1925.

The rising rate of women's crime is often cited as a significant American social problem. Several theories have been proposed in the last few years to explain why

TABLE 16.3 | Numbers of Inmates and Rates of Incarceration per 100,000 Population, 1925–1996

| YEAR | TOTAL | RATE | MALES | | FEMALES | |
			NUMBER	RATE	NUMBER	RATE
1925	91,669	79	88,231	149	3,438	6
1930	129,453	104	124,785	200	4,668	8
1935	144,180	113	139,278	217	4,902	8
1940	173,703	131	167,345	252	6,361	10
1945	133,649	98	127,609	193	6,040	9
1950	166,123	109	160,309	211	5,814	8
1955	185,780	112	178,655	217	7,125	8
1960	212,953	117	205,265	230	7,688	8
1965	210,895	108	203,327	213	7,568	8
1970	196,429	96	190,794	191	5,635	5
1975	240,593	111	231,918	220	8,675	8
1980	315,974	138	306,643	274	12,331	11
1985	480,568	200	458,972	380	21,296	19
1990	739,980	292	699,416	575	40,564	32
1994	1,016,760	389	956,691	753	60,069	45
1996	1,182,169	427	1,107,439	819	74,730	51

SOURCES: Lawrence A. Greenfield, "Women in Prison," *Bureau of Justice Statistics Special Report* (Washington DC: U.S. Government Printing Office, 1991); Kathleen Maguire and Ann L. Pastore, *Sourcebook of Criminal Justice Statistics, 1995* (Washington DC: U.S. Government Printing Office, 1996) 556; Tracy L. Snell, "Correctional Populations in the United States, 1993," *Bureau of Justice Statistics Report* (Washington DC: U.S. Government Printing Office, 1995) 9; Christopher J. Mumola, "Prisoners in 1996" (Washington, DC: U.S. Government Printing Office, 1997) 1, 5.

FIGURE 16.1 | Sentenced Prisoners in State and Federal Institutions 1925–1996

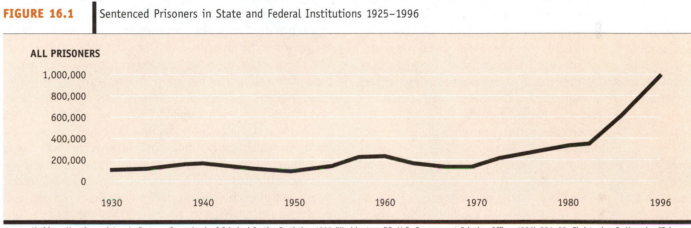

SOURCE: Kathleen Maguire and Ann L. Pastore, *Sourcebook of Criminal Justice Statistics, 1995* (Washington, DC: U.S. Government Printing Office, 1996) 554–55; Christopher J. Mumola, "Prisoners in 1996" (Washington, DC: U.S. Government Printing Office, 1997) 1–5.

women's crime has suddenly begun to rise after remaining stable for many decades. Women's rates of poverty have increased faster than men's since 1980, which probably accounts for the largest share of the increase.[60] Figures 16.1 and 4.4 illustrate the trends in incarceration for men, women, and all prisoners.

Upward Trends in Incarceration

The recent trends in corrections, as illustrated by these figures, show steady increases. With current sentencing strategies, these trends are likely to continue to move upward after the turn of the twenty-first century. One of the strongest criticisms of rehabilitation strategies in the 1970s was that they did not work. There were, in fact,

many failings of rehabilitation strategies. Yet, the prison population has soared beyond any modern world measures since the correctional philosophy shifted to punishment strategies. Not all of the increase can be attributed to philosophy of punishment, however. Other factors also increase rates of incarceration. Rising crime rates, reduced use of other correctional strategies such as probation or community treatment programs, and reduced judicial discretion also push the prison population upward.

Many people believe that the rise in the prison population reflects rising crime rates, but actually the rate of crime has declined since the changes in correctional policies first became evident in 1980. Current trends include a steady, or slightly declining, crime rate, although offenses are up among certain demographic groups such as the very young. Alternative correctional strategies have declined in recent years and new mandatory sentences reduce judicial decisionmaking and require prison terms for many offenses. These sentencing trends have influenced the size of the prison population. The belief among lawmakers that long, mandatory prison terms will serve as a deterrent has oriented many of the recent sentencing changes. The expansion of the prison population, the abandonment of rehabilitation, and the new longer prison sentences, all represent a get-tough attitude toward crime that have brought American corrections past the level of a million people imprisoned. Figures 16.1 and 4.4 illustrated changes in treatment strategies that began in 1980 and have ushered in an new era in corrections. The policymakers of the twenty-first century will be faced with the effects of these changes.

Summary

In 1893, the noted French sociologist Emile Durkheim was among the first to explain how social structure influences the type and importance of law and punishment in any society.[61] From Durkheim's point of view, there are two types of social solidarity: *mechanical* and *organic*. Mechanical solidarity prevails in primitive societies, where social life is relatively simple. The people are united by their common interests, values, and interpersonal ties. In organic solidarity societies, which are more characteristic of complex modern societies, a widely diversified labor force and a great variety of values, attitudes, and personal differences separate people. In mechanical solidarity **repressive law** prevails. This means that the law is used to enforce collective values. Punishments tend to be harsh, and they are used to preserve social solidarity. Severe sanctions are used in such societies to serve as an example to all members of society; deviance is not tolerated under repressive law strategies.

In organic solidarity societies, **restitutive law** supersedes repressive law. Under restitutive law the punishment is used to repair the harm done by the offender's actions. In such societies there is great emphasis on compensation, or amending the offense. The offender in such societies "pays a debt to society" for the wrongful action. Crimes are considered to be acts against the victim or the state, rather than against the collective conscience, or common values, of the entire society. The punishment in organic solidarity societies should be beneficial to the offender by promoting rehabilitation.

The history of punishment, as illustrated by the overview presented in this chapter, reflects many of the insights Durkheim articulated in his theories of law and social response to law violation. Punishments prior to the writings of Beccaria and Bentham reflected the community standards of mechanical solidarity. Wrongful behavior was severely sanctioned to serve as an example to all others. Very minor offenses (by contemporary standards) were punishable by torture and death because they offended the collective sentiments of the culture.

Beccaria and Bentham created a revolution in sentiment toward punishment, in part because their work coincided with other social structural changes that initiated transformation to organic solidarity and restitutive law. The Industrial Revolution brought the birth of modern, complex, highly diversified societies, with a shift away from the values of the group and new emphasis on the sanctity of the individual. The focus of punishment shifted away from torture and death in favor of restitution. As Foucault has said, the punishment shifted from the body of the offender to the inner soul of the prisoner.[62]

Modern American punishments exemplify the ideas presented by Durkheim over one hundred years ago. The primary purpose of contemporary punishments is to teach offenders a lesson so that they will refrain from future illegal activities. Underlying ideals of restitutive law imply that punishment is good for the offender and good for society. Crime is punished by sanctions intended to make the discomfort of punishment memorable enough for the offender that no future law violations will ensue. The philosophies of individual deterrence and selective incapacitation underlie the most recent sentencing guidelines, initiated to make punishments longer, more severe, and more consistently applied.

Most rehabilitative punishments have disappeared from American corrections. The underlying belief that punishment itself is rehabilitative, if the offender applies rational standards to the benefits of staying out of prison, is implied in both commonsense reactions to crime and current political rhetoric. As corrections shifted to a primarily punishment orientation in the 1980s, the number of prisoners incarcerated in the United States reached unprecedented levels. Current trends suggest that an increased use of imprisonment as the primary punishment strategy will continue into the twenty-first century.

Critical Thinking Questions

1. Several politicians have proposed that declines in crime rates are related to the increased use of prisons over the last two decades. Others say that the crime rate is not related to punishment strategies. Which position do you support? Why?
2. How do punishment strategies reflect the prevailing cultural forces of the times in which they are used? What cultural forces may be related to contemporary American punishment strategies?
3. What cultural forces were behind the decline of the reformatory movement?

4. Why did the Industrial Revolution have an impact on punishment strategies? What current "revolutions" may influence punishment in the future?

Suggested Readings

Michel Foucault, *Discipline and Punish: The Birth of the Prison,* tr. Alan Sheridan (New York: Vintage, 1977).

Douglas Hay, Peter Linebaugh, John G. Rule, E.P. Thompson, and Cal Winslow, *Albion's Fatal Tree: Crime and Society in Eighteenth Century England* (New York: Pantheon, 1975).

Dario Melossi and Massimo Pavarini, *The Prison and the Factory: Origins of the Penitentiary System,* tr. Glynis Cousin (London: Macmillan, 1977).

David J. Rothman, *The Discovery of Asylum: Social Order and Disorder in the New Republic* (Boston: Little, Brown, 1971).

Notes

1 Jeffrey Reiman, *The Rich Get Richer and the Poor Get Prison: Ideology, Crime, and Criminal Justice* (Boston: Allyn & Bacon, 1995).

2 Immanuel Kant, *The Metaphysical Elements of Justice,* tr. John Ladd (New York: Bobbs-Merrill, 1965).

3 For a discussion of the myth of leniency, or failure to prosecute or punish, see Victor E. Kappeler, Mark Blumberg, and Gary W. Potter, *The Mythology of Crime and Criminal Justice* (Prospect Heights, IL: Waveland, 1993), Ch. 10.

4 The Supreme Court, for example, upheld a life sentence for a Texas defendant who had stolen $228 through credit card fraud in 1980. See *Rummel v. Estelle* (1980) 445 U.S. 263.

5 Reiman, *The Rich Get Richer and the Poor Get Prison: Ideology, Crime, and Criminal Justice.*

6 See, for example, James Q. Wilson, *Thinking About Crime* (New York: Random House, 1975), or James Q. Wilson and Richard J. Herrnstein, *Crime and Human Nature* (New York: Simon & Schuster, 1985).

7 Ibid.

8 William Clinton, State of the Union Address, 25 January 1994.

9 Kyle Kercher, "Causes and Correlates of Crime Committed by the Elderly," in *Critical Issues in Aging Policy,* ed. Edgar F. Borgatta and R.J.W. Montgomery (Beverly Hills, CA: Sage, 1987).

10 Michael Gottfredson and Travis Hirschi, "The True Value of Lambda Would Appear To Be Zero: An Essay on Career Criminals, Criminal Careers, Selective Incapacitation, Cohort Studies, and Related Topics," *Criminology 24* (1986) 213–34.

11 Peter W. Greenwood and Allan Abrahamse, *Selective Incapacitation* (Santa Monica, CA: Rand Corporation, 1982).

12 Ibid.

13 Christy A. Visher, "Incapacitation and Crime Control: Does a 'Lock 'Em Up' Strategy Reduce Crime?" *Justice Quarterly 4* (1987) 514–15.

14 Lee Bowker, "Crime and the Use of Prisons in the United States: A Time Series Analysis," *Crime and Delinquency 27* (1981) 206–212.

15 Georg Rusche and Otto Kircheimer, *Punishment and Social Structure* (New York: Russell and Russell, 1939).

16 Edward H. Bierstadt, *What Do You Know About Crime?* (New York: Stokes, 1935) 87; Edward G. McGehee and William H. Hildebrand, *The Death Penalty* (Boston: DC Heath, 1964) 5.

17 Charlotte G. O'Kelly and Larry S. Carney, *Women and Men in Society: Cross-Cultural Perspectives on Gender Stratification,* 2nd ed. (Belmont, CA: Wadsworth, 1986), Ch. 5.

18 Stuart A. Queen and Robert W. Habenstein, *The Family in Various Cultures* (Philadelphia: JB Lippincott, 1974), Ch. 10.

19 See Dario Melossi and Massimo Pavarini, *The Prison and the Factory: Origins of the Penitentiary System,* tr. Glynis Cousin (London: The Macmillan Press, 1977).

20 Ibid., 14-15, 34.

21 Rusche and Kircheimer, *Punishment and Social Structure.*

22 Ibid., 15.

23 Michel Foucault, *Discipline and Punish: The Birth of the Prison,* tr. Alan Sheridan (New York: Vintage, 1977).

24 Douglas Hay, "Property, Authority, and the Criminal Law," in *Albion's Fatal Tree: Crime and Society in Eighteenth Century England,* ed. Douglas Hay et al. (New York: Pantheon, 1975) 19–21, 17–64.

25 Ibid., 14.

26 Ibid., 12–13.

27 Ibid., 28–31.

28 For discussion see: Rusche and Kircheimer, *Punishment and Social Structure.*

29 Melossi and Pavarini, *The Prison and the Factory: Origins of the Penitentiary System,* 48.

30 Ibid.

31 Harry Elmer Barnes, *The Story of Punishment* (Boston: Stratford, 1930) 117–22.

32 Robert Johnson, *Hard Time: Understanding and Reforming the Prison,* 2nd ed. (Belmont, CA: Wadsworth, 1996) 32–33.

33 David J. Rothman, *The Discovery of Asylum: Social Order and Disorder in the New Republic* (Boston: Little, Brown, 1971) 61.

34 Ibid., 81–93.

35 Ibid.

36 Barnes, *The Story of Punishment,* 144.

37 Ibid., 142–44; John P. Conrad, *Crime and Its Corrections* (Berkeley: University of California Press, 1965) 128.

38 Conrad, *Crime and Its Corrections,* 128.

39 James V. Bennett, "Evaluating a Prison," *Annals of the American Academy of Political and Social Science 293* (1954) 11.

40 Howard B. Gill, "Correctional Philosophy and Architecture," *Journal of Criminal Law, Criminology, and Police Science 53* (1962) 312–22.

41 Clarice Feinman, "Sex Role Stereotypes and Justice for Women," *Crime and Delinquency* (January 1979) 87–94. Most of the programs were still evident to some degree in women's corrections as late as the 1980s. Wisconsin, for example, advocated using women prisoners in the dairy industry in 1971 because they were believed to be empathetic to problems of swollen udders in cows. See Ruth M. Glick and Virginia V. Neto, "National Study of Women's Correctional Programs," in *The Criminal Justice System and Women: Women Offenders, Victims, and Workers,* ed. Barbara Raffel Price and Natalie J. Sokoloff (New York: Clark Boardman, 1982) 141–54.

42 Feinman, "Sex Role Stereotypes and Justice for Women"; Foucault, *Discipline and Punish: The Birth of the Prison;* Rothman, *The Discovery of Asylum: Social Order and Disorder in the New Republic.*

43 Kathleen Maguire and Ann L. Pastore, *Sourcebook of Criminal Justice Statistics, 1993* (Washington, D.C.: U.S. Government Printing Office, 1994) 600.

44 Johnson, *Hard Time: Understanding and Reforming the Prison* uses this concept throughout his book. See also Matthew Silberman, *A World of Violence* (Belmont CA: Wadsworth, 1995).

45 Johnson, *Hard Time: Understanding and Reforming the Prison,* 86.

46 James B. Jacobs, *Stateville: The Penitentiary in Mass Society* (Chicago: University of Chicago Press, 1977) 29–30.

47 Silberman (1995) 62; Desmond Ellis, Harold G. Grasmick, and Bernard Billman, "Violence in Prisons: A Sociological Analysis," *American Journal of Sociology 80* (1974) 16.

48 Silberman, *A World of Violence,* 62.

49 Johnson, *Hard Time: Understanding and Reforming the Prison,* 139. See also Jacobs, *Stateville: The Penitentiary in Mass Society.*

50 *Siegel v. Ragen* (1950) 180 F.2d 785, 788 (7th Cir.), *cert. denied,* 339 U.S. 990.

51 *Johnson v. Avery* (1969), 393 U.S. 483.

52 Johnson, *Stateville: The Penitentiary in Mass Society,* 140.

53 NBC Nightly News, 12 April 1995.

54 Silberman, *A World of Violence,* 62–63.

55 Johnson, *Stateville: The Penitentiary in Mass Society,* 132.

56 Reiman, *The Rich Get Richer and the Poor Get Prison: Ideology, Crime, and Criminal Justice,* Preface, 4th ed.

57 Ibid.

58 For discussion, see Reiman, *The Rich Get Richer and the Poor Get Prison: Ideology, Crime, and Criminal Justice.*

59 Allen J. Beck, "Prisoners in 1994," *Bureau of Justice Statistics Bulletin* (Washington DC: U.S. Government Printing Office, 1995) 5.

60 This phenomena is called the feminization of poverty. For discussion of the link between women's crime and poverty, see Darrell Steffensmeir and Cathy Streifel, "Trends in Female Crime, 1960–1990," or Martin Milkman and Sarah Tinkler, "Female Criminality: An Economic Perspective," both articles in *Female Criminality: The State of the Art,* ed. Concetta Culliver (New York: Garland, 1993).

61 Emile Durkheim, *The Division of Labor in Society,* tr. George Simpson (New York: The Free Press, 1964 [orig. pub. 1893]).

62 Foucault, *Discipline and Punish: The Birth of the Prison,* Part II.

chapter 17

Patterns of Incarceration

CHAPTER OUTLINE
COST OF CORRECTIONS
    Monetary Costs
    Social Costs
THE PRISON SYSTEM
    Prisons for Men
        Prison Classification
        Prison Culture
        Gangs in Prison
        Prison Violence
    Prisons for Women
        Incarcerated Mothers
    Jails
    Shock Incarceration (Boot Camps)
    Private Corrections
    Co-Corrections
    Community Corrections
        Community Corrections as an Alternative to Prison
        Costs of Community Corrections
ISSUES AND TRENDS
    AIDS
    Tuberculosis
    Mental Illness
    Geriatric Issues
    Correctional Officers
        Salaries in Corrections
        Job Satisfaction Among Correctional Officers
        Women in Correctional Work
        Sexual Harassment of Inmates
    Overcrowding
SUMMARY

KEY TERMS
recidivism
good-time policies
boot camps
shock incarceration
private corrections
prisonization
deprivation model
importation model
multiple classification
feminization of poverty
co-corrections
community corrections
intermediate sanctions
electronic monitoring
house arrest
diversion
de-institutionalization
capacity
rated capacity
operational capacity
design capacity

EVALUATIONS OF REHABILITATION STRATEGIES in the 1970s indicated that most programs had failed. **Recidivism,** or re-offense by released offenders, was not reduced by the rehabilitation programs initiated in the 1960s. A decade of failed programs convinced most prison administrators that a shift in philosophy was necessary. Whether the rehabilitation programs failed because the concept of rehabilitation was flawed, or because the programs did not meet the goals of rehabilitating offenders, has been a matter of debate since the shift back to punishment became apparent in the 1980s.[1]

Most of the interpretation of failures of rehabilitation originated with a 1974 study by Robert Martinson in which he investigated the outcome of 231 studies of rehabilitation and concluded that "nothing works."[2] Martinson's work, and a subsequent further report of the effectiveness of rehabilitation co-authored by Douglas Lipton and Judith Wilks, has been strongly criticized as simplistic and biased by overly pessimistic dismissal of many highly effective rehabilitation programs.[3] Regardless of the criticisms, Lipton, Martinson, and Wilks' report has become the foundation upon which most states abandoned rehabilitation and began more punitive treatment strategies. Policymakers and the public currently believe that the best treatment of criminals is punishment. Surveys of the American public, for example, indicate that only 13 percent of respondents believe that the purpose of prisons should be rehabilitation. Most people believe prisons should punish criminals and remove them from society.[4] Academics still debate the utilitarian benefits of punishment, but the mode of corrections has definitely shifted.

The philosophy of punishment has returned as the primary purpose of incarceration, and rehabilitation has nearly disappeared. When most people think about rehabilitation they imagine educational or vocational training programs in prison. Actually, the concept includes other programs less often linked to rehabilitation. Early release of prisoners who have proven their reform through good behavior in prison or **good-time policies,** parole, and reduced sentences of offenders who show remorse and willingness to change are all components of rehabilitation philosophies. With the return to punishment, such programs have declined in American corrections. More people are going into prison and fewer people are leaving early. As a result, the size of prison populations has sharply increased.

The increased prison population has brought many recent changes into corrections. Patterns of incarceration have changed. More women and minorities, for example, have been incarcerated since the changes began around 1980. The use of prisons and jails to house indigent people who are ill, such as those suffering from acquired immune deficiency syndrome (AIDS) or mental illness, has become a contemporary problem of corrections. And prison staffing problems, overcrowding, and prison violence have all been exacerbated with the expansion of the prison population. This chapter addresses each of these issues, and others facing contemporary prisons. Among the most important present-day considerations is the issue of costs of prisons.

Cost of Corrections

The cost of corrections could be calculated in a number of ways. There are, of course, the monetary costs. The amount of money necessary to sustain a system of corrections that incarcerates over 1 million people is enormous. The number of people entering American prisons is roughly 1100 new inmates every week, which means either that an equal number must be released, or that new prisons must be built to house the influx into the system.[5] Weekly releases do not equal weekly entrants into the system, sentences are longer than they were a decade ago, and the number of people incarcerated in the United States has grown at an alarming rate each year for nearly two decades. In 1996, there were 1.6 million people in prison or jail in the United States.[6] Thus, the financial costs are great—and they are increasing.

Monetary Costs

The financial costs of the justice system are not calculated or released as annual data like crime statistics. Data is available for yearly comparisons, but the numbers are

FIGURE 17.1 | Total Spending for Justice Activities by Level of Government

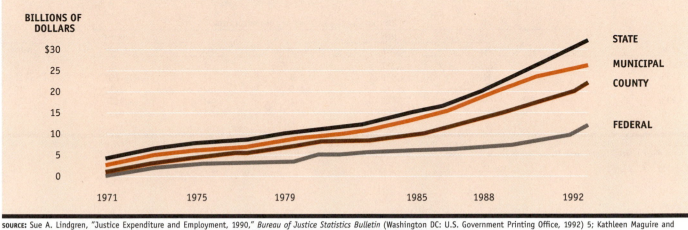

BILLIONS OF
DOLLARS

SOURCE: Sue A. Lindgren, "Justice Expenditure and Employment, 1990," *Bureau of Justice Statistics Bulletin* (Washington DC: U.S. Government Printing Office, 1992) 5; Kathleen Maguire and Ann L. Pastore, *Sourcebook of Criminal Justice Statistics, 1994* (Washington, DC: U.S. Government Printing Office, 1995) 4.

usually 5 or more years behind current expenditures. The current data on overall justice expenditures reflects 1990 and 1992 figures. In 1992, federal, state, and local governments spent $94 billion for civil and criminal justice activities. This was an increase of 162 percent over 1982 figures. Federal spending for justice activities between 1982 and 1992 increased faster than spending for all other government activities. In 1992, the federal government spent $367 on justice activities for every person living in the United States. The average state per-capita expenditure was $315 in 1992.[7]

While the federal government spends an enormous amount of money on justice activities, criminal justice is primarily a state and local concern. State and local governments increased spending for corrections activities by 359 percent between 1980 and 1992. At the federal level about 8 percent of justice expenditures is directed toward corrections, while courts, legal services, and federal police agencies drain most of the federal justice dollars. At the state level, however, 62 percent of justice expenditures involved corrections in 1992.[8] Figure 17.1 indicates increases in justice expenditures for each type of government between 1971 and 1992.

The states that spent the most money (over $1 million) on corrections in the 1992 data were California, Florida, Michigan, New York, Pennsylvania, and Texas. California spent more than any other state, with total corrections expenditures at over $4.9 million. The states that spent the least were Montana, North Dakota, South Dakota, Vermont, and Wyoming. Each of these states spent less than $50,000 on corrections, with North Dakota spending the least at $26,903 in 1992.[9] Of course, the relative factors of population size and density affect spending in these states.

A more important figure is the amount of money spent per inmate in each state. The average federal expenditure per inmate in 1990, which is the last year for which comprehensive calculations are available, was $14,456, while the states averaged $15,586 per inmate. The states that spent less than $10,000 per inmate in 1990 were Alabama, Arkansas, Idaho, Louisiana, Mississippi, Missouri, Nevada, and Oklahoma. Arkansas spent the least, at $7,557 per inmate. States that spent more than $20,000 per inmate in 1990 included Alaska, California, Maine, Minnesota, New Jersey, and Tennessee. Alaska spent the most, at $28,214 per inmate in 1990.[10]

Costs of incarceration are, of course, only part of the expenses involved in punishment. The cost of public defense of defendants who were too poor to hire an attorney increased 259 percent between 1971 and 1990. The per-capita costs of public defense in the states increased by 389 percent during the same years.[11] It is primarily the poor who are incarcerated in the United States, which means that governmental agencies assume the costs of defense, as well as prosecution and incarceration, of those who do not have the resources to fund their own defense. In 1992, 62 percent of inmates in state prisons had less than a high school education.[12] The average income of inmates prior to incarceration was less than $15,000 for 70 percent of inmates in 1991.[13]

Social Costs

Another view of costs focuses on the societal issues raised by punishment strategies. The United States has a higher percentage of its population in prison than any other country in the world, sentences are among the longest in the world, and the United States punishes behavior that is

TABLE 17.1 | Total Rates of Incarceration by Gender and Race, 1980–1996

| | | INCARCERATION RATE PER 100,000 POPULATION | | | | | |
| | | MEN | | | WOMEN | | |
YEAR	TOTAL	ALL	BLACK	WHITE	ALL	BLACK	WHITE
1980	139	275	1,111	168	11	45	6
1985	202	397	1,559	246	17	68	10
1990	297	575	2,376	339	32	125	19
1993	359	698	2,920	398	41	165	23
1996	427	819	3,250	461	51	n/a	n/a

SOURCE: Tracy L. Snell, "Correctional Populations in the United States, 1993," *Bureau of Justice Statistics Report* (Washington DC: U.S. Government Printing Office, 1995) 9; Christopher Mumola and Allen J. Beck, "Correctional Populations in the United States, 1996," *Bureau of Justice Statistics Report* (Washington DC: U.S. Government Printing Office, 1997) 3, 5, 9.

more commonly regulated through public health services in many parts of the world. People who are mentally ill, or addicted to drugs, for example, would be treated by public health authorities in most other countries, rather than processed as law violators, as is common in the United States. The costs of corrections include social problems that are indirectly related to corrections as well as financial expenditures.

The Prison System

The prison system in the United States is divided into multiple tiers. There are, for example, differences between state and federal corrections. Federal prisons are used to incarcerate people convicted of federal crimes, such as tax evasion, interstate trafficking of drugs, illegal transportation of goods across state lines, and many other crimes. State prisons house people convicted of violation of state laws. Federal corrections are managed by the Federal Bureau of Prisons, which ensures general consistency in the policies, staff qualifications, administration, and other aspects of prison governance throughout the country. State prisons are managed and organized in conjunction with the laws and policies of each state. As a result, there is considerable variation among the states with regards to organization, administration, and governance of state prisons.

The majority of prison inmates are held in state prisons, which have experienced unprecedented overcrowding and rising costs since about 1980. Many states have been experimenting with alternatives to traditional incarceration because of this overcrowding. Short, intensive incarceration in the form of **boot camps** or **shock incarceration** programs, for example, have been used in a number of states. Some states have also allowed private corrections corporations to handle the punishment of criminals. Rising costs of corrections often motivate the search for newer, more efficient mechanisms of punishment, including many community-based programs.

The majority of people in prison in the United States are African American men, who have the highest rate of incarceration of any demographic category in the United States. The rate of incarceration for black men was 3250 per 100,000 population in 1996, compared to 427 per 100,000 for the population as a whole.[14] Urban decay, export of manufacturing jobs outside of the United States, differentially harsh penalties for crack cocaine (which is sold by blacks) compared to powdered cocaine (sold by whites), and social service cutbacks in job training and educational programs have all had a significantly negative impact on opportunities for African American men. The result has been an extraordinary increase in the number of black men who use crime as their primary means of support.[15]

Men also have high rates of incarceration compared to women or to the population as a whole. The rate of incarceration for men in 1996 was 819 per 100,000 population. Men, as a group, are much more commonly involved in crime and account for 94 percent of the prison population in the United States.[16] Table 17.1 compares the rates of incarceration for various groups in the population.

Among the pertinent issues in contemporary corrections is programming that keeps inmates busy. Various programs have operated in the states since the beginning of the prison system. Prison industries, as discussed in Chapter 16, declined in the 1920s and 1930s because public sentiment opposed the use of forced labor in public areas, and because the cheap labor supplied by prisoners interfered with fair competition in the marketing of prison-made goods. In the 1980s, interest was revived in the use of prison labor for the benefit of private entrepreneurs, with little public opposition. Prison labor has been leased to various private industries in many states recently. Iowa, for example, uses inmates in telemarketing and in the mailing of tourism information. In other states, companies (for example, the Wahlers Company, which makes office furniture, and Utah Printing and Graphics) have employed prison labor throughout the country. Prisoners operate computer terminals, manufacture disk drives, make condensing units and airplane parts, and assemble a variety of other goods in prisons in many states.[17]

Virtually all prisons use inmates to work in some area of the prison as a required assignment. Some prisons, such as those in Illinois and Texas, utilize prisoners to produce or manufacture items that are used throughout the state by other prisons or state agencies. In Illinois, each prison specializes in the production of some commodity or food used throughout the state. The women's prison, for example, sews uniforms for a variety of state workers and makes flags flown over state buildings. Another prison butchers meat used by state institutions throughout the state; others process milk, soap, or fruit juice.[18] Texas prisons are similarly organized, and they are nearly self-supporting.

Among the programs offered most consistently in the states is education, which includes academic education and vocational or job training. As previously mentioned, most inmates have less than a high school education when they enter prison. Most have few marketable skills, and most have had interrupted or sporadic employment prior to incarceration. For obvious reasons, inmates who leave prison with more education than they had when they entered, or with skills they can use in the job market, are better equipped for successful re-entry into society. Evidence from research studies in the 1980s confirms that post-release success is related to inmates' enhanced marketability after leaving prison.[19] All states plus the Federal Bureau of Prisons offer educational programs. In some states, such as Illinois, inmates are tested upon entry into prison and are mandated to attend educational programs if their skills are below established levels.[20] Not all states offer the same programs; most states require inmates to pay for their own education beyond minimal levels; and advanced educational opportunities have declined in recent years. Table 17.2 lists the types of programs available and the number of inmates who participated in prison educational programs in 1993.

In 1995, a total of 521,970 new inmates were admitted into prisons in the United States and 455,139 were released. Prisoners are released for a variety of reasons, but most are released either conditionally (on parole), or unconditionally (sentence has been completed). About 33 percent of inmates left prison under conditions of parole in 1995.[21] *Parole* is an early release from prison with supervision. Inmates leave prison early when they have earned sufficient *good time,* or early release because they have accumulated time served without trouble to prison officials. Or, a parole board designates early release because they believe the offender is ready to return to society. Early release is, currently, a controversial concept because many politicians and the public believe it contributes to further crime among former inmates who have not been sufficiently punished. As a result, many

TABLE 17.2 | Educational Programs and Enrollments in State and Federal Prisons, 1993

TYPE OF PROGRAM	ENROLLMENT
Adult basic education	89,160
General education development (GED)	33,396
Vocational or technical training	65,594
Job readiness	7,609
Pre-release	15,859
Two-year college degree	33,590
Four-year college degree	3,656
Graduate work	202

SOURCE: Kathleen Maguire and Ann L. Pastore, *Sourcebook of Criminal Justice Statistics, 1994* (Washington DC: U.S. Government Printing Office, 1995) 560.

states have begun to curtail early releases or to limit good-time opportunities, at least for certain crimes. Within prisons this is controversial because the good-time policy has been an effective means of prison control. Inmates who know they can be released early for good behavior are more likely to behave in ways that lead to maximum accumulation of good-time leave. Threat of revoking good time has been an effective disciplinary measure in prisons for many years.

While it is true that about 80 percent of people in prison have served a prior sentence or have been under previous correctional supervision, it is doubtful that good-time policies or other early release programs are the reason for further criminal activities.[22] Insufficient job opportunities, few marketable skills, and widespread criminal opportunities probably contribute more significantly to re-entry into crime than release policies. Most prisons release offenders without sufficient planning for adjustment back into the community—with only a nominal sum of money and a change of clothes.[23] Conditional releases may be to a community-based center for a short period of time, or to the supervision of a parole officer. Without housing, food, or a job, and with insufficient funds to establish life in the community, temptations to re-kindle criminal contacts and return to crime are sometimes overwhelming.

Prisons for Men

In 1996, there were over 1 million men incarcerated in federal and state prisons, with an incarceration rate of 819 per 100,000 population.[24] Most men in prison are young; over 60 percent are under age 30 when they are admitted to prison.[25] The average educational level of new commitments to prison is less than a high school graduate, and most inmates have an annual income below the government-established poverty level at the time they are committed to prison.[26] The majority of men in prison are incarcerated for violent crimes, property crimes, or drug

The Impact of "Three Strikes" Laws on the California State Prison System

For several years, lawmakers and the general public have been concerned that serious offenders, or highly dangerous repeat offenders, are released from prison too early. Both state and federal laws have increased the penalties for violent offenders with "three strikes and you're out" laws, which are designed to remove serious offenders from society for long periods of time, and in many cases for life. Between 1993 and 1995, the federal government and twenty-four states enacted such laws, and several other states had introduced similar bills into state legislatures.

California expected that the first five years of the new law would bring in 40,000 inmates sentenced under a "two strikes" or "three strikes" provision. By December 31, 1996, however, only 26,074 offenders had been admitted into the California Department of Corrections (CDC) for either a two- or three-strikes sentence, and the original estimated impact of the law was revised downward. Nearly 90 percent of those admitted between 1993 and 1996 were sentenced under the two-strikes component of the law. The following table illustrates the characteristics of offenders sentenced under the new law.

The increasing trend of sentencing repeat offenders for longer time in prison will undoubtedly increase prison populations in all states that have three-strikes laws, but not by as much as most people have assumed. If California, which was the first state to enact such a law, is typical, the number of offenders given life sentences for the third strike will continue to be small. Still, nearly 50 percent of three-strikes offenders are over the age of 30 in California, which means average sentences of over 37 years amount to nearly a life sentence for most offenders, even if the number of offenders sentenced under such provisions is relatively small. Many states with three-strikes laws, including California, require that the offender serve all or most of the imposed sentence.

For corrections, the number of inmates serving exceptionally long sentences under the new three-strikes laws will increase slowly each year. In any given year, only a few thousand inmates are sentenced under these laws. The cumulative effect of such sentencing on corrections will be greatest as inmates age in the prison system.

Percentage Breakdown of Two- or Three-Strike Sentences in California 1993–1996

	TWO STRIKES	THREE STRIKES
SEX		
Male	94.9%	98.5%
Female	5.1	1.5
AGE		
Under 20	7.3	7.1
20–29	46.7	43.1
30–39	34.1	35.3
40–49	10.1	11.5
50+	1.7	3.0
RACE/ETHNICITY		
Black	37.1	43.9
Hispanic	32.7	27.1
White	26.5	25.3
Other	3.6	3.7
CURRENT OFFENSE		
Person	14.5	25.5
Property	41.1	38.8
Drugs	31.6	22.0
Other	12.8	13.8
SENTENCE LENGTH		
Life	0.2	0.5
Other than life	99.8	99.5
Average sentence	4.9 years	37.4 years

SOURCE: John Clark, James Austin, and D. Alan Henry, "'Three Strikes and You're Out': A Review of State Legislation," *National Institute of Justice Research in Brief* (Washington DC: U.S. Government Printing Office, 1997).

crimes (Box 17.1). Drug crime has been the fastest-growing category of crime among all inmates, but especially among African American men, for a decade. Commitments for violent crimes have dropped from 57 percent of inmates in 1980 to 46 percent in 1996. Property offenders dropped from 30 percent to 24 percent, and drug offenders increased from 8 to 23 percent between 1980 and 1996.[27]

Prison Classification

Most prisons for men are classified as maximum-, medium-, or minimum-security institutions. Within each institution there are further classifications of inmates according to the criteria of that institution. Most states have some special housing for inmates convicted of sex offenses, and many states have specially designated (death row) housing for inmates under the death penalty.

Maximum-security prisons are the most secure institutions, designed to hold the most dangerous, aggressive, or difficult-to-control inmates. Medium-security institutions hold inmates who are less dangerous, or more trustworthy, than maximum security inmates. In medium-security institutions, inmates have somewhat more freedom of movement than in maximum security. In minimum security, the cell, steel bars, and high walls are replaced by individual rooms or dormitories. Inmates have maximum freedom of movement and are trusted more openly than in either of the other security classifications. All prisons have internal classifications beyond the official security designation of the entire institution. A maximum security prison, for example, will have an honors section or other designated areas where the best-behaved maximum-security inmates are housed. Contrary to popular belief, the crime committed by the inmate is not always the determining factor in the security classification. Age, prior prison experience, gang membership, or other factors may be more important in determining security classification than the offender's crime. Murderers, for example, often have minimum or "honors" security classifications, even in maximum-security prisons, because they tend to be well-behaved inmates. Most murderers do not have a record of serious prior offenses (as is common with property offenders) and they generally serve long sentences. They behave well in prison in order to accumulate the greatest privileges; indeed, they are often model prisoners.

Prison Culture

The culture of prison life has intrigued researchers for several decades, and there are numerous studies that have illuminated the patterns of interaction among male prison inmates, as well as the origins of many cultural phenomena found in prisons for men. Researchers in this field are in general agreement that prisoners undergo a transformation when they enter prison. The means by which new inmates learn the rules, both formal and informal, within the prison is called prisonization. The process of **prisonization,** which was first articulated by sociologist Donald Clemmer, socializes inmates to the unique social organization of prison.[28]

Imprisonment is supposed to be painful for prisoners. They are subject to extreme physical, material, and emotional deprivations as a component of their punishment. Part of the effect of these deprivations is the creation of a subculture within prisons that changes the designation of valuable commodities and social hierarchies to which all people in free society are accustomed. How and why this subculture develops has been the subject of a wide variety of research studies.

Confinement, deprivation, sexual exploitation, violence, and bureaucratic indifference to the plight of inmates have all contributed to the development of prison subcultures that promote hierarchical inmate social systems. Whether these social systems originate from the conditions of confinement or whether inmates bring values and behavioral norms into the prison that foster the development of a prison subculture has been a matter of debate among theorists for many years.

One perspective, the **deprivation model,** suggests that inmates who are deprived of the many physical, emotional, and psychological securities that characterized their lives before prison develop alternative social arrangements in prison.[29] Gresham Sykes, who built upon the earlier work of Donald Clemmer, describes the inherent deprivations of imprisonment as the "pains of imprisonment."[30] Inmates who are cut off from family and friends lose emotional support and suffer boredom and loneliness. Inmate social hierarchies replace earlier emotional and psychological commitments. Material deprivations and loss of control over decisions about what to eat or wear, or when to sleep, cause inmates to look for mechanisms of control in other aspects of prison life, including distribution of valuable commodities such as cigarettes, items stolen from prison storage, or contraband smuggled into prison.

Heterosexual deprivations foster homosexual contacts, many of which are coercive, among prisoners who often find that being cut off from members of the opposite sex is among the most painful aspects of confinement. Inmates who are deprived of personal autonomy, who are regulated and watched 24 hours per day, and who have little control over their own fate, respond to these deprivations with aggression, violence, and brutality perpetrated against weaker inmates or staff, according to this model. The deprivation model explains the characteristics of prison subculture as adaptation among inmates whose confinement prevents social arrangements that normally occur outside of prison.

Another theoretical perspective, the **importation model,** says that male inmates are part of a criminal subculture before they enter prison. The skills and contacts necessary to commit robbery, burglary, and other types of crime are similar to the same skills and contacts that are necessary for survival in the prison subculture. This perspective, promoted by John Irwin, says that group loyalty, protection of fellow inmates in the face of authority, contempt for officials and regulations, and control of others through threat of violence and coercion are characteristic of the criminal world outside of prison. Inmates import these values and behavioral patterns into prison, from this perspective.[31]

Critics of the importation model point out that prison environments are widely variable, that not all prisoners adhere to inmate codes of behavior, and that characteristics both of inmates entering prison and criminal cultures outside of prison change regularly.[32] Many of the patterns of interaction in prison are common to patterns of interaction outside of prison, which means, according to critics, that these are social arrangements that transcend prison and the free world rather than patterns that are imported into the prison.

Probably neither the deprivation model nor the importation model completely explains prison subcultures. Rather, a combination of factors inherent in prison deprivations and the importation of values and attitudes from earlier criminal experience combine to create prison subculture. Regardless of the origins of this phenomenon, the effects of prison subculture are widespread, fairly consistent among most prisons in the United States, and very resistant to reformation. The tensions associated with extreme deprivation, long histories of aggressive behavior characteristic of many inmates, and the pervasive threat of force either from prison officials or from fellow prisoners all push anxiety up and personal security down for most inmates.

Gangs in Prisons

Among the most important current issues in men's prisons are gangs and violence. Gangs have been an escalating problem for many years. Street gangs in all urban areas have been increasing membership and expanding criminal activities in recent decades. As the crime component of street gangs has widened and diversified, more members of gangs have been committed to prisons. In addition, race-separatist gangs have increased membership since the mid-1980s, and they are a formidable threat in prisons. Gang affiliates inside prison have formed strong, cohesive interconnections and have taken over inmate social hierarchies in many prisons. A survey of all adult correctional facilities in the United States, Puerto Rico, and Canada in 1992 found the problem to be serious, growing, and insufficiently addressed at all levels of corrections.[33]

Racial conflicts in prison are often instigated by tensions among gangs. White-supremacist gangs such as the Aryan Brotherhood or the Aryan Nation have been especially problematic in some parts of the United States. About a third of wardens surveyed in the 1992 study advocated creation of a separate, centrally located, federal institution where all gang members could be sent. Over three-quarters of wardens surveyed believed that federal agencies should play a greater role in solving gang problems. Some prisons have dealt with the gang problem by balancing opposing gangs in each living unit or cell house. Other institutions use "bus therapy," which means instrumental gang members are transferred to a new institution every few days so that they build no ties in any single institution.[34]

Prison Violence

Prison violence, which is often related to gang activities, is a matter of great concern among all levels of men's corrections. Maintenance of control and prevention of brutality perpetrated against weaker inmates are, of course, primary concerns. In addition, protection of staff from the brutality of particularly dangerous and aggressive inmates is also imperative. Overcrowding and reduced program options in many prisons, combined with the younger average age of inmates and the solidarity of gangs, have pushed the potential for violence to unprecedented levels in many prisons. Lee Bowker suggests that these factors, combined with the dehumanizing character of the prison itself, have aggravated the prison environment to the level of a "controlled war." Bowker suggests that a number of factors contribute to the problems of violence in prisons:

> . . . (1) inadequate supervision by staff members; (2) architectural designs that promote rather than inhibit victimization; (3) the easy availability of deadly weapons; (4) the housing of violence-prone prisoners in close proximity to the relatively defenseless victims; and (5) a generally high level of tension produced by the close quarters and multiple crosscutting conflicts among both individuals and groups of prisoners. To these factors, we must add feedback systems through which prisoners feel the need to take revenge for real or imagined slights or past victimizations, the interrelationships among types of [violence], and the moral and administrative confusion that occurs when the aggressor becomes the victim. . . .[35]

In general, prisons for men are characterized by a high degree of aggression, overcrowding, and a disproportionately high number of poorly educated, low-income, and low-skilled inmates with few life successes prior to incarceration. In the last few years, prisons for men have incarcerated more young black men than any other ethnic group. Recurring problems with gangs and internal violence within prisons, and high recidivism among those released from prison, indicate that contemporary problems are ongoing.

Prisons for Women

In 1996, there were 74,730 women incarcerated in federal and state prisons. Women had an incarceration rate of 51 per 100,000 population, compared to 819 per 100,000 among men, in 1996.[36] As with men, African American women have a higher rate of incarceration than white women. The number of women in prison in the United States has been increasing faster than the number of men incarcerated and women inmates are often cited as the fastest-growing demographic category in American corrections.[37] But we have seen earlier that there are many misunderstandings about women's incarceration. In 1996, women constituted 6.3 percent of the prison population,

Women in prison are often supervised by male correctional officers. Female officers in prisons for male inmates are much less common.

although they were about 4 percent of prisoners in every prior decade between 1930 and 1990.[38] Rapid increases in the number of women incarcerated have had little overall effect on the gender distribution of the prison population because the number of women incarcerated is small relative to the number of men. Only a very small percentage of the prison population is female.

As with men, most women in prison are poor; they have low education, few marketable skills, and a high percentage are incarcerated for drug offenses. Unlike men, most women in prison are full-time caretakers of dependent children at the time they are incarcerated. Over two-thirds of women have dependent children under the age of 18 living with them before their incarceration.[39] Women are significantly less likely to be incarcerated for violent offenses than men, and they are much less likely than men to have served a prior sentence for any offense.[40]

Two-thirds of women in prison are incarcerated for low-level property offenses or drug crimes. Those women sentenced for violent crimes are more likely to have committed murder than any other violent crime. Women offenders in prison for murder are most likely to have murdered men, which is related to the fact that nearly half of women in prison have been victims of earlier physical or sexual abuse. Women who murder kill relatives or someone intimately known to them in 65 percent of cases.[41] Women murder in retaliation for years of abuse or in defense of themselves or their children more often than any other pattern.[42]

Most women's prisons in the United States are *multiple classification,* which means that they often house maximum, medium, minimum, mental health, and death row prisoners all in the same institution. The majority of states have fewer than three women's prisons and most have only one, which makes separate facilities for diverse security classifications impractical, especially for states with fewer than one hundred female inmates.[43] As a result, rehabilitative programming for women with multiple-security designations is problematic. The relatively low number of female inmates in each state has been used, historically, as a rationale for providing little or no programming in women's prisons.

Legal justifications for discriminating against women in the provision of fewer programming options than those available to men in the same states have rested primarily upon the high costs of providing the small number of incarcerated women with the options available to men.[44] Women have been a notoriously underserved prison population. The limited educational and vocational programs available commonly provide training in traditional women's employment fields such as hairdressing and secretarial skills, which prepare women for wages in the range of government poverty levels in most areas.[45] Women have very low rates of violence in prison compared to men; they are usually incarcerated for low-level property or drug offenses and few violent crimes; they have significantly lower recidivism than men; and they show greater potential for reform than men. Programming in women's prison has the potential of reducing recidivism even further by enhancing post-release success of women offenders.[46]

About 80 percent of women inmates have a history of drug use, which is often related in one way or another to their involvement in crime.[47] For women offenders, drug use is commonly symptomatic of prior physical and sexual abuse. Treatment that does not address both issues is unlikely to be successful. Unfortunately, "by all indications few drug-abusing women offenders actually receive treatment, either in custody or in the community, and little information is available on how programs for women offenders determine needs, plan treatment, and perform services." [48]

In addition to use of drugs to relieve the pains of brutal life experiences, many women offenders are incarcerated for drug sales used to supplement inadequate resources for the support of themselves and their children. As social service programs for women and children were being cut throughout the 1980s, the number of women who used drug crime to supplement incomes increased significantly. The problem of insufficient income for support of their families is a recurring theme among women offenders, especially among those who receive little or no support from absent fathers of their children.[49] Rare are the prison programs that train women in other than traditional low-paying "women's" occupations, which are inadequate for support of their families after release. Most programs for women do not address the special familial and economic needs of incarcerated women.

Incarcerated Mothers

Among the most pressing needs of incarcerated women is maintaining contact with their children while in prison and planning for post-release reunion with their families. Family issues are the most salient problems facing most incarcerated women.[50] A few programs have begun to address the unique family problems of incarcerated women in some states. Pregnant inmates in Massachusetts, for example, are housed in a separate facility that allows inmates to keep their babies after birth while the inmate undergoes drug rehabilitation and counseling. At Bedford Hills, New York, qualified inmates with infants may keep their babies with them in prison for up to 18 months. In Georgia, some inmates are furloughed for 30 days before

and 30 days after the birth of their infants. California offers many women in community corrections the opportunity to keep their children with them while they complete their sentences.[51]

Problems of poverty are more strongly associated with women's crime than with the offense patterns of men. Women very rarely commit violent predatory crimes, such as serial murder, assault of strangers, or gang-related violence. Rising rates of incarceration of women are more closely tied to the *feminization of poverty* (the trend since 1980 that the poor in the United States are most commonly women and their dependent children) than any other factor. Programs aimed at alleviating poverty and serious attention to sexual exploitation of women and children would significantly reduce increased incarceration of women. As is the case with male inmates, current punishment strategies rarely address the root causes of women's crime.[52]

Jails

In the United States, most jails are locally operated facilities used to hold prisoners for a variety of reasons. They are used, for example, to hold people who have been accused of crimes, but who have not yet been convicted and who are awaiting trial; they hold indigent people who are sick, mentally ill, or who have been picked up drunk or under the effects of drugs; and they hold people who have been convicted of a crime and have a sentence of less than 1 year or are awaiting transfer to a prison. Less often, jails are also used to hold juveniles in temporary custody; to re-admit parole, probation, and bail-bond violators; to hold witnesses for protective custody; and sometimes as the center for community-based programs such as electronic monitoring or specialized supervision.[53]

Historically, jails have been notoriously neglected, unsafe, and unsanitary places, which were subject to few regulations or controls. In many ways these stereotypes are still true. Jails are overcrowded, often understaffed, and the staff frequently is not trained to deal with the problems of those in custody. Many of the practical problems with jails are attributable to the fact that they are locally funded and locally managed. Elected local officials have neglected funding for jails for many decades because of public opposition. As a consequence, jails have been badly neglected in most jurisdictions.

People held in jails are commonly not yet convicted, or they are serving time for relatively minor offenses. Jails often have rigid security, few programming options, and limited opportunities for recreation, job training, or substance abuse treatment. Thus, those who have been convicted of the least serious offenses are often held under the most inhumane conditions.

People held in jails are, generally, released after a relatively short time. Some are held only for a few hours, a

TABLE 17.3 | Percent of Jail Inmates by Race and Sex: 1990, 1995

	1990	1995
SEX		
Males	91%	90%
Females	9	10
RACE		
White	42	39
Black	43	44
Hispanic	14	15
Other	1	2

SOURCE: Darrell K. Gilliard and Allen J. Beck, "Prison and Jail Inmates 1995," *Bureau of Justice Statistics Bulletin* (Washington DC: U.S. Government Printing Office, 1996) 10.

few days, or a few months. Inmates rarely remain in jail for longer than 1 year. Because the population is relatively transient, the number of people incarcerated in jail is counted in two ways. First, there are midyear counts, which include the number inmates held in jails on June 30 of a given year. Second, average daily counts are calculated to give the average number of people held in jail on any given day. The average daily count is used to reveal any obscure abnormality in the jail population (such as a riot that might lead to the arrest of an unusually large number of people on June 30), which might distort the midyear 1-day counts.

Jails in the United States held 541,913 inmates on June 30, 1995. The jail population increased by 4.2 percent between July 1, 1994, and June 30, 1995. Among the reasons for the increase were overall increases in arrests, a decreased tendency to release individuals who had been arrested, increased sentencing to jails after conviction, and an increased number of people held in local jails because of overcrowding in state and federal prisons.[54]

In 1995, one out of every 205 adult men and one out of every 1,936 adult women were held in a local jail. Forty-four percent of the jail population was black and 90 percent was male. The largest jail populations in the nation are in Los Angeles, New York City, Chicago, Harris County, Texas, and Dallas, Texas. Since 1983, Texas has expanded the use of jails more than any other jurisdiction in the United States, although they showed a slight decline in jail population between 1994 and 1995.[55] Table 17.3 illustrates the demographic characteristics of jail inmates for 1990 and 1995.

Shock Incarceration (Boot Camps)

Among the correctional options that have recently developed in many states are shock incarceration units, or boot camps. These facilities incarcerate young, first offenders for a short, intense period of "strict military-style discipline, unquestioning obedience to orders, and highly structured days filled with drills and hard work."[56] Offenders are sent to these facilities instead of a traditional prison in the belief that discipline, hard work, and physical training will have a reforming effect on them. Implicit in this treatment philosophy is the belief that many offenders end up in prison because they lack discipline and self-control. An intense "crash course" in personal responsibility, from this perspective, may turn a person toward a productive future.

Oklahoma opened the first boot camp prison in 1984. In 1993, over 14,000 prisoners participated in boot camp programs in thirty-four states and two federal units. Georgia and New York use this option most frequently, with seven facilities in Georgia and four in New York. Incarceration in boot camps is usually for 3- to 6-month periods, although California has a 10-month program. Most shock incarceration facilities are exclusively for young men, but twelve states and the Federal Bureau of Prisons have either allowed women to participate in male programs or have special facilities for female inmates.[57]

In New York State, the average age of men entering boot camp incarceration is 25, and for women, the average age is 27. Both men and women generally have less than a high school education before entering the program and most have been arrested one time before their conviction. Sixty-six percent of men and 82 percent of women in boot camp programs were convicted and sentenced to prison for drug offenses in 1992 and 1993. New York combines shock incarceration with extensive educational programming, substance abuse treatment, and intensive community supervision for 6 months after completion of the program. The New York Department of Correctional Services estimates that the program saved the state $305.3 million in reduced custody and capital construction costs between 1987 and 1993.[58]

Evaluations of boot camp programs have been mixed. They are considerably less expensive than traditional prisons. This is true even when intensive follow-up services such as job placement, counseling, and parole supervision are added into the expense of facility operation. Recidivism, which is usually measured by rates of reincarceration, is lower in only three participating states, however. In New York State, boot camp graduates have a recidivism rate of 30 percent as compared to 36 percent of all prison releases. Recidivism rates are similar in Illinois and Louisiana. In Florida, Georgia, Louisiana, Oklahoma, South Carolina, and Texas there are virtually no differences in recidivism among boot camp inmates and traditional prison inmates. The most successful programs are those that combine drug rehabilitation, educational programming, and post-release follow-up supervision with the boot camp discipline.[59]

While the failure of some jurisdictions to reduce recidivism with boot camps may signal failure of the concept of shock incarceration to skeptics, there are some important distinctions between those programs that show evidence of success and those that do not. Some programs are too new for evaluation. Minnesota, for example, had only seven offenders under supervision when the last national comparisons were calculated by the National Institute of Justice in 1993. Like many other states, Massachusetts designed a program comparable to the successful New York State model, but appropriations for the post-release follow-up phase of the program stalled in the legislature. Only a few states, such as Illinois and Minnesota, have developed an assessment process to match services to offender needs. Those programs with overriding emphasis on discipline and military training and the least educational or drug treatment services show the lowest success rates. Discipline without skill-building and therapeutic community treatment after release shows the lowest post-release success among program participants.[60]

Private Corrections

Among the recent trends in corrections is the use in a number of states of private correctional corporations to incarcerate offenders. Privately run prisons are owned, managed, and staffed by profit-driven corporations in seventeen states. At the end of 1995, there were eighty-nine private prisons owned and operated by fifteen corporations. The largest prison corporations in the United States are the Corrections Corporation of America, which operates twenty-one prisons, and Wackenhut Corrections Corporation, which owns nineteen prisons. Both corporations own and operate prisons in several states. Texas uses private corrections most extensively, with thirty-three private prisons run by thirteen different companies.[61]

Modern use of private corrections began in 1984 with the opening of the Houston (Texas) Processing Center by the Corrections Corporation of America. Since 1984, the number of private prisons operating for profit has increased annually.[62] The growth in this industry is attributable to a number of factors. First, during the 1980s political rhetoric repeatedly called for a reduction in the use of government to fund and manage programs that could be run more efficiently by private companies. The proliferation of private delivery services that could provide overnight package or letter delivery, growth in private waste and trash disposal services, medical services, police or security systems, and other services that had previously been operated or controlled almost exclusively by government opened avenues for further expansion of private companies to replace government services. Among these services were corrections.

Second, many people believe that attention to the business of corrections increases incentives for performance among service providers. If contract renewal is dependent upon low recidivism, for example, the business motivation to reform offenders drives rehabilitation pro-

grams. Third, the high costs of corrections have motivated many state governments to search for more efficient and cost-effective strategies for maintaining expanding prison populations. Private corporations may be able to manage the costs of incarceration more efficiently than notoriously inefficient state governments, according to many supporters.

Whether the private prisons are able to provide better services more cheaply than state governments has not yet been established. As the studies began to assess the comparative costs in the late 1980s, there was almost no evidence that private enterprise could deliver correctional services more cheaply than state governments.[63] Still, the growth of the corrections industry into the 1990s spurred increased interest in this option.

Many critics have argued against the use of private corporations to run prisons, even if they do eventually prove to be cost-effective. Arguments against the concept of private prisons stress that punishment for profit is unethical. This reasoning points out that the executive branch of government is charged with punishment of law violators, not a corporation with an interest in profiting from the illegal actions of the convicted offender. Defenders of the concept of private corrections counter with the argument that both the federal and state governments have failed in most correctional strategies, regardless of the prevalence of rehabilitative or retributive strategies in any given era. If government has failed, proponents argue, the time for an alternative has arrived—in the form of private corrections.[64] Regardless of the arguments for and against the proliferation of correctional strategies, they are an established variation in corrections. Current trends indicate continued growth in this industry as we move into the twenty-first century.

Co-Corrections

As the rate of incarceration of women has increased since 1980, most states and the federal prison system have been left with an alarming shortage of prison space for convicted women. As a result, many women have been sent to specially reserved sections of men's prisons. The incarceration of both men and women in the same facility is referred to as **co-corrections.** Most states eliminated the housing of men and women in the same facilities in the 1870s, but a renewed interest in this style of confinement arose in 1971 when the first federal co-correctional institution was opened at Fort Worth, Texas.[65] There are, currently, thirty-two state and federal facilities that house both men and women in the same institution.[66] In most cases, a relatively small number of women are incarcerated in a male prison in order to reduce overcrowding in women's prisons. One prison in Ohio, however, houses men in a women's facility.[67]

Many prisons in the United States are built with tiers of cells stacked around a central area of the prison. This model is based upon the original design of the Auburn, New York, prison, which was opened in 1817.

Some increase in the use of co-corrections in the 1980s was sparked by several research studies that indicated that the social character of co-correctional institutions was considerably "softer" than that of single-sex institutions, regardless of the security classifications of the institutions studied. Men in co-correctional institutions were found to be less violent, less aggressive, and more relaxed than in exclusively male prisons. Similarly, studies of women in co-corrections indicated that the more "normal" atmosphere of the prison softened the demeanor and language of women inmates and reduced tension among all inmates.[68] This was true even when programming and security restrictions prohibited the intermingling of the sexes. In the mid-1980s, about half of co-correctional institutions allowed some integration of male and female prisoners for meals, recreation, educational programming, or special events.[69] By the end of the 1980s, however, crowding and security problems led to more restrictions in co-correctional institutions.

In Illinois, for example, the first permanent placement of women inmates in a male prison was established at the Logan Correctional Center in 1988. The closing of county jail pre-release programs and a 50 percent reduction in community corrections options for women by the Department of Corrections led to a significant increase in the population of women in the only women's prison in the state. To alleviate overcrowding, 72 women were transferred to Logan, where 797 men were incarcerated. In the first 11 months that the women were in the Logan facility, seven pregnancies were reported. This led to a significant reduction in the programming options available to women inmates and an increased attention to security. Pregnant inmates were charged with "public indecency" or "sexual misconduct," lost 1 year of "good time," and were either placed in segregation for 375 days or transferred back to the women's facility at Dwight, Illinois.[70] (No penalties for male partners of the pregnant women were reported.) Such problems are not isolated to Illinois. Many states report similar problems with security, programming, and staff abuses.[71]

Contemporary co-corrections have strayed from the ideals of "normalcy" promoted by early proponents of this concept.[72] Because the small number of women present in such facilities makes separate programming costly,

Electronic monitors worn on the leg or wrist of convicted offenders provide an effective and inexpensive means of monitoring behavior among those who are most likely to be reformed through community corrections.

Community Corrections

The basic ideal of community corrections is to keep out of prisons offenders who are not dangerous and who would be better reformed in their communities with appropriate support services and effective programs. "The term **community corrections** describes community-based alternatives to the incarceration of offenders in state prisons."[74] Many people do not belong in prison, in spite of the fact that they have been convicted of a crime. Non-dangerous first offenders of minor crimes, people with substance-abuse problems, many drunk drivers, mothers of small children, and many juvenile offenders are more likely to refrain from future offenses if they are counseled and supported with services that address their specific problems than if they are sent to prison. Imprisonment of such individuals breaks family ties, results in loss of employment, and may ultimately destroy future life options for people who have little likelihood of further, or more serious, criminal behavior. In general, community corrections are based on two program orientations. They tend to be oriented either toward change of the offender or control of offenders. Highly specific programs, such as drug rehabilitation or counseling programs for domestic batterers, are designed to help offenders overcome particular problems that may be the root cause of their criminal activities. These programs aim to change the offender and thus prevent future crime.

The second orientation, control of offenders, is often referred to as **intermediate sanctions.** These programs are designed to keep offenders within the custody of justice authorities without sending them to prison. **House arrest** or **electronic monitoring** would be classified as intermediate sanctions, aimed at punishment through control of offenders' movements without the more intense deprivations of imprisonment. These programs have various designs and are often used in conjunction with other punishments, such as community service, fines, or treatment programs. With electronic monitoring, for example, offenders are fitted with an electronic cuff on a wrist or ankle that will signal an official in a central location if offenders travel outside of the restricted area to which they have been confined for the duration of the sentence. House arrest is similarly monitored with electronic devices surrounding the home, telephone contacts that randomly check to make sure the offender is at home, daily or weekly unannounced visits from surveillance staff, or other checks designed to assure that the offender does not leave home. Box 17.2 outlines some of the commonly used community corrections options.

Community Corrections as an Alternative to Prison
Alternatives to incarceration that are based in the community in which the offender resides appear to be as ef-

and security risks of intermingling the sexes are problematic for institutions, women prisoners have more limited opportunities for education, recreation, or other activities in co-corrections than in exclusively female prisons. Male prisoners in co-corrections tend to have a larger share of programming options and more freedom within the institutions, but all prisoners are subject to greater control and custody requirements in co-correctional institutions.[73]

Types of Community Corrections Programs

Intensive supervision	Either probation or parole supervision that intensely supervises the offenders' activities. Contact and supervision by probation or parole staff is intended to guide the offender toward appropriate life decisions and to prevent his or her involvement in activities that would hinder reform.
House arrest	Offenders suffer loss of freedom through confinement to their homes. Some programs require only curfews for night and weekend activities, others require the offender to stay at home for 24-hour detention.
Electronic monitoring	Often used with house arrest, this system monitors offenders' movements through electronic devices that signal officials if he or she leaves a designated area.
Urine screening	Either scheduled or random testing of offenders' urine to determine whether alcohol or drugs have been used.
Fines	A monetary amount either required or assessed for certain offenses. This penalty is often criticized because it differentially penalizes the poor.
Community service	The offender must work, without compensation, for a specified number of hours in activities that are beneficial to the community.
Halfway houses and work release centers	These facilities house offenders who are required to work, go to school, seek employment, or participate in specific programs, such as job training or drug treatment. Offenders are often sent to a halfway house or work release center as a condition of early release from prison. In this case, the supervision and limited freedom in these facilities help ex-offenders bridge the transition between prison and the community.
Treatment programs	These programs commonly specialize in a specific type of treatment for problems such as substance abuse, sexual adjustment, emotional adjustment, or domestic battery. They can be either residential programs or outpatient services. If the offender reports to the center daily, but is not required to live there, the program is sometimes called *day reporting*.

This table was adapted from Todd Clear, "Correction Beyond Prison Walls," in *Criminology*, ed. Joseph F. Sheley (Belmont, CA: Wadsworth, 1991) 399–417.

---

fective as traditional prison confinement, if the offenders are matched with appropriate programs.[75] In many cases, community-based programs are highly effective in reducing recidivism. And, the programs are considerably cheaper than imprisonment, which has motivated many jurisdictions to experiment with a variety of community correctional programs. As a result, many new community-based correctional options have been developed in recent years.

Juvenile offenders, for example, are frequently sentenced to community correctional programs. **Diversion,** which means the offender is diverted from prison to some socially beneficial activity, is based on the philosophy that incarceration of juveniles who have committed minor crimes will do more harm than good. With this strategy, offenders are sentenced to job training programs, drug or alcohol rehabilitation programs, community service, or other activities that both divert the offender from further inappropriate behavior and away from the harmful crimi-

nalizing environment of prison. Most diversion programs are designed for youthful offenders.

Community service programs have often been used to draw the attention of celebrities or socially elite offenders to the realities of the less fortunate, although they are even more commonly applied to "ordinary" people. Community service programs require that offenders donate a specified number of hours to a community service project. Former baseball star Pete Rose, for example, was required to give 1000 hours of assistance to physical education teachers in inner-city schools after serving a 5-month prison sentence for income tax evasion. After actress Zsa Zsa Gabor was convicted of hitting a police officer, the judge ordered her to pay a $13,000 fine and perform 120 hours of community service in a shelter for homeless women. When she announced that she gave the women in the shelter beauty tips, the judge increased the community service component of her sentence by 60 hours. In another case, ex-presidential aid and Marine officer

Oliver North was sentenced to 1200 hours of community service to Washington-area youth groups for his part in the Iran-Contra cover-up. It is estimated that between 200,000 and 500,000 people receive community service assignments as all or part of their sentence each year.[76]

Costs of Community Corrections

Community corrections programs are more cost-effective than many other correctional options. The electronic monitoring program administered from the Cook County Jail in Chicago, for example, supervises 1200 participants at any one time. Keeping an offender on the electronic monitor costs $22 per day per participant, compared to $40 per day to keep an offender in the Cook County Jail.[77] The Program for Female Offenders in Pittsburgh, Pennsylvania, provides services for women convicted of both felonies and misdemeanors who live in the center with their children at a cost of $41 per day. The program offers job training, life skills training, parenting education, and child care.[78] Similarly, the Council on Prostitution Alternatives in Portland, Oregon, provides intensive counseling, addiction treatment, sexual abuse counseling, and education on life skills, parenting, and health concerns for women with prostitution convictions—all at a cost of $1.95 per day per client.[79] The Illinois Sheriff's Work Alternative Program (SWAP) costs the state nothing, but offenders are charged a $25 registration fee and the offenders pay $1 per hour they work. Participants include drunk drivers, juveniles with misdemeanor offenses, senior citizens convicted of driving without auto insurance, and other minor offenders. Work assignments include cleaning trash from streets and roads, shoveling snow, raking leaves, and other work beneficial to the county. Over 32,000 offenders participated in SWAP between 1985 and 1995, with a 3 percent recidivism rate among drunk drivers and an overall 20 percent recidivism rate for all other offenders. Minor offenders sentenced to jail have a recidivism rate of over 70 percent in Illinois.[80]

With rising costs of incarceration, overcrowding at all levels of corrections, and continued research documenting the benefits of keeping non-dangerous, minor offenders out of prison, it is likely that community corrections will continue as a viable alternative to imprisonment. Many programs were cut in the 1980s, but a resurgence of interest in cheaper alternatives for minor offenders in the 1990s has revived some programs and sparked innovation of many alternatives to incarceration.

Issues and Trends

In addition to large increases in the size of the prison population at all levels, many other problems have confronted correctional authorities in recent decades. The number of inmates suffering from debilitating disease or mental ill-ness has become a matter of growing concern. The virtual absence of facilities to treat the current health problems of many inmates before crime occurs contributes, in a high percentage of cases, to the actions that lead to incarceration. Health care costs of inmates trigger controversial reactions in many states, where people believe that inmates should not be entitled to better health care than that which is available to other poor people who are not in prison. The counterargument is, of course, that the problem is not that prisoners have too much health care but rather that many poor families do not have enough.

Rising health care costs are a matter of concern in all parts of the country. Most states have added AIDS treatment to the usual roster of health treatments for inmates. In 1995, there were nearly 5099 confirmed cases of AIDS in U.S. prisons, and another 24,226 inmates were HIV-positive, which means they were carriers of the virus that causes AIDS.[81] Other increasingly common additions to the list of health treatments are obstetrics and gynecology. As women's incarceration has increased, the number of women entering prison pregnant has also increased. Each year about 6 percent of women entering prison are pregnant at the time they are incarcerated.[82] Other current issues include the number of elderly inmates who will begin to need geriatric care in the next few years.

AIDS

The human immunodeficiency virus (HIV), with the subsequent development of the AIDS infection, is spread widely through the sharing of contaminated needles among intravenous drug users or through sexual contact. With the rising rates of incarceration of drug offenders, the number of prisoners who are either HIV-positive or have AIDS has also increased.

In addition to high-risk behavior prior to incarceration, sexual contact among inmates in prison further increases risk of exposure to the HIV virus. Because sexual contact between inmates is prohibited behavior in prison, precautionary measures, such as the use of condoms, are unlikely for most inmates. Nationally, the percentage of inmates who are known to be HIV-positive is relatively low; less than 3 percent of male inmates and just over 4 percent of female inmates are HIV-positive. Yet 34 percent of prison deaths in 1995 were AIDS-related.[83]

Symptoms of fully developed AIDS may take several years to appear, from first exposure to outbreak of the disease. Without precautionary measures, particularly among male inmates whose sexual behavior in prison is among the most likely to increase risk of infection, the spread of AIDS in prison is a problem with explosive potential.[84] Estimates of men who engage in homosexual activity in prison range from 30 to 60 percent, thus increasing the potential spread of the disease.[85] Some researchers have suggested that current estimates of the problem are much too low. Perry Smith, for example, reports that 17 percent of male inmates and 18 percent of female inmates are HIV-positive in New York correctional institutions.[86] Without comprehensive testing upon entry into prison, and subsequent periodic testing among already-incarcerated inmates, the exact proportions of either the presence of the disease or patterns of spread will not be ascertained. Currently all 50 states and the District of Columbia test inmates for HIV on some basis, but only Rhode Island and Wyoming test inmates currently in custody. Some jurisdictions only test inmates who show symptoms of AIDS, or those who request testing.[87]

Risk of spread of AIDS among prisoners is only one of the potential problems of AIDS in prison. Presence of the disease increases risk of exposure among correctional staff and health care professionals who treat inmates with AIDS. Costs of treatment are notoriously high, and litigation by inmates or custodial staff over conditions and exposure in prison are a continuing concern. Currently, the regions of the country with the greatest known presence of AIDS in prison are the Northeast and the South, but the numbers of cases in all areas are increasing.[88]

Eleven states have 500 or more inmates who are known to be HIV positive. There has been a 38 percent increase in the number of HIV-positive inmates since 1991, although the prison population has increased 36 percent during the same years. There were one hundred AIDS-related deaths for every 100,000 state prison inmates in 1995.[89]

Tuberculosis

Earlier in this century, tuberculosis (TB) was a serious, usually fatal disease. It was nearly eliminated as a public health threat after the development of anti-tuberculous drugs in the 1940s. Tuberculosis, which is a disease of the lungs, is highly contagious because the tubercle bacilli that cause the disease are propelled through the air during coughing by an infected person with an active form of the disease. Current outbreaks of TB are an extraordinary health problem because the most active strains of the disease have become stronger and more resistant to antibiotic treatment.[90]

In addition, treatment has become very costly, as high as $200,000 per patient, as strains of TB have become stronger.[91] The recent resurgence of the disease is associated with three phenomena: use of crack cocaine, AIDS-related health conditions, and incarceration in any prison or jail.[92] Prisoners, of course, have high incidence of all three risk factors. This is especially problematic for jail inmates, who are often detained in large holding tanks that accommodate ten or more inmates at a time. Coughing by one infected inmate exposes all others in the immediate vicinity, including custodial staff. Overcrowding in virtually all American prisons and jails increases exposure and threat of serious epidemic outbreaks.

Without proper treatment, which can take from 1 to 4 years, TB in the current stronger form is usually fatal. It can spread from the lungs to any part of the body, most commonly causing disease in the internal organs, lymph nodes, bones, joints, genitals, or skin. At advanced stages coughing is profuse, which increases the potential of contagion, and the disease rapidly becomes fatal.[93]

There were an estimated 48,017 cases of TB in state and federal prisons, and another 13,424 jail inmates who tested positive for TB in 1993.[94] Scattered data from the states indicate that the problem is very serious. New York State, for example, experienced a 700 percent increase in the rate of TB-infected inmates in the correctional system between 1976 and 1986.[95] Similarly, crowded conditions at Cook County Jail in Illinois led to a serious outbreak there. New York City has opened an isolation unit at Rikers Island to house TB-infected inmates.[96] The problem of TB in correctional facilities is serious, deadly, and increasing.

Mental Illness

An important social problem in the nineteenth century was the practice of incarcerating schizophrenic people, those with other serious mental disorders such as bipolar disorder (manic depression), and epileptics in jails. Through the efforts of nineteenth-century social reformers like Dorthea Dix, the use of jails to house people with mental or physical disorders significantly declined in the late nineteenth century. The U.S. Census of 1880, for example, found that 0.7 percent of jail inmates were seriously mentally ill. One out of every 148 jail prisoners was seriously mentally ill at that time.[97] In 1992, the percentage of the jail population who were seriously mentally ill was 7.2, or 1 out of every 14 jail inmates. On any given day in 1992, there were 31,000 seriously disturbed individuals held in U.S. jails. Nearly 30 percent of mentally ill people in jails were held without criminal charges because no psychiatric services were available. Mentally ill people who are criminally charged in most communities are accused of "trespassing" or "disorderly conduct" rather than serious criminal charges.[98]

A chronic shortage of facilities to treat the mental health problems of the poor has been worsening; this situation is largely responsible for the increased use of jails to hold people with mental illnesses. Sixty-nine percent of jails report that the problems are getting worse. Flathead County, Montana, for example, has been placing mentally ill inmates in a "soft cell" for 20 years. This is a cell, reminiscent of those described by Dorthea Dix in the 1830s, that is completely padded, with a grate in the floor for a toilet, and where meals are passed through a slot in the door. Kentucky offers the fewest psychiatric services, with 81 percent of Kentucky jails holding uncharged, seriously mentally ill individuals. Only five states—Connecticut, Delaware, New Jersey, Pennsylvania, and Rhode Island—as

Among the many costs of "three strikes and you're out" sentencing requirements will be the incarceration of elderly inmates.

well as the District of Columbia, currently hold no mentally ill people in jails.[99]

The problem of the mentally ill in jails began with the **de-institutionalization** movement of the 1970s. The treatment philosophy of that era proposed that institutionalization of people who were able to function in society with support and guidance was inappropriate. Institutionalized, yet competent, people could be better served by community-based treatment programs, which were both more humane and less expensive. As a result, mental hospitals, institutional homes for children and handicapped adults, and many juvenile correctional institutions were closed in the 1970s. The philosophy was sound, but during the 1980s economic support of services for these individuals was withdrawn when most social programs were severely curtailed. Correctional facilities have suffered the fallout from the de-institutionalization movement.

Correctional staff in jails are ill-equipped to handle the special needs of the mentally ill. Without treatment, the conditions of the mentally ill in jail commonly deteriorate. They are often the victims of abuse, torment, beatings, and rape by other inmates. Exposure to deadly diseases such as AIDS and TB is a chronic problem. Correctional staff frequently resent the responsibility of caring for the mentally ill, and they usually are not trained to deal with the disor-

ders presented. Most corrections officers receive less than 3 hours of training in the treatment of all special problems of inmates. Thus, mistreatment by staff is problematic. The breadth of this problem has increased in recent years.

Geriatric Issues

There is some controversy over the age at which prisoners should be classified as elderly. By most designations, the age of 65 is used, because it is the age of eligibility for Social Security benefits and a commonly recognized point of retirement. Prison inmates, however, often show signs of advanced age before stereotypes of their physical age would predict.[100] Factors such as drug use, alcohol abuse, nicotine addiction, poor diets, inadequate health care, and many conditions associated with poverty or social deprivation cause premature aging among most people who are long-term incarcerates. As a consequence, the U.S. Department of Justice uses the age of 50, which is the age at which many older inmates require special care, as the designation of elderly prison inmates.[101]

In 1994, there were 27,674 inmates over age 50, and 701 inmates over age 75 in American prisons. Between 1990 and 1994, there was an increase in U.S. prisons of more than 8500 inmates who were over the age of 50.[102] With current sentencing strategies, which require life sen-

Race and Sex of Correctional Officers and Job Satisfaction

Numerous research studies in the 1980s indicated that both male and female minority correctional officers and female officers of any ethnicity had lower job satisfaction than white male officers. Minority officers complained of racial discrimination and female officers described widespread sexual harassment throughout all types of corrections. Most studies indicated that women and minority officers believed that white male officers resisted their presence in corrections as the result of "unqualified affirmative action hiring." Even when job performance was highly effective, minority and women officers believed white officers and supervisors judged their work more critically.

A study by Dana Britton, published in 1997, indicates that many of the problems reported in earlier studies are still evident, but that some important factors influence the level of job satisfaction experienced by female and minority correctional officers. First, black male and female officers are less satisfied with their jobs than white male officers, regardless of the size, security classification, or other facts about the institution within which they work. Minority male officers do report that they feel highly effective in their work with inmates and that job stress is relatively low. Most of minority male officers' dissatisfaction appears to be related to co-worker or supervisor interaction.

Second, white women have job satisfaction that is higher than that among white men. Female job dissatisfaction is more predominant among minority women than among white women. Interestingly, even when white women report experiencing sexual harassment and discrimination in assignments or promotions, they report a high level of job satisfaction. Britton suggests that opportunities to work under any circumstances may push white women's job satisfaction up, even when working conditions are unpleasant. Minority women, however, may find that intrinsic rewards of working do not outweigh discrimination and sexual harassment, because they reported much lower levels of job satisfaction in Britton's study. Over time, minority male officers feel significantly less stress and see themselves as more effective in working with inmates. The opposite outcome occurs with women officers. Over time, women feel more stress and less satisfaction in their jobs.

SOURCE: Dana M. Britton, "Perceptions of the Work Environment Among Correctional Officers: Do Race and Sex Matter?" *Criminology 35* (1997) 85–105.

---

tences for repeat offenders in many states, further annual increases are likely. Most elderly inmates have aged while in the system, rather than having entered corrections at a late age. In 1992, for example, only 1.3 percent of persons representing new commitments to prison were over age 55.[103]

The new sentencing strategies that require life sentences for certain offenses, plus the "three strikes and you're out" strategy, are likely to push the number of elderly prisoners higher in the near future. Medical costs for incarceration of elders will present a singular problem for corrections. Health problems such as hypertension, diabetes, heart disease, emphysema, cancer, and the mental and physical deterioration of aging are problems of the incarcerated elderly, just as they are among other older Americans. Treatment of the diseases of aging is considerably more expensive than the average costs for younger inmates. Estimates of yearly costs of medical care indicate that care of the elderly in prison will triple the average per capita expenditure for prison health care in the states.[104]

In addition to increased medical costs, facility modifications are also necessary. Housing that accommodates wheelchairs and the addition of nursing facilities are likely changes as the numbers of elders begins to rise. California currently offers the most comprehensive care of the elderly in prison, although no state has developed full plans of accommodation.[105] Future issues are likely to include debate over costs of incarceration of the elderly and facility redesign to adapt to the needs of elderly inmates.

Correctional Officers

Most people who work in corrections are white men. This is true at all levels of employment and in every type of institution, in both the federal and state systems. There have been some increases in the employment of women and minorities as correctional officers since the 1970s, but there has also been considerable resistance from traditional correctional staff to these changes. According to Robert Johnson, who has written extensively about the effects of staff on the nature of the prison environment, the employment of women and minorities has been viewed by traditionalists as symbolic of a loss of control held by prison authorities. Employment of women and minorities is often interpreted as just another intrusion of the courts into the running of prisons (Box 17.3). This is true even

| | STATE ADULT CORRECTIONAL SYSTEMS | | FEDERAL ADULT CORRECTIONAL SYSTEM |
	CORRECTIONAL OFFICERS	WARDENS	CORRECTIONAL OFFICERS
Total	205,453	1,359	26,761
White male	122,167	946	13,898
White female	19,864	124	4,637
Black male	32,838	181	3,228
Black female	13,812	48	1,726
Hispanic male	10,931	52	1,969
Hispanic female	1,982	8	548
Percent male	81%	87%	73%
Percent female	19	13	27
Percent white	69	79	69
Percent black	23	17	18
Percent Hispanic	6	4	9

SOURCE: Kathleen Maguire and Ann L. Pastore, *Sourcebook of Criminal Justice Statistics* (Washington, DC: U.S. Government Printing Office, 1995) 94, 96, 112.

when the hiring of minorities and women has not been court ordered.[106] Table 17.4 describes the representation of men, women, and minorities in various types of correctional work.

Salaries in Corrections

The occupation of correctional officer has traditionally been a low-paid job, with little skill or education required. Salaries remain low, relative to other high-risk occupations, in most parts of the country, and educational requirements continue to be minimal. Data from the American Correctional Association in 1995 indicate that the lowest-paid, entry-level correctional officers are in Arkansas, where starting salaries can be as low as $12,272. The highest minimal starting salaries are in Alaska and New Jersey, with $31,572 and $31,805, respectively. Most states set minimal entry-level salaries for correctional officers in the range of $15,000 to $20,000. Starting salaries for wardens average $40,272.[107]

In federal corrections, both the minimal starting salaries of correctional officers and wardens are higher than state averages. Entry-level minimal salaries for wardens are $68,667 and correctional officers minimally start at $24,585.[108] Higher salaries in the federal system attract better-educated correctional officers than are typically employed in the states. Forty-three percent of federal correctional officers have completed high school and about 16 percent have a college degree or better.[109]

Job Satisfaction Among Correctional Officers

Correctional officers, generally, are in a no-win job. They are charged with the security of the institution, but frequently have little real power with which to maintain control. They are on the lowest rung of the occupational ladder in the institution, which means they often lack power or influence in the staff hierarchy, and they are resented by the inmates whom they must control. Inmates commonly refer to correctional officers as "hacks" or "screws," which, of course, implies disdain. As a result of the tenuous status of correctional officers, reciprocal relationships often develop between them and inmates. Inmate social hierarchies wield considerable control within institutions. Correctional officers bring in contraband, ignore rule infractions, allow certain inmates additional privileges, or otherwise "bend" the rules for the benefit of particular prisoners, in order to increase favor among inmates who rule themselves within their own hierarchies.[110] Lenient enforcement of certain rules makes governance easier, and also serves to create favor with inmates that may protect officers in the event of a riot.

Research studies have indicated for over 30 years that job satisfaction among correctional officers is generally very low. They are charged with governance of those people whom society has rejected; the occupation is potentially very dangerous and requires acute attention to the private lives of people for whom they have little respect. Disrespect, disdain, frequent violence either among inmates or perpetrated by staff against inmates, and claustrophobic confinement with some of the most tragic people in the country promote job stress, depression, high absenteeism, frequent job turnover, and high levels of cynicism.[111]

Women in Correctional Work

Among other issues of current importance in correctional employment is the entrance of women into the ranks of correctional officers. Correctional work has been traditionally male. Currently, women are employed as less than 20 percent of correctional officers in state prisons, and a high percentage of female officers are in women's prisons.[112] The factor that has most significantly prevented women's entrance into correctional work has been the issue of privacy for male inmates. A number of lawsuits alleging violation of inmates' privacy prevented women from entering the ranks of correctional officer in many states until the mid-1980s.[113] Women were prevented from full duty by the issue of privacy, which has hindered advancement of women through officer ranks. By contrast, privacy for women inmates has generally not prohibited male guards from full officer responsibilities. Women correctional officers in male prisons, for example, have often been prohibited from supervising men in showers, but male correctional officers in women's prisons have not generally been prohibited from supervising women in showers or any other areas of the prison.

Women correctional officers have often reported that the work environment has been hostile to their advancement. They complain of sexual harassment by male co-workers more often than harassment by male inmates. This pattern has been documented in numerous research studies and appears to prevail in treatment of female correctional officers by administration, supervisors, and co-workers. The work environment often includes both offensive sexual comments or behaviors and non-sexual gendered "put-downs" that devalue the work done by women. Differences in job performance, as documented by several research studies, have indicated that women correctional officers tend to be better communicators than male officers, and they are less prone to use violence to solve problems of control in the institution. Female officers also tend to command more respect from male inmates than is typically the case with male correctional officers.[114]

Sexual Harassment of Inmates

In addition to issues of sexual harassment of female officers by male correctional officers, the issue of male officers abusing and harassing female inmates has also arisen in recent years. Issues of abuse of prisoners under all types of confinement has been a problem for the entire history of corrections. The problem of male guards abusing female inmates, however, is especially troublesome because a high proportion of female inmates have suffered physical and sexual abuse before they were incarcerated. In fact, prior abuse is more often linked to women's violent crime than most other life events. Nearly half of all women incarcerated have been raped, physically assaulted, or sexually abused by a spouse, friend, relative, co-worker, or someone else known to them, prior to incarceration (compared to 12 percent of male inmates).[115] The inescapability of abuse becomes a haunting fact of life that hinders post-release success or treatment for substance abuse if physical and sexual assault continue while women are incarcerated.

Several cases involving female inmates who have challenged correctional policies that permit exploitation and abuse have attracted national attention. The problem, however, is as old as the history of women's corrections. The horrible conditions at Auburn and Sing Sing prisons in New York State in 1820, where women were beaten, raped, and sometimes killed by guards and male inmates, prompted the chaplain of the prison to write that to be a woman prisoner in one of these facilities was "worse than death."[116]

Two cases of abuse of female inmates by male correctional officers that were sanctioned by the institutions within which they occurred made national headlines in recent years. In 1992, in Georgia, fourteen correctional officers, correctional officials, and the deputy warden of the Georgia Women's Correctional Institution at Hardwick were indicted for abuse of female inmates that included charges of sexual exploitation, rape, prostitution, sodomy, and drug dealing. In 1990, in Iowa, 14 inmates filed suit against the state to stop the practice of "four pointing," where female inmates were stripped naked, their hands and feet tied to the four posts of a cot in a spread-eagle position and left in an open area for several hours where all passersby could view them. According to the lawsuit, the practice was a disciplinary measure used for inmates who had had epileptic seizures, talked to an attorney regarding sexual abuse by male guards, and for minor misbehaviors that were symptoms of emotional disorders. The suit also described this practice for menstruating women who were not provided with any sanitary protection in the four-pointed position or in isolation cells, where they were also held without clothes. Inmates further complained of shower supervision by male guards, as well as handcuff restraints required in showers. In 1991, the case was settled out of court when the prison agreed to discontinue, temporarily, the practice of four-pointing and to make other changes at the institution, which included allowing inmates to be released from handcuffs while showering and separation of mentally ill inmates from the general population.[117]

While these celebrated cases made national headlines, women inmates complain that both physical and sexual abuse is common, harassment is routine, and that they are generally powerless to stop such mistreatment.[118] Similar cases in Texas, Hawaii, and other states in the early 1990s have drawn the attention of many theorists in the field, although little real change in prison policies seems to have resulted from such cases.[119] While abuse of men in prison is also common, the sexualized nature of mistreatment of women by male correctional officers and officials forms a unique pattern that often merges with other sexualized mistreatment of the women prior to their incarceration.

Punishment for Crime in Sweden

In Sweden, prison is one of the least-used punishments for crime. In 1992, there were almost 170,000 people punished for crimes, but only 5600 were in the correctional system (compared to just under 1 million in the United States that year). Almost all offenders sent to prison in Sweden are released early on a "conditional release," which is similar to the American system of parole. Sentences to prison in Sweden are light by comparison to American standards and inmates serve only a small fraction of their sentences. The following sentences do not include the early release provisions to which most prisoners are entitled:

Murder	More than 7 years
Manslaughter	More than 5 years
Aggravated robbery	From 3 to 5 years
Serious drug crime	From 3 to 5 years
Rape	More than 2 years
Aggravated assault	More than 1 year
Simple robbery/fraud	More than 1 year
Aggravated theft	9 months
Theft, simple fraud	From 3 to 5 months
Simple assault	3 months
Drunk driving	From 1 to 2 months

In Sweden there are 77 prisons and 30 jails. On any given day there are about 5000 inmates in the system, with about 10 percent on furlough or work release. Women or youthful offenders rarely serve prison sentences in Sweden. Most offenders are unemployed men with less than a high school education, who have poor health, often with drug or alcohol problems. The average amount of time an offender actually serves in a Swedish prison is about 3 months.

Recidivism is about 60 percent within 3 years of release, although the most likely time of recidivism is within the first year of release. Young men have the highest recidivism. As in the United States, women have relatively low recidivism.

SOURCE: Jan Carling, *Crime and Law in Sweden* (Stockholm: Statistics Sweden, 1994).

Overcrowding

The upward expansion of prison populations for two decades has meant that facilities in most parts of the country commonly house more inmates than they were designed to hold. This problem is a significant issue for modern corrections, although there has been some improvement through the 1990s as prison building projects have been initiated. The number of people under correctional supervision in the United States increased by three million between 1980 and 1993; between 1985 and 1995 the number of people incarcerated in state and federal prisons increased by 113 percent.[120] This influx of prisoners has overcrowded virtually all prisons (Box 17.4).

While the general statement that prisons are overcrowded is accurate, the exact parameters of overcrowding are, actually, difficult to discern. The reason for this is that there are several measures of *capacity,* or the number of inmates that an institution can hold. **Rated capacity** refers to the number of inmates a rating official assigns to institutions within a particular jurisdiction. **Operational capacity** is the number of inmates that can be accommodated with the staff, programs, and services in a particular institution. And **design capacity** refers to the number of inmates that architects intended to be held in a particular facility. States do not uniformly report capacity to the U.S. Department of Justice when addressing issues of overcrowding. Conservative figures estimate that state

prisons are overcrowded at a rate of 114 percent of capacity; higher estimates put the overcrowding at 125 percent of capacity in 1995. The federal prison system was operating at 126 percent of capacity in 1995.[121]

Overcrowding has meant that cells designed for one or two inmates hold more. Dormitory-style housing is common in some minimum-security prisons. Educational or recreational programs have been suspended or eliminated in many parts of the country because supervision of larger numbers of inmates has become problematic. One of the most pressing concerns about overcrowding is the potential for increased violence as tension and frustration increase in the cramped conditions. Illinois, for example, experienced a 45 percent increase in their prison population between 1985 and 1990. During the same period, assaults against correctional officers by inmates increased by 109 percent.[122] Some research has indicated that it is not the number of new inmates in prison that causes the rates of violence to go up, but rather that an influx of *young* inmates in overcrowded conditions results in increased violence. Older inmates are generally not as emotionally volatile as younger prisoners.[123]

Overcrowding and Early Release

Contrary to popular belief, large numbers of inmates are *not* released early because of overcrowding in state prisons. While the practice is more prevalent in some states than others, it is generally not the pattern throughout the United States. The average amount of time served before release from prison has not changed significantly since 1985, indicating that untimely early release is not common. Overcrowding is more often addressed by housing sentenced inmates in local jails until space is opened in state prisons. In 1995, for example, over 32,000 inmates were held in local jails because of overcrowding in state facilities. Louisiana housed the largest number of inmates awaiting prison space in local jails in 1995.[124]

Many people believe that early release of inmates to alleviate overcrowding threatens public safety. In general, early release of prisoners means that their prison time is shortened by only a few weeks or months. The release of inmates under such conditions has little or no effect on public safety, but it does alleviate overcrowding and it forestalls prison building. In Illinois, for example, since 1980 inmates who qualify for *meritorious good time* (*MGT*) have been released from prison 90 days before their scheduled release. The state estimates that it saved $98.7 million, (about $7000 per inmate) with this policy. Re-arrest of early released inmates accounted for only 0.05 percent of adult arrests between 1980 and 1991. In addition, almost all of the re-arrests of early released inmates have been in the minor misdemeanor categories.[125]

Summary

Trends in American corrections indicate that upward incarceration rates that began around 1980 are likely to persist into the twenty-first century. Many of the problems of incarceration, such as overcrowding, health issues, and rising costs are likely to be exacerbated as the trend toward longer sentences and required lifetime incarceration for repeat violent offenders begins to multiply the current effects of contemporary sentencing policies. As the costs of prison building escalate and correctional budgets further expand, some of the more successful alternative programs (New York's model of boot camp prisons) and many intermediate sanctions (house arrest) are likely to become more commonly adopted options.

Throughout the history of corrections, the pendulum of incarceration policies has swung back and forth between the philosophies of rehabilitation and punishment. The current emphasis is on punishment strategies, with reform efforts taking a low priority. As the high costs of these efforts begin to affect the economy of the nation, a shift back to reform is likely. Exactly when the pendulum will begin the return swing toward reform and rehabilitation is a question for the twenty-first century.

When Martinson and his colleagues publicized their findings that "nothing works" with rehabilitation strate-

gies in 1974,[126] correctional policies shifted, and a new era of punishment was evident by 1980. As new theorists point to the human and economic costs of current alternatives to the rehabilitation strategies of the 1970s and publicize findings that "punishment doesn't work," it is likely that the pendulum will begin to redirect policies once more to reform.

The problem with either punishment or reform strategies is that both fail to address significant societal issues that are associated with crime and ultimately with incarceration of convicted offenders. Economic inequalities that make crime profitable for wealthy offenders (see Chapter 6), the realities of urban decay, declining American manufacturing jobs, rising rates of poverty, and an increasing chasm between those with economic security and a marginalized underclass, make the problem of crime a pervasive American dilemma. "Nothing works" in American corrections because solving American social problems is beyond the scope of correctional strategies. As the pendulum swings back to reform at some point in the twenty-first century, failure to address underlying American social problems will be predictive of future failures in corrections.

Critical Thinking Questions

1. Present arguments for and against the use of shock incarceration as a means of reforming criminals. Which side do you support and why?
2. Should male correctional officers supervise female inmates? Should female correctional officers supervise male inmates? Is there any difference in the use of opposite-sex correctional officers in either male or female institutions?
3. Do you think the expense and management problems inherent in geriatric corrections are worth the sentencing option that sends third-time offenders to prison for life? Why or why not?
4. What do you think should be done about the problem of gangs in prisons?

Suggested Readings

Robert Johnson, *Hard Time: Understanding and Reforming the Prison,* 2nd ed. (Belmont, CA: Wadsworth, 1996).

Lucien X. Lombardo, *Guards Imprisoned: Correctional Officers at Work* (New York: Elsevier, 1981, 1989).

Marilyn D. McShane and Wesley Krause, *Community Corrections* (New York: Macmillan, 1993).

Alida V. Merlo and Joycelyn M. Pollock, eds., *Women, Law, and Social Control* (Boston: Allyn & Bacon, 1995).

Notes

1 See Robert Johnson, *Hard Time: Understanding and Reforming the Prison*, 2nd ed.(Belmont, CA: Wadsworth, 1996) 268–70.

2 Robert Martinson, "What Works? Questions and Answers About Prison Reform," *The Public Interest* 35 (1974) 22–54.

3 Douglas Lipton, Robert Martinson, and Judith Wilks, *The Effectiveness of Correctional Treatment: A Survey of Treatment Evaluation Studies* (New York: Praeger, 1975).

4 Kathleen Maguire and Ann L. Pastore, *Sourcebook of Criminal Justice Statistics, 1994* (Washington, DC: U.S. Government Printing Office, 1995) 177.

5 Christopher Mumola and Allen J. Beck, "Prisoners in 1996," *Bureau of Justice Statistics Bulletin* (Washington, DC: U.S. Government Printing Office, 1997) 1; Allen J. Beck and Darrel K. Gilliard, "Prisoners in 1994," *Bureau of Justice Statistics Bulletin* (Washington, DC: U.S. Government Printing Office, 1995) 3.

6 Mumola and Beck, "Prisoners in 1996," 2.

7 Maguire and Pastore, *Sourcebook of Criminal Justice Statistics, 1994*, 4, 11.

8 Ibid., 5–6.

9 Maguire and Pastore, *Sourcebook of Criminal Justice Statistics, 1994*, 6–10.

10 Kathleen Maguire and Ann L. Pastore, *Sourcebook of Criminal Justice Statistics, 1993* (Washington, DC: U.S. Government Printing Office, 1994) 13.

11 Sue A. Lindgren, "Justice Expenditure and Employment, 1990," *Bureau of Justice Statistics Bulletin* (Washington, DC: U.S. Government Printing Office, 1992) 5.

12 Maguire and Pastore, *Sourcebook of Criminal Justice Statistics, 1994*, 551.

13 Allen Beck et al., "Survey of State Prison Inmates, 1991," *Bureau of Justice Statistics Bulletin* (Washington, DC: U.S. Government Printing Office, 1993) 3.

14 Christopher Mumola and Allen J. Beck, "Correctional Populations in the United States, 1996," *Bureau of Justice Statistics Report* (Washington, DC: U.S. Government Printing Office, 1997) 3, 9.

15 Linnet Myers, "Decade of Destruction: Losing a Generation of Youths to Crack," *Chicago Tribune*, 31 December 1995, 1-1, 1-6; Samuel Walker, *Sense and Nonsense about Crime and Drugs: A Policy Guide*, 3rd ed. (Belmont CA: Wadsworth, 1994), Chs. 1, 13; Steven F. Messner and Richard Rosenfeld, *Crime and the American Dream* (Belmont CA: Wadsworth, 1994), Ch. 5.

16 Mumola and Beck, "Prisoners in 1996," 5.

17 Todd. R. Clear and George F. Cole, *American Corrections* (Monterey, CA: Brooks/Cole, 1986) 333–38.

18 Illinois Department of Corrections, Fact Sheet, May 1994.

19 Paul Gendreau and Robert R. Ross, "Revivification of Rehabilitation: Evidence from the 1980s," *Justice Quarterly* 4 (1987) 395; Francis T. Cullen and Paul Gendreau, "The Effectiveness of Correctional Rehabilitation: Reconsidering the 'Nothing Works' Debate," in *The American Prison: Issues in Research and Policy*, ed. Lynn Goodstein and Doris Layton Mackenzie (New York: Plenum, 1989) 23–44.

20 Mark Myrent and Maureen Hickey, "Educating Inmates: Illinois' Approach," *The Compiler* (Fall 1991) 10–12.

21 Mumola and Beck, "Prisoners in 1996," 12.

22 Caroline Wolf Harlow, "Comparing Federal and State Prison Inmates, 1991," *Bureau of Justice Statistics* (Washington, DC: U.S. Government Printing Office, 1994) 6.

23 For discussion, see Johnson, *Hard Time: Understanding and Reforming the Prison*, 287–88.

24 Mumola and Beck, "Prisoners in 1996," 5, 9.

25 Kathleen Maguire and Ann L. Pastore, *Sourcebook of Criminal Justice Statistics, 1995* (Washington, DC: U.S. Government Printing Office, 1996) 567.

26 Ibid.; and Beck et al., "Survey of State Prison Inmates, 1991," 3.

27 Mumola and Beck, "Prisoners in 1996," 10.

28 Donald Clemmer, *The Prison Community* (New York: Holt, Rinehart and Winston, 1965).

29 Ibid.

30 Gresham Sykes, *The Society of Captives: A Study of a Maximum Security Prison* (Princeton, NJ: Princeton University Press, 1958).

31 John Irwin, *Prisons in Turmoil* (Boston: Little, Brown, 1980); see also John Irwin and Donald R. Cressey, "Thieves, Convicts, and Inmate Culture," *Social Problems* 10 (1962) 142–55.

32 For an overview of the criticisms, see John Irwin, "Prison," *Contemporary Sociology* 5 (1976) 424–26.

33 George W. Knox, "Preliminary Results of the 1992 Adult Corrections Survey," Gang Crime Research Center (Chicago, IL: Chicago State University, 1992).

34 Ibid., 3–7.

35 Lee H. Bowker, "Victimizers and Victims in American Correctional Institutions," in *The Pains of Imprisonment*, ed. Robert Johnson and Hans Toch (Prospect Heights, IL: Waveland, 1982) 63–74, 64.

36 Mumola and Beck, "Prisoners in 1996," 5.

37 Tracy L. Snell, "Women in Prison," *Bureau of Justice Statistics Special Report* (Washington, DC: U.S. Government Printing Office, 1994); Mumola and Beck, "Prisoners in 1996," 6.

38 Derived from Maguire and Pastore, *Sourcebook of Criminal Justice Statistics, 1994*, 540.

39 Snell, "Women in Prison"; Beck et al., "Survey of State Prison Inmates, 1991," 10.

40 Beck et al., "Survey of State Prison Inmates, 1991", 12.

41 Tracy L. Snell, "Correctional Populations in the United States, 1991," *Bureau of Justice Statistics* (Washington, DC: U.S. Government Printing Office, 1993) 3.

42 See Snell, "Correctional Populations in the United States, 1991"; also, Pauline B. Bart and Eileen Geil Moran, *Violence Against Women: The Bloody Footprints* (Newbury Park, CA: Sage, 1993).

43 Maguire and Pastore, *Sourcebook of Criminal Justice Statistics, 1994*, 537.

44 For excellent discussion of this issue, see Geoffrey P. Alpert, "Women Prisoners and the Law: Which Way Will the Pendulum Swing?" in *The Criminal Justice System and Women: Women Offenders, Victims, Workers*, ed. Barbara Raffel Price and Natalie J. Sokoloff (New York: Clark Boardman, 1982) 171–82.

45 See Clarice Feinman, *Women in the Criminal Justice System*, 2nd ed. (New York: Praeger, 1986); Joycelyn M. Pollock-Byrne, *Women, Prison and Crime* (Pacific Grove, CA: Brooks/Cole, 1990); Myrent and Hickey, "Educating Inmates: Illinois' Approach," 11. For a discussion of women's wages in the paid labor force, see Barbara Resnick and Irene Padavic, *Women and Men at Work* (Thousand Oaks, CA: Pine Forge Press, 1994).

46 Ibid.

47 Snell "Correctional Populations in the United States, 1991," 31.

48 Jean Wellish, Michael Prendergast, and M. Douglas Anglin, "Drug-Abusing Women Offenders: Results of a National Survey," *Office of Justice Programs* (Washington, DC: U.S. Government Printing Office, 1994) 1–2.

49 Ibid.; also, Pollock-Byrne, *Women, Prison and Crime*. See also James A. Inciardi, Dorothy Lockwood, and Anne E. Pottieger, *Women and Crack-Cocaine* (New York: Macmillan, 1993).

50 Alida V. Merlo and Joycelyn M. Pollock, eds., *Women, Law, and Social Control* (Boston: Allyn & Bacon, 1995), Part III.

51 Arlene Levinson, "Prison For Pregnant Women Opens," *Peoria Journal Star*, 12 December 1988, B-7; Jim Bencivenga, "Prison Inequities," *Chicago Tribune*, 11 December 1988, 6-9; James Austin, Barbara Bloom, and Trish Donahue, "Female Offenders in the Community: An Analysis of Innovative Strategies and Programs" (San Francisco: National Council on Crime and Delinquency, 1992).

52 For discussion, see Pollock-Byrne, *Women, Prison and Crime*; Bart and Moran, *Violence Against Women:The Bloody Footprints*; Merlo and Pollock, *Women, Law, and Social Control*.

53 Craig A. Perkins, James J. Stephan, and Allen J. Beck, "Jails and Jail Inmates, 1993–1994," *Bureau of Justice Statistics Bulletin* (Washington, DC: U.S. Government Printing Office, 1995) 2; Darrell K. Gilliard and Allen J. Beck, "Prison and Jail Inmates, 1995," *Bureau of Justice Statistics Bulletin* (Washington, DC: U.S. Government Printing Office, 1996) 1.

54 Perkins et al., "Jails and Jail Inmates, 1993–1994," 1–2.

55 Gilliard and Beck, "Prison and Jail Inmates, 1995," 6–12.

56 Cherie L. Clark, David W. Aziz, and Doris L. MacKenzie, "Shock Incarceration in New York: Focus on Treatment," National Institute of Justice (Washington, DC: U.S. Government Printing Office, 1994) 1.

57 Maguire and Pastore, *Sourcebook of Criminal Justice Statistics, 1994*, 99.

58 Clark et al., "Shock Incarceration in New York: Focus on Treatment," 8–9.

59 Ernest L. Cowles and Thomas C. Castellano, *"Boot Camp" Drug Treatment and Aftercare Intervention: An Evaluation Review*, National Institute of Justice Research Report (Washington, DC: U.S. Government Printing Office, 1995) 26–31; Clark et al., "Shock Incarceration in New York: Focus On Treatment," 9; Doris Layton MacKenzie, Robert Brame, David McDowall, and Claire Souryal, "Boot Camp Prisons and Recidivism in Eight States," *Criminology* 33 (1995) 327–58.

60 Cowles and Castelanno, *"Boot Camp" Drug Treatment and Aftercare Intervention: An Evaluation Review*, 116–20.

61 Maguire and Pastore, *Sourcebook of Criminal Justice Statistics, 1995*, 97–100.

62 Ibid.

63 See, for example, American Correctional Association, "Private Sector Operation of a Correctional Institution" (Washington, DC: U.S. Department of Justice, 1985); John D. Donahue, "Prisons for Profit: Public Justice, Private Interests" (Washington, DC: Economic Policy Institute, 1988).

64 See, for example, Patrick Anderson, Charles R. Davoli, and Laura J. Mortiarty, "Private Corrections: Feast or Fiasco?" *The Prison Journal* 65 (1985) 34.

65 Feinman, *Women in the Criminal Justice System*, 2nd ed., 65.

66 Maguire and Pastore, *Sourcebook of Criminal Justice Statistics, 1994*, 101. This excludes prisons operated by the U.S. Army, Navy, and Air Force, which generally house fewer than fifteen women in any given year.

67 Ibid.

68 See discussions in Pollock-Byrne, *Women, Prison and Crime*, 100–101, and Feinman, *Women in the Criminal Justice System*, 2nd ed., 64–71.

69 Ibid.

70 The Citizens Assembly Serving the Illinois General Assembly, *The Citizens' Council on Women Annual Report, 1989*, 127–30.

71 Ibid., 129.

72 Pollock-Byrne, *Women, Prison and Crime*.

73 Ibid., 68–69.

74 Marilyn D. McShane and Wesley Krause, *Community Corrections* (New York: Macmillan, 1993) 4.

75 Vince Fallin, "Gaining Support For Sentencing Options," in *Intermediate Punishment: Community-Based Sanctions*, ed. American Correctional Association (Laurel, MD: 1990) 5. Vince Fallin is the Deputy Commissioner, Probation Division, Georgia Department of Corrections.

76 Examples and statistics are drawn from McShane and Krause, *Community Corrections*, 184–85.

77 Kristi Turnbaugh, "Electronic Monitoring," *The Compiler* (Winter/Spring, 1995) 7.

78 James Austin et al., "Female Offenders in the Community: An Analysis of Innovative Strategies and Programs," 43.

79 Ibid., 52.

80 Kristi Turnbaugh, "Sheriff's Work Alternative Program: Paying Back the Community," *The Compiler* (Winter/Spring 1995) 4–7.

81 Laura Maruschak, "HIV in Prisons and Jails, 1995," *Bureau of Justice Statistics Bulletin* (Washington, DC: U.S. Government Printing Office, 1997) 1.

82 Maguire and Pastore, *Sourcebook of Criminal Justice Statistics, 1994*, 551; Beck et al., "Survey of State Prison Inmates, 1991", 10.

83 Maruschak (1997), 5.

84 High-risk sexual behavior includes anal sex with an infected partner. Since most prison sex among male inmates is of this type, risk of exposure to AIDS is high.

85 See Wayne S. Wooden and Jay Parker, *Men Behind Bars: Sexual Exploitation in Prison* (New York: Plenum, 1982).

86 Perry F. Smith, "HIV Infection Among Women Entering the New York State Correctional System," *American Journal of Public Health 81* (1991) 35.

87 Peter M. Brien and Caroline Wolf Harlow, "HIV in Prisons and Jails, 1993," *Bureau of Justice Statistics Bulletin* (Washington, DC: U.S. Government Printing Office, 1995) 5.

88 Maguire and Pastore, *Sourcebook of Criminal Justice Statistics, 1994*, 583.

89 Maruschak, "HIV in Prisons and Jails, 1995," 1.

90 New Grolier Multimedia Encyclopedia for Macintosh (1994).

91 Robert D. McFadden, "A Drug-Resistant TB Results in 13 Deaths in New York Prisons," *New York Times*, 16 November 1991, 1.

92 New Grolier Multimedia Encyclopedia for Macintosh (1994).

93 Ibid.

94 Cheryl A. Crawford, "Health Care Needs in Corrections: NIJ Responds," *National Institute of Justice Journal* (November 1994) 32; Snell, 1993, 66.

95 Mile M. Braun et al., "Increasing Incidence of Tuberculosis in a Prison Inmate Population," *Journal of the American Medical Association 261* (1989) 393.

96 Jan Elvin, "TB Comes Back, Poses Special Threat to Jails, Prisons," *National Prison Project Journal 7* (1992) 1.

97 Sidney M. Wolfe, "Criminalizing the Seriously Mentally Ill: The Abuse of Jails as Mental Hospitals," in *Health Letter: Public Citizen Health Research Group 8* (1992) 1–3, 9.

98 Ibid.

99 Ibid.

100 Peter C. Kratcoski and George A. Pownall, "Federal Bureau of Prisons Programming for Older Inmates," *Federal Probation 53* (1989) 30.

101 Maguire and Pastore, *Sourcebook of Criminal Justice Statistics, 1995*, 565.

102 Ibid.

103 Ibid., 569.

104 Larry E. Sullivan, *The Prison Reform Movement—Forlorn Hope* (Boston: Twayne, 1990) 135.

105 Joan B. Morton, "Training Staff to Work with Elderly and Disabled Inmates," *Corrections Today 55* (1993) 1.

106 Johnson, *Hard Time: Understanding and Reforming the Prison*, 2nd ed., 224–25.

107 Maguire and Pastore, *Sourcebook of Criminal Justice Statistics, 1995*, 94.

108 Ibid.

109 Maguire and Pastore, *Sourcebook of Criminal Justice Statistics, 1994*, 112; educational levels for state correctional officers are not available.

110 See Johnson, *Hard Time: Understanding and Reforming the Prison*, 2nd ed., Ch. 7.

111 There are numerous studies to support these generalizations. See, for example, Donald Clemmer, *The Prison Community* (Boston: Christopher Publishing, Lucien X, 1940); Lombardo, *Guards Imprisoned: Correctional Officers at Work* (New York: Elsevier, 1981, 1989); Hans Toch, *Living in Prison: The Ecology of Survival* (New York: Free Press, 1977).

112 Women were generally employed only in juvenile or women's institutions until the 1970s, although staff were still predominantly male even in these facilities.

113 See: *Forts v. Ward* (1979) 621 F.2d. 1210 (2nd Cir.); *Bowling v. Enomoto* (1981 514 F. Supp. 201; *Avery v. Rerrin* (1979) 473 F. Supp. 90; *Gunther v. Iowa* (1980) 612 F.2d. 1079, cert. denied 446 U.S. 996 (8th Cir.); and concerning pat searches, see: *Smith v. Fairman* (1983) 678 F.2d. 52, cert. denied 461 U.S. 907 (7th Cir.); *Sam'i v. Mintzes* (1983) 544 F. Supp. 416; *Madyun v. Franzen* (1983) 704 F. 2d. 954; and *Bagley v. Watson* (1983) 579 F. Supp. 1099 (D.C. Ore.). The cases were cited in Linda L. Zupan, "The Progress of Women Correctional Officers in All-Male Prisons," in *The Changing Roles of Women in the Criminal Justice System: Offenders, Victims, and Professionals*, 2nd ed., ed. Imogene L. Moyer (Prospect Heights, IL: Waveland, 1992) 323–43.

114 Joanne Belknap, "Women in Conflict: An Analysis of Women Correctional Officers," in *The Criminal Justice System and Women: Offenders, Victims and Workers*, 2nd ed., ed. Barbara Raffel Price and Natalie J. Sokoloff (New York: McGraw-Hill, 1995) 404–420; Nancy C. Jurik, "Striking a Balance: Female Correctional Officers, Gender Role Stereotypes, and Male Prisoners," *Sociological Inquiry 58* (1986) 291–304; Cheryl Bowser Petersen, "Doing Time with the Boys: An Analysis of Women Correctional Officers in an All-Male Facility," in *The Criminal Justice System and Women*, ed. Barbara Raffel Price and Natalie J. Sokoloff (New York: Clark Boardman, 1984) 437–60; Zupan, "The Progress of Women Correctional Officers in All-Male Prisons"; Joycelyn M. Pollock, "Women in Corrections: Custody and the 'Caring Ethic,'" in *Women, Law, and Social Control*, ed. Alida V. Merlo and Joycelyn M. Pollock (Boston: Allyn & Bacon, 1995) 97–116.

115 Snell, "Women in Prison," 5.

116 David W. Lewis, *From Newgate to Dannemora: The Rise of the Penitentiary in New York, 1796–1848* (Ithaca, NY: Cornell University Press, 1965) 73–75, 162–63; as quoted in Clarice Feinman, "Sex Role Stereotypes and Justice for Women," in *The Criminal Justice System and Women*, ed. Barbara Raffel Price and Natalie J. Sokoloff (New York: Clark Boardman, 1984) 131–39.

117 Associated Press Wire Service, October 1992; United States District Court, Southern District of Iowa, Case number 89-863-A, *Laura Brooks et al. v. Terry E. Brandstad, Paul Grossheim, and Barbara Olk*, filed April 10, 1990; Chris Osher, "Inmates Settle Suit over Nude Punishments," *Des Moines Register*, 24 April 1991, 2.

118 See, for example, Barbara Raffel Price and Natalie J. Sokoloff, eds., *The Criminal Justice System and Women* (New York: Clark Boardman, 1982); William R. Blount, Joseph B. Kuhns III, and Ira J. Silverman, "Intimate Abuse Within an Incarcerated Female Population: Rates, Levels, Criminality, a Continuum, and Some Lessons About Self-Identification," in *Female Criminality: The State of the Art*, ed. Concetta C. Culliver (New York: Garland, 1993), 413–68.

119 Merlo and Pollock, *Women, Law, and Social Control*, 166.

120 Beck and Gilliard, "Prisoners in 1994," 2; Gilliard and Beck, "Prison and Jail Inmates, 1995," 2.

121 Gilliard and Beck, "Prison and Jail Inmates, 1995," 8.

122 Jeffrey Austin, "A Record Year for Criminal Justice," Illinois Criminal Justice Information Authority, *The Compiler* (Fall 1991) 16.

123 Sheldon Olson, Dennis Barrick, and Lawrence Cohen, "Prison Overcrowding and Disciplinary Problems: An Analysis of the Texas Prison System," *Journal of Applied Behavioral Science 19* (1983) 163–76.

124 Gilliard and Beck, "Prison and Jail Inmates, 1995," 7.

125 Illinois Criminal Justice Information Authority, "Shorter Prison Terms and Public Safety," *The Compiler* (Winter/Spring 1995) 3.

126 Martinson, "What Works? Questions and Answers About Prison Reform," (1974); Lipton et al., *The Effectiveness of Correctional Treatment: A Survey of Treatment Evaluation Studies*.

part 6

Conclusion

UNLIKE THE STUDY OF CRIME, which has no obvious end point, this book must come to a close. Chapter 18 presents eight concluding themes to our study of American crime and criminal justice. This chapter is not a summary of previous chapters, but rather an exit message. That is, these eight themes can be seen as insights to be thought about now and for years to come.

This book began with the promise to provide answers and raise questions. You should already have an ample supply of each. Now, as you read the final chapter, try to recall the key information and main lessons of the previous chapters. The eight themes discussed in Chapter 18 will help you do this.

For updated information on current themes in criminology, consult the Wadsworth web site at http://www.wadsworth.com/cj.html

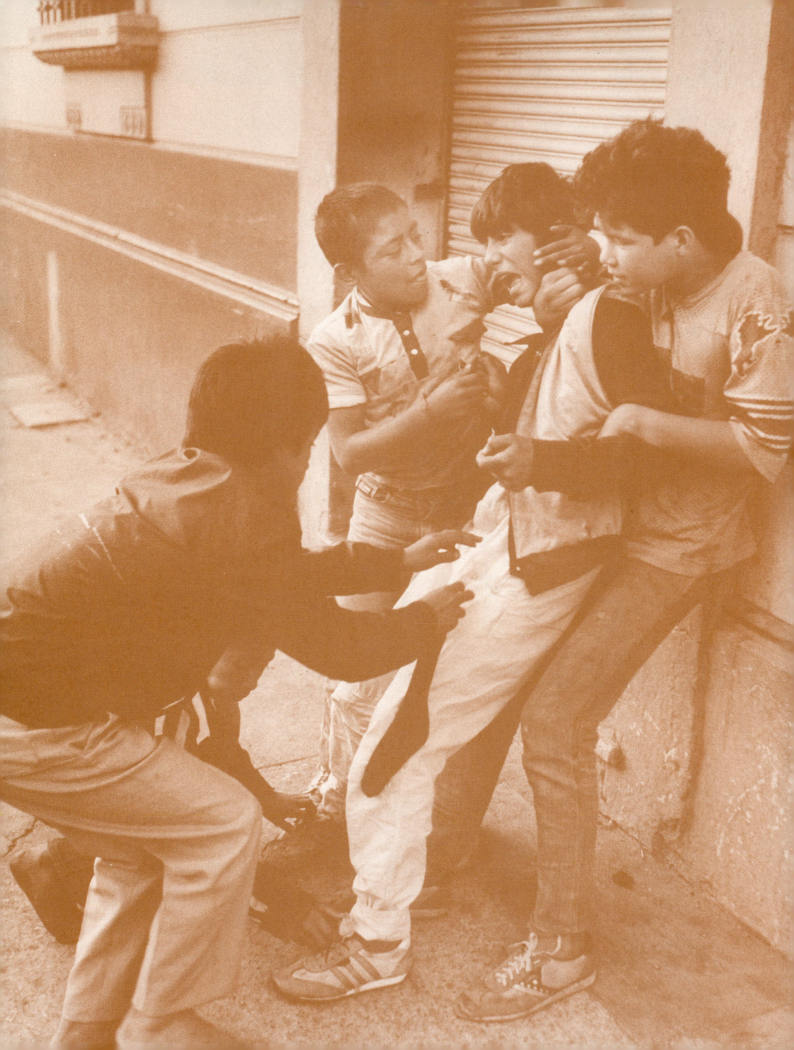

chapter 18

Current Themes in Criminology

CHAPTER OUTLINE
CURRENT THEMES
Theme 1 Crime Is Disproportionately a Male Enterprise
Theme 2 Crime Crosscuts Class and Race
Theme 3 Guilt Is an Insufficient Deterrent to Crime
Theme 4 Many Types of Serious Wrongdoing Are Not Adequately Addressed
Theme 5 Crime Is Individually Chosen and Structurally Determined
Theme 6 Commitment to Ideology Can Handicap Crime Policy
    Definition of "Serious Crime"
    Ideological Gridlock
    Ideological Triage
Theme 7 Results of Criminal Justice "Toughness" Are Unclear
Theme 8 Future Crime Patterns in the United States

KEY TERMS
clearance rate
definition of the situation
ideology
ideological triage
selective incapacitation
historical inertia

IN PREVIOUS CHAPTERS WE have examined a broad range of crime-related topics: the nature and extent of criminal behavior in the United States, popular beliefs about crime, scientific definitions and theories of crime, major types of crime, and the criminal justice system. The presentation and discussion of each of these topics was *shaped by the scientific literature. Through their research, sociologists and criminologists have learned a great deal about crime, and this book is an attempt to integrate and review the most important findings. There is no need to repeat or even summarize what has been stated earlier. Instead, the research findings already discussed can be used as a base from which to draw some general conclusions.*

Current Themes

This final chapter provides an overall assessment of fundamental issues. Specifically, we discuss eight significant themes regarding American patterns of crime and criminal justice. These concluding themes can be seen as "talking points"—key crime-related topics about which an informed citizen is likely to have views.

Theme 1: Crime Is Disproportionately a Male Enterprise

Despite the attention given to recent increases in female crime, the one common thread among street crime, organized crime, corporate crime, white-collar crime, and political crime is that the offenders are typically men. Whether we consider interpersonal violence or stealing crimes, most serious criminal behavior is committed by men. This conclusion is supported first by police statistics (UCR), which indicate that men are most likely to be arrested for committing index crimes. For example, only 15 percent of all those arrested for murder, rape, robbery, and aggravated assault are women.[1] Women constitute 27 percent of those arrested for the second set of four index crimes, burglary, larceny-theft, motor vehicle theft, and arson.[2]

Victimization studies (NCVS) also suggest that men are more frequent serious criminal offenders. Victim studies show that, for crimes that involve contact between victim and offender, men are far more likely than women to be identified as perpetrators.[3] NCVS data also indicate that women are ten times more likely than men to be victims of violence inflicted by an intimate partner.[4] Of major measures of crime, only self-report studies that track relatively minor criminal offenses fail to find greater male involvement in crime.[5]

Big-time crime is also typically a male enterprise. This includes acts of corporate violence that injure or kill tens of thousands of Americans annually.[6] When companies operate unsafe work settings or produce dangerous products, it is usually the result of decisions made by male executives (as recently as 1990, women held only 2.6 percent of the 6502 top jobs at Fortune 500 companies[7]). Also included here are acts of corporate greed. Corporate price-fixing and fraud result in the stealing of billions of

dollars. Again, the perpetrators are typically men. Finally, acts of state violence and political corruption, the misdeeds of those "running the country," are most often committed by men as well. Thus, serious crime is mainly a male activity.

Theme 2: Crime Crosscuts Class and Race

Popular stereotypes have long suggested that poor people and minority group members commit a disproportionately high amount of crime in the United States. Historically, this category was referred to as the "dangerous class."[8] While the relationship between social class and crime has been explored in numerous studies, the findings have not always been consistent. In general, research is influenced by how crime is measured. There are two considerations here. First, what measure of crime is used—police statistics (UCR data) or self-report studies? Second, what types of crime are examined—street crime or crimes of the powerful? These points require elaboration.

Early investigation found that members of the lower socioeconomic classes were most likely to engage in criminal behavior. These studies typically used police statistics to define and measure criminal behavior. The poor were (and are) most likely to get caught up in the criminal justice system. The advent of self-report measures of criminal activity, however, led to a reassessment of the relationship between class and crime. Self-report studies tend to show that law violation exists across class boundaries, that a high proportion of people, regardless of class position, admit to law breaking.[9]

Many sociologists and criminologists argue that differential law enforcement helps account for the high crime rates of members of the lower class. The poor, more frequently than members of the middle or upper classes, are suspected, watched, arrested, prosecuted, convicted, and incarcerated for crime commission.[10] Law-enforcement practices contribute to the appearance of a criminogenic lower class, when in fact crime is spread throughout all socioeconomic levels.

There is a second question central to studying the relationship between class and crime: What types of criminal behavior are considered? When the focus is on street crime, then the poor are found to be the most frequent offenders. However, when white-collar crimes are examined, it is found that the poor are infrequent offenders. Individuals from all social classes engage in crime, but the type of crime chosen often varies by class standing of the offender. For example, robbery, embezzlement, and price-fixing are all forms of stealing; however, robbery tends to be a lower-class activity, embezzlement a middle-class crime, and price-fixing an upper-class offense.

Race is of fundamental importance in analyzing American social relations. This is particularly true with regard to evaluating crime patterns. For example, it is a fact that African Americans have a disproportionately high rate of participation in index crimes (as well as a high rate of victimization for these crimes). This finding appears in both police statistics and victim studies.[11] Why are blacks comparatively more likely than other Americans to engage in serious conventional crimes such as murder, robbery, and burglary? Numerous answers to this question have been advanced. Conservatives typically argue that the instability of urban black family life hinders proper socialization of children. This view suggests that the one-parent family structure common in some black communities is ill-equipped to instill proper values and norms. Liberals reject this thinking, preferring to describe African American crime as the product of institutional patterns of discrimination. Those who advance the liberal position place special emphasis on educational and economic discrimination.

William Julius Wilson, a prominent expert on race relations in the United States, offers a comprehensive, non-ideological explanation. He argues that the decline of manufacturing jobs available to inner-city blacks has contributed to a variety of social patterns (unemployment, attraction to the drug trade, breakdown of the family) that have resulted in high rates of violent crimes and stealing offenses among urban blacks.[12]

Before concluding that blacks are more crime-prone than other racial or ethnic groups, it should be observed that white Americans commit the overwhelming share of the crimes of the powerful. White-collar, corporate, and political crimes are offenses most often committed by whites. Moreover, as we have noted repeatedly in previous chapters, these offenses are far more costly to society than conventional crimes. Hence, while there are distinct and important race-associated patterns of criminality, crime is not a problem reducible to any one racial or ethnic group in society. Even the associations between race and patterns of crime are related to macro structural forces. There is no evidence to link race and crime directly. In conclusion, as it does with class, crime crosscuts racial boundaries.

Theme 3: Guilt Is an Insufficient Deterrent to Crime

It is clear that guilt feelings fail to prevent millions of serious crimes each year. Why is sense of guilt not a more ef-

fective crime deterrent? Many sociologists suggest that contemporary American culture provides numerous rationalizations for criminal behavior. Currently, dominant cultural patterns support a "therapeutic ethic" that elevates victimization and simultaneously depresses notions of responsibility and guilt. The end result is that no *type* of criminal offender is swayed by guilt feelings.[13] This does not mean that guilt feelings never prevent crimes, nor does it mean that guilt feelings never overwhelm offenders after they have committed criminal acts. It simply means that most offenders find ways of escaping or neutralizing their sense of guilt. This applies for all types of offenders.

Chapters 5 through 8 examined several categories of criminal activity, including interpersonal violence, low-level stealing, organized crime, corporate wrongdoing, and political lawlessness. To evaluate the effectiveness of guilt feelings, let us consider a representative offense for each of the categories identified: murder, shoplifting, selling illegal drugs, price-fixing, and illegal wiretapping. With regard to offenders who commit these crimes, the research literature offers support for these broad characterizations:

- Murderers often blame their victim for precipitating the act.
- Shoplifters state that store losses are covered by insurance.
- Drug dealers argue that there is no moral difference between selling whiskey and cocaine.
- Corporate executives who fix prices claim that smart business demands it and that all companies do it.
- Government officials or employees who break the law think that they are doing so for a higher purpose.

For many people, a personal sense of guilt can be easily defeated in contemporary American society. This is one explanation for America's high crime rate. It is probably not the most important factor, but it appears to be a significant one.

Theme 4: Many Types of Serious Wrongdoing Are Not Adequately Addressed

There is both *recognized* and *unrecognized* serious crime in the United States. The former is usually defined in terms of the familiar index crimes. These are the offenses that receive special attention and scrutiny by the police, the media, and the general public. Despite the fact that these crimes are identified as serious wrongs, evidence demonstrates that the police are only minimally successful at detecting index crimes and apprehending the offenders. For every one index crime known to the police, there are about three others that actually take place. What is more, these offenses frequently go unsolved. Law-enforcement agencies use the term **clearance rate** to refer to a situation where "at least one person is arrested, charged, and turned over for prosecution."[14] Several of the index crimes have very low clearance rates. For instance, in only about 25 percent of all robbery cases are the police able to arrest the person or persons that they believe committed the crime. Even when the police make what they consider to be a good arrest, there is no assurance that the alleged offender will be prosecuted, convicted, or incarcerated. In fact, for some index crimes, rape being a prime example, there is a historical pattern of low rates of prosecution, conviction, and incarceration.

American criminal justice agencies have a less than stellar record of dealing with index crimes; they have an even worse record of responding to acts of wrongdoing that are prevalent yet receive little attention. Domestic abuse is such an example. While the media promotes domestic abuse as a popular issue for discussion, the problem often remains hidden. Sociologists and social workers, however, know that the incidence of spousal and child abuse is widespread. As recently as 1992, the United States Surgeon General ranked abuse by husbands or male partners as the leading cause of injury to women between 15 and 44 years of age.[15] Elder abuse is also a serious problem. It is estimated that there are 1.5 million cases of physical or emotional abuse of elderly persons each year in the United States.[16] Despite the widespread incidence of domestic abuse cases, these crimes have not usually been given high priority by police, prosecutors, or judges.

Not all serious wrongdoing is defined as criminal. Jeffrey Reiman, a criminologist cited frequently in this book, argues that many harmful actions are either not defined as criminal, or there is lax enforcement of existing regulations. Consider his statement:

> **The criminal justice system fails to protect people from the most serious dangers by failing to define the dangerous acts of those who are well off as crimes . . . and by failing to enforce the law vigorously against the well-to-do when they commit acts that are defined as crimes. . . .[17]**

Shortcomings of the criminal justice system do not fully explain the persistence of serious wrongdoing in the United States. Even more fundamental than the workings of the criminal justice system is the ideological agenda of policymakers. This topic is taken up later in Theme 6.

Theme 5: Crime Is Individually Chosen and Structurally Determined

Many in society blame individuals for crime. They subscribe generally to the classical theory of criminal behavior, which states that crime is rational, freely chosen, and self-interested. Others reject this approach and favor the view that crime is behavior brought on by social-environmental influences. They believe that individuals are pressured or enticed into committing crimes. Sociologists, of course, have long argued that human behavior is more the product of social influence than individual will.

Neither the individualistic nor social-structural explanation of crime is satisfactory by itself. Both views are partly correct. Perhaps the use of a metaphor will make this point evident. Consider a person in a river attempting to swim from point A to point B. In determining whether or not the individual will be able to swim from one point to the other, two variables have overriding importance: the ability of the swimmer and the strength of the current. One cannot predict with certainty that a weak swimmer will be unsuccessful (he or she may be aided by a strong river current), nor is it inevitable that a person will be unable to swim successfully against a strong current. Everyday life is like this. Social structures, including poverty and institutionalized racism, might make conventional success difficult, but it is not impossible. If it were impossible, then no one raised in an urban ghetto would ever become successful. Individual determination and talent can overcome structural barriers. On the other hand, structural influence should not be underestimated. The opportunities and limitations associated with family life, formal education, and economic well-being help to shape a person's life. Social patterns, including patterns of crime, bear this out repeatedly. Hence, crime is not simply a result of individual will, nor is it solely the product of social forces. It is an outcome of both personal and social-structural considerations.

Theme 6: Commitment to Ideology Can Handicap Crime Policy

Sociologists have long emphasized the importance of a **definition of the situation.** Human behavior is influenced greatly by how various aspects of a social setting are defined. Ideology works as a sort of collective definition of the situation. An **ideology** is a set of ideas, usually not scientifically testable, that offers an interpretation of existing social arrangements, including social problems. Accordingly, ideology influences how people think about crime. In the United States, a commitment to ideology has shaped crime policy (Box 18.1).

Definition of "Serious Crime"
The most elementary aspect of America's dominant ideology of crime is the notion that interpersonal violence and lower-class stealing are the most serious crimes facing the nation. This view was institutionalized in 1930 when law-enforcement authorities began collecting national crime data. Murder, rape, aggravated assault, robbery, burglary, larceny, and motor vehicle theft were categorized as Part I index crimes (arson was added to the list

Ideology and the Cuban Boat People

In 1980, over 100,000 Cubans tried to cross ocean waters to come to the United States. These "boat people" consisted mainly of middle-class entrepreneurs and professionals, along with a small number of criminals and people with mental problems. Overall, U.S. government authorities praised the boat people as political freedom seekers. But Immigration and Naturalization personnel did classify 350 as having criminal backgrounds. Eventually, the total who were classified as criminal escalated to 7000. Sociologist Mark Hamm has examined this process and concluded that the political and economic forces defining the relationship between the United States and Cuba influenced the way in which thousands of boat people were classified. In short, ideology helped shape the categorization of individuals as criminals.

SOURCE: Mark Hamm, *The Abandoned Ones: The Imprisonment and Uprising of the Mariel Boat People* (Boston: Northeastern University Press, 1995).

in 1979). Today, these crimes continue to receive the most attention. Both the police and the public believe that index crimes are the most common and most serious crimes in America.

One of the consequences of fixing attention on interpersonal violence and lower-class stealing is that there is a tendency to describe crime as the behavior of *individuals,* particularly the young and the poor. The ideology of crime might be drastically different today if government authorities had initially identified additional or alternative crimes. Consider, for example, the possibility that in 1930 the following seven offenses had been introduced as the Part I index crimes: Sale of unsafe products, operation of dangerous work settings, illegal pollution, unauthorized government violence, political corruption, price-fixing, and false advertising. It could have happened. These crimes are serious offenses. They account for more deaths and injuries than do the actual index crimes, and they are much more costly financially. Of course, today we would be discussing a much different "typical" offender. The typical perpetrator of these crimes is middle-aged or elderly, affluent, and acting on behalf of a corporation or agency. Clearly, the original definition of serious crime had a pivotal influence on the development of our dominant ideology of crime.

Beyond the definition of serious crime, ideological perspectives also include proposals for crime prevention and reduction. As we shall now see, commitment to opposed ideological positions often results in ideological gridlock.

Ideological Gridlock

For the past several years there has been considerable discussion in the United States about political gridlock. For example, when a Democrat is in the White House and the Republicans control Congress, it is said that neither political party is able to legislate its agenda. Why do Democrats and Republicans attempt to block each other? Often it is done to gain a political advantage. Most politicians from each party are concerned with re-election and few are willing to allow their opponents a campaign edge. Meg Greenfield, a columnist for *Newsweek,* argues that this had been particularly true with regard to the budget deficit: "The basic premise of both parties seems to be that there is no more urgent obligation than cutting the deficit, except for the obligation to humiliate the other side whenever it attempts to."[18]

Consideration of political gain is not the only cause of gridlock. Democrats and Republicans are committed to opposed ideologies. Democrats tend to embrace a liberal ideology, while Republicans generally favor a conservative ideology. Liberals and conservatives disagree on many fundamental points, including causes of crime, crime control programs, and correctional strategies. Given their opposed ideological convictions, it is not surprising that politicians are often unable to agree on crime policy issues.

Ideological Triage

Gridlock does not always prevail. There are cases in which the two political parties agree. However, even when liberals and conservatives agree on a joint crime policy proposal, the proposal is not always in the best interest of society. At times, politicians practice something that can be thought of as **ideological triage.** *Triage* is a medical term referring to the practice of prioritizing patients on a "worst case first" basis—that is, the patient with the most serious health problems receives top consideration. Unfortunately, lawmakers occasionally practice a perverse form of public policy triage by agreeing to support the worst crime-related proposals. For example, partly galvanized by an exaggerated concern about drug offenses,

Prison chain gang labor was abandoned by most states in the 1930s because of public opposition. A recent resurgence of this type of prison labor has surfaced in many parts of the country where prisoners are routinely used to clean highways and maintain public areas.

both liberals and conservatives have united to support a general "get tough on crime" movement. Incarcerating more offenders for longer periods has become the dominant approach to crime. This strategy has been attacked as extremely costly without being particularly effective. For example, the shift to long, or life, sentences is inconsistent with the fact that most offenders mature out of criminal careers. Nevertheless, both liberals and conservatives want to be viewed as crime fighters and so the get-tough strategy is implemented.

Theme 7: Results of Criminal Justice "Toughness" Are Unclear

Many nations have responded to increasing crime rates with toughness. China, for instance, has initiated a program called "Strike Hard" to combat crime rates that have risen 10 percent annually over the past dozen years.[19] As the following indicates, Strike Hard measures are stark:

> **Trials are a bare formality, the verdict usually foreordained. Groups of convicted criminals are paraded before a "mass sentencing rally" in a public place. Then they are taken to a vacant field, where they kneel in neat rows and are shot in the head. Relatives often are required to pay for the bullets.[20]**

Toughness has also characterized America's response to crime. In fact, in terms of locking people up, no nation has been tougher than the United States over the past ten to fifteen years. America's prison population doubled between 1985 (502,507 inmates) and 1994 (1,053,738 inmates).[21] We have already dealt with the issue of increased incarceration in detail. Most relevant here is the bottom-line question of whether locking up more people for longer periods has yielded positive consequences. Proponents of tougher sentencing answer in the affirmative. They argue that, after a decade or more of get-tough policies, encouraging results are now evident. For instance, they point to the fact that police reports (UCR) of violent crime have decreased since 1992. Moreover, NCVS findings show that there were 1 million fewer violent crimes in the United States in 1995 than 1994.[22] Commenting on this decrease, President Bill Clinton stated: "I'm not declaring victory. . . . I'm just saying we're moving in the right direction and what we need to do is not abandon the present course, but to bear down and do more of it."[23] From this point of view, the overall answer to crime is to incarcerate more people for longer periods. Tough measures are showing positive results.

Critics of the get tough movement offer a completely different assessment. First, they contend that crime rate reductions are not as sizable as they should be. Despite a dramatic decrease in the number of people aged 15 to 30 (the crime-prone years) and an equally dramatic increase in the number of people incarcerated, the crime rate has not decreased proportionately since the introduction of get-tough policies. In fact, according to the federal government, violent crimes reported to the police increased 40 percent between 1985 and 1994.[24] Measuring crime, even interpersonal violent crime, is problematic, but, according to critics of get-tough measures, current findings do not indicate that increased incarceration has resulted in a major decrease in violent crime.

Second, critics of increased incarceration argue that the financial cost is excessive. Prison construction is expensive, as is general maintenance. Actual costs of incarceration vary greatly from state to state, but it is generally conceded that the sharp rise in the number of prison inmates has required significant increases in government expenditures.

A third problem identified by critics of get-tough policies is that the toughness strategy has frequently been misplaced. Despite calls for **selective incapacitation** (confining the most dangerous people), a majority of prison inmates are incarcerated for low-level stealing offenses, public-order infractions, or drug crimes. Violent offenders no longer make up a majority of prison inmates: "As a percentage of all State and Federal inmates, violent offenders fell from 57% in 1980 to 45% in 1993, . . ."[25] During the same period, drug offenders rose from 8 percent of total inmates in 1980 to 26 percent of total inmates in 1993.[26] Some criminologists question why many drug offenders are imprisoned at all, let alone kept in prison well beyond their crime-prone years. Even with nearly 2 million people locked up, many of the truly violent are not in jail or prison.

Finally, even if short-term trends become long-term patterns, critics of the get-tough movement reject the conclusion that more stern policies are necessarily the cause of recent crime reductions. They argue that crime is produced by a wide range of social and policy factors and that crime reduction is also a product of many factors.

Who is correct in this debate about increased incarceration, the proponents or the critics? Unfortunately, there are too many uncontrollable variables for social scientists to answer this question definitively at this time.

Gridlock is common to many social policy issues, including crime.

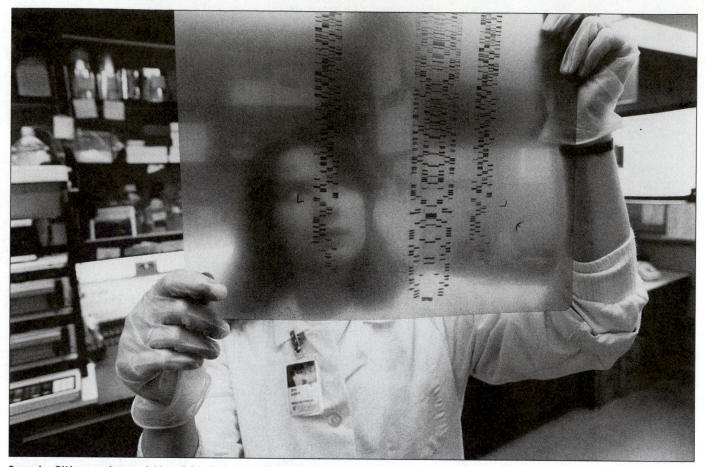

Some day DNA research may yield useful insights for understanding crime and criminals.

Theme 8: Future Crime Patterns in the United States

Americans appear willing to spend billions of dollars in the war on crime. Despite the amount of money spent on law enforcement, criminal prosecution, and prison construction and maintenance, government devotes comparatively little money to crime research. Alfred Blumstein, a national expert on crime and criminal justice, notes that $50 million is spent yearly on crime research, while dental research receives $165 million and $600 million is directed to mental health research.[27] Criminologists will require more research money in order to conduct the large-scale projects necessary to better understand present and future crime patterns.

Even with well-funded, first-rate research, crime in the United States is not likely to abate soon. Numerous social indicators suggest that conventional crime will increase in the decades ahead. These indicators include continued easy access to guns, media violence, illegal drug markets, family instability, gang warfare, racial/ethnic divisions, increasing wealth and income disparity, and more

frequent acts of terrorism. In addition, there is a demographic fact of extreme importance: The cohort of Americans aged 15 to 30 is now expanding, and evidence shows that members of this cohort have exceptionally high rates of violent crime participation.[28] As we move into the twenty-first century, interpersonal violent crime may become an even more acute social problem than it is now (Box 18.2).

Beyond all of the important social indicators just identified, there is also the phenomenon of **historical inertia.** Jeffrey Reiman maintains that there is no conspiracy to promote serious crime; rather, it continues as a result of historical inertia.[29] That is, the people who have the power to change existing social patterns are not motivated to do so, while those who are motivated to change current conditions are unable to do so. Hence, without effective intervention, the historical flow of social relations and social structural conditions will persist, and serious crime is likely to continue at high rates.

Of course, nothing in social life is absolutely certain. Dramatic social change is always possible. An example of this was the collapse of the Soviet Union in 1989. This de-

Juvenile Violence and Demography

Professor James Fox argues that there are currently two contradictory crime trends in the United States: The adult crime rate is declining, while the juvenile crime rate in increasing. The increase in juvenile violence has become pronounced For example, the overall murder rate between 1990 and 1994 showed a 4 percent reduction, but the murder rate during those same years rose 22 percent for teenagers aged 14 to 17. Most alarming to Fox and other criminologists is the fact that the teenage population has been declining. That pattern will reverse itself shortly. In the first decade of the next century, the teenage cohort is expected to increase 20 percent over present levels. We will see if social policies can effectively mitigate the predicted effects of demographics.

SOURCE: Roger Prybylski, "Breaking the Cycle of Juvenile Violence," *The Compiler* (Chicago: Illinois Criminal Justice Information Authority, 1997) 4–5.

velopment took social scientists by surprise. American society could likewise change in fundamental ways not currently foreseen by sociologists and criminologists. Consider these possibilities: (1) wealth and income will be redistributed more evenly in society; (2) the political focus in the United States will shift away from the individual or racial/ethnic categories to the community level; (3) an ethic of responsibility will displace the concept of individual rights and a culture of victimization as a guiding force in social life; and (4) the criminal justice system will be transformed from punitive to rehabilitative in nature. While most sociological and criminological indicators do not point in the direction of these changes, they are possible, and, if they occur, crime will likely be reduced significantly.

Critical Thinking Questions

1. Eight themes were identified and discussed in this chapter. Pick one with which you disagree. Give three detailed reasons for your disagreement.
2. What do you know now that you did not know before reading this book? Give at least five illustrations.
3. In your opinion, what is the most important question that criminologists have not yet been able to answer?

Notes

1 Kathleen Maguire and Ann Pastore, *Sourcebook of Criminal Justice Statistics, 1996* (Washington, DC: U.S. Government Printing Office, 1997) 380.
2 Ibid.
3 Michael Hindelang, "Sex Differences in Criminal Activity," *Social Problems 27* (1979) 143–56, 152.
4 Marianne Zawitz, "Violence Between Intimates," *Bureau of Justice Statistics Selected Findings, NCJ-149259* (Washington, DC: U.S. Government Printing Office, 1994).
5 Gresham Sykes and Francis T. Cullen, *Criminology,* 2nd ed. (New York: Harcourt Brace Jovanovich, 1992) 106–107.
6 Jeffrey Reiman, *The Rich Get Richer and the Poor Get Prison,* 4th ed. (Boston: Allyn & Bacon, 1995) 49–99.
7 Richard Schaefer, *Sociology,* 5th ed. (New York: McGraw-Hill, 1995) 319.
8 John Hagan, "Presidential Address: The Poverty of a Classless Criminology," *Criminology 30* (1992) 1–19.
9 Joseph Weis, "Social Class and Crime," in *Positive Criminology,* ed. Michael Gottfredson and Travis Hirschi (Beverly Hills, CA: Sage, 1987); Charles Tittle, Wayne Villemez, and Douglas Smith, "The Myth of Social Class and Criminality," *American Sociological Review 43* (1978) 643–56.
10 Reiman, *The Rich Get Richer and the Poor Get Prison,* 4th ed., 100–147.
11 Sykes and Cullen, *Criminology,* 2nd ed., 110; John Laub, "Data for Positive Criminology," in *Positive Criminology,* ed. Michael Gottfredson and Travis Hirschi (Beverly Hills, CA: Sage, 1987) 62; Michael Hindelang, "Race and Involvement in Common Law Personal Crimes," *American Sociological Review 43* (1978) 93–109.
12 William Julius Wilson, *The Truly Disadvantaged: The Inner City, the Underclass, and Public Policy* (Chicago: University of Chicago Press, 1987) 161.
13 Brendan Maguire, "Guilt Feelings and Crime," *Sociological Focus 21* (1988) 95–112; Brendan Maguire and Georgie Ann Weatherby, "Crime in and Beyond Weber's 'Iron Cage,'" *Michigan Sociological Review 9* (1995) 41–62.
14 *Uniform Crime Reports 1994,* 206.
15 Karin Swisher, *Domestic Violence* (San Diego: Greenhaven, 1996).
16 Mel Weith, "Elder Abuse: A National Tragedy," *FBI Law Enforcement Bulletin* (February 1994) 24–26.
17 Jeffrey Reiman, *The Rich Get Richer and the Poor Get Prison,* 4th ed., 8–9.
18 Meg Greenfield, "Habit-Forming Politics," *Newsweek,* 29 July 1996, 80.
19 George Wehrfritz, "Crime: 'You Die, I Live,'" *Newsweek,* 22 July 1996, 67.
20 Ibid.
21 Allen Beck and Darrell Gilliard, *Prisoners in 1994* (Washington, DC: U.S. Department of Justice, 1995) 1.
22 Brad Hahn, "Violent Crime Drops 9% in 1995," *Chicago Tribune,* 18 September 1996, 1-3.
23 Quoted in Hahn, 1996.
24 Howard Snyder, Melissa Sickmund, and Eileen Poe-Yamagata, *Juvenile Offenders and Victims: 1996 Update on Violence* (Washington, DC: Office of Juvenile Justice and Delinquency Prevention, 1996) 20.
25 Allen Beck and Darrell Gilliard, *Prisoners in 1994,* 10.
26 Ibid.
27 Quoted in Marie Simmetti Rosen, "LEN Interview: Prof. Alfred Blumstein," *Law Enforcement News XXI* (1995) 10–13, 13.
28 Alfred Blumstein, *Youth Violence, Guns, and Illicit Drug Markets* (Washington, DC: U.S. Department of Justice, 1996); Roger Przbylski, "With Higher Numbers of Children Entering Their Crime-Prone Years, More Needs To Be Done To Address Increasing Rates of Juvenile Violence," *The Compiler* (Summer 1996) 4–7.
29 Reiman, *The Rich Get Richer and the Poor Get Prison,* 4th ed., 148–71.

Photo Credits

Name Index

A

Abramaese, A., 316–317
Abrams, E., 107
Adams, B., 205–206
Adler, F., 249
Agnew, R., 255, 257
Akers, R., 257
Albanese, J., 99
Albert, M., 241–242
Albini, J., 149
Alpert, G., 270
Antonio, R., 230
Arnick, J., 293
Arthur, J., 253
Astone, N., 232–233
Austin, J., 336

B

Bakker, J., 102
Baldus, D., 300
Baldwin, L., 275
Ball, R., 36
Barber III, J., 293
Bass, R., 108
Bastian, L., 45, 47, 68, 120
Beccaria, C., 164, 165, 168, 170–171, 172–173, 174, 178, 187, 314, 319
Bechtel, H., 267
Beck, A., 51, 55, 116, 334, 341
Becker, G., 173–174
Becker, H., 23, 225, 226, 227
Bellah, R., 126
Bentham, J., 164, 165, 166, 168, 170–171, 172, 173, 174, 178, 187, 319
Bentham, S., 165
Berger, P., 4
Black, D., 303
Blasco, T., 165
Block, A., 149
Blumstein, A., 192, 366
Bohm, R., 246, 253
Bonger, W., 174, 246
Bowker, L., 317, 338
Braithwaite, J., 109, 232
Broli, L., 5
Bromley, M., 270
Brown, J., 297, 298
Brown, M., 189
Brownmiller, S., 73, 249
Burdine, C., 301
Burgess, E., 208
Burton, Jr., V., 231

Bush, G., 106
Butler, D., 177

C

Carling, J., 352
Casey, W., 106
Castillo, A., 104
Castro, F., 105
Ceretti, A., 5
Chaddock, G., 107
Chambliss, W., 24–25, 227, 250
Chesney-Lind, M., 249, 250
Chiricos, T., 248
Chodorow, N., 251
Christiansen, K., 193
Clark, J., 38–39, 336
Clarke, R., 176
Clear, T., 345
Clemmer, D., 337
Clinard, M., 252
Clinton, B., 364
Cloward, R., 255
Cohen, A., 255
Cohen, J., 192
Cohen, L., 214
Coleman, J., 174
Comte, A., 184
Cooney, M., 303
Copernicus, 184
Cornish, D., 176
Cottingham, E., 293
Cox, S., 270
Craytor, G., 293
Cressey, D., 149, 211, 212
Critchley, T., 264
Cuadrado, M., 276
Cullen, F., 193, 230, 231, 256
Cunanan, A., 13–14
Curran, D., 258
Currie, E., 39
Curry, G. D., 36

D

Dalton, K., 195
Daly, K., 249, 250
Darwin, C., 184
Davis, R., 78
DeBerry, Jr., M., 68, 120
Decker, S. H., 36
DeKeseredy, W., 255
Delone, M., 248
Dewey, J., 206

Dinh Diem, N., 105
Dinitz, S., 215–216
Dix, D., 347
Dixon, D., 95
Dolan, M., 293
Dole, E., 25
Donziger, S., 57
Dorsey, T., 120
Doyle, D., 231
Drummond, E., 19
Dugdale, R., 186
Dunaway, R., 231
Dunham, R., 270
Dunkley, M., 165
Dupont, J., 21
Durant, A., 167
Durant, W., 167
Durkheim, E., 17, 23, 48, 156, 208, 244, 328

E

Earls, F., 219
Eastwood, C., 160–161
Edgar, J., 117
Eitzen, D., 95
Elliott, M., 253
English, M., 108
Eppes, F., 293
Epstein, E., 189
Epstein, J., 101
Erikson, K., 225, 226, 227
Estrich, S., 72
Etzioni, A., 242
Evans, T., 231
Eysenck, H., 194

F

Fall, J., 108
Farrington, D., 192
Faulkner, W., 25
Fay, M., 210
Felson, M., 214, 215
Fermi, E., 186–187
Ferracuti, F., 218–219
Ferrero, W., 188
Ferri, E., 186–187, 188, 189–190
Figlio, R., 192
Finckenauer, J., 6
Fineman, H., 178
Fishman, G., 16
Fisse, B., 232
Fitch, J., 293
Fogelson, R., 267

Foster, J., 84
Foucault, M., 318
Fox, C., 166
Fox, J., 367
Franklin, B., 320
Freedman, E., 322
Freeman, L., 293
Freud, S., 143, 184, 197–199
Friedan, B., 242

G
Gacy, J., 183–184
Galileo, 184
Gall, F., 185
Gamage, J., 280
Garcia, M., 56
Garofalo, R., 186–187, 190–191
Garrison, B., 301
Garrison, J., 159
Gelles, R., 77
Gibbons, D., 6, 258
Gibbs, J., 175
Gideon, C., 305
Gilliard, D., 51, 55, 341
Gilligan, C., 128
Gilmore, G., 298
Glaser, D., 215, 216
Glueck, E., 191, 192
Glueck, S., 191, 192
Goldstein, H., 278
Gordon, D., 174–175, 246
Goring, C., 191
Gottfredson, M., 192, 199, 234, 235, 316
Gotti, J., 141
Green, D., 307
Greenberg, D., 176, 192
Greenfeld, L., 307, 327
Greenfield, M., 363
Greenwood, P., 316–317
Gregory, L., 177
Griffin, S., 249
Guerry, A., 185–186
Gusfield, J., 23

H
Hackett, G., 213
Hammett, T., 101
Harper, W., 206
Harring, S., 267
Haviland, J., 320
Hay, D., 319
Helmsley, L., 99
Henry, D., 336
Herrera, L., 297–298
Herrnstein, R., 192, 193
Hinderliter, R., 25
Hing-Yan Wong, Simon, 189
Hinrichs, D., 305
Hirschi, T., 192, 199, 228–229, 231, 234, 235, 316
Hooton, E., 191
Hoover, J., 268
Horowitz, I., 243–244
Howard, J., 320

I
Inwald, R., 273
Irwin, J., 337

J
Jacobs, J., 23, 323–324
Jeffery, C., 192
Jenkins, P., 149
Jesilow, P., 279
Johnson, H., 104
Johnson, L., 159
Johnson, R., 321, 323, 326
Jones, S., 265

K
Kaczynski, T., 47, 51
Kant, I., 314
Kappeler, V., 60
Katz, J., 250
Kelling, G., 271, 274
Kennedy, E., 291
Kennedy, J., 159
Kenney, D., 273
Kent, L., 231
Keough, L., 293
Kercher, K., 316
Khomeini, Ayatollah, 179
Killias, M., 57
King, Jr., M., 105–106, 242
King, R., 278
Kitsuse, J., 225, 226, 227
Kleck, G., 82
Knowles, J., 227
Kocieniewski, D., 293
Koss, M., 74
Kretschmer, E., 191
Kruttschnitt, C., 307

L
Land, K., 192
Lane, R., 267
Langan, P., 297, 298
Lawson, J., 99
LeBeau, J., 216
Lemert, E., 225, 226, 227, 230, 252
Letterman, D., 84
Levin, J., 280
Levin, Y., 190
Levy, S., 215
Liddle, M., 252
Liebeck, S., 305
Lindesmith, A., 190
Lindgren, S., 333
Liu, W., 236
Livingston, J., 15
Locke, J., 164, 165
Lombroso, C., 184, 185, 186, 188, 190, 191
Lundman, R., 267

M
MacKinnon, C., 140, 249, 254
Madison, J., 165
Maestro, M., 165
Maguire, B., 25, 267, 272
Maguire, K., 46, 51, 55, 67, 68, 70, 72, 82, 273, 307, 325, 327, 333, 350
Manning, P., 276–277
Manzie, S., 215
Marvell, T., 295
Marx, K., 48, 156, 185, 252
Mathers, R., 25
Matthews, R., 255

Matza, D., 219
McFarlane, R., 106
McKay, H., 208–211, 213–214, 216–217
McKillop, P., 213
McLanahan, S., 232–233
McNaughton, D., 19
Mearday, J., 263–264, 270
Mednick, S., 192
Meredith, J., 242
Merton, R., 127, 244–246, 251, 252, 256–257
Mesch, G., 16
Messerschmidt, J., 249–250, 254–255
Messner, S., 126–127, 128, 129
Michalowski, R., 15, 21–22, 248, 253
Milken, M., 175
Miller, J., 231
Millet, K., 145
Mills, C., 158, 243
Minor-Harper, S., 307
Mock, R., 301
Monahan, H., 293
Monkkonen, E., 267
Mooar, B., 293
Moody, C., 295
Moore, J., 280
Moore, T., 17
Moran, B., 77
Moran, R., 19
Morgan, F., 206
Morison, K., 273
Moynihan, D., 232, 234
Mumola, C., 116
Murray, C., 193
Myers, W., 151

N
Nader, R., 98
Nagin, D., 192
Natarajan, M., 276
Newton, 184
Nixon, R., 127
Nye, F. I., 37–38, 228, 229

O
Ohlin, L., 255
Olson, F., 105
O'Neal, S., 227
Owens, M., 27, 265

P
Paolucci, H., 165
Park, R., 206–207, 208
Parker, K., 16
Parsons, T., 158, 250
Pastore, A., 46, 51, 55, 67, 68, 70, 72, 82, 273, 307, 325, 327, 333, 350
Pedersen, D., 271
Peel, R., 19, 266
Peeler, C., 301
Pepinsky, H., 256
Petersilia, J., 175–176
Phillips, D., 85
Pierce, C., 206
Platt, T., 248
Poindexter, J., 106
Pollak, O., 251
Popper, K., 157
Potter, G., 149

Pratt, J., 265
Prybylski, R., 367

Q

Quadagno, J., 230
Quetelet, A., 185–186
Quinney, R., 246, 247, 252, 256

R

Radosh, P., 249, 250
Ragen, J., 323–324
Ramken, G., 117
Ray, A., 177
Ray, I., 186
Ray, M., 16
Reagan, R., 98, 106, 107, 178
Reaves, B., 269, 276
Reckless, W., 215–216, 228
Reibstein, L., 271
Reiman, J., 16, 44, 247, 248, 286, 316, 362, 366
Reiss, A., 219
Renda, M., 95
Renzetti, C., 258
Richardson, J., 267
Ritzer, G., 23
Robinson, J., 120
Rockefeller, J., 206, 207
Rockefeller, Sen. J., 232
Rodriguez, M., 279
Roosevelt, T., 268
Rosenfeld, R., 126–127, 128, 129
Rosenhan, D., 228
Roshier, B., 14
Ross, E., 301
Rousseau, J., 164, 165
Rowe, A., 176
Ruddick, S., 251
Rush, B., 320

S

Sackett,, 293
Sagarin, E., 196
Salinas y Gortari, C., 107
Sampson, R., 232, 233
Schaeffer, R., 84
Schafran, L., 294
Schneider, R., 105
Schwartz, M., 255
Schwendinger, H., 20–21, 248, 249
Schwendinger, J., 20–21, 248, 249

Sellin, T., 192, 300
Serpico, F., 277–278
Shaw, C., 207, 208–211, 213–214, 216–217
Sheldon, W., 191
Shields, J., 193
Short, J. F., 37–38
Simmons, S., 215
Simon, D., 95, 96
Simon, R., 249
Simpson, O., 77
Sinclair, U., 143
Situ, Y., 236
Skinner, B.F., 211–212
Small, A., 206, 208
Smith, D., 149
Smith, P., 254, 276
Snell, T., 298, 334
Sobal, J., 305
Speck, R., 193–194
Spitzer, S, 248
Stark, R., 231
Stebbins Wells, A., 275, 276
Steffensmeir, D., 99, 124
Steinmetz, S., 81
Stephens, G., 275
Stephenson, J., 254
Stewart, P., 141
Stone, O., 159
Straus, M., 77
Streifel, C., 99, 124
Sutherland, E., 5, 20, 92, 211, 213–214, 217
Sutton, W., 163–164
Sykes, G., 219, 337

T

Tannebaum, F., 225
Tarde, G., 212
Taylor, B., 37, 45, 47, 78
Terry, C., 270
Thomas, A., 280
Thompkins, W., 280
Tifft, L., 38–39
Tindal, N., 19
Tittle, C., 176
Topinard, P., 4
Trujillo, R., 105
Tuchman, G., 249

U

Uchtenhagen, A., 57

V

Valachi, J., 150
Van Den Berghe, P., 192
Verri, A., 165
Verri, P., 165
Versace, G., 14
Volavka, J., 192
Vollmer, A., 267
Voltaire, 164

W

Wade, J., 270
Walker, D., 273
Walker, L., 80
Walker, S., 137, 265–266
Wallace, A., 305
Wallerstein, J., 37
Ward, R., 324
Warr, M., 16
Weber, M., 156
Weitz, S., 250
Welch, R., 322
Wells, A., 275, 276
Werner, E., 215
White, D., 196
Whitman, C., 194
Whyte, W., 40
Wickersham, G., 277
Wilbanks, W., 118, 306
Williams, D., 223–224
Williams, J., 113
Williams, N., 223–224, 230
Williams, S., 113
Wilson, E., 192
Wilson, J., 192, 193, 271, 274
Wilson, O., 267
Wilson, W., 247
Wolfgang, M., 192, 218–219
Wright, J., 230
Wyle, C., 37

Y

Young, T., 248, 253–254, 256, 258

Z

Zimring, F., 5

Subject Index

A

Abortion, 144
About this book, 7–9
Absence of capable guardians, 214–215
Accused, The, 84
Achievements, 255
Acquaintance rape, 74
Acquittals, 52, 289
Action as amoral, 226–227
Adequacy
  of classical theory of criminology, 177–178
  of internal sources of crime, 200
  of labeling and social control theories, 234–235
  of social ecology and differential association theories, 216
  of theories of macro social causes of crime, 256–257
Administrative law, 287
Administrative sentencing, 295
Adoption studies, 193
African Americans. *See also* Race
  attitudes toward police, 279
  Civil Rights Movement, 242
  demographic patterns for homicide and, 70
  disruption of families and crime, 232
  environmental racism and, 103–104
  family structure of, 232
  first marshal in U.S., 265
  percentage of officers, 273
  policing and race, 279, 280
  race and property crimes, 118
  rate of incarceration for, 306
  rates of victimization for violent offenses, 48, 67
  recruitment as police officers, 272–273
  Tuskegee experiment, 105
  victimization rates for property crimes, 119
Against Our Will (Brownmiller), 73
Age
  arrests for public order crimes by, 136
  elder abuse, 81
  geriatric issues for prisons, 348–349
  property crimes and, 118, 119
  of victims of property crimes, 119
Agency
  differences between classicism and positivism, 187
  individual's responsibility for, 172, 173
  for labeling and social control theories, 230–231
  in macro social causes of crime, 251–252
  positivism and, 190

  problem of, 172
  in social ecology and differential association, 213–214
  society's responsibility for, 172
  theories of crime and, 158–159
Aggravated assault, 75
Aggregate statistics, 31
Aggressive behavior
  as learned, 218
  low blood sugar and low cholesterol, 196
  testosterone levels and, 194–195
AIDS
  prices for treatment of, 101
  in prisons, 346–347
America's Dumbest Criminals (Butler, Gregory, and Ray), 177
Amorality, 228–229
Analogous forms of social injury, 21–22
Anomie, 244
Anti-smoking groups, 24
Anti-stalking laws, 84
Anti-War Movement, 242–243
Appellate courts, 289
Arrests
  crimes cleared by, 51
  demographic percentages for, 71
  domestic violence and patterns of, 78–79
  myth of criminals who go to trial "get off," 52–53
  for property crimes, 118, 119, 124
  for public order crimes, 135, 136
  punishment after, 52–53
Arson, 115, 122–123
Aspirations, 255
Assault and battery, 74–76
  defined, 74–75
  hate crimes, 75–76
  myths and facts about domestic battery, 79
  patterns of, 75
Assessing criminal justice programs, 5–6
Assignments and situations for police, 274
Atavists, 188
Attachment, 229
Attitudes
  toward child abuse, 80
  toward controlling media violence, 83–85
  toward gun control, 82, 83
Auburn System, 320–321, 322, 343
Autonomic nervous system deficiency, 194

B

Battered woman syndrome defense, 79–80
Beat integrity, 273–274

Behavior freely chosen, 168–169
Beliefs. *See also* Myths
  crime versus criminology, 4
  debunking crime myths, 4–5, 43–62
  in value system, 229
Bell Curve, The (Herrnstein and Murray), 193
Benefits of crime, 48–49
B-girls, 143
Big House prisons and violence, 323–324
Biological factors and crime, 194–197. *See also* Brain
  autonomic nervous system deficiency, 194
  brain dysfunctions, 194
  dietary conditions, 195–196
  genetic influences on crime, 191–194
  hypoglycemia and criminal behavior, 196
  identification of criminals by physical features, 189–190
  low blood sugar and low cholesterol, 196
  phrenology, 185
  physical stigmata, 189
  radical feminist criminology, 249
  sex hormones, 194–195
Blacks. *See* African Americans
Blaming victims of domestic violence, 77–78
Bobbies, 266
Body type and crime, 191–192
Boot camps, 334, 341–342
Bootleggers, 142
Born criminals, 188
Brain
  dysfunctions of, 194
  IQ and crime, 193
  phrenology research, 185
  post-mortem exams of, 183–184
Bribery, 102, 278
  international efforts to stop, 107
"Broken Windows: Police and Neighborhood Safety" (Wilson and Kelling), 271
Broken windows, 271
Bundeskriminalamt, 39, 125
Bureaucratic and clerical duties of police, 270, 277
Burglary, 121–122
  defined, 115
  property crime and, 121–122
Business ethics and elite crime, 104

C

California "Three Strikes" laws, 336
Call girls, 143
Campus police, 269–270
Caning, 210

Capacity of prisons, 352
Capitalism
    corporate crime and, 247
    as crime producer, 246
    crimes of control and, 246
    crimes of economic domination and, 246
    crimes of government and, 246
    crimes of resistance and, 247
    Gordon's critique of crime and, 174–175
    instrumentalist theory of capitalist rule, 247
    predatory crimes and, 246–247
    state-defined crime and controls, 247–248
Capital offenses, 297
Career criminals, 114, 192
Carnival mirror image, 16
Cartography, 185
Causal relationships and theories of crime, 160
Caveats, 159
Central Intelligence Agency (CIA)
    corruption and drug crime, 139
    governmental crime and, 105–107
    pressures to reform, 108
Chain gang labor, 364
Chicago school of sociology, 206–208
    appreciation of Durkheim's theories, 208
    influence of Progressive Era on sociological
        discipline, 208
    searching for root causes, 208
Chicago Tribune crime coverage, 15
Child abuse, 80–81
    attitudes toward, 80
    intergenerational patterns of, 80
    trends in, 80–81
Child pornography, 141
Children and effects of media violence, 83
China. See People's Republic of China
Choice structuring, 176
CIA. See Central Intelligence Agency
Cities. See also Neighborhoods
    community policing, 273–275
    concentric zone model of, 209
    crime control in, 271
    as natural areas, 208–209
    neighborhoods and delinquency rates,
        209–210
Civil courts, 289
Civil Rights Movement, 242
Class distinctions. See also White-collar crime
    crime crosscutting race and, 360–361
    myth of crime as lower class phenomenon,
        47–48
    in property crimes, 126
Classical criminology, 163–181
    adequacy of, 177–178
    Beccaria as reformer and celebrity, 165
    Becker's economic model of crime, 173–174
    Bentham's influence on, 166
    classical theories of criminal justice, 170–171
    comprehensive nature of, 178
    core propositions of, 168–171
    current appeal of, 178–179
    intellectual climate during development of,
        164–166
    origins of, 164
    policy implications of, 172–173
    versus positivism, 186–187
Clearance rates, 33, 51–52, 361
Cocaine
    history of use, 143

    smuggling in, 140
    trends in use of, 138
Co-corrections, 342–343
Cognitive social learning, 212
Commitment, 229
Common law, 289
Community corrections, 344–346
    as alternative to prison, 344–346
    costs of, 346
    overview of, 344
    types of, 345
Community policing, 273–275
Community service, 271, 345
Competitive crime, 215
Compiler, The (Illinois Criminal Justice
        Information Authority), 39
Complainant, 135
Comprehensive nature
    of classical criminology, 178
    of internal sources of crime, 200
    of labeling and social control theories, 235
    of social ecology and differential association
        theories, 216–218
    of theories of macro social causes, 257
Computer crimes, 125
Concentric zone model, 209
Conflict theory of law creation, 24–25
Conformity, 245
Consensus theory of law creation, 23
Conservative strategies for property crime, 128
Constable, 264
Constitutional law, 288–289
Contractual services, 270
Controlling property crimes, 128–129
Convictions, 289
Core propositions
    of classical criminology, 168–171
    of early positivism, 186–190
    of micro social causes of crime, 208–213
    Mills' theory of, 158
    of social ecology and differential association,
        208–213
Corporate crime
    business ethics and elite crime, 104
    corporate accountability and, 109
    corporate deviance and, 101–102
    corporate dumping, 102–103
    dangers from faulty products and working
        conditions, 96–97
    as elite crime, 92–93, 94–95
    Marxist theory of crime and, 247
    price gouging, 101, 102, 104
    weighing profit versus harm, 97
Correctional officers, 349–351
    by race, gender, and type of institution, 350
    job satisfaction, 349, 350
    salaries for, 350
    sexual harassment of inmates by, 351
    women as, 350–351
Corrections, 313–329. See also Prisons
    co-corrections, 342–343
    costs of, 332–334
    deterrence, 314–315
    history of, 317–324
    incapacitation, 316–317
    modern era of, 324–328
    prison litigation, 325
    private, 342
    professional administration, 325

    rehabilitation, 315–316
    retribution, 314
    shift to custody and control, 325–327
    theories of punishment, 314–317
    upward trends in incarceration, 327–328
    for women, 322, 326–327
Corruption
    and drug crimes, 139
    gratuities and police, 278
Costs
    of community corrections, 346
    of corrections, 332–334
    of courts, 286
    of elite crime, 95–96
    of index crimes, 95
    of police, 267–268
    of prisons, 332–334
    of property crimes, 116–117
    of public order crimes, 135–136
    salaries for correctional officers, 350
    of violent crimes, 68
    weighing profit versus harm, 97
    of white-collar crime, 95
County police, 269
Courts, 285–310. See also Sentencing
    for administrative law, 287
    civil, 289
    constitutional law, 288–289
    contemporary issues for, 286
    costs of, 286
    criminal, 288, 289
    death penalty, 297–302
    federal, 290–291
    frivolous litigation in, 304–305, 325
    gender disparity in sentencing, 306–307
    issues and trends for, 291–302
    judges for, 291–294
    for judicial law, 287
    for legislative law, 287
    with limited jurisdictions, 290
    overloading of, 302–304
    prisoner's lawsuits, 305, 325
    for procedural law, 287–288
    racial disparity in sentencing, 305–306
    sentencing, 294–296
    state, 290
    trial and appellate, 289
    types of, 287–291
Credit card fraud, 124
Crime: Its Causes and Remedies (Lombroso), 188
Crime. See also Myths
    beliefs about, 4–5
    biological factors associated with, 194–197
    capitalism as producer of, 246
    of control, 246
    criminal behavior as learned, 211–212
    crosscutting class and race, 360–361
    as disproportionately male enterprise, 360
    of economic domination, 246
    economic model of, 173–174
    effects of environment on childhood and, 57
    Freudian interpretations of, 197–199
    future patterns of in U.S., 366–367
    Gordon's critique of capitalism and, 174–175
    of government, 246
    guilt as insufficient deterrent to, 361
    harms-based definition of, 20–23
    as individually chosen and structurally
        determined, 362

Crime (continued)
    labeling definition of, 18, 20, 22–23
    legalistic definition of, 17–18, 22–23
    measures for reducing, 59–60
    myth of getting tough with, 56–58
    myth of increasing, 45–46
    naturalistic definition of, 187
    as normal behavior, 210–211
    as outgrowth of routine activities, 214–215
    personal, 247
    produced by macro social forces, 246
    reducing drug-related, 57
    of resistance, 247
    socially determined, 213
    as social process, 224–225
    as social reaction to behavior, 224–225
    strengths and weaknesses of definitions, 22–23
    in Tanzania, 253
    techniques and rationalizations for, 212
    unrecognized, 361–362
Crime and Human Nature (Wilson and Herrnstein), 192
Crime and the American Dream (Messner and Rosenfeld), 126–127
Crime displacement, 176–177
Crime index, defined, 32
Crime in the United States (FBI), 30–35
Crime problem, 15–16
Crime rates
    additional sources of crime data, 39–40
    comparing American and German crime, 39
    defined, 30
    estimating scope of gang crime, 36
    example of statistics in Uniform Crime Reports, 35
    history of crime reporting, 30–31
    myth of increasing crime, 45–46
    myths of crime cannot be reduced, 59–60
    for violent crimes, 69
Crimes cleared, myths about, 51–52
Criminal anthropology, 188
Criminal behavior
    action as amoral, 226–227
    cognitive social learning and, 212
    differential identification theory of, 215–216
    hypoglycemia and, 196
    identity maintenance and, 215–216
    imitation and, 212
    as learned, 211–212
    religion and, 231
    sexual identification and, 198–199
    significant others and encouragement for, 212
    techniques and rationalizations for, 212
Criminal courts
    function of, 289
    key roles in criminal trials, 288
Criminal intent, 69
    determining for elite crime, 97
Criminality and Economic Conditions (Bonger), 246
Criminal justice
    eighteenth-century, 166–168
    in Iran, 179
    laws shape behavior, 170
    punishment as deterrent, 170–171
    social justice preceding, 248–249
Criminals. *See* Offenders
Criminal sexual assault laws, defined, 71

Criminology, 3–9, 163–181, 359–367. *See also* Nineteenth century criminology
    adequacy of classical theory of, 177–178
    assessing criminal justice programs, 5–6
    Beccaria as reformer and celebrity, 165
    Becker's economic model of crime, 173–174
    beliefs about crime versus, 4
    Bentham's influence on, 166
    classical theories of criminal justice, 170–171
    comprehensive nature of classical, 178
    core propositions of classical, 168–171
    crime as disproportionately male enterprise, 360
    crime as individually chosen and structurally determined, 362
    crime crosscuts class and race, 360–361
    current appeal of classical, 178–179
    debunking crime myths with, 4–5
    deterrence theory, 175–176
    developing policies on crime, 5
    eighteenth-century criminal justice, 166–168
    evaluation research and, 5–6
    future crime patterns in U.S., 366–367
    Gordon's critique of crime and capitalism, 174–175
    guilt as insufficient deterrent to crime, 361
    ideology as handicap to crime policies, 362–363
    individual responsibility for agency, 172, 173
    intellectual climate during development of, 164–166
    juvenile violence and demography, 367
    limitations of, 6–7
    in 19th century, 185–186
    origins of, 4
    origins of classical, 164
    policy implications of classical, 172–173
    rational choice theory, 176–177
    social responsibility for agency, 172
    some crimes not recognized, 361–362
    unclear outcomes of get-tough policies, 364–365
Criticisms
    of National Crime Victimization Survey, 35–37
    of Uniform Crime Reports (UCR), 34–35
Critiques
    of classical criminology, 177–179
    of positivism, 200
    of theories of crime, 159
Cuban boat people, 363
Cultural goals and social structural means, 244
Culture of prisons, 337–338
Current appeal
    of classical criminology, 178–179
    of internal sources of crime, 200
    of labeling and social control theories, 236
    of social ecology and differential association, 218–219
    of theories of macro social causes, 257–258

D

Dangerous class, 266–267
Dangers from faulty products and working conditions, 96–97
Darwinism. *See* Evolutionary theories
Date rape, defined, 74
Deadly force, 278
Death penalty

appellate review of, 299
costs of, 301–302
as Garofalo's total elimination policy, 191
for juveniles, 299
lethal injection, 302
morality and, 299–300
racial and social class discrimination, 300–301
statistics on, 298
Supreme Court rulings on, 297–298
Decriminalization of public order crimes, 146–147
Defense attorneys
    in death penalty cases, 300, 301
    role of in criminal trial, 288
Definite sentences, 295
Definition of a situation, 362
Definitions favorable for law violation, 212
Definitions of crime, 13–27
    actual conditions contributing to law creation, 25
    conflict theory, 24–25
    consensus theory, 23
    crime problem versus problem of crime, 15–16
    fear of crime in Israel, 16
    harms-based, 20–23
    labeling, 18, 20, 22–23
    legalistic, 17–18, 22–23
    media's role in perception of crime, 14–15
    models of law creation, 23–25
    moral entrepreneurship, 23–24
    strengths and weaknesses of, 22–23
    typical criminal, 16–17
De-institutionalization, 231, 348
Delinquency
    neighborhoods and rates of, 209–210
    as prior condition for drug addiction, 57
Demographic patterns
    in crime, 8
    for homicide, 70–71
    for property crimes, 119
    for rape, 74
    total arrests for property crimes, 118
Demographics, juvenile violence and, 367
Department of Justice, *Sourcebook of Criminal Justice Statistics,* 39
Deprivation model, 337
Descent of Man (Darwin), 185
Design capacity, 352
Detection of forgery, fraud, and embezzlement, 124–125
Determinate sentencing, 295–296
Deterrence, 175–176, 314–315
    general, 175, 294
    guilt as insufficient, 361
    optimal conditions for, 315
    punishment as deterrent, 170–171
    rates of recidivism and, 175
    specific, 175, 294
    as strategy for sentencing, 294
    types of, 315
Deviance
    as collective phenomenon, 255
    corporate, 101–102
    economic strain and, 255
    elite, 100–101
    etiology of, 225–226
    labeling theory and focus on causes of, 225–228

Differential association, 211–213. *See also* Micro social causes of crime; Social ecology
  adequacy of theory, 216
  agency as perceived in, 213–214
  communication within intimate personal groups, 212
  comprehensive nature of, 216–218
  crime as outgrowth of routine activities, 214–215
  criminal behavior as learned, 211–212
  current appeal of, 218–219
  defined, 208
  definitions favorable for law violation, 212
  example of, 213
  hot weather and domestic disputes, 216
  Internet as crime zone, 215
  Sutherland's development of theory, 211, 217–218
  techniques and rationalizations for criminal behavior, 212
  unfavorable definition of legal code, 212
  variations in, 212–213
Differential identification theory, 215–216
Direct instruction and criminal behavior, 211
Disintegrative shaming, 232
Dismissal, defined, 52
Diversion, 231, 345
Diversity and police recruitment, 272–273
Division of Labor in Society, The (Durkheim), 244
Domestic violence, 77–81. *See also* Child abuse
  arrest patterns and, 78–79
  battered woman syndrome defense, 79–80
  blaming victims of, 77–78
  elder abuse, 81
  mandatory reporting laws for, 78, 79
  overview, 77
  patterns of abuse, 80
  patterns of intimate murder, 78
  patterns of victimization, 77
Double failures, 255
Double standards of justice with elite crime, 94
Drug crimes. *See also specific drugs listed by name*
  corruption and, 139
  delinquency as prior condition for drug addiction, 57
  eradication of drug supplies, 137
  history of drug use in U. S., 143
  illegal drugs, 143–144
  interdiction of drug supplies, 137
  myth of drugs causing crime, 58–59
  offenders and, 137–138
  race and sentencing for, 306
  reducing, 57
  Swiss approach to prevention of addiction, 57
  trafficking drugs from Columbia, 140
  trends in drug use, 138
  victimization and, 139
Drug trafficking and organized crime, 149
Drunk Driving (Jacobs), 23
Drunk driving victims, 139

E

Early positivism, 186–190
Early release, 352–353
Economic benefits of crime, 48
Ectomorphs, 191
Educational programs and enrollments in prisons, 335

Ego
  defined, 197
  imbalance with id and superego, 198
Egoistic personality, 246
Eighteenth-century criminology, 166–168
Elder abuse, 81
Electronic monitoring, 344, 345
Elite crime, 91–111
  business ethics and, 104
  corporate accountability, 109
  as corporate and organizational crime, 92–93
  corporate deviance and, 101–102
  corporate dumping, 102–103
  dangers from faulty products and working conditions, 96–97
  determining criminal intent for, 97
  double standards of justice with, 94
  effects of, 94–95
  elite deviance, 100–101
  enforcing, 107–109
  environmental racism, 103–104
  environmental regulation and environmental crime, 101
  financial costs of, 95–96
  as governmental crime, 93, 105–107
  government support and subsidies to wealthy, 100
  offenders of, 99
  overview, 91–92, 110
  price gouging, 101, 102, 104
  sentencing trends for, 98
  social and economic contributors to, 98
  social harm as crime, 98–99
  trial and punishment for, 97–98
  victims of, 99–100
  weighing profit versus harm, 97
  as white-collar or occupational crime, 92
Elite deviance, 100–101
Elmira Reformatory, 321
Embezzlement, 99, 124–125
Endomorphs, 191
Enforced reparation, 191
Enforcing elite crime, 107–109
English policing, 264–265, 266
Environmental crime, 101
  environmental racism, 103–104
  environmental regulation and, 101
  Exxon *Valdex* oil spill, 108
  pollution and corporate crime, 96–97
Eradication of drug supplies, 137
Ethics of care and justice, 128
Etiology, 226
Evolutionary theories
  influence on 19th century criminology, 185
  influence on positivism, 184
  social ecologists and adaptation of, 208–209
Exclusionary rule, 52, 278
Expectations, 255
Experiments on U. S. citizens, 105
Exploitative crime, 215
Extent
  of property crimes, 116
  of public order crimes, 135–136
External social controls, 229
Exxon *Valdex* oil spill, 108

F

False consciousness, 248
False reports of rape, 74

Falsifiability of crime theories, 157–158
Family structure, 232–234
Family violence. *See* Domestic violence
FBI. *See* Federal Bureau of Investigation
Fear of crime in Israel, 16
Federal agencies employing police, 269
Federal Bureau of Investigation (FBI). *See also* Uniform Crime Reports (UCR)
  defining property crime, 115
  as federal police, 268
  harassment of Martin Luther King, Jr., 105–106
  Uniform Crime Reports, 31–35
Federal Bureau of Narcotics, 143–144
Federal courts, 289, 290–291
Federal police. *See* Federal Bureau of Investigation
Federal regulatory agencies
  enforcement laws, 107–108
  progress in enforcing laws, 108–109
  reforming the CIA, 108
Felicity calculus, 170, 171
Felonies
  defined, 18
  sentencing statistics for, 297–298
Felony-murder doctrine, 69
Female Offender, The (Lombroso and Ferrero), 188
Feminine Mystique, The (Friedan), 242
Feminist theory of crime, 249–251
  adequacy of, 257
  agency and, 252
  comprehensive nature of, 257
  current appeal of, 257–258
  gender-sensitive explanations required, 250–251
  including women in theories, 250
  liberal feminist criminology, 249
  Marxist feminist criminology, 249
  peacemaking criminology and, 256
  policy implications for, 254–255
  radical feminist criminology, 249
  socialist feminist criminology, 249–250
  society shaped by patriarchal relations, 250
  summary of, 251
  unfair treatment of women in justice system, 251
Feminization of poverty, 340
Fencing merchandise, 114
Fines, 345
Firestone case, 96
Fixed sentences, 173
Flat sentences, 295
Ford Pinto case, 96
Forgery, fraud, and embezzlement, 124–125
Forms of elimination, 191
"Four Noble Truths" of Guatama Buddha, 256
France, historical criminal procedure in, 318
Frankpledge system, 264
Fraud, 124–125
  gender and, 99
Free agents, 165, 187
Free will, 18
Freudian interpretations of crime, 197–199
  as explanation for crime, 197–199
  overview, 197, 199
  personality development, 197
  unconscious drives and behavior, 197
Frivolous litigation in courts, 304–305, 325

Functions of police, 270–272
Furman v. Georgia, 300

G

Gambling, 144, 149
Gangs, 36, 338
Gay rights, 242
Gender. *See also* Feminist theory of crime
  of correctional officers, 350
  disparity in sentencing by, 306–307
  feminist theory of crime and influence of,
    249–251
  forgery, fraud, and embezzlement and, 124
  moral orientation and, 128
  property crimes and, 118, 127
  prostitution and, 137
  public order crimes and, 136
  rates of incarceration by race and, 334
  sexism in courts, 291–294
  sexual harassment of inmates by correctional
    officers, 351
General deterrence, 175, 294
General strain theory, 255, 257
General Theory of Crime, A (Gottfredson and
  Hirschi), 234
Genetic influences on crime, 191–194
  adoption studies, 193
  body type theories, 191–192
  crime and human nature, 192–193
  XYY theory and, 193–194
Geriatric issues for prisons, 348–349
Germany
  recidivism in, 58
  theft in, 125
"Get tough" policies
  myth of, 56–58
  "Three Strikes" laws in California, 336
  unclear outcomes of, 364–365
Ghetto crime, 174
Good faith efforts of police, 53
Good-time policies, 295, 332, 335, 353
Governmental commissions on organized crime,
  150
Governmental crime. *See also* Central
    Intelligence Agency; Federal Bureau of
    Investigation
  assassination attempts, 105
  covert experiments on U. S. citizens, 105
  as elite crime, 93, 105–107
  government support and subsidies to wealthy,
    100
  Iran Contra affair, 106–107
  savings and loan scandals, 107–108
Gratuities and police corruption, 278
Greatest happiness principle, 170
Gregg v. Georgia, 299
Guilt as insufficient deterrent to crime, 361
Guilty but mentally ill (GBMI) test, 18
Guns
  attitudes toward gun control, 82, 83
  violent crimes and, 53–54, 82–83

H

Habits of the Heart (Bellah et al.), 126
Hackers, 125
Halfway houses, 345
Handgun Violence Prevention Act of 1994, 82
Harms-based definition of crime, 20–22, 254

Hate crimes, 75–76
Heroin
  history of use of, 143
  smuggling in, 140
  users and costs of, 138
Hidden crime, 99–100
Highway patrol, 268
Hispanics. *See also* Race
  as offenders of public order crimes, 137
  police recruitment and, 273
Historical inertia, 366
History of corrections, 317–324. *See also*
    Nineteenth-century criminology
  Big House prisons and violence, 323–324
  French policies before revolution of 1789, 318
  modern era, 324–328
  nineteenth-century American punishment,
    319–321
  nineteenth-century imprisonment of women,
    322
  punishments before Industrial Revolution,
    317–319
  twentieth-century corrections, 321–324
History of crime reporting, 30–31
History of policing, 264–267
  in colonial America, 265–266
  early English society, 264–265
  expansion of American police in mid-
    nineteenth century, 266–267
  London constabulary, 266
  reforms of 1920s to 1940s, 167
  significant events in American policing, 265
Homicide, 69–71
  defined, 69
  demographic patterns for, 70–71
  felony-murder doctrine, 69
  misdemeanor-manslaughter doctrine, 69–70
  patterns of, 303
  patterns of intimate murder, 78
  rates of, 70
  trends in murder rates, 70
Homosexuality
  civil rights and, 242
  in prisons, 337
House arrest, 344, 345
Hue and cry, 264
Human ecology, 206
Human nature and crime, 192–193
Human rights
  analogous forms of social injury and, 21–22
  crimes as violation of, 20–21
Hung jury, 52
Hypoglycemia and criminal behavior, 196

I

Id
  defined, 197
  imbalance with ego and superego, 198
  as inducement to commit crime, 228
Ideal type, 157
Identification
  by physical features, 189–190
  differential, 215–216
  sexual, 198–199
Identity maintenance, 215–216
Ideological triage, 363
Ideology, 248, 362–363
  Cuban boat people and, 363

  defined, 362
  defining serious crime and, 362–363
  ideological triage, 363
  political gridlock on, 363, 365
Illegal drugs, 143–144
Illinois Criminal Justice Information Authority, 39
Imitation of criminal behavior, 212
Importation model, 337
Incapacitation, 294, 316–317, 365
Incarcerated mothers, 340
Incarceration. *See* Prisons
Indeterminate sentencing, 295
Index crimes
  age of offenders for property crimes, 119
  average losses from, 95
  defined, 32
  determining "serious crime," 362–363
  elite crime versus, 94
  felony sentences imposed for, 297–298
  gender and property crimes, 118, 127
  myth of crime as lower class and, 47
  property crimes as, 120–123
  statistics for 1993, 51
  trends in, 46
India and women police, 276
Individualistic crime, 215, 251
Industrial Revolution, punishments before,
  317–319
Innovation, 245
Insanity defense, 19
Instrumentalist theory of capitalist rule, 247
Intensive supervision, 345
Intent
  criminal prosecution and, 17–18
  homicide and criminal, 69
Interdiction of drug supplies, 137
Intergenerational patterns of child abuse, 80
Intermediate sanctions, 344
Internal flaws, 184
Internal forces and criminal behavior. *See*
  Positivism
Internal social controls, 229
International Monetary Fund (IMF), 107
Internet as crime zone, 215
Involvement, 229
IQ and crime, 193
Iran Contra affair, 106–107
Irresistible impulse test, 18
Israel, 16

J

Jails, 340–341
Japan, 232
Job satisfaction for correctional officers, 349,
  350
Judges, 291–294
  characteristics of presidential appointments
    to federal, 292
  election of, 291
  qualifications of, 291
  role of in criminal trial, 288
  salaries of, 291
  sexism, racism, and bias, 291–294
Judicial law, 287
Jungle, The (Sinclair), 143
Juries, 52, 288
Jurisdictions
  courts with limited, 290

original jurisdiction, 290
 without death penalty, 298
Just desserts, 314
Juvenile crime
 delinquency rates and neighborhoods,
  209–210
 violence and demography of, 367

K

Kent State protest, 243
Klinefelter's syndrome (XYY theory), 193–194
Knapp Commission, 277–278

L

Labeling theory, 225–228
 action as amoral, 226–227
 adequacy of, 234–235
 agency for, 230
 crime as social process, 224–225
 defining crime with, 18, 20
 family structure and, 232–234
 influence of structural functionalism on, 225
 leaving etiology unexplored, 225–226
 low self-control and, 234
 policy implications for, 231–232
 power of labeling, 227–228
 self-report studies and, 225
 shaming, 232
 social control in China, 236
 societal changes leading to, 224
 summary of, 228
Labor demands and punishment, 318–319
Larceny-theft, 115, 120–121
Law creation
 actual conditions contributing to, 25
 conflict theory, 24–25
 consensus theory, 23
 moral entrepreneurship, 23–24
Law Enforcement Assistance Administration
  (LEAA), 265
Laws
 administrative, 287
 anti-stalking, 84
 California "Three Strikes," 336
 common law, 289
 constitutional, 288–289
 criminal sexual assault, 71
 enforcing federal regulatory, 107–108
 judicial, 287
 legislative, 287
 obscenity, 145
 procedural, 287–288
 regulating narcotics, 143–144
 as repressive, 328
 restitution and, 328
 seat belt laws, 25
 shaping behavior, 170
 truth in sentencing, 56
Left realism, 255–256
Legalistic definition of crime, 17–18
 free will and, 18
 intent and, 17–18
 knowledge and, 18
Legalization of marijuana, 147
Legislative law, 287
Liberal feminist criminology, 249
Liberal strategies for property crime, 128
Limitations of criminology, 6–7

London constabulary, 266
Looking-glass self, 228
Love Canal, 93
Low blood sugar, 196
Low cholesterol, 196
Low self-control, 199–200, 234

M

Macro social causes of crime, 241–260
 adequacy of theories, 256–257
 agency and, 251–252
 Anti-War Movement and, 242–243
 Civil Rights Movement and, 242
 comprehensive nature of theories, 257
 current appeal of theories, 257–258
 extensions of strain theory, 255
 feminist theory of crime, 249–251
 left realism, 255–256
 Marxist theory of crime, 246–249
 Merton's strain theory, 244–246, 255
 "new" sociology and, 243–244
 peacemaking criminology, 256
 policy implications of, 252–255
 postmodern criminology, 256
 socialism and crime in Tanzania, 253
Macro social forces, 158
Mandatory reporting laws for domestic violence,
  78, 79
Mandatory sentencing, 296
Mann Act, 143
Mapp v. Ohio, 265
Marijuana
 history of use, 143
 legalization of, 147
 publicizing dangers of, 143–144
 smuggling in, 140
 trends in use of, 138
Marijuana Tax Act, 144
Marxist theory of crime, 246–249
 adequacy of, 257
 agency and, 252
 background for, 246
 capitalism in, 246, 247–248
 comprehensive nature of, 257
 corporate crime and, 247
 current appeal of theories, 257–258
 ideology and false consciousness, 248
 left realism, 255–256
 Marxist feminist criminology, 249
 policy implications and, 253
 powerful commit most serious crimes, 248
 socialism and crime in Tanzania, 253
 social justice preceding criminal justice,
  248–249
 summary of, 249
Masculinity, violence and, 85
Massachusetts v. Sheppard, 53, 278
Massage parlors, 143
McKlesky v. Kemp, 300
Measuring crime, 29–42
 additional sources of crime data, 39–40
 comparing American and German crime, 39
 history of crime reporting, 30–31
 with National Crime Victimization Survey, 31,
  32, 35–37
 overview, 30, 40–41
 participant observation research, 40
 self-report surveys, 37–39

with Uniform Crime Reports, 29–35
 unreported crimes, 32–33
Mechanical solidarity, 328
Media, 83–85
 debate over controlling violence in, 83–85
 effects of violence on children, 83
 newspaper crime coverage, 15
 role in perception of crime, 14–15
 television police, 272
Men
 aggression and testosterone levels, 194–195
 average years for sentencing, 307
 childhood abuse and, 81
 in co-corrections prisons, 342–343
 crime as disproportionately male enterprise,
  360
 elder abuse and, 81
 elite crime and, 99
 job satisfaction as correctional officers, 349
 majority of judges in U.S. as, 292
 moral orientation of, 128
 Old Boy network in courts, 291
 prisons for, 335–338
 property crimes and, 118, 124, 127
 prostitution and, 137
 sentencing of, 307
 sexual harassment of inmates by correctional
  officers, 351
 victimization rates for property crimes, 119
 as victims of rape, 74
 violence and masculinity, 85
Mens rea, 17, 69
Mental incompetency
 guilty but mentally ill (GBMI) test, 18
 mental illness in prisons, 347–348
 M'Naghten case and insanity defense, 19
Meritorious good time, 353
Mesomorphs, 191
Methamphetamine, 138
Micro social causes of crime, 205–220,
  223–238. *See also* Differential association;
  Labeling; Social control; Social ecology
 action as amoral, 226–227
 adequacy of theories on, 234–235
 agency and, 213–214, 230–231
 city as a natural area, 208–209
 comprehensive nature of theories on,
  216–218, 235
 concentric zone model, 209
 core propositions of, 208–213
 crime as normal behavior, 210–211
 crime as social process, 224–225
 current appeal of theories on, 218–219, 236
 delinquency/crime varies by zone, 209–210
 development of Chicago school of sociology,
  206–208
 differential identification theory, 215–216
 family structure and, 232–234
 hot weather and domestic disputes, 216
 impact of self-report studies, 225
 influence of structural functionalism on
  theories, 225
 Internet as crime zone, 215
 labeling theory, 225–228
 low self-control, 234
 policy implications for theories on, 214,
  231–232
 Progressive Era and sociological discipline, 208

Micro social causes of crime (*continued*)
routine activities and crime, 214–215
searching for root causes, 208
shaming, 232
social control in China, 236
social ecology as theory of crime, 208–211
societal changes leading to labeling and
social control theories, 224
Micro social forces, 158, 206
Midwifery and abortion, 144
Miller v. California, 140
Minimum mandatory sentences, 56
Miranda v. Arizona, 265
Miranda warnings, 279
Misdemeanor-manslaughter doctrine, 18, 69–70
Mission impossible, 276–277
Missouri Plan, 291
M'Naghten rules, 18, 19
Models of law creation, 23–25
Modes of adaptation, 244–245
Moral entrepreneurship
defined, 23–24
seat belt laws as form of, 25
Morality
action as amoral, 226–227
death penalty and, 299–300
ethic of justice and care, 128
gender and moral orientation, 128
public order crimes and, 134–135
stealing and, 126–127
Moral offenses, 134
Motivated offenders, 214
Motor vehicle theft, 122
defined, 115
stopping, 117
Multiple classification prisons, 339
Muncy Act, 306–307
Municipal police, 269
Murder. *See* Homicide
Mutualistic crime, 215
Myths, 4–5, 43–62
of crime as bad for everyone, 48–49
of crime as lower class phenomenon, 47–48
of crime cannot be reduced, 59–60
of criminals, 49–51, 52–53, 66–67
of domestic battery, 79
of drugs causing crime, 58–59
of getting tough with crime, 56–58
of increasing crime, 45–46
of increasing criminal activities for women,
54–56
of most crimes being solved and offenders
punished, 51–52
of no relationship between guns and
violence, 53–54
of organized crime, 149
overview of, 44
about rape, 73
of violent crime, 46–47, 66

N

Narcotics laws, 143–144
National Crime Victimization Survey (NCVS), 31,
32, 35–37
criticisms of, 35–37
property crimes, 115
rates of victimization, 35, 68
sample table of crime rates, 37

scope of, 35
Uniform Crime Report data and, 37
National Incident-Based Reporting System
(NIBRS), 31
Natural area concept, 208–209
Naturalistic definition of crime, 187
Nature
of property crimes, 115
of public order crimes, 135–136
NCVS. *See* National Crime Victimization Survey
Negative peace, 256
Negative social relations, 255
Neighborhoods
community policing, 273–275
delinquency rates and, 209–210
as key force in social ecology, 213
"New" sociology, 243–244
New Sociology, The (Horowitz), 243
Newspaper crime coverage, 15
New York v. Ferber, 141
New Zealand, 189
NIBRS (National Incident-Based Reporting
System), 31
Nineteenth-century criminology, 185–186
American punishment and, 319–321
expansion of American police force, 266–267
imprisonment of women, 322
Non-index crimes, 123–125, 127

O

Obscenity laws, 145
Occupational crime, 92
Occupational Safety and Health Administration
(OSHA), 22, 98
Offenders. *See also* Biological factors and crime;
Positivism
behavior freely chosen by, 18, 168–169
career criminals, 192
categorizing in New Zealand and People's
Republic of China, 189
communication within intimate personal
groups, 212
crime as outgrowth of routine activities,
214–215
criminal behavior as learned, 211–212
definitions favorable for law violation, 212
drugs and, 137–138
of elite crime, 99
gender and race of public order, 136
identification by physical features, 189–190
as irrational, 177
low self-control, 199–200
as menace, 230–231
motivated, 214
myth of punishment for, 51–52
as part of subculture of violence, 218–219
of property laws, 117–118
for public order crimes, 136–138
rape victims blamed for actions of, 49
as rational, 168, 172
as reactors, 230
as seeking pleasure, 169–170
as self-interested, 168
as someone victim knows, 49–51
techniques and rationalizations for criminal
behavior, 212
typical, 16–17
using techniques of neutralization, 219

of violent crimes, 68–69
white-collar, 94
Old Boy network in courts, 291
On Crimes and Punishments (Beccaria), 164, 165
Operant conditioning, 211–212
Operational capacity, 352
Opium, 143
Opportunistic crimes, 114
Order keeping function of police, 271
Organic solidarity, 328
Organizational crime as elite crime, 92–93
Organized crime, 147–151
activities of, 147–149
Chinese, 151
defined, 136
drug trafficking and, 149
gambling, 149
governmental commissions on, 150
myth or realities of, 149
names for, 147
Prohibition and, 142
prosecution of, 150–151
prostitution and, 143, 149
public order crimes and, 147–151
waste industry and, 148
Original jurisdiction, 290
Origins of criminology, 4
OSHA (Occupational Safety and Health
Administration), 22, 98
Outsiders (Becker), 23
Overcrowding of prisons, 352–353
Overloading of courts, 302–304

P

Pain, seeking to avoid, 168
Pandering, 140
Parents, promoting low self-control in children,
234
"Park Smart Awareness Week," 117
Parole, 295, 335
Partial elimination, 191
Participant observation research, 40
Patent medicines, 143
Patrol, 270
Patterns of victimization
in domestic violence, 77
for intimate murder, 78
for violent crime, 67–68
Peacemaking criminology, 256
Pennsylvania System of punishment, 320, 321
People's Republic of China
categorizing offenders in, 189
Chinese organized crime, 151
social control of transients, 236
"Strike Hard" program, 364
Personal crimes, 247
Personality development and crime, 197
Phrenology, 185
Physical stigmata, 189
Pinkerton Detective Agency, 270
Plaintiff, 304
Plausibility of theories of crime, 157
Plea bargaining, 295–296, 303–304
Pleasure
motivation to seek, 168
search for resulting in crime, 169–170
PMS (premenstrual syndrome) and crime rates,
195

Police, 263–282
    campus, 269
    community policing, 273–275
    corruption of, 278
    costs of, 267–268
    data included in Uniform Crime Reports, 34
    employed by federal agencies, 269
    federal, 268
    functional awkwardness, 277
    history of policing, 264–267
    local, 269
    Manning's "mission impossible" thesis, 276–277
    in mid-nineteenth century, 266–267
    Miranda warnings, 279
    misconduct of, 277–279
    private, 270
    professionalism versus bureaucratization of, 277
    public relations and, 279
    race and, 280
    recruiting, 272–273
    role of, 270–272
    state law-enforcement agencies, 268–269
    statistics about, 275
    television, 272
    types of, 268–270
    women as, 275–276
Police brutality, 278
Policy implications
    of classical criminology, 172–173
    for labeling and social control theories, 231–232
    for positivism, 190–191
    of social ecology and differential association, 214
    of theories of macro social causes, 252–255
Political gridlock on ideology, 363, 365
Pollution and corporate crime, 96–97
Pope v. Illinois, 141
Pornography, 140–141, 144–146
Positive aspects of crime, 48–49
Positive peace, 256
Positivism, 183–202
    agency and, 190
    biological factors associated with crime, 194–197
    born criminals, 188
    categorizing offenders, 189
    classical criminology versus, 186–187
    core propositions of early, 186–190
    criminology in 19th century, 185–186
    critiquing, 200
    evolutionary thought and, 185
    Freudian interpretations of crime, 197–199
    genetic influences, 191–194
    identifying criminals by physical features, 189–190
    intellectual and social influences on, 184
    low self-control, 199–200
    policy implications for, 190–191
    positivism and, 184
    rejection of classical criminology, 187
    scientific study of crime, 187–188
    as theories explaining driven offenders, 184
    view of sentencing with, 187
Postmodernism, 256
Power as factor in property crimes, 126

Precedent, 287
Predatory crimes, 246–247
Predictability and theories of crime, 158
Premenstrual syndrome (PMS) and crime rates, 195
Presumptive sentencing, 296
Price gouging, 101, 102, 104
Primary deviation, 226
Prisoners
    historical numbers of men and women, 55
    lawsuits by, 305, 325
Prison industries, 322–323, 334–335
Prisonization, 337
Prisons, 331–355. *See also* Corrections
    AIDS in, 346–347
    co-corrections, 342–343
    community corrections, 344–346
    correctional officers of, 349–351
    costs of corrections, 332–334
    culture of, 337–338
    decline in property crime and, 116
    early release and overcrowding, 352–353
    educational programs and enrollments in, 335
    gangs in, 338
    geriatric issues for, 348–349
    impact of "Three Strikes" laws on California, 336
    incarcerated mothers, 340
    jails, 340–341
    for men, 335–338
    mental illness, 347–348
    monetary costs of, 332–333
    overview of, 334–335
    partial elimination and, 191
    prison industries, 322–323
    prison system, 334–346
    private corrections, 342
    rates of incarceration by gender and race, 334
    recidivism, 332
    shock incarceration (boot camps), 341–342
    social costs of, 333–334
    in Sweden, 352
    tuberculosis, 347
    types of, 336–337
    violence in, 338
    for women, 338–341
Private corrections, 342
Private police, 270
Probation, 295, 296
Problem of crime versus crime problem, 15–16
Procedural error, 288
Procedural law, 287–288
Professional administration for corrections, 325
Professional criminals, 114–115
Professional standards for police, 267, 277
Progressive Era, 208, 321–322
Prohibition, 141–142
Property crimes, 113–130
    age and, 118, 119
    arrests of men and women for, 124
    arson, 122–123
    burglary, 121–122
    computer crimes, 125
    controlling, 128–129
    costs of, 116–117
    defining, 114–115

    extent of, 116
    forgery, fraud, and embezzlement, 124–125
    gender and, 118
    increased imprisonment and rates of, 116
    index offenses, 120–123
    larceny-theft, 120–121
    moral values and stealing, 126–127
    motor vehicle theft, 122
    nature of, 115
    non-index offenses, 123–125
    offenders of, 117–118
    race and, 118
    rationales for class distinctions in property crimes, 126
    societal issues, 125–129
    stopping motor vehicle theft, 117
    total arrests by demographic categories, 118
    victims of, 119–120
Proportionate punishment, 171
Proprietary security, 270
Prosecution of organized crime, 150–151
Prosecutors in criminal trial, 288
Prostitution
    double standards of prosecution for, 137
    organized crime and, 143, 149
    as public order crime, 142–143
Protective statutes, 306
Public order crimes, 133–153
    abortion, 144
    arrests by race, gender, and age, 136
    decriminalizing, 146–147
    defining, 134
    drug crimes, 137, 139, 143–144
    gambling, 144
    history of regulating, 141–146
    legalization of marijuana, 147
    nature, extent, and costs of, 135–136
    number and rate of arrests for, 135
    offenders for, 136–138
    organized crime, 147–151
    pornography, 140–141, 144–146
    Prohibition, 141–142
    prostitution, 142–143
    standards of morality and, 134–135
    victims of, 138–141
Public relations and police, 279
Punishment. *See also* Prisons; Sentencing
    after arrests, 52–53
    in ancient Greece and Rome, 318
    Auburn System, 320–321, 322
    before Industrial Revolution, 317–319
    Big House prisons and violence, 323–324
    as deterrent, 170–171
    for drug offenses, 137
    eighteenth-century criminal justice, 166–168
    for elite crime, 97–98
    French criminal procedure before revolution of 1789, 318
    increased imprisonment and rates of property crimes, 116
    in Iran, 179
    labor demands and, 318–319
    minimum mandatory sentences, 56
    modern corrections, 324–328
    myths about, 51–53, 56–58
    nineteenth-century American, 319–321
    Pennsylvania System of, 320, 321
    recidivism and severe, 58

Punishment (*continued*)
  shift to custody and control, 325–327
  in Singapore, 210
  theories of, 314–317
  torture as, 319
  truth in sentencing laws, 56
  twentieth-century corrections, 321–324
  upward trends in incarceration, 327–328
  for white-collar crime, 108–109
Pure Food and Drug Act, 143
Purposeful actors, 165

Q

Qualifications of police officers, 273
Qualitative research on crime, 40
Quantitative statistics, 31
Quartering, 167

R

Race. *See also* African Americans; Hispanics
  arrests for public order crimes, 136
  Civil Rights Movement, 242
  of correctional officers, 350
  crime as normal behavior and, 210–211
  crime crosscutting class and, 360–361
  death penalty and racial discrimination,
    300–301
  job satisfaction as correctional officers and,
    349
  policing and, 279, 280
  property crimes and, 118
  of public order offenders, 133–153
  racial disparity in sentencing, 305–306
  rates of incarceration by gender and, 334
Racketeer Influence and Corrupt Organization
    Act (RICO), 151
Radical feminist criminology, 249
Rape, 71–74
  changes in legal codes and proceedings on,
    73–74
  demographic patterns for, 74
  false reports of, 74
  male victims of, 74
  media depiction of, 84
  myths and facts about, 73
  radical feminist criminology perspectives on,
    249
  reporting, 74
  societal stereotypes about, 72–73
  underreporting of, 71–72
  victims blamed for offender's actions, 49
Rated capacity, 352
Rates of crime
  for homicide, 70
  interpreting, 45
  trends in murder rates, 70
  for violent crimes, 46, 67, 70
Rates of victimization, 35
  for assault, 75
  for violent crime, 67
Rational choice theory, 176–177
Rationality of criminals, 168, 172, 177
Reactors, offenders as, 230
Real-life evidence and theories of crime, 157
"Real rape," 72
Reasoning actor, 165
Rebellion, 245
Recidivism

defined, 56
deterrence theory and rates of, 175
effects of on prison programs, 332
higher rates with more severe punishment, 58
in Sweden, 352
Recruiting police, 272–273
Reform
  Beccaria's role in criminal justice, 165
  Bentham's influence on criminology, 166
Reformatory system, 321
Regulating public order crimes, 141–146
Rehabilitation, 294, 315–316
Reintegrative shaming, 232
Religion and criminal justice in Iran, 179
Remanded cases, 291
Reporting rape, 74
Repression, 199
Repressive law, 328
Requisites, 176
Responsibility. *See also* Agency
  agency as individual's, 172, 173
  agency as society's, 172
  defined, 18
Restitutive law, 328
Retreatism, 245
Retribution
  as strategy for sentencing, 294–295
  as theory of punishment, 314
Rewards, 176
Rich Get Richer and the Poor Get Prison, The
    (Reiman), 44, 247
Right to bear arms, 53–54
Risk, rewards, and requisites, 176
Ritualism, 245
Robbery, 76
Rodney King case, 277, 278
Rohyphnol, 138
Routine activities of social life, 214
Rules of Sociological Method, The (Durkheim), 48

S

Salaries for correctional officers, 350
Savings and loan scandals, 107–108
Scared Straight programs, 6, 7
Scientific method, 184
Scientific study of crime, 187–188
Search warrants, 52
Seat belt laws, 25
Secondary deviation, 226
Selective incapacitation, 294, 316–317, 365
Self-fulfilling prophecies, 228
Self-interest of criminals, 168
Self-report surveys, 37–39
  benefits and problems of research using,
    38–39
  labeling and social control theories responses
    to, 225
  use of, 37–38
Sentencing. *See also* Punishment
  determinate, 295–296
  deterrence strategy for, 294
  for elite crime, 98
  fixed sentences, 173
  gender disparity in, 306–307
  incapacitation strategy for, 294
  indeterminate, 295
  mandatory, 296
  minimum mandatory sentences, 56

positivists view of, 187
racial disparity in, 305–306
rehabilitation strategy for, 294
retribution as strategy for, 294–295
statistics on felony, 297–298
strategies for, 294–295
trends in, 296–297
truth in sentencing laws, 56
types of, 295–296
Sentencing disparity, 291
Sex crimes, 49
Sex hormones and crime, 194–195
Sexism
  in courts, 291–294
  job satisfaction as correctional officers and,
    349
  sexual harassment of inmates by correctional
    officers, 351
Sexual identification and criminal behavior,
    198–199
Sexual Politics (Millet), 145
Shakedowns, 278
Shaming, 232
Shire reeve, 264
Shock incarceration programs, 334, 341–342
Shoplifting, 114–115
Shopping by police, 278
Simple assault, 75
Simplicity and theories of crime, 156–157
Singapore's punishment of crime, 210
Single-parent families, 232–233
Sisters in Crime (Adler), 249
Situations in policing, 274
Social bond, 229
Social contract theory of society, 168
Social control theory, 228–230, 231
  adequacy of, 235
  adolescents and work, 230
  agency for, 230–231
  constraints on individual's actions, 229
  crime as social process, 224–225
  crime as social reaction to conforming
    behavior, 224–225
  family structure and, 232–234
  inducements for committing crimes,
    228–229
  influence of structural functionalism on, 225
  low self-control, 234
  overview of, 228, 229
  policy implications for, 231–232
  religion and criminal behavior, 231
  self-report studies and, 225
  shaming, 232
  social control in China, 236
  societal changes leading to, 224
Social costs of prisons, 333–334
Social determinism, 230
Social disorganization, 209
Social ecology, 208–211. *See also* Micro social
    causes of crime; Social ecology
  adequacy of theory, 216
  agency as perceived in, 213–214
  city as a natural area, 208–209
  comprehensive nature of, 216–218
  concentric zone model, 209
  crime as normal behavior, 210–211
  crime as outgrowth of routine activities,
    214–215

current appeal of, 218–219
delinquency/crime varies by zone, 209–210
hot weather and domestic disputes, 216
Social harm as crime, 98–99
Social influence, leading to labeling and social control theories, 224
Social influences, 81–85, 125–129. *See also* Macro social causes of crime; Micro social causes of crime
anti-stalking laws, 84
for elite crime, 98
guns and violent crimes, 82–83
intellectual background of classical criminology, 164–166
justifiable stealing, 127
liberal and conservative strategies for property crime, 128
media violence, 83–85
micro and macro causes, 8, 158
morality and public order crimes, 134–135
moral values and stealing property, 126–127
power as factor in property crimes, 126
rationales for class distinctions in property crimes, 126
sale of drugs and social trends, 138
social views on white-collar crime, 20–21
society shaped by patriarchal relations, 250
violence and masculinity, 85
Social injury, 21–22
Socialist feminist criminology, 249–250
Social justice preceding criminal justice, 248–249
Social protests, 242–243
"Social Structure and Anomie" (Merton), 244
Social System, The (Parsons), 158
Sociobiology (Wilson), 192
Sociological Imagination, The (Mills), 243
Sociology. *See also* Macro social causes of crime; Micro social causes of crime
criminal theories and, 206–208
definition of a situation, 362
developing the discipline of, 208
influence of structural functionalism on, 225
influence of structural functionalism on criminology, 225
"new" sociology and macro social causes of crime, 243–244
Solidarity, 328
Sourcebook of Criminal Justice Statistics (U. S. Department of Justice), 39
Specific deterrence, 175, 294
Split sentences, 295
Stalking, defined, 84
Stare decisis, 287
State courts, 290
State law-enforcement agencies, 268–269
highway patrol, 268
state police, 269
sworn officers, 269
State police, 269
Stateville (Jacobs), 323–324
Statistics
additional sources of crime data, 39–40
aggregate and quantitative, 31
changing trends in violent crimes, 68
comparing American and German crime, 39
distorting crime trends with, 30
on full-time police employees, 275

on gang-related crime, 36
with National Crime Victimization Survey, 31, 32, 35–37
on ownership of guns, 82
from participant observation research, 40
for property crimes, 115
self-report surveys, 37–39
trends in child abuse, 80–81
trends in murder rates, 70
in Uniform Crime Reports, 29–35
of violent crime in Sweden, 72
Status-frustration, 255
Stealing, 127
Stereotyping
of criminals, 16–17
sexual assault and blaming victims, 49
Stonewall Inn, 242
Strain theory, 244–246, 255
adequacy of, 256–257
agency and, 251
anomie and, 244
comprehensive nature of, 257
crime produced by macro social forces, 246
cultural goals and social structural means, 244
current appeal of theories, 257–258
extensions of, 255
modes of adaptation, 244–245
policy implications for, 252–253
summary of, 246
Strategies for sentencing, 294–295
Street Corner Society (Whyte), 40
Street crime, 91
Street level drug enforcement, 137
Street walkers, 143
"Strike Hard" program, 364
Structural functionalism, 225
Structuralist theory, 247, 248–249
Subculture of Violence, The (Wolfgang and Ferracuti), 218–219
Success goals, 244
Suitable targets, 214
Superego, 197, 198
Suspended sentences, 295
Sweden
prisons in, 352
theft in, 125
violent crime in, 72
Switzerland, 57
Sworn officers, 269

T

Taboos in Criminology (Sagarin), 196–197
Tanzania, 253
Techniques and rationalizations for criminal behavior, 212
Techniques of neutralization, 219
Television
crime as portrayed on, 14–15
police on, 272
Theft
computerized detection of, 125
larceny-theft, 115, 120–121
moral values and, 126–128
motor vehicle, 115, 117, 122
property crime and, 144–145
in Sweden, 125
Theoretical adequacy, 159

Theories of Crime (Curran and Renzetti), 258
Theories of crime, 155–160. *See also* Positivism
background for, 158
causal relationships and, 160
choosing "right," 150
core propositions for, 158
critiques of, 159
differential association as, 208
each person as theorist, 156
falsifiability, 157–158
micro and macro social forces, 158
plausibility, 157
policy implications, 159
position on agency (responsibility), 158–159
predictability, 158
real-life evidence, 157
simplicity and, 156–157
social ecology as, 208–211
understanding, 160–161
Theories of punishment, 314–317
deterrence, 314–315
incapacitation, 294, 316–317
rehabilitation, 315–316
retribution, 314
Third world markets and corporate dumping, 103
Threats of violence, 125
Three Rs: risk, rewards, and requisites, 176
"Three Strikes" laws in California, 336
Tobacco industry
advertising for, 22, 106
marketing in third world countries, 103
Torts, 289
Torture, 167, 319
Total elimination, death penalty as, 191
Transients in China, 236
Transmitted behavior, 186
Treatment programs, 345
Trends in child abuse, 80–81
Trial courts, 289
Trials
and punishment for elite crime, 97–98
right to speedy and public, 173
as speedy, public, and fair, 170, 171
Truth in sentencing laws, 56
Tuberculosis in prisons, 347
Twentieth-century criminology. *See also* Criminology
corrections, 321–324
future crime patterns in United States, 366–367
police reforms of 1920s to 1940s, 167
Twins, 193
Typical criminals, 16–17

U

Unconscious drives and behavior, 197
Understanding theories of crime, 160–161
Unfavorable definition of legal code, 212
Unfounded rape, 74
Uniform Crime Reports (UCR), 29–35
crime rates, 35
crimes "cleared" by arrest, 33
criticisms of, 34–35
detail included with, 33–34
evolution of, 30–31
examples of reports, 34, 35
first publication of, 30

Uniform Crime Reports (UCR) (continued)
  National Crime Victimization Survey data
    and, 37
  Part II offenses, 32–33
  Part I offenses, 31–32
  rate of violent crimes, 69
  rates of victimization, 68
  volume and rate of violent crime, 46
United States
  circuit courts in, 290
  comparing crime rates for Germany and, 39
  district courts in, 290
  future crime patterns in, 366–367
  nineteenth-century punishment in, 319–321
  twentieth-century corrections in, 321–324
United States Bureau of Justice Assistance (BJA),
    84
United States Coast Guard (USCG), 268
United States Department of Justice, 39
United States Supreme Court, 290–291
United States v. Behrman, 143
United States v. Leon, 52–53
University of Chicago, 206–208
Unreported crimes, 32–33
Unsafe working conditions, 96–97
Urine screening, 345
Utilitarian principle, 168

V
Vagrancy, 24, 236
Vice, 134
Victimization
  decreasing rates of, 47
  decreasing trends in, 45
  drug crimes and, 139
  of drunk driving, 139
  for elite crime, 99–100
  offenders and victims of violent crimes,
    68–69
  patterns in domestic violence, 77
  pornography and, 140–141
  of property crimes, 119–120
  for robbery, 76
  trends in child abuse, 80–81
  victims blamed for, 49
  in violent crimes, 67–68
Victimless crimes, 134
  failure to report, 33
Victims
  myths of criminals as stranger to, 49–51, 66
  of property crimes, 119–120
  of public order crimes, 138–141
  reasons for not reporting crimes, 32–33
  of violent crimes, 68–69

Violence
  in Big House prisons, 323–324
  juvenile, 367
  masculinity and, 85
  in prisons, 338
Violent crimes, 65–88
  assault and battery, 74–76
  changing statistical trends in, 68
  child abuse, 80–81
  costs of, 68
  domestic violence, 77–80
  elder abuse, 81
  guns and, 53–54, 82–83
  homicide, 69–71
  media violence, 83–85
  misperceptions of, 66–67
  myths of all crime as, 46–47
  offenders and victims, 68–69
  overview of, 66, 86
  patterns of victimization, 67–68
  rape, 71–74
  rates of, 46, 70
  robbery, 76
  societal trends and, 81–85
  in Sweden, 72
Volstead Act, 142
Volume of crime, defined, 45

W
Walnut Street Jail, 320
Watch/ward system, 265
Weather and domestic disputes, 216
Webb v. U.S., 143
Web site on crime, 1
Weighing profit versus harm, 97
Welfare fraud, 125
Welfare to wealthy, 100
Whistleblowers, 109
White-Collar Crime (Sutherland), 92
White-collar crime
  danger of, 96–97
  debunking myth of crime as lower class
    phenomena, 47–48
  elite crime as, 92
  Firestone case, 96
  Ford Pinto case, 96
  Gordon's critique of crime and capitalism,
    174–175
  powerful commit most serious crimes, 248
  social views on, 20–21
  unsafe working conditions and, 96
Wild beast theory, 18
Wilding, 213
Women. See also Feminist theory of crime; Rape

  arrests of for property crimes, 124
  battered woman syndrome defense, 79–80
  childhood abuse and, 81
  Civil Rights Movement, 242
  in co-corrections prisons, 342–343
  as correctional officers, 349, 350–351
  corrections for, 322, 326–327
  crime as disproportionately male enterprise,
    360
  demographic patterns for homicide of, 71
  elder abuse and, 81
  elite crime and, 99
  gender and property crimes, 118, 127
  gender-sensitive explanations required for
    crime, 250–251
  health care costs for incarcerated, 346
  history of contraception and abortion in U.S.,
    144
  incarcerated mothers, 340
  including in criminology theories, 250
  larceny-theft by, 121
  moral orientation of, 128
  myth of increasing criminal activities for,
    54–56
  myths about domestic battery, 79
  Old Boy network in courts, 291
  as police, 275–276
  as police officers, 273
  pornography and sexual violence toward,
    144–146
  premenstrual syndrome (PMS) and crime
    rates, 195
  prisons for, 338–341
  prostitution and, 137
  rates of victimization for African American,
    48
  sentencing for, 306–307
  sexism in courtroom, 292–294
  sexual harassment of imprisoned, 351
  societal stereotypes about rape, 72–73
  unfair treatment of in justice system, 251
  as victims of domestic violence, 77–78, 79
  as victims of property crimes, 119
  violence and masculinity, 85
Women and Crime (Simon), 249
Work release centers, 345
World Bank, 107

X
XYY theory, 193–194

Y
Young v. American Mini Theaters, 141